Volume 1 • 2005

WHAT DO I READ NEXT?

A Reader's Guide
to Current
Genre Fiction

- Fantasy
- Popular Fiction
- Romance
- Horror
- Mystery
- Science Fiction
- Historical
- Inspirational
- Western

ISSN 1052-2212

Volume 1 • 2005

WHAT DO I READ NEXT?

A Reader's Guide
to Current
Genre Fiction

- Fantasy
- Popular Fiction
- Romance
- Horror
- Mystery
- Science Fiction
- Historical
- Inspirational
- Western

NEIL BARRON
TOM BARTON
DANIEL S. BURT
MELISSA HUDAK
D.R. MEREDITH
KRISTIN RAMSDELL
TOM AND ENID SCHANTZ

THOMSON
™
GALE

Detroit • New York • San Francisco • San Diego • New Haven, Conn. • Waterville, Maine • London • Munich

THOMSON

GALE

What Do I Read Next? 2005. Volume 1

Project Editor
Beverly Baer

Editorial
Dana Ferguson
Kathy Meek

Editorial Support Services
Tom Potts

Data Capture
Katrina Coach
Beverly Jendrowski
Elizabeth Pilette
Beth Richardson

Manufacturing
Drew Kalasky

LIBRARY OF CONGRESS CATALOG CARD NUMBER 82-15700
ISBN 0-7876-9021-X
ISSN 1052-2212

Printed in the United States of America
10 9 8 7 6 5 4 3 2 1

Contents

Introduction

Thousands of books are published each year intended for devoted fans of genre fiction. Dragons, outlaws, lovers, murderers, monsters, and aliens abound on our own world or on other worlds, throughout time—all featured in the pages of fantasy, western, romance, mystery, horror, science fiction, historical, inspirational, and popular fiction. Given the huge variety of titles available each year, added to the numbers from previous years, readers can be forgiven if they're stumped by the question "What do I read next?" And that's where this book comes in.

Designed as a tool to assist in the exploration of genre fiction, *What Do I Read Next?* guides the reader to both current and classic recommendations in nine widely read genres: Mystery, Romance, Western, Fantasy, Horror, Science Fiction, Historical, Inspirational, and Popular Fiction. *What Do I Read Next?* allows readers quick and easy access to specific data on recent titles in these popular genres. Plus, each entry provides alternate reading selections, thus coming to the rescue of librarians and booksellers, who are often unfamiliar with a genre, yet must answer the question frequently posed by their patrons and customers "What do I read next?"

Details on 1,212 Titles

Volume 1 of this year's edition of *What Do I Read Next?* contains entries for titles published mostly in late 2004 and early 2005. These entries are divided into sections for Mystery, Romance, Western, Fantasy, Horror, Science Fiction, Historical, Inspirational, and Popular Fiction. Experts in each field compile the entries for their respective genres. The experts also discuss topics relevant to their genres in essays that appear at the beginning of each section.

The criteria for inclusion of specific titles vary somewhat from genre to genre. In genres such as Romance and Mystery, where large numbers of titles are published each year, the inclusion criteria are more selective, and the experts attempted to select the recently published books they considered the best. In genres such as Horror and Western, where the amount of new material is relatively small, a broader range of titles is represented, including many titles published by small or independent houses and some young adult books.

The entries are listed alphabetically by main author in each genre section. Most provide the following information:

- **Author or editor's name** and real name if a pseudonym is used. Co-authors, co-editors, and illustrators are also listed where applicable.

- **Book title.**
- **Date and place of publication; name of publisher.**
- **Series name.**
- **Story type:** Specific categories within each genre, identified by the compiling expert. Definitions of these types are listed in the "Key to Genre Terms" section.
- **Subject(s):** Gives the subject matter covered by the title.
- **Major character(s):** Names and brief descriptions of up to three characters featured in the title.
- **Time period(s):** Tells when the story takes place.
- **Locale(s):** Tells where the story takes place.
- **What the book is about:** A brief plot summary.
- **Where it's reviewed:** Citations to reviews of the book, including the source of the review, date of the source, and the page on which the review appears. Reviews are included from genre-specific sources such as *Locus* and *Affaire de Coeur*, as well as more general reviewing sources such as *Booklist* and *Publishers Weekly*.
- **Other books by the author:** Titles and publication dates of other books the author has written, useful for those wanting to read more by a particular author.
- **Other books you might like:** Titles by other authors written on a similar theme or in a similar style. These titles further the reader's exploration of the genre.

Indexes Answer Readers' Questions

The nine indexes in *What Do I Read Next?* used separately or in conjunction with each other, create many pathways to the featured titles, answering general questions or locating specific titles. For example:

"Are there any new Eve Dallas books?"

The SERIES INDEX lists entries by the name of the series of which they are a part.

"I like Regency Romances. Can you recommend any new ones?"

The GENRE INDEX breaks each genre into story types or more specialized areas. In the Romance genre for example, there is a story type heading "Regency." For the definitions of story types, see the "Key to Genre Terms."

"I'm looking for a story set in Paris."

The GEOGRAPHIC INDEX lists titles by their locale. This can help readers pinpoint an area in which they may have a particular interest, such as their hometown, another country, or even Cyberspace.

"Do you know of any science fiction stories set during the 23rd century?"

The TIME PERIOD INDEX is a chronological listing of the time settings in which the main entry titles take place.

"What books are available that feature teachers?"

The CHARACTER DESCRIPTION INDEX identifies the major characters by occupation (e.g. Accountant, Editor, Librarian) or persona (e.g. Cyborg, Noblewoman, Stowaway).

"Has anyone written any new books with Sherlock Holmes in them?"

The CHARACTER NAME INDEX lists the major characters named in the entries. This can help readers who remember some information about a book, but not an author or title.

"What has Debra White Smith written recently?"

The AUTHOR INDEX contains the names of all authors featured in the entries and those listed under "Other books you might like."

"I want to read a book that's similar to Michael Chabon's The Amazing Adventures of Kavalier & Clay."

The TITLE INDEX includes all main entry titles and all titles recommended under "Other books by the author" and "Other books you might like" in one alphabetical listing. Thus a reader can find a specific title, new or old, then go to that entry to find out what new titles are similar.

"I'm interested in books that depict military life."

The SUBJECT INDEX is an alphabetical listing of all the subjects covered by the main entry titles.

The indexes can also be used together to narrow down or broaden choices. A reader interested in Mysteries set in New York during the 19th century would consult the TIME PERIOD INDEX and GEOGRAPHIC INDEX to see which titles appear in both. Time Travel is a common theme in Science Fiction but occasionally appears in other genres such as Fantasy and Romance. Searching for this theme in other genres would enable a reader to cross over into previously unknown realms of reading experiences. And with the AUTHOR and TITLE indexes, which include all books listed under "Other books by the author" and "Other books you might like," it is easy to compile an extensive list of recommended reading, beginning with a recently published title or a classic from the past.

Also Available Online

The entries in this book can also be found in the online version of *What Do I Read Next?* on GaleNet. This electronic product encompasses over 100,000 books, including genre fiction, mainstream fiction, and nonfiction. All the books included in the online version are recommended by librarians or other experts, award winners, or appear on bestseller lists. The user-friendly functionality allows users to refine their searching by using several criteria, while making it easy to identify similar titles for further research and reading. The online version is updated with new information two times a year. For more information about *What Do I Read Next?* Online or GaleNet, please contact Gale Group, Inc.

Suggestions Are Welcome

The editors welcome any comments and suggestions for enhancing and improving *What Do I Read Next?* Please address correspondence to the Editors, *What Do I Read Next?*, at the following address:

Gale Group
27500 Drake Rd.
Farmington Hills, MI 48331-3535
Phone: 248-699-GALE
Toll-free: 800-347-GALE
Fax: 248-699-8054

About the Genre Experts

Neil Barron Barron, the coordinator of the Science Fiction, Fantasy, and Horror Fiction sections, is the editor of the reader guides *Anatomy of Wonder: A Critical Guide to Science Fiction* (Libraries Unlimited, 5th ed., 2004) and *Fantasy and Horror: A Critical and Historical Guide to Literature, Illustration, Film, TV, Radio, and the Internet* (Scarecrow Press, 1999). He welcomes comments at writeneil@charter.net.

Tom Barton Barton (Popular Fiction) is a reference librarian at the Rebecca Crown Library, Dominican University in River Forest, Illinois. A former journalist and community organizer, Barton lives in the West Beverly neighborhood of Chicago.

Daniel S. Burt Burt (Historical Fiction) is a writer and college literature professor who teaches graduate literature courses at Wesleyan University in Middletown, Connecticut, where he was dean for nine years. He is the author of *The Chronology of American Literature* (Houghton Mifflin, 2004), *What Historical Novel Do I Read Next?* Volumes 1-3 (Gale, 1997-2003), *The Novel 100* (Facts on File, 2003), *The Literary 100* (Facts on File, 2001), *The Biography Book* (Greenwood/Oryx, 2001), and the forthcoming *Drama 100* (Facts on File, 2006). He lives with his wife on Cape Cod, Massachusetts.

Melissa Hudak Hudak (Inspirational Fiction) is a medical librarian for Methodist Medical Center in Peoria, Illinois. She was previously employed in public libraries and wrote a column on inspirational literature for *Library Journal*.

D.R. Meredith Meredith (Western Fiction) is a full time writer of western historical novels and three mystery series. The award-winning Sheriff series are western mysteries set in rural Texas. *The Sheriff and the Panhandle Murders* and *The Sheriff and the Branding Iron Murders* were actually first published as Westerns (Walker, 1984 and 1985). *Murder by Impulse* (Ballantine, 1988) and *Murder by Deception* (Ballantine, 1989) were both nominated for the Anthony Award. Her latest title in the Megan Clark series is *By Hook or by Book* (Berkley, 2000). In addition to writing, she is book review editor for *Roundup Magazine*, reviews western literature for the *Amarillo Globe-News*, is a speaker at writers' conferences, colleges and universities, libraries, and civic clubs, and is Liaison Chairperson for the American Crime Writers League. She is a member of Western Writers of America, Mystery Writers of America, and Sisters in Crime.

Kristin Ramsdell Ramsdell (Romance Fiction) is a librarian at California State University, Hayward and is a nationally known speaker and consultant on the subject of romance fiction. Besides writing articles about the romance genre, she writes a romance review column for *Library Journal* and is the author of *Romance Fiction: A Guide to the Genre* (Libraries Unlimited, 1999) and its predecessor, *Happily Ever After: A Guide to Reading Interests in Romance Fiction* (Libraries Unlimited, 1987). She was named Librarian of the Year by Romance Writers of America in 1996.

Tom & Enid Schantz This couple (Mystery Fiction) has been in the mystery business for nearly 35 years. From 1970 to 1980 they ran a rare and out of print mail order business as The Aspen Bookhouse and later as The Rue Morgue Mystery Bookshop. Between 1980 and 2000, they operated a retail mystery bookstore, The Rue Morgue, in Boulder, Colorado. During that same period, they edited a monthly publication, *The Purloined Letter*, which reviews all new mystery titles. They have written a monthly crime fiction column for the *Denver Post* since 1982. In the 1970s, they operated The Aspen Press, which published books of detective stories and items of Sherlockiana. In 1997, they founded The Rue Morgue Press, which continues to publish reprints of classic mysteries from the turn of the century to the 1960s. They continue to operate a mail order book business as The Rue Morgue, which specializes in vintage mystery fiction, and are the recipients of the 2001 Raven from the Mystery Writers of America in honor of their distinguished contribution to mystery bookselling and publishing.

Contributors

John Charles Charles (Romance Fiction), a reference librarian and retrospective fiction selector for the Scottsdale Public Library, was named 2002 Librarian of the Year by the Romance Writers of America. Charles reviews books for *Library Journal*, *Booklist*, and *VOYA* (*Voice of Youth Advocates*) and co-authors *VOYA's* annual "Clueless: Adult Mysteries with Young Adult Appeal" column. John Charles is co-author of *The Mystery Readers' Advisory: The Librarian's Clues to Murder and Mayhem* (ALA, 2001). Along with co-author Shelley Mosley, Charles has twice been the recipient of the Romance Writers of America's Veritas Award.

Don D'Ammassa D'Ammassa (Science Fiction and Fantasy) has been reading SF and fantasy for almost 40 years and has been the book reviewer for the *Chronicle*, formerly the *Science Fiction Chronicle*, for many years. He has had fiction published in fantastic magazines and anthologies and has contributed essays to a variety of reference books dealing with fantastic literature. D'Ammassa is the author of the novels *Blood Beast*, *Servants of Chaos*, and the forthcoming *Scarab*.

Stefan Dziemianowicz Dziemianowicz (Horror Fiction) is a medical editor for a New York-based law book publisher. He authored the definitive study, *The Annotated Guide to Unknown and Unknown Worlds* (Starmont House, 1991) and is also the author of *Bloody Mary and Other Tales for a Dark Night* (Barnes and Noble, 2000). He has co-edited numerous horror and mystery anthologies—among them the Bram Stoker Award-winning *Horrors! 365 Scary Stories* (Barnes and Noble, 1998). Dziemianowicz also writes features on horror fiction for *Publishers Weekly*.

Shelley Mosley Mosley (Romance Fiction), a library manager and romance genre specialist for the Glendale (AZ) Library System, was named 2001 Librarian of the Year by the Romance Writers of

America. She writes romantic comedies with Deborah Mazoyer under the pen name Deborah Shelley. Their book, *Talk about Love*, was a Holt Medallion finalist for Best First Book. With John Charles, also a *What Do I Read Next?* contributor, she has won two Romance Writers of America's Veritas Awards. In addition to two newspaper columns, she reviews romance for *Booklist*. Mosley has written articles for *Wilson Library Bulletin*, *Library Journal*, *Romance Writer's Report*, and *VOYA*.

Key to Genre Terms

The following is a list of terms used to classify the story type of each novel included in What Do I Read Next? *along with brief definitions of the terms. To find books that fall under a particular story type heading, see the Genre Index.*

Action/Adventure ❙ Minimal detection; not usually espionage, but can contain rogue police or out of control spies.

Adult ❙ Fiction dealing with adult characters and mature, developed ideas.

Adventure ❙ The character(s) must face a series of obstacles, which may include monsters, conflict with other travelers, war, interference by supernatural elements, interference by nature, and so on.

Alternate History ❙ A story dealing with how society might have evolved if a specific historical event had happened differently, e.g., if the South had won the American Civil War.

Alternate Intelligence ❙ Story featuring an entity with a sense of identity and able to self-determine goals and actions. The natural or manufactured entity results from a synergy, generally unpredictable, of individual elements. This subgenre frequently involves a computer-type intelligence.

Alternate Universe ❙ More accurately, in most cases, alternate history, in which the South won the Civil War, the Nazis triumphed, etc. The idea is a venerable one in SF.

Alternate World ❙ The story starts out in the everyday world, but the main character is transported to an alternate/parallel world by supernatural means.

Amateur Detective ❙ Detective work is performed by a non-professional rather than by police or a private detective.

Americana ❙ A romance set in the present that features themes that are particularly American; often focuses on small-town life.

Ancient Evil Unleashed ❙ The evils may take familiar forms, like vampires undead for centuries, or malevolent ancient gods released from bondage by careless humans, or ancient prophecies wreaking havoc on today's world. The so-called *Cthulhu Mythos* originated by H.P. Lovecraft, in which *Cthulhu* is prominent among a pantheon of ancient evil gods, is a specific variation of this.

Anthology ❙ A collection of short stories by different authors, usually sharing a common theme.

Apocalyptic Horror ❙ Traditionally, horrors that signal or presage the end of the world, or the world of the characters, and the establishment of a new, possibly very sinister order.

Arts ❙ Fiction that incorporates some aspect of the arts, whether it be music, painting, drama, etc.

Biblical Fiction ❙ Novels that take their plots or characters from the Bible.

Black Magic ❙ Magic directed toward malevolent ends, as distinct from white magic, which is directed toward benevolent ends. Witch-craft is commonly thought of as a black art. Voodoo consists of mysterious rites and practices, including sorcery, magic and conjuration, and often has evil goals.

Carnival-Circus Horror ❙ Derived from its setting, especially the freakish world of the sideshow, in which the distorted or horrific is the norm and is sometimes used as a distorting mirror to reveal hidden selves.

Chase ❙ A traditional Western in which the action of the plot is based on some form of pursuit.

Child-in-Peril ❙ The innocence of childhood is often used to heighten the intensity and unpredictability of evil.

Collection ❙ A book of short stories by a single author.

Coming-of-Age ❙ A story in which the primary character is a young person, usually a teenager. The growth of maturity is chronicled.

Contemporary ❙ A story set in the present.

Contemporary/Exotic ❙ Set in the present but with an especially unusual or exotic setting, e.g., the tent of a desert sheik or a boat on the Amazon.

Contemporary/Fantasy ❙ A contemporary story that makes use of fantasy or supernatural elements.

Contemporary/Innocent ❙ Story set in the present that contains little or no sex.

Contemporary/Mainstream ❙ A story set in the present that would be more properly categorized as general fiction rather than a work in a specific genre.

Contemporary Realism ❙ An accurate representation of characters, settings, ideas, themes in the present day. Not idealistic in nature.

Curse ❙ Words said when someone wishes evil or harm on someone or something, such as a witch's or prophet's curse.

Cyberpunk ❙ Usually applied to the stories by a group of writers who became prominent in the mid-1980s, such as William Gibson and his *Necromancer* (1984). The "cyber" is derived from cybernetics, nominally the study of control and communications in machines. These books also feature a downbeat, punk sensibility reminiscent of the hardboiled school of detective fiction writers.

Disaster ❙ A tale recounting some event or events seriously disruptive of the social fabric but not as serious as a holocaust.

Domestic ❙ Fiction relating to household and family matters. Concerned with psychological and emotional needs of family members.

Doppelganger ❙ A double or alter ego, popularized in the works of E.T.A. Hoffmann, Edgar Allan Poe, and Robert Louis Stevenson.

Dystopian ▌ The antonym of utopian, sometimes called anti-utopian, in which traditionally positive utopian themes are treated satirically or ironically and the mood is downbeat or satiric.

End of the World ▌ A story that concerns the last events following some sort of disaster.

Erotic Horror ▌ Sexuality and horror are often argued to be inextricably linked, as in Bram Stoker's *Dracula* and Sheridan Le Fanu's "Carmilla," although others have argued that they are antithetical. Sexuality became increasingly explicit in the 1980s, sometimes verging on the pornographic, as in Brett Easton Ellis' *American Psycho*.

Espionage ▌ Involving the CIA, KGB, or other organizations whose main focus is the collection of information from the other side. Can be either violent or quiet.

Espionage Thriller ▌ Plot contains a high level of action and suspense relating to espionage.

Ethnic ▌ A work in which the ethnic background of the characters is integral to the story. Usually the focus is on an American ethnic minority group (e.g., African American, Asian American, Native American, Latino) and the two main characters are members of this group.

Evil Children ▌ The presumed innocence of a child is replaced with adult-like malevolence and cunning, contradicting the reader's usual expectations.

Family Saga ▌ Stories focusing on the problems or concerns of a family; estrangement and reunion are common themes.

Fantasy ▌ A story that contains some fantasy or supernatural elements.

Femme Fatale ▌ A seductress for whom men abandon careers, families, and responsibilities and who feels no pity or compunction in return; a common figure in history and literature.

First Contact ▌ Any story about the initial meeting or communication of humans with extraterrestrials or aliens. The term may take its name from the eponymous 1945 story by Murray Leinster.

Future Shock ▌ A journalistic term derived from Alvin Toffler's 1970 book and which refers to the alleged disorientation resulting from rapid technological change.

Futuristic ▌ A story with a science fiction setting. Often these stories are set on other planets, aboard spaceships or space stations, or on Earth in an imaginary future or, in some cases, past.

Gay/Lesbian Fiction ▌ Stories portraying homosexual characters or themes.

Generation Starship ▌ If pseudoscientific explanations involving faster-than-light drives are rejected, then the time required for interstellar travel will encompass many human generations.

Genetic Manipulation ▌ Sometimes called genetic engineering, this assumes that the knowledge exists to shape creatures, human or otherwise, using genetic means, as in *Brave New World* (1932).

Ghost Story ▌ The spirits of the dead, who can be benevolent, as in Charles Dickens, or malevolent, as in the tales of M.R. James.

Gothic ▌ A story with a strong mystery suspense plot that emphasizes mood, atmosphere, and/or supernatural or paranormal elements. Unexplained events, ancient family secrets, and a general feeling of impending doom often characterize these tales. These stories are most often set in the past.

Gothic Family Chronicle ▌ A story often covering several generations of a family, many of whose members are typically evil, perverted, or loathsome, and in which family violence is common. The family may live in a decaying mansion suggestive of those in 18th-century Gothic novels.

Hard Science Fiction ▌ Stories in which the author adheres with varying degrees of rigor to scientific principles believed to be true at the time of writing, principles derived from hard (physical, biological) rather than soft (social) sciences.

Haunted House ▌ Literally, a house visited by ghosts, usually with evil intentions in horror fiction, but sometimes the subject of comedy.

Historical ▌ Set in an earlier time frame than the present.

Historical/American Civil War ▌ Set during the American Civil War, 1861-1865.

Historical/American Revolution ▌ Set during the American Revolutionary period.

Historical/American West ▌ Set in the Western portion of the United States, usually during the second half of the 19th century. Stories often involve the hardships of pioneer life (Indian raids, range wars, climatic disasters, etc.) and the main characters (most often the hero) can be of Native American extraction.

Historical/American West Coast ▌ Set in the American Far West (California, Oregon, Washington, or Alaska). Stories often focus on the Gold Rush and the tension between Spanish Land Grant families and immigrants from the Pacific Rim, usually China.

Historical/Americana ▌ A story dealing with themes unique to the American experience.

Historical/Ancient Egypt ▌ A novel set during the time of the pharaohs from the fourth century B.C. to the first century A.D. and the absorption of Egypt into the Roman Empire.

Historical/Ancient Greece ▌ Set during the flowering of the ancient Greek civilization, particularly during the age of Pericules in the 5th century B.C.

Historical/Ancient Rome ▌ Covering the history of Rome from its founding and the Roman Republic before Augustus through the decline and fall of the Roman Empire in the fifth century.

Historical/Antebellum American South ▌ Set in the American Old South (prior to the Civil War).

Historical/Canadian West ▌ Set in the western or frontier portions of Canada, usually during the 19th century. Stories most often revolve around the hardships of frontier life.

Historical/Colonial America ▌ Set in America before the American Revolution, 1620-1775. Stories featuring the Jamestown Colony, the Salem Witch Trials, and the French and Indian Wars are especially popular.

Historical/Depression Era ▌ Set mainly in America during the period of economic hardship brought on by the 1929 Stock Market Crash that continued throughout the 1930s.

Historical/Edwardian ▌ Set during the reign of Edward VII of England, 1901-1910.

Historical/Elizabethan ▌ A novel set during the reign of Elizabeth I of England (1558-1603). There is some overlap with the last part of the Historical Renaissance category but the emphasis is British.

Historical/Exotic ▌ Setting is an unusual or exotic place.

Historical/Fantasy ▌ A historical work that makes use of fantasy or supernatural elements.

Historical/French Revolution ▌ Set during the French Revolution, 1789-1795.

Historical/Georgian ▌ Set during the reigns of the first three "Georges" of England. Roughly corresponds to the 18th century.

Stories often focus on the Jacobite Rebellions and the escapades of Bonnie Prince Charlie.

Historical/Mainstream ❙ Historical fiction that would be more properly categorized as fiction rather than a specific genre.

Historical/Medieval ❙ Set during the Middle Ages, approximately the fifth through the fifteenth centuries. Stories feature battles, raids, crusades, and court intrigues; plot-lines associated with the Battle of Hastings (1066) are especially popular.

Historical/Napoleonic Wars ❙ Set between 1803-1815 during the wars waged by and against France under Napoleon Bonaparte.

Historical/Post-American Civil War ❙ Set in the years following the Civil War/War Between the States, generally from 1865 into the 1870s.

Historical/Post-American Revolution ❙ Set in the years immediately following the Civil War, 1865-1870s.

Historical/Post-French Revolution ❙ Set during the years immediately following the French Revolution; stories usually take place in France or England.

Historical/Pre-History ❙ Set in the years before the Middle Ages.

Historical/Regency ❙ A novel that is set during the Regency period (1811-1820).

Historical/Renaissance ❙ Novel set in the years of the Renaissance in Europe, generally lasting from the 14th through the 17th centuries.

Historical/Roaring Twenties ❙ Usually has an American setting and takes place in the 1920s.

Historical/Russian Revolution ❙ These stories are set around and during the 1917 Russian Revolution.

Historical/Seventeenth Century ❙ A work of fiction set during the 17th century. Stories of this type often center around the clashes between the Royalists and the Cromwellians and the Restoration.

Historical/Victorian ❙ Set during the reign of Queen Victoria, 1837-1901. This designation does not include works with a predominately American setting.

Historical/Victorian America ❙ Set in America, usually the Eastern part, during the Victorian Period, 1837-1901.

Historical/War of 1812 ❙ Set during the British-U.S. conflict which lasted from 1812 to 1814.

Historical/World War I ❙ Set during the First World War, 1914-1918.

Historical/World War II ❙ Set in the years of the Second World War, 1939-1945.

Holiday Themes ❙ Fiction that focuses on or is set during a particular holiday or holiday season (e.g., Christmas, Valentine's Day, Mardi Gras).

Horror ❙ Refers to stories in which interest in the events, the intellectual puzzle characteristic of much of SF, is subordinated to a feeling of terror or horror by the reader, which could result from a variety of causes, including a disaster or an invasion of earth.

Humor ❙ Story with an amusing story line.

Immortality ❙ Usually includes extreme longevity, resulting from fountains of youth, elixirs, or something with a pseudoscientific basis.

Indian Culture ❙ These novels center on the lives, customs, and cultures of characters who are American Indians or who lived among the Indians.

Indian Wars ❙ Often traditional Westerns, these stories are set during the period of the Indian wars and rely on this warfare for plots, characters, and themes.

Inspirational ❙ A novel with an uplifting, often Christian theme, and usually considered "innocent."

Invasion of Earth ❙ An extremely common theme, often paralleling historical events and reflecting fears of the time. Most invasions are depicted as malign, only occasionally benign.

Legal ❙ Main focus is on a lawyer, though it does not always involve courtroom action.

Legend ❙ A story based on a legend, myth, or fairy tale that has been rewritten.

Lesbian/Contemporary ❙ A story with lesbian protagonists set in the present.

Lesbian/Historical ❙ Historical fiction with lesbian protagonists.

Light Fantasy ❙ There is a great deal of humor throughout the story and it is almost guaranteed to have a happy ending.

Literary ❙ Relates to the nature and knowledge of literature; can be applied to setting or characters.

Lost Colony ❙ Stories centering around a colony on another world that loses contact with or is abandoned by its parent civilization and the type of society that evolves under those conditions. Conflict usually arises when contact is re-established between the colony and its home world.

Magic Conflict ❙ The main conflict of the story stems from magical interference. Protagonists may be caught in the middle of a conflict between sorcerers or may themselves be engaged in conflict with other sorcerers.

Magic Realism ❙ A style of prose fiction writing in which the author blends the realism of describing ordinary places and incidents with fantastic, dreamlike, or mythical events and does not differentiate between the real and the magical.

Man Alone ❙ A lone man, alienated from the society that would normally support him, faces overwhelming dangers.

Medical ❙ Stories in which medical themes are dominant.

Military ❙ Stories have a military theme; may deal with life in the armed forces or military battles.

Modern ❙ Reflection of the present time period.

Mountain Man ❙ Any story in which the principal characters are mountain men and women, living in mountain areas remote from civilization and depending upon their own resourcefulness for survival.

Multicultural ❙ A romance in which the ethnic background of the characters is integral to the story.

Mystery ❙ Usually a story where a crime occurs or a puzzle must be solved.

Mystical ❙ Fiction dealing with spiritual elements. Miraculous or supernatural characteristics of events, characters, settings, and themes.

Nature in Revolt ❙ Tales in which normally docile plants or animals suddenly turn against humankind, sometimes transformed (giant crabs resulting from radioactivity, predatory rats, plagues, blobs that threaten London or Miami, etc.).

Occult ❙ An adjective suggesting fiction based on a mystical or secret doctrine, but sometimes referring to supernatural fiction generally. Implies that there is a reality beyond the perceived world that only adepts can penetrate.

Paranormal ❙ Novel contains supernatural elements. Story may include ghosts, UFOs, aliens, demons, and haunted houses among other unexplained phenomena.

Parody ▮ A narrative that follows the form of the original but usually changes its sense to nonsense, thus making fun of the original or its ideas.

Police Procedural ▮ A story in which the action is centered around a police officer.

Political ▮ The novel deals with political issues that are skewed by the use and presence of fantastic elements.

Possession ▮ Domination, usually of humans, by evil spirits, demons, aliens, or other agencies in which one's own volition is replaced by an outside force.

Post-Disaster ▮ Story set in a much degraded environment, frequently involving a reduction in population and the resulting loss of access to processes, resources, technology, etc.

Post-Holocaust ▮ The events following a world-wide disaster, often the result of human folly rather than natural events (collision with a meteor, etc.).

Post-Nuclear Holocaust ▮ The events following a world-wide nuclear disaster.

Private Detective ▮ Usually detection, involving a professional for hire.

Psychic Powers ▮ Parapsychological or paranormal powers.

Psychological ▮ Fiction dealing with mental or emotional responses.

Psychological Suspense ▮ Tales in which the psychological exploration and quirks of characters generate suspense and plot.

Quest ▮ The central characters are on a journey filled with dangers to reach some worthwhile goal.

Ranch Life ▮ The basic cowboy story, in which the plot and characters are inextricably bound up in the workings of a ranch.

Reanimated Dead ▮ These can take many forms, such as mummies and zombies (often the result of Voodoo).

Regency ▮ A light romance involving the British upper classes, set during the Regency Period, 1811-1820. During this time, the Prince of Wales acted as Prince Regent because of the incapacity of his father, George III. In 1820, "Prinny" became George IV. These stories, in the style of Jane Austen, are essentially comedies of manners and the emphasis is on language, wit, and style. Georgette Heyer set the standard for the modern version of this genre. This designation is also given to stories of similar type that may not fit precisely within the Regency time period.

Reincarnation ▮ A tale in which the horror arises in connection with the reincarnation of one of the characters.

Religious ▮ Religion of any sort plays a primary role in the plot.

Revenge ▮ A character who has suffered an unjust loss returns to take vengeance. This is one of the most common traditional themes.

Robot Fiction ▮ From the Jewish Golem to the traditional clanking bucket of bolts to the human-like android, robots in various guises have been among us for centuries. The term comes from Karl Capek's play, *R.U.R.*, which stands for Rossum's Universal Robots. Robots are often surrogates for humans and may be treated seriously or comically.

Romance ▮ Stories involving love affairs and love stories; deals with the emotional attachments of the characters.

Romantic Suspense ▮ Romance with a strong mystery suspense plot. This is a broad category including works in the tradition of Mary Stewart, as well as the newer women-in-jeopardy tales by writers such as Mary Higgins Clark. These stories usually have contemporary settings but some are also set in the past.

Saga ▮ A multi-generational story that usually centers around one particular family and its trials, tribulations, successes, and loves.

Satanism ▮ Suggests worship of evil rather than benevolent gods, the antithesis of conventional theism, whether Christianity or other religions. Evil demons are Satan writ small and usually lack the awful majesty of their parent.

Satire ▮ Fiction written in a sarcastic and ironic way to ridicule human vices or follies; usually using an exaggeration of characteristics to stress a point.

Science Fantasy ▮ A somewhat vague term in which there are "rational" elements from SF and "magical" or "fanciful" elements from fantasy, which hopefully cohere in a plausible story.

Science Fiction ▮ Although the story has been classified in another genre, there are strong elements of science fiction.

Serial Killer ▮ A multiple murderer, going back to Bluebeard and up to Ed Gein, who inspired Robert Bloch's *Psycho*.

Series ▮ A number of books united either by continuing characters and situations or by a common theme. Series books may appear under a single author's name or each book in the series may be by a different author.

Small Town Horror ▮ The coziness and intimacy of a small community is disrupted by some sort of horrific happening, suggesting an unjustified placidity and complacency on the part of the citizens.

Space Colony ▮ A permanent space station, usually orbiting Earth but in principal located in deep space or near other planets or stars.

Space Opera ▮ Intergalactic adventures; westerns in space; a specialized form of the genre type Adventure.

Supernatural Vengeance ▮ Punishment inflicted by God or a god-like creature, whether justly or capriciously.

Sword and Sorcery ▮ Often a muscle-bound swordsman, who is innocent of thought and common sense, up against evil sorcerers and sorceresses, who naturally lose in the end because they are evil.

Techo-Horror ▮ Suggests a catastrophe with horrific elements resulting from a scientific miscalculation or technological hubris; Victor Frankenstein's unnamed monster or a plague resulting from a laboratory mishap.

Techno-Thriller ▮ Stories in which a technological development, such as an invention, is linked to a series of suspenseful (thrilling) events.

Theological ▮ Stories in which religion or religious belief plays an important role.

Time Travel ▮ A story in which characters from one time are transported either literally or in spirit to another time period. The time shifts are usually between the present and another historical period.

Traditional ▮ Traditional stories may deal with virtually any time period or situation, but they are related by shared conventions of setting and characterization.

Trail Drive ▮ Any story in which a cattle drive (or, more rarely, a drive of sheep or horses) is a major plot component.

UFO ▮ Unidentified Flying Objects, literally, although sometimes used more generally to refer to any object of mysterious origin or intent.

Urban ▮ Stories set in large cities; usually the tone of the novel is gritty and realistic and may involve issues such as drugs and gangs.

Utopia ▮ A large, often influential, story type that takes its name from Thomas More's 1516 book. Usually refers to a society considered better by the author, even if not perfect. Aldous Huxley's *Island* (1962) is a utopia, whereas his more famous *Brave New World* (1932) is a dark twin, a dystopia.

Vampire Story ❚ Based on mythical bloodsucking creatures possessing supernatural powers and various forms, both animal and human. The concept can be traced far back in history, long before Bram Stoker's famous novel, *Dracula*.

Wagon Train ❚ A book that deals with wagon trains traveling across the American West.

Werewolf Story ❚ *Were* is Old English for man, suggesting the ancient lineage of a creature that once dominated a world in which witches and sorcerers were equally feared. Sometimes used to refer to any shape shifter, whether wolves or other animals.

Wild Talents ❚ The phrase comes from Charles Fort's writings and usually refers to parapsychological powers such a telepathy, psychokinesis, and precognition, collectively called psychic or psi phenomena.

Witchcraft ❚ Characters either profess to be or are stigmatized as witches or warlocks, and practitioners of magic associated with witchcraft. This can include black magic or white magic (e.g., Wicca).

Young Adult ❚ A marketing term for publishers; one or more of the central characters is a teenager often testing his or her skills against adversity to achieve a greater degree of maturity and self-awareness. A category used by librarians to shelve books of likely appeal to teenage readers.

Young Readers ❚ A novel with characters, plot, and vocabulary primarily aimed at juveniles.

Award Winners

Mystery Awards
by Tom and Enid Schantz

The Anthony The Anthony was presented at Boucher-con, the World Mystery Convention, in October 2004 in Toronto for books published in 2003. The award, like the convention itself, is named for the late mystery editor, writer, reviewer Anthony Boucher. It is second in prestige in the United States only to the Edgar, which is given out in the spring by the Mystery Writers of America. The knock on the Anthony is that it is too often a popularity contest where many of the voters will not have read the nominated books. Nominations and final voting are by the members of the convention.

Best Novel: *Every Secret Thing* by Laura Lippman

Best First Novel: *Monkeewrench* by P.J. Tracy

Best Paperback Original: *Deadly Legacy* by Robin Burcell

Best Short Story: "Doppelganger" by Rhys Bowen

Best Young Adult Mystery: *Harry Potter and the Order of the Phoenix* by J.K. Rowling

Best Historical Mystery: *For the Love of Mike* by Rhys Bowen

Best Critical/Non-Fiction Work: *Make Mine a Mystery* by Gary Warren Niebuhr

Best Fan Publication: *Mystery Scene* edited by Kate Stine

The Barry This award is named for the late fan reviewer Barry Gardner, a former contributor to *What Do I Read Next?*. Voting is by subscribers to *Deadly Pleasures*, a fanzine edited by George Easter. The award traditionally leans toward dark, gritty novels. The 2004 awards (for books published in 2003) were presented at Bouchercon in Toronto in October 2004.

Best Novel: *Every Secret Thing* by Laura Lippman

Best First Novel: *Monkeewrench* by P.J. Tracy

Best British Crime Novel: *The Distant Echo* by Val McDermid

Best Paperback Original: *Tough Luck* by Jason Starr

Best Mystery Short Story: "Rogues Gallery" by Robert Barnard

The Dilys Named for Dilys Winn, the founder of Murder Ink, the world's first brick and mortar mystery bookstore, this award is voted upon by members of the Independent Mystery Booksellers Association and given to the book they most enjoyed selling in 2004. The winner was announced in February 2005 at Left Coast Crime in El Paso.

The winner: *Darkly Dreaming Dexter* by Jeff Lindsay

Runners-up: *The Enemy* by Lee Child, *Something Rotten* by Jasper Fforde, *The Intelligencer* by Leslie Silbert, *Birds of a Feather* by Jacqueline Winspear, and *Shadow of the Wind* by Carlos Ruiz Zafon

The Hammett Given by the North American Branch of the International Association of Crime Writers, with nominees chosen by the organization's nominating committee, with final selection done by a rotating panel of outside judges.

The winner: *The Seduction of Water* by Carol Goodman

Killer Books Five mysteries to die for are selected each month by the members of the Independent Mystery Booksellers Association. Emphasis is on non-bestsellers. Most, but not all, of the selections are originally published in the calendar year the picks are made, but there is a special category for overlooked earlier titles, or "ones that almost got away."

October 2004 Picks (first month): *The Alto Wore Tweed* by Mark Schweizer, *Blitz* by Ken Bruen, *The Damascened Blade* by Barbara Cleverly, *Cosmic Clues* by Manjiri Prahbu, *Confessions of a Death Maiden* by Ruth Francisco

November 2004 Picks: *Bitch Creek* by William Tapply, *Hot Plastic* by Peter Craig, *Bye, Bye Love* by Virginia Swift, *Good Morning, Midnight* by Reginald Hill, *The Castlemaine Murders* by Kerry Greenwood

December 2004 Picks: *Queer Street* by Curt Colbert, *The Coroner's Lunch* by Colin Cotterill, *Last Seen in Aberdeen* by M.G. Kincaid, *The Surrogate Thief* by Archer Mayor, *Death by Discount* by Mary Vermillion

January 2005 Picks: *Speak Now* by Margaret Dumas, *Thumbprint* by Friedrich Glauser, *The Famous Flower of Serving Men* by Deborah Grabien, *Innocence* by Karen Novak, *Wiley's Shuffle* by Lono Waiwaiole

The Macavity Named for the mystery cat in T.S. Eliot's *Old Possum's Book of Practical Cats*, this award is nominated and voted on by members of Mystery Readers International. Awards for books first published in 2003 were announced at Bouchercon in Toronto in October 2004.

Best Novel: *The House Sitter* by Peter Lovesey

Best First Mystery Novel: *Maisie Dobbs* by Jacqueline Winspear

Best Bio/Critical Work: *Make Mine a Mystery* by Gary Warren Niebuhr

Best Mystery Short Story: "The Grass Is Always Greener" by Sandy Balzo

Nero Wolfe Award Presented annually by members of the Wolfpack, the Nero Wolfe Society.

The Winner: *Fear Itself* by Walter Mosley

Runners-up: *The Vanished Man* by Jeffery Deaver, *Fat Ollie's Book* by Ed McBain, *Burning Garbo* by Robert Eversz, *Where the Truth Lies* by Rupert Holmes

The Shamus Nominations and final voting are by members of the Private Eye Writers of America (PWA). The 2004 awards (for books published in 2003) were announced at a private luncheon in Toronto in October 2004 during, but not part of, Bouchercon. The award is given to books in which the investigator is a paid operative—lawyer, private eye, journalist, etc.—who is not a member of a professional city, state or national police force.

Best Novel: *The Guards* by Ken Bruen

Best First Novel: *Black Maps* by Peter Speigelman

Best Paperback Original: *Cold Quarry* by Andy Straka

Best Short Story: "Lady on Ice" by Loren D. Estleman

Romance Awards
by Kristin Ramsdell

As romance fiction has attained increased recognition as a legitimate literary genre, various publications, organizations, and groups have developed to support the interests of its writers and readers. As part of this mission, a number of these offer awards to recognize the accomplishments of the practitioners. Some awards are juried and are presented for excellence in quality and style of writing; others are based on popularity and are selected by the readers. Usually awards are given for a particular work by a particular writer; however, some awards are presented for a body of work produced over a number of years (a type of career award) and others are given for various types of contributions to romance fiction in general. The Romance Writers of America, *Romantic Times*, *Affaire de Coeur*, and RRA-L listserv are the sponsors of most of the awards listed below.

Romance Writers of America Awards A number of awards for excellence in romance fiction writing are presented by the Romance Writers of America at the annual RWA conference in July. The awards presented in 2004 are listed in Volume 2 of *What Do I Read Next? 2004*. The winners of the awards to be presented at the 2005 conference in Reno, Nevada, have not yet been determined and were not available as of this writing.

Affaire de Coeur Awards Reader/Writer Poll Awards are awarded to romances published in a given year on the basis of a readers' poll conducted by *Affaire de Coeur* magazine. The categories can vary from year to year. The awards given for books published in 2002 and announced in 2003 were listed in Volume 1 of *What Do I Read Next? 2004*. Since that time, no further awards have been given.

Romantic Times Bookclub *Reviewer's Choice Awards* Presented by *Romantic Times Bookclub Magazine* for outstanding romances published in the previous year. Selection is done by the *RT* romance reviewers. Categories may vary from year to year. The awards for books published in 2003 were published in Volume 2 of *What Do I Read Next? 2004* and will not be repeated here. The awards for books published in 2004 were presented at the *Romantic Times* Annual Booklovers Convention in St. Louis, Missouri, April 28-May 1, 2005, and are not available as of this writing.

RRA-L Awards Selected by the members of the RRA-L (Romance Readers Anonymous) electronic mailing list, these awards are usually published on the list in midwinter. The awards for books published in 2004 are listed below. Note: RRA-L has streamlined its awards, this year offering awards in only four categories.

Best Romance Novel of 2004: *Bet Me* by Jennifer Crusie

Best Romance Novella of 2004: "Winterfair Gifts" by Lois McMaster Bujold in *Irresistible Forces*

Best Debut Romance Novel of 2004: *A Secret Passion* by Sophia Nash

Best Romance Novel Outside the Genre in 2004: *Angel-Seeker* by Sharon Shinn

Awards information courtesy of Romance Writers of America, *Romantic Times* Publishing Group, *Affaire de Coeur*, and the RRA-L listserv.

Western Awards
by D.R. Meredith

WILLA Literary Awards The WILLA Literary Awards, named in honor of Pulitzer Prize winner Willa Cather, honor contemporary and historical books that capture the diversity and broad roles of women in the American West. It is sponsored by Women Writing the West, a non-profit association of writers and other professionals who promote remembering the women's West. The winning entries are chosen by professional librarians and historians. Winners for 2003, announced in October 2004 are:

Best Contemporary Fiction: *All over Creation* by Ruth Ozeki

Finalists: *Desert Wives* by Betty Webb, *Unpaid Dues* by Barbara Seranella

Best Historical Fiction: *Silver Lies* by Ann Parker

Finalists: *Fireweed: A Woman's Saga in Gold Rush America* by Carolyn Evans Campbell, *Matchless* by Jane Candia Coleman

Best Original Paperback: *Deliverance Valley* by Gladys Smith

Finalist: *The Scout* by Lynna Banning

Best Children and Young Adult Fiction: *Rodzina* by Karen Cushman

Finalists: *Meadowlark* by Mary Peace Finley, *Words West: Voices of Young Pioneers* by Ginger Wadsworth

WWW is a non-profit association of writers and other professionals, writing and promoting the women's West. Membership is open to any person worldwide who shares these interests. For more information about the WILLA Awards or WWW, please visit www.womenwritingthewest.org.

Fantastic Fiction Awards
by Neil Barron

Locus provides full listings of dozens of awards given throughout the year and provides a comprehensive historical and current list on its Web site, www.locusmag.com/sfawards, often before the monthly issues are published. This volume lists the awards given later in 2004. Because awards are given the year following the year of publication, and normally after the editorial deadline for this volume, most books listed here are discussed in earlier volumes of *WDIRN?*.

Hugo Awards Given at the world SF convention (worldcon) held over Labor Day weekend each year and chosen by the votes of those attending or supporting the convention. The 2004 (62nd) convention was held in Boston. Glasgow will host it in 2005 (when there will also be a North American SF Convention in Seattle) and Los Angeles (Anaheim) in 2006. Awards are given in thirteen categories, of which only two are relevant for this guide.

Best Novel: *Paladin of Souls* by Lois McMaster Bujold

Runners-up: *Ilium* by Dan Simmons, *Singularity Sky* by Charles Stross, *Blind Lake* by Robert Charles Wilson, *Humans* by Robert J. Sawyer

Best Related Book: *The Chesley Awards for Science Fiction & Fantasy Art: A Retrospective* by John Grant, Elizabeth L. Humphrey, and Pamela D. Scoville

Runners-up: *The Thackery T. Lambshead Pocket Guide to Eccentric & Discredited Diseases* by Jeff VanderMeer and Mark Roberts, *Spectrum 10: The Best in Contemporary Fantastic Art* by Cathy and Arnie Fenner, *Dreamer of Dun: The Biography of Frank Herbert* by Brian Herbert, *Scores: Reviews 1993-2003* by John Clute, *Master Story Teller: The Fiction of L. Ron Hubbard* by William J. Widder

Locus Poll These books are chosen by the readers and staff of the most important monthly devoted to fantastic fiction, with reader ballots tabulated usually in the August issue. For the 34th annual awards, 629 ballots were received, 407 of them online. Fifteen categories are used, of which seven are given here, limited to the top five in each category.

SF Novel: *Ilium* by Dan Simmons, *Pattern Recognition* by William Gibson, *Quicksilver* by Neal Stephenson, *Darwin's Children* by Greg Bear, *The Speed of Dark* by Elizabeth Moon

Fantasy Novel: *Paladin of Souls* by Lois McMaster Bujold, *Monstrous Regiment* by Terry Pratchett, *The*

Light Ages by Ian R. MacLeod, *The Dark Tower V: Wolves of the Calla* by Stephen King, *1610: A Sundial in a Grave* by Mary Gentle

First Novel: *Down and Out in the Magic Kingdom* by Cory Doctorow, *Veniss Underground* by Jeff Vander-Meer, *The Time Traveler's Wife* by Audrey Niffenegger, *The Etched City* by K.J. Bishop, *Paper Mage* by Leah R. Cutter

Young Adult Novel: *The Wee Free Men* by Terry Pratchett, *Abhorsen* by Garth Nix, *The Merlin Conspiracy* by Diana Wynne Jones, *Swan Sister* edited by Ellen Datlow and Terri Windling, *A Stir of Bones* by Nina Kiriki Hoffman

Anthology: *The Year's Best Science Fiction: Twentieth Annual Collection* edited by Gardner Dozois, *Legends II* edited by Robert Silverberg, *The Year's Best Fantasy and Horror: Sixteenth Annual Collection* edited by Ellen Datlow and Terri Windling, *McSweeney's Mammoth Treasury of Thrilling Tales* edited by Michael Chabon, *The Dark: New Ghost Stories* edited by Ellen Datlow

Collection: *Changing Planes* by Ursula K. Le Guin, *GRRM: A Retrospective* by George R.R. Martin, *Bradbury Stories: 100 of His Finest Tales* by Ray Bradbury, *Custer's Last Jump and Other Collaborations* by Howard Waldrop, *Roma Eterna* by Robert Silverberg

World Fantasy Awards Reader ballots generate a list of candidates, and a panel of judges selects additional candidates and the winners. Fantasy is defined to include horror as well. The winners are announced at a convention held over Halloween each year. The 2004 convention was held in Tempe, AZ, and the 2005 will be held in Madison, WI.

Best Novel: *Tooth and Claw* by Jo Walton

Runners-up: *The Etched City* by K.J. Bishop, *Fudoki* by Kij Johnson, *The Light Ages* by Ian R. MacLeod, *Veniss Underground* by Jeff Vandermeer

Best Anthology: *Strange Tales* edited by Rosalie Parker

Runners-up: *Gathering the Bones* edited by Jack Dann, Ramsey Campbell and Dennis Etchison; *The Dark: New Ghost Stories* edited by Ellen Datlow; *Trampoline: An Anthology* edited by Kelly Link; *The Thackery T. Lambshead Pocket Guide to Eccentric & Discredited Diseases* edited by Jeff VanderMeer and Mark Roberts

Best Collection: *Bibliomancy* by Elizabeth Hand

Runners-up: *Ghosts of Yesterday* by Jack Cady, *The Two Sams* by Glen Hirshberg, *GRRM: A Retrospective* by George R.R. Martin, *More Tomorrow & Other Stories* by Michael Marshall Smith

Life Achievement Award: Stephen King (author), Gahan Wilson (cartoonist)

Popular Fiction Awards
by Tom Barton

Medal for Distinguished Contribution to American Letters Sponsored by the National Book Foundation, the award is given out annually to an author whose total body of work has made a significant contribution to American literature.

2002 Winner: Judy Blume

National Book Award   The National Book Award, sponsored by the National Book Foundation, was established in 1950. The award is given out each year for a work judged to be commendable. Nominees are submitted by publishers and the winner is determined by a panel of independent judges.

2004 Winner: *The News from Paraguay* by Lily Tuck

Finalists: *Ideas of Heaven: A Ring of Stories* by Joan Silber, *Madeleine Is Sleeping* by Sarah Shun-Lien Bynum, *Our Kind* by Kate Walbert, *Florida* by Christine Schutt

Man Booker Prize   Great Britain's major literary prize is awarded annually to the author of a full length novel. The prize was established in 1968 by Booker PLC, an international food company, and the Book Trust and Publishers Association. The Man Group took over sponsorship for the prize in 2002.

2004 Winner: *The Line of Beauty* by Alan Hollinghurst

Finalists: *Bitter Fruit* by Achmat Dangor, *Cloud Atlas* by David Mitchell, *The Electric Michelangelo* by Sarah Hall, *The Master* by Colm Toibin, *I'll Go to Bed at Noon* by Gerard Woodward

Nobel Prize in Literature   The Nobel Prize in Literature is awarded by the Swedish Academy. The selection is based on a writer's total body of work.

2004 Winner: Elfriede Jelinek

Mystery in Review
by
Tom and Enid Schantz

John Dunning, whose 1992 bibliomystery *Booked to Die* signaled, and perhaps ignited, the hypermodern collecting field in crime and mystery fiction, is fond of saying that one of the major problems in the genre is the need by authors to publish a book a year, whether or not they have a decent idea, or the time to smooth out the wrinkles in their story. This, he claims, leads to a lot of inferior mysteries finding their way into bookstores. Dunning himself refuses to sign a contract in advance and delivers each new book not only on spec but according to his own timetable, a situation that makes it very difficult for his publisher to promote his books onto the holy grail of the publishing industry, *The New York Times* bestseller list.

There's no doubt that publishers prefer this book a year timetable. When Diane Mott Davidson's culinary mysteries first hit the bottom slots of the *Times* list, she was doing a book a year for Bantam, a time schedule that clashed with her own internal muse. As a result, she negotiated a new contract that called for a book every 18 months, but when Bantam showed signs of being uneasy with that schedule, Davidson bolted to William Morrow. Her first book for Morrow, *Double Shot*, earned good reviews and once again found its way onto the *Times* list, albeit still near the bottom and still only for a relatively short duration.

Dunning himself continues to garner good reviews, but the mega-seller still eludes him. Whether that's the result of his erratic schedule or the fact that bibliomysteries don't necessarily attract a large book-buying audience remains to be seen. Still, his sales are very good and his publisher outwardly appears to accept his eccentric ways. It also might be argued that none of Dunning's subsequent books has been as good as that first Cliff Janeway mystery. One non-series book published during this period, *Two O'Clock, Eastern Wartime*, appears to have been carved out of a manuscript predating *Booked to Die*. Although it contains much to admire, there were times when you felt as if a vital piece of information had accidentally been excised. Still,

there's a fine line between working over a manuscript and overworking one. Of course it's difficult sometimes to say when a book—or any piece of art—is actually finished. Another artistic absolutist, surrealist painter Salvador Dali, said no painting is ever actually finished, but suggested anyone spending more than a week on a single canvas risks extinguishing some of the original fire that first inspired it.

The mistake both Dali and Dunning make is to extrapolate from their own personal experiences a model for the work process for other writers and artists. Certainly, a lot of major mysteries, including books by perennial bestsellers and award nominees, exhibit technical flaws, sloppy writing, or substandard plots. While in some cases an extra year might have led to a better book, it probably wouldn't have led to a book *that* much better. Many of these writers are actually doing the very best they can. An extra month, year or decade might well be meaningless. These writers are on the bestseller list because there's some spark, some almost indefinable aspect to their writing, that strikes a responsive chord with readers. However, sometimes these writers continue to make the lists because a bad habit, like smoking, is hard to kick. Patricia Cornwell's best work is long behind her—one might argue (and we do) that she actually peaked three-fourths of the way through her first book, *Post Mortem*—but forests are still being decimated on a regular basis to record the joyless life of Dr. Kay Scarpetta. Good reviews might help make a newcomer, but the Cornwells of the mystery world survive, and prosper, on their past successes. In fact, so few reviewers tackled Cornwell's latest effort, *Trace*, that believers in conspiracy theories might well suspect collusion, though an unconscious collective boredom is no doubt a more reasonable explanation.

Of course, a good many mysteries are what a former customer of ours called bathtub reading. If it got him through a long soak, it was worth what he paid for it. And if it got a little waterlogged in the process, well, that's no great loss. Any number of paperback originals, and more than a handful of hardcovers as well, fit into this category. The writers here aren't trying to hit one out of the park. A well placed single or a good old-fashioned Texas Leaguer keeps their fans happy and helps pay the rent or mortgage.

Besides, there are quite a few writers out there who are perfectly capable of turning out excellent, perhaps even flawless, books on an annual basis. Peter Lovesey immediately springs to mind, and if his name is absent from our list of the twenty-five best mysteries of the last six months of 2004, it is because 2004 is one of those rare years in which Lovesey has not produced a novel. Fortunately for the mystery reading public, several grizzled veterans did produce excellent books. Our selection of the twenty-five best mysteries:

The Seniors. Writers falling into this category have already produced a body of work that would earn them a bust in the Mystery Writers Hall of Fame, if such a place existed.

Hark! by Ed McBain. S.S. Van Dine claimed a mystery series goes stale after six books, and he proved that for himself when he stopped at a dozen. But the 87th Precinct series is likely to hit ten times that number before this Italian-American writer with an Irish pseudonym finally lets the boys hand in their badges. If anything, this series is getting better. We're not much on author readings, but if you ever get the chance, go hear McBain read from his books. His delivery will resonate with every line you read. It's an experience you won't soon forget.

The Burnt Orange Sunrise by David Handler. Handler won an Edgar, a lot of praise and only modest sales for his first major series featuring celebrity ghostwriter Stuart ''Hoagy'' Hoag. His new series features a Jewish intellectual couch potato who reviews movies for a living and his athletic black cop girlfriend, who share a small ramshackle house on the Connecticut shore. In less capable hands, the relationship would be trite and contrived. Here it's pure magic.

A Dead Man in Trieste by Michael Pearce. There's a hint of Eric Ambler in this unusual tale of murder and intrigue set in Trieste in 1906 as Seymour of the Special Branch looks into the disappearance of the British consul. The child of East End immigrants, Seymour isn't as engaging a figure as the Mamur Zapt from Pearce's other early twentieth-century series, but you will find the same quiet, intelligent wit that earned that earlier series an almost cult following. Unfortunately, ''cult'' in this case translates into tiny. A former editor for his previous publisher said Pearce's books were among their worst sellers, but the new publisher for the Mamur Zapt series, Poisoned Pen Press, has more faith in him, as does Carroll & Graf, who is launching the Seymour series.

Garden of Beasts by Jeffery Deaver. In a departure from his usual breakneck contemporary thrillers, Deaver takes us back to Berlin just before the outbreak of World War II.

It's a marvelously detailed and suspenseful portrait of a world gone mad—or at least of a world led into darkness by madmen.

The Judgment of Caesar by Steven Saylor. Gordianus the Finder finds himself once again embroiled in a Roman civil war when he transports his wife to her native Egypt to take a cure in the waters of the Nile. Neither of the two rivals for the throne of Rome, Julius Caesar or Pompey, are terribly fond of Gordianus, though both realize that he has his uses. Saylor knows his history but, more importantly, he knows how to use history without ever slowing down or cluttering his story.

The Castlemaine Murders by Kerry Greenwood. You might wonder how a writer many of you have probably never heard of can find her way on a list of established veterans. Australian readers, who have been gobbling up her books for years, could probably tell you why. The first attempt to bring her out (in mass market paperback) in the U.S. flopped, perhaps proving what some editors claim is an aversion by American readers for books that aren't set in either Britain or the U.S. But the new Poisoned Pen Press editions of the Phryne Fisher books seem to be finally attracting the attention of cozy connoisseurs.

Thumbprint by Friedrich Glauser. Although this tale of a traveling salesman's murder in Switzerland was first published in 1936 in Europe, it didn't appear in the U.S. until 2004, from another small press, Bitter Lemon. But the author's five *noir* novels, featuring a moody police sergeant, have long been popular in Europe, and the German equivalent of the Edgar is named for him.

California Girl by T. Jefferson Parker. Although not as focused and possibly less powerful than the author's Edgar-winning *Silent Joe*, this ambitious tale of two intertwined families set against the background of Orange County in the 1960s is just as absorbing. Parker is well on his way to establishing himself as one of the premier mystery novelists of his generation. For our money, he and his even more overlooked colleague John Shannon, author of the Jack Liffey mysteries, surpass bestselling Michael Connelly in chronicling the Southern California dream turned nightmare.

Carnage on the Committee by Ruth Dudley Edwards. Edwards has one of the wickedest pens to come out of England since Evelyn Waugh and maybe the early Robert Barnard. She uses it to great advantage in this marvelously comic tale in which members of a major literary award committee are bumped off one by one, and their pretensions and misguided political correctness meet an equally savage fate.

Flesh and Blood by John Harvey. Some people will never forgive Harvey for abandoning his series about Charlie Resnick, the jazz-loving Nottingham copper. We're not big fans of serial-killer books, but Harvey is the rare talent who can keep up our interest in this overworked subgenre. Too often writers fall back on the serial-killer formula because it absolves them from the more difficult plotting that a traditional detective novel requires. We also applaud Harvey for completing the Resnick series while it was still fresh and moving on to a new, equally intriguing character, and his publisher, Carroll & Graf, for marketing the new series.

Skinny Dip by Carl Hiaasen. If Hiaasen isn't the funniest mystery writer ever, we'd love to read his superior. He's at his satirical best in this tale of an heiress who teams up with a retired cop to gain revenge on her crooked (and supremely inept) marine biologist of a husband after he inexplicably tries to drown her. Hiaasen may be mellowing over the years, for not only is he successfully interjecting engaging romantic entanglements (see also his previous book, *Basket Case*) into his comedy, but he's even creating endearing villains.

Wolves Eat Dogs by Martin Cruz Smith. Earlier in this introduction we suggested that a number of bestselling writers have gone stale and remain at the top of the lists solely on the basis of their early reputations. That doesn't include Smith, one of the most consistently dependable writers in the genre. His series about world-weary Russian policeman Arkady Renko has kept up with the times, and here he paints a chilling picture of the nuclear wasteland that is Chernobyl.

Bitch Creek by William G. Tapply. The author is best known for his series featuring Boston lawyer Brady Coyne. Brady likes fishing as much as he likes discreetly prying into the secrets of Boston's Brahmins, but Tapply's new hero, Stoney Calhoun, just likes fishing and is getting a steady paycheck that lets him do just that. However, he has no idea what the money is for, having lost his memory when he was allegedly struck by lightning. Like us, we suspect you'll enjoy getting to know Stoney almost as much as he will himself.

The Juniors. The writers in this group made strong debuts, avoided sophomore slumps, and are quickly (often at a book-a-year clip) establishing themselves as the genre's heirs apparent to the veterans above.

The Damascened Blade by Barbara Cleverly. Cleverly's third novel, set in India in the 1920s, won the coveted Ellis Peters Dagger from the British Crime Writers Association. It's set in an area very much in the news today, the Afghanistan border, and is a thoroughly engrossing look at colliding cultures, coupled with a well-wrought detective puzzle. It's also from a smaller publisher, Carroll & Graf.

Blitz by Ken Bruen. This Irish writer is actually more a second year junior since not all of his books have yet come out in the U.S. That's going to change very quickly. If you think British mysteries are all tea and vicars, you haven't been paying attention lately. Bruen

writes them as tough and gritty as Dennis Lehane or George Pelecanos, especially in this laconic yet almost lyrical tale of a hated London cop with his own peculiar sense of honor.

The Warlord's Son by Dan Fesperman. The author, who was a correspondent in Afghanistan, paints a vivid picture of life in the forbidding mountains on the Afghan-Pakistan border as a burned-out journalist enlists the aid of a black-sheep Pakistani to aid him tracking down news about the world's No. 1 fugitive. This is thriller writing at the highest level.

The Sophomores. Any writer who collected great reviews for their debut novels no doubt fears falling prey to the infamous sophomore jinx. These writers didn't.

The Lake of Sorrows by Erin Hart. ''May you die in Ireland'' is both a curse and a wish, depending on circumstances. Hart makes good use of local color in this complex and engaging second case for American pathologist Nora Gavin.

The Famous Flower of Serving Men by Deborah Grabien. After one mostly supernatural novel, Grabien has now published two highly original novels of mystery and detection. There is still much of the otherworldly here, as a woman director- producer seeks to unravel the mystery surrounding a ghost who inhabits a London theater she inherited from a distant relative. It seems that this Victorian-era theater was built on the site of a prison whose inmates were burned alive during the Peasants' Rebellion of 1381. The author ably moves from this dark past to the much brighter though dangerous present.

Hot Plastic by Peter Craig. Our favorite criminals have always been con artists, and Craig has come up with a most unusual trio of grifters in this comic novel set in 1983. It reads like a collaboration between Jim Thompson and Donald E. Westlake

The Freshmen. These debut novels have a freshness to them, often coupled with a an original character or plot. That gives us hope that you can still turn the old game on its ear.

The Midnight Band of Mercy by Michael Blaine. Contemporary writers have mined Hell's Kitchen in New York City for a wealth of material, but the New York of 1893 was just as rough and brutal, perhaps even more so, than the modern city. The title refers to a group of well-bred women who are chloroforming thousands of stray cats. When a Jewish boxer turned reporter looks into this unusual practice, he uncovers a number of scandals, including a budding eugenics movement. This title is from Soho Press, our favorite mystery publisher because it isn't afraid to embrace unusual titles.

The Coroner's Lunch by Colin Cotterill. This is another offering from Soho Press. One of the rules of modern publishing is that mysteries have to be set in either the United States or Britain. Soho continually defies this conventional wisdom by publishing mysteries featuring a wide range of locales. Set in 1976 in the newly formed People's Republic of Laos, this most unusual book features as its detective a 72-year-old doctor who has been pressed into service as the new nation's chief—and only—state medical examiner. He had hoped that his years of indifferent service to the Communist Party might have earned him a quiet retirement. Instead, he finds himself involved in a murder involving high-ranking party officials, as well as neighboring Vietnam. The dead reveal their secrets to the doctor, and not always as a result of an autopsy, in this sometimes mystical first novel.

Speak Now by Margaret Dumas. Set in modern-day San Francisco, this book has a nice old-fashioned touch. A wealthy heiress returns from England with a new husband on her arm only to discover a body in the bathtub of her hotel suite. She begins to wonder if her husband's naval career was as uninteresting as he claims. Maybe she'd been right to avoid commitment in the past. It all adds up to good fun well told, and it's another find by Poisoned Pen Press.

Skinny-Dipping by Claire Matturro. If Janet Evanovich's Stephanie Plum had gone to law school and tamed her big hair, she might well have turned out like Sarasota attorney Lilly Cleary. Besides, we're not sure we've ever read a book in which the murder weapon was tainted marijuana.

And it shouldn't come as a surprise that our pick for the best of the best is also a first novel.

Darkly Dreaming Dexter by Jeff Lindsay. Mystery bookstore owners (see awards section) picked this title as the book they most enjoyed selling in 2004. We suspect this is only the first of many awards with which the author of this strikingly original novel is going to be able to decorate his mantle. The antihero title character is a sociopath who kills because he can't help it, although his adoptive father, a cop, has trained him to kill only other serial killers. He's also taught him how to avoid capture and how to be an otherwise relatively decent human being, if one can overlook his one tiny little character flaw. Lindsay's triumph is that the reader is able to do just that, in no small part thanks to Dexter's attachment to his family and his wry sense of humor.

But we'd also be remiss if we didn't tell you we recently discovered that we missed one of the best books of 2002, *The Alto Wore Tweed* by Mark Schweitzer.

The Baritone Wore Chiffon, its hilarious sequel, also deals with Episcopalian church politics, small-town police work, and Raymond Chandler's typewriter, but was published in 2004 and so makes our current list. The collection of mock blurbs on the first page is alone worth the price of the book. Because it was published in trade paperback by a firm that primarily issues church choral music publications, you might have to look hard to find a copy, but you'll be glad you did. We suspect some smart New York editor is going to snap up this sparkling series.

Of course that implies that there is such a thing as a smart New York editor. If you look at our picks, you'll find that nearly half of them were published by smaller houses either courageous enough to take a chance on an unknown writer with an original voice or smart enough to pick up a talented discard. New York is looking for potential bestsellers, and who can blame them, or books that can be marketed without exerting a lot of time, effort or money. It's often tough to find a marketing hook for a truly original book. Don't get us wrong. We sympathize with those marketers. After all, a really original mystery is the toughest kind to write up when we are doing entries for *What Do I Read Next?*, since their very uniqueness makes it incredibly difficult to come up with five other similar books readers might also enjoy.

Some independent booksellers are predicting the end of mass market paperbacks as the market changes. The big chains, the big discount stores, and Amazon.com have cornered the book market in the United States through their ability to use a calculator. Discounting is the name of the game and mass market paperbacks just can't be profitably marked down. By the time a $6.99 mass market paperback is discounted by 20 percent, the retailer is making only $1.40 on the book, but selling it takes as much effort as selling a discounted $25 hardcover, which yields a $5 profit, or a discounted $14.00 quality trade paperback, which yields $2.80. If you think that the new John Grisham is priced at $27.95 because of his big contract, think again. Only a handful of people pay the full fare on these monster bestsellers. If retailers (and this includes supermarkets and discount department stores, as well as Amazon and the chains) offer big books at 20, 30 or even 40 percent off, they want them to carry the highest price possible.

Part of the problem with many mass market paperbacks—i.e., rack-size paperbacks that are sold in various outlets in addition to bookstores—is that there's really nothing mass about them at all. Many have print runs in the 15,000 to 25,000 copy range, and a 40 percent return rate isn't unheard of. But the only thing that's returnable is the cover, and publishers require that retailers destroy the stripped unsold books. Why? Because it costs too much to ship whole copies back, especially when you figure that a book that's in transit twice is twice as likely to end up dinged and thus unsaleable. So that 15,000 copy print run is now effectively a 9,000 copy edition. Of course, trade paperbacks and hardcovers also get damaged when they're returned, but because of their higher unit cost, people at all ends tend to handle them a bit more carefully and publishers usually remainder them at a reduced price to retailers.

We're not ready to signal the end to mass market paperbacks ourselves. They offer a chance for new writers to prove themselves before publishers commit to the cost of bringing them out in more expensive editions. And they offer convenient, portable, disposable entertainment for travelers and other readers who don't intend to keep their books. Remember that old customer we told you about who just wanted a book that would entertain him during a long soak in the tub? He might not be so inclined to splash about with a trade paperback in his hands. Quality paperbacks do have their place in the publishing world, although there have been some misfires. Several years ago Berkley tried an experiment where they simultaneously brought out new mysteries in hardcover and trade paperback, following them a year later with a mass market edition. This had to be one of the most baffling marketing ploys in recent years. The trade paperbacks cut into both their hardcover and mass market sales and left customers used to the old system scratching their heads and tightening the grip on their wallets.

The place for trade paperbacks is in reprints of books that have a solid but relatively small audience. Gay and lesbian mysteries traditionally have fallen into this category. They have been joined in recent years by reprints of historical mysteries, as well as vintage mysteries from the past, books translated from other languages, and so-called literary mysteries. This is truly the place for the trade paperback in a sensible marketplace. It's too bad the marketplace is often anything but sensible. Of course, trade paperbacks are also the format of choice for any number of small presses who are bringing out original mysteries but whose print runs and budgets don't permit case binding their titles. It's also likely to be the choice of those new vanity presses who utilize Print on Demand technology. (Yes, we know, not all POD books are subsidized by their authors, but an alarming number are.)

The bottom line is that it isn't the format of the book that's in danger. It's the independent bookstore that stocks them (and can't afford to discount them) whose future is in jeopardy. And we don't see any chance of that situation changing.

While we're talking about things in the book world that irk us, we might as well mention Elizabeth George. No, she doesn't personally irritate us. We've met her, even had dinner with her, and found her to be a funny, engaging woman whose first published novel, *A Great Deliverance*, remains a great favorite of ours. But there is a tendency on the part of people who have been successful as writers to think they know more about the genre, in particular its history, than they really do.

Case in point: in her introduction to *A Moment on the Edge: 100 Years of Crime Stories by Women*, George rightly suggests that literature is ''whatever lasts.'' Dickens might have been considered a writer of potboilers by his contem-

poraries, but he's still being read today. Where George does err is in her assertion that the Golden Age of mystery fiction (roughly that period between the world wars) was dominated in England by the polite traditional mystery, mostly written by women, whereas the more violent, hard-boiled form of the genre, typified by Dashiell Hammett and Raymond Chandler, reigned supreme on this side of the Atlantic. Ironically, this common misconception is even refuted in one of the introductory notes to the individual stories in that anthology by the knowledgeable critic Jon L. Breen, who was understandably bemused by George's thesis when he got his contributor's copy. English writer Minette Walters, again another personal and professional favorite of ours, made precisely the same error in a lecture and book-signing tour she did in the U.S. several years ago to promote her latest mystery.

The fact is that the traditional mystery dominated the literary landscape in America as well as in England. S.S. Van Dine scored several *New York Times* bestsellers with his very erudite, if nearly insufferable, sleuth Philo Vance, while countless other writers, both male and female, dominated the publishers' lists with books that would be equally at home in Britain. Ellery Queen, Rex Stout, John Dickson Carr, Mary Roberts Rinehart, and Mignon G. Eberhart come immediately to mind. It was not until the post World War II era that hard-boiled fiction rose to prominence and enjoyed great sales in the United States, with writers ranging in ability from Mickey Spillane to Ross Macdonald.

Sadly, several writers who helped shaped those eras wrote the final the end to their life stories in 2004, including Hugh B. Cave, who saw a rebirth of interest in his work, however limited, in his 90s; Lange Lewis, whose charming mysteries from the 1940s and 1950s were reprinted in the 1980s to the delight of modern readers; Lucy Freeman, who was a pioneer in psychological suspense; Anna Clarke, who bridged the gap between Agatha Christie and Walters in the English mystery; and Joseph Hansen, who turned the genre on its ear by making a gay man his sleuth.

But the loss we mourn the most is that of a fan. William F. Deeck, compiler of indexes and a tireless laborer on any number of mystery reference books edited by other authors, died from cancer shortly after missing a Malice Domestic convention (he was one of its founders) for the first time. He was a man of great wit and intelligence who was as passionate about his large collection of mystery fiction as he was about introducing his friends, including us, to forgotten and often truly obscure classics. His tongue-in-cheek presentation on the writings of James Corbett, perhaps the single worst wordsmith in the history of the genre, remains one of the single greatest, and funniest, moments in the history of mystery conventions.

Mystery Titles

1

ALINA ADAMS (Pseudonym of Alina Sivorinovsky)

On Thin Ice
(New York: Berkley, 2004)

Story type: Amateur Detective
Series: Bex Levy. Book 2
Subject(s): Sports/Ice Skating; Television
Major character(s): Rebecca ''Bex'' Levy, Researcher, Detective—Amateur
Time period(s): 2000s
Locale(s): New York, New York; Poconos, Pennsylvania

Summary: Bex, a researcher for a sports network, is alerted by an ice-skating coach that one of her pupils, 13-year-old Jeremy Hunt, has a phenomenal talent that could take him all the way to the top. The only problem is that his father doesn't want him to compete in the Nationals. Bex meets with Jeremy and, at his request, talks to his father, who can't be budged and who then disappears with Jeremy. Meanwhile, Bex is working on another story, which takes her to the Poconos in search of the missing partner of a failed Olympic medalist. Eventually, the two stories turn out to be connected, but before Bex has all the answers, there's a murder. The author, who under her real name has published several nonfiction books on ice skating, knows her subject well and provides much fascinating information on the sport.

Where it's reviewed:
Romantic Times, October 2004, page 84

Other books by the same author:
Murder on Ice, 2003

Other books you might like:
Kathy Brandt, *The Hannah Sampson Series,* 2003-
Charlotte Elkins, *The Lee Ofsted Series,* 1989-
Victoria Houston, *The Lew Ferris Series,* 2000-
Roberta Isleib, *The Cassie Burdette Series,* 2002-
Twist Phelan, *The Hannah Dain Series,* 2002-

2

SUSAN WITTIG ALBERT

The Tale of Hill Top Farm
(New York: Berkley, 2004)

Story type: Historical/Edwardian; Amateur Detective
Series: Beatrix Potter. Book 1
Subject(s): Authors and Writers; Rural Life; Animals
Major character(s): Beatrix Potter, Historical Figure, Detective—Amateur
Time period(s): 1900s (1905)
Locale(s): Near Sawrey, England (Lake District)

Summary: In 1905, beloved children's book author Beatrix Potter unexpectedly loses her fiance and buys Hill Top Farm in the Lake District with the income from her writing and a small inheritance. Her career as a writer and illustrator had flourished from the beginning, starting with *The Tale of Peter Rabbit* in 1902, and she longs for independence from her parents. The villagers aren't sure what to make of a single woman and a Londoner attempting to run a farm on her own. Beatrix soon wins them over with her gentle but determined ways and by small acts of kindness, such as reading to the schoolchildren. When a villager dies a suspicious death, she turns detective, aided by an assortment of talking animal companions, ranging from rabbits to hedgehogs to mice. It's a new, very cozy historical series from the creator of the China Bayles herbal mysteries set in the Texas hill country. The author also writes a series of Victorian mysteries with her husband, Bill Albert, as Robin Paige. Recipes for authentic Edwardian treats are included.

Where it's reviewed:
Library Journal, October 1, 2004, page 62
Publishers Weekly, September 13, 2004, page 62
Romantic Times, October 2004, page 82

Other books by the same author:
A Dilly of a Death, 2003
An Unthymely Death and Other Gardening Mysteries, 2003 (short stories)
Indigo Dying, 2002

Blood Root, 2001
Mistletoe Man, 2000

Other books you might like:
Emily Brightwell, *The Mrs. Jeffries Series*, 1993-
Sydney Hosier, *The Mrs. Hudson Series*, 1996-
Kate Kingsbury, *The Pennyfoot Hotel Series*, 1993-
Sam McCarver, *The Case of the Second Seance*, 2000
Amy Myers, *The Auguste Didier Series*, 1986-

3

MIKE ASHLEY, Editor

The Mammoth Book of Roaring Twenties Whodunnits

(New York: Carroll & Graf, 2004)

Story type: Anthology; Historical/Roaring Twenties
Subject(s): Short Stories
Time period(s): 1920s

Summary: This anthology of short murder mysteries from the age of bright young things contains 24 stories from mostly contemporary authors, such as Peter Lovesey, Gillian Linscott, Max Allan Collins, Annette Meyers, H.R.F. Keating, and others, who have written original stories set in this period, specifically for this volume. There are also a handful of vintage stories from authors who originally wrote during that era, such as Hulbert Footner, Cornell Woolrich, and others less well-known. Several stories feature actual historical figures, such as Amy Myers' ''Valentino's Valediction,'' about the legendary film star, and Christine Matthews' ''For the Benefit of Mr. Means,'' about Fatty Arbuckle. As the editor points out in his introduction, the 1920s gave birth to the so-called Golden Age of detective fiction and, as such, furnishes the ideal background for mystery short stories.

Other books by the same author:
The Mammoth Book of Roman Whodunnits, 2003 (editor)
The Mammoth Book of Egyptian Whodunnits, 2002 (editor)
The Mammoth Book of More Historical Whodunnits, 2001 (editor)
The Mammoth Book of Locked-Room Mysteries and Impossible Crimes, 2000 (editor)
The Mammoth Book of Shakespearean Whodunnits, 1997

Other books you might like:
James Anderson, *The Affair of the Blood-Stained Egg Cozy*, 1975
Carola Dunn, *The Daisy Dalrymple Series*, 1994-
Kerry Greenwood, *The Phryne Fisher Series*, 1989-
Annette Meyers, *The Olivia Brown Series*, 1999-
Walter Satterthwait, *Escapade*, 1995

4

MARIAN BABSON

Please Do Feed the Cat

(New York: St. Martin's Minotaur, 2004)

Story type: Amateur Detective; Humor
Subject(s): Animals/Cats; Authors and Writers; Small Town Life

Major character(s): Lorinda Lucas, Writer (mystery novelist), Detective—Amateur
Time period(s): 2000s
Locale(s): Brimful Coffers, England

Summary: Mystery novelist Lorinda Lucas returns to her cottage in the English village of Brimful Coffers after an arduous book tour of the U.S. She is shocked to find her neighbor's cat Roscoe in a half-starved condition and in her own kitchen, being helped by her two cats, Had-I and But-Known, to devour the food left in their bowls. Soon her neighbor and fellow writer Freddie, another member of the small enclave of mystery writers that has settled in the village, is over to fill her in on the details. Roscoe's owner, who writes thrillers under the name Macho Magee, has been taken over by a control freak named Cassie, a chick lit writer who has moved in with him and put Roscoe on a diet. Then there is a murder when a hit-and-run accident turns out to be deliberate. The author pokes gentle fun at writers, the publishing business, and village life, and adds comforting details about food and cats as well. Although her recent books aren't part of any of her series, they all involve cats and their relationships with their owners.

Where it's reviewed:
Publishers Weekly, October 25, 2004, page 32

Other books by the same author:
The Cat Who Wasn't a Dog, 2003
The Cat Next Door, 2002
To Catch a Cat, 2000
The Company of Cats, 1999
Canapes for the Kitties, 1997

Other books you might like:
Garrison Allen, *The Big Mike Series*, 1994-
Lilian Jackson Braun, *The Cat Who Series*, 1966-
Rita Mae Brown, *The Mrs. Murphy Series*, 1990-
Carole Nelson Douglas, *The Midnight Louie Series*, 1992-
Shirley Rousseau Murphy, *The Joe Grey Series*, 1996-

5

SANDRA BALZO

Uncommon Grounds

(Waterville, Maine: Five Star, 2004)

Story type: Amateur Detective; Humor
Subject(s): Small Town Life; Restaurants; Secrets
Major character(s): Maggy Thorsen, Restaurateur (coffee house owner), Detective—Amateur
Time period(s): 2000s
Locale(s): Brookhills, Wisconsin

Summary: Maggy Thorsen, in the process of divorcing her unfaithful husband, joins two of her close women friends in opening a gourmet coffee shop, Uncommon Grounds. On the very day they open their doors, one of the partners, Patricia Harper, is found dead, apparently electrocuted by the espresso machine. Local sheriff Jake Pavlik soon discovers that Patricia's death was no accident, which sets Maggy off in a parallel investigation to find out who would want to kill Patricia, and why. The small-town ambience is nicely done, and the author tells her story with an engaging sense of humor and some genuine insight into what it takes to run this type of small business. First mystery.

Where it's reviewed:
Mystery News, December 2004/January 2005, page 21
Publishers Weekly, October 18, 2004, page 51
Romantic Times, January 2005, page 82

Other books you might like:
Susan Wittig Albert, *The China Bayles Series*, 1992-
Laura Childs, *The Theodosia Browning Series*, 2001-
Cleo Coyle, *The Clare Cosi Series*, 2003-
Diane Mott Davidson, *Double Shot*, 2004
Linda French, *Coffee to Die For*, 1998

6

JO BANNISTER

The Depths of Solitude
(New York: St. Martin's Minotaur, 2004)

Story type: Psychological Suspense; Private Detective
Series: Brodie Farrell. Book 4
Subject(s): Small Town Life; Revenge; Friendship
Major character(s): Elspeth Brodie Farrell, Detective—Private; Jack Deacon, Police Officer (detective superintendent); Daniel Hood, Teacher
Time period(s): 2000s
Locale(s): Dimmock, England

Summary: Brodie Farrell has carved out a career for herself finding things for clients, running an agency called Looking for Something? She and her friend Daniel Hood have been on the outs for some time, but she's shocked to find his house up for sale and Daniel nowhere to be found. Further, his family seems remarkably unconcerned over his disappearance. Then Brodie becomes the target of someone who clearly is out to get her: her car is vandalized and her handbag stolen. She turns to another friend, Supt. Jack Deacon of the local police, for help. The author writes several other series, including an ensemble series of police procedurals featuring Frank Shapiro and his colleagues.

Where it's reviewed:
Library Journal, December 1, 2004, page 95
Publishers Weekly, November 8, 2004, page 39

Other books by the same author:
Reflections, 2003
True Witness, 2002
Echoes of Lies, 2001

Other books you might like:
Marjorie Eccles, *The Gil Mayo Series*, 1988-
Ann Granger, *The Alan Markby/Meredith Mitchell Series*, 1991-
Patricia Hall, *The Laura Ackroyd/Michael Thackeray Series*, 1993-
Susan B. Kelly, *The Allison Hope/Nick Trevellyan Series*, 1990-
Michelle Spring, *The Laura Principal Series*, 1994-

7

CYNTHIA BAXTER

Putting on the Dog
(New York: Bantam, 2004)

Story type: Amateur Detective
Series: Jessica Popper. Book 2
Subject(s): Animals/Dogs; Dog Shows; Wealth
Major character(s): Jessica Popper, Veterinarian, Detective—Amateur; Nick Burby, Detective—Private, Boyfriend (of Jessica)
Time period(s): 2000s
Locale(s): Bromptons, New York (the Hamptons, on Long Island)

Summary: Jessica is recruited to run the ''Ask the Vet'' booth for a week at a gala charity dog show on Long Island, accompanied, of course, by her one-eyed Dalmatian, Lou, and her tailless Westie, Max. No sooner does she arrive than a sneaky paparazzo is killed when a giant ice sculpture falls on him. The police write it off as accidental but suspicious Jess wonders if it might just be murder. Her boyfriend, private eye Nick Burby, shows up to keep her company, but he has a rival in a handsome movie star who's taken a fancy to Jess. Dog lovers will relish the antics of Jess' canine companions, who frequently steal the show, as well as the considerable doggie lore that's woven into the story.

Where it's reviewed:
Publishers Weekly, August 15, 2004, page 48
Romantic Times, October 2004, page 84

Other books by the same author:
Dead Canaries Don't Sing, 2004

Other books you might like:
Lydia Adamson, *The Dr. Deirdre Nightingale Series*, 1994-
Patricia Guiver, *The Delilah Doolittle Series*, 1997-
Barbara Moore, *The Gordon Christy Series*, 1983-1986
Lillian M. Roberts, *The Andi Pauling Series*, 1996-
Karen Ann Wilson, *The Samantha Holt Series*, 1994-

8

M.C. BEATON (Pseudonym of Marion Chesney)

The Deadly Dance
(New York: St. Martin's Minotaur, 2004)

Story type: Amateur Detective; Humor
Series: Agatha Raisin. Book 15
Subject(s): Small Town Life; Animals/Cats; Romance
Major character(s): Agatha Raisin, Detective—Private
Time period(s): 2000s
Locale(s): Carsley, England (Cotswolds)

Summary: Long a shameless snoop in the small Cotswolds village to which she retired after a career in public relations, Agatha has made it official: she has opened her own private detective agency. Her cases run more toward missing cats and joy-riding teenagers than serious crimes until a wealthy divorcee hires Agatha to investigate death threats made against her daughter. Even better, the case gives her a chance to work with her old friend, Sir Charles Fraith, upon whom the love-hungry Agatha develops a hopeless crush. Agatha is a truly original character, cranky yet kindhearted, overbearing yet vulnerable, and always comically in denial of her real feelings. The author writes another contemporary series about Hamish Macbeth, a village constable in the Scottish Highlands, and has, under her real name, begun a light-hearted Edwardian mystery series.

Where it's reviewed:
Library Journal, July 2004, page 64

Other books by the same author:
Agatha Raisin and the Case of the Curious Curate, 2003
Agatha Raisin and the Haunted House, 2003
Agatha Raisin and the Day the Floods Came, 2002
Agatha Raisin and the Love from Hell, 2001
Agatha Raisin and the Fairies of Fryfam, 2000

Other books you might like:
Robert Barnard, *A Little Local Murder*, 1983
Janie Bolitho, *The Rose Trevelyan Series*, 1997-
Simon Brett, *The Fethering Series*, 2000-
Hazel Holt, *The Mrs. Malory Series*, 1989-
Joyce Porter, *The Honorable Constance Ethel Morrison-Burke Series*, 1970-1979

9

CAROL LEA BENJAMIN

Fall Guy
(New York: William Morrow, 2004)

Story type: Private Detective
Series: Rachel Alexander & Dash. Book 7
Subject(s): Animals/Dogs; Suicide; City and Town Life
Major character(s): Rachel Alexander, Detective—Private, Animal Trainer (dogs); Dashiell, Animal (pit bull)
Time period(s): 2000s
Locale(s): New York, New York

Summary: Like many another New York writer, Benjamin has incorporated the aftermath of 9/11 in her latest book. Private detective Rachel Alexander met NYPD officer Timothy O'Fallon in a post-9/11 support group where she was doing pet therapy with her pit bull Dashiell. She exchanged only a few words with him at the time, so she is surprised beyond belief when he dies and names her executor of his will, even though he is survived by two siblings. As she investigates the situation, she comes to wonder if O'Fallon's death was really a suicide, as ruled by the cops, and if it's connected in any way to O'Fallon's roommate, a drifter he befriended whose own aunt was murdered. The author is an authority on dog training.

Where it's reviewed:
Booklist, September 1, 2004, page 67
Publishers Weekly, August 2, 2004, page 55
Romantic Times, September 2004, page 85

Other books by the same author:
The Long Good Boy, 2001
The Wrong Dog, 2000
Lady Vanishes, 1999
A Hell of a Dog, 1998
The Dog Who Knew Too Much, 1997

Other books you might like:
Laurien Berenson, *The Melanie Travis Series*, 1995-
Lawrence Block, *The Bernie Rhodenbarr Series*, 1977-
Melissa Cleary, *The Jackie Walsh Series*, 1992-
Susan Conant, *The Holly Winter Series*, 1989-
Virginia Lanier, *The Jo Beth Sidden Series*, 1995-2003

10

LAURIEN BERENSON

Jingle Bell Bark
(New York: Kensington, 2004)

Story type: Amateur Detective
Series: Melanie Travis. Book 11
Subject(s): Animals/Dogs; Christmas; Dog Shows
Major character(s): Melanie Travis, Teacher (special education), Detective—Amateur
Time period(s): 2000s
Locale(s): Stamford, Connecticut

Summary: In addition to her roles as a teacher and mother to eight-year-old Davey, Melanie trains and shows Standard Poodles, in particular her budding champion puppy, Eve. She's preparing for an upcoming show, getting ready for Christmas, dealing with her ex-husband, and trying to find time to spend with her fiance, when Henry Pruitt, Davey's school bus driver, dies under mysterious circumstances. He leaves behind two homeless, aging golden retrievers, whom Melanie takes to her Aunt Peg's kennel for safekeeping. Then Henry's heartless children show up, determined to sell the dogs on eBay, and Melanie learns some things about Henry's past that may lead her to his killer.

Where it's reviewed:
Publishers Weekly, August 9, 2004, page 235
Romantic Times, October 2004, page 87

Other books by the same author:
Best in Show, 2003
Hot Dog, 2002
Once Bitten, 2001
Unleashed, 2000
Hush Puppy, 1999

Other books you might like:
Carol Lea Benjamin, *The Rachel Alexander and Dash Series*, 1996-
Susan Conant, *The Holly Winter Series*, 1989-
Patricia Guiver, *The Delilah Doolittle Series*, 1997-
Virginia Lanier, *The Jo Beth Sidden Series*, 1995-2003
Leslie O'Kane, *The Allie Babcock Series*, 1998-

11

STEVE BERRY

The Romanov Prophecy
(New York: Ballantine, 2004)

Story type: Action/Adventure
Subject(s): Russians; Russian Empire; Political Thriller
Major character(s): Miles Lord, Lawyer; Akilina Petrovna, Entertainer (circus performer)

Time period(s): 2000s; 1910s (1916-1918)
Locale(s): Moscow, Russia

Summary: Miles Lord, an African-American lawyer from Atlanta, is tapped for an unusual mission. The people of post-Soviet Russia have voted to restore the monarchy after a series of weak governments. Miles, who speaks Russian fluently and is an expert on the country's history, is recruited by a shadowy group of Western businessmen to perform a background check on the tsarist candidate they favor, chosen from a group of distant relatives of Nicholas II. When Miles discovers evidence that two of Nicholas' children survived the massacre of the Romanovs by Lenin in 1918, he becomes the target of assassins and goes on the run with Akilina Petrovna, a Russian circus performer. Miles may even be "the Raven," prophesied by Rasputin to be the ultimate savior of Russia's royal house.

Where it's reviewed:
Library Journal, July 2004, page 66
Publishers Weekly, August 9, 2004, page 230

Other books by the same author:
The Amber Room, 2003

Other books you might like:
Boris Akunin, *The Winter Queen*, 2003
Tom Bradby, *The White Russian*, 2003
Brian Garfield, *The Romanov Succession*, 1974
Adam Hall, *Quiller Balalaika*, 2003
Robert Harris, *Archangel*, 1999

12

CLAUDIA BISHOP (Pseudonym of Mary Stanton)

Buried by Breakfast
(New York: Berkley, 2004)

Story type: Amateur Detective
Series: Hemlock Falls. Book 12
Subject(s): Hotels and Motels; Food; Small Town Life
Major character(s): Sarah "Quill" Quilliam, Innkeeper, Detective—Amateur; Margaret "Meg" Quilliam, Cook, Detective—Amateur
Time period(s): 2000s
Locale(s): Hemlock Falls, New York

Summary: The Inn at Hemlock Falls in upstate New York is uncharacteristically busy for March. The judge and jury on a high-profile trial are being sequestered there, and despite their relatively small numbers, they keep Meg and Quill on their toes with their demands. Then a group of Civil War buffs, calling themselves Friends of the Dead, start picketing a local developer who plans to relocate the town's Civil War cemetery so he can build a golf course on its site. Finally, the judge is murdered, and another murder follows. Recipe included.

Where it's reviewed:
Romantic Times, December 2004, page 86

Other books by the same author:
A Puree of Poison, 2003
Fried by Jury, 2003
Just Desserts, 2002
Marinade for Murder, 2000

A Steak in Murder, 1999

Other books you might like:
Mary Daheim, *The Judith McMonigle Flynn Series*, 1991-
Jean Hager, *The Tess Darcy Series*, 1994-2000
Parnell Hall, *Cozy*, 2001
Tamar Myers, *The Magdalena Yoder Series*, 1994-
Tim Myers, *The Lighthouse Inn Series*, 2001-

13

ETHAN BLACK (Pseudonym of Bob Reiss)

At Hell's Gate
(New York: Simon & Schuster, 2004)

Story type: Police Procedural; Psychological Suspense
Series: Conrad Voort. Book 5
Subject(s): Treasure; Salvage; Revenge
Major character(s): Conrad Voort, Detective—Homicide
Time period(s): 2000s
Locale(s): New York, New York

Summary: NYPD homicide detective Conrad Voort comes from wealth and privilege, the much-decorated scion of an old New York family that boasts three centuries of police officers and to whom Voort is utterly devoted. He and his fiancee, Camilla, are kayaking on the East River one day when they discover a corpse floating in the water. The deceased was searching for the wreck of a British supply ship that was sunk during the Revolutionary War, reportedly with a fortune in gold on board. Voort's investigation leads him to a ruthless group of foreign mercenaries who abduct him and scare him into leaving town temporarily with Camilla. However, a sense of duty to his job and his family, who are being threatened by his enemy, leads him to return incognito to New York to seek revenge. The author is a journalist who has also published mainstream fiction and nonfiction under his real name.

Where it's reviewed:
Booklist, June 1, 2004, page 1706
Publishers Weekly, August 2, 2004, page 52

Other books by the same author:
Dead for Life, 2003
All the Dead Were Strangers, 2001
Irresistible, 2000
The Broken Hearts Club, 1999

Other books you might like:
Michael Connelly, *The Harry Bosch Series*, 1992-
Jeffery Deaver, *The Lincoln Rhyme Series*, 1997-
Christopher Newman, *The Joe Dante Series*, 1986-
Ridley Pearson, *The Lou Boldt Series*, 1988-
John Sandford, *The Lucas Davenport Series*, 1989-

14

MICHAEL BLAINE

The Midnight Band of Mercy
(New York: Soho, 2004)

Story type: Historical/Victorian
Subject(s): Ethics; Journalism; Social Conditions

Major character(s): Max Greengrass, Detective—Amateur, Journalist (newspaper reporter)
Time period(s): 1890s (1893)
Locale(s): New York, New York

Summary: New York City in 1893 is not a pretty place to live, full of suffering, disease, and corruption, but it's his life blood for hard-drinking Max Greengrass, a stringer—or space rater—for the *New York Herald*. Max, a former boxer and the son of Jewish immigrants who changed their name to fit in, has lost touch with his faith and ethnicity, and spends his days scrambling for stories in hopes of eventually being hired as a reporter with a steady paycheck. He gets the break he's always dreamed of when he runs across four dead cats arranged neatly in front of a Greenwich Village brothel and discovers they are among thousands of strays being chloroformed by a mysterious group of well-bred women who call themselves the Midnight Band of Mercy. Their strange story turns into something much larger and transforms the cynical Max into a bit of a crusading muckraker when he learns its ultimate scope. He eventually uncovers scandals involving a heartless church which owns slums all over the city, baby farming, a primitive form of eugenics, insurance fraud, crooked lawyers and cops, murder, and much more, all of which put his own life in danger. First mystery.

Where it's reviewed:
Booklist, September 1, 2004, page 54
Library Journal, September 1, 2004, page 136
New York Times Book Review, September 26, 2004, page 24
Publishers Weekly, August 2, 2004, page 51

Other books by the same author:
The Desperate Season, 1999 (mainstream fiction)

Other books you might like:
Caleb Carr, *The Alienist*, 1994
David Liss, *A Spectacle of Corruption*, 2004
Maan Meyers, *The House on Mulberry Street*, 1996
Troy Soos, *The Marshall Webb Series*, 2001-
Will Thomas, *Some Danger Involved*, 2004

15

NERO BLANC (Pseudonym of Cordelia Frances Biddle and Steve Zettler)

Wrapped Up in Crosswords
(New York: Berkley, 2004)

Story type: Amateur Detective; Private Detective
Series: Belle Graham. Book 9
Subject(s): Animals/Dogs; Games; Christmas
Major character(s): Belle Graham, Editor (crossword puzzles), Detective—Amateur; Rosco Polycrates, Detective—Private, Spouse (of Belle)
Time period(s): 2000s
Locale(s): Newcastle, Massachusetts

Summary: It's Christmas and Rosco and two of his cop friends are dressed up in Santa Claus suits, collecting children's gifts from local merchants. They're pulled over by the police, who don't recognize them and suspect them to be three convicts recently escaped from a nearby Boston prison. In fact, the criminals are nearby, stocking up at a gun shop for their next adventure. Two of them are captured, but the third remains at large until he crashes a Christmas party where Belle, Rosco, and their two dogs are in attendance, and he's captured by one of the dogs. This time the crossword puzzles scattered throughout are used more as messages between lovebirds Belle and Rosco, and there's a new feature: dogs who talk to each other about their owners.

Where it's reviewed:
Publishers Weekly, October 25, 2004, page 32
Romantic Times, January 2005, page 87

Other books by the same author:
Anatomy of a Crossword, 2004
A Crossworder's Gift, 2003
Corpus de Crossword, 2003
A Crossword to Die For, 2002
A Crossworder's Holiday, 2002 (short stories)

Other books you might like:
Helen Chappell, *The Holly and Sam Westcott Series*, 1996-
Parnell Hall, *The Puzzle Lady Series*, 1999-
David Handler, *The Berger & Mitry Series*, 2001-
Carolyn Hart, *The Death on Demand Series*, 1987-
Patricia Moyes, *A Six-Letter Word for Death*, 1983

16

ELEANOR TAYLOR BLAND

A Cold and Silent Dying
(New York: St. Martin's Minotaur, 2004)

Story type: Police Procedural
Series: Marti MacAlister. Book 12
Subject(s): African Americans; Mothers and Daughters; Serial Killers
Major character(s): Marti MacAlister, Detective—Homicide; Matthew "Vic" Jessenovik, Detective—Homicide; Gail Nicholson, Police Officer (lieutenant)
Time period(s): 2000s
Locale(s): Lincoln Prairie, Illinois (suburb of Chicago)

Summary: Black former Chicago cop Marti MacAlister finds herself at odds with her new boss, Lt. Gail Nicholson, an ambitious woman who is also African American and who regards Marti as a potential competitor who has been successful purely by chance. Marti's best friend, Sharon, is having difficulty dealing with her teenage daughter, and then her psychopathic ex-husband turns up again, gunning for both Sharon and Marti. When a homeless woman dies under suspicious circumstances, Lt. Nicholson is inclined to ignore it, but Marti senses that the woman's death could be the work of a serial killer and takes up the investigation, even though it could cost her her job.

Where it's reviewed:
Library Journal, December 1, 2004, page 94
Publishers Weekly, November 8, 2004, page 38

Other books by the same author:
Fatal Remains, 2003
Windy City Dying, 2002
Whispers in the Dark, 2001
Scream in Silence, 2000
Tell No Tales, 1999

Other books you might like:
Nora DeLoach, *The Candi Covington Series*, 1997-2000
Terris McMahon Grimes, *The Theresa Galloway Series*, 1996-
Judith Smith-Levine, *The Starletta Duvall Series*, 1996-
Valerie Wilson Wesley, *The Tamara Hayle Series*, 1994-
Paula L. Woods, *The Charlotte Justice Series*, 1999-

17

MEREDITH BLEVINS

The Vanished Priestess

(New York: Forge, 2004)

Story type: Amateur Detective; Humor
Series: Annie Szabo. Book 2
Subject(s): Gypsies; Family; Circus
Major character(s): Annie Szabo, Journalist, Widow(er); Mina Szabo, Gypsy
Time period(s): 2000s
Locale(s): Sonoma County, California

Summary: Annie married a handsome young Gypsy who left her a young widow when he died in a motorcycle accident. He also left her his eccentric family, especially his strong-willed mother Mina, a fortune-teller, and his crazy alcoholic sister Capri, who have become a permanent part of her life. Now Mina has moved her trailer onto Annie's property, at the same time that Annie's close friend and neighbor, Margo Spanger, dies and her partner Lili goes missing. Margo had used her considerable wealth to fund a New Age circus which in turn supported a women's shelter, where Annie's own daughter has taken up residence. With Margo's death the circus and the shelter both threaten to fall apart, and Annie is determined to get to the bottom of things. Filled with the same energy and colorful characters as its predecessor, this mystery is a celebration of family, love, laughter, craziness, and Gypsy life.

Where it's reviewed:
Library Journal, October 1, 2004, page 62
Romantic Times, October 2004, page 87

Other books by the same author:
The Hummingbird Wizard, 2003

Other books you might like:
Rosemary Aubert, *The Ellis Portal Series*, 1997-
Joe Gores, *32 Cadillacs*, 1992
Pip Granger, *Not All Tarts Are Apple*, 2002
Edward D. Hoch, *The Iron Angel*, 2003
  short stories
Martin Cruz Smith, *The Roman Grey Series*, 1971-1972

18

KATE BORDEN (Pseudonym of Kate Grilley)

Death of a Trickster

(New York: Berkley, 2004)

Story type: Amateur Detective
Series: Cobb's Landing. Book 2
Subject(s): Small Town Life; Halloween

Major character(s): Peggy Turner, Political Figure (town mayor), Detective—Amateur
Time period(s): 2000s
Locale(s): Cobb's Landing, New England

Summary: Hardware store owner and struggling single mom Peggy Turner took over the job of mayor of Cobb's Landing when her husband died some years ago. It's a quaint, historic village with serious financial problems, which are beginning to go away since the town has been turned into a tourist attraction, a sort of New England version of Williamsburg. The annual pumpkin float race is barely under way when Luigi Alsop, one of the town elders, disappears. Then the police chief's son is found dead, and Peggy sets out to solve the mystery of what happened. Under her real name, the author writes a series set in the Caribbean featuring radio station manager Kelly Ryan.

Other books by the same author:
Death of a Tart, 2004

Other books you might like:
Donna Andrews, *Revenge of the Wrought Iron Flamingos*, 2001
Laura Childs, *The Theodosia Browning Series*, 2001-
Sarah Graves, *The Jacobia Tiptree Series*, 1998-
Leslie Meier, *The Lucy Stone Series*, 1993-
Tim Myers, *The Harrison Black Series*, 2004-

19

C.J. BOX

Trophy Hunt

(New York: Putnam, 2004)

Story type: Action/Adventure; Psychological Suspense
Series: Joe Pickett. Book 4
Subject(s): American West; Nature; Wilderness
Major character(s): Joe Pickett, Game Warden
Time period(s): 2000s
Locale(s): Twelve Sleep County, Wyoming

Summary: Cattle, moose, and human corpses are being discovered in the Wyoming landscape, all eerily mutilated and giving rise to speculation by the locals that alien visitors from space are responsible. Crop circles and other weird phenomena follow, until Joe Pickett, who is definitely not a believer in otherworldly forces, reluctantly interviews Cleve Garrett, a professed expert on paranormal events. Meanwhile, Joe continues to gather his own evidence and clues from human witnesses, including his own family and a developmentally disabled fisherman. Like the other books in this impressive series, it's strongly grounded in the natural landscape of the American West.

Where it's reviewed:
Booklist, May 1, 2004, page 1502
Mystery News, August/September 2004, page 14
People Weekly, July 19, 2004, page 46
Publishers Weekly, June 21, 2004, page 46

Other books by the same author:
Winterkill, 2003
Savage Run, 2002
Open Season, 2001

Other books you might like:
Gregory Bean, *The Harry Starbranch Series*, 1995-
Peter Bowen, *The Gabriel Du Pre Series*, 1994-
James D. Doss, *The Shaman Laughs*, 1995
Michael McGarrity, *The Kevin Kerney Series*, 1996-
Clinton McKinzie, *The Edge of Justice*, 2002

20

GERRY BOYLE

Home Body

(New York: Berkley, 2004)

Story type: Amateur Detective
Series: Jack McMorrow. Book 8
Subject(s): Country Life; Adolescence; Runaways
Major character(s): Jack McMorrow, Journalist (freelance reporter), Detective—Amateur; Roxanne Masterson, Social Worker
Time period(s): 2000s
Locale(s): Prosperity, Maine; Portland, Maine

Summary: Jack and his pregnant girlfriend Roxanne are in Portland for the day when they save a runaway teenage boy from a savage beating by a street gang. They try to get him to a hospital, but the boy—known only as Rocky—escapes. The shelter where he'd been staying reports that there have been no inquiries about him, and soon the reporter in Jack is trying to find out what Rocky's story is. Although they keep running into Rocky, it's clear he doesn't want to be helped, and when Jack finally does find his family, Rocky's stepfather accuses him of molesting the boy.

Where it's reviewed:
Booklist, May 15, 2004, page 1500
Publishers Weekly, May 31, 2004, page 55

Other books by the same author:
Pretty Dead, 2003
Cover Story, 2000
Borderline, 1998
Potshot, 1997
Lifeline, 1996

Other books you might like:
Brendan DuBois, *The Lewis Cole Series*, 1994-
Jeremiah Healy, *The John Francis Cuddy Series*, 1984-
William Landay, *Mission Flats*, 2003
Archer Mayor, *The Joe Gunther Series*, 1988-
William G. Tapply, *The Brady Coyne Series*, 1984-

21

SIMON BRETT

The Hanging in the Hotel

(New York: Berkley, 2004)

Story type: Amateur Detective; Humor
Series: Fethering. Book 5
Subject(s): Small Town Life; Hotels and Motels; Friendship
Major character(s): Carole Seddon, Civil Servant (retired), Detective—Amateur; Jude Nichol, Friend, Detective—Amateur

Time period(s): 2000s
Locale(s): Fethering, England (West Sussex)

Summary: Starchy Carole Seddon, retired from the Home Office, is still settling into life in her adopted village of Fethering. She's become friends with her free-wheeling New Age neighbor Jude, who is helping out a friend by waitressing at the Hopwicke Country House Hotel, an elegant converted Edwardian mansion. Business at the Hopwicke has declined drastically since 9/11, and owner Suzy Longthorne has had to downgrade her guest list to include a local men's club known for their indiscreet partying. When one of them is found hanged in his room, Jude and Carole disbelieve the official verdict of suicide and get to work sleuthing. There's plenty of wry social commentary worked into the complicated plot of this sparkling mystery of manners. The author has also written other series featuring the perpetually out-of-work London-based actor Charles Paris and the resourceful widow Mrs. Pargeter, but he has really hit his stride with the Fethering mysteries.

Where it's reviewed:
Booklist, August 2004, page 1823
Mystery News, October/November 2004, page 21
Publishers Weekly, July 19, 2004, page 148

Other books by the same author:
Murder in the Museum, 2003
The Torso in the Town, 2002
Death on the Downs, 2001
The Body on the Beach, 2000

Other books you might like:
Robert Barnard, *A Little Local Murder*, 1983
M.C. Beaton, *The Agatha Raisin Series*, 1992-
Hazel Holt, *The Mrs. Malory Series*, 1989-
Marianne Macdonald, *Blood Lies*, 2002
Colin Watson, *The Flaxborough Series*, 1960-1982

22

EMILY BRIGHTWELL (Pseudonym of Cheryl Arguile)

Mrs. Jeffries Stalks the Hunter

(New York: Berkley, 2004)

Story type: Historical/Victorian
Series: Mrs. Jeffries. Book 19
Subject(s): Victorian Period; Servants; Social Classes
Major character(s): Mrs. Jeffries, Housekeeper, Widow(er); Gerald Witherspoon, Police Officer (inspector)
Time period(s): 1870s
Locale(s): London, England

Summary: The premise of this long-running series of light historicals is that Inspector Witherspoon's successes at Scotland Yard can be largely attributed to the sleuthing skills of his shrewd housekeeper Mrs. Jeffries. A policeman's widow, she solves the inspector's cases while letting him think he actually did. This time Sir Edmund Leggett, about to make a profitable marriage that he hopes will rid him of debt, is being stalked by a young woman whose attentions he finds both irritating and flattering. When he's murdered at his own engagement party, suspicion falls upon his stalker, who disappears. Once again Witherspoon ''solves'' the case, thanks to the intrepid Mrs. Jeffries.

Other books by the same author:
Mrs. Jeffries Sweeps the Chimney, 2004
Mrs. Jeffries Pleads Her Case, 2003
Mrs. Jeffries Pinches the Post, 2001
Mrs. Jeffries Weeds the Plot, 2000
Mrs. Jeffries Rocks the Boat, 1999

Other books you might like:
Martin Davies, *Mrs. Hudson and the Spirits' Curse*, 2004
Kate Kingsbury, *The Pennyfoot Hotel Series*, 1993-
Robin Paige, *The Kathryn Ardleigh Series*, 1994-
Paula Paul, *The Alexandra Gladstone Series*, 2002-
Anne Perry, *The Thomas and Charlotte Pitt Series*, 1979-

23

KEN BRUEN

Blitz
(New York: St. Martin's Press, 2004)

Story type: Police Procedural
Series: Brant. Book 4
Subject(s): Crime and Criminals; Homosexuality/Lesbianism; Law Enforcement
Major character(s): Brant, Police Officer (detective sergeant); Roberts, Police Officer (chief inspector); Falls, Police Officer (woman police constable)
Time period(s): 2000s
Locale(s): London, England

Summary: The title refers to the nickname of a psychopath who worships serial killers and decides to put himself in the history books by murdering eight cops. His final target is Brant, a thuggish cop who once roughed him up. Brant is crude and cruel and so despised by his fellow coppers at his South East London station that they readily welcome a gay officer into the precinct when he announces that he'd draw the line at having sex with Brant. If there's a good side to Brant— and you have to dig deep to find it—it's that he supports his fellow cops, including the gay newcomer, his colleague Inspector Roberts, and black female officer Falls, even though he's a self-proclaimed bigot. Near burnout, he's teetering on an edge from which even he doesn't dare glance down. In a world where retribution often has to take the place of justice, Brant is a necessary evil, a fact that his fellow cops eventually come to not only accept but to appreciate and perhaps even emulate. The first three short novels in this quartet were collected in *The White Trilogy*. The author also writes a series about alcoholic ex-Guard turned Galway private detective, Jack Taylor, as well as several equally gritty postmodern stand-alones not yet published in the U.S.

Where it's reviewed:
Library Journal, June 1, 2004, page 197
Publishers Weekly, May 31, 2004, page 55

Other books by the same author:
The Coming of the Tinkers, 2004 (Jack Taylor series)
The Guards, 2003 (Jack Taylor series)
The Magdalen Martyrs, 2003 (published only in England)

The White Trilogy, 2003 (contains *The McDead* (2000), *Taming the Alien* (1999), and *A White Arrest* (1998))
London Boulevard, 2002 (published only in England)

Other books you might like:
John Harvey, *The Charlie Resnick Series*, 1989-1998
Bill James, *The Harpur and Iles Series*, 1985-
Quintin Jardine, *The Robert Skinner Series*, 1993-
Val McDermid, *The Tony Hill/Carol Jordan Series*, 1995-
Ian Rankin, *The John Rebus Series*, 1987-

24

FIONA BUCKLEY (Pseudonym of Valerie Anand)

The Siren Queen
(New York: Scribner, 2004)

Story type: Historical/Elizabethan
Series: Ursula Blanchard. Book 8
Subject(s): Kings, Queens, Rulers, etc.; Espionage; History
Major character(s): Ursula Blanchard, Spy, Widow(er)
Time period(s): 16th century (1569)
Locale(s): Yorkshire, England

Summary: An illegitimate daughter of Henry VIII, Ursula is occasionally employed as a spy by her half-sister, Queen Elizabeth I. Ursula agree to go to London with her family when the Duke of Norfolk urges her to meet a potential husband for Meg, her daughter who will soon be 14. However, Ursula is dismayed to learn that the duke and an Italian banker, Roberto Ridolfi, may be hatching a secret plot against Elizabeth. She resumes her familiar role as sleuth and gains access to the correspondence between the duke and Ridolfi, which confirms her suspicions that they are plotting to place Mary, Queen of Scots on the throne. Meanwhile, Meg and her suitor, Edmund Dean, have taken a fancy to each other, but their romance sets off a potentially disastrous chain of events, which tests Ursula's loyalty to the queen to its utmost.

Where it's reviewed:
Booklist, November 1, 2004, page 466
Library Journal, November 1, 2004, page 62
Mystery News, December 2004/January 2005, page 18
Publishers Weekly, October 4, 2004, page 73

Other books by the same author:
The Fugitive Queen, 2003
A Pawn for a Queen, 2002
Queen of Ambition, 2001
Queen's Ransom, 2000
To Ruin a Queen, 2000

Other books you might like:
Judith Cook, *The Slicing Edge of Death*, 1993
P.C. Doherty, *The Prince Lost to Time*, 1995
Kathy Lynn Emerson, *The Susanna, Lady Appleton Series*, 1997-
Karen Harper, *The Elizabeth I Series*, 1999-
Edward Marston, *The Queen's Head*, 1988

25

ALAFAIR BURKE

Missing Justice

(New York: Holt, 2004)

Story type: Legal
Series: Samantha Kincaid. Book 2
Subject(s): Missing Persons; Law; Politics
Major character(s): Samantha Kincaid, Lawyer (deputy district attorney)
Time period(s): 2000s
Locale(s): Portland, Oregon

Summary: When a city judge goes missing and then is found dead near a construction site, her husband, a prominent surgeon who might have been motivated by the fact his wife was having an affair, is a possible suspect. So too is a poor black drug addict whose plea to gain custody of his children was up before the judge just before she died. Samantha, newly promoted to the department's serious crimes unit, must sort out these suspects to get to the truth, even if it means exposing high-level corruption that her superiors might not welcome. The author is a former deputy district attorney in Portland.

Where it's reviewed:
Booklist, May 1, 2004, page 1502
Deadly Pleasures, Summer/Fall 2004, page 41
Library Journal, May 15, 2004, page 119
Mystery News, June/July 2004, page 19
Publishers Weekly, May 31, 2004, page 55

Other books by the same author:
Judgment Calls, 2003

Other books you might like:
Linda Fairstein, *The Alexandra Cooper Series*, 1996-
Jonnie Jacobs, *The Kali O'Brien Series*, 1996-
Perri O'Shaughnessy, *The Nina Reilly Series*, 1995-
Lisa Scottoline, *The Rosato & Associates Series*, 1993-
Kate Wilhelm, *The Barbara Holloway Series*, 1991-

26

LESLIE CAINE (Pseudonym of Leslie O'Kane)

Death by Inferior Design

(New York: Dell, 2004)

Story type: Amateur Detective; Humor
Series: Erin Gilbert. Book 1
Subject(s): Competition; Adoption
Major character(s): Erin Gilbert, Interior Decorator, Detective—Amateur; Steve Sullivan, Interior Decorator
Time period(s): 2000s
Locale(s): Crestview, Colorado (thinly disguised Boulder)

Summary: When interior designer Erin Gilbert shows up to do a surprise makeover on a client's bedroom while his wife is away, she discovers that a local magazine editor has set up a competition between her and Steve Sullivan. Steve, her chief rival, is doing a similar makeover on a room in a neighbor's house. Both will get coverage in the magazine, but the winner will be hired to do an expensive family room makeover in the editor's own house. Erin's prepared to make the best of it, but the discovery of her own baby picture hidden in the paneling of the room she's about to redo sends her off on a quest for her birth parents, whom she figures must be connected with the client. Then murder strikes, and Erin begins to realize that her own life is in danger. Numerous decorating tips are mixed into the story. Under her own name, the author has written equally light-hearted series featuring Allie Babcock, a Boulder dog psychologist, and Mollie Masters, a greeting card designer living in an upstate New York suburb. First mystery under this pseudonym.

Where it's reviewed:
Publishers Weekly, September 13, 2004, page 64
Romantic Times, November 2004, page 88

Other books you might like:
Kate Collins, *Mum's the Word*, 2004
Jerrilyn Farmer, *The Madeline Bean Series*, 1998-
Sarah Graves, *The Jacobia Tiptree Series*, 1998-
Maddy Hunter, *The Emily Andrew Series*, 2003-
Dean James, *Decorated to Death*, 2004

27

MARION CHESNEY

Hasty Death

(New York: St. Martin's Minotaur, 2004)

Story type: Historical/Edwardian; Traditional
Series: Lady Rose Summer. Book 2
Subject(s): Social Classes; Women's Rights
Major character(s): Captain Harry Cathcart, Detective—Private; Lady Rose Summer, Clerk, Detective—Amateur
Time period(s): 1900s
Locale(s): London, England

Summary: Lady Rose Summer has determined to throw off the shackles of her privileged upbringing and join the working class. After becoming a proficient typist and training her lady's maid, Daisy, to become one also, she sets off for London with Daisy where the two of them take a furnished room and find jobs in an office. Their spartan existence is nowhere near as satisfying as Rose had expected, but her working days are cut short when an acquaintance is murdered and she is required to reenter high society to solve the crime. She's helped by dashing Captain Harry Cathcart, as well as Superintendent Kerridge of Scotland Yard. The author is better known to mystery readers as M.C. Beaton, author of the Hamish Macbeth and Agatha Raisin series.

Where it's reviewed:
Deadly Pleasures, Summer/Fall 2004, page 45
Library Journal, July 2004, page 64
Publishers Weekly, June 28, 2004, page 34
Romantic Times, September 2004, page 90

Other books by the same author:
Snobbery with Violence, 2003

Other books you might like:
Clare Curzon, *Guilty Knowledge*, 2000
Dianne Day, *The Fremont Jones Series*, 1995-
Robert Goddard, *Past Caring*, 1986
Kate Kingsbury, *The Pennyfoot Hotel Series*, 1993-
Gillian Linscott, *Dead Man Rising*, 2002

28

LAURA CHILDS (Pseudonym of Gerry Schmitt)

Bound for Murder

(New York: Berkley, 2004)

Story type: Amateur Detective
Series: Carmela Bertrand. Book 3
Subject(s): Crafts; Stores, Retail; Weddings
Major character(s): Carmela Bertrand, Store Owner (scrapbooking shop), Detective—Amateur
Time period(s): 2000s
Locale(s): New Orleans, Louisiana

Summary: After Carmela's impetuous husband of one year walked out of their house in New Orleans' Garden District and never came back, she opened up a small scrapbooking shop in the French Quarter and put everything she had into making it a success. One night she's assembling the place settings for a pre-wedding party at the elegant Bon Tiempe restaurant when she discovers the groom's body with a butcher knife stuck in his shoulder. After the grief-stricken bride asks her to investigate, she puts her business on hold and gets to work. Recipes from the restaurant are included. The author also writes the Theodosia Browning tea-shop series set in historic Charleston, South Carolina.

Where it's reviewed:
Mystery News, December 2004/January 2005, page 28
Romantic Times, January 2005, page 87

Other books by the same author:
Photo Finish, 2004
Keepsake Crimes, 2002

Other books you might like:
Susan Wittig Albert, *The China Bayles Series*, 1992-
Monica Ferris, *The Betsy Devonshire Series*, 1999-
Janis Harrison, *The Bretta Solomon Series*, 1999-
Carolyn Hart, *The Death on Demand Series*, 1987-
Tamar Myers, *The Abigail Timberlake Series*, 1996-

29

LAURA CHILDS (Pseudonym of Gerry Schmitt)

The Jasmine Moon Murder

(New York: Berkley, 2004)

Story type: Amateur Detective
Series: Theodosia Browning. Book 5
Subject(s): American South; Restaurants; Food
Major character(s): Theodosia Browning, Store Owner (tea shop), Detective—Amateur
Time period(s): 2000s
Locale(s): Charleston, South Carolina

Summary: Theo loves her life as owner of the Indigo Tea Shop in Charleston's picturesque historic district, and as hard as she works, she still likes to contribute some of her time to the city's worthy causes. This time she and her staff are serving up tea and treats at the first Ghost Crawl at Charleston's Jasmine Cemetery, but the event is interrupted when a re-search cardiologist (who is also the uncle of Theo's boyfriend Jory) dies suddenly. Although she promises the investigating

officer that she won't meddle in murder again, Theo can't refuse when Jory begs her to step in. Lots of tea lore and tempting recipes are included. The author also writes a series of scrapbooking mysteries set in New Orleans.

Where it's reviewed:
Deadly Pleasures, Summer/Fall 2004, page 50
Library Journal, September 1, 2004, page 121
Mystery News, August/September 2004, page 29
Publishers Weekly, August 23, 2004, page 40
Romantic Times, September 2004, page 91

Other books by the same author:
Shades of Earl Grey, 2003
The English Breakfast Murder, 2003
Gunpowder Green, 2002
Death by Darjeeling, 2001

Other books you might like:
Susan Wittig Albert, *The China Bayles Series*, 1992-
Sandra Balzo, *Uncommon Grounds*, 2004
Cleo Coyle, *The Clare Cosi Series*, 2003-
Yasmine Galenorn, *Ghost of a Chance*, 2003
Tamar Myers, *The Abigail Timberlake Series*, 1996-

30

JILL CHURCHILL (Pseudonym of Janice Young Brooks)

A Midsummer Night's Scream

(New York: William Morrow, 2004)

Story type: Amateur Detective; Humor
Series: Jane Jeffry. Book 15
Subject(s): Actors and Actresses; Theater; Friendship
Major character(s): Jane Jeffry, Widow(er), Detective—Amateur; Shelley Nowack, Friend (of Jane), Detective—Amateur
Time period(s): 2000s
Locale(s): Chicago, Illinois (suburban Chicago)

Summary: Jane Jeffry is a widow whose late husband had the consideration to get himself killed before he could carry out his plans to run off with another woman, leaving Jane with their three children, now mostly grown. Jane's best friend, Shelley Nowack, has bought an old theater with her husband and donated it to the drama department of the local university. Even though Jane is busy working on a novel and learning needlepoint, she agrees to help Shelley judge the caterers she's auditioning for her husband's business and to supply snacks for the theater volunteers. When a cast member is found dead, Jane and Shelley disagree with the police verdict that it was an accident and turn sleuths again to find the killer. The author also writes the equally cozy Grace and Favor historical series about Lily and Robert Brewster, once-wealthy siblings trying to scrape by during the Depression.

Where it's reviewed:
Booklist, November 15, 2004, page 564
Publishers Weekly, October 18, 2004, page 51

Other books by the same author:
Bell, Book and Scandal, 2003
The House of Seven Mabels, 2002
Mulch Ado about Nothing, 2000
A Groom with a View, 1999

The Merchant of Menace, 1998

Other books you might like:
Diane Mott Davidson, *The Goldy Bear Schulz Series*, 1990-
Monica Ferris, *Crewel Death*, 1990
Judy Fitzwater, *Dying to Get Published*, 1998
Joan Hess, *A Conventional Corpse*, 2000
Valerie Wolzien, *The Susan Henshaw Series*, 1987-

31

MARY HIGGINS CLARK
CAROL HIGGINS CLARK, Co-Author

The Christmas Thief
(New York: Simon & Schuster, 2004)

Story type: Amateur Detective
Series: Christmas. Book 3
Subject(s): Christmas; Humor; Country Life
Major character(s): Alvirah Meehan, Detective—Amateur; Regan Reilly, Detective—Private
Time period(s): 2000s
Locale(s): Stowe, Vermont

Summary: This collaborative holiday lagniappe from this well-known mother and daughter concerns the theft of the Rockefeller Center Christmas tree before it can be cut down and transported to Manhattan. It seems the towering blue spruce had been picked over 12 years ago as the hiding place for a stash of diamonds bought by con artist Packy Noonan with the proceeds of a scam that sent him to prison—but not before he managed to conceal his loot. Now he's out and determined to retrieve it. Alvirah and Willy Meehan are in Stowe for the weekend, along with Regan Reilly, her NYPD homicide cop fiance Jack, Regan's parents, and Opal Fogarty, one of Packy's victims. They all join forces to track down the tree thief. Separately, Mary Higgins Clark is the author of numerous bestselling novels of suspense and the creator of lottery winner Alvirah Meehan, and daughter Carol is the author of the Regan Reilly series.

Where it's reviewed:
Entertainment Weekly, December 10, 2004, page 98
People Weekly, December 6, 2004, page 58
Publishers Weekly, October 25, 2004, page 31

Other books by the same author:
He Sees You When You're Sleeping, 2001
Deck the Halls, 2000

Other books you might like:
Nero Blanc, *A Crossworder's Gift*, 2003
Jane Haddam, *Not a Creature Was Stirring*, 1990
Lee Harris, *The Christmas Night Murder*, 1994
Leslie Meier, *Mail-Order Murder*, 1993
    also published as *Mistletoe Murder*
Valerie Wolzien, *Tis the Season to Be Murdered*, 1994

32

BARBARA CLEVERLY

The Damascened Blade
(New York: Carroll & Graf, 2004)

Story type: Historical
Series: Joe Sandilands. Book 3
Subject(s): Identity, Concealed; Blackmail; Serial Killers
Major character(s): Joe Sandilands, Police Officer (Scotland Yard commander)
Time period(s): 1920s (1922)
Locale(s): India

Summary: Commander Joe Sandilands of Scotland Yard is still in India, this time visiting his old army friend James Lindsay in a remote outpost of the empire near the Afghan border. To his dismay, he's assigned to look after Lily Coblenz, a headstrong American heiress who is determined to see the real India regardless of the dangers. And dangers there are, as the peace with Afghanistan is broken, a Pathan prince dies, and Joe and James are given exactly a week to find and execute the prince's killer before there's an all-out war. As well-plotted as a Golden Age puzzler, this third book in the series is also peopled with convincing characters of various nationalities and bursting with atmosphere and period detail.

Where it's reviewed:
Booklist, July 2004, page 1823
Library Journal, July 2004, page 63
New York Times Book Review, August 8, 2004, page 15
Publishers Weekly, June 14, 2004, page 46

Other books by the same author:
Ragtime in Simla, 2002
The Last Kashmiri Rose, 2001

Other books you might like:
Rennie Airth, *River of Darkness*, 1999
H.R.F. Keating, *The Murder of the Maharajah*, 1980
Laurie R. King, *The Game*, 2004
Michael Pearce, *The Mamur Zapt Series*, 1988-
Charles Todd, *The Ian Rutledge Series*, 1996-

33

MARGARET COEL

Wife of Moon
(New York: Berkley, 2004)

Story type: Amateur Detective
Series: Father John O'Malley/Vicky Holden. Book 10
Subject(s): Indian Reservations; American West; Photography
Major character(s): Father John O'Malley, Religious (priest), Detective—Amateur; Vicky Holden, Lawyer, Indian (Arapaho); Adam Lone Eagle, Lawyer, Indian (Arapaho)
Time period(s): 2000s; 1900s (1907)
Locale(s): Wind River Reservation, Wyoming

Summary: This historian-turned-author is always at her best when she explores the history of the Arapaho people, as she does in this story which goes back to the arrival of photographer Edward S. Curtis on the Wind River Reservation in 1907. In an attempt to document a vanishing way of life,

Curtis staged a realistic attack on a village, but it went awry when the chief's daughter was murdered and her killer was never found. Now the photographs are on display at the museum on the mission reservation, and history seems to repeat itself when a descendant of the same tribal chief is murdered and the museum curator disappears. Father John and Vicky Holden are drawn into the mystery, while he is preparing for a visit to his mission from a potential presidential candidate and Vicky is being romanced by fellow attorney Adam Lone Eagle.

Where it's reviewed:
Booklist, September 1, 2004, page 68
Library Journal, September 1, 2004, page 122
Publishers Weekly, August 9, 2004, page 234
Romantic Times, September 2004, page 85

Other books by the same author:
Killing Raven, 2003
The Shadow Dancer, 2002
The Thunder Keeper, 2001
The Spirit Woman, 2000
The Lost Bird, 1999

Other books you might like:
James D. Doss, *The Shaman Series*, 1994-
Jean Hager, *The Molly Bearpaw Series*, 1992-
Tony Hillerman, *The Joe Leaphorn/Jim Chee Series*, 1970-
Mardi Oakley Medawar, *Murder on the Red Cliff Rez*, 2002
Aimee Thurlo, *The Ella Clah Series*, 1995-
    David Thurlo, co-author

34

NANCY J. COHEN

Died Blonde

(New York: Kensington, 2004)

Story type: Amateur Detective; Humor
Series: Marla Shore. Book 6
Subject(s): Hair; Psychic Powers; Romance
Major character(s): Marla Shore, Hairdresser, Detective—Amateur; Dalton Vail, Detective—Homicide
Time period(s): 2000s
Locale(s): Palm Haven, Florida

Summary: When Marla left the salon run by Carolyn Sutton to open her own business, her former boss never forgave her and the women became archrivals, especially as Marla's clients left Hairstyle Heaven with her. Now Carolyn is dead, and it's Marla who finds the body. Naturally she goes to work trying to find out who killed the woman, who had many enemies. She's encouraged by psychic Wilda Cleaver, who tells Marla that Carolyn's spirit is imploring her to solve the murder. Also, finally, Marla and her longtime boyfriend, homicide cop Dalton Veil, become officially engaged.

Where it's reviewed:
Library Journal, October 1, 2004, page 64
Publishers Weekly, November 8, 2004, page 39
Romantic Times, December 2004, page 89

Other books by the same author:
Highlights to Heaven, 2003
Body Wave, 2002

Murder by Manicure, 2001
Hair Raiser, 2000
Permed to Death, 1999

Other books you might like:
Jennifer Apodaca, *The Samantha Shaw Series*, 2002-
Nancy Bartholomew, *The Sierra Lavatoni Series*, 1998-
Sophie Dunbar, *The Claire Claiborne Series*, 1993-
Anne George, *Murder on a Bad Hair Day*, 1996
Sarah Strohmeyer, *The Bubbles Yablonsky Series*, 2001-

35

CURT COLBERT

Queer Street

(New York: Uglytown, 2004)

Story type: Private Detective; Historical
Series: Jake Rossiter. Book 3
Subject(s): Homosexuality/Lesbianism; City and Town Life; Humor
Major character(s): Jake Rossiter, Detective—Private; Miss Jenkins, Assistant
Time period(s): 1940s (1949)
Locale(s): Seattle, Washington

Summary: Jake Rossiter is a wisecracking private eye in the best Raymond Chandler tradition, although he investigates cases and uses language that are far too racy to have been published in the 1940s. His sidekick, Miss Jenkins, has moved up from being his secretary in the first book of the series to being his junior partner here, and in the process she seems to have developed amorous designs on him. They've been called in to investigate the murder of a female impersonator at the Garden of Allah, a notoriously exclusive gay nightclub in Seattle. It's their misfortune that the cops pick that night to raid the joint and they're hauled off to jail with the rest of the patrons, a very colorful lot. There are many additional plot threads, characters, and themes, including police corruption and the Red scare, all handled with comedic zest and a solid knowledge of the era.

Other books by the same author:
Sayonaraville, 2003
Rat City, 2001

Other books you might like:
Andrew Bergman, *The Jack LeVine Series*, 1974-
Max Allan Collins, *Majic Man*, 1999
Stuart M. Kaminsky, *The Toby Peters Series*, 1977-
Ken Kuhlken, *The Tom Hickey Series*, 1991-
Eddie Muller, *The Distance*, 2001

36

KATE COLLINS (Pseudonym of Linda Tsoutsouris)

Mum's the Word

(New York: Signet, 2004)

Story type: Amateur Detective
Series: Abby Knight. Book 1
Subject(s): Small Town Life; Gardens and Gardening

Major character(s): Abby Knight, Store Owner (flower shop owner), Detective—Amateur; Marco Salvare, Police Officer (former), Saloon Keeper/Owner (bar owner)
Time period(s): 2000s
Locale(s): New Chapel, Indiana

Summary: Life dealt Abby Knight a double whammy when she flunked out of law school and got jilted by her fiance, but she's pulled herself together, returned to her home town in Indiana, and bought a small flower shop, Bloomers. All is going well until one morning when a young man in a black SUV rams into her cherished vintage Corvette and flees the scene. The plates are registered to a city councilman, but it was probably his nephew who was driving. Then Abby finds a dead body in her apartment and turns to handsome former cop Marco Salvare to see if there's a link between the murder and the man who damaged her car. Under her own name, the author has written a number of romance novels.

Where it's reviewed:
Romantic Times, November 2004, page 86

Other books you might like:
Susan Wittig Albert, *The China Bayles Series*, 1992-
Laura Childs, *The Theodosia Browning Series*, 2001-
Janis Harrison, *The Bretta Solomon Series*, 1999-
Denise Swanson, *The Scumble River Series*, 2000-
Heather Webber, *A Hoe Lot of Trouble*, 2004

37

MAX ALLAN COLLINS

Road to Purgatory
(New York: William Morrow, 2004)

Story type: Historical/World War II
Series: O'Sullivan Family. Book 2
Subject(s): Organized Crime; Fathers and Sons; World War II
Major character(s): Michael O'Sullivan Jr., Military Personnel, Veteran
Time period(s): 1940s (1942); 1920s (1922)
Locale(s): Bataan, Philippines; Chicago, Illinois; Rock Island, Illinois

Summary: In 1998, the author published a graphic novel, *The Road to Perdition*, that was the basis for the acclaimed 2002 Tom Hanks/Paul Newman film. It detailed the struggles of a renegade mob hit man and his young son to avenge himself against the likes of gangsters Al Capone and Frank Nitti in 1930s Chicago. In this sequel, the son, Michael O'Sullivan, Jr., is grown up and going by the name Michael Satariano, after the Italian-American couple who adopted and raised him. He's a soldier in World War II, fighting in the savage battle for Bataan, and when it's over he returns to the home front a decorated war hero, ready to pick up the fight against crime. He infiltrates the Capone gang and becomes the right-hand man to Nitti, Capone's heir. A side story flashes back to 1922 Rock Island, when Michael O'Sullivan, Sr., covers up a crime committed by his surrogate father to protect his own murderous son. The author has written dozens of mysteries, many of them what he calls true-crime fiction, including the Nathan Heller series about a 1940s private detective based in Chicago but involved in many celebrity cases and another set

against various historical disasters, as well as numerous movie tie-ins and novelizations.

Where it's reviewed:
Deadly Pleasures, Summer/Fall 2004, page 5
Entertainment Weekly, November 26, 2004, page 125
Mystery News, December 2004/January 2005, page 26
Publishers Weekly, November 22, 2004, page 39

Other books by the same author:
The London Blitz Murders, 2004
The Lusitania Murders, 2002
Angel in Black, 2001 (Nathan Heller series)
The Pearl Harbor Murders, 2001
The Hindenburg Murders, 2000

Other books you might like:
W.R. Burnett, *Goodbye Chicago*, 1981
Loren D. Estleman, *Jitterbug*, 1998
Joe Gores, *Hammett*, 1975
Craig Holden, *The Jazz Bird*, 2002
Eddie Muller, *The Billy Nichols Series*, 2002-

38

ROSE CONNORS

Maximum Security
(New York: Scribner, 2004)

Story type: Legal; Psychological Suspense
Series: Marty Nickerson. Book 3
Subject(s): Law; Small Town Life; Trials
Major character(s): Marty Nickerson, Lawyer; Harry Madigan, Lawyer
Time period(s): 2000s
Locale(s): Cape Cod, Massachusetts

Summary: Former prosecutor Marty Nickerson has gone into private practice as a defense lawyer with former public defender Harry Madigan, and now their relationship has become personal, as well as professional. Then Harry asks her to represent Louisa Rawlins, an old girlfriend charged with the murder of her wealthy husband who died in a boating accident and left her with $1 million in life insurance. The author's own experience as a trial lawyer and familiarity with the Cape Cod setting provide an authentic background to the story.

Where it's reviewed:
Booklist, August 2004, page 1904
Romantic Times, August 2004, page 85

Other books by the same author:
Temporary Sanity, 2003
Absolute Certainty, 2002

Other books you might like:
Alafair Burke, *Judgment Calls*, 2003
Jonnie Jacobs, *The Kali O'Brien Series*, 1996-
Perri O'Shaughnessy, *The Nina Reilly Series*, 1995-
Lisa Scottoline, *The Rosato & Associates Series*, 1993-
Kate Wilhelm, *The Barbara Holloway Series*, 1991-

39

RICK COPP

The Actor's Guide to Adultery

(New York: Kensington, 2004)

Story type: Humor; Amateur Detective
Series: Jarrod Jarvis. Book 2
Subject(s): Homosexuality/Lesbianism; Actors and Actresses; Weddings
Major character(s): Jarrod Jarvis, Actor, Detective—Amateur
Time period(s): 2000s
Locale(s): Los Angeles, California

Summary: Former child actor Jarrod Jarvis has led a quiet life since his career ended in the 1980s, living in the Hollywood Hills with his cop boyfriend, Charlie, and taking an occasional guest role on television shows. He's disturbed to learn that Wendell Butterworth, a man who stalked him as a child, is out on parole, and is further alarmed when his best friend and agent Laurette Taylor announces that she's marrying a promiscuous soap opera actor, Juan Carlos Barranco. Jarrod and Charlie attend the ceremony at Hearst Castle, where an uninvited—and unwelcome—guest drinks poisoned champagne and collapses into the wedding cake. Jarrod is convinced that Barranco is behind it and makes up his mind to prove it, following the man everywhere—and, at the same time, being stalked again himself by the creepy Butterworth. The author, a film and television writer, definitely has the goods on the Hollywood lifestyle and tells his story in a nice breezy fashion.

Where it's reviewed:
Mystery News, December 2004/January 2005, page 21
Publishers Weekly, October 4, 2004, page 73

Other books by the same author:
The Actor's Guide to Murder, 2003

Other books you might like:
Michael Craft, *The Mark Manning Series*, 1997-
Dean James, *The Simon Kirby-Jones Series*, 2002-
Grant Michaels, *The Stan Kraychik Series*, 1990-
Lev Raphael, *The Nick Hoffman Series*, 1995-
John Morgan Wilson, *The Benjamin Justice Series*, 1996-

40

PATRICIA CORNWELL

Trace

(New York: Putnam, 2004)

Story type: Psychological Suspense
Series: Kay Scarpetta. Book 13
Subject(s): Serial Killers; Medicine; Psychology
Major character(s): Kay Scarpetta, Consultant (forensic), Doctor (former medical examiner); Lucy Farinelli, Detective—Private, Relative (Kay's niece); Pete Marino, Police Officer (retired)
Time period(s): 2000s
Locale(s): Richmond, Virginia

Summary: Former medical examiner Kay Scarpetta temporarily returns to the Richmond office from which she was fired to help investigate the death of a teenager. She and her former partner, retired cop Pete Marino, find Kay's replacement a most unpleasant person and the office in a shambles. The bad guy here is a whacked-out psychopath named Edgar Allan Pogue who preys on women who have the flu. A dead teenager may have been one of his victims, and Kay and Marino sift through the scant evidence to find a link. Meanwhile, Kay's niece Lucy, who is running a detective agency of her own, is concerned about her roommate, who's been assaulted, and runs a parallel investigation into that.

Where it's reviewed:
Booklist, August 2004, page 1868
Entertainment Weekly, September 10, 2004, page 267
Library Journal, September 15, 2004, page 48
Mystery News, October/November 2004, page 24
People Weekly, September 13, 2004, page 56

Other books by the same author:
Blow Fly, 2003
The Last Precinct, 2000
Black Notice, 1999
Point of Origin, 1998
Unnatural Exposure, 1997

Other books you might like:
Linda Fairstein, *The Alexandra Cooper Series*, 1996-
Thomas Harris, *The Hannibal Lecter Series*, 1981-
Iris Johansen, *The Eve Duncan Series*, 1998-
Kathy Reichs, *The Tempe Brennan Series*, 1997-
Karin Slaughter, *The Sara Linton Series*, 2001-

41

COLIN COTTERILL

The Coroner's Lunch

(New York: Soho, 2004)

Story type: Police Procedural
Series: Dr. Siri Paiboun. Book 1
Subject(s): Communism; Medicine; Cultures and Customs
Major character(s): Siri Paiboun, Doctor (medical examiner)
Time period(s): 1970s (1976)
Locale(s): Vientiane, Laos

Summary: While a medical student in Paris in the late 1920s, Dr. Siri Paiboun, an admittedly ordinary man, embraced communism because he spied a female classmate, an ardent party member, in a tight sweater. Forty-seven years later, aged 72 and now a widower, Siri is looking forward to a pension from the party for his years of mediocre, half-hearted service to the cause. The party has other ideas. In 1976, the Pathet Lao controls Laos but most of the educated class have fled the country. Even though he has no training and even less inclination, Siri is appointed state coroner. Aided by a mildly retarded technician and a clever nurse, Siri finds himself looking into a series of seemingly unrelated deaths involving both party higher-ups, as well as the neighboring Vietnamese. The sights, smells, and colors of Laos practically jump off the pages of this inspired, often wryly witty first novel. There's just a touch of mysticism as the dead reveal their secrets to Siri in a most unconventional manner.

Where it's reviewed:
Booklist, October 1, 2004, page 313
Publishers Weekly, November 22, 2004, page 42

Other books you might like:
John Burdett, *Bangkok 8*, 2003
Martin Limon, *The Ernie Bascom/George Sueno Series*, 1992-
Francine Mathews, *The Secret Agent*, 2002
Eliot Pattison, *The San Tao Yun Series*, 1999-
Christopher West, *The Inspector Wang Series*, 1998-

42

CLEO COYLE

Through the Grinder

(New York: Berkley, 2004)

Story type: Amateur Detective
Series: Clare Cosi. Book 2
Subject(s): Food; Restaurants; City and Town Life
Major character(s): Clare Cosi, Restaurateur (coffee house owner), Detective—Amateur; Mike Quinn, Detective—Police; Bruce Bowman, Crime Suspect (of being a murderer)
Time period(s): 2000s
Locale(s): New York, New York (Greenwich Village)

Summary: With her marriage over long ago and her daughter Joy grown and moved out of her house in the New Jersey suburbs, Clare decides to make a big change in her life. Years ago she had been manager of the historic Village Blend coffee house, and now its owner has enticed her back with the promise of a part ownership and rent-free living in the two-bedroom apartment above the shop. Business is good, and there's a new man, Bruce Bowman, in Clare's life, who seems perfect in every way. Suddenly, though, her customers are dying, all after drinking a cup of her special coffee blend. Throw in a handsome police detective (who suspects Bowman in the murders), a cat named Java, lots of coffee lore, and some enticing recipes using coffee, and you have the ultimate cozy, although this one is a little darker than its predecessor.

Where it's reviewed:
Mystery News, December 2004/January 2005, page 12
Romantic Times, November 2004, page 88

Other books by the same author:
On What Grounds, 2003

Other books you might like:
Sandra Balzo, *Uncommon Grounds*, 2004
Laura Childs, *The Theodosia Browning Series*, 2001-
Diane Mott Davidson, *Double Shot*, 2004
Linda French, *Coffee to Die For*, 1998
Barbara Jaye Wilson, *The Brenda Midnight Series*, 1997-

43

PETER CRAIG

Hot Plastic

(New York: Hyperion, 2004)

Story type: Humor; Action/Adventure

Subject(s): Crime and Criminals; Fathers and Sons
Major character(s): Jerry Swift, Con Artist; Kevin Swift, Con Artist, Teenager; Colette, Con Artist, Runaway
Time period(s): 1980s (1983)
Locale(s): United States

Summary: The time is 1983, and charming con artist Jerry Swift and his obsessive-compulsive son Kevin are crisscrossing the country running credit card scams, staying in cheap hotel rooms, and stealing the occasional car. When Kevin gets sick, Jerry hires a seductive young runaway, Colette, to take care of him while he's out working his scams. When it's time for them to move on (one step ahead of the law), Colette decides to join them and proves a worthy addition to the team. Kevin falls for her, even though she's now sleeping with his father, and their lives all get terribly complicated from this point on. Oddball characters, intriguing con games, and smart, funny writing make this a standout in its subgenre.

Where it's reviewed:
Booklist, February 15, 2004, page 1040
Entertainment Weekly, March 2004, page 120
Library Journal, March 1, 2004, page 108
Publishers Weekly, January 19, 2004, page 52

Other books by the same author:
The Martini Shot, 1998

Other books you might like:
Judson Jack Carmichael, *The Scared Stiff*, 2002
Eric Garcia, *Matchstick Men*, 2002
Pete Hautman, *Ring Game*, 1997
Philip Reed, *Bird Dog*, 1997
Ross Thomas, *The Fourth Durango*, 1989

44

ISIS CRAWFORD (Pseudonym of Barbara Block)

A Catered Wedding

(New York: Kensington, 2004)

Story type: Amateur Detective
Series: Bernie and Libby Simmons. Book 2
Subject(s): Catering Business; Sisters; Weddings
Major character(s): Bernadette ''Bernie'' Simmons, Caterer, Detective—Amateur; Libby Simmons, Caterer, Detective—Amateur
Time period(s): 2000s
Locale(s): New York, New York

Summary: When Bernie left Los Angeles and her loser boyfriend, she fled to New York where she went to work for her sister Libby, who owns a catering company called A Little Taste of Heaven. Their newest client is Leeza Sharp, a pretty young woman from Missouri who's about to marry an Estonian businessman about twice her age and means to have the most lavish wedding money can buy. Just hours before the ceremony, Leeza is shot through the chest with an arrow, and Libby and Bernie go to work looking for her killer. Recipes included. Under her own name, the author wrote a series about pet store owner Robin Light.

Where it's reviewed:
Publishers Weekly, November 8, 2004, page 39

Romantic Times, January 2005, page 86

Other books by the same author:
A Catered Affair, 2004

Other books you might like:
Diane Mott Davidson, *The Goldy Bear Schulz Series*, 1990-
Deborah Donnelly, *The Carnegie Kincaid Series*, 2002-
Jerrilyn Farmer, *Killer Wedding*, 2000
Janis Harrison, *A Deadly Bouquet*, 2002
Valerie Wolzien, *Weddings Are Murder*, 1998

45

BILL CRIDER

A Bond with Death

(New York: St. Martin's Minotaur, 2004)

Story type: Amateur Detective; Humor
Series: Sally Good. Book 3
Subject(s): Academia; College Life; Witches and Witchcraft
Major character(s): Sally Good, Professor, Detective—Amateur
Time period(s): 2000s
Locale(s): Houston, Texas (suburban)

Summary: Sally Good, chairman of the English department at a small suburban community college, doesn't know whether to be amused or irritated when a colleague starts a rumor that she is descended from one of the Salem witches, Sarah Good. In reality, the so-called witch is her ex-husband's ancestor, not hers, and she'd like to know what this tenuous connection to a woman who was certainly falsely convicted of a crime 400 years ago has to do with her job performance anyway. Unfortunately, the man responsible for the rumor, who had been denied tenure and dismissed for his poor performance, is murdered, and Sally becomes the chief suspect. The author writes several other series, including one about laid-back small-town Texas sheriff Dan Rhodes and another about another college professor, Carl Burns.

Where it's reviewed:
Booklist, October 15, 2004, page 392
Publishers Weekly, November 1, 2004, page 47

Other books by the same author:
A Knife in the Back, 2002
Murder Is an Art, 1999

Other books you might like:
Donna Andrews, *The Meg Langslow Series*, 1999-
Joanne Dobson, *The Karen Pelletier Series*, 1997-
Jane Isenberg, *The Bel Barrett Series*, 1999-
M.D. Lake, *The Peggy O'Neill Series*, 1989-
Lev Raphael, *The Nick Hoffman Series*, 1995-

46

DEBORAH CROMBIE

In a Dark House

(New York: William Morrow, 2004)

Story type: Police Procedural; Traditional
Series: Gemma James/Duncan Kincaid. Book 10

Subject(s): Missing Persons; Kidnapping; Arson
Major character(s): Gemma James, Police Officer (detective inspector); Duncan Kincaid, Police Officer (superintendent)
Time period(s): 2000s
Locale(s): London, England

Summary: A series of arsons among the Victorian-era warehouses of South London's Southwark district reveal the charred body of a woman burned beyond recognition and murdered before the fire was started. Duncan and Gemma (who are lovers, as well as partners) are called in to investigate, and they discover a tangled web of evil-doing, including an abducted ten-year-old girl and two missing women. The kidnapped child had been a pawn in her parents' bitter divorce, and her disappearance may be connected with the murder of the woman. It takes all the detectives' patience and skill to unravel the complex relationships of the people involved and get to the truth, while little Harriet's life hangs in the balance.

Where it's reviewed:
Library Journal, June 1, 2004, page 109
Publishers Weekly, October 4, 2004, page 74
Texas Monthly, October 2004, page 68

Other books by the same author:
Now May You Weep, 2003
And Justice There Is None, 2002
A Finer End, 2001
Kissed a Sad Goodbye, 1999
Dreaming of the Bones, 1997

Other books you might like:
Elizabeth George, *The Thomas Lynley Series*, 1988-
Caroline Graham, *The Inspector Tom Barnaby Series*, 1987-
Erin Hart, *The Nora Garvin Series*, 2003-
Jill McGown, *The Inspector Lloyd/Judy Hill Series*, 1983-
Janet Neel, *The John McLeish/Francesca Wilson Series*, 1988-

47

LAURA CRUM

Forged

(New York: St. Martin's Minotaur, 2004)

Story type: Amateur Detective
Series: Gail McCarthy. Book 8
Subject(s): Animals/Horses; Ranch Life; Veterinarians
Major character(s): Gail McCarthy, Veterinarian, Detective—Amateur
Time period(s): 2000s
Locale(s): Harkins Valley, California

Summary: Veterinarian Gail McCarthy lives a life of quiet contentment on her small ranch with her horses, dogs, and live-in lover Blue. Her life is disrupted when Dominic Castillo, the master farrier who had an appointment to shoe one of her horses, is found shot in the stomach in her barn. Before he dies, he tells her he was cleaning his gun, but neither Gail nor Matt Johnson, the cop who's investigating the case, believes him. In fact, Gail is convinced that Johnson suspects her of the crime, and it looks as if she's going to have to conduct her own investigation in order to clear herself.

Where it's reviewed:
Romantic Times, August 2004, page 89

Other books by the same author:
Hayburner, 2003
Breakaway, 2001
Slickrock, 1999
Roped, 1998
Roughstock, 1997

Other books you might like:
Christine Andreae, *The Lee Squires Series*, 1992-
Carolyn Banks, *The Robin Vaughan Series*, 1993-
Sinclair Browning, *The Trade Ellis Series*, 1999-
Earlene Fowler, *The Benni Harper Series*, 1994-
Jody Jaffe, *The Natalie Gold Series*, 1995-

48

CLARE CURZON (Pseudonym of Eileen-Marie Duell Buchanan)

A Meeting of Minds
(New York: St. Martin's Minotaur, 2004)

Story type: Police Procedural
Series: Mike Yeadings. Book 17
Subject(s): Small Town Life; Neighbors and Neighborhoods; Law Enforcement
Major character(s): Mike Yeadings, Police Officer (detective superintendent); Rosemary ''Z'' Zycynski, Police Officer (detective sergeant)
Time period(s): 2000s
Locale(s): Henley-on-Thames, England (Thames Valley)

Summary: Mike Yeadings of the Thames Valley Police and his team are called to a car park one chilly November morning where the body of a woman, stylishly wrapped in a heavy fur coat, has been discovered in a parked car. Sergeant Zycynski (known to all as Z) realizes that the woman is a neighbor of hers, living in the same upscale apartment house to which she's recently relocated. Sheila Winter lived with her aging mother and kept to herself, and Z has no clue as to how she came to be dead, an apparent suicide, wearing nothing but her fur coat.

Where it's reviewed:
Publishers Weekly, August 23, 2004, page 40
Romantic Times, October 2004, page 87

Other books by the same author:
The Body of a Woman, 2003
Don't Leave Me, 2002
Cold Hands, 2001
All Unwary, 1998
Close Quarters, 1997

Other books you might like:
Jo Bannister, *The Frank Shapiro Series*, 1993-
Marjorie Eccles, *The Gil Mayo Series*, 1988-
Peter Lovesey, *The Peter Diamond Series*, 1991-
Kay Mitchell, *The John Morrissey Series*, 1990-

Janet Neel, *The John McLeish/Francesca Wilson Series*, 1988-

49

JUDITH CUTLER

Staying Power
(New York: St. Martin's Minotaur, 2004)

Story type: Police Procedural
Series: Kate Power. Book 2
Subject(s): Abuse; Children; Sexism
Major character(s): Kate Power, Police Officer (detective sergeant)
Time period(s): 1990s
Locale(s): Birmingham, England

Summary: After the death of her married lover, Kate left the London force for a post in Birmingham, where she is the only woman in the CID and the target of considerable sexual harassment from her male colleagues. While on holiday, she meets Alan Grafton, a handsome young exporter of leather goods, and is shocked when, only days later, he's found hanging from a bridge with her business card in his pocket. Alan had not seemed the sort to commit suicide, and she determines to find out what really happened. The author also writes a series about Birmingham college lecturer Sophie Rivers.

Where it's reviewed:
Booklist, June 1, 2004, page 1706
Publishers Weekly, May 17, 2004, page 37
Romantic Times, August 2004, page 90

Other books by the same author:
Power on Her Own, 2003
Dying for Power, 1998 (Sophie Rivers series)
Dying for Millions, 1997 (Sophie Rivers series)
Dying on Principle, 1996 (Sophie Rivers series)
Dying to Write, 1996 (Sophie Rivers series)

Other books you might like:
Deborah Crombie, *The Duncan Kincaid/Gemma James Series*, 1993-
Marjorie Eccles, *The Gil Mayo Series*, 1988-
Priscilla Masters, *The Joanne Piercy Series*, 1995-
Jill McGown, *The Inspector Lloyd/Judy Hill Series*, 1983-
Jennie Melville, *The Charmian Daniels Series*, 1962-

50

MARY DAHEIM

This Old Souse
(New York: William Morrow, 2004)

Story type: Amateur Detective; Humor
Series: Judith McMonigle Flynn. Book 20
Subject(s): Neighbors and Neighborhoods; Hotels and Motels; Secrets
Major character(s): Judith McMonigle Flynn, Innkeeper, Detective—Amateur
Time period(s): 2000s
Locale(s): Seattle, Washington

Summary: Judith takes a break from the chores at Hillside Manor, her Seattle bed-and-breakfast, to do some snooping in the neighborhood where her cousin Renie grew up. Renie had always admired a run-down Spanish-style mansion on Moonfleet Street, which the cousins thought had been deserted since 1947. Apparently, though, Dick and Jane Bland and Jane's sister Sally have been living a reclusive existence there all along, or so their talkative milkman tells Renie and Judith. When Judith finds the milkman, very dead, in the trunk of her car, they discover that the mysterious residents of the house very much don't want this crime to be solved. The author also writes a long-running series about small-town Washington newspaper editor Emma Lord.

Where it's reviewed:
Booklist, August 2004, page 1904
Library Journal, August 2004, page 60
Publishers Weekly, July 19, 2004, page 148
Romantic Times, September 2004, page 89

Other books by the same author:
Hocus Croakus, 2003
The Silver Scream, 2002
Suture Self, 2001
A Streetcar Named Expire, 2000
Creeps Suzette, 1999

Other books you might like:
Claudia Bishop, *The Hemlock Falls Series*, 1994-
Jo Dereske, *The Miss Zukas Series*, 1994-
Jean Hager, *The Tess Darcy Series*, 1994-2000
Tamar Myers, *The Magdalena Yoder Series*, 1994-
Tim Myers, *Innkeeping with Murder*, 2001

51

JEANNE M. DAMS

Winter of Discontent

(New York: Forge, 2004)

Story type: Amateur Detective; Traditional
Series: Dorothy Martin. Book 9
Subject(s): Christmas; Museums; World War II
Major character(s): Dorothy Martin, Expatriate, Detective—Amateur
Time period(s): 2000s
Locale(s): Sherebury, England

Summary: When she was widowed, Indiana-born retired schoolteacher Dorothy Martin realized her lifelong dream of moving to England, where she settled in the medieval cathedral town of Sherebury, and met and married the county's chief constable, Alan Nesbitt (now retired). Christmas is only weeks away, and Dorothy is in the midst of her usual preparations when Bill Fanshawe, curator of the local museum and a World War II veteran and former POW, is found dead in the museum basement. In their youth, Bill and Dorothy's best friend, Jane Langland, had been sweethearts, but the war and the passage of time had turned the romance into friendship. Partly for Jane's sake, Dorothy determines to find who killed Bill and why, poring over the few clues she has and information she gathers from talking to Bill's friends, past and pres-ent. The author also writes a series set in turn-of-the-century Indiana about a Swedish immigrant servant, Hilda Johansson.

Where it's reviewed:
Publishers Weekly, November 1, 2004, page 47

Other books by the same author:
Sins out of School, 2003
To Perish in Penzance, 2001
Killing Cassidy, 2000
The Victim in Victoria Station, 1999
Malice in Miniature, 1998

Other books you might like:
M.C. Beaton, *The Agatha Raisin Series*, 1992-
Simon Brett, *The Fethering Series*, 2000-
Hamilton Crane, *The Miss Seeton Series*, 1968-
  begun by Heron Carvic
Hazel Holt, *The Mrs. Malory Series*, 1989-
Betty Rowlands, *The Melissa Craig Series*, 1989-

52

DIANE MOTT DAVIDSON

Double Shot

(New York: William Morrow, 2004)

Story type: Amateur Detective; Domestic
Series: Goldy Bear Schulz. Book 12
Subject(s): Cooks and Cooking; Food; Family
Major character(s): Goldy Bear Schulz, Caterer, Detective—Amateur
Time period(s): 2000s
Locale(s): Aspen Meadow, Colorado

Summary: Goldy's obnoxious, abusive ex-husband, Dr. John Richard Korman (aka ''the Jerk''), has just been released from prison where he served time for aggravated assault and is now back in Aspen Meadow searching for a trophy home in which to settle with his newest trophy girlfriend. When Goldy is felled by a masked assailant while she's preparing the food for a gala luncheon, she immediately suspects Korman but has no proof. Next he confronts her with an angry request to change his visitation time with their teenage son Arch, and soon after that he's found dead, with Goldy's missing gun next to him. This makes her the prime suspect in his murder and forces her to turn detective in order to clear herself. As usual, she throws herself into her cooking as therapy for her troubled soul, and the mouthwatering recipes she concocts are found at the back of the book. All the series regulars return here, including the Jerk's other ex-wife, Marla, now Goldy's best friend, and her young assistant Julian.

Where it's reviewed:
Library Journal, October 2004, page 65
Publishers Weekly, September 13, 2004, page 61
Romantic Times, November 2004, page 85

Other books by the same author:
Chopping Spree, 2002
Sticks & Scones, 2001
Tough Cookie, 2001
Prime Cut, 1998
The Grilling Season, 1997

Other books you might like:
Susan Wittig Albert, *The China Bayles Series*, 1992-
Isis Crawford, *A Catered Murder*, 2003
Jerrilyn Farmer, *The Madeline Bean Series*, 1998-
Katherine Hall Page, *The Faith Sibley Fairchild Series*, 1990-
Virginia Rich, *The Eugenia Potter Series*, 1982-
    continued by Nancy Pickard, 1993-

53

MARTIN DAVIES

Mrs. Hudson and the Spirits' Curse
(New York: Berkley, 2004)

Story type: Historical/Victorian; Amateur Detective
Subject(s): Victorian Period; Servants; Social Conditions
Major character(s): Mrs. Hudson, Housekeeper, Detective—Amateur; Flotsam "Flottie", Servant (scullery maid), Sidekick; Sherlock Holmes, Detective—Private
Time period(s): 1880s
Locale(s): London, England

Summary: Kind-hearted Mrs. Hudson has taken a young orphan girl, Flotsam, under her wing, whisking her off the streets and from a life of thieving to train as a first-class scullery maid and to teach her to read and write as well. When their employer dies, the family solicitor puts Mrs. Hudson in touch with a pair of gentlemen who have just taken lodgings in Baker Street and are in need of a housekeeper. They are, of course, Sherlock Holmes, the world's first consulting detective, and his friend and assistant Dr. Watson. She's no sooner taken charge of the household than a young man recently returned from the Far East shows up begging Holmes to help him thwart a Sumatran curse that's been placed upon him. (Readers of the canon will recognize the oft alluded to case of the giant rat of Sumatra.) Mrs. Hudson has great respect for Holmes' deductive powers—indeed, she considers them almost equal to her own—but she feels he lacks her common sense. With the help of Flottie, now a respectable young woman of 14 who is devoted to her in every way, Mrs. Hudson initiates her own investigation, even as Holmes and Watson conduct theirs. The story is narrated by Flottie and is both an affectionate homage to the Holmes canon, with its swirling, choking pea-soup fogs and the cozy gaslit chambers at 221B, and a sly feminist spin upon it. First mystery.

Where it's reviewed:
Publishers Weekly, November 8, 2004, page 39

Other books you might like:
Carole Nelson Douglas, *The Irene Adler Series*, 1990-
Laurie R. King, *The Mary Russell/Sherlock Holmes Series*, 1994-
Barrie Roberts, *Sherlock Holmes and the Crosby Murder*, 2002
Lora Roberts, *The Affair of the Incognito Tenant*, 2004
Alan Vanneman, *Sherlock Holmes and the Giant Rat of Sumatra*, 2002

54

LINDSEY DAVIS

Scandal Takes a Holiday
(New York: Mysterious, 2004)

Story type: Historical/Ancient Rome
Series: Marcus Didius Falco. Book 16
Subject(s): Ancient History; Roman Empire; Kidnapping
Major character(s): Marcus Didius Falco, Detective—Private
Time period(s): 1st century (76)
Locale(s): Rome, Roman Empire

Summary: When Infamia, the gossip columnist for the Rome *Daily Gazette*, disappears mysteriously, his employers retain Marcus Didius Falco to find the missing scribe. Falco learns that Infamia had been investigating a group of pirates responsible for kidnapping wealthy Roman women and holding them for ransom. After poking around, Falco discovers the man is really the victim of a far more sinister conspiracy, involving not only the government but some of Falco's own more unsavory relatives. The historical background is sound enough, but the author makes frequent use of deliberate and humorous anachronisms in the characters' speech to lighten things up.

Where it's reviewed:
Booklist, September 1, 2004, page 68
Publishers Weekly, July 12, 2004, page 47

Other books by the same author:
The Accusers, 2004
The Jupiter Myth, 2003
A Body in the Bathhouse, 2002
Ode to a Banker, 2001
Three Hands in the Fountain, 1999

Other books you might like:
Ron Burns, *Roman Nights*, 1991
Jane Finnis, *Get Out or Die*, 2004
John Maddox Roberts, *The SPQR Series*, 1990-
Steven Saylor, *The Roma Sub Rosa Series*, 1991-
David Wishart, *The Marcus Corvinus Series*, 1995-

55

JEFFERY DEAVER

Garden of Beasts
(New York: Simon & Schuster, 2004)

Story type: Historical/World War II; Espionage
Subject(s): World War II; Nazis; Spies
Major character(s): Paul Schumann, Murderer (hit man), Spy
Time period(s): 1930s (1936)
Locale(s): Berlin, Germany; New York, New York

Summary: Mob hit man Paul Schumann is recruited by military intelligence to take out one of Hitler's top men. If he refuses, the electric chair awaits him. If he accepts, he gets his freedom and a chance to stay clean for life. So he's soon posing as a journalist attached to the 1936 U.S. Olympic team bound for Germany, but before he even arrives at his destination he arouses the suspicions of a German spy aboard the ship. When he arrives in Berlin to meet his contact, things immediately begin to go wrong. He's quite unprepared for the horrors of the Third Reich. After he instinctively tries to protect a Jewish bookseller from a group of thuggish Stormtroopers, he becomes a man on the run, helped by an opportunistic but Nazi-hating German black marketeer, Otto Webber. He finds an ally in his landlady, a young woman named Kathe Richter with whom he begins a tentative affair. As Schumann continues to pursue his target and is in turn pursued by the German police and the German high command, the plot twists pile up, with many real-life characters of the day—from Hitler and Heinrich Himmler to Jesse Owens—making cameo appearances. Most unforgettable is the portrait of the making of a genuine hero from the most unpromising material. The author has written many contemporary thrillers, including a series about paralyzed criminalist Lincoln Rhyme, but this is his first historical.

Where it's reviewed:
Booklist, May 1, 2004, page 1504
Deadly Pleasures, Summer/Fall 2004, page 6
Library Journal, May 15, 2004, page 113
Mystery News, August/September 2004, page 9
Publishers Weekly, May 3, 2004, page 166

Other books by the same author:
The Vanished Man, 2003 (Lincoln Rhyme series)
The Stone Monkey, 2002 (Lincoln Rhyme series)
The Blue Nowhere, 2001
Speaking in Tongues, 2000
The Empty Chair, 2000 (Lincoln Rhyme series)

Other books you might like:
Alan Furst, *The Polish Officer*, 1995
Jack Gerson, *Death's Head Berlin*, 1987
Joseph Kanon, *The Good German*, 2001
Philip Kerr, *March Violets*, 1990
Robert Wilson, *The Company of Strangers*, 2001

56

NELSON DEMILLE, Editor

The Best American Mystery Stories 2004
(New York: Houghton Mifflin, 2004)

Story type: Anthology
Series: Best American Mystery Stories. Book 8
Subject(s): Short Stories

Summary: The 20 stories here come from such veteran mystery writers as Richard Lupoff and Dick Lochte and from well-known writers outside the genre, such as Joyce Carol Oates and Stephen King, as well as a number of newcomers and lesser-known writers. Reportedly series editor Otto Penzler selects a wide range of meritorious tales, from which the celebrity guest editor, in this case bestselling thriller writer DeMille, picks the 20 finalists. If so, this may explain why so few of the works chosen are actually detective stories but are better classified as suspense, crime, and even supernatural. Lupoff contributes a double—perhaps triple—pastiche, ''The Incident of the Impecunious Chevalier,'' in which Sherlock Holmes calls upon Edgar Allan Poe's Auguste Dupin to help him track down a jeweled black bird. Jeffrey Robert Bowman's ''Stonewalls'' is a historical set during the Civil

War dealing with Stonewall Jackson's death from friendly fire. Christopher Cloake, Jeff Abbott, Scott Wolven, and William J. Carroll, Jr., also contribute stories.

Where it's reviewed:
Booklist, October 1, 2004, page 4
Library Journal, June 1, 2004, page 109
Publishers Weekly, August 30, 2004, page 35

Other books you might like:
Lawrence Block, *Blood on Their Hands*, 2003
    editor
Ed Gorman, *The World's Finest Mystery and Crime Stories Series*, 2000-
    Martin H. Greenberg, co-editor
Tony Hillerman, *The Oxford Book of American Detective Stories*, 1997
    editor
Janet Hutchings, *The Cutting Edge: Best and Brightest Mysteries of the 90s*, 1998
    editor
Herbert Maurice Van Thal, *The Mammoth Book of Great Detective Stories*, 2001
    editor

57

FORREST DEVOE JR. (Pseudonym of Max Phillips)

Into the Volcano
(New York: HarperCollins, 2004)

Story type: Espionage
Series: Mallory & Morse. Book 1
Subject(s): Spies; Russians; Humor
Major character(s): Jack Mallory, Spy, Military Personnel (ex-soldier); Laura Morse, Spy, Martial Arts Expert
Time period(s): 1960s (1962)
Locale(s): Istanbul, Turkey; Cannes, France

Summary: Conceived as an homage to the 1960s spy novel, this stylish and intentionally derivative thriller introduces special agents Jack Mallory and Laura Morse, operatives for the shadowy Consultancy. He's a randy former soldier from Texas and she's an aloof, beautiful karate expert from an old-line Boston family. They're sent to Istanbul, where a fellow spy has been killed in a spectacular fashion, and ordered to track down two of their opposite numbers, the Russian assassin Piotr Nemerov and a diabolically clever arms dealer, Anton Rauth, who is improbably headquartered in an extinct South Seas volcano. There are futuristic gadgets and fantastic plots galore, none of them meant to be taken too seriously. First thriller by a literary novelist and *noir* publisher.

Where it's reviewed:
Booklist, September 15, 2004, page 211
Mystery News, December 2004/January 2005, page 23

Other books you might like:
Len Deighton, *The Harry Palmer Series*, 1962-1976
    the anonymous hero was called Harry Palmer in the movie versions
Ian Fleming, *The James Bond Series*, 1954-1966
Donald Hamilton, *The Matt Helm Series*, 1960-1993
Mabel Maney, *The Jane Bond Series*, 2001-

Peter O'Donnell, *The Modesty Blaise Series*, 1965-1996

58

P.C. DOHERTY

The Hangman's Hymn

(New York: St. Martin's Minotaur, 2004)

Story type: Historical/Medieval
Series: Canterbury Tales. Book 5
Subject(s): Witches and Witchcraft; Middle Ages
Major character(s): Simon Cotterill, Carpenter
Time period(s): 14th century (1358)
Locale(s): Gloucester, England

Summary: Geoffrey Chaucer's classic *Canterbury Tales* provides the framework and characters for this series set in medieval England, with each of the pilgrims, en route from London to Canterbury, taking turns entertaining the rest of the company with their personal stories. Here it is the carpenter's turn. Simon Cotterill was a young apprentice carpenter near Gloucester when his future father-in-law ran him out of town and he joined the local hangman's crew, after one of them met a horrible end. The executioners' next macabre assignment is hanging three women accused of being witches, but they are too frightened to finish the job and simply leave them hanging, but not yet dead. The leader of the coven is out for revenge, and it's up to the carpenter to set things right. Chaucer himself, as one of the pilgrims, has a minor role in the framework story. The prolific author has written dozens of historical mysteries from various periods and under various pseudonyms.

Where it's reviewed:
Publishers Weekly, November 15, 2004, page 44

Other books by the same author:
Ghostly Murders, 1997
A Tournament of Murders, 1996
A Tapestry of Murders, 1995
An Ancient Evil, 1994

Other books you might like:
Gertrude Clancy, *Death Is a Pilgrim*, 1993
    Joseph Clancy, co-author
Duane Crowley, *Riddle Me a Murder*, 1986
Susanna Gregory, *The Matthew Bartholomew Series*, 1996-
Paul Harding, *The Brother Athelstan Series*, 1991-
    pseudonym of P.C. Doherty
Candace Robb, *The Owen Archer Series*, 1993-

59

JAMES D. DOSS

The Witch's Tongue

(New York: St. Martin's Minotaur, 2004)

Story type: Police Procedural; Humor
Series: Charlie Moon. Book 9
Subject(s): American West; Indian Reservations; Native Americans

Major character(s): Charlie Moon, Police Officer (retired), Rancher; Daisy Perika, Shaman, Relative (Charlie's aunt); Lila McTeague, FBI Agent
Time period(s): 2000s
Locale(s): Ute Reservation, Colorado; Granite Creek, Colorado

Summary: Tall, lanky tribal investigator Charlie Moon tried retiring from police work to become a full-time rancher but the job just won't let him quit. A series of strange events near Granite Creek requires his attention: a small private museum is broken into; a man disappears into Spirit Canyon, leaving behind a battered wife who isn't sure whether to be relieved or sad; the owner of an antiques store is wounded when a sniper fires through his window; and an Apache assaults a police officer. To top it off, Charlie's aunt, Daisy Perika, a shaman and tribal elder, dreams of being buried alive. Neither the local police nor the FBI, in the person of Special Agent Lila McTeague, can connect these events, so they turn to Charlie. The author writes with grace and humor, treating native beliefs and customs with respect, as well as a certain amount of wit.

Where it's reviewed:
Library Journal, September 15, 2004, page 214
Publishers Weekly, August 23, 2004, page 40

Other books by the same author:
Dead Soul, 2003
White Shell Woman, 2002
Grandmother Spider, 2001
The Night Visitor, 1999
The Shaman's Game, 1998

Other books you might like:
Margaret Coel, *The Father John O'Malley/Vicky Holden Series*, 1995-
Kathleen O'Neal Gear, *Bone Walker*, 2001
    W. Michael Gear, co-author
Tony Hillerman, *The Joe Leaphorn/Jim Chee Series*, 1970-
Jake Page, *The Stolen Gods*, 1993
Aimee Thurlo, *The Ella Clah Series*, 1995-
    David Thurlo, co-author

60

CAROLE NELSON DOUGLAS

Cat in an Orange Twist

(New York: Forge, 2004)

Story type: Amateur Detective
Series: Midnight Louie. Book 16
Subject(s): Animals/Cats; Humor; Homosexuality/Lesbianism
Major character(s): Midnight Louie, Animal (cat), Detective—Amateur; Temple Barr, Public Relations, Detective—Amateur
Time period(s): 2000s
Locale(s): Las Vegas, Nevada

Summary: Petite PR consultant Temple Barr is taking a breather between dead bodies to work on her shoe wardrobe and take a job coordinating publicity events for a trendy new furniture showroom. The main event is a visit from high-powered domestic diva Amelia Wong, who claims to have been receiving death threats. When terrorists do attack at the gala grand opening, it's designer Simon Foster who's the victim. Since he's the life partner of Temple's dear friend, choreographer Danny Dove, she takes it personally and determines to find his killer. Meanwhile, Midnight Louie, a sleek black cat who fancies himself a private detective (despite his lack of paying clients), is on the case, along with his daughter Midnight Louise, both of whom fear for Temple's life. The author also writes a historical series featuring Irene Adler, a contemporary of Sherlock Holmes.

Where it's reviewed:
Publishers Weekly, July 15, 2004, page 42
Romantic Times, August 2004, page 89

Other books by the same author:
Cat in a Neon Nightmare, 2003
Cat in a Midnight Choir, 2002
Cat in a Leopard Spot, 2001
Cat in a Kiwi Con, 2000
Cat in a Jeweled Jumpsuit, 1999

Other books you might like:
Garrison Allen, *The Big Mike Series*, 1994-
Marian Babson, *The Diamond Cat*, 1994
Lilian Jackson Braun, *The Cat Who Series*, 1966-
Rita Mae Brown, *The Mrs. Murphy Series*, 1990-
Shirley Rousseau Murphy, *The Joe Grey Series*, 1996-

61

CAROLE NELSON DOUGLAS

Spider Dance
(New York: Forge, 2004)

Story type: Historical/Victorian
Series: Irene Adler. Book 8
Subject(s): Victorian Period; Women; Conspiracies
Major character(s): Irene Adler, Detective—Amateur, Singer; Sherlock Holmes, Detective—Private; Nellie Bly, Journalist, Historical Figure
Time period(s): 1880s (1889)
Locale(s): New York, New York

Summary: The author has taken a minor but memorable figure from the Sherlock Holmes canon—Irene Adler, the New Jersey-born opera singer who bested the great detective in the short story "A Scandal in Bohemia"—and reinvented her as the wily heroine of a convoluted series moving from England to Paris and lately to New York. Irene is still searching for the identity of her birth mother, a search in which both Sherlock Holmes and the adventurous reporter Nellie Bly join her. The story is narrated, as usual, by Nell Huxleigh, Irene's faithful secretary and companion. Another major character is the legendary entertainer Lola Montez, and part of the action goes back to the Gold Rush days in California where Lola first made her mark. There are hints that this may be the last book in the series. The author also writes a long-running, more whimsical contemporary series featuring feline detective Midnight Louie.

Where it's reviewed:
Publishers Weekly, November 29, 2004, page 27
Romantic Times, January 2005, page 85

Other books by the same author:
Femme Fatale, 2003
Castle Rouge, 2002
Chapel Noir, 2001
Irene's Last Waltz, 1994 (also published as *Another Scandal in Bohemia*)
Irene at Large, 1992 (also published as *A Soul of Steel*)

Other books you might like:
Caleb Carr, *The Alienist*, 1994
J.D. Christilian, *Scarlet Women*, 1996
Paula Cohen, *Gramercy Park*, 2002
Arthur Conan Doyle, *The Sherlock Holmes Series*, 1887-1927
Laurie R. King, *The Mary Russell/Sherlock Holmes Series*, 1994-

62

JOAN DRUETT

A Watery Grave
(New York: St. Martin's Minotaur, 2004)

Story type: Historical/Victorian
Series: Wiki Coffin. Book 1
Subject(s): Ships; Voyages and Travels; Maoris
Major character(s): William "Wiki" Coffin, Linguist, Sailor
Time period(s): 1830s (1838)
Locale(s): Hampton Roads, Virginia; *Swallow*, At Sea

Summary: Wiki Coffin, a half-Maori, half-American linguist and navigator, is part of the 1838 United States South Seas Exploring Expedition which sailed from Virginia in several ships bound for the opposite side of the world. Because of his heritage and the rampant bigotry of the time, Wiki is falsely accused of murder just before the ships sail. He is exonerated in time to join the expedition, on the condition that he allow the local sheriff to deputize him to find the real killer, whom he suspects to be on Wiki's ship. This unusual and intriguing mystery is the fiction debut of New Zealander Joan Druett, author of many nonfiction works on maritime history.

Where it's reviewed:
Booklist, September 1, 2004, page 68
Library Journal, August 2004, page 59
Publishers Weekly, July 26, 2004, page 41

Other books you might like:
Max Byrd, *Shooting the Sun*, 2004
Barbara Hambly, *The Benjamin January Series*, 1997-
Patrick O'Brian, *The Aubrey/Maturin Series*, 1970-2004
Wilder Perkins, *The Bartholomew Hoare Series*, 1998-2001
Richard Zimler, *Hunting Midnight*, 2003

63

BRENDAN DUBOIS

Buried Dreams
(New York: St. Martin's Minotaur, 2004)

Story type: Amateur Detective
Series: Lewis Cole. Book 5
Subject(s): Beaches; History; Archaeology

Major character(s): Lewis Cole, Journalist (magazine columnist), Detective—Amateur
Time period(s): 2000s
Locale(s): Tyler, New Hampshire

Summary: Lewis Cole used to work for the Department of Defense, and when he left government work he signed a nondisclosure form that required him to keep his past and the terms of his leaving secret. Now he lives in a beachfront house on the New Hampshire coast, from which he writes an occasional magazine column and spends the rest of his time doing pretty much as he pleases. By chance he befriends Jon Ericson, an amateur archaeologist who combs the beaches after each storm, hoping to turn up evidence of a Viking settlement he's convinced once existed on the site. When he calls Lewis one day with the news that he's finally found his proof, Lewis rushes to see it but instead finds Jon dead. The author has written several stand-alone mysteries as well this very pleasant, low-key series.

Where it's reviewed:
Booklist, May 15, 2004, page 1600
Publishers Weekly, May 31, 2004, page 54

Other books by the same author:
Killer Waves, 2002
The Shattered Shell, 1999
Black Tide, 1995
Dead Sand, 1994

Other books you might like:
Gerry Boyle, *The Jack McMorrow Series*, 1993-
Philip R. Craig, *The J.W. Jackson Series*, 1989-
William Landay, *Mission Flats*, 2003
William G. Tapply, *The Brady Coyne Series*, 1984-
Randy Wayne White, *The Doc Ford Series*, 1990-

64

MARGARET DUMAS

Speak Now

(Scottsdale, Arizona: Poisoned Pen Press, 2004)

Story type: Amateur Detective
Subject(s): Theater; Marriage; Secrets
Major character(s): Charley Van Leeuwen, Director (theatrical), Heiress
Time period(s): 2000s
Locale(s): San Francisco, California

Summary: Returning to San Francisco from a year of studying repertory theater in England, wealthy heiress Charley Van Leeuwen surprises her friends by bringing back a husband, handsome retired Navy meteorologist Jack Fairfax. The newlyweds themselves are in for a big surprise when they find the bathtub in their luxurious hotel suite occupied by a dead body. It quickly becomes apparent that Jack may not have told Charley everything about his past. She gamely endures a series of frightening events and even struggles to stage a play and keep her repertory theater going. A sort of hybrid of the sophisticated comic husband-wife detective novel and the spy caper, it's the author's first novel, short-listed for the British Crime Writers Association Debut Dagger.

Where it's reviewed:
Booklist, September 1, 2004, page 68
Library Journal, June 1, 2004, page 109
Mystery News, December 2004/January 2005, page 15
Publishers Weekly, September 6, 2004, page 50

Other books you might like:
Dorothy Cannell, *The Ellie and Ben Haskell Series*, 1984-
P.M. Carlson, *The Maggie Ryan Series*, 1985-1991
Dashiell Hammett, *The Thin Man*, 1934
Takis Iakovou, *The Nick and Julia Lambros Series*, 1996-1998
  Judy Iakovou, co-author
Joanne Pence, *The Angelina Amalfi Series*, 1993-

65

CAROLA DUNN

A Mourning Wedding

(New York: St. Martin's Minotaur, 2004)

Story type: Historical; Amateur Detective
Series: Daisy Dalrymple. Book 13
Subject(s): Social Classes; Weddings; Family Life
Major character(s): Daisy Dalrymple, Journalist, Detective—Amateur; Alec Fletcher, Police Officer (inspector), Spouse (of Daisy)
Time period(s): 1920s (1924)
Locale(s): London, England

Summary: Daisy, now in the early stages of pregnancy, and her policeman husband, Inspector Alec Fletcher, accept an invitation to the gala wedding of their friend Lucy Fotheringay at her grandfather's country home, Haverhill. The festivities are marred by the discovery of the bride's great-aunt, strangled to death in her bed, and then her uncle's dead body in the conservatory. Along with her husband, Daisy begins investigating the myriad family members to see who could be responsible for these disturbing events.

Other books by the same author:
Die Laughing, 2003
Mistletoe and Murder, 2002
The Case of the Murdered Muckraker, 2002
To Davy Jones Below, 2001
Rattle His Bones, 2000

Other books you might like:
James Anderson, *The Affair of the Blood-Stained Egg Cozy*, 1975
K.K. Beck, *The Iris Cooper Series*, 1984-
Kerry Greenwood, *The Phryne Fisher Series*, 1989-
Laurie R. King, *Justice Hall*, 2002
Jacqueline Winspear, *The Maisie Dobbs Series*, 2003-

66

MICHAEL ALLEN DYMMOCH

The Fall

(New York: St. Martin's Minotaur, 2004)

Story type: Psychological Suspense

Mystery

Subject(s): Organized Crime; Federal Witness Security Program

Major character(s): Joanne Lessing, Photographer, Single Parent

Time period(s): 2000s

Locale(s): Chicago, Illinois (suburbs)

Summary: Professional photographer and single mother Joanne Lessing is taking pictures of Canadian geese at a suburban Chicago park when she happens to witness a hit-and-run accident when one car sideswipes another and flees the scene. Of course, she photographs the incident and of course she turns the photos over to the police, who identify the driver as a Mafia hit man whom the FBI has been hunting for years. When an elderly man in the witness protection program is killed the same day in the same neighborhood, the FBI wants Joanne to testify and offers to place her and her teenage son in the witness protection program. Not wanting to endanger herself or her son, Joanne refuses, even though she's become romantically involved with the FBI agent on the case. The author has also written a series featuring Chicago cop John Thinnes and gay Chicago psychiatrist Jack Caleb.

Where it's reviewed:
Booklist, August 2004, page 1904
Drood Review of Mystery, June/July 2004, page 11
Publishers Weekly, July 12, 2004, page 47

Other books by the same author:
The Feline Friendship, 2003
Incendiary Designs, 1998
The Death of Blue Mountain Cat, 1995
The Man Who Understood Cats, 1993

Other books you might like:
Jan Burke, *The Irene Kelly Series*, 1993-
Barbara D'Amato, *The Cat Marsala Series*, 1990-
Libby Fischer Hellmann, *The Ellie Foreman Series*, 2002-
Wendy Hornsby, *The Maggie MacGowen Series*, 1992-
Stephen White, *The Program*, 2001

67

MARTIN EDWARDS

The Coffin Trail

(Scottsdale, Arizona: Poisoned Pen Press, 2004)

Story type: Traditional

Series: Hannah Scarlett & Daniel Kind. Book 1

Subject(s): Rural Life

Major character(s): Daniel Kind, Historian, Television Personality; Hannah Scarlett, Police Officer (detective chief inspector)

Time period(s): 2000s

Locale(s): Brackdale, England (Lake District)

Summary: Oxford historian Daniel Kind has been swept off his feet by Miranda, a vibrant young woman to whom he shows Tarn Cottage in a beautiful, remote valley in the Lake District. She impulsively decides they should sell their houses and buy the cottage, where they can start a new life together working from home. Daniel goes along with the plan, although he is a little uneasy because of his history with the place. The cottage was the home of a young autistic friend of

his, Barrie Gilpin, who was suspected of murdering a young woman and arranging her body on an ancient pagan site called the Sacrifice Stone some 20 years earlier. Barrie died before there could be an investigation, but now the local police have set up a cold case unit headed up by DCI Hannah Scarlett, a protegee of Daniel's policeman father, who made the original arrest. Daniel's interest in helping her solve the case is colored by his desire to clear Barrie of the crime. The author, a prolific editor, anthologist, and writer of nonfiction, has also written a series featuring Liverpool lawyer Harry Devlin.

Where it's reviewed:
Booklist, September 15, 2004, page 212
Mystery News, December 2004/January 2005, page 12
Publishers Weekly, August 1, 2004, page 55

Other books by the same author:
The First Cut Is the Deepest, 1999
The Devil in Disguise, 1998
Eve of Destruction, 1996 (published in the US in 1998)
Yesterday's Papers, 1994
All the Lonely People, 1991 (published in the US in 2004)

Other books you might like:
Stephen Booth, *The Ben Cooper/Diane Fry Series*, 2000-
Deborah Crombie, *The Duncan Kincaid/Gemma James Series*, 1993-
Reginald Hill, *The Dalziel/Pascoe Series*, 1970-
Val McDermid, *A Place of Execution*, 2000
Peter Robinson, *The Inspector Alan Banks Series*, 1987-

68

RUTH DUDLEY EDWARDS

Carnage on the Committee

(Scottsdale, Arizona: Poisoned Pen Press, 2004)

Story type: Amateur Detective; Humor

Series: Robert Amiss. Book 10

Subject(s): Literature; Authors and Writers; Publishing

Major character(s): Robert Amiss, Writer (aspiring mystery novelist), Detective—Amateur; Baroness Jack Troutbeck, Administrator (mistress of college), Detective—Amateur

Time period(s): 2000s

Locale(s): London, England; Cambridge, England

Summary: Having given up the British civil service for good, Robert Amiss is now an aspiring mystery novelist and a member of the judging panel for the prestigious (and lucrative) Knapper-Warburton Literary Prize. When the panel's chairperson dies mysteriously, Robert immediately calls upon his old friend, Baroness ''Jack'' Troutbeck, to fill in, knowing full well what kind of mischief she will make (and how much she will loathe doing the necessary reading). For one thing, the famously politically incorrect baroness firmly believes the prize should be awarded on literary merit, not upon the author's ethnicity, gender, or politics. For another, she's fully capable of shamelessly manipulating the committee members any way she wants. Even as she rides roughshod over them, the judges are being murdered one by one, until all of them are placed under guard by the police. The author herself has ridden roughshod over any number of cherished British institutions in her career, from elite men's clubs to academia to the

Church of England, taking no prisoners as she does so. The publishing industry itself, as well as literary prizes, are skewered here.

Where it's reviewed:
Publishers Weekly, October 25, 2004, page 31

Other books by the same author:
The Anglo-Irish Murders, 2002
Publish and Be Murdered, 1999
Murder in a Cathedral, 1997
Ten Lords A-Leaping, 1996
Matricide at St. Martha's, 1994

Other books you might like:
Robert Barnard, *Death of an Old Goat*, 1974
Sarah Caudwell, *The Hilary Tamar Series*, 1981-2000
Martha Grimes, *Foul Matter*, 2003
Andrew Taylor, *The William Dougal Series*, 1982-
Donald E. Westlake, *The Hook*, 2000

ANTHONY EGLIN

The Blue Rose
(New York: St. Martin's Minotaur, 2004)

Story type: Amateur Detective
Subject(s): Gardens and Gardening; Country Life
Major character(s): Kate Sheppard, Antiques Dealer, Detective—Amateur; Alex Sheppard, Architect, Detective—Amateur
Time period(s): 2000s
Locale(s): Wiltshire, England

Summary: One day while driving through the Wiltshire countryside, Kate and Alex spot a lovely old house, known locally as The Parsonage, that is exactly the house of their dreams, from its exquisite architectural detailing to its two-acre walled garden. They buy it, move in, and are busy renovating the overgrown garden when Kate discovers a rosebush bearing sapphire-blue blooms—the Holy Grail of rose fanciers and breeders. The discovery could bring them millions, as horticulturists have been trying unsuccessfully for decades to develop such a bloom. However, when word of it leaks out, their life turns into a nightmare that includes unprincipled plant breeders, kidnapping, theft, and even murder. First mystery.

Where it's reviewed:
Library Journal, November 1, 2004, page 60
Publishers Weekly, November 1, 2004, page 47

Other books you might like:
Susan Kenney, *Garden of Malice*, 1983
Barbara Michaels, *Vanish with the Rose*, 1992
Sheila Pim, *Common or Garden Crime*, 1945 reprinted 2001
Ann Ripley, *The Louise Eldridge Series*, 1994-
John Sherwood, *The Celia Grant Series*, 1984-1996

EARL EMERSON

Pyro
(New York: Ballantine, 2004)

Story type: Psychological Suspense; Action/Adventure
Subject(s): Arson; Fires; Politics
Major character(s): Paul Wollf, Fire Fighter
Time period(s): 2000s
Locale(s): Seattle, Washington

Summary: Seattle fire lieutenant Paul Wollf is the son of a fire fighter who died in a fire set by an arsonist, setting off a series of events that left his mother in a deep depression and his brother in jail for murder. Paul has a special hatred of arsonists, even more so when a pyromaniac starts setting fires across the city and he and his crew are nearly killed. He's an angry, volatile, risk-taking man whom the department mistrusts but doesn't know how to let go. Once Paul realizes he's been targeted by the arsonists, he begins suspecting everyone. The author, a Seattle fire fighter himself, based this book on two actual serial arsonists and set it in his own firehouse. He has also written a series about Seattle private eye Thomas Black and another about firefighter Mac Fontana.

Where it's reviewed:
Booklist, May 1, 2004, page 1504
Deadly Pleasures, Summer/Fall 2004, page 24
Library Journal, June 1, 2004, page 120
Mystery News, August/September 2004, page 24
Publishers Weekly, July 5, 2004, page 36

Other books by the same author:
Into the Inferno, 2003
Vertical Burn, 2002

Other books you might like:
Suzanne Chazin, *The Fourth Angel*, 2001
Peter Lance, *First Degree Burn*, 1997
Ridley Pearson, *Beyond Recognition*, 1997
Shelley Reuben, *Spent Matches*, 1996
Don Winslow, *California Fire and Life*, 1999

71

K.J. ERICKSON

Alone at Night
(New York: St. Martin's Minotaur, 2004)

Story type: Police Procedural
Series: Mars Bahr. Book 4
Subject(s): Missing Persons; Fathers and Sons; Kidnapping
Major character(s): Marshall ''Mars'' Bahr, Detective—Police, Divorced Person; Nettie Frisch, Detective—Police
Time period(s): 2000s (2003); 1980s (1984)
Locale(s): Minneapolis, Minnesota; Redstone, Minnesota

Summary: Mars and his partner Nettie have left the Minneapolis Police Department to join the Cold Case Unit with the State of Minnesota. Mars needs a change of pace, and Nettie needs to test a database she's developing. They decide that their first project will be working on the probable abductions of three convenience-store workers, in particular that of Andrea Bergstad in 1984 from a store in Redstone, Minnesota. The narrative moves back and forth between the present and the past, detailing the two investigations prompted by Andrea's disappearance.

Where it's reviewed:
Booklist, July 2004, page 1824
Deadly Pleasures, Spring/Fall 2004, page 43

Other books by the same author:
The Last Witness, 2003
The Dead Survivors, 2002
Third Person Singular, 2001

Other books you might like:
Barbara D'Amato, *The Suze Figueroa/Norm Bennis Series*, 1996-
Tami Hoag, *Dust to Dust*, 2001
David Housewright, *The Holland Taylor Series*, 1995-
John Sandford, *The Lucas Davenport Series*, 1989-
Steve Thayer, *The Weatherman*, 1995

72

JANET EVANOVICH

Metro Girl
(New York: HarperCollins, 2004)

Story type: Humor; Action/Adventure
Subject(s): Boats and Boating; Missing Persons; Romance
Major character(s): Alexandra Barnaby, Mechanic (former), Young Woman; Sam Hooker, Sports Figure (NASCAR driver)
Time period(s): 2000s
Locale(s): Miami, Florida; Key West, Florida; At Sea

Summary: After getting a frantic call from her younger brother, ''Wild'' Bill Barnaby, Alex leaves Baltimore for Miami, where he was last seen. Someone else is looking for Bill: his friend Sam Hooker, a race car driver whose boat, *The Happy Hooker*, Bill has borrowed without permission. Alex, pert, blonde, and sexy, is a sister under the skin to the author's wildly popular series character Stephanie Plum. Like Alex, Stephanie can't drive a car without destroying it (although Alex would be able to rebuild its engine). There's definite chemistry between Alex and Sam, lots of bad guys, some exciting boating sequences in international waters, and even a plot (involving Cuban gold and the long-ago missile crisis).

Where it's reviewed:
Booklist, November 1, 2004, page 443
Entertainment Weekly, November 5, 2004, page 85
Publishers Weekly, November 8, 2004, page 36

Other books by the same author:
Ten Big Ones, 2004
Hard Eight, 2002
Visions of Sugar Plums, 2002
Seven Up, 2001
Hot Six, 2000

Other books you might like:
Nancy Bartholomew, *The Sierra Lavatoni Series*, 1998-
Tim Dorsey, *The Serge O. Storms Series*, 1999-
Carl Hiaasen, *Skinny Dip*, 2004

Claire Matturro, *Skinny-Dipping*, 2004
Sarah Strohmeyer, *The Bubbles Yablonsky Series*, 2001-

73

NANCY FAIRBANKS (Pseudonym of Nancy Herndon)

Holy Guacamole!
(New York: Berkley, 2004)

Story type: Amateur Detective
Series: Carolyn Blue. Book 6
Subject(s): Food; Travel; Opera
Major character(s): Carolyn Blue, Journalist (food writer), Detective—Amateur
Time period(s): 2000s
Locale(s): El Paso, Texas

Summary: Faculty wife and dedicated foodie Carolyn Blue has been fortunate in being able to coordinate her writing assignments with her husband's academic travels. For this book, however, she and Jason are staying at home in El Paso, where they've been invited to join the executive committee of the local opera company. At a post-production party, the artistic director, Vladislav Gubenko, dies after eating some of his favorite guacamole, and soon Carolyn is again on the trail of a murderer. Many recipes for Mexican food and drink are included, along with bits of history pertaining to border cuisine. Under her real name, the author writes a series about small-town Texas police officer Elena Jarvis.

Where it's reviewed:
Romantic Times, December 2004, page 85

Other books by the same author:
The Perils of Paella, 2004
Chocolate Quake, 2003
Death a l'Orange, 2002
Crime Brulee, 2001
Truffled Feathers, 2001

Other books you might like:
Michael Bond, *The Monsieur Pamplemousse Series*, 1983-
Maddy Hunter, *The Emily Andrew Series*, 2003-
Peter King, *The Gourmet Detective*, 1994
Joanne Pence, *The Angelina Amalfi Series*, 1993-
Phyllis Richman, *The Chas. Wheatley Series*, 1997-

74

KATHARINE FARRER

The Cretan Counterfeit
(Lyons, Colorado: Rue Morgue Press, 2004)

Story type: Police Procedural; Traditional
Series: Richard Ringwood. Book 2
Subject(s): Archaeology; Museums; Marriage
Major character(s): Richard Ringwood, Police Officer (detective inspector); Claire Liddicote Ringwood, Spouse (of Richard)
Time period(s): 1950s
Locale(s): London, England

Summary: Richard Ringwood and his new wife Claire, a fellow Oxford graduate, delight in reading between the lines of the *Times* obituaries. One particularly dismissive notice catches their attention, that of the death of wealthy amateur archaeologist Sir Alban Worrell. Soon afterwards, a young woman who wrote a spirited defense of Sir Alban in response to the obituary is nearly killed in a knife attack. Ringwood conducts a thorough investigation which introduces him to several of the archaeologists and other people associated with Sir Alban's dig in Corfu, including a volatile Cretan restaurateur. Originally published in England in 1954, the book makes its first American appearance here.

Other books by the same author:
The Missing Link, 1952 (reprinted 2004)

Other books you might like:
Nicholas Blake, *The Nigel Strangeways Series*, 1935-1968
Clyde B. Clason, *Murder Gone Minoan*, 1939
    reprinted 2003
Ngaio Marsh, *The Roderick Alleyn Series*, 1934-1982
Dorothy L. Sayers, *The Lord Peter Wimsey Series*, 1923-1937
Josephine Tey, *The Alan Grant Series*, 1929-1952

75

KATHARINE FARRER

The Missing Link
(Lyons, Colorado: Rue Morgue Press, 2004)

Story type: Police Procedural; Traditional
Series: Richard Ringwood. Book 1
Subject(s): Academia; Babies; Gypsies
Major character(s): Richard Ringwood, Police Officer (detective inspector); Clare Liddicote, Scholar, Fiance(e)
Time period(s): 1950s
Locale(s): Oxford, England

Summary: Young Inspector Richard Ringwood of Scotland Yard is interrupted while on holiday courting his prospective bride, Clare Liddicote, to investigate the kidnapping of an infant from its pram in the yard of an Oxford don. It turns out that Richard went to school with John Link, the frantic father, and he enlists Clare's aid in tracking down the kidnapper, knowing that their chances of finding the child alive decrease with each hour that goes by. A prophecy from an old gypsy woman, a suspect herself in the kidnapping, is more confusing than enlightening. Both the city and the university provide the backdrop to the proceedings, which end in an exciting and terrifying chase in which Richard finally meets his adversary face to face in a most unlikely place. This is the author's first novel, originally published in England in 1952 and making its first American appearance.

Other books you might like:
Margery Allingham, *The Albert Campion Series*, 1930-1968
Nicholas Blake, *The Nigel Strangeways Series*, 1935-1968
Ngaio Marsh, *The Roderick Alleyn Series*, 1934-1982
Dorothy L. Sayers, *Gaudy Night*, 1935
Josephine Tey, *The Alan Grant Series*, 1929-1952

76

MONICA FERRIS (Pseudonym of Mary Monica Kuhlfeld)

Crewel Yule
(New York: Berkley, 2004)

Story type: Amateur Detective
Series: Betsy Devonshire. Book 8
Subject(s): Crafts; Christmas; Sewing
Major character(s): Betsy Devonshire, Store Owner (needlework shop), Detective—Amateur
Time period(s): 2000s
Locale(s): Nashville, Tennessee; Excelsior, Minnesota

Summary: Since taking over her late sister's needlework shop, Crewel World, in the small Minnesota town of Excelsior, Betsy Devonshire has thrown herself into the business. She's attending a needlework convention in Nashville just before Christmas, when a fellow shop owner plunges nine floors to her death. Everyone at first assumes it is an accident, but Betsy soon begins to wonder. Belle Hammermill had many enemies, several of whom are at the convention, and eventually Betsy and her assistant, Godwin, add up the clues to a murder. A pattern for a crewel Christmas ornament is included.

Where it's reviewed:
Library Journal, June 1, 2004, page 109
Publishers Weekly, September 27, 2004, page 41
Romantic Times, November 2004, page 88

Other books by the same author:
Cutwork, 2004
Hanging by a Thread, 2003
A Murderous Yarn, 2002
Unravelled Sleeve, 2001
A Stitch in Time, 2000

Other books you might like:
Susan Wittig Albert, *The China Bayles Series*, 1992-
Donna Andrews, *Revenge of the Wrought Iron Flamingos*, 2001
Lizbie Brown, *The Elizabeth Blair Series*, 1992-
Laura Childs, *The Carmela Bertrand Series*, 2003-
Tamar Myers, *The Abigail Timberlake Series*, 1996-

77

DAN FESPERMAN

The Warlord's Son
(New York: Knopf, 2004)

Story type: Action/Adventure
Subject(s): Political Thriller; Cultures and Customs; Terrorism
Major character(s): Stanford J. ''Skelly'' Kelly, Journalist (war correspondent); Najeeb Ajam, Guide, Linguist (translator)
Time period(s): 2000s (2001)
Locale(s): Peshawar, Pakistan; Afghanistan

Summary: The author turns his attention from Eastern Europe, the scene of his earlier thrillers, to war-torn Afghanistan in the wake of September 11, 2001. Skelly, a burned-out former war correspondent now covering the suburban beat of a Midwestern daily, wants to close out his career on a high note and is given the coveted opportunity to go abroad to cover the war on terror. His first stop is Peshawar, Pakistan, where he hires a young American-educated translator, Najeeb, to be his "fixer" and arrange for him to get into Afghanistan. Najeeb can't tell Skelly that he's been forced to be an informer for his government and has been cast out of his tribe for betraying his own father. Further, he's frantic over the disappearance of his girlfriend Daliya, who is also being ostracized for refusing to fall in with an arranged marriage. Eventually Skelly and Najeeb make their way into Afghanistan, where the search for bin Laden is in full force, and forge an unlikely friendship in the process. The author is himself a war correspondent who was stationed in Afghanistan.

Where it's reviewed:
Booklist, September 1, 2004, page 60
Entertainment Weekly, September 17, 2004, page 86
Library Journal, September 1, 2004, page 130
Publishers Weekly, August 16, 2004, page 43

Other books by the same author:
The Small Boat of Great Sorrows, 2003
Lie in the Dark, 1999

Other books you might like:
Cheryl Benard, *Moghul Buffet*, 1998
John Le Carre, *Absolute Friends*, 2003
Eliot Pattison, *Beautiful Ghosts*, 2004
Martin Cruz Smith, *Wolves Eat Dogs*, 2004
Steven E. Wilson, *Winter in Kandahar*, 2003

78

SHARON FIFFER

Buried Stuff

(New York: St. Martin's Minotaur, 2004)

Story type: Amateur Detective
Series: Jane Wheel. Book 4
Subject(s): Collectors and Collecting; Antiques; Archaeology
Major character(s): Jane Wheel, Antiques Dealer, Detective—Amateur; Charley Wheel, Scientist (geologist), Spouse (of Jane); Tim Lowry, Antiques Dealer, Detective—Amateur (homosexual)
Time period(s): 2000s
Locale(s): Evanston, Illinois; Kankakee, Illinois

Summary: In an attempt to streamline her life and get rid of the incredible amount of stuff she's collected over the years, Jane Wheel has finally worked up the courage to hold her very first garage sale. She's relieved when the event is called to a halt by a phone call from her mother Nellie, who wants Jane and her geologist husband Charley to rush down to Kankakee. It seems her parents' neighbor, Fuzzy Neilson, has found some bone fragments buried on his farm, and he wants Charley to see if they are of any archaeological significance. Jane's best friend Tim, a gay antiques dealer, decides to come along, with the idea of helping to boost Kankakee's economy by having the pretty little river town host the World's Largest Garage Sale. When a very recent body turns up on the Neilson farm, Jane and Tim turn detective again.

Where it's reviewed:
Booklist, November 15, 2004, page 565
Library Journal, November 1, 2004, page 60

Other books by the same author:
The Wrong Stuff, 2003
Dead Guy's Stuff, 2002
Killer Stuff, 2001

Other books you might like:
Elaine Flinn, *Tagged for Murder*, 2004
Susan Holtzer, *Something to Kill For*, 1994
Toni L.P. Kelner, *Tight as a Tick*, 1998
Deborah Morgan, *The Jeff Talbot Series*, 2001-
Tamar Myers, *The Abigail Timberlake Series*, 1996-

79

ELAINE FLINN

Tagged for Murder

(New York: Avon, 2004)

Story type: Amateur Detective
Series: Molly Doyle. Book 2
Subject(s): Antiques; Sisters; Children
Major character(s): Molly Doyle, Antiques Dealer, Detective—Amateur
Time period(s): 2000s
Locale(s): Carmel, California

Summary: Former high-powered Manhattan antiques dealer Molly Doyle has started all over again after being unwittingly involved in an fake antiques scandal dreamed up by her ex-husband and his girlfriend. Her friend and mentor Max Roman has given her a rundown shop to manage in Carmel, California, that she's transformed into a smart little gem filled with treasures. Right now she's shocked and saddened by the murder of a friend and colleague, Trudy Collins. Then she has a surprise visitor in the person of her selfish sister Carrie, whom she hasn't seen in 15 years and who only stays long enough to leave her 12-year-old daughter with Molly before vanishing again. Emma becomes very dear to Molly, who turns detective when another dealer is murdered, one who is possibly connected with Molly's family.

Other books by the same author:
Dealing in Murder, 2003

Other books you might like:
Sharon Fiffer, *The Jane Wheel Series*, 2001-
Susan Holtzer, *Something to Kill For*, 1994
Toni L.P. Kelner, *Tight as a Tick*, 1998
Deborah Morgan, *The Jeff Talbot Series*, 2001-
Tamar Myers, *The Abigail Timberlake Series*, 1996-

80

JOANNE FLUKE

Sugar Cookie Murder

(New York: Kensington, 2004)

Story type: Amateur Detective
Series: Hannah Swensen. Book 6
Subject(s): Christmas; Cooks and Cooking; Small Town Life

Major character(s): Hannah Swensen, Baker, Detective—
Amateur
Time period(s): 2000s
Locale(s): Lake Eden, Minnesota

Summary: Hannah Swensen, owner of The Cookie Jar Bakery
in the small Minnesota town of Lake Eden, is back in a new
case with a Christmas background. She's compiled a cookbook of recipes from local residents and is introducing it at a
festive holiday party at the town's community center. Among
the many guests are recently divorced Martin Dubinski and
his brand-new trophy wife Brandi, a former Las Vegas show-
girl. During the proceedings, Hannah notices that her
mother's antique silver cake knife has gone missing, and then
it's discovered protruding from the chest of a very dead
Brandi. Together with her family, friends, and a handsome
homicide detective, Hannah goes on a search for the killer.
Many recipes, for everything from soups, salads, and appe-
tizers to entrees and side dishes to desserts are included, over
80 in all, making it nearly as much a cookbook as a mystery.

Where it's reviewed:
Publishers Weekly, September 6, 2004, page 49
Romantic Times, November 2004, page 86

Other books by the same author:
Fudge Cupcake Murder, 2004
Lemon Meringue Pie Murder, 2003
Blueberry Muffin Murder, 2002
Strawberry Shortcake Murder, 2001
Chocolate Chip Cookie Murder, 2000

Other books you might like:
JoAnna Carl, *The Chocolate Cat Caper*, 2002
Laura Childs, *The Theodosia Browning Series*, 2001-
Isis Crawford, *A Catered Murder*, 2003
Diane Mott Davidson, *The Goldy Bear Schulz Series*, 1990-
Nancy Fairbanks, *The Carolyn Blue Series*, 2001-

G.M. FORD

Red Tide

(New York: William Morrow, 2004)

Story type: Action/Adventure
Series: Frank Corso. Book 4
Subject(s): Biological Warfare; Terrorism
Major character(s): Frank Corso, Journalist (crime writer);
Meg Dougherty, Photographer
Time period(s): 2000s
Locale(s): Seattle, Washington

Summary: Frank and Meg are attending the opening of her
one-woman photography show when the gallery is evacuated
because of a toxic spill in the area. It turns out to be a terrorist
attack in which a mutated strain of the Ebola virus has been let
loose in a nearby bus tunnel, killing a hundred people. It's just
the beginning of a nightmarish chain of events that could lead
to the destruction of the human race, if a way to stop an even
more lethal strain of the virus can't be found. Frank, a
disgraced journalist with nerves of steel and a tenacious
curiosity, is just the man to find that way. The author has

written a series about Seattle private eye Leo Waterman and
his band of homeless helpers.

Where it's reviewed:
Booklist, June 1, 2004, page 1706
Mystery News, August/September 2004, page 22
Publishers Weekly, June 21, 2004, page 43

Other books by the same author:
A Blind Eye, 2003
Black River, 2002
Fury, 2001

Other books you might like:
Lee Child, *The Jack Reacher Series*, 1997-
Michael Connelly, *The Harry Bosch Series*, 1992-
Jeffery Deaver, *The Devil's Teardrop*, 1999
Earl Emerson, *Into the Inferno*, 2003
James W. Hall, *The Thorn Series*, 1987-

82

CHRISTOPHER FOWLER

Full Dark House

(New York: Bantam, 2004)

Story type: Police Procedural; Historical/World War II
Subject(s): World War II; Theater; Opera
Major character(s): Arthur Bryant, Detective—Police; John
May, Detective—Police
Time period(s): 2000s; 1940s (1940)
Locale(s): London, England

Summary: In the present day, elderly police detective Arthur
Bryant is caught in an explosion at the Peculiar Crimes Unit
headquarters in London, and his longtime partner, John May,
investigates, with the help of their younger colleague, Detective Sergeant Janice Longbright. The heart of the story, however, is a lengthy flashback to the first case the men solved
together during the early days of the Blitz, when a series of
murders took various members of the cast of a production of
Orpheus in the Underworld at the Palace Theater. First mystery by an English author known for his tales of urban horror.

Where it's reviewed:
Booklist, May 1, 2004, page 1506
Deadly Pleasures, Summer/Fall 2004, page 1506
Library Journal, June 1, 2004, page 108
Publishers Weekly, May 3, 2004, page 175

Other books you might like:
Robert Barnard, *Out of the Blackout*, 1984
Max Allan Collins, *The London Blitz Murders*, 2004
John Lawton, *Black Out*, 1995
Ngaio Marsh, *Night at the Vulcan*, 1951
Jill Paton Walsh, *A Presumption of Death*, 2003
based on characters by Dorothy L. Sayers

83

MARGARET FRAZER (Pseudonym of Gail Frazer)

A Play of Isaac

(New York: Berkley, 2004)

Story type: Historical/Medieval
Series: Joliffe. Book 1
Subject(s): Middle Ages; Theater; Actors and Actresses
Major character(s): Joliffe, Actor
Time period(s): 15th century (1434)
Locale(s): Oxford, England

Summary: The author of the Dame Frevisse mysteries begins a new series, set in the same time period (1434). This series features a struggling family of actors, headed by their patriarch, Joliffe, who was introduced in the Frevisse series and comes into his own here. The players are performing in Oxford during the Corpus Christi festival. In the audience is Lewis, a young man with Down syndrome (known as an Eden-child to his contemporaries, who believed such people were touched by God). He invites them to be guests in his home, where his wealthy parents welcome them and offer food and lodging in return for two additional performances. The murder of an unwelcome guest and then widespread food poisoning at a banquet puts Joliffe and the other actors under suspicion, forcing him to turn detective to clear their names.

Where it's reviewed:
Romantic Times, October 2004, page 86

Other books by the same author:
The Bastard's Tale, 2003
The Clerk's Tale, 2002
The Squire's Tale, 2000
The Reeve's Tale, 1999
The Maiden's Tale, 1998

Other books you might like:
Alys Clare, *The Abbess Helewise Series*, 1999-
C.L. Grace, *The Kathryn Swinbrooke Series*, 1993-
Edward Marston, *The Nicholas Bracewell Series*, 1988-
Kate Sedley, *The Roger the Chapman Series*, 1991-
Leonard Tourney, *The Players' Boy Is Dead*, 1980

84

ERLE STANLEY GARDNER

The Danger Zone and Other Stories

(Virginia Beach, Virginia: Crippen & Landru, 2004)

Story type: Collection
Subject(s): Short Stories
Time period(s): 1930s

Summary: Ten of the 11 stories in this collection originally appeared in pulp magazines in the 1930s. They feature a variety of lesser known but colorful sleuths from the creator of Perry Mason, including the unconventional private eye Snowy Shane, gentleman burglar George Brokay, and ex-convict Slicker Williams. Each story relies on an ingenious (sometimes preposterous) gimmick for its convoluted plot and moves with lightning speed. Part of the publisher's Lost Classics line, the collection is the first of several featuring

various of this prolific author's lesser-known pulp characters. Editor Bill Pronzini contributes an informative introduction.

Where it's reviewed:
Booklist, June 1, 2004, page 1707

Other books by the same author:
Honest Money & Other Short Novels, 1992 (short stories)
Dead Men's Letters, 1990 (short stories)
The Blonde in Lower Six, 1990 (short stories)
The Adventures of Paul Pry. Vols. 1-2, 1989-1992 (short stories)
The Amazing Adventures of Lester Leith, 1980 (short stories)

Other books you might like:
Joseph Commings, *Banner Deadlines*, 2004
    short stories
Norbert Davis, *The Adventures of Max Latin*, 1988
    short stories
Maxwell Grant, *Norgil the Magician*, 1977
    short stories
Maxim Jakubowski, *The Mammoth Book of Pulp Action*, 2001
    editor
Craig Rice, *Murder, Mysteries and Malone*, 2002
    short stories

85

FRIEDRICH GLAUSER

Thumbprint

(London: Bitter Lemon, 2004)

Story type: Police Procedural
Series: Sergeant Studer. Book 1
Subject(s): Law Enforcement; Cultures and Customs
Major character(s): Studer, Police Officer (sergeant)
Time period(s): 1930s (1936)
Locale(s): Gerzenstein, Switzerland

Summary: Studer, a lowly sergeant in the Criminal Investigation Department of the cantonal police, is investigating the murder of a traveling salesman in the forest of Gerzenstein. Although a suspect has confessed to the murder, Studer is skeptical of his story. He digs deeper and uncovers a nightmare of envy, sexual abuse, and corruption that belies the tranquil appearance of the Swiss countryside and quaint villages where the events occur. First published in 1936, this is the first of five crime novels featuring Sergeant Studer to be published in the U.S. The author is a cult figure in Europe after whom the German equivalent of the Edgar award is named. Translated from the German by Mike Mitchell.

Where it's reviewed:
Mystery News, December 2004/January 2005, page 22

Other books you might like:
Friedrich Duerenmatt, *The Pledge*, 1959
Henning Mankell, *The Kurt Wallander Series*, 1997-
Gunter Ohnemus, *The Russian Passenger*, 2004
Georges Simenon, *The Inspector Maigret Series*, 1931-1972
Maj Sjowall, *The Martin Beck Series*, 1967-1976
    Per Wahloo, co-author

86

CHRISTINE GOFF

Death Takes a Gander

(New York: Berkley, 2004)

Story type: Amateur Detective
Series: Birdwatcher's Mysteries. Book 4
Subject(s): Animals/Birds; American West; Wildlife Conservation
Major character(s): Angela Dimato, Government Official (U.S. Fish & Wildlife agent), Detective—Amateur
Time period(s): 2000s
Locale(s): Elk Park, Colorado

Summary: Rookie Fish & Wildlife agent Angela Dimato answers a call from the senior agent who is training her, but when she arrives at Barr Lake, she finds him dead and a swan behaving strangely. The official verdict is suicide, but Angela isn't so sure. Then, during the first annual Ice Fishing Jamboree at Elk Park, hundreds of poisoned dead and dying geese are found on the ice. Meanwhile, guests at the nearby Drummond Hotel are falling ill, presumably from food poisoning. When she starts getting too nosy, Angela's boss takes her off the case, but she's not one to let that stop her from her investigation. All the books in this series are set in and around Elk Park (presumably based on Estes Park) which adjoins Rocky Mountain National Park, and feature a variety of protagonists and various species of birds.

Where it's reviewed:
Romantic Times, December 2004, page 90

Other books by the same author:
A Nest in the Ashes, 2001
Death of a Songbird, 2001
A Rant of Ravens, 2000

Other books you might like:
Donna Andrews, *Murder with Puffins*, 2000
J.S. Borthwick, *The Case of the Hook-Billed Kites*, 1982
Ann Cleeves, *A Bird in the Hand*, 1983
Jessica Speart, *Bird Brained*, 1999
Judith Van Gieson, *Raptor*, 1990

87

ED GORMAN, Editor
MARTIN H. GREENBERG, Co-Editor

The World's Finest Mystery and Crime Stories: Fifth Annual Collection

(New York: Forge, 2004)

Story type: Anthology
Series: World's Finest Mystery and Crime Stories. Book 5
Subject(s): Short Stories

Summary: These two veteran editors, who have produced countless anthologies between them, have selected 32 stories from around the world for this latest installment in the series. Essays on the state of the mystery in Britain, the U.S., Canada, and Germany, and on mystery fandom, as well as a yearbook of the short story, round out the volume. Notable contributors include Liza Cody, Joyce Carol Oates, Sharyn McCrumb, Rhys Bowen, Peter Robinson, Edward D. Hoch, Dick Lochte, Doug Allyn, and Brendan DuBois. All the stories are reprinted from their first appearances in magazines and original mystery anthologies and are mostly American and British, with a few writers from other countries included. In addition to his achievements as an anthologist and editor, Ed Gorman has written many mystery novels, most recently a series set in America's heartland at mid-century featuring small-town lawyer Sam McCain.

Where it's reviewed:
Publishers Weekly, September 20, 2004, page 49

Other books by the same author:
The World's Finest Mystery and Crime Stories: Fourth Annual Collection, 2003 (Martin H. Greenberg, co-editor)
The World's Finest Mystery and Crime Stories: Third Annual Collection, 2002 (Martin H. Greenberg, co-editor)
The World's Finest Mystery and Crime Stories: Second Annual Collection, 2001
The World's Finest Mystery and Crime Stories: First Annual Collection, 2000

Other books you might like:
Michael Connelly, *The Best American Mystery Stories 2003*, 2003
Otto Penzler, series editor
James Ellroy, *The Best American Mystery Stories 2002*, 2002
Otto Penzler, series editor
Tony Hillerman, *The Oxford Book of American Detective Stories*, 1997
editor
Herbert Maurice Van Thal, *The Mammoth Book of Great Detective Stories*, 2001
editor
Donald E. Westlake, *The Best American Mystery Stories 2000*, 2000
Otto Penzler, series editor

88

DEBORAH GRABIEN

The Famous Flower of Serving Men

(New York: St. Martin's Minotaur, 2004)

Story type: Amateur Detective
Series: Murder, Music and Ghosts of the Past. Book 2
Subject(s): Theater; Ghosts; Actors and Actresses
Major character(s): Penelope ''Penny'' Wintercraft-Hawkes, Director (theatrical), Detective—Amateur; Rupert Dudley ''Ringan'' Laine, Singer (folk singer)
Time period(s): 2000s
Locale(s): London, England

Summary: When Penny is bequeathed a London theater by a French aunt she scarcely knew, as well as the funds to renovate it, she's elated, as it will give her acting company a permanent base and a chance to branch out a bit. Of course, there turns out to be a catch: the theater is inhabited by a vengeful ghost from medieval times determined to right some ancient wrongs. Penny and Ringan realize they have to lay this desperate spirit to rest before they can get on with their lives, and they set out to learn exactly who their ghost is and what her sad history might have been. The story is nicely creepy, with the darkness balanced by the intriguing portrait of bright, talented young urbanites enjoying their lives to the full. It's the second in a series featuring the ghosts of characters in old folk ballads. Besides an earlier mystery with supernatural overtones, the author has written fantasy and romance novels.

Where it's reviewed:
Booklist, November 15, 2004, page 565
Library Journal, November 1, 2004, page 60
Publishers Weekly, October 11, 2004, page 59

Other books by the same author:
The Weaver and the Factory Maid, 2003
Eyes in the Fire, 1989

Other books you might like:
Kate Ellis, *The Wesley Peterson Series*, 1999-
Erin Hart, *Haunted Ground*, 2003
Dorothy MacArdle, *The Uninvited*, 1942
Sharyn McCrumb, *The Songcatcher*, 2001
Sarah Stewart Taylor, *O' Artful Death*, 2003

89

C.L. GRACE (Pseudonym of P.C. Doherty)

A Feast of Poisons
(New York: St. Martin's Minotaur, 2004)

Story type: Historical/Medieval
Series: Kathryn Swinbrooke. Book 7
Subject(s): Middle Ages; Small Town Life; Politics
Major character(s): Kathryn Swinbrooke, Doctor, Detective—Amateur; Colum Murtagh, Spouse (of Kathryn)
Time period(s): 15th century (1473)
Locale(s): Walmer, England; Canterbury, England

Summary: Physician Kathryn Swinbrooke and her new husband Colum Murtagh are visiting the village of Walmer while the local lord, Henry Beauchamp, and emissaries of Louis XI of France meet on important business. During the course of the negotiations, the village blacksmith and his wife, who had been known to step out on him with other men, are both poisoned in different ways. Kathryn doesn't believe it possible that they murdered each other, and neither does the village healer. Much is riding on the state meeting, but Kathryn finds time to investigate what turns out to be the first in a series of poisonings. Under this and other pseudonyms, as well as his real name, the author has written a number of historical series spanning many centuries.

Where it's reviewed:
Booklist, June 1, 2004, page 1707
Publishers Weekly, May 3, 2004, page 175
Romantic Times, August 2004, page 92

Other books by the same author:
A Maze of Murders, 2003
Saintly Murders, 2001
The Book of Shadows, 1996
The Merchant of Death, 1995
The Eye of God, 1994

Other books you might like:
P.C. Doherty, *Dove Amongst the Hawks*, 1990
Robert Farrington, *The Henry Morane Series*, 1971-1978
Margaret Frazer, *The Dame Frevisse Series*, 1992-
Sheri Holman, *A Stolen Tongue*, 1997
Kate Sedley, *The Roger the Chapman Series*, 1991-

90

CAROLINE GRAHAM

A Ghost in the Machine
(New York: St. Martin's Minotaur, 2004)

Story type: Police Procedural; Traditional
Series: Inspector Barnaby. Book 7
Subject(s): Small Town Life; Inheritance; Humor
Major character(s): Tom Barnaby, Police Officer (chief inspector)
Time period(s): 2000s
Locale(s): Forbes Abbot, England

Summary: This talented author is back after a five-year absence with a new Inspector Barnaby mystery, welcome news for admirers of her series of classic village cozies with a bite. Mallory Lawson and his wife Kate seem locked into their unfulfilling jobs and demanding mortgage when his Aunt Carey dies, leaving them a lovely house in the tiny village of Forbes Abbot and the freedom to pursue the life they've always longed for. When the aunt's financial advisor is murdered and another death follows, Inspector Barnaby steps in. Eccentric characters and complex relationships abound, along with generous helpings of humor and suspense. Graham is one of the top-ranking practitioners of the traditional British detective novel.

Where it's reviewed:
Booklist, August 2004, page 1905
Library Journal, August 2004, page 60
Publishers Weekly, July 12, 2004, page 47
Romantic Times, October 2004, page 84

Other books by the same author:
A Place of Safety, 1999
Faithful Unto Death, 1998
Written in Blood, 1995
Death in Disguise, 1993
Death of a Hollow Man, 1993

Other books you might like:
Robert Barnard, *The Charlie Peace/Mike Odhams Series*, 1989-
Colin Dexter, *The Inspector Morse Series*, 1975-
Peter Lovesey, *The Peter Diamond Series*, 1991-
Ngaio Marsh, *The Roderick Alleyn Series*, 1934-1982
Susannah Stacey, *The Robert Bone Series*, 1987-

91

KERRY GREENWOOD

The Castlemaine Murders
(Scottsdale, Arizona: Poisoned Pen Press, 2004)

Story type: Historical; Private Detective

Series: Phryne Fisher. Book 13
Subject(s): Homosexuality/Lesbianism; Chinese; Gold Discoveries
Major character(s): Phryne Fisher, Detective—Private; Lin Chung, Businessman, Lover (of Phryne)
Time period(s): 1920s (1928); 1850s
Locale(s): St. Kilda, Australia; Castlemaine, Australia

Summary: Phryne Fisher is the free-spirited daughter of a baronet who early on fled her domineering father to strike out on her own, with a healthy trust fund to smooth over life's rough edges. Now she's settled in St. Kilda with her two adopted daughters, loyal servants, her lover Lin Chung, and her younger sister Eliza, who has just joined this unconventional household to escape an unwelcome arranged marriage. Eliza, however, has become aloof, condescending, and terribly unhappy, burdened with two great secrets that eventually come out in the open. Phryne has little time to deal with Eliza's problems, however, after she discovers a mummified corpse during an outing to an amusement park and her investigations into its history put her and her entire family into terrible danger. Meanwhile, Lin has been charged by his family with settling a blood feud going back to the Australian gold rush of the 1850s, and both he and Phryne end up in Castlemaine, once the site of the great gold fields that drew fortune hunters from the world over. The two story lines converge neatly, each hinging on the general lawlessness of that colorful period in Australia's history. The background on Chinese immigrants in the 1850s and 1920s is especially well detailed.

Where it's reviewed:
Publishers Weekly, August 23, 2004, page 40

Other books by the same author:
Murder in Montparnasse, 2004
Away with the Fairies, 2001
Death Before Wicket, 1999
Raisins and Almonds, 1997
Urn Burial, 1996

Other books you might like:
K.K. Beck, *The Iris Cooper Series*, 1984-
Carola Dunn, *The Daisy Dalrymple Series*, 1994-
Laurie R. King, *The Mary Russell/Sherlock Holmes Series*, 1994-
Lucy Sussex, *The Scarlet Rider*, 1996
Jacqueline Winspear, *The Maisie Dobbs Series*, 2003-

92

KERRY GREENWOOD

Murder in Montparnasse
(Scottsdale, Arizona: Poisoned Pen Press, 2004)

Story type: Historical; Private Detective
Series: Phryne Fisher. Book 12
Subject(s): World War I
Major character(s): Phryne Fisher, Detective—Private
Time period(s): 1920s (1928); 1910s (1918)
Locale(s): St. Kilda, Australia; Paris, France

Summary: Stylish, flamboyant, pleasure-loving, and shrewdly intelligent, the Hon. Phryne Fisher has led a full and exciting

life, including a stint driving an ambulance in France during World War I. Now, ten years later, she's approached by a couple of former soldiers who unknowingly witnessed a murder while celebrating the end of the war in Paris with several comrades. Now two of the group are dead, and the survivors fear for their lives as well. As it happens, Phryne herself was in the same spot in Montparnasse on the day in question, and while memories flood over her she determines to find out who is stalking the men. A strong cast of supporting characters round out the story, from her Chinese lover, Lin Chung, to a very proper butler to a sympathetic police detective. Except for the first, which was published in paperback in the U.S. some years ago, none of the books in this refreshing series has been available in this country until now. The publisher promises to issue them all in time.

Where it's reviewed:
Booklist, June 1, 2004, page 1707
Library Journal, June 1, 2004, page 106
Mystery News, August/September 2004, page 14
Publishers Weekly, May 3, 2004, page 175

Other books by the same author:
Away with the Fairies, 2001
Death Before Wicket, 1999
Raisins and Almonds, 1997
Urn Burial, 1996
Ruddy Gore, 1995

Other books you might like:
K.K. Beck, *The Iris Cooper Series*, 1984-
Carola Dunn, *The Daisy Dalrymple Series*, 1994-
Laurie R. King, *The Mary Russell/Sherlock Holmes Series*, 1994-
Walter Satterthwait, *Masquerade*, 1998
Jacqueline Winspear, *The Maisie Dobbs Series*, 2003-

93

MARTHA GRIMES

Winds of Change
(New York: Viking, 2004)

Story type: Police Procedural; Traditional
Series: Inspector Jury. Book 19
Subject(s): Children; Abuse; Kidnapping
Major character(s): Richard Jury, Police Officer (detective chief inspector); Melrose Plant, Professor, Sidekick
Time period(s): 2000s
Locale(s): London, England

Summary: When the body of a sexually abused five-year-old girl who had been shot in the back, turns up near a house known to be a hangout for pedophiles, Richard Jury is outraged and launches an investigation. He discovers that the man who heads up the ring is the father of another little girl who had disappeared mysteriously from her country home and has never been found. In his search for the killer, Jury is aided by his aristocratic friend, Melrose Plant, who at one point goes undercover as a gardener to unearth the information Jury needs. As usual, the book's title is taken from the name of a pub, in this case one where Jury and Plant meet frequently to puzzle out the case. The author has also written a number of non-series mysteries.

Where it's reviewed:
Booklist, August 2004, page 1870
Publishers Weekly, July 26, 2004, page 41
Romantic Times, November 2004, page 86

Other books by the same author:
The Grave Maurice, 2002
The Blue Last, 2001
The Lamorna Wink, 1999
The Stargazey, 1998
The Case Has Altered, 1997

Other books you might like:
Deborah Crombie, *The Duncan Kincaid/Gemma James Series*, 1993-
Elizabeth George, *The Thomas Lynley Series*, 1988-
Teri Holbrook, *A Far and Deadly Cry*, 1995
P.D. James, *The Adam Dalgliesh Series*, 1962-
Ruth Rendell, *The Inspector Wexford Series*, 1964-

94

BATYA GUR

Bethlehem Road Murder

(New York: HarperCollins, 2004)

Story type: Police Procedural
Series: Michael Ohayon. Book 5
Subject(s): Judaism; Cultural Conflict; Arab-Israeli Wars
Major character(s): Michael Ohayon, Police Officer (chief superintendent)
Time period(s): 2000s
Locale(s): Jerusalem, Israel

Summary: Michael Ohayon, a Moroccan-born Israeli Jew, was a medieval scholar before turning to police work. He has justifiably been compared to P.D. James' Adam Dalgliesh in terms of his education, temperament, and intelligence, and he is well suited to the challenges that his politically charged job offers him. This time he's investigating the murder of a young Yemenite-Jewish woman in the Arab quarter of West Jerusalem. The setting allows the author to explore the entire history of the Israeli state, including tensions between Ashkenazis and Mizrahis, ongoing conflicts between Jews and Arabs, and a fascinating account of the kidnapping of Yemenite children in the 1950s. Translated from the Hebrew by Vivian Eden.

Where it's reviewed:
Library Journal, November 1, 2004, page 62
New York Times Book Review, December 12, 2004, page 26
Publishers Weekly, November 8, 2004, page 39
Romantic Times, January 2005, page 87

Other books by the same author:
Murder Duet, 1999
Murder on a Kibbutz, 1995
Literary Murder, 1993
The Saturday Morning Murder, 1988

Other books you might like:
Jonathan Kellerman, *The Butcher's Theater*, 1988
Harry Kemelman, *Monday the Rabbi Took Off*, 1972

Donna Leon, *The Guido Brunetti Series*, 1992-
Robert Rosenberg, *The Avram Cohen Series*, 1993-
Roger L. Simon, *Raising the Dead*, 1988

95

PARNELL HALL

And a Puzzle to Die On

(New York: Bantam, 2004)

Story type: Amateur Detective; Humor
Series: Puzzle Lady. Book 6
Subject(s): Birthdays; Hobbies; Games
Major character(s): Cora Felton, Aged Person, Detective—Amateur; Sherry Carter, Divorced Person, Relative (niece of Cora)
Time period(s): 2000s
Locale(s): Bakerhaven, Connecticut

Summary: Sweet-faced, grandmotherly Cora Felton is beloved by the many puzzle fans who read her syndicated crossword column, but its real author is her niece, Sherry Carter, who shuns publicity. In reality Cora is a sarcastic, chain-smoking, hard-drinking (until recently) old bird who couldn't solve a crossword puzzle if her life depended on it, much less construct one. Crime solving is really her forte. Sherry is planning a gala birthday celebration for Cora, who has reached an age when birthdays only annoy her, and she's delighted when she's asked to look into a decades-old murder case in which the man serving time for the crime may actually be innocent. The author also writes a comic private eye series featuring hapless New York investigator Stanley Hastings, as well as a courtroom series with lawyer Steve Winslow.

Where it's reviewed:
Booklist, November 1, 2004, page 466
Mystery News, December 2004/January 2005, page 26
Publishers Weekly, October 25, 2004, page 32
Romantic Times, November 2004, page 86

Other books by the same author:
With This Puzzle, I Thee Kill, 2003
A Puzzle in a Pear Tree, 2002
Puzzled to Death, 2001
Last Puzzle and Testament, 2000
A Clue for the Puzzle Lady, 1999

Other books you might like:
Nero Blanc, *The Crossword Murder*, 1999
Monica Ferris, *The Betsy Devonshire Series*, 1999-
Carolyn Hart, *The Henrie O Series*, 1993-
Stefanie Matteson, *The Charlotte Graham Series*, 1990-
Patricia Moyes, *A Six-Letter Word for Death*, 1983

96

BARBARA HAMBLY

Dead Water

(New York: Bantam, 2004)

Story type: Historical/Antebellum American South
Series: Benjamin January. Book 8
Subject(s): African Americans; Slavery; American South

Major character(s): Benjamin January, Slave (former), Detective—Amateur
Time period(s): 1830s (1835)
Locale(s): New Orleans, Louisiana

Summary: Benjamin January is a free black man, the son of slaves who was freed by a benefactor and educated in Paris. A doctor as well as a musician, he and his new wife, Rose, are entering a welcome period of stability and prosperity in their lives. They have bought a beautiful house at the edge of the French Quarter, where Rose has realized her lifelong dream of opening a school for young women of color. When their bank is wiped out by an employee who has stolen all its assets, their only course of action, if they don't want to lose their house, is to find him and recover the money. To this end they pose as slaves to Benjamin's white friend, a lovable scoundrel named Hannibal Sefton, and board a Mississippi riverboat in search of the thief.

Where it's reviewed:
Booklist, July 2004, page 1798
Deadly Pleasures, Summer/Fall 2004, page 48
Publishers Weekly, July 5, 2004, page 41
Romantic Times, August 2004, page 86

Other books by the same author:
Days of the Dead, 2003
Wet Grave, 2002
Die upon a Kiss, 2001
Sold Down the River, 2000
Graveyard Dust, 1999

Other books you might like:
Ron Burns, *Enslaved*, 1990
David Fulmer, *Chasing the Devil's Tail*, 2001
Ann McMillan, *The Narcissa Powers Series*, 1998-
Miriam Grace Monfredo, *The North Star Conspiracy*, 1993
Robert Skinner, *The Wesley Farrell Series*, 1997-

97

STEVE HAMILTON

Ice Run

(New York: St. Martin's Minotaur, 2004)

Story type: Private Detective
Series: Alex McKnight. Book 6
Subject(s): Feuds; Secrets; Family Problems
Major character(s): Alex McKnight, Detective—Private; Natalie Reynaud, Police Officer (constable)
Time period(s): 2000s
Locale(s): Paradise, Michigan (Upper Peninsula); Sault Ste. Marie, Michigan

Summary: Former ballplayer turned Detroit cop turned occasional private eye Alex McKnight has been in an uncharacteristically upbeat mood lately. He's also eating salads and limiting his beer consumption, and he's even colored his hair. The reason: he's fallen in a big way for Natalie Reynaud, the Ontario police officer he met in *Blood Is the Sky*. In fact, they've arranged to meet for a romantic weekend at a historic hotel in nearby Sault Ste. Marie, despite the major snowstorm that's threatening the Upper Peninsula. They make their rendezvous, but it's ruined by a message to their hotel room that

sets off a disastrous chain of events involving old family secrets from Natalie's past and some violent confrontations in the present.

Where it's reviewed:
Booklist, May 1, 2004, page 1508
Deadly Pleasures, Summer/Fall 2004, page 22
Library Journal, June 1, 2004, page 107
Publishers Weekly, May 24, 2004, page 48

Other books by the same author:
Blood Is the Sky, 2003
North of Nowhere, 2002
The Hunting Wind, 2001
Winter of the Wolf Moon, 2000
A Cold Day in Paradise, 1998

Other books you might like:
C.J. Box, *Savage Run*, 2002
Lee Child, *The Jack Reacher Series*, 1997-
William Kent Krueger, *The Cork O'Connor Series*, 1998-
Chuck Logan, *Absolute Zero*, 2002
Michael McGarrity, *The Kevin Kerney Series*, 1996-

98

DAVID HANDLER

The Burnt Orange Sunrise

(New York: St. Martin's Minotaur, 2004)

Story type: Traditional; Humor
Series: Berger & Mitry. Book 4
Subject(s): Winter; Hotels and Motels; Romance
Major character(s): Mitch Berger, Critic (film), Widow(er); Desiree Mitry, Police Officer (trooper), Artist
Time period(s): 2000s
Locale(s): Dorset, Connecticut

Summary: Mitch Berger, a New York film critic, widower, and world-class couch potato, has improbably found happiness with Desiree Mitry, a tall, athletic, African-American artist whose day job is trooper in the picturesque New England town they both now call home. One of Dorset's many historical attractions is Astrid's Castle, a fantastic hilltop edifice built in the 1920s by a Wall Street financier for his mistress and since turned into a lavish country inn. The millionaire's daughter, Ada Geiger, went on to become a legendary photographer and film director and is returning to the U.S. after a long self-imposed exile. A star-studded homecoming is planned for her at Astrid's Castle, and Mitch, an ardent admirer of Ada's, is pleased that he and Des are on the guest list for the smaller reception the night before the big event. Then a raging blizzard cuts the castle off from the outside world and traps the guests, mostly family and close friends, there for the duration. Events take a horrifying turn when first the innkeeper's wife is found dead, and then Ada herself is strangled. Des efficiently takes charge, but the killings continue. It's a familiar plot, and all the more pleasurable for that, especially in the hands of this gifted storyteller, who also wrote a delightful series about celebrity ghostwriter Stewart Hoag.

Where it's reviewed:
Publishers Weekly, September 6, 2004, page 49

Other books by the same author:
The Bright Silver Star, 2003
The Hot Pink Farmhouse, 2002
The Cold Blue Blood, 2001

Other books you might like:
Lawrence Block, *The Burglar in the Library*, 1997
Philip R. Craig, *The J.W. Jackson Series*, 1989-
Aaron Elkins, *The Gideon Oliver Series*, 1982-
Parnell Hall, *Cozy*, 2001
Dashiell Hammett, *The Thin Man*, 1934

99

ERIN HART

Lake of Sorrows

(New York: Doubleday, 2004)

Story type: Amateur Detective
Series: Nora Gavin. Book 2
Subject(s): Archaeology; Rural Life; Treasure
Major character(s): Nora Gavin, Doctor (pathologist), Detective—Amateur; Cormac Maguire, Archaeologist, Detective—Amateur
Time period(s): 2000s
Locale(s): County Offaly, Ireland

Summary: American pathologist Nora Gavin returns to the misty peat bogs of Ireland and the scene of another murder—two, actually, one ancient and one modern. Workers have dug up a long-buried but well-preserved body in a place known as the Lake of Sorrows, where the acid peat bogs inhibit decay and make it difficult to tell how long ago death occurred. The body has sustained multiple wounds, suggesting the primitive ''triple-death'' ritual in which a victim is murdered in three separate ways. Then a second corpse, much more recent, is unearthed shortly after her arrival, also suggesting murder by triple death. Nora's lover, archaeologist Cormac Maguire, is also on the scene, and their volatile relationship is tested by an investigation that threatens to endanger them both.

Where it's reviewed:
Library Journal, September 1, 2004, page 125
Publishers Weekly, August 16, 2004, page 41

Other books by the same author:
Haunted Ground, 2003

Other books you might like:
John Brady, *A Carra King*, 2001
Kate Ellis, *The Wesley Peterson Series*, 1999-
Ann C. Fallon, *The James Fleming Series*, 1990-
Bartholomew Gill, *Death in Dublin*, 2003
Patrick McGinley, *Bogmail*, 1981

100

JOHN HARVEY

Flesh & Blood

(New York: Carroll & Graf, 2004)

Story type: Police Procedural
Series: Frank Elder. Book 1

Subject(s): Law Enforcement; Crime and Criminals; Relationships
Major character(s): Frank Elder, Police Officer (retired detective inspector)
Time period(s): 2000s
Locale(s): Nottinghamshire, England; Cornwall, England

Summary: Since his retirement two years ago to Cornwall from the Nottinghamshire police force following his wife's infidelity, Frank Elder has been haunted by nightmares of a 16-year-old schoolgirl who had gone missing 14 years earlier. Two men, both suspects in the case, were imprisoned after being convicted a year later of the murder and rape of another young girl. Now one of them, Shane Donald, is out of prison and has escaped the halfway house to which he's been assigned. Then another schoolgirl goes missing and turns up murdered. Unable to endure his enforced retirement any longer, Elder returns to Nottinghamshire, where he resumes his search for the first missing girl. Charlie Resnick, the protagonist of Harvey's earlier 10-book series, makes a cameo appearance here. The book, however, belongs to Frank Elder, a complex, troubled man whose relationship with his teenage daughter (whom he fears may be the killer's next target) and his understanding of the criminal mind are crucial to the plot. It's a superb beginning to a new series from one of England's most underrated crime writers.

Where it's reviewed:
Booklist, May 1, 2004, page 1504
Deadly Pleasures, Summer/Fall 2004, page 37
Library Journal, July 2004, page 64
New York Times Book Review, July 25, 2004, page 19

Other books by the same author:
True Light, 2002
Last Rites, 1998
Still Waters, 1998
Easy Meat, 1996
Cold Light, 1994

Other books you might like:
Stephen Booth, *The Ben Cooper/Diane Fry Series*, 2000-
Reginald Hill, *The Dalziel/Pascoe Series*, 1970-
Bill James, *The Colin Harpur/Desmond Iles Series*, 1985-
Ian Rankin, *The John Rebus Series*, 1987-
Peter Robinson, *The Inspector Alan Banks Series*, 1987-

101

ROBIN HATHAWAY

Satan's Pony

(New York: St. Martin's Minotaur, 2004)

Story type: Amateur Detective
Series: Jo Banks. Book 2
Subject(s): Doctors; Small Town Life; Hotels and Motels
Major character(s): Jo Banks, Doctor, Detective—Amateur
Time period(s): 2000s
Locale(s): Bayfield, New Jersey

Summary: Although she had vowed to give up medicine when she left her practice in Manhattan after a little girl who was a patient of hers died, Jo now finds herself running a small clinic out of a motel in southern New Jersey. Her transportation of choice is a motorbike, and she's the target of much derision when a gang of Harley-riding bikers, calling themselves Satan's Apostles, descends upon her motel. One of them, Pi, turns out to be a childhood friend whose career as a mathematician was cut short when he dropped out of MIT. When one of his fellow bikers ends up dead in the parking lot, Pi is the chief suspect. However, Jo, convinced that he is a basically gentle man who could never have committed a murder, sets out to clear him. The author also writes a similarly cozy and engaging series about an old-fashioned Philadelphia physician, Dr. Fenimore.

Where it's reviewed:
Library Journal, October 1, 2004, page 64
Publishers Weekly, September 13, 2004, page 62

Other books by the same author:
Scarecrow, 2003

Other books you might like:
Kate Gallison, *The Mother Lavinia Grey Series*, 1995-
Lora Roberts, *The Liz Sullivan Series*, 1994-
Beth Sherman, *The Anne Hardaway Series*, 1998-
Virginia Swift, *The Mustang Sally Series*, 2000-
Nancy Tesler, *The Carrie Carlin Series*, 1997-

102
STEVEN F. HAVILL

Convenient Disposal
(New York: St. Martin's Minotaur, 2004)

Story type: Police Procedural
Series: Posadas County. Book 12
Subject(s): Small Town Life; American West; Mexican Americans
Major character(s): Estelle Reyes-Guzman, Police Officer (undersheriff); Bill Gastner, Police Officer (retired)
Time period(s): 2000s
Locale(s): Posadas County, New Mexico

Summary: With her predecessor Bill Gastner retired, but still a presence in the community, his former assistant Estelle continues the kind of humane and conscientious police work that was his trademark. She's called to the local middle school to help defuse a fight over a boy between two tough-girl students, Carmen Acosta and Deena Hurtado. Then she receives another call, to the Acosta home, after Carmen has been badly beaten and taken to the hospital. The question is: who is responsible? It's more likely to be another family member than Deena. Bill Gastner steps in to help Estelle sort things out in another solid entry in a sensitively written and often overlooked series.

Where it's reviewed:
Booklist, November 1, 2004, page 466
Publishers Weekly, October 18, 2004, page 51

Other books by the same author:
A Discount for Death, 2003
Scavengers, 2002
Bag Limit, 2001
Dead Weight, 2000
Out of Season, 1999

Other books you might like:
P.M. Carlson, *The Marty Hopkins Series*, 1992-1995
Nancy Herndon, *The Elena Jarvis Series*, 1995-
J.A. Jance, *The Joanna Brady Series*, 1993-
Mary Logue, *The Claire Watkins Series*, 1999-
Charlene Weir, *The Susan Wren Series*, 1992-

103
CARL HIAASEN

Skinny Dip
(New York: Knopf, 2004)

Story type: Humor; Action/Adventure
Subject(s): Revenge; Ecology; Pollution
Major character(s): Joey Perrone, Spouse; Mick Stranahan, Police Officer (retired); Karl Rolvaag, Detective—Homicide
Time period(s): 2000s
Locale(s): Broward County, Florida; Everglades, Florida

Summary: Chaz Perrone is the most unlikely marine biologist you can imagine. Employed by the government to monitor water samples, Chaz is uncertain as to which direction the Gulf Stream flows and more interested in his own sexual prowess than in the flora and fauna of the Everglades. In reality he gets generous kickbacks from a ruthless agribusiness polluter to swap out the samples. When he thinks his heiress wife Joey has caught on to the scam, he books an anniversary cruise on the *Sun Duchess* and unceremoniously flips her overboard one night. Unfortunately for Chaz, Joey was captain of her college swim team and survives by clinging to a stray bale of Jamaican pot. She is fished out of the sea by retired cop Mick Stranahan, who's been even more unlucky in love than Joey has. Together this appealing duo hatch a hilarious scheme to wreak revenge on the hapless Chaz, who repeatedly tries to kill the people who wise up to him and repeatedly fails. Skink, the reclusive ex-governor of Florida and roadkill connoisseur who has gone berserk in the Everglades, makes a welcome cameo appearance. Another inspired creation is Tool, the polluter's hulking, hairy henchman who swipes painkiller patches from the frail residents of nursing homes to calm the agony of a bullet lodged in his butt, but ends up being reformed by one of his victims, who appeals to the better nature that lurks deep within him. It's one of Hiaasen's best books, demonstrating that his skill at creating sympathetic characters has now outstripped his gift for portraying despicable villains.

Where it's reviewed:
Booklist, May 1, 2004, page 1514
Deadly Pleasures, Summer/Fall 2004, page 27
Library Journal, June 1, 2004, page 122
Publishers Weekly, May 10, 2004, page 34

Other books by the same author:
Basket Case, 2002
Sick Puppy, 2000
Lucky You, 1997
Stormy Weather, 1995
Strip Tease, 1993

Other books you might like:
G.D. Gearino, *Counting Coup*, 1997
David Handler, *The Berger & Mitry Series*, 2001-
Elmore Leonard, *Be Cool*, 1999
Donald E. Westlake, *Trust Me on This*, 1988
Randy Wayne White, *The Doc Ford Series*, 1990-

104

REGINALD HILL

Good Morning, Midnight

(New York: HarperCollins, 2004)

Story type: Psychological Suspense; Police Procedural
Series: Dalziel and Pascoe. Book 23
Subject(s): Family; Suicide; Relationships
Major character(s): Andy Dalziel, Police Officer (detective superintendent); Peter Pascoe, Police Officer (detective inspector)
Time period(s): 2000s
Locale(s): Yorkshire, England

Summary: When a prominent corporate executive, Paul Maciver, shoots himself at the desk of his locked study in his Yorkshire family estate, police detectives Andy Dalziel and Peter Pascoe investigate. The case turns out to be a knotty one; not only had the victim's father shot himself under almost identical circumstances ten years earlier, but Dalziel had been the investigating officer. Further, it begins to look as if the death was not a suicide but an ingeniously executed murder. Dalziel and Pascoe must dig deep into the past of the Maciver family and their corporation, which has been involved in questionable arms dealing. Mordantly witty and intelligently written, the book is a nifty update of the old-fashioned locked-room mystery set against a background of modern-day corporate shenanigans. The author also writes a series about black private detective Joe Sixsmith and has written a number of books under the pseudonym Patrick Ruell.

Where it's reviewed:
Booklist, September 1, 2004, page 68
Library Journal, September 1, 2004, page 125
New York Times Book Review, October 24, 2004, page 27
Publishers Weekly, August 16, 2004, page 45

Other books by the same author:
Death's Jest Book, 2003
Dialogues of the Dead, 2002
Arms and the Women, 1999
On Beulah Height, 1998
The Wood Beyond, 1995

Other books you might like:
Colin Dexter, *The Inspector Morse Series*, 1975-
P.D. James, *The Adam Dalgliesh Series*, 1962-
Peter Lovesey, *The Peter Diamond Series*, 1991-
Ruth Rendell, *The Inspector Wexford Series*, 1964-
Peter Robinson, *The Inspector Alan Banks Series*, 1987-

105

SAM HILL

Buzz Riff

(New York: Carroll & Graf, 2004)

Story type: Humor; Private Detective
Series: Top Kiernan. Book 2
Subject(s): American South; Crime and Criminals; History
Major character(s): Top Kiernan, Detective—Private
Time period(s): 2000s
Locale(s): Athens, Georgia

Summary: Top Kiernan normally has two jobs: he runs an Internet research firm from his home in an old schoolhouse in Athens, Georgia, and he works undercover as an operative for Shaw's Mercantile Marine. His company isn't doing so well since his office manager (and former lover) was fired and took half his client list with her, and Shaw's won't touch him because they think he's become too high-risk. So he reluctantly takes a job with a racist client to find the Confederate battle flag used to bind Stonewall Jackson's wounds when he was fatally shot in May 1863. The $20,000 retainer will bring his mortgage payments up to date and keep him out of the hole until he can regroup. Not too surprisingly the job pits him against Civil War collectors, outlaw bikers, the ATF, the KKK, and assorted right-wingers and religious nuts. It does, however, get his adrenaline going—which is what Top Kiernan lives for.

Where it's reviewed:
Booklist, August 2004, page 1905
Library Journal, September 1, 2004, page 121

Other books by the same author:
Buzz Monkey, 2003

Other books you might like:
Steve Brewer, *Bullets*, 2004
Tim Dorsey, *Triggerfish Twist*, 2002
Pete Hautman, *The Mortal Nuts*, 1996
Philip Reed, *Bird Dog*, 1997
Ben Rehder, *Buck Fever*, 2002

106

TONY HILLERMAN

Skeleton Man

(New York: HarperCollins, 2004)

Story type: Police Procedural
Series: Joe Leaphorn/Jim Chee. Book 17
Subject(s): Native Americans; Indian Reservations; American West
Major character(s): Jim Chee, Police Officer (sergeant, tribal police), Indian (Navajo); Joe Leaphorn, Detective—Private (retired lieutenant), Indian (Navajo); Bernadette "Bernie" Manuelito, Police Officer (Border Patrol), Indian (Navajo)
Time period(s): 2000s
Locale(s): Grand Canyon, Arizona; Navajo Reservation, New Mexico

Summary: The title refers both to the Hopi guardian spirit of the underworld who takes away mortals' fear of death and to some skeletal remains at the bottom of the Grand Canyon, the result of a midair crash between two passenger planes nearly 50 years ago over the national landmark. The remains belong to a courier who had an attache case of rare diamonds chained to his wrist. The search for his arm is central to the story, as DNA testing on it will determine who is heir to the gems. One of the diamonds has turned up in the possession of a small-time crook who tries to pawn it for a pittance. Joe Leaphorn, now retired, joins his longtime colleague Jim Chee on the case, accompanied by Chee's fiancee, Bernie Manuelito.

Where it's reviewed:
Booklist, September 15, 2004, page 179
Entertainment Weekly, November 26, 2004, page 123
New York Times Book Review, November 28, 2004, page 17
People Weekly, December 6, 2004, page 55
Publishers Weekly, October 18, 2004, page 50

Other books by the same author:
The Sinister Pig, 2003
The Wailing Wind, 2002
Hunting Badger, 1999
The First Eagle, 1998
The Fallen Man, 1996

Other books you might like:
Margaret Coel, *The Father John O'Malley/Vicky Holden Series*, 1995-
James D. Doss, *The Shaman Series*, 1994-
Kirk Mitchell, *Cry Dance*, 1999
Jake Page, *The Stolen Gods*, 1993
Aimee Thurlo, *The Ella Clah Series*, 1995-
   David Thurlo, co-author

107

MADDY HUNTER (Pseudonym of Mary Mayer Holmes)

Pasta Imperfect
(New York: Pocket, 2004)

Story type: Amateur Detective; Humor
Series: Emily Andrew. Book 3
Subject(s): Travel; Old Age; Authors and Writers
Major character(s): Emily Andrew, Tour Guide, Detective—Amateur
Time period(s): 2000s
Locale(s): Rome, Italy; Florence, Italy; Pisa, Italy

Summary: After stepping in one year to lead a senior tour group in Switzerland, Emily has become the Iowa-based travelers' official guide. This year they're off to Italy, thanks to a special discount package that allows Emily to bring her family along as well. What she doesn't realize is that her seniors will be sharing their itinerary with a group of vicious, pre-published romance writers who are competing for a book contract. Disaster follows, of course: first their hotel burns down, then Emily's wardrobe is raided by the writers, and then bodies start turning up, dressed in her clothes. Another fresh, laugh-out-loud funny entry in this frothy series.

Where it's reviewed:
Deadly Pleasures, Summer/Fall 2004, page 49

Mystery News, August 9, 2004, page 16
Romantic Times, August 2004, page 91

Other books by the same author:
Alpine for You, 2003
Top o' the Mournin', 2003

Other books you might like:
Sarah Caudwell, *Thus Was Adonis Murdered*, 1981
Janet Evanovich, *The Stephanie Plum Series*, 1994-
Joan Hess, *The Maggody Series*, 1987-
Fred Hunter, *Ransom at Sea*, 2003
Emily Toll, *The Lynn Montgomery Series*, 2002-

108

J.A. JANCE

Day of the Dead
(New York: William Morrow, 2004)

Story type: Psychological Suspense
Series: Diana Ladd/Brandon Walker. Book 3
Subject(s): American West; Indian Reservations; Serial Killers
Major character(s): Diana Ladd, Writer (novelist); Brandon Walker, Police Officer (retired sheriff)
Time period(s): 2000s
Locale(s): Tucson, Arizona; Tohono O'Odham Reservation, Arizona

Summary: Restless in his retirement, former sheriff Brandon Walker is pleased to receive an invitation to join The Last Chance, a group devoted to solving cold case crimes. To his surprise the first case he deals with is one dating back to 1970 when he was a rookie homicide cop, involving the murder of a 15-year-old Tohono O'Odham (Papago) girl at the hands of a pair of serial killers who were never caught. Brandon's own adopted daughter belongs to the same tribe, and much information on the Tohono O'Odham culture and reservation is woven into the story, which also features Walker's Pulitzer Prize-winning novelist wife Diana Ladd, whose past is entwined with that of the killers. This series is darker and more graphically violent than the author's other two, which feature Cochise County sheriff Joanna Brady and retired Seattle cop J.P. Beaumont respectively.

Where it's reviewed:
Booklist, June 1, 2004, page 1670
Deadly Pleasures, Summer/Fall 2004, page 38
Library Journal, June 1, 2004, page 122
Mystery News, August/September 2004, page 28
Publishers Weekly, April 12, 2004, page 34

Other books by the same author:
Kiss of the Bees, 2000
Hour of the Hunter, 1992

Other books you might like:
Sinclair Browning, *The Trade Ellis Series*, 1999-
David Cole, *The Laura Winslow Series*, 2000-
Thomas Harris, *The Silence of the Lambs*, 1988
Richard Parrish, *The Joshua Rabb Series*, 1993-
Betty Webb, *The Lena Jones Series*, 2001-

109

IRIS JOHANSEN

Blind Alley

(New York: Bantam, 2004)

Story type: Psychological Suspense
Series: Eve Duncan. Book 5
Subject(s): Serial Killers; Mothers and Daughters; Adolescence
Major character(s): Eve Duncan, Artist (forensic sculptor)
Time period(s): 2000s
Locale(s): Atlanta, Georgia

Summary: Eve Duncan makes her living by reconstructing the faces of murder victims, using their skulls as a starting point. It may not be the happiest job in the world, but she does get some satisfaction from giving victims' families closure by helping to identify their loved ones' remains. However, she's shocked when the face that her skillful fingers fashion over the skull of a newly discovered victim is almost identical to that of her adopted daughter, Jane. Then she learns that a serial killer named Aldo has been slaying young women with similar features all over Europe because they resemble a young woman, dead for 2,000 years, whom he somehow holds responsible for his father's death. Eve, whose biological daughter was lost to a serial killer, fears that Jane will be Aldo's next target. The author has also written a number of stand-alone suspense novels.

Where it's reviewed:
Booklist, August 2004, page 1871
Entertainment Weekly, September 17, 2004, page 84
Publishers Weekly, August 23, 2004, page 37
Romantic Times, October 2004, page 85

Other books by the same author:
Body of Lies, 2002
The Search, 2000
The Killing Game, 1999
The Face of Deception, 1998

Other books you might like:
Patricia Cornwell, *The Kay Scarpetta Series*, 1990-
Barbara Michaels, *Be Buried in the Rain*, 1985
Barbara Parker, *The Gail Connor Series*, 1994-
Kathy Reichs, *The Tempe Brennan Series*, 1997-
J.D. Robb, *The Eve Dallas Series*, 1995-

110

DOLORES JOHNSON

Taking the Wrap

(New York: St. Martin's Minotaur, 2004)

Story type: Amateur Detective
Series: Mandy Dyer. Book 7
Subject(s): Identity; Family; Humor
Major character(s): Mandy Dyer, Businesswoman (owner of a dry cleaners), Detective—Amateur
Time period(s): 2000s
Locale(s): Denver, Colorado

Summary: Mandy Dyer inherited a dry-cleaning establishment (and the building's sizable mortgage) from her uncle and has made a go of the business. Her step-cousin Laura, a photographer, inherited enough money to set up her own studio. The two women are great friends, although too busy to spend much time together, but Mandy can't say no when Laura asks a favor of her. It seems somebody switched coats with her at a restaurant, and she wants to locate the owner so they can make the swap. The only clue is a dry-cleaning tag that Mandy knows is meaningless, but she agrees to make a few inquiries. Then the woman who took Laura's coat is found dead, and Laura herself is nearly killed by a hit-and-run driver. A light, good-natured read.

Where it's reviewed:
Booklist, September 1, 2004, page 69
Library Journal, November 1, 2004, page 60
Mystery News, October/November 2004, page 28
Romantic Times, January 2005, page 86

Other books by the same author:
Buttons and Foes, 2002
Homicide and Old Lace, 2000
Wash, Fold and Die, 1999
A Dress to Die For, 1998
Hung Up to Die, 1997

Other books you might like:
Donna Andrews, *The Meg Langslow Series*, 1999-
Jo Dereske, *The Miss Zukas Series*, 1994-
Christine Jorgensen, *The Stella the Stargazer Series*, 1994-
Leslie O'Kane, *The Allie Babcock Series*, 1998-
Sharon Short, *The Josie Toadfern Series*, 2003-

111

SHARON KAHN

Which Big Giver Stole the Chopped Liver?

(New York: Scribner, 2004)

Story type: Amateur Detective; Humor
Series: Ruby the Rabbi's Wife. Book 5
Subject(s): Small Town Life; Judaism; Reunions
Major character(s): Ruby Rothman, Widow(er), Computer Expert
Time period(s): 2000s
Locale(s): Eternal, Texas

Summary: Ruby's longtime nemesis, Essie Sue Margolis, has launched a renovation drive for Temple Rita after a small population increase in the tiny town of Eternal. Among the fundraising activities she's scheduled is a reunion of all the temple's former congregants, highlighted by a festive luncheon. Unfortunately the centerpiece of the table, a map of Texas molded in chopped liver, has been replaced by a dead body. It's up to the resourceful Ruby to find out what has happened.

Where it's reviewed:
Booklist, August 2004, page 1904
Library Journal, August 2004, page 60
Publishers Weekly, July 19, 2004, page 147
Romantic Times, September 2004, page 89

Other books by the same author:
Don't Cry for Me, Hot Pastrami, 2002
Hold the Cream Cheese, Kill the Lox, 2002
Never Nosh a Matzo Ball, 1999
Fax Me a Bagel, 1998

Other books you might like:
Kinky Friedman, *Meanwhile, Back at the Ranch*, 2002
Harry Kemelman, *The Rabbi David Small Series*, 1964-1996
Camille Minichino, *The Gloria Lamerino Series*, 1997-
Serita Stevens, *The Fanny Zindel Series*, 1991-
James Yaffe, *A Nice Murder for Mom*, 1988

112

STUART M. KAMINSKY

The Last Dark Place
(New York: Forge, 2004)

Story type: Police Procedural
Series: Abe Lieberman. Book 8
Subject(s): Gangs; Bar Mitzvah/Bat Mitzvah; Law Enforcement
Major character(s): Abe Lieberman, Detective—Homicide; Bill Hanrahan, Detective—Homicide; Sister Agatha, Religious (nun); Tom Green, Police Officer (sheriff)
Time period(s): 2000s
Locale(s): Chicago, Illinois; Yuma, Arizona

Summary: Known as the Rabbi and the Priest, odd-couple Chicago police partners Abe Lieberman and Bill Hanrahan are a study in contrasts. Lieberman is Jewish, methodical, philosophical, and intensely moral, while Hanrahan is an impulsive Irish Catholic who is driven by guilt, alcoholism, and his marriage to a woman outside his own culture and faith with ties to an Asian mob. As Lieberman is attempting to extradite a professional assassin from Arizona, the man is shot down at the Yuma airport by an elderly janitor. As he tries to find who ordered the hit, Lieberman is also called upon to stop a gang war between Hispanics and Asians and figure out how he's going to pay for his grandson's upcoming bar mitzvah. Meanwhile, Hanrahan has his hands full with the rape of a young police officer's wife and the thuggish relative who's threatening his pregnant wife. The author writes several other series, about Sarasota process server Lew Fonesca, 1940s Hollywood private eye Toby Peters, and Moscow policeman Porfiry Rostnikov.

Where it's reviewed:
Mystery News, December 2004/January 2004, page 24
Publishers Weekly, October 11, 2004, page 59

Other books by the same author:
Not Quite Kosher, 2002
The Big Silence, 2000
Lieberman's Day, 1995
Lieberman's Law, 1995
Lieberman's Thief, 1995

Other books you might like:
Barbara D'Amato, *The Suze Figueroa/Norm Bennis Series*, 1996-
Joe Gash, *The Terry Flynn/Karen Kovac Series*, 1984-
Hugh Holton, *The Larry Cole Series*, 1994-2002

113

STUART M. KAMINSKY

Now You See It
(New York: Carroll & Graf, 2004)

Story type: Historical; Private Detective
Series: Toby Peters. Book 24
Subject(s): Movie Industry; Magicians; Actors and Actresses
Major character(s): Toby Peters, Detective—Private; Harry Blackstone, Magician; Phil Pevsner, Detective—Private (former homicide detective)
Time period(s): 1940s (1944)
Locale(s): Hollywood, California

Summary: The magician Harry Blackstone joins Toby's long list of illustrious clients when he comes to him with a big problem: someone is threatening to kill him if he doesn't give up his closely guarded professional secrets. Attempts are made on his life in a way that suggest a fellow magician is behind them, but when somebody else gets murdered, Blackstone himself becomes a suspect. Toby has taken in his brother, retired cop Phil Pevsner, as a partner in his detective agency, and the two men work together to solve this tricky mystery. Regulars from previous books also make appearances, including dentist Sheldon Minck and Toby's eccentric landlady Irene Plaut, which only adds to the fun. Period color abounds, nicely defining wartime Hollywood, and each chapter is headed by instructions on how to do a simple magic trick. The prolific and always entertaining author writes two other series, one featuring Russian policeman Porfiry Rostnikov and the other starring philosophical Chicago cop Abe Lieberman.

Where it's reviewed:
Booklist, October 1, 2004, page 313
Publishers Weekly, September 13, 2004, page 61

Other books by the same author:
Mildred Pierced, 2003
To Catch a Spy, 2002
A Few Minutes Past Midnight, 2001
A Fatal Glass of Beer, 1997
Dancing in the Dark, 1996

Other books you might like:
George Baxt, *The Greta Garbo Murder Case*, 1992
Andrew Bergman, *The Big Kiss-Off of 1944*, 1974
Max Allan Collins, *Angel in Black*, 2001
Terence Faherty, *Kill Me Again*, 1996
Daniel Stashower, *Elephants in the Distance*, 1989

114

STEPHANIE KANE

Seeds of Doubt
(New York: Scribner, 2004)

Story type: Legal; Psychological Suspense
Series: Jackie Flowers. Book 3
Subject(s): Law; Learning Disabilities; Phobias
Major character(s): Jackie Flowers, Lawyer (defense attorney)
Time period(s): 2000s

Locale(s): Denver, Colorado

Summary: Jackie Flowers, a young defense attorney who battles dyslexia and a paralyzing fear of heights, works very hard for her clients, relying on a network of friends to help her when she needs it. She's prevailed upon by an old boyfriend from her public defender days to take the case of Rachel Boyd, who is free after serving 30 years for the murder of a playmate when she was just a child. Now residing with her brother, a wealthy banker, Rachel becomes a suspect in the murder of his gardener's child. Jackie not only takes Rachel as a client but shelters her in her own home until the trial starts. Although she believes Rachel to be innocent, she becomes concerned when the woman strikes up a friendship with a troubled adolescent girl who is Rachel's neighbor. The author is a Denver trial lawyer.

Where it's reviewed:
Booklist, September 15, 2004, page 212
Publishers Weekly, September 17, 2004, page 36

Other books by the same author:
Extreme Indifference, 2003
Blind Spot, 2000

Other books you might like:
Alafair Burke, *The Samantha Kincaid Series*, 2003-
Jonnie Jacobs, *The Kali O'Brien Series*, 1996-
Perri O'Shaughnessy, *The Nina Reilly Series*, 1995-
Marianne Wesson, *The Cinda Hayes Series*, 1997-
Kate Wilhelm, *The Barbara Holloway Series*, 1991-

115

H.R.F. KEATING

A Dreaming Detective

(New York: St. Martin's Minotaur, 2004)

Story type: Police Procedural
Series: Harriet Martens. Book 4
Subject(s): Law Enforcement; Women
Major character(s): Harriet Martens, Police Officer (detective superintendent)
Time period(s): 2000s
Locale(s): Birchester, England

Summary: Harriet Martens began her law enforcement career in London but transferred to Birchester because it was so difficult to be a woman in a large metropolitan crime unit. Now an experienced and successful police officer, she's been nicknamed the Hard Detective because of her tough stance on crime. However, her new chief constable is determined to see her fail and assigns her to a very cold case. Her investigation will be into the 1960s murder of Krishna Kumaramangalam, the so-called Boy Preacher, in the ballroom of a hotel that's about to be demolished. She's instructed to use DNA results to determine the killer's identity, but they don't support evidence she's turned up in interviews. It's a no-win situation for Harriet: if she fails, her chief can get rid of her, and if she succeeds, he can take all the credit. The author has also written a long-running series about Bombay detective Ganesh Ghote, as well as numerous stand-alone mysteries.

Where it's reviewed:
Publishers Weekly, December 6, 2004, page 46

Other books by the same author:
A Detective under Fire, 2004
A Detective in Love, 2002
The Hard Detective, 2000

Other books you might like:
Judith Cutler, *The Kate Power Series*, 2003-
Frances Fyfield, *The Helen West Series*, 1989-
Lucy Harkness, *The Happy Pigs*, 2002
Lynda La Plante, *Prime Suspect*, 1993
Gay Longworth, *The Jessie Driver Series*, 2003-

116

LEE CHARLES KELLEY

To Collar a Killer

(New York: Avon, 2004)

Story type: Amateur Detective
Series: Jack Field. Book 3
Subject(s): Animals/Dogs; Small Town Life; Holidays
Major character(s): Jack Field, Animal Trainer (dogs), Detective—Amateur; Jamie Cutter, Doctor (medical examiner), Fiance(e) (of Jack)
Time period(s): 2000s
Locale(s): Perseverance, Maine

Summary: While at a Fourth of July picnic, kennel owner and former cop Jack Field takes time away from the crowd to play fetch with a Welsh corgi who surprises him by bringing back a bloodstained yachting cap instead of the tennis ball he'd thrown her. When he goes to investigate, he finds a drowned man washed up on the rocks clutching the tennis ball. To his surprise, the police think he killed the man, having found a plausible motive, and it quickly becomes clear to Jack that someone is trying to frame him for murder. Even his fiancee, assistant state medical examiner Jamie Cutter, is disturbed by the evidence that is piling up against him. Dog lovers will relish the canine lore woven into the story, as well as the author's notes and recommended reading at the end of the book.

Other books by the same author:
Murder Unleashed, 2004
A Nose for Murder, 2003

Other books you might like:
Carol Lea Benjamin, *The Rachel Alexander and Dash Series*, 1996-
Laurien Berenson, *The Melanie Travis Series*, 1995-
Susan Conant, *The Holly Winter Series*, 1989-
Virginia Lanier, *The Jo Beth Sidden Series*, 1995-2003
Leslie O'Kane, *The Allie Babcock Series*, 1998-

117

DIANA KILLIAN (Pseudonym of Diane Browne)

Verse of the Vampyre

(New York: Pocket, 2004)

Story type: Amateur Detective
Series: Grace Hollister. Book 2
Subject(s): Theater; Literature; Vampires

Major character(s): Grace Hollister, Teacher, Detective—Amateur; Peter Fox, Antiques Dealer, Thief (reformed jewel thief)
Time period(s): 2000s
Locale(s): Lake District, England

Summary: American scholar and Anglophile Grace Hollister is extending her sabbatical in England's Lake District, where she is working on a book about Lord Byron and consulting for a local theater company which is producing the play *The Vampyre*, written by Byron's physician. She is also helping her friend Peter Fox, a former jewel thief turned antiques dealer, in his shop, but lately he has been trying to avoid her. Could it be that he is in some way connected with a series of jewel thefts that have taken place in the area? The police think so, and Grace means to find out. There are also rumors of a vampire loose in the district, fueled by the discovery of a corpse drained of its blood, and a series of mysterious accidents have befallen members of the theater company.

Other books by the same author:
High Rhymes and Misdemeanors, 2003
The Art of Dying, 2001

Other books you might like:
Nora Kelly, *In the Shadow of King's*, 1984
Susan Kenney, *Garden of Malice*, 1983
Sharyn McCrumb, *The Windsor Knot*, 1990
Barbara Michaels, *The Dancing Floor*, 1997
Audrey Peterson, *Elegy in a Country Graveyard*, 1990

118

M.G. KINCAID (Pseudonym of Moira Maus)

Last Seen in Aberdeen
(New York: Pocket, 2004)

Story type: Police Procedural
Series: Seth Mornay. Book 2
Subject(s): Missing Persons; Smuggling; Law Enforcement
Major character(s): Seth Mornay, Police Officer (detective sergeant); Claire Gillespie, Police Officer (constable)
Time period(s): 2000s
Locale(s): Aberdeen, Scotland; Cordiff, Scotland

Summary: When a young boy goes missing in northern Scotland, Seth Mornay and his partner, Constable Claire Gillespie, at first assume it was a kidnapping for ransom, but when the child's body is found in a horse trailer in a traffic pileup, the case becomes a homicide. However, there are precious few leads and Mornay and Claire find their task is made more difficult by departmental politics. Mornay, a moody ex-Marine with many demons in his past, also has personal issues to deal with: his estranged fisherman father may be smuggling heroin, a woman in a coma may be carrying his baby, he's being threatened with blackmail, and he's still being dogged by repercussions of a previous case. In fact, it may be best to read the first book in the series, *The Last Victim in Glen Ross*, in order to be up to speed on Mornay and his problems before starting the second in this fine new series.

Where it's reviewed:
Romantic Times, December 2004, page 86

Other books by the same author:
The Last Victim in Glen Ross, 2003

Other books you might like:
Val McDermid, *The Distant Echo*, 2003
Denise Mina, *The Garnethill Trilogy*, 1999-2002
Ian Rankin, *The John Rebus Series*, 1987-
Manda Scott, *No Good Deed*, 2002
Graham Thomas, *Malice in the Highlands*, 1998

119

KATE KINGSBURY (Pseudonym of Doreen Roberts)

Fire When Ready
(New York: Berkley, 2004)

Story type: Historical/World War II
Series: Lady Elizabeth Hartleigh Compton. Book 7
Subject(s): World War II; Small Town Life; Arson
Major character(s): Lady Elizabeth Hartleigh Compton, Noblewoman, Widow(er)
Time period(s): 1940s
Locale(s): Sitting Marsh, England

Summary: During the dark days of World War II, with many of the men of Sitting Marsh away at the front, leaving their loved ones at home, Lady Elizabeth is firm about doing her bit to keep morale high and look out for the public welfare. However, she's totally unable to get the locals to accept the presence of a new munitions factory in the village, and she's perturbed when its owner confides in her that he's been receiving death threats in the post. When a fire breaks out in the factory, killing not only the owner but a charwoman, Elizabeth is not as certain as the police that it was an accident, especially when she learns that the victims were locked in an office inside and unable to escape. So, as usual, Elizabeth takes up the investigation herself. The author has also written a long-running series set in the Edwardian period at the Pennyfoot Hotel, a seaside resort.

Where it's reviewed:
Romantic Times, January 2005, page 82

Other books by the same author:
Berried Alive, 2004
Paint by Murder, 2003
Dig Deep for Murder, 2002
A Bicycle Built for Murder, 2001
For Whom Death Tolls, 2001

Other books you might like:
Robert Barnard, *Out of the Blackout*, 1984
Joanna Cannan, *Death at the Dog*, 1941 reprinted 2000
Peter Dickinson, *Hindsight*, 1983
Elizabeth Foxwell, *The Sunken Sailor*, 2004 editor, collaborative novel
Jill Paton Walsh, *A Presumption of Death*, 2003 based on characters by Dorothy L. Sayers

120

CHRISTINE KLING

Cross Current
(New York: Ballantine, 2004)

Story type: Amateur Detective; Action/Adventure
Series: Seychelle Sullivan. Book 2
Subject(s): Refugees; Boats and Boating; Haitians
Major character(s): Seychelle Sullivan, Shipowner (tugboat operator), Detective—Amateur
Time period(s): 2000s
Locale(s): Fort Lauderdale, Florida; At Sea

Summary: Like her father before her, Seychelle operates a tugboat on the Gulf Stream waters, docked outside of Fort Lauderdale. One day she's out on the water when she runs across a fishing boat containing a dead woman and a small Haitian girl named Solange, whose father is American. Seychelle is touched by Solange's plight, but in her attempts to protect her she runs afoul of the border patrol, the police, and the murderer, who is still after Solange. There are numerous other colorful characters, including two men with whom tall, beautiful Seychelle is romantically involved.

Where it's reviewed:
Booklist, September 1, 2004, page 69
Publishers Weekly, October 4, 2004, page 71
Romantic Times, October 2004, page 82

Other books by the same author:
Surface Tension, 2002

Other books you might like:
Nevada Barr, *The Anna Pigeon Series*, 1993-
James W. Hall, *The Forests of the Night*, 2005
Vicki Hendrix, *Iguana Love*, 1999
John D. MacDonald, *The Travis McGee Series*, 1964-1985
Randy Wayne White, *The Doc Ford Series*, 1990-

121

J.A. KONRATH

Whiskey Sour
(New York: Hyperion, 2004)

Story type: Police Procedural
Series: Jack Daniels. Book 1
Subject(s): Serial Killers; City and Town Life; Humor
Major character(s): Jacqueline Daniels, Detective—Homicide
Time period(s): 2000s
Locale(s): Chicago, Illinois

Summary: A serial killer known as the Gingerbread Man is leaving the mutilated bodies of young women in his wake, and Lt. Jacqueline "Jack" Daniels, head of the Chicago PD Violent Crimes Unit, is lying awake nights trying to figure out how to stop him before she becomes his next victim. Since she has chronic insomnia, this is nothing new for her; she's sacrificed her personal life for the demands of the job. This debut mystery is an odd hybrid of grim urban serial killer fiction and light-hearted humor, with colorful, well-drawn secondary characters, including Jack's in-your-face elderly mom.

Where it's reviewed:
Deadly Pleasures, Summer/Fall 2004, page 41
Library Journal, May 1, 2004, page 144
Mystery News, June/July 2004, page 20
Mystery Scene, Summer 2004, page 84
Publishers Weekly, April 26, 2004, page 45

Other books you might like:
Paul Bishop, *The Fey Croaker Series*, 1994-
Janet Evanovich, *The Stephanie Plum Series*, 1994-
Linda Fairstein, *The Alexandra Cooper Series*, 1996-
Elmore Leonard, *Rum Punch*, 1992
Ed McBain, *The 87th Precinct Series*, 1956-

122

MICHAEL KORTYA

Tonight I Said Goodbye
(New York: St. Martin's Minotaur, 2004)

Story type: Private Detective
Subject(s): Missing Persons; Russians; Organized Crime
Major character(s): Lincoln Perry, Detective—Private; Joe Pritchard, Detective—Private
Time period(s): 2000s
Locale(s): Cleveland, Ohio; Myrtle Beach, South Carolina

Summary: Lincoln Perry and Joe Pritchard were once partners on the Cleveland police force; Perry was fired for drinking and Pritchard retired a year later. The two reunited to form their own private detective agency. Now they've been hired by seventyish John Weston, whose son Wayne—also a private detective—has been found dead with his wife and daughter gone missing. The police think it's a murder/suicide, but Wayne's father refuses to believe the official verdict. He's right not to, of course, as Perry and Pritchard discover as they follow a trail that leads them to Myrtle Beach, South Carolina, and to the Russians, an ex-Marine, and the cops. This is an accomplished debut by a young writer, still a college student, who won the 2003 St. Martin's/Private Eye Writers of America prize for best first P.I. novel.

Where it's reviewed:
Library Journal, September 1, 2004, page 125
Publishers Weekly, August 30, 2004, page 32

Other books you might like:
Loren D. Estleman, *The Amos Walker Series*, 1980-
George Pelecanos, *The Derek Strange/Terry Quinn Series*, 2001-
Bill Pronzini, *The Nameless Detective Series*, 1971-
Rick Riordan, *The Tres Navarre Series*, 1997-
Les Roberts, *The Milan Jacovich Series*, 1988-

123

ROCHELLE KRICH

Grave Endings
(New York: Ballantine, 2004)

Story type: Psychological Suspense
Series: Molly Blume. Book 3
Subject(s): Orthodox Judaism; Weddings

Major character(s): Molly Blume, Writer (true crime writer), Divorced Person
Time period(s): 2000s
Locale(s): Los Angeles, California

Summary: Molly, a true crime writer, is in the midst of preparations for her upcoming wedding to her rabbi boyfriend, Zack, when she's asked to identify a locket found on the body of an actor and recovering drug addict, Roland Greeley, dead of an apparent overdose. The locket belonged to Molly's best friend Aggie Lasher, who was murdered six years earlier, and it contains a sacred red thread with the power to protect the wearer from evil. Aggie was a social worker at a shelter for abused women, and Molly had bought her the locket on a trip to Israel. The police suspect Greeley of having murdered Aggie, but Molly's instincts tell her otherwise. The author has also written several stand-alone suspense novels and a series featuring LAPD detective Jessie Drake.

Where it's reviewed:
Booklist, August 2004, page 1905
Library Journal, October 15, 2004, page 54
Publishers Weekly, August 9, 2004, page 230
Romantic Times, October 2004, page 81

Other books by the same author:
Dream House, 2003
Blues in the Night, 2002

Other books you might like:
Jan Burke, *The Irene Kelly Series*, 1993-
Denise Hamilton, *The Eve Diamond Series*, 2001-
Libby Fischer Hellmann, *An Eye for Murder*, 2002
Faye Kellerman, *The Rina Lazarus/Peter Decker Series*, 1986-
Mary Willis Walker, *The Molly Cates Series*, 1994-

124

MICHAEL KURLAND, Editor

Sherlock Holmes: The Hidden Years

(New York: St. Martin's Minotaur, 2004)

Story type: Anthology; Private Detective
Series: Sherlock Holmes
Subject(s): Short Stories
Major character(s): Sherlock Holmes, Detective—Private
Time period(s): 1890s (1891-1894)

Summary: The 11 original stories in this anthology all take place during Sherlock Holmes' so-called ''missing years.'' This is the period between his supposed death in 1891 at Reichenbach Falls at the hands of his arch-enemy Professor Moriarty and the day he suddenly reappeared in London, confessing to his grief-stricken colleague Dr. Watson that he had simply faked his own death. Contributors include Carolyn Wheat, Rhys Bowen, Bill Pronzini, Peter Beagle, Carole Bugge, Richard Lupoff, and the editor himself, all presenting different theories as to where Holmes might actually have been during those years. The locales range from Tibet to Borneo to Alaska to Switzerland to New Orleans, and the writers all have a good deal of fun with the premise, as will the reader.

Where it's reviewed:
Publishers Weekly, October 11, 2004, page 59

Other books by the same author:
My Sherlock Holmes, 2003 (editor)
The Great Game, 2001
Death by Gaslight, 1982
The Infernal Device, 1979

Other books you might like:
Mike Ashley, *The Mammoth Book of New Sherlock Holmes Adventures*, 1999
    editor
Martin H. Greenberg, *Holmes for the Holidays*, 1996
    Jon L. Lellenberg, Carol-Lynn Waugh, co-editors
Martin H. Greenberg, *Murder, My Dear Watson*, 2002
    Jon L. Lellenberg, Daniel Stashower, co-editors
Martin H. Greenberg, *The New Adventures of Sherlock Holmes*, 1999
    Jon L. Lellenberg, Carol-Lynn Waugh, co-editors
Marvin Kaye, *The Resurrected Holmes*, 1997
    editor

125

JANET LAPIERRE

Death Duties

(McKinleyville, California: Perseverance, 2004)

Story type: Private Detective
Series: Port Silva. Book 8
Subject(s): Mothers and Daughters; Small Town Life
Major character(s): Patience Mackellar, Detective—Private, Widow(er); Verity Mackellar, Detective—Private
Time period(s): 2000s
Locale(s): Port Silva, California

Summary: The small northern California coastal town of Port Silva has been the setting (or starting point) for all the novels in this loosely connected and sensitively written series. However, in this and its predecessor (*Keepers*) a new mother-daughter detective team has carried the story line, with old series regulars making only cameo appearances. Patience Mackellar is a retired policeman's widow who has continued her late husband's private detective agency, welcoming her daughter Verity, who's putting a troubled marriage behind her, as her new partner. This time they are hired by Christina Larson to put to rest rumors of pedophilia that drove her grandfather, Edgar Larson, to commit suicide 30 years earlier.

Where it's reviewed:
Mystery News, October/November 2004, page 28

Other books by the same author:
Keepers, 2001
Baby Mine, 1999
Old Enemies, 1993
Grandmother's House, 1991
The Cruel Mother, 1990

Other books you might like:
Susan Dunlap, *The Veejay Haskell Series*, 1983-
Laurie R. King, *A Darker Place*, 1999
Mary Kittredge, *Murder in Mendocino*, 1987
Marcia Muller, *Point Deception*, 2001

Gillian Roberts, *Whatever Doesn't Kill You*, 2001

126

LAURA LEVINE

Killer Blonde

(New York: Kensington, 2004)

Story type: Humor; Amateur Detective
Series: Jaine Austen. Book 3
Subject(s): Authors and Writers; Writing; Modern Life
Major character(s): Jaine Austen, Writer (ghostwriter), Detective—Amateur
Time period(s): 2000s
Locale(s): Los Angeles, California

Summary: It's not the assignment she would have chosen, but Jaine is in no position to turn down a $3,000-a-week gig ghostwriting a book for Beverly Hills hostess SueEllen Kingsley, who wants to share her hospitality secrets with an adoring public. Although she comes to detest SueEllen, who's shallow, selfish and domineering, Jaine becomes quite fond of her employer's hapless stepdaughter Heidi, a shy, overweight girl whom SueEllen takes delight in humiliating. When SueEllen is found dead in her bubble bath, electrocuted by her own hair dryer, the police suspect Heidi, and Jaine sets to work trying to clear the teenager.

Where it's reviewed:
Mystery News, August/September 2004, page 30

Other books by the same author:
Last Rites, 2003
This Pen for Hire, 2002

Other books you might like:
Jennifer Apodaca, *Dating Can Be Murder*, 2002
Judy Fitzwater, *The Jennifer Marsh Series*, 1998-
Lindsay Maracotta, *The Dead Hollywood Moms Society*, 1996
Marlys Millhiser, *The Charlie Greene Series*, 1992-
Sarah Strohmeyer, *The Bubbles Yablonsky Series*, 2001-

127

ROY LEWIS

Headhunter

(New York: Carroll & Graf, 2004)

Story type: Traditional; Amateur Detective
Series: Arnold Landon. Book 14
Subject(s): Serial Killers; Archaeology
Major character(s): Arnold Landon, Archaeologist, Detective—Amateur
Time period(s): 2000s
Locale(s): North Shields, England

Summary: When the headless torso of a young boy is discovered in the Tyne River, the police are stymied, unable to identify the victim or know where to start in finding the killer. So Operation Headhunter is launched, with Interpol becoming involved and eventually casting its net for a serial killer. Meanwhile, Arnold Landon, who is working on a dig where an ancient Roman chariot has been unearthed, finds a stash of pornographic material and is drawn into the case. His involvement causes him to also become a target for the killer. The author writes two other series, one featuring solicitor Eric Ward and one with police inspector John Crow.

Other books by the same author:
Dead Secret, 2001
The Ghost Dancer, 1999
A Short-Lived Ghost, 1995
Angel of Death, 1995
The Cross Bearer, 1994

Other books you might like:
Aaron Elkins, *The Gideon Oliver Series*, 1982-
Kate Ellis, *The Wesley Peterson Series*, 1999-
Erin Hart, *Haunted Ground*, 2003
Jessica Mann, *The Tamara Hoyland Series*, 1982-
John Trench, *Dishonoured Bones*, 1955

128

JEFF LINDSAY

Darkly Dreaming Dexter

(New York: Doubleday, 2004)

Story type: Psychological Suspense; Humor
Series: Dexter Morgan. Book 1
Subject(s): Serial Killers; Brothers and Sisters; Psychology
Major character(s): Dexter Morgan, Scientist, Serial Killer
Time period(s): 2000s
Locale(s): Miami, Florida

Summary: Dexter Morgan was adopted at the age of four after having undergone an unspeakably traumatic experience. His adoptive father, a policeman, soon realizes that Dexter isn't like other boys; he is a psychopath who kills because he can't help it. Knowing that Dexter can never be rehabilitated, Harry Morgan teaches his son to choose who he kills (only really bad people), and to kill so efficiently that he'll never be caught. Harry has also taught Dexter how to behave like a real human being, so he's become quite a likable fellow. He's a good brother to his adopted sister Deborah, who has followed in Harry's footsteps and become a cop. Dexter, who also works for the Miami police as a blood spatter technician (although he hates blood), wants to help Deborah get ahead, so when a serial killer whose work is eerily like Dexter's own starts making headlines, he determines to help Deborah bag him. Although he may not be quite human himself, Dexter is an astute observer of the human condition in general and police department politics in particular. The book, despite its grisly subject matter, is often hilarious, stylishly narrated in Dexter's wry, self-deprecating, and totally original voice. First novel.

Where it's reviewed:
Booklist, May 15, 2004, page 1602
Deadly Pleasures, Summer/Fall 2004, page 4
Library Journal, June 15, 2004, page 59
New York Times Book Review, July 25, 2004, page 19
Publishers Weekly, April 29, 2004, page 36

Other books you might like:
Lawrence Block, *Hit Man*, 1998
Blake Crouch, *Desert Places*, 2004

Peter Lovesey, *The Reaper*, 2001
Carol O'Connell, *The Kathleen Mallory Series*, 1994-
T. Jefferson Parker, *Silent Joe*, 2001

129

LAURA LIPPMAN

By a Spider's Thread

(New York: William Morrow, 2004)

Story type: Private Detective
Series: Tess Monaghan. Book 8
Subject(s): Missing Persons; Family Problems; Marriage
Major character(s): Tess Monaghan, Detective—Private, Journalist (former newspaper reporter)
Time period(s): 2000s
Locale(s): Baltimore, Maryland

Summary: Tess' newest client is Mark Rubin, a Baltimore furrier and Orthodox Jew whose wife Natalie has inexplicably disappeared with their three children. He insists that their marriage was perfect and there was no reason for his wife to leave, but Tess knows from experience that husbands are often the last to know if their wives are unhappy. Part of the book is told from Natalie's point of view as she travels on rural roads in the Midwest with Zeke, a cunning, violent man who poses a huge threat to Natalie's children.

Where it's reviewed:
Library Journal, August 2004, page 60
Mystery News, August/September 2004, page 20
Romantic Times, September 2004, page 85

Other books by the same author:
Every Secret Thing, 2003
The Last Place, 2002
In a Strange City, 2001
The Sugar House, 2000
In Big Trouble, 1999

Other books you might like:
Linda Barnes, *The Carlotta Carlyle Series*, 1987-
Ruth Birmingham, *The Sunny Childs Series*, 1998-
Sue Grafton, *The Kinsey Millhone Series*, 1982-
Marcia Muller, *The Sharon McCone Series*, 1977-
Katy Munger, *The Casey Jones Series*, 1997-

130

CONSTANCE LITTLE
GWENYTH LITTLE, Co-Author

The Black House

(Lyons, Colorado: Rue Morgue Press, 2004)

Story type: Humor; Amateur Detective
Subject(s): Rural Life; Winter
Major character(s): Henry Debbon, Lawyer, Detective—Amateur
Time period(s): 1950s (1950)
Locale(s): New York

Summary: Henry Debbon didn't exactly want to play bodyguard to his boss's beautiful redheaded stepdaughter Diana, and he especially didn't want to get shot at or have his clothes

taken away from him. Nor did he bargain on having most of his fellow workers follow him to the house he inherited from his aunt in upstate New York. When the old house (painted black) is cut off from the rest of the world by a winter snowstorm, it's up to Henry to figure out who is drinking the sherry he sets out for his deceased aunt and which of his unwelcome guests is a potential murderer. First published in 1950, this is the first book by these Australian-born sisters to have a male protagonist.

Other books by the same author:
The Black Coat, 1948 (reprinted 2001)
The Black Piano, 1948 (reprinted 2004)
The Black Goatee, 1947 (reprinted 2004)
The Black Stocking, 1946 (reprinted 2000)
Great Black Kanba, 1944 (reprinted 1998)

Other books you might like:
Donna Andrews, *The Meg Langslow Series*, 1999-
Elizabeth Dean, *The Emma Marsh Series*, 1939-1944 reprinted 1998-2001
Joan Hess, *The Claire Malloy Series*, 1986-
Charlotte MacLeod, *The Sarah Kelling Series*, 1979-1998
Craig Rice, *Home Sweet Homicide*, 1944 reprinted 2002

131

MARY LOGUE

Bone Harvest

(New York: Ballantine, 2004)

Story type: Police Procedural
Series: Claire Watkins. Book 4
Subject(s): Small Town Life; Mothers and Daughters; Law Enforcement
Major character(s): Claire Watkins, Police Officer (deputy sheriff), Single Parent
Time period(s): 2000s
Locale(s): Fort St. Antoine, Wisconsin (Pepin County)

Summary: After she lost her husband, Claire fled the big city for rural Wisconsin to become a deputy sheriff in Pepin County. She and her daughter Meg have thrived there and she's found a new love in the person of Rich Haggard, who wants to marry her, despite the inherent dangers in her job. A series of events begins which will eventually shatter the quiet community. First some lethal pesticides are stolen, then they are used to wipe out a flower bed, then a little girl's pet chickens, and then to poison the lemonade at the local Fourth of July picnic. Claire discovers that the crimes are linked to the slaughter 50 years ago of the Schuler family, who were innocent victims of anti-German sentiment following World War II. Each of the seven corpses had a finger removed, and now the fingerbones are turning up with each new crime. Anxious for her daughter's safety, Claire sends Meg away until the would-be killer is caught. A sensitive, beautifully written entry in this strong series.

Where it's reviewed:
Booklist, April 1, 2004, page 1353
Mystery News, June/July 2004, page 16
Publishers Weekly, May 24, 2004, page 44

Romantic Times, June 2004, page 89

Other books by the same author:
Glare Ice, 2001
Dark Coulee, 2000
Blood Country, 1999

Other books you might like:
P.M. Carlson, *The Marty Hopkins Series*, 1992-1995
K.C. Greenlief, *The Lark Swenson/Lacey Smith Series*, 2002-
J.A. Jance, *The Joanna Brady Series*, 1993-
William Kent Krueger, *The Cork O'Connor Series*, 1998-
Charlene Weir, *The Susan Wren Series*, 1992-

132

GAY LONGWORTH

The Unquiet Dead

(New York: St. Martin's Minotaur, 2004)

Story type: Police Procedural
Series: Jessie Driver. Book 2
Subject(s): Law Enforcement; Relationships
Major character(s): Jessie Driver, Police Officer (detective chief inspector)
Time period(s): 2000s
Locale(s): London, England

Summary: Stubborn, scrappy, clever Jessie Driver has to prove herself every day in the male-dominated CID where she works, and life doesn't get any better for her when her new department head, a woman, turns out to be anything but supportive of her. It doesn't help, either, that Jessie is never one to take the tactful approach in any situation. A search for the runaway daughter of a film star takes Jessie into the creepy environs of the abandoned Marshall Street Baths in Soho, once a playground for local kids and now infested with rats, drug addicts, and desperate homeless people. There she chances upon the mummified remains of a man which go back to the 1980s, and this discovery connects her not only with the baths' caretaker but an Anglican priest who specializes in exorcisms. The departmental rivalries, Jessie's ongoing relationship with a rock star whom she met on her previous case, and her forceful personality itself are at least as absorbing as the complex and well-clued plot.

Where it's reviewed:
Publishers Weekly, November 8, 2004, page 39

Other books by the same author:
Dead Alone, 2003

Other books you might like:
Judith Cutler, *The Kate Power Series*, 2003-
Frances Fyfield, *The Helen West Series*, 1989-
Lucy Harkness, *The Happy Pigs*, 2002
Lynda La Plante, *Prime Suspect*, 1993
Priscilla Masters, *The Joanne Piercy Series*, 1995-

133

MARGARET MARON

High Country Fall

(New York: Mysterious, 2004)

Story type: Amateur Detective
Series: Deborah Knott. Book 10
Subject(s): American South; Rural Life; Small Town Life
Major character(s): Deborah Knott, Judge, Detective—Amateur
Time period(s): 2000s
Locale(s): Cedar Gap, North Carolina; Colleton County, North Carolina

Summary: Deborah is not prepared for all the fuss her large extended family is making about her recent engagement to Deputy Sheriff Dwight Bryant, so she welcomes the chance to get away from all the relatives and hold court in the small rural community of Cedar Gap, high in the Blue Ridge Mountains. A local physician has been murdered and his daughter's boyfriend has been arrested for the crime. Even though she is not at all convinced of the man's guilt, Deborah has no choice but to rule that the case can proceed. When another murder takes place, she realizes there is a lot of investigating to do if justice is to be done. There's also a handsome district attorney on hand who's taking her mind off Dwight. In addition to several non-series books and short story collections, the author has also written a series featuring Manhattan police detective Sigrid Harald.

Where it's reviewed:
Booklist, May 1, 2004, page 1515
Deadly Pleasures, Summer/Fall 2004, page 47
Library Journal, June 2004, page 64
Publishers Weekly, June 21, 2004, page 46

Other books by the same author:
Slow Dollar, 2002
Uncommon Clay, 2001
Storm Track, 2000
Home Fires, 1998
Killer Market, 1997

Other books you might like:
Phillip DePoy, *The Fever Devlin Series*, 2003-
Anne Underwood Grant, *The Sydney Teague Series*, 1998-
Charlaine Harris, *The Lily Bard Series*, 1996-
Joan Hess, *The Claire Malloy Series*, 1986-
Sharyn McCrumb, *The Ballad Series*, 1990-

134

EDWARD MARSTON (Pseudonym of Keith Miles)

The Counterfeit Crank

(New York: St. Martin's Press, 2004)

Story type: Historical/Elizabethan
Series: Nicholas Bracewell. Book 14
Subject(s): Theater; Actors and Actresses
Major character(s): Nicholas Bracewell, Producer (book holder)
Time period(s): 16th century (1590s)

Locale(s): London, England

Summary: Problems once again beset the London theater group, Westfield's Men, and its book holder, Nicholas Bracewell, must find ways to set things right. Their playwright has fallen ill, many of the actors have lost their meager salaries gambling, and worst of all, their costumes have been stolen, forcing them to perform in ill-fitting substitutes. As usual, it's a colorful and entertaining evocation of the period and the world of the theater from a prolific writer. Miles has, under his own name and two pseudonyms, created a number of mystery series set in various time periods and locales, most notably the Domesday Book series set in the England of William the Conqueror and a more recent series set in Restoration London.

Where it's reviewed:
Booklist, July 2004, page 1824
Drood Review of Mystery, May/June 2004, page 5
Library Journal, August 2004, page 60
Publishers Weekly, July 19, 2004, page 148

Other books by the same author:
The Vagabond Clown, 2004
The Bawdy Basket, 2002
The Devil's Apprentice, 2001
The Wanton Angel, 1999
The Fair Maid of Bohemia, 1997

Other books you might like:
P.F. Chisholm, *The Sir Robert Carey Series*, 1994-
Judith Cook, *The Slicing Edge of Death*, 1993
Philip Gooden, *The Sleep of Death*, 2000
Simon Hawke, *The Smythe/Shakespeare Series*, 2000-
Leonard Tourney, *Time's Fool*, 2004

135

SUJATA MASSEY

The Pearl Diver

(New York: HarperCollins, 2004)

Story type: Amateur Detective
Series: Rei Shimura. Book 7
Subject(s): Missing Persons; Japanese Americans; Restaurants
Major character(s): Rei Shimura, Antiques Dealer, Detective—Amateur
Time period(s): 2000s
Locale(s): Washington, District of Columbia

Summary: Half-Japanese, half-American antiques dealer Rei Shimura, who spent many years as an expatriate in Japan, seems to be back in the U.S. for good after a visit to her family in San Francisco. She's settled in Washington, D.C., where she and her lawyer boyfriend, Hugh Glendinning, are making tentative wedding plans. Rei is pleased and surprised when restaurateur Marshall Zanger hires her to furnish the upscale Japanese restaurant he's opening. In the middle of all this, Rei's cousin Kendall, who is working with her to prepare for the opening night festivities, disappears without a trace. Then Rei becomes involved with tracing the disappearance 30 years earlier of a Japanese war bride who had been a pearl diver in her native Japan.

Where it's reviewed:
Booklist, July 2004, page 1825
Library Journal, August 2004, page 59
New York Times Book Review, August 22, 2004, page 15
Publishers Weekly, July 19, 2004, page 148
Romantic Times, September 2004, page 85

Other books by the same author:
The Samurai's Daughter, 2003
The Bride's Kimono, 2001
The Floating Girl, 2000
The Flower Master, 1999
Zen Attitude, 1998

Other books you might like:
Dale Furutani, *The Toyotomi Blades*, 1999
Susanna Jones, *The Earthquake Bird*, 2001
Patricia McFall, *Night Butterfly*, 1992
James Melville, *The Inspector Otani Series*, 1979-
Laura Joh Rowland, *The Sano Ichiro Series*, 1994-

136

CLAIRE MATTURRO

Skinny-Dipping

(New York: William Morrow, 2004)

Story type: Legal; Humor
Series: Lilly Cleary. Book 1
Subject(s): Doctors; Law; Trials
Major character(s): Lilly Bell Rose Cleary, Lawyer
Time period(s): 2000s
Locale(s): Sarasota, Florida

Summary: Lilly is the only female partner in a Sarasota law firm, specializing in medical malpractice suits. She's six feet tall, a devout vegetarian, and blessed with a wry outlook on life and an appreciation of the weirdness around her, as well as an appetite for romance. When one of her doctor clients dies from some tainted marijuana and she and another physician are shot at, she's got to figure out what's going on before it's too late. She's also torn, romantically, between a handsome lawyer and an equally handsome detective, and her life is further complicated by her eccentric law partners and some equally offbeat animals, including an unusual Rottweiler and an incontinent ferret. Written by a former lawyer, this debut mystery novel is as strong on the law as it is rich with comedy.

Where it's reviewed:
Publishers Weekly, September 20, 2004, page 44
Romantic Times, November 2004, page 85

Other books you might like:
Tim Dorsey, *The Serge O. Storms Series*, 1999-
Janet Evanovich, *Metro Girl*, 2004
Carl Hiaasen, *Skinny Dip*, 2004
Lisa Scottoline, *Killer Smile*, 2004
Randy Wayne White, *The Doc Ford Series*, 1990-

137

ARCHER MAYOR

The Surrogate Thief

(New York: Mysterious, 2004)

Story type: Police Procedural
Series: Joe Gunther. Book 15
Subject(s): Law Enforcement; Crime and Criminals; Relationships
Major character(s): Joe Gunther, Police Officer, Widow(er)
Time period(s): 2000s
Locale(s): Brattleboro, Vermont

Summary: Gunther's investigations have become somewhat larger in scope since he was made a special agent with the newly created Vermont Bureau of Investigation, a promotion from his former job as Brattleboro chief of police. He's handed an opportunity to right a very old wrong when the murder of a shopkeeper 32 years earlier is reopened after the same gun turns up in a fresh homicide. Gunther, who was assigned the original case but was distraught at the time over his wife's imminent death from cancer, did something that's haunted him ever since: he let the crime go unsolved. Now new technology makes his task easier, but the killer he's pursuing will do anything to keep from getting caught.

Where it's reviewed:
Library Journal, June 2004, page 109
Publishers Weekly, September 13, 2004, page 62

Other books by the same author:
Gatekeeper, 2003
The Sniper's Wife, 2002 (features Willy Kunkle, one of Gunther's team)
Tucker Peak, 2001
The Marble Mask, 2000
Occam's Razor, 1999

Other books you might like:
Gerry Boyle, *The Jack McMorrow Series*, 1993-
Brendan DuBois, *The Lewis Cole Series*, 1994-
Donald Harstad, *The Carl Houseman Series*, 1998-
William Landay, *Mission Flats*, 2003
Robert B. Parker, *The Jesse Stone Series*, 1997-

138

ED MCBAIN (Pseudonym of Evan Hunter)

Hark! A Novel of the 87th Precinct

(New York: Simon & Schuster, 2004)

Story type: Police Procedural; Humor
Series: 87th Precinct. Book 54
Subject(s): Crime and Criminals; Literature
Major character(s): Steve Carella, Police Officer
Time period(s): 2000s
Locale(s): Isola, New York (thinly disguised Manhattan)

Summary: The Deaf Man, a recurring villain in this long-running series who was apparently left for dead in *Mischief* (1993), resurfaces in this book, bigger and badder than ever. He's still very much a mystery man, with none of the detectives at the 87th Precinct knowing what he looks like or even if he's really deaf. All they know is that he's the smartest and deadliest thief they've ever dealt with. Here he tantalizes Steve Carella and the rest of the gang with clues in the form of anagrams and quotations from Shakespeare, hinting at some crime he's yet to commit. Story lines from recent books—Fat Ollie's novel, the impending marriages of Carella's sister and mother—also continue here. The author also writes a series about Florida lawyer Matthew Hope and has done several stand-alones, besides writing mainstream fiction under his real name.

Where it's reviewed:
Booklist, July 2004, page 41
Mystery News, August/September 2004, page 23
New York Times Book Review, August 22, 2004, page 15
Publishers Weekly, July 19, 2004, page 148

Other books by the same author:
Fat Ollie's Book, 2003
The Frumious Bandersnatch, 2003
Money, Money, Money, 2001
The Last Dance, 2000
Big Bad City, 1999

Other books you might like:
William Caunitz, *One Police Plaza*, 1984
Ed Dee, *The Anthony Ryan/Joe Gregory Series*, 1994-
William Heffernan, *The Paul Devlin Series*, 1988-
Christopher Newman, *The Joe Dante Series*, 1986-
Lawrence Sanders, *The Edward X. Delaney Series*, 1973-1985

139

RALPH MCINERNY

Green Thumb

(New York: St. Martin's Minotaur, 2004)

Story type: Amateur Detective; Private Detective
Series: Knight Brothers. Book 8
Subject(s): Universities and Colleges; Sports/Golf; Humor
Major character(s): Roger Knight, Professor, Detective—Amateur; Philip Knight, Detective—Private, Relative (Roger's brother)
Time period(s): 2000s
Locale(s): South Bend, Indiana

Summary: One morning when Phil is playing golf with his friend Jimmy, the men discover an unconscious body on the green of the third hole. The man, Mortimer Sadler, dies at the hospital and the autopsy reveals that he was poisoned with deadly nightshade. Sadler, an unpopular but very generous donor to Notre Dame, was visiting South Bend for an informal reunion with some classmates. When Roger, a professor at the university, teams up with his brother, private detective Phil Knight, to get to the bottom of things, they discover a number of Sadler's college friends had reason to dislike him. But which one wanted him dead?

Where it's reviewed:
Booklist, November 15, 2004, page 565

Other books by the same author:
Irish Coffee, 2003
Celt and Pepper, 2002

Emerald Aisle, 2001
The Book of Kills, 2000
Irish Tenure, 1999

Other books you might like:
Bill Crider, *The Carl Burns Series*, 1988-
William De Andrea, *The Niccolo Benedetti Series*, 1979-
M.D. Lake, *The Peggy O'Neill Series*, 1989-
Francis M. Nevins, *The Loren Mensing Series*, 1975-
Sally S. Wright, *The Ben Reese Series*, 1997-

140
RALPH MCINERNY

Requiem for a Realtor
(New York: St. Martin's Minotaur, 2004)

Story type: Amateur Detective
Series: Father Dowling. Book 23
Subject(s): Marriage; Catholicism; Ethics
Major character(s): Father Roger Dowling, Religious (parish priest), Detective—Amateur
Time period(s): 2000s
Locale(s): Fox River, Illinois

Summary: When a non-parishioner comes to Father Dowling for advice concerning his marriage, he does his best to help the man, whose wife wants to leave him for a member of the church, a wealthy dentist. Unable to offer the kind of help the troubled husband wants, Father Dowling is dismayed when one of the three parties is killed in a hit-and-run accident which he knows may really be murder. The priest has an ethical obligation not to pass on information obtained in confidence to the police, so he can only watch while the investigation proceeds.

Where it's reviewed:
Booklist, August 2004, page 1906
Publishers Weekly, June 28, 2004, page 35

Other books by the same author:
Last Things, 2003
Prodigal Father, 2002
Triple Pursuit, 2001
Grave Undertakings, 2000
The Tears of Things, 1996

Other books you might like:
G.K. Chesterton, *The Father Brown Series*, 1911-1935
Margaret Coel, *The Father John O'Malley/Vicky Holden Series*, 1995-
Andrew M. Greeley, *The Blackie Ryan Series*, 1985-
William X. Kienzle, *The Father Robert Koesler Series*, 1979-2001
Brad Reynolds, *The Father Mark Townsend Series*, 1996-

141
PAT MCINTOSH

The Harper's Quine
(New York: Carroll & Graf, 2004)

Story type: Historical/Medieval
Series: Gil Cunningham. Book 1

Subject(s): Law; Middle Ages; Cultures and Customs
Major character(s): Gilbert Cunningham, Lawyer; Maistre Pierre, Artisan (master mason)
Time period(s): 15th century (1492)
Locale(s): Glasgow, Scotland; Isle of Bute, Scotland

Summary: Newly minted lawyer Gil Cunningham, whose family still expects him to become a priest, discovers the body of a young woman in Glasgow Cathedral. He recognizes the woman as the runaway wife of a nobleman, John Semphill. Gil and his friend Maistre Pierre, a French master mason who is helping with the construction of a new building at the cathedral, are asked to find the woman's murderer, an investigation that leads them to the Semphill household and eventually to the Isle of Bute. Along the way, Gil finds himself increasingly attracted to the mason's lovely and intelligent daughter, Alys. First mystery.

Where it's reviewed:
Deadly Pleasures, Summer/Fall 2004, page 58
Library Journal, July 2004, page 63
Publishers Weekly, July 12, 2004, page 47

Other books you might like:
C.L. Grace, *A Feast of Poisons*, 2004
Sheri Holman, *A Stolen Tongue*, 1997
Alanna Knight, *The Dagger in the Crown*, 2001
Candace Robb, *A Trust Betrayed*, 2001
Kate Sedley, *The Roger the Chapman Series*, 1991-

142
DEON MEYER

Heart of the Hunter
(New York: Little, Brown, 2004)

Story type: Action/Adventure; Espionage
Subject(s): Kidnapping; Spies; Apartheid
Major character(s): Thobela "Tiny" Mpayipheli, Revolutionary (former), Maintenance Worker
Time period(s): 2000s
Locale(s): Cape Town, South Africa

Summary: In a former life, Tiny, a hulking, gentle giant of a man who is the descendant of proud Xhosa warriors, was an assassin trained by the KGB in the war against apartheid in South Africa. Today he's a janitor in a Cape Town motorcycle shop and has settled down with a woman he loves deeply and her young son, whom he is teaching how to farm. His violent past is brought back to him when the daughter of an old friend comes to him for help. Her father has been kidnapped, and in exchange for his life his captors want a computer disc delivered to them that contains the names of double agents and moles within the government. Tiny has 72 hours to delivery, and he sets off on a dangerous journey that will test skills he thought he had put aside long ago. This is the first of this Grand Prix-winning South African's novels to be published in the U.S. Translated from the Afrikaans by K.L. Seegers.

Where it's reviewed:
Booklist, July 2004, page 1825
Library Journal, May 15, 2004, page 115
Mystery News, October/November 2004, page 19
Publishers Weekly, July 19, 2004, page 146

Other books you might like:
Peter Abrahams, *A Night of Their Own*, 1965
Wessel Ebersohn, *The Yudel Gordon Series*, 1979-1981
John Le Carre, *The Tailor of Panama*, 1996
James McClure, *The Lt. Kramer/Sgt. Zondi Series*, 1971-1991
Gillian Slovo, *Red Dust*, 2003

143

MARK MILLS

Amagansett
(New York: Putnam, 2004)

Story type: Historical
Subject(s): Social Classes; World War II; Emigration and Immigration
Major character(s): Conrad Labarde, Fisherman, Veteran (World War II); Tom Hollis, Police Officer (assistant police chief)
Time period(s): 1940s (1947)
Locale(s): Amagansett, New York (Long Island)

Summary: Following World War II, fisherman Conrad Labarde, the son of Basque immigrants, returns to the working-class town of Amagansett on Long Island's south shore and resumes his livelihood. One day he hauls in the body of Lillian Wallace, a Manhattan socialite with whom he has a history. Disgraced assistant police chief Tom Hollis is assigned the investigation. Although Labarde is initially the prime suspect, Hollis uncovers evidence that implicates the young woman's wealthy family, as well as her former boyfriend. This debut mystery novel explores the displacement of working-class immigrants as the Hamptons become settled by the rich and privileged, and the conflicts between year-round residents and summer people.

Where it's reviewed:
Booklist, August 2004, page 1907
Library Journal, July 2004, page 72
New York Times Book Review, August 29, 2004, page 12
Publishers Weekly, July 12, 2004, page 44

Other books you might like:
Thomas Cook, *Breakheart Hill*, 1995
David Guterson, *Snow Falling on Cedars*, 1994
Michael Malone, *Uncivil Seasons*, 1984
Nina Revoyr, *Southland*, 2003
Michael C. White, *A Brother's Blood*, 1996

144

JAMES C. MITCHELL

Choke Point
(New York: St. Martin's Minotaur, 2004)

Story type: Private Detective
Series: Brinker. Book 2
Subject(s): Deserts; American West; Mexicans
Major character(s): Brinker, Detective—Private
Time period(s): 2000s
Locale(s): Tucson, Arizona; Nogales, Mexico

Summary: Tender-hearted private detective Brinker, a former INS agent wounded during a border sweep, is approached by Los Angeles reporter April Lennox with a problem. She had been contacted by a man in Mexico who promised her a juicy story about ''oppression and murder'' and arranged to meet her in Tucson on the night of a riot following a basketball game. He didn't show up, but a man was shot dead in the streets during the revelry, and April fears he may have been her informant. She wants Brinker to go to Mexico and investigate, but before he can make up his mind to help her, she crosses the border herself and doesn't return. Much of the book takes place in Nogales, Mexico, home to many *maquiladoras*, or U.S. owned factories employing low-paid Mexican labor.

Other books by the same author:
Lovers Crossing, 2003 (Shamus Award nominee)

Other books you might like:
Sinclair Browning, *The Trade Ellis Series*, 1999-
David Cole, *The Laura Winslow Series*, 2000-
Allana Martin, *The Texana Jones Series*, 1996-
Janice Steinberg, *Death Crosses the Border*, 1995
Judith Van Gieson, *North of the Border*, 1988

145

SKYE KATHLEEN MOODY

The Good Diamond
(New York: St. Martin's Minotaur, 2004)

Story type: Police Procedural
Series: Venus Diamond. Book 7
Subject(s): Crime and Criminals; Treasure; Smuggling
Major character(s): Venus Diamond, Government Official (U.S. Fish and Wildlife agent)
Time period(s): 2000s
Locale(s): Yellowknife, Northwest Territories, Canada; Pasayten, Washington; New York, New York

Summary: Moody turns her attention here to the international diamond trade and its link to arms smuggling. When a man named Big Jim Hardy is murdered in Canada's Northwest Territories after having discovered a 384-carat blue-green diamond the size of a baseball, he leaves Venus' name written in blood at the crime scene. Initially seized as a suspect, Venus is able to identify Big Jim as a former colleague, Buzz Radke, who was an undercover agent with the feds working on diamond smuggling. Outraged by his death, Venus' search for the killer takes her from Canada to a chicken farm in Washington state that is really headquarters for a racist paramilitary community to the diamond markets of New York City.

Where it's reviewed:
Booklist, August 2004, page 1906
Library Journal, August 2004, page 60

Other books by the same author:
Medusa, 2003
K Falls, 2001
Habitat, 1999
Wildcrafters, 1998
Blue Poppy, 1997

Other books you might like:
Nevada Barr, *The Anna Pigeon Series*, 1993-
Gerald Browne, *11 Harrowhouse*, 1972
John B. Robinson, *The Sapphire Sea*, 2003
Jessica Speart, *The Rachel Porter Series*, 1997-
Robin White, *Siberian Light*, 1997

146

HARKER MOORE

A Mourning in Autumn

(New York: Mysterious, 2004)

Story type: Police Procedural
Series: Jimmy Sakura. Book 2
Subject(s): Japanese Americans; Serial Killers; Blindness
Major character(s): Jimmy Sakura, Detective—Homicide
Time period(s): 2000s
Locale(s): New York, New York

Summary: A new serial killer preys on young women in Manhattan, who are snatched from clubs and gruesomely butchered. Once again Jimmy Sakura investigates, along with his partners from the NYPD and his blind wife, Hanae, who nearly became a victim in the last such case Jimmy worked on. She has compensated for her blindness with a kind of inner vision that complements her husband's own almost detached determination to find the killer. The characters are interesting and their relationships offer many insights into Japanese culture.

Where it's reviewed:
Booklist, May 1, 2004, page 1514
Library Journal, July 2004, page 63
Publishers Weekly, June 28, 2004, page 34

Other books by the same author:
A Cruel Season for Dying, 2003

Other books you might like:
E.V. Cunningham, *The Sgt. Masao Masuto Series*, 1967-1984
Dale Furutani, *The Ken Tanaka Series*, 1996-
Leslie Glass, *The April Woo Series*, 1993-
Sujata Massey, *The Rei Shimura Series*, 1997-
James Melville, *The Supt. Otani Series*, 1979-

147

DEBORAH MORGAN

Four on the Floor

(New York: Berkley, 2004)

Story type: Amateur Detective
Series: Jeff Talbot. Book 4
Subject(s): Antiques; Phobias; Automobiles
Major character(s): Jeff Talbot, Antiques Dealer (picker), Detective—Amateur
Time period(s): 2000s
Locale(s): Seattle, Washington

Summary: Former FBI agent turned antiques picker Jeff Talbot is delighted to learn that his cherished 1948 Chevy woodie has been restored after being wrecked in a serious accident. However, when he and his butler, Greer, pick it up, they find four dead men in the vintage station wagon, including shop owner Louie Stella, an informant from Jeff's FBI days. The deaths turn out to be homicides and the answers are to be found somewhere in Jeff's past. His housebound, agoraphobic wife Sheila joins him in searching through all the things he's saved and collected over the years in hopes of finding a clue to the murders. An appendix of source materials and websites pertaining to vintage automobiles and other antiques and collectibles discussed in the book is included.

Other books by the same author:
The Marriage Casket, 2003
The Weedless Widow, 2002
Death Is a Cabaret, 2001

Other books you might like:
Sharon Fiffer, *The Jane Wheel Series*, 2001-
Elaine Flinn, *The Molly Doyle Series*, 2003-
Susan Holtzer, *Something to Kill For*, 1994
Toni L.P. Kelner, *Tight as a Tick*, 1998
Tamar Myers, *The Abigail Timberlake Series*, 1996-

148

PHILIPPA MORGAN

Chaucer and the House of Fame

(New York: Carroll & Graf, 2004)

Story type: Historical/Medieval
Subject(s): Middle Ages; War
Major character(s): Geoffrey Chaucer, Historical Figure, Writer (poet)
Time period(s): 14th century (1370)
Locale(s): France

Summary: The poet Geoffrey Chaucer, at the bidding of the king's son, John of Gaunt, undertakes a delicate mission to France to persuade an influential nobleman, the Comte de Guyac, to remain loyal to England. The Hundred Years War is still raging and England is in danger of losing its prized territory, Aquitaine, to France, if Chaucer does not prevail in his mission. It also means he will once again see his former lover, Rosamund, now married to de Guyac. When he arrives at the castle, there is little time for the past when the comte is killed during a boar hunt and it soon becomes evident that his death was no accident. Beset by factions at the castle intent on sabotaging his mission, Chaucer must solve the murder before he can return to England and be reunited with his family. First mystery.

Where it's reviewed:
Booklist, September 1, 2004, page 70
Publishers Weekly, August 2, 2004, page 55

Other books you might like:
Ann Benson, *The Burning Road*, 1999
Gertrude Clancy, *Death Is a Pilgrim*, 1993
    Joseph Clancy, co-author
Duane Crowley, *Riddle Me a Murder*, 1986
Paul Harding, *The Brother Athelstan Series*, 1991-
Candace Robb, *The Owen Archer Series*, 1993-

149

JOHN MORTIMER

Rumpole and the Penge Bungalow Murders

(New York: Viking, 2004)

Story type: Legal
Series: Rumpole of the Bailey. Book 12
Subject(s): Law; World War II; Humor
Major character(s): Horace Rumpole, Lawyer
Time period(s): 2000s; 1940s
Locale(s): London, England

Summary: Just as Sherlock Holmes frequently alluded to triumphs in his past, so throughout this series has the elderly acerbic barrister Horace Rumpole, particularly to the illustrious title case (his very first), which took place in the years immediately after World War II. Alarmed that the young barristers he works with are only vaguely familiar with that period and totally ignorant of the case, Rumpole writes a memoir which sheds light on his postwar years as a young "white wig" attorney defending (brilliantly, of course) a young man accused of shooting his father and their next-door neighbor, both former RAF pilots. The story also reveals how the young Rumpole came to meet his formidable wife Hilda, or "She Who Must Be Obeyed," and other bits of Rumpolean history. Lively, witty, and full of colorful characters, it's a must-read for fans of this brilliantly entertaining series.

Where it's reviewed:
Booklist, October 15, 2004, page 362
Publishers Weekly, November 1, 2004, page 47

Other books by the same author:
Rumpole and the Primrose Path, 2003 (short stories)
Rumpole Rests His Case, 2002
Rumpole and the Angel of Death, 1996
Rumpole and the Age of Miracles, 1988 (short stories)
Rumpole's Last Case, 1987 (short stories)

Other books you might like:
Sarah Caudwell, *The Hilary Tamar Series*, 1981-2000
Henry Cecil, *Brief Tales from the Bench*, 1972
Michael Gilbert, *Anything for a Quiet Life*, 1990
Cyril Hare, *Tragedy at Law*, 1942
Arthur Train, *The Mr. Tutt Series*, 1920-1941

150

FIONA MOUNTAIN

Pale as the Dead

(New York: St. Martin's Minotaur, 2004)

Story type: Amateur Detective
Series: Natasha Blake. Book 1
Subject(s): Genealogy; Art; History
Major character(s): Natasha Blake, Genealogist, Detective—Amateur
Time period(s): 2000s
Locale(s): Snowshill, England (Cotswolds); London, England; Oxford, England

Summary: Natasha became a genealogist partly because she knew so little about her own history, having been adopted as an infant by a couple who knew almost nothing about her birth mother. Her expertise is locating people's ancestors, not contemporary missing persons, but agrees when she's asked to find a beautiful young woman, Bethany, who's disappeared. Bethany was obsessed with Lizzie Siddal, wife to Pre-Raphaelite artist Dante Gabriel Rossetti, and both Natasha and Bethany's lover, Adam, fear the missing woman may have emulated Siddal, whose short, tragic life was ended by an overdose of laudanum. First novel.

Where it's reviewed:
Booklist, June 1, 2004, page 1708
Publishers Weekly, June 21, 2004, page 46
Romantic Times, September 2004, page 90

Other books you might like:
Deborah Grabien, *The Weaver and the Factory Maid*, 2003
Mollie Hardwick, *The Dreaming Damozel*, 1990
Erin Hart, *Haunted Ground*, 2003
Rett MacPherson, *The Torie O'Shea Series*, 1997-
Sarah Stewart Taylor, *O' Artful Death*, 2003

151

MARCIA MULLER

The Dangerous Hour

(New York: Mysterious, 2004)

Story type: Private Detective
Series: Sharon McCone. Book 23
Subject(s): Politics; Secrets; City and Town Life
Major character(s): Sharon McCone, Detective—Private
Time period(s): 2000s
Locale(s): San Francisco, California

Summary: Since Sharon branched out to form her own detective agency, her business has continued to thrive and she's added a number of new employees. The agency is threatened when one of her most recently hired operatives, Julia Rafael, is accused of stealing a credit card from Alex Aguilar, a politically ambitious city supervisor on track to become San Francisco's first Latino mayor. When Sharon looks into the matter, however, she comes to believe that Julia is innocent and that it's Aguilar who has something to hide. Elena Oliverez, the museum curator who was featured in an earlier series by the author, makes a cameo appearance here, and the ending promises some big changes ahead in Sharon's personal life. The author has also written two stand-alone mysteries, as well as another short-lived series featuring art expert Joanna Stark.

Where it's reviewed:
Booklist, February 1, 2004, page 140
Deadly Pleasures, Summer/Fall 2004, page 48
Library Journal, June 1, 2004, page 106
Publishers Weekly, June 7, 2004, page 351
Romantic Times, August 2004, page 86

Other books by the same author:
Dead Midnight, 2002
Listen to the Silence, 2000
A Walk through the Fire, 1999

While Other People Sleep, 1998
Both Ends of the Night, 1997

Other books you might like:
Linda Barnes, *The Carlotta Carlyle Series*, 1987-
Janet Dawson, *The Jeri Howard Series*, 1990-
Sue Grafton, *The Kinsey Millhone Series*, 1982-
Linda Grant, *The Catherine Sayler Series*, 1988-
Karen Kijewski, *The Kat Colorado Series*, 1988-

152

TIM MYERS

Booked for Murder

(New York: Berkley, 2004)

Story type: Amateur Detective
Series: Lighthouse Inn. Book 5
Subject(s): Hotels and Motels; Small Town Life; American South
Major character(s): Alex Winston, Innkeeper, Detective—Amateur
Time period(s): 2000s
Locale(s): Elkton Falls, North Carolina

Summary: Alex Winston has realized his dream of operating a bed and breakfast in the foothills of the Blue Ridge Mountains—Hatteras West, a replica of the famous lighthouse on North Carolina's Outer Banks. As hard as he and his assistant, Elise Danton, have worked, though, they're still troubled by a shortage of paying guests. Now they are hosting a throng of sightseers who've come to view the fabled Carolina Rhapsody Emerald, which its owner has requested they display in one of the guest rooms. When the guard is found dead and the gem turns out to be a fake, and then one of his guests is shot, Alex learns that there is a curse associated with the emerald. As the story develops, so does the tentative relationship between Alex and Elise. The author also writes an equally cozy series about Harrison Black, a young man who's inherited his beloved aunt's candle shop.

Other books by the same author:
Room for Murder, 2003
Murder Checks Inn, 2002
Reservations for Murder, 2002
Innkeeping with Murder, 2001

Other books you might like:
Claudia Bishop, *The Hemlock Falls Series*, 1994-
Mary Daheim, *The Judith McMonigle Flynn Series*, 1991-
Jean Hager, *The Tess Darcy Series*, 1994-2000
Parnell Hall, *Cozy*, 2001
Tamar Myers, *The Magdalena Yoder Series*, 1994-

153

TIM MYERS

Snuffed Out

(New York: Berkley, 2004)

Story type: Amateur Detective
Series: Harrison Black. Book 2
Subject(s): Small Town Life; Crafts; Animals/Cats

Major character(s): Harrison Black, Store Owner (candle shop), Detective—Amateur
Time period(s): 2000s
Locale(s): Micah's Ridge, North Carolina

Summary: When his beloved Aunt Belle died and left him her candle shop, At Wick's End, Harrison learned that she also owned the riverfront building in which it and a number of other boutiques are located. He also learned to his dismay that the building is heavily mortgaged, that the rents are fixed at bargain rates, and that if he doesn't give shopkeeping a trial of at least five years, he loses everything. Determined to make a go of it, Harrison plunges full tilt into making and selling candles. As landlord of the complex as well, he's the one who rushes to check the circuit box when there's a blackout in the building. He finds one of his tenants, pottery store owner Aaron Gaston, dead on the floor of his shop in a puddle of water with evidence that's he's been electrocuted by his own pottery wheel. However, Harrison knows that Gaston never used the electric wheel and that the apparent accident must have been rigged. Recipes and candle-making tips are included. The author also writes another cozy series, also set in rural North Carolina, about innkeeper Alex Winston.

Other books by the same author:
At Wick's End, 2004

Other books you might like:
Susan Wittig Albert, *The China Bayles Series*, 1992-
Laura Childs, *The Carmela Bertrand Series*, 2003-
Monica Ferris, *The Betsy Devonshire Series*, 1999-
Joanne Fluke, *The Hannah Swenson Series*, 2000-
Carolyn Hart, *The Death on Demand Series*, 1987-

154

SHARAN NEWMAN

The Witch in the Well

(New York: Forge, 2004)

Story type: Historical/Medieval
Series: Catherine LeVendeur. Book 10
Subject(s): Middle Ages; Judaism; Legends
Major character(s): Catherine LeVendeur, Scholar
Time period(s): 12th century (1149)
Locale(s): Vielleteneuse, France

Summary: With her husband Edgar off to Lombardy, Catherine is spending the summer with her brother's family in their castle in the country. An old woman appears out of nowhere to a hunting party and is brought back to the castle, near death. As Catherine attends her, the crone warns her in a dying message that the water up on which the castle depends is threatened and that Catherine's mother's life is in danger. Catherine learns that there is an old legend that if the spring dries up the family dies. Some in the castle think the woman is a demon who has cursed them, but Catherine sees her message more as a warning. Then the woman's body vanishes mysteriously. Although Catherine doesn't believe in the family legends, she knows she must get to the truth of what is happening as more people die. This one is a little lighter than previous installments in the series, which deal more with Catherine's secret Jewish heritage.

Where it's reviewed:
Romantic Times, January 2005, page 85

Other books by the same author:
The Outcast Dove, 2003
Heresy, 2002
To Wear the White Coat, 2000
The Difficult Saint, 1999
Cursed in the Blood, 1998

Other books you might like:
Ann Benson, *The Burning Road*, 1999
Alys Clare, *The Abbess Helewise Series*, 1999-
Catherine Jinks, *The Inquisitor*, 2002
Ellis Peters, *The Brother Cadfael Series*, 1977-1994
Caroline Roe, *The Isaac of Girona Series*, 1998-

155

CAROL O'CONNELL

Winter House

(New York: Putnam, 2004)

Story type: Police Procedural
Series: Kathleen Mallory. Book 8
Subject(s): Serial Killers; Law Enforcement
Major character(s): Kathleen Mallory, Detective—Homicide; Riker, Detective—Homicide; Charles Butler, Psychologist
Time period(s): 2000s
Locale(s): New York, New York

Summary: Kathy Mallory, a former street child whose survival instincts were honed by her precarious life, was adopted by a kind-hearted cop and his wife and became a police officer herself. Mallory is aided in her work by her street smarts and willingness to think outside the box. Her newest case seems routine at first: a burglar is killed with an ice pick by the elderly woman whose mansion he broke into. The woman turns out to be Nedda Winter, who was thought to have perished with the rest of her family nearly 60 years ago, all of them killed in the same house with perhaps the very same weapon. The burglar turns out to be a serial killer whom Mallory had put away and who is mysteriously out on bail. Series regulars, such as psychologist Charles Butler and Mallory's partner, Detective Riker, are on hand to help her solve the puzzle.

Where it's reviewed:
Booklist, October 14, 2004, page 393
Publishers Weekly, September 27, 2004, page 36

Other books by the same author:
Deaf Famous, 2003
Crime School, 2002
Shell Game, 2000
Stone Angel, 1997
Killing Critics, 1996

Other books you might like:
Robin Burcell, *The Kate Gillespie Series*, 2001-
Patricia Cornwell, *The Kay Scarpetta Series*, 1990-
Linda Fairstein, *The Alexandra Cooper Series*, 1996-
Lynn S. Hightower, *The Sonora Blair Series*, 1995-
Laurie R. King, *The Kate Martinelli Series*, 1993-

156

STUART PALMER

The Puzzle of the Blue Banderilla

(Lyons, Colorado: Rue Morgue Press, 2004)

Story type: Amateur Detective; Humor
Series: Hildegarde Withers. Book 8
Subject(s): Bullfighting; Mexicans; Trains
Major character(s): Hildegarde Withers, Teacher (grade school), Detective—Amateur; Oscar Piper, Detective—Homicide
Time period(s): 1930s
Locale(s): Mexico City, Mexico; New York, New York

Summary: When Inspector Oscar Piper, off on a junket to Mexico, witnesses a murder aboard a train bound for Mexico City, he telegraphs his old friend Hildegarde Withers in Manhattan with a query about the perfume the victim sniffed before dropping dead. Hildy, of course, heads south of the border to come to Oscar's aid. They can't understand why anyone would want to kill a harmless Mexican customs inspector and so assume that the intended victim is really a rich American woman whose husband seems devoted to her. There are plenty of other suspects, and then there is a second murder when a spectator at a bullfight dies from a blue banderilla driven through his back. Originally published in 1937, this is one of the most successful in this series of lighthearted mysteries, many of which were turned into popular movies.

Other books by the same author:
Hildegarde Withers: Uncollected Riddles, 2002 (previously uncollected short stories)
The Puzzle of the Red Stallion, 1936
The Puzzle of the Silver Persian, 1934
The Puzzle of the Pepper Tree, 1933
Murder on the Blackboard, 1932

Other books you might like:
Frances Crane, *The Turquoise Shop*, 1941
reprinted 2004
Craig Rice, *Home Sweet Homicide*, 1944
reprinted 2002
Kelley Roos, *The Frightened Stiff*, 1942
reprinted 2004
Charlotte Murray Russell, *The Message of the Mute Dog*, 1942
reprinted 2001
Margaret Scherf, *The Gun in Daniel Webster's Bust*, 1949
reprinted 2004

157

ROBERT B. PARKER

Melancholy Baby

(New York: Putnam, 2004)

Story type: Private Detective
Series: Sunny Randall. Book 4
Subject(s): Adoption; Divorce; Psychology

Major character(s): Sunny Randall, Detective—Private, Divorced Person
Time period(s): 2000s
Locale(s): Boston, Massachusetts

Summary: Sunny is unexpectedly devastated when she learns that her ex-husband (by choice) is about to remarry. To help her move on with her life, she consults a woman psychologist, Dr. Silverman (surely Susan Silverman of the author's Spenser books) for support. She also takes a case helping a college student, Sarah Markham, discover if she is indeed adopted, as she suspects, and if so, who her birth parents are. Sunny's probing into the case has some immediate disastrous consequences, but she has her cop father, her gay bartender friend Spike, and her bull terrier Rosie to fall back on. This bestselling author also writes a long-running series about tough Boston private eye Spenser, another about small-town Massachusetts police chief Jesse Stone, and occasional stand-alones.

Where it's reviewed:
Booklist, September 1, 2004, page 6
Library Journal, September 15, 2004, page 50
New York Times Book Review, October 3, 2004, page 30
Publishers Weekly, August 30, 2004, page 35

Other books by the same author:
Shrink Rap, 2002
Perish Twice, 2000
Family Honor, 1999

Other books you might like:
Linda Barnes, *The Carlotta Carlyle Series*, 1987-
Ruth Birmingham, *The Sunny Childs Series*, 1998-
Sue Grafton, *The Kinsey Millhone Series*, 1982-
Marcia Muller, *The Sharon McCone Series*, 1977-
Sara Paretsky, *The V.I. Warshawski Series*, 1982-

158

T. JEFFERSON PARKER

California Girl
(New York: William Morrow, 2004)

Story type: Psychological Suspense
Subject(s): Brothers; Coming-of-Age; Relationships
Major character(s): Nick Becker, Detective—Homicide; Andy Becker, Journalist (newspaper reporter); David Becker, Religious (minister)
Time period(s): 2000s; 1960s (1968)
Locale(s): Orange County, California

Summary: The three Becker brothers have a history with the Vonn family, going back to their high school days in the 1950s. It was set off by a rumble between the brothers of each family in an orange packing house, which the Beckers won. In 1968, on his first homicide case with the Orange County sheriff's department, rookie cop Nick finds, in the same packing house, the decapitated body of the Vonns' younger sister Janelle, who had gone on to become a beauty queen. There's plenty of nostalgic evocation of California's recent past as the orange groves give way to tract homes and strip malls and hippies and flower children invade the turf of the John Birch

Society. The author also writes a series about maverick Orange County deputy sheriff Merci Rayborn.

Where it's reviewed:
Booklist, September 15, 2004, page 180
Entertainment Weekly, October 1, 2004, page 78
Library Journal, June 1, 2004, page 109
Publishers Weekly, September 13, 2004, page 56

Other books by the same author:
Silent Joe, 2001 (Edgar Award winner)
Where Serpents Lie, 1998
The Triggerman's Dance, 1996
Summer of Fear, 1993
Pacific Beat, 1991

Other books you might like:
Peter Duchin, *Good Morning, Heartache*, 2003
    John Morgan Wilson, co-author
Dennis Lehane, *Mystic River*, 2001
George Pelecanos, *Hard Revolution*, 2000
Nina Revoyr, *Southland*, 2003
John Shannon, *The Jack Liffey Series*, 1996-

159

MICHAEL PEARCE

A Dead Man in Trieste
(New York: Carroll & Graf, 2004)

Story type: Historical/Edwardian; Espionage
Series: Sandor Seymour. Book 1
Subject(s): Spies; World War I; International Relations
Major character(s): Sandor Seymour, Police Officer (Special Branch), Spy
Time period(s): 1910s (1910)
Locale(s): Trieste, Italy

Summary: The port city of Trieste, although technically located in Italy, is part of the Austro-Hungarian Empire and its only outlet to the sea. Halfway between the top of Italy and the Balkans, it's a melting pot of the entire European continent with residents of all nationalities living uneasily together and various nationalist movements fomenting unrest. The British consul has gone missing, and Sandor Seymour of Special Branch is sent on a mission to find him. Sandor's chief qualifications are his mixed Polish-Hungarian ancestry (he was born of an immigrant family in London's East End) and his proficiency in numerous languages. Set during the years just before the Great War, it's a promising new historical series from the creator of the delightful Mamur Zapt mysteries, set in colonial Egypt during roughly the same time period.

Where it's reviewed:
Library Journal, November 1, 2004, page 58
New York Times Book Review, December 26, 2004, page 22
Publishers Weekly, October 4, 2004, page 73

Other books by the same author:
A Cold Touch of Ice, 2004
Death of an Effendi, 2004
The Face in the Cemetery, 2004
The Mingrelian Conspiracy, 2003
The Last Cut, 1998

Other books you might like:
R. Wright Campbell, *Circus Couronne*, 1997
Erskine Childers, *The Riddle of the Sands*, 2003
Michael Gilbert, *Ring of Terror*, 1995
Jody Shields, *Fig Eater*, 2000
Sarah Smith, *Knowledge of Water*, 1996

160

MICHAEL PEARCE

Death of an Effendi

(Scottsdale, Arizona: Poisoned Pen Press, 2004)

Story type: Historical/Edwardian
Series: Mamur Zapt. Book 12
Subject(s): Politics; Cultures and Customs; Russians
Major character(s): Gareth Owen, Police Officer (head of secret police)
Time period(s): 1900s (1909)
Locale(s): Cairo, Egypt

Summary: Effendis are the Egyptian elite, very important people who, during this period in the country's history, are often foreigners. Gareth Owen, the British head of the Cairo secret police—or Mamur Zapt—is assigned to guard one such effendi, a maverick Russian financier named Tvardovsky, who is entertaining a group of Egyptian investors on a hunting party. When he's shot dead, apparently by one of the hunters, Owen is dismayed when Tvardovsky's body is removed from the scene and another Russian arrested before a proper investigation can be conducted.

Where it's reviewed:
Booklist, June 1, 2004, page 1709
Publishers Weekly, May 3, 2004, page 175

Other books by the same author:
The Fig Tree Murder, 2003
The Mingrelian Conspiracy, 2003
The Snake Catcher's Daughter, 2003
The Camel of Destruction, 2002
The Last Cut, 1998

Other books you might like:
Conrad Allen, *Murder on the Marmora*, 2004
Barbara Cleverly, *The Last Kashmiri Rose*, 2001
Laurie R. King, *The Game*, 2004
Eric Lawlor, *Murder on the Verandah*, 1999
Elizabeth Peters, *Guardian of the Horizon*, 2004

161

JOANNE PENCE

Courting Disaster

(New York: Avon, 2004)

Story type: Amateur Detective
Series: Angelina Amalfi. Book 11
Subject(s): Food; Greek Americans; Restaurants
Major character(s): Angelina Amalfi, Journalist (former food columnist), Detective—Amateur
Time period(s): 2000s
Locale(s): San Francisco, California

Summary: Culinary freelancer Angie Amalfi, still between jobs, has made a deal with her controlling mother: if Serafina is allowed to plan Angie's engagement party to homicide cop Paavo Smith, Angie will be given free reign with the wedding. The problem is that Serafina won't even tell her where the party is being held. Angie gets sidetracked when her neighbor, Stan, falls for a beautiful and very pregnant waitress at a nearby Greek restaurant and she becomes a suspect when the waiter who is the baby's father is killed. Recipes for Greek delicacies are included.

Where it's reviewed:
Romantic Times, December 2004, page 85

Other books by the same author:
If Cooks Could Kill, 2003
Bell, Book and Candle, 2001
To Catch a Cook, 2000
A Cook in Time, 1999
Cook's Night Out, 1998

Other books you might like:
Camilla Crespi, *The Simona Griffo Series*, 1991-
Diane Mott Davidson, *The Goldy Bear Schulz Series*, 1990-
Nancy Fairbanks, *The Carolyn Blue Series*, 2001-
Joanne Fluke, *The Hannah Swenson Series*, 2000-
Phyllis Richman, *The Chas. Wheatley Series*, 1997-

162

ANNE PERRY

A Christmas Visitor

(New York: Ballantine, 2004)

Story type: Historical/Victorian
Series: Christmas. Book 2
Subject(s): Christmas; Victorian Period; Social Classes
Major character(s): Henry Rathbone, Inventor, Scientist (mathematician)
Time period(s): 1850s
Locale(s): Lake District, England

Summary: As if it weren't enough to write three separate historical series, one set in the 1850s, one in the 1880s, and another during the Great War, the author is now offering her readers a Christmas novella each year, featuring a minor character from one or another of her regular series. This time Henry Rathbone, from the William Monk series, takes center stage. He is summoned to a snowbound estate in the Lake District where the Dreghorn family has reunited for the holidays. One of the three brothers dies accidentally just before Christmas, and his widow—Rathbone's godchild—asks him to investigate. As he does so, it begins to look more and more as if the death was no accident, and as if the murderer may have another target in mind.

Where it's reviewed:
Entertainment Weekly, December 10, 2004, page 101

Other books by the same author:
Shoulder the Sky, 2004 (World War I setting)
A Christmas Journey, 2003 (novella)
Seven Dials, 2003 (Thomas and Charlotte Pitt series)
Death of a Stranger, 2002 (William Monk series)
Southampton Row, 2002 (Thomas and Charlotte Pitt series)

Other books you might like:

John Dickson Carr, *Scandal at High Chimneys*, 1959
Evelyn Hervey, *The Governess*, 1983
Alanna Knight, *The Inspector Faro Series*, 1988-
Peter Lovesey, *The Sergeant Cribb/Constable Thackeray Series*, 1970-1976
Robin Paige, *The Kathryn Ardleigh Series*, 1994-

163

ANNE PERRY

Shoulder the Sky

(New York: Ballantine, 2004)

Story type: Historical/World War I
Series: Joseph Reavley. Book 2
Subject(s): World War I; Espionage; Conspiracies
Major character(s): Joseph Reavley, Professor, Religious (chaplain); Matthew Reavley, Spy; Judith Reavley, Driver, Linguist (translator)
Time period(s): 1910s (1915)
Locale(s): Ypres, Belgium; London, England

Summary: With trench warfare in full swing, chaplain Joseph Reavley is gallantly ministering to the soldiers on the front in Ypres while his sister Judith volunteers nearby as a driver and translator to a general with whom she is falling in love. Brother Matthew, meanwhile, is an intelligence officer back in London, still trying to determine the identity of the shadowy figure called the Peacemaker, who killed their parents and is trying to undermine the war effort and establish his own world order. The murder of a war correspondent near Ypres offers another piece to this complicated puzzle. This is the second of five projected volumes taking place against the backdrop of the Great War by the author, who also writes two long-running detective series set at different periods in the Victorian era. The central character is based on her own maternal grandfather.

Where it's reviewed:
Booklist, July 2004, page 1800
Library Journal, September 1, 2004, page 126
Publishers Weekly, July 26, 2004, page 41
Romantic Times, October 2004, page 82

Other books by the same author:
No Graves as Yet, 2003

Other books you might like:
Clare Curzon, *Guilty Knowledge*, 2000
Michael Gilbert, *Into Battle*, 1977
Robert Goddard, *In Pale Battalions*, 1988
Laurie R. King, *The Beekeeper's Apprentice*, 1994
Charles Todd, *The Ian Rutledge Series*, 1996-

164

MANJIRI PRABHU

The Cosmic Clues

(New York: Dell, 2004)

Story type: Private Detective
Series: Sonia Samarth. Book 1

Subject(s): Astrology; Cultures and Customs
Major character(s): Sonia Samarth, Detective—Private, Astrologer
Time period(s): 2000s
Locale(s): Pune, India

Summary: Although presented as a novel, this is really a collection of loosely connected short stories, featuring one of the more original sleuths around. Sonia Samarth operates Stellar Investigations in Pune, India, a private detective agency based on the principles of Vedic astrology, a not so outlandish idea in a place where just about everyone keeps their horoscope handy. Sonia is quick to point out that she uses astrology—which she considers a true science—only as a map to help guide her investigations; otherwise, she employs all the standard detective tools, including interviews, surveillance, and lots of legwork. However, if a horoscope tells her that the accused is not capable of committing a crime, Sonia knows she has to look elsewhere. The stories are true puzzles in the grand old tradition that reaches back to Edgar Allan Poe and Arthur Conan Doyle. Tying them all together is the master criminal, a mysterious figure known as the Owl, whose presence is felt throughout the book. It's all good fun, made even more enjoyable by an evocative portrait of life in modern India. First mystery.

Where it's reviewed:
Library Journal, June 1, 2004, page 109

Other books you might like:
Barbara Cleverly, *The Joe Sandilands Series*, 2002-
Steven Forrest, *Stalking Anubis*, 2003
H.R.F. Keating, *The Ganesh Ghote Series*, 1964-
Paul Mann, *The George Sansi Series*, 1993-
Alexander McCall Smith, *The No. 1 Ladies' Detective Agency Series*, 1998-

165

BILL PRONZINI

The Alias Man

(New York: Walker, 2004)

Story type: Psychological Suspense
Subject(s): Crime and Criminals; Women; Revenge
Major character(s): Jessie Keene, Antiques Dealer, Widow(er); Sarah Collins, Store Owner (bookstore); Morgan Cord, Teacher (high school)
Time period(s): 2000s
Locale(s): Los Alegres, California; Santa Fe, New Mexico; Vancouver, British Columbia, Canada

Summary: Three women—Sarah, Jessie, and Morgan—discover they have something in common besides a superficial resemblance to one another: a husband who is not really who they thought he was when they married him. He has disappeared from each of their lives, taking all their money after several otherwise uneventful years of marriage. They nickname this shadowy figure the Alias Man and travel across the country trying to track him down and expose his crimes. In the process, they learn something about themselves and the weaknesses that made them all vulnerable to him. In addition to numerous stand-alones and short story collections, the author has written a long-running series about a nameless San Francisco private detective.

Where it's reviewed:
Booklist, May 15, 2004, page 1602
Library Journal, June 1, 2004, page 1231
Publishers Weekly, June 7, 2004, page 33

Other books by the same author:
Step to the Graveyard Easy, 2002
In an Evil Time, 2001
Nothing but the Night, 1999
A Wasteland of Strangers, 1997
Blue Lonesome, 1996

Other books you might like:
Lawrence Block, *After the First Death*, 1994
Lee Child, *The Jack Reacher Series*, 1997-
Harlan Coben, *Tell No One*, 2001
Michael Connelly, *Void Moon*, 2000
Peter Robinson, *The First Cut*, 2004

166

XIAOLONG QIU

When Red Is Black

(New York: Soho, 2004)

Story type: Police Procedural
Series: Inspector Chen. Book 3
Subject(s): China; Communism; Cultures and Customs
Major character(s): Chen Cao, Police Officer (inspector); Yu Guangming, Detective—Police
Time period(s): 2000s
Locale(s): Shanghai, China

Summary: Inspector Chen Cao of the Shanghai Police is taking an uncharacteristic vacation, in part to take a lucrative assignment translating a business proposal for a glitzy retail complex to be built in the city. So it falls to his partner, Detective Yu, to investigate when a dissident woman novelist, Yin Lige, is found murdered in her apartment. Although a neighbor confesses to the crime, something doesn't quite add up for Yu, and it's only when Chen is able to take part in the investigation that the truth emerges. The politics and culture of modern Shanghai are vividly evoked by this Anthony Award-winning novelist, a native of Shanghai who currently lives and teaches in the U.S.

Where it's reviewed:
Booklist, May 1, 2004, page 1519
Deadly Pleasures, Summer/Fall 2004, page 55
Mystery News, August/September 2004, page 9
Publishers Weekly, April 26, 2004, page 44

Other books by the same author:
A Loyal Character Dancer, 2002
Death of a Red Heroine, 2000

Other books you might like:
Eliot Pattison, *The Inspector Shan Series*, 1999-
Lisa See, *The Flower Net*, 1997
James Thayer, *The Gold Swan*, 2002
Shuo Wang, *Playing for Thrills*, 1997
Christopher West, *The Inspector Wang Series*, 1998-

167

LEV RAPHAEL

Tropic of Murder

(McKinleyville, California: Perseverance, 2004)

Story type: Amateur Detective; Humor
Series: Nick Hoffman. Book 6
Subject(s): Academia; Homosexuality/Lesbianism; Vacations
Major character(s): Nick Hoffman, Professor (untenured), Detective—Amateur
Time period(s): 2000s
Locale(s): Michiganapolis, Michigan; Serenity Island, Caribbean

Summary: Academic infighting and the appointment of an unpopular department chair have led gay professor Nick Hoffman and his partner Stefan to take their spring break at a Club Med on the Caribbean island of Serenity. Trouble follows them, however, in the form of some people involved in an investigation Nick has undertaken for a graduate student, but these problems are trumped by the murder of the resort manager. The author gets in some very funny digs at academia. Nick's employer, the fictitious State University of Michigan, not only has a Canadian Studies program but is considering launching a White Studies program, and the departmental politics are as savage as they are hilarious. The author has also written several mainstream novels, one of which, *The German Money* (2003), has mystery elements.

Where it's reviewed:
Booklist, September 1, 2004, page 69
Library Journal, August 2004, page 59

Other books by the same author:
Burning Down the House, 2001
Little Miss Evil, 2000
The Death of a Constant Lover, 1999
The Edith Wharton Murders, 1997
Let's Get Criminal, 1995

Other books you might like:
Robert Barnard, *Death of an Old Goat*, 1974
Robert Bernard, *Deadly Meeting*, 1970
Michael Craft, *Desert Winter*, 2003
Joanne Dobson, *The Karen Pelletier Series*, 1997-
Ruth Dudley Edwards, *Matricide at St. Martha's*, 1994

168

BEN REHDER

Flat Crazy

(New York: St. Martin's Minotaur, 2004)

Story type: Humor
Series: John Marlin. Book 3
Subject(s): Rural Life; Animals; Poaching
Major character(s): John Marlin, Game Warden
Time period(s): 2000s
Locale(s): Blanco County, Texas

Summary: Quietly competent game warden John Marlin may be the only sane individual in Blanco County. There's his old nemesis, Duke Waldrop, at loose ends since the bunny-huggers in the state made canned hunts with exotic wild animals illegal. There are two good ol' boys, Red O'Brien and Billy Don Craddock, who've come up with a get-rich-quick scheme involving a mysterious wild animal being sighted in the county, dubbed a chupacabra by the locals. And there is a visiting movie maker who's shooting a porn film with Chinese dwarves. When a corpse shows up with odd fang-like marks in its neck, it's up to Marlin to figure out who—or what—is to blame.

Where it's reviewed:
Deadly Pleasures, Summer/Fall 2004, page 50
Mystery News, October/November 2004, page 22
Publishers Weekly, August 16, 2004, page 46

Other books by the same author:
Bone Dry, 2003
Buck Fever, 2002

Other books you might like:
Bill Crider, *The Sheriff Dan Rhodes Series*, 1986-
Kinky Friedman, *Meanwhile, Back at the Ranch*, 2002
Pete Hautman, *Short Money*, 1995
Carl Hiaasen, *Native Tongue*, 1991
Elmore Leonard, *Out of Sight*, 1996

169

RUTH RENDELL

The Rottweiler

(New York: Crown, 2004)

Story type: Psychological Suspense
Subject(s): Serial Killers; Antiques; City and Town Life
Major character(s): Inez Ferry, Antiques Dealer, Landlord
Time period(s): 2000s
Locale(s): London, England

Summary: There's a serial killer on the prowl in London, or to be more precise, a serial garroter, who strangles young women and takes some small keepsake from each body as a grisly souvenir. Because his first victim had bite marks on her neck (which later proves to be totally unrelated), the media have named the killer the Rottweiler. Then the items taken from his victims start to turn up in Inez Ferry's cluttered antiques shop, and it becomes clear that the killer is in some way associated with either Inez's shop or the flats that she lets in the building above. He could be one of her tenants, or a customer, or even an employee. Perhaps not as suspenseful as some of Rendell's psychological chillers, it's still absorbing and disturbing, typical of the outstanding body of work the author has created over the years. She also writes a series of police procedurals featuring Inspector Wexford.

Where it's reviewed:
Entertainment Weekly, November 19, 2004, page 88
New York Times Book Review, December 12, 2004, page 26

Other books by the same author:
Adam and Eve and Pinch Me, 2002
Piranha to Scrufy, 2000 (short stories)
A Sight for Sore Eyes, 1999
Blood Lines, 1996 (short stories)
The Keys to the Street, 1996

Other books you might like:
Freda Davis, *A Fine and Private Place*, 2001
Elizabeth George, *A Great Deliverance*, 1988
Frances Hegarty, *The Play Room*, 1991
Minette Walters, *The Shape of Snakes*, 2001
Laura Wilson, *My Best Friend*, 2001

170

CYNTHIA RIGGS

Jack in the Pulpit

(New York: St. Martin's Minotaur, 2004)

Story type: Amateur Detective
Series: Victoria Trumbull. Book 4
Subject(s): Small Town Life; Clergy; Stalking
Major character(s): Victoria Trumbull, Aged Person, Detective—Amateur
Time period(s): 2000s
Locale(s): West Tisbury, Massachusetts (Martha's Vineyard)

Summary: *Jack in the Pulpit*, a prequel to the earlier books in this charming series, tells how Victoria befriends the town's new police chief, Casey O'Neill, and how her granddaughter Elizabeth comes to live with her. When the feud between the outgoing pastor of the local church and his successor, both of whom are named Jack, escalates into open warfare, and then four people from the parish die from eating poisoned food left at their houses, Casey turns to the elderly Victoria for advice. Victoria believes there is a link, but she's also having to cope with the arrival of Elizabeth, who is fleeing an abusive husband. With lots of information on the flora and fauna of the island (in particular poisonous mushrooms), the book is the next best thing to a visit to Martha's Vineyard.

Where it's reviewed:
Booklist, May 1, 2004, page 1516
Deadly Pleasures, Summer/Fall 2004, page 44
Library Journal, May 1, 2004, page 144
Mystery News, August/September 2004, page 27
Publishers Weekly, April 19, 2004, page 43

Other books by the same author:
The Cemetery Yew, 2003
The Cranefly Orchid Murders, 2002
Deadly Nightshade, 2001

Other books you might like:
Philip R. Craig, *The J.W. Jackson Series*, 1989-
Francine Mathews, *The Merry Folger Series*, 1994-
Stefanie Matteson, *The Charlotte Graham Series*, 1990-
David Osborne, *Murder on Martha's Vineyard*, 1989
Katherine Hall Page, *The Body in the Lighthouse*, 2003

171

DAVID ROBERTS

The More Deceived

(New York: Carroll & Graf, 2004)

Story type: Historical/Depression Era
Series: Lord Edward Corinth/Verity Browne. Book 5
Subject(s): Civil War/Spanish; Social Classes; Politics

Major character(s): Lord Edward Corinth, Nobleman; Verity Browne, Journalist, Activist
Time period(s): 1930s (1937)
Locale(s): *Queen Mary*, At Sea

Summary: Lord Edward Corinth is an English aristocrat who has fallen for commoner Verity Browne, a communist journalist who's made it clear she's not interested in bourgeois concepts like marriage. It's 1937 and communism is the political flavor of the year among British bohemians, many of whom are supporting the Republican cause in the Spanish Civil War. The British government knows that war with Germany is certain, a war that England is woefully unprepared to fight. Someone in the government appears to be leaking news about England's lack of preparedness to Winston Churchill, currently on the political outs. When the Foreign Office asks Edward to make a few discreet inquiries into these leaks, he little realizes that he's about to fall under the spell of one of the most charismatic politicians of the century. Instead of investigating Churchill, Edward finds himself looking into the murder of government officials loyal to the future prime minister. Meanwhile, Verity continues to report on the war in Spain, but her life may be in danger when she learns of a secret plan to attack the undefended town of Guernica.

Where it's reviewed:
Booklist, November 15, 2004, page 566
Library Journal, November 1, 2004, page 62
Publishers Weekly, October 11, 2004, page 59

Other books by the same author:
Dangerous Sea, 2003
Hollow Crown, 2003
Sweet Poison, 2001
The Bones of the Buried, 2001

Other books you might like:
James Anderson, *The Affair of the 39 Cufflinks*, 2003
Robert Barnard, *Skeleton in the Grass*, 1988
Carola Dunn, *The Daisy Dalrymple Series*, 1994-
Robert Goddard, *Closed Circle*, 1993
James Woods, *The General's Dog*, 2000

172

GILLIAN ROBERTS (Pseudonym of Judith Greber)

Till the End of Tom

(New York: Ballantine, 2004)

Story type: Amateur Detective; Humor
Series: Amanda Pepper. Book 12
Subject(s): Weddings; Schools/High Schools
Major character(s): Amanda Pepper, Teacher (high school), Fiance(e) (of Mackenzie); C.K. Mackenzie, Student—Graduate (criminology), Police Officer (former)
Time period(s): 2000s
Locale(s): Philadelphia, Pennsylvania

Summary: After taking an early departure from a dreary faculty meeting at Philly Prep, the high school where she teaches, Amanda stumbles across a dead body at the foot of the school's elegant marble staircase. It's Tomas Severin, who belonged to one of Philadelphia's oldest and most prominent families, and it turns out that he slipped and fell after ingesting

a cup of poisoned tea on the school premises. With the help of her fiance, C.K. Mackenzie, a former cop who's now working on his doctorate in criminology, Amanda investigates—as best she can, what with her family and his bugging her about their upcoming wedding plans. With its dry wit and perceptive characterizations, this has consistently been one of the most engaging cozy series. Recently the author has begun a second series featuring an odd-couple pair of women private eyes, Emma Howe and Billie August.

Where it's reviewed:
Booklist, September 1, 2004, page 69
Library Journal, September 1, 2004, page 122
Publishers Weekly, September 20, 2004, page 49

Other books by the same author:
Claire and Present Danger, 2003
Helen Hath No Fury, 2000
Adam and Evil, 1999
The Bluest Blood, 1998
The Mummer's Curse, 1996

Other books you might like:
Donna Andrews, *The Meg Langslow Series*, 1999-
Joanne Dobson, *The Karen Pelletier Series*, 1997-
Joan Hess, *The Claire Malloy Series*, 1986-
Nancy Martin, *The Blackbird Sisters Series*, 2002-
Nancy Pickard, *The Jenny Cain Series*, 1984-1995

173

MADELEINE E. ROBINS

Petty Treason

(New York: Forge, 2004)

Story type: Historical/Napoleonic Wars; Private Detective
Series: Sarah Tolerance. Book 2
Subject(s): Social Classes; Prostitution; Politics
Major character(s): Sarah Tolerance, Detective—Private
Time period(s): 1810s (1810)
Locale(s): London, England

Summary: When Sarah Brereton ran off with her brother's fencing master and returned to London nearly 12 years later, she took the name of Tolerance to avoid embarrassing her socially prominent family. As a fallen woman, her career choices were limited to harlotry or millinery; instead, she reinvented herself as a private enquiry agent and took lodgings at her aunt's brothel (Mrs. Brereton is another of the Fallen). Her qualifications for this calling are her wits, her ambiguous social standing, her skill with the sword, and her willingness to dress in men's clothing when advantageous. Sarah's newest case involves the murder of the dissolute Chevalier d'Aubigny, beaten to death in his bedchambers in a tightly sealed house. Almost all who knew him could be a suspect, and her search for his killer takes her from the brothels of London's shadowy underworld to the no less kinky royal family itself. Note to readers: Sarah's Regency England is not the historical one. Here George III has been off the throne for some years due to his madness and his wife Charlotte has become his regent.

Where it's reviewed:
Library Journal, September 1, 2004, page 126

Publishers Weekly, August 16, 2004, page 46
Romantic Times, September 2004, page 89

Other books by the same author:
Point of Honour, 2003

Other books you might like:
T.F. Banks, *The Thief-Taker*, 2001
Stephanie Barron, *The Jane Austen Series*, 1996-
Wilder Perkins, *The Bartholomew Hoare Series*, 1998-2001
Kate Ross, *The Julian Kestrel Series*, 1993-1997
Rosemary Stevens, *The Beau Brummell Series*, 2000-

174

PETER ROBINSON

The First Cut

(New York: HarperCollins, 2004)

Story type: Psychological Suspense
Subject(s): Serial Killers; Memory Loss; Psychology
Major character(s): Kirsten, Student—College; Martha Browne, Writer
Time period(s): 1980s (1987)
Locale(s): Whitby, England (Yorkshire)

Summary: Kirsten is a young university student on the eve of graduating when, walking home from a party, she becomes the first victim of the man who will become famous as the "Student Slasher." Miraculously, Kirsten survives the multiple stab wounds inflicted upon her, although she is mutilated in painful ways that aren't always visible and has almost no recollection of the assault. Meanwhile, a woman named Martha Browne, who says she is a writer, checks into a bed and breakfast in the small village of Whitby on the Yorkshire coast, where she embarks on a mysterious research project. This chilling stand-alone thriller was originally published in Canada and the U.K. as *Caedmon's Song* in 1991 and is finally being published in the U.S. The author's works also include the acclaimed Inspector Alan Banks series about a Yorkshire police detective.

Where it's reviewed:
Library Journal, July 2004, page 65
Publishers Weekly, July 26, 2004, page 36

Other books by the same author:
Playing with Fire, 2004
Close to Home, 2003
Aftermath, 2001
Cold Is the Grave, 2000
In a Dry Season, 1999

Other books you might like:
Freda Davis, *A Fine and Private Place*, 2001
Lucy Harkness, *The Happy Pigs*, 2002
Manda Scott, *No Good Deed*, 2002
Minette Walters, *The Shape of Snakes*, 2001
Laura Wilson, *My Best Friend*, 2001

175

CAROLINE ROE (Pseudonym of Medora Sale)

Consolation for an Exile

(New York: Berkley, 2004)

Story type: Historical/Medieval
Series: Isaac of Girona. Book 8
Subject(s): Middle Ages; Judaism; Cultures and Customs
Major character(s): Isaac of Girona, Doctor, Handicapped (blind)
Time period(s): 14th century (1355)
Locale(s): Girona, Spain; Granada, Spain

Summary: Isaac lives in a time and a place where, for a period, Jews, Christians, and Muslims coexist in comparative harmony. He has taken a young Muslim, Yusuf Ibn Hasan, as his apprentice, but Yusuf is called away to return to Granada by his relative, the emir. Isaac is seeing a new patient who complains of insomnia and nightmares. As Isaac is looking for a psychological basis for the man's troubles, the man dies, forcing Isaac to turn detective again. Under her own name, the author wrote a contemporary series about Toronto police detective John Sanders and his photographer girlfriend Harriet Jeffries.

Where it's reviewed:
Publishers Weekly, October 4, 2004, page 73
Romantic Times, December 2004, page 88

Other books by the same author:
A Poultice for a Healer, 2003
A Draught for a Dead Man, 2002
A Potion for a Widow, 2001
Solace for a Sinner, 2000
An Antidote for Avarice, 1999

Other books you might like:
Ann Benson, *The Burning Road*, 1999
Umberto Eco, *The Name of the Rose*, 1983
Susanna Gregory, *An Order for Death*, 2001
Arturo Perez-Reverte, *The Flanders Panel*, 1994
Richard Zimler, *The Last Kabbalist of Lisbon*, 1998

176

PRISCILLA ROYAL

Tyrant of the Mind

(Scottsdale, Arizona: Poisoned Pen Press, 2004)

Story type: Historical/Medieval
Subject(s): Monasticism; Nuns; Middle Ages
Major character(s): Eleanor, Religious (nun)
Time period(s): 13th century (1271)
Locale(s): Wales

Summary: Eleanor, now prioress of the East Anglian Priory of Tyndale, returns to her home, the castle of Wynethorpe, located on the Welsh border. It's winter and bitter cold, and Eleanor, along with her traveling companions Sister Anne and Brother Thomas, has been summoned to care for her ailing young nephew Richard, the bastard son of her brother Robert. A neighbor is found stabbed to death, with Robert standing over his body with a bloody knife. The castle is cut off from the outside world by severe weather and Eleanor is forced to prove her brother's innocence by tracking down the real murderer.

Where it's reviewed:
Library Journal, November 1, 2004, page 60
Publishers Weekly, November 15, 2004, page 44

Other books by the same author:
Wine of Violence, 2003

Other books you might like:
Alys Clare, *The Abbess Helewise Series*, 1999-
Margaret Frazer, *The Dame Frevisse Series*, 1992-
Paul Harding, *The Brother Athelstan Series*, 1991-
Ellis Peters, *The Brother Cadfael Series*, 1977-1994
Peter Tremayne, *The Sister Fidelma Series*, 1994-

177

S.J. ROZAN

Absent Friends

(New York: Delacorte, 2004)

Story type: Psychological Suspense
Subject(s): Friendship; Death; City and Town Life
Major character(s): Laura Stone, Journalist
Time period(s): 2000s (2001)
Locale(s): New York, New York

Summary: The author of a popular series featuring New York private detectives Lydia Chin and Bill Smith has produced a multilayered stand-alone crime novel set, again, in New York, in the aftermath of the destruction of the World Trade Center on September 11, 2001. Among those who died that day was fire Captain James McCaffery, initially acclaimed as a hero. Newspaper reporter Harry Randall finds evidence linking Mc-Caffery with a 1979 shooting on Staten Island and suggests that he diverted mob money to the widow of the shooter, Mark Keegan (who in turn was killed while serving time for the murder). Family and friends of McCaffery are outraged at the story, and when Randall dies in a suspicious fall from the Verrazano Narrows Bridge, his much younger girlfriend, Laura Stone, resolves to continue his investigation no matter where it takes her. Told in numerous flashbacks and from multiple points of view, it's an ambitious novel that successfully depicts the turmoil and heartbreak of post 9/11 New York.

Where it's reviewed:
Booklist, September 1, 2004, page 7
Library Journal, September 15, 2004, page 50
People Weekly, October 18, 2004, page 49
Publishers Weekly, September 6, 2004, page 45
Romantic Times, December 2004, page 90

Other books by the same author:
Winter and Night, 2002
Reflections in the Sky, 2001
Stone Quarry, 1999
A Bitter Feast, 1998
No Colder Place, 1997

Other books you might like:
Lawrence Block, *Small Town*, 2003
Harlan Coben, *Just One Look*, 2004

Michael Connelly, *The Narrows*, 2004
Dennis Lehane, *Mystic River*, 2001
T. Jefferson Parker, *California Girl*, 2004

178

KIRK RUSSELL

Night Game

(San Francisco: Chronicle, 2004)

Story type: Police Procedural
Series: John Marquez. Book 2
Subject(s): Endangered Species; Poaching; Animals/Bears
Major character(s): John Marquez, Game Warden
Time period(s): 2000s
Locale(s): Sierra Nevadas, California; Sacramento, California

Summary: John Marquez is a former DEA agent who now works with a covert Special Operations Unit for the California Department of Fish and Game. Headquartered in Sacramento, he and his team are working undercover to locate bear poaching and bear farming rings in the Sierra Nevada Mountains, in which bear bile and paws are harvested to satisfy the demands of Chinese medical practitioners. The investigation is complicated by his history with the local game warden, who is now dating a member of a well-known poaching family, and becomes more complicated when the warden's wife is killed and he's a suspect in still another murder. The author does a remarkable job in describing the wilderness settings in which most of the action takes place.

Where it's reviewed:
Booklist, September 15, 2004, page 214
Library Journal, October 1, 2004, page 65

Other books by the same author:
Shell Games, 2003

Other books you might like:
Nevada Barr, *Blood Lure*, 2001
C.J. Box, *The Joe Pickett Series*, 2001-
Skye Kathleen Moody, *The Venus Diamond Series*, 1996-
Jessica Speart, *A Killing Season*, 2002
David Rains Wallace, *The Turquoise Dragon*, 1985

179

JONATHAN SANTLOFER

Color Blind

(New York: William Morrow, 2004)

Story type: Psychological Suspense
Series: Kate McKinnon. Book 2
Subject(s): Serial Killers; Art; City and Town Life
Major character(s): Kate McKinnon, Art Historian, Police Officer (former); Floyd Brown, Detective—Homicide
Time period(s): 2000s
Locale(s): New York, New York

Summary: Two horribly eviscerated bodies have turned up in the Bronx, each with a garishly colored oil painting left at the scene. NYPD homicide detective Floyd Brown seeks the help of his former partner Kate McKinnon, now retired from the force and settled into a comfortable life as an art historian and

PBS television host. At first Kate resists, but when the third victim is her own husband, a wealthy lawyer whom she loves madly, she can no longer refuse. Once again she must get into the mind of the psychopathic serial killer in order to discover his identity. The depiction of the New York art world is convincing; the subject matter is often gruesome and the descriptions graphic. Not for squeamish readers.

Where it's reviewed:
Library Journal, September 1, 2004, page 141
Publishers Weekly, September 6, 2004, page 46

Other books by the same author:
The Death Artist, 2002

Other books you might like:
Michael Connelly, *The Harry Bosch Series*, 1992-
Linda Fairstein, *The Alexandra Cooper Series*, 1996-
Thomas Harris, *The Silence of the Lambs*, 1988
Jonathan Kellerman, *The Alex Delaware Series*, 1985-
Karin Slaughter, *The Sara Linton Series*, 2001-

180

STEVEN SAYLOR

The Judgment of Caesar

(New York: St. Martin's Minotaur, 2004)

Story type: Historical/Ancient Rome
Series: Roma Sub Rosa. Book 10
Subject(s): Ancient History; Roman Empire; Kings, Queens, Rulers, etc.
Major character(s): Gordianus the Finder, Detective—Private; Julius Caesar, Historical Figure, Ruler; Cleopatra, Historical Figure, Ruler
Time period(s): 1st century B.C. (48 B.C.)
Locale(s): Alexandria, Egypt

Summary: Despite the dangers involved as Cleopatra and her brother Ptolemy engage in a bitter rivalry for control of Egypt, Gordianus agrees to accompany his beloved wife (and former slave) Bethesda to her native Alexandria so that she can bathe in the sacred waters of the Nile and perhaps be cured of the mysterious malady which has greatly weakened her. Before their ship makes port, it's threatened by Gordianus' enemy, Pompey the Great, who has sworn to see him dead. Pompey's fleet is in turn defeated by Julius Caesar, who has arrived in Alexandria to impose a Roman peace on Egypt and decide which sibling, Cleopatra or Ptolemy, is to rule the country. When both Caesar and Cleopatra are nearly poisoned, Gordianus' own adopted son Meto is accused of the crime. In the meantime, Bethesda has disappeared into the Nile and Gordianus fears he may have lost her forever. Possibly the best book in this splendid series, it delves deeply into the personal life of its hero at the same time that it examines the public lives of the historical figures whom Gordianus is in a unique position to observe. The author has also written two stand-alone mysteries.

Where it's reviewed:
Booklist, May 1, 2004, page 1518
Library Journal, June 1, 2004, page 108
Mystery News, August/September 2004, page 25
Publishers Weekly, May 10, 2004, page 40

Other books by the same author:
A Mist of Prophecies, 2002
Last Seen in Massilia, 2000
Rubicon, 1999
The House of the Vestals, 1997 (short stories)
A Murder on the Appian Way, 1996

Other books you might like:
Ron Burns, *Roman Shadows*, 1992
Lindsey Davis, *The Marcus Didius Falco Series*, 1989-
Joan O'Hagan, *Roman Death*, 1988
John Maddox Roberts, *The SPQR Series*, 1990-
Marilyn Todd, *The Claudia Seferius Series*, 1995-

181

HAROLD SCHECHTER

The Mask of Red Death

(New York: Ballantine, 2004)

Story type: Historical/Victorian America
Series: Edgar Allan Poe. Book 3
Subject(s): Native Americans; American West; Serial Killers
Major character(s): Edgar Allan Poe, Historical Figure, Writer; Kit Carson, Scout, Historical Figure
Time period(s): 1840s (1845)
Locale(s): New York, New York

Summary: A child killer who scalps his victims is on the loose in Manhattan, and suspicion falls on the Crow Indian Chief Wolf Bear, one of the attractions in P.T. Barnum's American Museum. An angry mob, about to lynch the chief, is stopped by the timely arrival of Kit Carson. Poe, a young journalist and friend of P.T. Barnum, is living in New York with his young wife and her mother (also Poe's aunt). He teams up with Carson to track down the real killer and protect Wolf Bear.

Where it's reviewed:
Deadly Pleasures, Summer/Fall 2004, page 61
Library Journal, July 2004, page 64
Publishers Weekly, May 31, 2004, page 54

Other books by the same author:
The Hum Bug, 2001
Nevermore, 1999

Other books you might like:
George Egon Hatvary, *The Murder of Edgar Allan Poe*, 1997
Stephen Marlowe, *The Lighthouse at the End of the World*, 1995
Manny Meyers, *The Last Mystery of Edgar Allan Poe*, 1978
Randall Silvis, *On Night's Shore*, 2000
Dwight Steward, *Evermore*, 1978
  Barbara Steward, co-author

182

MARGARET SCHERF

The Gun in Daniel Webster's Bust

(Lyons, Colorado: Rue Morgue Press, 2004)

Story type: Amateur Detective; Humor
Series: Henry & Emily Bryce. Book 1
Subject(s): Antiques; City and Town Life; Romance

Mystery

Major character(s): Emily Murdock, Interior Decorator, Detective—Amateur; Henry Bryce, Interior Decorator, Detective—Amateur
Time period(s): 1940s (1949)
Locale(s): New York, New York

Summary: Emily Murdock owns an interior decorating store in Manhattan which specializes in refinishing old furniture. Her chief employee is Henry Bryce, who's fond of Emily but not so sure he wants to marry her, having had an unfortunate first marriage to a woman who cried a lot and threw hot coffee in his face. The question is put aside when their most disagreeable customer is murdered and, shortly after, they discover a gun in a bust of Daniel Webster, which has been requisitioned as a stage prop for a Broadway play. First published in 1949, it's a lighthearted comedy of manners and the first in a four-book series. The author also wrote a series about a small-town Montana Episcopal minister, Martin Buell, another about pathologist Grace Severance, and a number of stand-alone mysteries, all with a light comic touch.

Other books by the same author:
The Diplomat and the Gold Piano, 1965
Glass on the Stairs, 1954
The Green Plaid Pants, 1951

Other books you might like:
Delano Ames, *The Jane & Dagobert Brown Series*, 1948-1959
Frances Crane, *The Pat & Jean Abbot Series*, 1941-1962
Dashiell Hammett, *The Thin Man*, 1934
Frances Lockridge, *The Mr. & Mrs. North Series*, 1940-1963
   Richard Lockridge, co-author
Kelley Roos, *The Jeff & Haila Troy Series*, 1940-1966

183

MARK SCHWEIZER

The Baritone Wore Chiffon

(Hopkinsville, Kentucky: St. James Music Press, 2004)

Story type: Humor
Series: Hayden Konig. Book 2
Subject(s): Episcopalians; Music and Musicians; Clergy
Major character(s): Hayden Konig, Police Officer (police chief), Musician (choir director and organist)
Time period(s): 2000s
Locale(s): St. Germaine, North Carolina; York, England

Summary: Hayden Konig, a very wealthy individual (thanks to a gadget he invented for the phone company), would never have to work again if he didn't want to. Instead, he fills his days with being the full-time (albeit soft-hearted) police chief of his small North Carolina town, as well as part-time choir director and organist at St. Barnabas, the local Episcopal church. He's also acquired Raymond Chandler's typewriter and works diligently at becoming a mystery writer of the hard-boiled variety. When he returns to St. Germaine after a short jaunt to England, he's alarmed to learn that the new priest is planning a Clown Eucharist, that the altar guild has gone feng shui, and that a performance of the Edible Last Supper is being planned. He also has to deal with a murder. Eccentric characters and broad social satire, not to mention

outrageous excerpts from Hayden's work in progress, make this cleverly conceived and executed comedic mystery as hilarious as its predecessor.

Other books by the same author:
The Alto Wore Tweed, 2002

Other books you might like:
Jim Brewster, *The Vicar of Afton*, 2002
Joan Coggin, *Who Killed the Curate?*, 1944
   reprinted 2001
Ruth Dudley Edwards, *Murder in a Cathedral*, 1997
Kate Gallison, *Bury the Bishop*, 1995
Peter Lovesey, *The Reaper*, 2001

184

SHARON SHORT

Death by Deep Dish Pie

(New York: Avon, 2004)

Story type: Amateur Detective; Humor
Series: Josie Toadfern. Book 2
Subject(s): Small Town Life; Food; Holidays
Major character(s): Josie Toadfern, Businesswoman (laundromat owner), Detective—Amateur
Time period(s): 2000s
Locale(s): Paradise, Ohio

Summary: The biggest business in the small Ohio town of Paradise is the Breitenstrater Pie Factory, sponsor of the annual Fourth of July pie-eating contest. Like the rest of the town, Josie—who owns a laundromat and has made a name for herself as a stain removal expert—is looking forward to the event, but it's spoiled for everyone when one of the Breitenstraters dies after eating a pie meant for his brother. The police call it a heart attack, but Josie thinks otherwise, and is determined to get the pie tested.

Where it's reviewed:
Romantic Times, September 2004, page 89

Other books by the same author:
Death of a Domestic Diva, 2003

Other books you might like:
Monica Ferris, *The Betsy Devonshire Series*, 1999-
Joanne Fluke, *The Hannah Swenson Series*, 2000-
Dolores Johnson, *The Mandy Dyer Series*, 1997-
Denise Swanson, *The Scumble River Series*, 2000-
Valerie S. Valmont, *Death, Lies and Apple Pies*, 1997

185

STEVEN SIDOR

Skin River

(New York: St. Martin's Minotaur, 2004)

Story type: Psychological Suspense
Subject(s): Crime and Criminals; Small Town Life
Major character(s): Buddy Bays, Saloon Keeper/Owner, Criminal (former)
Time period(s): 2000s
Locale(s): Gunnar, Wisconsin

Summary: Trying hard to forget his past as a small-time crook in Chicago, where he specialized in armed robbery, fiftyish Buddy Bays is making a go of his tavern in the small town of Gunnar, Wisconsin, where he's made a few friends and learned to enjoy the quiet life. One day, however, he discovers a severed hand while out fishing, and suddenly he's a suspect in the murder of a college student. Fearing that his old life has come back to haunt him, he returns to Chicago to see if he's indeed being set up for a crime he didn't commit. It's a suspenseful, often grisly debut novel with an atmospheric, menacing north woods setting.

Where it's reviewed:
Booklist, August 2004, page 1907
Library Journal, August 2004, page 60

Other books you might like:
C.J. Box, *The Joe Pickett Series*, 2001-
Steve Hamilton, *The Alex McKnight Series*, 1998-
William Kent Krueger, *The Cork O'Connor Series*, 1998-
Chuck Logan, *The Phil Broker Series*, 1996-
Clinton McKinzie, *The Antonio Burns Series*, 2002-

186

JULIE SMITH

Louisiana Lament

(New York: Forge, 2004)

Story type: Private Detective
Series: Talba Wallis. Book 3
Subject(s): American South; African Americans; Poetry
Major character(s): Talba Wallis, Detective—Private, Writer (poet and performance artist); Eddie Valentine, Detective—Private
Time period(s): 2000s
Locale(s): New Orleans, Louisiana

Summary: Talba is a young, hip, African-American computer whiz who works days as a private eye and nights as a performance poet known as the Baroness de Pontalba. Eddie is her much older mentor and boss, as irascible as he is kind-hearted, and the two of them make an unbeatable team. When Talba gets a call from her half-sister Janessa, she and Eddie wind up investigating the murder of a mysterious socialite and patroness of the arts, Allyson Brower. The woman is found shot to death in her own swimming pool with her daughter Cassie, also dead from multiple stab wounds. Janessa, who had been hired to paint murals in Allyson's house, is the chief suspect in the murders. Another major player in the story is Talba's mother Miz Clara, with whom she still lives. Talba began as a minor character in the author's long-running series about New Orleans police detective Skip Langdon.

Where it's reviewed:
Booklist, May 1, 2004, page 1519
Deadly Pleasures, Summer/Fall 2004, page 46

Other books by the same author:
Louisiana Bigshot, 2002
Louisiana Hotshot, 2001

Other books you might like:
Ace Atkins, *Leavin' Trunk Blues*, 2000
Charlotte Carter, *The Nanette Hayes Series*, 1997-

D.J. Donaldson, *The Andy Broussard Series*, 1988-
Sophie Dunbar, *The Claire Claiborne Series*, 1993-
Dick Lochte, *The Neon Smile*, 1995

187

MARTIN CRUZ SMITH

Wolves Eat Dogs

(New York: Simon & Schuster, 2004)

Story type: Police Procedural
Series: Arkady Renko. Book 5
Subject(s): Russians; Nuclear Power Plants; Nuclear Waste Disposal
Major character(s): Arkady Renko, Police Officer
Time period(s): 2000s
Locale(s): Moscow, Russia; Pripyat, Ukraine (site of the nuclear power plant, Chernobyl)

Summary: The embattled Russian policeman Arkady Renko has survived the transition from a communist state to one, equally corrupt, in which power is now in the hands of billionaire entrepreneurs and criminals instead of party officials. He's as cynical and contrary as ever. So, when he's asked to confirm the official verdict of suicide when billionaire Pasha Ivanov is found dead on the pavement below his luxurious high-rise condominium in Moscow, he does just the opposite. Even though the apartment was locked, Renko is puzzled as to why the dead man is clutching a salt shaker and why there is a layer of salt on a closet floor. Then another executive is found dead near Chernobyl, shut down since the 1986 meltdown that rendered the landscape around the nuclear power plant an eerie radioactive wasteland. Arkady arrives there to find the area—called the Zone of Exclusion—still sparsely populated, not only by scientists studying the site but stubborn Ukrainians who refuse to leave their homes. The author has also written a number of exceptional non-series thrillers.

Where it's reviewed:
Booklist, September 1, 2004, page 8
Library Journal, October 15, 2004, page 56
Mystery News, October/November 2004, page 24
New York Times Book Review, November 14, 2004, page 50
Publishers Weekly, September 6, 2004, page 43

Other books by the same author:
Havana Bay, 1999
Red Square, 1992
Polar Star, 1989
Gorky Park, 1981

Other books you might like:
Robert Harris, *Archangel*, 1999
Stuart M. Kaminsky, *The Porfiry Rostnikov Series*, 1981-
Philip Kerr, *Dead Meat*, 1995
John Le Carre, *Our Game*, 1995
Robin White, *Siberian Light*, 1997

188

TROY SOOS

Burning Bridges

(New York: Kensington, 2004)

Story type: Historical/Victorian America; Amateur Detective
Series: Marshall Webb. Book 3
Subject(s): Social Conditions; Drugs; Homeless People
Major character(s): Marshall Webb, Journalist, Detective—Amateur; Rebecca Davies, Activist, Detective—Amateur
Time period(s): 1890s (1894)
Locale(s): New York, New York

Summary: Muckraking journalist Marshall Webb has finally earned a permanent spot on the staff of *Harper's Weekly*, and his sweetheart, Rebecca Davies, is still running her shelter for abused and homeless women, Colden House. Marshall is on the scene when a prominent Brooklyn businessman who opposes consolidating his city with Manhattan is shot after delivering a fiery speech. When Marshall investigates the murder, he learns some shameful secrets about the man's business holdings. Rebecca is puzzled when a young society woman who sought shelter at Colden House after a night of revelry, reeking of opium and alcohol, suddenly disappears. Her search for the missing woman takes Rebecca into the city's many opium dens. The author also wrote a series set in the 1920s with a baseball background.

Where it's reviewed:
Romantic Times, November 2004, page 87

Other books by the same author:
The Gilded Cage, 2002
Island of Tears, 2001

Other books you might like:
Michael Blaine, *The Midnight Band of Mercy*, 2004
Rhys Bowen, *The Molly Murphy Series*, 2001-
Caleb Carr, *The Alienist*, 1994
Maan Meyers, *The House on Mulberry Street*, 1996
Victoria Thompson, *The Sarah Brandt Series*, 1999-

189

DANA STABENOW

A Taint in the Blood

(New York: St. Martin's Minotaur, 2004)

Story type: Private Detective
Series: Kate Shugak. Book 14
Subject(s): Mothers and Daughters; Animals/Dogs
Major character(s): Kate Shugak, Detective—Private, Single Parent; Jim Chopin, Police Officer (state trooper)
Time period(s): 2000s
Locale(s): Anchorage, Alaska

Summary: Charlotte Bannister Muravieff, part of a prominent Anchorage family, hires Kate to prove that her mother, Victoria, was innocent of the crime for which she was convicted and imprisoned over 30 years ago. Now dying of cancer, Victoria was found guilty of setting fire to her own house while her two sons were inside, burning one of them to death. Kate's task is made even more difficult by Victoria's refusal

to talk about the case, although she had initially pleaded not guilty. Still involved in raising her adopted teenage son, Kate conducts a steamy romance with state trooper Jim Chopin. Her family, friends, and faithful dog Mutt are also very much on hand. The author, a native Alaskan, also writes a series about Alaska state trooper Liam Campbell.

Where it's reviewed:
Booklist, September 1, 2004, page 70
Publishers Weekly, August 30, 2004, page 35
Romantic Times, October 2004, page 81

Other books by the same author:
A Grave Denied, 2003
A Fine and Bitter Snow, 2002
The Singing of the Dead, 2001
Midnight Come Again, 2000
Hunter's Moon, 1999

Other books you might like:
Nevada Barr, *The Anna Pigeon Series*, 1993-
Val Davis, *Return of the Spanish Lady*, 2001
Sue Henry, *The Alex Jensen/Jessie Arnold Series*, 1991-
Stan Jones, *White Sky, Black Ice*, 1999-
Marcia Simpson, *The Liza Romero Series*, 2000-

190

RICHARD STARK (Pseudonym of Donald E. Westlake)

Nobody Runs Forever

(New York: Mysterious, 2004)

Story type: Psychological Suspense
Series: Parker. Book 22
Subject(s): Crime and Criminals; Money
Major character(s): Parker, Criminal, Thief
Time period(s): 2000s
Locale(s): Rutherford, Massachusetts

Summary: After a scheme to liberate a shipment of dental gold goes haywire when one of the conspirators is found to be wearing a wire, Parker lets himself be talked into another heist. This one is a bank job in western Massachusetts, where a transfer of assets between two merging banks is to take place, and a bank insider will be helping them. A lot could go wrong, of course. The crew of crooks Parker is working with are either inept or psychotic, and one of them is emotionally involved with the inside contact, a banker's wife. The story is told in the author's usual clean, cool prose, and whether one cares for amoral protagonists or not, it's almost impossible to put the book down. As Richard Stark, the author has also written several books featuring actor and part-time bank robber Grofield, and under his real name, a series featuring the hapless crook Dortmunder, as well as numerous outstanding non-series crime novels.

Where it's reviewed:
Booklist, September 1, 2004, page 7
Library Journal, November 1, 2004, page 63
Publishers Weekly, October 11, 2004, page 59

Other books by the same author:
Breakout, 2002
Firebreak, 2001
Flashfire, 2000

Backflash, 1999
Comeback, 1997

Other books you might like:
Lawrence Block, *The Bernie Rhodenbarr Series*, 1977-
Lawrence Block, *The John Keller Series*, 1998-
Anthony Bourdain, *Gone Bamboo*, 1997
Max Allan Collins, *The Quarry Series*, 1976-1977
Patricia Highsmith, *The Tom Ripley Series*, 1955-1980

191

T.S. STRIBLING

Dr. Poggioli: Criminologist
(Norfolk, Virginia: Crippen & Landru, 2004)

Story type: Collection; Amateur Detective
Series: Dr. Henry Poggioli. Book 3
Subject(s): Short Stories
Major character(s): Henry Poggioli, Psychologist (professor), Detective—Amateur
Time period(s): 1930s
Locale(s): Caribbean

Summary: The author, who won a Pulitzer Prize for his mainstream novels about race relations in the American South, also wrote a number of detective short stories featuring psychologist-detective Dr. Henry Poggioli, set in various locales in the Caribbean. Poggioli often becomes a detective by accident, motivated by his desire to see social and racial justice done, and is always conflicted by the enjoyment he gets from solving a crime versus the horror of the crime itself. After the publication of the first volume of Poggioli stories and before another series written for *Ellery Queen's Mystery Magazine*, the author wrote eight more, which are collected here for the first time. The collection is edited and introduced by Arthur Vidro and includes a complete checklist of Dr. Poggioli stories.

Other books by the same author:
Best Dr. Poggioli Detective Stories, 1975
Clues of the Caribbees, 1929

Other books you might like:
G.K. Chesterton, *The Incredulity of Father Brown*, 1926
    short stories
Carter Dickson, *The Department of Queer Complaints*, 1940
    short stories
C. Daly King, *The Complete Curious Mr. Tarrant*, 2003
Helen McCloy, *The Pleasant Assassin and Other Cases of Dr. Basil Willing*, 2002
Clayton Rawson, *The Great Merlini: The Complete Stories of the Magician Detective*, 1979

192

CRISTINA SUMNERS

Thieves Break In
(New York: Bantam, 2004)

Story type: Amateur Detective
Series: Kathryn Koerney. Book 2
Subject(s): Clergy; Episcopalians; Castles

Major character(s): Kathryn Koerney, Religious (Episcopal priest), Detective—Amateur; Tom Holden, Police Officer (chief)
Time period(s): 2000s
Locale(s): Oxford, England; Harton, New Jersey

Summary: Kathryn is on the faculty of the seminary at Harton (read Princeton) University and works as an associate at St. Margaret's Episcopal Church. As she is about to leave for Oxford for a much-anticipated holiday visiting her cousin Rob Hillman, Kathryn receives word that he has fallen to his death under suspicious circumstances. She asks her good friend Tom Holden, the (married) local police chief, to travel with her and help solve the crime. Tom, who is not-so-secretly in love with Kathryn, is glad to accompany her and together they search the grounds of Datchworth Castle, where Rob worked for a baronet. Among the secrets they turn up is one that could lead right to the murderer. The author is an ordained minister.

Where it's reviewed:
Romantic Times, November 2004, page 85

Other books by the same author:
Crooked Heart, 2002

Other books you might like:
Michelle Blake, *The Lily Connors Series*, 2000-
Kate Gallison, *The Mother Lavinia Grey Series*, 1995-
D.M. Greenwood, *The Theodora Braithwaite Series*, 1991-
Isabelle Holland, *The Claire Aldington Series*, 1983-
Julia Spencer-Fleming, *The Clare Fergusson Series*, 2002-

193

DENISE SWANSON (Pseudonym of Denise Swanson Stybr)

Murder of a Pink Elephant
(New York: Signet, 2004)

Story type: Amateur Detective
Series: Scumble River. Book 6
Subject(s): Small Town Life; Bands; Schools/High Schools
Major character(s): Skye Denison, Psychologist (high school)
Time period(s): 2000s
Locale(s): Scumble River, Illinois

Summary: Back in her home town of Scumble River after life on the outside didn't work out, Skye is busy with her job as a high school psychologist, establishing a relationship with Simon Reid, the town coroner, and dealing with her eccentric family. One of them is her older brother Vince, who plays in a rock band called Pink Elephant. With Valentine's Day coming up, Skye arranges for the band to play at the high school dance. The band members, however, seem to be at odds with each other, and then a fire breaks out during the dance, leaving the lead singer dead and the police chief looking at Vince as his chief suspect. To top it all off, the high school students are acting weird and Skye suspects drugs, and a shady developer is trying to buy up local farmland to build an amusement park.

Other books by the same author:
Murder of a Barbie and Ken, 2003
Murder of a Snake in the Grass, 2003
Murder of a Sleeping Beauty, 2002
Murder of a Sweet Old Lady, 2001

Murder of a Small-Town Honey, 2000

Other books you might like:
Kate Collins, *Mum's the Word*, 2004
Kat Goldring, *The Willi Gallagher Series*, 2001-
Rett MacPherson, *The Torie O'Shea Series*, 1997-
Valerie S. Malmont, *The Tori Miracle Series*, 1994-
Beth Sherman, *The Anne Hardaway Series*, 1998-

194

VIRGINIA SWIFT (Pseudonym of Virginia Scharff)

Bye, Bye Love

(New York: HarperCollins, 2004)

Story type: Amateur Detective
Series: Mustang Sally. Book 3
Subject(s): American West; Country Music; Environment
Major character(s): Sally Alder, Professor (history), Detective—Amateur
Time period(s): 2000s
Locale(s): Laramie, Wyoming

Summary: Sally Alder, a former hippie who still plays guitar and sings with a local band, is a respectable history professor at the local university. She is thrilled when she's approached by one of her music idols, country singer Thomas ''Stone'' Jackson about the company his ex-wife, legendary folk singer Nina Cruz, is keeping on a nearby ranch. Nina has taken up with a group of vegan eco-terrorist animal rights activists. Sally arrives at the ranch to check things out during a winter storm and finds Nina has been shot in a suspicious hunting accident. When a second shooting fells a member of Sally's band, she starts sleuthing in earnest.

Where it's reviewed:
Booklist, September 1, 2004, page 70
Library Journal, October 1, 2004, page 62
Publishers Weekly, September 27, 2004, page 40

Other books by the same author:
Bad Company, 2002
Brown-Eyed Girl, 2000

Other books you might like:
Sarah Andrews, *Tensleep*, 1994
C.J. Box, *Savage Run*, 2002
Karen Kijewski, *Honky Tonk Kat*, 1996
Clinton McKinzie, *The Edge of Justice*, 2002
Cecelia Tishy, *The Kate Banning Series*, 1997-

195

JON TALTON

Dry Heat

(New York: St. Martin's Minotaur, 2004)

Story type: Police Procedural
Series: David Mapstone. Book 3
Subject(s): American West; History; Law Enforcement
Major character(s): David Mapstone, Police Officer (deputy sheriff), Historian (former history professor); Lindsey Adams, Police Officer, Spouse (David's wife)
Time period(s): 2000s

Locale(s): Phoenix, Arizona; San Francisco, California

Summary: Former cop and failed history professor David Mapstone—dubbed the History Cop—has been deputized by the Maricopa County sheriff's department to investigate old crimes, or cold cases, where his knowledge of his hometown's history is a real asset. He's helped by his wife, computer whiz Lindsey Adams, and other cold-case specialists in the department. They're investigating how an FBI badge missing since 1948 has turned up on the body of a homeless, drowned man in a decaying suburb of Phoenix. Their efforts are hampered by FBI stonewalling, departmental rivalries, and even the Russian mafia.

Other books by the same author:
Camelback Falls, 2003
Concrete Desert, 2001

Other books you might like:
Sinclair Browning, *The Trade Ellis Series*, 1999-
Edwin Gage, *Phoenix No More*, 1978
J.A. Jance, *The Joanna Brady Series*, 1993-
Raymond Ring, *Arizona Kiss*, 1991
Betty Webb, *The Lena Jones Series*, 2001-

196

WILLIAM G. TAPPLY

Bitch Creek

(New York: Lyons, 2004)

Story type: Amateur Detective
Series: Stoney Calhoun. Book 1
Subject(s): Fishing; Memory Loss; Outdoor Life
Major character(s): Stoney Calhoun, Fisherman, Amnesiac
Time period(s): 2000s
Locale(s): Bitch Creek, Maine

Summary: Stoney Calhoun lost his memory after being struck by lightning and has a steady income somehow as a result of the accident. After leaving the hospital he headed to rural Maine, where he has settled into a nice little house by the creek of the title and taken a job working as a fishing guide for Kate Balaban, the owner of a bait and tackle shop. He has no idea who he was or what he did in his former life, except that the government wants him never to remember it. When a tourist from Florida and Stoney's best friend both disappear on a fishing expedition, Stoney helps the police look for them, and discovers in the process that he was some kind of trained investigator. The author, who also writes a series about maverick Boston lawyer/detective Brady Coyne, as well as numerous books on fishing, weaves a great deal of fly fishing lore and wilderness expertise into the narrative. First in an intriguing new series.

Where it's reviewed:
Booklist, September 15, 2004, page 214
Library Journal, September 1, 2004, page 121
Publishers Weekly, August 16, 2004, page 46

Other books by the same author:
Shadow of Death, 2003
A Fine Line, 2002
Past Tense, 2001
Scar Tissue, 2000

Muscle Memory, 1999

Other books you might like:
Gerry Boyle, *The Jack McMorrow Series*, 1993-
Brendan DuBois, *The Lewis Cole Series*, 1994-
William Landay, *Mission Flats*, 2003
Archer Mayor, *The Joe Gunther Series*, 1988-
Jenny Siler, *Flashback*, 2004

197

SARAH STEWART TAYLOR

Mansions of the Dead

(New York: St. Martin's Minotaur, 2004)

Story type: Amateur Detective
Series: Sweeney St. George. Book 2
Subject(s): Art; History; Academia
Major character(s): Sweeney St. George, Art Historian (professor), Detective—Amateur
Time period(s): 2000s
Locale(s): Boston, Massachusetts

Summary: Sweeney St. George is an art history professor who specializes in graveyard art, especially from 19th-century New England. She's a woman with a sad and complicated past. At nearly 30, Sweeney is a forceful character and full-blown eccentric who is also preeminent in her field. When one of her students is found dead in his dorm room, ritualistically adorned with 19th-century mourning jewelry, the police call Sweeney in for a consultation. It's a delicate case, as Brad Putnam comes from a wealthy and prominent New England family. As the family's secrets are revealed, so too are more of Sweeney's. It's an absorbing follow-up to the author's striking first novel *O' Artful Death*.

Where it's reviewed:
Booklist, May 1, 2004, page 1524
Library Journal, July 2004, page 64
Romantic Times, September 2004, page 91

Other books by the same author:
O' Artful Death, 2003

Other books you might like:
Dana Cameron, *The Emma Fielding Series*, 2002-
Nicholas Kilmer, *The Fred Taylor Series*, 1995-
Jane Langton, *Murder at the Gardner*, 1988
John Malcolm, *The Gwen John Sculpture*, 1986
Iain Pears, *The Jonathan Argyll Series*, 1991-

198

BETSY THORNTON

Dead for the Winter

(New York: St. Martin's Minotaur, 2004)

Story type: Amateur Detective
Series: Chloe Newcombe. Book 4
Subject(s): Small Town Life; American West; Deserts
Major character(s): Chloe Newcombe, Activist (victim advocate), Detective—Amateur
Time period(s): 2000s
Locale(s): Old Dudley, Arizona

Summary: Old Dudley is a very thinly disguised version of the author's home town of Old Bisbee, a former mining town in southern Arizona's Cochise County. In recent years, it's become a haven for artists, former hippies, and other free spirits, who have fondly dubbed the hilly, picturesque hamlet "The Town Too Dumb to Die." Chloe Newcombe (like the author) works as a victim advocate there, and is ironically assigned to represent the widow of a murder victim whom she had briefly dated before learning that he was married. She is determined to find out who murdered him but her search is hampered by the local sheriff who, because of Chloe's history with the dead man, suspects her. The eccentric little town and the surrounding desert are players in the story as much as the characters, all of whom are skillfully drawn.

Where it's reviewed:
Booklist, October 1, 2004, page 315
Library Journal, November 1, 2004, page 62

Other books by the same author:
Ghost Towns, 2002
High Lonesome Road, 2001
The Cowboy Rides Away, 1996

Other books you might like:
Sinclair Browning, *The Trade Ellis Series*, 1999-
David Cole, *The Laura Winslow Series*, 2000-
J.A. Jance, *The Joanna Brady Series*, 1993-
Judith Van Gieson, *The Claire Reynier Series*, 2000-
Betty Webb, *The Lena Jones Series*, 2001-

199

AIMEE THURLO
DAVID THURLO, Co-Author

Thief in Retreat

(New York: St. Martin's Minotaur, 2004)

Story type: Amateur Detective
Series: Sister Agatha. Book 1
Subject(s): Convents; Monasticism; Legends
Major character(s): Sister Agatha, Religious (nun); Tom Green, Police Officer (sheriff)
Time period(s): 2000s
Locale(s): Bernalillo, New Mexico

Summary: As an extern nun in the convent of the Sisters of the Blessed Adoration in New Mexico, Sister Agatha, unlike her cloistered sisters, is allowed to leave the grounds from time to time to run errands on her candy-red Harley. Because of her experience as a former journalist, she's called upon by the archbishop to investigate some mysterious thefts of southwestern folk art pieces from the Retreat, a former monastery now being run as a conference hotel by the archdiocese. There are also legends of a ghost walking the halls of the Retreat. Sister Agatha teams up with Sheriff Tom Green, a friend from her former life, and the curator to investigate a growing number of suspects. The authors also write a series featuring Navajo tribal investigator Ella Clah and another about Lee Nez, another tribal police officer who is also a vampire.

Where it's reviewed:
Publishers Weekly, November 22, 2004, page 41

Other books by the same author:
Bad Faith, 2002

Other books you might like:
Veronica Black, *The Sister Joan Series*, 1990-
Carolina Garcia-Aguilera, *A Miracle in Paradise*, 1999
Sister Carol Anne O'Marie, *The Sister Mary Helen Series*, 1984-
Monica Quill, *The Sister Mary Teresa Dempsey Series*, 1984-
Winona Sullivan, *The Sister Cecile Buddenbrooks Series*, 1993-

200

DAVID THURLO
AIMEE THURLO, Co-Author

Blood Retribution

(New York: Forge, 2004)

Story type: Police Procedural
Series: Lee Nez. Book 2
Subject(s): Werewolves; Native Americans; Vampires
Major character(s): Lee Nez, Police Officer (tribal), Vampire (Navajo nightwalker); Diane Lopez, FBI Agent
Time period(s): 2000s (2002)
Locale(s): Navajo Reservation, New Mexico

Summary: Lee Nez was transformed into a vampire, or Navajo nightwalker, over 50 years ago. He is now an officer with the New Mexico state police and is working with FBI agent Diane Lopez in a case involving turquoise smuggling across the Mexican border. So far two police officers have been killed by the smugglers, whom Lee and Diane discover to be werewolves, or Navajo skinwalkers, able to shapeshift and impossible to imprison. Their only option is to eliminate the entire pack, but Lee's resolve wavers when one of the skinwalkers turns out to look very much like his dead wife. She has information that could help them, but Lee can't be sure where her loyalties lie. They could also benefit from the help of one of two vampires bent on killing Lee, who claims to want to start a new, crime-free life—but can he be trusted? The supernatural elements don't overwhelm the mystery, and the usual careful attention is paid to Navajo culture and customs and the breathtaking New Mexico landscape. The authors also write two other series, one about tribal police detective Ella Clah, and the other about a Roman Catholic nun, Sister Agatha, both also set in New Mexico.

Where it's reviewed:
Booklist, September 1, 2004, page 70
Publishers Weekly, September 13, 2004, page 62

Other books by the same author:
Second Sunrise, 2002

Other books you might like:
Margaret Coel, *The Ghost Walker*, 1996
Jean Hager, *Night Walker*, 1990
Tony Hillerman, *Skinwalkers*, 1987
Barbara Moore, *The Wolf Whispered Death*, 1986
Martin Cruz Smith, *Nightwing*, 1977

201

LEONARD TOURNEY

Time's Fool

(New York: Forge, 2004)

Story type: Historical/Elizabethan
Subject(s): Theater; Relationships; Blackmail
Major character(s): William Shakespeare, Historical Figure, Writer
Time period(s): 17th century (1603)
Locale(s): London, England

Summary: Shakespeare himself is the narrator of this historical mystery, the first from the author in ten years, and one can hope that it's the start of a new series from him. Will's former lover, the famous Dark Lady of his sonnets who is now riddled with the pox and totally without funds, is trying to blackmail him over their relationship. Before her scheme goes anywhere, she dies trying to escape a suspicious fire. That's only the start of Will's troubles: he's beset by robbers and framed in the death of a young boy he's accused of having improper relations with. His newfound prosperity threatens to evaporate unless he can find out exactly who is trying to destroy him. The author also wrote an earlier eight-part Elizabethan series featuring village constable Matthew Stock and his loyal wife Joan.

Where it's reviewed:
Publishers Weekly, May 3, 2004, page 174

Other books by the same author:
Frobisher's Savage, 1994
Witness of Bones, 1992
Knaves Templar, 1991
Old Saxon Blood, 1988
The Bartholomew Fair Murders, 1986

Other books you might like:
Judith Cook, *The Slicing Edge of Death*, 1993
Philip Gooden, *Mask of Night*, 2004
Simon Hawke, *The Smythe/Shakespeare Series*, 2000-
Tony Hays, *Murder on the Twelfth Night*, 1993
Faye Kellerman, *The Quality of Mercy*, 1989

202

PETER TREMAYNE (Pseudonym of Peter Berresford Ellis)

Whispers of the Dead

(New York: St. Martin's Minotaur, 2004)

Story type: Collection; Historical/Medieval
Series: Sister Fidelma. Book 13
Subject(s): Short Stories; Dark Ages; Christianity
Major character(s): Sister Fidelma, Religious (former nun), Scholar
Time period(s): 7th century (ca. 666)

Summary: Fidelma, formerly a nun but now primarily a *dalaigh*, or advocate of the ancient law courts of Ireland, is featured in these 15 short stories, three of which were written just for this collection. Most are set in Ireland, although ''The Lost Eagle''—the only one in which her usual companion, Brother Eadulf, also appears—takes place in Canterbury.

Another secondary character, Fidelma's mentor, Abbot Laisran of Durrow, appears in several of the tales, and several more focus on particular aspects of Brehon law. There is a useful introduction explaining the role of women in Ireland (a remarkably enlightened country at that time), the absence of celibacy among its clergy, and other background.

Where it's reviewed:
Library Journal, August 2004, page 60
Publishers Weekly, June 28, 2004, page 35

Other books by the same author:
The Haunted Abbot, 2004
Smoke in the Wind, 2003
Our Lady of Darkness, 2002
Act of Mercy, 2001
The Monk Who Vanished, 2001

Other books you might like:
Alys Clare, *The Abbess Helewise Series*, 1999-
Anthony Clarke, *Ordeal at Lichfield*, 1998
Margaret Frazer, *The Dame Frevisse Series*, 1992-
Martin H. Greenberg, *Murder Most Medieval*, 2004 editor
Sharan Newman, *Death Comes as Epiphany*, 1993

203

ELAINE VIETS

Dying to Call You
(New York: Signet, 2004)

Story type: Amateur Detective; Humor
Series: Helen Hawthorne. Book 3
Subject(s): Computers; Work; Missing Persons
Major character(s): Helen Hawthorne, Fugitive, Detective—Amateur
Time period(s): 2000s
Locale(s): Fort Lauderdale, Florida

Summary: On the lam since she assaulted her no-good ex-husband with a crowbar, Helen has taken a series of low-paying jobs, for which she's paid in cash, settled into a retro Fort Lauderdale apartment, and generally managed to fly under the law enforcement radar. She doesn't miss much about her old life in St. Louis except the six-figure salary she once pulled down. Now she's working as a telemarketer with the Tank Titan Septic System Cleaner company. One day while she's on the phone to the home of Henry Asporth, she overhears a violent argument, then a scream, then nothing. She uses the office computer to find out more about Asporth, learning he'd moved in with a much younger woman who then disappeared. The author also writes a series about St. Louis reporter Francesca Vierling.

Where it's reviewed:
Romantic Times, October 2004, page 82

Other books by the same author:
Murder between the Covers, 2003
Shop Till You Drop, 2003

Other books you might like:
Carole Berry, *The Bonnie Indermill Series*, 1987-
Janet Evanovich, *The Stephanie Plum Series*, 1994-

Sarah Graves, *The Jacobia Tiptree Series*, 1998-
Sparkle Hayter, *The Robin Hudson Series*, 1994-
Lora Roberts, *The Liz Sullivan Series*, 1994-

204

LONO WAIWAIOLE

Wiley's Shuffle
(New York: St. Martin's Minotaur, 2004)

Story type: Psychological Suspense
Series: Wiley. Book 2
Subject(s): Crime and Criminals; Revenge; Prostitution
Major character(s): Wiley, Gambler, Criminal
Time period(s): 2000s
Locale(s): Las Vegas, Nevada; Los Angeles, California; Portland, Oregon

Summary: Wiley, who's part Hawaiian, lives on the fringes of society. His best friends are hookers and porn dealers, and he makes his living, such as it is, playing a little poker and robbing an occasional drug dealer. He's still mourning the murder of his daughter (see *Wiley's Lament*) and getting by as best he can when a sadistic pimp named Dookie kidnaps a call girl, Miriam, whom he considers a friend. He and his best buddy Leon go after the pair, on a chase that leads them from Las Vegas to Los Angeles and back to Portland, where they all live. Whatever his shortcomings, there's a strong streak of loyalty in Wiley's makeup and even if all the characters are criminals, some are definitely worse than others. The story is noir, violent, and driven by action, as well as character.

Where it's reviewed:
Booklist, June 1, 2004, page 1709
Drood Review of Mystery, May/June 2004, page 13
Publishers Weekly, May 31, 2004, page 55

Other books by the same author:
Wiley's Lament, 2003

Other books you might like:
Ken Bruen, *The Jack Taylor Series*, 2003-
Tim Dorsey, *The Serge O. Storms Series*, 1999-
Brian Hodge, *Wild Horses*, 1999
Jenny Siler, *Easy Money*, 1999
Richard Stark, *The Parker Series*, 1962-

205

BETTY WEBB

Desert Shadows
(Scottsdale, Arizona: Poisoned Pen Press, 2004)

Story type: Private Detective
Series: Lena Jones. Book 3
Subject(s): Racism; Publishing; American West
Major character(s): Lena Jones, Detective—Private
Time period(s): 2000s
Locale(s): Scottsdale, Arizona

Summary: Lena Jones is a private detective and former police officer with a troubled past. As a child she was abandoned and nearly killed by her own mother, rescued by strangers, and raised in foster homes. Now she works on her own, with a

Pima Indian partner, Jimmy Sisiwan. Always searching for answers to the mystery of her own past, she takes other cases as well. This time she goes to bat for Jimmy's cousin Owen, who is suspected of murdering a racist local publisher, Gloriana Alden-Taylor, who's poisoned at a regional publishing expo. The case introduces her not only to the victim's family but to right-wing, racist hate groups, as well as to a serial killer on Arizona's death row.

Where it's reviewed:
Booklist, July 2004, page 1826
Publishers Weekly, June 21, 2004, page 47

Other books by the same author:
Desert Wives, 2003
Desert Noir, 2002

Other books you might like:
Sinclair Browning, *The Trade Ellis Series*, 1999-
David Cole, *The Laura Winslow Series*, 2000-
J.A. Jance, *The Joanna Brady Series*, 1993-
John Shannon, *Terminal Island*, 2004
Judith Van Gieson, *The Neil Hamel Series*, 1988-

206

HEATHER WEBBER

A Hoe Lot of Trouble
(New York: Avon, 2004)

Story type: Amateur Detective
Series: Nina Quinn. Book 1
Subject(s): Gardens and Gardening; Small Town Life; Divorce
Major character(s): Nina Quinn, Landscaper, Detective—Amateur
Time period(s): 2000s
Locale(s): Freedom, Ohio

Summary: Having just kicked out her cheating husband, Nina throws herself into her thriving landscaping business, Taken by Surprise (they do surprise garden makeovers for unsuspecting clients). She's crushed when the man who had been her mentor, Farmer Joe, dies under mysterious circumstances. Her other problems include: valuable landscaping equipment that keeps disappearing and her stepson (who stayed behind after the divorce) has joined a gang. Since the police won't investigate Farmer Joe's death, it's up to her to prove that it was a murder. First mystery.

Where it's reviewed:
Deadly Pleasures, Summer/Fall 2004, page 47
Romantic Times, September 2004, page 92

Other books you might like:
Diane Mott Davidson, *The Goldy Bear Schulz Series*, 1990-
Mary Freeman, *The Rachel O'Connor Series*, 1999-
Janis Harrison, *The Bretta Solomon Series*, 1999-
Julie Wray Hermann, *The Korine McFaile Series*, 2000-
Ann Ripley, *The Louise Eldridge Series*, 1994-

207

VALERIE WILSON WESLEY

Dying in the Dark
(New York: Ballantine, 2004)

Story type: Private Detective
Series: Tamara Hayle. Book 7
Subject(s): African Americans; Adolescence; Homosexuality/Lesbianism
Major character(s): Tamara Hayle, Detective—Private, Single Parent
Time period(s): 2000s
Locale(s): Newark, New Jersey

Summary: Black private eye Tamara Hayle, back after a four-year absence, is asked by Cecil Jones, the teenage son of an old friend, Celia Jones, to investigate his mother's murder. Tamara, who hadn't seen Celia in years, reluctantly agrees, but when Cecil is murdered, she throws herself into the case. Celia had a complicated life, including a domineering ex-husband and ex-lovers of both sexes, all of whom had a grudge against her. The trail may lead even further back into Celia's past, to the days when she and Tamara were still friends. Tamara has a teenage son herself and is concerned about his future, as well as her own when he leaves for college.

Where it's reviewed:
Booklist, September 1, 2004, page 70
Essence, August 2004, page 122
Romantic Times, October 2004, page 84

Other books by the same author:
The Devil Riding, 2000
Easier to Kill, 1998
No Hiding Place, 1997
Where Evil Sleeps, 1996
Devil's Gonna Get Him, 1995

Other books you might like:
Eleanor Taylor Bland, *The Marti McAlister Series*, 1992-
Grace F. Edwards, *The Mali Anderson Series*, 1997-
Barbara Neely, *The Blanche White Series*, 1992-
Pamela Thomas-Graham, *The Nikki Chase Series*, 1998-
Paula L. Woods, *The Charlotte Justice Series*, 1999-

208

MARIANNE WESSON

Chilling Effect
(Boulder: University Press of Colorado, 2004)

Story type: Legal; Psychological Suspense
Series: Lucinda Hayes. Book 3
Subject(s): Law; Trials; Freedom of Speech
Major character(s): Lucinda ''Cinda'' Hayes, Lawyer
Time period(s): 2000s
Locale(s): Boulder, Colorado

Summary: First Amendment issues are the framework in this latest case for liberal Boulder lawyer Cinda Hayes, who must delve into the unsavory world of child pornography and snuff films. She reluctantly agrees to represent a woman who is suing the producer of a film that she claims incited a man to murder her young daughter. The killer, who committed the act after continuously watching a snuff film in which a child was involved, has been found criminally insane and the mother feels the lawsuit is the only redress she has. It's a complex case that requires all of Cinda's legal expertise and raises timely concerns about the laws governing free speech.

Where it's reviewed:
Library Journal, September 1, 2004, page 122
Publishers Weekly, August 9, 2004, page 235

Other books by the same author:
Suggestion of Death, 2000
Render Up the Body, 1998

Other books you might like:
Linda Fairstein, *The Alexandra Cooper Series*, 1996-
Jonnie Jacobs, *The Kali O'Brien Series*, 1996-
Stephanie Kane, *The Jackie Flowers Series*, 2000-
Baine Kerr, *Harmful Intent*, 1999
Perri O'Shaughnessy, *The Nina Reilly Series*, 1995-

209

RANDY WAYNE WHITE

Tampa Burn

(New York: Putnam, 2004)

Story type: Action/Adventure
Series: Doc Ford. Book 11
Subject(s): Fathers and Sons; Kidnapping; Nature
Major character(s): Marion ''Doc'' Ford, Scientist (marine biologist), Single Parent; Sighurdhr Tomlinson, Genius, Hippie; Lake Fuentes, Teenager
Time period(s): 2000s
Locale(s): Sanibel Island, Florida; Everglades National Park, Florida; Tampa, Florida

Summary: Way back in Doc's murky past as a CIA agent in Central America, he had an affair with a woman named Pilar Fuentes, who bore him a son named Lake, now a teenager and only recently known to Doc. Although they've met, they stay in touch mostly via e-mail. Now Lake has been kidnapped and is being held hostage by a very nasty hit man employed by his mother's former husband. Pilar turns to Doc to save the boy, which presents a problem for his current girlfriend, Dewey, who suspects he is still carrying a torch for Pilar. He enlists the aid of his hippie genius friend Tomlinson to rescue Lake, who is still being allowed to e-mail him and is dropping subtle hints as to his location. After a somewhat slow start they're off on an exciting chase through the Everglades and the inland waterways near Tampa, with new, intriguing revelations about both Doc and Tomlinson's past histories thrown in.

Where it's reviewed:
Booklist, May 15, 2004, page 1580
Publishers Weekly, April 25, 2004, page 41

Other books by the same author:
Everglades, 2003
Twelve Mile Limit, 2002
Shark River, 2001
Ten Thousand Islands, 2000
The Mangrove Coast, 1998

Other books you might like:
James W. Hall, *The Thorn Series*, 1987-
Carl Hiaasen, *Skinny Dip*, 2004
John D. MacDonald, *The Travis McGee Series*, 1964-1985
Laurence Shames, *The Key West Series*, 1992-
Les Standiford, *The John Deal Series*, 1993-

210

JOHN MORGAN WILSON

Moth and Flame

(New York: St. Martin's Minotaur, 2004)

Story type: Amateur Detective
Series: Benjamin Justice. Book 6
Subject(s): Homosexuality/Lesbianism; Journalism; City and Town Life
Major character(s): Benjamin Justice, Journalist (disgraced), Homosexual
Time period(s): 2000s
Locale(s): West Hollywood, California

Summary: Benjamin Justice was a Pulitzer Prize-winning journalist who had to return his award when it was discovered that he had fabricated sources. Now, several years and too many bottles later, he is HIV positive, has gone through the difficult breakup of a relationship, and is trying to come to terms with his past. To that end, he is writing his memoirs, but his funds are running low so he accepts a freelance job vacated when another writer is murdered while in the midst of writing a booklet. Although Benjamin tries to stay away from investigating his predecessor's murder, it soon becomes clear that it's connected with a controversy he turns up while doing research for the booklet on buildings of historical significance in North Hollywood. The Edgar-winning author also co-writes, with bandleader Peter Duchin, a series set in 1960s California.

Other books by the same author:
Blind Eye, 2003
The Limits of Justice, 2000
Justice at Risk, 1999
Revision of Justice, 1997
Simple Justice, 1996

Other books you might like:
Michael Craft, *The Mark Manning Series*, 1997-
Joseph Hansen, *The Dave Brandstetter Series*, 1970-1991
Michael Nava, *The Henry Rios Series*, 1986-2001
R.D. Zimmerman, *The Todd Mills Series*, 1995-
Mark Richard Zubro, *The Tom & Scott Series*, 1988-

Romance Fiction in Review
by
Kristin Ramsdell

"Romance has been elegantly defined as the off-spring of fiction and love."
—Benjamin Disraeli

"Romance Fiction: Have We Got a Story for You!"
—Strategic Committee on Image, Romance Writers of America

And what stories there were this year—not only between the covers of the books, but also within the industry itself! Romance Writers of America's (RWA) new slogan for the romance genre hit the nail on the head, and while the romance news of 2004 wasn't all good, by any means, it is definitely worthy of a "story."

Romance Statistics

Statistically speaking, the story for 2003 was mixed. The numbers have been crunched, the results tallied, and according to RWA's annual ROMStat report [Hall, Olivia. "2003 ROMStat Report." *Romance Writers' Report* 24 (October 2004): 28-31.], the genre gained in a few areas, but lost in many others. While the overall popular fiction market gained slightly (1.6%)in total unit sales, romance dropped from 225,799,000 units sold in 2002 to 223,940,000 in 2003 for a loss of 0.8%. The number of romance titles released in 2003 was down as well, sliding from 2,169 in 2002 to 2,093 for a loss of 3.5%. Unfortunately, the total dollar sales for the genre also declined to $1.41 billion, down from $1.63 billion in 2002; and while that may look like quite a drop, it still is a huge share of the industry's revenue pie.

Despite losing some market share in 2003, romance still beat out the other popular fiction categories, accounting for 33.8% (down from 34.6% in 2002) of the total number of units sold. 2003 was an especially good year for the Mystery/Suspense/Thriller group, which gained 2.5% (after posting a loss of 13% the year before), to claim a market share of 25.6%. The other winner in the mix was the General

Fiction category, which rose by 0.8% to garner a respectable 24.9% of total market sales. (This, however, was not so substantial a gain as last year's rise from 17% to 24.1%.) Science Fiction/Fantasy dipped by 0.5% and accounted for 6% of the market; while the group that includes the rest of the genres (Religious, Occult, Historical, Western, Male Adventure, Adult, Movie Tie-ins) continued its slide from the year before, dropping by 2.2% to claim only 9.7% of 2003 total market sales. As always, it must be mentioned that the way a book is labeled and marketed by its publisher determines the category into which it falls. Often this is accurate; however, it is not uncommon for books to be mislabeled for a variety of reasons, as readers who have ever picked up a General Fiction title only to discover it was really Suspense or Romance, know well.

Although print is still the primary publication format for Romance, as well as the other popular fiction genres, audio, and to a lesser extent downloadable e-books, are a growing presence in the industry. Currently, these statistics are not broken out separately, and are, therefore, not included in the Romance stats; but the fact that Ipsos BookTrends (a major statistical gathering source for the industry) is beginning to include them indicates their increasing popularity. (Ask any public librarian about the circulation statistics for their books-on-tape collection.) Although the mass market paperback remains the primary publishing format for the romance genre, it is beginning to lose share to trade paperbacks. Mass market paperbacks fell from 53.5% of the market to 48% in 2003, and trade sales jumped from 13.5% to 24.9% to continue its upward streak of the previous year. Hardcover sales edged up slightly from 5.7% to 7.1%.

A few major houses continue to dominate romance publishing, and as usual, Torstar [Harlequin, Mills & Boon, MIRA, Red Dress, Silhouette, Steeple Hill, LUNA (fantasy)] tops the charts with 54.5% of the total title releases, an increase of 3.5% from the year before. Kensington (Brava, Citadel, Dafina, Encanto, Kensington, Pinnacle, Zebra), however, dropped from 219 titles in 2002 to 164 in 2003, to claim a still respectable 7.7% of the market. Pearson (Berkley, NAL, Dutton, Jove, Onyx, Putnam, Signet, Topaz, Viking) is close behind with 154 titles, accounting for almost 7.4% of total releases, followed by the energetic Dorchester (104 titles/almost 5% market share) and dependable Harper/Avon (94 titles/4.5% market share). Avalon, Bertlesmann (Ballantine, Bantam, Broadway, Crown, Dell, Delacorte, Doubleday, Fawcett, Knopf, Ivy Random House, WaterBrook), BET/Arabesque, Ellora's Cave, Five Star, Genesis, Pocket/Sonnet/Atria, St. Martin's, and Warner together released almost 17.5% of the titles in 2003, and Baker Books, Barbour, Tyndale House and several others that published fewer than 20 books that year, made up the rest. Although romance publishing remains the domain of the large publishers, smaller presses continue to add to the diversity and quality of the genre; and while some do fall by the wayside (e.g., Imajinn recently declared bankruptcy), others continue to add their unique contributions to the mix.

Subgenre Statistical Details

Once again, Contemporary Romance rules, accounting for 1,371 of the total titles published in 2003 and ramping up its share of the market from 61.7% last year to almost 65.5%. Of this group, almost 55% were series romances and 45% were single title releases, roughly the same proportions as the year before. Hardcover releases rose 35%, from 31 in 2002 to 42 in 2003, but reprints of older titles declined slightly from 135 the year before to 112, for a welcome drop of 16%.

Historicals continue to be the perennial bridesmaid to the Contemporary subgenre's bride, but as Contemporaries rise slightly in popularity, Historicals slide even further in the rankings. Dropping from 580 titles released in 2002 to 479 in 2003, Historicals made up 22.9% of the total, down by 3.8% from 26.7%. Only 10 Historicals were published in hard cover, a drop of almost 63%; but reprints, while still numerous, dropped by 7% from 55 to 51 for the year.

Although Regencies are included in the figures for Historicals, because they are obviously historically set, these tales of manners and custom set during the British Regency (1811-1820) have long been considered their own subgenre, and it makes sense to discuss them as such. The number of Regency titles released actually rose 4.5% in 2003 (from 93 in 2002 to 96 in 2003), and accounted for 20% of the Historical and 4.6% of the total romance market. Both of these percentages are increases from the year before and will be welcome news to the fans of this niche, but beloved, subgenre. 10% of the Regencies published in 2003 were reprints.

The various Alternative Realities Romance subgroups (Paranormals, Time Travels, Fantasy, and Futuristics) continue to rise. This year, the jump was a meteoric 36% increase in the number of titles released (88 in 2002 to 120 in 2003), resulting in the subgenre's claiming an impressive 5.7% of the overall romance market.

As usual, the ROMStat report does not tally separate statistics for the Romantic Suspense and Gothic Romance subgenres. Generally, Romantic Suspense titles often will be included within the Contemporary groups (although the number of historical mysteries seems to be growing), and Gothics of the paranormal variety will be counted within that group. Hall does mention, however, that the Romantic Suspense category seems to be disappearing, at least insofar as the publishers are concerned, because many stories of this type are now being marketed under other headings, e.g., Suspense, Mystery, Romance. As a result, it is difficult to get an accurate count of these particular subgenres, even though they are still going strong.

Like Romantic Suspense, Multicultural Romance is not tallied separately. Nevertheless, the subgenre is definitely growing. BET increased its number of Arabesque titles by 4.8% (from 62 in 2002 to 65 in 2003) and Genesis released 18 titles in 2003 to lay claim together to almost 4% of the total romance market in 2003. With Dafina's new mass market Romance line (launched August 2004), the growing number of multicultural writers who are making the leap from ethnically specific houses (such as BET and Genesis) to the general romance publishers, and the increasing regularity with which ethnically diverse characters routinely appear in romances of all types, it is a given that this subgenre is on a roll and is actually much larger than the figures above would indicate.

On the other hand, popular though it has been, Inspirational Romance took a bit of a tumble in 2003, falling almost 24% from 153 titles released in 2002 to 117 in 2003, to account for 5.6% of the market—down from 7% in 2002. On the positive side, only one of these titles was a reprint. As usual, Torstar's Steeple Hill lines account for a large number of these, with the rest being produced by various religious publishers (Barbour, Baker, Tyndale, Harvest House, Multnomah) and an occasional release from WaterBrook.

The number of anthologies skyrocketed from 61 titles in 2002 to a stunning 104 in 2003 for an increase of 70%. Forty-five were Contemporary (three were in the series lines, forty-two were single titles), twenty-one were Historicals, and eleven were Inspirationals. Although no anthologies were listed specifically as paranormal or multicultural, a number of these were published; I assume they were counted along with either the Contemporary or Historical subgenres.

That about sums it up for the 2003 statistics. (For more details, please see Libby Hall's article mentioned above.) But what about the figures for the most recent year? Although we are well into 2005 and it might seem logical to assume that the stats for 2004 should be ready, it takes time for the industry to produce the figures and it takes time to pull out the data for the genre. I expect to see them in Fall 2005. However, in the meantime we do have the books; and while they won't provide the same information as the numbers, they can tell us a lot about what was really going on in the genre during 2004.

The Romance Genre in Detail

As in past years, the romance genre continued to progress in its accustomed way, building upon past successes, discarding things that no longer achieved the desired results, and tapping into the current culture to see what new and different trends might work for the genre. To some extent, each subgenre follows its own path, evolving in ways unique to its type; nevertheless, there can be some trends that cut across subgenre lines and apply to the genre as a whole. Some of these are worth noting.

Humor, popular across the board for a number of years, was still ubiquitous, although the fact that Harlequin has decided to cancel its humorous Flipside series, especially since publishers' decisions are almost always driven by the bottom line, might make one wonder. Nevertheless, humor abounded in the books of 2004, and while it varied from subtle to slapstick and inhabited the Contemporary subgenre more than any other, humorous Regencies and hilarious vampire stories were not unknown.

Sex is still hot and is getting hotter, as any current reader of the genre will tell you. And it's not just in the lines that focus on explicit sex (e.g., Brava, Ellora's Cave, Red Sage, Blaze). Stories in most other romance lines are becoming steamier and more graphic; and while there are some that don't seem to be affected, specifically those that are sweet or inspirational in nature, the trend toward the more erotic seems entrenched.

Trilogies and other linked books remained popular in 2004 and are likely to do so in coming years. Harlequin/Silhouette continued their various continuity series (often a series of twelve books linked by theme or place, written by different authors). Numerous other publishers featured series of various lengths but commonly trilogies by a single author, most often linked by characters or place.

Vampires, werewolves, and all things magical abounded in the genre last year. Although most often confined to the Alternative Realities subgenre, things mystical, magical, and unexplained often appeared—and were welcomed—where least expected.

Just as paranormal elements are infiltrating romances across the board, culturally, ethnically, and sexually diverse characters are doing the same. Although the culture-specific lines/publishers (e.g., Arabesque, Dafina, Genesis, Encanto) produce stories that focus on particular groups and cultures, diversity of all kinds is becoming the norm in the genre as a whole. Bi-racial characters and gay/lesbian characters are less uncommon than before, and given the diversity of our population, this trend is likely to continue.

2004 was the year of the "take-charge" heroine. Larger than life, independent, and self-sufficient, these modern-day Wonder Women are carving out a new place for themselves in the romance genre and are changing it as they go. In much the same way that Scarlett O'Hara gave heroines permission to be something other than just good and sweet (like Me-

lanie), these action-packed stories feature heroines who are the unapologetic heroes of their own stories, and when they get the guy in the process, it's on their terms, no one else's.

Finally, genre blending remains alive and well, as the traditional lines between both the subgenres and the larger fiction genres blend and change. More stories seem to be targeting the crossover reader (Romance/Fantasy, Romance/Mystery, Romance/Science Fiction, Romance/Horror, Romance/Women's Fiction), and while this is generally a good thing because it expands readership, it does make it more and more difficult to categorize the various novels—and it makes Romance more difficult to define.

The Subgenres

Contemporary Romance, as always the most popular of the subgenres, continues to dominate the market, dividing its offerings between the series lines and single titles. Although series titles are still more numerous, single titles are gradually gaining ground, and if things continue in the same vein, the balance will switch in the near future. Note: Since series have always been an important part of Harlequin's bottom line, it will be interesting to see how their losses for the first three quarters of 2004 and a predicted loss for the fourth quarter (*Publishers Weekly*, November 1, 2004, page 6), which are partially blamed on a softening in the North American market, affect this dynamic.

Currently, the word is out that there will be major changes in July 2005 to the Harlequin lines—Flipside (sassy humor) will be cancelled, Temptation (sensual) will no longer be available in North America, Historicals will be available to the North American market by direct mail only, Romance (sweet) is being renovated, and, on the positive side, Blaze (sexy) will go from four to six titles a month. Stay tuned.

As expected, the traditional core of home, family, and marriage-centered romances, especially in the series, remained secure. However, with the increasing interest in modern, sassy, urban-set chick lit-type romances with heroines still in search of themselves (Dorchester launched its new Making It line in September which joined Kensington's Strapless, Pocket's Down Town Press, and Harlequin's Red Dress Ink.) and the stunning popularity of action-oriented stories featuring tough, capable, take-charge heroines (e.g., Silhouette's new Bombshell line, Dorchester's 2176 futuristic five book series, Christine Feehan's paranormal GhostWalker books), it is clear that readers are open to something less traditional, and the genre is more than willing to oblige.

Although there is still plenty of good reading within the series, single titles seems to be where the market is heading; and, while the bandwagon syndrome is always a factor, as a group they are amazingly diverse. Settings can vary from small town or rural America (Geralyn Dawson's *My Long, Tall Texas Heartthrob* or Marcia Evanick's *A Berry Merry*

Christmas) to the big city (Roxanne St. Claire's *Killer Curves* or Heather Swain's *Lucious Lemon*); and some even manage to include both to varying degrees (Carly Alexander's *The Eggnog Chronicles* or Janet Dailey's *Calder Promise*). Styles are as varied as the settings, and while it is common to find a heartwarming tale in a small town setting (*Bright Eyes* by Catherine Coulter) or a smart, upbeat story in an urban setting (*The Babe Magnet* by Robin Wells), there are some that vary the format with delightful results (*Sweetheart, Indiana* by Suzanne Simmons or Lori Soard's *The Lipstick Diaries*).

Humor in all its incarnations abounds and everything from subtle to slapstick can show up between the covers of the current crop of Contemporaries. Themes and plot patterns run the gamut, and while reunions (Jeanette Baker's *Chesapeake Tide* and Jerri Corgiat's *Follow Me Home*) and weddings (Janelle Taylor's *Dying to Marry* and Shirley Jump's *The Bride Wore Chocolate*) are still popular, stories that are edgier and a bit bolder when it comes to subject matter are not uncommon (Kathy Love's *Getting What You Want* tackles alcoholism, obesity, and self-esteem issues).

Characters also vary widely, and everything from the traditional ranchers, widows/widowers, and single parents to the more atypical accountants, mythical characters (e.g., tooth fairy), time travelers, and witches can be found. Genre blending continues to make its presence felt, as elements from other subgenres—magic, mythical characters, ghosts, mystery—appear in Contemporaries with increasing regularity (*Blue Dahlia* by Nora Roberts and Emily Carmichael's *The Cat's Meow*).

Finally, the Contemporary subgenre not only continues to launch its writers into other genres or subgenres, but it also is becoming a new home to writers from other categories testing the classic contemporary waters.

Although still second in popularity, Historicals continue to lose ground to Contemporaries and now account for less than 25 percent of all Romances published. Naturally varied, Historicals may be set during any time in the past and in any earthly location. However, in practice, most take place during the eighteenth and nineteenth centuries or the Middle Ages, and are most often set in North America, the British Isles, or, occasionally, France (Deborah John's *Maiden of Fire*). Although the years surrounding the British Regency (1811-1820) are still by far the most popular time period (almost 20% of the Historicals included in this volume fall into this category) and Scotland still has a wild cachet, other times and places are not ignored. The Victorian Period, both in England and America, remain popular, as books such as *He Said Never* by Patricia Wadell and Kate Rothwell's *Somebody Wonderful* demonstrate; and the American West, so popular a number of years ago, has not been forgotten (Jodi Thomas' *A Texan's Luck*). Plots and styles vary, and anything from Anne Stuart's darkly intense medieval, *Hidden Honor* and Lynn Kerstan's sensual, evil-laden *Dangerous Deceptions* to Barbara Metzger's lively Regency romp, *A Pefect Gentleman* can be alive

and well within the genre. As usual, humor, to varying degrees, is present, most often appearing in Historicals set during the Regency (Barbara Metzger's *A Perfect Gentleman*). A number of Historicals, however, do have their darker sides, and Janet Tanner's *Forgotten Destiny* and Lynn Kerstan's book mentioned above are only two of the many examples. As in the recent past, books in series or with linked characters are all the rage, and Jodi Thomas' Wife Lottery series, Lynn Kerstan's Black Phoenix trilogy, Jo Goodman's Compass Club series, Rebecca Hagan Lee's Free Fellows League series, Sasha Lord's Scottish medieval Wild trilogy, Jacqueline Navin's Mayfair Brides series, Patricia Rice's Magic series, Anne Robins' Perfect series, and Patricia Waddell's Gentlemen's Club series are only a few of the many examples. Sensuality, as noted above, is on the rise across the genre, and Historicals, long considered a hotbed of romantic explicitness, are running true to form. Of course, there are still some of the sweeter kind, but, in general, the trend is toward the sexier variety.

Although Regencies did relatively well in 2003, the future is unclear, to say the least. Zebra and Signet continue to produce Regencies of the traditional sort—well- written, witty, and focused on the courtship conundrums of upper-class British society of the early 1800s—but rumors about the permanence of the Signet line persist. In the meantime, however, 2004 produced a delightful crop of stories—elegant, literate, and altogether charming. Sweet, rather than sensual, the traditional Regency is light, often humorous, and committed to accurately depicting the world of the British Regency *ton*. Lively, often wryly humorous, these comedies of manners range from fast- paced romps (Mona Gedney's *On the Twelfth Day of Christmas*)to more serious, measured tales (Jeanne Savery's *The Christmas Matchmaker*) and include, among others, stories focused on the Napoleonic Wars (Kate Huntington's *The General's Daughter*), the social whirl of the London Season (Sharon Stancavage's *An Enchanting Minx*), or the ultimate goal of a Regency romance—a suitable marriage (Laura Paquet's *An Honorable Match*). As has been the case for a number of years, Regency writers are leaving the genre for the larger, less restrictive and more lucrative Historical market; and with the shrinking of the lines and the general uncertainty surrounding the subgenre, one can hardly blame them. Obviously, this diminishes the traditional Regency market; however, it also has the effect of making the Historical subgenre richer. Since these writers generally continue to set their stories during the Regency period and readers will often follow them across subgenres, it may not reflect a loss of readership at all—simply a realignment.

Alternative Realities romances continued their upward trend, following traditional paths, as well as blazing new trails. Several new lines were launched this year, joining Dorchester's longstanding Love Spell imprint. Harlequin's new fantasy line, LUNA, got off to a good start; and Tor's promising new paranormal romance line was successfully launched with Constance O'Day-Flannery's shapechanger romance *Shifting Love*, followed by Patricia Simpson's chilling tale of ancient evil *The Dark Lord*. In addition, books with supernatural elements were forthcoming from most of the major romance houses. Although vampires, werewolves, and witches are still favored as characters, they have been joined by a number of others with varying powers and missions. Of particular interest is *Master of the Night*, Angela Knight's complex, dark tale of alternative universes that includes both vampires and witches dedicated to protecting humankind. As usual, stories can range from the off beat and funny (MaryJanice Davidson's *Undead and Unemployed* and Lynsay Sands' *Tall, Dark, and Hungry*) to the dark and intense (Patricia Simpson's *The Dark Lord*) and the sensuality levels can vary widely. Stories based on fairy tales and legends could also be found, and P.C. Cast's revisionist version of Persephone and Hades, *Goddess of Spring* (third in her Goddess Summoning series), and Claire Delacroix's short story "An Elegy for Melusine" in the anthology *To Weave a Web of Magic* are only two examples. Futuristics (Patti O'Shea's *The Power of Two* and Susan Grant's *The Scarlett Empress*, both part of the 2176 five-book series), time travels (Jude Deveraux's *Always*), and stories with indeterminate times or fictional settings (Linda Winstead Jones' *The Sun Witch* and Emma Holly's *The Demon's Daughter*) were not ignored. In addition, a number of anthologies featuring supernatural or paranormal stories saw print, *Hot Blooded*, *Man of My Dreams*, and *To Weave a Web of Magic* are only three of the many examples.

Ever popular, Romantic Suspense, whether labeled as Mystery, Suspense, Fiction, or something else entirely, continues to attract readers. Although the conventions of this subgenre require both romance and mystery/suspense plotlines, from there on nothing is standard. While often contemporary, fast-paced, and seriously realistic (Karen Rose's *I'm Watching You*, Beverly Barton's *As Good as Dead*, or Hunter Morgan's *She'll Never Live*), the subgenre also has room for stories with a touch of sass and humor (Jane Graves' *Light My Fire*, Jane Blackwood's *A Hard Man Is Good to Find*, or Harley Jane Kozak's *Dating Is Murder*), those with historical or unusual contemporary settings (Jo Goodman's *Beyond a Wicked Kiss* or Nora Roberts' *Northern Lights*), or those with a touch of the paranormal (Lori Handeland's *Blue Moon* or Eileen Wilks' *Tempting Danger*).

Books with Gothic elements continue to do well; and while few currently are labeled "Gothic," a number that meet the criteria, at least to some degree, can be found within the Paranormal and Historical ranks. Janet Tanner's *Forgotten Destiny* is only one example.

Multicultural Romance, whether in separate imprints, or part of a publisher's regular lines, continues to expand. As usual, African-American romance, thanks to BET's Arabesque line, Genesis, and Dafina's new mass market romance line is going strong. Add to that, the fact that a

number of authors are now writing romances for the general market as well, and it seems clear that the popularity of African-American romance is definitely on the rise. Books featuring characters from other cultural backgrounds were not nearly so well represented, although stories featuring Native Americans, Hispanics, and Asians were all part of the year's offerings. Lindsay McKenna's *First Born* (Native American), Alisa Valdes-Rodriguez' *Playing with Boys* (Hispanic), and Maureen Tan's *A Perfect Cover* (Vietnamese/African-American) are only three of the many examples. While it doesn't have the ethnic aspects of most multicultural romances, *Dark Harvest*, Karen Harper's suspenseful tale of an undercover agent within a threatened Amish community certainly qualifies in the multicultural sense and is worth mentioning. Finally, it is noteworthy that a number of romances featured cross-cultural/racial protagonists and casually included ethnically, culturally, and sexually diverse characters in a variety of roles, reflecting America's increasingly diverse population and the growing diversity and sophistication of the romance readership.

Inspirational Romance continued to be popular, and while the 2003 figures were not stellar, the subgenre seemed to meet the needs of its devoted fans and is looking to expand into new areas in the future. (For example: Leisure recently launched an Inspirational line (Julie Marshall's *Haven*); Steeple Hill is attempting to appeal to the young, modern, hip woman with their recently launched Steeple Hill Cafe imprint and plans a new Romantic Suspense line.) As in the past, Steeple Hill, with its Love Inspired series, plus the single title lines, dominates the market. However, a number of smaller, religious presses (Baker, Multnomah, Tyndale, etc.), plus several imprints from larger secular houses, added a substantial number of titles to the list. Although the majority of these sweet, conservative Christian romances are family and child oriented, often with small town settings, it is clear that the subgenre is trying to reach beyond this traditional audience, especially with the new focus on inspirational chick lit. How well this will succeed is anybody's guess, but with chick lit's current popularity, if the authors can hit the right mix of faith and worldliness, it just might have a chance.

Anthologies continued to be popular in 2004, and they seemed to be just as diverse as in past years. Christmas, of course, garnered its fair share. Among the Christmas books were *Shadows of Christmas Past* (heartwarming and slightly paranormal), *One Starry Christmas* (Christmas in the old West), *Jingle All the Way* (Contemporary), and *The Christmas Visit* (English and Welsh/Historical). The magical and the paranormal were represented by *Moon Shadows*, *Man of My Dreams*, and *To Weave a Web of Magic*. Erotic novellas abounded (*Bad Boys with Expensive Toys*, *Bad Boys Down Under*, and *Strangers in the Night*) and there were even sexy anthologies with a paranormal twist (*Men at Work* and *Hot Blooded*). Several anthologies featuring Regency weddings (*With This Ring* and *Wedding Belles*) contrasted startlingly with the chilling, snow-laden, suspenseful *Silent Night*, and LuAnn Lane's sizzling trilogy of baseball-linked stories, *Hot Summer Nights*. Most unusual was *More than Words* a collection of stories written by noted Harlequin authors and based on true accounts of unsung heroines who contributed to society. It also seemed as though more authors than ever were writing books linked by characters, place, or theme. Julia London's Lear Sisters trilogy, Kathy Love's Stepp Sisters trilogy, Annette Mahon's Secret series, Jodi Thomas' Wife Lottery series, Jennifer Greene's Scent of Lavender series, Catherine Anderson's Coulter Family series, Marcia Evanick's Misty Harbor series, and Alison Kent's Smithson Group 5 series are only a few of the growing numbers.

Romance in Review

Romance continues to be regularly reviewed in print in the quarterly romance column in *Library Journal*, the ''Forecasts'' section of *Publishers Weekly*, *Booklist*, and in a number of newspapers throughout the country. In addition, many of these reviews are picked up by various indexing services, such as EbscoHosts' Academic Search Premier, InfoTrac's Expanded Academic ASAP, or bookseller's Web sites, such as Amazon.com and Barnes & Noble, and reprinted or posted to their Web sites. Nevertheless, the most comprehensive coverage still is provided by the genre-specific publications, such as *Romantic Times Book Club*, *Affaire de Coeur*, and *Rendezvous*. Online romance reviews sites are becoming increasingly popular; and while most of them, like any Web source, need to be viewed with a critical eye, they are certainly worth checking out. All about Romance (www.likesbooks.com), A Romance Review (www.aromancereview.com/news/), Romance Reviews Today (www.romrevtoday.com) and The Romance Reader (www.theromancereader.com) are only several of the many currently online. Finally, there are the listservs. RRA-L (Romance Readers Anonymous) was one of the first lists (established 1992), and it remains one of the primary forums for romance readers to discuss the genre and share their views and recommendations. It also has a Web site (www.toad.net/~dolma/) which, among other things, lists the RRA-L Award winners from their establishment in 1994 to the present and provides links to RRA-L's archives. Fiction-L is another list of interest to readers and librarians that, while not specifically devoted to romance, does focus on the genre on a regular basis. For more information see their Web site at (www.webrary.org/rs/flbklistmenu.html).

Romance News of Interest

While each year there are any number of excellent regional and local workshops, conventions, celebrations, and meetings that readers, writers, librarians, and others interested in the romance genre can attend, the annual conference of the Romance Writers of America is the most important. The 2004 conference was held in Dallas, Texas, in July, and although the romance writers had to share the turf with a major Mary Kay conference, it was, as always, a good conference, and the Librarians' and Booksellers' Day that has preceded the conference for the past six years was a resounding success. Because these events were discussed more thoroughly in *What Do I Read Next? 2004. Vol. 2*, the details will not be repeated here. Scheduled to be present at the July 2005 RWA conference Librarians' and Booksellers' Day in Reno, Nevada, are authors Nora Roberts, Susan Elizabeth Phillips, Suzanne Brockmann, Jennifer Greene, Linda Howard, Jayne Ann Krentz, and Maggie Osborne, editors Monique Patterson, Anna Genoese, and Beth de Guzman, and librarians John Charles and Joanne Hamilton-Selway. The annual RWA Literacy Autographing event will take place just afterwards. The purpose of this event is to attract local librarians and booksellers and help them become familiar with the romance genre. The cost for the event is minimal and it is an excellent opportunity to mingle with some of the major players in the industry—and pick up some free books and other goodies, besides! For more information, see the RWA website (www.rwanational.org).

The RWA Strategic Committee on Image, mentioned in *What Do I Read Next? 2004. Vol. 2*, continues its work, not the least of which was a successful recommendation to the RWA Board to establish an annual grant which would be awarded to scholars doing research in the area of popular romance fiction. The committee established to administer these grants has met and as of this writing has selected the first recipient. As a member of this committee, I can say that the pool was encouraging and the choice was difficult but excellent; however, because the grant has not officially been awarded as of this writing, I cannot announce the name at this time.

In spite of the fact that the grants committee mentioned above had several excellent research projects to judge, the actual number of scholarly publications seeing print remains slim. One book of particular interest is Juliet Flesch's *From Australia with Love: A History of Modern Australian Popular Romance Novels* (Curtin University Books, 2004), a revision of her Ph.D. dissertation that makes for surprisingly good reading. Although it focuses on Australia, there is much that is relevant for us all. In addition, readers familiar with Janice Radway's original study of romance readers might be interested in Helen Wood's article that revisits Radway's theories, ''What Reading the Romance Did for Us'' [*European Journal of Cultural Studies* 7 (May 2004): 147-154]. Although dissertations studying the genre are few and far between, one from late 2003 might be of interest to readers, ''Hearts of Darkness: The Racial Politics of Popular Romance'' by Stephanie Carol Burley (University of Maryland, College Park, 2003). As usual, the popular press continues to cover the genre with varying degrees of respect and from a number of approaches; an example that looks at things from a financial point of view is Tomas Kellner's discussion of several best selling writers, including Nora Roberts, ''Who Needs a Muse'' (*Forbes*, November 15,

2004, pages 200-203). Finally, librarians will be interested to know that Joyce Saricks' new readers' advisory column, ''At Leisure'', appears in *Booklist* and covers romance, as well as other genres.

The Future

So what lies ahead? Will it be more of the same or something different? As a practical matter, the romance genre usually builds on past successes and heads in new directions when they become relevant and are likely to attract readers (and dollars to the publishers' bottom lines). So with the warning that the future is uncertain and nothing is guaranteed, let's take a look at where the genre might be going in 2005.

First and foremost, genre blending and the new directions in which the writerss (and publishers) are taking the genre is beginning to raise questions about what the romance genre really is. Although in its infancy, this discussion is addressing a real issue and is likely to continue. As alluded to above, genre blending, the phenomenon of elements from various genres or subgenres merging across boundaries that is driving the above concerns, will continue. Chick lit, with its sassy, urban style, will continue to attract readers, as well as impacting other romance lines.

Sex will continue to sell, and while sex for its own sake or without the emotional involvement of the characters doesn't work in romance, romances are likely to get hotter. Action-oriented stories with take-charge, bombshell-type heroines will continue strong, and there will be more diversity insofar as ethnicity, cultural background, and sexual orientation is concerned among both primary and secondary characters. Multicultural romance will continue to thrive, and there will be a general trend toward more diverse characters in all the romance subgenres.

In addition, African-American writers, in particular, will break out of the ethnic lines and head in a more mainstream direction. Inspirationals will continue to hold their niche and some lines will try to broaden their readership by branching out in more secular directions. All things paranormal will continue strong, although there will be new directions; humor in a variety of forms will be pervasive; and given Harlequin's miscalculation of the American market, there will be some revamping of lines, and perhaps less reliance on the traditional series romance scenarios. Single titles will increase, and the series will lose market share. Finally, trilogies and other linked stories will become increasingly popular as writers (and publishers) see the benefit of producing related stories, all of which readers will want to buy.

Will any of these things happen? That remains to be seen. What is certain, however, is that when it comes to romance, 2005 is going to be a very interesting year.

Recommendations for Romance

Reading tastes vary greatly. What makes a book appeal to one person may make another reject it. By the same token, two people may like the same book for totally different reasons. Obviously, reading is a highly subjective and personal undertaking. For this reason, the recommended readings attached to each entry have tried to cast as broad a net as was reasonably possible. Suggested titles have been chosen on the basis of similarity to the main entry in one or more of the following areas: historical time period, geographic setting, theme, character types, plot pattern or premise, writing style, or overall mood or ''feel.'' All suggestions may not appeal to the same person, but it is to be hoped that at least one would appeal to most.

Because romance reading tastes do vary so widely and readers (and writers) often apply vastly differing criteria in determining what makes a romance good, bad, or exceptional, I cannot claim that the following list of recommendations consists solely of the ''best'' recently published romance novels. (In fact many of these received no awards or special recognition at all.) It is simply a selection of books that the romance contributors, John Charles and Shelley Mosley, and I found particularly interesting; perhaps some of these will appeal to you, too.

Deceiving Miss Dearborn by Laurie Bishop

A Hard Man Is Good to FFind by Jane Blackwood

My Pleasure by Connie Brockway

To Weave a Web of Magic edited by Claire Delacroix

Too Close to the Sun by Diana Dempsey

Under a Lucky Star by Diane Farr

Mind Game by Christine Feehan

All She Ever Wanted by Barbara Freethy

To Tempt a Texan by Georgina Gentry

The Scarlet Empress by Susan Grant

Wild in the Moonlight by Jennifer Greene

Her Scandalous Affair by Candice Hern

American Idle by Alesia Holliday

The Sun Witch by Linda Winstead Jones

Dangerous Deceptions by Lynn Kerstan

Secrets of a Summer Night by Lisa Kleypas

First Born by Lindsay McKenna

The Duel by Barbara Metzger

The Heiress of Hyde Park by Jacqueline Navin

Night of Sin by Julia Ross

Courting Trouble by Nonnie St. George

Sweetheart, Indiana by Suzanne Simmons

The Dark Lord by Patricia Simpson

A Perfect Cover by Maureen Tan

A.K.A. Goddess by Evelyn Vaughn

For Further Reference

Review Journals

Booklist, *Library Journal*, and to a lesser extent *Publishers Weekly*, continue their coverage of the romance genre. *Library Journal* publishes a quarterly romance review column—January, April 15, August, and November 15; *Booklist* has a separate romance fiction category in each issue, as do the other genres; and *Publishers Weekly* has some romance reviewers who are generally, though unfortunately not always, conversant with the genre. Though some reviews appear in these publications, most romance reviews still appear in sources—both print and online—that specialize in the romance genre. Several of the more important of these sources are listed below.

Affaire de Coeur (www.affairedecoeur.com) includes reviews, articles, and information on the world of romance fiction, in general. 3976 Oak Hill Road, Oakland, CA 94605-4931; phone, (510) 569-5675; fax, (510) 632-8868. Subscriptions, Monthly, $35 a year (U.S. First Class Rates); $65 for 2 years (U.S. First Class Rates); $30 a year (U.S. Third Class Rates); $55 for 2 years (U.S. Third Class Rates); $65 a year (Canadian Rates); $5 a single copy, U.S.

All about Romance (www.likesbooks.com) contains selected, graded, and sometimes hostile reviews.

Amazon.com (www.amazon.com) includes some published reviews, as well as readers' comments. Quite comprehensive.

Barnes and Noble (www.barnesandnoble.com) includes some published reviews as well as readers' comments.

Rendezvous: A Monthly Review of Contemporary and Historical Romances, Mysteries, and Women's Fiction (www.rendezvousreviews.com/) includes reviews of most romances published each month. Published by Love Designers Writers' Club, Inc., 1507 Burnham Avenue, Calumet City, IL 60409; phone, (708) 862-9797. Subscriptions, Monthly, $45 a year; $24 for 6 month; $4 single copy.

The Romance Reader (www.theromancereader.com) has a good selection of ranked, sometimes personally harsh reviews.

Romance Reviews Today (www.romrevtoday.com) has a comprehensive election of reviews.

Romantic Times Book Club (www.romantictimes.com) includes reviews of most romances published each month, articles, and information about the world of romance fiction. Also includes miscellaneous news and reviews of books in other genres and mainstream women's fiction. Note: Name changed from *Romantic Times* mid-year in 2002. Published by: *Romantic Times* Publishing Group, 55 Bergen Street, Brooklyn Heights, NY 11201; phone, (718) 237-1097; fax, (718) 624-4231. Subscriptions, Monthly, $29.95 for 1 year (Fourth Class U.S. Rates); $59.90 for 2 years (Fourth Class U.S. Rates); $54 for 1 year (First Class U.S. Rates); $108 for 2 years (First Class U.S. Rates); $65 for 1 year (Canadian and Mexican Rates); $130 for 2 years (Canadian and Mexican Rates); $65 for 1 year (International Rates); $130 for 2 years (International Rates; $99 for 1 year (International Airmail Rates); $198 for 2 years (International Airmail Rates).

Book Suppliers/Web Sites/Book Clubs

In addition to going to the general Web sites of online book suppliers like Amazon.com and traditional bookstores such as Borders and Barnes & Noble, readers can now order books directly from some individual publishers' Web sites. Many of these Web sites also feature reviews, information on any subscription book clubs the publisher has, and ways for readers to connect with each other. Services vary from Web site to Web site; several of the more popular are listed below.

Publishers

Avalon Books. www.avalonbooks.com/

BET Books (BET/Arabesque). www.bet.com/Books/

Five Star. www.galegroup.com/fivestar/

HarperCollins/Avon Books. www.harpercollins.com/hc/features/romance/

Dorchester Publishing (Leisure and Love Spell). http://www.dorchesterpub.com/. See Web site for book club information.

Harlequin/Silhouette/MIRA/Red Dress Ink/Steeple Hill/LUNA/HQN. eharlequin.com

Kensington Books (Zebra, Dafina, Brava, Strapless). www.kensingtonbooks.com. See Web site for book club information.

Book Suppliers

Amazon.com. www.amazon.com

Barnes & Noble. www.barnesandnoble.com

Borders (teamed with Amazon). www.borders.com

Book Clubs and Mail Order Services

Harlequin Book Club. Provides books in the Harlequin and Silhouette series on a monthly subscription basis. Write, phone, or check the Web site for series descriptions and price information. http://www.bookclubdeals.com/harlequinbookclub.html; P.O. Box 5190, Buffalo, NY 14240-5190; or http://www.bookclubdeals.com/harlequinbookclub.html; P.O. Box 615, Fort Erie, Ontario L2A 5X3.

Rhapsody: The Romance Lover's Book Club. Offered through Booksonline.com, a direct marketer created through a partnership between Doubleday Direct, Inc. and Book- of-the-Month club Holdings LLC, Rhapsody provides romances from a variety of sources on a subscription basis. Check the Web site, phone, or write for more information. http://www.rhapsodybookclub.com

Conferences

Numerous conferences are held each year for writers and readers of romance fiction. Two of the more important national ones are listed below. For a more complete listing, particularly of regional or local conferences designed primarily for romance writers, consult the *Romance Writers' Report*, a monthly publication of The Romance Writers of America.

Annual RT Book Lovers Convention is sponsored by *Romantic Times Book Club*. The 21st Annual RT Book Lovers Convention was held on March 24-28, 2004, in New York City. (This organization also sponsors a number of romance-related tours for readers and writers.) The 22nd Annual Book Lovers Convention took place April 27-May 1, 2005, in St. Louis, Missouri. The dates and location of the 23rd Annual Book Lovers Convention were not available as of this writing.

RWA Annual Conference is sponsored by Romance Writers of America and usually held in July. The 2004 Conference was held July 28-31 in Dallas, Texas. The 2005 Conference is scheduled for July 27-30 in Reno, Nevada.

Romance Titles

211

CARLY ALEXANDER (Pseudonym of Rosalind Noonan)

The Eggnog Chronicles
(New York: Kensington, 2004)

Story type: Contemporary
Subject(s): Christmas; Holidays; Relationships
Major character(s): Jane Conner, Journalist (obituary writer); Ricki Conner, Store Owner (Christmas shop); Emma Dombrowski, Banker (supervisor)
Time period(s): 2000s
Locale(s): New York, New York; Nag's Head, North Carolina

Summary: This collection of linked stories follows a pair of sisters and a friend on their varied journeys—together and apart—through the holidays and gives them each a happy ending. Included are: Jane's story, "Hooks, Premises, and Killer Endings;" Ricki's story, "Signs and Symbols;" and Emma's story, "A Christmas Sky." Although two of the stories have an urban, chick lit feel, Ricki's story is overflowing with small-town charm.

Where it's reviewed:
Romantic Times, October 2004, page 104

Other books by the same author:
Ghosts of Boyfriends Past, 2003

Other books you might like:
Marcia Evanick, *A Berry Merry Christmas*, 2004
    small-town ambience
Marcia Evanick, *Christmas on Conrad Street*, 2002
    Christmas in a small Maine town
Alesia Holliday, *Shop 'til Yule Drop*, 2004
Lynn Messina, *Fashionistas*, 2003
    chick lit/no holiday theme
Lori Soard, *The Lipstick Diaries*, 2004
    no holiday theme

212

LAURA MARIE ALTOM

Sleep Tight
(New York: Dorchester, 2004)

Story type: Paranormal; Contemporary/Fantasy
Subject(s): Fairies; Fairy Tales; Single Parent Families
Major character(s): Arabella Antoinette Moody, Mythical Creature (tooth fairy), Single Parent; Daniel Eli Wentworth IV, Mythical Creature (boogie man), Wealthy
Time period(s): 2000s
Locale(s): Clairemonte Falls, Texas

Summary: Arabella Antoinette Moody, also known as Belle, is a hardworking single mom. As the Tooth Fairy, she collects teeth and sells them to wing makers, who then grind them into the powder used to make fairy wings iridescent. Wealthy Daniel Eli Wentworth IV has a problem. He's turning into a boogie man. His mother, a former orgasm fairy, gets the two together in hopes that Belle's goodness can save Daniel, and together they can make Valentine fairies. This funny, fractured fairy tale has a decidedly dark edge.

Where it's reviewed:
Romantic Times, September 2004, page 131

Other books by the same author:
Babies and Badges, 2004
Kissing Frogs, 2004
Blue Moon, 2003
Inherited: One Baby!, 2003
Bad Luck Bride, 2002

Other books you might like:
Karen Fox, *Buttercup Baby*, 1998
    fairies
Karen Harbaugh, *Cupid's Darts*, 1998
Mary Alice Kruesi, *Second Star to the Right*, 1999
    Tinkerbell
Judi McCoy, *I Dream of You*, 2001
    genie

Nora Roberts, *Jewels of the Sun*, 1999
fairies and ghosts

213

CATHERINE ANDERSON (Pseudonym of Adeline Catherine Anderson)

Bright Eyes

(New York: Signet, 2004)

Story type: Contemporary
Series: Coulter Family. Book 4
Subject(s): Murder; Family Relations; Trust
Major character(s): Natalie Patterson, Restaurateur (dinner club owner), Divorced Person; Zeke Coulter, Store Owner (ranch supply store), Rancher
Time period(s): 2000s
Locale(s): Crystal Falls, Oregon

Summary: Divorced mother of two, singer and songwriter Natalie Patterson has her hands full trying to make a go of her supper club and deal with her wacky relatives. When her 12-year-old son decides to take his frustration over his father's neglect out on the house and garden of the rancher next door, Zeke Coulter comes storming into her life and things will never be the same. A murder adds some interest, but the emphasis is clearly on the developing relationship between Nattie and Zeke. Issues of trust and self-esteem are central to this heartwarming, sometimes humorous story that makes good use of secondary characters.

Where it's reviewed:
Rendezvous, June 2004, page 15
Romantic Times, June 2004, page 113

Other books by the same author:
Blue Skies, 2003 (Coulter Family. Book 3)
Always in My Heart, 2002
Sweet Nothings, 2002 (Coulter Family. Book 2)
Phantom Waltz, 2001 (Coulter Family. Book 1)
Seventh Heaven, 2000

Other books you might like:
Jerri Corgiat, *Sing Me Home*, 2004
Colleen Faulkner, *Taming Ben*, 2000
another confirmed bachelor
Barbara Freethy, *The Sweetest Thing*, 1999
heartwarming
JoAnn Ross, *Far Harbor*, 2000

214

MARY KAY ANDREWS

Hissy Fit

(New York: HarperCollins, 2004)

Story type: Humor; Contemporary
Subject(s): Humor; Weddings; Antiques
Major character(s): Keeley Murdock, Bride (jilted), Interior Decorator; Will Mahoney, Wealthy, Businessman
Time period(s): 2000s
Locale(s): Madison, Georgia

Summary: Interior designer Keeley Murdock throws a hissy fit that shocks Madison, Georgia, when she catches her maid-of-honor and groom-to-be in a compromising position. Despite her rumored, mercurial temperament, Keeley does good work, and Will Mahoney wants only the best to decorate the lavish home he's bought to impress a television personality he intends to wed. Of course, he's never met this media celebrity, but Will's a stubborn man, so he's not going to let that little fact stand in his way.

Where it's reviewed:
Booklist, August 2004, page 1895
Entertainment Weekly, September 3, 2004, page 79
Library Journal, July 2004, page 66
Publishers Weekly, July 5, 2004, page 36

Other books by the same author:
Little Bitty Lies, 2003
Savannah Blues, 2002

Other books you might like:
Judith Arnold, *The Wrong Bride*, 1999
Holly Jacobs, *A Day Late and a Bride Short*, 2003
Shirley Jump, *The Bride Wore Chocolate*, 2004
Ann Kline, *The Ride to Dinah's Wedding*, 2003
Pam McCutcheon, *My Favorite Husband*, 2003

215

ADELE ASHWORTH (Pseudonym of Adele Budnick)

Duke of Sin

(New York: Avon, 2004)

Story type: Historical/Victorian
Subject(s): Blackmail; Seduction
Major character(s): Vivian Rael-Lamont, Businesswoman (florist), Widow(er); William Raleigh, Nobleman (Duke of Trent)
Time period(s): 1850s (1856-1857)
Locale(s): Penzance, England

Summary: In order to keep her own scandalous past a secret, Vivian Rael-Lamont must find some way to retrieve a valuable Shakespearean sonnet from William Raleigh, the "Duke of Sin." When Vivian first meets with the reclusive William, who is rumored to have murdered his wife, she is quite surprised to find he is more than willing to sell the sonnet to her, but his price is her "company." With no other choice, Vivian agrees to his terms, hoping that somehow she can get hold of the sonnet before she becomes too emotionally involved with the dangerously seductive William.

Where it's reviewed:
Romantic Times, November 2004, page 38

Other books by the same author:
When It's Perfect, 2002
Someone Irresistible, 2001
Winter Garden, 2000
Stolen Charms, 1999
My Darling Caroline, 1998

Other books you might like:
Christina Dodd, *In My Wildest Dreams*, 2001
Jane Goodger, *The Perfect Wife*, 2000

Judith Ivory, *The Indiscretion*, 2001
Lisa Kleypas, *Lady Sophia's Lover*, 2002
Linda Francis Lee, *Swan's Grace*, 2000

216

DAWN ATKINS (Pseudonym of Daphne Atkeson)

Very Truly Sexy

(Toronto: Harlequin, 2004)

Story type: Contemporary
Subject(s): Sexual Behavior; Writing
Major character(s): Elizabeth Samuels, Journalist (entertainment column); Adam Rafael Jarvis, Businessman (magazine vp)
Time period(s): 2000s
Locale(s): Phoenix, Arizona; San Francisco, California

Summary: When *Man's Man* magazine buys out *Phoenix Rising*, entertainment writer Beth Samuels quickly discovers that her column ''On the Town'' is the first thing the new publisher wants to scrap. The only way Beth can keep her job is if she adds a bit more sizzle to her writing, but she feels a little bit rusty in that department since it has been more than a year since her last date. Deciding she needs a little research to inspire her, Beth picks up the first hot guy she spots in a local bar, not realizing that the sexy man she plans on spending the night with just happens to be her new boss!

Other books by the same author:
The Perfect Life, 2004
Wilde for You, 2004
Friendly Persuasion, 2003
Room. . .but Not Bored!, 2003
Wedding for One, 2003

Other books you might like:
Carrie Alexander, *The Chocolate Seduction*, 2003
Kristin Hardy, *My Sexiest Mistake*, 2002
Leslie Kelly, *Suite Seduction*, 2000
Joanne Rock, *Girl Gone Wild*, 2004
Vicki Lewis Thompson, *Truly, Madly, Deeply*, 2002

217

JEANETTE BAKER

Chesapeake Tide

(Don Mills, Ontario: MIRA, 2004)

Story type: Contemporary
Subject(s): Mothers and Daughters; Environment; Reunions
Major character(s): Elizabeth Jane Delacourte, Scientist (genetic biologist), Parent (of a teenage girl); Russell Tremayne Hennessey, Businessman (fishing business), Parent (of a teenage girl)
Time period(s): 2000s
Locale(s): Los Angeles, California; Marshyhope Creek, Maryland

Summary: High school sweethearts Russ Hennessey and Libby Delacourte return to Marshyhope Creek the same sultry summer—Libby to see her ailing mother and Russ to be closer to his teenage daughter, Tess, and revitalize the family

fishing business. The atmosphere in town gets a little hotter as they revisit their past relationship and work together to discover what is responsible for some serious local pollution. Environmental issues, local fishing concerns, teenage angst, old secrets, and small town dynamics work together to provide an intriguing, emotionally rewarding read.

Where it's reviewed:
Rendezvous, June 2004, page 15
Romantic Times, June 2004, page 113

Other books by the same author:
The Delaney Woman, 2003
Blood Roses, 2002
Spellbound, 2001
Nell, 1999
Irish Lady, 1998

Other books you might like:
Kathleen Eagle, *What the Heart Knows*, 1999
   rekindled love/different setting
Lorraine Heath, *Hard Lovin' Man*, 2003
Emilie Richards, *Rising Tides*, 1997
   family issues and old secrets
Nora Roberts, *Rising Tides*, 1998
   similar setting
Nora Roberts, *Sea Swept*, 1998

218

KATHLEEN BALDWIN

Lady Fiasco

(New York: Zebra, 2004)

Story type: Regency
Subject(s): Courtship; Accidents; Sports/Swimming
Major character(s): Fiona Hawthorn, Noblewoman (daughter of a baron), Debutante; Tyrell, Nobleman (Earl of Westmont)
Time period(s): 1810s
Locale(s): England

Summary: Trouble seems to follow free-spirited Fiona Hawthorn wherever she goes. However, instead of discouraging the Earl of Westmont, Fiona's childhood friend, he refuses to believe that the trouble is the result of a curse or jinx. The accidents are real, the jinx, however, is not; someone is definitely out to cause Fiona trouble, and it takes a bit of doing to uncover the villain. A humorous Regency with plenty of interesting secondary characters and a dash of real danger as well.

Where it's reviewed:
Romantic Times, September 2004, page 115

Other books by the same author:
Cut from the Same Cloth, 2005
Mistaken Kiss, 2005

Other books you might like:
Mary Balogh, *The Famous Heroine*, 1996
Mary Blayney, *The Captain's Mermaid*, 2004
Marion Chesney, *The Dreadful Debutante*, 1995
Martha Kirkland, *An Uncommon Courtship*, 2000
Sharon Stancavage, *An Enchanting Minx*, 2004

219

BEVERLY BARTON (Pseudonym of Beverly Beaver)

As Good as Dead

(New York: Zebra, 2004)

Story type: Contemporary; Romantic Suspense
Subject(s): Serial Killers; Murder; Twins
Major character(s): Reve Sorrell, Twin (of Jazzy Talbot), Socialite; Jacob Butler, Police Officer (sheriff); Jazzy Talbot, Twin (of Reve Sorrell), Businesswoman
Time period(s): 2000s
Locale(s): Cherokee Pointe, Tennessee

Summary: Learning that Jazzy Talbot could possibly be her twin, Reve Sorrell heads for rural Cherokee Pointe to see for herself. Although they look alike—red hair and all—they are as different as night and day; nevertheless, they join forces to discover the truth of their pasts. Then a serial killer, who has been adorning the murdered bodies of redheads with black ribbons around their necks, becomes aware of Jazzy and Reve. It is only a matter of time before one—or both—of them becomes the next victim. A handsome sheriff adds the romantic interest to this story that follows *The Fifth Victim* and *The Last to Die*.

Where it's reviewed:
Rendezvous, September 2004, page 34
Romantic Times, September 2004, page 126

Other books by the same author:
The Last to Die, 2004
The Fifth Victim, 2003
What She Doesn't Know, 2002
After Dark, 2000
Keeping Annie Safe, 1999

Other books you might like:
Margaret Allison, *The Last Curve*, 1999
Lisa Jackson, *The Night Before*, 2003
Karen Rose, *Have You Seen Her?*, 2004
Maggie Shayne, *Forgotten Vows*, 1994
Katherine Sutcliffe, *Bad Moon Rising*, 2003

220

LOUISE BERGIN

A Worthy Opponent

(New York: Signet, 2004)

Story type: Regency
Subject(s): Courtship; Friendship
Major character(s): Judith Shelton, Gentlewoman; Peregrine Campion, Gentleman
Time period(s): 1810s
Locale(s): Cheshire, England

Summary: Judith Shelton knows that in order to provide a secure financial future for her younger brother and sister she must marry money. Therefore, the ever-practical Judith devises a plan to ensnare the romantic interest of Viscount Westfall. The only obstacle is Peregrine Campion, who is determined to do whatever he must to keep Judith from sinking her fortune-hunting claws into his friend; even if it means using himself as romantic bait.

Where it's reviewed:
Romantic Times, June 2004, page 110

Other books by the same author:
The Spinster and the Wastrel, 2004

Other books you might like:
Kate Huntington, *The Captain's Courtship*, 1999
Laura Matthews, *A Rival Heir*, 2002
Elizabeth Powell, *A Reckless Bargain*, 2002
Regina Scott, *Utterly Devoted*, 2002
Rhonda Woodward, *A Spinster's Luck*, 2002

221

ELIZABETH BEVARLY

The Thing about Men

(New York: Avon, 2004)

Story type: Contemporary
Subject(s): Child Custody; Family; Television Programs
Major character(s): Claire Willoughby, Writer, Television Personality; Ramsey Sage, Government Official (DEA intelligence agent)
Time period(s): 2000s
Locale(s): Nashville, Tennessee; Belmont, Tennessee

Summary: Claire Willoughby is a nationally known lifestyle expert whose television show and magazine *Simple Pleasures* teaches millions about the joys of going back to the basics, but she doesn't know the first thing about children. So when her number one fan leaves Claire custody of her baby, Anabel Claire Sage, Claire immediately begins searching for someone better suited to raising the child. At first it would seem that someone would be Ramsey Sage, Anabel's uncle, but once she meets the tall, dark, and totally dangerous-looking Ramsey, Claire begins to think that even she knows more about raising a kid than him!

Where it's reviewed:
Romantic Times, January 2004, page 89

Other books by the same author:
Taming the Beastly MD, 2003
The Ring on Her Finger, 2003
Take Me, I'm Yours, 2002
Taming the Prince, 2002
The Secret Life of Connor Monahan, 2001

Other books you might like:
Jennifer Crusie, *Faking It*, 2003
Jennifer Greene, *Where Is He Now?*, 2003
Luanne Jones, *Sweethearts of the Twilight Lanes*, 2001
Karen Kendall, *Someone Like Him*, 2003
Julie Ortolon, *Dear Cupid*, 2001

222

ELIZABETH BEVARLY

Undercover with the Mob

(Toronto: Harlequin, 2004)

Story type: Contemporary; Humor
Subject(s): Crime and Criminals; Secrets
Major character(s): Natalie Dorset, Teacher (high school); John ''Jack'' Miller, Government Official (witness protection program)
Time period(s): 2000s
Locale(s): Louisville, Kentucky; New York, New York

Summary: Knowing how her landlady likes to embellish her stories, Natalie Dorset doesn't really believe her gorgeous new neighbor, Jack Miller, is a member of the mob. Sure Jack dresses in black, talks like he is connected, and is extremely secretive, but that doesn't mean he is a hit man. Then Natalie overhears Jack talking about taking care of a ''little problem'' and suddenly it's possible that Jack really might kill people for a living. Natalie always hoped that one day she would find a good guy for herself, but now it seems she is falling for a wiseguy!

Where it's reviewed:
Romantic Times, October 2004, page 112

Other books by the same author:
The Thing about Men, 2004
Taming the Beastly MD, 2003
The Ring on Her Finger, 2003
Take Me, I'm Yours, 2002
Taming the Prince, 2002

Other books you might like:
Stephanie Bond, *Seeking Single Male*, 2000
Jennifer Crusie, *Tell Me Lies*, 1998
Jacquie D'Alessandro, *In over His Head*, 2003
Kristin Gabriel, *Bullets over Boise*, 1998
Julie Kenner, *Undercover Lovers*, 2002

223

DONNA BIRDSELL

The Painted Rose

(New York: Berkley Sensation, 2004)

Story type: Historical/Georgian; Gothic
Subject(s): Beauty; Grief
Major character(s): Lady Sarah Essington, Noblewoman (daughter of the Earl of Darby), Handicapped (facially scarred); Lucien Delacourte, Artist (painter), Teacher (tutor)
Time period(s): 1770s (1777)
Locale(s): Whitford, England

Summary: Psychologically unable to paint after his wife and daughter are killed in a Paris fire, artist Lucien Delacourte goes to Elmstone House in the English countryside to serve as a tutor to the mysterious, veiled Lady Sarah Essington. Two badly wounded hearts are healed in this gothically tinged, emotionally rich story that deals with art, beauty, self-forgiveness, and the true meaning of love. First novel.

Where it's reviewed:
Romantic Times, October 2004, page 42

Other books you might like:
Gabriella Anderson, *Ever Yours*, 2003
  gothic touches
Miranda Jarrett, *Sunrise*, 2000
  emotionally wounded protagonists
Allison Lane, *Kindred Spirits*, 2002
  Regency treatment
Edith Layton, *To Wed a Stranger*, 1997
  physical appearance issues
Mary Jo Putney, *One Perfect Rose*, 1997

224

LAURIE BISHOP

Deceiving Miss Dearborn

(New York: Signet, 2004)

Story type: Regency
Subject(s): Farm Life; Memory Loss
Major character(s): Annabelle Dearborn, Gentlewoman; Gregory Alden Swain, Nobleman
Time period(s): 1810s
Locale(s): England

Summary: Upon discovering a badly injured man, who has no idea of his true identity, hiding in her barn, Annabelle Dearborn offers him a place to stay and a job. Initially Annabelle's mystery man, who comes up with the name ''John Wakefield'' for himself, seems to be a solution to some of the problems Annabelle faces as she tries to run her family's manor house on a very restricted budget. The only problem is that once ''John'' regains his memory, Annabelle risks losing not only a valuable employee, but also a man she now loves.

Where it's reviewed:
Romantic Times, May 2004, page 118

Other books by the same author:
The Best Laid Plans, 2003

Other books you might like:
Louise Bergin, *The Spinster and the Wastrel*, 2004
Susannah Carleton, *A Twist of Fate*, 2003
Elisabeth Fairchild, *Breach of Promise*, 2000
Carla Kelly, *The Lady's Companion*, 1996
Melynda Beth Skinner, *The Blackguard's Bride*, 2003

225

JANE BLACKWOOD (Pseudonym of Jane Goodger)

A Hard Man Is Good to Find

(New York: Kensington, 2004)

Story type: Humor; Romantic Suspense
Subject(s): Humor; Murder; Newspapers
Major character(s): Jaimie McLane, Editor, Journalist; Harry Crandall, Publisher, Editor (managing)
Time period(s): 2000s
Locale(s): Nortown, Connecticut

Summary: Harry Crandall has just been named publisher and managing editor of the *Nortown Journal*, but the staff wonders why. After all, Harry is a Pulitzer Prize-winning senior reporter from the *New York Times*, and Nortown is well on its way to becoming a ghost town. Jaimie McLane, the paper's editor, is dying of curiosity, and determined to discover the secret behind Harry's sudden job change. There are other mysteries to solve as well, like who killed a small boy and his puppy, and Jaimie has to get close to Harry before she can expect him to share any of his confidences.

Where it's reviewed:
Booklist, November 15, 2004, page 567
Romantic Times, December 2004, page 113

Other books by the same author:
The Sexiest Dead Man Alive, 2004

Other books you might like:
Sheryl Anderson, *Killer Heels*, 2004
Lori Foster, *Unexpected*, 2003
Harley Jane Kozak, *Dating Is Murder*, 2005
Sarah Mason, *Playing James*, 2004
Vicki Lewis Thompson, *The Nerd Who Loved Me*, 2004

226

ANNETTE BLAIR

A Christmas Baby
(New York: Zebra, 2004)

Story type: Historical/Regency; Holiday Themes
Series: Rogue. Book 4
Subject(s): Christmas; Babies
Major character(s): Larkin McAdams, Guttersnipe (innkeeper's daughter), Parent; Ashford Blackburne, Nobleman (Earl of Blackburne)
Time period(s): 1810s (1818)
Locale(s): England

Summary: When Ash Blackburne wins a wager and ends up marrying the innkeeper's fiercely resistant daughter in order to gain his inheritance, the stage is set for disaster. The Christmas holidays are on the horizon, and a Christmas miracle just might be in store. Light, lively, and sensual entertainment—with a few more weighty issues dealt with—that will appeal to fans of the period.

Where it's reviewed:
Romantic Times, October 2004, page 48

Other books by the same author:
An Unmistakable Rogue, 2003
An Unforgettable Rogue, 2002
Thee I Love, 1999

Other books you might like:
Shannon Donnelly, *Under the Kissing Bough*, 2001
Diane Farr, *Once upon a Christmas*, 2000
Mona Gedney, *On the Twelfth Day of Christmas*, 2004
Cynthia Pratt, *A Duke for Christmas*, 2004
Debbie Raleigh, *The Christmas Wish*, 2001
    Devil's Daughters. Book 1

227

SANDY BLAIR (Pseudonym of Annette Blair)

A Man in a Kilt
(New York: Zebra, 2004)

Story type: Paranormal; Time Travel
Subject(s): Castles; Ghosts; Marriage
Major character(s): Katherine Elizabeth Pudding, Caterer; Duncan Angus MacDougall, Laird, Spirit
Time period(s): 2000s; 15th century (1408)
Locale(s): New York, New York; Drasmoor, Scotland

Summary: Katherine Elizabeth ''Beth'' Pudding doesn't care if Blackstone Castle, the estate she recently inherited, is haunted; she is just happy to finally have a home of her own. After meeting Duncan Angus MacDougall, the castle's resident spirit, Beth is even more thrilled to discover her very own personal ghost is a sexy Scottish Highlander. Then a boating accident sends Beth back in time, and now the only way she can return to the present is by breaking the curse that trapped Duncan in the first place, but that could mean losing Duncan forever.

Where it's reviewed:
Booklist, September 1, 2004, page 71
Romantic Times, September 2004, page 42

Other books you might like:
Terri Brisbin, *The Queen's Man*, 1999
Lisa Cach, *The Changeling Bride*, 1999
Virginia Farmer, *Sixpence Bride*, 2000
Anne Kelleher, *Love's Labyrinth*, 2000
Tess Mallory, *Highland Dream*, 2001

228

MARY BLAYNEY

The Captain's Mermaid
(New York: Zebra, 2004)

Story type: Regency
Subject(s): Courtship; Relationships; Freedom
Major character(s): Lavinia Stewart, Gentlewoman; William Chartwell, Military Personnel (captain), Sea Captain
Time period(s): 1810s (1811-1812)
Locale(s): Sussex, England (Talford)

Summary: Free-spirited, unconventional Lavinia Stewart and by-the-book Captain William Chartwell spar their way to respect and then to love in this lively Regency featuring humor and a cast of memorable characters, including several young children. A hero with a mysterious past, a compassionate heroine, and good description combine to produce a heartwarming story as refreshing as a sea breeze.

Where it's reviewed:
Romantic Times, September 2004, page 115

Other books by the same author:
A Husband for Mama, 2003 (anthology; Julia Parks, Debbie Raleigh, co-authors)
The Pleasure of His Company, 2003
His Heart's Delight, 2002

His Last Lover, 2002
Father Christmas, 1989

Other books you might like:
Wilma Counts, *The Trouble with Harriet*, 2001
Valerie King, *A Rogue's Deception*, 2002
Martha Kirkland, *An Uncommon Courtship*, 2000
Evelyn Richardson, *The Gallant Guardian*, 1998

229

ELIZABETH BLOOM (Pseudonym of Beth Saulnier)

See Isabelle Run

(New York: Time Warner, 2005)

Story type: Romantic Suspense; Humor
Subject(s): Humor; Murder; Suspense
Major character(s): Isabelle Leonard, Bride (jilted), Waiter/
   Waitress; Maxwell Collins, Businessman (executive)
Time period(s): 2000s
Locale(s): New York, New York (Manhattan)

Summary: Bodies are piling up at Becky Belden's mega
corporation, Multimedia, and they're all employees. Isabelle
Leonard, a jilted bride stuck with a lease on an apartment she
can't afford, is grateful when the Martha Stewartesque Becky
offers her a job. Then the organizational mortality rate begins
to make Isabelle nervous. Things get even worse when she,
too, becomes the target of the eccentric killer. On top of
everything, her new boyfriend, Maxwell Collins, might be
one of the bad guys. An impressive debut novel.

Other books you might like:
Jane Blackwood, *A Hard Man Is Good to Find*, 2004
Janet Evanovich, *To the Nines*, 2003
Harley Jane Kozak, *Dating Is Murder*, 2005
Sarah Mason, *Playing James*, 2004
Vicki Lewis Thompson, *The Nerd Who Loved Me*, 2004

230

TERESA BODWELL

Loving Mercy

(New York: Kensington, 2005)

Story type: Historical/American West
Subject(s): American West; Cattle Drives; Grief
Major character(s): Mercy Clarke, Rancher, Widow(er);
   Thaddeus Buchanan, Gambler, Veteran (Civil War)
Time period(s): 1860s (1867)
Locale(s): Abilene, Kansas; Fort Victory, Colorado

Summary: Widowed rancher Mercy Clarke needs to drive her
cattle to Abilene; get top money for them; and then take the
funds to her nefarious neighbor, who's ready to take over her
land and make it part of his. He'll marry her or kill her—he
doesn't care, as long as he gets the property. Meanwhile, Civil
War veteran Thaddeus Buchanan hasn't seen his sister since
he went off to war. He needs a guide to get from Kansas to her
home in Colorado. Although Mercy's willing to travel alone,
she begrudgingly accepts a fee from Thad, little knowing the
dangers facing them on the trail ahead. An exciting debut
novel.

Where it's reviewed:
Booklist, December 1, 2004, page 640
Romantic Times, January 2005, page 38

Other books you might like:
Georgina Gentry, *To Tame a Texan*, 2003
Rachelle Morgan, *Mustang Annie*, 2000
Maggie Osborne, *The Promise of Jenny Jones*, 1997
Nancy J. Parra, *A Wanted Man*, 2002
Jodi Thomas, *When a Texan Gambles*, 2003
   Wife Lottery. Book 2

231

BARBARA BRETTON

Chances Are

(New York: Berkley, 2004)

Story type: Contemporary
Subject(s): Secrets; Weddings; Family Relations
Major character(s): Maddy Bainbridge, Single Parent, Bride;
   Aidan O'Malley, Bridegroom
Time period(s): 2000s
Locale(s): Paradise Point, New Jersey

Summary: No one in Paradise Point, New Jersey, has more
help planning her wedding than single mom Maddy Bainbridge. Her mother, aunts, cousins, and friends are all in on
the act. Maddy has a good idea of what kind of wedding she
wants. Unfortunately, so do her friends and relatives. One of
them has a terrible secret that has the potential to cast a
shadow over Maddy's ceremony, not to mention her future.
However, secrets are hard to keep when PBS is taping a
documentary about Maddy's family and town.

Where it's reviewed:
Booklist, October 1, 2004, page 315
Romantic Times, September 2004, page 117

Other books by the same author:
Sentimental Journey, 2004
Girls of Summer, 2003
One and Only, 2003
Shore Lights, 2003
A Soft Place to Fall, 2001

Other books you might like:
Roz Denny Fox, *Someone to Watch over Me*, 2003
Mary Alice Monroe, *Skyward*, 2003
Francis Ray, *Like the First Time*, 2004
Kathryn Shay, *After the Fire*, 2003
   Hidden Cove. Book 1

232

CONNIE BROCKWAY

My Pleasure

(New York: Pocket, 2004)

Story type: Historical/Regency
Subject(s): Secrets; Seduction; Sports/Fencing
Major character(s): Helena Nash, Companion, Gentlewoman;
   Ramsey Munro, Teacher (fencing)
Time period(s): 1800s (1805)

Locale(s): London, England; Scotland

Summary: The only pleasure Helena Nash gets from her job as lady's companion to the horribly demanding Alfreda Tilpot is that it lets her help play matchmaker between Lady Tilpot's niece Flora and Flora's secret lover Oswald. While delivering a missive between the two young lovers, a disguised Helena stumbles across Ramsey Munro in one of Vauxhall Gardens' dark and dangerous corners. Four years earlier, Ram had been one of three young gentlemen who had pledged their support to any of the Nash sisters should they ever need it. Now it seems Helena, who has unknowingly attracted the unwanted attentions of a mysterious admirer, needs his help, and Ram is determined to provide it whether the stubborn lady wants it or not!

Where it's reviewed:
Booklist, November 1, 2004, page 469
Publishers Weekly, September 27, 2004, page 43
Romantic Times, October 2004, page 41

Other books by the same author:
My Seduction, 2004
Bridal Favors, 2002
Once upon a Pillow, 2002
Bridal Season, 2001
McClairen's Isle: The Ravishing One, 2000

Other books you might like:
Celeste Bradley, *The Pretender*, 2003
Liz Carlyle, *The Devil You Know*, 2003
Gaelen Foley, *Lady of Desire*, 2003
Lynn Kerstan, *The Golden Leopard*, 2002
Julia London, *Highlander Unbound*, 2004

233

LAURIE BROWN

The Christmas Wedding
(New York: Zebra, 2004)

Story type: Historical/Victorian; Holiday Themes
Subject(s): Christmas
Major character(s): Matilda "Matty" Maxwell, Heiress—Lost, Noblewoman (granddaughter of a duke); Davies Preston, Nobleman (Viscount Bathers), Agent (for the queen)
Time period(s): 19th century
Locale(s): England; Turnabout, Tennessee (Westgate Farm)

Summary: Shocked to be told that she is actually the granddaughter of an English duke, Tennessee bred Matty Maxwell is not about to believe the messenger, Whitehall agent Davies Preston, Viscount Bathers—no matter how charming he is. In fact, she thinks he is running a scam on the old duke. When the sanctimonious locals threaten to take her children from her because of her "sins," she reluctantly heads for England and an entirely new life. Humor, sensuality, and a dash of danger add to this holiday romp.

Where it's reviewed:
Romantic Times, October 2004, page 48

Other books by the same author:
The Night We Kissed, 2003

The Truth about Cassandra, 2003

Other books you might like:
Gabriella Anderson, *A Matter of Pride*, 2001
    humor/no holiday link/Regency treatment
Meredith Bond, *Wooing Miss Whately*, 2004
    Regency treatment
Tracy Cozzens, *A 5th Avenue Christmas*, 2003
Anna DeForest, *A Cowboy for Christmas*, 2003
Lynn Kerstan, *Marry in Haste*, 1998
    humor/no holiday link/Regency treatment

234

LISA CACH

Dream of Me
(New York: Love Spell, 2004)

Story type: Historical/Fantasy
Subject(s): Dreams and Nightmares; Revenge; Seduction
Major character(s): Lucia, Royalty (Princess of Maramures); Theron, Demon (incubus)
Time period(s): 15th century (1423; 1429-1430)
Locale(s): Transylvania; Moldavia, Fictional Country; Maramures, Fictional Country

Summary: After Vlad Draco breaks his promise to Theron, the demon decides to exact his revenge by seducing Vlad's innocent fiancee, Princess Lucia of Maramures. Now, even though she has been kept in an isolated castle and wears a magical pendant, Lucia finds her dreams being haunted by a sexy stranger who promises that he can fulfill her every sensual desire. As Theron slowly wears down Lucia's resistance, he begins to introduce her to the pleasures of sex. However, he never expected that sweet Lucia would be the one to finally teach him the meaning of love.

Where it's reviewed:
Booklist, September 15, 2004, page 218
Romantic Times, October 2004, page 33

Other books by the same author:
Come to Me, 2004
Dr. Yes, 2003
Dating Without Novocain, 2002
George and the Virgin, 2002
The Wildest Shore, 2001

Other books you might like:
Susan Carroll, *The Night Drifter*, 1999
Tracy Fobes, *Forbidden Garden*, 2000
Emma Holly, *Hunting Midnight*, 2003
Susan Krinard, *To Catch a Wolf*, 2003
Karen Marie Moning, *To Tame a Highland Warrior*, 1999

235

SUSANNAH CARLETON (Pseudonym of Susan A. Lantz)

A Rake's Redemption
(New York: Signet, 2004)

Story type: Regency
Subject(s): Courtship; Music and Musicians

Major character(s): Sarah Mallory, Noblewoman; Theodore Middleford, Nobleman (Viscount Dunnley)
Time period(s): 1810s (1814)
Locale(s): London, England; Hampshire, England

Summary: Theo Middleford, Viscount Dunnley, is ready to give up his rakish ways and get married, but first he needs to find a suitable bride. While the Season offers plenty of eligible young ladies, Theo finds Sarah Mallory, the ''Welsh Beauty,'' to be the most intriguing of the bunch. When the two of them are caught in a potentially compromising situation, Theo convinces Sarah to become his fiancee until the scandal blows over, hoping in the meantime their pretend engagement might turn into a much more permanent relationship.

Where it's reviewed:
Romantic Times, November 2004, page 108

Other books by the same author:
A Twist of Fate, 2003
The Marriage Campaign, 2003
A Scandalous Journey, 2002

Other books you might like:
Laurie Bishop, *The Best Laid Plans*, 2003
Elisabeth Fairchild, *The Rakehell's Reform*, 1997
April Kihlstrom, *An Outrageous Proposal*, 1998
Amanda McCabe, *Scandal in Venice*, 2001
Elizabeth Powell, *The Reluctant Rogue*, 2003

236

EMILY CARMICHAEL (Pseudonym of Emily Krokosz)

The Cat's Meow
(New York: Bantam, 2004)

Story type: Contemporary/Fantasy; Humor
Subject(s): Animals/Cats; Memory Loss; Change
Major character(s): McKenna Wright, Lawyer (defense attorney), Amnesiac; Tom Markham, Lawyer (assistant district attorney); Nefertiti ''Titi'', Animal (cat)
Time period(s): 2000s
Locale(s): Sedona, Arizona

Summary: When high-powered, workaholic defense attorney McKenna Wright loses her memory in a car accident—and with it her memory of all things legal—she ends up without a job, but with a cat who talks to her! Of course, Titi has always been able to talk; it's just that McKenna hasn't been listening. Serious issues about what is important in life intertwine with humor, romance (in the form of attractive Assistant DA Tom Markham), and a dash of danger in this lively story featuring a meddlesome, take-charge cat with a mind of her own. Spin-off of *Finding Mr. Right* and *Diamond in the Ruff*.

Where it's reviewed:
Rendezvous, October 2004, page 28
Romantic Times, November 2004, page 126

Other books by the same author:
Becoming Georgina, 2003
Diamond in the Ruff, 2001
Jezebel's Sister, 2001
A Ghost for Maggie, 1999

Finding Mr. Right, 1998

Other books you might like:
Victoria Alexander, *Santa Paws*, 1997
  holiday anthology with matchmaking dogs
Adrienne Burns, *It Takes Two*, 2000
Jennifer Crusie, *Crazy for You*, 2000
  humor and animals
Jo Ann Ferguson, *Mistletoe Kittens*, 1999
  Regency anthology with matchmaking kittens
Susan Krinard, *Bewitched*, 1997
  Halloween anthology featuring cats

237

TORI CARRINGTON (Pseudonym of Lori Karayianni and Tony Karayianni)

Where You Least Expect It
(Toronto: Harlequin, 2004)

Story type: Contemporary
Subject(s): Family; Secrets
Major character(s): Penelope Moon, Store Owner (bookseller); Aidan Kendall, Teacher
Time period(s): 2000s
Locale(s): Old Orchard, Ohio

Summary: Aidan Kendall knows better than to get involved with Penelope Moon. On the run from his past, Aidan has gotten used to never becoming a permanent part of any place he stays, but now he has found a town he wants to call home and a woman he wants to get to know better. The only problem is that once Penelope learns the truth about his past, it could ruin any chance Aidan might have of a future with her.

Where it's reviewed:
Romantic Times, March 2004, page 89

Other books by the same author:
Flavor of the Month, 2003
Red-Hot and Reckless, 2003
Night Fever, 2003
Just between Us, 2003
Going Too Far, 2003

Other books you might like:
Maureen Child, *Loving You*, 2001
Amy J. Fetzer, *Taming the Beast*, 2001
Jennifer Greene, *Where Is He Now?*, 2003
Virginia Kantra, *The Temptation of Sean MacNeill*, 2000
Ruth Wind, *Rio Grande Wedding*, 1999

238

P.C. CAST

Goddess of Spring
(New York: Berkley Sensation, 2004)

Story type: Contemporary/Fantasy
Series: Goddess Summoning. Book 3
Subject(s): Mythology; Ancient History
Major character(s): Carolina ''Lina'' Santoro, Baker (bakery owner), Time Traveler (to mythological times); Hades, Deity (god of the Underworld)

Time period(s): 2000s
Locale(s): Tulsa, Oklahoma; Underworld, Mythical Place

Summary: A fervent plea to the goddess Demeter for help with her baking so her bakery will be saved zaps Lina Santoro into Demeter's mythological realm. Lina finds that she has temporarily traded bodies with the goddess Persephone (Demeter's daughter) and Persephone is going to save her restaurant. Of course, that means Lina is expected to go to the Land of the Dead to bring a little spring to the Underworld—and to help the god Hades get his kingdom back on track. He thinks she is really Persephone, and when the chemistry between the two begins to sizzle, Lina finds herself with problems of a completely different kind. This is a creative reinterpretation of the Persephone/Hades myth with a humorous, lively air, and another in Cast's series in which modern day women trade lives and bodies with ancient goddesses (the high priestess of the Celtic goddess Epona in *Goddess by Mistake* and Undine, daughter of the sea god Lir, in *Goddess of the Sea*).

Where it's reviewed:
Romantic Times, August 2004, page 120

Other books by the same author:
Goddess of the Sea, 2003 (Goddess Summoning. Book 2)
Goddess by Mistake, 2001 (Goddess Summoning. Book 1)

Other books you might like:
Jessica Bryan, *Across a Wine Dark Sea*, 1991
  more mythology
Marilyn Campbell, *Stolen Dreams*, 1994
  science fiction with a mythical twist
Maura Seger, *Silver Zephyr*, 1984
Deborah Smith, *Alice at Heart*, 2002
  Waterlilies. Book 1
Deborah Smith, *Diary of a Radical Mermaid*, 2004
  Waterlilies. Book 2

239

JANET CHAPMAN

Tempting the Highlander

(New York: Pocket Star, 2004)

Story type: Contemporary; Time Travel
Series: Highlander. Book 4
Subject(s): Time Travel; Magic; Abuse
Major character(s): Catherine Daniels, Runaway (from an abusive ex-husband); Robbie McBain, Time Traveler, Foster Parent (of four teenage boys); Pendaar "Father Daar", Religious (druidh), Time Traveler
Time period(s): 2000s
Locale(s): Pine Creek, Maine

Summary: Robbie McBain, an eight-year-old in the previous book in this series, is now an adult with four teenage wards of the court as foster children. He also has a large logging operation to run, and the responsibility of acting as guardian to his father and the other Highland warriors who were dragged from their medieval existence and dropped in rural Maine 35 years earlier. Now the group's settled existence is about to be threatened as the wizard Pendaar's spell nears its end, and it is up to Robbie to go back in time to find the book of spells that Daar needs to keep the Highlanders from being zapped back to the Middle Ages. In addition, Robbie needs a housekeeper to cook and generally keep tabs on the boys. Enter Catherine Daniels, on the run from her abusive ex-husband with her two children in tow, and in need of a job and protection. It's a perfect match, in more ways than one.

Where it's reviewed:
Romantic Times, September 2004, page 128

Other books by the same author:
The Seductive Imposter, 2004
Charming the Highlander, 2003 (Highlander. Book 1)
Loving the Highlander, 2003 (Highlander. Book 2)
Wedding the Highlander, 2003 (Highlander. Book 3)

Other books you might like:
Diana Gabaldon, *Outlander*, 1991
  classic Highlander time travel romance
Lynn Kurland, *My Heart Stood Still*, 1998
Karen Marie Moning, *The Dark Highlander*, 2004
  another traveling Highlander
Karen Marie Moning, *Kiss of the Highlander*, 2001
  more time traveling Highlanders
Christina Skye, *Christmas Knight*, 1998

240

MEG CHITTENDEN

Snap Shot

(New York: Berkley Sensation, 2004)

Story type: Contemporary; Romantic Suspense
Subject(s): Murder; Photography
Major character(s): Diana Gordon, Detective—Private, Photographer; Connor Callahan, Doctor (chiropractor), Widow(er)
Time period(s): 2000s
Locale(s): Port Findlay, Washington

Summary: Shot while in pursuit of a man she suspected of defrauding an insurance company, PI Diana Gordon has had enough and heads for Port Findlay, Washington, and a new career as a photographer. Unfortunately, trouble seems to be stalking her; and when the head of the local Arts Alliance is found murdered, suddenly Port Findlay seems chillingly dangerous. A sexy chiropractor adds romantic interest to this lively, complex, suspenseful mystery that has a few unexpected twists.

Where it's reviewed:
Romantic Times, September 2004, page 86

Other books by the same author:
More than You Know, 2003
Dying to See You, 2000
Don't Forget to Die, 1999
Dead Beat and Deadly, 1998
This Time Forever, 1990 (reincarnation)

Other books you might like:
Susan Andersen, *All Shook Up*, 2001
Karen Harper, *Dark Harvest*, 2004
  another wounded heroine
Jill Marie Landis, *Lovers' Lane*, 2003
Nora Roberts, *River's End*, 1999

Alicia Scott, *The Quiet One*, 1996

241

EDIE CLAIRE

Meant to Be

(New York: Warner Forever, 2004)

Story type: Contemporary
Subject(s): Mystery; Inheritance; Family Relations
Major character(s): Meara O'Rourke, Adoptee, Teacher;
Fletcher Black, Artist (sculptor)
Time period(s): 2000s
Locale(s): Pennsylvania

Summary: When Meara O'Rourke's biological mother dies
and she inherits half ownership of a historic Pennsylvania
estate, she finds herself in conflict with her mother's stepson,
Fletcher Black, who has always thought the estate would
belong to him. Mystery surrounds Meara's adoption, and as
the pieces of the puzzle fall into place, the relationship between Meara and Fletch takes on a new and more romantic,
but sweet, dimension. Emotionally involving and complex.

Where it's reviewed:
Romantic Times, June 2004, page 113

Other books by the same author:
Long Time Coming, 2003

Other books you might like:
Diane Chamberlain, *Summer's Child*, 2000
Barbara Delinsky, *The Passions of Chelsea Kane*, 1992
Kay Hooper, *Amanda*, 1995
Anne Stuart, *Shadow Lover*, 1999
    gothic touches
Phyllis Whitney, *Woman Without a Past*, 1991

242

KATE CLEMENS (Pseudonym of Mary Mackey)

Sweet Revenge

(New York: Zebra, 2004)

Story type: Contemporary; Humor
Subject(s): Revenge; Murder; Humor
Major character(s): Nora Wynn, Businesswoman, Divorced
Person (Sam's ex-wife); Sam Gallo, Director (documen-
tary films)
Time period(s): 2000s
Locale(s): Los Angeles, California

Summary: Known far and wide as the Queen of Revenge,
businesswoman Nora Wynn's specialty is arranging for revenge fantasies. However, when the fantasies start to turn real
and people end up dead, she is forced to go to her former
husband, Sam Gallo, for help. This lively story of rekindled
love is both funny and frightening, but definitely delightful.

Where it's reviewed:
Booklist, April 15, 2004, page 1429

Other books by the same author:
The Stand In, 2003

Other books you might like:
Susan Andersen, *Baby, Don't Go*, 2000
Jennifer Crusie, *Manhunting*, 2003
Jennifer Crusie, *Strange Bedpersons*, 2003
Rachel Gibson, *It Must Be Love*, 2000
Jane Heller, *Crystal Clear*, 1999

243

KRESLEY COLE

The Price of Pleasure

(New York: Pocket, 2004)

Story type: Historical/Victorian; Historical/Exotic
Subject(s): Shipwrecks; Missing Persons; Behavior
Major character(s): Victoria Anne Dearbourne, Noblewoman
(granddaughter of an earl), Orphan; Grant Sutherland, Sea
Captain, Gentleman
Time period(s): 1850s
Locale(s): Oceania (unnamed island); England; At Sea

Summary: When Captain Grant Sutherland is hired by the
aging Earl of Belmont to search for his shipwrecked family
who were lost in the South Seas eight years earlier, he is
thrilled when he actually discovers the earl's granddaughter,
Victoria Dearbourne, on an island in southern Oceania. Spirited, clever Tori is legitimately wary of strangers, and it takes
days and a lot of running about the island before Grant can
even get close enough to tell her who he is and what his
mission is. Funny, sexy, and fast-paced, this adventurous
romance takes a freedom-loving, independent heroine, pairs
her with an dashing, but honorable, hero, and sweeps them
from the primitive, unregimented tropics to uptight Victorian
England—with all the expected cultural conflicts and romantic results. This novel is linked to *The Captain of All Pleasures*; the heroes of both stories are brothers.

Where it's reviewed:
Romantic Times, July 2004, page 38

Other books by the same author:
If You Dare, 2005
The Captain of All Pleasures, 2003

Other books you might like:
Candice Proctor, *Beyond Sunrise*, 2003
    island adventure
Mary Jo Putney, *The Bartered Bride*, 2002
Gina Robins, *Always and Forever*, 1992
    similar re-entry issues/American South
Katherine Sutcliffe, *Dream Fever*, 1991
Katherine Sutcliffe, *Notorious*, 2002
    exotic adventure

244

JERRI CORGIAT

Follow Me Home

(New York: Onyx, 2004)

Story type: Contemporary; Americana
Series: O'Malley Sisters. Book 2
Subject(s): Small Town Life; Reunions; Family Relations

Major character(s): Alcea O'Malley Addams, Divorced Person, Baker; Dakota Jones, Heir (to business), Writer
Time period(s): 2000s
Locale(s): Cordelia, Missouri (Ozarks)

Summary: When her ex-husband's bank forecloses on her house, Alcea is at her wits' end. Her money is gone, her home is gone, and she has no job! Then Dakota Jones, the one boy from high school she never forgot, strides back into town to settle his grandfather's estate and literally crashes into her life, with not unexpected results. A multitude of likable secondary characters, including many from the first volume in the series, and a typically difficult teenager, add to this multilayered story. This is a tender romance with a lot of down-home charm and small town appeal.

Where it's reviewed:
Romantic Times, November 2004, page 117

Other books by the same author:
Sing Me Home, 2004 (O'Malley Sisters. Book 1)

Other books you might like:
Kathleen Eagle, *What the Heart Knows*, 1999
    emotionally involving/rekindled love
Barbara Freethy, *Just the Way You Are*, 2000
Luanne Jones, *The Dixie Belle's Guide to Love*, 2002
    down-home charm/more humor
Debbie Macomber, *Dakota Born*, 2000
Karen White, *Falling Home*, 2002
    small town ambience/rekindled love

245

JANET DAILEY

Calder Promise
(New York: Kensington, 2004)

Story type: Contemporary; Romantic Suspense
Series: Calder. Book 8
Subject(s): Courtship; Marriage
Major character(s): Laura Calder, Socialite (recent college graduate); Boone Rutledge, Wealthy, Businessman; Sebastian Dunshill, Nobleman (Earl of Crawford)
Time period(s): 2000s
Locale(s): Europe; Montana; Texas

Summary: While on a post-graduation tour of Europe, young Laura Calder meets two men who vie for her hand—bad boy Boone Rutledge and handsome, debonnaire, and titled Sebastian Dunshill. Old enmities surface in this family-rich story that treats its readers to a taste of glittering European society, as well as wealthy American ranch life. Mystery, a bit of suspense, and a few twists add interest. This story stands on its own, but fans of the series will especially enjoy re-meeting characters from earlier books.

Where it's reviewed:
Romantic Times, July 2004, page 114

Other books by the same author:
Shifting Calder Wind, 2003 (Calder. Book 7)
Green Calder Grass, 2002 (Calder. Book 6)
A Capital Holiday, 2001
Calder Pride, 1999 (Calder. Book 5)

This Calder Sky, 1981 (Calder. Book 1)

Other books you might like:
Barbara Bickmore, *Beyond the Promise*, 1996
    family issues
Kathleen Eagle, *The Last True Cowboy*, 1998
Joan Johnston, *The Cowboy*, 2000
    family issues
Nora Roberts, *Montana Sky*, 1996

246

CLAUDIA DAIN
DEE DAVIS, Co-Author
EVELYN ROGERS, Co-Author

Silent Night
(New York: Leisure, 2004)

Story type: Contemporary; Romantic Suspense
Subject(s): Winter; Suspense
Time period(s): 2000s
Locale(s): United States (isolated, rural settings)

Summary: This trio of wintry thrillers that are more suspense than romance focuses on the threatened heroine of the women-in-jeopardy variety and uses snow and isolation to up the ante. Included are "Tracked," Claudia Dain's frightening tale of abandonment and pursuit; "Still of the Night," Dee Davis' complex story of a woman fleeing her husband's killers; and "Wounded," Evelyn Rogers' gripping story of a woman who finds an injured stranger on her isolated property during a snowstorm.

Where it's reviewed:
Romantic Times, October 2004, page 97

Other books you might like:
Dee Davis, *After Twilight*, 2001
Christine Feehan, *The Shadows of Christmas Past*, 2004
    two wintery novellas; Susan Sizemore, co-author
Ginna Gray, *The Witness*, 2001
Karen Robards, *Wait Until Dark*, 2001
    chilling anthology

247

CAROLYN DAVIDSON
CAROL FINCH, Co-Author
LYNNA BANNING, Co-Author

One Starry Christmas
(Toronto: Harlequin, 2004)

Story type: Historical/American West; Holiday Themes
Subject(s): Christmas; Romance
Time period(s): Indeterminate Past
Locale(s): United States

Summary: This sweet series of heartwarming Christmas novellas set in the American West includes: *Stormwalker's Woman*, Carolyn Davidson's puppy-filled story of the healing power of love; *Home for Christmas*, Carol Finch's story of a former bounty hunter who falls for the woman he was sent to bring home for Christmas; and *Hark, the Harried Angels*, a charming story of a reclusive hero who finds love with his caring Russian neighbor by Lynna Banning.

Where it's reviewed:
Rendezvous, November 2004, page 19
Romantic Times, November 2004, page 44

Other books by the same author:
One Christmas Wish, 2000 (holiday anthology)

Other books you might like:
Millie Criswell, *A Western Family Christmas*, 2001
　holiday anthology
Hannah Howell, *A Stockingful of Joy*, 1999
Ruth Ryan Langan, *Christmas Miracle*, 1992
Linda Lael Miller, *Springwater Christmas*, 1999

248

MARYJANICE DAVIDSON

Undead and Unemployed
(New York: Berkley Sensation, 2004)

Story type: Contemporary/Fantasy; Paranormal
Subject(s): Vampires; Humor
Major character(s): Betsy Taylor, Vampire (vampire queen); Eric Sinclair, Vampire (vampire king)
Time period(s): 2000s
Locale(s): Minneapolis, Minnesota; St. Paul, Minnesota

Summary: Shoes, sex, and vampires are the focus of this lively, sometimes hilarious story. Betsy Taylor, queen of the vampires and designer shoe maven, and her sexy consort, Eric Sinclair, king of the vampires, are hunting for a killer who has been targeting vampires. Following *Undead and Unwed*, this lively story is sexy, wicked, and just plain fun.

Where it's reviewed:
Rendezvous, August 2004, page 34
Romantic Times, August 2004, page 120

Other books by the same author:
The Royal Treatment, 2004
Undead and Unwed, 2004
By Any Other Name, 1998

Other books you might like:
Laura Marie Altom, *Kissing Frogs*, 2004
　humor and fairy tales
Barbara Boswell, *Magic Slippers*, 1996
　funny, modern anthology featuring shoes
Christine Feehan, *Dark Symphony*, 2003
　dark, not funny, vampires
Lynsay Sands, *Love Bites*, 2004
Lynsay Sands, *Single White Vampire*, 2003
　humorous vampires

249

GERALYN DAWSON (Pseudonym of Geralyn Dawson Williams)

My Long, Tall Texas Heartthrob
(New York: Pocket Star, 2004)

Story type: Contemporary; Americana

Subject(s): Small Town Life; Babies; Romance
Major character(s): Tess Anderson, Agent (talent manager), Child-Care Giver (to newborn twin nieces); Nicholas Sutherland, Lawyer, Philanthropist
Time period(s): 2000s
Locale(s): Cedar Dell, Texas

Summary: As she has always done, LA agent Tess Anderson runs to her sister's rescue and ends up in sleepy Cedar Dell, Texas, caring for newborn twin girls, and fighting her feelings for rich, sexy, macho Nick Sutherland. Funny, sexy, and sprinkled with memorable secondary characters and a lot of Texas small town flavor.

Where it's reviewed:
Rendezvous, June 2004, page 16

Other books by the same author:
My Big Old Texas Heartache, 2003
The Pink Magnolia Club, 2002
The Bad Luck Wedding Night, 2001
Sizzle All Day, 2000
Simmer All Night, 1999

Other books you might like:
Leanne Banks, *Some Girls Do*, 2003
Lorraine Heath, *Hard Lovin' Man*, 2003
Lorraine Heath, *Smooth Talkin' Stranger*, 2003
Pamela Morsi, *Doing Good*, 2002
　sassy humor
Susan Elizabeth Phillips, *Heaven, Texas*, 1995
　humorous

250

CLAIRE DELACROIX
LYNN KURLAND, Co-Author
PATRICIA A. MCKILLIP, Co-Author
SHARON SHINN, Co-Author

To Weave a Web of Magic
(New York: Berkley, 2004)

Story type: Historical/Fantasy; Anthology
Subject(s): Legends; Mythology; Romance

Summary: Offering a unique combination of fantasy and romance, this quartet of novellas from some of the best writers in the field will appeal to fans of both genres. This anthology includes: *The Gorgon in the Cupboard*, veteran fantasy writer Patricia McKillip's story of a painter in search of a muse; *The Tale of Two Swords*, Lynn Kurland's lively medieval with non-stop adventure; *Fallen Angel*, Sharon Shinn's compelling fantasy set in her angel-filled world of Samaria; and *An Elegy for Melusine*, Claire Delacroix's version of a classic legend.

Where it's reviewed:
Romantic Times, July 2004, page 104

Other books by the same author:
The Sorceress, 1994 (magical medieval/Melusine is a character)

Other books you might like:
Madeline Baker, *Enchanted Crossings*, 1994
Jo Beverley, *Irresistible Forces*, 2004
　fantasy anthology

Romance

Michele Hauf, *Seraphim*, 2004
Lynn Kurland, *This Is All I Ask*, 1997
 medieval adventure

251

DIANA DEMPSEY

Too Close to the Sun

(New York: Onyx, 2004)

Story type: Contemporary
Subject(s): Family Problems; Responsibility; Business Enterprises
Major character(s): Gabriela ''Gabby'' DeLuca, Vintner (assistant winemaker); Will Henley, Businessman, Financier
Time period(s): 2000s
Locale(s): Napa Valley, California

Summary: Disillusioned by love, Napa Valley native Gabby DeLuca focuses all her considerable abilities on restoring her family's reputation for making quality wines. When the owner of the winery her family works for decides to let her incompetent son take over the management, things go from bad to worse for all concerned. In addition, a private-equity firm that wants to buy the winery, represented by attractive and persistent Will Henley, just adds to the conflict. Emotionally rich, romantic, and well-written, this story focuses on issues of family responsibility, integrity, and being true to one's self.

Where it's reviewed:
Rendezvous, July 2004, page 25
Romantic Times, October 2004, page 90

Other books by the same author:
Catch the Moon, 2003
Falling Star, 2002

Other books you might like:
Barbara Freethy, *Love Will Find a Way*, 2002
Shirl Henke, *Bouquet*, 1994
Nora Roberts, *The Villa*, 2001
Katherine Stone, *Bed of Roses*, 1998
Lisa Ann Verge, *Sweet Harvest*, 1992

252

JANELLE DENISON
NINA BANGS, Co-Author
MARYJANICE DAVIDSON, Co-Author

Men at Work

(New York: Berkley Sensation, 2004)

Story type: Paranormal; Anthology
Subject(s): Work; Sexuality; Paranormal
Time period(s): 2000s
Locale(s): United States

Summary: Sexy, physically hard-working men are the heroes of the three novellas in this lively, funny, highly sensual anthology by some of the genre's hottest writers. Included are: *Slow Hands*, Janelle Denison's sizzling reunion story of two former sweethearts; *Color Me Wicked*, Nina Bangs' magical romp in an amusement park instigated by a wickedly

mischievous cosmic troublemaker; and *The Fixer Upper*, MaryJanice Davidson's steamy tale of an obnoxious hunk, a nifty ghost, and a life-changing role-swap.

Where it's reviewed:
Romantic Times, December 2004, page 124

Other books you might like:
Nina Bangs, *An Original Sin*, 1999
 more ''cosmic'' trouble
Colleen Faulkner, *Tempting Zach*, 2000
 another hardworking hero/sweeter
Lori Foster, *Bad Boys to Go*, 2003
 anthology: Janelle Denison, Nancy Warren, co-authors
Lori Foster, *I Love Bad Boys*, 2002
 sensual anthology; Janelle Denison, Donna Kauffman, co-authors
Lori Foster, *Perfect for the Beach*, 2004
 anthology; Janelle Denison, Erin McCarthy, MaryJanice Davidson, Kayla Perrin, and Morgan Leigh, co-authors

253

JUDE DEVERAUX

Always

(New York: Pocket, 2004)

Story type: Time Travel; Contemporary/Fantasy
Series: Forever. Book 3
Subject(s): Time Travel; Psychic Powers; Kidnapping
Major character(s): Darci Monroe Montgomery, Psychic; Jack Hallbrooke, FBI Agent (undercover); Adam Montgomery, Professor
Time period(s): 2000s; 1840s (1843)
Locale(s): United States

Summary: Wrapping up her Forever trilogy but cannily leaving opportunities for future series, Deveraux takes psychic Darci Montgomery and FBI Agent Jack Hallbrooke on a search for a kidnapper that lands them in another time, 1843 to be exact. There Darci surprisingly loses her powers and Jack must deal with a lady named Lavender. Complex and filled with references and characters from the earlier volumes in the series, this story will be more easily understood if those books have been read.

Where it's reviewed:
Romantic Times, November 2004, page 126

Other books by the same author:
Forever and Always, 2003 (Forever. Book 2)
Forever, 2002 (Forever. Book 1)
The Mulberry Tree, 2002
The Summerhouse, 2001
Temptation, 2000

Other books you might like:
Kristin Hannah, *Once in Every Life*, 1993
Constance O'Day-Flannery, *Time After Time*, 2001
Antoinette Stockenberg, *Beyond Midnight*, 1996
Antoinette Stockenberg, *Embers*, 1994

254

SHANNON DONNELLY
JENNIFER MALIN, Co-Author
DONNA SIMPSON, Co-Author

With This Ring
(New York: Zebra, 2004)

Story type: Anthology; Regency
Subject(s): Courtship
Time period(s): 1800s
Locale(s): England

Summary: Three different regency novellas explore the romantic delights of courtship. In Shannon Donnelly's *Stolen Away*, Audrey Colbert's efforts to match up her beautiful cousin Chloe with the Marquis of Arncliffe become somewhat complicated once Audrey realizes she wants to marry the handsome nobleman herself. Miranda Granville expects to one day wed her best friend's brother, Lord Julian Ellsworth, until Andrew Owen convinces Miranda that they are much better suited—both musically and romantically—in Jennifer Malin's *A Perfect Duet*. Sorrow Marchand must find a way to let Bertram Carlyle know that when he marries her he is not only getting a new bride, but also a somewhat "unique" new family in Donna Simpson's *Sorrow's Wedding*.

Where it's reviewed:
Romantic Times, June 2004, page 110

Other books you might like:
Anne Barbour, *A Wedding Bouquet*, 2004
Jo Ann Ferguson, *A Valentine Waltz*, 2004
Elena Greene, *His Blushing Bride*, 2001
Alice Holden, *On Bended Knee*, 2003
Valerie King, *My Darling Bride*, 1998

255

STEPHANIE DOYLE

Who Wants to Marry a Heartthrob?
(Toronto: Harlequin, 2004)

Story type: Contemporary; Humor
Subject(s): Contests; Television
Major character(s): Bridget Connor, Assistant; Richard Wells, Advertising
Time period(s): 2000s
Locale(s): New York, New York; Pennsylvania

Summary: After a botched bit of cosmetic surgery leaves advertising executive Richard Wells one contestant short for his new reality dating television show, "Who Wants to Marry a Heartthrob?," Richard coerces his assistant Bridget Connor into filling in for the missing woman. Even though everyone believes she will be the first to be eliminated, Bridget still sees participating as a chance to show Richard that she isn't just the perfect assistant; she is a woman too. When it actually seems that Bridget might have a chance of winning dreamy soap opera star Brock Brickman as her husband, Bridget is forced to stop and think just how far she is willing to go to teach Richard a lesson!

Where it's reviewed:
Romantic Times, September 2004, page 104

Other books by the same author:
One True Love, 2003
Baily's Irish Dream, 2002
Down Home Diva, 2001
Undiscovered Hero, 1997

Other books you might like:
Elizabeth Bevarly, *That Boss of Mine*, 2004
Samantha Connelly, *I Will Survive*, 2004
Kate Hoffman, *Sweet Revenge*, 1999
Holly Jacobs, *I Waxed My Legs for This?*, 2001
Wendy Wax, *7 Days and 7 Nights*, 2003

256

BARBARA DUNLOP

Out of Order
(Toronto: Harlequin, 2004)

Story type: Contemporary
Subject(s): Careers; Law
Major character(s): Shelby Jacobs, Receptionist; Dallas Williams, Lawyer
Time period(s): 2000s
Locale(s): Chicago, Illinois

Summary: Shelby Jacobs had no idea that her latest boss was running guns and pirating software, but fortunately for Shelby, lawyer Dallas Williams just happens to be at the police station when she is being booked. Dallas manages to get Shelby cleared of the charges, but he immediately regrets helping her out when Shelby turns up the next day as the new receptionist for his law firm. He wants someone sophisticated and elegant, not wild and fun like Shelby, as his receptionist; but Shelby has finally found a job she really likes, and she isn't giving it up for anyone, not even her sexy new boss!

Where it's reviewed:
Romantic Times, August 2004, page 98

Other books by the same author:
The Wish List Wife, 2003
Too Close to Call, 2003
A Groom in Her Stocking, 2002
Next to Nothing, 2002
Forever Jake, 2001

Other books you might like:
Jennifer Crusie, *Strange Bedpersons*, 2003
Stephanie Doyle, *One True Love*, 2003
Dorien Kelly, *Do-Over*, 2003
Cindi Myers, *Life According to Lucy*, 2004
Jill Shalvis, *Natural Blond Instincts*, 2003

257

CASSIE EDWARDS

Wind Walker
(New York: Signet, 2004)

Story type: Historical/American West

Subject(s): Native Americans; Kidnapping; American West
Major character(s): Maggie Tolan, Adventurer, Captive (kidnapped); Wind Walker, Indian (Cheyenne), Widow(er)
Time period(s): 1860s (1868)
Locale(s): Wyoming

Summary: Leaving her native Boston and heading West for the excitement of the frontier, Maggie Tolan learns firsthand the dangers of adventure. She is kidnapped by a crazed local rancher who is looking for a replacement for his late wife. Fortunately, Maggie's uncle seeks the aid of Wind Walker, a Cheyenne warrior who will stop at nothing until he rescues Maggie. Filled with romance and Native American lore.

Where it's reviewed:
Romantic Times, June 2004, page 37

Other books by the same author:
Proud Eagle, 2004
Nightwolf, 2003
Savage Dance, 1997
White Fire, 1997
Wild Splendor, 1993

Other books you might like:
Genell Dellin, *Cherokee Warriors: The Captive*, 1994
Genell Dellin, *Cherokee Warriors: The Loner*, 2002
Kathleen Harrington, *Cherish the Dream*, 1990
Karen Kay, *Lone Arrow's Pride*, 2002
Karen Kay, *Soaring Eagle's Embrace*, 2003

258

MARCIA EVANICK

A Berry Merry Christmas
(New York: Zebra, 2004)

Story type: Contemporary; Holiday Themes
Series: Misty Harbor. Book 4
Subject(s): Christmas; Small Town Life
Major character(s): Amber McAllister, Businesswoman (berry and jam business), Widow(er); Ian McNeal, Businessman (marketing and advertising)
Time period(s): 2000s
Locale(s): Misty Harbor, Maine

Summary: When her husband is killed in a car accident, Amber McAllister leaves the fast-paced life in Boston and heads for sleepy Misty Harbor, Maine, where she joins her rather unconventional aunt in making a success of her berry jam and jelly business, It's the Berries. When things take off because of the marketing plan that Ian McNeal, Amber's late husband's business partner, has created, Amber is swamped. Ian rides to the rescue, and before long the business is on target and so is the romantic relationship between Amber and Ian. Interesting secondary characters and lots of small town atmosphere shine in this holiday-centered book that continues Evanick's Misty Harbor series.

Where it's reviewed:
Romantic Times, October 2004, page 90

Other books by the same author:
Blueberry Hill, 2003 (Misty Harbor. Book 3)
Catch of the Day, 2002 (Misty Harbor. Book 1)

Christmas on Conrad Street, 2002 (Misty Harbor. Book 2)

Other books you might like:
Pamela Browning, *Baby Christmas*, 2000
Kathleen Creighton, *A Christmas Love*, 1992
Teresa Hill, *Twelve Days*, 2000
Fern Michaels, *Family Blessings*, 2004
Fern Michaels, *Jingle All the Way*, 2004
    holiday anthology

259

DIANE FARR (Pseudonym of Diane Farr Golling)

Under a Lucky Star
(New York: Signet, 2004)

Story type: Historical/Regency
Subject(s): Courtship
Major character(s): Cynthia Fitzwilliam, Noblewoman; Derek Whittaker, Gentleman, Secretary
Time period(s): 1800s (1803; 1806)
Locale(s): England

Summary: One kiss with Cynthia Fitzwilliam, one of the Season's fairest beauties, convinces Derek Whittaker that they are perfect for each other, but Derek realizes that a nobleman's secretary such as himself doesn't have a chance with a lady like Cynthia. Three years later when Derek and Cynthia cross paths again, Derek has come up in the world, but Cynthia lives up to her nickname of "Frost Fair" by trying to freeze him out of her life. Derek knows that Cynthia is the only woman for him; now all he has to do is find some way to melt her cold facade with the warmth of his love.

Where it's reviewed:
Booklist, April 15, 2004, page 1429
Publishers Weekly, March 15, 2004, page 60
Romantic Times, April 2004, page 34

Other books by the same author:
Under the Wishing Star, 2003
Duel of Hearts, 2002
The Fortune Hunter, 2002
Falling for Chloe, 2000
Once upon a Christmas, 2000

Other books you might like:
Elizabeth Boyle, *Stealing the Bride*, 2003
Candice Hern, *Once a Scoundrel*, 2003
Sabrina Jeffries, *The Dangerous Lord*, 2000
Rebecca Hagan Lee, *Barely a Bride*, 2003
Teresa Medeiros, *One Night of Scandal*, 2003

260

CHRISTINE FEEHAN
MAGGIE SHAYNE, Co-Author
EMMA HOLLY, Co-Author
ANGELA KNIGHT, Co-Author

Hot Blooded
(New York: Jove, 2004)

Story type: Paranormal; Anthology
Subject(s): Paranormal; Seduction

Time period(s): 2000s
Locale(s): United States

Summary: This sizzling quartet of novellas focuses on the darker side of the paranormal romantic environment. Included are *Dark Hunger*, Christine Feehan's latest Carpathian tale; *Awaiting Moonrise*, Maggie Shayne's magical werewolf romance; *The Night Owl*, a sexy vampire tale by Emma Holly; and *Seduction's Gift*, Angela Knight's vampire tale laced with humor.

Where it's reviewed:
Rendezvous, September 2004, page 16
Romantic Times, September 2004, page 128

Other books by the same author:
Dark Symphony, 2003
Fantasy, 2002 (anthology; Sabrina Jeffries, Emma Holly, and Elda Minger, co-authors)

Other books you might like:
Emma Holly, *Hunting Midnight*, 2003
Susan Krinard, *Prince of Wolves*, 1994
Maggie Shayne, *Twilight Hunger*, 2002

261

CHRISTINE FEEHAN

Mind Game

(New York: Jove, 2004)

Story type: Contemporary; Paranormal
Series: Ghostwalker. Book 2
Subject(s): Paranormal; Psychic Powers; Suspense
Major character(s): Dahlia LeBlanc, Psychic (''ghostwalker''); Nicolas Trevane, Psychic (''ghostwalker'')
Time period(s): 2000s
Locale(s): Louisiana (bayou)

Summary: Feehan's work builds on the premise from *Shadow Game*—that there are a number of super-psychic people who have been trained to enhance their powers, but at great mental risk to themselves. This episode sends ghostwalker Nico Trevane to the Louisiana bayou in search of Dahlia LeBlanc to bring her back so she can be taught to live with her psychic abilities. Others are searching for Dahlia, too, and after a bloody battle, Nico and Dahlia escape, only to find themselves in even more danger. Lots of fast-paced action.

Where it's reviewed:
Rendezvous, August 2004, page 34
Romantic Times, August 2004, page 118

Other books by the same author:
Wild Rain, 2004
Dark Melody, 2003
Dark Symphony, 2003
The Twilight Before Christmas, 2003
Shadow Game, 2003

Other books you might like:
Suzanne Brockmann, *Over the Edge*, 2001
Susan Grant, *The Legend of Banzai Maguire*, 2004
Liz Maverick, *The Shadow Runners*, 2004
    2176. Book 3

Lindsay McKenna, *First Born*, 2004
Patti O'Shea, *The Power of Two*, 2004
    2176. Book 4

262

CHRISTINE FEEHAN
SUSAN SIZEMORE, Co-Author

The Shadows of Christmas Past

(New York: Pocket Star, 2004)

Story type: Contemporary; Holiday Themes
Subject(s): Christmas; Animals; Werewolves
Time period(s): 2000s

Summary: Veteran authors Christine Feehan and Susan Sizemore join forces to provide a Christmas anthology that is not an ordinary holiday read. Although both novellas focus on animals and each has a uniquely gifted veterinarian heroine, each author adds her own paranormal twist for different, but equally rewarding, results. In Feehan's heartwarming *Rocky Mountain Miracle*, an empathic veterinarian who can link minds with animals is snowbound with two feuding brothers and ends up healing more than the horses. Sizemore's unusual *A Touch of Harry*, concerns a veterinarian who takes in a tranquilized wolf who is not what he seems, and finds love and fulfillment where she least expects it.

Where it's reviewed:
Library Journal, November 15, 2004, page 47
Romantic Times, November 2004, page 128

Other books by the same author:
The Twilight Before Christmas, 2003 (Christmas fantasy)

Other books you might like:
Janet Chapman, *Wedding the Highlander*, 2003
    Christmas magic of a different kind
Linda Howard, *Christmas Kisses*, 1996
Sherrilyn Kenyon, *Stroke of Midnight*, 2004
    paranormal anthology
Susan Krinard, *Prince of Shadows*, 1996
    werewolf

263

JO ANN FERGUSON

The Perfect Bride

(New York: Zebra, 2004)

Story type: Regency
Subject(s): Courtship; Sisters
Major character(s): Bianca Dunsworthy, Gentlewoman; Lucian Wandersee, Nobleman (earl)
Time period(s): 1810s
Locale(s): London, England; Dunstonbury, England

Summary: Her discovery of a wounded nobleman outside her cottage inspires Bianca Dunsworthy to play matchmaker between the nobleman who turns out to be Lucian, the Earl of Wandersee, and Bianca's shy younger sister Primrose. While Lucian appreciates the fact that Bianca has taken him into her home and cared for his wounds, he really has no romantic interest at all in Primrose. To distract Bianca from her plan,

Lucian tries a bit of matchmaking of his own, only to find that he doesn't want to pair Bianca up with any man but himself.

Where it's reviewed:
Booklist, September 15, 2004, page 218
Romantic Times, October 2004, page 50

Other books by the same author:
Digging Up Trouble, 2004
Lord Pierson Reforms, 2004
Faire Game, 2003
Grave Intentions, 2003
Greatest Possible Mischief, 2003

Other books you might like:
Susannah Carleton, *A Scandalous Journey*, 2002
Valerie King, *A Country Flirtation*, 1998
Debbie Raleigh, *Lord Carlton's Courtship*, 2000
Donna Simpson, *A Rake's Redemption*, 2002
Rhonda Woodward, *A Hint of Scandal*, 2003

264

AMY J. FETZER

Tell It to the Marines
(New York: Brava, 2004)

Story type: Contemporary
Subject(s): Military Life; Adventure and Adventurers; Sexuality
Time period(s): 2000s

Summary: This trio of super sexy stories by Fetzer features tough, courageous, heroic Marines who have been sent to exotic locales to rescue their heroines from danger, only to find themselves in danger of a different kind. Brave, resourceful heroines are definitely the equals of their would-be rescuers in this fast-paced, set of adventures. Included are "Hot Conflict," "Landing Zone," and "Hot Target."

Where it's reviewed:
Romantic Times, December 2004, page 49

Other books by the same author:
Alias, 2004 (Silhouette Bombshell)
The Irish Knight, 2002
Taming the Beast, 2001
The Irish Enchantress, 2001
Renegade Heart, 2000

Other books you might like:
Robyn Amos, *Hero at Large*, 2000
    Year of Living Dangerously. Book 5
Suzanne Brockmann, *Over the Edge*, 2001
    military adventure
Judith Leon, *Code Name: Dove*, 2003
    Silhouette Bombshell
Merline Lovelace, *The Spy Who Loved Him*, 2001
    Year of Living Dangerously. Book 7
Lindsay McKenna, *First Born*, 2004

265

FLO FITZPATRICK

Ghost of a Chance
(New York: Zebra, 2004)

Story type: Contemporary; Romantic Suspense
Subject(s): Ghosts; Theater; Plays
Major character(s): Kiely Davlin, Dancer (choreographer); Rafe Montez, Actor; Don Mueller, Spirit, Actor (former)
Time period(s): 2000s
Locale(s): Dallas, Texas

Summary: As a favor to an old friend, and lured by the promise of real Tex-Mex and single, straight men, dancer and choreographer Kiely Davlin goes to Dallas to help with the revival of an old melodrama, *Bad Business on the Brazos*. Kiely ends up in a haunted theatre with a ghost that only she can see. Sexy Rafe Montez adds zing to this funny, sometimes wacky, romance that features a cast of unique characters and a real murder mystery.

Where it's reviewed:
Library Journal, August 2004, page 55
Romantic Times, August 2004, page 118

Other books you might like:
Alice Alfonsi, *Eternal Love*, 1998
    ghosts and some fun
Emily Carmichael, *A Ghost for Maggie*, 1999
    humor and more ghosts
Judi McCoy, *You're the One*, 1992
    ghostly humor and an old murder
Angie Ray, *Ghost of My Dreams*, 1996
Antoinette Stockenberg, *Emily's Ghost*, 1992

266

JACEY FORD (Pseudonym of Beverly Brandt)

Dangerous Curves
(New York: Berkley Sensation, 2004)

Story type: Contemporary; Romantic Suspense
Subject(s): Suspense; Murder; Loyalty
Major character(s): Raine Robey, Businesswoman (security company co-owner), Computer Expert; Calder Preston, FBI Agent, Lover (Raine's former)
Time period(s): 2000s
Locale(s): Atlanta, Georgia

Summary: Leaving the FBI when she comes under suspicion of murder, computer expert Raine Robey and two other former FBI agents form their own corporate security company, Partners in Crime. Struggling to make ends meet, Raine reluctantly accepts an unofficial job from her old boss and former lover, Calder Preston, and ends up involved in an investigation that is far more dangerous than she had ever imagined—and far more romantic, as well. Car theft, kidnappings, murder, and a killer with a technological bent combine in this chilling, fast-paced adventure. First novel under the pseudonym Jacey Ford by romance novelist Beverly Brandt.

Where it's reviewed:
Rendezvous, June 2004, page 27

Romantic Times, June 2004, page 123

Other books you might like:
Jasmine Cresswell, *Decoy*, 2004
Christiane Heggan, *Scent of a Killer*, 2004
Lisa Jackson, *The Morning After*, 2004
Merline Lovelace, *Call of Duty*, 1998
Mariah Stewart, *Dead Wrong*, 2004

267

LORI FOSTER

Just a Hint—Clint

(New York: Kensington, 2004)

Story type: Romantic Suspense; Humor
Series: Visitation. Book 4
Subject(s): Suspense; Humor; Kidnapping
Major character(s): Julie Rose, Heiress, Crime Victim (kidnapped); Clint Evans, Mercenary, Hero
Time period(s): 2000s
Locale(s): Cincinnati, Ohio

Summary: Four kidnappers are holding Julie Rose hostage in a remote cabin. They've abused her, and now they're going to rape her before they kill her. Suddenly an unarmed man walks into their camp, picking off the kidnappers as effortlessly as if they were pieces of lint. Julie has no idea why she's been kidnapped, and her rescuer, Clint Evans, is determined to find out. An imperfect woman and a flawed man make the perfect couple in this sexy, often humorous romantic suspense.

Where it's reviewed:
Booklist, October 1, 2004, page 316
Romantic Times, October 2004, page 89

Other books by the same author:
The Secret Life of Bryan, 2004
When Bruce Met Cyn. . ., 2004
Say No to Joe, 2003
Unexpected, 2003
Never Too Much, 2002

Other books you might like:
Susan Andersen, *All Shook Up*, 2001
Gena Hale, *Sun Valley*, 2002
Harley Jane Kozak, *Dating Is Murder*, 2005
Jayne Ann Krentz, *Eclipse Bay*, 2000
Vicki Lewis Thompson, *The Nerd Who Loved Me*, 2004

268

BARBARA FREETHY

All She Ever Wanted

(New York: Signet, 2004)

Story type: Contemporary; Romantic Suspense
Subject(s): Murder; Friendship; Mystery
Major character(s): Natalie Bishop, Doctor; Cole Parish, Editor (newspaper)
Time period(s): 2000s
Locale(s): San Francisco, California

Summary: Shocked when a popular novel is published that seems to tell the exact story of the death of one of her sorority sisters and then implicates her as the killer, medical resident Natalie Bishop is determined to get to the bottom of things. With the help of Cole Parish, the brother of the girl who died and her first love, she does just that. Emotionally involving and intellectually satisfying.

Where it's reviewed:
Romantic Times, December 2004, page 118

Other books by the same author:
Golden Lies, 2004
Summer Secrets, 2003
Love Will Find a Way, 2002
Some Kind of Wonderful, 2001
Almost Home, 2000

Other books you might like:
Georgia Bockoven, *Things Remembered*, 1998
 reunions
Barbara Bretton, *At Last*, 2000
 reunions
Sandra Brown, *Breath of Scandal*, 1996
Luanne Jones, *Sweethearts of the Twilight Lanes*, 2001
Erica Spindler, *Shocking Pink*, 2001

269

MONA GEDNEY

The Affair at Greengage Manor

(New York: Zebra, 2004)

Story type: Regency
Subject(s): Children; Reunions; Courtship
Major character(s): Alexandra Lytton, Gentlewoman, Governess; Richard Browning, Gentleman, Guardian (of five children)
Time period(s): 1810s
Locale(s): England

Summary: When Alexandra's carriage is held up and one of the highwaymen is wounded and turns out to be a young boy, Alexandra discovers that he is the eldest of five orphaned children. She sets out to help them find their uncle who is supposed to be their guardian. Of course, their orderly, proper uncle, Richard Browning, knows nothing of this. Once the shock has worn off after Alexandra and the five children appear at his door, he knows that his life is about to change— a lot. A spoiled fiancee adds interest to this light, lively Regency that does a nice job with a standard plot.

Where it's reviewed:
Library Journal, August 2004, page 55
Romantic Times, August 2004, page 47

Other books by the same author:
A Love Affair for Lizzie, 2004
On the Twelfth Day of Christmas, 2004
An Icy Affair, 2002
Lady Hilary's Halloween, 2001
A Dangerous Arrangement, 1998

Other books you might like:
Catherine Blair, *A Family for Gillian*, 2001

Monique Ellis, *An Uncommon Governess*, 1998
Victoria Hinshaw, *Cordelia's Corinthian*, 2004
Kate Huntington, *Mistletoe Mayhem*, 2000
    holiday theme
Evelyn Richardson, *The Gallant Guardian*, 1998

270

MONA GEDNEY

On the Twelfth Day of Christmas

(New York: Zebra, 2004)

Story type: Regency; Holiday Themes
Subject(s): Holidays; Reunions; Courtship
Major character(s): Violet Leigh, Gentlewoman; Travis Halliday, Gentleman
Time period(s): 1810s
Locale(s): England

Summary: Resigned to the fact that she is tall, dark, and plain—unlike the rest of her beautiful family—Violet Leigh is caught off guard when she is wooed by the handsome and highly eligible Travis Halliday. When gossips whisper that he is simply in the market for a rich wife, she abruptly declines his offer. Thus spurned, he heads for the West Indies and out of her life. Now, two years later, he is back, and Violet comes face to face with him during the Christmas holidays at a country house party—with lively results. A mischievous monkey, a persistent unwanted suitor, a spoiled, mean-spirited other woman, and a host of other supporting characters add to this holiday romp that takes at least one unexpected twist.

Where it's reviewed:
Rendezvous, October 2004, page 35
Romantic Times, October 2004, page 50

Other books by the same author:
A Love Affair for Lizzie, 2004
The Affair at Greengage Manor, 2004
An Icy Affair, 2002
Lady Diana's Daring Deed, 2000
A Dangerous Arrangement, 1998

Other books you might like:
Diane Farr, *Once upon a Christmas*, 2000
Paula Tanner Girard, *A Father for Christmas*, 1996
Kate Huntington, *Mistletoe Mayhem*, 2000
Kate Huntington, *A Rogue for Christmas*, 2001
Donna Simpson, *A Matchmaker's Christmas*, 2002

271

GEORGINA GENTRY (Pseudonym of Lynne Murphy)

To Tempt a Texan

(New York: Kensington, 2005)

Story type: Historical/American West; Humor
Subject(s): Humor; American West; Saloons
Major character(s): Lacey Van Schuyler Durango, Journalist, Editor (*Crusader*); Blackie O'Neal, Saloon Keeper/Owner, Rake
Time period(s): 19th century

Locale(s): Whiskey Flats, Oklahoma; Pretty Prairie, Oklahoma

Summary: They are as different as night and day. Blackie O'Neal is a rascally saloon owner who supported the South. Lacey Van Schuyler Durango, a Union sympathizer who owns and edits the *Crusader*, is an ardent reformer pushing for temperance. Lacey wants to change the name of their town to Pretty Prairie. Blackie prefers Whiskey Flats, and they even hold an election over this issue. The main thing that Lacey and Blackie are clashing over is a prime piece of Oklahoma land. Blackie will stop at nothing to get this property away from "damnyankee Iron Corset," and vice versa. The Battle of the Sexes was never so much fun.

Where it's reviewed:
Romantic Times, February 2005, page 34

Other books by the same author:
To Tame a Rebel, 2004
To Tame a Texan, 2003
To Tame a Savage, 2002
Warrior's Heart, 2001
Apache Tears, 1999

Other books you might like:
Lorraine Heath, *Hard Lovin' Man*, 2003
Constance O'Banyon, *Heart of Texas*, 2004
Maggie Osborne, *Shotgun Wedding*, 2003
Bobbi Smith, *Brazen*, 2004
Jodi Thomas, *To Wed in Texas*, 1999

272

RACHEL GIBSON

The Trouble with Valentine's Day

(New York: Avon, 2005)

Story type: Contemporary; Humor
Subject(s): Trust; Guilt; Small Town Life
Major character(s): Kate Hamilton, Detective—Private; Rob Sutter, Businessman
Time period(s): 2000s
Locale(s): Gospel, Idaho

Summary: Private detective Kate Hamilton, en route to her grandfather's house in Gospel, Idaho, for some much needed R-and-R, stops at a ski lodge in Sun Valley. On a whim, and for the first time, Kate tries to pick up a guy in the bar. Much to her horror, he not only soundly rejects her, but also gives her a lecture. When Kate gets to her grandfather's house, his friend, Rob Sutter, turns out to be none other than the hunk from the bar. Kate prays that Rob won't share the story of their encounter. She's also determined to prove to Rob that she's not a bimbo, something that's even harder than it sounds.

Where it's reviewed:
Romantic Times, February 2005, page 97

Other books by the same author:
Daisy's Back in Town, 2004
See Jane Score, 2003
Lola Carlyle Reveals All, 2002
True Confessions, 2001

Truly, Madly Yours, 1999

Other books you might like:
Jane Blackwood, *A Hard Man Is Good to Find*, 2004
Gena Hale, *Sun Valley*, 2002
Harley Jane Kozak, *Dating Dead Men*, 2004
Suzann Ledbetter, *South of Sanity*, 2001
Sandi Kahn Shelton, *What Comes After Crazy*, 2005

273

JO GOODMAN (Pseudonym of Joanne Dobrzanski)

Beyond a Wicked Kiss
(New York: Zebra, 2004)

Story type: Historical/Regency; Romantic Suspense
Series: Compass Club. Book 4
Subject(s): Mystery; Spies
Major character(s): Ria Ashby, Teacher (headmistress, girls' school), Ward; Evan "West" Marchman, Nobleman (Duke of Westphal), Guardian
Time period(s): 1790s (1798); 1810s (1818)
Locale(s): England

Summary: When Evan Marchman unexpectedly becomes the Duke of Westphal, he not only acquires the substantial responsibilities of the estate, he also gains a lovely 24-year-old ward! Ria Ashby is a ward with a problem. One of the girls from the school where she is headmistress is missing and she badly needs West's help. West, always a spy at heart, obliges; and thus begins a dangerous and romantic adventure that takes them into the coils of the secret society, now led by men who, as boys, were the archenemies of the Compass Club years earlier. Although this story nicely stands on its own, readers will probably want to read the stories in order since this one does complete the quartet. Politics, intrigue, and suspense add to this fast-paced, sensual adventure.

Where it's reviewed:
Romantic Times, August 2004, page 42

Other books by the same author:
All I Ever Needed, 2003 (Compass Club. Book 3)
Everything I Wanted, 2003 (Compass Club. Book 2)
Let Me Be the One, 2002 (Compass Club. Book 1)
More than You Wished, 2001
Tempting Torment, 2001

Other books you might like:
Jo Beverley, *Forbidden Magic*, 1998
Lynn Kerstan, *Dangerous Deceptions*, 2004
   Black Phoenix. Book 1
Lynn Kerstan, *Heart of the Tiger*, 2003
   Cat. Book 2
Stephanie Laurens, *The Lady Chosen*, 2003
   Bastion Club. Book 1
Stephanie Laurens, *The Perfect Lover*, 2003

274

SUSAN GRANT

The Scarlet Empress
(New York: Love Spell, 2004)

Story type: Futuristic
Series: 2176. Book 5
Subject(s): Politics; Adventure and Adventurers; Futuristic Fiction
Major character(s): Bree "Banzai" Maguire, Military Personnel (U.S. Air Force captain), Pilot; Cameron "Scarlet" Tucker, Military Personnel (U.S. Air Force), Pilot
Time period(s): 22nd century (2176)
Locale(s): Earth

Summary: In this, the final installment of this riveting series, Banzai's partner, Cam Tucker, is captured by a pair of Rim Riders and taken back to the city and Prince Kyber. Of course, Cam has no idea that the rugged rider she had gotten to know and like on the trip back is actually the prince in disguise. Cam's main goal is to find Banzai, and it is one that leads her into greater danger than she had ever imagined. Politics, lots of action, and romance are here in full measure.

Where it's reviewed:
Romantic Times, December 2004, page 124

Other books by the same author:
The Legend of Banzai Maguire, 2004 (2176. Book 1)
The Star Princess, 2003
Contact, 2002
The Star Prince, 2001
Once a Pirate, 2000

Other books you might like:
Megan Sybil Baker, *An Accidental Goddess*, 2002
Justine Davis, *Lord of the Storm*, 1994
Liz Maverick, *The Shadow Runners*, 2004
Kathleen Nance, *Day of Fire*, 2004
   2176. Book 2
Patti O'Shea, *The Power of Two*, 2004
   2176. Book 4

275

PATRICIA GRASSO

To Love a Princess
(New York: Zebra, 2004)

Story type: Historical/Regency; Gothic
Subject(s): Marriage
Major character(s): Amber Kazanov, Royalty (princess), Bastard Daughter (of the czar); Miles Montgomery, Nobleman (Earl of Stratford)
Time period(s): 1820s
Locale(s): England; Russia

Summary: When she learns of her uncle's plans to marry her off to a slave trader who plans to breed her with one of his own slaves and then sell their babies, Amber Kazanov flees Russia and seeks shelter with her cousin, Prince Rudolf Kazanov in London. Knowing she will never be safe unless she marries, she enlists the aid of Rudolf, who knows of just the man for her. However, Miles Montgomery is still in love with his late wife and, although he needs an heir, he's wary of marriage—partly because of facial scars from the fire that killed his wife. Amber sees through the scars to the wounded man beneath and eventually they put the past behind them and find love.

Where it's reviewed:
Romantic Times, November 2004, page 41

Other books by the same author:
To Catch a Countess, 2004 (Douglas Sisters. Book 3)
To Charm a Prince, 2003 (Douglas Sisters. Book 2)
To Tame an Angel, 2002 (Douglas Sisters. Book 1)
To Tame a Duke, 2001
Violets in the Snow, 1998

Other books you might like:
Gabriella Anderson, *Forever Yours*, 2003
Susan Carroll, *The Bride Finder*, 1998
Christina Dodd, *Move Heaven and Earth*, 2003
Candice Hern, *The Bride Sale*, 2002
Stephanie Laurens, *On a Wicked Dawn*, 2002

276

JANE GRAVES

Light My Fire
(New York: Ivy, 2004)

Story type: Contemporary; Romantic Suspense
Series: DeMarco Brothers. Book 4
Subject(s): Murder; Guilt
Major character(s): Sandy DeMarco, Store Owner (florist); Ethan Millner, Lawyer
Time period(s): 2000s
Locale(s): Tolosa, Texas

Summary: Defense attorney Ethan Millner, a clever, hotshot lawyer who's made an art of defending the guilty and winning, smashes his car, barely misses a DUI conviction, and ends up with a reckless driving charge. The judge sentences him to 40 hours of community service on a neighborhood crime-watch patrol so he can see the other side of things. That, of course, is bad enough; but when his partner turns out to be Sandy DeMarco, ardent crime-watch supporter and from a family of cops, he knows this is going to be no picnic. When they find a body on one of their rounds and the chief suspect turns out to be Sandy's assistant, things take an interesting new twist as Ethan goes to his defense—and riles a number of people in the process. Murder, humor, and passion.

Where it's reviewed:
Rendezvous, November 2004, page 28
Romantic Times, November 2004, page 121

Other books by the same author:
Flirting with Disaster, 2003 (DeMarco Brothers. Book 3)
Wild at Heart, 2002 (DeMarco Brothers. Book 2)
I Got You, Babe, 2001 (DeMarco Brothers. Book 1)

Other books you might like:
Susan Andersen, *Head over Heels*, 2002
Susan Andersen, *Hot and Bothered*, 2004
Rachel Gibson, *It Must Be Love*, 2000

Linda Howard, *Open Season*, 2001
suspense/not necessarily funny
JoAnn Ross, *Magnolia Moon*, 2003
Callahan Brothers Trilogy. Book 3

277

CARMEN GREEN

Kissed
(New York: Dafina, 2004)

Story type: Contemporary; Multicultural
Subject(s): African Americans; Marriage; Work
Major character(s): Cheryl Crawford, Spouse (of an ambassador), Teacher; Justin Crawford, Diplomat (ambassador)
Time period(s): 2000s
Locale(s): Ecuador; United States

Summary: A successful ambassador's commitment to his work causes his wife to pursue her own dreams—and they don't necessarily include him. Justin is determined to win Cheryl back, but with an old boyfriend appearing on the scene and Justin's job in jeopardy, it will take all of his considerable abilities—and a fair amount of soul searching—to accomplish his goal. Another of Green's stories about the Crawfords.

Other books by the same author:
Doctor, Doctor, 2002
Island Bliss, 2002
Endless Love, 2000
Keeping Secrets, 1998
Silken Love, 1997

Other books you might like:
Rochelle Alers, *Private Passions*, 2001
Donna Hill, *Say Yes*, 2004
Donna Hill, *A Scandalous Affair*, 2000
Candice Poarch, *Bargain of the Heart*, 2002
Tracey Tillis, *Flashpoint*, 1997

278

JENNIFER GREENE (Pseudonym of Alison Hart)

Wild in the Moment
(New York: Silhouette, 2004)

Story type: Contemporary
Subject(s): Family; Small Town Life
Major character(s): Daisy Campbell, Divorced Person; Teague Larson, Carpenter, Contractor
Time period(s): 2000s
Locale(s): White Hills, Vermont

Summary: Daisy Campbell has rotten luck when it comes to men. So when a blizzard strands Daisy with a sexy stranger, she tries very hard to resist her natural inclination to indulge in a one night fling. Temptation wins out though and Daisy and the stranger, who turns out to be Teague Larson, give into their desire for each other. Neither Daisy nor Teague expect their brief affair to last, so both of them are quite surprised when their wild moment of passion turns into a permanent kind of love.

Where it's reviewed:
Romantic Times, December 2004, page 98

Other books by the same author:
Wild in the Moonlight, 2004
Where Is He Now?, 2003
Wild in the Field, 2003
Woman Most Likely To, 2002
Rock Solid, 2001

Other books you might like:
Elizabeth Bevarly, *The Secret Life of Connor Monahan*, 2001
Patricia Coughlin, *Tall, Dark, and Difficult*, 2001
Kathleen Korbel, *Some Men's Dreams*, 2003
Barbara McCauley, *Reese's Wild Wager*, 2001
Ruth Wind, *Beautiful Stranger*, 2000

279

JENNIFER GREENE (Pseudonym of Alison Hart)

Wild in the Moonlight
(New York: Silhouette, 2004)

Story type: Contemporary
Series: Scent of Lavender. Book 2
Subject(s): Farm Life; Sisters
Major character(s): Violet Campbell, Businesswoman (Herb Haven); Cameron Lachlan, Scientist (agricultural chemist)
Time period(s): 2000s
Locale(s): White Hills, Vermont

Summary: Cameron Lachlan wants Violet Campbell's lavender. Violet has developed several new strains of the herb that Cameron's employer, the French perfume company Jeunesse, wants for their products, and Cameron intends on talking Violet into selling her rights to him. While Cameron may have begun negotiations with Violet thinking he is only interested in her lavender, the more he gets to know the surprisingly complex Violet, the more he realizes lavender isn't the only thing he desires.

Where it's reviewed:
Romantic Times, June 2004, page 103

Other books by the same author:
Where Is He Now?, 2003
Wild in the Field, 2003
Woman Most Likely To, 2002
Millionaire M.D., 2001
Rock Solid, 2001

Other books you might like:
Elizabeth Bevarly, *The Secret Life of Connor Monahan*, 2001
Patricia Coughlin, *The Cupcake Queen*, 2002
Kristin Gabriel, *Send Me No Flowers*, 1999
Charlotte Maclay, *Courting Cupid*, 1999
Ruth Wind, *Beautiful Stranger*, 2000

280

MARIA GREENE

Captain Hawkins' Dilemma
(New York: Zebra, 2004)

Story type: Regency
Subject(s): Courtship; Inheritance; Marriage
Major character(s): Eliza Lytton, Gentlewoman, Scholar (bluestocking); Leo Hawkins, Military Personnel (captain), Nobleman (son of a viscount)
Time period(s): 1810s
Locale(s): England

Summary: Knowing that she must marry in order to gain her inheritance, but not about to wed the dull, chauvinistic, older man who is pursuing her, intelligent, fiery Eliza Lytton decides to head north and deliver her father's 15 years worth of Egyptian research notes to her uncle who lives in the Lake District. Of course, she needs a man to guard her and her companions on the trip. When she advertises for an ''unattached gentleman,'' Captain Leo Hawkins applies and the stage is set for a lively, funny, romantic romp that sweeps its characters through some singularly picturesque country.

Where it's reviewed:
Romantic Times, August 2004, page 47

Other books by the same author:
Double Deception, 2004
Lord Sandhurst's Surprise, 2003
The Ashcroft Curse, 2003
A Christmas Blessing, 2002
The Ghost and Mrs. Wenthaven, 2002

Other books you might like:
Lynn Kerstan, *Francesca's Rake*, 1992
Valerie King, *My Lady Valiant*, 2002
    more traveling togetherness
Jennifer Malin, *Lord St. Leger's Find*, 2003
Joan Overfield, *The Viscount's Vixen*, 1992

281

AMELIA GREY (Pseudonym of Gloria Dale Skinner)

A Hint of Seduction
(New York: Berkley Sensation, 2004)

Story type: Historical/Regency
Subject(s): Courtship; Mystery
Major character(s): Catherine Reynolds, Debutante, Gentlewoman; John Wickenham-Thickenham-Fines, Nobleman (Earl of Chatwin)
Time period(s): 1810s
Locale(s): London, England

Summary: Publicly in London for the Season, but actually there to locate her real father, Catherine Reynolds gets things off to a rousing start by being thrown from her horse. She then ''borrows'' the horse of the wickedly attractive Earl of Chatwin, the man who caused her horse to rear in the first place. Naturally, the earl wants his horse back; but even more, he wants to find the lovely hoyden who stole it. A lively story filled with wit, adventure, and romance set during the glittering Regency Period.

Where it's reviewed:
Rendezvous, August 2004, page 19
Romantic Times, September 2004, page 39

Other books by the same author:
A Little Mischief, 2003
Never a Bride, 2001

Other books you might like:
Loretta Chase, *The Last Hellion*, 1998
Candice Hern, *Once a Scoundrel*, 2003
Amanda Quick, *Reckless*, 2000
Amanda Quick, *Scandal*, 1991
Julia Quinn, *The Viscount Who Loved Me*, 2000

282

DEBORAH HALE

Highland Rogue

(Toronto: Harlequin, 2004)

Story type: Historical/Victorian
Subject(s): Secrets; Sisters
Major character(s): Claire Brancaster Talbot, Businesswoman, Heiress; Ewan Geddes, Businessman
Time period(s): 1870s (1875)
Locale(s): London, England; South Carolina

Summary: Claire Brancaster Talbot is convinced that the American stranger courting her naive half-sister Tessa is nothing but a fortune hunter. So Claire decides to present the cad with a more tempting target: herself. When Claire finally meets Tessa's new beau, she discovers he is none other than Ewan Geddes, a former servant at her family's Scottish estate. Now the only flaw in Claire's plan is that she is no longer certain if she is really trying to keep Tessa safe from Ewan or if she is trying to keep Ewan for herself.

Where it's reviewed:
Booklist, October 1, 2004, page 316
Romantic Times, October 2004, page 46

Other books by the same author:
The Last Champion, 2004
The Wizard's Ward, 2004
Beauty and the Baron, 2003
Lady Lyte's Little Secret, 2003
Border Bride, 2002

Other books you might like:
Christina Dodd, *In My Wildest Dreams*, 2001
Susan King, *Taming the Heiress*, 2003
Constance Laux, *Diamond Rain*, 1999
Julianne MacLean, *To Marry the Duke*, 2003
Patricia Waddell, *The Lady's Proposal*, 2001

283

LORI HANDELAND

Blue Moon

(New York: St. Martin's Paperbacks, 2004)

Story type: Contemporary; Paranormal
Subject(s): Werewolves; Humor
Major character(s): Jessie McQuade, Police Officer; Will Cadotte, Professor (Native American totem expert), Werewolf; Edward Mandenauer, Hunter (jager-sucher & werewolf hunter)
Time period(s): 2000s
Locale(s): Miniwa, Wisconsin (north woods)

Summary: A rash of strange wolf attacks near the small north woods town of Miniwa shatters the peace of police officer Jessie McQuade's existence. When a noted wolf hunter, the obsessed Edward Mandenauer, arrives to help track the rogue wolves down—and she is assigned to help him—things go from bad to worse for Jessie. Then there is sexy Will Cadotte, an Ojibwe professor of American Indian culture and expert on totems, who is much more than he seems. Lively humor nicely intertwines with the paranormal in this highly sensual romance that is likely the beginning of a werewolf series.

Where it's reviewed:
Rendezvous, October 2004, page 42
Romantic Times, October 2004, page 30

Other books you might like:
Christine Feehan, *Dark Melody*, 2003
  vampires
Sherrilyn Kenyon, *Night Pleasures*, 2002
Susan Krinard, *Prince of Shadows*, 1996
  werewolves
Lynsay Sands, *Single White Vampire*, 2003
  humor and vampires
Maggie Shayne, *Twilight Hunger*, 2002

284

KRISTIN HARDY (Pseudonym of Kristin Lewotsky)

Turn Me On

(Toronto: Harlequin, 2004)

Story type: Contemporary
Subject(s): Seduction; Television
Major character(s): Sabrina Pantolini, Producer; Stefos Costas, Director
Time period(s): 2000s
Locale(s): Los Angeles, California; New York, New York; Chicago, Illinois

Summary: Sabrina Pantolini knows her new cable documentary series ''True Sex'' will be the hottest thing on television, but then she loses her director just as the pilot is about to be filmed. When Stef Costas offers to be her new director, Sabrina reluctantly accepts since she still isn't completely convinced that either one of them is over their brief, but memorable, affair from eight years ago. Sabrina wants to believe that she can keep their new relationship strictly business, but working with Stef soon convinces her that they might not be romantically through with each other just yet.

Where it's reviewed:
Romantic Times, August 2004, page 97

Other books by the same author:
As Bad as Can Be, 2003
Scoring, 2003
Slippery When Wet, 2003
My Sexiest Mistake, 2002

Other books you might like:
Jamie Denton, *Sleeping with the Enemy*, 2002
Alison Kent, *Bound to Happen*, 2002
Joanne Rock, *Girl's Guide to Hunting and Kissing*, 2003
Vicki Lewis Thompson, *Truly, Madly, Deeply*, 2002
Cathy Yardley, *Working It*, 2003

285

KAREN HARPER

Dark Harvest

(Don Mills, Ontario: MIRA, 2004)

Story type: Contemporary; Romantic Suspense
Series: Maplecreek. Book 2
Subject(s): Amish; Prejudice; Cultural Conflict
Major character(s): Kat Lindley, Imposter (posing as an Amish woman), Police Officer (undercover); Luke Brand, Widow(er), Farmer (Amish)
Time period(s): 2000s
Locale(s): Maplecreek, Ohio

Summary: Severely wounded by the crazed father of an abused child she had tried unsuccessfully to save, recovering cop Kat Lindley heads for rural Maplecreek, Ohio, to heal. When the local Amish community becomes the target of a series of violent hate crimes, Kat goes undercover as Katie Kurtz and, in addition to the inevitable violence and danger, finds a love and a sense of belonging she had never expected. Fast-paced, intriguing, and filled with cultural details about the Amish.

Where it's reviewed:
Rendezvous, May 2004, page 33
Romantic Times, June 2004, page 124

Other books by the same author:
The Baby Farm, 1999
The Empty Cradle, 1998
Black Orchid, 1996
Dark Road Home, 1996
Wings of the Morning, 1993

Other books you might like:
Annette Blair, *Thee I Love*, 1999
Sharon da Vita, *The Marriage Promise*, 2000
Tami Hoag, *Still Waters*, 1996
   Amish setting—suspense
Jessamyn West, *The Friendly Persuasion*, 1945
Penelope Williamson, *The Outsider*, 1996

286

SHIRLEY HARRISON

The Pleasure Principle

(Washington, D.C.: BET, 2004)

Story type: Contemporary; Multicultural
Subject(s): African Americans; Mystery; Reunions
Major character(s): Natalie Goodman, Accountant (CPA); David Spenser, Lawyer
Time period(s): 2000s
Locale(s): Atlanta, Georgia

Summary: CPA Natalie Goodman and attorney David Spenser renew their past relationship with quite romantic results when he returns to Atlanta for a family visit. David helps Natalie when she ends up the target of a firm she's been auditing—a firm that has a lot to hide. Sensual.

Where it's reviewed:
Romantic Times, May 2004, page 108

Other books by the same author:
The Proposition, 2002
Dangerous Fortune, 2001

Other books you might like:
Rochelle Alers, *Just Before Dawn*, 2000
Donna Hill, *A Scandalous Affair*, 2000
Linda Hudson-Smith, *Sass*, 2003
Candice Poarch, *Tender Escape*, 2000
Angela Winters, *Sudden Love*, 2000

287

SHIRLEY HARRISON

Sweet Justice

(Washington, D.C.: BET, 2004)

Story type: Contemporary; Multicultural
Subject(s): African Americans; Murder; Trust
Major character(s): Aislyn St. Clair, Television Personality (interview show host); Eric Morgan, Businessman, Real Estate Agent
Time period(s): 2000s
Locale(s): Georgia

Summary: When Aislyn St. Clair's friend and roommate Tamara Landry is found dead, it at first seems to be a simple accident. However, something just doesn't seem right, and as Aislyn searches further, she begins to think that her boyfriend's faithless brother might have been involved, a circumstance that places a lot of pressure on their growing relationship. Issues of trust and family are part of this sensual, suspenseful romance.

Where it's reviewed:
Rendezvous, October 2004, page 30
Romantic Times, November 2004, page 123

Other books by the same author:
The Pleasure Principle, 2004
The Proposition, 2002
Dangerous Fortune, 2001
Picture Perfect, 1999

Under a Blue Moon, 1999

Other books you might like:
Rochelle Alers, *No Compromise*, 2002
Leslie Esdaile, *Through the Storm*, 2002
Evelyn Palfrey, *Dangerous Dilemmas*, 2002
Candice Poarch, *Tender Escape*, 2000

288

LAUREN HENDERSON, Editor
CHRIS MANBY, Co-Editor
SARAH MLYNOWSKI, Co-Editor

Girls Night In
(New York: Red Dress Ink, 2004)

Story type: Contemporary; Anthology
Subject(s): Romance; Careers; Love
Time period(s): 2000s

Summary: This diverse collection of 21 short stories by some of chick lit's best known writers was put together as a fund-raising vehicle for War Child, a humanitarian organization that helps young victims of war. Contributing authors are: Meg Cabot, Carole Matthews, Alisa Valdes-Rodriguez, Sophie Kinsella, Jill A. Davis, Emily Barr, Jessica Adams, Sarah Mlynowski, Isabel Wolff, Lauren Henderson, Megan McCafferty, Louise Bagshawe, Lisa Jewell, Marian Keyes, Lynda Curnyn, Stella Duffy, Anna Maxted, Adele Lang, Jennifer Weiner, Jenny Colgan, and Chris Manby.

Where it's reviewed:
Romantic Times, September 2004, page 51

Other books you might like:
Carly Alexander, *The Eggnog Chronicles*, 2004
Lynda Curnyn, *Confessions of an Ex-Girlfriend*, 2001
Sarah Mlynowski, *Milkrun*, 2001
Melissa Senate, *See Jane Date*, 2001
Lori Soard, *The Lipstick Diaries*, 2004

289

VIRGINIA HENLEY

Insatiable
(New York: Signet, 2004)

Story type: Historical/Elizabethan; Paranormal
Subject(s): Psychic Powers; Courtship; Kings, Queens, Rulers, etc.
Major character(s): Catherine Seton Spencer, Noblewoman; Patrick Hepburn, Nobleman (Lord Stewart), Psychic
Time period(s): 17th century (1603)
Locale(s): London, England (court of Elizabeth I); Scotland

Summary: Patrick Hepburn is a psychic. Although King James used this Hepburn family gift as an excuse to label them "witches" and seize their lands, he relies on Patrick's "sight" for political gain. For the use of Patrick's gift, James promises him a landed English noblewoman of his choice. Patrick has seen visions of Cat Spencer, Queen Elizabeth I's talented but scandalous clothing designer. Cat refuses to believe that Patrick wants her for anything but her properties, and, against his advice, gets herself involved in court intrigue

that could be seen as treason. Dangerous liaisons and political machinations add to the thrills of this steamy historical, set in the final year of the powerful monarch.

Where it's reviewed:
Romantic Times, November 2004, page 37

Other books by the same author:
Bold Conquest, 2003
Undone, 2003
Ravished, 2002
The Border Hostage, 2001
The Marriage Prize, 2000

Other books you might like:
Denise Domning, *Lady in White*, 1999
Ruth Ryan Langan, *Conor*, 1999
May McGoldrick, *The Dreamer*, 2001
Tori Phillips, *One Knight in Venice*, 2001
Haywood Smith, *Border Lord*, 2001

290

CANDICE HERN

Her Scandalous Affair
(New York: Avon, 2005)

Story type: Historical/Regency
Subject(s): Stealing; Secrets; Romance
Major character(s): Lady Isabel Weymouth, Noblewoman; Richard Mallory, Nobleman (Viscount Mallory)
Time period(s): 1810s (1814)
Locale(s): England

Summary: Commanded by his grandmother to retrieve a ruby brooch, a family heirloom which has been missing for years, Viscount Richard Mallory heads for London where it has supposedly been seen. Startled to find the Mallory Heart so soon—and located on the bosom of the charming Lady Isabel Weymouth—Richard decides to steal it from her room. When Isabel, knowing it has always belonged to *her* grandmother, steals it back, the game is on; and as Richard and Isabel match wits, their hearts also become engaged. Old scandals and current danger combine in this well-written, cleverly-plotted story that explores the issue of true love versus social expectations, features appealing characters that touch the emotions, and delivers a satisfactory ending that neatly ties up all loose ends.

Where it's reviewed:
Romantic Times, December 2004, page 40

Other books by the same author:
Once a Gentleman, 2004 (Ladies' Fashionable Cabinet. Book 3)
Once a Dreamer, 2003 (Ladies' Fashionable Cabinet. Book 1)
Once a Scoundrel, 2003 (Ladies' Fashionable Cabinet. Book 2)
The Bride Sale, 2002
The Best Intentions, 1999

Other books you might like:
Mary Balogh, *Thief of Dreams*, 1998
Allison Lane, *A Clandestine Courtship*, 1998

Allison Lane, *Lord Avery's Legacy*, 1998
Mary Jo Putney, *One Perfect Rose*, 1997
Evelyn Richardson, *Fortune's Lady*, 2002

291

ANNE HERRIES (Pseudonym of Linda Sole)

A Wicked Wench

(New York: Severn House, 2004)

Story type: Historical/Georgian
Subject(s): Marriage
Major character(s): Arabella Tucker, Gentlewoman, Impoverished; Nan Tucker, Gentlewoman, Impoverished; Gervase Winston, Nobleman (Marquis of Roxbourne)
Time period(s): 1750s (1756)
Locale(s): London, England

Summary: Two gently-born, but impoverished, sisters come to London to find husbands and find romance, scandal, and, eventually, love as they negotiate the treacherous waters of the London social scene. A heroine who is a bit more saucy than she should be finds herself in deep trouble when the man of her dreams proves unworthy, and she ends up being rescued by a man she had rejected before. Realistic and romantic.

Where it's reviewed:
Booklist, June 1, 2004, page 1710

Other books by the same author:
A Damnable Rogue, 2003
A Matter of Honor, 2002
Captive of the Harem, 2002
The Sheikh, 2002
The Marriage Chests, 1993

Other books you might like:
Jo Beverley, *Tempting Fortune*, 1995
Christina Dodd, *A Well Pleasured Lady*, 1997
Jane Feather, *The Diamond Slipper*, 1997
Stephanie Laurens, *A Promise in a Kiss*, 2001
Kat Martin, *Innocence Undone*, 2001

292

DONNA HILL

Say Yes

(New York: Dafina, 2004)

Story type: Contemporary; Multicultural
Subject(s): African Americans
Major character(s): Regina Everette, Store Owner (bookstore), Divorced Person (mother of two); Parker Heywood, Artist, Teacher; Antoinette ''Toni'' Davis, Social Worker
Time period(s): 2000s
Locale(s): New York, New York

Summary: Things are finally coming together for Regina Everette. She is out of a loveless marriage, has opened her own bookstore, and has found a man she adores, Parker Heywood. Things begin to unravel when Gina's ex, as well as their children, want to put the marriage back together and Parker's teenage daughter, Tracy, comes to live with him and doesn't want Gina in her dad's life. Gina begins to wonder if she and

Parker will make it after all. Two additional romance plots (those of Gina's friends, Toni and Victoria) add depth to this book that explores some serious relationship issues. Sequel to *If I Could*.

Where it's reviewed:
Romantic Times, October 2004, page 101

Other books by the same author:
Getting Hers, 2005
In My Bedroom, 2005
Divas, Inc., 2004
An Ordinary Woman, 2003
If I Could, 2000

Other books you might like:
Rochelle Alers, *Lessons of a Low Country Summer*, 2004
   more mainstream
Rochelle Alers, *Rosie's Curl and Weave*, 1999
   anthology/includes a story by Hill
Sandra Kitt, *Family Affairs*, 2004
Francis Ray, *Like the First Time*, 2004
Kimberly White, *Forever After*, 2004

293

SANDRA HILL

Wet and Wild

(New York: Dorchester, 2004)

Story type: Humor; Time Travel
Series: Viking II. Book 4
Subject(s): Humor; Vikings; Time Travel
Major character(s): Alison MacLean, Military Personnel (lieutenant), Doctor; Ragnor Magnusson, Time Traveler, Warrior (Viking)
Time period(s): 11th century (1010); 2000s
Locale(s): Coronado Island, California; Norselands, Scandinavia

Summary: Navy Lieutenant Alison MacLean finds herself inexplicably drawn to SEAL trainee Torolf Magnusson. Considering she's surrounded by testosterone-laden males, she finds this odd and annoying. Torolf isn't Torolf, however. After an accident erases Torolf's memory, he goes AWOL, and his almost identical half-brother, Ragnor, is transported from the 11th-century Norselands to take his place. Humor abounds as Ragnor out-SEALs the SEALs and adjusts to life a thousand years in the future.

Where it's reviewed:
Romantic Times, October 2004, page 31

Other books by the same author:
A Tale of Two Vikings, 2004 (Viking I. Book 7)
The Cajun Cowboy, 2004
A Very Virile Viking, 2003 (Viking II. Book 3)
Frankly, My Dear, 2003
Tall, Dark, and Cajun, 2003

Other books you might like:
Connie Flynn, *The Dragon Hour*, 1996
Teresa Medeiros, *Breath of Magic*, 1996
Angie Ray, *A Knight to Cherish*, 1999
Eugenia Riley, *Bushwhacked Bride*, 1999

Christina Skye, *Christmas Knight*, 1998

294
VICTORIA HINSHAW

Cordelia's Corinthian
(New York: Zebra, 2004)

Story type: Regency
Subject(s): Courtship; Country Life; Children
Major character(s): Cordelia "Corey" Bransford, Gentlewoman (impoverished), Governess (by default); Lord Matthew Allerton, Nobleman, Military Personnel (captain)
Time period(s): 1810s
Locale(s): Dorset, England (Lodesham Hall)

Summary: Looking forward to a quiet, restful summer at her cousin's country estate before she is forced to look for a paid position in the fall in order to support her parents, Cordelia Bransford is surprised to find herself suddenly the de facto governess to her cousin's three young children when their nurse is called away. That isn't the only thing that disrupts her plans—the Quorn Quartet, a group of four men she knew in their wilder salad days, is gathering for a resumption of their boyhood angling contest, and Lord Matthew Allerton, the one of the group she was most attracted to, is with them and is determined to make Corey take his advances seriously. A hero trying to recover physically and emotionally from war, a heroine who is wary of casual flirtation and rakish charm, and a plethora of children and secondary characters make this a lighthearted Regency romp.

Where it's reviewed:
Romantic Times, May 2004, page 118

Other books by the same author:
An Ideal Match, 2004
The Eligible Miss Elliot, 2003
The Fontainbleau Fan, 2002

Other books you might like:
Catherine Blair, *A Family for Gillian*, 2001
Gail Eastwood, *The Persistent Earl*, 1995
Monique Ellis, *An Uncommon Governess*, 1998
Carla Kelly, *Mrs. Drew Plays Her Hand*, 1998
Evelyn Richardson, *The Gallant Guardian*, 1998

295
ALESIA HOLLIDAY

American Idle
(New York: Dorchester, 2004)

Story type: Contemporary; Humor
Subject(s): Television Programs; Humor
Major character(s): Jules Vernon, Television (production coordinator); Sam Blake, Carpenter
Time period(s): 2000s
Locale(s): Los Angeles, California (Hollywood area)

Summary: Being production coordinator of a new reality TV show sounds like the dream job to Jules Vernon—until she has to deal with all the difficult, oddball people associated with the program. Only quiet, sexy carpenter Sam Blake is different. He is like the calm in the storm and somehow he seems to be there whenever she needs him. Funny, fast-paced, and over-the-top at times, this hilarious contemporary takes dead-on potshots at the entertainment industry. This is an excellent first book in Dorchester's chick lit line, Making It.

Where it's reviewed:
Library Journal, August 2004, page 55
Romantic Times, August 2004, page 124

Other books by the same author:
Nice Girls Finish First, 2005

Other books you might like:
Jennifer Crusie, *Welcome to Temptation*, 2000
Rachel Gibson, *Truly, Madly Yours*, 1999
    lively humor
Kasey Michaels, *This Can't Be Love*, 2004
Lisa Plumley, *Perfect Switch*, 2004
    humor in the entertainment world
Lisa Plumley, *Perfect Together*, 2003
    humor in the entertainment world

296
EMMA HOLLY

The Demon's Daughter
(New York: Berkley, 2004)

Story type: Historical/Fantasy; Paranormal
Subject(s): Paranormal; Demons
Major character(s): Roxanne McAllister, Outcast, Bastard Daughter; Adrian Philips, Detective—Police (inspector), Cyborg
Time period(s): Indeterminate Past
Locale(s): Avvar, Fictional Country (Aedlyne Empire)

Summary: While on duty trying to keep the peace between the demons and humans of Avvar, Inspector Adrian Philips is wounded and ends up bleeding in Roxanne McAllister's roof garden. Roxanne nurses him back to health and they fall in love in the process. Although both are outcasts in their own ways—he because his strength is a result of demon technology, she because she is the illegitimate daughter of an infamous singer—it wouldn't be easy for them to be part of each other's worlds. Class issues, passion, and a fascinating world are part of this highly sensual romance that is both heartwarming and explicitly sexy.

Where it's reviewed:
Rendezvous, October 2004, page 38
Romantic Times, November 2004, page 47

Other books by the same author:
Catching Midnight, 2003
Hunting Midnight, 2003
Beyond Seduction, 2002
Beyond Innocence, 2001
In the Flesh, 2000

Other books you might like:
Christine Feehan, *Dark Symphony*, 2003
Angela Knight, *Master of the Moon*, 2005
Angela Knight, *Master of the Night*, 2004

Susan Sizemore, *I Thirst for You*, 2003

297

HANNAH HOWELL
LYNSAY SANDS, Co-Author

The Eternal Highlander

(New York: Kensington, 2004)

Story type: Historical/Medieval; Paranormal
Subject(s): Paranormal; Marriage
Time period(s): 15th century (1474-1476)
Locale(s): Scotland

Summary: This duet of two linked stories tells of two women who wed Highland cousins who need to marry outside their increasingly cursed supernatural race in order to ensure that their bloodline will continue. "Nightriders" by Hannah Howell starts things off with the story of Bridget Callan and Carthal MacNachton, and "The Highland Bride" by Lynsay Sands concludes things with Eva Caxton and Connall Mac-Adie. Passionate, violent, and compelling.

Where it's reviewed:
Library Journal, August 2004, page 55
Rendezvous, September 2004, page 21

Other books you might like:
Christine Feehan, *Dark Symphony*, 2003
    vampires/not historical
Sherrilyn Kenyon, *Night Pleasures*, 2002
Susan King, *Laird of the Wind*, 1998
Susan Krinard, *To Catch a Wolf*, 2003
Susan Krinard, *Touch of the Wolf*, 1999

298

KATE HUNTINGTON (Pseudonym of Kathy Chwedyk)

The General's Daughter

(New York: Zebra, 2004)

Story type: Regency
Subject(s): Courtship; Sisters
Major character(s): Marian Randall, Gentlewoman, Nurse; Adam Lyonbridge, Military Personnel (major)
Time period(s): 1810s (1812-1814)
Locale(s): Spain; Portugal; England

Summary: Marian Randall has spent most of her life nursing wounded English soldiers, but after her regimental surgeon father is killed, Marian discovers her real father is General Grimsby. The general insists that Marian give up her nursing duties, and he charges Major Adam Lyonbridge, who is engaged to Marian's new half sister Isabelle, with the task of accompanying his new daughter home. While traveling to England, Adam gradually learns more about Marian, only to discover that he would gladly trade his fiancee, Isabelle, for maddeningly stubborn, yet all too intriguing, Marian.

Where it's reviewed:
Romantic Times, April 2004, page 118

Other books by the same author:
His Lordship's Holiday Surprise, 2003

Town Bronze, 2003
The Merchant Prince, 2002
A Rogue for Christmas, 2001
Mistletoe Mayhem, 2000

Other books you might like:
Catherine Blair, *Athena's Conquest*, 2001
Wilma Counts, *The Willful Miss Winthrop*, 2000
Shannon Donnelly, *A Much Compromised Lady*, 2002
Evelyn Richardson, *Lord Harry's Daughter*, 2001
Donna Simpson, *Miss Truelove Beckons*, 2001

299

LISA JACKSON

See How She Dies

(New York: Zebra, 2004)

Story type: Contemporary; Romantic Suspense
Subject(s): Kidnapping; Inheritance; Family Relations
Major character(s): Adria Nash, Adoptee, Heiress—Lost (possible); Zachary Danvers, Wealthy, Contractor
Time period(s): 2000s
Locale(s): Portland, Oregon

Summary: When her adopted father dies and leaves her a tape telling her that he thinks she is actually London Danvers, the legendary heiress who was kidnapped as a child, Adria Nash heads for Oregon to discover who she really is. Of course, her half-siblings don't believe her; many have come forward claiming to be London over the years. There is something about Adria, however, that is different, making some of them wonder if she really could be London. Unfortunately, her mother's killer thinks she might be London, too, and is plotting a similar fate for her. Zachary Danvers adds the romantic interest in this dark, chilling, fast-paced story that is an updated, rewritten version of *Treasures* (1994).

Where it's reviewed:
Romantic Times, August 2004, page 116

Other books by the same author:
The Morning After, 2004
The Impostress, 2003
The Night Before, 2003
Cold Blooded, 2002
Wild and Wicked, 2002

Other books you might like:
Christiane Heggan, *The Enemy Within*, 2000
Kay Hooper, *Amanda*, 1995
Nora Roberts, *River's End*, 1999
Anne Stuart, *Shadow Lover*, 1999
    similar theme
Phyllis Whitney, *Woman Without a Past*, 1991
    long-lost heiress theme

300

TRISH JENSEN

Phi Beta Bimbo

(New York: Love Spell, 2005)

Story type: Humor; Contemporary

Subject(s): Humor; Identity, Concealed; Self-Confidence
Major character(s): Leah Smith, Sociologist; Mark Colson, Businessman (security)
Time period(s): 2000s
Locale(s): Great Falls, Minnesota; Tyson's Corner, Minnesota

Summary: Sociologist Leah Smith has a theory—a buxom blonde bimbo with no marketable skills will get hired before a qualified (but flat-chested) brunette. Leah disguises herself as a blonde bombshell, ''Candi Devereaux,'' and applies for a job using both identities. Sure enough, Candi is practically hired on the spot. Ironically, so is Leah. Security expert Mark Colson knows that Candi and Leah are the same person, but he lets her play her part to the fullest in hopes of finding out whether or not she's a corporate spy.

Where it's reviewed:
Romantic Times, January 2005, page 112

Other books by the same author:
Without a Clue, 2005
Here Comes Santa Claus, 2001 (anthology)
Stuck with You, 2001
Against His Will, 2000
The Harder They Fall, 1997

Other books you might like:
Rachel Gibson, *The Trouble with Valentine's Day*, 2005
Shirley Jump, *The Bride Wore Chocolate*, 2004
Kathy Love, *Getting What You Want*, 2004
Susan Elizabeth Phillips, *Nobody's Baby but Mine*, 1997
Pat White, *Ring around My Heart*, 2004

301

DEBORAH JOHNS (Pseudonym of Deborah Johns Schumaker)

Maiden of Fire
(New York: Zebra, 2004)

Story type: Historical/Medieval
Subject(s): Trials; Religion; Inquisition
Major character(s): Claire of Foix, Religious (novice); Aimery, Nobleman (Count of Segni)
Time period(s): 14th century (1314; 1331)
Locale(s): France

Summary: Chosen as a child and trained in the arts of spell-binding by a Templar knight, Claire of Foix is a noviate at the Convent of St. Magdalene. She finds herself enmeshed in a web of religious and political intrigue that promises both danger and love in this lush, colorful tale set against the backdrop of the Grand Inquisition in 14th-century France. Using the trial of William Belibaste in 1331 as a background, this historically rich story draws upon details of the shadowy Cathar sect and the Templar Knights society to create a complex tale of passion, betrayal, and religious prejudice.

Where it's reviewed:
Rendezvous, July 2004, page 20
Romantic Times, August 2004, page 41

Other books you might like:
Katherine Deauville, *Eyes of Love*, 1996
Gayle Feyrer, *The Prince of Cups*, 1995

Tori Phillips, *One Knight in Venice*, 2001
 Italian Inquisition
Haywood Smith, *Dangerous Gifts*, 1999
Susan Wiggs, *Dancing on Air*, 1996
 more religious fanaticism

302

SUSAN JOHNSON
KATHERINE O'NEAL, Co-Author
PAM ROSENTHAL, Co-Author

Strangers in the Night
(New York: Brava, 2004)

Story type: Historical; Anthology
Subject(s): Romance; Erotica; Relationships

Summary: This sizzling trio of sexually explicit novellas pairs three wickedly delicious heroes with independent heroines, sets them down in very different situations, and lets the seductive games begin. Included are *Natural Attraction*, Susan Johnson's lusty Georgian tale of a wicked viscount who meets his match in a bold, smart, cross-dressing heroine; *Fool Me Once*, Katherine O'Neal's unique Mexican-set story of a pair of con artists, their outrageous scam, and numerous celebrities from the Thirties; and *A House East of Regent Street*, Pam Rosenthal's sexy Regency story of two people who both want the same house (a former brothel) and will do just about anything to get it.

Where it's reviewed:
Romantic Times, December 2004, page 51

Other books by the same author:
Temporary Mistress, 2000

Other books you might like:
Katherine O'Neal, *My One and Only*, 2000
 exotic setting
Pam Rosenthal, *Almost a Gentleman*, 2000
Robin Schone, *The Lover*, 2000
Bertrice Small, *Delighted*, 2002
 erotic historical anthology

303

JOAN JOHNSTON

The Rivals
(New York: Pocket, 2004)

Story type: Contemporary; Romantic Suspense
Series: Bitter Creek. Book 5
Subject(s): Missing Persons; Feuds; Suspense
Major character(s): Sarah Barndollar, Police Officer (deputy sheriff), Single Parent; Drew DeWitt, Lawyer
Time period(s): 2000s
Locale(s): Jackson, Wyoming (Teton County)

Summary: When the third young girl goes missing in Teton County in just over a year and she just happens to be the illegitimate daughter of U.S. Attorney General Clay Black-thorne and the granddaughter of his archrival, King Grayhawk, Deputy Sheriff Sarah Barndollar has her hands full. She must not only solve the crime, but deal with sexy and persistent Drew DeWitt, one of the Blackthorne cousins. Plots, espionage, bitter rivalries, and complex family dynamics are all part of this fast-paced mystery, part of Johnston's popular Bitter Creek series about the rival Blackthorne and Grayhawk families.

Where it's reviewed:
Rendezvous, August 2004, page 26
Romantic Times, September 2004, page 126

Other books by the same author:
The Price, 2003
Hawke's Way Grooms, 2002
Sisters Found, 2002
The Loner, 2002
Hawke's Way Brides, 2001

Other books you might like:
Janet Dailey, *This Calder Range*, 1989
    Calder. Book 1
Janet Dailey, *This Calder Sky*, 1981
    Calder. Book 2
Linda Howard, *Mackenzie's Mountain*, 1989
Jayne Ann Krentz, *Eclipse Bay*, 2000
    family feuds laced with murder and humor
Nora Roberts, *Montana Sky*, 1996

304

LINDA WINSTEAD JONES

The Sun Witch
(New York: Berkley, 2004)

Story type: Fantasy; Paranormal
Series: Sisters of the Sun. Book 1
Subject(s): Witches and Witchcraft; Sisters; Kidnapping
Major character(s): Sophie Frye, Witch, Single Parent; Kane Varden, Veteran (rebellion), Revolutionary
Time period(s): Indeterminate
Locale(s): Columbyana, Fictional Country

Summary: In the 365th year of the reign of the Beckyts, Kane Varden and his brother, rebels against an evil emperor, are caught in an ambush. Unable to save his brother, Kane is wounded and left for dead. Sophie Frye is a witch, and she wants a child. Unfortunately, she and her sisters are under a curse that causes anyone who loves them to die young. Sophie finds Kane and heals him. She's sure that she can mate with him and leave him without any emotional attachment. However, when Kane returns to the site of their tryst a year later, and sees Sophie with their baby, he insists they marry. Nothing will convince him otherwise. To make matters worse, the infant is kidnapped, and no power, human or otherworldly, will keep Kane and Sophie from saving their child.

Where it's reviewed:
Booklist, December 1, 2004, page 641
Romantic Times, December 2004, page 120

Other books by the same author:
Truly, Madly, Dangerously, 2005
A Touch of the Beast, 2004
Fever, 2004
Running Scared, 2004
On Dean's Watch, 2003

Other books you might like:
Jo Beverley, *Forbidden Magic*, 1998
Susan Carroll, *Midnight Bride*, 2001
Susan King, *Waking the Princess*, 2003
Ruth Ryan Langan, *The Knight and the Seer*, 2003
Nora Roberts, *Dance upon the Air*, 2001
    Three Sisters Island Trilogy. Book 1

305

SHIRLEY JUMP

The Bride Wore Chocolate
(New York: Zebra, 2004)

Story type: Humor; Contemporary
Subject(s): Humor; Weddings; Courtship
Major character(s): Candace Woodrow, Businesswoman (Gift Baskets to Die For), Fiance(e); Michael Vogler, Wealthy, Advertising
Time period(s): 2000s
Locale(s): Boston, Massachusetts

Summary: Chocoholic Candace Woodrow wakes up in Michael Vogler's bed three weeks before her wedding. The problem is, Michael's not the groom-to-be. Michael figures that Candace is up for grabs until the final ''I dos,'' so he wages an all-out courtship to keep her from the walk to the wrong altar. Rapid fire dialogue and hilarious situations make this first book in a trilogy a treat for anyone with a funny bone. Decadent chocolate recipes with inventive directions accompany each chapter.

Where it's reviewed:
Booklist, September 1, 2004, page 72
Romantic Times, September 2004, page 122

Other books by the same author:
The Daddy's Promise, 2004
The Bachelor's Dare, 2003
The Virgin's Proposal, 2003

Other books you might like:
Mary Kay Andrews, *Hissy Fit*, 2004
Judith Arnold, *The Wrong Bride*, 1999
Holly Jacobs, *A Day Late and a Bride Short*, 2003
Ann Kline, *The Ride to Dinah's Wedding*, 2003
Pam McCutcheon, *My Favorite Husband*, 2003

306

SHIRLEY JUMP

The Devil Served Tortellini
(New York: Kensington, 2005)

Story type: Humor; Ethnic
Subject(s): Humor; Italian Americans; Weight Control
Major character(s): Maria Pagliano, Young Woman; Dante Del Rosso, Cook (chef), Restaurateur
Time period(s): 2000s
Locale(s): Boston, Massachusetts

Summary: Antonio Lombardi, captain of the football team, not to mention the sexiest guy in high school, has personally called Maria Pagliano and asked her if she's coming to the reunion. Maria's packed on a few pounds since graduation, so she joins Chubby Chums for guidance and support. Chef Dante Del Rosso doesn't think Maria needs to lose weight. In fact, he thinks she's perfect just the way she is. A relationship with a man who creates fine, calorie-laden dishes for a living can be really tricky for a woman on a strict diet.

Other books by the same author:
Kissed by Cat, 2005
The Angel Craved Lobster, 2005
Her Frog Prince, 2004
The Bride Wore Chocolate, 2004
The Daddy's Promise, 2004

Other books you might like:
Beverly Brandt, *True North*, 2001
Sue Civil-Brown, *Next Stop, Paradise*, 2001
Millie Criswell, *What to Do about Annie*, 2001
Lisa Plumley, *Reconsidering Riley*, 2002
Deborah Shelley, *My Favorite Flavor*, 2000

307

DONNA KAUFFMAN
NANCY WARREN, Co-Author
ERIN MCCARTHY, Co-Author
MARYJANICE DAVIDSON, Co-Author
LUCY MONROE, Co-Author

Merry Christmas, Baby
(New York: Brava, 2004)

Story type: Contemporary; Holiday Themes
Subject(s): Christmas; Anthology
Time period(s): 2000s

Summary: Six sexy short stories by Brava's established and up-and-coming authors focus on romance during the holiday season in a wide variety of settings. From a yacht on the Caribbean to a Chicago highrise rooftop during a blizzard, these stories will please readers who like their romantic reading on the erotic side. Included are ''Making Waves'' by Donna Kauffman, ''Let It Snow'' by Nancy Warren, ''You, Actually'' by Erin McCarthy, ''Undercover Claus'' by MaryJanice Davidson, ''Silver Bella'' by Lucy Monroe, and ''Snow Day'' by Susanna Carr.

Where it's reviewed:
Romantic Times, October 2004, page 89

Other books you might like:
MaryJanice Davidson, *The Royal Treatment*, 2004
    no holiday theme
Lori Foster, *Bad Boys on Board*, 2003
    anthology; Donna Kauffman, Nancy Warren, co-authors
Lori Foster, *Jingle Bell Rock*, 2003
Shannon McKenna, *Bad Boys Next Exit*, 2004
    anthology; with a holiday story by Kauffman: Donna Kauffman, E.C. Sheedy, co-authors
Elda Minger, *Christmas with Eve*, 1996
    sex and humor

308

DORIEN KELLY

In Like Flynn
(Toronto: Harlequin, 2004)

Story type: Contemporary; Humor
Subject(s): Business; Family
Major character(s): Annie Rutherford, Businesswoman (vice president); Daniel Flynn, Consultant, Writer
Time period(s): 2000s
Locale(s): Ann Arbor, Michigan; Clifden, Ireland

Summary: As vice president of Long Range Planning for Donovan Enterprises, Annie Rutherford helped put the Donovan pizza chain on the U.S. map, and now Annie is ready to take the company overseas. The only problem is that the company's CEO has just returned from a vacation in Ireland and now wants to open a chain of pubs. Hoping that her boss will eventually get distracted and forget about his new idea, Annie agrees to work with his consultant, Daniel Flynn, only to find she is the one becoming distracted by a certain sexy Irishman.

Where it's reviewed:
Romantic Times, November 2004, page 101

Other books by the same author:
Hot Nights in Ballymuir, 2004
Do-Over, 2003
The Girl Most Likely to. . ., 2003
The Girl Least Likely to. . ., 2003
The Last Bride in Ballymuir, 2003

Other books you might like:
Jennifer Crusie, *Anyone but You*, 2003
Stephanie Doyle, *One True Love*, 2003
Kristin Gabriel, *Dangerously Irresistible*, 2001
Charlotte Maclay, *Courting Cupid*, 1999
Cathy Yardley, *Working It*, 2003

309

JULIE KENNER

Aphrodite's Flame
(New York: Love Spell, 2004)

Story type: Contemporary; Paranormal
Subject(s): Family
Major character(s): Isole Frost, Counselor; Mordichai Black, Hero (superhero)
Time period(s): 2000s
Locale(s): New York, New York; Los Angeles, California; Olympus, Fictional Country

Summary: Isole ''Izzy'' Frost is determined to prove she received her promotion to Re-Assimilation Counselor based on her skills and not on her family connections. Convincing her first client, notorious outcast Hieronymous Black, to give up his evil ways, will be quite a challenge. Mordichai ''Mordi'' Black is certain that his father's much celebrated return to the side of good is just a facade for his next plot against humankind. Proving to Izzy that she is wrong about Hieronymous won't be easy, especially since Izzy's special powers let her know everything Mordi is thinking—even how much he likes her!

Where it's reviewed:
Romantic Times, August 2004, page 120

Other books by the same author:
Stolen Kisses, 2004
The Spy Who Loves Me, 2004
Aphrodite's Secret, 2003
Silent Confessions, 2003
Silent Desires, 2003

Other books you might like:
P.C. Cast, *Goddess of the Sea*, 2003
Karen Fox, *Prince of Charming*, 2000
Kristin Grayson, *Utterly Charming*, 2000
Sherrilyn Kenyon, *Night Pleasures*, 2002
Judi McCoy, *Say You're Mine*, 2002

310

ALISON KENT

The Samms Agenda
(New York: Brava, 2004)

Story type: Contemporary; Romantic Suspense
Series: Smithson Group 5. Book 3
Subject(s): Spies; Adventure and Adventurers
Major character(s): Katrina Flurry, Journalist (society columnist); Julian Samms, Spy (Smithson Group)
Time period(s): 2000s
Locale(s): Florida

Summary: Shocked when the man she'd been dating in order to get information for her urban lifestyle column turns out to be a mobster, Katrina Flurry is even more stunned to realize that she has become a target for murder. When Julian Samms is assigned by the Smithson Group to keep her safe, and they end up on the run from the would-be assassin, they have an unexpected romantic relationship. There is lively, passionate action in this third installment in Kent's sexy Smithson Group series.

Where it's reviewed:
Romantic Times, December 2004, page 50

Other books by the same author:
The Beach Alibi, 2005 (Smithson Group 5. Book 4)
The McKenzie Artifact, 2005 (Smithson Group 5. Book 5)
The Bane Affair, 2004 (Smithson Group 5. Book 1)
The Shaughnessey Accord, 2004 (Smithson Group 5. Book 2)

Other books you might like:
Nina Bangs, *From Boardwalk with Love*, 2003
    B.L.I.S.S. Book 1
Suzanne Brockmann, *Bodyguard*, 1999
    sex and lively action
Suzanne Brockmann, *The Defiant Hero*, 2001
Lisa Cach, *Dr. Yes*, 2003
    B.L.I.S.S. Book 2
Lynsay Sands, *The Loving Daylights*, 2003
    B.L.I.S.S. Book 3

311

ALISON KENT

The Shaughnessey Accord
(New York: Brava, 2004)

Story type: Contemporary; Romantic Suspense
Series: Smithson Group 5. Book 2
Subject(s): Spies; Adventure and Adventurers
Major character(s): Glory Brighton, Restaurateur (sandwich shop); Tripp Shaughnessey, Spy (Smithson Group), Detective (undercover)
Time period(s): 2000s
Locale(s): New York

Summary: Independent Glory Brighton has no idea that her sandwich shop is under surveillance by the neighboring Smithson Group or that Smithson is not an engineering company but is really a cover for a group of crime fighters. When the sandwich shop is taken over by thugs while Glory and Smithson "engineer" Tripp Shaughnessey are necking in the storage room, she finds herself in an adventure that is both dangerous and exhilarating. This short, individually published novella, is the second episode in Kent's explicitly sexy, action-oriented Smithson Group 5 (SG-5) series.

Where it's reviewed:
Romantic Times, November 2004, page 114

Other books by the same author:
The Beach Alibi, 2005 (Smithson Group 5. Book 4)
The McKenzie Artifact, 2005 (Smithson Group 5. Book 5)
The Bane Affair, 2004 (Smithson Group 5. Book 1)
The Samms Agenda, 2004 (Smithson Group 5. Book 3)

Other books you might like:
Nina Bangs, *From Boardwalk with Love*, 2003
    B.L.I.S.S. Book 1
Suzanne Brockmann, *Bodyguard*, 1999
    sex and action
Lisa Cach, *Dr. Yes*, 2003
    B.L.I.S.S. Book 2
Shannon McKenna, *Standing in the Shadows*, 2003
Lynsay Sands, *The Loving Daylights*, 2003
    more sexy spies, with humor

312

SHERRILYN KENYON
MAGGIE SHAYNE, Co-Author
SUZANNE FORSTER, Co-Author
VIRGINIA KANTRA, Co-Author

Man of My Dreams
(New York: Jove, 2004)

Story type: Contemporary; Paranormal
Subject(s): Magic; Paranormal; Anthology

Summary: This collection of novellas by well-known authors sweeps readers from futuristic worlds and the faery realm to contemporary Santa Barbara and small-town America in a diverse quartet of nicely-written romances, both supernatural and otherwise. Included are *Fire and Ice*, Sherrilyn Kenyon's futuristic tale of a princess who marries an assassin and ends up being his salvation; *Daydream Believer*, Maggie Shayne's chilling, yet not too dark, story of a psychic, a cop, and a serial killer; *Shocking Lucy*, Suzanne Forster's sizzling story of a reluctant bride and an electrifying electrician; and *Midsummer Night's Magic*, Virginia Kantra's magical retelling of the story of Tam Lin.

Where it's reviewed:
Rendezvous, October 2004, page 18
Romantic Times, November 2004, page 129

Other books you might like:
Suzanne Forster, *Come Midnight*, 1997
Virginia Kantra, *All a Man Can Be*, 2003
Robin D. Owens, *Heart Duel*, 2004
Maggie Shayne, *Forever Enchanted*, 1997
Josepha Sherman, *Childe of Faerie, Childe of Earth*, 1992
    young adult/fairies and mortals

313

SHERRILYN KENYON
AMANDA ASHLEY, Co-Author
L.A. BANKS, Co-Author
LORI HANDELAND, Co-Author

Stroke of Midnight

(New York: St. Martin's Paperbacks, 2004)

Story type: Anthology; Paranormal
Subject(s): Werewolves; Paranormal
Time period(s): 2000s

Summary: This quartet of paranormal short stories by some of the genre's best-known writers focuses on werewolves, shapeshifters, and the strange things that happen at the stroke of midnight. Included are ''Winter Born,'' Sherrilyn Kenyon's sizzling were-panther tale; ''Born of the Night,'' a dark, mysterious captive-in-love-with-captor story by Amanda Ashley; ''Make It Last Forever,'' L.A. Banks' story of a young woman whose fate rests in the hands of a sexy, uncommon biker; and ''Red Moon Rising,'' a mesmerizing tale of a writer stalked by a Navajo skinwalker by Lori Handeland.

Where it's reviewed:
Romantic Times, November 2004, page 126

Other books by the same author:
Man of My Dreams, 2004 (paranormal anthology)
Night Pleasures, 2002

Other books you might like:
Amanda Ashley, *After Sundown*, 2003
Lori Handeland, *Blue Moon*, 2004
Susan Krinard, *Prince of Wolves*, 1994

314

LYNN KERSTAN

Dangerous Deceptions

(New York: Signet, 2004)

Story type: Historical/Regency
Series: Black Phoenix. Book 1
Subject(s): Identity, Concealed; Secrets; Abuse

Major character(s): Kate Falshaw, Actress (''Gaetana''), Spy (for the Black Phoenix); Jarrett Dering, Nobleman (Lord Dering), Spy (for the Black Phoenix)
Time period(s): 1810s
Locale(s): Lake District, England (Paradise resort)

Summary: Sent to Paradise, an exclusive pleasure resort in the Lake District, to uncover the truth about some disturbingly dark activities that seem to be centered there, Jarrett Dering and Kate Falshaw embark on a plan that becomes more dangerous and more romantic as it progresses. Chilling danger, unexpected twists, and exquisite sensuality are highlights of this fast-paced story that does an exceptional job of revealing the darker, sometimes evil, side of the glittering Regency period.

Where it's reviewed:
Romantic Times, November 2004, page 38

Other books by the same author:
Heart of the Tiger, 2003 (Cat. Book 2)
The Silver Lion, 2003 (Cat. Book 3)
The Golden Leopard, 2002 (Cat. Book 1)
Lord Dragoner's Wife, 1999
Marry in Haste, 1998

Other books you might like:
Mary Balogh, *One Night for Love*, 1999
    dark, with a touch of violence
Jo Beverley, *The Dragons' Bride*, 2001
Jo Beverley, *Forbidden Magic*, 1998
    dark and with a touch of magic
Christina Dodd, *A Well Pleasured Lady*, 1997
Anne Stuart, *To Love a Dark Lord*, 1994

315

VALERIE KING (Pseudonym of Valerie Bosna)

An Adventurous Lady

(New York: Zebra, 2004)

Story type: Regency
Subject(s): Neighbors and Neighborhoods; Treasure, Buried
Major character(s): Evelina Wesley, Gentlewoman; Rotherstone, Nobleman (Earl of Rotherstone)
Time period(s): 1810s (1817)
Locale(s): Maybridge, England

Summary: After finding a treasure map hidden in the attic of Wildings Hall, the first thing Evelina Wesley can think of is how much fun it would be to search for the smuggler's long lost booty. Then Evelina discovers the treasure is most likely buried somewhere at Blacklands, the estate of her misanthropic neighbor, the Earl of Rotherstone. Convincing the unsociable nobleman to let her and her friends onto his grounds won't be easy, but to Evelina's surprise, the handsome earl turns out to be much more charming, and much less cranky, than rumor has led her to believe.

Where it's reviewed:
Booklist, October 15, 2004, page 394
Romantic Times, November 2004, page 108

Other books by the same author:
A Daring Courtship, 2003

A Rogue's Wager, 2003
A Rogue's Deception, 2002
A Rogue's Embrace, 2002
A Rogue's Embrace, 2002

Other books you might like:
Catherine Blair, *Athena's Conquest*, 2001
Shannon Donnelly, *A Much Compromised Lady*, 2002
Barbara Metzger, *Miss Westlake's Windfall*, 2001
Joy Reed, *Mr. Jeffries and the Jilt*, 2003
Jeanne Savery, *An Independent Lady*, 2003

316

GWEN KIRKWOOD

Children of the Glens
(New York: Severn House, 2004)

Story type: Contemporary; Saga
Series: Maxwell Family. Book 3
Subject(s): Greed; Farm Life; Animals/Cows
Major character(s): Gerda Fritz-Allan, Femme Fatale, Con Artist; Ewan Maxwell, Farmer
Time period(s): 1960s (1962); 1970s
Locale(s): Lochandee, Scotland

Summary: Gold-digging femme fatale Gerda Fritz-Allan knows that she's beautiful, so she uses her stunning looks to trap dairy farmer Ewan Maxwell, whom she thinks is wealthy, into marriage. Her machinations and greed put the family lands, and even the lives of others, at risk. This is part of the continuing saga of the Maxwell family and their beloved Lochandee.

Other books by the same author:
A Tangled Web, 2003 (Maxwell Family. Book 2)
Laird of Lochandee, 2002 (Maxwell Family. Book 1)
Fairlyden at War, 1993
The Family of Fairlyden, 1992
Fairlyden, 1991

Other books you might like:
Nancy Cato, *All the Rivers Run*, 1922
John Galsworthy, *The Forsythe Saga*, 1922
Dorothy Garlock, *A Place Called Sweetwater*, 2003
Dee Holmes, *The Caleb Trees*, 2000
Colleen McCullough, *The Thorn Birds*, 1977

317

LISA KLEYPAS

Secrets of a Summer Night
(New York: Avon, 2004)

Story type: Historical/Regency
Subject(s): Social Classes; Wealth; Courtship
Major character(s): Annabelle Peyton, Impoverished, Noblewoman; Simon Hunt, Wealthy, Businessman
Time period(s): 1840s
Locale(s): London, England

Summary: Annabelle Peyton's family is of noble birth, but poor as church mice. Her lack of a dowry has resulted in three failed seasons for Annabelle. During this fourth one, it's imperative that she find a wealthy nobleman to wed. She joins forces with Society's three other "wallflowers" to come up with a plan to snag husbands for all of them. Simon Hunt, a self-made businessman, has plenty of money, but not one drop of noble blood. He's determined to marry the beautiful Annabelle, who seems more interested in every foolish, foppish duke and earl, but not him. There's lots of matchmaking fun as Annabelle takes on Society, and Society takes on Annabelle.

Where it's reviewed:
Romantic Times, November 2004, page 37

Other books by the same author:
Where's My Hero?, 2003 (anthology)
Worth Any Price, 2003
Lady Sophia's Lover, 2002
Suddenly You, 2001
Where Dreams Begin, 2000

Other books you might like:
Jennifer Ashley, *The Pirate Next Door*, 2003
Pamela Britton, *Seduced*, 2003
Nicole Byrd, *Widow in Scarlet*, 2003
Lorraine Heath, *Love with a Scandalous Lord*, 2003
Stephanie Laurens, *The Lady Chosen*, 2003

318

ANGELA KNIGHT

Master of the Night
(New York: Berkley, 2004)

Story type: Contemporary/Fantasy; Paranormal
Subject(s): Vampires; Seduction; Espionage
Major character(s): Erin Grayson, FBI Agent, Witch (latent); Reece Champion, Businessman, Vampire
Time period(s): 2000s
Locale(s): United States

Summary: Centuries ago, Merlin and Nimue were sent from the Mageverse, an alternate universe, to Earth to establish a group of immortals, vampires, and witches, who were charged to guard and protect humankind. Their children were born mortal but with the latent ability to be changed by existing vampires or Majae (witches) through sex. Reece Champion is a vampire, but he is a also a wealthy businessman and, incidentally, works with the FBI and CIA. Currently, he is the target of Agent Erin Grayson, who thinks he has links to a murderous cult who killed her partner and wants to get information from him. Erin is a latent—although she doesn't know it, and Reece knows the consequences of making love to her. Evil, passion, and seduction are part of this chilling story that creates a fascinating world based on alternative Grail lore, first introduced in a short story "Seduction's Gift" in the anthology *Hot Blooded*, also published in 2004.

Where it's reviewed:
Rendezvous, October 2004, page 39
Romantic Times, October 2004, page 29

Other books by the same author:
Master of the Moon, 2005
Jane's Warlord, 2004
The Forever Kiss, 2004

Other books you might like:
Jo Beverley, *Irresistible Forces*, 2004
    anthology
Christine Feehan, *Dark Secret*, 2005
Sherrilyn Kenyon, *Seize the Night*, 2005
Karen Marie Moning, *The Immortal Highlander*, 2004
Mary Jo Putney, *Kiss of Fate*, 2004
    another guardian-type series/historical

319

HARLEY JANE KOZAK

Dating Is Murder

(New York: Doubleday, 2005)

Story type: Humor; Romantic Suspense
Series: Dating Mysteries. Book 2
Subject(s): Humor; Television Programs; Murder
Major character(s): Wollstonecraft "Wollie" Shelley, Detective—Amateur, Artist; Simon Alexander, FBI Agent
Time period(s): 2000s
Locale(s): Los Angeles, California; Encino, California; San Pedro, California

Summary: Once again, Wollie Shelley is without a man. Doc, the love of her life, has terminated their relationship to be near his daughter. Now a strange, handsome man is following her as she searches for her missing math tutor. Whether dealing with her dysfunctional family, painting a mural of scientifically accurate frogs, or starring in "Biological Clock," an aptly named reality television show, this entertaining amateur sleuth provides lots of laughs.

Other books by the same author:
Dating Dead Men, 2004 (Dating Mysteries. Book 1)

Other books you might like:
Susan Andersen, *Baby, I'm Yours*, 1998
Sue Civil-Brown, *Catching Kelly*, 2000
Janet Evanovich, *Ten Big Ones*, 2004
Rachel Gibson, *It Must Be Love*, 2000
Sherryl Woods, *Ask Anyone*, 2002
    Trinity Hunter. Book 2

320

ALLISON LANE
EDITH LAYTON, Co-Author
LYNN KERSTAN, Co-Author
BARBARA METZGER, Co-Author
CARLA KELLY, Co-Author

Wedding Belles

(New York: Signet, 2004)

Story type: Anthology; Regency
Subject(s): Courtship; Weddings
Time period(s): 19th century
Locale(s): England

Summary: All the romance of weddings is captured in this sparkling Regency story collection. Richard Hughes vows to wed a woman used to a life of modest means, but then he meets Georgina Whittaker, an heiress in desperate need of his help, in Allison Lane's "For Richer or Poorer." Terrence Powell has done everything he can think of to break up his brother Leslie's forthcoming marriage to Joanna Littleton, but meeting the bride's sister Valerie soon has Terrence wondering about a wedding of his own in Edith Layton's "A Marriage of True Minds." In Lynn Kerstan's "The Marriage Scheme," Julia Flyte finds herself being pushed into marrying either her guardian's eldest son or the youngest, but it is really the middle son who is the perfect match for her. In Barbara Metzger's "A Match Made in Heaven—or Hell," St. Peter and the Devil wager on whether one woman can reform a wounded war hero and rake. In Carla Kelly's "A Hasty Marriage," Englishwoman Ann Utley runs from the very thought of marriage until she finds herself falling in love with an American sea captain who shares her taste for adventure.

Where it's reviewed:
Romantic Times, May 2004, page 118

Other books you might like:
Shannon Donnelly, *With This Ring*, 2004
Elena Greene, *His Blushing Bride*, 2001
Alice Holden, *On Bended Knee*, 2003
Lynn Kerstan, *A June Betrothal*, 1993
Patricia Rice, *A Wedding Bouquet*, 1996

321

CONNIE LANE (Pseudonym of Connie Laux)

The Duke's Scandalous Secret

(New York: Pocket, 2004)

Story type: Historical/Regency
Subject(s): Secrets; Scandal; Gambling
Major character(s): Lady Lynette Overton, Noblewoman; Thomas Flanders, Nobleman (Duke of Ravensfield)
Time period(s): 1810s
Locale(s): England

Summary: Lady Lynette Overton knows she is being stalked—and she knows she should leave London. So when the opportunity falls in her lap to take a wager that she can discover what is keeping the notorious Duke of Ravensfield at his estate and away from society, she jumps at the chance. Of course, the fact she has been in love with the duke since she first saw him as a young girl aids her decision. When her coach conveniently breaks down near his estate one dark and stormy night, her plan is successfully launched. Lively and sensual.

Where it's reviewed:
Romantic Times, September 2004, page 41

Other books by the same author:
Guilty Little Secrets, 2003
The Viscount's Bawdy Bargain, 2003
Romancing Riley, 2002
Reinventing Romeo, 2000

Other books you might like:
Candace Camp, *So Wild a Heart*, 2002
Christina Dodd, *Rules of Surrender*, 2000
Jo Goodman, *Beyond a Wicked Kiss*, 2004
Candice Hern, *Once a Dreamer*, 2003
Betina Krahn, *The Last Bachelor*, 1994

322

REBECCA HAGAN LEE

Hardly a Husband

(New York: Berkley, 2004)

Story type: Historical/Regency
Series: Free Fellows League. Book 3
Subject(s): Courtship; Marriage; Freedom
Major character(s): Sarah Eckersley, Gentlewoman (vicar's daughter); Jarrod Shepherdston, Nobleman (Marquess of Shepherdston)
Time period(s): 1810s (1813)
Locale(s): England

Summary: Evicted from the vicarage upon the death of her father and threatened with an undesirable marriage, Sarah Eckersley heads for London with an impossible task. She must convince the man of her dreams, Jarrod, Marquess of Shepherdston to marry her, and she only has 30 days to do it. Light and charming.

Where it's reviewed:
Rendezvous, August 2004, page 21
Romantic Times, October 2004, page 45

Other books by the same author:
Truly a Wife, 2005 (Free Fellows League. Book 4)
Merely the Groom, 2004 (Free Fellows League. Book 2)
Barely a Bride, 2003 (Free Fellows League. Book 1)
Always a Lady, 2002 (Marquess of Templeston Heirs. Book 3)
A Hint of Heather, 2000

Other books you might like:
Connie Brockway, *My Seduction*, 2004
Karen Hawkins, *The Seduction of Sara*, 2001
Julia Justiss, *My Lady's Pleasure*, 2002
Amanda Quick, *Mistress*, 1994
Barbara Dawson Smith, *Never a Lady*, 1994

323

CATHIE LINZ (Pseudonym of Cathie Baumgardner)

The Marine Meets His Match

(New York: Silhouette, 2004)

Story type: Contemporary
Subject(s): Books and Reading; Military Life
Major character(s): Serena Anderson, Store Owner (bookseller); Radoslaw Kozlowski, Military Personnel (U.S. Marine captain)
Time period(s): 2000s
Locale(s): North Carolina

Summary: The only way U.S. Marine Captain Rad Kozlowski can escape the unwanted attentions of his commanding officer's very determined daughter is by inventing a fiancee for himself. However, Rad mistakenly uses the first name that comes to his mind, which just happens to be Serena Anderson, a bookseller he met earlier that day. In order to convince Serena to pretend to be his loving fiancee, Rad, who happens to own the building in which Serena's bookstore is located, offers her a cut in her rent if she plays along with his little charade. Serena really could use the break in rent, but her ''professional'' arrangement with Rad becomes complicated once she realizes she might be falling in love with him.

Where it's reviewed:
Booklist, September 1, 2004, page 72
Library Journal, August 2004, page 55
Romantic Times, September 2004, page 110

Other books by the same author:
Cinderella's Sweet-Talking Marine, 2004
Her Millionaire Marine, 2004
Sleeping Beauty and the Marine, 2003
A Prince at Last, 2002
Married to a Marine, 2002

Other books you might like:
Elizabeth Bevarly, *When Jayne Met Erik*, 1996
Jennifer Crusie, *The Cinderella Deal*, 1996
Jennifer Greene, *Kiss Your Prince Charming*, 1999
Holly Jacobs, *A Day Late and a Bride Short*, 2003
Laura Wright, *Cinderella and the Playboy*, 2002

324

HOLLY LISLE

Midnight Rain

(New York: Onyx, 2004)

Story type: Contemporary; Romantic Suspense
Subject(s): Paranormal; Stalking; Murder
Major character(s): Phoebe Rain, Abuse Victim, Psychic (tarot card reader); Alan MacKerrie, Doctor
Time period(s): 2000s
Locale(s): Fort Lauderdale, Florida

Summary: There is no way the threatening call that tarot card reader Phoebe Rain receives could be from her abusive ex-husband. After all, he is miles away in a coma—or is he? Phoebe is psychic, and she knows someone is stalking her and she is terrified. Eventually, she turns to her skeptical neighbor, Dr. Alan MacKerrie for help—with the expected romantic results. Ghosts, visions, and other paranormal events are part of this chilling story that is unusual, frightening, and romantic.

Where it's reviewed:
Romantic Times, November 2004, page 125

Other books by the same author:
Gods Old and Dark, 2004 (World Gates. Book 3)
The Wreck of Heaven, 2003 (World Gates. Book 2)
Memory of Fire, 2002 (World Gates. Book 1)
Vengeance of Dragons, 2000 (Secret Texts. Book 2)
Diplomacy of Wolves, 1999 (Secret Texts. Book 1)

Other books you might like:
Heather Graham, *Tall, Dark, and Deadly*, 1999
Linda Howard, *Kill and Tell*, 1998
Lisa Jackson, *Wishes*, 1998
Karen Robards, *Wait Until Dark*, 2001
    chilling anthology
Alicia Scott, *The Quiet One*, 1996

325

JULIA LONDON

Beauty Queen

(New York: Berkley Sensation, 2004)

Story type: Contemporary; Humor
Series: Lear Sisters Trilogy. Book 2
Subject(s): Politics; Self-Acceptance; Humor
Major character(s): Rebecca Lear, Single Parent, Divorced Person; Matt Parrish, Lawyer (litigator)
Time period(s): 2000s
Locale(s): Ruby Falls, Texas; Austin, Texas; Colorado

Summary: Former beauty queen Rebecca Lear, a divorced mother, is unemployed. Her self-esteem in shambles from a two-timing husband, she agrees to be a political campaign strategist as a favor for a friend. Much to her surprise, Matt Parrish, a stranger she accused of stealing her quesadilla, and who thinks she's whacky, is on the campaign, too. Clever banter and witty repartee fill this book about a woman whose beauty is more than skin deep and the man who, against his better judgment, comes to adore her.

Where it's reviewed:
Booklist, April 1, 2004, page 1355
Publishers Weekly, March 22, 2004, page 68

Other books by the same author:
Material Girl, 2003 (Lear Sisters. Book 1)
The Secret Lover, 2002 (Rogues of Regent Street. Book 4)
The Beautiful Stranger, 2001 (Rogues of Regent Street. Book 3)
The Dangerous Gentleman, 2000 (Rogues of Regent Street. Book 1)
The Ruthless Charmer, 2000 (Rogues of Regent Street. Book 2)

Other books you might like:
Lilian Darcy, *Cinderella After Midnight*, 2002
Rachel Gibson, *Lola Carlyle Reveals All*, 2002
Connie Lane, *Dirty Little Lies*, 2004
Nora Roberts, *Considering Kate*, 2001
Susan Wiggs, *Passing through Paradise*, 2002

326

JULIA LONDON

Miss Fortune

(New York: Berkley, 2004)

Story type: Contemporary; Humor
Series: Lear Sisters Trilogy. Book 3
Subject(s): Conduct of Life; Growing Up; Fathers and Daughters
Major character(s): Rachel Lear, Student—Graduate (doctoral); Flynn Oliver, Investigator, Gentleman (English)
Time period(s): 2000s
Locale(s): Providence, Rhode Island

Summary: When her wealthy father threatens to cut her funding off unless she gets her life together, Rachel Lear decides to shape up, get a job, and put some love into her life. After her Wicca friend casts a spell and gorgeous Brit Flynn Oliver

shows up—and doesn't seem inclined to go away—her life takes on a whole new heady glow. An appealing heroine, a hero on a mission of his own, and a cast of well-drawn characters take London's often humor-laiden Lear Sisters Trilogy to its expected, romantic conclusion.

Where it's reviewed:
Library Journal, November 15, 2004, page 46
Romantic Times, November 2004, page 111

Other books by the same author:
Beauty Queen, 2004 (Lear Sisters Trilogy. Book 2)
Material Girl, 2003 (Lear Sisters Trilogy. Book 1)
The Secret Lover, 2002 (Rogues of Regent Street. Book 4)
The Beautiful Stranger, 2001 (Rogues of Regent Street. Book 3)
The Ruthless Charmer, 2000 (Rogues of Regent Street. Book 2)

Other books you might like:
Rachel Gibson, *Truly, Madly Yours*, 1999
Susan Elizabeth Phillips, *Heaven, Texas*, 1995
Nora Roberts, *Hidden Riches*, 1994
   art, mystery, and romance
Suzanne Simmons, *Sweetheart, Indiana*, 2004

327

SASHA LORD (Pseudonym of Rebecca Saria)

In a Wild Wood

(New York: Signet, 2004)

Story type: Historical/Medieval; Historical/Fantasy
Series: Wild Trilogy. Book 2
Subject(s): Twins; Psychic Powers
Major character(s): Lady Matalia McTaver, Royalty (daughter of a princess); Brogan O'Bannon, Nobleman (exiled earl's son), Twin
Time period(s): Indeterminate Past
Locale(s): Scotland

Summary: When wild, independent Matalia McTaver, daughter of Kalial and Ronin from *Under a Wild Sky* and heir to her mother's forest kingdom, captures a wandering Scots warrior in the forest, she is attracted to him and decides to use him to satisfy her sexual curiousity. Unfortunately for Matalia, when they are discovered and Brogan O'Bannon turns out to be a Scottish earl's exiled son, they are forced to wed. Brogan takes Matalia home with him to Kirkcauldy in an effort to take his rightful place in his family. However, family rivalries, jealousies, and real danger lurk at Kirkcauldy and Matalia has her hands full trying to stay alive and win Brogan's love. This book contains lots of rough, explicit sex, and is not for readers who prefer their sensuality on the gentle side.

Where it's reviewed:
Romantic Times, August 2004, page 38

Other books by the same author:
Across a Wild Sea, 2005 (Wild Trilogy. Book 3)
Under a Wild Sky, 2004 (Wild Trilogy. Book 1)

Other books you might like:
Virginia Henley, *A Year and a Day*, 1998
   bawdy and sexy

Emma Holly, *Hunting Midnight*, 2003
Johanna Lindsey, *Fires of Winter*, 1980
Johanna Lindsey, *A Gentle Feuding*, 1984
    Scottish sensuality
Bertrice Small, *A Memory of Love*, 2000
    erotic

328

KATHY LOVE

Wanting What You Get

(New York: Kensington, 2004)

Story type: Contemporary
Series: Stepp Sisters. Book 2
Subject(s): Self-Acceptance; Alcoholism; Sisters
Major character(s): Ellie Stepp, Librarian; Mason Sweet, Alcoholic, Political Figure (mayor)
Time period(s): 2000s
Locale(s): Millbrook, Maine

Summary: Mayor Mason Sweet of Millbrook, Maine, is handsome, successful. . .and an alcoholic. He drowns his troubles, as well as his memories, in a bottle at every given opportunity. Ellie Stepp is the town librarian. One of the pariah Stepp sisters, the overweight woman stayed in Millbrook despite her horrible adolescence. Mason barely noticed Ellie in high school, but now that he's been in a wedding party with her, he finds himself attracted to her ample curves. However, after they start dating, he insists on keeping their relationship quiet, and what's left of Ellie's self-esteem evaporates. A couple who shouldn't be together vow to make it work in this emotion-filled romance.

Where it's reviewed:
Romantic Times, November 2004, page 113

Other books by the same author:
Getting What You Want, 2004 (Stepp Sisters. Book 1)

Other books you might like:
Barbara Bretton, *Shore Lights*, 2003
Mary Alice Monroe, *Skyward*, 2003
Christie Ridgway, *Mad Enough to Marry*, 2002
Kathryn Shay, *After the Fire*, 2003
Kim Watters, *Home at Last*, 2003

329

KATIE MACALISTER (Pseudonym of Marthe Arends)

You Slay Me

(New York: Onyx, 2004)

Story type: Contemporary/Fantasy
Subject(s): Dragons; Magic; Murder
Major character(s): Aisling Gray, Courier; Drake Vireo, Mythical Creature (dragon)
Time period(s): 2000s
Locale(s): Paris, France

Summary: Brand new courier Aisling Gray arrives in Paris with the gold statue she is supposed to deliver, only to find her client has been murdered mere minutes earlier. Aisling doesn't really believe Drake Vireo, the sexy stranger linger-

ing at the scene of the crime, is an Interpol detective, but before she can stop him, Drake disappears along with her statue. All of Aisling's efforts to clear her name with the police become even more complicated once she learns that not only is she one of the Guardians to the portals of Hell, but that Drake is really a dragon and she is supposed to be his new mate!

Where it's reviewed:
Booklist, September 1, 2004, page 73
Romantic Times, September 2004, page 128

Other books by the same author:
Sex and the Single Vampire, 2004
The Corset Diaries, 2004
The Trouble with Harry, 2004
A Girl's Guide to Vampires, 2003
Men in Kilts, 2003

Other books you might like:
Gail Crease, *Poseidon's Kiss*, 1999
Donna Fletcher, *Wedding Spell*, 1999
Kristin Grayson, *Simply Irresistible*, 2002
Sherrilyn Kenyon, *Fantasy Lover*, 2002
Karen Marie Moning, *The Dark Highlander*, 2002

330

DEBBIE MACOMBER

When Christmas Comes

(Don Mills, Ontario: MIRA, 2004)

Story type: Contemporary; Holiday Themes
Subject(s): Christmas; Communication
Major character(s): Emily Springer, Widow(er), Teacher (kindergarten); Ray Brewster, Professor (history)
Time period(s): 2000s
Locale(s): Leavenworth, Washington (near the Cascades); Boston, Massachusetts

Summary: When Emily Springer's daughter Heather says she can't come home to Washington for Christmas, Emily decides to leave the West Coast and pay her a surprise visit in Boston. However, Heather is really heading to Florida with a motorcycle gang and Emily is stuck for two weeks in a condo (she swapped houses with a history professor who wanted peace and quiet over the holidays), in a town she doesn't know. When the professor's brother, Ray Brewster, arrives to check up on him, Emily's life takes a decided turn for the more romantic. Romance is also blossoming across the country when Emily's friend Faith decides to surprise Emily and finds the professor there, instead. Holiday cheer and humor abound in this heartwarming Christmas story.

Where it's reviewed:
Rendezvous, October 2004, page 31
Romantic Times, November 2004, page 115

Other books by the same author:
311 Pelican Court, 2003 (Cedar Cove. Book 3)
The Snow Bride, 2003
204 Rosewood Lane, 2002 (Cedar Cove. Book 2)
A Gift to Last, 2002
16 Lighthouse Road, 2001 (Cedar Cove. Book 1)

Romance

Other books you might like:
Pamela Browning, *Baby Christmas*, 2000
Marcia Evanick, *A Berry Merry Christmas*, 2004
   Misty Harbor. Book 4
Teresa Hill, *Twelve Days*, 2000
Fern Michaels, *Family Blessings*, 2004
Sheila Rabe, *All I Want for Christmas*, 2000

331

ANNETTE MAHON

The Secret Beau

(New York: Avalon, 2004)

Story type: Multicultural; Holiday Themes
Series: Secret. Book 4
Subject(s): Small Town Life; Grief; Forgiveness
Major character(s): Kim Ascension, Banker (teller); Greg
   Yamamoto, Veterinarian, Imposter
Time period(s): 2000s
Locale(s): Malino, Hawaii

Summary: Kim Ascension needs a boyfriend to take to the wedding of the woman who stole her fiance. Kim promised to be her bridesmaid when they were in college, and even though the bride has shown a stunning lack of ethics, Kim's determined to follow through on that long ago vow. Greg Yamamoto passed up a lucrative veterinary practice in Honolulu to care for his dying mother. Now that he's back in Malino, and he's agreed to pose as Kim's boyfriend, the town matchmakers are rubbing their hands in glee. Heartwarming small town fare.

Where it's reviewed:
Library Journal, August 2004, page 56

Other books by the same author:
The Secret Santa, 2003
The Secret Wedding, 2002
The Secret Admirer, 2001
Just Friends, 1998
Chase Your Dreams, 1997

Other books you might like:
Belmont Delange, *Romancing the Holidays. Volume 1*, 2003
   anthology
Debbie Macomber, *These Christmas Angels*, 2003
Luanne Rice, *Silver Bells*, 2004
Deborah Shelley, *Talk about Love*, 1999
LaVyrle Spencer, *Small Town Girl*, 1998

332

LISA MANUEL

Mostly Mayhem

(New York: Zebra, 2004)

Story type: Historical/Regency
Series: Mostly Trilogy. Book 2
Subject(s): Mystery; Social Conditions; Secrets
Major character(s): Tess James Hardington, Widow(er), Single Parent (to her sister's daughter); Charles Emerson, Military Personnel (former army captain)

Time period(s): 1820s (1825)
Locale(s): London, England

Summary: Tess Hardington is caring for her late sister's young daughter while trying to secretly save prostitutes from a serial abductor, and possibly a murderer, who is plaguing the city. The widowed Tess realizes that she must marry soon in order to keep her uncle from taking control of her life and her funds. So when a love from her past reappears, Tess strikes a matrimonial bargain with Charles Emerson—with ultimately romantic results. Mystery, secrets, danger, and greed are elements in this lively romance that is set just after the British Regency period.

Where it's reviewed:
Rendezvous, August 2004, page 21
Romantic Times, September 2004, page 42

Other books by the same author:
Mostly Married, 2004 (Mostly Trilogy. Book 1)

Other books you might like:
Liz Carlyle, *A Woman of Virtue*, 2001
Kimberly Cates, *Angel's Fall*, 1996
Katherine Kingsley, *No Greater Love*, 1992
Lisa Kleypas, *Someone to Watch over Me*, 1999
Betina Krahn, *The Last Bachelor*, 1994

333

JULIE MARSHALL (Pseudonym of Bobbi Smith)

Haven

(New York: Leisure, 2005)

Story type: Contemporary/Innocent; Inspirational
Subject(s): Change; Faith; Catholicism
Major character(s): Jenny Emerson, Young Woman (pregnant); Darrell Miller, Convict (ex-con); Dorothy Pennington, Spouse, Store Owner (boutique co-owner)
Time period(s): 2000s
Locale(s): United States

Summary: *Haven* centers on the lives of people living within the parish boundaries of Our Lady of Perpetual Help. This sweetly gentle story concerns an ex-con trying to get his life back on track, a young single mother-to-be determined to keep her baby, and a woman dumped by her husband for a younger woman. With the help of the parish priest, caring, helpful Joe Myers, and a dash of faith everything comes out right. Less dogmatic than many inspirationals, but somewhat simplistic.

Where it's reviewed:
Romantic Times, January 2005, page 105

Other books you might like:
Robin Lee Hatcher, *The Forgiving Hour*, 1999
Jan Karon, *At Home in Mitford*, 1999
Jan Karon, *A Light in the Window*, 1995
Diane Noble, *The Last Storyteller*, 2004
Kate Welsh, *Never Lie to an Angel*, 1999

Romance

334

FRANCINE MATTHEWS

As You Wish

(Washington, D.C.: BET, 2004)

Story type: Ethnic; Multicultural
Subject(s): African Americans; Grief; Foster Children
Major character(s): Katrina Prescott, Widow(er), Foster Parent; Devlin Graham, Bounty Hunter, Wealthy
Time period(s): 2000s
Locale(s): Harborport, New Jersey

Summary: After Katrina Prescott's cruel husband and unborn baby are killed in a car accident, she begins working with foster kids. The youth center needs money, so Katrina goes to bounty hunter turned businessman Devlin Graham for financial assistance. Devlin doesn't want to help; he wants to buy the property that the center sits on and develop it for a nice profit. Meantime, Katrina's epileptic seizures are increasing in frequency and intensity, and her dead husband shows up very much alive, with murder on his mind.

Where it's reviewed:
Booklist, November 15, 2004, page 568
Romantic Times, December 2004, page 118

Other books by the same author:
Blown, 2005
The Secret Agent, 2002
The Cutout, 2001
Death in a Cold, Hard Light, 1998 (a Merry Folger mystery)
Death in a Mood Indigo, 1997 (a Merry Folger mystery)

Other books you might like:
Rochelle Alers, *No Compromise*, 2002
Gwynne Forster, *Once in a Lifetime*, 2002
Lori Foster, *Say No to Joe*, 2003
Mildred Riley, *Bad to the Bone*, 2003
Linda Randall Wisdom, *Small-Town Secrets*, 2002

335

AMANDA MCCABE
ALLISON LANE, Co-Author
EDITH LAYTON, Co-Author
BARBARA METZGER, Co-Author
SANDRA HEATH, Co-Author

Regency Christmas Magic

(New York: Signet, 2004)

Story type: Anthology; Regency
Subject(s): Christmas; Magic
Time period(s): 19th century
Locale(s): England

Summary: Five different Regency tales celebrate the magic and romance of Christmas. A naval captain finds himself bewitched by a Jamaican beauty when they meet in "Upon a Midnight Clear" by Amanda McCabe. A chaperone trying to successfully get her charge to the altar without a scandal finds her efforts not only complicated by the spirited girl, but also by her own scandalous feelings for a handsome nobleman in Allison Lane's "The Ultimate Magic." An ex-soldier be-comes bewitched by one of a pair of dancing sisters he has been hired to guard in Edith Layton's "Two Dancing Daughters." In Barbara Metzger's "The Enchanted Earl," a young widow wishes for a magician for her Christmas party and fate sends her a plethora of choices, including a wizard who just might be the man of her dreams. Two people who once shared a romantic moment years ago are reunited with the help of a unique dress in Sandra Heath's "The Green Gauze Gown."

Where it's reviewed:
Romantic Times, October 2004, page 50

Other books you might like:
Mary Balogh, *A Regency Christmas Feast*, 1999
Elisabeth Fairchild, *A Regency Christmas Present*, 1999
Sandra Heath, *Regency Christmas Wishes*, 2003
Edith Layton, *A Regency Christmas Carol*, 1997
Anthea Malcolm, *A Christmas Delight*, 1991

336

PAM MCCUTCHEON

Caught in the Act

(New York: Kensington, 2005)

Story type: Humor; Romantic Suspense
Subject(s): Humor; Burglary; Identity, Concealed
Major character(s): Nicole Dreyfuss, Librarian, Fiance(e) (fake); Scott Richmond, Wealthy, Fiance(e) (fake)
Time period(s): 2000s
Locale(s): Denver, Colorado

Summary: When Nicole Dreyfuss' teenaged sister, Chrissie, steals the Richmond family jewels and fences them so she can go to Juilliard, Nicole goes to the Richmond estate. Scott Richmond, the charming, happy-go-lucky heir, won't take the money she offers him. After all, he helped Chrissie steal the jewels in the first place. Now that the jewels have been purchased by Society's elite, Scott and Nicole need to get them back. What better way to get into the houses of the rich than to pretend to be a newly engaged couple seeking advice from their experienced neighbors? Jewels, real and fake, and a whole slew of suspects make this madcap sequel to *My Favorite Husband* a winner.

Other books by the same author:
Belle of the Ball, 2003 (Three Graces. Book 1)
My Favorite Husband, 2003
Enchantment: Hope Chest, 2001
Here Comes the. . .Baby, 1998
Reluctant Rogue, 1997

Other books you might like:
Claire Cross, *Third Time Lucky*, 2003
Dixie Kane, *Chasing Lily*, 2003
Connie Lane, *Dirty Little Lies*, 2004
Suzann Ledbetter, *North of Clever*, 2001
Lori Wilde, *License to Thrill*, 2003

337

MAUREEN MCKADE (Pseudonym of Maureen Webster)

Arouse Suspicion
(New York: Berkley, 2004)

Story type: Contemporary; Romantic Suspense
Subject(s): Murder
Major character(s): Danielle "Danni" Hawkins, Detective—Private (former police detective); Nick Sirocco, Writer (former Army Ranger)
Time period(s): 2000s
Locale(s): New York, New York

Summary: Estranged from her father, Paddy, P.I. Danni Hawkins doesn't question the fact that he committed suicide—until Nick Sirocco walks into her office and changes her mind. A mystery writer who owes a debt to the cop that made him go straight as a young boy, a daughter who felt she was always second best in her father's eyes, and a killer who will stop at nothing to keep the truth from coming out combine in a cleverly plotted romantic thriller.

Where it's reviewed:
Romantic Times, November 2004, page 119

Other books by the same author:
To Find You Again, 2004
His Unexpected Wife, 2001
Outlaw's Bride, 2001
Mail Order Bride, 2000
A Dime Novel Hero, 1998

Other books you might like:
Mary Lynn Baxter, *Hot Texas Nights*, 1996
   another threatening killer
Patricia Potter, *Twisted Shadows*, 2004
Karen Rose, *I'm Watching You*, 2004
E.C. Sheedy, *Perfect Evil*, 2003
Karen Young, *In Confidence*, 2004

338

LINDSAY MCKENNA

First Born
(New York: Silhouette, 2004)

Story type: Contemporary; Multicultural
Series: Morgan's Mercenaries
Subject(s): Military Life; Interpersonal Relations
Major character(s): Annie Dazen, Military Personnel (chief warrant officer), Pilot (helicopter); Jason Trayhern, Military Personnel (chief warrant officer), Pilot (helicopter)
Time period(s): 2000s
Locale(s): Fort Campbell, Kentucky; Afghanistan

Summary: With one last chance to avoid a bad conduct discharge, Apache helicopter pilot Jason Trayhern is assigned to Annie Dazen's combat team in the hope that he can adjust his arrogant, loner attitude and not be a further blot on his legendary father's reputation. It won't be easy under any circumstances and Annie has only one month to make Jason part of her team before they head into combat in Afghanistan. Annie is intuitive, and her instincts tell her that Jason deserves a second chance—and she gives it to him. Adventure, danger, and romance are part of this action-packed military romance, part of McKenna's popular Morgan's Mercenaries saga. Multicultural aspects (Annie's Apache heritage and culture are influences) are integral to this story.

Where it's reviewed:
Rendezvous, May 2004, page 23
Romantic Times, June 2004, page 115

Other books by the same author:
Daughter of Destiny, 2004
Sister of Fortune, 2004
Protecting His Own, 2002 (Morgan's Mercenaries)
Man with a Mission, 2001 (Morgan's Mercenaries)
Man Alone, 2000 (Morgan's Mercenaries)

Other books you might like:
Suzanne Brockmann, *Flashpoint*, 2004
Suzanne Brockmann, *Over the Edge*, 2001
Merline Lovelace, *Call of Duty*, 1998
   military life
Merline Lovelace, *Dark Side of Dawn*, 2001
   military life
Merline Lovelace, *In Love and War*, 2003
   anthology

339

SHANNON MCKENNA

Return to Me
(New York: Brava, 2004)

Story type: Contemporary; Romantic Suspense
Subject(s): Reunions; Mystery
Major character(s): Ellen Kent, Innkeeper (bed and breakfast owner); Simon Riley, Photojournalist
Time period(s): 2000s
Locale(s): La Rue, Oregon (La Rue River Valley)

Summary: When Simon Riley roars back into town after a 17-year absence looking for all the world like a Hell's Angel, his main goal is to investigate his uncle's suspicious death and lay some old ghosts to rest. When he finds his teenage love, Ellen Kent, they both realize that the fire is still there, even though Ellen has a good life and is engaged to be married. Danger, as well as passion, flares when Simon begins to delve into the past; and there is one who will stop at nothing to see that the truth remains hidden, even if it means death for Ellen. Explicit sex.

Where it's reviewed:
Romantic Times, June 2004, page 75

Other books by the same author:
Standing in the Shadows, 2003
Behind Closed Doors, 2002

Other books you might like:
Lori Foster, *Bad Boys on Board*, 2003
Lori Foster, *Too Much Temptation*, 2002
Susan Johnson, *Hot Legs*, 2004
Donna Kauffman, *Walk on the Wild Side*, 2001
Nancy Warren, *Drive Me Crazy*, 2004

340

LUANN MCLANE

Hot Summer Nights

(New York: New American Library, 2004)

Story type: Contemporary; Collection
Subject(s): Small Town Life; Sexuality; Sports/Baseball
Time period(s): 2000s
Locale(s): Sander's City, Midwest (on the Ohio River)

Summary: This collection of three steamy novellas set during the equally steamy summer in the small Midwestern town of Sander's City focuses on baseball, sex, and romance as three couples find love during those hot, summer nights. *Hot August Night* pairs a high school principal with a former pro baseball player who fulfills her desperate need for a baseball coach. *Heat Wave* takes a newly divorced drama teacher and a team manager and urges them down the path to love. In *Hotshot*, a PE teacher finds unexpected love with a sexy pitcher. All three stories are written by McLane and while they are all linked, each stands on its own. Explicit sex.

Other books by the same author:
Taking Care of Business, 2005

Other books you might like:
Lori Foster, *Hot and Bothered*, 2001
     erotic anthology
Lori Foster, *I Love Bad Boys*, 2002
     erotic anthology
Lori Foster, *Too Much Temptation*, 2002
Lynn Kurland, *Opposites Attract*, 2000

341

MARLISS MELTON

Forget Me Not

(New York: Warner Forever, 2004)

Story type: Contemporary
Series: SEAL Team Twelve. Book 1
Subject(s): Memory Loss; Reunions; Prisoners of War
Major character(s): Helen Renault, Widow(er) (presumed); Gabriel Renault, Military Personnel (Navy SEAL lieutenant), Amnesiac
Time period(s): 2000s
Locale(s): Virginia

Summary: Declared dead after being missing in action for a year, Navy SEAL Gabe Renault suddenly washes up on a North Korean beach, alive but with no memory of the mission that went wrong or his time in a prison camp. He also has no memory of his wife, Helen, or his teenage stepdaughter Mallory. Now home to recover, he has to get used to his ''new'' family and they must readjust to him. Problems, both personal and military, abound as Helen and Gabe begin to forge a new relationship; but as his memory begins to return, danger lurks because someone doesn't want Gabe to remember. Melton also writes as Marliss Moon.

Where it's reviewed:
Romantic Times, December 2004, page 118

Other books you might like:
Suzanne Brockmann, *Identity Unknown*, 2000
     another Navy SEAL with amnesia
Suzanne Brockmann, *Unsung Hero*, 2000
Merline Lovelace, *Call of Duty*, 1998
     military theme
Fern Michaels, *About Face*, 2003
     memory loss/mystery
Sharon Sala, *Remember Me*, 1999
     amnesia/emotionally compelling

342

BARBARA METZGER

The Duel

(New York: Signet, 2005)

Story type: Historical/Regency; Humor
Subject(s): Humor; Guilt; Sisters
Major character(s): Athena Renslow, Young Woman; Ian Maddox, Nobleman (Earl of Marden), Wealthy
Time period(s): 1800s
Locale(s): London, England

Summary: Ian Maddox, Earl of Marden, gets involved in a duel. Instead of hitting the other duelist, one of the bullets goes wild, and a young boy is shot from his horse, striking his head on a rock as he falls, making his injuries even worse. Not sure if the lad will live or die, Ian brings him to his London townhouse and sends for the boy's sister. Athena Renslow turns out to be older than Ian expected, and since she spends the night, albeit innocently, in a bachelor's home, her reputation is shot. Now, everyone's after Ian, London's most notorious rake, to marry Athena. Everyone, that is, except the would-be bride.

Where it's reviewed:
Romantic Times, February 2005, page 34

Other books by the same author:
A Perfect Gentleman, 2004
Love, Louisa, 2004
Wedded Bliss, 2004
The Diamond Key, 2003
Lady Sparrow, 2002

Other books you might like:
Celeste Bradley, *Fallen*, 2003
Suzanne Enoch, *London's Perfect Scoundrel*, 2003
Lisa Kleypas, *Suddenly You*, 2001
Kasey Michaels, *Someone to Love*, 2001
Lynsay Sands, *The Reluctant Reformer*, 2002

343

BARBARA METZGER

A Perfect Gentleman

(New York: Signet, 2004)

Story type: Historical/Regency; Humor
Subject(s): Humor; Mystery; Social Classes
Major character(s): Ellianne Kane, Detective—Amateur; Stony Wellstone, Nobleman (viscount), Impoverished

Time period(s): 1800s
Locale(s): London, England

Summary: Viscount Stony Wellstone is out of money, and his young, widowed stepmother is used to living in high style. By a quirk of fate, the handsome, charming nobleman is hired to escort single women to parties and balls so their brothers and cousins don't have to do it. The women never know their debonair date is paid to escort them, and Stony becomes a high demand escort. Ellianne Kane wants to hire Stony as her escort. Not that she needs a date, but Stony can get her into society events so she can find her missing sister. This rollicking Regency romp, with its quirky cast of secondary characters, is sure to entertain.

Where it's reviewed:
Booklist, October 1, 2004, page 317
Library Journal, August 2004, page 56
Romantic Times, October 2004, page 42

Other books by the same author:
A Debt to Delia, 2002
The Painted Lady, 2002
Miss Westlake's Windfall, 2001
A Worthy Wife, 2000
Saved by Scandal, 2000

Other books you might like:
Pamela Britton, *Scandal*, 2002
Suzanne Enoch, *The Rake*, 2002
Amanda Quick, *The Paid Companion*, 2004
Jaclyn Reding, *The Pretender*, 2002
Lynsay Sands, *The Reluctant Reformer*, 2002

344

FERN MICHAELS

Family Blessings
(New York: Atria, 2004)

Story type: Contemporary; Holiday Themes
Subject(s): Christmas; Family
Major character(s): Loretta Cisco, Businesswoman (retired CEO of candy company), Widow(er); Ezra Danford, Widow(er)
Time period(s): 2000s
Locale(s): Allegheny Mountains, Pennsylvania

Summary: As if the fact that a tornado destroyed the home she's lived in for years weren't enough—and right before Thanksgiving, too—Loretta Cisco's beloved grandchildren are all behaving strangely. Are they having marital problems? Or is it something else? Secrets, miscommunications, and misperceptions are at the heart of this story which radiates small-town charm and nicely solves all problems. Light, lively, and filled with heartwarming family interactions, this short novella is just right for the holidays.

Other books by the same author:
No Place Like Home, 2002
Charming Lily, 2001
Plain Jane, 2001
What You Wish For, 2000
Heart of the Home, 1997

Other books you might like:
Janet Dailey, *Maybe This Christmas*, 2003
Marcia Evanick, *A Berry Merry Christmas*, 2004
   Misty Harbor. Book 4
Teresa Hill, *Twelve Days*, 2000
Debbie Macomber, *When Christmas Comes*, 2004
Luanne Rice, *Silver Bells*, 2004

345

FERN MICHAELS
LINDA LAEL MILLER, Co-Author
THERESA ALAN, Co-Author
JANE BLACKWOOD, Co-Author

Jingle All the Way
(New York: Zebra, 2004)

Story type: Anthology; Holiday Themes
Subject(s): Christmas; Short Stories
Time period(s): 2000s

Summary: The magic of the Christmas holidays shines through in this quite diverse, delightful quartet of novellas by some of the genre's best know writers. Included are: *A Bright Red Ribbon*, veteran romance author Fern Michaels' blizzard-set heartwarming story of a dog, a wheelchair-bound hero, and an appealing heroine; *The 24 Days of Christmas*, Linda Lael Miller's emotionally compelling reunion romance with a charming secondary love story; *Santa Unwrapped*, Theresa Alan's smart, modern story that features a sassy heroine and a wheelchair-bound Santa hero; and *Maybe This Christmas*, Jane Blackwood's magical holiday tale.

Where it's reviewed:
Library Journal, November 15, 2004, page 48
Romantic Times, November 2004, page 114

Other books by the same author:
Family Blessings, 2004

Other books you might like:
Judith Arnold, *'Tis the Season*, 2000
Janet Dailey, *Maybe This Christmas*, 2003
Donna Kauffman, *Merry Christmas, Baby*, 2004
Sheila Rabe, *All I Want for Christmas*, 2000

346

TANYA MICHAELS

Not Quite as Advertised
(Toronto: Harlequin, 2004)

Story type: Contemporary; Humor
Subject(s): Business; Competition
Major character(s): Jocelyn ''Joss'' McBride, Advertising (executive); Hugh Brannon, Advertising (executive)
Time period(s): 2000s
Locale(s): Dallas, Texas; Houston, Texas

Summary: Joss McBride should be used to coming in second to Hugh Brannon. After all not only had her ex-lover managed to steal an account she had spent weeks slaving over, he also edged her out of a promotion she richly deserved. After their employer is indicted for fraud, Joss and Hugh part company to go work at different advertising firms, but now an unexpected business merger brings the two back together as co-workers again. This time around Joss is determined to prove to the oh-so-sexy Hugh that his winning streak is through.

Where it's reviewed:
Romantic Times, November 2004, page 101

Other books by the same author:
Hers for the Weekend, 2004
Sheer Decadence, 2004
The Maid of Dishonor, 2003
Who Needs Decaf?, 2003

Other books you might like:
Stephanie Bond, *It Takes a Rebel*, 2003
Dorien Kelly, *Do-Over*, 2003
Mary Leo, *Stick Shift*, 2004
Cindi Myers, *Life According to Lucy*, 2004
Jill Shalvis, *Natural Blond Instincts*, 2003

347

ELIZABETH MINOGUE

The Prince
(New York: Berkley, 2004)

Story type: Historical/Medieval; Historical/Fantasy
Subject(s): Revenge; Middle Ages; Fantasy
Major character(s): Rose of Valinor, Royalty (princess); Florian of Venya, Royalty (prince), Sorcerer (sorcerer pirate)
Time period(s): Indeterminate Past
Locale(s): Venya, Fictional Country; Valinor, Fictional Country

Summary: Orphaned and stripped of his royal heritage when his uncle, Richard, kills his parents, Prince Florian of Venya lives for the day when he will reclaim his land and his throne. Now the exiled Princess Rose of Valinor, Richard's niece, comes to him for help; but Florian, cynical and suspicious, questions her motives. Ultimately, they join forces, and while all is not resolved, the pair find love, and go a long way toward accomplishing their goals. An interesting blend of realism and fantasy.

Where it's reviewed:
Rendezvous, November 2004, page 25
Romantic Times, November 2004, page 38

Other books you might like:
Katherine Deauville, *Daggers of Gold*, 1993
Juliana Garnett, *The Baron*, 1999
Lisa Jackson, *Wild and Wicked*, 2002
Karyn Monk, *The Rose and the Warrior*, 2000
Anne Stuart, *Lord of Danger*, 1993

348

MARGARET MOORE
TERRI BRISBIN, Co-Author
GAIL RANSTROM, Co-Author

The Christmas Visit
(Toronto: Harlequin, 2004)

Story type: Anthology; Holiday Themes
Subject(s): Christmas
Time period(s): Indeterminate Past

Summary: This diverse trio of Christmas novellas from three of Harlequin's popular historical writers makes use of English and Welsh settings and provides plenty of heartwarming, romantic holiday atmosphere. Included are *Comfort and Joy*, Margaret Moore's compelling beauty-and-the beast story of healing and love; *Love at First Step*, Terri Brisbin's unusual tale with a prostitute heroine; and *A Christmas Secret*, Gail Ranstrom's sexy Regency with more than its share of intriguing secrets. There's something for everyone in this collection.

Other books you might like:
Suzanne Barclay, *The Knights of Christmas*, 1997
    historical anthology
Nancy Butler, *A Regency Christmas Eve*, 2000
    Regency anthology
Sandra Heath, *Regency Christmas Wishes*, 2003
Ruth Ryan Langan, *One Christmas Night*, 2003
    historical anthology
Susan Spencer Paul, *'Tis the Season*, 2001
    historical anthology

349

HUNTER MORGAN (Pseudonym of Colleen Faulkner)

She'll Never Live
(New York: Zebra, 2004)

Story type: Contemporary; Romantic Suspense
Series: She'll Never. . . Trilogy. Book 3
Subject(s): Serial Killers; Murder; Small Town Life
Major character(s): Claire Drummond, Police Officer (police chief), Single Parent (of teenage daughter); Graham Simpson, Widow(er), Store Owner (office supply); Ashley Drummond, Teenager
Time period(s): 2000s
Locale(s): Albany Beach

Summary: There's a serial killer loose in Albany Beach, and it's up to Police Chief Claire Drummond to find him. The clever Bloodsucker is part of the community and Claire knows he could be any of a dozen men—maybe even the one she is romantically interested in. Lots of realistic small town atmosphere, assorted teenagers, including Claire's 15-year-old daughter, and a calculating, insane killer result in a chilling thriller.

Where it's reviewed:
Rendezvous, September 2004, page 39

Other books by the same author:
She'll Never Know, 2004 (She'll Never. . . Trilogy. Book 2)
She'll Never Tell, 2004 (She'll Never. . . Trilogy. Book 1)

The Other Twin, 2003

Other books you might like:
Beverly Barton, *As Good as Dead*, 2004
Beverly Barton, *The Fifth Victim*, 2003
Lisa Jackson, *The Morning After*, 2004
S.K. McClafferty, *Be Very Afraid*, 2004
Karen Rose, *I'm Watching You*, 2004

350

CINDI MYERS (Pseudonym of Cynthia Myers)

What Phoebe Wants

(Toronto: Harlequin, 2004)

Story type: Contemporary
Subject(s): Self-Confidence
Major character(s): Phoebe Frame, Office Worker (medical transcriptionist); Jeff Fischer, Computer Expert
Time period(s): 2000s
Locale(s): Houston, Texas

Summary: After Phoebe Frame's husband dumps her for a younger model, her lecherous boss tries to add a few new ''duties'' to her job and her car is taken hostage by the dealer. Phoebe decides she is no longer going to be taken advantage of by any man. A change in hair color and a change in attitude give Phoebe the confidence to start standing up to anyone, including Jeff Fischer, the young sexy computer expert who has been hired to train Phoebe on a new system at work. Even though Phoebe might think that the last thing she needs in her life is another man trying to tell her what to do, Jeff is determined to prove to Phoebe that he really is the only man for her.

Where it's reviewed:
Romantic Times, July 2004, page 95

Other books by the same author:
Life According to Lucy, 2004
Rumor Has It, 2004
Just 4 Play, 2003
Say You Want Me, 2003
It's a Guy Thing, 2002

Other books you might like:
Carrie Alexander, *The Chocolate Seduction*, 2003
Stephanie Bond, *Seeking Single Male*, 2000
Kristin Gabriel, *Seduced in Seattle*, 2002
Holly Jacobs, *I Waxed My Legs for This?*, 2001
Bev Katz Rosenbaum, *Wanted: An Interesting Life*, 2004

351

JACQUELINE NAVIN

The Heiress of Hyde Park

(New York: Berkley, 2004)

Story type: Historical/Regency
Series: Mayfair Brides. Book 2
Subject(s): Social Classes; Missing Persons; Inheritance
Major character(s): Trista Josephine Nash, Heiress—Lost, Artisan (milliner); Lord Roman Aylesgarth, Nobleman; Lady May Hayworth, Noblewoman (daughter of an earl)

Time period(s): 1810s
Locale(s): London, England

Summary: When the nobleman she loves is forced to marry for money, Trista Nash flees, adopts the personna of widowed Trista Fairhaven. and sets about making a new life as a milliner for herself and her unborn son. Her life is turned upside down when Lady May Hayworth, sister to the late Earl of Woolrich, informs Trista that she is the daughter of the earl and a very wealthy heiress. The repercussions of this are enormous as Trista is thrown into the same social circles as Lord Roman Aylesgarth, her son's father, and he seems intent on pursuing her. Deception, passion, and a touch of villainy are the order of the day in this second installment in a trilogy in which Lady May Hayworth locates the illegitimate children of her late brother, the Earl of Woolrich, and makes sure they have the inheritance and social position they deserve.

Where it's reviewed:
Rendezvous, August 2004, page 22
Romantic Times, August 2004, page 41

Other books by the same author:
The Beauty of Bond Street, 2005
The Princess of Park Lane, 2003
The Bliss, 2002
Meet Me at Midnight, 2001
The Sleeping Beauty, 2001

Other books you might like:
Mary Balogh, *The Secret Pearl*, 1997
Patricia Grasso, *Violets in the Snow*, 1998
    Cinderella story/magical elements
Mary Jo Putney, *The Bargain*, 1999
Julia Quinn, *An Offer from a Gentleman*, 2001
Gayle Wilson, *Lady Sarah's Son*, 2001

352

BRENDA NOVAK

Cold Feet

(Toronto: Harlequin, 2004)

Story type: Romantic Suspense
Subject(s): Family; Murder; Secrets
Major character(s): Madison Lieberman, Real Estate Agent; Caleb Trovato, Writer (true crime)
Time period(s): 2000s
Locale(s): Seattle, Washington

Summary: Madison Lieberman always believed that her father could never have been the ''Sandpoint Strangler,'' but then she discovers a box containing items from some of the killer's victims hidden in her parents' house. True crime writer Caleb Trovato spent years trying to solve the Sandpoint Strangler murders before giving up, but now the disappearance of his ex-wife's younger sister has Caleb convinced that there is some connection between the two. Caleb is certain that Madison is the key to everything, but getting her to trust him with her secrets won't be easy.

Other books by the same author:
A Husband of Her Own, 2003
Sanctuary, 2003
Taking the Heat, 2003

A Baby of Her Own, 2002
Shooting the Moon, 2002

Other books you might like:
Catherine Coulter, *The Cove*, 1996
Suzanne Forster, *Every Breath She Takes*, 1999
Jayne Ann Krentz, *Eclipse Bay*, 2000
Carla Neggers, *The Harbor*, 2003
Anne Stuart, *Still Lake*, 2002

353

CONSTANCE O'DAY-FLANNERY

Shifting Love
(New York: Tor, 2004)

Story type: Contemporary/Fantasy; Paranormal
Subject(s): Psychic Powers; Fantasy; Love
Major character(s): Magdalene ''Maggie'' O'Shea, Supernatural Being (shapeshifter), Store Owner; Julian McDonald, Wealthy, Businessman (venture capitalist)
Time period(s): 2000s
Locale(s): Philadelphia, Pennsylvania

Summary: Growing up as a shapechanger, Maggie uses her abilities to get what she wants; but when one of her boyfriends throws himself off a mountain because she isn't serious about him, her life takes a bizarre turn. Captured by a mysterious shapechanger, Marcus Bocelli, and taught that her powers are far greater than she had thought, she learns that she must work for a mysterious foundation and atone for misusing her gifts by healing wounded, heartbroken men so they can get on with their lives and learn to love again. The key, of course, is never to fall in love with them—something that is not a problem until Julian McDonald becomes her next assignment. There's something different about this man because the foundation is very interested in him—and Maggie wants to know why. A fascinating premise combines with interesting characters to produce a sensual, romantic story.

Where it's reviewed:
Romantic Times, November 2004, page 125

Other books by the same author:
Time After Time, 2001
Anywhere You Are, 1999
Sunsets, 1996
Seasons, 1995
Timeless Passion, 1986

Other books you might like:
Jo Beverley, *Irresistible Forces*, 2004
    paranormal anthology
Susan Carroll, *The Night Drifter*, 1999
Christine Feehan, *Dark Melody*, 2003
    darker
Christine Feehan, *Dark Symphony*, 2003
    darker

354

PATTI O'SHEA

The Power of Two
(New York: Love Spell, 2004)

Story type: Futuristic
Series: 2176. Book 4
Subject(s): Adventure and Adventurers; Futuristic Fiction
Major character(s): Cai Randolph, Military Personnel (captain); Jake Tucker, Military Personnel (captain)
Time period(s): 22nd century (2176)
Locale(s): Unified Colonies of Earth, Earth

Summary: The techie half of the Quantum Brain Tandem Project, Cai Randolph has been mentally linked to Captain Jake Tucker through nanoprobes in their brains for years. She processes and synthesizes information at top speed and then feeds it to him mentally while he and his Special Forces operatives are on missions. Though mental partners and friends, Cai and Jake have never met; but that all changes when Cai has the chance to physically go with the group. Jake gets the shock of his life—and is furious at the deception—when he realizes that Cai is not the computer he'd always thought, but a beautiful, live, sexy woman with a mind of her own. Now together on a dangerous quest, one that could lead Cai to information about her missing parents or destroy her mind, their relationship develops in new, and more romantic, directions. The 2176 series is set in the future, during the time of the United Colonies of Earth (U.C.E.).

Where it's reviewed:
Romantic Times, November 2004, page 128

Other books by the same author:
Ravyn's Flight, 2002

Other books you might like:
Susan Grant, *Contact*, 2002
Susan Grant, *The Legend of Banzai Maguire*, 2004
    2176. Book 1
Susan Krinard, *Kinsman's Oath*, 2004
Liz Maverick, *The Shadow Runners*, 2004
Kathleen Nance, *Day of Fire*, 2004
    2176. Book 2

355

DIANA PALMER
CARLA NEGGERS, Co-Author
EMILIE RICHARDS, Co-Author
BRENDA NOVAK, Co-Author
SUSAN MALLERY, Co-Author

More than Words
(Toronto: Harlequin, 2004)

Story type: Anthology; Contemporary
Subject(s): Charity; Healing; Social Issues
Time period(s): 2000s

Summary: This collection of stories is based on the true experiences of women who have made extraordinary contributions to society. In ''The Greatest Gift'' by Diana Palmer, a homeless woman and her children collect food for others in need. Carla Neggers' "Close Call" has a prosecutor and a police officer find love in an inn owned by a woman who's escaped her abusive spouse. "Hanging by a Thread" by Emilie Richards concerns a troubled teen who moves in with a childless couple. In "Small Packages" by Brenda Novak, a woman divorced from an abusive man offers to adopt a single man's baby. A widower hides from the world behind his bookcase in "Built to Last" by Susan Mallery.

Where it's reviewed:
Booklist, September 15, 2004, page 225
Romantic Times, October 2004, page 89

Other books by the same author:
Renegade, 2004

Other books you might like:
Susan Mallery, *Someone Like You*, 2004
Carla Neggers, *Night's Landing*, 2004
Brenda Novak, *A Family of Her Own*, 2004
Emilie Richards, *Wedding Ring*, 2004

356

DIANA PALMER

Renegade

(Toronto: Harlequin, 2004)

Story type: Romantic Suspense; Contemporary
Subject(s): Rape; Child Abuse; Trust
Major character(s): Tippy Moore, Model ("The Georgia Fire-fly"), Abuse Victim (of child molestation and rape); Cash Grier, Police Officer (police chief)
Time period(s): 2000s
Locale(s): Jacobsville, Texas

Summary: Police chief and former Texas Ranger Cash Grier doesn't trust women. The woman his widowed father married turned the family against Cash, causing him to be exiled to a military school at a young age. Actress/model Tippy Moore, "The Georgia Firefly," can't stand to have a man touch her—her mother's boyfriend had raped her repeatedly when she was a child. Trusting, healing, and forgiving are all hard to come by in this book about two people so damaged by traumatic childhoods that they have to learn together how to build a normal, loving relationship.

Where it's reviewed:
Booklist, August 2004, page 1910
Library Journal, August 2004, page 56
Publishers Weekly, August 30, 2004, page 33

Other books by the same author:
A Hero's Kiss, 2003 (anthology)
Lawless, 2003
A Man of Means, 2002
Desperado, 2002
Texas Ranger, 2001

Other books you might like:
Catherine Anderson, *Seventh Heaven*, 2000
Lori Foster, *When Bruce Met Cyn...*, 2004
Nora Roberts, *Carolina Moon*, 2000
Debra Salonen, *Back in Kansas*, 2001
Sheri Whitefeather, *Skyler Hawk: Lone Brave*, 2000

357

LAURA PAQUET

An Honorable Match

(New York: Zebra, 2004)

Story type: Regency
Subject(s): Courtship; Marriage
Major character(s): Lady Sarah Harrison, Noblewoman (daughter of an earl), Impoverished; Lord William Cates, Nobleman (son of a duke), Diplomat
Time period(s): 1810s
Locale(s): London, England; Yorkshire, England

Summary: When the profligate Duke of Cambermere impulsively marries his mistress instead of his fiancee, it is up to his younger brother, Lord William Cates, to go to Yorkshire and break the news to Lady Sarah Harrison. However, William doesn't stop there; in an effort to salvage his own family's badly tarnished reputation and to help Lady Sarah save face, he proposes marriage—which she summarily refuses. Sarah won't marry someone who pities her and, in any case, she needs to marry money. She does, however, convince William to take her and her mother with him to London where she can use the upcoming Season to find someone to wed. Funny, charming, and typically Regency.

Where it's reviewed:
Romantic Times, September 2004, page 115

Other books by the same author:
Mr. McAllister Sets His Cap, 2003
Miss Scott Meets Her Match, 2002
Lord Langdon's Tutor, 2000

Other books you might like:
Patricia Bray, *The Irish Earl*, 2000
Lynn Collum, *The Wedding Charm*, 2001
Candice Hern, *A Garden Folly*, 1997
Kate Huntington, *The Captain's Courtship*, 1999
Evelyn Richardson, *Lady Alex's Gamble*, 1995

358

LAURA PAQUET

A Rakish Spy

(New York: Zebra, 2004)

Story type: Regency
Subject(s): Espionage; Family; Schools
Major character(s): Charlotte Gregory, Teacher (schoolmistress); Francis Burnham, Nobleman (Viscount Finchwood)
Time period(s): 1810s
Locale(s): London, England; Gillington, England

Summary: After spending a year hopelessly trying to lose himself in cards and drink, a wounded Francis Burnham, Viscount Finchwood, is delighted to be given another chance to serve his country when he is asked to break up a ring of French spies and smugglers working out of Hampshire. While Finch's family connections will help him out with his mission, he will also need a local assistant; and schoolmistress Charlotte Gregory seems perfect for the job. The only difficulty is that Finch's rakish reputation has preceded him, and convincing Charlotte that she will be safe working with him won't be easy, especially once Finch finds he isn't completely immune to his charming and intelligent new partner.

Where it's reviewed:
Romantic Times, July 2004, page 42

Other books by the same author:
Mr. McAllister Sets His Cap, 2003
Miss Scott Meets Her Match, 2002
Lord Langdon's Tutor, 2000

Other books you might like:
Blair Bancroft, *The Indifferent Earl*, 2001
Nadine Miller, *The Yorkshire Lady*, 2001
Julia Parks, *His Saving Grace*, 2002
Evelyn Richardson, *The Scandalous Widow*, 2004
Melynda Beth Skinner, *The Blue Devil*, 2001

359

NANCY J. PARRA

The Marryin' Kind
(New York: Avalon, 2005)

Story type: Historical/Americana
Series: Morgan Brothers. Book 5
Subject(s): Trust; Secrets; Family Relations
Major character(s): Madeline Morgan, Spinster; Trevor Montgomery, Gunfighter
Time period(s): 1860s
Locale(s): Boltonville, Wisconsin

Summary: Twenty-three-year-old Maddie Morgan's father decrees that none of his younger daughters can begin courting until she gets married. Her brother suggests Maddie tell everyone that she's been secretly engaged to his friend, Evan Montgomery, who hasn't been heard from since he left to fight in the War Between the States. News of the engagement spreads quickly, and soon Maddie is living in the empty Montgomery place. Two years later, Evan's brother Trevor, a gunfighter, decides to come home, but when he gets there, he's shocked to find Maddie in residence. Trevor can't figure out why this woman who claims to be engaged to his brother is living in their house, especially since Evan would be the last person on earth to tie himself down to one female. Worse than that, Trevor is attracted to Maddie himself.

Other books by the same author:
Wyoming Wedding, 2004 (Morgan Brothers. Book 4)
Loving Lana, 2003 (Morgan Brothers. Book 3)
A Wanted Man, 2002 (Morgan Brothers. Book 2)
Saving Samantha, 2002 (Morgan Brothers. Book 1)

Other books you might like:
Lori Copeland, *Bridal Lace and Buckskin*, 2003
Georgina Gentry, *To Tame a Texan*, 2003
Lorraine Heath, *A Rogue in Texas*, 1999
Linda Lael Miller, *Skye*, 2000
Jodi Thomas, *When a Texan Gambles*, 2003

360

DIANE PERKINS

The Improper Wife
(New York: Warner, 2004)

Story type: Historical/Regency
Subject(s): Marriage
Major character(s): Maggie Delaney, Gentlewoman; John Grayson, Military Personnel (captain)
Time period(s): 1810s (1814; 1816-1817)
Locale(s): England

Summary: Maggie Delaney thinks her husband, Captain John Grayson, is dead. Therefore when a very pregnant Maggie arrives at Grayson's London townhouse, she is quite surprised to find that not only is Grayson not dead, he isn't even the man she married. At first all Grayson wants to do is find some way of gracefully getting rid of his new "wife," but the more time he spends with Maggie, the more Grayson begins to think that being married to her might not be so bad after all.

Where it's reviewed:
Booklist, November 15, 2004, page 568
Publishers Weekly, October 18, 2004, page 53
Romantic Times, November 2004, page 38

Other books you might like:
Nicole Byrd, *Dear Imposter*, 2003
Suzanne Enoch, *London's Perfect Scoundrel*, 2003
Katherine Greyle, *Major Wycliff's Campaign*, 2001
Madeline Hunter, *The Saint*, 2003
Kathryn Smith, *A Seductive Offer*, 2002

361

CANDICE POARCH (Pseudonym of Candice Poarch Baines)

Loving Delilah
(Washington, D.C.: BET, 2004)

Story type: Romantic Suspense; Ethnic
Series: Coree Island. Book 3
Subject(s): African Americans; Murder; Adoption
Major character(s): Delilah Benton, Writer (aspiring); David Washington, Doctor (pediatrician)
Time period(s): 2000s
Locale(s): Coree Island, North Carolina; Morehead City, North Carolina; Raleigh, North Carolina

Summary: Delilah Benton, a proposal manager for a security company, flees to Coree Island after her two-timing boyfriend, who happens to also be her boss, fires her to please the "other woman." Soon, pediatrician David Washington begins to fall for Delilah, and after she moves into his guest house, things really begin to heat up. Then David's ex-fiancee makes an appearance, and wants to join his practice. All of this pales in light of the fact that someone's trying to kill Delilah, and they'll stop at nothing to do it.

Where it's reviewed:
Booklist, November 15, 2004, page 569
Romantic Times, December 2004, page 115

Other books by the same author:
Courage under Fire, 2003
Lighthouse Magic, 2003 (Coree Island. Book 2)
Bargain of the Heart, 2002
The Last Dance, 2001 (Nottoway. Book 4)
Shattered Illusions, 2000 (Coree Island. Book 1)

Other books you might like:
Rochelle Alers, *No Compromise*, 2002
Roxanne St. Claire, *Tropical Getaway*, 2003
Janelle Taylor, *Dying to Marry*, 2004
Alice Wootson, *Aloha Love*, 2005
Karen Young, *Someone Knows*, 2002

362

CYNTHIA PRATT

A Duke for Christmas

(New York: Zebra, 2004)

Story type: Regency; Holiday Themes
Subject(s): Christmas; Courtship; Widows/Widowers
Major character(s): Sophie Lindel Banner, Widow(er); Dominic Swift, Nobleman (Duke of Saltaire)
Time period(s): 1810s
Locale(s): England

Summary: Widowed and returning to England, Sophie Banner is met at the dock by Dominic Swift, Duke of Saltaire, the man she rejected for her late husband; only this time, their relationship is about to take a very different turn. Although the path to love is not smooth and various difficulties arise, the result of this lively, charming Regency with its holiday setting is worth the wait.

Where it's reviewed:
Rendezvous, October 2004, page 35
Romantic Times, October 2004, page 50

Other books by the same author:
The Black Mask, 2003

Other books you might like:
Mary Balogh, *Christmas Belle*, 1994
Diane Farr, *Once upon a Christmas*, 2000
Emma Jensen, *His Grace Endures*, 1998
Patricia Oliver, *Broken Promises*, 2001
    similar situation
Joan Smith, *The Kissing Bough*, 1994

363

LUANNE RICE

Silver Bells

(New York: Bantam, 2004)

Story type: Holiday Themes; Paranormal
Subject(s): Christmas; Grief; Family Relations
Major character(s): Catherine Tierney, Widow(er), Librarian; Christy Byrne, Widow(er), Single Parent
Time period(s): 2000s
Locale(s): New York, New York (Manhattan)

Summary: Widower Christy Byrne grows Christmas trees in Nova Scotia, then takes them to Manhattan during the holiday season to sell. When his son Danny runs away after they fight, Christy searches for him, but to no avail. After a year, he returns to Manhattan, hoping to find his son. Widow Catherine Tierney has been helping Danny and giving him access to the private library where she works. Now his dad's back, and she's falling for him. Should she tell Christy about his son and lose Danny's trust or keep Danny's secret and lose his father?

Where it's reviewed:
Romantic Times, November 2004, page 91

Other books by the same author:
Dance with Me, 2004
Safe Harbor, 2003
The Perfect Summer, 2003
The Secret Hour, 2003
True Blue, 2002

Other books you might like:
Judith Arnold, *'Tis the Season*, 2000
Janet Dailey, *Maybe This Christmas*, 2003
Debbie Macomber, *The Christmas Basket*, 2002
Annette Mahon, *The Secret Santa*, 2003
Judi McCoy, *Heaven Sent*, 2003

364

PATRICIA RICE

This Magic Moment

(New York: Signet, 2004)

Story type: Historical/Georgian; Historical/Fantasy
Series: Magic. Book 4
Subject(s): Psychic Powers; Magic
Major character(s): Lady Christina Malcolm Childe, Psychic, Noblewoman; Lord Harry Winchester, Nobleman (Duke of Sommersville)
Time period(s): 1750s (1755)
Locale(s): England

Summary: With the sudden deaths of both his father and his elder brother, carefree Lord Harry Winchester becomes the new Duke of Sommersville and inherits the crumbling estate and all the problems that go with it. Needing money to set things to rights, Harry has no choice but to marry his long-time fiancee, Christina Malcolm Childe. Christina has assets other than her dowry. Like all the Malcolm women she has special gifts, and Christina can see auras and sometimes, ghosts. Appalled that her fun-loving Harry's aura has turned dark, she decides to get to the root of his depression and make things right once more. Danger lurks in the ancient estate, and if Christina and Harry don't get to the bottom of things soon, neither of them may survive the next "accident." A malicious villain, family spectres, and a dash of magic add to this charming romance.

Where it's reviewed:
Library Journal, August 2004, page 56
Romantic Times, August 2004, page 37

Other books by the same author:
McCloud's Woman, 2003 (McCloud Brothers. Book 2)
The Trouble with Magic, 2003 (Magic. Book 3)

Must Be Magic, 2002 (Magic. Book 2)
All a Woman Wants, 2001
Merely Magic, 2000 (Magic. Book 1)

Other books you might like:
Jo Beverley, *Forbidden Magic*, 1998
Susan Carroll, *Midnight Bride*, 2001
    family ghosts and gifts
Kimberly Cates, *Magic*, 1998
    magic and time travel
Elizabeth Lowell, *Untamed*, 1993
Mary Jo Putney, *Kiss of Fate*, 2004
    magic and paranormal gifts

365

LINDA L. RICHARDS

Mad Money

(Don Mills, Ontario: MIRA, 2004)

Story type: Romantic Suspense; Contemporary
Series: Madeleine Carter. Book 1
Subject(s): Murder; Mystery; Kidnapping
Major character(s): Madeline Carter, Stock Broker, Detective—Amateur; Steve Rundle, Salesman
Time period(s): 2000s
Locale(s): New York, New York (Manhattan); Los Angeles, California; Malibu, California

Summary: After stockbroker Madeline Carter's friend is shot before her very eyes at the New York Stock Exchange, she moves to Los Angeles. Life isn't easier there. A bad insider's tip from a former lover causes her to lose her money. Then he, along with her landlord's daughter, are kidnapped. Madeline is determined to find both of them, even if it means putting her own life on the line. This is the first book in a new series about Madeleine Carter, financial wizard turned sleuth.

Where it's reviewed:
Booklist, November 15, 2004, page 569
Romantic Times, December 2004, page 88

Other books you might like:
Sheryl Anderson, *Killer Heels*, 2004
Janet Evanovich, *Ten Big Ones*, 2004
Dixie Kane, *Chasing Lily*, 2003
Jayne Ann Krentz, *Light in Shadow*, 2003
Sharon Sala, *Out of the Dark*, 2003

366

NORA ROBERTS

Blue Dahlia

(New York: Jove, 2004)

Story type: Contemporary/Fantasy; Paranormal
Series: In the Garden Trilogy. Book 1
Subject(s): Gardens and Gardening; Ghosts
Major character(s): Stella Rothchild, Widow(er), Businesswoman (nursery manager); Logan Kitridge, Landscaper (landscape architect)
Time period(s): 2000s
Locale(s): Memphis, Tennessee

Summary: Tragically widowed but determined to get on with her life and raise her two sons, Stella Rothchild, complete with a degree and experience in nursery management, returns home to Memphis and lands a job as manager of the In the Garden Nursery, located on the lovely old Harper estate. As a condition of her job, she, her sons, and their dog move into the Harper Mansion, with heartwarming and sometimes hilarious results. Clashes with landscape architect Logan Kitridge set off sparks which eventually lead to romance, and a tormented ghost with unresolved issues result in a lively, intricately plotted story.

Where it's reviewed:
Library Journal, November 15, 2004, page 46
Romantic Times, November 2004, page 126

Other books by the same author:
Key of Valor, 2004 (Key Trilogy. Book 3)
Face the Fire, 2002 (Three Sisters Island Trilogy. Book 3)
Dance upon the Air, 2001 (Three Sisters Island Trilogy. Book 1)
Heaven and Earth, 2001 (Three Sisters Island Trilogy. Book 2)
The Villa, 2001

Other books you might like:
Sue Civil-Brown, *Carried Away*, 1997
    more ghosts
Jennifer Malin, *Eternally Yours*, 2002
    more ghosts
Marilyn Pappano, *First Kiss*, 2000
Patricia Rice, *This Magic Moment*, 2004
    historical
Antoinette Stockenberg, *Beyond Midnight*, 1996
    historical ghosts

367

NORA ROBERTS
JILL GREGORY, Co-Author
RUTH RYAN LANGAN, Co-Author
MARIANNE WILLMAN, Co-Author

Moon Shadows

(New York: Jove, 2004)

Story type: Anthology; Fantasy
Subject(s): Magic; Paranormal; Fantasy

Summary: Linked by myth, magic, and the mysterious moon, this stunning quartet of exceptional paranormal short stories will please fantasy fans and garner new readers. Included are: ''Wolf Moon,'' an unusual werewolf story by Nora Roberts; ''The Moon Witch,'' Jill Gregory's story of a courageous princess determined to save her sister by bearding an evil sorceress in her den; ''Blood on the Moon,'' a story of vengeance and love amid the Scottish Highlands by Ruth Ryan Langan; and ''West of the Moon,'' Marianne Willman's story of a strong heroine who rescues her love from the coils of the Faery realm.

Where it's reviewed:
Rendezvous, September 2004, page 17
Romantic Times, October 2004, page 29

Other books by the same author:

Once upon a Midnight, 2003 (anthology; Jill Gregory, Ruth Ryan Langan, and Marianne Willman, co-authors)

Once upon a Kiss, 2002 (anthology; Jill Gregory, Ruth Ryan Langan, and Marianne Willman, co-authors)

Once upon a Rose, 2001 (anthology; Jill Gregory, Ruth Ryan Langan, and Marianne Willman, co-authors)

Once upon a Castle, 1998 (anthology; Jill Gregory, Ruth Ryan Langan, and Marianne Willman, co-authors)

Once upon a Star, 1998 (anthology; Jill Gregory, Ruth Ryan Langan, and Marianne Willman, co-authors)

368

NORA ROBERTS

Northern Lights

(New York: Putnam, 2004)

Story type: Romantic Suspense
Subject(s): Family; Murder
Major character(s): Megan Galloway, Pilot (bush pilot); Nate Burke, Police Officer (police chief)
Time period(s): 2000s
Locale(s): Lunacy, Alaska

Summary: Guilt-ridden over his partner's death, Baltimore police detective Nate Burke accepts a job offer from the small town of Lunacy, Alaska, thinking that a new beginning is just what he needs. After arriving in Lunacy, Nate discovers the small town's many quirky inhabitants, including bush pilot Meg Galloway, offer more than enough challenges to keep him busy. When the body of Meg's father, who disappeared almost 20 years earlier, is found, it threatens the gradually blossoming romance between Nate and Meg; and forces Nate to find a way to keep Meg safe from a killer who is determined to keep old secrets from being discovered.

Where it's reviewed:
Booklist, September 1, 2004, page 7
Library Journal, October 1, 2004, page 72
Publishers Weekly, September 6, 2004, page 44
Romantic Times, October 2004, page 96

Other books by the same author:
Key of Valor, 2004
Birthright, 2003
Key of Light, 2003
Key of Knowledge, 2003
Chesapeake Blue, 2002

Other books you might like:
Catherine Coulter, *The Cove*, 1996
Linda Howard, *Open Season*, 2001
Jayne Ann Krentz, *Deep Waters*, 1997
Dinah McCall, *Jackson Rule*, 1996
Mariah Stewart, *Devlin's Light*, 1997

369

ANNE ROBINS (Pseudonym of Alice Duncan)

A Perfect Romance

(New York: Zebra, 2004)

Story type: Historical
Series: Perfect. Book 2
Subject(s): Mystery; Stealing; Survival
Major character(s): Loretta Linden, Socialite (activist), Survivor; Malachai Quarles, Sea Captain
Time period(s): 1910s (1914)
Locale(s): San Francisco, California

Summary: A *Titanic* survivor committed to helping others, socialite activist Loretta Linden encounters the dashing, earring-bedecked sea captain Malachai Quarles at one of the Ladies' Benevolence League's soup kitchens one night while he is looking for one of his crew, and sparks fly. Missing treasure, a dash of humor, and good sexual tension add to this lively story that does a good job of creating a clear sense of time and place in early 20th-century San Francisco. Second in a series about *Titanic* survivors.

Where it's reviewed:
Romantic Times, November 2004, page 41

Other books by the same author:
A Perfect Stranger, 2004 (Perfect. Book 1)

Other books you might like:
Emily Bradshaw, *The Heart's Journey*, 1992
Deborah Camp, *My Wild Rose*, 1992
Lori Copeland, *Angel Face and Amazing Grace*, 1997
Jude Deveraux, *Temptation*, 2000
   another activist heroine
Nan Ryan, *A Lifetime of Heaven*, 1994

370

JOANNE ROCK

Girl Gone Wild

(Toronto: Harlequin, 2004)

Story type: Contemporary
Subject(s): Cooks and Cooking; Newspapers; Seduction
Major character(s): Giselle Cesare, Cook (executive chef); Hugh Duncan, Journalist
Time period(s): 2000s
Locale(s): Miami, Florida

Summary: With her over-protective brothers temporarily away from home, Giselle Cesare decides now is the perfect time to indulge in a little fling, and that journalist Hugh Duncan is her ticket to a week of sensual delights. The only problem is that Hugh has been sent by his editor to write about Club Paradise, Miami's latest sexy new singles club, of which Giselle is a part owner. When Hugh insists on digging into the club's, and Giselle's, scandalous past, Giselle tries to tempt Hugh into giving up his story in return for a taste of her favors.

Where it's reviewed:
Romantic Times, May 2004, page 83

Other books by the same author:
The Wedding Knight, 2004
Girl's Guide to Hunting and Kissing, 2003
Sex and the Single Girl, 2003
One Naughty Night, 2003
Wild and Wicked, 2003

Other books you might like:
Stephanie Bond, *Manhunting in Mississippi*, 2003
Tori Carrington, *Red-Hot and Reckless*, 2003
Kristin Hardy, *Slippery When Wet*, 2003
Alison Kent, *Wicked Games*, 2003
Julie Elizabeth Leto, *Just Watch Me*, 2002

371

JOANNE ROCK

The Knight's Redemption
(Toronto: Harlequin, 2004)

Story type: Historical/Medieval
Subject(s): Castles; Legends; Middle Ages
Major character(s): Ariana Glamorgan, Noblewoman; Roarke Barret, Knight
Time period(s): 13th century (1260)
Locale(s): Wales; France

Summary: English knight Roarke Barret has recently been granted a Welsh estate by the king, but Roarke must immediately find a Welsh lass to wed if he wants to keep his new prize. Ariana Glamorgan intends on breaking the curse of spinsterhood that has haunted the Glamorgan women for more than a century by pretending to be her cousin Ceara and tricking Roarke into marrying her. She believes her plan should work perfectly, unless of course, Roarke discovers her little deception first.

Where it's reviewed:
Booklist, September 1, 2004, page 73
Romantic Times, September 2004, page 38

Other books by the same author:
Date with a Diva, 2004
Girl Gone Wild, 2004
The Wedding Knight, 2004
Her Final Fling, 2004
One Naughty Night, 2003

Other books you might like:
Terri Brisbin, *The Dumont Bride*, 2001
Teresa Medeiros, *The Bride and the Beast*, 2001
Amanda Quick, *Desire*, 1994
Tina St. John, *Lord of Vengeance*, 1999
Jayel Wylie, *This Dangerous Magic*, 2002

372

KAREN ROSE

I'm Watching You
(New York: Warner Forever, 2004)

Story type: Contemporary; Romantic Suspense
Subject(s): Murder; Serial Killers

Major character(s): Kristen Mayhew, Lawyer (prosecutor); Abe Reagan, Detective—Police
Time period(s): 2000s
Locale(s): Chicago, Illinois

Summary: When ace prosecutor Kristen Mayhew loses a particularly difficult murder case and the son of a mob boss walks free, she is chilled to learn that she has acquired an admirer—a "helpful" one who is going to make sure the killers she couldn't convict get their just desserts. When this vigilante killer targets the mobster's son, he vows revenge, and Kristen is faced not only with a crazed serial killer, but a powerful criminal who has the means to make good his threats. This dark, fast-paced thriller is threaded throughout with the growing love between Kristen and Detective Abe Reagan.

Where it's reviewed:
Rendezvous, September 2004, page 39
Romantic Times, October 2004, page 81

Other books by the same author:
Have You Seen Her?, 2004
Don't Tell, 2003

Other books you might like:
Margaret Allison, *The Last Curve*, 1999
Beverly Barton, *The Fifth Victim*, 2003
Tami Hoag, *Guilty as Sin*, 2003
Patricia Potter, *Cold Target*, 2004
Karen Robards, *The Beachcomber*, 2003

373

JOANN ROSS

Out of the Storm
(New York: Pocket Star, 2004)

Story type: Contemporary; Romantic Suspense
Series: Stewart Sisters. Book 3
Subject(s): Politics; Murder; Suspense
Major character(s): Laurel Stewart, Journalist (investigative reporter); Joe Gannon, Detective—Police (lieutenant)
Time period(s): 2000s
Locale(s): Washington, District of Columbia; Somersett, South Carolina

Summary: On suspension because a story she researched and published proved to be false, journalist Laurel Stewart is worried when her roommate, Chloe, disappears while on her way to South Carolina. Seriously concerned, she heads south and ends up in coastal Somersett where she connects with police lieutenant Joe Gannon who has an unsolved mystery of his own. Last in the Stewart Sisters trilogy, this story nicely ties up a number of loose ends.

Other books by the same author:
Out of the Blue, 2004 (Stewart Sisters. Book 2)
Magnolia Moon, 2003 (Callahan Brothers. Book 3)
Out of the Mist, 2003 (Stewart Sisters. Book 1)
Legends Lake, 2001
Far Harbor, 2000

Other books you might like:
Dixie Browning, *Rocky and the Senator's Daughter*, 1996

Patricia Rice, *Carolina Girl*, 2004
  McCloud Brothers Trilogy. Book 3
Patricia Rice, *McCloud's Woman*, 2003
  McCloud Brothers Trilogy. Book 2
Karen Rose, *Have You Seen Her?*, 2004
  more chilling
Mariah Stewart, *Carolina Mist*, 1996

374

JULIA ROSS (Pseudonym of Jean Ross Ewing)

Night of Sin
(New York: Berkley, 2005)

Story type: Historical/Regency
Subject(s): Fossils; Adventure and Adventurers; Healing
Major character(s): Anne Marsh, Gentlewoman (clergyman's daughter); Lord Jonathan Devoran St. George, Nobleman (son of a duke), Adventurer
Time period(s): 1810s
Locale(s): England; India

Summary: When a thief on the run slips a priceless "dragon's" fang fossil into Anne Marsh's marketing basket just before he is murdered, Anne suddenly finds herself caught up in a bizarre and deadly clash between two men who both want the same thing but for vastly different reasons. An innocent, but naively passionate heroine, a dragon-hunting hero tormented by the past, and a rich cast of secondary characters, both ordinary and exotic, combine in a complex plot that is introspective, action-oriented, thought-provoking, highly sensual, and well-written.

Where it's reviewed:
Romantic Times, January 2005, page 33

Other books by the same author:
The Wicked Lover, 2004
The Seduction, 2002
My Dark Prince, 2000
Flowers under Ice, 1999
Illusion, 1998

Other books you might like:
Julia Justiss, *My Lady's Pleasure*, 2002
Lynn Kerstan, *The Golden Leopard*, 2002
  exotic and well-written
Lynn Kerstan, *Heart of the Tiger*, 2003
Lynn Kerstan, *The Silver Lion*, 2003
Mary Jo Putney, *River of Fire*, 1996

375

KATE ROTHWELL (Pseudonym of Margaret K. Rothwell)

Somebody Wonderful
(New York: Zebra, 2004)

Story type: Historical/Victorian America
Subject(s): Social Classes; Romance; Irish Americans
Major character(s): Timona "Timmy" Calverson, Young Woman; Michael McCann, Police Officer
Time period(s): 1880s (1882)
Locale(s): New York, New York

Summary: When Irish cop Mick McCann rescues Timona Calverson from a street beating, he is shocked to realize that the unconscious "he" is a "she"—and a very attractive she at that! Although strong, the attraction is put on hold when Mick realizes that she is from a very different social circle from his, and, of course, they would never suit. Timmy, naturally, has different ideas, and their journey toward love is lively, humorous, and delightful. Serious social and class issues are addressed.

Where it's reviewed:
Rendezvous, June 2004, page 14
Romantic Times, July 2004, page 32

Other books you might like:
Betina Krahn, *Sweet Talking Man*, 2000
Linda Francis Lee, *Swan's Grace*, 2000
Candace McCarthy, *Irish Linen*, 1996
Meagan McKinney, *The Merry Widow*, 2000
Penelope Williamson, *The Passions of Emma*, 1997
  more serious approach to class and social issues

376

SHARON SALA

Missing
(Don Mills, Ontario: MIRA, 2004)

Story type: Contemporary; Romantic Suspense
Subject(s): Suspense; Healing; Drugs
Major character(s): Ally Monroe, Handicapped (lame); Wesley Holden, Military Personnel (colonel), Invalid (post traumatic stress syndrome)
Time period(s): 2000s
Locale(s): Blue Creek, West Virginia; Fort Benning, Georgia

Summary: Ally Monroe, lame, unwed, and housekeeper for her widowed father and two grown brothers, dreams of something better than her current, bleak existence. Wes Holden, emotionally damaged by the war in the Middle East and then the senseless killing of his wife and child once he arrives home, seeks solace and healing in the hills of West Virginia—where he finds Ally and begins his road to recovery. As Wes begins to come back to life, he also realizes that danger lurks in the hills—danger that will threaten Ally unless he takes action. Classic wounded hero tale, with a dash of the wounded heroine.

Where it's reviewed:
Romantic Times, November 2004, page 122

Other books by the same author:
Amber by Night, 2003
Whipporwill, 2003
Dark Water, 2002
The Way to Yesterday, 2002
Remember Me, 1999

Other books you might like:
Linda Castillo, *The Perfect Victim*, 2002
Nina Coyle, *Sharon's Hope*, 1996
  religious aspects
Ginna Gray, *For the Love of Grace*, 1995
Kathleen Korbel, *A Soldier's Heart*, 2002
  PTSD issues

Dinah McCall, *Jackson Rule*, 1996
  another badly wounded hero

377

LYNSAY SANDS

Tall, Dark, and Hungry
(New York: Love Spell, 2004)

Story type: Contemporary/Fantasy
Series: Argeneau Family. Book 3
Subject(s): Vampires
Major character(s): Terri Simpson, Professor, Friend; Bastien Argeneau, Vampire, Businessman
Time period(s): 2000s
Locale(s): New York

Summary: When Terri Simpson flies in from England to be the maid of honor at her cousin and best friend's wedding, she has no idea that she is landing right in the middle of an ancient family of vampires. Not only is cousin Kate marrying a vampire, Lucien Argeneau, but she has also become one herself—something that Terri knows nothing about. Things become complicated when Terri needs to stay in the family penthouse with Bastien Argeneau, Lucien's love-wary brother and the chemistry between them heats up. Other family members, wedding plans gone awry, and a few serious issues amid the fun result in a lively story that nicely continues Sands' humorous vampire romance series.

Where it's reviewed:
Romantic Times, July 2004, page 120

Other books by the same author:
Love Bites, 2004 (Argeneau Family. Book 2)
Single White Vampire, 2003 (Argeneau Family. Book 1)
The Reluctant Reformer, 2002
What She Wants, 2002
Lady Pirate, 2001

Other books you might like:
Janet Chapman, *Wedding the Highlander*, 2003
  another paranormal "family"
Christine Feehan, *Dark Melody*, 2003
  vampires/darker
Christine Feehan, *Lover Beware*, 2003
  paranormal anthology
Lori Handeland, *Blue Moon*, 2004
  werewolves with a dash of humor
Sandra Hill, *A Very Virile Viking*, 2003

378

JEANNE SAVERY (Pseudonym of Jeanne Savery Casstevens)

The Christmas Matchmaker
(New York: Zebra, 2004)

Story type: Regency
Subject(s): Family; Holidays
Major character(s): Penelope Garth, Widow(er); Vincent Beverly, Gentleman
Time period(s): 1810s
Locale(s): England

Summary: When Vincent Beverly finds a near frozen woman and her young child on the way to his cousin's houseparty, he does the only thing he can: he brings them along with him. Vincent's cousin Georgi immediately recognizes the woman as the former Penelope Tennytree, now Penelope Garth, a recent war widow, not acknowledged by her father. Even though Vincent suspects Georgi will do everything she can to reunite the estranged family, he never imagined that his mischievous cousin would try playing matchmaker between him and the lovely Penelope.

Where it's reviewed:
Booklist, October 1, 2004, page 317
Romantic Times, October 2004, page 50

Other books by the same author:
My Lady Housekeeper, 2004
An Independent Lady, 2003
The Reluctant Rake, 2003
The Family Matchmaker, 2003
Miss Seldon's Suitors, 2002

Other books you might like:
Catherine Blair, *A Viscount for Christmas*, 2000
Kate Huntington, *Mistletoe Mayhem*, 2000
Julia Parks, *A Gift for a Rogue*, 2002
Joy Reed, *A Home for the Holidays*, 1998
Donna Simpson, *A Matchmaker's Christmas*, 2002

379

AMANDA SCOTT

Highland Princess
(New York: Warner Forever, 2004)

Story type: Historical/Medieval
Subject(s): Middle Ages; Marriage; Twins
Major character(s): Lady Mairi MacDonald, Noblewoman; Lachlan Maclean, Nobleman, Warrior (Highlander)
Time period(s): 14th century (1366)
Locale(s): Scotland (Scottish Isles)

Summary: Although Lady Mairi is supposed to marry her much older uncle for political reasons, when Highland warrior Lachlan Maclean meets her, he knows she is the one for him. Mairi is similarly attracted, but when she approaches her father about the matter, he says no—until Lachlan kidnaps him and convinces him otherwise. Lots of action and exceptionally well-done historical detail are part of this complex romance.

Where it's reviewed:
Rendezvous, October 2004, page 27
Romantic Times, November 2004, page 39

Other books by the same author:
The Hidden Heiress, 2002 (Secret Clan. Book 2)
Border Storm, 2001
The Abducted Heiress, 2001 (Secret Clan. Book 1)
Border Fire, 2000
Highland Fling, 1995

Other books you might like:
Suzanne Barclay, *Lion's Legacy*, 1996
Juliana Garnett, *The Laird*, 2002
Samantha James, *A Promise Given*, 1998

Romance

Susan King, *Laird of the Wind*, 1998
Sue-Ellen Welfonder, *Knight in My Bed*, 2002

380

SUZANNE SIMMONS (Pseudonym of Suzanne Simmons Guntrom)

Sweetheart, Indiana

(New York: Berkley, 2004)

Story type: Contemporary; Romantic Suspense
Subject(s): Inheritance; Small Town Life; Humor
Major character(s): Gillian Charles, Socialite, Heiress; Samuel Law, Lawyer
Time period(s): 2000s
Locale(s): Sweetheart, Indiana

Summary: Born and raised in the rarified atmosphere of upper-class New York society, the last place Gillian Charles ever expected to be was in a small Midwestern town of fewer than 12,000 people. Big cities are definitely more her style. However, her grandfather has willed her the entire town of Sweetheart, Indiana, and in order for her to inherit all the rest of his vast holdings, she must go to Sweetheart by the first week in May; live there for the next six months; handle all the affairs related to the town properties; and work closely with Sam Law, the stubborn, but vastly appealing attorney overseeing the whole thing. What her beloved grandfather had in mind when he set this up, Gillian has no idea, but before it's over, she intends to find out what he meant by calling this his "last gift to Gillian." A sexy, funny, sassy story with a dash of mystery and suspense, this book has links to characters in *Lip Service*.

Where it's reviewed:
Romantic Times, August 2004, page 109

Other books by the same author:
Goodnight, Sweetheart, 2005
Lip Service, 2001
Lady's Man, 1999
No Ordinary Man, 1998
Paradise Man, 1997

Other books you might like:
Susan Andersen, *Baby, I'm Yours*, 1998
Patricia Coughlin, *The Cupcake Queen*, 2002
Jennifer Crusie, *Welcome to Temptation*, 2000
Rachel Gibson, *Truly, Madly Yours*, 1999
    similar idea
Jayne Ann Krentz, *Deep Waters*, 1997

381

PATRICIA SIMPSON

The Dark Lord

(New York: Tor, 2005)

Story type: Contemporary/Fantasy; Paranormal
Series: Forbidden Tarot. Book 1
Subject(s): Mythology; Archaeology; Good and Evil
Major character(s): Rae Lambert, Professor (mathematics); Michael Gregory, Architect; Simeon Avare, Supernatural Being

Time period(s): 2000s
Locale(s): Egypt; Alameda, California

Summary: When her mentor wills her half of his estate, including a wonderful old house in Alameda, Rae Lambert is forced to share the estate with her mentor's son, Michael Gregory, her childhood love. Something is not right, though, and as Rae struggles to figure out why her mentor was killed, she is forced to choose between two men, the charming, but mysterious, Simeon Avare and the often difficult Michael. An ancient deck of cursed tarot cards, a drought, an impulsive woman, and the unleashing of an evil power that has been waiting for its chance at revenge are core elements of this gripping paranormal romantic suspense.

Where it's reviewed:
Romantic Times, January 2005, page 119

Other books by the same author:
The Night Orchid, 1994
The Legacy, 1992
Whisper of Midnight, 1991

Other books you might like:
Amanda Ashley, *After Sundown*, 2003
Shannon Drake, *The Awakening*, 2003
Tracy Fobes, *Forbidden Garden*, 2000
Jill Jones, *Circle of the Lily*, 1998
Nora Roberts, *Face the Fire*, 2002
    Three Sisters Island Trilogy. Book 3

382

LORI SOARD

The Lipstick Diaries

(Waterville, Maine: Five Star, 2004)

Story type: Contemporary/Mainstream
Subject(s): Friendship; Diaries
Major character(s): Kate Tyler, Tour Guide ("haunted" history); Sarah, Store Owner (New Age shop); Rebecca, Nurse
Time period(s): 2000s
Locale(s): New Orleans, Louisiana; Greenfield, Indiana

Summary: Friends since the seventh grade, Kate, Becca, and Sarah leave their adopted home, New Orleans, and head back to Greenfield, Indiana, to save Kate's younger sister, Jen, from making the mistake of her life—marrying the jerk who cheated on Kate when they were in high school. Of course, it all doesn't go the way they expect. Small town atmosphere and lots of family dynamics highlight this lively story that combines a chick lit sass with satisfying romance.

Other books by the same author:
Housebreaking a Husband, 2002

Other books you might like:
Gila Berkowitz, *The Brides*, 1992
Barbara Bretton, *At Last*, 2000
Colleen Faulkner, *Marrying Owen*, 2000
Luanne Jones, *Sweethearts of the Twilight Lanes*, 2001
Debbie Macomber, *Three Brides, No Groom*, 1997

Romance

383

ROXANNE ST. CLAIRE

Killer Curves
(New York: Pocket, 2005)

Story type: Romantic Suspense; Contemporary
Subject(s): Identity, Concealed; Forgiveness; Transplants
Major character(s): Celeste Bennett, Wealthy, Public Relations; Beau Lansing, Sports Figure (race car driver)
Time period(s): 2000s
Locale(s): New York, New York

Summary: The stepdaughter of a wealthy candidate for the U.S. Senate, Celeste Bennett is on her third fiance. NASCAR champion Beau Lansing is interested in Celeste for another reason—he wants her kidney, not for himself, but for her natural father, who will die without it. Celeste's father deserted her mother before she was born, and Celeste has never forgiven him. Beau convinces Celeste to take a job at her dad's company so she can get to know him. She agrees, but only if she's incognito. The problem is, someone knows who Celeste really is, and for some reason, they're trying to kill her.

Where it's reviewed:
Booklist, December 1, 2004, page 642
Romantic Times, February 2005, page 105

Other books by the same author:
When the Earth Moves, 2005
French Twist, 2004
Like a Hurricane, 2004
The Fire Still Burns, 2004
Tropical Getaway, 2003

Other books you might like:
Pamela Britton, *Dangerous Curves*, 1996
Catherine George, *The Right Choice*, 1996
Patricia Hagan, *Race to the Altar*, 2001
Kathryn Shay, *Trust in Me*, 2003
Crystal Wilson-Harris, *Cherish*, 1998

384

NONNIE ST. GEORGE (Pseudonym of Nonnie Saad)

Courting Trouble
(New York: Zebra, 2004)

Story type: Regency
Subject(s): Courtship; Sisters
Major character(s): Arabella Swann, Heiress; August Warburton, Nobleman (Duke of St. Fell)
Time period(s): 1810s
Locale(s): London, England

Summary: Arabella Swann vows that when she marries it will be for love, and certainly not to some man chosen for her by her father like the arrogant, smug, totally conceited, fortune hunting, yet all-too-handsome-for-his-own-good Duke of St. Fell. Used to getting any woman he wants, St. Fell is certain Arabella will eventually succumb to his charms, especially once she gives up her foolish dreams of romance. Then another rival for Arabella's affections begins courting the sharp-tongued, opinionated lady, and the naturally cynical St.

Fell is forced into flirting with romance if he wants to win Arabella's love.

Where it's reviewed:
Romantic Times, May 2004, page 118

Other books by the same author:
The Ideal Bride, 2003

Other books you might like:
Diane Farr, *Falling for Chloe*, 2000
Candice Hern, *A Garden Folly*, 1997
Emma Jensen, *Best Laid Schemes*, 1998
Regina Scott, *Utterly Devoted*, 2002
Rhonda Woodward, *A Spinster's Luck*, 2002

385

JENNIFER ST. GILES (Pseudonym of Jenni Leigh Grizzle)

The Mistress of Trevelyan
(New York: Pocket, 2004)

Story type: Gothic; Historical/Victorian America
Subject(s): Children; Family; Murder
Major character(s): Titania ''Ann'' Lovell, Governess; Benedict Trevelyan, Businessman (shipping company)
Time period(s): 1870s (1873)
Locale(s): San Francisco, California

Summary: Despite the rumors she has heard about the reclusive Benedict Trevelyan and the mysterious death of his wife, Ann Lovell applies for and, to her great surprise, secures the position of tutor to his two young boys. Ann arrives at Trevelyan Manor determined to bring some joy and light back into the lives of her two new students only to quickly become caught up in the house's many dark secrets. She finds herself encountering many different kinds of dangers in her new position, but the greatest danger of all might be her growing desire for the dark and brooding Benedict.

Where it's reviewed:
Library Journal, August 1, 2004, page 56
Publishers Weekly, July 19, 2004, page 150
Romantic Times, August 2004, page 42

Other books you might like:
Catherine Coulter, *The Countess*, 2000
Tracy Fobes, *Forbidden Garden*, 2000
Evelyn Rogers, *The Ghost of Carnal Cove*, 2002
Colleen Shannon, *The Wolf of Haskell Hall*, 2001
Karen White, *Whispers of Goodbye*, 2001

386

TINA ST. JOHN (Pseudonym of Tina Haack)

Heart of the Hunter
(New York: Ivy, 2004)

Story type: Historical/Medieval
Subject(s): Quest; Magic; Legends
Major character(s): Lady Ariana of Clairmont, Noblewoman; Braedon ''The Hunter'' Le Chasser, Guide
Time period(s): 13th century (1275)
Locale(s): London, England; France

Summary: Ariana of Clairmont has dangerous knowledge of the legendary Dragon Chalice, information that she hopes will ransom her brother. Heading for France, she runs into a bit of trouble and is rescued by the man who ends up being her guide—and eventually something far more important. Danger, passion, and a dash of magic intertwine in this fast-paced story.

Where it's reviewed:
Romantic Times, June 2004, page 35

Other books by the same author:
Black Lion's Bride, 2002
White Lion's Lady, 2001
Lady of Valor, 2000
Lord of Vengeance, 1999

Other books you might like:
Suzanne Barclay, *Knight's Ransom*, 1996
Elizabeth Bonner, *A Vow to Keep*, 1993
Marsha Canham, *In the Shadow of Midnight*, 1994
Claire Delacroix, *The Sorceress*, 1994
Amanda Quick, *Mystique*, 1995
    lighter with more humor

387

SHARON STANCAVAGE

An Enchanting Minx

(New York: Zebra, 2004)

Story type: Regency
Subject(s): Courtship; Identity, Concealed
Major character(s): Jane Ravenwood, Noblewoman (granddaughter of a duke); Richard Hughes, Nobleman (Marquess of Blackmoore)
Time period(s): 1810s
Locale(s): London, England

Summary: Deciding that she wants to give her 25-year-old niece, Jane Ravenwood, a London season, providing she hide the fact that she is Welsh and her father is a wealthy merchant—after all being from Wales isn't at all the thing and her fortune would only attract fortune hunters—the Dowager Countess of Stockmorton is certain they can manage the deception. When Jane attracts the attention of the quite eligible, but moody, Marquess of Blackmoore, a man who is currently squiring her cousin about, she knows she will be hard pressed to keep her secret. A heroine who longs to just be herself and a hero with a secret past eventually find love amid the glittering social whirl of Regency England.

Where it's reviewed:
Romantic Times, September 2004, page 115

Other books by the same author:
Bath Intrigue, 2005
Emily's Christmas Wish, 2003

Other books you might like:
Kathleen Baldwin, *Lady Fiasco*, 2004
Diane Farr, *The Nobody*, 1999
Candice Hern, *An Affair of Honor*, 1996
Georgette Heyer, *Arabella*, 1949
Judith A. Lansdowne, *Annabella's Diamond*, 1999

388

ANNE STUART (Pseudonym of Anne Kristine Stuart Ohlrogge)

Hidden Honor

(Don Mills, Ontario: MIRA, 2004)

Story type: Historical/Medieval
Subject(s): Identity, Concealed; Kings, Queens, Rulers, etc.; Pilgrims and Pilgrimages
Major character(s): Elizabeth of Bredon, Noblewoman; Peter de Montselm, Knight (former), Religious (monk); William Fitzroy, Royalty (prince), Bastard Son
Time period(s): 13th century
Locale(s): England

Summary: Elizabeth of Bredon is looking forward to joining the Convent of Saint Anne. Before her life is completely free of men, Elizabeth must first travel to the shrine with a group of monks, knights, and Prince William Fitzroy, King John's bastard son. Elizabeth has heard the rumors about wicked William, who is on pilgrimage to atone for his many sins, and she intends on keeping as far away from him as possible on their journey. The only problem with her plan is that Elizabeth soon discovers the dark and dangerous prince not only has enough charm to tempt any woman into sinning, he is also not quite the man she first expected.

Where it's reviewed:
Library Journal, August 1, 2004, page 58
Romantic Times, August 2004, page 37

Other books by the same author:
Into the Fire, 2003
Still Lake, 2002
The Widow, 2001
Lady of Fortune, 2000
Shadows at Sunset, 2000

Other books you might like:
Jo Beverley, *Lord of Midnight*, 2002
Glynnis Campbell, *My Hero*, 2002
Christina Dodd, *Once a Knight*, 1996
Blythe Gifford, *The Knave and the Maiden*, 2004
Madeline Hunter, *By Possession*, 2000

389

HEATHER SWAIN

Lucious Lemon

(New York: Downtown, 2004)

Story type: Contemporary
Subject(s): Pregnancy; Restaurants; Grief
Major character(s): Ellie "Lemon" Manelli, Restaurateur (owner of Lemon), Cook (chef); Eddie, Businessman (olive oil importer), Wealthy
Time period(s): 2000s
Locale(s): New York, New York

Summary: Lemon Manelli finally has it all—her own restaurant, a family who loves her, and a wonderful boyfriend, Eddie. When an unexpected pregnancy threatens her dreams, she stubbornly refuses to slow down, give up on her goals, or surrender her independence by getting married. However, once again life throws her a curve, and Lemon is forced to reassess things and figure out what is really important to her. Funny, sexy, and serious, this is chick lit with a satisfying ending.

Where it's reviewed:
Romantic Times, October 2004, page 102

Other books by the same author:
Eliot's Banana, 2003

Other books you might like:
Carly Alexander, *The Eggnog Chronicles*, 2004
Millie Criswell, *The Trouble with Mary*, 2002
    restaurants/different treatment
Alesia Holliday, *American Idle*, 2004
Cathy Yardley, *L.A. Woman*, 2002

390

MAUREEN TAN

A Perfect Cover
(New York: Silhouette, 2004)

Story type: Contemporary; Romantic Suspense
Subject(s): Vietnamese Americans; Murder
Major character(s): Lacie Reed, Investigator (special agent), Spy; Anthony Beauprix, Detective—Police
Time period(s): 2000s
Locale(s): New Orleans, Louisiana

Summary: Vietnamese born and American bred, special agent Lacie Reed is one of the best in the business, especially when it comes to undercover work. Her biracial heritage (African American/Vietnamese) and her small size allow her to disguise herself in any number of ways and her quick thinking has gotten her out of trouble more than once. Now in New Orleans at the request of an old family friend, she is on the trail of a killer who is preying on the Vietnamese community. Her work is dangerous, and as it becomes more and more complex, she realizes that there is more behind these murders than she had expected. Her romantic relationship with police Detective Anthony Beauprix is beautifully done, and the issues that this well-written romance address are important and well-handled.

Where it's reviewed:
Library Journal, August 2004, page 58
Romantic Times, September 2004, page 108

Other books you might like:
Christine Feehan, *Mind Game*, 2004
Katherine Greyle, *Playing with Matches*, 2004
    anthology/Asian-American heroines/not suspense
Jessica Hall, *Into the Fire*, 2004
    more Louisiana murders
Metsy Hingle, *Flash Point*, 2003
    more New Orleans killings/psychic aspects
Katherine Sutcliffe, *Bad Moon Rising*, 2003
    another New Orleans killer

391

JANET TANNER

Forgotten Destiny
(New York: Severn House, 2004)

Story type: Historical; Gothic
Subject(s): Memory Loss; Secrets; Slavery
Major character(s): Davina Grimes, Amnesiac; Richard Wells, Single Parent
Time period(s): 1800s
Locale(s): England

Summary: Davina Grimes is injured so badly in a carriage accident that she can't even remember her own name for two years. Her grandparents arrange to have her married to John Paterson. John is older and wealthy, but he repulses Davina, who discovers his money comes from the illegal slave trade. To complicate matters, a handsome stranger stops her on the street and calls her "Rowan." As her memory returns, she realizes just how bad things are, and that she and her infant son are in mortal danger. A delightfully dark Gothic.

Where it's reviewed:
Booklist, October 1, 2004, page 317

Other books by the same author:
Shadows of the Past, 2003
Tucker's Inn, 2003
Morwennan House, 2002
All That Glisters, 2001
Hostage to Love, 2001

Other books you might like:
Debra Lee Brown, *The Virgin Spring*, 1995
Kristin Hannah, *Waiting for the Moon*, 1995
Miranda Jarrett, *Sunrise*, 2000
Lisa Kleypas, *Someone to Watch over Me*, 1999
Susan Wiggs, *Miranda*, 1996

392

JANELLE TAYLOR

Dying to Marry
(New York: Kensington, 2004)

Story type: Romantic Suspense; Contemporary
Subject(s): Weddings; Social Classes; Suspense
Major character(s): Lizbeth Morrow, Bride, Photographer; Dylan Dunhill III, Bridegroom, Wealthy
Time period(s): 2000s
Locale(s): Troutville, New Jersey

Summary: Someone wants to stop the wedding of wealthy "Up Hill" Dylan Dunhill to "Down Hill" barmaid/photographer Lizbeth Morrow, and they're willing to resort to murder if necessary. Everyone's a suspect when attempt after attempt is made on the wedding party. Snobbery turns deadly in this novel of love and suspense.

Where it's reviewed:
Romantic Times, November 2004, page 123

Other books by the same author:
Someday Soon, 2004

Don't Go Home, 2003
Lakota Flower, 2003
Night Moves, 2002
In Too Deep, 2001

Other books you might like:
Susan Andersen, *Head over Heels*, 2002
Justine Dare, *Avenging Angel*, 2002
Jayne Ann Krentz, *Soft Focus*, 1999
Merline Lovelace, *After Midnight*, 2003
Linda Randall Wisdom, *Small-Town Secrets*, 2002

393

SIMONA TAYLOR (Pseudonym of Roslyn Carrin)

Wonderful and Wild

(Washington, D.C.: BET, 2004)

Story type: Contemporary; Multicultural
Subject(s): African Americans; Writing
Major character(s): Mahalia "Hailie" Derwood, Writer; Darius Grant, Artist (illustrator)
Time period(s): 2000s
Locale(s): Casuarinas, California (writer's colony)

Summary: When noted fantasy/horror novelist Hailie Derwood decides to write a graphic novel, she hires Darius Grant to illustrate it. Despite the fact that he is seven years her junior, the attraction is instantaneous—and the results are predictable. An autistic child is part of this mix.

Where it's reviewed:
Rendezvous, April 2004, page 27
Romantic Times, May 2004, page 108

Other books by the same author:
Love Me All the Way, 2003
Mesmerized, 2000
Soul's Desire, 2000
Night Heat, 1999

Other books you might like:
Jo Beverley, *In Praise of Younger Men*, 2001
    anthology featuring older heroines & younger heroes
Adrienne Byrd, *Unforgettable*, 2004
Shirley Harrison, *The Pleasure Principle*, 2004
Pamela Morsi, *Courting Miss Hattie*, 1991
    classic older heroine/younger hero romance
Kimberly White, *Forever After*, 2004

394

JODI THOMAS (Pseudonym of Jodi Koumalats)

A Texan's Luck

(New York: Jove, 2004)

Story type: Historical/American West
Series: Wife Lottery. Book 3
Subject(s): American West; Robbers and Outlaws; Revenge
Major character(s): Lacy Larson, Crime Victim, Bride; Walker Larson, Military Personnel (captain), Bridegroom
Time period(s): 1880s (1886; 1888)
Locale(s): Cottonwood, Texas; Cedar Point, Texas

Summary: Captain Walker Larson doesn't want a wife, but his father has gotten him one by proxy through a bride lottery. He doesn't even meet her until she shows up at his outpost three years after the proxy marriage and demands that their union be consummated. Since he's in the process of evacuating the fort, Walker reluctantly and speedily obliges her. Two years pass, and Walker is ordered to return to Lacy—and his hometown—to protect her from a sadistic killer she helped put away. Much to his surprise, she doesn't want his protection. Or him.

Where it's reviewed:
Romantic Times, November 2004, page 37

Other books by the same author:
When a Texan Gambles, 2003 (Wife Lottery. Book 2)
The Texan's Wager, 2002 (Wife Lottery. Book 1)
The Texan's Dream, 2001
Twilight in Texas, 2001
To Wed in Texas, 1999

Other books you might like:
Claudia Dain, *A Kiss to Die For*, 2003
Georgina Gentry, *To Tame a Texan*, 2003
Beth Henderson, *At Twilight*, 2004
Nancy J. Parra, *A Wanted Man*, 2002
Bobbi Smith, *Hunter's Moon*, 2003

395

COLLEEN THOMPSON

Fatal Error

(New York: Leisure, 2004)

Story type: Contemporary; Romantic Suspense
Subject(s): Murder; Missing Persons; Stealing
Major character(s): Susan Maddox, Teacher; Luke Maddox, Businessman (owns car dealership), Computer Expert
Time period(s): 2000s
Locale(s): Clementine, Texas

Summary: Susan Maddox's life has been a nightmare since her husband, Brian, disappeared along with the banker's wife and a fortune in fraudulent loans. When no one can find Brian, the word is out that Susan actually killed her husband—and now the school board is threatening to terminate her teaching contract. In an effort to find out what is really going on, she joins forces with her husband's brother and high school crush, Luke, and together they try to sort it all out. Passion, mystery, and a healthy dose of rekindled love make for a lively story.

Where it's reviewed:
Library Journal, November 15, 2005, page 47
Romantic Times, November 2004, page 121

Other books you might like:
Barbara Delinsky, *A Woman Betrayed*, 1991
Stephanie Mittman, *Head over Heels*, 1999
    sweeter
Patricia Rice, *Nobody's Angel*, 2002
Sharon Sala, *Dark Water*, 2002
Karen Young, *In Confidence*, 2004

396

VICKI LEWIS THOMPSON

Nerd Gone Wild

(New York: St. Martin's Paperbacks, 2005)

Story type: Humor; Contemporary
Series: Nerd. Book 3
Subject(s): Humor; Inheritance; Identity, Concealed
Major character(s): Ally Jarrett, Heiress, Photographer (wildlife); Mitchell Carruthers, Bodyguard, Detective—Private (former)
Time period(s): 2000s
Locale(s): Porcupine, Alaska

Summary: When her wealthy grandmother dies, Ally Jarrett goes to Porcupine, Alaska, to learn to be a wildlife photographer. Her grandmother's assistant and executor of her will, nerdy Mitchell Carruthers, follows Ally up north, because, unbeknownst to her, he's also her bodyguard. An evil uncle, whom Ally trusts implicitly, has plans to go to Alaska and relieve her of her fortune. Ally's annoyed that Mitch is in Porcupine, but the more she's around him, the more she sees through his geeky facade. Roadkill casserole, lots of hot sex, and tons of snow make the trip to Porcupine an unforgettable one.

Where it's reviewed:
Romantic Times, February 2005, page 98

Other books by the same author:
Every Woman's Fantasy, 2004
Killer Cowboy Charm, 2004
Old Enough to Know Better, 2004
The Nerd Who Loved Me, 2004
Nerd in Shining Armor, 2003

Other books you might like:
Elizabeth Bloom, *See Isabelle Run*, 2005
Rachel Gibson, *The Trouble with Valentine's Day*, 2005
Trish Jensen, *Phi Beta Bimbo*, 2005
Shirley Jump, *The Bride Wore Chocolate*, 2004
Pam McCutcheon, *Caught in the Act*, 2005

397

VICKI LEWIS THOMPSON

The Nerd Who Loved Me

(New York: St. Martin's Paperbacks, 2004)

Story type: Humor; Contemporary
Subject(s): Humor; Child Custody; Gifted Children
Major character(s): Lainie Terrell, Dancer, Single Parent; Harry Ambrewster, Accountant, Babysitter
Time period(s): 2000s
Locale(s): Las Vegas, Nevada

Summary: While accountant Harry Ambrewster is babysitting Vegas dancer Lainie Terrell's genius four-year-old son, Dexter, Dexter's estranged father, Joey, goes into a rage and tries to smash in the door to get him. Escaping through a window and down a tree, Harry takes Dexter to his mother's house, where Joey can't find him. Then, to further thwart Joey, Harry and Lainie take off for Sedona, where she discovers an overly enthusiastic condo salesman, a six foot rattlesnake, and the real reason why Joey wants her son. Funny, fast-paced fiction.

Where it's reviewed:
Booklist, August 2004, page 1910
Publishers Weekly, June 21, 2004, page 48
Romantic Times, August 2004, page 107

Other books by the same author:
Behind the Red Doors, 2003
Nerd in Shining Armor, 2003
Acting on Impulse, 2002
Double Exposure, 2002
Truly, Madly, Deeply, 2002

Other books you might like:
Patti Berg, *Something Wild*, 2004
Sandra Hill, *The Cajun Cowboy*, 2004
Connie Lane, *Guilty Little Secrets*, 2003
Susan Elizabeth Phillips, *Nobody's Baby but Mine*, 1997
Pat White, *Got a Hold on You*, 2003

398

ALISA VALDES-RODRIGUEZ

Playing with Boys

(New York: St. Martin's Press, 2004)

Story type: Ethnic; Multicultural
Subject(s): Friendship; Hispanic Americans; Writing
Major character(s): Alexis Lopez, Agent, Public Relations; Vladimir Menendez, Singer (rap star)
Time period(s): 2000s
Locale(s): Los Angeles, California

Summary: Agent-publicist Alexis Lopez represents the group Chimpances del Norte, and she wants them to break into mainstream stardom. Alexis has similar aspirations for former Spanish language soap opera star Marcella Bosch, and Salvadoran mom Olivia Reyes has written just the script to make it happen. As Alexis, Marcella, and Olivia begin to bond, Alexis starts another relationship, this one romantic, with sexy Cuban rapper Vladimir Menendez, known to his fans as ''Goya.'' The witty writing, the many references to Latino culture, and the wonderful metaphors and one-liners make this book highly entertaining.

Where it's reviewed:
Romantic Times, September 2004, page 50

Other books by the same author:
The Dirty Girls Social Club, 2003

Other books you might like:
Julia Alvarez, *How the Garcia Girls Lost Their Accents*, 1999
Julia Alvarez, *Yo!*, 1999
Denise Chavez, *Loving Pedro Infante*, 2000
Sandra Cisneros, *Caramelo*, 2002
Esmeralda Santiago, *The Turkish Lover*, 2004

399

EVELYN VAUGHN (Pseudonym of Yvonne Jocks)

A.K.A. Goddess

(Toronto: Harlequin, 2004)

Story type: Romantic Suspense; Contemporary
Subject(s): Mythology; Secrets; Treasure
Major character(s): Magdalene ''Maggi'' Singer, Professor (mythology); Alexander ''Lex'' Rothschild Stuart III, Businessman, Boyfriend (Maggi's former); Rhys Pritchard, Religious (former priest), Researcher
Time period(s): 2000s
Locale(s): United States; France; England

Summary: Maggi Singer isn't just a mythology professor; she is a Grailkeeper, one of an ancient line of women charged with the protection of nine sacred, secret Goddess artifacts. When the Messaline Chalice becomes the target of the Comitatus, a secret society of men intent on destroying all the goddess grails they can find, Maggi must not only locate the chalice, but keep it safe. Both Lex Stuart, an old lover with whom Maggi shares a complicated history, and Rhys Pritchard, a new friend who may want a more personal relationship, offer their help, but Maggi isn't sure which man she can believe or trust.

Where it's reviewed:
Romantic Times, August 2004, page 100

Other books by the same author:
Buried Secrets, 2003
The Player, 2003
Forest of the Night, 1996
Beneath the Surface, 1995
Burning Times, 1994

Other books you might like:
Melissa James, *Who Do You Trust?*, 1992
Jayne Ann Krentz, *Midnight Jewels*, 1992
Rachel Lee, *Under Suspicion*, 2001
Christina Skye, *Bride of the Mist*, 1996
Gayle Wilson, *Midnight Remembered*, 2000

400

PATRICIA WADDELL

He Said Never

(New York: Zebra, 2004)

Story type: Historical/Victorian
Series: Gentlemen's Club. Book 4
Subject(s): Marriage
Major character(s): Prudence Tamhill, Heiress, Ward (of the Duke of Worley); Benjamin Edward Exeter, Nobleman (Viscount Rathbone)
Time period(s): 1860s (1867)
Locale(s): London, England

Summary: Intrigued when he finds Prudence Tamhill walking unchaperoned in the park, the Viscount Rathbone is even more puzzled when she adamantly refuses his offer to escort her back to her home. Although she ultimately relents, she has piqued his interest in more ways than one—an interest that eventually compromises them and ends in a wedding. The classic plot in which a forced marriage turns into a marriage of love is enhanced by Prudence's search to resolve the mystery of her past. Sensual and filled with lively dialogue.

Where it's reviewed:
Romantic Times, October 2004, page 47

Other books by the same author:
He Said No, 2004 (Gentlemen's Club. Book 2)
He Said Now, 2004 (Gentlemen's Club. Book 3)
He Said Yes, 2003 (Gentlemen's Club. Book 1)
A Stylish Marriage, 2002
Diamond in the Rough, 2002

Other books you might like:
Pamela Britton, *Seduced*, 2003
    earlier time/mystery
Christina Dodd, *Rules of Attraction*, 2001
Victoria Malvey, *A Proper Affair*, 2001
Patricia Rice, *All a Woman Wants*, 2001
Barbara Dawson Smith, *Her Secret Affair*, 1998

401

NANCY WARREN

Bad Boys Down Under

(New York: Brava, 2004)

Story type: Contemporary
Subject(s): Business Enterprises; Sports/Surfing; Erotica
Time period(s): 2000s
Locale(s): San Francisco, California; Australia

Summary: An Australian surf and boogie board company and a California marketing firm come together to form the setting for this trio of closely linked stories by Nancy Warren that, in true Brava fashion, are sexy, fast-paced, and sassy. Included are ''Sizzling in Sydney,'' the fiery story of the macho CEO of Crane's Surf and Boogie Boards, Cameron Crane, and marketing whiz Jennifer Talbot; ''Surfer Boy,'' in which advertising expert Lise Atwater is expected to turn gorgeous surfer Steve Jackson into the promotion's spokesperson; and ''The Great Barrier,'' the story of conservative finance expert (and Jen Talbot's former fiance), Mark Forsythe, and party girl (and Cameron Crane's half sister), Bronwyn Spencer, that neatly wraps everything up.

Where it's reviewed:
Rendezvous, June 2004, page 21

Other books by the same author:
Drive Me Crazy, 2004
By the Book, 2003
Fringe Benefits, 2003
Hot Off the Press, 2003

Other books you might like:
Jennifer Crusie, *Fast Women*, 2001
    sexy, but funny
Lori Foster, *Bad Boys on Board*, 2003
    erotic anthology; Donna Kauffman, Nancy Warren, co-authors

Lori Foster, *I Love Bad Boys*, 2002
   erotic anthology; Janelle Denison, Donna Kauffman, co-authors
Lori Foster, *Perfect for the Beach*, 2004
   erotic anthology of six short stories
Elda Minger, *The Dare*, 2003

402

NANCY WARREN
MARYJANICE DAVIDSON, Co-Author
KAREN KELLEY, Co-Author

Bad Boys with Expensive Toys
(New York: Brava, 2004)

Story type: Contemporary
Subject(s): Relationships; Sexuality
Time period(s): 2000s

Summary: Sexy heroes and their varied expensive ''toys'' are the focus of the latest Bad Boys anthology from Brava that will appeal to fans who like their romances hot, modern, and lively. Included are *The Fourteen Million Dollar Poodle*, Nancy Warren's steamy, funny tale of a labor negotiator and a nanny; *The World Is Too Darned Big*, MaryJanice Davidson's fast-paced tale of an engineering geek and a kick-butt heroine; and *Anything You Can Do. . .*, Karen Kelley's sizzling battle of the sexes between a wealthy entreprenuer and a rich designer.

Where it's reviewed:
Romantic Times, November 2004, page 115

Other books by the same author:
Drive Me Crazy, 2004

Other books you might like:
Lori Foster, *Bad Boys on Board*, 2003
Lori Foster, *Bad Boys to Go*, 2003
Donna Kauffman, *Walk on the Wild Side*, 2001
Janice Maynard, *Wildest Dreams*, 2003

403

ROBIN WELLS

The Babe Magnet
(New York: Love Spell, 2004)

Story type: Contemporary
Subject(s): Babies; Parenthood; Marriage
Major character(s): Stevie Stedquest, Radio Personality (parenting expert); Holt Landen, Consultant (helps struggling companies), Single Parent (of Isabelle); Isabelle Landen, Baby
Time period(s): 2000s
Locale(s): New Orleans, Louisiana

Summary: When business consultant Holt Landen ends up with a baby he never knew he had, he goes to the local talk show parenting guru for advice and ends up proposing! It's a marriage of convenience, of course; but baby Isabelle has other ideas in this funny, fast-paced contemporary romp that will keep readers engaged.

Where it's reviewed:
Romantic Times, June 2004, page 117

Other books by the same author:
Wild about You, 2003
Ooh, La La!, 2002
Baby, Oh Baby!, 2001

Other books you might like:
Barbara Freethy, *Some Kind of Wonderful*, 2001
Jennifer Greene, *Millionaire M.D.*, 2001
Kate Little, *Jingle Bell Baby*, 1996
   Christmas theme
Kasey Michaels, *Love to Love You Baby*, 2001
Paula Detmer Riggs, *Daddy by Accident*, 1997

404

PAT WHITE

Ring around My Heart
(New York: Dorchester, 2004)

Story type: Humor; Contemporary
Subject(s): Sports/Wrestling; Humor; Self-Acceptance
Major character(s): Alexandra Hayes, Public Relations, Single Parent; Timothy Lucas Silverspoon, Sports Figure (wrestler)
Time period(s): 2000s
Locale(s): St. Louis, Missouri; Sycamore, Illinois; Cincinnati, Ohio

Summary: Public relations expert Alexandra Hayes is offered a nice chunk of money to transform wild and crazy wrestler ''Loverboy Luke Silver'' into someone socially presentable. As a single mother, she can use the cash. Unfortunately, Loverboy likes his crude, scantily clothed, villainous persona, and the last thing he wants to be seen as is one of the good guys. A Pygmalion story with a ringside setting.

Where it's reviewed:
Romantic Times, September 2004, page 117

Other books by the same author:
Got a Hold on You, 2003

Other books you might like:
Sue Civil-Brown, *Catching Kelly*, 2000
Kasey Michaels, *Love to Love You Baby*, 2001
Susan Elizabeth Phillips, *Heaven, Texas*, 1995
Lisa Plumley, *Perfect Together*, 2003
Sheila Rabe, *A Prince of a Guy*, 2001

405

DIANE WHITESIDE (Pseudonym of Karla Massey)

The Irish Devil
(New York: Brava, 2004)

Story type: Historical/Victorian America; Historical/American West
Subject(s): Relationships; Secrets; Survival
Major character(s): Viola Ross, Widow(er), Businesswoman; William Donovan, Wealthy
Time period(s): 1870s

Locale(s): Arizona

Summary: Widowed and abandoned in Arizona, plucky Viola Ross struggles to make ends meet. Ultimately, in order to avoid marriage to a man she loathes, she makes an outrageous proposal to sexy William Donovan, an Irishman who is strong and powerful enough to keep her safe. She will become his mistress for three months in exchange for his protection, and a financial stake for her future. Romance soon follows, but so does the danger, as a killer's lust drives him down a deadly path. Highly sensual.

Where it's reviewed:
Rendezvous, July 2004, page 22
Romantic Times, August 2004, page 42

Other books you might like:
Susan Johnson, *Forbidden*, 1991
    sensual
Susan Johnson, *Force of Nature*, 1996
    sensual
Nan Ryan, *Love Me Tonight*, 1994
    sensual
Nan Ryan, *You Belong to My Heart*, 1996
Shelly Thacker, *Into the Sunset*, 1999
    sensual

406

EILEEN WILKS

Tempting Danger
(New York: Berkley, 2004)

Story type: Contemporary; Romantic Suspense
Subject(s): Murder; Werewolves
Major character(s): Lily Yu, Detective—Police; Rule Turner, Werewolf, Royalty (werewolf prince)
Time period(s): 2000s
Locale(s): San Diego, California

Summary: Police Detective Lily Yu finds herself working with a werewolf prince in order to find a brutal murderer who is terrorizing San Diego. Danger, temptation, and trust are all part of this taut romantic thriller with a paranormal twist.

Other books by the same author:
Meeting at Midnight, 2004
Midnight Choices, 2003
Midnight Promises, 2000
Night of No Return, 2000

Other books you might like:
Sherrilyn Kenyon, *Night Play*, 2004
Susan Krinard, *Prince of Shadows*, 1996
    werewolves/different approach
Rebecca York, *Crimson Moon*, 2005
Rebecca York, *Edge of the Moon*, 2005
Rebecca York, *Killing Moon*, 2003

407

JILL WINTERS

Raspberry Crush
(New York: NAL, 2004)

Story type: Contemporary
Subject(s): Murder; Reunions
Major character(s): Belinda "Billy" Cabot, Computer Expert (former web designer), Baker (cake decorator); Seth Lannigan, Businessman, Consultant (owns consulting firm)
Time period(s): 2000s
Locale(s): Churchill, Massachusetts

Summary: Trying to make ends meet as a cake decorator after losing her web design job, Billy Cabot is shocked and thrilled when her old flame Seth Lannigan walks back into her life. The results are ultimately romantic, but the road to the happy ending is lively, funny, and filled with a bit of suspense. Quirky characters, a dash of murder, and lots of sizzle add to this upbeat, modern romance.

Where it's reviewed:
Romantic Times, September 2004, page 122

Other books by the same author:
Blushing Pink, 2003
Plum Girl, 2002

Other books you might like:
Jennifer Crusie, *Tell Me Lies*, 1998
Barbara Freethy, *The Sweetest Thing*, 1999
Rachel Gibson, *Truly, Madly Yours*, 1999
Lisa Plumley, *Perfect Together*, 2003
Lisa Plumley, *Reconsidering Riley*, 2002

408

JOAN WOLF

White Horses
(Don Mills, Ontario: MIRA, 2004)

Story type: Historical/Regency
Subject(s): Smuggling; Circus; War
Major character(s): Gabrielle Robichon Rieux, Businesswoman (equestrian circus owner), Smuggler (for the Crown); Leo Standish, Military Personnel (colonel), Nobleman (Earl of Branford)
Time period(s): 1810s (1813)
Locale(s): France; England; Spain

Summary: Gabrielle's late father, owner of the famous Cirque Equestre, had long supported the English cause against Napoleon by helping transport money by means of the circus. Now, it is up to Gabrielle to take a shipment of gold to the Duke of Wellington in Portugal. However, to do so, the British insist upon an escort in the form of handsome Colonel Leo Standish—and they must pretend to be married to make the subterfuge work! Sparks fly between the pair, but so do more passionate feelings. Many obstacles plague their romance, but all does work out well in the end.

Where it's reviewed:
Romantic Times, August 2004, page 38

Other books by the same author:
Silverbridge, 2002
The Royal Bride, 2001
The Gamble, 1998
The Arrangement, 1997
The Guardian, 1997

Other books you might like:
Mary Balogh, *Beyond the Sunrise*, 1992
    spies/Napoleonic wars
Jane Feather, *Velvet*, 1994
Ruth Owen, *Midnight Mistress*, 1994
    Napoleonic Wars
Mary Jo Putney, *Petals in the Storm*, 1993

409

RHONDA WOODWARD

Moonlight and Mischief

(New York: Signet, 2004)

Story type: Regency
Subject(s): Courtship; Family
Major character(s): Mariah Thorncroft, Gentlewoman; Nicholas Morley, Nobleman (Earl of Haverstone)
Time period(s): 1810s (1816)
Locale(s): London, England; Chippenham, England

Summary: Mariah Thorncroft is tired of men who are only interested in her money. So when the Earl of Haverstone invites Mariah and her family to a house party, Mariah vows to ignore the flirtatious nobleman since he seems exactly like the wastrels and fortune hunters with whom she is already familiar. The only problem is that Mariah soon finds it isn't quite so easy to banish the handsome earl from her thoughts as first she imagined!

Where it's reviewed:
Booklist, November 15, 2004, page 570
Romantic Times, December 2004, page 47

Other books by the same author:
A Hint of Scandal, 2003
The Wagered Heart, 2003
A Spinster's Luck, 2002

Other books you might like:
Diane Farr, *Falling for Chloe*, 2000
Candice Hern, *A Garden Folly*, 1997
Emma Jensen, *Best Laid Schemes*, 1998
Amanda McCabe, *The Errant Earl*, 2002
Sophia Nash, *A Secret Passion*, 2004

410

ALICE WOOTSON

Aloha Love

(Washington, D.C.: BET, 2005)

Story type: Ethnic; Multicultural
Subject(s): African Americans; Crime and Criminals; Drugs
Major character(s): Jeanine Stewart, Pilot (helicopter), Rescuer (trained); Chris Harris, Architect
Time period(s): 2000s

Locale(s): Hilo, Hawaii; Haleakala, Hawaii; Lahaina, Hawaii

Summary: After Jeanine Stewart is told by her trusted mechanic that her helicopter is in great shape, it crashes. Fortunately, neither she nor her passenger, architect Chris Harris, is injured. The cause of the accident turns out to be a faulty replacement part from a rejected government order which should have been destroyed, not re-sold. Intrigue and conspiracies abound as Jeanine and Chris find themselves caught in the middle of an investigation by a mysterious federal agent whose motives appear unclear at best.

Where it's reviewed:
Romantic Times, January 2005, page 113

Other books by the same author:
Kindred Spirits, 2004
To Love Again, 2004
Escape to Love, 2003
Trust in Me, 2002
Home for Christmas, 2001

Other books you might like:
Susan Andersen, *Head over Heels*, 2002
Candice Poarch, *Loving Delilah*, 2004
Mildred Riley, *Bad to the Bone*, 2003
Roxanne St. Claire, *Tropical Getaway*, 2003
Janelle Taylor, *In Too Deep*, 2001

411

COURTNI WRIGHT

Espresso for Two

(New York: Arabesque, 2004)

Story type: Ethnic; Multicultural
Subject(s): African Americans; Fires; Neighbors and Neighborhoods
Major character(s): Brandi Owens, Store Owner (bookstore); Sam Carlson, Restaurateur (coffee shop owner), Divorced Person
Time period(s): 2000s
Locale(s): Washington, District of Columbia

Summary: Brandi Owens, owner of Over the Rainbow bookshop, and Sam Carlson, owner of Where Worlds Meet, the coffee shop next door, have been friends for six years. Now, their friendship is growing into something deeper. They've even decided to combine their stores. Then a big chain tries to buy out Brandi, and an arsonist nearly turns their dreams to ashes. A modern David and Goliath tale.

Where it's reviewed:
Booklist, September 15, 2004, page 228
Romantic Times, October 2004, page 89

Other books by the same author:
The Music of Love, 2003 (Dory-Phyfer. Book 3)
A Charmed Love, 2002 (Dory-Phyfer. Book 1)
Uncovered Passion, 2002 (Dory-Phyfer. Book 2)
Recipe for Love, 2001
All That Matters, 2000

Other books you might like:
Rochelle Alers, *Private Passions*, 2001
Anita Bunkley, *Relative Interest*, 2003

Romance

Francine Matthews, *As You Wish*, 2004
Doreen Rainey, *Can't Deny Love*, 2003

Francis Ray, *Someone to Love Me*, 2003

The Year in Westerns
by
D.R. Meredith

The trend I've noticed and have no explanation for is the number of Westerns concerning ranchers as survivors seeking revenge for the murder of their families. Among the more than eighty-five Westerns over this six month period there are twenty- two with the theme of revenge. Of course, revenge is always a good theme for a Western or a mystery, for that matter, but it seems there are more than usual, and the theme is stronger than usual. The victims are almost always the innocent whose existence poses no risk for the murderers, and whose deaths are particularly gruesome. The innocent victims far outnumber those whose professions put them at risk, such as sheriffs, federal marshals, police officers, and Pinkerton agents. One could almost call this trend the development of the *noir* Western analogous to the *noir* or hard-boiled mystery and the *film noir*. These books are gritty, realistic, sometimes dark, as opposed to what I think of as the John Wayne Westerns, or those in which the innocent such as women and children are not generally the victims, and the blood does not seem so real. An example of the John Wayne Western would be *A Soldier Returns* by Fred Grove, in which a galvanized Yankee wants to marry a woman who must first obtain a divorce. They return to the soldier's home town where he learns that he has not been forgiven for volunteering to serve in the Union Army in the West in order to escape a Union prison for the duration of the war. His home is attacked by the Klu Klux Klan, so there is no shortage of violence, but the intensity of the violence is overshadowed by the psychological character of the protagonist. The violence is an outgrowth of the situation the character finds himself in, rather than the strongest element and the motivating factor in the novel. One is more caught up in the soldier's guilt over serving in the Union army, and his hurt over the attitude of the town. The violence springs naturally from the plot.

Another John Wayne Western is *War at Fire Creek* by Cameron Judd, in which two immigrant brothers search for the uncle who came to America years before. Is there violence? Yes, the brothers join their newly discovered uncle in a range war with another rancher, but the uncle's attempts to prevent his nephews from involving themselves in the violence is the stronger element. That is not to suggest that these John Wayne Westerns are weak in action. There is enough action for any reader; it is just that it is more meaningful than gratuitous. *The Palo Duro Trail*, written in the style of Ralph Compton by Jory Sherman, is a case in point. The book features a cattle drive from Texas to Wyoming, with swollen rivers, stampedes, Comanches, and disloyal companions providing all the action one could wish. So it is with *Trouble's Messenger* by Max Brand. The protagonist is an eastern greenhorn who has trained since childhood to fight and kill a certain Blackfoot chief. There is lots of action with the greenhorn defending himself with his fists rather than guns. Then comes his challenge to the death to the Blackfoot chief. That is violent, but the clever twist ending demonstrates the wiliness that age has imparted to the Blackfoot that enables him to win the match without killing the young man. The reader is caught up in the obsession of the young man to kill the Blackfoot no mater what the cost to himself. One can almost pity him that someone had so twisted his life that revenge is his driving force without him focusing much on what he is to be killing for.

Two more examples of the John Wayne Westerns are both about Wyatt Earp in Tombstone, so we have the unremitting violence of that cursed place culminating in the gunfight at the O.K. Corral. What we have in both books is the Earps defending themselves against the Cowboys, criminals who are the visible manifestation of the corruption in Tombstone. *Tombstone Travesty* by Jane Candia Coleman is a fictionalized autobiography in which Allie, Virgil Earp's wife, recounts the events in Tombstone to correct a book supposedly dictated by her that vilified the Earps, particularly Wyatt. The reader sees the situation in Tombstone through Allie's eyes, and the corruption and wrongness of the town is more emphasized than the violence. To Allie, the violence is justified, and the reader accepts her view. In

Trouble in Tombstone by Richard S. Wheeler, Wyatt is pondering the events in Tombstone from the perspective of an aged man close to death. He sees that the town was about politics, elected offices, personal power supported by the violence of the Cowboys. The events were driven by politics, not monetary corruption as he assumed at the time. Wyatt sees himself as a tool of justice, and is satisfied that he did the right thing at the time. The reader agrees. Both books are psychological novels which happen to be about historical events that occurred at a particular time in a particular place, which happened to be in the West. The two books by Coleman and Wheeler are examples of an evolution in the Western, in which violence is still present and must be present, sometimes omnipresent, but not the strongest element in the story. The violence is certainly not the point of the stories; human motivation and human reactions are.

Now to discuss the *noir* Western. They are more violent, and the violence is the motivation of the characters. That is not to say that *noir* are bad, or feature inferior writing. To the contrary, some of the *noir* Westerns, like certain traditional Westerns, are very good. One example is *A Bad Day to Die* by J. Lee Butts. The protagonist is motivated by the violent murder of his family and seeks the killer in revenge. A friend persuades him to join the Texas Rangers, thus placing vengeance in a legal context. Suddenly the violence is not the only motivation; obtaining justice for his family by following the rule of law is. His conflict between the desire to manipulate the Rangers for his own vengeance, and supporting the efforts of legal justice becomes the point upon which the story balances. There is also a similar shift of focus in *Vengeance Rider* by Joseph A. West in the style of Ralph Compton. The protagonist has a seriously ill daughter who can be helped at a clinic in Switzerland. To earn the money to take her, he plans to ride in a horse race where the first prize is $10,000. Before the race, outlaws kill his hired hand and steal the horse. He tracks the killers to avenge his employee, yes, but his stronger motivation is to take back his horse and win that race. The violent death of the hired hand provided the springboard for the plot, but it is the stolen horse that keeps the suspense going. An ailing Doc Holliday appears in the story as a friend of the protagonist to help him take back his horse and kill the murderers. Doc Holliday's motivation is concern for the sick daughter, as well as anger that these worthless killers had placed her life in danger. Unlike some *noir* Westerns, both these books end happily. In contrast, *Judgement Day* by Frank Roderus ends unhappily. In this book a man is in love with a beautiful young schoolgirl, an idealized love by an immature young man prone to compulsive actions that proves to be the catalyst for tragedy. It is a perfect portrait of a man who is not quite a boy, but has the passions of a man and little ability to control those passions. Driven by sexual hunger, wounding humiliation, and a wrongful sense of pride, this likeable young man commits a violent act, a senseless act that an older, more mature man might not have made. The book is gritty with a ominous feeling about it. It is dark in mood, but wonderfully written. Roderus nails his

young character perfectly. While a violent act does not precipitate the action nor provide the motivation, minor defeats and a series of self-destructive acts by the young suitor escalate into horrible violence, that is never described on the page, but inferred. It is a most powerful book.

In *West of Rock River* by John D. Nesbitt, a young rancher helps his neighbors chase the murderers of their brother. Thus we have an act of violence as impetus to the revenge plot, and several other violent acts occur during the course of the story. The violence is graphic, the sense of place is strong, and the mood is dark, but Nesbitt leaves the reader with the hope of a happy ending. Not a stated happy ending nor a promise of a happy ending, but only a hope. Also, although action, including violent action, is present and provided the initial motivation for this young rancher to leave his wife and child, we soon learn that he is not at all sorry to be riding with the neighbors even though the murdered brother was not a friend. The murder only provided an excuse, not a motivation. The rancher is angry with his wife, and his leaving is a way of punishing her. The reasons for his anger are learned gradually over the course of the book, and the reader is sympathetic, and agrees with his conviction that a wronged man has a right to get even. As he gradually begins to understand himself, he realizes he must forgive his wife however hard that may be for him. And he doesn't know if he will succeed, and if he does, the relationship will not return to its former status. This story is almost too realistic and dark. As in the Western by Roderus, Nesbitt's story engages the reader to an almost painful degree because he can empathize so deeply with the characters.

Another *noir* Western is *Chasing Destiny* by Stephen Overholser. In fact, properly marketed this novel could be Overholser's breakout book because it will appeal to a wider audience than just the Western reader. The two characters, Destiny and Michael, are runaways hunting for Destiny's father, so she may prove to the sheriff that he wasn't killed escaping from a robbery and murder he allegedly committed. Both characters are 12-years-old, both abused, Michael desperate to change his situation, while Destiny wants to restore her situation to what is, in her circumstances, normal. That they must fight the domination of adults that they meet on the way to the mining town where Destiny believes her father may be, is a given. They are younger, physically weaker than adults, vulnerable, and in Michael's case, innocent. Destiny's life has been too horrible for her to retain much innocence. As in *noir* novels of any genre, this one is painfully realistic. There is no glass wall between the character and the reader. The fears, hurts, and hopes of Destiny and Michael assault us in our most vulnerable place: our hearts. Once more, the springboard of the plot is an act of violence, the killing of Destiny's father, but it is not revenge that drives her; it is hope that someone else is killed instead of him. Once more, the ending is unflinchingly realistic, although the reader doesn't know immediately that things will work out happily.

I consider these *noir* Westerns to be a positive in the genre. No type of literature, genre or not, can remain static. That is the way to the extinction of literature. In fact, the poor sales and precarious position of most Westerns on publishers' lists may, in my opinion, be because the Western remained unchanged for so long. Once the generation that learned the craft by writing for the pulps passed away, many imitators appeared who lacked the ability to write beneath the surface of the Western. Because so many were writing the "typical" Western—lots of action, black and white characters and not very interesting ones at that, and large helpings of cold steel and hot lead—the new editors believed that formula Westerns were what the Western was. Consequently, for decades the good Western, the literate Western, the *Travels of Jamie McPheeters* type of Western were lost among the mediocre—if such books were classified as Westerns at all. Finally, the Elmer Keltons, the Louis L'Amours, the Richard S. Wheelers, the Larry McMurtrys, and the Ed Gormans began to change the genre. The layered Western, the Western with meaning buried under meaning; ambiguous actions by characters that might be and might not be bad; and motivations springing from the human condition, not simply a knee-jerk reaction to violence, became more prevalent and thus began to be imitated. This evolution of the Western may be the saving of the genre from extinction.

Now I must switch hats from editor to reader and select the top twenty-five Westerns preceded by my usual disclaimer. These are my top twenty-five favorites out of those listed in this volume. This does not mean that I am infallible. It does not mean that my judgment is the final arbitrator of what is good and what is bad in Westerns. It does not mean you should avoid reading those books not included on my list. I have tripped over my own assertions too many times for my recommendations to be foolproof. Feel free to disagree after reading several on the list. You might feel so-and-so's book is the next Pulitzer Prize winner, and I should have included it on my list. You might be right and I might be wrong and both possibilities exist. Everyone has their own personal criteria as to what constitutes a good book, and that is why there are over 50,000 books published in the United States each year. So readers will have choices. These are mine. Happy Reading.

1. *Trouble in Tombstone* by Richard S. Wheeler is a superb psychological Western exploring what really went wrong for the Earps in Tombstone.

2. *Chasing Destiny* by Stephen Overholser is another superb psychological Western that is an outstanding example of the *noir* Western. One could flip the positions of these two books by Wheeler and Overholser, and still be right.

3. *Judgment Day* by Frank Roderus is the epitome of the *noir* Western, and should be studied by any writer aspiring to create a different kind of book. Roderus maintains the realism of the story by not compromising the painful ending in favor of a happy one.

4. *The Riders of the Purple Sage: The Restored Edition* by Zane Grey is a classic published as Grey wrote it, not degraded by editing that was perhaps appropriate for the time of the original publication, although I would argue with that position. There is nothing graphic in this novel that would make it unsuitable for adults at the time of the original publication. The original editing resulted in removing the motivation for many of the actions taken by the characters. If you read the original years ago, as most of us did, read this restored edition and enjoy the story all over again.

5. *Tombstone Travesty* by Jane Candia Coleman is another wonderful psychological Western about the Earps, this one told from a woman's point of view, differing from the male point of view in *Trouble in Tombstone* by Richard S. Wheeler.

6. *When the Sky Rained Dust* by Patrick Dearen is a story about the Depression, another trend in Westerns that has shown up in recent months. Despite no gunfights or chases on horseback, this book about the Dust Bowl is very Western. Although those on either coast suffered financial depression, the inhabitants of the Great Plains and the Southwest were attempting to survive against the aggression of nature. The black dusters were a phenomenon restricted to the heart of the West, and some of the character displayed by Westerners, charity to neighbors and strangers; toughness in the face of adversity; survival in desolate lonely places, were honed by enduring those dust storms. This is an extraordinary novel in terms of its realism, yet there is hope, too.

7. *Territorial Rough Rider* by Tim Champlin paints a vivid picture of Teddy Roosevelt's Rough Riders and their experiences in Cuba. There is a faint r of Stephen Crane's *The Red Badge of Courage* as the protagonist struggles fear of cowardice. The assault on San Juan Hill is realistic, gritty, graphic, best example of a Western that includes elements of the *noir* without bei totally dark.

8. *Following the Harvest* by Fred Harris is another realistic Western that also includes some *noir* elements. The harvest referred to is the wheat harvest on the Great Plains. It is dark in that the young teenager, who accompanies the harvest crew employed by his father, feels responsible for trying to prevent his father's drinking. The book is realistic in that Harris does not avoid including the dangers inherent in operating harvesters. It is also a coming-of-age novel in that the protagonist grows up on the trek from Texas to South Dakota.

9. *East of the Border* by Johnny Boggs is a mixture of humor and realism that exists without a sense of incongruity. The realism is not the violence of a gunfight or a massacre, but Boggs' describing the historical figures of Wild Bill Hickok, Buffalo Bill Cody, and Texas Jack Omohundro with all their warts visible.

10. *West of Rock River* by John D. Nesbitt is a *noir* Western that begins dark and gradually lightens with the protagonist's resolution to forgive his wife and try to restore their relationship to some kind of contentment. While there is graphic violence, it is not the primary motivation for action.

11. *Blood River* by Jory Sherman is a very violent, very graphic *noir* Western novel. Hope and forgiveness are secondary to the grief and thirst for revenge felt by the young protagonist. Although the setting lacks authenticity for the time period—the Comanches were not still raiding and killing in 1876, and Amarillo, Texas, didn't exist until 1889—the book paints a very accurate picture of the deprecations suffered by settlers in Indian attacks.

12. *Wife of Moon* by Margaret Coel, a Father John O'Malley mystery set on the Arapaho Reservation, is a modern story of revenge, but one with a tie to the past and a complex plot that explores other experiences besides murder. The cultural conflict with the Arapaho tribe is vividly described, and as is the conflict within both Father O'Malley and the woman Arapaho lawyer about their love for one another.

13. *A Bad Day to Die* by J. Lee Butts begins with a murder of a family after which the husband, again a rancher, swears revenge and begins following the killers. His attitude changes gradually when he joins the Texas Rangers to lend legitimacy to his hunt.

14. *Vengeance Rider* by Joseph A. West, written in the style of Ralph Compton, begins with an act of violence, but revenge is less a motivation than the desperate need to save his daughter by taking back the horse he hopes will win $10,000 in a coming horse race.

15. *Blood for Brother* by Mackey Murdock is a realistic Western without being *noir*. The struggle of the Confederate veteran to overcome his wounds engages the reader.

16. *Bad Night at Dry Creek* by Cameron Judd is another realistic Western with beautiful characterization. Although revenge is a theme, it is revenge of the bad guys on the good guys, and even at that, greed is a stronger motivation than revenge.

17. *Devil's Kin* by Charles G. West is a revenge novel through and through. The violent murder of a mother and child is the impetus for the plot. However, the characters are sympathetic, at least the husband and father is. When he finds the bodies, his whole world implodes. All that he loved is gone. One can't help being sympathetic.

18. *Trouble's Messenger* by Max Brand is less about revenge than about obsession with revenge. A clever twist to the ending prevents the story from being completely *noir*.

19. *Voices in the Hill* by Steve Frazee is a collection of the author's best short stories. The title story is particularly good.

20. *Silver Yoke* by Roland Cheek is a rousing and humorous story of revenge containing very little graphic violence.

21. *Dead Man's Canyon* by Ralph Cotton is a clever tale of twins with a twist ending. Good writing and good characters lift this traditional Western way above average.

22. *A Soldier Returns* by Fred Grove is good story with psychological overtones.

23. *Evil Breed* by Charles G. West is about vengeance leading to evil actions. An Army captain is determined to hang our hero, even though he has been ordered to release him. He hires the most brutal bounty hunter to track him down.

24. *The Witch's Tongue* by James D. Doss is the latest volume in what I consider to be the best Western mystery series. In this addition to the Charlie Moon series, a Southern Ute woman shaman, who sees and speaks with figures from Ute folklore, is balanced by her amiable nephew, a rancher and occasional investigator for the Southern Utes.

25. *Donovan's Dove* by Joseph A. West is a hilarious romp. A gambler wins a gold watch and a prostitute from an outlaw, then must flee for his life because the outlaw wants the gold watch back. The gambler is welcome to the prostitute.

For More Information about Western Fiction

The Western Writers of America maintain a database of bookstores willing to stock and/or order Western titles. For information on the database, or to add your favorite bookstore to it, write to Candy Moulton, Editor, *Roundup Magazine*, Box 29 Star Route, Encampment, WY 82325.

For general information on what's happening in Western writing, subscribe to *Roundup Magazine* at the above address. *Roundup* is the official publication of the Western Writers of America and includes reviews of Western fiction and nonfiction done by yours truly. In addition, there is a series of features on Writers of the 20th Century, a section on what's doing in Hollywood by Miles Hood Swarthout, and articles on new directions in Western writing.

For the computer literate, there is no source like amazon.com for finding out-of-print Westerns, or just titles by a favorite that you are missing. Remember also to periodically check for titles in your local used bookstores, estate sales, flea markets, garage sales, and your local Friends of the Library book sale. And speaking of libraries, if the title you want is in hardback, ask your local library to get it for you on interlibrary loan. Some libraries will order original paperbacks on interlibrary loan, but you will need to ask. As a last resort, contact a rare book dealer for some desired title you want, but be prepared to pay dearly. I found one of my first printing, original paperbacks, used, for $108. I didn't make a whole lot more than that when I wrote it.

Western Titles

RUDOLFO ANAYA

Serafina's Stories

(Albuquerque: University of New Mexico Press, 2004)

Story type: Historical/American West; Indian Culture
Subject(s): American West; Folk Tales; Indians of North America
Major character(s): Serafina, Indian (Pueblo), Storyteller; Governor, Government Official (governor of Santa Fe); Gaspar Garcia, Guard (at the governor's palace)
Time period(s): 17th century (1680)
Locale(s): Santa Fe, New Mexico

Summary: In this Southwestern version of the story of Scheherazade, 12 Pueblo Indians are brought before the governor of Santa Fe. The 12 are accused of plotting a rebellion against the Spanish and the Catholic Church. One of the 12 is a young girl named Serafina who pleads with the governor to exchange a story for the life of each prisoner. The governor agrees and enjoys Serafina's first story so much that he releases an Indian. Each night Serafina tells a story, most familiar to the governor and the reader, as the stories are Pueblo versions of European folk tales such as Cinderella, Beauty and the Beast, and Faust among others. The governor grows to love Serafina as a daughter. His guard, Gaspar Garcia, also falls in love with her. When the governor's enemies inform the Inquisition that Serafina is a witch, Gaspar proposes marriage, because as the wife of a Spaniard she would be safe from the religious persecution of the Inquisition. She turns him down, trusting the governor to protect her. He does, but perhaps not in the way she expects. A wonderful story of cultural conflicts and the yearning to be free.

Where it's reviewed:
Roundup Magazine, June 2005, page 32

Other books by the same author:
Tortuga, 2004
My Land Sings, 2001
Shaman Winter, 2000
Zia Summer, 1996

Bless Me, Ultima, 1972 (reprinted 1999)

Other books you might like:
William J. Buchanan, *Diablo the Devil Steer*, 2004
Ralph M. Flores, *The Horse in the Kitchen*, 2004
Kent Haruf, *Eventide*, 2004
Richard D. Jensen, *Tristeza*, 2004
Lisa Sandlin, *In the River Province*, 2004

RUDOLFO ANAYA

Tortuga

(Albuquerque: University of New Mexico Press, 2004)

Story type: Modern; Man Alone
Subject(s): American West; Crime and Criminals; Hospitals
Major character(s): Tortuga, Teenager, Accident Victim (paralyzed); Filomon, Driver (ambulance); Ismelda, Care Giver (of Tortuga)
Time period(s): 2000s (2004)
Locale(s): Agua Bendita, New Mexico

Summary: An ambulance driver named Filomon takes a paralyzed 16-year-old boy to the hospital in the desert near the town of Agua Bendita following an accident. Tortuga Mountain, so named because it is believed to resemble a sea turtle, looms over the town. According to old Mexican folk beliefs, the mountain is magic and the water that flows from it can cure the sick. The boy begins to call himself Tortuga because of the plaster casts that encase him from head to toe, like a turtle's shell. He no longer believes in magic or miracles, despite Filomon's tales, until dreams about the healing power of the holy river begin to restore his faith.

Where it's reviewed:
Roundup Magazine, December 2004, page 32

Other books by the same author:
My Land Sings, 2001
Shaman Winter, 2000
Zia Summer, 1996
Heart of Aztlan, 1988

Bless Me, Ultima, 1972

Other books you might like:
William J. Buchanan, *Diablo the Devil Steer*, 2004
Ralph M. Flores, *The Horse in the Kitchen*, 2004
Kent Haruf, *Eventide*, 2004
Richard D. Jensen, *Tristeza*, 2004
Lisa Sandlin, *In the River Province*, 2004

414

ROBERT J. AVRECH

The Hebrew Kid and the Apache Maiden
(Los Angeles: Seraphic, 2005)

Story type: Historical/American West; Quest
Series: Hebrew Kid. Book 1
Subject(s): Judaism; Frontier and Pioneer Life; Religious Traditions
Major character(s): Ariel Isaacson, Immigrant (Jewish); John Henry "Doc" Holliday, Historical Figure, Gambler; Lozen, Indian (Apache), Relative (Chief Victorio's sister)
Time period(s): 1870s (1874)
Locale(s): Arizona

Summary: Ariel Isaacson and his family flee Russia to America in search of religious tolerance rather than the religious persecution they experience from the Cossacks. Forced to leave their home in a small town in Arizona Territory, the Isaacsons find themselves in the desert Apache country on their way to Tombstone. The family is kidnapped by a band of Apaches led by Lozen, the sister of Victorio, the most feared Apache leader. Ariel tells Lozen that his father is a holy man who talks to God. Lozen takes them to her village where she demands that Ariel's father heal a sick baby. If the baby dies, so does Ariel's father. His mother's broth saves the baby, and the Isaacson family is released. Lozen follows them and she and Ariel become good friends as they exchange knowledge about their different beliefs. When Ariel's sister is kidnapped by scalp hunters, it is Lozen and Victorio who track down the villainous men. Then Doctor John Henry Holliday, dentist, gambler, and shootist, arranges enough men to allow Ariel to celebrate his bar mitzvah. This is the first in a series about observant Jewish youngsters in the American West.

Where it's reviewed:
Roundup Magazine, June 2005, page 32

Other books you might like:
Frederic Bean, *The Red River*, 1998
Thomas Eidson, *The Missing*, 2003
Richard D. Jensen, *Tristeza*, 2004
Louis L'Amour, *Hondo*, 2004
Richard S. Wheeler, *Rendezvous*, 1997
  Skye's West. Book 9

415

JON R. BAUMAN

Santa Fe Passage
(New York: St. Martin's Press, 2004)

Story type: Traditional; Saga

Subject(s): American West; Mexican Americans; War
Major character(s): Matthew Collins, Scout (on the Santa Fe Trail), Businessman (in Santa Fe); Edward Waterman, Businessman (Matthew's partner)
Time period(s): 19th century (1822-1846)
Locale(s): Santa Fe, New Mexico

Summary: Orphaned Matthew Collins runs away from what amounts to indentured servitude in 1822. He joins a freight caravan and becomes a teamster, then a scout on the Santa Fe Trail. His skirmish with a band of Comanche leaves him with his hair and a deep respect for the ferocity of that tribe's warriors. Eventually, Matthew partners up with Edward Waterman and the two become prosperous businessmen in Santa Fe. Matthew has a preference for Mexican culture and customs, and marries the daughter of a Mexican landowner. In a decision that has future unforeseen consequences, Matthew becomes a Mexican citizen, not out of conviction but out of expediency. His business will be stronger if he is a Mexican citizen. Then, in 1846, comes the Mexican War and the arrival of American troops. Matthew is caught between the two countries, between his heart and his head. He must choose, and his decision will impact his marriage, his family, his partner, and his business.

Where it's reviewed:
Publishers Weekly, October 18, 2004, page 50

Other books you might like:
Jane Candia Coleman, *Moving On*, 1999
T.T. Flynn, *Night of the Comanche Moon*, 2000
Jovita Gonzales, *Caballero*, 1996
  Eve Raleigh, co-author
Jeff Shaara, *Gone for Soldiers*, 2000
Norman Zollinger, *Chapultepec*, 1995

416

WIN BLEVINS

Beauty for Ashes
(New York: Forge, 2004)

Story type: Historical/American West; Quest
Series: Rendezvous. Book 2
Subject(s): Fur Trade; Frontier and Pioneer Life
Major character(s): Sam Morgan, Trapper; Gideon Poor Boy, Mountain Man, Sidekick (of Sam); Meadowlark, Indian (Crow woman), Lover (of Sam Morgan)
Time period(s): 1820s (1824-1825)
Locale(s): Henry's Fork, Wyoming; Wind River Village, Wyoming; Cache Valley, Utah

Summary: Sam Morgan, a boy who has run away from his home in Pennsylvania, is serving out his apprenticeship as a mountain man. A member of General Ashley's brigade that traps beaver in the foothills of the Rocky Mountains, Sam enjoys his friends, principal among them the mountain man Gideon Poor Boy, a mixed breed with a French father and a Cree Indian mother. Sam also has his pet coyote, Coy, but more than anything he wants to return to the Wind River Village of the Crow and propose to Meadow Lark. Gideon, Third Wing, and Jim Beckworthe join Sam on this trip up the Wind River. Once Sam and his companions reach the village, he finds he must become more Crow than white man. Before Sam can marry Meadow Lark, he accompanies his three friends and Meadow Lark's brother, Blue Horse, on a hunting trip. They stumble into a Lakota Sioux band, and Sam survives with nothing but his horse and his coyote. His friends are dead and he must start his life over, outfit himself, and accumulate goods to present to Meadow Lark's family, or she will not be allowed to marry him.

Where it's reviewed:
Publishers Weekly, October 28, 2004, page 49
Roundup Magazine, December 2004, page 34

Other books by the same author:
So Wild a Dream, 2003 (Rendezvous. Book 1)
Ravenshadow, 1999
The Rock Child, 1998
Stone Song, 1995 (Spur Award winner)
Charbonneau: A Man of Two Dreams, 1985

Other books you might like:
Frederic Bean, *The Red River*, 1998
Don Coldsmith, *South Wind*, 1998
W. Michael Gear, *Coyote Summer*, 1997
W. Michael Gear, *The Morning River*, 1996
Richard S. Wheeler, *Rendezvous*, 1997
    Skye's West. Book 9

417

JOHNNY D. BOGGS

East of the Border

(Waterville, Maine: Five Star, 2004)

Story type: Historical/American West; Saga
Subject(s): Actors and Actresses; Humor; Theater
Major character(s): Texas Jack Omohundro, Scout (for the U.S. Army), Actor (amateur); James Butler ''Wild Bill'' Hickok, Gunfighter, Historical Figure; William F. ''Buffalo Bill'' Cody, Entertainer, Historical Figure
Time period(s): 1870s (1873)
Locale(s): Richmond, Virginia; New York, New York; Lexington, Kentucky

Summary: This hilarious story by Johnny D. Boggs offers an account of one season's tour of the east coast by the Buffalo Bill Combination. The Wild West stage melodrama is owned by Buffalo Bill Cody, who relishes being on stage and away from his wife. Touring gives him the opportunity to indulge his fondness for drink and loose women. Wild Bill Hickok, famous scout and gambler, is only performing in the show because he needs the money. Texas Jack Omohundro, a scout, drover, and relatively untalented actor, falls in love with the show's leading lady, Guiseppina Morlacchi, only to suffer the agonies of jealousy when Wild Bill gets too familiar with her on stage. Wild Bill, in fact, causes no end of trouble with his bouts of drinking and his outbursts of violence. The story is told in separate sections from the point of view of each of the three characters.

Where it's reviewed:
Roundup Magazine, June 2005, page 32

Other books by the same author:
Dark Voyage of the Mittie Stephens, 2004

Purgatoire, 2003
The Big Fifty, 2003
Lonely Trumpet, 2002
The Despoilers, 2002

Other books you might like:
Bill Brooks, *Law for Hire: Defending Cody*, 2003
Bill Brooks, *Law for Hire: Protecting Hickok*, 2003
Randy Lee Eickhoff, *And Not to Yield*, 2004
Richard Jensen, *Ride the Wild Trail*, 2003
Bruce Olds, *Bucking the Tiger*, 2001

418

FRANK BONHAM

The Phantom Bandit

(Waterville, Maine: Five Star, 2005)

Story type: Traditional; Collection
Subject(s): American West; Short Stories; Civil War
Time period(s): 19th century (post-Civil War)
Locale(s): West

Summary: A collection of eight stories written for the pulps in the 1940s and 1950s, these tales are some of Bonham's finest short works. In ''A River Man Goes to War'' two partners in a riverboat are on opposite side during the Civil War. ''Wanted!'' tells the story of a former army captain convicted of embezzling, who escapes from prison to track down the man who is really guilty. A Dakota Territory rancher is in danger of losing his ranch, but refuses to aid in capturing wild mustangs for their hides. The title story is a fictionalized account of the famous robber and would-be poet, Black Bart. These stories showcase the varied settings used by Bonham, from stagecoaches to mining.

Where it's reviewed:
Roundup Magazine, June 2005, page 34

Other books by the same author:
Outcasts of Rebel Creek, 2004
Stage Trails West, 2002
The Last Mustang, 2001
One Ride Too Many, 1997
The Canon of Maverick Brands, 1997

Other books you might like:
Max Brand, *The Lost Valley*, 2002
Ralph M. Flores, *The Horse in the Kitchen*, 2004
John Jakes, *The Funeral of Tanner Moody*, 2004
    Elmer Kelton, Robert J. Randisi, and others, co-authors
Annie Proulx, *Bad Dirt*, 2004
Cherry Wilson, *The Throwback*, 2002

419

MAX BRAND

Trouble's Messenger

(Waterville, Maine: Five Star, 2005)

Story type: Traditional; Revenge
Subject(s): Indians of North America; American West
Major character(s): Peter Messenger, Martial Arts Expert (bent on vengeance); Henry Lessing, Frontiersman, Friend

(of Peter Messenger); Summer Day, Chieftain, Shaman (of the Blackfoot)

Time period(s): 19th century (pre-Civil War)
Locale(s): Ft. Lippewan, Washington

Summary: Fur trapper and mountain man Henry Lessing bets Louis Despart, owner of Ft. Lippewan, that Peter Messenger, the pale young man watching the Blackfoot gathered around the fort, is no greenhorn. Lessing wins a revolver from Despart when Messenger defeats two Blackfoot warriors without using a weapon. Peter is waiting for Summer Day, a Blackfoot chief and shaman. From childhood, Peter has been trained in the martial arts for the purpose of killing Summer Day to avenge the murder of a white man years before. Lessing befriends Peter and tries to get him to let the past go, but Peter challenges Summer Day to the death. However, Summer Day has not lived so many years without learning a few tricks of his own.

Where it's reviewed:
Roundup Magazine, June 2005, page 33

Other books by the same author:
Hawks and Eagles, 2004
Mountain Storms, 2004
The Golden Cat, 2004
The Range Finder, 2004
Peter Blue, 2003

Other books you might like:
Will Cade, *Henry Kidd, Outlaw*, 2003
Thomas Eidson, *The Missing*, 2003
Stephen Overholser, *Track of a Killer*, 2003
Troy D. Smith, *The Trail Brothers*, 2003
Gary Svee, *The Peacemaker's Vengeance*, 2003

420

PETER BRANDVOLD

Staring Down the Devil

(New York: Berkley, 2004)

Story type: Traditional; Chase
Series: Lou Prophet. Book 5
Subject(s): Gold Discoveries; Crime and Criminals
Major character(s): Lou Prophet, Bounty Hunter, Guide (to a Russian countess); Natasha Roskov, Noblewoman (Russian countess); Ed Champion, Outlaw, Thief
Time period(s): 19th century (post-Civil War)
Locale(s): Broken Knee, Arizona; Denver, Colorado

Summary: Lou Prophet, bounty hunter extraordinary, is flat broke and drunk. After being thrown out of the Slap and Tickle saloon and brothel, he lands at the feet of Countess Natasha Roskov and her manservant. The countess offers Lou $2,000.00 to find her sister, who discovered a treasure trove in Arizona, then disappeared. Lou refuses, having too much pride to work for foreigners who boss him around. When an accidental meeting with the love of his life, even if they don't intend to marry, leads to her leaving him money on his pillow, a humiliated Lou takes the countess up on her offer. Someone else is interested in the countess when he notices that she owns her own stagecoach. Curious about why the countess wants to hire Lou and believing that robbing her will be

lucrative, Ed Champion rounds up his gang and they follow Lou and the countess. Lou isn't surprised, since a beautiful woman and treasure are always going to attract low-down men. Lou figures he will deal with the problem before Champion can cause too much trouble.

Where it's reviewed:
Roundup Magazine, June 2005, page 33

Other books by the same author:
.45-Caliber Revenge, 2004
The Devil Gets His Due, 2004 (Lou Prophet. Book 4)
Once Late with a .38, 2003
Riding with the Devil's Mistress, 2003 (Lou Prophet. Book 3)
The Romantics, 2001

Other books you might like:
Robert J. Conley, *The Gunfighter*, 2001
Thomas Eidson, *The Missing*, 2003
Stephen Overholser, *Track of a Killer*, 2003
Cotton Smith, *Sons of Thunder*, 2003
Richard S. Wheeler, *The Bounty Trail*, 2004

421

TERRY BURNS

Mysterious Ways

(Colorado Springs, Colorado: RiverOak, 2005)

Story type: Traditional
Subject(s): American West; Crime and Criminals
Major character(s): Amos Taylor, Imposter (disguised as a preacher), Thief; Judy Valentine, Gentlewoman (from Boston); Joseph Washington, Aged Person, Handicapped (blind)
Time period(s): 1860s (1868)
Locale(s): Quiet Valley, Texas

Summary: Amos Taylor meets Judy Valentine when he robs the stage in which she is riding. Not the type of outlaw who mistreats women, Amos refrains from robbing Judy, an act she thinks very mannerly. Amos drives off in the stage, dons a parson's black suit and collar, and returns to "pretend" to find the passengers. When the party with the "parson" arrives in Quiet Valley, Amos is forced to preach a sermon at the schoolhouse as the town has no regular preacher. Amos is scared out of his mind since he has never even been in a church. Seeing Joseph Washington across the street at the jail, Amos figures to get some advice, since Joseph is not only the cook and handyman at the jail, he is also the unofficial chaplain. Joseph senses immediately that Amos is masquerading, but agrees to help since the outlaw will be preaching the gospel. Thus Amos finds himself the town's preacher, in love with Judy Valentine, and the object of Joseph's preaching, a heck of a fix for an outlaw to find himself in.

Where it's reviewed:
Roundup Magazine, February 2005, page 34

Other books by the same author:
To Keep a Promise, 2002

Other books you might like:
Max Brand, *The Lost Valley*, 2002
Sandra Chastain, *The Mail Order Groom*, 2002

Fred Grove, *Destiny Valley*, 2000
Stephen Overholser, *Shadow Valley Rising*, 2002
Troy D. Smith, *Caleb's Price*, 2001

422

J. LEE BUTTS

A Bad Day to Die
(New York: Berkley, 2004)

Story type: Historical/American West; Chase
Subject(s): Crime and Criminals; Law Enforcement; American West
Major character(s): Lucius "By God" Dodge, Lawman (Texas Ranger); Boz Tatum, Lawman (Texas Ranger); Slayton Bone, Rancher, Thief
Time period(s): 1870s (1878)
Locale(s): Lampasas, Texas

Summary: Lucius Dodge witnesses the deaths of his father and brother at the hands of Slayton Bone's hired killers. After burying his family, Lucius grabs his father's rifle and takes his revenge by killing Bone, without the benefit of any legal authority. Soon after, he saves Texas Ranger Boz Tatum from being beaten to death. Boz persuades Lucius to join the Rangers and hunt down Bone's hired killers legally. Lucius accepts, pins on a badge, and becomes one of the West's most respected lawmen. Lucius narrates his own story with side-splitting humor.

Where it's reviewed:
Roundup Magazine, June 2005, page 33

Other books by the same author:
Brotherhood of Blood, 2004
Hell in the Nations, 2003
Lawdog: Life and Times of Hayden Tilden, 2001

Other books you might like:
Tim Champlin, *Territorial Rough Rider*, 2004
Tim Champlin, *The Tombstone Conspiracy*, 1999
Ed Gorman, *Texas Rangers*, 2004
John Jakes, *The Funeral of Tanner Moody*, 2004
Elmer Kelton, *The Buckskin Line*, 1999
   Texas Rangers. Book 1

423

WILL CADE

Sawyer's Quest
(New York: Leisure, 2005)

Story type: Traditional; Man Alone
Subject(s): American West; Books and Reading; Crime and Criminals
Major character(s): Billy Sawyer, Clerk (in a general store); Laurel Sawyer, Handicapped (born with club feet), Relative (Billy Sawyer's daughter); Framp Rupert, Relative (Billy's brother-in-law), Alcoholic
Time period(s): 19th century (post-Civil War)
Locale(s): Rockfield, Kansas; Dodge City, Kansas

Summary: A tornado strikes Rockfield, Kansas, just as Charles Oliver Farnsworth, a wealthy and very famous author, is speaking at the library. Farnsworth escapes the tornado, but loses a metal box holding the only manuscript of his new book. Billy Sawyer loses something more valuable: his home and the general store where he works. He and his crippled daughter, Laurel Sawyer, seek shelter from Laurel's uncle, Framp Rupert, a man loyal to his family, but a little weak in the honesty department. Rupert finds Farnsworth's manuscript and plans to extort money from the author for its return. Billy wants to return the box to Farnsworth, and hopes that the author feels generous enough to give him a reward, so that Billy can take Laurel to a famous surgeon who can correct her club feet. Billy takes the box from its hiding place and starts for Dodge City where Farnsworth is supposed to be. He is chased by Framp Rupert and several other hardcases who think it is worth a lot of money.

Where it's reviewed:
Roundup Magazine, June 2005, page 34

Other books by the same author:
Henry Kidd, Outlaw, 2003
Stalker's Creek, 2002
Genesis Rider, 2000
Larimont, 1999
The Gallowsman, 1999

Other books you might like:
Tim Champlin, *Fire Bell in the Night*, 2004
Henry Chappell, *Blood Kin*, 2004
Robert J. Conley, *The Gunfighter*, 2001
Loren D. Estleman, *Port Hazzard*, 2003
Gary Svee, *The Peacemaker's Vengeance*, 2003

424

TIM CHAMPLIN

The Last Campaign
(New York: Leisure, 2005)

Story type: Indian Wars; Chase
Subject(s): Indians of North America; Indian Removal
Major character(s): Russell Norwood, Courier (for the U.S. Army); Geronimo, Indian (Apache renegade), Historical Figure; Henry Lawton, Military Personnel (captain in U.S. Army)
Time period(s): 1880s (1886)
Locale(s): Sierra Madre Mountains, Mexico

Summary: Courier Russell Norwood is sent after Captain Henry Lawton, who has been hunting Geronimo in the Sierra Madre Mountains of northern Mexico for four months. Norwood is leading a pack train of supplies for Lawton and his men. Accompanied by several calvarymen, Indian scouts, and the infamous scout Tom Horn, Norwood catches up with Lawton, and finds himself caught fighting Geronimo. In fact, when push comes to shove, it is Norwood, Lawton, and Horn who finally catch up with Geronimo and his band. Now the question becomes who will survive the encounter?

Where it's reviewed:
Roundup Magazine, June 2005, page 35

Other books by the same author:
Fire Bell in the Night, 2004
White Lights Roar, 2003

Raiders of the Western & Atlantic, 2002
A Trail to Wounded Knee, 2001
By Flare of Northern Lights, 2001

Other books you might like:
Giff Cheshire, *Comanche Prairie*, 2003
Fred Grove, *A Distance of Ground*, 2000
Ernest Haycox, *Bugles in the Afternoon*, 2003
R.C. House, *Warhawk*, 1994
Terry C. Johnston, *Buffalo Palace*, 1996

425

TIM CHAMPLIN

Territorial Rough Rider

(Waterville, Maine: Five Star, 2004)

Story type: Historical/Mainstream; Saga
Subject(s): Spanish-American War
Major character(s): Peter Ormond, Postal Worker (temporary job), Drifter; Charley Gunderson, Foreman (of a ranch); Millard Johnson, Servant, Cook (for Rough Riders)
Time period(s): 1890s (1898)
Locale(s): Prescott, Arizona; San Antonio, Texas; San Juan Hill, Cuba

Summary: Tired of his father always demeaning him, Peter Ormond steals the old man's gold coin collection worth $50,000. It is an impulsive act committed while Peter is drunk after his father's birthday party. Peter catches a train back to Prescott, Arizona, already regretting the theft and planning to send the coins back to his father. All the coins except four are stolen from him when he falls asleep on the train. He believes his life is over as soon as his father tracks him down, so he joins his friend, Charley Gunderson, driving wild mustangs to a buyer. Before he can saddle his horse, his father's black body servant, Millard Johnson, confronts him, demanding he return the coins. Peter explains the coins were stolen and advises Millard to go back to Boston. Knowing the elder Ormond will fire him, if not worse, Millard joins the mustang drive. When a band of horse thieves steals the mustangs and begins shooting everyone they see, Peter and his two friends escape on a military train where they join Teddy Roosevelt's Rough Riders as a way to protect themselves from the outlaws. Before they know it, they are in Cuba, where they learn that war isn't as glamorous as Roosevelt paints it.

Where it's reviewed:
Roundup Magazine, December 2004, page 34

Other books by the same author:
Fire Bell in the Night, 2004
White Lights Roar, 2003
Raiders of the Western & Atlantic, 2002
A Trail to Wounded Knee, 2001
By Flare of Northern Lights, 2001

Other books you might like:
Will Cade, *Henry Kidd, Outlaw*, 2003
P.H. Holt, *Silver Creek*, 2003
Stephen Overholser, *Track of a Killer*, 2003
Troy D. Smith, *The Trail Brothers*, 2003
Joseph A. West, *Me and Johnny Blue*, 2000

426

ROLAND CHEEK

The Silver Yoke

(Columbia Falls, Montana: Skyline, 2004)

Story type: Traditional; Revenge
Series: Valediction for Revenge. Book 6
Subject(s): Crime and Criminals; Gold Discoveries; Miners and Mining
Major character(s): Jethro Spring, Mine Owner, Fugitive (falsely accused of murder); Angus MacFarlane, Businessman (manager of a mine); Otto Mannschlieter, Engineer (mining)
Time period(s): 19th century (post-Civil War)
Locale(s): Leadville, Colorado

Summary: Abandoning his homestead in Wyoming when his battle against rancher Bill Burroughs to keep his land and marry Burroughs' intended bride leads him into a tactic that kills his mentor and his lover's father, Jethro becomes a notable drunk in Leadville, Colorado, where he owns a gold mine. Found in a snowbank dead drunk by Angus MacFarlane, manager for the Peace and Prosperity Mine, who saves his life, Jethro meets John Burroughs, brother of his nemesis, Bill Burroughs, and president of the greedy and soul-destroying Amalgamated Minerals and Mining Company, better known as A Double M. Burroughs wants to buy Jethro's mine. Jethro despises the Burroughses and refuses to sell. Determined to bring the A Double M to its knees, Jethro sobers up and hires irascible mining engineer Otto Mannschlieter, who in turn hires Angus MacFarlane, fired by John Burroughs. Jethro's mines are rich, so now he has the money to bring down the Burroughses and help free the woman he loves from their possession.

Where it's reviewed:
Roundup Magazine, April 2005, page 34

Other books by the same author:
Crisis on the Stinkingwater, 2004 (Valediction for Revenge. Book 5)
Gunnar's Mine, 2003 (Valediction for Revenge. Book 4)
Lincoln County Crucible, 2002 (Valediction for Revenge. Book 3)
Bloody Merchant's War, 2001 (Valediction for Revenge. Book 2)
Echoes of Vengeance, 2000 (Valediction for Revenge. Book 1)

Other books you might like:
James Carlos Blake, *Under the Skin*, 2003
Henry Chappell, *Blood Kin*, 2004
Henry Chappell, *The Callings*, 2002
Elmer Kelton, *The Buckskin Line*, 1999
    Texas Rangers. Book 1
Richard S. Wheeler, *Goldfield*, 1995

427

MARGARET COEL

Wife of Moon
(New York: Berkley, 2004)

Story type: Modern; Mystery
Series: Father John O'Malley/Vicky Holden. Book 10
Subject(s): Law Enforcement; Indians of North America; Crime and Criminals
Major character(s): Father John O'Malley, Religious (Roman Catholic priest), Detective—Amateur; Vicky Holden, Lawyer (for Crow Nation), Indian (Arapaho); Adam Lone Eagle, Lawyer, Indian (Arapaho)
Time period(s): 2000s
Locale(s): Wind River Reservation, Wyoming

Summary: The Arapaho museum located at St. Francis Mission on the Wind River Reservation is hosting an exhibit of Edward S. Curtis' early 20th-century photographs of Plains Indians. Naturally, every Arapaho on the reservation comes to the museum to view the photographs to see if one of their ancestors is featured. The exhibit is a roaring success until someone shoots a descendent of one of the tribal chiefs in a Curtis photograph. When the new curator disappears, everyone assumes his guilt except Father O'Malley. He believes that is too easy a solution, but before he can do much about finding the murderer and the curator, United States senator and presumptive presidential candidate Jaime Evans, who, it turns out, is a descendent of a figure in the Curtis photograph, prepares to visit the mission. Vicky Holden, long in love with Father O'Malley who returns her feelings, but like Vicky doesn't by voice or action confess his love, is both trying to ignore her romantic longing for a life with the priest, and decide what to do with suitor Adam Lone Eagle. The murder and the missing curator distract her from her dilemma. Another wonderful mixture of mystery and Arapaho life.

Where it's reviewed:
Publishers Weekly, August 9, 2004, page 234
Roundup Magazine, December 2004, page 33

Other books by the same author:
Killing Raven, 2003 (Father John O'Malley/Vicky Holden. Book 9)
The Shadow Dancer, 2002 (Father John O'Malley/Vicky Holden. Book 8)
The Thunder Keeper, 2001 (Father John O'Malley/Vicky Holden. Book 7)
The Spirit Woman, 2000 (Father John O'Malley/Vicky Holden. Book 6)
The Lost Bird, 1999 (Father John O'Malley/Vicky Holden. Book 7)

Other books you might like:
Frederic Bean, *Murder at the Spirit Cave*, 1999
James D. Doss, *The Shaman's Bones*, 1997
  Charlie Moon. Book 1
James D. Doss, *The Shaman's Game*, 1998
  Charlie Moon. Book 2
Kathleen O'Neal Gear, *The Visitant*, 1999
  W. Michael Gear, co-author
Tony Hillerman, *The Sinister Pig*, 2003

428

JANE CANDIA COLEMAN

Tombstone Travesty
(Waterville, Maine: Five Star, 2004)

Story type: Historical/American West; Saga
Subject(s): Women; Crime and Criminals; Law Enforcement
Major character(s): Allie Earp, Spouse (of Virgil Earp); Wyatt Earp, Lawman (U.S. deputy marshal), Historical Figure; Josie Earp, Spouse (of Wyatt Earp), Actress
Time period(s): 19th century; 20th century (1865-1929)
Locale(s): Dodge City, Kansas; Tombstone, Arizona

Summary: In this fictionalized autobiography of Virgil Earp's wife, Allie Earp, an aged Allie narrates the story of her life and the Earps to a niece. From Allie becoming an orphan after the Civil War, her marriage to Virgil Earp without benefit of clergy, the days in Tombstone, and into the 20th century with Wyatt's death in 1929, Allie corrects the story she supposedly told to an author who published a book full of lies about her and the Earps, especially her relationship with Wyatt. She calls Tombstone a town of death and relates stories about Wyatt and Josie Earp, whom the Earp family called Sadie. This is a different portrait of Wyatt Earp, his brothers, and the Tombstone days than the conventional one, and well worth reading.

Where it's reviewed:
Roundup Magazine, June 2005, page 35

Other books by the same author:
Lost River, 2003
Matchless, 2003
Country Music, 2002
Mountain Time, 2001
Borderlands, 2000

Other books you might like:
Matt Braun, *Doc Holliday*, 1997
Matt Braun, *Wyatt Earp*, 1994
Randy Lee Eickhoff, *The Fourth Horseman*, 1997
Preston Lewis, *Mix-Up at the O.K. Corral*, 1996

429

RALPH COMPTON
DAVID ROBBINS, Co-Author

Bucked Out in Dodge
(New York: Signet, 2004)

Story type: Traditional; Trail Drive
Subject(s): American West; Crime and Criminals; Civil War
Major character(s): Jess Donner, Cowboy; Steve Ellsworth, Friend (of Jess, Stu, and Heck), Cowboy; Stu Wilkins, Cowboy
Time period(s): 19th century (post-Civil War)
Locale(s): Dodge City, Kansas

Summary: Barely 16 and on his first cattle drive, Jess Donner is looking forward to Dodge City, the end of the drive and the Babylon of the West according to the trail boss. With his friends, Stu Wilkins, Steve Ellsworth, and Heck Myers, Jess plans to drink some, gamble some, and romance the women

Western

for hire. First their trail boss tells them the story of how one of his friends was shot dead by Dave Mather, a lowdown murderer, who shot him right in front of Bat Masterson, the peace officer of Dodge City. The trail boss warns Jess and his friends to avoid meeting with the law by keeping to the letter of the law. The boys promise, but they all end up romancing the same lady of the evening, which doesn't set well with some of the troublemakers. Not that Jess is surprised; every saloon has some troublemakers. Jess figures he and his friends are in a little bit of a tight spot, but with a little luck, and if everyone can just refrain from shooting, there is a chance that he and his buddies might get out alive.

Where it's reviewed:
Roundup Magazine, June 2005, page 35

Other books by the same author:
Nowhere, Texas, 2004
The Palo Duro Trail, 2004
Vengeance Trail, 2004
The Abilene Trail, 2003
Demon's Pass, 2000

Other books you might like:
Frederic Bean, *Law of the Gun*, 1993
Zane Grey, *Top Hand*, 2004
Lauran Paine, *Open Range*, 2003
Troy D. Smith, *The Trail Brothers*, 2003
Richard S. Wheeler, *The Bounty Trail*, 2004

430

RALPH COMPTON
JORY SHERMAN, Co-Author

The Palo Duro Trail
(New York: Signet, 2004)

Story type: Traditional; Trail Drive
Subject(s): American West; Cattle Drives
Major character(s): Felix Dagstaff, Rancher; Jimmy Gough, Cowboy (works for Felix); Jo Finnerty, Young Woman (daughter of cattle drive cook)
Time period(s): 19th century (post-Civil War)
Locale(s): Quitaque, Texas; Cheyenne, Wyoming

Summary: When Felix Dagstaff agrees to lead a cattle drive from his home ranch in Quitaque, Texas, through Indian Territory, Colorado, and finally Cheyenne, Wyoming, he didn't know it would mean fighting Mother Nature, as well as treacherous actions from his own crew. Dagstaff battles torrential rains, flooded rivers, ankle deep mud, and, as if Nature weren't enough, the Comanches and a hired killer shadow him along the trail. A marvelous picture of a cattle drive with action, tragedy, and love to round it out.

Where it's reviewed:
Roundup Magazine, June 2005, page 35

Other books by the same author:
Nowhere, Texas, 2004
Vengeance Rider, 2004
The Abilene Trail, 2003
Demon's Pass, 2000
Death Rides a Chestnut Mare, 1999

Other books you might like:
Ralph Cotton, *Between Hell and Texas*, 2004
John Holt, *Hunted*, 2003
Robert J. Horton, *The Hanging X*, 2003
Lauran Paine, *Open Range*, 2003
Troy D. Smith, *The Trail Brothers*, 2003

431

RALPH COMPTON
JOSEPH A. WEST, Co-Author

Vengeance Rider
(New York: Signet, 2004)

Story type: Traditional; Revenge
Subject(s): American West; Crime and Criminals; Animals/Horses
Major character(s): Buck Fletcher, Rancher; Port Austin, Outlaw, Murderer; John Henry "Doc" Holliday, Historical Figure, Gambler
Time period(s): 1880s (1886)
Locale(s): Two-Bit Creek, South Dakota

Summary: Buck Fletcher owns a race horse that he hopes can win a $10,000.00 prize. He and his wife want to use the money to go to a Swiss clinic to seek treatment for their ailing daughter. Six outlaws kill one of Buck's hired hands and steal the horse. Buck goes after them, but is ambushed and, during the firefight, kills a young man. The man's two brothers track Buck to a saloon where he kills one. The other brother is killed by an old friend of Buck, Doctor John Henry Holliday, dentist, gambler, and legendary gunman. Despite the fact that he is ill himself (he would die the following year), Doc offers to accompany Buck on his manhunt, out of friendship and concern for Buck's daughter. Fast draws and thundering pistols punctuate the action as Buck and Doc track down the killers.

Where it's reviewed:
Roundup Magazine, June 2005, page 35

Other books by the same author:
Nowhere, Texas, 2004
The Palo Duro Trail, 2004
The Abilene Trail, 2003
Death Rides a Chestnut Mare, 1999
The Deadwood Trail, 1999

Other books you might like:
Max Brand, *Tales of the Wild West*, 2000
Grey Judson, *Down to Marrowbone*, 2000
Louis L'Amour, *Hondo*, 2004
W.W. Lee, *Rustler's Venom*, 1990
Jason Manning, *The Black Jacks*, 1997

432

RALPH COTTON

Dead Man's Canyon
(New York: Signet, 2004)

Story type: Traditional; Chase

Subject(s): Indians of North America; Crime and Criminals; Twins

Major character(s): Blake Carly, Outlaw, Twin (of Abel); Abel Carly, Twin (of Blake); Sam Burrack, Lawman (Arizona Ranger)

Time period(s): 19th century (post-Civil War)

Locale(s): Taos, New Mexico; Benton Wells, Arizona

Summary: When Blake Carly shoots the sheriff of Benton Wells, Arizona, and rides out of town, his innocent twin, Abel, goes after him, hoping to protect his twin from being caught and hanged. Neither one of the Carly twins counts on being tracked all the way into New Mexico by Arizona Ranger Sam Burrack. With only one horse left, Blake tells Abel they must ambush Burrack, or they both will be taken back to Arizona and hanged, but Abel refuses. When Burrack hears a gun shot and finds the twins, one is dead and the other is crying over the body. The remaining twin introduces himself as Abel Carly and confesses to killing Blake in self-defense. Since the Carly brothers are identical twins, Burrack has no idea if the survivor is Abel or Blake, but he's not taking any chances. He takes the last Carly brother back to Arizona in handcuffs, hoping to determine on the way who his prisoner is—Abel or Blake.

Where it's reviewed:
Roundup Magazine, December 2004, page 34

Other books by the same author:
Gunman's Song, 2004
Hell's Riders, 2004
Blood Money, 2002
Blood Rock, 2001
Devil's Due, 2001

Other books you might like:
Robert J. Conley, *The Gunfighter*, 2001
Fred Grove, *The Years of Fear*, 2002
Stephen Overholser, *Track of a Killer*, 2003
Frank Roderus, *Lewisville Flats*, 2002
Richard S. Wheeler, *Restitution*, 2001

433

M. ALLEN CUNNINGHAM

The Green Age of Asher Witherow

(Denver: Unbridled Books, 2004)

Story type: Historical/American West; Saga

Subject(s): Gold; Miners and Mining

Major character(s): Asher Witherow, Miner (coal); Thomas Morton, Miner (coal); Anna Flood, Friend (of Asher Witherow)

Time period(s): 1860s (1861-1869)

Locale(s): Nortonville, California

Summary: Coal mining in Nortonville, California, in the 1860s is dangerous, causing death not only from tunnels collapsing and accidents with explosives, but illnesses such as Black Lung, a terminal condition that results from breathing coal dust. A young Welsh immigrant, Asher Witherow, begins his career as a coal miner when he is ten years old. He and another boy, Thomas Morton, become good friends by benefit of their closeness in age, as well as sharing the brutal

misery of coal mining. Thomas shows Asher how to see in the dark, a skill which doesn't save Thomas from falling into a pit of muck, a mixture of coal dust and mud that ignites and burns him to death. Asher witnesses the accidental death, but tells no one, not even his friend, Anna Flood, because he feels survivor's guilt and believes he should have been able to rescue Thomas. When the body is found, the miners blame an eccentric preacher until Asher finally confronts the harm his continued silence is causing.

Where it's reviewed:
Library Journal, August 2004, page 66

Other books you might like:
Tim Champlin, *By Flare of Northern Lights*, 2001
Tim Champlin, *Wayfaring Strangers*, 2000
Frances Fuller Victor, *Women of the Gold Rush*, 1998
Richard S. Wheeler, *Goldfield*, 1995
Richard S. Wheeler, *Sun Mountain*, 1999

434

BEN DAITZ

Delivery

(Albuquerque: University of New Mexico Press, 2004)

Story type: Modern; Revenge

Subject(s): Drugs; Crime and Criminals; Cerebral Palsy

Major character(s): Junior Shiflett, Drug Dealer (small-time), Addict; Clarisse Shiflett, Spouse (of Junior Shiflett), Abuse Victim (beaten by Junior); Matt Dorgan, Doctor (in family practice), Widow(er)

Time period(s): 1980s (1985)

Locale(s): Mogote, New Mexico; Albuquerque, New Mexico

Summary: When Dr. Matt Dorgan delivers Junior and Clarisse Shiflett's son, the baby has severe cerebral palsy, seizures, and is brain damaged. There is no cure for his condition; and limited treatment. Clarisse lives in a small, decrepit trailer house outside of town caring for her son and dreaming at night that she has killed the baby. She has no car and no human contact except Junior, the young social worker Pilar Castillo, and medical personnel during her frequent trips to the emergency room with her baby. Pilar tries to persuade Clarisse to leave Junior before his escalating violence toward her leads to his killing her. In the meantime, Junior has an opportunity to set up his first major marijuana distribution deal. He must have money for his investment in a inventory of the drug. He decides to sue Dr. Dorgan for medical malpractice, claiming that his son's condition is a result of the doctor's mistakes during delivery. The scenes of Clarisse's increasing depression are balanced by descriptions of the beautiful landscape of New Mexico. The relationships between the Anglo and Hispanic residents of Mogote provide a social background for this gritty tale about the modern West where the desolate landscape mirrors the sterile lives of Junior and Clarisse.

Where it's reviewed:
Roundup Magazine, December 2004, page 34

Other books you might like:
Sandra Babb, *Where Names Are Unknown*, 2004

James Lee Burke, *Bitterroot*, 2001
    Billy Bob Holland. Book 3
James Lee Burke, *In the Moon of Red Ponies*, 2004
    Billy Bob Holland. Book 4
Michael McGarrity, *Everyone Dies*, 2003
    Kevin Kerney. Book 9
Bobby R. Woodall, *Clearwater*, 2003

435

PHYLLIS DE LA GARZA

Silk and Sagebrush

(Unionville, New York: Silk Label, 2004)

Story type: Historical/American West; Collection
Subject(s): Women; Short Stories
Locale(s): West

Summary: These fictionalized biographies of many famous and infamous women who impacted American history or culture include Elizabeth Custer, Carry Nation, Julia Bulette, Calamity Jane, Kate Bender, and Anna Surratt. A brief paragraph provides a historical context for each story, and introduces the characters.

Where it's reviewed:
Roundup Magazine, February 2005, page 35

Other books by the same author:
Bounty Hunter's Daughter, 2000
Camels West, 1999
Clarissa of the Overland Express, 1999
Apache Kid, 1995

Other books you might like:
Zane Grey, *The Desert Crucible*, 2003
Stan Lynde, *Vigilante Moon*, 2003
Clay Reynolds, *The Vigil*, 2001
Lisa Waller Rogers, *Get Along, Little Dogies*, 2001
Gladys Smith, *Deliverance Valley*, 2003

436

PATRICK DEAREN

When the Sky Rained Dust

(Austin, Texas: Eakin, 2004)

Story type: Saga; Historical/Depression Era
Subject(s): American West; Depression (Economic)
Major character(s): Josh Watson, Teenager (14-year-old); Shan Burke, Teenager (14-year-old); Luke Watson, Farmer (destitute), Parent (Josh's father)
Time period(s): 1930s (1934)
Locale(s): Pettit, Texas

Summary: The Great Depression has joined with the worst drought in the 20th century to bring the farmers in Central Texas to their knees. Their livestock is starving, their fields are bare, cracked dirt, and Black Dusters sweep across the land at the rate of several a month. Luke Watson mortgages his farm to pay for his small daughter's surgery. With no crops to sell, no food for his livestock or family, Luke is desperate. Now the bank has foreclosed on his property. He will lose everything! Luke's son, Josh Watson, knows that

times are hard, and food consists of beans and cornbread and eggs from their chickens, but he loves his family and Shan, the girl on the next farm. They ride horses and steal kisses and go to the barn dances until Shan tells him her father has sold everything and they'll be moving. Then Luke Watson sells the family's cows, including Josh's pet, and Josh is angry and resents his father. When he receives a letter from Shan, he goes to stay with her family the rest of the summer, but Shan has found another boyfriend. When his father falls off the windmill, Josh goes home, knowing that he was wrong to blame his dad for nature's actions.

Where it's reviewed:
Roundup Magazine, February 2005, page 35

Other books by the same author:
Comanche Peace Pipe, 2001
Hidden Treasure of the Chisos, 2001
On the Pecos Trail, 2001
Cowboy of the Pecos, 1996
When Cowboys Die, 1995

Other books you might like:
Sandra Babb, *Where Names Are Unknown*, 2004
Louise Erdrich, *Four Souls*, 2004
Ralph M. Flores, *The Horse in the Kitchen*, 2004
Elmer Kelton, *The Time It Never Rained*, 1973
Bruce Murkoff, *Waterborne*, 2004

437

JAMES D. DOSS

The Witch's Tongue

(New York: St. Martin's Minotaur, 2004)

Story type: Modern; Mystery
Series: Charlie Moon. Book 9
Subject(s): American West; Indians of North America; Crime and Criminals
Major character(s): Charlie Moon, Police Officer (tribal investigator), Rancher; Daisy Perika, Shaman (Ute Nation), Relative (Charlie Moon's aunt); Lila McTeague, FBI Agent
Time period(s): 2000s
Locale(s): Granite Creek, Colorado; Ute Reservation, Colorado

Summary: A Ute man disappears in Spirit Canyon; Daisy Perika, a Ute shaman and Charlie's aunt, dreams she hears the owl hoot, the harbinger of death. A private museum belonging to the wealthy Cassidy family is burgled of a collection of antique cameos and several rare coins. An Apache assaults a Southern Ute police officer, who happens to be white, and a sniper shoots through the window of an antiques store and kills the owner while Charlie Moon is standing next to him. Charlie is too busy with his enormous ranch, the Columbine, that he inherited from an elderly white woman, to want to want to be involved investigating the antiques dealer's murder, or serving as middle man to the burglar so he can return the cameos and coins to the Cassidys for a reward. However, tribal Chief Oscar Sweetwater tells Charlie to investigate the assault case because the Apache's lawyer is suing the tribe. Then Charlie is supposed to learn what happened in the Spirit

Canyon disappearance case. In the meantime, Daisy Perika is conducting secret rituals over what to do with a horned star pendant once belonging to the most famous Navajo shaman. Then the newest FBI Special Agent, Lila McTeague, arrives in Colorado to investigate a dead body found in a shallow grave on the Ute Reservation, and pulls Charlie into that investigation which turns out to related to the other odd crimes. It seems he may never get back to his ranch, but being ordered to aid Lila keeps Charlie in Agent McTeague's vicinity, which he considers ample compensation.

Where it's reviewed:
Publishers Weekly, August 23, 2004, page 40
Roundup Magazine, February 2005, page 35

Other books by the same author:
Dead Soul, 2003 (Charlie Moon. Book 8)
White Shell Woman, 2002 (Charlie Moon. Book 7)
Grandmother Spider, 2001 (Charlie Moon. Book 6)
The Night Visitor, 1999 (Charlie Moon. Book 5)
The Shaman's Game, 1998 (Charlie Moon. Book 4)

Other books you might like:
Frederic Bean, *Murder at the Spirit Cave*, 1999
Margaret Coel, *Killing Raven*, 2003
Tony Hillerman, *The Sinister Pig*, 2003
Kirk Mitchell, *Sky Woman Falling*, 2004
Aimee Thurlo, *The Blackening Song*, 2002
    David Thurlo, co-author

438

DEBORAH L. DUVALL

Rabbit Goes Duck Hunting

(Albuquerque: University of New Mexico Press, 2004)

Story type: Traditional; Indian Culture
Series: Grandmother Stories. Book 5
Subject(s): Folk Tales; Animals/Rabbits; Indians of North America
Major character(s): Ji-Stu, Animal (rabbit); Otter, Animal (Ji-Stu's friend); Chief, Animal (leader of wood ducks)
Time period(s): Indeterminate Past
Locale(s): Smokey Mountains, Tennessee

Summary: When Ji-Stu sees an enormous wood duck surrounded by hundred of smaller wood ducks, the mischievous rabbit knows he is looking at the Chief of All Wood Ducks. Excited by his discovery Ji-Stu runs down the riverbank looking for his best friend, Otter. When he tells Otter of his discovery, the other animal is not sure whether he ought to believe him. Rabbits, after all, are the tricksters of the animal world. When the two friends return to the spot of discovery Chief is gone, and Otter is sure Ji-Stu tricked him. He catches a small wood duck for his lunch and ignores Ji-Stu. Ji-Stu jumps in the river to catch his own wood duck when Chief lands on him, and the wily rabbit ropes him with a grape vine. Chief flies away and Ji-Stu must pull his best trick ever to save himself. A book for all ages.

Where it's reviewed:
Roundup Magazine, February 2005, page 35

Other books by the same author:
Rabbit and the Bears, 2004 (Grandmother Stories. Book 4)

How Medicine Came to the People, 2003 (Grandmother Stories. Book 2)
How Rabbit Lost His Tail, 2003 (Grandmother Stories. Book 3)
The Great Ball Game of the Birds and Animals, 2002 (Grandmother Stories. Book 1)
Talaquah: Cherokee Nation, 1999

Other books you might like:
Patrick Dearen, *Comanche Peace Pipe*, 2001
Patrick Dearen, *Hidden Treasure of the Chisos*, 2001
James Rice, *Victor Lopez at the Alamo*, 2001
Melinda Rice, *Fire on the Hillside*, 2001
Lisa Waller Rogers, *Get Along, Little Dogies*, 2001

439

DOROTHY WARD ERSKINE

North with De Anza

(Albuquerque: University of New Mexico Press, 2004)

Story type: Historical/American West; Indian Culture
Subject(s): Indians of North America; Conquest
Major character(s): Don Juan Bautista de Anza, Military Personnel (captain in Spanish army), Historical Figure; Pedro Peralta, Child (12-year-old), Immigrant (to California); Jaime Alviso, Friend (of Pedro Peralta), Immigrant (to California)
Time period(s): 1770s (1775-1776)
Locale(s): Tubac, Arizona; San Francisco Bay, California

Summary: Captain Don Juan Bautista de Anza arrives in Tubac with 20 families from the south. Ten more families will join the rest in Tubac. Pedro Peralta and his friend Jaime Alviso are two of the youngsters going to California with their families. Both are 12-years-old and believe the journey of 2,000 miles is the most exciting time of their lives. Despite the Apache bands that shadow their expedition and occasionally steal horses and other domestic animals, the snows in the mountains, and the treacherous crossing of the Colorado River, Pedro and Jaime are thoroughly enjoying themselves. Upon reaching San Gabriel, California, Captain de Anza clashes with Comandante Rivera who is planning to make war on the Indians. The captain is against it because the Indians badly outnumber the Spanish in California. Finally, Anza leaves for the north over the objections of the comandante. He selects Pedro to accompany him to San Francisco Bay to survey it. A captivating story of Anza, an explorer who ranks with Lewis and Clark.

Where it's reviewed:
Roundup Magazine, June 2005, page 35

Other books you might like:
Win Blevins, *So Wild a Dream*, 2003
Emerson Hough, *The Covered Wagon*, 2000
Jane Kirkpatrick, *All Together in One Place*, 2000
    Kinship and Courage. Book 1
Jane Kirkpatrick, *No Eye Can See*, 2001
    Kinship and Courage. Book 2
Robert J. Randisi, *Lancaster's Orphans*, 2004

440

T.T. FLYNN

Reunion at Cottonwood Station

(New York: Leisure, 2004)

Story type: Traditional; Collection
Subject(s): American West; Crime and Criminals; Short Stories
Time period(s): 19th century (post-Civil War)
Locale(s): West

Summary: Four novellas that represent Flynn's best work in that literary form are all action filled, with wonderful characters every reader will love. In *Brothers of the Owlhoot*, a young man searches for his fugitive brother, while in *Rodeo's "A" Man*, a top rodeo rider is hunting the men who unjustly sent him to prison. *Outlawed* tells the story of an innocent young man mistaken for the West's most desperate outlaw. The title story recounts the tale of a stage full of passengers who must fight together when the Apache attack an isolated stagecoach station.

Where it's reviewed:
Roundup Magazine, June 2005, page 36

Other books by the same author:
Hell's Canon, 2002
Rawhide, 2002
Night of the Comanche Moon, 2000
The Devil's Lode, 1999
Long Journey to Deep Canon, 1998

Other books you might like:
Phyllis de la Garza, *Silk and Sagebrush*, 2004
Ed Gorman, *The Long Ride Back*, 2004
Louis L'Amour, *Bowdrie*, 2004
Les Savage Jr., *The Devil's Corral*, 2003
Dale L. Walker, *Westward*, 2003
    editor

441

STEVE FRAZEE

Voices in the Hill

(New York: Leisure, 2005)

Story type: Traditional; Collection
Subject(s): American West; Short Stories
Time period(s): 19th century (post-Civil War)
Locale(s): West

Summary: Five of Frazee's best short stories are collected for the first time in paperback. The title story revolves around an old miner who has worked underground so long that he claims to understand the sounds of the earth. The old man knows the sounds portend a terrible calamity, but will anyone believe that he really does hear the voices in the hill? "Low Smoke" finds two companions on the run who are hired by a former Confederate general with a lovely daughter. One man loves her and the other is interested only for a time. Twisted selfishness and blind loyalty make a powerful character study. "McCorkhill's War" shifts the scene to the Civil War, and an endless hatred between a Union corporal and a Confederate

private. All the stories are full of action and suspense with three dimensional characters worth knowing.

Where it's reviewed:
Roundup Magazine, June 2005, page 36

Other books by the same author:
Tower of Rocks, 2004
Nights of Terror, 2003
Hidden Gold, 2001
Ghost Mine, 2000
The Way through the Mountain, 1999

Other books you might like:
Ricardo L. Garza, *Brother Bill's Bait Bites Back and Other Tales from the Raton*, 2004
Ed Gorman, *The Long Ride Back*, 2004
John Jakes, *The Funeral of Tanner Moody*, 2004
    Elmer Kelton, Robert J. Randisi, and others, co-authors
Les Savage Jr., *The Devil's Corral*, 2003
Jon Tuska, *Stories of the Golden West. Book 4*, 2004
    editor

442

ED GORMAN

Branded

(New York: Berkley, 2004)

Story type: Traditional; Chase
Subject(s): American West; Crime and Criminals
Major character(s): Andy Malloy, Clerk (in his father's general store), Relative (Tom Malloy's son); Tom Malloy, Alcoholic, Store Owner (general store); Ken Burkett, Lawman (sheriff)
Time period(s): 19th century (post-Civil War)
Locale(s): West

Summary: Andy Malloy knows his father has a fierce temper when he is sober and a worse one when he is drunk, which is most of the time. When Andy arrives home and finds his stepmother dead, he suspects his father, Tom Malloy, of murdering her. When his father denies the crime, Andy believes him, but not without doubt. Andy and Tom ride to Sheriff Ken Burkett's office, so Tom can turn himself in, but Burkett hates Tom Malloy and plans to use this occasion to see him hanged. Andy tells his dad to run, and Burkett throws him in jail as a material witness. Dalia Evans, daughter of the best lawyer in town, loves Andy and persuades her father to help him. Burkett then pays the town drunk to kill Tom Malloy. Andy and Dalia don't believe the drunk's story that Tom Malloy had drawn on him, but can't persuade him to tell the judge who hired him to murder Tom. In fact, Andy suspects that Burkett will kill the drunk as soon as he can do it unseen. Andy doesn't intend to let that happen, even if he has to kill Burkett himself.

Where it's reviewed:
Roundup Magazine, June 2005, page 36

Other books by the same author:
Texas Rangers, 2004 (editor)
The Long Ride Back, 2004
Gun Truth, 2003
Night of Shadows, 2002

Lawless, 2000

Other books you might like:
Dave Austin, *Man on the Border*, 2004
Dick Clason, *The Ranger and the Green Derby*, 2004
Stan Lynde, *Saving Miss Julia*, 2004
Stephen Overholser, *West of the Border*, 2004
Frank Roderus, *Old Marsden*, 1999

443

ED GORMAN, Editor
MARTIN H. GREENBERG, Co-Editor

Texas Rangers

(New York: Berkley, 2004)

Story type: Traditional; Anthology
Subject(s): American West; Crime and Criminals; Law Enforcement
Locale(s): Texas

Summary: This anthology of short stories on the Texas Rangers includes such authors as Louis L'Amour, Elizabeth Fackler, Robert Randisi, and James Reasoner. The stories cover every era, from L'Amour's "Down Sonora Way," about the 19th-century Rangers, to Larry D. Sweazy's "The Promotion," about the present day Rangers. Two stories are different from the traditional Ranger plot of fighting Comanches and chasing outlaws. "After the Great War" by Gary Lovisi is about a young man who returns from WWI with a buddy. When the buddy is killed, the young man joins the Rangers determined to find his friend's killer, and learns about anti-Semitism as a motive for murder. "The End of Autumn" by Russell Davis is a poignant story of a Ranger's last gunfight and his courage facing his own death.

Where it's reviewed:
Roundup Magazine, February 2005, page 35

Other books by the same author:
The Blue and the Gray Undercover, 2001 (editor)
Lawless, 2000
Storm Riders, 1999
The Fatal Frontier, 1997 (Martin H. Greenberg, co-editor)
Gunslinger, 1995 (editor)

Other books you might like:
Max Brand, *Tales of the Wild West*, 2000
Elmer Kelton, *Badger Boy*, 2001
   Texas Rangers. Book 2
Elmer Kelton, *The Buckskin Line*, 1999
   Texas Rangers. Book 1
W.W. Lee, *Rustler's Venom*, 1990
Jason Manning, *The Black Jacks*, 1997

444

LOREN ZANE GREY

Lassiter

(New York: Leisure, 2004)

Story type: Traditional; Man Alone
Subject(s): American West; Crime and Criminals

Major character(s): Lassiter, Gunfighter, Avenger; Allie Kerrington, Rancher; Joe Rudd, Rancher, Thief (cattle rustler)
Time period(s): 19th century (post-Civil War)
Locale(s): Wayfield, Arizona

Summary: Zane Grey's son builds a story around Lassiter, a character that his father created in his novel *Riders of the Purple Sage*. Loren Zane Grey recounts Lassiter's early years before he became a gunman and an implacable enemy of Mormons, whom Lassiter believes enticed his young sister into joining their religion. Lassiter had been a drifter at a young age, and, now a man full grown, he joins a close friend in a cattle ranch in Arizona. He has barely reached the area of the ranch when Joe Rudd rides up. Lassiter had testified against Rudd in a rustling case, and has no desire to be the man's neighbor. Once a rustler, always a rustler. Nor does Lassiter want to join in a fight against Allie Kerrington, who is an honest woman and rancher so far as he can tell. One thing Lassiter knows for sure: when his cattle start disappearing, he knows exactly whom to confront. He will meet Joe Rudd with his six-gun loaded and ready to send a bullet through the miscreant's heart.

Where it's reviewed:
Roundup Magazine, June 2005, page 36

Other books you might like:
B.M. Bower, *The Terror*, 2003
Max Brand, *The Runaways*, 2003
P.H. Holt, *Silver Creek*, 2003
Stephen Overholser, *Track of a Killer*, 2003
Lauran Paine, *The White Bird*, 1999

445

ZANE GREY

Riders of the Purple Sage: The Restored Edition

(Waterville, Maine: Five Star, 2005)

Story type: Ranch Life; Historical/American West
Subject(s): Mormons; Religious Traditions
Major character(s): Jane Withersteen, Rancher (inherited ranch); Elder Tull, Religious (elder in Mormon church), Rancher (greedy for Jane's land); Lassiter, Gunfighter, Avenger (for sister's death)
Time period(s): 1870s (1871)
Locale(s): Cottonwoods, Utah

Summary: Faithful Mormon Jane Withersteen, owner of a vast ranch and other properties, falls in love with a Gentile, Bern Venters. Elder Tull wants Jane for his second wife so he may claim her inheritance. Bishop Dyer commands Jane to marry Tull but she refuses. The shadowy figure known only as Lassiter rides into Jane's yard in time to rescue Venters from the Mormons, who plan to whip him and run him out of Utah. Lassiter has come to Jane for information about the location of his sister's grave. His sister was enticed into leaving her home and her husband by the Mormons. They took her child by a Mormon man and gave her away. It was this as much as illness that killed Lassiter's sister. For that Lassiter will avenge his sister, then find her daughter and take her from the Mormons. Jane, through loyalty to her religion, refuses to tell

Western

Lassiter the name of the man who shamed his sister. Not until Elder Tull and Bishop Dyer set her servants to spying on her, and the two men and others begin defrauding her of all that she possesses does Jane realize that the Mormons intend to make her a pauper and force her to marry Elder Tull. This is *Riders of the Purple Sage* restored to the story Grey actually wrote, but that has not been published until now, compiled from Grey's handwritten manuscript. This version is longer, richer in characterization, and restores scenes that reveal motive behind actions. It is a magnificent read, for both newcomers and those who have always loved the story.

Where it's reviewed:
Roundup Magazine, June 2005, page 37

Other books by the same author:
The Maverick Queen, 2004
Top Hand, 2004
The Desert Crucible, 2003
Tonto Basin, 2003
Open Range, 2001

Other books you might like:
Jane Candia Coleman, *Last River*, 2003
Robert J. Horton, *The Hanging X*, 2003
Lauran Paine, *The Running Iron*, 2000
F.M. Parker, *The Predators*, 1990
Conrad Richter, *The Sea of Grass*, 1937

446

FRED GROVE

A Soldier Returns

(Waterville, Maine: Five Star, 2004)

Story type: Historical/American West
Subject(s): Mexicans; War; Civil War
Major character(s): Jesse Alden Wilder, Prisoner (of Union army), Military Personnel (captain, Confederate army); Susan Andrews Lattimore, Parent (of Apache captive), Lover (of Jesse Wilder); B.L. Sawyer, Lawyer (for Susan Lattimore)
Time period(s): 1860s (1867-1869)
Locale(s): Tucson, Arizona; Petersberg, Tennessee

Summary: Wounded during the Battle of Franklin, Jesse Alden Wilder wakes up in a Union prison hospital. After several weeks of watching his fellow prisoners die of hunger and abuse from prison guards, Jesse volunteers to join the Union army and fight Indians in the West. After being mustered out, Jesse returns home to find himself shunned as a galvanized Yankee. Disinherited by his father, Jesse returns to the West and fights with the Juaristas in liberating Mexico, then undertakes several rescue missions for the army. He arrives in Tucson and shortly thereafter Susan Andrews Lattimore hires him to rescue her son who has been captured by the Apaches. The two fall in love and travel to Petersberg, Tennessee, to visit Jesse's family farm and hire B.L. Sawyer to obtain a divorce for Susan. Jesse is still shunned as a traitor, and becomes a target of the Ku Klux Klan, along with his neighbors. Finally, Jesse is accepted and leads the fight against the riders in white.

Where it's reviewed:
Roundup Magazine, December 2004, page 35

Other books by the same author:
Spring of Valor, 2003
The Years of Fear, 2002
Red River Stage, 2001
A Distance of Ground, 2000
Destiny Valley, 2000

Other books you might like:
Tim Champlin, *Raiders of the Western & Atlantic*, 2002
Tim Champlin, *The Tombstone Conspiracy*, 1999
Andrew J. Fenady, *Double Eagles*, 2002
Kevin McCalley, *The Other Side*, 2000
Cotton Smith, *Pray for Texas*, 2000

447

FRED HARRIS

Following the Harvest

(Norman: University of Oklahoma Press, 2004)

Story type: Traditional; Modern
Subject(s): American West; Family Relations; Farm Life
Major character(s): Will Haley, Worker (on wheat-harvesting crew), Teenager; Bob Haley, Farmer, Alcoholic; Jim Gruber, Farmer
Time period(s): 1940s (1943)
Locale(s): Vernon, Oklahoma; Cheyenne, Wyoming; Rhame, North Dakota

Summary: Will Haley looks forward to being a member of his father's wheat-harvesting crew. His cousins also hire on as crew. Will is excited about the summer except for his fear about his father's drinking. Bob Haley is never a mean drunk but he is a drunk, and Will fears his father might get hurt on some of the machinery. One of Will's cousins, Spider, is a lazy whiner who is not liked by the other crew members. The other, Emmett, is a harder worker and more dependable, but like Bob Haley and his drinking, Emmett also has a secret that is exposed on the journey north. Will discovers that each of the crew members has a secret that they must confront. By the time the harvest crew reaches the end of the journey, no one remains unchanged, and not all return to Oklahoma.

Where it's reviewed:
Publishers Weekly, September 27, 2004, page 37
Roundup Magazine, December 2004, page 36

Other books by the same author:
Easy Pickin's, 2000
Coyote Revenge, 1999

Other books you might like:
Sandra Babb, *Where Names Are Unknown*, 2004
Patrick Dearen, *When the Sky Rained Dust*, 2004
Ralph M. Flores, *The Horse in the Kitchen*, 2004
Elmer Kelton, *The Day It Never Rained*, 1973
Giles Tippette, *Southwest of Heaven*, 1999

Western

448

STEVEN F. HAVILL

Convenient Disposal

(New York: St. Martin's Minotaur, 2004)

Story type: Modern; Mystery
Series: Posadas County. Book 12
Subject(s): American West; Crime and Criminals; Mexican Americans
Major character(s): Estelle Reyes-Guzman, Police Officer; Carmen Acosta, Teenager (in middle school), Crime Victim (murdered); Kevin Ziegler, Government Official (county manager)
Time period(s): 2000s
Locale(s): Posadas County, New Mexico

Summary: When Carmen Acosta is brutalized, then murdered with a hat pin shoved in her ear, Undersheriff Estelle Reyes-Guzman knows that the murderer is a vicious individual too dangerous to roam free. The easy answer seems to be that Kevin Ziegler, a mild-mannered Clark Kent man who has disappeared, is the murderer, and indeed, many of the residents of Posadas County already believe him guilty. Estelle smells liquor and cigarette smoke in Ziegler's abandoned pickup, and the county manager neither drank or smoked. However, like Clark Kent, Kevin Ziegler is not who he seems to be. The original protagonist, retired Sheriff Bill Gaston, now a brand inspector, hovers on the edges of the story, ready to help out Estelle, whom he treats as a daughter. Estelle Reyes-Guzman is a big girl now, balancing her career with her life as a wife and mother, and doesn't really need the retired sheriff's help, or so she believes.

Where it's reviewed:
Publishers Weekly, October 18, 2004, page 51

Other books by the same author:
A Discount for Death, 2003 (Posadas County. Book 10)
Scavengers, 2002 (Posadas County. Book 9)
Bag Limit, 2001 (Posadas County. Book 8)
Before She Dies, 2001 (Posadas County. Book 7)
Dead Weight, 2000 (Posadas County. Book 6)

Other books you might like:
Frederic Bean, *Murder at the Spirit Cave*, 1999
Margaret Coel, *Killing Raven*, 2003
James D. Doss, *Dead Soul*, 2003
  Charlie Moon. Book 8
Tony Hillerman, *The Sinister Pig*, 2003
Michael McGarrity, *Slowkill*, 2004
  Kevin Kerney. Book 9

449

WILL HENRY

Blind Canon

(Waterville, Maine: Five Star, 2005)

Story type: Traditional; Collection
Subject(s): Gold Discoveries; Miners and Mining; Crime and Criminals
Time period(s): 19th century (post-Civil War)

Locale(s): West

Summary: Two long novellas by Will Henry, one humorous and one revealing the worst traits of man, reel in the reader like a fisherman reeling in a trout. In *Bandits of Tehuantlrux*, two good friends plan to return prosperity to the cantina owned by one. Since the river flooded, the village has rebuilt on the other side, leaving Porfirio and his cantina isolated on the other side. He has only two regular customers, and neither of them have any money. Then one of the customers suggests that they become bandits to raise money to save the cantina. The title story concerns a gold mine owned by a mixed blood Sioux who was adopted by Sitting Blue. The other miners, greedy for his rich strike, pass a law stating that only American citizens may own or operate a mining property. The mixed-blood Sioux has no intention of losing his mine.

Where it's reviewed:
Roundup Magazine, April 2005, page 36

Other books by the same author:
The Hunkpapa Scout, 2004
Winter Shadows, 2003
The Legend of Sotoju Mountain, 2002
Ghost Wolf of Thunder Mountain, 2000
Tumbleweeds, 1999

Other books you might like:
Max Brand, *Jokers Extra Wild*, 2002
Walt Coburn, *Coffin Ranch*, 2002
T.T. Flynn, *The Devil's Lode*, 1999
Wayne D. Overholser, *Wheels Roll West*, 2002
Cherry Wilson, *The Throwback*, 2002

450

JANET MUIRHEAD HILL

Starlight Comes Home

(Norris, Montana: Raven, 2004)

Story type: Modern; Ranch Life
Series: Starlight. Book 6
Subject(s): Animals/Horses; Coming-of-Age
Major character(s): Miranda Stevens, Teenager (13-year-old), Animal Lover (especially horses); Chris Bergman, Teenager (13-year-old), Friend (of Miranda); Starlight, Animal (Miranda's favorite horse)
Time period(s): 2000s
Locale(s): Shady Hills, Montana

Summary: The last volume in the series featuring Miranda Stevens and her horse, Starlight, finds Miranda a teenager. The teen years bring conflict and confusion to Miranda. She finds that she likes Chris Bergman as more than just a friend, but realizes that liking a boy is a little frightening. She also discovers that her horse, Starlight, is no longer the first priority of her life, and that discovery makes her feel a little guilty, especially after Starlight disappears from his stable. Growing up is exciting and scary at the same time, and Miranda is afraid if she and Chris become girlfriend and boyfriend, they won't be real friends anymore. A refreshing story about a girl's coming-of-age.

Where it's reviewed:
Roundup Magazine, April 2005, page 36

Other books by the same author:
Starlight Shines for Miranda, 2004 (Starlight. Book 5)
Starlight's Shooting Star, 2003 (Starlight. Book 4)
Starlight, Star Bright, 2003 (Starlight. Book 3)
Miranda and Starlight, 2002 (Starlight. Book 1)
Starlight's Courage, 2002 (Starlight. Book 2)

Other books you might like:
William J. Buchanan, *Diablo the Devil Steer*, 2004
Ralph M. Flores, *The Horse in the Kitchen*, 2004
Fred Harris, *Following the Harvest*, 2004
Lisa Lenard-Cook, *Coyote Morning*, 2004
Tillie Olsen, *Yonnondio from the Thirties*, 2004

451

TONY HILLERMAN

Skeleton Man

(New York: HarperCollins, 2004)

Story type: Modern; Mystery
Series: Joe Leaphorn/Jim Chee. Book 17
Subject(s): American West; Indians of North America; Crime and Criminals
Major character(s): Jim Chee, Police Officer (sergeant), Indian (Navajo); Joe Leaphorn, Detective—Private (retired police lieutenant), Indian (Navajo); Billy Tuve, Indian (Navajo)
Time period(s): 2000s
Locale(s): Window Rock, New Mexico; Navajo Reservation, New Mexico

Summary: In 1956, two planes collide in the air above the Grand Canyon. Two items are never found: a courier's arm and a diamond-filled security case attached to that arm. The whereabouts of both are still unknown after nearly 50 years. Joe Leaphorn, a retired lieutenant in the Navajo police, works intermittently as a private detective if he finds a case interesting or if he is paid. Leaphorn investigates the possible link between a diamond stolen in an old robbery, and another one stolen in a recent robbery, and what, if anything, the two stolen diamonds have to do with the jewels lost in the plane crash. Sergeant Jim Chee is personally investigating the case against Billy Tuve for possibly trying to hock a jewel from a current robbery. Chee involves himself because Tuve is the cousin of his best friend, a fellow Navajo policeman. Tuve claims an old man gave him the jewel when they accidently met at an isolated Navajo shrine. Chee must verify the alibi, and he is not too happy that Leaphorn's investigation may be related. Leaphorn, is after all, retired and has no authority to stick his nose into current police investigations. On the other hand, Leaphorn is handy in a tight situation, which this case is. Hillerman creates another exciting tale of everyone's favorite Navajo cops, filled with Navajo lore and personal relationships, particularly Chee's engagement to fellow cop Bernie Manuelito.

Where it's reviewed:
Publishers Weekly, October 18, 2004, page 50
Roundup Magazine, February 2005, page 38

Other books by the same author:
The Sinister Pig, 2003 (Joe Leaphorn/Jim Chee. Book 16)

The Wailing Wind, 2002 (Joe Leaphorn/Jim Chee. Book 15)
Hunting Badger, 1999 (Joe Leaphorn/Jim Chee. Book 14)
The First Eagle, 1998 (Joe Leaphorn/Jim Chee. Book 13)
The Fallen Man, 1996 (Joe Leaphorn/Jim Chee. Book 12)

Other books you might like:
Johnny D. Boggs, *Spark on the Prairie*, 2003
   Western Heritage Award winner
Margaret Coel, *The Shadow Dancer*, 2002
   Father John O'Malley/Vicky Holden. Book 8
James D. Doss, *The Witch's Tongue*, 2004
   Charlie Moon. Book 9
Kathleen O'Neal Gear, *The Visitant*, 1999
   W. Michael Gear, co-author
Aimee Thurlo, *Plant Them Deep*, 2003
   Ella Clah. Book 9

452

PERRY HOLMES

Mountains Against the Sun

(New York: Leisure, 2004)

Story type: Traditional; Revenge
Subject(s): Crime and Criminals; American West
Major character(s): Frank Allard, Rancher; Ben Lenifee, Outlaw, Murderer; Amos Burns, Lawman (sheriff), Crime Victim (bullet wound)
Time period(s): 1870s (1875)
Locale(s): Mountain Pass, Utah

Summary: When young Deputy Sheriff Tom Yeager brings in Jack Slade and hangs him, a vicious cycle of bloodshed and vengeance begins. Although Sheriff Amos Burns sends Yeager out of the county, Slade's gang shoots him in the head, killing him instantly. Frank Allard, Tom's best friend, vows to hunt down Yeager's killers. Burns warns him that the killers are holed up in Winona Basin, with guards posted at the only two entrances. The leader of the clan of killers is Ben Lenifee, and to Ben, family is everything, even if a family member is guilty of shooting a man when his back is turned. Frank, however, is determined to identify his friend's killer and return him to Mountain Pass for hanging.

Where it's reviewed:
Roundup Magazine, June 2005, page 36

Other books you might like:
Daniel Alef, *Pale Truth*, 2000
Will Cade, *Genesis*, 2000
Elmer Kelton, *Cloudy in the West*, 1997
Frank Roderus, *Old Marsden*, 1999
Jim R. Woolard, *Blood at Dawn*, 2001

453

JOHN JAKES
ELMER KELTON, Co-Author
ROBERT J. RANDISI, Co-Author

The Funeral of Tanner Moody

(New York: Leisure, 2004)

Story type: Traditional; Saga

Subject(s): American West; Crime and Criminals
Major character(s): Tanner Moody, Lawman, Outlaw; Bat Masterson, Lawman (marshal), Journalist
Time period(s): 1900s (1902-1903)
Locale(s): Fort Worth, Texas

Summary: Framed by a series of newspaper articles allegedly written by Bat Masterson, each story about Tanner Moody is written by a different author about different periods of Tanner's life. Dropping into the White Horse Saloon in Fort Worth, Bat learns that Tanner Moody is dead and a wake is being held for him. Bat had known Tanner, so he attends the wake where he meets a number of people who had known Tanner at various times in his life. "Poor Ole Moody" by Marthayn Pelegrimas tells the story of Moody's relationship with Elvira Clifford, a childhood friend who loves him all his life but never tells him so. "Straw Boss" by Elmer Kelton tells of Don Felipe Talamantes, a rancher from Mexico who raids Texas cattle ranchers until he runs into Tanner Moody who doesn't approve of rustling. Peter Brandvold in "Love and Bullets" tells the story of Tanner's turning outlaw in his early twenties. Each story is beautifully written and is integrated with the other stories without any feeling of a hodge podge collection with no coherence.

Where it's reviewed:
Roundup Magazine, December 2004, page 36

Other books by the same author:
Bold Frontier, 2001
Heaven and Hell, 2000
American Dreams, 1998
Homeland, 1993
Arena, 1963

Other books you might like:
Sallie Bissell, *Call the Devil by His Oldest Name*, 2004
James Carlos Blake, *Pistoleer*, 1995
James Carlos Blake, *Wildwood Boys*, 2000
Henry Chappell, *The Callings*, 2002
Clay Reynolds, *The Tentmaker*, 2002

454

WILL JAMES

The American Cowboy

(Missoula, Montana: Mountain Press, 2005)

Story type: Ranch Life; Historical/American West
Subject(s): Cowboys/Cowgirls
Major character(s): Bill the First, Rancher; Bill the Second, Rancher (Bill's son); Bill the Third, Rancher (son of Bill the Second)
Time period(s): 19th century; 20th century (1836-1940)
Locale(s): West

Summary: James presents the history of the American cowboy by following a fictional family through three generations. The first Bill, a boy at the time of the Alamo and San Jacinto, is orphaned when a band of Apaches scalps his family and burns their cabin while he is away rounding up milk cows. On his own at ten years old, Bill is taken in by a petty thief with whom he lives until grown. Then he begins rounding up the wild longhorns and driving them to market in Missouri. After

the Civil War Bill drives the cattle to the Kansas markets, then further north where he settles, marries, and has a son, Bill the Second. After Bill the First's death, Bill the Second takes over the ranch. There are few Indians to fight, but still plenty of rustlers. The cattle changes to pure bred animals, with few longhorns remaining. By the time Bill the Third is born, open range is gone and pastures are fenced. Still, just as in his father and grandfather's day, there are rustlers, droughts, blizzards, and rough land no one but the cowboys want. This is a good, fast moving story with nothing to slow it down—just as cowboys are.

Where it's reviewed:
Roundup Magazine, April 2005, page 36

Other books by the same author:
My First Horse, 2003
The Dark Horse, 2003
Look-See with Uncle Bill, 2002
Cowboy in the Making, 2001
Smokey the Cowhorse, 2000

Other books you might like:
Ralph Cotton, *Between Hell and Texas*, 2004
Zane Grey, *The Maverick Queen*, 2004
Wayne C. Lee, *Son of a Gunman*, 2003
Kent Myers, *The Work of Wolves*, 2004
Cotton Smith, *Winter Kill*, 2004

455

CRAIG JOHNSON

The Cold Dish

(New York: Viking, 2005)

Story type: Modern; Mystery
Subject(s): Crime and Criminals; Indians of North America
Major character(s): Walt Longmire, Police Officer (sheriff); Victoria Moretti, Police Officer (deputy sheriff); Henry Standing Bear, Indian (Cheyenne), Friend (of Sheriff Longmire)
Time period(s): 2000s
Locale(s): Absaroka County, Wyoming

Summary: As the sheriff of Absaroka County, a rural county in a mostly rural state, Walt Longmire often has little to do on patrol except enjoy the drive and the passing scenery. That changes when young Cody Pritchard is found shot to death near the Cheyenne reservation. Pritchard was one of four boys accused of raping a young Cheyenne girl. This could be a revenge killing. Certainly, Deputy Victoria Moretti believes that revenge is the motive, but Sheriff Longmire isn't so sure. His best friend, Henry Standing Bear, denies that the Cheyenne had anything to do with Pritchard's murder. Then the second of the accused rapists is murdered, and Longmire is faced with the strong possibility that his best friend from childhood, Henry Standing Bear, has deliberately lied to him and is protecting a killer.

Where it's reviewed:
Publishers Weekly, December 13, 2004, page 48
Roundup Magazine, June 2005, page 36

Other books by the same author:
Father Hunger, 2004 (Margot Maine, co-author)

Western

Decentralization, 2003
Grounding the State, 2003
Water Wise, 2003

Other books you might like:
Frederic Bean, *Murder at the Spirit Cave*, 1999
Peter Bowen, *Thunder Horse*, 1999
James Lee Burke, *In the Moon of Red Ponies*, 2004
Kirk Mitchell, *Spirit Sickness*, 2001
Aimee Thurlo, *Wind Spirit*, 2004
    David Thurlo, co-author

456

CAMERON JUDD

Bad Night at Dry Creek
(New York: Leisure, 2004)

Story type: Traditional; Man Alone
Subject(s): Crime and Criminals; American West
Major character(s): Charley Hanna, Lawman (marshal); Noah Murphy, Outlaw (thief); Sarah Redding, Widow(er)
Time period(s): 19th century (post-Civil War)
Locale(s): Dry Creek, Colorado

Summary: Marshal Charley Hanna is trying to cope with his mother's impending death and his feelings for Sarah Redding, a young widow. The last thing he needs is a deathbed confession from Willy Murphy, who is dying of a gunshot wound inflicted by his own brother, outlaw gang leader Noah Murphy. Willy confesses to robbing a bank with Noah and his gang, then hiding the money, but he doesn't tell Charley where it is buried before he dies. Charley's confrontation with Noah is delayed by the death of Charley's mother. At her funeral, a shady gambler announces the story to the town, and accuses Charley of plotting to keep the money for himself, which turns the townsfolk against him. Noah doesn't believe Charley's denial of any knowledge of the money's whereabouts, either. Noah threatens to destroy the town if Charley does not give up the secret, and he murders a group of men who attempt to find it. Now Charley must defend himself, Sarah, and a town that no longer trusts him.

Where it's reviewed:
Roundup Magazine, April 2005, page 36

Other books by the same author:
Beggars Gulch, 2004
War at Fire Creek, 2004
Overmountain Men, 2003
Shootout in Dodge City, 2003
Border Men, 1992

Other books you might like:
Will Cade, *Henry Kidd, Outlaw*, 2003
Jason Manning, *The Outlaw Trail*, 2003
Stephen Overholser, *Track of a Killer*, 2003
Jory Sherman, *Texas Dust*, 2004
S.J. Stewart, *Beyond the Verde River*, 2003

457

CAMERON JUDD

War at Fire Creek
(New York: Pocket, 2004)

Story type: Traditional; Ranch Life
Series: Carrigan Brothers. Book 3
Subject(s): American West; Feuds; Relatives
Major character(s): Liam Carrigan, Relative (nephew of Patrick), Cowboy; Joseph Carrigan, Relative (nephew of Patrick), Cowboy; Patrick Carrigan, Rancher
Time period(s): 1870s (1879)
Locale(s): Fire Creek, Montana

Summary: Liam and Joseph Carrigan, brothers and Irish immigrants, are in Montana Territory where they believe their Uncle Patrick ranches. The Carrigan brothers have never met Patrick since he left Ireland and disappeared in America. Arriving at the little town of Fire Creek, they attend a magic show where an alleged ghost machine shows an image of a man who looks like the brothers' dead father. A few cowboys in the audience threaten the Carrigans, and peacemaker Joseph persuades his brother to leave and help him find the photographer who took the picture. From the photographer they learn that their uncle is in a range war with powerful rancher Bret Ellison that amounts to a blood feud. Ever the peacemaker, Joseph tries to settle the feud and is captured by Ellison instead. Patrick offers himself in exchange for Joseph. Now the two brothers need to rescue Patrick before he meets his maker with Ellison's help. So the brothers clean their guns and prepare for a showdown that will end the life of Ellison or the Carrigans.

Where it's reviewed:
Roundup Magazine, February 2005, page 36

Other books by the same author:
Revenge on Shadow Trail, 2003 (Carrigan Brothers. Book 2)
Shootout in Dodge City, 2002 (Carrigan Brothers. Book 1)
Kenton's Challege, 2001
Brazos, 2000
Border Men, 1992

Other books you might like:
Roland Cheek, *Crisis on the Stinkingwater*, 2004
Douglas Hirt, *Ketcham's Land*, 2002
John D. Nesbitt, *Black Hat Butte*, 2003
Lauran Paine, *Open Range*, 2003
Les Savage Jr., *Bloody Quarter*, 1999

458

ELMER KELTON

Jericho's Road
(New York: Forge, 2004)

Story type: Traditional; Chase
Series: Texas Rangers. Book 6
Subject(s): American West; Crime and Criminals
Major character(s): Andy Pickard, Lawman (Texas Ranger); Farley Brackett, Lawman (Texas Ranger), Military Per-

sonnel (former Confederate soldier); Jericho Jackson, Rancher (on Texas-Mexico border)
Time period(s): 19th century (post-Civil War)
Locale(s): Nueces Strip, Texas; Mexico

Summary: Texas Rangers Andy Pickard and Farley Brackett are sent to the Nueces Strip along the Texas-Mexico border which is in a state close to war between the Anglo Texans and the Mexicans. Jericho Jackson owns, or at least controls, an enormous ranch on the Texas side of the Rio Grande. His counterpart in Mexico is Guadalupe Chavez. The two men hate one another, Jericho because he hates Mexicans in general, and Chavez because the Texans defeated the Mexicans at the Battle of San Jacinto. Both men rustle one another's cattle and kill one another's men when given the opportunity. In addition, there is smuggling back and forth across the Rio Grande. Andy and Farley, along with several other Rangers are expected to bring peace to the border by forcing Jericho and Chavez to keep to their own side of the Rio Grande, an assignment that leads to death on both sides of the river.

Where it's reviewed:
Roundup Magazine, December 2004, page 35

Other books by the same author:
Texas Vendetta, 2004 (Texas Rangers. Book 5)
Ranger's Trail, 2002 (Texas Rangers. Book 4)
Badger Boy, 2001 (Texas Rangers. Book 2)
The Way of the Coyote, 2001 (Texas Rangers. Book 3)
The Buckskin Line, 1999 (Texas Rangers. Book 1)

Other books you might like:
Dave Austin, *Man on the Border*, 2004
Dick Clason, *The Ranger and the Green Derby*, 2004
Kat Goldring, *Death Medicine*, 2003
Leslie Scott, *Terror Stalks the Border*, 2002
Edwin Shrake, *The Borderland*, 2000

459

J. LEA KORETSKY

Domino

(New York: Regent, 2004)

Story type: Modern; Mystery
Series: Dalton Keys. Book 4
Subject(s): Crime and Criminals; Homosexuality/Lesbianism; American West
Major character(s): Dalton Keys, Police Officer (U.S. marshal); Isaiah DuBois, Police Officer (U.S. marshal), Homosexual
Time period(s): 2000s
Locale(s): Flagstaff, Arizona

Summary: To avoid a scandal that would embarrass the U.S. Marshal's Service, Deputy U.S. Marshal Isaiah DuBois is transferred out of the San Bernardino, California, office to patrol southwestern Arizona. DuBois is black and gay and was indiscreet and unwise in his personal relationships. U.S. Marshal Dalton Keys is a friend of DuBois, and hopes the reassignment will offer the other officer opportunities to repair his reputation. Dalton intends to look out for DuBois, but he is unable to save his friend from becoming a murder victim. Angry and grieving, as well as determined that the

Marshal's Service will look as long as it takes to track down the killer, Dalton searches through DuBois' recent case notes. The dead man had been investigating truck-hijacking and drug-smuggling rings, both of which were very dangerous targets, both of which are becoming common occurrences along the borders between California, Arizona, and New Mexico. It is an ugly fact of life in the modern West. Dalton reconstructs DuBois' investigation, questions the dead man's informants, and finally witnesses a truck-hijacking himself. At this point, he discovers just how dangerous hijackers and drug smugglers are.

Where it's reviewed:
Library Journal, November 1, 2004, page 60

Other books by the same author:
Sweat Box, 2004
Eternity Look, 2003
Wall of Darkness, 2002

Other books you might like:
Frederic Bean, *Murder at the Spirit Cave*, 1999
James D. Doss, *The Witch's Tongue*, 2004
D.R. Meredith, *Murder by Deception*, 2004
Kirk Mitchell, *Spirit Sickness*, 2001
Pari Noskin Taichert, *The Clovis Incident*, 2004

460

LISA LENARD-COOK

Coyote Morning

(Albuquerque: University of New Mexico Press, 2004)

Story type: Modern; Quest
Subject(s): American West; Animals/Coyotes; Environment
Major character(s): Alison Lomez, Divorced Person (single mother); Rachel Lomez, Child (Alison's daughter); Natalie Harold, Activist
Time period(s): 2000s
Locale(s): Valle Bosque, New Mexico

Summary: Alison Lomez glances out her window to see a coyote sitting by her seven-year-old daughter, Rachel. Alison is terrified that the coyote will attack Rachel, but her daughter climbs on the school bus and the coyote trots off. Rachel doesn't understand why her mother is so upset, or all the villagers either. The coyote, whom she names Chris after her father, is Rachel's friend. Natalie Harold, a transplant from New York, has lived in the village for 30 years and has never seen a coyote, although it is her dearest wish. She writes letters to the *Valle Bosque Beacon* defending the coyote which outrages most of the old timers. Written in the form of letters to the editor, *Coyote Morning* features the opinions of nearly every faction in Valle Bosque: Ralph Sandoval, animal control; Indians and Indian wannabes; university professors; and Rachel. How to coexist with wild animals such as the coyote who are adapting to human environments is a problem recognizable to anyone in the West.

Where it's reviewed:
Library Journal, October 1, 2004, page 70
Roundup Magazine, December 2004, page 36

Other books by the same author:
Dissonance, 2001

Other books you might like:
B.M. Bower, *The Terror*, 2003
Richard Hoyt, *Pony Girls*, 2004
Kent Myers, *The Work of Wolves*, 2004
Ben Rehder, *Bone Dry*, 2003
Linda Sandifer, *The Daughters of Luke McCall*, 2000

461

FRANK B. LINDERMAN

Indian Why Stories

(Lincoln: University of Nebraska Press, 2004)

Story type: Traditional; Indian Culture
Subject(s): American West; Folklore; Indians of North America
Major character(s): Napa, Mythical Creature; War Eagle, Shaman (Chippewa tribe), Storyteller
Time period(s): Indeterminate Past
Locale(s): Blackfoot Reservation, Montana

Summary: Napa is a strange figure in Blackfoot, Cree, and Chippewa folklore whom they credit with creating the world, but making many mistakes while he does. Napa is not God, or Manitou as the Indians call the Deity. In fact, he sometimes appears as a thief, a liar, a clown, or an animal. He is the featured player in these why stories, so-called because they explain to Indian children why things are the way they are: why chipmunks have stripes on their backs; why Blackfeet never kill mice; why otter skins became great medicine. War Eagle, a shaman, gathers the children in his lodge in the evenings after the first frost, and tells them the why stories. Many of the stories are similar to Greek fables, or fairy tales. For example, he tells the story of a race between a deer and an antelope; reminiscent of the story of the tortoise and the hare. These are fascinating stories that tell us much about the Indians' view of creation.

Where it's reviewed:
Roundup Magazine, April 2005, page 36

Other books by the same author:
Indian Old Man Stories, 2003
Plenty-Coups: Chief of the Crows, 2003
Pretty Shield, 2003

Other books you might like:
Don Coldsmith, *The Pipestone Quest*, 2004
Will Cook, *Until Day Breaks*, 2004
Deborah L. Duvall, *Rabbit and the Bears*, 2004
Deborah L. Duvall, *Rabbit Goes Duck Hunting*, 2004
Billy Moore, *Little Brother Real Snake*, 2004

462

L.J. MARTIN

McKeag's Mountain

(New York: Pinnacle, 2004)

Story type: Revenge; Ranch Life
Subject(s): American West; Crime and Criminals
Major character(s): Bertoldus Prager, Rancher (greedy), Thief; Dan McKeag, Rancher, Crime Victim (of Bertoldus

Prager); Roan McKeag, Teenager (Dan McKeag's nephew)
Time period(s): 1870s (1877)
Locale(s): Helena, Montana; Deer Lodge, Montana

Summary: Bertoldus Prager wants McKeag's Mountain and the Lucky Seven ranch owned by Dan McKeag. Prager wants the ranch so badly that he hires seven gunslingers to kill Dan and run off his hands. One of the seven hard cases sends his saloon girlfriend to shoot Dan, collects his blood money, and rides off. Dan isn't dead, although a coffin is buried in a grave with his name on the tombstone. His brother-in-law Paddy and Rose Ballard, a widow who owns a saloon hide him away. Thinking Dan is dead, Prager sends his men over to the Lucky Seven where they kill all the ranch hands but the foreman, Old Tom, and Dan's nephew, Roan McKeag. Besides the ranch hands, Prager's men also kill Dan's wife. It is the killers' last mistake. Dan and Paddy ride hell-for-leather with their six guns loaded, determined to kill all those responsible, including Prager.

Where it's reviewed:
Roundup Magazine, June 2005, page 36

Other books by the same author:
O'Rourke's Revenge, 2005
Wolf Mountain, 2004
Blood Mountain, 2003
Strandhan, 2003
Condor Canyon, 2000

Other books you might like:
Lyle Brandt, *Justice Gun*, 2003
J. Lee Butts, *Brotherhood of Blood*, 2004
Ralph Cotton, *Gunman's Song*, 2004
Ford Pendleton, *Gunmaster*, 2003
Jory Sherman, *Texas Dust*, 2004

463

MICHAEL MCGARRITY

Slowkill

(New York: Dutton, 2004)

Story type: Modern; Mystery
Series: Kevin Kerney. Book 9
Subject(s): Animals/Horses; Crime and Criminals; Horse Racing
Major character(s): Kevin Kerney, Police Officer (chief), Rancher (raises quarter horses); Alice Spalding, Divorced Person, Handicapped (Alzheimer's); Ellie Lowrey, Police Officer (sergeant)
Time period(s): 2000s
Locale(s): Santa Fe, New Mexico; San Luis Obispo, California; Santa Barbara, California

Summary: Kevin Kerney travels to a quarter horse breeding ranch outside of San Luis Obispo, California, to buy breeding stock for his own operation. He shares the ranch's guest house with millionaire Clifford Spalding who plans to buy a horse for his wife. Kerney finds the man dead and himself suspected of murder by Sergeant Ellie Lowrey. Although both the Santa Fe Police Department and the New Mexico State Police vouch for him, Lowrey is still suspicious because Spalding's beautiful second wife spends most of her time in Santa Fe. Kerney decides he will do a little investigating of his own, starting with Alice Spalding, the murder victim's first wife. Alice Spalding is in the beginning stages of Alzheimer's disease, but still is able to function most of the time. Her life for the last 35 years has been devoted to discovering the whereabouts of her son whom everyone else says died in Vietnam. Kerney wonders why she is so sure her son is alive, and why everyone ignores her. Then he discovers that everyone has been lying to the old woman about searching for her son on the orders of Clifford Spalding. The autopsy report shows that Spalding died of lack of adequate doses of a thyroid hormone, a prescription that his second wife filled for him in Santa Fe at her lover's pharmacy. The lover has fled Santa Fe and is a fugitive. All Kerney has to do is ship four horses back to New Mexico, find the missing lover, and charge him with murder, while at the same time avoid becoming a murder victim himself.

Where it's reviewed:
Roundup Magazine, February 2005, page 36

Other books by the same author:
Everyone Dies, 2003
The Big Gamble, 2002
Under the Color of Law, 2001
The Judas Judge, 1999
Hermit's Peak, 1998

Other books you might like:
Frederic Bean, *Murder at the Spirit Cave*, 1999
Carol Caverly, *Dead in Hog Heaven*, 2000
    Thea Barlow. Book 3
Elizabeth Dearl, *Diamondback*, 2000
    Taylor Madison. Book 1
J.A. Jance, *Exit Wounds*, 2003
Joe Wise, *Cannibal Plateau*, 1997

464

D.R. MEREDITH

Tome of Murder

(New York: Berkley, 2005)

Story type: Modern; Mystery
Series: Megan Clark. Book 4
Subject(s): American West; Crime and Criminals; Indians of North America
Major character(s): Megan Clark, Archaeologist (specializes in ancient mummies), Librarian (assistant reference librarian); Ryan Stevens, Historian (western American history), Museum Curator; Spotted Tongue, Warrior (Comanche), Detective—Amateur
Time period(s): 1860s (1868); 2000s
Locale(s): Amarillo, Texas; Palo Duro Canyon, Texas

Summary: Past and present connect in Palo Duro Canyon outside the town of Canyon, Texas. It is a pleasant late summer afternoon in 1868 until Spotted Tongue, Comanche warrior, discovers the dead body of his second wife, Little Flower, murdered by a blow to her head. Spotted Tongue sinks to his knees in grief, because he loved Little Flower more than a warrior should love any woman. Soon anger takes

him over and he swears to find his wife's killer, and challenge him to a fight to the death. For one Comanche to kill another Comanche is against all tradition, and the murderer carries evil about with him. First Spotted Tongue must bury Little Flower, then he would hunt—and kill—the murderer. Nearly 140 years later, Megan Clark, Ryan Stevens, and the rest of the Murder by the Yard group are enjoying a picnic in Palo Duro Canyon, in celebration of the first anniversary of the reading club. The group takes a walk up a small side canyon where Megan's two dogs unearth a human skeleton. As a paleopathologist, Megan is the only person in the Texas Panhandle qualified to study the skeleton and determine cause of death. She is in her element, involved in another murder case, despite the police warning her away, and Ryan fearing that Megan will push her luck one step too far, and hers will be the next body dug up.

Where it's reviewed:
Roundup Magazine, June 2005, page 36

Other books by the same author:
Murder by Reference, 2005 (John Lloyd Branson. Book 4)
Murder by Deception, 2004 (John Lloyd Branson. Book 2)
Murder by Masquerade, 2004 (John Lloyd Branson. Book 3)
Murder by Impulse, 2003 (John Lloyd Branson. Book 1)
Murder Past Due, 2002 (Megan Clark. Book 3)

Other books you might like:
Frederic Bean, *Murder at the Spirit Cave*, 1999
Peter Bowen, *Badlands*, 2003
Margaret Coel, *Killing Raven*, 2003
Debra Magpie Earling, *Perma Red*, 2002
Tony Hillerman, *The Sinister Pig*, 2003

465

MAJOR MITCHELL

Mokelumne Gold

(Baltimore: PublishAmerica, 2004)

Story type: Traditional; Man Alone
Subject(s): American West; Crime and Criminals
Major character(s): Leonida Garcia, Fiance(e) (of Shawn), Heiress (of a California land grant); Shawn Kilkenney, Doctor; Josiah Russell, Lawman (retired Texas Ranger), Investigator (for Judge Hansen)
Time period(s): 1850s (1852)
Locale(s): San Francisco, California; Dogtown, California

Summary: A rich gold strike is found in the Mokelumne River on Dona Leonida Garcia's rancho. Leonida insists that all the people on her land share in the good fortune. Ten percent of the money is set aside to pay the fee of attorney James Sattler, who is representing Leonida in a court battle to keep her property. Sattler, unbeknownst to Leonida, is crooked and is cheating her. In the meantime, one of Leonida's employees, Josiah Russell, is appointed by a judge to look into the murder of Ambrose Brice, a very unsavory character. Leonida is also in love with Dr. Shawn Kilkenney, although he left her after she ordered a man hanged. The three plot lines—the gold discovery, Brice's murder, and Leonida and Shawn's love story—are intertwined in a historical saga about the gold rush and the clash between Americans and the Mexican rancheros.

Where it's reviewed:
Roundup Magazine, June 2005, page 37

Other books by the same author:
The Dona, 2001
The Manhunter, 1998

Other books you might like:
Dan Cushman, *Blood on the Saddle*, 2003
Bennett Foster, *The Mexican Saddle*, 2003
John Holt, *Hunted*, 2003
Wayne D. Overholser, *Wild Horse River*, 2003
Lauran Paine, *Open Range*, 2003

466

BILLY MOORE

Little Brother Real Snake

(Montgomery, Alabama: Junebug, 2004)

Story type: Historical/American West; Indian Culture
Subject(s): Indians of North America; Animals/Eagles; Coming-of-Age
Major character(s): Red Squirrel, Indian (Comanche); Wild Fire, Indian (Comanche warrior), Parent (father of Pale Moon); Pale Moon, Indian (Comanche)
Time period(s): Indeterminate Past
Locale(s): Llando Estacado, Texas

Summary: Red Squirrel, tall but still skinny as a small boy, accompanies warrior chieftain Wild Fire and other men of his band to hunt. Red Squirrel is a daydreamer, always dreaming of brave acts he will commit to be worth of wearing the eagle feathers in his hair and marrying Pale Moon, Wild Fire's daughter and his friend since childhood. Losing track of the rest of the hunters, Red Squirrel stumbles upon an Apache, his people's worst enemy. Wild Fire is riding toward the Apache without seeing him. Red Squirrel attaches the Apache, kills him, and takes his scalp, but his act nauseates him. Although Wild Fire gives him eagle feathers for his bravery, and his band honors him, Red Squirrel feels he is a coward or he wouldn't have become sick in front of all the hunters, although his band thinks him modest. He refuses to wear Wild Fire's feathers because a real warrior catches an eagle and plucks his own feathers. He leaves the village and builds an eagle trap, but two unfriendly boys who don't like him put a snake in it. Red Squirrel removes the snake without killing it, and an eagle drops two feathers in the trap from high above.

Where it's reviewed:
Roundup Magazine, February 2005, page 36

Other books by the same author:
Cracker's Mule, 2002

Other books you might like:
Don Coldsmith, *The Pipestone Quest*, 2004
Will Cook, *Until Day Breaks*, 2004
Louise Erdrich, *Four Souls*, 2004
Will Henry, *White Shadows*, 2002
Elmer Kelton, *The Way of the Coyote*, 2001

467

MACKEY MURDOCK

Blood for Brother

(Waterville, Maine: Five Star, 2005)

Story type: Traditional
Subject(s): American West; Crime and Criminals; Cattle Drives
Major character(s): Rawls Slaton, Rancher, Military Personnel (discharged, Confederate Army); Marcus Slaton, Rancher (Rawls' brother); Ramon Lopez, Rancher, Neighbor (of the Slatons)
Time period(s): 1860s (1865-1866)
Locale(s): Plum Grove, Texas

Summary: Rawls Slaton returns from the Civil War with a nervous condition that leaves an arm and a leg weak and slow to move, and with partial amnesia. Arriving at the ranch he and his brother Marcus own, he finds Marcus gone and his sister-in-law Bess about to have a baby. Bess doesn't seem to care about Marcus' absence, but Rawls hunts his brother down in Plum Grove. He finds Marcus very drunk and about to board a stagecoach with a prostitute. Rawls hauls him back to the ranch, with Marcus resisting all the way. Although Rawls feels almost helpless because of his infirmity, he realizes someone has to take charge, run the ranch, and care for Bess and the baby. Rounding up some wild longhorns, Rawls sets out to drive them to Abilene, accompanied by a neighbor, Ramon Lopez, and Marcus. Rawls must deal with his physical disabilities, as well as harsh terrain, bad weather, his brother's unreliability, and a band of Comancheros that begins to follow them.

Where it's reviewed:
Roundup Magazine, April 2005, page 37

Other books by the same author:
Chute, 2002
Forgotten War, 2002
Last of the Old-Time Texans, 2000

Other books you might like:
Paul Bagdon, *The Stranger from Medina*, 2004
Stephen Bly, *The Next Roundup*, 2003
James David Buchanan, *Welcome, Suckers*, 2003
Dudley Dean, *Song of the Gun*, 20003
Ed Gorman, *Gun Truth*, 2003

468

JOHN D. NESBITT

West of Rock River

(Fort Worth: Texas Christian University Press, 2004)

Story type: Traditional; Revenge
Subject(s): American West; Crime and Criminals
Major character(s): Fred Durham, Rancher (Moon and Tip's brother); Vance Coolidge, Rancher; Tip Durham, Rancher (Fred and Moon's brother)
Time period(s): 19th century (post-Civil War)
Locale(s): Rock River, Wyoming

Summary: In a Western that asks deeper questions than usual about human motives, a man is forced to reevaluate his priorities. When Moon Durham is murdered, his brothers, Tip and Fred, ask Vance Coolidge to help track down his killers. Vance leaves his wife and infant behind on his ranch to help the Durhams. He believes strongly that people who have been wronged deserve the chance to get even. He doesn't voice this belief to his wife, Josie, because he believes she is having an affair, and, in spite of his hurt and anger, does not want her to think he is punishing her. On the trail, Vance begins to think that forgiveness and going on with one's life are more important than punishment. As he looks down the barrel of a killer's gun, he wonders if he will ever make it back alive to forgive Josie.

Where it's reviewed:
Roundup Magazine, June 2005, page 37

Other books by the same author:
Black Hat Butte, 2003
Red Wind Crossing, 2003
Man from Wolf River, 2001
North of Cheyenne, 2000
One-Eyed Cowboy Wild, 1994

Other books you might like:
Peter Brandvold, *Once Late with a .38*, 2003
Tim Champlin, *White Lights Roar*, 2003
Jane Candia Coleman, *Lost River*, 2003
Tom Franklin, *Hell at the Breech*, 2003
Bobby R. Woodall, *Clearwater*, 2003

469

DAN O'BRIEN

The Indian Agent

(Guilford, Connecticut: Lyons, 2004)

Story type: Saga; Indian Culture
Subject(s): Indians of North America; Indian Reservations
Major character(s): Valentine T. McGillycuddy, Doctor, Historical Figure (Indian agent); Fanny McGillycuddy, Spouse (of Valentine), Historical Figure; Red Cloud, Historical Figure, Indian (Sioux war chief)
Time period(s): 19th century (1879-1893)
Locale(s): Pine Ridge Indian Reservation, South Dakota; Wounded Knee, South Dakota; Rapid City, South Dakota

Summary: A sequel to *The Contract Surgeon*, this novel continues the fictionalized biography of Dr. Valentine T. McGillycuddy. Valentine is appointed the new Indian agent for the Sioux living on the Pine Ridge Indian Reservation, to replace the one who was completely corrupt. The Sioux, encouraged by the war chief Red Cloud, are near to fleeing the reservation. Valentine arrives with his wife, Fanny, in 1879. He wins the trust of the imperious, arrogant Red Cloud, as well as the rest of the Sioux. He demands the government keep its word to provide the Sioux with provisions. With the huge buffalo herds nearly wiped out, the Sioux have lost their principal food supply, so government rations are essential to prevent starvation. Valentine teaches the Sioux agriculture, although they hate farming, and establishes an Indian police force. Valentine's life is complicated by Fanny's illness and enemies back in Washington who undercut his support in the Bureau of Indian Affairs. He is relieved of his duties in 1887, and becomes the president of the School of Mines in Rapid City. Without Valentine's steadying influence, the Sioux fall back into their old ways and adopt the Ghost Dance religion. The Army is called in by the settlers, but the officer in charge waits too long before sending for Valentine. He arrives at Wounded Knee unable to prevent the massacre.

Where it's reviewed:
Publishers Weekly, October 4, 2004, page 68

Other books by the same author:
Buffalo for the Broken Heart, 2001
The Contract Surgeon, 1999 (Western Heritage Award for fiction winner)
Brendan Prairie, 1997
Equinox, 1997

Other books you might like:
Frederick J. Chiaventone, *Moon of Bitter Cold*, 2002
Don Coldsmith, *The Pipestone Quest*, 2004
Anne Linzer, *Ghost Dancing*, 2002
Mardi Oakley Medawar, *Murder on the Red Cliff Rez*, 2002
Aimee Thurlo, *Shooting Chant*, 2001
    David Thurlo, co-author

470

TILLIE OLSEN

Yonnondio from the Thirties

(Lincoln: University of Nebraska Press, 2004)

Story type: Historical/Depression Era
Subject(s): Depression (Economic); Poverty; Drought
Major character(s): Mazie Holbrook, Child (10-year-old), Abuse Victim (beaten by parents); Anna Holbrook, Parent (Mazie's mother), Abuse Victim (spousal abuse); Jim Holbrook, Miner (coal), Bully (beats wife and children)
Time period(s): 1930s (1930-1932)
Locale(s): Wyoming; Zell, South Dakota; Omaha, Nebraska

Summary: Mazie Holbrook lives in a nameless coal mining town in Wyoming with her parents, Jim and Anna Holbrook, and three brothers. Her father works in a coal mine and lives in a company house. Many of his fellow miners die in mining accidents or of Black Lung. The Holbrooks are desperately poor and often hungry as the family is too big for Jim's salary to support. He feels angry about this, but it is the Depression and there are hardly any jobs, so he drinks and beats his children and Anna. When his friend dies, Jim decides to move to a farm in South Dakota when April arrives, but they are caught in a snowstorm just short of their destination. As a tenant farmer, Jim learns that his share of a crop is not enough to pay his debts. Once more the Holbrooks move, this time to Omaha where Jim finds work on first a road crew, then in a slaughter house. *Yonnondio from the Thirties* is a grim reminder of the poverty and hardship of the Great Depression in the West.

Where it's reviewed:
Roundup Magazine, February 2005, page 37

Other books by the same author:
Tell Me a Riddle, 1984

Other books you might like:
Sandra Babb, *Where Names Are Unknown*, 2004
Patrick Dearen, *When the Sky Rained Dust*, 2004
Ralph M. Flores, *The Horse in the Kitchen*, 2004
Elmer Kelton, *The Time It Never Rained*, 1973
Kent Myers, *The Work of Wolves*, 2004

471

STEPHEN OVERHOLSER

Chasing Destiny

(Waterville, Maine: Five Star, 2005)

Story type: Traditional; Chase
Subject(s): American West; Crime and Criminals
Major character(s): Destiny Eckstrum, Relative (daughter of Bobby), Runaway (to avoid an orphanage); Michael Jenning, Friend (of Destiny), Runaway (from his father); Noah Locke, Mountain Man, Hunter (of buffalo)
Time period(s): 1890s (1894)
Locale(s): Columbia, Colorado; Owl Canon, Colorado

Summary: Old Noah Locke shoots Bobby Eckstrum from 1,000 yards when Bobby flees the Lazy S after robbing and murdering its owner. Two problems arise: Bobby's face is so damaged that he has to be identified by his clothing, and the money is not on his body. Bobby's daughter, 12-year-old Destiny Eckstrum, doesn't believe her father could rob or kill anyone. She tells the sheriff that it had to be her Uncle Loy who was shot, not her father. Her father is still alive and she intends to find him. Accompanied by Michael Jenning, who is fleeing his brutal father, Destiny walks toward the mountains and a mining town where she believes her father may be hiding. Road agents, a Chinese man hiding in a cave, a big mastiff named Boy, and the appearance of Noah Locke are milestones on Michael and Destiny's journey. If they can stay alive long enough to reach the mining camp she heard her father mention, Destiny hopes to find out the truth about her father.

Where it's reviewed:
Roundup Magazine, April 2005, page 38

Other books by the same author:
West of the Moon, 2004
Fire in the Rainbow, 2003
Shadow Valley Rising, 2002
Double-Cross, 2001
Cold Wind, 1999

Other books you might like:
Tim Champlin, *Wayfaring Strangers*, 2000
Tim Champlin, *White Lights Roar*, 2003
Steve Frazee, *Nights of Terror*, 2003
Tom Piccirilli, *Coffin Blues*, 2004
Richard S. Wheeler, *Vengeance Valley*, 2004

472

MARY E. PENSON

Billy Bardin and the Witness Tree

(Fort Worth: Texas Christian University Press, 2004)

Story type: Modern; Quest
Subject(s): Trees; Family Life
Major character(s): Billy Bardin, Teenager (14-year-old); William Bardin, Surveyor, Farmer (retired); Roger Fassig, Teenager, Friend (of Billy's)
Time period(s): 2000s
Locale(s): Arlington, Texas

Summary: Based on a true story, *Billy Bardin and the Witness Tree* tells of young Billy Bardin's quest to save a 500-year-old oak tree that was the point from which all property in Arlington, Texas, was surveyed. Grandpa William Bardin, Billy's namesake, was a surveyor and the previous owner of the land upon which the Witness Tree stood. When Grandpa sold his property he inserted a clause in the bill of sale that forbade any commercial building within 26 feet of the tree. Kmart plans to build a superstore on Grandpa's old property, but the present owner refuses to sell to the giant retailer. Kmart merely moves their planned store to the spot where the Witness Tree stood. They offer Grandpa a small fortune for the site, but Grandpa refuses to budge. He tells Billy about the tree and about Kmart, so Billy and his friend, Roger Fassig, take on the project of saving the tree, the most important landmark in the entire county.

Where it's reviewed:
Roundup Magazine, February 2005, page 36

Other books by the same author:
You're an Orphan, Molly Brown, 1998

Other books you might like:
Patrick Dearen, *Hidden Treasure of the Chisos*, 2001
Patrick Dearen, *On the Pecos Trail*, 2001
Billy Moore, *Little Brother Real Snake*, 2004
Melinda Rice, *Fire on the Hillside*, 2001
Melinda Rice, *Secrets in the Sky*, 2001

473

J. MARK POWELL
L.D. MEAGHER, Co-Author

The Curse of Cain

(New York: Forge, 2005)

Story type: Saga; Historical/American West
Subject(s): Crime and Criminals
Major character(s): Basil Tarleton, Murderer (psychotic), Criminal; Jack Tanner, Detective (undercover); John Wilkes Booth, Actor, Murderer
Time period(s): 1860s (1865)
Locale(s): Washington, District of Columbia; Richmond, Virginia

Summary: In February 1865, Confederate Congressman Robert Sandiford hires Basil Tarleton to assassinate President Abraham Lincoln. Overhearing the plan is Sandiford's "Man," a crooked gambler known as Kincaid. Jack Tanner, agent of the Confederate Provost Guard in Richmond arrests the gambler for fleecing the attorney general's nephew in a crooked card game. Kincaid tells all, and the two prepare an ambush at the stable where Tarleton's horse is. Tarleton arrives early at the stable, kills Kincaid, and leaves before Tanner's arrival. Tanner hurries to President Jefferson Davis with news of the conspiracy, and is assigned to hunt down Tarleton and stop him by whatever means necessary, as Davis refuses to condone assassinating Lincoln. Jack, with his own grudge against the Yankees, dons the clothing of a draftsman and takes the road to Washington, D.C. and a meeting with one of the South's most notorious spies: Kathleen O'Leary. With her help and a great deal of luck, the two of them should be able to dispose of Tarleton and prevent the assassination of Lincoln. Unfortunately, Tanner knows nothing of another plot to kill Lincoln; Tanner thinks John Wilkes Booth is just an actor and ardent supporter of the South.

Where it's reviewed:
Roundup Magazine, June 2005, page 37

Other books by the same author:
The Curse of Cain, 2005 (L.D. Meagher, co-author)

Other books you might like:
Tim Champlin, *Lincoln's Ransom*, 1999
James Rhodes, *Hardscrabble Valley*, 2003
Cotton Smith, *Sons of Thunder*, 2003
Jack Stanford, *Jayhawker Crossing*, 1994
Glendon Swarthout, *The Shootist*, 1998

474

ANNIE PROULX

Bad Dirt

(New York: Scribner, 2004)

Story type: Modern; Collection
Series: Wyoming Stories. Book 2
Subject(s): Short Stories
Time period(s): 2000s
Locale(s): Wyoming

Summary: This is the second collection of short stories by Proulx about life in modern Wyoming that range from ''What Kind of Furniture Would Jesus Pick,'' in which a rancher seeks to save the land that has been in his family for generations from the ravages of debt and the effects of years-long drought to ''Man Crawling Out of Trees,'' in which a retired couple from New England find their marriage is breaking up from the loneliness of harsh terrain and the unfriendly locals.

Where it's reviewed:
Publishers Weekly, October 4, 2004, page 68

Other books by the same author:
Cider, 2003
When Curly Won a Cathouse, 2003
Old Ace in the Hole, 2002
Close Range, 1999 (Wyoming Stories. Book 1)

Other books you might like:
Frederic Bean, *Murder at the Spirit Cave*, 1999
Peter Bowen, *Thunder Horse*, 1999
James Lee Burke, *In the Moon of Red Ponies*, 2004

Kent Myers, *The Work of Wolves*, 2004
David Marion Wilkinson, *Oblivion's Altar*, 2002

475

ROBERT J. RANDISI

Backshooter

(New York: Leisure, 2005)

Story type: Traditional; Revenge
Subject(s): American West; Crime and Criminals
Major character(s): Kyle Maddux, Lawman (marshal), Crime Victim (shot and disabled); Glenn Wilkes, Detective—Private (Pinkerton agent); Joe Hannibal, Lawman (marshal after Maddux)
Time period(s): 19th century (post-Civil War)
Locale(s): Cromwell, Oklahoma; Ceremony, New Mexico

Summary: While facing down three outlaws, Kyle Maddux is shot in the back by a fourth man. Three years later, he has been forced to resign as sheriff because of the wound, and he is still wondering who shot him. Then he learns of someone who is killing other lawmen by shooting them in the same manner. Glenn Wilkes, a Pinkerton agent hired by the family of one of the dead lawmen, contacts Kyle. He wants him and Joe Hannibal, the current sheriff of Cromwell, to help him track down the killer. Although his wife threatens to leave him if he returns to his old profession, Kyle feels the familiar thrill of the hunt and sets off for Texas with Wilkes and Hannibal. He still has a bullet in his back and feels the need for vengeance.

Where it's reviewed:
Roundup Magazine, June 2005, page 38

Other books by the same author:
Vengeance Creek, 2005
Blood of Angels, 2004
Widowmaker, 2004
Leaving Epitaph, 2004
Curtains of Blood, 2002

Other books you might like:
Jon Chandler, *Tom Horn*, 2002
Will Cook, *The Devil's Roundup*, 2002
Ed Gorman, *Night of Shadows*, 2002
Cotton Smith, *Brothers of the Gun*, 2002
Gary Svee, *Single Tree*, 1994

476

ROBERT J. RANDISI

Invitation to a Hanging

(New York: Pocket, 2004)

Story type: Traditional; Man Alone
Series: Widowmaker. Book 2
Subject(s): American West; Crime and Criminals
Major character(s): John Locke, Bounty Hunter (former), Lawman (former); Nina Ballinger, Journalist (owns newspaper); Ignacio Colon, Outlaw, Murderer
Time period(s): 1880s (1886)
Locale(s): Fredericksburgh, Texas; Tombstone, Arizona

Summary: John Locke has been a bounty hunter, a gun-for-hire, a former marshal at Tombstone, but he has never been a *bastonero*, or Master of Ceremonies, at a hanging. Ignacio Colon, a murderous outlaw, has been tried and condemned to hang, and the Fredericksburgh town council wants Locke to keep the peace since Colon's gang will undoubtedly be riding into town to break him out of jail. After talking to Colon, Locke accepts the town council's offer because Ignacio Colon is about as worthless a man as Locke has ever met. He meets Nina Ballinger, the owner of the local paper, to hire her to print up invitations to the hanging, which she agrees to do if Locke will grant her an interview about his days in Tombstone. Locke does not talk about Tombstone—ever—but he persuades her anyway. The whole situation makes Locke uneasy; the whole town seems to be holding its breath and the town council seems to be up to something.

Where it's reviewed:
Roundup Magazine, February 2005, page 36

Other books by the same author:
Lancaster's Orphans, 2004
Leaving Epitaph, 2004 (The Sons of Daniel Shaye. Book 1)
Boot Hill, 2002 (editor)
Miracle of the Jacal, 2002
White Hats, 2002

Other books you might like:
Troy Boucher, *Prince of the Plains*, 2002
Tim Champlin, *The Tombstone Conspiracy*, 1999
Phyllis de la Garza, *Bounty Hunter's Daughter*, 2000
Fred Grove, *Drums Without Warriors*, 2002
Jason Manning, *Gun Justice*, 1999

477

ROBERT J. RANDISI

Leaving Epitaph

(New York: HarperCollins, 2004)

Story type: Traditional; Revenge
Series: Sons of Daniel Shaye. Book 1
Subject(s): Crime and Criminals; American West
Major character(s): Daniel Shaye, Lawman (sheriff); Ethan Langer, Thief (bank robber), Outlaw; Matthew Shaye, Relative (Daniel's son), Lawman (deputy)
Time period(s): 1880s (1889)
Locale(s): Epitaph, Texas; Salina, Kansas; Oklahoma City, Oklahoma

Summary: In the course of robbing the bank in Epitaph, Texas, Ethan Langer runs down Sheriff Dan Shaye's wife and kills her. Shaye and his three sons, Thomas, Matthew, and James, track Langer to Salina, Kansas, where Langer is meeting up with his brother, Aaron, who has just robbed a bank in South Dakota. Ethan is being haunted by the ghost of Shaye's wife, whom he imagines laughing at him. The Langer brothers head for a showdown with the Shayes and the sheriff of Salina, but as in most revenge stories, there is a price to be paid.

Where it's reviewed:
Roundup Magazine, February 2005, page 35

Other books by the same author:
Invitation to a Hanging, 2004 (The Widowmaker. Book 1)

Lancaster's Orphans, 2004
Boot Hill, 2002 (editor)
Miracle of the Jacal, 2002
Tin Star, 2002 (editor)

Other books you might like:
Will Cade, *Henry Kidd, Outlaw*, 2003
Jason Manning, *The Outlaw Trail*, 2003
Stephen Overholser, *Track of a Killer*, 2003
Frank Roderus, *Left to Die*, 2000
Troy D. Smith, *The Trail Brothers*, 2003

478

BEN REHDER

Flat Crazy

(New York: St. Martin's Minotaur, 2004)

Story type: Modern; Mystery
Series: Blanco County. Book 3
Subject(s): Humor; Hunting
Major character(s): John Marlin, Game Warden; Billy Don Craddock, Hunter (incompetent), Sidekick (of Red O'Brien); Duke Waldrip, Convict (ex-con), Con Man
Time period(s): 2000s
Locale(s): Blanco County, Texas

Summary: As is usual, the game warden of Blanco County, Texas, John Marlin, is up to his neck in improbable problems. The whole county is sure they have seen a mysterious beast called a *chupacabra*. No one has ever seen one, so know one knows what the beast looks like, but that doesn't stop everyone from describing it. Marlin just hopes hunting season ends without any idiots heading to the woods to make a trophy out of a *chupacabra*—whatever that may be. Meanwhile, two bumbling friends who are always causing unintentional trouble, Billy Don Craddock and Red O'Brien, are laying plans to catch the mysterious creature. When a body with fang marks on its throat is found in the woods, county tension begins to bubble. Ex-con Duke Waldrip, out of prison but not rehabilitated, sells phony trophies and arranges hunts of exotic animals. It's a good con game until a savvy hunter sniffs out the scam and Duke must try to cover his tracks. Full of eccentric characters and over the top situations, Rehder's mysteries are worth a read.

Where it's reviewed:
Publishers Weekly, August 16, 2004, page 46

Other books by the same author:
Bone Dry, 2003
Buck Fever, 2002

Other books you might like:
Frederic Bean, *Murder at the Spirit Cave*, 1999
James D. Doss, *The Witch's Tongue*, 2004
D.R. Meredith, *Murder by Deception*, 2004
Pari Noskin Taichert, *The Clovis Incident*, 2004
Aimee Thurlo, *Walking Bear*, 2003
    David Thurlo, co-author

479

FRANK RODERUS

Judgment Day

(New York: Berkley, 2004)

Story type: Traditional; Man Alone
Subject(s): American West; Cowboys/Cowgirls
Major character(s): Johnny Ackerman, Cowboy; Edwin Foster, Teacher; Sarah Young, Teenager (16-year-old), Girlfriend (of Johnny)
Time period(s): 19th century (post-Civil War)
Locale(s): Redhorse Butte, Montana

Summary: Although Redhorse Butte is pretty much a one horse town, Johnny Ackerman calls it home. He was born there and plans to die there. Now grown, and a trained cowboy, he is planning to propose to Sarah Young, the girl he's loved since childhood. His plans are thrown into disarray when good-looking Edwin Foster, the new schoolmaster, catches Sarah's eye. Driven by jealousy, Johnny decides to put Edwin in his place. Most of his attempts to humiliate Edwin end up humiliating Johnny instead. Sarah is furious at first, but relents a little later on. Convinced that all's right between them, Johnny goes to the school to pick up Sarah and gets the shock of his life.

Where it's reviewed:
Roundup Magazine, June 2005, page 38

Other books by the same author:
Wrangler, 2005
Billy Roy and the Good News, 2004
Dead Man's Journey, 2002
Lewisville Flats, 2002

Other books you might like:
Jane Candia Coleman, *Lost River*, 2003
Ed Gorman, *Night of Shadows*, 2002
Stephen Overholser, *Chasing Destiny*, 2005
Glendon Swarthout, *The Shootist*, 1998
Joseph A. West, *Donovan's Dove*, 2004

480

LES SAVAGE JR.

Trail of the Silver Saddle

(Waterville, Maine: Five Star, 2005)

Story type: Traditional; Collection
Subject(s): American West; Short Stories
Time period(s): 19th century (post-Civil War)
Locale(s): West

Summary: A trio of short novels showcases the talents of Les Savage, Jr. Known for his skill in writing psychological novels, Savage was ahead of his time. In *Whip Master*, a man guilty of inciting the Taos Rebellion that killed several citizens of New Mexico Territory is hired as a teamster on a freight wagon train going to Santa Fe. Then the U.S. Army receives word that the wagons are carrying guns and powder to Southern sympathizers to use for barter with the Apaches to attack New Mexico settlements and the U.S. military. In *Secret of the Santiago*, the heir of a lost Spanish mine tries to learn the secret of his inheritance, but murder and false accusations lead to his running from the law. In *Trail of the Silver Saddle*, a Pinkerton agent is assigned to find the owner of a financial empire in Texas who has disappeared. The agent is rightly nervous because the first two Pinkerton men assigned to the case were murdered.

Where it's reviewed:
Roundup Magazine, June 2005, page 38

Other books by the same author:
The Beast in Canada Diablo, 2004
The Ghost Horse, 2004
The Devil's Corral, 2003
West of Laramie, 2003
Danger Rides the River, 2002

Other books you might like:
James Carlos Blake, *Wildwood Boys*, 2000
Tim Champlin, *Raiders of the Western & Atlantic*, 2002
T.T. Flynn, *The Devil's Lode*, 1999
Steve Frazee, *Nights of Terror*, 2003
Lewis B. Patten, *Guns of Vengeance*, 2003

481

JORY SHERMAN

The Baron Honor

(New York: Forge, 2005)

Story type: Traditional; Saga
Series: Grass Kingdom. Book 6
Subject(s): American West; Mexican Americans; War
Major character(s): Martin Baron, Rancher (son of ranch founder), Lawman (joins Texas Rangers); Anson Baron, Rancher (Martin's son); Miguel Aguilar, Rancher
Time period(s): 1860s (1862)
Locale(s): Baronsville, Texas

Summary: The blood hasn't dried and the bodies are still lying on Baron land from war between the Barons and Miguel Aguilar, when Martin Baron tells his son, Anson, that he has joined the Texas Rangers to help protect the state while war rages in the east between the Union and the Confederacy. Anson Baron is angry with his father for running away and leaving him to pick up the pieces and rebuild the burned ranch house. Martin has a habit of leaving the ranch in a mess to go somewhere to do something he considers important. Anson knows he must catch a wild white bull to breed up the Baron herd. There are also other difficulties for the Baron family. Miguel Aguilar has escaped an ambush and swears to avenge himself on the Barons. The vaqueros desert the Baron ranch, and a band of Apaches plan to take the Baron land by killing everyone living there. The Barons find themselves forced to consider who is loyal to them and who waits for their downfall.

Where it's reviewed:
Roundup Magazine, June 2005, page 38

Other books by the same author:
Blood River, 2005
Abilene Gundown, 2004
Texas Dust, 2004
Song of the Cheyenne, 2003

Ballad of Pinewood Lake, 2001

Other books you might like:
Jane Candia Coleman, *Lost River*, 2003
T.T. Flynn, *Night of the Comanche Moon*, 2000
Larry McMurtry, *Lonesome Dove*, 1985
Frank Roderus, *Old Marsden*, 1999
Norman Zollinger, *Riders to Cibola*, 1977

482
JORY SHERMAN

Blood River
(New York: Berkley, 2005)

Story type: Ranch Life; Revenge
Subject(s): American West; Indians of North America
Major character(s): Chip Morgan, Rancher (on frontier), Avenger (against Comanches and Utes); Mercy Morgan, Frontierswoman (Chip's mother); Bear, Indian (mixed-blood Ute), Friend (of Chip)
Time period(s): 1870s (1876)
Locale(s): Palo Duro Canyon, Texas; Blood River, Colorado

Summary: When the Comanche begin scalping all the whites in Palo Duro Canyon and burning their homes, Chip Morgan's father wants to move the family to Colorado. His mother, Mercy Morgan, resists until the Carrero family and all their Mexican vaqueros are killed and mutilated by the Indians. Among the dead is Nora, the girl Chip planned to marry, and the sight of her body is one he will never forget. The Morgans relocate to Colorado, build a cabin, and start over, but they turn out to be no safer there. The Utes are on the warpath, but Chip isn't worried because of his friendship with a mixed-blood Ute named Bear and his family. Bear, however, is an outcast because he killed a prominent Ute to defend his wife. When one of the Morgans' hired men desecrates a sacred Ute shrine, the Utes attack the Morgans' cabin. They carry off Chip's father and mutilate Mercy, although Bear stops them from actually killing her. When spring comes, Chip rides off determined to kill the Ute chieftain or die trying.

Where it's reviewed:
Roundup Magazine, June 2005, page 39

Other books by the same author:
The Baron Honor, 2005
Abilene Gundown, 2004
Texas Dust, 2004
Baron War, 2004 (Grass Kingdom. Book 5)
Song of the Cheyenne, 2003

Other books you might like:
Richard Curtis, *Blood Cut*, 2003
Dan Cushman, *Blood on the Saddle*, 2003
James D. Doss, *Dead Soul*, 2003
    Charlie Moon. Book 8
Elmer Kelton, *The Buckskin Line*, 1999
Louis L'Amour, *Bowdrie*, 2004

483
MARC SIMMONS
RONALD KIL, Illustrator

Friday, the Arapaho Boy
(Albuquerque: University of New Mexico Press, 2004)

Story type: Indian Culture; Young Readers
Series: Children of the West
Subject(s): Indians of North America; Fur Trade
Major character(s): Black-spot, Indian (Arapaho); Tom Fitzpatrick, Mountain Man (a fur trapper), Historical Figure
Time period(s): 1830s (1831-1832)
Locale(s): Cimarron River, Oklahoma; Taos, New Mexico; St. Louis, Missouri

Summary: In 1831, drought hits the plains of Colorado, Kansas, and Oklahoma, leaving the Arapahos hungry. A nine-year-old boy named Black-spot goes hunting for prairie dogs, from which his mother can make a fine stew, but finds his village gone when he returns. Efforts to track his tribe are thwarted by roaming bands of Kiowa or Apache, enemies of his people. Mountain man Tom Fitzpatrick finds the boy almost dead and nurses him back to health. The boy is afraid to talk, and Fitzpatrick names him Friday, after the day on which he found him. Friday accompanies Fitzpatrick to Taos, then to St. Louis, where Fitzpatrick leaves him at a boarding school. After finding Friday's tribe, Fitzpatrick returns to find that Friday can now speak perfect English. The young man eventually becomes a great chief and peacemaker, and a liaison between his people and the whites.

Where it's reviewed:
Roundup Magazine, February 2005, page 36

Other books by the same author:
Millie Cooper's Ride, 2002
Little Lion of the Southwest, 1997
Coronado's Land, 1996
When Six Guns Ruled, 1990
Murder on the Santa Fe Trail, 1987

Other books you might like:
Phyllis de la Garza, *Camels West*, 1999
Patrick Dearen, *Comanche Peace Pipe*, 2001
    Lone Star Heroes. Book 1
Deborah L. Duvall, *Rabbit and the Bears*, 2004
Billy Moore, *Little Brother Real Snake*, 2004
Melinda Rice, *Fire on the Hillside*, 2001

484
COTTON SMITH

Winter Kill
(New York: Leisure, 2004)

Story type: Traditional; Ranch Life
Subject(s): American West; Crime and Criminals
Major character(s): Titus Branson, Rancher; Bass Manko, Singer (in a saloon), Friend (of Cade Branson); Cade Branson, Rancher (Titus Branson's son)
Time period(s): 19th century (post-Civil War)
Locale(s): Deer Creek, Texas

Summary: Titus Branson is a sick old man who blames everyone else for his troubles. His inherent cruelty is increased by a worsening case of consumption. Branson's eldest son, John, observes a man he thinks is saloon singer Bass Manko near a herd of his father's cattle shortly before they go missing. Bass is Titus' son Cade's best friend, and Cade warns Bass when Titus sends some men after him, with an eye to hanging him. Cade and Bass hold off Titus' men, and Titus disinherits his son. The sheriff makes Cade and Bass his deputies, so they can help him track down rustlers who have been striking at local small ranchers. To Cade's consternation, he realizes that someone on his father's ranch is responsible for the rustling. Nonstop action is a hallmark of Smith's writing.

Where it's reviewed:
Roundup Magazine, December 2004, page 36

Other books by the same author:
The Thirteenth Bullet, 2004
Sons of Thunder, 2003
Spirit Rider, 2003
Brothers of the Gun, 2002
Behold a Red Horse, 2001

Other books you might like:
Claire David, *Winter Range*, 2000
Fred Grove, *A Distance of Ground*, 2000
Douglas Hirt, *Ketcham's Land*, 2002
Lauran Paine, *The Running Iron*, 2000
Lewis B. Patton, *Ride the Red Trail*, 2001

485

MARK SPRAGG

An Unfinished Life

(New York: Knopf, 2004)

Story type: Ranch Life; Modern
Subject(s): American West; Abuse; Family Relations
Major character(s): Jean Gilkyson, Widow(er), Single Parent (to Griff); Griff Gilkyson, Child (9-year-old); Einar Gilkyson, Rancher, Grandparent (to Griff)
Time period(s): 2000s
Locale(s): Ishawooa, Wyoming

Summary: Jean Gilkyson was driving when a car wreck killed her husband, and his father, Einar Gilkyson, blames her, and has had nothing to do with her or his granddaughter, Griff, for ten years. Jean would rather do anything than go back home to Ishawooa, Wyoming, to live with Einar, but she is out of money and her current boyfriend likes to use his fists on her. She is terrified of him, and it is her fear as much as lack of money that drives her to Einar's ranch. Einar is very reluctant to take in Jean and Griff, but they are kin, and one can't refuse help to kin. Although Einar has little use or affection for Griff, the little girl loves the ranch, his log cabin, and his best friend and fellow Vietnam vet, Mitch. Mitch is terribly scarred from a grizzly attack, but Griff is not repulsed by Mitch's scars nor her grandfather's coldness. She loves everything about her new life, and Einar finds himself unable to resist his precocious granddaughter. Jean, on the other hand, has still not gained his forgiveness. Although Jean would rather not be treated like a pariah, she has a more serious worry and is

busily trying to win the sheriff's affection in order to protect herself from the brutal boyfriend she left behind. A strong sense of place and strong characters add to the strength of this offering.

Where it's reviewed:
Publishers Weekly, August 9, 2004, page 231

Other books by the same author:
The Fruit of Stone, 2002

Other books you might like:
James Carlos Blake, *Under the Skin*, 2003
C.J. Box, *Savage Run*, 2002
Louise Erdrich, *The Master Butchers Singing Club*, 2003
Max Evans, *Now and Forever*, 2003
Bruce Murkoff, *Waterborne*, 2004

486

JACK BRITTON SULLIVAN

The Lutheran

(Thomaston, Maine: Dan River, 2004)

Story type: Traditional; Revenge
Subject(s): American West; Crime and Criminals
Major character(s): Threadbare the Lutheran, Bounty Hunter, Murderer; Dampier Mox, Salesman (sells Bibles); Billy, Orphan, Frontierswoman
Time period(s): 1820s (1826-1829); 1840s (1844)
Locale(s): Great Salt Flats, Utah; San Antonio, Texas

Summary: Billy is taken in by a family six months after she loses her parents. While traveling east from Oregon hunting for dryer air, Billy's new family and their sickly son are killed by Threadbare the Lutheran. A mystic figure filled with hate and anger, the Lutheran kills to relieve his hatred. He is a bounty hunter tracking Dampier Mox, a young Bible salesman who killed a man in self-defense, although the locals chose not to believe it and sent a posse after him. The Lutheran kills the posse, then pursues Dampier and Billy. Together they escape the Great Salt Flats, but Dampier knows that Threadbare the Lutheran will always be searching for him. After the couple marry and Billy gives birth to twins, the Lutheran kidnaps the younger of the twins and turns him into a killer. As the years pass, the boy, Torq, is captured by Mexican officers and sentenced to hang. Torq escapes and continues to kill, his soul as twisted as the Lutheran's, as desolate as the harsh land into which he was born. He and the Lutheran meet up again at Billy's, the Lutheran to end his game with Billy and Dampier. Instead Torq challenges him, one twisted soul against another. They reckon without Billy who has waited years to destroy the Lutheran. An unusual story with a hint of the supernatural.

Where it's reviewed:
Roundup Magazine, December 2004, page 37

Other books you might like:
D.L. Birchfield, *Field of Honor*, 2004
Margaret Coel, *The Thunder Keeper*, 2001
     Father John O'Malley/Vicky Holden. Book 6
James D. Doss, *Dead Soul*, 2003
     Charlie Moon. Book 8
Debra Magpie Earling, *Perma Red*, 2002

Aimee Thurlo, *Tracking Bear*, 2003
  David Thurlo, co-author

487

JON TALTON

Dry Heat

(New York: St. Martin's Minotaur, 2004)

Story type: Modern; Mystery
Series: David Mapstone. Book 3
Subject(s): American West; Crime and Criminals
Major character(s): David Mapstone, Police Officer (deputy sheriff), Historian (amateur); Lindsey Mapstone, Police Officer, Spouse (David's wife); John Pilgrim, FBI Agent, Crime Victim (murdered in 1948)
Time period(s): 2000s
Locale(s): Phoenix, Arizona

Summary: In 1948 FBI Agent John Pilgrim was murdered in Phoenix. He was the only FBI agent ever to be murdered in the state of Arizona—until Deputy Sheriff David Mapstone pulls a homeless man out of a swimming pool and finds an FBI badge on him. Although the Pilgrim case was never solved, most law enforcement knew which gang was responsible but could not prove it. The gang still operates and David wonders if it also murdered this newest man. When Lindsey Mapstone, David's wife and a Phoenix police officer, uncovers proof that this particular gang did, indeed, murder John Pilgrim, she becomes its next target. The race is on between the gang and David Mapstone. The prize is his wife's life. A gritty picture of modern Phoenix.

Where it's reviewed:
Publishers Weekly, November 22, 2004, page 42

Other books by the same author:
Camelback Falls, 2003 (David Mapstone. Book 1)
Concrete Desert, 2001 (David Mapstone. Book 2)

Other books you might like:
Frederic Bean, *Murder at the Spirit Cave*, 1999
Margaret Coel, *The Shadow Dancer*, 2002
  Father John O'Malley/Vicky Holden. Book 8
James D. Doss, *The Witch's Tongue*, 2004
  Charlie Moon. Book 9
J.A. Jance, *Exit Wounds*, 2003
  Sheriff Joanna Brady. Book 10
D.R. Meredith, *Tome of Murder*, 2005
  Megan Clark. Book 4

488

BETSY THORNTON

Dead for the Winter

(New York: St. Martin's Minotaur, 2004)

Story type: Modern; Mystery
Series: Chloe Newcombe. Book 4
Subject(s): American West; Crime and Criminals
Major character(s): Chloe Newcombe, Activist (victim's advocate), Detective—Amateur; Terry Barnett, Carpenter, Crime Victim (murdered); Heather Stephens, Artist, Spouse (of Terry)
Time period(s): 2000s
Locale(s): Cochise County, Arizona

Summary: As a victim's advocate, Chloe Newcombe is assigned to help Heather Stephens cope with her husband Terry Barnett's murder. Chloe feels guilty, since she had hired Barnett to build a bookcase for her, and ended up having dinner with him. He was handsome and charismatic and Chloe had been attracted to him—until he told her he was married. Feeling like a fool, Chloe dropped him like the proverbial hot potato. Now she has to concentrate on helping Heather. During the autopsy on Barnett, the pathologist finds the carpenter had been shot before he was left in a burning barn, so now Chloe has to worry if Heather discovered Barnett's infidelities and took an alternative to divorce. As Chloe traces the tangled relationships of Cochise County, she finds that Heather isn't the only one with a motive. The merciless desert environment and isolation of the communities in this vast county add stress to people's relationships.

Where it's reviewed:
Publishers Weekly, August 30, 2004, page 35

Other books by the same author:
Ghost Towns, 2002 (Chloe Newcombe. Book 3)
High Lonesome Road, 2001 (Chloe Newcombe. Book 2)

Other books you might like:
Elizabeth Dearl, *Twice Dead*, 2001
  Taylor Madison. Book 2
J.A. Jance, *Exit Wounds*, 2003
Michael McGarrity, *Everyone Dies*, 2003
  Kevin Kerney. Book 8
Skye Kathleen Moody, *K Falls*, 2001
Jon Talton, *Concrete Desert*, 2001

489

DONLEY WATT

Dancing with Lyndon

(Fort Worth: Texas Christian University Press, 2004)

Story type: Modern; Quest
Subject(s): American West; Politics
Major character(s): Thomas Patterson, Lawyer (criminal defense), Political Figure (running for judge); Mary Lee Patterson, Spouse (of Thomas), Parent (of Tommy); Tommy Patterson, Teenager (14-year-old)
Time period(s): 1940s (1948)
Locale(s): Cottonwood, Texas

Summary: This novel of life in a small East Texas town centers around Lyndon Johnson's campaign for the United States Senate in 1948. Attorney Thomas Patterson is campaigning for election as a district judge, and he desperately wants an endorsement from either the governor or Johnson. A stiff and logical man who eschews all emotion as irrational, Thomas doesn't realize that his dreamy romantic wife, Mary Lee, is extremely unhappy and dissatisfied with their marriage. Their son, Tommy, is tired of being caught in the middle of the unspoken battle between his parents. In desperation, Mary Lee consults a gypsy fortune teller who predicts a change in her life and someone to show her the way. She doesn't wait long for change. A black client whom Thomas successfully defended against a charge of raping a white girl, suddenly kills himself. Thomas sees his campaign falling apart because Cottonwood sees the man's suicide as an admission of guilt. Racism boils over as the town accuses Thomas of defending a black man he knew was guilty. In a bid to save his campaign, Thomas and Mary Lee drive to a barbecue where Lyndon Johnson is scheduled to speak. Thomas hopes for an endorsement, but he is too innocent to be in Texas politics in 1948, when loyalty and honesty were words as empty as a politician's promise. A truly wonderful story about politics in Texas, where deals are made at barbecues, cowboy bands play country and western music, and no one turns down a dance with LBJ.

Where it's reviewed:
Roundup Magazine, February 2005, page 37

Other books by the same author:
Reynolds, 2002
Haley, Texas, 1959, 1999

Other books you might like:
James Carlos Blake, *Under the Skin*, 2003
Mike Blakely, *Summer of the Pearls*, 2000
Joe R. Lansdale, *Sunset and Sawdust*, 2004
D.R. Meredith, *Murder by Deception*, 2004
  John Lloyd Branson. Book 2
Janice Woods Windle, *Will's War*, 2001

490

CHARLES G. WEST

Bloody Hills

(New York: Signet, 2004)

Story type: Traditional; Revenge
Subject(s): American West; Crime and Criminals
Major character(s): Billy Ray Blevins, Outlaw, Murderer; Clay Culver, Scout (for the U.S. Army); Rachel Andrews, Spouse (of murdered schoolmaster), Employer (hires Clay)
Time period(s): 1870s (1875)
Locale(s): Dry Folk, South Dakota; Black Hills, South Dakota

Summary: Billy Ray Blevins is a short, skinny kid who is a deadly shot. He discovers that he enjoys killing and guns down several people. He first kills a young cowboy over a wager, then kills the schoolmaster after the man objects to Billy Ray forcibly fondling his wife, then the local sheriff when he attempts to arrest him. Billy Ray leaves town, one step ahead of a posse, and searches for a place to hide out. Rachel Andrews is determined to avenge her husband's death, so she teams up with Deputy Sheriff Lon Fortson to hunt down Billy Ray. Neither of them have any tracking skills, so they hire army scout Clay Culver to help them. A problem arises when the Sioux go on the warpath and begin trailing them. Billy Ray, meanwhile, has found a kindred spirit, an old reprobate named Henry, who is also a stone-cold killer. They kidnap and abuse Rachel. When Culver finds her, he fears she will never recover from the ordeal, provided the Sioux don't get them.

Where it's reviewed:
Roundup Magazine, June 2005, page 39

Other books by the same author:
Devil's Kin, 2005
Hangman's Song, 2005
Evil Breed, 2003
Hero's Stand, 2003
Savage Cry, 2002

Other books you might like:
James Carlos Blake, *Under the Skin*, 2003
Peter Brandvold, *Riding with the Devil's Mistress*, 2003
Stan Lynde, *Saving Miss Julia*, 2004
John D. Nesbitt, *Red Wind Crossing*, 2003
Frank Roderus, *Old Marsden*, 1999

491

CHARLES G. WEST

Devil's Kin

(New York: Signet, 2005)

Story type: Traditional; Revenge
Subject(s): American West; Crime and Criminals
Major character(s): Jordan Gray, Farmer; Jed Ramey, Lawman (deputy U.S. marshal); Johnny Spratte, Lawman (deputy sheriff), Outlaw (joins gang of killers)
Time period(s): 19th century (post-Civil War)
Locale(s): Oklahoma; Fort Smith, Arkansas

Summary: Leach, Snake, and Roach ride into Jordan Gray's homestead, murder his wife and son, and burn his cabin. Jordan buries his dead family after returning from riding with a posse looking for these same killers. He reports the crime to the sheriff, who frets about rounding up another posse. The sheriff's deputy, Johnny Spratte, had been consorting with three rough-looking strangers the night before, and Jordan remembers that it was Spratte who led the posse in the wrong direction, and who insisted that the killers had left the territory. Jordan deduces that Spratte has thrown in with the killers for whatever reason, and rides back to his cabin to pick up the trail from there. Meanwhile, the three outlaws and Johnny Spratte rob the bank in Fort Smith and kill two people. U.S. Deputy Marshal Jed Ramey, reputed to be the meanest lawman in Arkansas and the Indian Nations, rounds up a posse to chase down the killers. With poor descriptions from eye witnesses, Ramey mistakenly arrests Jordan Gray. As Jed Ramey's deputy unties Jordan's hands and feet, Jordan escapes. Using the deputy's rifle, Jordan takes the two lawmen's horses and heads for Indian Territory after Johnny and his partners, while being doggedly pursued by Jed Ramey.

Where it's reviewed:
Roundup Magazine, June 2005, page 39

Other books by the same author:
Hangman's Song, 2005
Bloody Hills, 2004
Evil Breed, 2003
Hero's Stand, 2003
Savage Cry, 2002

Other books you might like:
Ed Gorman, *Night of Shadows*, 2002

Stephen Overholser, *Chasing Destiny*, 2005
Bill Pronzini, *Borgade's Crossing*, 2004
Jory Sherman, *Bloody River*, 2005
Gary Svee, *Vengeance Peacemaker*, 2003

492

JOSEPH A. WEST

Donovan's Dove

(New York: Signet, 2004)

Story type: Traditional; Man Alone
Subject(s): American West; Crime and Criminals; Gambling
Major character(s): Zeke Donovan, Gambler, Drifter; Ike Vance, Gambler, Murderer; Nancy Brown, Prostitute
Time period(s): 1870s (1879)
Locale(s): Deadwood, South Dakota; Tombstone, Arizona

Summary: Zeke Donovan stirs up a pot of trouble for himself when he wins $250.00, a prized pocket watch, and a prostitute named Nancy from Ike Vance in a card game. Ike takes exception to the loss of his watch and Nancy, but particularly the watch. Donovan himself prefers the watch to the rest of his winnings, and takes it as a sign of bad luck when the sheriff runs him and Nancy out of town to avoid a showdown with Vance. Donovan is good at running—he's been doing it all his life—and it's a good skill for a man who's a terrible shot to have. He can't seem to outrun Nancy however, but when she is shot by some bushwhackers, he stays to help her. Eventually they end up in Tombstone, but there they run straight into Vance and three gunslinger pals of his.

Where it's reviewed:
Roundup Magazine, February 2005, page 37

Other books by the same author:
Johnny Blue and the Texas Rangers, 2004
Johnny Blue and the Hanging Judge, 2001
Me and Johnny Blue, 2000

Other books you might like:
Matt Braun, *Doc Holliday*, 1997
Ralph Cotton, *Hell's Riders*, 2004
Ken Hodgson, *God's Pocket*, 2004
Tom Piccirilli, *Coffin Blues*, 2004
Richard S. Wheeler, *The Bounty Trail*, 2004

493

JOSEPH A. WEST

Johnny Blue and the Texas Rangers

(New York: Signet, 2004)

Story type: Traditional; Chase
Series: Johnny Blue. Book 3
Subject(s): Crime and Criminals; Humor
Major character(s): Johnny Blue Dupree, Cowboy (African American), Sidekick (of narrator); Doc Fortune, Con Artist, Thief; Me, Narrator (unnamed), Friend (of Johnny Blue)
Time period(s): 1880s (1888)
Locale(s): San Antonio, Texas; Santa Alana, Mexico

Summary: Johnny Blue and his sidekick, an unnamed narrator referred to only as "me" have a series of comic misadventures. They include angering the inhabitants of a small town by shooting the statue of a war hero in the posterior; partnering with Doc Fortune, con man *extraordinaire*, to find a hidden cashbox containing $30,000.00 worth of gold coins, the original thief of which takes exception to their interference; trying to establish a bicycle factory; and dodging the U.S. Army and the Mexican *federales* for various and sundry hanging offenses. After a time, me and Johnny Blue decide to head to Florida until things cool off in Texas. Besides, me has a plan for rescuing Geronimo. . . .

Where it's reviewed:
Roundup Magazine, February 2005, page 37

Other books by the same author:
Donovan's Dove, 2004
Johnny Blue and the Hanging Judge, 2001
Me and Johnny Blue, 2000

Other books you might like:
Robert J. Conley, *Barjack*, 2000
Robert J. Conley, *Broke Loose*, 2000
Preston Lewis, *The Demise of Billy the Kid*, 1995
Ellen Recknor, *Leaving Missouri*, 1997
Ellen Recknor, *Me and the Boys*, 1995

494

RICHARD S. WHEELER

Trouble in Tombstone

(New York: Signet, 2004)

Story type: Traditional; Man Alone
Subject(s): American West; Crime and Criminals
Major character(s): Wyatt Earp, Lawman (in Tombstone), Historical Figure; John Henry "Doc" Holliday, Historical Figure, Gambler; John Behan, Lawman (sheriff), Friend (of the gang)
Time period(s): 1880s (1881)
Locale(s): Tombstone, Arizona

Summary: This is not just another book about the shootout at the O.K.Corral; this a psychological profile of the Earp brothers, particularly Wyatt, who is the narrator; John Behan; Doc Holliday; and by extension, the town of Tombstone. The Earps arrive in Tombstone hoping to make their fortunes, and soon own some mining claims, faro games, city lots, and whatever else looks like a moneymaker. They are also lawmen, with Virgil becoming city marshal after the previous lawman is gunned down in the street. The Earps try to break the Cowboys' hold on Tombstone, but it is a constant battle and they are outnumbered twenty to one. The threats from the Clantons and McLaury finally erupts into the infamous gunfight, followed by Morgan Earp's murder and Virgil Earp's disabling wound in his arm. The Earps leave Tombstone with Wyatt sending Virgil and the women to California with Morgan's body. Wyatt and Doc Holliday and a few other allies go after Morgan's murderers, and over time get all of them. Then Wyatt joins up with his wife Josie and outlives all his contemporaries at Tombstone, and often puzzles over the events when he is an old man. He decides the young Wyatt didn't understand the politics of Tombstone, or that votes and elected offices were more important than justice. This is a deeper study of Wyatt Earp the man than has ever been done, augmented by all the rip-snorting action of the best kind of Western novel.

Where it's reviewed:
Roundup Magazine, June 2005, page 39

Other books by the same author:
An Obituary for Major Reno, 2004
The Bounty Trail, 2004
The Exile, 2003
Restitution, 2001
Going Home, 2000

Other books you might like:
Matt Braun, *Wyatt Earp*, 1994
Bill Brooks, *Law for Hire: Saving Masterson*, 2004
    Law for Hire. Book 3
Richard Jensen, *Ride the Wild Trail*, 2003
Preston Lewis, *Mix-Up at the O.K. Corral*, 1996
Nelson Nye, *Gunfight at the O.K. Corral*, 2003

495
RICHARD S. WHEELER
Vengeance Valley
(New York: Pinnacle, 2004)

Story type: Traditional; Man Alone
Subject(s): Gold Discoveries; Crime and Criminals; Miners and Mining
Major character(s): Will Yancy, Mine Owner, Prospector (looking for gold); Alfred Noble, Mine Owner; Adelaide Kearney, Widow(er), Saloon Keeper/Owner
Time period(s): 19th century (post-Civil War)
Locale(s): Yancy City, Colorado

Summary: Will ''Hard Luck'' Yancy is the most knowledge-able prospector in Colorado, finding precious metals where other miners saw nothing. Yancy is cheated out of a silver mine by the unscrupulous syndicate headed by Alfred Noble. When Yancy finds a rich vein of gold behind the Sisters of Charity miner's hospital, he files claims for the property on either side of the hospital, and warns Sister Carmela, the head of the hospital, to watch out for Noble. Noble manages to cheat the Sisters out of their property anyway, and has the sheriff run Yancy out of town. He takes refuge in an old cliff dwelling where he discovers something more precious than gold. When Noble's mining operation destroys the only spring in the area, the syndicate sells the now worthless land to Yancy, who may have actually outsmarted them.

Where it's reviewed:
Roundup Magazine, February 2005, page 38

Other books by the same author:
Eclipse, 2002
Downriver, 2001
Restitution, 2001
Going Home, 2000
The Witness, 2000

Other books you might like:
Tim Champlin, *By Flare of Northern Lights*, 2001
Tim Champlin, *Wayfaring Strangers*, 2000
Steve Frazee Ghost, *Ghost Mine*, 2002
Cameron Judd, *Confederate Gold*, 1993
JoAnn Levy, *For California's Gold*, 2000

496
JEANNE WILLIAMS
The Hidden Valley
(Waterville, Maine: Five Star, 2004)

Story type: Historical/American Civil War; Saga
Series: Beneath the Burning Ground Trilogy. Book 2
Subject(s): American West; Slavery
Major character(s): Charlie Ware, Worker (freighter), Military Personnel (Confederate army); Dan O'Brien, Military Personnel (Union army); Jonathan Ware, Religious (Universalist minister), Parent (Charlie and Christy's father)
Time period(s): 1860s (1860-1862)
Locale(s): Kansas

Summary: Dan O'Brien loves Christy Ware and wants to marry her, but the time is not right. Kansas is in the midst of a drought and everyone believes war is coming. Christy's brother Charlie, has no such qualms, and marries Melissa, the daughter of a pro-slavery plantation owner. Universalist minister Jonathan Ware, Christy and Charlie's father, is a pacifist and an abolitionist as well. When the war does come, he enlists in the Kansas militia, hoping he will not actually have to fight. He is heartsick when Charlie joins the Confederate Army, and his other son, Thomas, enlists in the Union Army. Dan also becomes a Union soldier and the horrors he witnesses on the battlefield make him feel too dirty to ever marry Christy. This is a wonderful novel about a tortured time in history and the toll it takes on people, told through the eyes of the Ware family.

Where it's reviewed:
Roundup Magazine, February 2005, page 38

Other books by the same author:
The Underground River, 2004 (Beneath the Burning Ground Trilogy. Book 1)
Wind Water, 1997
Home Station, 1996
The Unplowed Sky, 1994
Home Mountain, 1990

Other books you might like:
James Carlos Blake, *Wildwood Boys*, 2000
Tim Champlin, *Raiders of the Western & Atlantic*, 2002
Tim Champlin, *The Tombstone Conspiracy*, 1999
Preston Lewis, *The Redemption of Jesse James*, 1999
Ellen Recknor, *Leaving Missouri*, 1997

Western

497

JEANNE WILLIAMS

The Underground River

(Waterville, Maine: Five Star, 2004)

Story type: Historical/American Civil War; Saga
Series: Beneath the Burning Ground Trilogy. Book 1
Subject(s): American West; Slavery
Major character(s): Christy Ware, Teenager (13-year-old); Dan O'Brien, Orphan (adopted by Parks family), Friend (of Christy Ware); Charlie Ware, Worker (freighter)
Time period(s): 1850s (1853-1858)
Locale(s): Clear Creek, Kansas

Summary: This is the first volume of a trilogy about the Kansas-Missouri border war as pro-slavery forces battled anti-slavery forces over whether Kansas Territory would become a slave state or a free state. The Ware family emigrates from Illinois to Kansas. The Wares are against slavery, but are not violent fanatics like John Brown and his family. Young Christy Ware, 13 when the family arrives in Kansas in 1853, grows up witnessing the horrible violence on both sides of the issue. Her own brother, Charlie Ware, works as a freighter for a pro-slavery family. Dan O'Brien, an Irish orphan adopted by the Parks family, is against slavery, and he and Christy discover an underground river where they can hide runaway slaves. Not until the Ware family becomes committed to abolition by risking their lives hiding slaves, does Christy realize how divided her neighbors are. Soon the Wares find themselves shunned by their pro-slavery neighbors and everyone in Kansas will have to take a stand for or against slavery, and prepare to defend their views, with their lives if necessary.

Where it's reviewed:
Roundup Magazine, February 2005, page 38

Other books by the same author:
Wind Water, 1997
Home Station, 1996
The Unplowed Sky, 1994
Home Mountain, 1990
No Roof but Heaven, 1990

Other books you might like:
Frederic Bean, *Lorena*, 1996
James Carlos Blake, *Wildwood Boys*, 2000
Tim Champlin, *Lincoln's Ransom*, 1999
Elizabeth Flacker, *Texas Lily*, 1999
Richard S. Wheeler, *The Deliverance*, 2003

Fantasy Fiction in 2004
by
Don D'Ammassa

Modern fantasy fiction has been dominated for the last ten years or more by two separate traditions which often overlap. The first of these is the result of the continuing popularity of the Lord of the Rings trilogy by J.R.R. Tolkien, which makes use of a setting in which humans are just one of many races existing in a magical world, interacting with elves, trolls, orcs, and other types in some combination. The plots involve the tensions among the races and often center on wars or the threat of war. The books themselves are often published as trilogies, a single continuing story spread over three volumes, which may or may not have some form of subsidiary resolution at the end of each book. The recent film versions have certainly stimulated fresh interest in Tolkien's work, but so far readers have been spared the flood of slavish imitations that followed the trilogy's first mass market paperback editions during the late 1960s.

The second form is a that of a disguised historical novel, usually a medieval style setting involving swords and sorcery, kings and nobles, court intrigues, castles and dragons. Sometimes there are other intelligent races besides humanity, sometimes there are not. The most popular plots involve quests—usually to obtain some form of magical artifact, efforts to protect or recover the throne, or wars against malevolent enemies who are usually aided by sorcery. In many cases, the fantastic elements are mere window dressing and occasionally virtually non-existent. It is usually quite easy to tell the heroes from the villains, even when the characterization is skillfully done, and there is often a strong romantic undercurrent.

Although the trilogy is the most common form of fantasy, writers like Robert Jordan, L.E. Modesitt Jr., Mercedes Lackey, Katherine Kurtz, and others have become very successful writing fantasy series that extend beyond three volumes. However, they rarely venture too far from the basic formula and vary among themselves quite significantly in quality. Unfortunately, it has become increasingly difficult to remain fresh and original when constrained to use the same setting and usually the same characters as well. There were a few very fine novels of this type in 2004, most notably *The Chernagor Pirates* by Dan Chernenko, *The Charnel Prince* by Greg Keyes, and *Exile's Return* by Raymond E. Feist, but most of the outstanding novels of 2004 were at least slightly outside the mainstream. Keyes, whose previous fantasy novels appeared as by J. Gregory Keyes, returns to the world of Everon, first introduced in *The Briar King*. This time he chronicles the efforts of a loyal knight as he is sent to find the missing heir to the throne, apparently kidnapped by forces hostile to the royal family. The third volume in Raymond Feist's Conclave of Shadows series has an unlikely hero, the deposed villain of the earlier books, who discovers a supernatural threat to the world and decides to help save the day. Feist manages to reclaim his character without removing his hard edges.

Dave Duncan and China Mieville were particularly innovative this past year, even though both produced what are essentially elaborate quest stories. Duncan's *The Jaguar Knights*, for example, is part of his King's Blades series set in a world where knights are magically bound to their masters. However, the latest title takes place in a foreign land whose culture is so different that even magic works in a different fashion and the inhabitants are not entirely human. When a band of warriors from that distant land stages an unexpected assault, an outcast Blade is assigned the job of locating their homeland and discovering what precipitated the attack. Mieville's *The Iron Council* takes place in the world of New Crobuzon, a city that is featured in his two previous novels. There magic and technology work side by side, as do humans and a variety of very non-traditional intelligent species. Another outsider, in this case one of a group of rebels, hijacks a train and an exciting chase through a bizarre landscape follows. Although not as polished as the two preceding titles, *The Year of Our War* by Steph Swainston, the author's debut novel, similarly mixes familiar and unfamiliar elements in a plot which involves an immortal hero, the return of the gods to Earth, and an invasion by giant insects.

As good as Swainston's novel is, the best first fantasy of the year was *Jonathan Strange & Mr. Norrell* by Susanna Clarke, the story of two rival magicians at work in a nineteenth-century England that closely resembles our own. Clarke's prose is masterful and she describes the complex rivalry in a sophisticated and entertaining fashion. Historical settings were unusually common in fantasy in 2004, resulting in several other excellent novels. Sara Douglass gave us *The Nameless Day*, previously published in Australia but available internationally only this past year, the first in the Crucible series which pits a clergyman in fourteenth-century Europe against a host of demons living disguised among humans. In *Rite of Conquest* by Judith Tarr, William the Conqueror is taught to make use of his innate magical talents while still a young man. *The Last Light of the Sun* by Guy Gavriel Kay is a Norse saga with magic. Jeff Barlough's *Strange Cargo* technically does not take place in our world but is set in an alternate nineteenth century, in which the last Ice Age has not yet receded and civilization is only possible along the continental coastland.

Books and libraries figured prominently in two of the year's new titles. A scholar happens upon a magical book which transforms her life in *Alphabet of Thorn* by Patricia A. McKillip, one of the author's cleverly understated fantasies. There is a group of librarians dedicated to protecting a storehouse of magical books from falling into the wrong hands in *The Destruction of the Books* by Mel Odom, sequel to the earlier *The Rover*. They are faced this time with the painful choice between destroying the books in their charge or having their secrets revealed to ambitious external forces.

Shadows in Darkness by Elaine Cunningham is her first novel not related to a role playing game system, and is a dramatic leap forward. The setting is contemporary America and the protagonist is a female private detective who discovers that magic is real and that her own future is bound by it. *The Runes of the Earth* by Stephen R. Donaldson also starts with a contemporary setting, although its main characters soon find themselves in a fantasy world. This is the first in a four-book sequence that follows the six books of the Thomas Covenant saga. *Dime Store Magic* by Kelley Armstrong is the first in a series about a coven of modern-day witches. A sequel, *Industrial Magic*, was less interesting but still entertaining. In *One King, One Soldier*, Alexander Irvine introduces a Korean War veteran who discovers that he has been selected for an even more imposing task, guardianship of the Holy Grail.

In the absence of a new Harry Potter book from J.K. Rowling, the best young adult fantasy novel of the year was *Gifts*, which is also an allegory meaningful to adults. All of the inhabitants of a village have varying magic powers, which each of them cultivates in order to maintain a balance of power that has provided generations of stability. When two young people from opposing factions declare their unwillingness to learn to use their magic, it threatens either to incite a general conflict or to cause everyone to question the wisdom of the way they and their ancestors have spent their lives.

Several disparate novels round out the year. Diana L. Paxson provides a prequel to the Avalon novels of the late Marion Zimmer Bradley with *Ancestors of Avalon*, which describes the flight by the last survivors of drowned Atlantis, their arrival in the British Isles, and their influence on the local culture in the time of King Arthur and Camelot. Paxson preserves the feminist slant of the original novels. John Wright, who made an impressive debut as a science fiction writer a couple of years back, tries his hand at fantasy with *The Last Guardian of Everness*, first volume in the War of Dreaming. The protagonist is a warrior who has served the powers of Light against the powers of Darkness. He begins to question things when he realizes that the former would oppose just as restrictive a rule over humanity as the latter, although with more benevolent motives. The warrior concludes that the human race is better off opposing Darkness without supernatural allies. The battle presumably will unfold in subsequent volumes in the series. Gene Wolfe continued the highly literate and sophisticated adventure story which started with *The Knight*, in which a young boy finds himself trapped in the body of a knight, and which is now concluded with *The Wizard*.

Three collections of short fantasy stories deserve special mention this year. *Innocents Aboard* by Gene Wolfe collects most of his fantasy and supernatural fiction. His witty, intelligent style and unique viewpoint are almost always outstanding. Pamela Sargent brings her sensitivity and fine storytelling talents to the stories collected in *Eye of Flame and Other Fantasies*. Robert E. Howard's Conan stories have been assembled into so many combinations that it is hard to single out any one title as his best, but the selection in *The Bloody Crown of Conan* includes many of his finest exploits. The anthology *Crossroads*, edited by Brett Cox and Andy Duncan, is a superior selection of original short stories of fantasy and the supernatural written by writers from the Southern half of the United States.

The two best fantasy novels of the year were fairly easy to choose in 2004. China Mieville has consistently produced exceptional work, creating unique settings and situations and telling his story in gripping prose, and *The Iron Council* is no exception. Dave Duncan has been steadily improving ever since he first started writing, and the King's Blades series has propelled him into the top rank of fantasy writers. *The Jaguar Knights* is his best work yet. It is significant that neither book is set in a standard fantasy world society and that both are told from the points of view of individuals cast in the role of outsiders. This might indicate that the genre is ready to evolve into something more original and thought provoking and less restricted by genre conventions.

The recommended titles listed below augur well for fantasy readers who have grown tired of the seemingly endless string of disguised historical novels that have dominated fantasy. There is a much greater degree of diversity than has existed since fantasy first began to function as a genre separate from science fiction, with which it is still closely associated. Authors and publishers seem increasingly willing to take a chance on a story that does not fit into existing patterns. This increase in diversity should not only prove rewarding to established readers but may also increase the genre's appeal to an even larger cross section of readers.

Recommended Titles

Entries for the following books are included in this volume.

Strange Cargo by Jeff Barlough

Jonathan Strange & Mr. Norrell by Susanna Clarke

Crossroads edited by Brett Cox and Andy Duncan

Shadows in Darkness by Elaine Cunningham

The Runes of the Earth by Stephen R. Donaldson

The Nameless Day by Sara Douglass

The Jaguar Knights by Dave Duncan

Exile's Return by Raymond E. Feist

The Bloody Crown of Conan by Robert E. Howard

One King, One Soldier by Alexander Irvine

The Charnel Prince by Greg Keyes

Gifts by Ursula K. Le Guin

The Iron Council by China Mieville

Ancestors of Avalon by Diana L. Paxson

Rite of Conquest by Judith Tarr

The Wizard by Gene Wolfe

The Last Guardian of Everness by John Wright

The entries for the following books can be found in *WDIRN? 2004. Volume 2.*

Dime Store Magic by Kelly Armstrong

The Chernagor Pirates by Dan Chernenko

The Last Light of the Sun by Guy Gavriel Kay

Alphabet of Thorn by Patricia A. McKillip

The Destruction of the Books by Mel Odom

Eye of Flame and Other Fantasies by Pamela Sargent

The Year of Our War by Steph Swainston

Innocents Aboard by Gene Wolfe

Fantasy Titles

Taking Time

(New York: Ace, 2004)

Story type: Time Travel; Mystery
Series: Emma Merrigan. Book 3
Subject(s): Time Travel
Major character(s): Emma Merrigan, Time Traveler; Redmond Longleigh, Businessman; Harry Graves, Businessman
Time period(s): 2000s
Locale(s): United States

Summary: Emma Merrigan has a unique ability to project herself into the past where she tracks down the causes of magical curses that affect people in the present. Her newest case is a particularly complex one, involving an entire family who continue to suffer for the deeds of their ancestors.

Where it's reviewed:
Chronicle, July 2004, page 44

Other books by the same author:
Behind Time, 2001
Out of Time, 2000
The Nether Scroll, 2000
Planeswalker, 1998
Cinnabar Shadows, 1995

Other books you might like:
Elaine Bergstrom, *The Door through Washington Square,* 1998
John Dickson Carr, *Fear Is the Same,* 1956
Jack Finney, *Time and Again,* 1970
John R. Maxim, *Time Out of Mind,* 1986
Chet Williamson, *Second Chance,* 2002

The First Stone

(New York: Bantam, 2004)

Story type: Sword and Sorcery; Magic Conflict
Series: Last Rune. Book 6
Subject(s): Magic
Major character(s): Travis Wilder, Sorcerer; Grace Beckett, Adventurer; Sareth, Sorcerer
Time period(s): Indeterminate
Locale(s): The Dominions, Fictional Country

Summary: Travis Wilder thought that he had escaped the wiles of sorcery forever, but his enemies have not been inactive. They have discovered that the secrets of a lost form of powerful sorcery can be learned from the blood of Wilder's daughter, so he must venture out to defeat them once again. *The First Stone* appears to be the final volume in this series.

Other books by the same author:
Gates of Winter, 2003
Blood of Mystery, 2002
The Dark Remains, 2001
The Keep of Fire, 1999
Beyond the Pale, 1998

Other books you might like:
David Eddings, *The Magician's Gambit,* 1983
Sarah A. Hoyt, *Any Man So Daring,* 2003
Andrew J. Offutt, *The Iron Lords,* 1979
Mickey Zucker Reichert, *The Return of Nightfall,* 2004
Sarah Zettel, *The Usurper's Crown,* 2003

Currant Events

(New York: Tor, 2004)

Story type: Humor; Quest

Series: Xanth. Book 28
Subject(s): Humor
Major character(s): Clio, Historian; Humfrey, Magician; Sherlock, Wizard
Time period(s): Indeterminate
Locale(s): Xanth, Fictional Country

Summary: When Clio sits down to write the next chapter in the history of Xanth, she discovers that part of the future has already been inscribed. She decides to consult with a powerful magician, but to get his cooperation, she must set out on a quest. Her adventures mix action with farcical humor in the manner of the previous novels in this long-running series.

Where it's reviewed:
Booklist, October 1, 2004, page 318
Library Journal, October 15, 2004, page 58
Publishers Weekly, August 30, 2004, page 37

Other books by the same author:
Cube Route, 2003
Up in a Heaval, 2002
Swell Foop, 2001
The Muse of Art, 1999
The Zombie Lover, 1998

Other books you might like:
John DeChancie, *Bride of the Castle*, 1994
Esther Friesner, *Elf Defense*, 1988
Craig Shaw Gardner, *The Other Sinbad*, 1991
Tom Holt, *The Divine Comedies*, 2003
Terry Pratchett, *The Truth*, 2000

501

KELLEY ARMSTRONG

Industrial Magic
(New York: Bantam, 2004)

Story type: Contemporary; Mystery
Series: Women of the Otherworld. Book 4
Subject(s): Magic; Wicca
Major character(s): Paige Winterbourne, Computer Expert, Witch; Lucas Cortez, Lawyer, Sorcerer; Benicio Cortez, Businessman, Sorcerer
Time period(s): 2000s
Locale(s): Miami, Florida

Summary: Paige Winterbourne is a progressive witch, on the side of good, trying to adapt the old ways to new conditions. When she learns that someone is murdering the older children of a rival coven's members, she gets drawn into a murder mystery that is complicated by the presence of dark magic, and her former romantic relationship with one of the key players.

Other books by the same author:
Dime Store Magic, 2004
Stolen, 2003
Bitten, 2001

Other books you might like:
Brenda Jordan, *The Brentwood Witches*, 1987
Graham Joyce, *Dark Sister*, 1992
Fritz Leiber, *Conjure Wife*, 1953

Josephine Pinckney, *Great Mischief*, 1948
John Updike, *The Witches of Eastwick*, 1984

502

SARAH ASH

Prisoner of the Iron Tower
(New York: Bantam, 2004)

Story type: Political; Sword and Sorcery
Series: Tears of Artamon. Book 2
Subject(s): Quest
Major character(s): Gavril Nagarian, Artist, Prisoner; Eugene of Tielen, Nobleman; Astasia Orlova, Noblewoman
Time period(s): Indeterminate
Locale(s): Azhkendir, Fictional Country

Summary: Although Gavril has finally been freed of a demonic force that possessed him in the opening volume of this series, his crimes while under that creature's control have destroyed his reputation, and he is imprisoned in an asylum. The man responsible for his incarceration has an ulterior motive; he seeks to control the power of that same demon.

Where it's reviewed:
Booklist, August 2004, page 1912
Library Journal, August 2004, page 73

Other books by the same author:
Lord of Snow and Shadows, 2003
The Lost Child, 1998
Songspinners, 1996
Moths to a Flame, 1995

Other books you might like:
Storm Constantine, *The Crown of Silence*, 2001
Louise Cooper, *Avatar*, 1992
David Eddings, *The Diamond Throne*, 1989
Mercedes Lackey, *Exile's Honor*, 2002
Sarah Zettel, *A Sorcerer's Treason*, 2002

503

JAMES BARCLAY

Demonstorm
(London: Gollancz, 2004)

Story type: Sword and Sorcery; Magic Conflict
Series: Legends of the Raven. Book 6
Subject(s): Magic
Major character(s): Dystran, Ruler; Hirad Coldheart, Barbarian, Warrior; Tessaya, Ruler
Time period(s): Indeterminate
Locale(s): Balaia, Fictional Country; Xetesk, Fictional Country

Summary: The war between the forces of Tessaya and Dystran seems to have reached a turning point at last. As Dystran looks at what appears to be inevitable defeat, he decides to resort to his most powerful and dangerous weapon, the magical power that keeps separate dimensions from interacting with one another. Will saving his armies result in the end of multiple worlds?

Where it's reviewed:
Chronicle, November 2004, page 43

Other books by the same author:
Light Stealer, 2003
Shadowheart, 2003
Elfsorrow, 2002
Nightchild, 2001
Noonshade, 2000

Other books you might like:
Jack L. Chalker, *Vengeance of the Dancing Gods*, 1985
Susan Dexter, *The Ring of Allaire*, 1981
Lyndon Hardy, *Master of the Five Magics*, 1980
R.A. Salvatore, *The Demon Wakens*, 1997
Tad Williams, *Otherland*, 1996

504

JEFFREY E. BARLOUGH

Strange Cargo
(New York: Ace, 2004)

Story type: Alternate History; Light Fantasy
Subject(s): Alternate History
Major character(s): Frederick Cargo, Traveler; Tim Christmas, Apprentice; Jane Wastefield, Traveler
Time period(s): 19th century
Locale(s): Alternate Universe

Summary: This unusual story is set in an alternate Earth where the ice age never ended and civilization is confined largely to the coastal regions. A group of travelers with varied purposes find their lives drawn together in an intricate web of magic, intrigue, and adventure.

Other books by the same author:
The House in the High Woods, 2001
Dark Sleeper, 2000

Other books you might like:
Poul Anderson, *Operation Luna*, 1999
Gregory Frost, *Lyrec*, 1984
Mary Gentle, *1610*, 2003
Barbara Hambly, *The Icefalcon's Quest*, 1998
J. Gregory Keyes, *The Empire of Unreason*, 2002

505

T.A. BARRON

Child of the Dark Prophecy
(New York: Philomel, 2004)

Story type: Historical; Legend
Series: Great Tree of Avalon. Book 1
Subject(s): Arthurian Legends
Major character(s): Tamwyn, Worker; Harlech, Warrior; Merlin, Wizard
Time period(s): Indeterminate Past
Locale(s): England

Summary: In the days before the rise of King Arthur and Camelot, a warrior, a roof thatcher, and several others have a series of magical adventures involving the mythical land of

Avalon and the doings of the famous wizard, Merlin, who will later become Arthur's adviser.

Other books by the same author:
The Tree Girl, 2001
The Wings of Merlin, 2000
The Fires of Merlin, 1999
The Mirror of Merlin, 1999
The Ancient One, 1992

Other books you might like:
Cary James, *King and Raven*, 1995
Robert Nye, *Merlin*, 1979
Nikolai Tolstoy, *The Coming of the King*, 1989
Jane Yolen, *Sword of the Rightful King*, 2003
Sarah Zettel, *In Camelot's Shadow*, 2004

506

NANCY VARIAN BERBERICK

Prisoner of Haven
(Renton, Washington: Wizards of the Coast, 2004)

Story type: Magic Conflict; Sword and Sorcery
Series: Age of Mortals. Book 4
Subject(s): Magic
Major character(s): Usha Majere, Prisoner; Dezra Majere, Prisoner; Madoc Diviner, Warrior
Time period(s): Indeterminate
Locale(s): Alternate Universe

Summary: Two women find themselves prisoners when their city falls under siege and is occupied by a foreign army. Although they are rivals and not friends, they are forced to put their personal differences aside in order to survive, and they discover a new strength through unity that helps them accomplish much more than survival.

Other books by the same author:
The Lioness, 2002
The Inheritance, 2001
Tears of the Night Sky, 1998 (Linda Baker, co-author)
The Panther's Hoard, 1994
A Child of Elvish, 1992

Other books you might like:
Lynn Abbey, *Daughter of the Bright Moon*, 1979
Stephen R. Donaldson, *The Mirror of Her Dreams*, 1986
Ru Emerson, *The Princess of Flames*, 1986
Anne Kelleher, *Silver's Edge*, 2004
Jo Walton, *The King's Name*, 2001

507

CARL BOWEN

A Day Dark as Night
(Stone Mountain, Georgia: White Wolf, 2004)

Story type: Sword and Sorcery; Magic Conflict
Subject(s): Magic
Major character(s): Harmonious Jade, Warrior; Dace, Military Personnel; Selene Chaisa, Noblewoman
Time period(s): Indeterminate
Locale(s): Alternate Universe

Fantasy

Summary: Harmonious Jade has been imbued by a god with superhuman powers, with which she carries out various tasks, often bloody and fatal to her quarry. She is curious about her own destiny, however, and travels to a dangerous city to pursue her private investigations.

Other books by the same author:
Silent Striders, 2001
Vampire, 2000

Other books you might like:
Simon R. Green, *The Bones of Haven*, 1992
Robert E. Howard, *Kull*, 1985
Richard A. Knaak, *The Shrouded Realm*, 1991
Harry Turtledove, *Conan of Venarium*, 2004
Karl Edward Wagner, *The Book of Kane*, 1985

508

CAITLIN BRENNAN

The Mountain's Call

(New York: LUNA, 2004)

Story type: Romance; Light Fantasy
Subject(s): Women
Major character(s): Valeria, Horse Trainer (equestrian); Kerrec, Horse Trainer; Evan, Barbarian, Nobleman
Time period(s): Indeterminate
Locale(s): Aurelian Empire, Fictional Country

Summary: Valeria has always had an affinity for horses and she aspires to be the first female rider, an elite group who serve the gods of the mountains. Her people forbid women to assume that role, however, so even when she wins the competition for that honor, it appears she will be denied.

Other books you might like:
Constance Ash, *The Horse Girl*, 1988
C.J. Cherryh, *Cloud's Rider*, 1996
Mary Herbert, *Lightning's Daughter*, 1991
Mercedes Lackey, *The River's Gift*, 1999
Jean Rabe, *The Finest Creation*, 2004

509

NOEL-ANNE BRENNAN

The Blood of the Land

(New York: Ace, 2004)

Story type: Sword and Sorcery; Political
Series: Land. Book 2
Subject(s): Magic
Major character(s): Rilsin Sae Becha, Government Official, Noblewoman; Prince Raphat, Nobleman; Sola Dira Mudrin, Inventor
Time period(s): Indeterminate
Locale(s): Saeditin, Fictional Country; Runchot, Fictional Country

Summary: Although Rilsin has triumphed and become the ruler of Saeditin, her troubles are not over. Her cousin has found allies in another country and is preparing to launch a war, and at the moment of crisis her own child is kidnapped.

Other books by the same author:
The Sword of the Land, 2003
Winter Reckoning, 1986

Other books you might like:
Lynn Abbey, *The Black Flame*, 1980
Dave Duncan, *Sky of Swords*, 2000
Doranna Durgin, *Wolverine's Daughter*, 2000
Judith Tarr, *The Lady of Han-Gilen*, 1987
Jo Walton, *The King's Name*, 2001

510

PATRICIA BRIGGS

Raven's Shadow

(New York: Ace, 2004)

Story type: Sword and Sorcery; Magic Conflict
Series: Raven. Book 1
Subject(s): Magic
Major character(s): Seraph, Sorceress; Tier, Military Personnel; Brewydd, Ruler
Time period(s): Indeterminate
Locale(s): Alternate Universe

Summary: An experiment in sorcery causes widespread devastation. In the aftermath, people are generally fearful of those who wield magic. Seraph is one of the last of these, whose destiny seems likely to be quick and unpleasant, until she enlists the aid of the soldier Tier.

Other books by the same author:
Dragon Blood, 2003
Dragon Bones, 2002
The Hob's Bargain, 2001
Steal the Dragon, 1995
Masques, 1993

Other books you might like:
Lynn Abbey, *Jerlayne*, 1999
Barbara Hambly, *The Armies of Daylight*, 1983
J.V. Jones, *A Cavern of Black Ice*, 1999
Larry Niven, *The Magic Goes Away*, 1978
Jennifer Roberson, *Legacy of the Sword*, 1986

511

TERRY BROOKS

Tanequil

(New York: Del Rey, 2004)

Story type: Sword and Sorcery; Magic Conflict
Series: Shannara. Book 13
Subject(s): Quest
Major character(s): Pen Ohmsford, Wizard; Tagwen, Mythical Creature (dwarf); Kermadec, Mythical Creature (troll)
Time period(s): Indeterminate
Locale(s): Shannara, Alternate Universe

Summary: Someone has kidnapped the High Druid of Shannara. A rescue operation sets out, consisting of a young wizard, a dwarf, and a troll, but their task is a difficult one. Even if they manage to succeed, that is only the first step in restoring peace to a world threatened by dark magic.

Where it's reviewed:
Booklist, June 1, 2004, page 1670
Library Journal, July 2004, page 75
Publishers Weekly, August 2, 2004, page 56

Other books by the same author:
Jarka Ruus, 2003
Antrax, 2001
The Ilse Witch, 2000
Angel Fire East, 1999
Running with the Demon, 1997

Other books you might like:
Louise Cooper, *The Outcast*, 1986
David Eddings, *The Seeress of Kell*, 1991
David Gemmell, *Waylander*, 1986
Robin Hobb, *Fool's Errand*, 2002
J.V. Jones, *The Barbed Coil*, 1997

512

JIM BUTCHER

Furies of Calderon
(New York: Ace, 2004)

Story type: Magic Conflict; Quest
Series: Codex Alera. Book 1
Subject(s): Quest
Major character(s): Gaius Sextus, Ruler; Tavi, Teenager; Amara, Spy
Time period(s): Indeterminate
Locale(s): Alera, Fictional Country

Summary: The people of Alera have been battling against hordes of unnatural creatures for generations, but the battle is going against them lately. The fact that their ruler is aging and has no apparent heir doesn't help. A teenager befriends a woman who appears to be a runaway slave only to discover she is actually a spy for the king, sent to identify those less than loyal.

Where it's reviewed:
Booklist, October 1, 2004, page 318
Chronicle, November 2004, page 41
Library Journal, September 15, 2004, page 52
Locus, September 2004, page 27
Publishers Weekly, September 27, 2004, page 42

Other books by the same author:
Death Masks, 2003
Summer Night, 2002
Fool Moon, 2001
Grave Peril, 2001
Storm Front, 2000

Other books you might like:
Susan Dexter, *The Wind-Witch*, 1994
Barbara Hambly, *Mother of Winter*, 1996
Naomi Kritzer, *Freedom's Gate*, 2004
Mickey Zucker Reichert, *The Legend of Nightfall*, 1993
Jane Welch, *The Lament of Abalone*, 1998

513

RICHARD LEE BYERS

The Rage
(Renton, Washington: Wizards of the Coast, 2004)

Story type: Sword and Sorcery; Magic Conflict
Series: Forgotten Realms: Year of Rogue Dragons. Book 1
Subject(s): Magic
Major character(s): Dorn Graybrook, Hunter, Mythical Creature (half-golem); Will Turnstone, Hunter; Kara, Traveler
Time period(s): Indeterminate
Locale(s): Faerun, Alternate Universe

Summary: Dorn Graybrook and his companions are professional dragon hunters, but they get more than they bargained for when a plague of madness infects the normally placid dragons of Faerun. Accompanied by a mysterious young woman they rescue from bandits, Dorn and his friends have a series of exciting adventures before discovering the reason for the change.

Other books by the same author:
Forbidden, 2003
The Black Bouquet, 2003
Dissolution, 2002
Forsaken, 2002
The Soul Killer, 1999

Other books you might like:
Katharine Kerr, *The Fire Dragon*, 2001
Richard A. Knaak, *The Day of the Dragon*, 2001
Dennis L. McKiernan, *Dragondoom*, 1990
Irene Radford, *The Renegade Dragon*, 1999
Lawrence Watt-Evans, *Dragon Venom*, 2003

514

RACHEL CAINE

Chill Factor
(New York: Roc, 2004)

Story type: Contemporary; Magic Conflict
Series: Weather Warden. Book 3
Subject(s): Magic; Disasters
Major character(s): Joanne Baldwin, Witch; Kevin, Teenager; David, Mythical Creature (djinn)
Time period(s): 2000s
Locale(s): Las Vegas, Nevada

Summary: Joanne Baldwin has had her human body restored after a brief stint as a djinn, but she might not have long to enjoy it. Most of the leaders of the secret organization of magicians who control the world's weather are dead, and a powerful djinn is planning to stir things up again.

Where it's reviewed:
Locus, November 2004, page 31

Other books by the same author:
Heat Stroke, 2004
Ill Wind, 2003

Other books you might like:
Emma Bull, *War for the Oaks*, 1987

Fantasy

Leah R. Cutter, *The Paper Mage*, 2003
Esther Friesner, *New York by Knight*, 1986
David Lee Jones, *The Unicorn Highway*, 2004
Gwyneth Jones, *Midnight Lamp*, 2003

515

JACQUELINE CAREY

Banewreaker

(New York: Tor, 2004)

Story type: Sword and Sorcery; Magic Conflict
Series: Sundering. Book 1
Subject(s): Quest
Major character(s): Tanaros Blacksword, Warrior; Satoris, Deity; Cerelinde, Noblewoman
Time period(s): Indeterminate
Locale(s): Alternate Universe

Summary: The world has been divided between two deities, each of whom believes the other to be evil. One of these is Satoris, whose chief defender is Tanaros Blacksword, a man grown bitter because of the death of his wife. When he is sent to rescue another woman, he discovers that he has not lost the capacity to love, and this discovery will alter the balance of power between the gods.

Where it's reviewed:
Chronicle, November 2004, page 40
Library Journal, October 15, 2004, page 57
Locus, November 2004, page 21
Publishers Weekly, September 13, 2004, page 63

Other books by the same author:
Kushiel's Avatar, 2003
Kushiel's Chosen, 2002
Kushiel's Dart, 2001

Other books you might like:
Stephen R. Donaldson, *The One Tree*, 1982
Jennifer Fallon, *Medalon*, 2000
L.E. Modesitt Jr., *Darksong Rising*, 1999
Jo Walton, *The King's Peace*, 2000
Lawrence Watt-Evans, *Night of Madness*, 2000

516

DEBORAH CHESTER

The Queen's Knight

(New York: Ace, 2004)

Story type: Sword and Sorcery; Magic Conflict
Series: Queen's Gambit. Book 3
Subject(s): Magic; Quest
Major character(s): Pheresa, Ruler (queen); Sir Talmor, Knight
Time period(s): Indeterminate
Locale(s): Mandria, Fictional Country

Summary: In order to rescue Queen Pheresa from her enemies, Sir Talmor is forced to reveal the fact that he has magical talents, which results in his banishment in disgrace. Pheresa doubly regrets the necessity, because she knows she will have

cause to rely on his loyalty in the future, as there is more than one plot against the throne.

Other books by the same author:
The King Betrayed, 2003
The Queen's Gambit, 2002
The Chalice, 2001
Realm of Light, 1997
Realm of Shadows, 1996

Other books you might like:
Anne Bishop, *Queen of Darkness*, 2000
Teresa Edgerton, *The Queen's Necklace*, 2001
Eileen Kernaghan, *The Snow Queen*, 2000
Katherine Kurtz, *In the King's Service*, 2003
Jo Walton, *The King's Peace*, 2000

517

SUSANNA CLARKE

Jonathan Strange & Mr. Norrell

(New York: Bloomsbury, 2004)

Story type: Historical; Magic Conflict
Subject(s): Magicians
Major character(s): Jonathan Strange, Magician; Mr. Norrell, Scholar, Magician; John Segundus, Magician
Time period(s): 1810s (1817); 1800s (1806)
Locale(s): England

Summary: In an alternate version of the early 19th century, a man emerges with magical powers that make him a celebrity. When a second magician appears, the two men form a partnership, but the younger man's ambitions and desire for greater power precipitate a crisis.

Where it's reviewed:
Booklist, July 2004, page 1797
Library Journal, August 2004, page 64
Locus, August 2004, page 19
New Yorker, September 13, 2004, page 89
Publishers Weekly, August 9, 2004, page 133

Other books you might like:
James P. Blaylock, *Homunculus*, 1986
Paul Di Filippo, *The Steampunk Trilogy*, 1996
Mark Frost, *The List of Seven*, 1993
Barbara Hambly, *Bride of the Rat God*, 1994
Christopher Priest, *The Prestige*, 1995

518

DAWN COOK

Lost Truth

(New York: Ace, 2004)

Story type: Light Fantasy; Magic Conflict
Series: Truth. Book 4
Subject(s): Magic; Gender Roles
Major character(s): Alissa, Sorceress; Keribdis, Sorceress, Teacher; Connen-Neute, Teacher
Time period(s): Indeterminate
Locale(s): The Hold, Mythical Place

Summary: Alissa is finally learning to master her magical powers but there is considerable disagreement among the faculty about who should be teaching her, and what she should be taught. Keribdis, a powerful and talented sorceress in her own right, forces the issue and violence ensues.

Other books by the same author:
Forgotten Truth, 2003
Hidden Truth, 2002
The First Truth, 2002

Other books you might like:
Deborah Christian, *The Truthsayer's Apprentice*, 1999
Dave Duncan, *Sir Stalwart*, 1999
Katharine Kerr, *The Red Wyvern*, 1997
Mindy L. Klasky, *The Glasswright's Apprentice*, 2001
Mercedes Lackey, *Owlsight*, 1998

519

BRUCE R. CORDELL

Lady of Poison

(Renton, Washington: Wizards of the Coast, 2004)

Story type: Sword and Sorcery; Magic Conflict
Series: Forgotten Realms: The Priests
Subject(s): Quest; Magic
Major character(s): Marrec, Warrior; Gunggari Ulmarra, Warrior; Gameliel, Sorcerer
Time period(s): Indeterminate
Locale(s): Alternate Universe

Summary: Evil sorcery is brewing once again, and the local priesthood may not be capable of holding back the minions of the Rotting Man and his unholy allies. Two itinerant warriors wander into the middle of the upheaval and prove instrumental in turning back the forces of evil. This is the author's first novel under his own name.

Other books you might like:
Ed Greenwood, *The Dragon's Doom*, 2003
Jeff Grubb, *The Last Guardian*, 2002
Scott McGough, *Champion's Trial*, 2003
Andrew J. Offutt, *The Shadow of Sorcery*, 1993
R.A. Salvatore, *Immortalis*, 2003

520

BEN COUNTER

Grey Knights

(Nottingham, England: Black Library, 2004)

Story type: Science Fiction; Magic Conflict
Series: Warhammer
Subject(s): Magic
Major character(s): Grand Master Mandulis, Military Personnel; Alaric, Religious; Gholic Valinov, Government Official (inquisitor)
Time period(s): Indeterminate Future
Locale(s): Outer Space

Summary: Although this novel involves space ships traveling to distant stars and using high tech weaponry, their opponents are demons and their minions. The Grey Knights are an elite corps used for particularly dangerous assignments, but this time they may finally have met their match.

Other books by the same author:
The Bleeding Chalice, 2003
Soul Drinker, 2002

Other books you might like:
Dan Abnett, *Sabbat Martyr*, 2003
Barrington J. Bayley, *Eye of Terror*, 2000
William King, *Space Wolf*, 2000
David Mason, *The Deep Gods*, 1973
Gav Thorpe, *Annihilation Squad*, 2004

521

F. BRETT COX, Editor
ANDY DUNCAN, Co-Editor

Crossroads

(New York: Tor, 2004)

Story type: Anthology
Subject(s): Short Stories; American South

Summary: This is an anthology of both original and reprinted stories by various writers from the southern region of the United States, designed to show the regional influence on their work. Among those contributing are Gene Wolfe, Michael Bishop, Fred Chappell, Scott Edelman, Kelly Link, and Michael Swanwick. The stories range from light contemporary fantasy to near horror.

Other books you might like:
Michael Bishop, *Brighten to Incandescence*, 2003
Fred Chappell, *Dagon*, 1968
Scott Edelman, *These Woods Are Haunted*, 2001
Kelly Link, *Stranger Things Happen*, 2001
Michael Swanwick, *Jack Faust*, 1997

522

ELAINE CUNNINGHAM

Shadows in the Darkness

(New York: Tor, 2004)

Story type: Contemporary; Mystery
Subject(s): Secrets
Major character(s): Gwen "GiGi" Gelman, Detective—Private; Carl Jamison, Criminal; Diane Cody, Businesswoman
Time period(s): 2000s
Locale(s): Providence, Rhode Island

Summary: After being scapegoated out of the police force, Gwen Gelman opens a private detective agency and is doing pretty well until she becomes involved with repeated cases of missing teenagers. The first one is found brutally murdered and the second seems to have disappeared off the face of the Earth. Her investigations will eventually uncover evidence that ancient magic still exists in the modern world, and that she has some talent in that area herself.

Where it's reviewed:
Booklist, October 15, 2004, page 394

Chronicle, October 2004, page 25
Library Journal, September 15, 2004, page 52
Locus, December 2004, page 31
Publishers Weekly, September 13, 2004, page 63

Other books by the same author:
Dark Journey, 2002
The Wizardwar, 2002
The Floodgate, 2001
The Magehound, 2000
Evermeet, 1998

Other books you might like:
Mignon Ballard, *An Angel to Die For*, 2001
Glen Cook, *Faded Steel Heat*, 1999
Diane Duane, *Stealing the Elf-King's Roses*, 2002
Esther Friesner, *Druid's Blood*, 1988
J. Michael Reaves, *Darkworld Detective*, 1982

523

ELLEN DATLOW, Editor
KELLY LINK, Co-Editor
GAVIN J. GRANT, Co-Editor

The Year's Best Fantasy and Horror: Seventeenth Annual Collection
(New York: St Martin's Griffin, 2004)

Story type: Anthology
Subject(s): Short Stories

Summary: This is the latest in an ongoing series of very large selections of the best short fiction of the previous year, accompanied by lengthy essays on the state of the two genres. Stories selected include tales by Kij Johnson, Nina Kiriki Hoffman, Stephen King, Marc Laidlaw, Lucius Shepard, Neil Gaiman, Ursula K. Le Guin, Karen Joy Fowler, and many others.

Other books by the same author:
The Dark, 2003
Lethal Kisses, 1996
Twists of the Tale, 1996
Little Deaths, 1994
Blood Is Not Enough, 1989

Other books you might like:
Nina Kiriki Hoffman, *Past the Size of Dreaming*, 2001
Kij Johnson, *Fudoki*, 2003
Stephen King, *Everything's Eventual*, 2002
Marc Laidlaw, *The 37th Mandala*, 1996
Lucius Shepard, *Two Trains Running*, 2004

524

STEPHEN R. DONALDSON

The Runes of the Earth
(New York: Putnam, 2004)

Story type: Magic Conflict; Alternate Universe
Series: Last Chronicles of Thomas Covenant. Book 1
Subject(s): Magic

Major character(s): Linden Avery, Doctor; Roger Covenant, Murderer; Stave, Warrior
Time period(s): 2000s
Locale(s): United States; The Land, Alternate Universe

Summary: Dr. Linden Avery is overseeing the care of the late Thomas Covenant's mentally ill wife when his son, Roger, arrives announcing that with the coming of maturity, he has decided to take charge of his mother. He subsequently kidnaps her and Avery's adopted child, and she pursues them into the alternate world of The Land, where Lord Foul is once again threatening to destroy the world.

Where it's reviewed:
Locus, October 2004, page 33

Other books by the same author:
Reave the Just, 1999
Chaos and Order, 1994
A Man Rides Through, 1987
The One Tree, 1982
Lord Foul's Bane, 1977

Other books you might like:
Terry Brooks, *The Sword of Shannara*, 1977
E.R. Eddison, *The Worm Ouroboros*, 1922
Robert Jordan, *The Eye of the World*, 1990
George R.R. Martin, *A Game of Thrones*, 1996
J.R.R. Tolkien, *The Fellowship of the Ring*, 1954

525

SARA DOUGLASS

The Nameless Day
(New York: Tor, 2004)

Story type: Historical; Quest
Series: Crucible. Book 1
Subject(s): Angels
Major character(s): Brother Thomas Neville, Religious; Prior Bertrand, Religious; Lady Margaret Rivers, Noblewoman
Time period(s): 14th century (1378-1379)
Locale(s): Germany; Italy

Summary: Brother Thomas Neville has a problem. Angels have appeared to him and directed him to accomplish unusual tasks, but devils have also been competing for his attention. As his progress across 14th-century Europe continues, he begins to wonder if he has correctly identified which are which. This novel was previously published in Australia in 2000.

Where it's reviewed:
Booklist, July 2004, page 1828
Library Journal, June 15, 2004, page 62
Publishers Weekly, June 21, 2004, page 47

Other books by the same author:
Gods' Concubine, 2004
Beyond the Hanging Wall, 2003
Hades' Daughter, 2003
Enchanter, 1996
Sinner, 1987

Other books you might like:
Gael Baudino, *Branch and Crown*, 1996

Ann Chamberlin, *The Merlin of Oak Wood*, 2001
Thomas Harlan, *The Shadow of Ararat*, 1999
Gail Van Asten, *Charlemagne's Champion*, 1990
Chelsea Quinn Yarbro, *The Soul of an Angel*, 1999

526

SARA DOUGLASS

Sinner
(New York: Tor, 2004)

Story type: Sword and Sorcery; Magic Conflict
Series: Wayfarer Redemption. Book 4
Subject(s): Quest
Major character(s): Caelum SunSoar, Ruler; Dragonstar SunSoar, Criminal, Rebel; Wolfstar SunSoar, Wizard
Time period(s): Indeterminate
Locale(s): Tencendor, Fictional Country

Summary: In a world where three intelligent races have lived in conflict for many years, the SunSoar family—endowed with superhuman powers—have finally defeated a monstrous enemy and brought peace to the land. Now a rebellious member of their own family threatens to bring fresh havoc. This novel was previously published in England in 1997.

Where it's reviewed:
Booklist, September 15, 2004, page 215

Other books by the same author:
Gods' Concubine, 2004
Beyond the Hanging Wall, 2003
Hades' Daughter, 2003
Crusader, 1997
Enchanter, 1996

Other books you might like:
James Barclay, *Light Stealer*, 2003
Raymond E. Feist, *A Darkness at Sethanon*, 1986
Maggie Furey, *Dhammara*, 1997
Naomi Kritzer, *Turning the Storm*, 2003
Tad Williams, *To Green Angel Tower*, 1993

527

DAVID DRAKE

Master of the Cauldron
(New York: Tor, 2004)

Story type: Sword and Sorcery; Magic Conflict
Series: Lord of the Isles. Book 6
Subject(s): Magic
Major character(s): Garric or-Reiss, Ruler; Cashel, Shepherd; Ilsa, Witch
Time period(s): Indeterminate
Locale(s): Sandrakkan, Fictional Country

Summary: In an effort to unite the various islands under his rule, a king and his entourage visit the island of Sandrakkan, where they become involved in a variety of local court intrigues. Not only does the local aristocracy want its independence, but they are prepared to use violence and treachery to ensure they have control of the local throne.

Other books by the same author:
Grimmer than Hell, 2003
The Far Side of the Stars, 2003
Paying the Piper, 2002
Mistress of the Catacombs, 2001
With the Lightnings, 1998

Other books you might like:
Ed Greenwood, *The Kingless Land*, 2000
L.E. Modesitt Jr., *Scepters*, 2004
Andre Norton, *The Warding of Witch World*, 1996
Andrew J. Offutt, *The Iron Lords*, 1979
R.A. Salvatore, *The Demon Apostle*, 1999

528

DAVE DUNCAN

The Jaguar Knights
(New York: Eos, 2004)

Story type: Sword and Sorcery; Quest
Series: King's Blades. Book 6
Subject(s): Quest
Major character(s): Sir Wolf, Knight; Dolores Hogwood, Government Official (inquisitor); Sir Lynx, Knight
Time period(s): Indeterminate
Locale(s): Chivial, Fictional Country; Tlixilia, Fictional Country

Summary: A remote outpost of Chivial is attacked by a horde of strangely dressed warriors and at least two inhuman creatures, aided by a form of sorcery previously unknown. An unpopular knight and a young female inquisitor are given the job of investigating the event, and then tracking down the source of the powerful new magic, in hope of gaining its secret.

Where it's reviewed:
Booklist, September 1, 2004, page 74
Publishers Weekly, July 12, 2004, page 48

Other books by the same author:
Paragon Lost, 2002
Sky of Swords, 2000
The Crooked House, 2000
Future Indefinite, 1997
Cursed, 1995

Other books you might like:
Steven Brust, *The Phoenix Guards*, 1991
L. Sprague de Camp, *The Clocks of Iraz*, 1971
Raymond E. Feist, *The King's Buccaneer*, 1992
Fritz Leiber, *Lean Times in Lankhmar*, 1996
Andrew J. Offutt, *Conan the Mercenary*, 1980

529

ROBERT EARL

The Burning Shore
(Nottingham, England: Black Library, 2004)

Story type: Sword and Sorcery; Military
Series: Warhammer
Subject(s): Magic

Major character(s): Florinn D'Artaud, Nobleman, Mercenary; Lorenzo, Mercenary; Mordicio, Mercenary
Time period(s): Indeterminate
Locale(s): Lustria, Fictional Country

Summary: A nobleman who ruined his reputation and exhausted his fortune decides to make a new life for himself as head of a band of mercenaries. The group travels to a distant part of Lustria for their first job, in a land covered by an immense and unforgiving jungle. First novel.

Other books you might like:
Del Dowdell, *The Warlord of Ghandor*, 1977
Richard A. Knaak, *Land of the Minotaurs*, 1996
Neil McIntosh, *Taint of Evil*, 2003
Andrew J. Offutt, *Shadowspawn*, 1987
Mike Sirota, *Flight from Berbora*, 1978

530

JENNIFER FALLON

Treason Keep
(New York: Tor, 2004)

Story type: Quest; Magic Conflict
Series: Hythrun Chronicles. Book 2
Subject(s): Magic
Major character(s): Tarja Tenragen, Nobleman; Hablet, Ruler (king); Damin Wolfblade, Nobleman
Time period(s): Indeterminate
Locale(s): Medalon, Fictional Country

Summary: The evil queen of Medalon has been defeated, but even worse may follow in her wake. A rival kingdom has mounted an invasion force, while scheming to form secret political alliances. At the same time, the protagonist must find a magical cure for his sister, who was mortally wounded at the conclusion of *Medalon*, the first volume in the series.

Where it's reviewed:
Booklist, November 15, 2004, page 571
Publishers Weekly, September 6, 2004, page 50

Other books by the same author:
Lord of the Shadows, 2003
Eye of the Labyrinth, 2002
The Lion of Senet, 2002
Medalon, 2000

Other books you might like:
Richard Lee Byers, *The Shattered Mask*, 2001
Storm Constantine, *The Way of Light*, 2001
Stephen R. Donaldson, *A Man Rides Through*, 1987
Paul S. Kemp, *Shadow's Witness*, 2000
Tad Williams, *Shadowmarch. Volume 1*, 2004

531

MICK FARREN

Kindling
(New York: Tor, 2004)

Story type: Alternate History; Magic Conflict
Subject(s): Alternate History

Major character(s): Argo Weaver, Teenager; Cordelia Blakeney, Noblewoman; Raphael Vega, Military Personnel
Time period(s): Indeterminate
Locale(s): Alternate Universe

Summary: In an alternate version of our world, Europe has been conquered by a barbaric nation ruled by a fanatical religious cult. They turn their attention to the New World where their supernatural beasts of war seem likely to annihilate anyone who opposes them. The best hope for resistance consists of four disparate people with unusual abilities.

Where it's reviewed:
Booklist, August 2004, page 1912
Library Journal, August 2004, page 73

Other books by the same author:
Underland, 2002
More than Mortal, 2001
Darklost, 2000
The Time of Feasting, 1996
The Feelies, 1990

Other books you might like:
Neal Barrett Jr., *The Leaves of Time*, 1971
William Gibson, *The Difference Engine*, 1991
    Bruce Sterling, co-author
J. Gregory Keyes, *Newton's Cannon*, 1998
Charles Stross, *The Atrocity Archives*, 2004
Roger Zelazny, *A Dark Traveling*, 1987

532

BILL FAWCETT, Editor

Masters of Fantasy
(New York: Baen, 2004)

Story type: Anthology
Subject(s): Short Stories

Summary: This book contains 12 all new short stories by prominent fantasy writers, each set in the recurring universe of one or another of their ongoing series. The contributors include Andre Norton, Mercedes Lackey, David Drake, Alan Dean Foster, Elizabeth Moon, Janny Wurts, and others.

Other books by the same author:
Cats in Space and Other Places, 2002
Cold Steel, 2002
Honor of the Regiment, 1993
Dangerous Interfaces, 1990
The Far Stars War, 1990

Other books you might like:
David Drake, *Lord of the Isles*, 1997
Alan Dean Foster, *The Moment of the Magician*, 1984
Mercedes Lackey, *Alta*, 2004
Elizabeth Moon, *Liar's Oath*, 1992
Janny Wurts, *Peril's Gate*, 2002

533

RAYMOND E. FEIST

Exile's Return

(New York: Eos, 2004)

Story type: Sword and Sorcery; Magic Conflict
Series: Conclave of Shadows. Book 3
Subject(s): Magic; Quest
Major character(s): Kaspar, Nobleman (duke), Expatriate; Jorgen, Child; McGoin, Warrior
Time period(s): Indeterminate
Locale(s): Midkemia, Alternate Universe

Summary: Duke Kaspar has been sent into exile after his despotic rule is brought to an end. Humbled, he seeks employment in various ways, eventually building a new life for himself, but in the process of doing so he discovers a new magical threat that could endanger all of Midkemia, and becomes an unlikely hero in order to save the day.

Other books by the same author:
King of Foxes, 2003
Talon of the Silver Hawk, 2003
Tear of the Gods, 2001
Krondor the Assassins, 1999
Krondor the Betrayal, 1999

Other books you might like:
Dave Duncan, *The Jaguar Knights*, 2004
Simon R. Green, *Blue Moon Rising*, 1991
George R.R. Martin, *A Game of Thrones*, 1996
R.A. Salvatore, *The Highwayman*, 2004
Lawrence Watt-Evans, *Dragon Weather*, 1999

534

CATHERINE FISHER

Snow-Walker

(New York: Greenwillow, 2004)

Story type: Young Adult; Sword and Sorcery
Subject(s): Magic
Major character(s): Gudrun, Mythical Creature; Jessa Horolfsdaughter, Expatriate; Skapti, Minstrel
Time period(s): Indeterminate
Locale(s): Europa, Alternate Universe

Summary: This is a combined edition of the complete trilogy consisting of *The Snow-Walker's Son*, *The Empty Hand*, and *The Soul Thieves*, originally published separately between 1994 and 1996. The magically powerful creature Gudrun threatens a world that resembles that of the Vikings, but is eventually defeated by a young girl and a bard.

Where it's reviewed:
Booklist, September 1, 2004, page 106
Publishers Weekly, November 15, 2004, page 61
School Library Journal, November 2004, page 143

Other books by the same author:
The Oracle Betrayed, 2004

Other books you might like:
Poul Anderson, *The Broken Sword*, 1954

Linda Evans, *Sleipnir*, 1994
H. Rider Haggard, *Eric Brighteyes*, 1891
Juliet Marillier, *Foxmask*, 2004
Lars Walker, *Wolf Time*, 1999

535

ESTHER FRIESNER, Editor

Turn the Other Chick

(New York: Baen, 2004)

Story type: Anthology
Series: Chicks in Chainmail. Book 5
Subject(s): Short Stories; Women Soldiers

Summary: This is the fifth anthology about assertive female warriors, primarily fantasies. The authors in this work are predominantely newer or lesser known writers, but there are stories by Harry Turtledove, J. Ardian Lee, Laura Frankos, Robin Bailey, Eric Flint, and other more familiar names. The themes range from adventure to humor.

Where it's reviewed:
Chronicle, November 2004, page 41

Other books by the same author:
Death and the Librarian, 2002
Up the Wall, 2000
To Storm Heaven, 1997
Wishing Season, 1996
The Sherwood Game, 1995

Other books you might like:
Lynn Abbey, *The Black Flame*, 1980
Jennifer Fallon, *The Lion of Senet*, 2002
Jessica Amanda Salmonson, *The Swordswoman*, 1982
Carol Severance, *Demon Drums*, 1992
Judith Tarr, *The Lady of Han-Gilen*, 1987

536

R. GARCIA Y ROBERTSON

White Rose

(New York: Forge, 2004)

Story type: Time Travel; Romance
Series: Lady Robyn. Book 2
Subject(s): Time Travel
Major character(s): Robyn Stafford, Time Traveler; Edward Plantagenet, Royalty, Historical Figure; Lady Elizabeth, Noblewoman
Time period(s): 15th century
Locale(s): England

Summary: Robyn Stafford has found a way to slip back through time to the 15th century, where she becomes romantically involved with the nobleman Edward Plantagenet. Her habits and preferences from the modern world clash with the environment in which she finds herself, but she becomes adept at finding a way through the intricacies of court intrigues.

Where it's reviewed:
Chronicle, October 2004, page 252

Locus, October 2004, page 62

Other books by the same author:
Lady Robyn, 2003
Knight Errant, 2001
Atlantis Found, 1997
The Virgin and the Dinosaur, 1996
The Spiral Dance, 1991

Other books you might like:
Elaine Bergstrom, *The Door through Washington Square*, 1998
John Dickson Carr, *The Devil in Velvet*, 1951
Louise Cooper, *The Outcast*, 1986
Thomas B. Costain, *Below the Salt*, 1957
Diana Gabaldon, *Voyager*, 1994

537

MARC GASCOIGNE, Editor
CHRISTIAN DUNN, Co-Editor

Swords of the Empire

(Nottingham, England: Black Library, 2004)

Story type: Anthology
Series: Warhammer
Subject(s): Short Stories
Time period(s): Indeterminate
Locale(s): Earth

Summary: This is a collection of six original stories set in the Warhammer shared universe series set on Earth during a dark age when sorcery and monsters both make life more dangerous. The contributors include Dan Abnett, C.L. Werner, Gordon Rennie, Jonathan Green, Robert Earl, and James Wallis.

Other books by the same author:
Lords of Valour, 2001 (Christian Dunn, co-editor)
Into the Maelstrom, 2000 (Andy Jones, co-editor)

Other books you might like:
Dan Abnett, *Ravenor*, 2004
Jonathan Green, *The Dead and the Damned*, 2002
Gordon Rennie, *Shadow Point*, 2003
James Wallis, *The Mark of Heresy*, 2003
C.L. Werner, *Blood Money*, 2003

538

LAURA ANNE GILMAN

Staying Dead

(New York: LUNA, 2004)

Story type: Romance; Mystery
Subject(s): Magic
Major character(s): Wren Valere, Detective—Private; Oliver Frants, Businessman; Sergei, Detective—Private
Time period(s): 20th century
Locale(s): New York, New York

Summary: In an alternate version of our world in which magic works, Wren Valere is an investigator with a special talent for finding things. When she is hired to find out what happened to a stolen magical artifact, she finds herself involved with demons, wizardry, and other magical occurrences.

Where it's reviewed:
Locus, September 2004, page 27

Other books you might like:
Emma Bull, *Finder*, 1994
Esther Friesner, *New York by Knight*, 1986
Laurell K. Hamilton, *Seduced by Moonlight*, 2004
Mike Resnick, *Stalking the Unicorn*, 1987
Will Shetterly, *Elsewhere*, 1991

539

CHRISTIE GOLDEN

On Fire's Wings

(New York: LUNA, 2004)

Story type: Romance; Quest
Subject(s): Quest
Major character(s): Kevla Bai-sha, Worker; Jashemi-kha-Tahmu, Nobleman, Rebel; Yeshi, Leader
Time period(s): Indeterminate
Locale(s): Arukan, Fictional Country

Summary: A young woman who is prone to prophetic dreams finds a new life for herself in the company of a rebel prince in a magical kingdom facing a supernatural threat. The two set out on a quest to find salvation for their people and fall in love during the course of their adventures.

Other books by the same author:
Lord of the Clans, 2001
Instrument of Fate, 1996
The Enemy Within, 1994
Dance of the Dead, 1992
Vampire of the Mists, 1991

Other books you might like:
Wayland Drew, *Dragonslayer*, 1981
Mick Farren, *Kindling*, 2004
Elizabeth Haydon, *Rhapsody*, 1999
L.E. Modesitt Jr., *Legacies*, 2002
Lawrence Watt-Evans, *Dragon Weather*, 1999

540

MARTIN H. GREENBERG, Editor
JOHN HELFERS, Co-Editor

Little Red Riding Hood in the Big Bad City

(New York: DAW, 2004)

Story type: Anthology
Subject(s): Short Stories; Fairy Tales

Summary: This anthology includes 17 stories, none published previously, each of which involves a traditional fairy tale character but in a modern, urban setting. The contributors provide varied interpretations of the concept. Included are stories by Alan Dean Foster, Tanya Huff, Fiona Patton, Jean Rabe, Michelle West, and others.

Other books by the same author:
Merlin, 1999
Elf Fantastic, 1997
Wizard Fantastic, 1997
Elf Magic, 1997
Against the King, 1992

Other books you might like:
Alan Dean Foster, *The Kingdoms of Light*, 2001
Tanya Huff, *Smoke and Shadows*, 2004
Fiona Patton, *The Golden Sword*, 2001
Jean Rabe, *Redemption*, 2002
Michelle West, *The Sun Sword*, 2004

541

MICHELE HAUF

Seraphim
(New York: LUNA, 2004)

Story type: Romance; Historical
Subject(s): Magic
Major character(s): Lucifer de Morte, Nobleman; Seraphim D'Ange, Warrior; Dominique San Juste, Traveler
Time period(s): 15th century (1433)
Locale(s): France

Summary: Amidst the chaos of 15th-century France, a band of marauders under an ambitious and magically empowered nobleman are busily establishing control over ever greater portions of the countryside. Their efforts are opposed by a mysterious knight who is actually a woman seeking vengeance for the murder of her family.

Where it's reviewed:
Library Journal, May 15, 2004, page 70

Other books you might like:
Gael Baudino, *Maze of Moonlight*, 1993
Jessica Bryan, *Across a Wine Dark Sea*, 1991
Ann Chamberlin, *The Merlin of St. Gilles' Well*, 1999
Sara Douglass, *The Nameless Day*, 2004
Gail Van Asten, *The Dark Sword's Lover*, 1990

542

ELIZABETH HAYDON

Elegy for a Lost Star
(New York: Tor, 2004)

Story type: Sword and Sorcery; Magic Conflict
Series: Symphony of Ages. Book 5
Subject(s): Magic
Major character(s): Rhapsody, Singer; Achmed, Ruler; Grunthor, Warrior
Time period(s): Indeterminate
Locale(s): Alternate Universe

Summary: Although part of a series, this volume is independent of the ongoing story line. The political situation in a magical world is rapidly deteriorating, and a number of innocent people get caught up in the ensuing chaos as the country slides toward war.

Where it's reviewed:
Booklist, August 2004, page 1913
Publishers Weekly, July 12, 2004, page 48

Other books by the same author:
Requiem for the Sun, 2003
Destiny, 2001
Prophecy, 2000
Rhapsody, 1999

Other books you might like:
Sarah Ash, *Songspinners*, 1996
Greg Bear, *The Serpent Mage*, 1986
Alan Dean Foster, *Spellsinger*, 1983
L.E. Modesitt Jr., *Darksong Rising*, 1999
Patricia Wrede, *The Harp of Imach Thyssel*, 1985

543

CORY J. HERNDON

The Fifth Dawn
(Renton, Washington: Wizards of the Coast, 2004)

Story type: Sword and Sorcery; Magic Conflict
Series: Magic the Gathering
Subject(s): Magic
Major character(s): Glissa, Mythical Creature (elf); Slobad, Mythical Creature (goblin); Bruenna, Wizard
Time period(s): Indeterminate
Locale(s): Mirrodin, Fictional Country

Summary: An elf, a goblin, and a human wizard make their way from one place to another, seeking allies in their battle against the evil sorcery that threatens to engulf the entire world. They are pursued by the magic and the minions of a powerful and furious enemy. First novel.

Other books you might like:
Clayton Emery, *Hazezon*, 2002
Simon R. Green, *Beyond the Blue Moon*, 2000
J. Robert King, *Onslaught*, 2002
Mercedes Lackey, *Exile's Honor*, 2002
Sarah Zettel, *The Firebird's Vengeance*, 2004

544

JAMES A. HETLEY

The Winter Oak
(New York: Ace, 2004)

Story type: Contemporary; Light Fantasy
Series: Oak. Book 2
Subject(s): Legends
Major character(s): Maureen Pierce, Witch; Brian Albion, Warrior; Fiona, Witch
Time period(s): 2000s
Locale(s): Maine; Mythical Place

Summary: Maureen Pierce and her sister have gained access to an alternate reality where magic works, and where Maureen is romantically involved with a local warrior. Her sister wants to return to our world, particularly when it becomes obvious that the malevolent witch Fiona is jealous of Maureen's growing magical talents.

Where it's reviewed:
Booklist, November 15, 2004, page 571
Library Journal, October 15, 2004, page 57
Locus, November 2004, page 66
Publishers Weekly, October 11, 2004, page 61

Other books by the same author:
The Summer Country, 2002

Other books you might like:
Emma Bull, *War for the Oaks*, 1987
Pamela Dean, *The Dubious Hills*, 1994
Craig Shaw Gardner, *The Dragon Sleeping*, 1994
Sarah A. Hoyt, *Ill Met by Moonlight*, 2001
Mickey Zucker Reichert, *The Lost Dragons of Barakhai*, 2002

545

MADELINE HOWARD

The Hidden Stars

(New York: Eos, 2004)

Story type: Sword and Sorcery; Magic Conflict
Series: Rune of Unmaking. Book 1
Subject(s): Magic
Major character(s): Sinderian, Noblewoman; Nione, Wizard; Ouriana, Ruler (empress)
Time period(s): Indeterminate
Locale(s): Alternate Universe

Summary: A magical war devastates the world and leaves Empress Ouriana as a despotic ruler because she is one of the few survivors capable of using sorcery. Others who lived have been transformed in horrible ways and the magic that accompanies them is unpredictable. Years later, there are signs and predictions that change is near, and that young Sinderian is destined to be the catalyst. First novel.

Where it's reviewed:
Library Journal, November 15, 2004, page 54
Publishers Weekly, October 4, 2004, page 34

Other books you might like:
Jacqueline Carey, *Kushiel's Dart*, 2001
Sara Douglass, *Enchanter*, 1996
Elizabeth Haydon, *Elegy for a Lost Star*, 2004
Laura Resnick, *In Legends Born*, 1998
Jo Walton, *The Prize in the Game*, 2002

546

ROBERT E. HOWARD

The Bloody Crown of Conan

(New York: Del Rey, 2004)

Story type: Collection; Sword and Sorcery
Subject(s): Short Stories
Major character(s): Conan, Barbarian
Time period(s): Indeterminate Past
Locale(s): Europe

Summary: This work contains three stories featuring Conan, the barbarian swordsman who battles monsters, men, and magic in a prehistoric Europe. Also included in this volume is a collection of synopses and other materials recovered from Howard's papers, plus background material and notes on the text. Conan was the prototype for all the barbarian heroes who have followed.

Where it's reviewed:
Chronicle, November 2004, page 45

Other books by the same author:
The Savage Tales of Solomon Kane, 2004
The Hour of the Dragon, 2001
Eons of the Night, 1986
The Worm of the Earth, 1979
Red Nails, 1977

Other books you might like:
L. Sprague de Camp, *Conan the Swordsman*, 1978
Lin Carter, co-author
John Jakes, *Brak the Barbarian*, 1968
Robert Jordan, *Conan the Victorious*, 1984
Andrew J. Offutt, *Conan the Mercenary*, 1980
Karl Edward Wagner, *The Book of Kane*, 1985

547

ROBERT E. HOWARD

The Savage Tales of Solomon Kane

(New York: Del Rey, 2004)

Story type: Sword and Sorcery; Collection
Subject(s): Short Stories
Major character(s): Solomon Kane, Adventurer

Summary: The 16 stories in this collection were originally published during the 1920s and 1930s, and are now gathered with a short biography of the author and other material. They retell the varied magical adventures of Solomon Kane, who travels through Europe and Africa, encountering and defeating various supernatural foes.

Where it's reviewed:
Chronicle, October 2004, page 26

Other books by the same author:
Eons of the Night, 1996
Trails in the Darkness, 1996
Cthulhu, 1988
Kull, 1985
Black Canaan, 1978

Other books you might like:
Poul Anderson, *Conan the Rebel*, 1981
L. Sprague de Camp, *Conan the Liberator*, 1980
Fritz Leiber, *Ill Met in Lankhmar*, 1995
Andrew J. Offutt, *Sign of the Moonbow*, 1977
Karl Edward Wagner, *The Book of Kane*, 1985

548

KIM HUNTER

Scabbard's Song

(London: Orbit, 2004)

Story type: Sword and Sorcery; Magic Conflict

Series: Red Pavilions. Book 3
Subject(s): Magic
Major character(s): Soldier, Military Personnel, Amnesiac; Humbold, Ruler; Drummond, Military Personnel
Time period(s): Indeterminate
Locale(s): Alternate Universe

Summary: Soldier still hasn't been able to remember his real identity, lost when he awakened on a battlefield. He is now the leader of an army designed to ensure the peace, but he has doubts about his allegiance, his past, and deep suspicions of some of those whom he encounters. All of this builds toward the revelation of his own personal truth.

Where it's reviewed:
Chronicle, November 2004, page 44

Other books by the same author:
Wizard's Funeral, 2002
Knight's Dawn, 2001

Other books you might like:
James Barclay, *Nightchild*, 2001
Elaine Cunningham, *The Wizardwar*, 2002
Sara Douglass, *Beyond the Hanging Wall*, 2003
Mickey Zucker Reichert, *The Western Wizard*, 1992
Freda Warrington, *The Obsidian Tower*, 2001

549

ALEXANDER C. IRVINE

One King, One Soldier
(New York: Del Rey, 2004)

Story type: Historical; Mystical
Subject(s): Legends
Major character(s): Lance Porter, Military Personnel; Jack Spicer, Writer (poet), Historical Figure; Arthur Rimbaud, Writer (poet), Historical Figure
Time period(s): 1950s
Locale(s): New York, New York; San Francisco, California

Summary: Lance Porter has just returned from fighting in the Korean War and hopes to visit the girl he loves. Unfortunately, he encounters instead an offbeat poet who insists that Lance is the Fisher King and is fated to protect the Holy Grail from those who have been seeking it. He is initially skeptical and then increasingly concerned that he is not up to the task before him.

Where it's reviewed:
Booklist, July 2004, page 1828
Library Journal, July 2004, page 75

Other books by the same author:
A Scattering of Jades, 2002

Other books you might like:
James P. Blaylock, *The Paper Grail*, 1991
Leonora Carrington, *The Hearing Trumpet*, 1974
Molly Cochran, *The Forever King*, 1992
     Warren Murphy, co-author
Susan Cooper, *The Dark Is Rising*, 1973
Susan Shwartz, *The Grail of Hearts*, 1992

550

ANNE KELLEHER

Silver's Edge
(New York: LUNA, 2004)

Story type: Romance; Sword and Sorcery
Subject(s): Legends
Major character(s): Nessa, Teenager; Delphinea, Noblewoman; Cecily, Ruler
Time period(s): Indeterminate
Locale(s): Alternate Universe

Summary: A conspiracy is afoot to seize power not only in the Shadowlands where humans dwell, but across the mystical gap in the land of the Sidhe as well. The fate of both worlds lies in the hands of three women, one a queen, one a noble, and the other a teenager, all of whom will display surprising strength before the battle is over.

Where it's reviewed:
Publishers Weekly, May 24, 2004, page 49

Other books by the same author:
Love's Labyrinth, 2000
The Ghost and Katie Coyle, 1999
A Once and Future Love, 1998

Other books you might like:
Marion Zimmer Bradley, *Lady of Avalon*, 1997
Jennifer Fallon, *Medalon*, 2000
Michele Hauf, *Seraphim*, 2004
Diana L. Paxson, *Ancestors of Avalon*, 2004
Jessica Amanda Salmonson, *The Swordswoman*, 1982

551

PAUL S. KEMP

Dawn of Night
(Renton, Washington: Wizards of the Coast, 2004)

Story type: Sword and Sorcery; Magic Conflict
Series: Erevis Cale. Book 3
Subject(s): Magic
Major character(s): Erevis Cale, Sorcerer; Jak, Adventurer; Magadon, Psychic
Time period(s): Indeterminate
Locale(s): Alternate Universe

Summary: Erevis Cale and his companions have been accumulating arcane knowledge in their travels around the world, and now he has become a powerful master of sorcery. With that power comes the responsibility to use it wisely, and his next choice is whether or not to trust an ambiguous god whose worshippers seem more likely to be criminals than respected members of society.

Other books by the same author:
Twilight Falling, 2003
Shadow's Witness, 2000

Other books you might like:
Lynn Abbey, *Simbul's Gift*, 1997
Robin Wayne Bailey, *Swords Against the Shadowlands*, 1998
Simon R. Green, *The God Killer*, 1991

Robert E. Howard, *The Bloody Crown of Conan*, 2004
Fritz Leiber, *Ill Met in Lankhmar*, 1995

552

J. GREGORY KEYES

The Charnel Prince

(New York: Del Rey, 2004)

Story type: Sword and Sorcery; Magic Conflict
Series: Kingdoms of Thorn and Bone. Book 2
Subject(s): Magic
Major character(s): Sir Neil MeqVren, Knight; Anne Dare, Noblewoman; Leovigild Ackenzac, Composer
Time period(s): Indeterminate
Locale(s): Crotheny, Fictional Country

Summary: Ancient legends have begun to prove themselves true with the appearance of supposedly mythical creatures in the forests of Crotheny. The queen is caught in a power struggle with a militant church hierarchy and the heir to the throne has disappeared under mysterious circumstances.

Where it's reviewed:
Booklist, August 2004, page 1913
Library Journal, August 2004, page 73
Locus, July 2004, page 60

Other books by the same author:
The Briar King, 2003
The Empire of Unreason, 2000
A Calculus of Angels, 1999
Newton's Cannon, 1998
The Blackgod, 1997

Other books you might like:
Steven Brust, *Issola*, 2001
Storm Constantine, *The Way of Light*, 2001
David Gemmell, *Ravenheart*, 2001
Simon R. Green, *Beyond the Blue Moon*, 2000
Diana L. Paxson, *Lady of Darkness*, 1983

553

ROSEMARY KIRSTEIN

The Language of Power

(New York: Del Rey, 2004)

Story type: Magic Conflict; Quest
Series: Steerswoman. Book 4
Subject(s): Quest
Major character(s): Rowan, Traveler, Scholar; Jannik, Wizard; Bel, Agent
Time period(s): Indeterminate
Locale(s): Alternate Universe

Summary: A master wizard has reportedly been destroying all life in remote parts of the world. Rowan, a Steerswoman, sets out to track him down and discover why he has been acting so oddly, a journey that will expose her to a series of strange experiences and occasional dangers.

Where it's reviewed:
Booklist, August 2004, page 1913

Library Journal, August 2004, page 73
Publishers Weekly, July 26, 2004, page 42

Other books by the same author:
The Lost Steersman, 2003
The Outskirter's Secret, 1989
The Steerswoman, 1989

Other books you might like:
Gayle Greeno, *Sunderlies Seeking*, 1998
Barbara Hambly, *The Icefalcon's Quest*, 1998
Robin Hobb, *Ship of Magic*, 1998
China Mieville, *The Scar*, 2002
Jennifer Roberson, *The Shapechanger's Song*, 2001

554

TRYSTAM KITH

A Cold Summer Night

(Waterville, Maine: Five Star, 2004)

Story type: Historical; Magic Conflict
Series: Trouble in the Forest. Book 1
Subject(s): Magic; Legends
Major character(s): Hugh deSteny, Lawman (sheriff), Knight (former); Robin Hood, Criminal; Chilton, Agent
Time period(s): Indeterminate Past
Locale(s): England

Summary: Kith's book is part one of an unusual two volume variation of the legend of Robin Hood. Hugh deSteny is an ex-crusader ordered by his liege lord to hunt down the outlaws in Sherwood Forest. This Robin Hood and his band are not the likable rebels helping the downtrodden, but rather creatures who have fallen under the influence of dark magic. First novel.

Other books you might like:
Parke Godwin, *Robin and the King*, 1993
Paul Hazel, *The Wealdwife's Tale*, 1993
Robert Holdstock, *Merlin's Wood*, 1994
Sarah A. Hoyt, *Ill Met by Moonlight*, 2001
Judith Tarr, *The Devil's Bargain*, 2002

555

MINDY L. KLASKY

The Glasswright's Master

(New York: Roc, 2004)

Story type: Sword and Sorcery; Magic Conflict
Series: Glasswright. Book 5
Subject(s): Magic
Major character(s): Rani Trader, Artisan; Halaravilli, Ruler (king); Father Siritalanu, Religious
Time period(s): Indeterminate
Locale(s): Morenia, Fictional Country; Sarmonia, Fictional Country

Summary: Foreign armies have conquered Morenia, so the king and his adviser, Rani Trader, are in temporary exile while they seek allies to help them regain the throne. Rani's life is further complicated by the machinations of the leaders of her guild, and by other foreigners interested in manipulating events to their own advantage.

Other books by the same author:
The Glasswright's Test, 2003
Season of Justice, 2002
The Glasswright's Progress, 2002
The Glasswright's Journeyman, 2002
The Glasswright's Apprentice, 2001

Other books you might like:
Simon R. Green, *Beyond the Blue Moon*, 2000
Gayle Greeno, *Sunderlies Seeking*, 1998
Mercedes Lackey, *Storm Rising*, 1996
L.E. Modesitt Jr., *Legacies*, 2002
Diana L. Paxson, *The Wind Crystal*, 1990

556

RICHARD A. KNAAK

The Well of Eternity
(New York: Pocket Star, 2004)

Story type: Sword and Sorcery; Magic Conflict
Series: WarCraft: War of the Ancients. Book 1
Subject(s): Magic
Major character(s): Krasus, Mythical Creature (dragon); Rhonin, Wizard; Broxigar, Mythical Creature (orc)
Time period(s): Indeterminate
Locale(s): Azeroth, Fictional Country

Summary: In a time long past, a horde of inhuman creatures were expelled from Azeroth and magically barred from returning. That barrier is about to be opened, and the world will be consumed unless three unlikely heroes can convince a demigod to act on their behalf.

Other books by the same author:
The Kingdom of Shadow, 2002
Legacy of Blood, 2001
The Day of the Dragon, 2001
The Citadel, 2000
Dragon Crown, 1994

Other books you might like:
James Barclay, *Noonshade*, 2000
Leonard Carpenter, *Conan the Hero*, 1989
Stephen R. Donaldson, *Lord Foul's Bane*, 1977
David Gemmell, *The Dark Prince*, 1991
Andrew J. Offutt, *Shadowspawn*, 1987

557

NAOMI KRITZER

Freedom's Gate
(New York: Bantam, 2004)

Story type: Sword and Sorcery; Adventure
Series: Dead Rivers. Book 1
Subject(s): Quest
Major character(s): Lauria, Spy, Courier; Kyros, Military Personnel; Tamar, Warrior
Time period(s): Indeterminate
Locale(s): Alternate Universe

Summary: Although his magical world has enjoyed comparative peace, a military leader of one of the civilized nations believes that the barbarians are preparing for another outbreak of war. He sends Lauria, his trusted assistant and spy, to pose as a worker in their camps and discover their plans. She is successful in infiltrating the enemy camp, but her own loyalties become less certain in the process.

Where it's reviewed:
Locus, August 2004, page 19

Other books by the same author:
Turning the Storm, 2003
Fires of the Faithful, 2002

Other books you might like:
Lynn Abbey, *Daughter of the Bright Moon*, 1979
Doranna Durgin, *Wolverine's Daughter*, 2000
Michele Hauf, *Seraphim*, 2004
Anne Kelleher, *Silver's Edge*, 2004
Carol Severance, *Reefsong*, 1991

558

MERCEDES LACKEY
JAMES MALLORY, Co-Author

To Light a Candle
(New York: Tor, 2004)

Story type: Magic Conflict; Sword and Sorcery
Series: Obsidian Trilogy. Book 2
Subject(s): Elves
Major character(s): Kellen, Knight, Magician; Idalia, Witch; Jermayan, Mythical Creature (elf), Knight
Time period(s): Indeterminate
Locale(s): Alternate Universe

Summary: The evil Demon Queen has begun her campaign to rule the disparate lands of a magical alternate reality under her banner. Humans and elves, formerly allies and now on bad terms, find it difficult to overcome long-standing animosities to fight together. A human knight and his sister, both possessing magical abilities of their own, find their lives caught up with that of an elven knight.

Where it's reviewed:
Library Journal, October 15, 2004, page 57

Other books by the same author:
Alta, 2004
Exile's Valor, 2003
Joust, 2003
The Outstretched Shadow, 2003 (James Mallory, co-author)
Chrome Borne, 1999

Other books you might like:
James P. Blaylock, *The Elfin Ship*, 1982
Elaine Cunningham, *Evermeet*, 1998
Ed Greenwood, *Elminster in Myth Drannor*, 1997
Stan Nicholls, *Warriors of the Tempest*, 2000
R.A. Salvatore, *The Icewind Trilogy*, 2000

Fantasy

559

ROBIN D. LAWS

Sacred Flesh

(Nottingham, England: Black Library, 2004)

Story type: Sword and Sorcery; Magic Conflict
Series: Warhammer
Subject(s): Magic
Major character(s): Angelika Fleischer, Criminal (looter); Franziskus, Traveler; Eugen, Traveler
Time period(s): Indeterminate
Locale(s): Old World, Alternate Universe

Summary: Angelika Fleischer supports herself by looting battlefields, of which there are unfortunately a large number in her part of the Old World. She accepts a job as escort for a group of pilgrims, during which she is involved in and eventually solves a murder mystery against a backdrop of sorcery and evil magic.

Where it's reviewed:
Chronicle, October 2004, page 27

Other books by the same author:
Honour of the Grave, 2003

Other books you might like:
Randall Garrett, *Too Many Magicians*, 1966
Richard A. Knaak, *Frostwing*, 1995
Jess Lebow, *The Darksteel Eye*, 2004
David Mason, *The Deep Gods*, 1973
Graham McNeill, *Ursun's Teeth*, 2004

560

URSULA K. LE GUIN

Gifts

(New York: Harcourt, 2004)

Story type: Young Adult; Magic Conflict
Subject(s): Magic
Major character(s): Gry, Teenager, Psychic; Orrec, Teenager, Psychic; Brantor Erroy, Psychic
Time period(s): Indeterminate
Locale(s): Alternate Universe

Summary: This thoughtful young adult novel is set in a village where everyone has one form or another of psychic powers, which creates an uneasy but stable balance of power. That all changes when two teenagers from different families decide not to use their powers to perpetuate the atmosphere of suppressed conflict.

Where it's reviewed:
Horn Book Magazine, September-October 2004, page 589
Locus, September 2004, page 66
Publishers Weekly, July 19, 2004, page 163

Other books by the same author:
Changing Planes, 2003
Tales from Earthsea, 2001
The Other Wind, 2001
The Telling, 2000
Tehanu, 1990

Other books you might like:
Susan Cooper, *The Dark Is Rising*, 1973
Alan Garner, *The Weirdstone of Brisingamen*, 1960
Paul Hazel, *The Wealdwife's Tale*, 1993
William Morris, *The Glittering Plain*, 1991
Jane Yolen, *The Wild Hunt*, 1995

561

JANE LINDSKOLD

Wolf Captured

(New York: Tor, 2004)

Story type: Adventure; Psychic Powers
Series: Wolf. Book 4
Subject(s): Magic
Major character(s): Firekeeper, Psychic; Blind Seer, Animal (wolf); Derian Carter, Adventurer
Time period(s): Indeterminate
Locale(s): Liglim, Fictional Country

Summary: Firekeeper is one of the few individuals who can actually speak to animals, some of whom are as intelligent as humans. She and two friends, one a wolf, are kidnapped by agents of a foreign nation which wishes to make use of her abilities, but she conceives a new idea, to free their animals from virtual slavery.

Where it's reviewed:
Library Journal, November 15, 2004, page 55
Publishers Weekly, October 25, 2004, page 32

Other books by the same author:
The Buried Pyramid, 2004
The Dragon of Despair, 2003
Wolf's Head, Wolf's Heart, 2002
Through Wolf's Eyes, 2001
Smoke and Mirrors, 1996

Other books you might like:
Dave Duncan, *The Jaguar Knights*, 2004
Doranna Durgin, *A Feral Darkness*, 2001
Kij Johnson, *The Fox Woman*, 2000
Mickey Zucker Reichert, *The Beasts of Barakhai*, 2001
Thomas Burnett Swann, *Wolfwinter*, 1972

562

REBECCA LOCKSLEY

The Three Sisters

(New York: Eos, 2004)

Story type: Romance; Magic Conflict
Subject(s): Magic
Major character(s): Wolf Madraga, Nobleman; Elena Starchild, Housewife; Yani, Warrior
Time period(s): Indeterminate
Locale(s): Yarmar, Fictional Country

Summary: An invading army has seized control of the nation of Yarmar, and its villainous leaders are also interested in possessing the beautiful Elena Starchild. Her two sisters, a warrior and a sorceress return to help rescue her. First novel.

Other books you might like:
Lynn Abbey, *The Black Flame*, 1980
Ru Emerson, *The Princess of Flames*, 1986
Richard Kirk, *Lords of the Shadows*, 1979
C.L. Moore, *Jirel of Joiry*, 1982
Jo Walton, *The King's Name*, 2001

563

ELIZABETH A. LYNN

Dragon's Treasure

(New York: Ace, 2004)

Story type: Magic Conflict; Political
Series: Dragon. Book 2
Subject(s): Magic
Major character(s): Karadur Atani, Nobleman, Mythical Creature (shapechanger); Maia Unamira, Healer; Lorimir Ness, Military Personnel
Time period(s): Indeterminate
Locale(s): Chingura, Fictional Country

Summary: The land of Chingura is ruled by a man with the ability to transform himself into a dragon. After his father's misrule, he is a comparatively benevolent king, but his animal side sometimes shows through. A healer from a poor village will eventually help him to come to terms with his own nature.

Where it's reviewed:
Booklist, September 1, 2004, page 75
Publishers Weekly, August 16, 2004, page 47

Other books by the same author:
Dragon's Winter, 1998
The Silver Horse, 1984
The Northern Girl, 1980
The Dancers of Arun, 1979
Watchtower, 1979

Other books you might like:
Carol Dennis, *Dragon's Queen*, 1991
Richard A. Knaak, *Firedrake*, 1989
Jennifer Roberson, *A Tapestry of Lions*, 2002
Christopher Rowley, *The Dragon at World's End*, 1997
Lawrence Watt-Evans, *Dragon Venom*, 2003

564

JENNIFER MACAIRE

The Secret of Shabaz

(Barrington, Illinois: Medallion, 2004)

Story type: Young Adult; Quest
Subject(s): Unicorns; Quest
Major character(s): Tania, Orphan; Shabaz, Mythical Creature (unicorn); Birchspring, Mythical Creature (elf), Aged Person
Time period(s): Indeterminate
Locale(s): Alternate Universe

Summary: An orphan girl, an elderly elf, and a unicorn who has lost his horn are the participants in a quest to defeat a dark lord who threatens to use his occult powers to overwhelm the land. Tania learns the secret of her heritage as they set out to

thwart the villain's plans. This is the author's first fantasy novel.

Other books by the same author:
The Promise, 2003
Virtual Murder, 2003

Other books you might like:
Lynn Abbey, *Unicorn and Dragon*, 1987
Peter S. Beagle, *The Last Unicorn*, 1968
Terry Brooks, *The Black Unicorn*, 1987
Elaine Cunningham, *The Unicorn Hunt*, 1995
John Lee, *The Unicorn War*, 1995

565

D.J. MACHALE

Black Water

(New York: Aladdin, 2004)

Story type: Young Adult; Alternate Universe
Series: Pendragon. Book 5
Subject(s): Quest
Major character(s): Bobby Pendragon, Teenager; Courtney Chetwynde, Teenager; Boom, Animal (cat)
Time period(s): 2000s
Locale(s): Alternate Universe

Summary: A teenaged boy with the ability to move from one reality to another believes that his purpose is to help the separate worlds remain free of an evil and ambitious man. His latest adventure involves the release of a plague whose existence may force him to reconsider how he deals with this power.

Other books by the same author:
The Never War, 2003
The Reality Bug, 2003
The Lost City of Faar, 2002
The Merchant of Death, 2002

Other books you might like:
K.A. Applegate, *Enter the Enchanted*, 1999
Eoin Colfer, *Artemis Fowl*, 2001
Bruce Coville, *Operation Sherlock*, 1986
Philip Jose Farmer, *The Maker of Universes*, 1965
John Peel, *The Book of Magic*, 1997

566

DIANA MARCELLAS

Twilight Rising, Serpent's Dream

(New York: Tor, 2004)

Story type: Contemporary; Magic Conflict
Series: Brierly Mefell. Book 3
Subject(s): Magic
Major character(s): Brierly Mefell, Sorceress; Ashdla Toldane, Teenager, Wizard; Megan Mefell, Child
Time period(s): 2000s
Locale(s): Alternate Universe

Summary: Brierly has been transported to a magical alternate world where she believes her daughter has been lost forever.

She discovers instead that the child has become a pawn in a sorcerous power struggle in which her own abilities will be tested once again.

Other books by the same author:
The Sealark's Song, 2002
Mother Ocean, Daughter Sea, 2001

Other books you might like:
James Clemens, *Wit'ch Fire*, 1998
Barbara Hambly, *The Witches of Wenshar*, 1987
Andre Norton, *Sorceress of the Witch World*, 1968
Jennifer Roberson, *Legacy of the Wolf*, 2001
R.A. Salvatore, *The Witch's Daughter*, 1991

567

ROBERT WAYNE MCCOY

The King of Ice Cream
(Waterville, Maine: Five Star, 2004)

Story type: Contemporary; Horror
Subject(s): Angels
Major character(s): Luke Yeager, Student—College, Teenager; Tina Jones, Student; Father Rosenzweig, Religious
Time period(s): 1990s (1992)
Locale(s): Mill Run, Kentucky

Summary: Although the citizens of Mill Run don't know it, buried beneath their town is a secret which could end life as they know it for the entire world. The ancient conflict that resulted in the fall of angels from Heaven may be about to repeat itself, and this time with a very different outcome. First novel.

Where it's reviewed:
Chronicle, November 2004, page 43
Publishers Weekly, August 30, 2004, page 38

Other books you might like:
James Blish, *Black Easter*, 1968
Thomas F. Monteleone, *The Blood of the Lamb*, 1992
James Morrow, *Towing Jehovah*, 1994
Richard Sears, *First Born*, 2000
Patrick J. Tilley, *Xan*, 1986

568

SCOTT MCGOUGH

Outlaw: Champions of Kanigawa
(Renton, Washington: Wizards of the Coast, 2004)

Story type: Sword and Sorcery; Magic Conflict
Series: Magic the Gathering
Subject(s): Magic; Secrets
Major character(s): Michiko, Teenager; Konda, Warlord; Mochi, Warrior
Time period(s): Indeterminate
Locale(s): Alternate Universe

Summary: In a magical world that strongly resembles ancient Japan, a young woman disobeys her father, a local warlord, and visits the local religious leaders, who help her contact the serpent spirits who dwell in the gap between worlds. With

their help, she hopes to avert a new wave of warfare that could devastate her people and bring down her father.

Other books by the same author:
Champion's Trial, 2003
Emperor's Fist, 2003
Assassin's Blade, 2002
Chainer's Torment, 2002

Other books you might like:
Kara Dalkey, *Genpei*, 2001
Kij Johnson, *The Fox Woman*, 2000
Jessica Amanda Salmonson, *The Golden Naginata*, 1982
Ree Soesbee, *The Crane*, 2000
Rich Wulf, *Wind of Justice*, 2003

569

CHINA MIEVILLE

Iron Council
(New York: Del Rey, 2004)

Story type: Magic Conflict; Quest
Series: New Crobuzon. Book 3
Subject(s): Magic; Quest
Major character(s): Cutter, Rebel; Pomeroy, Rebel; Ori, Worker
Time period(s): Indeterminate
Locale(s): New Crobuzon, Fictional Country

Summary: The city state of New Crobuzon is being transformed, and not for the better. The merchant class has become more avaricious and the rights of less fortunate citizens are increasingly restricted. A group of rebels steals a magical train and flees across the country, pursued by the authorities, giving rise to a spreading rebel spirit.

Where it's reviewed:
Booklist, June 1, 2004, page 1670
Library Journal, July 2004, page 75
Locus, September 2004, page 29
New York Times Book Review, July 18, 2004, page 19
Publishers Weekly, July 5, 2004, page 42

Other books by the same author:
Tain, 2003
The Scar, 2002
Perdido Street Station, 2001
King Rat, 1998

Other books you might like:
Dave Duncan, *The Jaguar Knights*, 2004
Jeffrey Ford, *The Physiognomy*, 1997
Mary Gentle, *Rats and Gargoyles*, 1990
Ursula K. Le Guin, *The Other Wind*, 2001
Ian R. MacLeod, *Light Ages*, 2003

570

JOHN MOORE

Heroics for Beginners
(New York: Ace, 2004)

Story type: Humor; Quest

Subject(s): Magic; Humor
Major character(s): Kevin Bigelow, Nobleman; Prince Logan, Royalty; Princess Rebecca, Royalty
Time period(s): Indeterminate
Locale(s): Deserae, Fictional Country

Summary: An evil magician menaces the kingdom of Deserae, so an incompetent hero decides to save the day and win the hand of the beautiful Princess Rebecca. Fortunately, he has a handbook that tells him everything he needs to become a hero. Sort of. A frequently humorous send up of quest adventures.

Other books by the same author:
Slay and Rescue, 1993

Other books you might like:
Robert Lynn Asprin, *Hit or Myth*, 1983
Esther Friesner, *Harpy High*, 1991
J. Calvin Pierce, *The Wizard of Ambermere*, 1993
Terry Pratchett, *The Rincewind Trilogy*, 2001
Lawrence Watt-Evans, *Ithanalin's Restoration*, 2002

571

ROBERT NEWCOMB

The Scrolls of the Ancients
(New York: Del Rey, 2004)

Story type: Sword and Sorcery; Magic Conflict
Series: Chronicles of Blood and Stone. Book 3
Subject(s): Magic
Major character(s): Tristan, Sorcerer, Twin (of Shailiha); Shailiha, Sorceress, Twin (of Tristan); Wigg, Wizard
Time period(s): Indeterminate
Locale(s): Eutracia, Fictional Country

Summary: Tristan and Shailiha have apparently fulfilled a prophecy by proving themselves capable of magic, but they learn of the existence of a third party with similar power. Misuse of this ability could have disastrous effects, so they set out to locate the other before it is too late.

Other books by the same author:
The Gates of Dawn, 2003
The Fifth Sorceress, 2002

Other books you might like:
Robert Jordan, *The New Spring*, 2004
George R.R. Martin, *A Storm of Swords*, 2000
L.E. Modesitt Jr., *The Wellspring of Chaos*, 2004
Melanie Rawn, *Exiles*, 1994
Tad Williams, *The Dragonbone Chair*, 1988

572

STAN NICHOLLS

The Covenant Rising
(New York: Eos, 2004)

Story type: Sword and Sorcery; Magic Conflict
Series: Dreamtime. Book 1
Subject(s): Magic
Major character(s): Reeth Caldason, Warrior; Kutch, Apprentice; Serrah Ardacris, Fugitive

Time period(s): Indeterminate
Locale(s): Bhealfa, Fictional Country

Summary: The protagonist is the last surviving member of a warrior race who was slaughtered through treachery many years earlier. His life is complicated by unpredictable fits of rage during which he is incapable of controlling himself, making things even more difficult when he crosses paths with a fugitive.

Where it's reviewed:
Chronicle, October 2004, page 26
Library Journal, October 15, 2004, page 57

Other books by the same author:
Warriors of the Tempest, 2000
Legion of Thunder, 1999
Bodyguard of Lightning, 1998

Other books you might like:
Jacqueline Carey, *Kushiel's Dart*, 2001
Kim Hunter, *Knight's Dawn*, 2001
Katharine Kerr, *The Fire Dragon*, 2001
Michael Moorcock, *Stormbringer*, 1984
Lawrence Watt-Evans, *The Spell of the Black Dagger*, 1993

573

DOUGLAS NILES

Wizards' Conclave
(Renton, Washington: Wizards of the Coast, 2004)

Story type: Sword and Sorcery; Magic Conflict
Series: Age of Mortals. Book 5
Subject(s): Magic; Quest
Major character(s): Dalamar, Wizard; Kalrakin, Adventurer; Jenna, Wizard
Time period(s): Indeterminate
Locale(s): Krynn, Alternate Universe

Summary: At the conclusion of a terrible war, new and powerful magic entered the world. The two most powerful wizards in the land set off on a quest to enter the stronghold of this new sorcery and secure it so that the dark power cannot be used corruptly by those who would seek to advance their own cause at the expense of others.

Other books by the same author:
The Goddess Worldweaver, 2003
Winterheim, 2003
The Golden Orb, 2002
The Messenger, 2001
The Puppet King, 1999

Other books you might like:
Nancy Varian Berberick, *Dalamar the Dark*, 2000
Wayland Drew, *Dragonslayer*, 1981
E.R. Eddison, *The Worm Ouroboros*, 1922
Richard A. Knaak, *The Citadel*, 2000
Chris Pierson, *Sacred Fire*, 2003

Fantasy

574
DIANA L. PAXSON

Ancestors of Avalon
(New York: Viking, 2004)

Story type: Historical; Magic Conflict
Subject(s): Magic
Major character(s): Tiriki, Religious; Damisa, Noblewoman; Micail, Noblewoman, Religious
Time period(s): Indeterminate Past
Locale(s): Avalon, Mythical Place

Summary: This book is a sequel to the Avalon series by the late Marion Zimmer Bradley. Three women, descendants of the survivors of lost Atlantis, consider their future in their new home in a magical version of the British Isles.

Where it's reviewed:
Booklist, June 1, 2004, page 1671
Chronicle, August 2004, page 24
Publishers Weekly, May 24, 2004, page 49

Other books by the same author:
The Book of the Stone, 2000
The Hallowed'Isle, 1999
The Dragons of the Rhine, 1995
The Earthstone, 1987
Brisingamen, 1984

Other books you might like:
A.A. Attanasio, *The Dragon and the Unicorn*, 1996
Marion Zimmer Bradley, *Lady of Avalon*, 1997
Gillian Bradshaw, *Hawk of May*, 1980
Juliet Marillier, *Daughter of the Forest*, 2000
Sarah Zettel, *In Camelot's Shadow*, 2004

575
JULIE ANNE PETERS

Luna
(New York: Little, Brown, 2004)

Story type: Young Adult; Light Fantasy
Subject(s): Magic
Major character(s): Regan, Teenager; Liam, Teenager; Luna, Teenager
Time period(s): 2000s
Locale(s): United States

Summary: Regan and Liam seem to be two ordinary teenagers, but Liam has a secret. At night, when the moon is full, he is magically transformed into a beautiful girl, in which guise he calls himself Luna. Regan is the only one who knows the secret, but Liam is determined to make Luna's existence known to everyone.

Other books you might like:
K.A. Applegate, *Mystify the Magician*, 2001
Bradley Denton, *Lunatics*, 1996
Michael Fessier, *Fully Dressed and in His Right Mind*, 1935
Lawrence Edward Watkin, *Darby O'Gill and the Little People*, 1959
Jane Yolen, *The Bagpiper's Ghost*, 2002

576
TERRY PRATCHETT

A Hat Full of Sky
(New York: HarperCollins, 2004)

Story type: Humor; Young Adult
Series: Discworld. Book 31
Subject(s): Magic
Major character(s): Tiffany Aching, Witch, Apprentice; Mistress Weatherwax, Witch; Rob Anybody, Thief
Time period(s): Indeterminate
Locale(s): Discworld, Alternate Universe

Summary: Young Tiffany Aching sets about her apprenticeship as a trainee witch, but she finds herself doing more housework than magic. As if that wasn't bad enough, there's an invisible entity dogging her footsteps and its intentions are far from clear, so she enlists the aid of a corps of tiny thieves.

Where it's reviewed:
Booklist, April 15, 2004, page 1451
Horn Book Magazine, July-August 2004, page 1460
School Library Journal, July 2004, page 111

Other books by the same author:
The Wee Free Men, 2003
The Night Watch, 2002
The Last Hero, 2001
The Rincewind Trilogy, 2001
Carpe Jugulum, 1998

Other books you might like:
Bruce Coville, *Jennifer Murdley's Toad*, 1992
Alan Garner, *Elidor*, 1965
Diana Wynne Jones, *Hexwood*, 1993
Norton Juster, *The Phantom Tollbooth*, 1961
Margery Sharp, *The Rescuers*, 1959

577
JEAN RABE

The Finest Creation
(New York: Tor, 2004)

Story type: Alternate Universe; Psychic Powers
Subject(s): Secrets
Major character(s): Gallant-Stallion, Animal (horse); Kalantha, Student; Meven, Student
Time period(s): Indeterminate
Locale(s): Alternate Universe

Summary: In an alternate reality, horses are given both intelligence and some magical abilities, and are charged with preserving the lives of certain individuals. Gallant-Stallion finds his fate tied to that of two young students, Meven and Kalantha, who are destined to be important figures in the future of the world, if they can survive long enough.

Where it's reviewed:
Booklist, November 1, 2004, page 471
Chronicle, November 2004, page 40
Library Journal, September 15, 2004, page 53
Publishers Weekly, October 11, 2004, page 61

Other books by the same author:
Eye of the Maelstrom, 2002
Redemption, 2002
Downfall, 2000
The Silver Stair, 1999
Red Magic, 1991

Other books you might like:
Constance Ash, *The Stalking Horse*, 1990
Mary Herbert, *Lightning's Daughter*, 1991
Mercedes Lackey, *The River's Gift*, 1999
Mary Stanton, *Piper at the Gate*, 1989
Judith Tarr, *A Wind in Cairo*, 1989

578

DAVID RANDALL

Clovermead

(New York: McElderry, 2004)

Story type: Young Adult; Light Fantasy
Subject(s): Magic
Major character(s): Clovermead Wickward, Teenager; Waxmelt, Aged Person; Lord Ursus, Nobleman
Time period(s): Indeterminate
Locale(s): Alternate Universe

Summary: Young Clovermead has been raised by a man whom she discovers is not really her father. She also learns that the story of her mother's death isn't accurate, so she sets out to discover her true history. At the same time, the minions of an evil aggressor threaten to subjugate the entire world. First novel.

Where it's reviewed:
Booklist, July 2004, page 1834
Locus, July 2004, page 31
Publishers Weekly, August 2, 2004, page 71
School Library Journal, July 2004, page 112

Other books you might like:
Lynn Abbey, *Jerlayne*, 1999
Susan Cooper, *Seaward*, 1983
Tamora Pierce, *First Test*, 1999
Sherwood Smith, *Wren's Quest*, 1993
Jane Yolen, *The Wizard's Map*, 1999

579

MICKEY ZUCKER REICHERT

The Return of Nightfall

(New York: DAW, 2004)

Story type: Sword and Sorcery; Magic Conflict
Series: Nightfall. Book 2
Subject(s): Magic
Major character(s): Sudian, Thief; Edward, Ruler (king); Varsah, Nobleman (duke)
Time period(s): Indeterminate
Locale(s): Alyndar, Fictional Country

Summary: Despite the contrary advice of his friend Sudian, the former thief, King Edward sets out to visit one of his questionably loyal vassals, Duke Varsah. When the king and

his entourage disappear, it is up to his advisor to discover the truth and rescue the monarch before the entire kingdom becomes unstable.

Where it's reviewed:
Booklist, September 1, 2004, page 75
Publishers Weekly, August 23, 2004, page 41

Other books by the same author:
The Lost Dragons of Barakhai, 2002
The Flightless Falcon, 2000
Prince of Demons, 1996
The Legend of Nightfall, 1993
By Chaos Cursed, 1991

Other books you might like:
David Feintuch, *The King*, 2002
Raymond E. Feist, *King of Foxes*, 2003
Fritz Leiber, *Swords Against Death*, 1970
George R.R. Martin, *A Game of Thrones*, 1996
Lawrence Watt-Evans, *Touched by the Gods*, 1997

580

JOEL ROSENBERG

Paladins

(New York: Baen, 2004)

Story type: Sword and Sorcery; Magic Conflict
Subject(s): Magic; Quest
Major character(s): Father Cully, Knight, Religious; Joshua Grayling, Nobleman; Bear, Warrior
Time period(s): Indeterminate
Locale(s): Alternate Universe

Summary: Father Cully has been away from the brotherhood of religious knights for a long period of time when two of his former cohorts come looking for him. It seems that there is fresh trouble rising in the world, and they convince him to return to his former discipline and help them save the day. This is the opening volume in an as yet unnamed series.

Where it's reviewed:
Booklist, September 15, 2004, page 216
Chronicle, October 2004, page 25

Other books by the same author:
Not Really the Prisoner of Zenda, 2003
The Last Jihad, 2003
Not Quite Scaramouche, 2001
The Crimson Sky, 1998
D'Shai, 1991

Other books you might like:
L. Sprague de Camp, *The Fallible Fiend*, 1973
David Drake, *Master of the Cauldron*, 2004
Dave Duncan, *The Jaguar Knights*, 2004
Robert E. Howard, *The Hills of the Dead*, 1979
Fritz Leiber, *Swords and Ice Magic*, 1977

Fantasy

581

SEAN RUSSELL

The Shadow Roads

(New York: Eos, 2004)

Story type: Magic Conflict; Sword and Sorcery
Series: Swans' War. Book 3
Subject(s): Magic
Major character(s): Elise Wills, Noblewoman; Hafydd, Knight; Toren, Warrior
Time period(s): Indeterminate
Locale(s): Ayr, Fictional Country

Summary: The power vacuum left when the King of Ayr died without designating a successor has spread across the land. Now it threatens to set off a renewed conflict among various sorcerers who have long hated one another and who could destroy much of the world if they let their hatred take form in a magical confrontation.

Where it's reviewed:
Chronicle, November 2004, page 41
Library Journal, September 15, 2004, page 53
Publishers Weekly, September 20, 2004, page 50

Other books by the same author:
The Isle of Battle, 2002
The One Kingdom, 2001
The Compass of the Soul, 1998
Beneath the Vaulted Hills, 1997
Sea Without a Shore, 1996

Other books you might like:
Dave Duncan, *The Jaguar Knights*, 2004
David Eddings, *The Sorceress of Darshiva*, 1989
George R.R. Martin, *A Storm of Swords*, 2000
Michael Moorcock, *The Bane of the Black Sword*, 1977
Lawrence Watt-Evans, *Touched by the Gods*, 1997

582

LISA SMEDMAN

Venom's Taste

(Renton, Washington: Wizards of the Coast, 2004)

Story type: Sword and Sorcery; Magic Conflict
Series: Forgotten Realms: House of Serpents. Book 1
Subject(s): Magic; Secrets
Major character(s): Arvin, Warrior; Zelia, Mythical Creature; Naulg, Criminal
Time period(s): Indeterminate
Locale(s): Alternate Universe

Summary: Restless gods and dark sorcery are bad enough unassisted, but when a cult of humans dedicates itself to advancing the cause of chaos and dissolution, even a reluctant hero like Arvin feels compelled to risk his life. Dodging criminals, fanatics, and inhuman enemies, he uncovers the heart of the cult's plans and sets about thwarting them in this first volume of a trilogy.

Other books by the same author:
The Apparition Trail, 2004

Tails You Lose, 2001
The Playback War, 2000
The Forever Drug, 1999
Blood Sport, 1998

Other books you might like:
Elaine Cunningham, *The Magehound*, 2000
L. Sprague de Camp, *The Pixilated Peeress*, 1991
David Gemmell, *Druss the Legend*, 1994
Michael Moorcock, *The Chronicles of Corum*, 1978
R.A. Salvatore, *The Lone Drow*, 2003

583

DANA STABENOW, Editor

Powers of Detection

(New York: Ace, 2004)

Story type: Anthology; Mystery
Subject(s): Short Stories; Mystery and Detective Stories

Summary: Each of the 12 original stories in this anthology involves a mystery which is solved in the context of one magical talent or another. The stories range from humorous to highly suspenseful. Among the contributors are Anne Bishop, Anne Perry, Simon R. Green, Sharon Shinn, and Charlaine Harris.

Where it's reviewed:
Chronicle, November 2004, page 44

Other books by the same author:
Red Planet Run, 1995
A Handful of Stars, 1991
The Second Star, 1991

Other books you might like:
Anne Bishop, *The Black Jewels Trilogy*, 2003
Laura Anne Gilman, *Staying Dead*, 2004
Simon R. Green, *Nightingale's Lament*, 2004
Charlaine Harris, *Club Dead*, 2003
Sharon Shinn, *Jenna Starborn*, 2002

584

JUDITH TARR

Rite of Conquest

(New York: Roc, 2004)

Story type: Historical; Magic Conflict
Subject(s): Coming-of-Age
Major character(s): William of Normandy, Nobleman; Mathilda of Flanders, Teacher; Harald Hardrada, Warrior
Time period(s): 11th century (1047-1066)
Locale(s): England; France

Summary: William of Normandy, a young man growing up in France, comes under the tutelage of Mathilda, a woman who knows the secrets of magic and imparts them to her student. As William matures, he uses that power to shape his own destiny as William the Conqueror during the invasion of the British Isles.

Where it's reviewed:
Booklist, September 15, 2004, page 215

Library Journal, September 15, 2004, page 52
Publishers Weekly, September 20, 2004, page 50

Other books by the same author:
Queen of the Amazons, 2004
Tides of Darkness, 2002
Pride of Kings, 2001
Kingdom of the Grail, 2000
White Mare's Daughter, 1998

Other books you might like:
Sara Douglass, *Gods' Concubine*, 2004
Thomas Harlan, *The Gate of Fire*, 2000
Marie Jakober, *The Black Chalice*, 2000
Guy Gavriel Kay, *The Last Light of Day*, 2004
Juliet Marillier, *Wolfskin*, 2003

585

ALAN F. TROOP

The Seadragon's Daughter
(New York: Roc, 2004)

Story type: Contemporary; Legend
Series: DelaSangre. Book 3
Subject(s): Legends
Major character(s): Peter DelaSangre, Mythical Creature
 (weredragon); Lorrel, Mythical Creature (weredragon);
 Chloe DelaSangre, Young Woman
Time period(s): 2000s
Locale(s): Miami, Florida (island off the coast)

Summary: Peter DelaSangre has concealed the fact that he can
turn into the form of a dragon. His hopes of living a quiet life
on an island off the coast of Florida are put in jeopardy when a
woman appears who is a member of a race of seagoing
shapeshifters he had thought long extinct.

Other books by the same author:
Dragon Moon, 2003
The Dragon DelaSangre, 2002

Other books you might like:
Joanne Bertin, *The Last Dragonlord*, 1998
Gordon R. Dickson, *The Dragon in Lyonesse*, 1998
Fred Saberhagen, *Dancing Bears*, 1996
Nancy Springer, *Madbond*, 1987
Lawrence Watt-Evans, *Dragon Weather*, 1999

586

GORDON VAN GELDER, Editor

In Lands That Never Were
(New York: Thunder's Mouth, 2004)

Story type: Anthology
Subject(s): Short Stories

Summary: The 12 stories in this anthology were all previously
published in *The Magazine of Fantasy & Science Fiction*.
Together they provide a good sampling of some of the variety
in the field, everything from sword and sorcery to light humor.
The contributors include R. Garcia y Robertson, Ellen Kushner, Ursula K. Le Guin, Fritz Leiber, Pat Murphy, and others.

Where it's reviewed:
Locus, September 2004, page 29

Other books by the same author:
One Lamp, 2003

Other books you might like:
R. Garcia y Robertson, *The Spiral Dance*, 1991
Ellen Kushner, *Swordspoint*, 1987
Ursula K. Le Guin, *Gifts*, 2004
Fritz Leiber, *Ill Met in Lankhmar*, 1995
Pat Murphy, *Nadya*, 1996

587

JEFF VANDERMEER

Secret Life
(Urbana, Illinois: Golden Gryphon, 2004)

Story type: Collection
Subject(s): Short Stories

Summary: The author writes very quirky fantasy stories set in
unusual landscapes and often related in very untraditional
storytelling structures. The 23 stories in this collection were
originally published between 1990 and 2004 and include most
of his best work, with brief introductions to each story.

Other books by the same author:
The City of Saints and Madmen, 2001
The Book of Lost Places, 1996
The Book of the Frog, 1989

Other books you might like:
John Crowley, *Novelties*, 1989
Paul Di Filippo, *Little Doors*, 2002
Jeffrey Ford, *The Beyond*, 2001
Mary Gentle, *Cartomancy*, 2004
Ursula K. Le Guin, *Tales from Earthsea*, 2001

588

DAVID WEBER

Windrider's Oath
(New York: Baen, 2004)

Story type: Sword and Sorcery; Magic Conflict
Series: Bahzell Bahnakson. Book 3
Subject(s): Magic
Major character(s): Bahzell Bahnakson, Barbarian, Diplomat
 (ambassador); Leeana Bowmaster, Teenager, Noble-
 woman; Kaeritha Seldansdaughter, Noblewoman
Time period(s): Indeterminate
Locale(s): Norfressa, Fictional Country

Summary: The representative of a horde of barbarians tries to
maintain his reputation in the court of a foreign king, but it
isn't long before he's in trouble involving wizards and the
revived dead. His problems are complicated by a mischievous
teenaged noblewoman, as well as a variety of villains who
wish to see him dead.

Where it's reviewed:
Locus, July 2004, page 59

Other books by the same author:
Empire from the Ashes, 2003
The Excalibur Alternative, 2002
The Apocalypse Troll, 1999
In Enemy Hands, 1997
Honor Among Enemies, 1996

Other books you might like:
Steven Brust, *The Phoenix Guards*, 1991
David Drake, *Lord of the Isles*, 1997
Dave Duncan, *The Jaguar Knights*, 2004
Mercedes Lackey, *Fiddler's Fair*, 1998
Janny Wurts, *The Fugitive Prince*, 1997

589

MICHELE M. WELCH

The Bright and the Dark

(New York: Bantam, 2004)

Story type: Magic Conflict; Quest
Subject(s): Magic
Major character(s): Elzith, Fugitive; Julian, Expatriate; Aron, Nobleman
Time period(s): Indeterminate
Locale(s): Alternate Universe

Summary: A young woman who fled her troubled country has visions of a terrible plague that will further weaken its people. Her life becomes entwined with that of an expatriate whose knowledge of powerful magics has made him the object of a search for those interested in exploiting his talents for their own advantage.

Other books by the same author:
Confidence Game, 2003

Other books you might like:
Maggie Furey, *Harp of Winds*, 1994
Sharon Green, *Convergence*, 1996
Katharine Kerr, *Daggerspell*, 1986
Mercedes Lackey, *Arrows of the Queen*, 1987
Jennifer Roberson, *Sword Born*, 1998

590

C.L. WERNER

Blood of the Dragon

(Nottingham, England: Black Library, 2004)

Story type: Sword and Sorcery; Magic Conflict
Series: Warhammer
Subject(s): Magic
Major character(s): Brunner, Bounty Hunter; Gobineau, Criminal; Corbus, Vampire
Time period(s): Indeterminate
Locale(s): Old World, Alternate Universe

Summary: Brunner, a bounty hunter, tracks down a noted highwayman in an obscure region, but his efforts to bring Gobineau back and claim his reward are hampered by two problems. First, he is caught in the conflict between two rival bands of humans in the area, and second, there's a particularly dangerous dragon upsetting things even further.

Where it's reviewed:
Chronicle, October 2004, page 27

Other books by the same author:
Witch Hunter, 2004
Blood & Steel, 2003
Blood Money, 2003

Other books you might like:
Robert Earl, *The Burning Shore*, 2004
Jonathan Green, *Magestorm*, 2004
Robert E. Howard, *The Savage Tales of Solomon Kane*, 2004
Fritz Leiber, *Farewell to Lankhmar*, 1988
Gordon Rennie, *Zavant*, 2002

591

RICHARD C. WHITE

Paths of Evil

(New York: Ibooks, 2004)

Story type: Sword and Sorcery; Magic Conflict
Subject(s): Magic; Quest
Major character(s): Morgan, Wizard; Layla, Warrior; Kore, Warrior
Time period(s): Indeterminate
Locale(s): Viridus, Fictional Country

Summary: A wizard teams up with a handful of warriors to track down the scattered parts of a magical device which could prove instrumental in defending the world of Viridus from a supernatural foe. They have various adventures at each stage of their journey, relying on the particular specialty of one or another of their company in each case. First novel.

Other books you might like:
Dave Duncan, *Cursed*, 1995
Raymond E. Feist, *Exile's Return*, 2004
David Gemmell, *The Swords of Night and Day*, 2004
Andrew J. Offutt, *The Shadow of Sorcery*, 1993
Lawrence Watt-Evans, *The Unwilling Warlord*, 1989

592

JACK WHYTE

The Lance Thrower

(New York: Forge, 2004)

Story type: Legend; Historical
Series: Camulod Chronicles. Book 8
Subject(s): Arthurian Legends
Major character(s): Arthur Pendragon, Ruler; Clothar, Scholar, Knight; Merlyn, Wizard
Time period(s): Indeterminate Past
Locale(s): England

Summary: The young Arthur Pendragon is still learning from Merlyn the Wizard when he undertakes a lengthy trip. He is accompanied by young Clothar, a student who will later change his name and be known as Sir Lancelot. Their friendship grows as they survive various adventures together.

Where it's reviewed:
Chronicle, November 2004, page 41

Other books by the same author:
Uther, 2000
The Fort at River's Bend, 1999
The Eagles' Brood, 1997
The Singing Sword, 1996
The Skystone, 1996

Other books you might like:
Parke Godwin, *Firelord*, 1980
Sanders Anne Laubenthal, *Excalibur*, 1973
Susan Shwartz, *The Grail of Hearts*, 1992
Nancy Springer, *I Am Mordred*, 1998
Jane Yolen, *Merlin*, 1997

593

KIM WILKINS

The Autumn Castle
(London: Gollancz, 2004)

Story type: Contemporary; Light Fantasy
Series: Europa Suite. Book 1
Subject(s): Magic
Major character(s): Christine Starlight, Invalid; Mayfridh, Sorceress; Immanuel Z, Artist
Time period(s): 2000s
Locale(s): Berlin, Germany

Summary: Christine Starlight is living with her artist boyfriend in Berlin, when her life is changed by an encounter with Mayfridh, an enchantress from another world. Their two lives become intertwined, and the situation becomes more complex when famous sculptor Immanuel Z takes an interest in them.

Other books by the same author:
Fallen Angel, 2002
The Resurrectionists, 2000
Grimoire, 1999
The Infernal, 1999

Other books you might like:
Emma Bull, *War for the Oaks*, 1987
Pamela Dean, *The Secret Country*, 1985
Laura Anne Gilman, *Staying Dead*, 2004
Laurell K. Hamilton, *Seduced by Moonlight*, 2004
Will Shetterly, *Dogland*, 1997

594

TAD WILLIAMS

Shadowmarch. Volume 1
(New York: DAW, 2004)

Story type: Sword and Sorcery; Magic Conflict
Series: Shadowmarch Trilogy. Volume 1
Subject(s): Magic
Major character(s): Barrick Eddon, Royalty (prince); Chert Blue Quartz, Mythical Creature (funderling); Yasammez, Demon
Time period(s): Indeterminate
Locale(s): Southmarch, Fictional Country

Summary: The king of Southmarch has been taken captive and the inexperienced members of his family are struggling to rule

in his stead. The task would be difficult in the best of times, but they are heavily beset by their enemies, including a rival human ruler, an embodied demon, and a race of inhuman creatures who are breaking through the barrier insulating them from the human world.

Where it's reviewed:
Booklist, October 15, 2004, page 395
Chronicle, November 2004, page 43
Publishers Weekly, April 28, 2004, page 14

Other books by the same author:
The War of the Flowers, 2003
Sea of Silver Light, 2001
Otherland, 1996
Caliban's Hour, 1994
Tailchaser's Song, 1985

Other books you might like:
David Feintuch, *The Still*, 1997
Raymond E. Feist, *A Darkness at Sethanon*, 1986
Robert Jordan, *Winter's Heart*, 2000
George R.R. Martin, *A Storm of Swords*, 2000
L.E. Modesitt Jr., *The Shadow Sorceress*, 2001

595

GENE WOLFE

The Wizard
(New York: Tor, 2004)

Story type: Magic Conflict; Light Fantasy
Series: Wizard Knight. Book 2
Subject(s): Magic; Quest
Major character(s): Able, Knight; Cloud, Mythical Creature (unicorn); Arnthor, Ruler
Time period(s): Indeterminate
Locale(s): Alternate Universe

Summary: A young boy from our world found himself in the body of a knight in another realm in the first book of this two-part novel, *The Knight*. Now he returns for another round of adventures after many years have passed, this time with a unicorn and the greater experience of maturity.

Where it's reviewed:
Locus, December 2004, page 23

Other books by the same author:
The Knight, 2004
Latro of the Mist, 2003
Return to the Whorl, 2001
In Green's Jungles, 2000
Strange Travelers, 2000

Other books you might like:
Peter S. Beagle, *Giant Bones*, 1997
James Branch Cabell, *Figures of Earth*, 1921
Paul Hazel, *Undersea*, 1982
Patricia A. McKillip, *Ombria in Shadow*, 2002
Sharon Shinn, *The Shape-Changer's Wife*, 1995

Fantasy

596

JOHN C. WRIGHT

The Last Guardian of Everness
(New York: Tor, 2004)

Story type: Sword and Sorcery; Contemporary
Series: War of the Dreaming. Book 1
Subject(s): Magic
Major character(s): Galen Waylock, Sorcerer; Raven Ravenson, Warrior; Wendy Ravenson, Housewife
Time period(s): 2000s
Locale(s): United States; Alternate Universe

Summary: Galen Waylock is a mystical guardian whose duty is to protect the world from the powers of darkness, which exist in another reality. When he contemplates asking help from the powers of light, he discovers that they would impose a more benevolent but equally restrictive rule over humanity, so he decides to forego their assistance.

Where it's reviewed:
Library Journal, August 2004, page 73
Locus, August 2004, page 29
Publishers Weekly, July 12, 2004, page 49

Other books by the same author:
The Golden Transcendence, 2003
The Phoenix Exultant, 2003
The Golden Age, 2002

Other books you might like:
E.R. Eddison, *The Worm Ouroboros*, 1922
Michael Moorcock, *The King of Swords*, 1971
Angus Wells, *Dark Magic*, 1992
Jonathan Wylie, *The Center of the Circle*, 1987
Roger Zelazny, *Nine Princes in Amber*, 1970

597

SARAH ZETTEL

The Firebird's Vengeance
(New York: Tor, 2004)

Story type: Sword and Sorcery; Magic Conflict
Series: Aglirta. Book 3
Subject(s): Magic
Major character(s): Bridget Lederle, Sorceress; Sakra, Sorcerer
Time period(s): Indeterminate
Locale(s): Isavalta, Fictional Country

Summary: Bridget Lederle leaves our world to enter one where magic not only works, but where she has the powers of a sorceress herself. There she also learns that her missing daughter is still alive, although she has fallen into the hands of an evil magician.

Where it's reviewed:
Library Journal, August 2004, page 72
Publishers Weekly, July 12, 2004, page 49

Other books by the same author:
The Usurper's Crown, 2003
A Sorcerer's Treason, 2002
The Quiet Invasion, 2000
Playing God, 1998
Reclamation, 1996

Other books you might like:
Stephen R. Donaldson, *Lord Foul's Bane*, 1977
Sara Douglass, *Beyond the Hanging Wall*, 2003
Mickey Zucker Reichert, *The Beasts of Barakhai*, 2001
Michelle West, *The Riven Shield*, 2003
Tad Williams, *The Dragonbone Chair*, 1988

598

MARC ZICREE
ROBERT CHARLES WILSON, Co-Author

Ghostlands
(New York: Eos, 2004)

Story type: Contemporary; Post-Disaster
Series: Magic Time. Book 3
Subject(s): Disasters; Magic
Major character(s): Cal Griffin, Lawyer, Survivor; Colleen Brooks, Survivor; Herman Goldman, Survivor
Time period(s): 2000s
Locale(s): United States

Summary: The band of survivors of the change that destroyed technology and brought dark magic back to the world has heard rumors of the possible source of the transformation. Their efforts to investigate and perhaps restore the old world are hindered when one of their number is kidnapped.

Where it's reviewed:
Library Journal, November 15, 2004, page 55
Publishers Weekly, November 29, 2004, page 27

Other books by the same author:
Angelfire, 2002 (Maya Kaathryn Bohnhoff, co-author)
Magic Time, 2001 (Barbara Hambly, co-author)

Other books you might like:
Gwyneth Jones, *Castles Made of Sand*, 2002
Madeleine E. Robins, *The Stone War*, 1999
Will Shetterly, *NeverNever*, 1993
Lisa Smedman, *The Lucifer Deck*, 1997
Lawrence Watt-Evans, *In the Empire of Shadow*, 1995

The Year in Horror 2004
by
Stefan Dziemianowicz

It was deja vu all over again for horror fiction in 2004—or at least so it seemed. In 1974, horror's man of the year was Stephen King, who that year saw the publication of *Carrie*, his first novel and the book now looked to as the jump-start of the horror publishing explosion of the late-twentieth century. Thirty years later King was once more horror's lead story, thanks to the publication of two novels that, for a very short period of time, were being touted as milestones marking the end of his career. *Song of Susannah* and *The Dark Tower* were, respectively, the sixth and seventh (and concluding) novels in his long-running The Dark Tower series, which King conceived while still in college in the 1960s, distilled into short stories in the early 1970s, reshaped as an introductory novel (*The Gunslinger*) in 1982, then watched assume a fulminant life all its own for the next two decades.

The seven volumes of The Dark Tower saga have been promoted as horror and dark fantasy fiction's Lord of the Rings equivalent, and while that may be a bit of an exaggeration they are an extraordinary achievement. Roland is a lone gunslinger in an alternate universe whose quest is to reach the Dark Tower, a nexus point between realities, and overthrow the evil Crimson King who threatens cosmic dissolution and chaos. The series began as an amalgam of themes from multiple popular fiction genres fashioned into a framework that could accommodate elements of just about every source that had influenced King as a writer, from the lyric poetry of Robert Browning to the spaghetti western films of Sergio Leone. As it evolved and expanded, the series became a touchstone for King's own development as a writer. Midway through, King began introducing characters and ideas from novels and stories he wrote outside the series. This gave an indication that he intended it as a unified field that ultimately would draw all of his fiction together, much the same way that Isaac Asimov, Robert Heinlein, and other speculative fiction writers had attempted to glue together their own diverse achievements through all-encompassing opuses written toward the end of their careers. Then, in the penultimate installment, King introduced himself as a character, an audacious twist that clarified his ambition for the saga to serve as not only a rousing tale of fantastic adventure, but also as a deeply personal meditation on creative inspiration and the significance of storytelling to the writer. Citing health reasons, including the near fatal automobile accident several years back that apparently hastened his completion of the series, King announced his retirement from writing. Then he quickly recanted (and, with Stuart O'Nan, wrote a road diary on the 2004 baseball season that yielded his third bestselling book of the year). It is likely that there will be more fiction from him in years to come, but it is unlikely that horror will ever see another magnum opus like The Dark Tower series.

The success of King's Dark Tower novels, which were the two top-selling horror titles of 2004, only called attention to the increasing prevalence of series books from other horror writers. By their nature, series books change the emphasis of horror fiction, if only because they assure readers in advance that characters will survive and cope with their horrifying experiences, shifting the emphasis from the horrifying phenomena to the characters themselves. The best series books suggest a broadly imagined story too big for the author to render adequately in a single book. The worst are nothing more than pulp writing, featuring resident characters who have so endeared themselves to readers that it hardly matters their latest adventure is simply a rehash of ones they've had before. Peter Straub's *In the Night Room*, his latest to feature his surrogate, writer Tim Underhill, was the best kind of series novel, which is to say its story (although a direct sequel to last year's *lost boy lost girl*) was conceived to stand on its own merits, independent of previous books in the author's oeuvre. An eerie tale of ghosts who aren't, and fictions that interpenetrate reality, it was yet another of Straub's masterful reconceptions of some of horror's stalest cliches for haunting literary fiction. Readers of F. Paul Wilson's *Crisscross*, his latest novel of urban mercenary Repairman Jack, benefited from familiarity with earlier books in the saga. However, Wilson has kept the series lively through his hero's subtle transformation to a harder, more desperate individual as his adventures draw him closer to a preordained showdown with the supernatural Otherness, which has dogged his steps for more than twenty years.

Books that introduced promising new series in 2004 include Dan Vining's *The Quick*, a blend of supernatural and hardboiled detective fiction, and Stephen Woodworth's *Through Violet Eyes*, a paranormal crime series about agents who can converse with the dead. Elaine Cunningham's *Shadows in the Darkness*, first in a series about an extraordinary private detective who is a supernatural changeling, at the very least, offers a non-conventional heroine who doesn't flinch at participating in the skin trade, if the job demands it. Other sequels and series books varied in quality. Caitlin Kiernan's *Murder of Angels* innovatively transported characters from the real-life world of its predecessor, *Silk*, to a dark fantasy world beyond death. Philip Rickman's sixth adventure featuring Anglican minister and occult investigator Merrily Watkins, *The Prayer of the Night Shepherd*, was an engrossing mix of British folklore and literary history surrounding the writing of Sir Arthur Conan Doyle's Sherlock Holmes standard, *The Hound of the Baskervilles*, while Simon Green's *Nightingale's Lament* added a third chapter to his Nightside series about an occult detective with a supernatural pedigree conducting investigations in a fantasy-laden corner of modern London. Kelley Armstrong's *Dime Store Magic* and *Industrial Magic* featured her strong heroine, witch Paige Winterbourne, in a series turning increasingly to soap opera. Lee Driver's *The Unseen* was another installment in her Chase Dagger occult detective series, while Daniel Hecht's *Land of Echoes* was the second novel to feature paranormal investigator Cree Black.

Alice Kimberly, in *The Ghost and Mrs. McClure*, started a series about a haunted bookstore whose resident ghost helps the proprietor solve crimes. Both Tanya Huff, resurrecting series vampire Henry Fitzroy in *Smoke and Shadows*, and Jim Butcher, whose wizard detective Harry Dresden appeared in his latest adventure, *Blood Rites*, built plots around horror emerging through the occult significance of escapades on movie sets. Other books to feature series detectives whose work brings them into contact with the occult included Lincoln Child and Douglas Preston's *Brimstone*, in which Special Agent Aloysius Pendergast unravels an occult conspiracy (with overtones of Dan Brown's *The Da Vinci Code*, no less) and Jay Russell's *Apocalypse Now, Voyager*, which brought back Marty Burns, a former child television star turned private eye, in another adventure laced with black comedy and Hollywood gossip.

Series fiction is most rampant among writers of vampire fiction, which is understandable given how easily immortal and seemingly indestructible vampires lend themselves to multi-book treatments. With the absence in 2004 of vampire fiction's poster child, Anne Rice—save for a rant on Amazon.com defending *Blood Canticle*, her 2003 novel (and supposedly the last in her long running saga of the Vampire Lestat), against reader criticisms—the throne was open to other writers. The best such book was Chelsea Quinn Yarbro's *Dark of the Sun*, her seventeenth novel since 1978 to feature the benevolent Count St. Germain, whose adventures are more about human nature and the bigotry and prejudices that have (mis)shaped the course of human history. Each book in the St. Germain canon jumps around to a different time and geographic location in the vampire's multi-thousand year lifetime, and Yarbro's meticulous research gives these books the rich texture of old-fashioned historical romances. Indeed, Yarbro's other book for 2004, *In the Face of Death*, was a vampire historical romance spun off from the St. Germain saga and set in the years around the American Civil War.

Lesser achievements in series vampire fiction in 2004 included L.A. Banks' *The Awakening* and *Hunted*, the second and third novels to feature Damali Richards, a hip-hop vampire huntress (whose career is sure to expand to fill the void created by the termination of television's Buffy the Vampire Slayer and its endless novelizations); Nigel Bennet and P.N. Elrod's *Siege Perilous*, another spinoff from television's Forever Knight series; Andrew Fox's *Bride of the Fat White Vampire*, second in a comic series about an obese vampire; Barb and J.C. Hendee's *Thief of Lives*, second novel set in an imaginary fantasy world; Trystam Kith's *Trouble in the Forest*, start of a series working a vampire variation on the Robin Hood legend; Mary Ann Mitchell's *The Vampire de Sade*, latest in her series of erotic horror novels featuring a modern avatar of the Marquis de Sade; Katherine Ramsland's *The Bloodhunters*, about a smoldering civil war between rival urban vampire factions; Susan Sizemore's *I Thirst for You*, a vampire romance; Karen Taylor's *Blood Red Dawn*, seventh novel in her Vampire Legacy series; and James Thompson's *Tainted Blood*, fourth in a series of books about a vampire exploring a scientific means to kick the blood-drinking habit. F. Paul Wilson's *Midnight Mass* wasn't a series book per se, but a fleshing out of the overly familiar idea he has developed in short stories and novellas written over the years about a vampire apocalypse that has reduced humanity to a vulnerable but rebellious feedstock.

The best-selling vampire novel of 2004 was also a series novel. Laurell K. Hamilton's *Incubus Dreams* was the twelfth novel in her series featuring Anita Blake, hardboiled vampire hunter on an alternate Earth that resembles our own, save that vampires and other supernatural beings enjoy the same rights as humans. It's been hard not to notice that Blake's popularity has increased as the series has gotten steamier with Anita, who once flirted with the supernatural but kept her distance, transforming through sexual dalliances with vampires and werewolves to a fiercely liberated woman with a darkly promiscuous side. Hamilton's books are the most prominent example of horror's recent cross-pollination with chick lit, a popular literary subgenre that promotes strong and spunky female characters and feminine concerns, ranging from the comically cliche to the dramatically serious.

Examples in 2004 included Charlaine Harris' *Dead to the World*, fourth novel in her series featuring ditzy psychic waitress Sookie Stackhouse in a world that seems a comic variation on that of Hamilton's novels; Lucy Ellman's *Dot in the Universe*, about a middle-age suicide who experiences successive reincarnations trying to find the fulfillment she lacked in her first life; Kim Harrison's *Dead Witch Walking*, first novel in a semi-comic series about a private eye who teams with supernatural clients to fight crime in an alternate world where the supernatural is common; and MaryJanice Davidson's *Undead and Unwed* and *Undead and Unemployed*, the first two novels in a series about a lovelorn vampire with a Prada fixation who works the night shift at Macy's in Minneapolis. At the far end of the same continuum as these books are novels and short stories marketed as paranormal romance fiction. Led by Christine Feehan, Sherrilyn Kenyon, Lynsay Sands, and other established romance writers, paranormal romances—which are essentially traditional gothic romances populated by amorous vampires, ghostly lovers, and other exotic and risque beings—are also increasing their market profile. They appear in the form of novels and multi-novella anthologies, such as *Hot Blooded* and *Midnight Thirst*. It was long thought that the abundance of modern gothic romance fiction in the 1960s helped cultivate the landscape where Stephen King and the authors who followed him flourished, so it is not hard to understand why this subgenre of romance fiction would be asserting itself so visibly.

One other significant growth area in horror in 2004 was fiction with an interest to black readers. Although horror, like any other emotion, is color-blind, horror fiction has been written overwhelmingly by white writers for white readers. Last year, Phyllis Alesia Perry was represented by *A Sunday in June*, second novel in a series exploring the black experience in America through a supernatural saga extending from the nineteenth through the twentieth century. Kensington's DaFina line, which markets to primarily black readers, broke out Brandon Massey's first novel, *Dark Corner*, about a supernatural legacy steeped in the slave experience of the American Civil War, and Robert Fleming's *Havoc After Dark*, a first collection of stories concerned with racial themes. Massey also edited *Dark Dreams*, a collection of horror and suspense fiction that complemented Angela C. Allen's *Dark Thirst*, a collection of vampire novellas, to showcase the work of black writers exclusively. These books shared many of the same contributors, and it will be interesting to see in years to come whether they remain an insular pocket of horror publishing or break out into the horror mainstream the way that Tananarive Due (whose

name was conspicuously present in most of the books) and Steve Barnes have.

A number of horror writers delivered fiction in 2004 that readers have come to expect of them. Dean R. Koontz produced two bestsellers, *The Taking* and *Life Expectancy*. The former concerns an alien invasion of Earth that manifests as violent meteorologic anomalies and worse horrors. The latter features a hero who has known since birth of several foreordained incidents which, at different points in his life, will threaten him and all he holds dear. Both are struck from the boilerplate Koontz has etched for the last three decades, with his patented inspirational message regarding the capacity of the good-hearted human beings who are generous in spirit to triumph over adversity. John Saul's *Black Creek Crossing* was yet another of his novels featuring teenagers victimized by supernatural threats. Richard Laymon died in 2001, but works unpublished in his lifetime continue to come out, including *The Lake*, another of his non-supernatural thrillers involving psychotic stalkers in pursuit of victims prone to having sex in all the wrong places.

Given horror's subversive nature, it is perhaps appropriate that much of the best work for the year either could not be easily categorized or found horror in unlikely themes. Several novels elaborated horrors related to the workplace. Ramsey Campbell's *The Overnight* tells of a modern chain bookstore built on a site cursed in ancient times. The horrors, when they manifest, do so ingeniously as glitches in modern retail technology, and an intensification of office politics and job dissatisfaction. James Hyne's *Kings of Infinite Space*, a witty satire of modern business, is about an overworked temp who discovers that the best way to climb the company ladder is to bargain with a feral race of former employees, who live beneath the office, to do his work. Christopher Fowler's *Breathe* is about a company that treats its employees as guinea pigs in order to test certain performance enhancing chemicals. *In The Resort*, Bentley Little exaggerates the worst aspects of resort hotels to a level of darkly comic grotesquerie. In contrast to these books, there is Jonathan Aycliffe's *A Garden Lost in Time*, a creepy ghost story written from a very contemporary sensibility. Greg Bear, in *Dead Lines*, offers a thoroughly modern variation on the traditional ghost story, in its account of ghosts who haunt the Earth because their astral dimension has become clogged with the flotsam of modern telecommunications and its electronic debris. Elizabeth Hand, in *Mortal Love*, examines the roots of artistic inspiration and finds them inextricably entwined with madness, death, and the supernatural in a story of a fantastic muse's malignant impact on succession of artists extending from the nineteenth to the late twentieth century. Much lighter in tone is Christopher Moore's *The Stupidest Angel*, a horror spoof in which a Christmas wish that comes true accidentally winds up reviving a town's dead as zombies.

Only a handful of first novels stood out in horror in 2004. John Harwood's *The Ghost Writer* is not just a fine first novel, but an excellent ghost story. It concerns a young man who finds his life dovetailing with events eerily encrypted in ghost stories written by his grandmother decades before. Nick Mamatas showed that there is still life left in the Cthulhu Mythos. His *Move under Ground* is a clever reappraisal of H.P. Lovecraft's cosmic forces of chaos and entropy as seen through the eyes of a disillusioned and paranoid Jack Kerouac and his beatnik buddies. Adam Nevill's *Banquet for the Damned* is a conventional tale of occult horrors promulgated by a renegade professor on a university campus, while Deborah LeBlanc's *Family Inheritance* and James Kidman's *Black Fire*, each in their own way, offer predictable treatments of the familiar theme of individuals wrestling with skeletons in the family closet. Disappointing trade debuts included Thomas Wheeler's *The Arcanum*, which features stereotypical representations of H.P. Lovecraft, Harry Houdini, Sir Arthur Conan Doyle, and other historical personalities fighting an occult conspiracy, and Allen C. Kupfer's *The Journal of Professor Abraham Van Helsing*, which rides the coattails of both Bram Stoker's vampire novel, *Dracula*, and the movie flop *Van Helsing* spun off from Stoker's creation. Kupfer's book is one of a significant number of books that exploites horror's popularity in film and television vehicles. These include the usual film novelizations (among them *The Journals of Eleanor Druse*, a spin-off from the very short-lived television series ''Stephen King's Kingdom Hospital''), but also unique archival compilations such as *The Complete Twilight Zone Scripts of Rod Serling*, *The Twilight Zone Scripts of Charles Beaumont*, and *Duel and The Distributor*, a collection of scripts and fiction by Richard Matheson. The most interesting spin-off from horror in visual media is Douglas Clegg's *The Attraction*, a short novel of the supernatural written partly in homage to horror B-movies.

Whereas novel-length fiction left much to be desired in the horror field in 2004, the year was once again abundant with superb single-author collections. Thomas F. Monteleone's *Fearful Symmetries* offers a thirty-year retrospective of a major author of the post-Stephen King era, while Douglas Clegg's *Machinery of Night* collects nearly all the short fiction written in the past fifteen years by one of horror's most talented newcomers. Conrad Williams' *Use Once, Then Destroy* is a solid first collection from a British writer of urban horror, and Stephen Gallagher's *Out of His Mind* is a long-overdue first collection from a writer known for his subtle blendings of mystery and supernatural horror. Lucius Shepard was a one-man novella factory in 2004 with his collections, *Trujillo* and *Two Trains Running* which, with the stand-alone novella *Viator*, showcases his uncanny talents for blending horror, fantasy, and science fiction in richly imagined fiction. Other excellent collections include Nancy Collins' compilation of weird westerns, *Dead Man's Hand*, Suzy McKee Charnas' *Stagestruck Vampires and Other Phantasms*, Joe R. Lansdale's retrospective collection *Bumper Crop* and miscellany *Mad Dog Summer and Other Stories*, John Farris'

Elvisland, Al Sarrantonio's *Hornets and Others*, David Morrell's *Nightscapes*, Christopher Fowler's *Demonized*, Tim Lebbon's *Fears Unnamed*, and a collaboration by Tim Powers and James Blaylock, *The Devils in the Details*. The quality of contents in these books attests to the enduring power and allure of the short horror story.

It was a more uneven year for horror anthologies, with only Barbara and Christopher Roden's *Acquainted with the Night* distinguishing itself among the small handful of all original anthologies. Jeanne Cavelos' *The Many Faces of Van Helsing*, yet another attempt to capitalize on the movie *Van Helsing*, feature mostly predictable vampire tales, while Peter Crowther's *Fourbodings* is uneven, with good novellas from Terry Lamsley and Mark Morris, but less memorable stories from other contributors. The better anthologies mix new and original stories: among them Kealan Patrick Burke's *Taverns of the Dead* (which collects horror stories set in drinking establishments), and Stephen Jones' revamped *The Mammoth Book of Vampires* and *The Mammoth Book of New Terror*. As always, two of the best anthologies are retrospective compilations of the previous year's horror fiction: Jones' *The Mammoth Book of Best New Horror. Volume 15*, and Ellen Datlow, Kelly Link, and Gavin Grant's *The Year's Best Fantasy and Horror: Seventeenth Annual Collection*. In addition to their sampling of fiction, these books feature summary essays on the year's yield in horror in all media that are indispensable annual time capsules.

In the past, it was fashionable to point out in the annual horror summary how an increasing number of horror titles each year was being published by specialty presses, which took up the slack when trade horror houses began abandoning horror lines and horror publishing in general in the late 1990s. With small publishers such as Ash Tree Press, Tartarus Press, PS Publishing, Sarob Press, Gauntlet, Cemetery Dance, Subterranean Press, Night Shade Books, Earthling, and Delirium Books (to name a few) publishing mixes of classic and new horror fiction as part of their annual programs, this is now a given. Increasingly, trade publishing houses are coming back to horror. Leisure, Pinnacle, Onyx, and other mass market publishers have revived their horror lines. Publishers of trade hardcover fiction continue to promote as general fiction novels and collections of short fiction whose plots and contents acknowledge the pervasive of horror in popular culture for the past three decades. The result, as Stephen Jones put it in his introduction to *The Mammoth Book of Best New Horror. Volume 15*, is that ''There's too much stuff.''

Already there are some in the horror media who equate abundance with renaissance, and who look to the clogged book racks and swelling specialty dealer catalogs as proof that horror is returning to the flush years it enjoyed in the 1980s and early 1990s. However, a significant difference separates now from then. Decades ago, the horror explosion was predicated on the belief that the best-selling popularity of Stephen King, Anne Rice, Dean Koontz, Peter Straub, and Clive Barker indicated a mass reading audience hungry for horror. The fallacy of that assumption was disproved in time and the publishers responded accordingly. Today, horror's expansion is both paradoxical and perplexing.

It is not happening under the delusion that publishers are grooming authors destined to achieve Stephen King-type sales. If anything, in the last five years the declining number of weeks for horror books on the bestseller list have indicated a change in reader interest in horror. What's more, a lot of authors whose books once drove the mass market and trade publishing lines are now safely ensconced at the specialty houses who embraced their work during horror's market downturn. So even as horror presents the image of robust health, there is still a good deal of uncertainty about the mass of ''product'' out there, its quality, and the audience buying it. The years ahead will determine whether horror has learned its lesson and is finding its proper level, or whether the boom that seems to be picking up steam is just a prelude to another dispiriting bust.

Recommended Reading

Entries for the following books are included in this volume.

Taverns of the Dead edited by Kealan Patrick Burke

The Overnight by Ramsey Campbell

Machinery of Night by Douglas Clegg

Dead Man's Hand by Nancy Collins

Out of His Mind by Stephen Gallagher

The Ghost Writer by John Harwood

The Mammoth Book of Best New Horror. Volume 15 edited by Stephen Jones

Fearful Symmetries by Thomas F. Monteleone

Acquainted with the Night edited by Barbara and Christopher Roden

Trujillo by Lucius Shepard

In the Night Room by Peter Straub

The entries for the following books can be found in *WDIRN? 2004. Volume 2.*

The Year's Best Fantasy and Horror: Seventeenth Annual Collection edited by Ellen Datlow, Kelly Link, and Gavin Grant

Elvisland by John Farris

Mortal Love by Elizabeth Hand

Kings of Infinite Space by James Hynes

Move under Ground by Nick Mamatas

Hornets and Others by Al Sarrantonio

Use Once, Then Destroy by Conrad Williams

Horror Titles

599

ANGELA C. ALLEN, Editor

Dark Thirst

(New York: Pocket, 2004)

Story type: Anthology; Vampire Story
Subject(s): African Americans; Supernatural; Vampires

Summary: Allen's anthology contains six all new novella-length vampire stories written by black writers. Omar Tyree's ''Human Heat: The Confessions of an Addicted Vampire,'' is the narrative of a young black man seduced and initiated by a female vampire. Monica Jackson's ''The Ultimate Diet'' is a semi-comic story of a woman who chooses vampirism as a weight-loss measure. In Angela C. Allen's ''Vampire Noir,'' a black female vampire grapples with the Mafia on the streets of New York City.

Other books you might like:
Robert Fleming, *Havoc After Dark*, 2004
Brandon Massey, *Dark Corner*, 2004
Brandon Massey, *Dark Dreams*, 2004
    editor
Sheree R. Thomas, *Dark Matter: A Century of Speculative Fiction from the African Diaspora*, 2000
    editor
Sheree R. Thomas, *Dark Matter: Reading the Bones*, 2003
    editor

600

SCOTT ALLIE, Editor

The Dark Horse Book of Witchcraft

(Milwaukie, Oregon: Dark Horse, 2004)

Story type: Anthology; Witchcraft
Subject(s): Short Stories; Witches and Witchcraft

Summary: These eight stories and one interview have themes relating to witchcraft and black magic. All but one of the stories is animated in graphic novel style, including ''Mac-beth,'' in which Tony Millionaire illustrates a portion of William Shakespeare's classic play, and ''The Troll Witch,'' a vignette from the Hellboy series by Mike Mignola. ''Mother of Toads'' reproduces the full text of Clark Ashton Smith's pulp tale of a sexually seductive witch and includes the illustrations by Gary Gianni.

Other books by the same author:
The Dark Horse Book of Hauntings, 2003

Other books you might like:
Clive Barker, *Tapping the Vein*, 1989
Ray Bradbury, *The Autumn People*, 1965
Joe R. Lansdale, *Weird Business*, 1995
    Richard Klaw, co-editor
Joss Whedon, *Tales of the Vampires*, 1994

601

KELLEY ARMSTRONG

Industrial Magic

(New York: Bantam, 2004)

Story type: Occult
Series: Women of the Otherworld. Book 4
Subject(s): Horror; Witches and Witchcraft; Supernatural
Major character(s): Paige Winterbourne, Computer Expert, Witch; Lucas Cortez, Lawyer, Sorcerer; Benicio Cortez, Businessman, Sorcerer
Time period(s): 2000s
Locale(s): Miami, Florida

Summary: Paige interrupts her plans to start a new witch coven in her town to assist her boyfriend Lucas, a sorcerer and uneasy heir imminent of the powerful Cortez Cabal. Someone has begun stalking and killing teenagers in the many supernatural family cabals that secretly proliferate around the world. While some suspect that it is the work of assassins hoping to promote civil war among the supernatural species, Paige and Lucas ultimately are aware that the killings are part of a ritual to obtain awesome magic powers for those committing them. This sequel to *Dime Store Magic* is the fourth novel in a series featuring supernatural beings who mingle secretly with normal humanity.

Other books by the same author:
Haunted, 2005
Dime Store Magic, 2004
Stolen, 2003
Bitten, 2001

Other books you might like:
L.A. Banks, *The Hunted*, 2004
Nancy A. Collins, *In the Blood*, 1992
Laurell K. Hamilton, *The Lunatic Cafe*, 1996
Tanya Huff, *Smoke and Mirrors*, 2004
Anne Rice, *The Witching Hour*, 2004

602

DAVID G. BARNETT, Editor

Damned: An Anthology of the Lost

(Orlando, Florida: Necro Publications, 2004)

Story type: Anthology
Subject(s): Horror; Short Stories; Supernatural

Summary: These 12 stories by various authors are concerned with issues of heaven and hell, angels and demons, and salvation and damnation. Included are Brian Hodge's vampire tale ''When the Bough Doesn't Break;'' Gary Braunbeck's ''That and the Rain,'' about a man who can psychically steal the memories of others; and Mehitobel Wilson's ''Close,'' about the eerie revelations that come to a hotel employee whose perversion is to hide under the beds of patrons. Most of the stories are hardcore horror fiction. Published in a signed limited edition.

Other books you might like:
Peter Crowther, *Heaven Sent: 18 Glorious Tales of the Angels*, 1995
    Martin H. Greenberg, co-editor
Edward E. Kramer, *Dante's Disciples*, 1996
    Peter Crowther, co-editor
John Pelan, *Darkside*, 1996
    editor
Shane Ryan Staley, *Dark Testament*, 2002
    editor

603

GREG BEAR

Dead Lines

(New York: Random House, 2004)

Story type: Occult
Subject(s): Afterlife; Death; Ghosts
Major character(s): Peter Russell, Writer (former screenwriter); Stanley Weinstein, Businessman; Joseph Adrian Benoliel, Wealthy
Time period(s): 2000s
Locale(s): Los Angeles, California

Summary: Still grieving over the death of his daughter and a good friend, and despondent over his messy divorce, former screenwriter Peter Russell takes a job promoting Trans, a super cellphone that can transmit data from anywhere in the world. When Peter begins seeing ghostly figures trying to contact him, he discovers that Trans taps into an energy source accessed from the astral dimension, and that the two-way flow of energy has caused the world of the dead to become clogged with spam and other computer detritus, making it impossible for ghosts to move on to the hereafter.

Other books by the same author:
Quantico, 2005
Darwin's Children, 2003
Vitals, 2002
Darwin's Radio, 1999
Dinosaur Summer, 1998

Other books you might like:
Daniel H. Gower, *The Orpheus Process*, 1992
Dean R. Koontz, *Hideaway*, 1992
Tim Powers, *Expiration Date*, 1996
Dean Wesley Smith, *Laying the Music to Rest*, 1989

604

AMBER BENSON
CHRISTOPHER GOLDEN, Co-Author
JOSE R. NIETO, Illustrator

Ghosts of Albion: Astray

(Burton, Michigan: Subterranean, 2004)

Story type: Occult
Series: Ghosts of Albion. Book 1
Subject(s): Ghosts; Folklore; Supernatural
Major character(s): Tamara Swift, Writer; William Swift, Banker; John Nichols, Doctor
Time period(s): 19th century
Locale(s): Blackbriar, England

Summary: William and Tamara Swift, who have sorcerous powers and associate regularly with the ghosts of renowned figures of British history, investigate a mysterious incident in rural Blackbriar, in which the newborn children of unwed mothers have all been replaced by supernatural changelings. Attempts to solve the mystery put them in the middle of a conflict between warring supernatural entities of English folklore. First published story in a projected series of novels based on a fantasy-playing game dramatized online at a website for the BBC. Published as a signed limited edition hardcover.

Other books you might like:
Alice Askew, *Aylmer Vance: Ghost-Seer*, 1998
    Claude Askew, co-author
Douglas Clegg, *The Necromancer*, 2003
Elizabeth Hand, *Mortal Love*, 2004
Kim Newman, *Seven Stars*, 2000
Brian Stableford, *The Hunger and Ecstasy of Vampires*, 1996

605

SIMON BESTWICK

A Hazy Shade of Winter

(Ashcroft, British Columbia: Ash-Tree Press, 2004)

Story type: Collection

Subject(s): Horror; Short Stories; Supernatural

Summary: Bestwick's first collection contains 13 stories of horror and the supernatural, all but five original to the volume. The title story is a tale of Christmas horror, in which a visitor to an unfamiliar town witnesses the pursuit and murder of a beast whom the townspeople treat as the ultimate incarnation of evil. ''Until My Darkness Goes'' tells of a man who buys a used book of ghost stories, only to discover it is imbued with the malevolent influence of its misogynistic and murderous former owner. ''Severance'' is a tale of deadly office politics. Introduction by Joel Lane.

Where it's reviewed:
All Hallows 37, October 2004, page 118

Other books you might like:
Steve Duffy, *The Night Comes On*, 1998
Terry Lamsley, *Under the Crust*, 1993
Joel Lane, *The Earth Wire and Other Stories*, 1994
Tim Lebbon, *Horrors Unnamed*, 2004
Phil Locascio, *Howling Hounds*, 2004

606

KEALAN PATRICK BURKE, Editor

Quietly Now
(Baltimore: Cemetery Dance, 2004)

Story type: Anthology
Subject(s): Horror; Short Stories; Supernatural

Summary: The stories and essays in this collection pay tribute to Charles L. Grant, a long-time fiction writer and editor in the horror field and one of the most dedicated promulgators of dark fantasy fiction in the 1970s and 1980s. The book contains three reprints, including Stephen King's ''Nona,'' which appeared in Grant's Shadows anthology series, plus 17 stories written especially for the book, all of which extend the tradition of quiet horror that Grant promoted. Contributors include Kim Newman, F. Paul Wilson, Steve Rasnic Tem, and Chet Williamson among others. Also included are appreciations by Joe R. Lansdale, Peter Straub, Douglas Winter, and others, and an introduction by Hank Wagner. Published only as a limited edition hardcover signed by all of the contributors.

Other books by the same author:
Taverns of the Dead, 2004

Other books you might like:
Charles L. Grant, *Shadows*, 1978
    editor
Richard Matheson, *Robert Bloch: Appreciations of the Master*, 1995
    Ricia Mainhardt, co-editor
William F. Nolan, *The Bradbury Chronicles*, 1991
    Martin H. Greenberg, co-editor
Claudia O'Keefe, *Ghosttide*, 1993
    editor
Peter Straub, *Peter Straub's Ghosts*, 1995
    editor

607

KEALAN PATRICK BURKE, Editor

Taverns of the Dead
(Baltimore: Cemetery Dance, 2004)

Story type: Anthology
Subject(s): Saloons; Short Stories; Supernatural

Summary: This is an anthology of 27 reprint and original stories of horror and the supernatural, all of which feature barroom and tavern settings. Neil Gaiman's ''Shoggoth's Old Peculiar'' is a semi-comic tale of a traveler who doesn't realize he has stepped into a pub steeped in Lovecraftian horrors. In Chet Williamson's ''The Smoke in Mooney's Pub,'' the smoldering political hatreds of Irish patrons taint the air of a bar where a traditional band plays, driving the musicians to individual acts of murder and madness. Terry Lamsley's ''The Snug,'' tells of a haunted pub whose patrons become caught up in the ghostly re-enactment of a mass murder.

Other books by the same author:
Quietly Now, 2004

Other books you might like:
Arthur C. Clarke, *Tales from the White Hart*, 1957
L. Sprague de Camp, *Tales from Gavagan's Bar*, 1953
    Fletcher Pratt, co-author
Michel Parry, *Spaced Out*, 1997
    editor
Michel Parry, *Strange Ecstasies*, 1973
    editor

608

JIM BUTCHER

Blood Rites
(New York: Roc, 2004)

Story type: Occult
Series: Dresden Files. Book 6
Subject(s): Occult; Movie Industry; Supernatural
Major character(s): Harry Dresden, Detective—Police, Wizard; Arturo Genosa, Director (film); Thomas, Vampire
Time period(s): 2000s
Locale(s): Chicago, Illinois

Summary: At the request of a vampire friend, police detective and wizard Harry Dresden investigates a rash of gruesome deaths on the set of a pornographic film. The deaths are the handiwork of someone secretly using an occult spell forbidden by the Council of Wizards. Much to Harry's dismay, it appears that Mavra, his old vampire enemy, has a hand in the nefarious killings.

Other books by the same author:
Death Masks, 2003
Summer Night, 2002
Fool Moon, 2001
Grave Peril, 2001
Storm Front, 2000

Other books you might like:
Ramsey Campbell, *Ancient Images*, 1989
Jonathan Carroll, *A Child Across the Sky*, 1989
Dale Hoover, *65mm*, 1994
Tanya Huff, *Smoke and Shadows*, 2004
Theodore Roszak, *Flicker*, 1991

609

A.S. BYATT

Little Black Book of Stories

(New York: Knopf, 2004)

Story type: Collection
Subject(s): Short Stories; Suspense; Supernatural

Summary: Byatt's collection contains five literary tales of the macabre in which supernatural and horrific experiences illuminate aspects of the characters' lives. In ''The Thing in the Forest,'' two schoolgirls see an inexplicable and monstrous creature, an experience that shapes the paths their lives take from that point on. ''Raw Material'' concerns a teacher who greatly misinterprets the grotesque source of inspiration for his star pupil's short stories. ''The Stone Woman'' tells of an alienated woman whose growing disaffection is mirrored in her transformation into a statue. In ''The Pink Ribbon,'' a man meets the young ghost of his still living but increasingly senile wife. First published in the United Kingdom in 2003.

Other books by the same author:
Elementals: Stories of Fire and Ice, 1998
The Djinn in the Nightingale's Eye, 1994
The Matisse Stories, 1993
Angels and Insects, 1992
Sugar and Other Stories, 1987

Other books you might like:
Margaret Atwood, *Wilderness Tips*, 1991
Rachel Ingalls, *The End of Tragedy*, 1987
Shirley Jackson, *The Lottery: Adventures of the Daemon Lover*, 1949
Alison Lurie, *Women and Ghosts*, 1994
Joyce Carol Oates, *Haunted*, 1994

610

PAT CADIGAN

The Twilight Zone: Upgrade/Sensuous Cindy

(New York: Black Flame, 2004)

Story type: Collection
Series: Twilight Zone
Subject(s): Horror; Short Stories; Supernatural

Summary: These two short novels are based on teleplays for stories that ran on the modern revival of Rod Serling's classic television program, ''The Twilight Zone.'' In *Upgrade*, a distraught woman who fantasizes an ideal life with an ideal family awakens in the middle of her imagined life and finds it both seemingly inescapable and not quite as ideal as she thought. In *Sensuous Cindy*, a man is seduced by an erotic virtual program unaware of its dangers.

Other books you might like:
Martin H. Greenberg, *New Stories from the Twilight Zone*, 1991
   editor
John Helfers, *The Twilight Zone: Deep in the Dark*, 1994
Jay Russell, *The Twilight Zone: Memphis/The Pool Guy*, 2004
Carol Serling, *Return to the Twilight Zone*, 1994
   editor
J. Michael Straczynski, *Tales from the New Twilight Zone*, 1989
   editor

611

RAMSEY CAMPBELL

The Overnight

(Harrogate, England: PS Publishing, 2004)

Story type: Ancient Evil Unleashed
Subject(s): Books and Reading; Horror; Supernatural
Major character(s): Woody Blake, Businessman; Wilf, Worker; Jill, Worker
Time period(s): 2000s
Locale(s): Fenny Meadows, England

Summary: Strange things are happening at Texts, the new chain bookstore built in the Fenny Meadows industrial park: books are disarranging themselves on shelves, videos are showing ghostly images when played, and an unusual amount of chaos on the job is antagonizing the employees. Eerie fogs that nightly envelope the park and other strange events suggest that something unnatural has been stirred up at the still developing site and is exerting itself in increasingly less subtle ways on the store and its patrons. Horrors come to a head on the night the manager persuades his employees to stay overnight in preparation for a corporate inspection the following day.

Other books by the same author:
The Darkest Part of the Woods, 2003
Pact of the Fathers, 2001
Silent Children, 2000
The Last Voice They Hear, 1998
The House on Nazareth Hill, 1996

Other books you might like:
Lisa Cantrell, *Torments*, 1989
Christopher Fowler, *Rune*, 1991
Stephen King, *The Shining*, 1977
Melisand March, *The Site*, 1989
William Browning Spencer, *Resume with Monsters*, 1995

612

JEANNE CAVELOS, Editor

The Many Faces of Van Helsing

(New York: Ace, 2004)

Story type: Anthology; Vampire Story
Subject(s): Horror; Short Stories; Vampires
Major character(s): Abraham Van Helsing, Vampire Hunter

Summary: Cavelos edited this anthology of 21 tales of horror and fantasy featuring vampire hunter Abraham Van Helsing, arch-nemesis of the evil vampire Count Dracula. The stories cover the span of Van Helsing's life from childhood to adulthood and include Thomas Tessier's ''The Infestation at Ralls,'' about a vampire infestation at a girls' school; J.A. Kornrath's ''The Screaming,'' in which Van Helsing intervenes in a house of unspeakable horrors; and Christopher Golden's ''Venus and Mars,'' in which Van Helsing takes on vampire prostitutes.

Other books you might like:

P.N. Elrod, *Dracula in London*, 2001
    editor
Martin H. Greenberg, *Dracula: Prince of Darkness*, 1992
    editor
Martin H. Greenberg, *Vampire Detectives*, 1995
    editor
Kevin Ryan, *Van Helsing*, 2004
Bram Stoker, *Dracula*, 1897

613

SUZY MCKEE CHARNAS

Stagestruck Vampires and Other Phantasms

(San Francisco: Tachyon, 2004)

Story type: Collection; Vampire Story
Subject(s): Horror; Supernatural; Vampires

Summary: These four stories of fantasy and the supernatural, include ''The Vampire Tapestry,'' the foundation of the author's renowned novel of the same title, in which a psychotherapist begins to realize that her patient is an ageless vampire; ''Boobs,'' which equates lycanthropy with nascent teenage female sexuality; and ''Beauty and the Opera or the Phantom Beast,'' a variation on the theme of *The Phantom of the Opera*. The book also includes two essays, among them ''The Stagestruck Vampire,'' in which the author discusses the process of adapting her fiction for the stage.

Other books by the same author:

Music of the Night, 2000
Moonstone and Tiger Eye, 1992
The Vampire Tapestry, 1980
Listening to Brahms, 1978

Other books you might like:

Kim Antieau, *Trudging to Eden*, 1994
Carol Emshwiller, *The Start of the End of It All*, 1991
James Tiptree, *Her Smoke Rose Up Forever*, 1985
Lisa Tuttle, *A Nest of Nightmares*, 1985
Chelsea Quinn Yarbro, *Apprehensions and Other Delusions*, 2003

614

R. CHETWYND-HAYES, Editor
STEPHEN JONES, Co-Editor

Great Ghost Stories: Tales of Mystery and Madness

(New York: Carroll & Graf, 2004)

Story type: Anthology; Ghost Story
Subject(s): Ghosts; Short Stories; Supernatural

Summary: This anthology of 25 stories of horror and the supernatural, both new and reprint, spans two centuries and includes ''Brickett Bottom'' by Amyas Northcote, about a spectral house that abducts unwary visitors; ''The Water Ghost of Harrowby Hall'' by John Kendrick Bangs, in which a man must devise a way to outsmart the ghost that has cursed his family for generations with fatal appearances; and ''On the Brighton Road'' by Richard Middleton, an afterlife fantasy with a twist ending. Chetwynd-Hayes, who contributes a story of his own, died in 2001. A deluxe hardcover edition of this volume was also published by Cemetery Dance.

Other books you might like:

Michael Cox, *The Oxford Book of English Ghost Stories*, 1986
    Michael Gilbert, co-editor
Richard Dalby, *The Mammoth Book of Ghost Stories*, 1995
    editor
Brad Leithauser, *The Norton Book of Ghost Stories*, 1994
    editor
Robert Phillips, *Triumph of the Night*, 1989
    editor
Robert Weinberg, *The Mists from Beyond*, 1993
    Stefan Dziemianowicz, Martin H. Greenberg, co-editors

615

RICHARD CHIZMAR, Editor

Shivers III

(Baltimore: Cemetery Dance, 2004)

Story type: Anthology
Series: Shivers. Book 3
Subject(s): Horror; Short Stories; Supernatural

Summary: Eighteen reprint and original stories make up the contents of the third volume in this annual non-theme horror anthology series. Douglas Clegg's ''Becoming Men'' pits juvenile delinquents against disciplinarians at a military style boot camp in a story full of deceit and paranoia. Thomas F. Monteleone's ''Horn of Plenty'' offers a variation on the vampire theme in its account of a musical instrument that draws sustenance from its owner. J.F. Gonzalez's ''The Lingering Scent of Brimstone'' tells of the unusual deal with satanic forces a couple makes to protect their young child.

Other books by the same author:

Shivers II, 2003
Shivers, 2002
Night Visions 10, 2001
The Best of Cemetery Dance, 1998
The Earth Strikes Back, 1994

Horror

Other books you might like:

Kenneth E. Abner Jr., *Terminal Fright*, 1998
editor

George Hatch, *Guignoir and Other Furies*, 1991
editor

Brian Hopkins, *13 Horrors*, 2003
editor

Elizabeth E. Monteleone, *Borderlands 5*, 2003
Thomas F. Monteleone, co-editor

John Pelan, *A Walk on the Darkside*, 2004
editor

616

DOUGLAS CLEGG

Afterlife

(New York: Onyx, 2004)

Story type: Wild Talents
Subject(s): Children; Mothers; Supernatural
Major character(s): Julie Hutchinson, Nurse; Matt Hutchinson, Teenager; Michael Diamond, Psychic
Time period(s): 2000s
Locale(s): Rellingford, New Jersey; New York, New York

Summary: After her husband's murder, Julie discovers that he may have led a secret life tied to a childhood past he never told her about. His latent psychic powers qualified him for study in Project Daylight, a top secret military experiment to study the powers of remote seeing. Bizarre dreams in which her husband communicates to her and ghostly presences in an abandoned apartment to which he owned a key lead her to seek help from a nationally known psychic. She discovers to her great dismay that the psychic was not only a participant in Project Daylight but supposedly died violently in it.

Other books by the same author:
The Abandoned, 2005
The Attraction, 2004
The Hour Before Dark, 2002
Naomi, 2000
Purity, 1999

Other books you might like:
Beth Amos, *Cold White Fury*, 1996
John Arbucci, *Blood of the Innocents*, 1991
Jack Caravela, *The Gifted*, 1991
John Farris, *The Fury*, 1976
Stephen King, *Firestarter*, 1980

617

DOUGLAS CLEGG

The Attraction

(North Webster, Indiana: Delirium, 2004)

Story type: Ancient Evil Unleashed
Subject(s): College Life; Horror; Supernatural
Major character(s): Josh, Student; Bronwyn Shapiro, Student; Charlie Goodrow, Mechanic
Time period(s): 1970s
Locale(s): Naga, Arizona

Summary: Horseplay by a carful of college students on spring break leads to the destruction of a glass museum case containing the body of the Flesh Scraper, an avatar of the Aztec god Xipe Totec. Brought to horrible life by the incident, the Flesh Scraper pursues them by night across the desert as they struggle to reach civilization. Published as a signed limited edition hardcover.

Other books by the same author:
Afterlife, 2004
The Hour Before Dark, 2002
Naomi, 2000
Purity, 1999
You Come When I Call You, 1996

Other books you might like:
Warren Newton Beath, *Shock Lines*, 1993
Chris Curry, *Trickster*, 1993
Lisa Dean, co-author
Stephen Gallagher, *Valley of Lights*, 1987
Charles L. Grant, *The Nestling*, 1982
Ashley McConnell, *Days of the Dead*, 1992

618

DOUGLAS CLEGG

The Machinery of Night

(Baltimore: Cemetery Dance, 2004)

Story type: Collection
Subject(s): Horror; Short Stories; Supernatural

Summary: Thirty-nine poems, fragments, short stories, and novellas representing most of the shorter works written by the author are included in this collection. Stories vary in their approach to horror themes from the humorous to the surreal and include ''People Who Love Life,'' in which a spurned lover's affection is so strong that it raises his unrequited love from the grave; ''Ice Palace,'' about a fraternity initiation prank that breaks its participants into a bizarre fantasy world drawn from their fears and anxieties; and ''Purity,'' a short novel of psychological suspense narrated by a young man who believes he possesses a supernatural pedigree. Commentary by the author on most of the stories is included. This volume includes the full contents of the author's International Horror Guild Award-winning *The Nightmare Chronicles*.

Other books by the same author:
The Abandoned, 2005
Afterlife, 2004
The Attraction, 2004
The Hour Before Dark, 2002
The Nightmare Chronicles, 1999

Other books you might like:
Glenn Hirshberg, *The Two Sams*, 2003
Stephen King, *Skeleton Crew*, 1987
Thomas F. Monteleone, *Fearful Symmetries*, 2004
Michael Marshall Smith, *More Tomorrow and Other Stories*, 2003
Peter Straub, *Houses Without Doors*, 1990
editor

619

NANCY A. COLLINS

Dead Man's Hand

(Atlanta, Georgia: Two Wolf Press, 2004)

Story type: Collection
Subject(s): Horror; Short Stories; Supernatural

Summary: Subtitled "Five Tales of the Weird West," this book collects five novellas incorporating classic and contemporary western themes into supernatural fiction. *Hell Come Sundown*, the one story original to the book, features a quasi-vampiric gunslinger hero summoned by a young boy to dispose of the monster under his bed. *Lynch* is a variation on the Frankenstein theme, while *Walking Wolf* is a coming-of-age story about a young werewolf in the wild west. *The Tortuga Hill Gang's Last Ride* is a serio-comic story of an outlaw band that allows a semi-human monster, who has come to know them through dime novel fiction, join them in their adventures.

Other books by the same author:
Knuckles and Tales, 2001
Avenue X, 2000
Midnight Blue, 1995
Nameless Sins, 1994
Wild Blood, 1993

Other books you might like:
Joe R. Lansdale, *Dead in the West*, 1986
Tim Lebbon, *Dead Man's Hand*, 2004
S.P. Somtow, *Moon Dance*, 1989
Steve Vernon, *Long Horn, Big Shaggy*, 2004

620

MATTHEW COSTELLO

Missing Monday

(New York: Berkley, 2004)

Story type: Science Fiction
Subject(s): Memory; Mystery; Time Travel
Major character(s): Janna Wade, Office Worker; Caryn Stern, Professor; Mark Swan, Scientist
Time period(s): 2000s
Locale(s): New York, New York; Banff, Alberta, Canada; Lynnfield, North Carolina

Summary: Janna Wade awakens one morning to find that she has no memory of the past 24 hours. Her efforts to recollect her blanked-out interval dovetail with other peculiar events involving a number of people that piece together as clues in a vast scientific conspiracy. The conspiracy concerns covering up a program by which time travelers from the future, seeking a fresh start in life, take up residence in the past and lead lives that don't always work out as pleasantly as intended.

Other books by the same author:
Unidentified, 2002
Poltergeist: The Legacy, 2000
See How She Runs, 1994
Garden, 1993
Homecoming, 1992

Other books you might like:
Jack Finney, *Time and Again*, 1970
Dean R. Koontz, *Lightning*, 1988
Patrick O'Leary, *Door Number Three*, 1995
Bernard Taylor, *Charmed Life*, 1992
F. Paul Wilson, *Legacies*, 1998

621

RALPH ADAMS CRAM

Black Spirits and White

(Surrey, England: Tartarus, 2004)

Story type: Collection
Subject(s): Horror; Short Stories; Supernatural

Summary: This book of eight stories contains Cram's sole collection of short fiction, *Black Spirits and White*, first published in 1895, plus two previously uncollected tales. Cram became a well-known architect and leading exponent of the Gothic revival, and five of the six stories from the early collection feature buildings haunted by restless spirits, including "In Kropfsberg Keep," "Sister Maddalena," and "The White Villa." "The Dead Valley" is an atmospheric tale of a dead and abandoned landscape. The gothic novella *The Decadent* was originally published on its own in 1893. This limited edition book features a general overview of Cram and his writing by Stefan Dziemianowicz and a bibliographic history of Cram's fiction by Douglas A. Anderson.

Other books you might like:
E.F. Benson, *The Collected Ghost Stories of E.F. Benson*, 1992
Julian Hawthorne, *The Rose of Death and Other Mysterious Delusions*, 1997
M.R. James, *The Best Ghost Stories of M.R. James*, 1946
W.C. Morrow, *The Monster Maker and Other Stories*, 2000
Edgar Allan Poe, *Poetry, Tales and Selected Essays*, 1996

622

PETER CROWTHER, Editor

Fourbodings

(Baltimore: Cemetery Dance, 2004)

Story type: Anthology
Subject(s): Horror; Short Stories; Supernatural

Summary: Four leading British horror writers supply previously unpublished novellas of horror and the supernatural. Terry Lamsley's *So Long Gerry* is the story of a haunted apartment. Mark Morris' *Stumps* is the tale of an unholy survival infesting the lands bordering on the new home a family buys in rural England. Simon Clark's *Langthwaite Road* is concerned with the legacy of supernatural horrors associated with a roadway notorious for its fatalities.

Other books by the same author:
Taps and Sighs, 2000
Destination Unknown, 1996
Blue Motel, 1994
Narrow Houses, 1992
Touch Wood, 1992

Other books you might like:
Mike Ashley, *The Mammoth Book of Short Horror Novels*, 1988
  editor
Richard Chizmar, *Trick or Treat*, 2001
  editor
Bentley Little, *Four Dark Nights*, 2002
  editor
William Sheehan, *Night Visions 11*, 2004
  editor
Charles G. Waugh, *13 Short Horror Novels*, 1987
  Martin H. Greenberg, co-editor

623

ELAINE CUNNINGHAM

Shadows in the Darkness

(New York: Tor, 2004)

Story type: Occult
Series: Changeling. Book 1
Subject(s): Kidnapping
Major character(s): Gwen ''GiGi'' Gelman, Detective—Private; Ryan Cody, Lawyer; Ian Forest, Businessman
Time period(s): 2000s
Locale(s): Providence, Rhode Island

Summary: When private eye GiGi Gelman takes the case of an apparent child kidnapping, her investigations lead her into the seamy underworld of child pornography and gentlemen's clubs that cater to tastes in adolescents. When data she turns up begins dovetailing unexpectedly with aspects of her own past, much of which is shrouded in mystery even to her, GiGi can't help but suspect that knowledgeable individuals have manipulated her into the case to serve their inscrutable ends. This appears to be the first novel in a series whose heroine will discover that she is a changeling with supernatural powers raised as a human being.

Other books by the same author:
The Windwalker, 2003
Dark Journey, 2002
The Wizardwar, 2002
Haldor Lillenas: The Marvelous Music Maker, 1992
Under the Lucky Bean Tree, 1991

Other books you might like:
Kelley Armstrong, *Bitten*, 2001
Jack Caravela, *The Gifted*, 1991
Scott Ciencin, *The Vampire Odyssey*, 1992
Laurell K. Hamilton, *Incubus Dreams*, 2004
Karen E. Taylor, *Blood Secrets*, 1994

624

FRANK DARABONT
BERNI WRIGHTSON, Illustrator

Walpuski's Typewriter

(Baltimore: Cemetery Dance, 2004)

Story type: Occult
Subject(s): Demons; Supernatural; Writing

Major character(s): Howard Walpuski, Writer (horror); Iggy Feinwold, Agent; Cyril Pratt, Repairman
Time period(s): 2000s
Locale(s): Hollywood, California

Summary: When horror writer Howard Walpuski takes his typewriter to an eerie store for repair work, it comes back possessed by a demon that promises to generate best-selling novels as long as Walpuski agrees to feed it fresh meat. Walpuski revels in the success the bargain brings him until the demon increases its demands to live kills, and eventually bigger game than the animals the writer initially thought would satisfy it. This darkly comic first novel is by a writer best known as the director of *The Shawshank Redemption* and *The Green Mile*, both written by Stephen King on whose career this story is a comic riff. Published as a signed limited edition hardcover.

Other books you might like:
Fredric Brown, *What Mad Universe*, 1949
Simon Clark, *Darkness Demands*, 2001
L. Ron Hubbard, *Typewriter in the Sky*, 1951
Stephen King, *The Dark Half*, 1989
Richard Laymon, *The Stake*, 1991

625

MARYJANICE DAVIDSON

Undead and Unemployed

(New York: Berkley Sensation, 2004)

Story type: Vampire Story
Subject(s): Satire; Supernatural; Vampires
Major character(s): Betsy Taylor, Vampire; Eric Sinclair, Vampire; Marc, Health Care Professional
Time period(s): 2000s
Locale(s): St. Paul, Minnesota

Summary: In her second adventure after *Undead and Unwed*, newly turned vampire and fashion fetishist Betsy Taylor lands a plum night shift job in retail that allows her to indulge her vampire nature, as well as her passion for shoes. Soon after, though, she is challenged by the presence of something unholy and unforeseen in her new house, and a trendy gang of vampire slayers who compel her to enlist the aid of other vampires in the neighborhood.

Other books by the same author:
Undead and Unwed, 2004

Other books you might like:
Anne Billson, *Suckers*, 1993
Lionel Fenn, *The Mark of the Moderately Vicious Vampire*, 1989
Charlaine Harris, *Dead Until Dark*, 2001
Floyd Kemske, *Human Resources*, 1995
Christopher Moore, *Bloodsucking Fiends*, 1995

626

ARTHUR CONAN DOYLE

The Captain of the Polestar
(Ashcroft, British Columbia: Ash-Tree Press, 2004)

Story type: Collection
Subject(s): Horror; Short Stories; Supernatural

Summary: This omnibus collection of 38 stories represents all the short weird fiction written by the author best known as the creator of Sherlock Holmes. The contents, which are arranged in chronological order of publication include ''The Parasite,'' about an incident of supernatural possession brought about by an experiment in mesmerism; ''Lot 249,'' in which a reanimated Egyptian mummy goes on the rampage; and ''The Horror of the Heights,'' in which an air traveler discovers that the upper atmosphere abounds with monsters of the ether. Also included are several Sherlock Holmes stories that touch on occult themes. Edited and with an introduction by Barbara and Christopher Roden; foreword by Michael M. Dirda.

Other books by the same author:
Round the Fire Stories, 1908
Round the Red Lamp, 1894
The Great Keinplatz Experiment, 1894
The Captain of the Polestar and Other Tales, 1890
Mysteries and Adventures, 1889

Other books you might like:
John Buchan, *The Watcher by the Threshold*, 2005
W.W. Jacobs, *The Monkey's Paw and Other Tales of Mystery and the Macabre*, 1998
M.R. James, *The Collected Ghost Stories of M.R. James*, 1931
Richard Marsh, *The Haunted Chair and Other Stories*, 1997
Arthur Quiller-Couch, *The Horror on the Stair and Other Weird Tales*, 2000

627

JOHN MEADE FALKNER

The Nebuly Coat
(Ashcroft, British Columbia: Ash-Tree Press, 2004)

Story type: Occult
Subject(s): Horror; Occult; Supernatural
Major character(s): Arthur Westray, Architect; Euphemia Joliffe, Landlord; Sharnall, Musician
Time period(s): 19th century
Locale(s): Cullerne, England

Summary: Architect Arthur Westray reluctantly travels to the remote town of Cullerne to help restore Cullerne Minster, a church fallen, like the town, into abysmal disrepair. While undertaking the project, the new Lord Blandamer—whose family coat of arms, the Nebuly Coat, adorns the church's transept—offers to underwrite Westray's work. This noble effort cheers the townfolk until mysteries concerning Blandamer's inheritance and inexplicable deaths suggest that something sinister, and possibly supernatural, is afoot. Originally published in 1903, this new limited edition of the novel features an introduction by Mark Valentine.

Other books by the same author:
Moonfleet, 1898
The Lost Stradivarius, 1895

Other books you might like:
Peter Ackroyd, *Hawksmoor*, 1985
Jonathan Aycliffe, *A Shadow on the Wall*, 2000
H.B. Gregory, *Dark Sanctuary*, 2001
Phil Rickman, *Candle Night*, 1991
Francis Brett Young, *Cold Harbour*, 1926

628

PAUL FINCH

Darker Ages
(Carmarthenshire, Wales: Sarob, 2004)

Story type: Collection
Subject(s): Horror; Short Stories; Middle Ages
Time period(s): 11th century

Summary: Finch's two historical novellas of supernatural horror are both set in the 11th century. *The Blood Month* tells of a pair of warriors who flee to Greenland in the wake of the defeat of Christian Viking King Olaf, only to encounter a supernatural horror that thrives in the darkness of the Arctic winter. *Twilight in the Orm-Garth* is set in the aftermath of the Norman conquest of England and concerns a terrible being that embodies England's primitive past and one family's efforts to fight it. Published in a limited edition, with an introduction by Mike Ashley.

Other books by the same author:
The Extremist and Other Tales of Conflict, 2004
Cape Wrath, 2002
After Shocks, 2001
The Shadows Beneath, 2000

Other books you might like:
William Hope Hodgson, *The House on the Borderland*, 1908
Gordon Honeycombe, *The Dragon under the Hill*, 1973
Robert E. Howard, *Bran Mak Morn*, 1969
Adrian Ross, *The Hole of the Pit*, 1914

629

JOHN B. FORD, Editor
PAUL KANE, Co-Editor

Top International Horror
(Wiltshire, England: Rainfall, 2004)

Story type: Anthology
Subject(s): Horror; Short Stories; Supernatural

Summary: Subtitled ''Contest Winners 2003,'' this book features 17 stories posted on the Internet and chosen on the basis of the number of votes readers cast for each. ''Third Shift'' by Kevin Anderson concerns a business whose cheap labor supply for night work turns out to be ghouls. Bruce Golden's ''The Withering'' is set in a future where criminals are punished with injections that cause them to wither and deteriorate even while still alive. ''Three Silver Bullets'' by John Ludlow is a traditional werewolf story.

Other books you might like:

Richard Chizmar, *Shivers II*, 2003
  editor
Peter Enfantino, *Quick Chills*, 1990
  editor
Victor Heck, *The Asylum: The Quiet Ward*, 2003
  editor
L.H. Maynard, *Darkness Rising. Volume 1*, 2001
  M.P.N. Sims, co-editor
Elizabeth A. Saunders, *When the Black Lotus Blooms*, 1990
  editor

630

CHRISTOPHER FOWLER

Breathe: Everyone Has to Do It

(Surrey, England: Telos, 2004)

Story type: Satire
Subject(s): Employment; Horror; Labor Conditions
Major character(s): Ben Harper, Security Officer; Miranda Jameson, Office Worker; Meera Mangeshkar, Office Worker
Time period(s): 2000s
Locale(s): London, England

Summary: Ben Harper takes a position as Chief Health and Safety Officer of the SymaxCorp and is witness to strange behavior among the personnel, ranging from zombie-like dedication to outrageously self-destructive acts. Too late, he discovers that the company pipes an unorthodox chemical mix into the office atmosphere to increase worker productivity, and that something has gone horribly wrong with it.

Other books by the same author:

The Water Room, 2004
Plastic, 2003
Calabash, 2000
Soho Black, 1998
Disturbia, 1997

Other books you might like:

Ramsey Campbell, *The Overnight*, 2004
Thomas M. Disch, *The Businessman*, 1984
Floyd Kemske, *Human Resources*, 1995
David Prill, *The Unnatural*, 1995
William Browning Spencer, *Resume with Monsters*, 1995

631

ANDREW FOX

Bride of the Fat White Vampire

(New York: Ballantine, 2004)

Story type: Vampire Story
Subject(s): Horror; Short Stories; Vampires
Major character(s): Jules Duchon, Vampire; Rory "Doodlebug" Richelieu, Vampire; Preston, Vampire
Time period(s): 2000s
Locale(s): New Orleans, Louisiana

Summary: A transvestite vampire, Doodlebug, is coerced against his will into solving the mystery of who is serially mutilating young female vampires of the High Krewe of Vlad Tepes, one of the most powerful vampire clans in all New Orleans. Doodlebug's only hope is to reconstitute his friend Jules Duchon, another vampire who, despondent over the loss of his beloved vampire girlfriend Maureen, had himself translated into 187 white rats. Doodlebug restores Jules and promises that he will resurrect Maureen from the pile of dust she was reduced to if he will help, but Jules finds himself hampered by his dependence on a vampire enemy for assistance and the absence of one renegade rat who represents a crucial part of his anatomy. This satirical vampire tale is a direct sequel to the author's first novel, *Fat White Vampire Blues*.

Other books by the same author:

Fat White Vampire Blues, 2003

Other books you might like:

Poppy Z. Brite, *Lost Souls*, 1992
Nancy A. Collins, *Sunglasses After Dark*, 1989
Laurell K. Hamilton, *Guilty Pleasures*, 1993
Charlaine Harris, *Dead Until Dark*, 2001
David Sosnowski, *Vamped*, 2004

632

STEPHEN GALLAGHER

Out of His Mind

(Harrogate, England: PS Publishing, 2004)

Story type: Collection
Subject(s): Horror; Short Stories; Supernatural

Summary: *Out of His Mind* consists of 21 well-crafted stories of supernatural and non-supernatural horror by a writer known for his subtle approach. "The Drain" tells of a trio of juvenile delinquents pursued through a sewer pipe by a creature who may be an otherworldly monster or merely a figment of their own guilty and fearful imaginations. In "The Jigsaw," a man fails to appreciate that the image he sees in a strange jigsaw puzzle is a premonition of his impending death. Several of the stories build on scenarios involving teenagers and children, including "Magpie," a nasty tale of revenge.

Other books by the same author:

White Bizango, 2002
Red Red Robin, 1995
Nightmare with Angel, 1992
The Boat House, 1991
Rain, 1990

Other books you might like:

Stephen King, *Night Shift*, 1978
Robert R. McCammon, *Blue World*, 1989
Thomas F. Monteleone, *Fearful Symmetries*, 2004
Michael Marshall Smith, *More Tomorrow and Other Stories*, 2003
F. Paul Wilson, *Soft and Others*, 1989

633

R. PATRICK GATES

The Prison

(New York: Pinnacle, 2004)

Story type: Haunted House
Subject(s): Horror; Prisoners and Prisons; Supernatural
Major character(s): Tim Saget, Guard; John Thompson, Guard; Jim Henderson, Guard
Time period(s): 2000s
Locale(s): New Rome, Massachusetts

Summary: Decades ago, when it was an insane asylum, The Hill was infamous for an uprising among the patients that resulted in the deaths of many staff and the destruction of much of the facility. Now rebuilt as the New Rome Correctional Institute, The Hill is besieged by strange events, spectral manifestations, and increasingly unruly behavior among the inmates, all of which suggests that the same evil force that instigated the asylum uprising is gathering enough power to push the prisoners to rebel.

Other books by the same author:
Jumpers, 1997
Deathwalker, 1995
Tunnelvision, 1991
Grimm Memorials, 1990
Fear, 1988

Other books you might like:
Thomas Baum, *Out of Body*, 1997
Stephen King, *The Green Mile*, 1997
Nina Romberg, *Shadow Walkers*, 1993
J.N. Williamson, *The Night Seasons*, 1991

634

JEFF GELB, Editor
MICHAEL GARRETT, Co-Editor

Strange Bedfellows

(New York: Kensington, 2004)

Story type: Anthology
Series: Hot Blood. Book 12
Subject(s): Horror; Sexuality; Short Stories

Summary: These 19 tales of erotic horror and suspense were written especially for this compilation. Selections include Greg Kihn's ''Abomination,'' about a crime implicating a pair of Siamese twins in an act of sexual deviance, and Graham Masterton's ''Camelot,'' in which a man's sexually vivacious lover becomes trapped in a world on the other side of her mirror.

Other books by the same author:
Fatal Attraction, 2003
Hot Blood X, 1998
Crimes of Passion, 1997
Kiss and Kill, 1997
Fear the Fever, 1996

Other books you might like:
Nancy A. Collins, *Dark Love*, 1995
  Edward E. Kramer, Martin H. Greenberg, co-editors
Ellen Datlow, *Little Deaths*, 1994
  editor
Linda Lovecraft, *The Devil's Kisses*, 1976
  editor
John Pelan, *Darkside*, 1996
  editor
Michele Slung, *I Shudder at Your Touch*, 1991
  editor

635

WALTER GREATSHELL

Xombies

(New York: Berkley, 2004)

Story type: Science Fiction
Subject(s): Horror; Scientific Experiments
Major character(s): Lulu Pangloss, Young Woman; Fred Cowper, Military Personnel; Alice Langhorne, Doctor
Time period(s): 2000s
Locale(s): Pawtucket, Rhode Island; Arctic

Summary: A scientific experiment to produce longevity goes awry, and instead produces a virus that incubates in females and causes the dead to become reanimated and violent. Lulu, a woman who shows unnatural immunity to the virus, flees with others to the Arctic to escape the chaos convulsing the world. However, she discovers that the very company that first created the virus has established a foothold there and is interested in trying to distill an antidote from her.

Other books you might like:
Alex Garland, *28 Days Later*, 2003
Brian Keene, *Rising*, 2004
Philip Nutman, *Wet Work*, 1993
John Russo, *Night of the Living Dead*, 1974
John Skipp, *Book of the Dead*, 1989
  Craig Spector, co-editor

636

SIMON R. GREEN

Nightingale's Lament

(New York: Ace, 2004)

Story type: Occult
Series: Nightside. Book 3
Subject(s): Detection; Music and Musicians; Supernatural
Major character(s): John Taylor, Detective—Private; Cathy Barrett, Secretary; Rossignol, Singer
Time period(s): 2000s
Locale(s): London, England

Summary: Private detective John Taylor is hired to investigate Rossignol, a popular nightclub singer whose songs regularly drive patrons of Caliban's Cavern to suicide. The many obstacles to John's investigation created by management, bodyguards, and others in Rossignol's life lead John to suspect that her career is tied in with larger power struggles in the

Horror

Nightside, a secret part of London where the occult and supernatural beings are a regular part of the landscape. Taylor, a private eye with a talent for finding things, is the offspring of a union between a mortal and a being from the Nightside.

Other books by the same author:
Hex and the City, 2005
Agents of Light and Darkness, 2003
Something from the Nightside, 2003

Other books you might like:
Nancy A. Collins, *A Dozen Black Roses*, 1996
Christopher Fowler, *Roofworld*, 1988
Laurell K. Hamilton, *Guilty Pleasures*, 1993
John Shirley, *Constantine*, 2005
Dan Vining, *The Quick*, 2004

637

LAURELL K. HAMILTON

Incubus Dreams

(New York: Berkley, 2004)

Story type: Vampire Story
Series: Anita Blake, Vampire Hunter. Book 12
Subject(s): Horror
Major character(s): Anita Blake, Vampire Hunter; Jean-Claude, Vampire; Richard Zeeman, Werewolf
Time period(s): 2000s
Locale(s): St. Louis, Missouri

Summary: Anita Blake, a law enforcement agent in an alternate world where humans and supernatural beings coexist, investigates serial killings of strippers that appear to be the work of one or more vampires. Her professional duties are complicated by her involvement with two lovers, one a vampire and the other a werewolf. Also, she has an increasingly promiscuous sensuality that sharpens her own supernatural powers, even as it plunges her more deeply into the inhuman world she opposes through her work.

Other books by the same author:
Cerulean Sins, 2003
Narcissus in Chains, 2001
Obsidian Butterfly, 2000
Blue Moon, 1998
Burnt Offerings, 1998

Other books you might like:
Kelley Armstrong, *Industrial Magic*, 2004
L.A. Banks, *Minion*, 2003
Nancy A. Collins, *A Dozen Black Roses*, 1996
Charlaine Harris, *Dead to the World*, 2004
Susan Sizemore, *Heroes*, 2003

638

CHARLAINE HARRIS

Dead to the World

(New York: Ace, 2004)

Story type: Vampire Story
Series: Southern Vampire. Book 4

Subject(s): Supernatural; Vampires; Witches and Witchcraft
Major character(s): Sookie Stackhouse, Waiter/Waitress; Eric Northman, Vampire, Amnesiac; Marnie Stonebrook, Witch
Time period(s): 2000s
Locale(s): Bon Temps, Louisiana; Shreveport, Louisiana

Summary: The night that her vampire boyfriend, Bill, leaves town on a secret project for the vampire hierarchy, Sookie comes upon Eric, a vampire leader, wandering naked and amnesiac on the road to her house. Investigating, she traces Eric's problem to a group of were-witches who have taken to drinking vampire blood in the hope of vaulting to the top of the supernatural hierarchy. Sookie's plans to thwart the witches and crush their revolt are complicated by the disappearance of her brother Jason, which she suspects is somehow tied in with her involvement in these affairs. This supernatural romantic comedy series is set in a world where vampires and other supernatural creatures coexist with humanity.

Other books by the same author:
Club Dead, 2003
Living Dead in Dallas, 2002
Dead Until Dark, 2001

Other books you might like:
Anne Billson, *Suckers*, 1993
MaryJanice Davidson, *Undead and Unemployed*, 2004
Laurell K. Hamilton, *Cerulean Sins*, 2003
Tanya Huff, *Smoke and Mirrors*, 2004
Katherine Ramsland, *The Blood Hunters*, 2004

639

M. JOHN HARRISON

The Course of the Heart

(San Francisco: Night Shade, 2004)

Story type: Occult
Subject(s): Occult; Schools; Supernatural
Major character(s): Lucas Medlar, Teacher; Pam Stuyvesant, Artist; Yaxley, Vagrant
Time period(s): 1990s
Locale(s): London, England

Summary: Lucas, Pam, and the unnamed narrator are all affected by differing sensations of the Pleroma, an occult realm of sensuality which they first became aware of from an unspoken ritual enacted during their school years at Cambridge. Intruding upon their lives in the mundane world, the transcendent Pleroma is responsible for the despondence, dysfunction, and distress that have shaped their lives ever since. First American edition of a novel originally published in the United Kingdom in 1992.

Other books by the same author:
Light, 2002
Signs of Life, 1997
The Luck in the Head, 1991
The Centauri Device, 1974
The Committed Men, 1971

Other books you might like:
Ramsey Campbell, *Incarnate*, 1983
Douglas Clegg, *Goat Dance*, 1989

J.K. Jeter, *Dark Seeker*, 1987
Lucius Shepard, *Kalimantan*, 1992
Donna Tartt, *The Secret History*, 1992

640

JOHN HARWOOD

The Ghost Writer

(Orlando, Florida: Harcourt, 2004)

Story type: Ghost Story
Subject(s): Ghosts; Mothers and Sons; Writing
Major character(s): Gerard Freeman, Librarian, Young Man; Alice Jessel, Young Woman, Handicapped (crippled); Phyllis Freeman, Widow(er)
Time period(s): 2000s
Locale(s): Mawson, Australia; London, England

Summary: Although Gerard's mother regales him with accounts of the idyllic childhood she spent at her family's home in Staplefield, England, she vows that she will never return there, and forcefully tries to dissuade her son from ever looking into her family's history. Then curious Gerard runs across published ghost stories by a writer who signs herself V.H., and whom he suspects was his grandmother. Assuming that these stories might deal in symbolic fashion with a tragedy that so transformed his mother's sentiments, Gerard travels to London to investigate, even though a death that might be his own has been foretold in his grandmother's fiction. First novel.

Where it's reviewed:
All Hallows 37, October 2004, page 138

Other books you might like:
Ramsey Campbell, *Nazareth Hill*, 1996
Jonathan Carroll, *Voice of Our Shadow*, 1983
Dennis McFarland, *A Face at the Window*, 1997
Peter Straub, *In the Night Room*, 2004
Lisa Tuttle, *My Death*, 2004

641

S.E. HINTON

Hawkes Harbor

(New York: Tor, 2004)

Story type: Vampire Story
Subject(s): Horror; Supernatural; Vampires
Major character(s): Jamie Sommers, Sailor, Thief; Grenville Hawkes, Vampire; Louisa Kahne, Doctor
Time period(s): 1960s; 1970s
Locale(s): Hawkes Harbor, Delaware

Summary: Orphaned as a young boy, Jamie Sommers leads a hardscrabble life as a full-time sailor and petty thief. Years after he has been institutionalized for his irremediable violent outbursts, Jamie undergoes therapy. He reveals how, on one of his adventures, he plundered a casket he thought to be full of treasure, only to discover that it was the coffin of a vampire who has held him in supernatural thrall ever since.

Other books by the same author:
Taming the Star Runner, 1988

Tex, 1979
Rumble Fish, 1975
That Was Then, This Is Now, 1971
The Outsiders, 1967

Other books you might like:
Gary Bowen, *Diary of a Vampire*, 1995
John Peyton Cooke, *Out for Blood*, 1991
Elizabeth Engstrom, *Black Ambrosia*, 1988
William Tedford, *Liquid Diet*, 1992
Sidney Williams, *Night Brothers*, 1989

642

TANYA HUFF

Smoke and Shadows

(New York: DAW, 2004)

Story type: Occult
Subject(s): Occult; Movie Industry; Supernatural
Major character(s): Henry Fitzroy, Vampire; Tony Foster, Filmmaker, Lover (Henry's former); Arra Pelindrake, Filmmaker, Wizard
Time period(s): 2000s
Locale(s): Vancouver, British Columbia, Canada

Summary: Arra Pelindrake's special effects on the set of the television program "Darkest Night" accidentally open a gate that admits the evil influence of a Shadowlord, who promptly kills a member of the cast and engages in other fiendish mischief. With the help of his former lover, vampire Henry Fitzroy, production assistant Tony Foster engages the services of Pelindrake, who is also secretly a wizard, to help close the gate and prevent further dangerous incursions of the supernatural. This novel features characters who appeared in the author's previous series of books featuring Fitzroy as their recurring hero.

Other books by the same author:
Blood Debt, 1997
Blood Pact, 1993
Blood Lines, 1992
Blood Trail, 1992
Blood Price, 1991

Other books you might like:
Jim Butcher, *Blood Rites*, 2004
Ramsey Campbell, *Ancient Images*, 1989
Jonathan Carroll, *A Child Across the Sky*, 1989
Dale Hoover, *65mm*, 1994
Theodore Roszak, *Flicker*, 1991

643

STEPHEN JONES, Editor

The Mammoth Book of Best New Horror.
Volume 15

(New York: Carroll & Graf, 2004)

Story type: Anthology
Subject(s): Horror; Short Stories; Supernatural

Horror

Summary: These 25 stories of horror and the supernatural were chosen by the editor as representative of the best horror fiction published in 2003. Included are Steve Rasnic Tem's "The Bereavement Photographer," a poignant story of a man paid to photograph the dead for family mementos; Steve Nagy's "The Hanged Man of Oz," which treats urban legends around the filming of *The Wizard of Oz* as dark truths; and Glen Hirshberg's "Dancing Men," in which the horrors of the Nazi holocaust manifest in a bizarre and subtly fantastic form to the grandson of a survivor of the concentration camps. The book includes a lengthy essay surveying the year's yield in horror in a variety of media, and an annual necrology compiled by the editor and Kim Newman.

Other books by the same author:
By Moonlight Only, 2003
Keep Out the Night, 2002
The Mammoth Book of Vampire Stories by Women, 2001
Dark Detectives, 1999
White of the Moon, 1999

Other books you might like:
Ramsey Campbell, *Gathering the Bones*, 2003
  Jack Dann, Dennis Etchison, co-editors
Ellen Datlow, *The Year's Best Fantasy and Horror: Seventeenth Annual Collection*, 2004
  Gavin Grant, Kelly Link, co-editors
John Pelan, *A Walk on the Darkside*, 2004
Barbara Roden, *Acquainted with the Night*, 2004
  Christopher Roden, co-editor
William Sheehan, *Night Visions 11*, 2004
  editor

644

STEPHEN JONES, Editor

The Mammoth Book of New Terror

(New York: Carroll & Graf, 2004)

Story type: Anthology
Subject(s): Horror; Short Stories; Supernatural

Summary: Jones' anthology contains 26 varied stories of horror and the supernatural, three original to the book. Contents include Christopher Fowler's "Turbo-Satan," in which a man discovers a method for accessing an infernal dimension through his cell phone; David J. Schow's "Wake-Up Call," about a future where the state turns criminals into long-lasting, physically insensitive zombies to serve out their prison sentences; and Terry Lamsley's "Under the Crust," about an ancient infectious evil festering in the atmosphere of a remote town.

Other books by the same author:
By Moonlight Only, 2003
Keep Out the Night, 2002
The Mammoth Book of Vampire Stories by Women, 2001
Dark Detectives, 1999
White of the Moon, 1999

Other books you might like:
Richard Chizmar, *The Best of Cemetery Dance*, 1998
  editor

Peter Crowther, *Narrow Houses*, 1992
  editor
Dennis Etchison, *Cutting Edge*, 1986
  editor
David G. Hartwell, *Foundations of Fear*, 1992
  editor
Kirby McCauley, *Dark Forces*, 1980
  editor

645

STEPHEN JONES, Editor

The Mammoth Book of Vampires. New Edition

(New York: Carroll & Graf, 2004)

Story type: Anthology; Vampire Story
Subject(s): Vampires; Short Stories; Supernatural

Summary: This revised edition of a vampire anthology, originally published in 1992, features three new stories and several new reprints. Selections include Sydney J. Bounds' "A Taste for Blood," a tongue-in-cheek story of a hospital that transfuses patients with vampire blood; John Burke's "The Devil's Tritone," in which a musician and his family become caught up in strange rituals of the dead in a remote town; and Hugh B. Cave's "Stragella," about a shipwreck that teems with vampiric life forms.

Other books by the same author:
By Moonlight Only, 2003
Keep Out the Night, 2002
The Mammoth Book of Vampire Stories by Women, 2001
Dark Detectives, 1999
White of the Moon, 1999

Other books you might like:
Poppy Z. Brite, *Love in Vein*, 1994
  editor
Ellen Datlow, *Blood Is Not Enough*, 1989
  editor
Martin H. Greenberg, *A Taste for Blood*, 1992
Alan Ryan, *Vampires*, 1987
Leonard Wolf, *Blood Thirst: 100 Years of Vampire Fiction*, 1997

646

TAMARA SILER JONES

Ghosts in the Snow

(New York: Bantam/Spectra, 2004)

Story type: Occult
Series: Dubric Bryerly. Book 1
Subject(s): Detection; Ghosts; Supernatural
Major character(s): Dubric Bryerly, Detective—Private; Nella, Servant; Lars, Royalty
Time period(s): Indeterminate
Locale(s): Faldorrah, Mythical Place

Summary: A continuing series of women are being slaughtered at Castle Faldorrah, and security chief Dubric Bryerly is the only one who sees their grisly ghosts enjoining him to find their murderer. This is no easy task since the murderer appears to be invisible, and since Nella, the linen maid whom Dubric thinks is the likely next candidate, is being shielded by someone with authority who may also be concealing evidence crucial to his investigation. First novel and first in a series featuring Bryerly as the hero.

Other books by the same author:
Threads of Malice, 2005

Other books you might like:
Trystam Kith, *Trouble in the Forest*, 2004
Lucius Shepard, *The Golden*, 1993
Chet Williamson, *Mordenheim*, 1994
David Niall Wilson, *To Sift through Bitter Ashes*, 1997

647

CAITLIN R. KIERNAN

The Dry Salvages

(Burton, Michigan: Subterranean, 2004)

Story type: Science Fiction
Subject(s): Aliens; Science Fiction; Space Exploration
Major character(s): Audrey Cather, Scientist; Joakim Hamilton, Scientist; Umachandra Murdin, Scientist
Time period(s): 23rd century
Locale(s): Paris, France; Piros, Planet—Imaginary

Summary: The starship *Montelius* voyages to Piros, a planet 15 light years from Earth, to study artifacts of what appears to be the first known non-human civilization in the universe. When they rendezvous with *Gilgamesh*, the exploratory ship that first discovered the planet, the officers of the *Montelius* find half the crew missing and the other half driven insane by a horror encountered on the planet's surface. Writing decades later, extrasolar exopaleontologist Audrey Cather reveals what the *Montelius* crew discovers when it makes its own fact-finding mission to the surface of Piros. Published as a signed limited edition hardcover.

Other books by the same author:
Murder of Angels, 2004
Low Red Moon, 2003
The Five of Cups, 2003
Threshold, 2001
Silk, 1998

Other books you might like:
Arthur C. Clarke, *2001: A Space Odyssey*, 1968
Alan Dean Foster, *Alien*, 1979
Brian Lumley, *The House of Doors*, 1990
Christopher Pike, *The Season of Passage*, 1992

648

CAITLIN R. KIERNAN

Murder of Angels

(New York: Roc, 2004)

Story type: Occult
Subject(s): Music and Musicians; Occult; Supernatural
Major character(s): Daria Parker, Musician; Nikki Ky, Young Woman; Marvin Gale, Care Giver

Time period(s): 2000s
Locale(s): San Francisco, California

Summary: Daria, Nikki, and their friends have still not recovered entirely from their experiment to open a door to the supernatural that resulted in the death of their friend, Spyder Baxter, in the author's first published novel, *Silk*. Influenced by dreams and reality warps in which Spyder talks to her directly from the realm beyond death, Nikki plunges off the Golden Gate Bridge and awakens in the afterlife where Spyder hopes to use her as a pawn to draw out a formidable supernatural adversary dubbed The Dragon. Meanwhile, in the realm of the living, Daria struggles to retrieve a talisman that is crucial to Nikki's role and for preventing The Dragon's incursion into our own world.

Other books by the same author:
The Dry Salvages, 2004
Low Red Moon, 2003
The Five of Cups, 2003
Threshold, 2001
Silk, 1998

Other books you might like:
Poppy Z. Brite, *Drawing Blood*, 1993
Sephera Giron, *Borrowed Flesh*, 2004
Rick Hautala, *Beyond the Shroud*, 1996
Kathe Koja, *Bad Brains*, 1992
Lucius Shepard, *Kalimantan*, 1992

649

STEPHEN KING

The Dark Tower

(New York: Donald M. Grant/Scribner, 2004)

Story type: Ancient Evil Unleashed
Series: Dark Tower. Book 7
Subject(s): Death; Good and Evil; Supernatural
Major character(s): Roland Deschain, Gunfighter; Donald Callahan, Religious; Eddie Dean, Addict, Spouse
Time period(s): 2000s
Locale(s): Lowell, Maine; New York, New York; Algul Sient, Mythical Place

Summary: In this final installment of the Dark Tower series, which has taken more than 30 years for the author to complete, otherworldly gunslinger Roland Deschain and his ka-tet of human companions from alternate earths converge upon the Dark Tower, the nexus of all universes. There they fight the Crimson King, who hopes to disrupt the universal order and plunge the cosmos into chaos. En route to his destiny at the Dark Tower, Roland assists in a variety of climax building adventures, including the thwarting of a vampire takeover in modern Manhattan, the battle with an inhuman offspring whose blood is a mingling of his own and the Crimson King's, and a meeting with writer Stephen King, whose fictional renderings of Roland's adventures give the plot a metafictional spin. This book not only concludes the epic series but unifies characters and themes throughout the author's work for most of the last three decades.

Other books by the same author:
Song of Susannah, 2004

Wolves of the Calla, 2003
The Waste Lands, 1991
The Drawing of the Three, 1987
The Gunslinger, 1982

Other books you might like:
Clive Barker, *The Great and Secret Show*, 1989
Raymond E. Feist, *Faerie Tale*, 1988
Robert Jordan, *The Dragon Reborn*, 1991
Kim Newman, *Seven Stars*, 2000
J.R.R. Tolkien, *The Return of the King*, 1956

650

RUSSELL KIRK

Ancestral Shadows

(Grand Rapids, Michigan: Eerdmans, 2004)

Story type: Collection
Subject(s): Horror; Short Stories; Supernatural

Summary: These 19 tales of ghosts and the supernatural are by a writer best known as a conservative thinker and political commentator. Selections include ''The Peculiar Demesne of Archvicar Gerontion,'' a man's account of how he outwitted supernatural possession by a black magic practitioner in Africa; ''Sorworth Place,'' in which a traveler in Scotland becomes caught up in the acting out of a centuries-old supernatural curse; and ''An Encounter by Mortstone Pond,'' an uncharacteristically poignant tale of an adult soldier who meets his innocent childhood self while visiting his family's old home. Editor Vigen Guroian, in his introduction, links the metaphysical and religious aspects of the author's fiction to his political beliefs.

Other books by the same author:
What Shadows We Pursue, 2003
Off the Sand Road, 2002
The Watchers at the Strait-Gate, 1984
The Princess of All Lands, 1979
The Surly Sullen Bell, 1962

Other books you might like:
Charles Birkin, *A Haunting Beauty*, 2000
Robert M. Coates, *The Hour After Westerly*, 1957
Shirley Jackson, *Just an Ordinary Day*, 1997
Gerald Kersh, *On an Odd Note*, 1958
Joyce Carol Oates, *Haunted*, 1995

651

TRYSTAM KITH

A Cold Summer Night

(Waterville, Maine: Five Star, 2004)

Story type: Vampire Story
Series: Trouble in the Forest. Book 1
Subject(s): Folk Tales; Supernatural; Vampires
Major character(s): Robin Hood, Vampire; Marian De Beauchamp, Noblewoman; Hugh deSteny, Lawman (sheriff), Knight (former)
Time period(s): 11th century
Locale(s): Nottingham, England

Summary: This book is a vampire variation on the legend of Robin Hood. It presupposes that Robin Hood and his Merry Men are roving vampires who prey upon woodsmen and their families and that their nemesis, the Sheriff of Nottingham, has fought their type before during the Holy Crusades.

Other books by the same author:
A Bright Winter Sun, 2004

Other books you might like:
Parke Godwin, *Robin and the King*, 1993
Richard Kluger, *The Sheriff of Nottingham*, 1992
Robin McKinley, *The Outlaws of Sherwood*, 1989
Jennifer Roberson, *Lady of the Forest*, 1992
Jane Yolen, *Briar Rose*, 1992

652

DEAN R. KOONTZ

Life Expectancy

(New York: Bantam, 2004)

Story type: Occult
Subject(s): Faith; Future; Supernatural
Major character(s): Jimmy Tock, Cook; Lorrie Hicks, Spouse; Punchinello Beezo, Criminal
Time period(s): 1970s; 2000s
Locale(s): Snow Village, Colorado

Summary: On the night of his birth, Jimmy Tock's grandfather, who dies shortly afterward, foretells five dates in the future, corresponding to Jimmy's 20th, 23rd, 28th, 29th, and 30th years, when he will faces challenges to his life and sunny disposition. These challenges, each of which proves to have a beneficial outcome for Jimmy, are invariably twined with the activities of the Beezos, a local family with a circus pedigree who constantly stir up in trouble in town, and whose fates tie up with Jimmy's in ways more intimate than can be imagined.

Where it's reviewed:
Publishers Weekly, November 15, 2004, page 41

Other books by the same author:
Velocity, 2005
The Taking, 2004
Odd Thomas, 2003
The Face, 2003
By the Light of the Moon, 2002

Other books you might like:
Ray Bradbury, *Something Wicked This Way Comes*, 1962
Stephen King, *The Regulators*, 1996
Robert R. McCammon, *Gone South*, 1992
Dan Simmons, *The Hollow Man*, 1992
Bernard Taylor, *Charmed Life*, 1992

653

RICHARD LAYMON

The Lake

(New York: Leisure, 2004)

Story type: Psychological Suspense
Subject(s): Accidents

Major character(s): Deana West, Teenager; Leigh West, Parent (Deana's mother); Mace Harrison, Police Officer
Time period(s): 2000s
Locale(s): San Francisco, California

Summary: Shortly after Deana's boyfriend is mowed down by a car, Deana and her mother find themselves being pursued by the driver. Clues and echoes of the tragedy take Leigh back to her own teenage years, and an incident in which her own boyfriend was accidentally killed. Leigh's boyfriend's mother never forgave Leigh for her son's death, and now Leigh is wondering if her past and present miseries might somehow be related. The author died in 2001 but this unpublished novel was found among his papers.

Other books by the same author:
Amara, 2002
Night in the Lonesome October, 2001
No Sanctuary, 2001
Among the Missing, 1999
The Travelling Vampire Show, 1999

Other books you might like:
John Farris, *The Axman Cometh*, 1989
Stephen Gallagher, *Down River*, 1989
Rick Hautala, *Impulse*, 1996
Stephen King, *Rose Madder*, 1995
Dean R. Koontz, *Intensity*, 1996

654

TIM LEBBON

Dead Man's Hand

(Gladstone, Mississippi: Necessary Evil, 2004)

Story type: Occult
Series: Assassin. Book 1
Subject(s): Angels; Good and Evil; Supernatural
Major character(s): Doug, Store Owner; Gabriel, Gunfighter; Temple, Gunfighter
Time period(s): 19th century
Locale(s): Deadwood, South Dakota

Summary: Two gunslinging opponents, Gabriel and Temple, possibly an angel and a demon, act out their personal vendetta on the streets of Deadwood, ultimately drawing Wild Bill Hickock into their bloody gunfight. First book in a series to be written by diverse writers, published as a signed limited edition chapbook.

Other books by the same author:
Desolation, 2005
Changing of Faces, 2003
Until She Sleeps, 2002
Face, 2001
The Nature of Balance, 2001

Other books you might like:
Nancy A. Collins, *Dead Man's Hand*, 2004
Stephen King, *The Dark Tower*, 1982
Joe R. Lansdale, *Dead in the West*, 1986
S.P. Somtow, *Moon Dance*, 1989
Michael Szymanski, *Weird Trails*, 2002

655

DEBORAH LEBLANC

Family Inheritance

(New York: Leisure, 2004)

Story type: Occult
Subject(s): Demons; Horror; Supernatural
Major character(s): Jessica LeJeune, Businesswoman; Eli, Shaman; Todd Guidry, Patient
Time period(s): 2000s
Locale(s): Baton Rouge, Louisiana; Memphis, Tennessee

Summary: Jessica, who has been endowed since youth with the ability to heal by touch, is plagued with headaches and horrifying visions coincident with her brother Todd becoming institutionalized for violent behavior. At the same time, Eli, a shaman in the bayous of Baton Rouge, has visions of Jessica and their shared destiny. Eli and Jessica realize that both are hosts to Maikana, a demonic being who has endowed them with their powers and driven Todd mad, and that Todd's salvation lies in their working together to exorcise the demon. First novel.

Other books you might like:
Nancy A. Collins, *Tempter*, 1990
Stephen Gallagher, *White Bizango*, 2002
Brian Hodge, *The Darker Saints*, 1995
Abigail McDaniels, *Althea*, 1995
Lucius Shepard, *Louisiana Breakdown*, 2003

656

EDWARD LEE

Infernal Angel

(New York: Leisure, 2004)

Story type: Occult
Subject(s): Hell; Horror; Sisters
Major character(s): Cassie Heydon, Patient; Walter Grey, Young Man; Angelese, Angel
Time period(s): 2000s
Locale(s): Mephistopolis, Mythical Place

Summary: As an Etheress, or identical twin who failed to commit suicide when her sister succeeded, Cassie Heydon wields awesome powers in Mephistopolis, the biblical Hell to which she travels from Earth to retrieve her sister's soul. Recognizing that her power is crucial to his plans to relocate Hell to Earth, Lucifer becomes involved in a cagey cat-and-mouse game designed to draw Cassie into his clutches. This is a mass market edition of a novel originally published as a signed limited edition hardcover in 2003, and a sequel to *City Infernal*.

Other books by the same author:
Flesh Gothic, 2005
Messenger, 2004
Monstrosity, 2002
City Infernal, 2001
Stickmen, 1999

Other books you might like:
Michael Cisco, *The Tyrant*, 2003

Brett Savory, *The Distance Travelled*, 2001
Shane Ryan Staley, *Dark Testament*, 2002
   editor
Jeffrey Thomas, *Letters from Hades*, 2003

657
EDWARD LEE

Messenger
(New York: Leisure, 2004)

Story type: Occult
Subject(s): Horror; Supernatural
Major character(s): Jane Ryan, Postal Worker; Steve Higgins, Police Officer; Alexander Dhevic, Scholar, Occultist
Time period(s): 2000s
Locale(s): Danelleton, Florida

Summary: Over the years, the town of Danelleton has been plagued by serial killings which appear to be linked to the local post office. Postal inspector Jane Ryan investigates and, with the help of occultist Alexander Dhevic, discovers that the legacy of murder and mayhem are related to an ancient talisman secreted on the premises.

Other books by the same author:
Infernal Angel, 2003
Monstrosity, 2002
Stickmen, 1999
Creekers, 1994
Incubi, 1991

Other books you might like:
Clive Barker, *The Great and Secret Show*, 1989
Thomas M. Disch, *The Sub: A Study in Witchcraft*, 1999
Charles L. Grant, *The Black Carousel*, 1995
Bentley Little, *The Mailman*, 1990
William Browning Spencer, *Resume with Monsters*, 1995

658
BENTLEY LITTLE

The Resort
(New York: Signet, 2004)

Story type: Occult
Subject(s): Horror; Hotels and Motels; Satire
Major character(s): Lowell Thurman, Businessman; Patrick Schlaegel, Critic; Ryan Thurman, Child
Time period(s): 2000s
Locale(s): Tucson, Arizona

Summary: Shortly after checking into The Reata, a remote resort in the Arizona desert, the Thurman family are subjected to peculiar and seemingly inescapable problems. The staff is surly, the accommodations are full of strange and often gruesome surprises, and certain organized activities have a ritualistic character. The discovery of the ruins of a previous version of the resort prompts concern that the Thurmans and other guests have wandered into the domain of a malignant influence that uses the grounds to attract sacrifices necessary to prolong its unholy existence. The novel mixes black comedy with horror.

Other books by the same author:
The Policy, 2003
The Return, 2002
The Association, 2001
The Town, 2000
The Walking, 2000

Other books you might like:
Michael Green, *The Jimjams*, 1994
Nancy Holder, *Dead in the Water*, 1994
Stephen King, *The Shining*, 1977
Robert Marasco, *Burnt Offerings*, 1973
T.M. Wright, *The Island*, 1988

659
PHIL LOCASCIO

Howling Hounds
(Carmarthenshire, Wales: Sarob, 2004)

Story type: Collection
Subject(s): Horror; Short Stories; Supernatural

Summary: These 13 stories of horror and the supernatural are by a writer whose work appears predominately in small press publications. Several of the stories revolve around psychologically disorienting timeslips, including "Bendable Rulers," in which a man piecing together fragmented memories realizes he may have murdered his wife, and "The Boy in the Corner," about the horrible impact a man's near-death as a child has on events in his adult life. Published as a limited edition hardcover.

Other books you might like:
Simon Bestwick, *A Hazy Shade of Winter*, 2004
Alison Davies, *Small Deaths*, 2003
Paul Finch, *After Shocks*, 2001
Joel Lane, *The Earth Wire and Other Stories*, 1994
Ashley McConnell, *Days of the Dead*, 1992

660
H.P. LOVECRAFT

The Dreams in the Witch House and Other Weird Stories
(New York: Penguin, 2004)

Story type: Collection
Subject(s): Horror; Short Stories; Supernatural

Summary: These 21 stories of horror, fantasy, and the supernatural are by a writer from the pulp era generally regarded as the most important horror writer of the early 20th century. Selections include "In the Vault," a grisly tale of supernatural revenge; "The Shunned House," about a vampiric influence that infests an infamous dwelling; "Dreams in the Witch House," about the unfortunate tenant of a house once inhabited by a witch whose presence is still very much alive in it; and "The Shadow out of Time," in which a man of the 20th century exchanges personalities with an extraplanetary entity. Edited and introduced by S.T. Joshi.

Other books by the same author:
The Thing on the Doorstep and Other Weird Stories, 2001
The Call of Cthulhu and Other Weird Stories, 1999
Dagon and Other Macabre Tales, 1965
At the Mountains of Madness and Other Novels, 1964
The Dunwich Horror and Others, 1963

Other books you might like:
Robert Bloch, *The Early Fears*, 1994
August Derleth, *The Mask of Cthulhu*, 1958
Frank Belknap Long, *The Hounds of Tindalos*, 1946
Donald Wandrei, *The Eye and the Finger*, 1944
Henry S. Whitehead, *Jumbee and Other Uncanny Tales*, 1944

661

BRIAN LUMLEY

Brian Lumley's Freaks
(Burton, Michigan: Subterranean, 2004)

Story type: Collection
Subject(s): Horror; Short Stories; Supernatural

Summary: Lumley's collection consists of five short stories, most of which depict mutants and monsters sympathetically as the victims of predatory "normal" humans. "In the Glow Zone" and "Mother Love" both feature genetic freaks of nuclear apocalypse. "Somebody Calling," the book's one previously unpublished story, details the peculiar psychic bond between a man and his deformed twin sister. "Problem Child" is the first-person narrative of a supernatural offspring blissfully unaware of his uncanny pedigree. Published as a signed limited edition hardcover.

Other books by the same author:
The House of the Temple, 2004
The Whisperer and Other Voices, 2001
The Second Wish and Other Exhalations, 1995
Fruiting Bodies and Other Fungi, 1993
The Horror at Oakdeene and Others, 1977

Other books you might like:
Groff Conklin, *Science Fiction Adventures in Mutation*, 1955
    editor
Dean R. Koontz, *Strange Highways*, 1995
David Langford, *Irrational Numbers*, 1994
Frank Belknap Long, *The Rim of the Unknown*, 1972
Richard Matheson, *Born of Man and Woman*, 1954

662

BRANDON MASSEY, Editor

Dark Dreams
(New York: DaFina, 2004)

Story type: Anthology
Subject(s): Horror; Short Stories; Suspense

Summary: These 20 stories (several previously unpublished) of horror and suspense are all by black writers. Linda Addison's "Power" is a voodoo variant, and Steven Barnes and Tananarive Due's "Danger Word" an apocalyptic tale of science fiction horrors. Virtually all of the stories touch in some way on the black experience in America and around the world, including Robert Fleming's "But Beautiful and Terrifying," in which a black GI finds a parallel to his treatment in the American South and the treatment of Jews in Nazi Germany.

Other books you might like:
Angela C. Allen, *Dark Thirst*, 2004
    editor
Tananarive Due, *The Good House*, 2003
Robert Fleming, *Havoc After Dark*, 2004
Sheree R. Thomas, *Dark Matter: A Century of Speculative Fiction from the African Diaspora*, 2000
    editor
Sheree R. Thomas, *Dark Matter: Reading the Bones*, 2003
    editor

663

ELIZABETH MASSIE

The Fear Report
(Modesto, California: Bloodletting, 2004)

Story type: Collection
Subject(s): African Americans; Short Stories; Supernatural

Summary: Thirty stories make up the contents of this retrospective collection by a Southern writer whose works are often inflected with the gothic and grotesque. Selections include "Stephen," a Bram Stoker Award-winning tale of a health care worker who falls in love with a grotesquely disfigured patient; "Hooked on Buzzer," a study of psychopathology; and the vampire tale, "Day Is Done, Gone the Sun."

Other books by the same author:
Wire Mesh Mothers, 2001
Welcome Back to the Night, 2000
Shadow Dreams, 1996
Southern Discomfort, 1993
Sineater, 1992

Other books you might like:
Poppy Z. Brite, *Swamp Foetus*, 1993
Dawn Dunn, *Pink Marble and Never Say Die*, 2001
Brian Hodge, *Lies and Ugliness*, 2002
Stephen Mark Rainey, *Fugue Devil and Other Weird Horror*, 1993
Mehitobel Wilson, *Dangerous Red*, 2003
    editor

664

RICHARD MATHESON

Duel and The Distributor
(Colorado Springs, Colorado: Gauntlet, 2004)

Story type: Collection
Subject(s): Short Stories

Summary: Matheson's work contains two short stories and the screenplays adapted from them. "Duel," about a desperate man in a car being pursued across a vacant stretch of desert by a murderous tractor-trailer, served as a vehicle for the Steven Spielberg film of the same name, which was one of the most popular made-for-television movies in history. The book also

Horror

features an interview with Dennis Weaver, the star of the film. "The Distributor," which never was filmed, is a classic tale of small-town paranoia concerning a man whose job it is to sow discord and distress among otherwise peaceful townspeople. Published as an oversized signed limited edition hardcover.

Other books by the same author:
Darker Places, 2004
Richard Matheson's Kolchak Scripts, 2004
Come Fygures, Come Shadowes, 2003
Offbeat: Uncollected Stories, 2002
Nightmare at 20,000 Feet, 2000

Other books you might like:
Charles Beaumont, *The Twilight Zone Scripts of Charles Beaumont. Volume 1*, 2004
Richard Chizmar, *Screamplays*, 1999
   Martin H. Greenberg, co-editor
Earl Hamner, *The Twilight Zone Scripts of Earl Hamner*, 2003
George Clayton Johnson, *Writing for the Twilight Zone*, 1980
Rod Serling, *As Timeless as Infinity*, 2004

665

DEREK MCCORMACK

The Haunted Hillbilly

(Brooklyn, New York: Soft Skull, 2004)

Story type: Vampire Story
Subject(s): Country Music; Homosexuality/Lesbianism; Vampires
Major character(s): Nudie, Vampire; Hank, Musician; Audrey, Spouse
Time period(s): 2000s
Locale(s): Nashville, Tennessee

Summary: In a world where clothes make the man, Nudie, a gay vampire couturier who once dressed Elvis Presley, casually seduces Hank, a country western singer, who under his influence and fashion sense excels at the Grand Ole Opry. This short novel follows the arc of their relationship as Hank's success breeds tension that ultimately leads to Nudie's withdrawal of affection and Hank's sorry decline.

Other books by the same author:
Dark Rides, 2004
Wish Book, 2004

Other books you might like:
Poppy Z. Brite, *Lost Souls*, 1992
Clark Hays, *The Cowboy and the Vampire*, 1999
   Kathleen McFall, co-author
Gail Peterson, *The Making of a Monster*, 1993
Anne Rice, *The Vampire Lestat*, 1985
S.P. Somtow, *Valentine*, 1992

666

ROBERT WAYNE MCCOY

The King of Ice Cream

(Waterville, Maine: Five Star, 2004)

Story type: Apocalyptic Horror
Subject(s): Angels; Small Town Life; Supernatural
Major character(s): Luke Yeager, Student—College, Teenager; Todd Baxter Pierce, Student; Russell Tucker, Guard
Time period(s): 1990s
Locale(s): Mill Run, Kentucky

Summary: Forces of evil tied to the second fall of the angels, which necessitated the biblical Deluge, reside beneath an ice cream parlor in the small Kentucky town of Mill Run. Although bound safely for centuries by the power of King Solomon and the Ark of the Covenant, they have attracted rogue powers related to the angels' proclivity for mating with human beings. Now, the prevention of their unleashing worldwide cataclysm will depend on Luke Yeager, a student who is also a Paladin trained especially to help maintain the cosmic balance of good and evil. First novel.

Other books you might like:
Garry Kilworth, *Archangel*, 1993
Stephen King, *The Gunslinger*, 1982
Chandler McGrew, *The Darkening*, 2004
Joseph Nassise, *Riverwatch*, 2001
Bryan Smith, *House of Blood*, 2004

667

CHANDLER MCGREW

The Darkening

(New York: Dell, 2004)

Story type: Apocalyptic Horror
Subject(s): Horror; Good and Evil; Supernatural
Major character(s): Dylan Barnes, Martial Arts Expert; Lucy Devereau, Detective—Private; Crank, Spy
Time period(s): 2000s
Locale(s): Needland, Maine; Ruredaga, Alabama; Atlanta, Georgia

Summary: Imminent apocalypse is slowly darkening the world, as otherworldly beings known as the Old Ones attempt to destroy it. The planet's only hope hinges on the efforts of a secret society with religious underpinnings, Rex Deus, to bring together Dylan, Lucy, and other mortals who are unaware of personal sensitivities and powers that make them crucial warriors in the cosmic battle to come.

Other books by the same author:
Night Terror, 2003
Cold Heart, 2002

Other books you might like:
James Herbert, *The Dark*, 1980
Stephen King, *The Stand*, 1978
Tim F. LaHaye, *Left Behind*, 1995
   Jerry B. Jenkins, co-author
Alan Rodgers, *Night*, 2001
F. Paul Wilson, *Nightworld*, 1992

668

MARY ANN MITCHELL

The Vampire de Sade

(New York: Leisure, 2004)

Story type: Vampire Story
Series: Marquis de Sade Vampire. Book 5
Subject(s): Horror; Supernatural; Vampires
Major character(s): Louis Sade, Vampire; Marie Laveau, Witch (voodoo queen); Liliana, Child
Time period(s): 2000s
Locale(s): New Orleans, Louisiana

Summary: Seeking fresh blood, Louis Sade, the modern persona of the vampire Marquis de Sade, travels to New Orleans, where he meets his match in Marie Laveau, the voodoo queen with whom he dangerously dallied in the past. In this series, a vampire version of the Marquis de Sade cuts a swath of bloodlust, pain, and erotic horror through contemporary America and Europe.

Other books by the same author:
Tainted Blood, 2003
Cathedral of Vampires, 2002
Ambrosial Flesh, 2001
Quenched, 2000
Sips of Blood, 1999

Other books you might like:
C. Dean Anderson, *I Am Dracula*, 1993
Kathryn Meyer Griffith, *Vampire Blood*, 1991
Mara McCuniff, *The Vampire Memoirs*, 1990
Anne Rice, *Blood Canticle*, 2003
Michael Romkey, *I, Vampire*, 1990

669

THOMAS F. MONTELEONE

Fearful Symmetries

(Baltimore: Cemetery Dance, 2004)

Story type: Collection
Subject(s): Horror; Short Stories; Supernatural

Summary: This retrospective collection of 26 stories of horror, suspense, and the supernatural, spans the years 1982 to 2002. Stories range in theme and approach from the Bradburyesque nostalgia of ''Yesterday's Child'' to the Lovecraftian horrors of ''Yog Sothoth, Superstar,'' and the erotic horrors of ''Triptych di Amore,'' a historical vampire tale. Published as a limited edition hardcover with an introduction by Rick Hautala.

Other books by the same author:
A Little Brown Book of Bizarre Stories, 2004
Rough Beasts and Other Mutations, 2003
Eye of the Virgin, 2002
Benediction, 2001
Dark Stars and Other Illuminations, 1981

Other books you might like:
Charles L. Grant, *Tales from the Nightside*, 1981
Rick Hautala, *Bedbugs*, 1999

Bob Leman, *Feesters in the Lake and Other Stories*, 2002
Al Sarrantonio, *Hornets and Others*, 2004
F. Paul Wilson, *Soft and Others*, 1989

670

THOMAS F. MONTELEONE

A Little Brown Book of Bizarre Stories

(Hampton Falls, New Hampshire: Borderlands, 2004)

Story type: Collection
Subject(s): Horror; Short Stories; Supernatural

Summary: This slim collection of seven stories of fantasy and horror is published in an edition uniform with editions of other books from the publisher with a similar name. Contents include ''The Pleasure of Her Company,'' about a Marilyn Monroe fan whose necrophilic tastes secure him the ultimate memento of his obsession, and ''Present Perfect,'' a self-reflective story of the strange manuscripts a science fiction editor receives and (usually) rejects.

Other books by the same author:
Fearful Symmetries, 2004
Rough Beasts and Other Mutations, 2003
Eye of the Virgin, 2002
Benediction, 2001
Dark Stars and Other Illuminations, 1981

Other books you might like:
Gary A. Braunbeck, *A Little Orange Book of Odd Stories*, 2003
Craig Shaw Gardner, *A Little Purple Book of Peculiar Stories*, 2003
Joe R. Lansdale, *A Little Green Book of Monster Stories*, 2003
John Maclay, *A Little Red Book of Vampire Stories*, 2002
Peter Straub, *A Little Blue Book of Rose Stories*, 2003

671

CHRISTOPHER MOORE

The Stupidest Angel

(New York: William Morrow, 2004)

Story type: Reanimated Dead
Subject(s): Angels; Christmas; Supernatural
Major character(s): Lena Marquez, Spouse; Tucker Case, Pilot; Theo Crowe, Police Officer
Time period(s): 2000s
Locale(s): Pine Cove, California

Summary: Subtitled ''A Heartwarming Tale of Christmas Terror,'' this horror spoof tells of an inept archangel. The archangel grants a child's wish that the Santa Claus he saw killed in cold blood be resuscitated for Christmas, unaware that the snuffed Santa was simply ordinary Dale Pearson in a holiday costume. Suddenly, Dale is a reanimated zombie and the rest of the recently departed of Pine Cove are rising from the dead and causing their share of Yuletide fear.

Other books by the same author:
Fluke; or, I Know Why the Winged Whale Sings, 2003
The Lust Lizard of Melancholy Cove, 1998
Bloodsucking Fiends, 1995

Horror

Coyote Blue, 1994
Practical Demonkeeping, 1991

Other books you might like:
Robert Devereaux, *Santa Steps Out*, 1998
Gordon Houghton, *Damned If You Do*, 2000
David Morrell, *The Hundred-Year Christmas*, 1983
Philip Nutman, *Wet Work*, 1993
Del Stone Jr., *Dead Heat*, 1996

672

DAVID MORRELL

Nightscape

(Burton, Michigan: Subterranean, 2004)

Story type: Collection
Subject(s): Horror; Supernatural; Suspense

Summary: These eight tales of horror and suspense are from a writer best known for his suspense thrillers and the novel that inspired the films *First Blood* and *Rambo*. "If I Should Die Before I Wake" takes its account of a doctor trying to attend to the sick, as well as his family during the flu pandemic of 1918 to a devastating surprise ending. "Nothing Will Hurt You" and "Rio Grande Gothic" are both novel serial killer stories, while "Remains to Be Seen" is a grisly fable of life under a military regime in a third-world country.

Other books by the same author:
The Protector, 2003
Black Evening, 1999
The Hundred-Year Christmas, 1983
Totem, 1979
Testament, 1975

Other books you might like:
Rick Hautala, *Bedbugs*, 1999
Stephen King, *Skeleton Crew*, 1987
Dean R. Koontz, *Strange Highways*, 1995
F. Paul Wilson, *The Barrens and Others*, 2000
Chelsea Quinn Yarbro, *Apprehensions and Other Delusions*, 2003

673

J.E. MUDDOCK

The Shining Hand and Other Tales of Terror

(Seattle: Midnight House, 2004)

Story type: Collection
Subject(s): Horror; Short Stories; Supernatural

Summary: These 23 stories of horror and the supernatural, many drawn from popular continental folk legends, are by a Victorian writer better known for the detective tales he wrote under the pseudonym Dick Donovan. "The Strange Story of Major Weir" is an account of a dwelling haunted relentlessly by the evil spirits of a sorcerer and a witch. In "A Night with the Dead," an angel intervenes to save a young boy from the living dead who arise in the crypt he has taken refuge in. "Some Experiences with a Head" tells of a ghoulish scien-

tific experiment to determine whether consciousness persists in the head of an newly decapitated victim. This volume reproduces the contents of the author's 1899 collection *Tales of Terror*, but adds in the novella *The Prophecy*, narrated by a diplomat whose love for a Brazilian woman is thwarted by a supernatural curse that the woman will die if she ever dares to marry. Edited and introduced by John Pelan.

Other books by the same author:
The Corpse Light and Other Tales of Terror, 1999
Tales of Terror, 1899
Stories Weird and Wonderful, 1889
The Man-Hunter, 1888

Other books you might like:
Ambrose Bierce, *Can Such Things Be?*, 1893
W.W. Jacobs, *The Lady of the Barge*, 1902
Clive Pemberton, *The Weird 'O It*, 1906
Tod Robbins, *Who Wants a Green Bottle*, 1926
Bram Stoker, *Dracula's Guest and Other Weird Stories*, 1914

674

ANDREW NEIDERMAN

Deficiency

(New York: Pocket Star, 2004)

Story type: Science Fiction
Subject(s): Doctors; Horror; Scientific Experiments
Major character(s): Terri Barnard, Doctor; Curt Levitt, Lawyer; Hyman Templeman, Doctor
Time period(s): 2000s
Locale(s): Centerville, New York

Summary: In Centerville, patients are showing up at the Community General Hospital on death's doorstep, all mysteriously drained of their natural vitamin resources. Dr. Terri Barnard's investigations uncover a medical experiment that has gone awry and produced a being who practices an unusual form of vampirism to draw the sustenance he needs from his victims.

Other books by the same author:
The Baby Squad, 2003
Dead Time, 2002
Under Abduction, 2002
Amnesia, 2001
Curse, 2000

Other books you might like:
Mark Burnell, *Glittering Savages*, 1995
Mary K. Hanner, *Rapid Growth*, 1993
Roxanne Longstreet, *The Undead*, 1993
Douglas Preston, *Relic*, 1995
    Lincoln Child, co-author
Steven Spruill, *Rulers of Darkness*, 1995

675

ADAM L.G. NEVILL

Banquet for the Damned

(Harrogate, England: PS Publishing, 2004)

Story type: Occult
Subject(s): Horror; Occult; Supernatural

Major character(s): Eliot Coldwell, Writer, Professor; Hart Miller, Anthropologist; Dante, Musician
Time period(s): 2000s
Locale(s): St. Andrews, Scotland

Summary: A festering evil is emerging in the university town of St. Andrews and causing sickness, disappearance, and death among its students. Visiting anthropologist Hart Miller finds a common link among the students whom he talks to: contact with visiting lecturer Eliot Coldwell, author of a countercultural text, *The Banquet of the Damned*, dismissed by most serious scholars for its occult proclivities. While Hart investigates the mystery of St. Andrews, Dante, a rock musician inspired by Coldwell, is en route to the town to pay homage to his mentor and possibly become party to a rendezvous that could break the horrors afflicting the town out into the world at large. The author has also written erotica under the pseudonym Lindsey Gordan; this is the first novel to be published under his own name. A signed limited edition hardcover with an introduction by Ramsey Campbell.

Other books you might like:
Douglas Clegg, *Goat Dance*, 1989
L. Ron Hubbard, *Typewriter in the Sky*, 1951
Fritz Leiber, *Conjure Wife*, 1953
Al Sarrantonio, *October*, 1990

676

SCOTT NICHOLSON

The Manor

(New York: Pinnacle, 2004)

Story type: Occult
Subject(s): Artists and Art; Horror; Supernatural
Major character(s): Mason Jackson, Artist; Anna Galloway, Paranormal Investigator; William Roth, Filmmaker
Time period(s): 2000s
Locale(s): Beechy Gap, North Carolina

Summary: A century ago, after completing the construction of Korban Manor, family patriarch Ephram Korban committed suicide. His modern descendants have turned Korban Manor into an artists' retreat. This year's attendees are victim to spectral manifestations, strange experiences, and terrible deaths, all of which suggest that Ephram's influence still persists and is using them to bring about his resurrection.

Other books by the same author:
Harvest, 2003
The Red Church, 2002
Thank You for the Flowers, 1998

Other books you might like:
Jack Cady, *The Well*, 1980
Bentley Little, *The Resort*, 2004
Michael O'Rourke, *Darkling*, 1994
Mike Sirota, *Demon Shadows*, 1990

677

KEVIN L. O'BRIEN, Editor

Eldritch Blue: Love and Sex in the Cthulhu Mythos

(Aurora, Colorado: Lindisfarne, 2004)

Story type: Anthology
Subject(s): Horror; Short Stories; Supernatural

Summary: Twenty stories explore, as the subtitle of this anthology suggests, the sexual aspects of the Cthulhu Mythos, a shared world of occult lore spun-off from H.P. Lovecraft's cosmic horror fiction. The majority of contributors are fan writers, but the book also includes Ramsey Campbell's ''The Faces at Pine Dunes,'' about a man whose romantic relationship is impacted by the visions he sees at a vacation retreat, and Lovecraft's own ''The Thing on the Doorstep,'' in which a man discovers that the wife he has married is merely the shell of a woman infested with an extradimensional entity.

Other books you might like:
Edward P. Berglund, *Disciples of Cthulhu*, 1975
     editor
Ramsey Campbell, *New Tales of the Cthulhu Mythos*, 1980
     editor
Stephen Jones, *Shadows over Innsmouth*, 1994
     editor
Robert M. Price, *The Shub Niggurath Cycle*, 1994
     editor
Thomas M.K. Stratman, *Cthulhu's Heirs*, 1994
     editor

678

FRANCES OLIVER

Children of Epiphany

(Ashcroft, British Columbia: Ash-Tree Press, 2004)

Story type: Occult
Subject(s): Islands; Mothers and Daughters; Supernatural
Major character(s): Tamsin, Teenager; Lisa, Artist; Robert, Writer
Time period(s): 1980s
Locale(s): Melaniki, Greece

Summary: Tamsin's mother gladly accepts an offer from the wealthy Signor Morelli to live rent-free in Pirgos, a historic family watchtower in a remote and largely abandoned part of the Aegean island of Melaniki. Only after they have moved there does Tamsin learn from Hugo, an expatriate who also lives on the island, of the legend of the Children of Epiphany, who are born between Christmas and the Epiphany. Because they have no souls they must drain them vampirically from those who do. According to Hugo, the caretakers of Tamsin's insane next-door neighbor, who are employed by Signor Morelli, are themselves Children of Epiphany, leading Tamsin to wonder if there is not some dark design in his plans to maneuver her family there. Reissue of a novel originally published in England in 1983.

Where it's reviewed:
All Hallows 37, October 2004, page 149

Horror

Other books by the same author:
Dancing on Air, 2004

Other books you might like:
Ramsey Campbell, *Pact of the Fathers*, 2001
John Fowles, *The Magus*, 1966
Graham Joyce, *House of Lost Dreams*, 1994
Jack Ketchum, *She Wakes*, 1989

679

JOHN PELAN, Editor

A Walk on the Darkside
(New York: Roc, 2004)

Story type: Anthology
Subject(s): Horror; Short Stories; Supernatural

Summary: This anthology contains 21 stories of horror and the supernatural, all but one original to the volume. Don Tumasonis' ''Crossroads'' tells of a musician's deal with infernal beings to achieve fame as a blues player. Mark Samuels' ''The Vanishing Point'' is an apocalyptic fantasy set in a strange realm where the living and the dead mingle. Both Steve Rasnic Tem's ''An Ending'' and Caitlin R. Kiernan's ''La Mer de Reves'' are surreal fantasies spun from the failing coherence and dwindling vitality of aging protagonists.

Other books by the same author:
The Darker Side, 2002
The Last Continent, 1999
Darkside, 1996

Other books you might like:
Richard Chizmar, *Shivers III*, 2004
  editor
Brian Hopkins, *13 Horrors*, 2003
  editor
Stephen Jones, *Dark Terrors 5*, 2000
  editor
Elizabeth E. Monteleone, *Borderlands 5*, 2003
  Thomas F. Monteleone, co-editor
William Sheehan, *Night Visions 11*, 2004
  editor

680

TOM PICCIRILLI, Editor

The Devil's Wine
(Baltimore: Cemetery Dance, 2004)

Story type: Anthology
Subject(s): Horror; Poetry; Supernatural

Summary: This compilation of macabre verse by 19 writers in the horror field, includes works by Ray Bradbury, Stephen King, Peter Straub, Jack Cady, and the editor. The poems, which number in the hundreds, deal with a variety of horror and fantasy themes. Published in a deluxe hardcover edition.

Other books you might like:
Linda D. Addison, *Animated Objects*, 1987
Bruce Boston, *Sensuous Debris*, 1995

August Derleth, *Fire, Sleet and Candelight*, 1965
  editor
Stephen Jones, *Now We Are Sick*, 1994
  Neil Gaiman, co-editor

681

SARAH PINBOROUGH

The Hidden
(New York: Leisure, 2004)

Story type: Occult
Subject(s): Horror; Memory; Supernatural
Major character(s): Rachel Wright, Editor, Amnesiac; Mike Flynn, Teacher; Elizabeth Ray, Child
Time period(s): 2000s
Locale(s): London, England

Summary: Recovering from an amnesiac interval for which she can't remember two months of her life, Rachel Wright is terrorized by visions of people on the other side of the glass in mirrors who warn her about nemeses called the Soulcatchers. Who the Soulcatchers are, and why they are haunting Rachel, is a mystery whose solution lies with people and friends who have returned from near-death experiences, and the diary of an 11-year-old girl whose family has been brutally slaughtered. First novel.

Other books you might like:
Clive Barker, *Weaveworld*, 1987
Graham Masterton, *Mirror*, 1989
T.L. Parkinson, *The Man Upstairs*, 1991
Simon Rees, *The Devil's Looking-Glass*, 1985

682

STEVEN PIZIKS

Exorcist: The Beginning
(New York: Pocket Star, 2004)

Story type: Occult; Ancient Evil Unleashed
Subject(s): Archaeology; Priests; Supernatural
Major character(s): Lankester Merrin, Religious (Catholic priest); Sarah Novack, Doctor; Trenton Jeffries, Archaeologist
Time period(s): 1940s
Locale(s): Derati, Kenya

Summary: Lankester Merrin is a Catholic priest who has fallen away from his faith after witnessing firsthand the atrocities of World War II. He agrees to assist in an archaeological dig that has discovered an ancient Byzantine church buried in the wilds of Kenya centuries ahead of any known Christian presence in the region. Horrifying events and inexplicable supernatural manifestations beset the expedition, leading to the realization that the church was interred to cover a potent source of evil which the expedition's digging has helped to release. Novelization of a screenplay by Alexi Hawley, based on a story by William Wisher and Caleb Carr, this story is the basis of a 2004 film by Renny Harlin that purports to give the background of events that precede the story of William Peter Blatty's novel, *The Exorcist*.

Other books by the same author:
Identity, 2003
In the Company of Mind, 1998

Other books you might like:
William Peter Blatty, *The Exorcist*, 1971
William Peter Blatty, *Legion*, 1972
Max Allan Collins, *The Mummy*, 1999
Joe Donnelly, *The Shee*, 1991
David Seltzer, *The Omen*, 1976

683

DOUGLAS PRESTON
LINCOLN CHILD, Co-Author

Brimstone

(New York: Warner, 2004)

Story type: Occult; Mystery
Subject(s): Conspiracies; Mystery; Occult
Major character(s): Aloysius Pendergast, FBI Agent; Vincent D'Agosta, Police Officer; Laura Hayward, Police Officer
Time period(s): 2000s
Locale(s): New York, New York; Florence, Italy

Summary: Special agent Pendergast, whose work often brings him into contact with weird and occult nemeses, investigates the bizarre death of a high profile art critic whose body is found incinerated in a locked room with the only clue to his killer a cloven hoof burned into the floor. Investigations into a possible satanic pact the man made in his youth uncover a wide international espionage ring with ties to illegal international munitions, members of which employed a stolen Stradivarius violin and a grimoire of ancient occult knowledge as part of its machinations.

Other books by the same author:
Dance of Death, 2005
Still Life with Crows, 2003
The Cabinet of Curiosities, 2002
Reliquary, 1997
Relic, 1995

Other books you might like:
Dan Brown, *The Da Vinci Code*, 2003
Michael Crichton, *Prey*, 2002
Daniel Easterman, *The Judas Testament*, 1994
Umberto Eco, *Foucault's Pendulum*, 1989

684

PHIL RICKMAN

The Prayer of the Night Shepherd

(London: Macmillan, 2004)

Story type: Ancient Evil Unleashed; Mystery
Series: Merrily Watkins. Book 6
Subject(s): Mystery; Occult; Small Town Life
Major character(s): Merrily Watkins, Religious; Jane Watkins, Housekeeper; Ben Foley, Innkeeper
Time period(s): 2000s
Locale(s): Ledwardine, England

Summary: Retired from producing television programs for the BBC, Ben Foley buys Stanner Hall, a declining Victorian inn where Sir Arthur Conan Doyle was reputed to have stayed while researching his Sherlock Holmes stories. Convinced that a local legend about a supernatural hound was the basis for Holmes' famous adventure *The Hound of the Baskervilles*, Foley, for a publicity stunt, invites a weird group of Doyle enthusiasts who hope to make psychic contact with the author. Their delvings stir up murder and mayhem with apparent origins in a curse from the past. This attracts the interest of Merrily Watkins, an Anglican minister with New Age proclivities who occasionally freelances as a psychic sleuth. Merrily's interest is particularly piqued because her daughter, Jane, works at the inn and is among the first to find herself in harm's way.

Other books by the same author:
The Lamp of the Wicked, 2002
A Crown of Lights, 2001
The Cure of Souls, 2001
Midwinter of the Spirit, 1999
The Wine of Angels, 1998

Other books you might like:
Ramsey Campbell, *The Long Lost*, 1994
Joe Donnelly, *Stone*, 1990
James Herbert, *Shrine*, 1983
Peter James, *Prophecy*, 1992
Kim Newman, *Jago*, 1992

685

BARBARA RODEN, Editor
CHRISTOPHER RODEN, Co-Editor

Acquainted with the Night

(Ashcroft, British Columbia: Ash-Tree Press, 2004)

Story type: Anthology
Subject(s): Horror; Short Stories; Supernatural

Summary: Barbara and Christopher Roden edited this anthology of 27 stories of horror and the supernatural, all original to the volume. Included are Glen Hirshberg's "Safety Clowns," about the strange supernatural retribution that befalls an ice-cream truck operation whose salesmen deal drugs to the underaged; Reggie Oliver's "The Devil's Number," presented as an unpublished episode from the life of Casanova in which the notorious rake unwittingly helps an agent of Satan to secure virgins for sacrifice; Joel Lane's "Beyond the River," in which gross commercialization at a publishing house corrupts the delicate fantasy world in one of the children's books it publishes; and Rick Kennet's "The Cross Talk," a sad afterlife fantasy.

Other books by the same author:
Shadows and Silence, 2000
Midnight Never Comes, 1997

Other books you might like:
Ramsey Campbell, *Gathering the Bones*, 2003
    Jack Dann, Dennis Etchison, co-editors
Ellen Datlow, *The Dark*, 2003
    editor

Stephen Jones, *By Moonlight Only*, 2003
  editor
Stephen Jones, *The Mammoth Book of Best New Horror. Volume 15*, 2004
  editor
John Pelan, *A Walk on the Darkside*, 2004
  editor

686

HANS RODIONOFF
ENRIQUE BRECCIA, Illustrator

Lovecraft

(New York: DC Comics, 2004)

Story type: Occult
Subject(s): Graphic Novel; Horror; Supernatural
Major character(s): Howard Phillips Lovecraft, Writer, Historical Figure; Sonia Greene, Businesswoman; Sarah Lovecraft, Aged Person
Time period(s): 1920s
Locale(s): Providence, Rhode Island

Summary: This is a lurid graphic novel rendering of the life of horror writer H.P. Lovecraft, adapted by Keith Giffen from a screenplay by Rodionoff. In this liberally imagined version, Lovecraft inherits from his insane father the *Necronomicon*, a book of forbidden occult lore that was supposed to have been destroyed. To his dismay, Lovecraft discovers that the alien monsters the book describes are very real, and intent on breaking through to his life, affecting his art and his relationships with his wife and family. Introduction by filmmaker John Carpenter.

Other books you might like:
Clive Barker, *Tapping the Vein*, 1989
Neil Gaiman, *Endless Nights*, 2003
Alan Moore, *The League of Extraordinary Gentlemen*, 2002

687

MICHAEL ROMKEY

American Gothic

(New York: Del Rey, 2004)

Story type: Vampire Story
Subject(s): Horror; Supernatural; Vampires
Major character(s): Nathaniel Peregrine, Vampire; Helen Fairweather, Wealthy; Michael Lavalle, Doctor
Time period(s): 1860s; 1910s
Locale(s): New Orleans, Louisiana; Cap Misere, Haiti

Summary: A vampire for nearly half a century, Nathaniel Peregrine wallows in despair over the ennui and boredom of his lonely immortal life until he meets vivacious Helen Fairweather on a trip to Haiti. His only hope for enjoying her mortal love is the research of Dr. Michael Lavalle, a specialist in blood diseases who believes he can help Nathaniel recover from his vampirism.

Other books by the same author:
The Vampire's Violin, 2003
The London Vampire Panic, 2001

Vampire Hunter, 1998
The Vampire Virus, 1997
The Vampire Princess, 1995

Other books you might like:
Hugh B. Cave, *The Evil*, 1981
Marie Kiraly, *Leanna: Possession of a Woman*, 1996
George R.R. Martin, *Fevre Dream*, 1982
Anne Rice, *Interview with the Vampire*, 1976
Jane Toombs, *Under the Shadow*, 1992

688

JAY RUSSELL

Apocalypse Now, Voyager

(Northborough, Massachusetts: Earthling Publications, 2004)

Story type: Occult
Subject(s): Horror; Occult; Supernatural
Major character(s): Marty Burns, Detective—Private; Vibiana, Witch; Guy Preston, Actor
Time period(s): 2000s
Locale(s): Los Angeles, California

Summary: Marty Burns, a hard-boiled detective whose work in the stranger fringes of Hollywood often brings him into contact with the supernatural, becomes a witness to a woman's murder of her lover and redemptive supernatural resurrection. The novella is loaded with an abundance of film and television references, as befits a series hero who was once a child television star. Introduction by Paul McAuley. Published as a signed limited edition chapbook.

Other books by the same author:
Greed and Stuff, 2001
Brown Harvest, 1999
Burning Bright, 1997
Blood, 1996
Celestial Dogs, 1996

Other books you might like:
Dennis Etchison, *Shadow Man*, 1993
Tanya Huff, *Smoke and Mirrors*, 2004
David J. Schow, *Bullets of Rain*, 2003
Dan Vining, *The Quick*, 2004

689

JAY RUSSELL

The Twilight Zone: Memphis/The Pool Guy

(New York: Black Flame, 2004)

Story type: Collection
Series: Twilight Zone
Subject(s): Horror; Short Stories; Supernatural

Summary: These two short novels are based on teleplays for stories that ran on the modern revival of Rod Serling's classic television program, "The Twilight Zone." In *Memphis*, a dying man who finds himself back in Memphis, Tennessee, on the day before Martin Luther King's assassination must determine if his actions on the fateful day will help give him a second chance in life. In *The Pool Guy*, a pool cleaner must determine if visions of his own death are a warning that he figure out a way to avert it.

Other books by the same author:
Brown Harvest, 2001
Greed and Stuff, 2001
Waltzes and Whispers, 1999
Burning Bright, 1997
Celestial Dogs, 1996

Other books you might like:
Pat Cadigan, *The Twilight Zone: Upgrade/Sensuous Cindy*, 2004
Russell Davis, *The Twilight Zone: A Gathering of Shadows*, 2003
Martin H. Greenberg, *New Stories from the Twilight Zone*, 1991
    editor
John Helfers, *The Twilight Zone: Deep in the Dark*, 1994
Carol Serling, *Journeys to the Twilight Zone*, 1993
    editor

690

LUCIUS SHEPARD

Trujillo

(Harrogate, England: PS Publishing, 2004)

Story type: Collection
Subject(s): Fantasy; Short Stories; Supernatural

Summary: This book contains 11 short stories and novellas by a writer known for haunting tales of alienation in lands imagined and real. ''Only Partly There'' is a ghost story set in the ruins of the World Trade Center collapse. ''A Walk in the Garden'' tells of American soldiers in Iraq after the fall of Saddam Hussein who stumble into recently opened caves that offer access to an Islamic Paradise that can be accessed only by way of Hell. ''Crocodile Rock'' involves a human who can shapeshift into a ravenous reptile. The title story, the capstone of a quintet of exercises in magic realism, is set in a town in contemporary Honduras. Published in a signed limited edition with an introduction by Michael Swanwick.

Other books by the same author:
Two Trains Running, 2004
Viator, 2004
Beast of the Heartland, 1999
The Ends of the Earth, 1991
The Jaguar Hunter, 1987

Other books you might like:
Lisa Goldstein, *Travellers in Magic*, 1994
Kim Newman, *Back in the USA*, 1997
    Eugene Byrne, co-author
John Shirley, *Darkness Divided*, 2001
Dan Simmons, *Lovedeath*, 1993
Michael Marshall Smith, *More Tomorrow and Other Stories*, 2003

691

LUCIUS SHEPARD

Viator

(Portland, Oregon: Nightshade, 2004)

Story type: Science Fiction
Subject(s): Horror; Salvage; Shipwrecks
Major character(s): Thomas Wilander, Businessman; Arlene Dauphinee, Store Owner; Pete Halmus, Appraiser
Time period(s): 2000s
Locale(s): Kaliaska, Alaska

Summary: Thomas Wilander hopes to turn his floundering life around when he lands the job of salvaging the *Viator*, a ship that ran aground mysteriously off the coast of Alaska. Once aboard the beached ship, Wilander discovers that the four colleagues he shares salvaging duties with all were chosen by the same temp agency and an employer whose intentions appear to involve a secret scheme. Worse, a strange influence aboard the ship—possibly the same one that caused its wreck—appears to be shaping the reality of the men the longer they work on board.

Other books by the same author:
Floater, 2003
Louisiana Breakdown, 2003
Aztechs, 2002
Colonel Rutherford's Colt, 2002
The Golden, 1993

Other books you might like:
Jack Cady, *The Jonah Watch*, 1981
Harlan Ellison, *Deathbird Stories*, 1975
James Lovegrove, *The Hope*, 1990
Erin Patrick, *Moontide*, 2002
Dan Simmons, *Worlds Enough and Time*, 2002

692

DAVID B. SILVA

All the Lonely People

(North Webster, Indiana: Delirium, 2004)

Story type: Occult
Subject(s): Illness; Small Town Life; Supernatural
Major character(s): Chase Hanford, Saloon Keeper/Owner; Chester Dugan, Drifter; James Cleaver, Accountant
Time period(s): 2000s
Locale(s): Sacramento, California; Corning, California

Summary: Shortly after a stranger shows up at the Last Stop Tavern and exposes patrons at the bar to sharp light from a Native American spirit box, the local community begins to fall apart. People take sick, begin acting psychotically, and generally lose their grip on life. Chase Hanford, owner of the tavern, seeks out the stranger who owns the box in a desperate struggle against time to find out why it has had such devastating effects and whether it is possible to reverse them. Published as a signed limited edition hardcover.

Other books by the same author:
Night in Fog, 1998
The Disappeared, 1995

The Presence, 1994
Come Thirteen, 1988
Child of Darkness, 1986

Other books you might like:
Jay Bonansinga, *Sick*, 1995
Douglas Clegg, *Dark of the Eye*, 1994
Mary K. Hanner, *Rapid Growth*, 1993
Stephen King, *Insomnia*, 1994
Richard Matheson, *A Stir of Echoes*, 1958

693

BRYAN SMITH

House of Blood

(New York: Leisure, 2004)

Story type: Occult
Subject(s): Good and Evil; Horror; Supernatural
Major character(s): Chad Robbins, Young Man; Dream Weaver, Young Woman; Alicia Jackson, Young Woman
Time period(s): 2000s
Locale(s): Chattanooga, Tennessee

Summary: In this literary equivalent of a splatter film, an ancient evil entity known as The Master controls an eerie house on the outskirts of Chattanooga. There he manipulates hapless men and women into bizarre games for his amusement. An unsuspecting carful of young men and women returning home from an aborted vacation in Florida become lost in the woods near the house. The group finds themselves subjected to shapeshifters and other monsters in their struggles to escape alive from The Master's challenges.

Other books you might like:
Jack Cady, *The Well*, 1980
Tom Elliott, *The Dwelling*, 1988
Scott Nicholson, *The Manor*, 2004
Al Sarrantonio, *House Haunted*, 1991

694

ELEANOR SMITH

Satan's Circus

(Ashcroft, British Columbia: Ash-Tree Press, 2004)

Story type: Collection
Subject(s): Horror; Short Stories; Supernatural

Summary: *Satan's Circus* consists of 13 tales of horror and suspense by a British writer of the first half of the 20th century best known for her journalism and society stories. This book reprints the 1932 edition of her sole collection of short fiction, embellished with another two previously uncollected fantasies. The title story concerns a circus run by vampires. In ''Mrs. Raeburn's Waxwork,'' the soul of an executed criminal haunts a wax museum that features her effigy. ''Lyceum'' tells of a dramatist who discovers that people whom he glimpses at the theater one evening are fictional representations waiting to be incarnated in a work for the stage. Edited and with an introduction by Christopher Roden.

Other books by the same author:
Lover's Meeting, 1940

Other books you might like:
E.F. Benson, *Visible and Invisible*, 1924
Marjorie Bowen, *Twilight and Other Supernatural Romances*, 1998
D.K. Broster, *Couching at the Door*, 1942
Margery Lawrence, *Nights of the Round Table*, 1926
H. Russell Wakefield, *They Return at Evening*, 1928

695

SHANE RYAN STALEY, Editor

New Dark Voices

(North Webster, Indiana: Delirium, 2004)

Story type: Anthology
Subject(s): Horror; Short Stories; Supernatural

Summary: The authors of these three novellas are promoted by the editor (who is also the publisher) as rising new stars of horror. John Urbancik's *Beneath Midnight* sets its protagonist's eerie subterranean exploration of a strange town against the backdrop of a visiting carnival. Michael Oliveri's *To Travel Among Men* is a postapocalyptic fantasy about a man's search for normality in a world devolving into savagery and chaos. Gene O'Neill's *White Tribe* tells of a small band of survivors of a California earthquake fighting something monstrous liberated from underground by the seismic activity. Introduction by Brian Keene. Published as a signed limited edition hardcover.

Other books by the same author:
Dark Testament, 2002

Other books you might like:
Dana Anderson, *Cafe Purgatorium*, 1991
   Charles de Lint, Ray Garton, co-authors
Bentley Little, *Four Dark Nights*, 2002
   Douglas Clegg, Tom Piccirilli, and Christopher Golden, co-authors
Mark McLaughlin, *The Gossamer Eye*, 2002
   Rain Graves, David Niall Wilson, co-authors
William Sheehan, *Night Visions 11*, 2004
David Whitman, *Appalachian Galapagos*, 2003
   Weston Ochse, co-author

696

FRANCIS STEVENS (Pseudonym of Gertrude Barrows Bennett)

The Nightmare and Other Tales of Dark Fantasy

(Lincoln: University of Nebraska Press, 2004)

Story type: Collection
Subject(s): Horror; Short Stories; Supernatural

Summary: This book contains eight tales of science fantasy by a writer whose career flourished in pulp fiction magazines between 1917 and 1920 and whose work is memorable for its blend of science fiction, supernatural, and lost race elements. The title story is set on an uncharted island where radiation has caused monstrous mutations in animal and plant life. ''Serapion'' is the story of a seance that gets out of hand and ends up channeling a malevolent supernatural being. ''Behind the Curtain'' is a Poe-esque tale of psychological horror, and ''Sunfire'' a tale of science and sorcery set in a lost city in Brazil. Edited and with an introduction by Gary Hoppenstand.

Other books by the same author:
The Citadel of Fear, 1970
Claimed, 1966
The Heads of Cerberus, 1952

Other books you might like:
Inez Haynes Gilmore, *Angel Island*, 1988
A. Merritt, *The Fox Woman and Other Stories*, 1949
C.L. Moore, *Northwest of Earth*, 1954
Sam Moskowitz, *Under the Moons of Mars*, 1970
  editor
Jane Rice, *The Idol of the Flies and Other Stories*, 1946

697

PETER STRAUB

In the Night Room

(New York: Random House, 2004)

Story type: Occult
Subject(s): Horror; Supernatural; Writing
Major character(s): Tim Underhill, Writer; Willy Bryce Patrick, Writer (of children's books); Mitchell Faber, Businessman, Fiance(e) (of Willy)
Time period(s): 2000s
Locale(s): Hendersonia, New Jersey; Milhaven, Wisconsin; New York, New York

Summary: Children's book writer Willy Patrick is disturbed by intense memories of her dead daughter when she bumps into another writer, Tim Underhill, at a local book signing. Tim is disturbed by Willy's presence, as he realizes she is one of his own imaginary creations. Tim and Willy's relationship progresses, but both are endangered by Willy's disgruntled fiance, Mitchell, another of Tim's creations, whom Tim realizes is linked in an eerie and inexplicable way to serial killer Joseph Kalendar.

Where it's reviewed:
Publishers Weekly, October 4, 2004, page 70

Other books by the same author:
lost boy lost girl, 2003
Mr. X, 1999
The Hellfire Club, 1996
The Throat, 1993
Mrs. God, 1990

Other books you might like:
Emmanuel Carrere, *Bravoure*, 1984
Jonathan Carroll, *The Land of Laughs*, 1980
Stephen King, *The Dark Half*, 1989
Richard Matheson, *Created By*, 1993
William Browning Spencer, *Zod Wallop*, 1995

698

CHARLES STROSS

The Atrocity Archives

(Urbana, Illinois: Golden Gryphon, 2004)

Story type: Collection
Subject(s): Horror; Science Fiction; Supernatural
Major character(s): Bob, Computer Expert

Summary: *The Atrocity Archives* has two quirky novella-length blends of horror and hard science fiction, both featuring Bob, a computer geek employed by a secret British espionage agency known as the Laundry. In the title story, Bob saves the world from monsters of a Lovecraftian cast who find access to our universe through a portal opened by Nazi soldiers using nascent computer technology of the mid-century to escape to an alternate dimension. In *The Concrete Jungle*, Bob and colleagues try to prevent a zombie onslaught against the Laundry, mobilized by an evil genius.

Other books by the same author:
Iron Sunrise, 2004
The Family Trade, 2004
Singularity Sky, 2003
Festival of Fools, 2002
Toast and Other Rusted Futures, 2002

Other books you might like:
Robert Bloch, *Strange Eons*, 1978
Yvonne Navarro, *Hellboy*, 2004
Joseph Pulver, *Nightmare's Disciple*, 1999
Michael Shea, *The Colour out of Time*, 1984
William Browning Spencer, *Resume with Monsters*, 1995

699

KOJI SUZUKI

Dark Water

(New York: Vertical, 2004)

Story type: Collection
Subject(s): Horror; Short Stories; Supernatural

Summary: These seven stories of the supernatural with a framing prologue and epilogue are by a writer popularized as the Japanese Stephen King. The title story concerns a woman who moves into an apartment whose previous tenant murdered her child, and who finds herself unconsciously embarked on the same horrifying path. ''Adrift'' concerns a group of swimmers who are menaced by a strange entity trapped in a bottle. Several of the other stories have aquatic settings and themes.

Other books by the same author:
Loop, 1998
Spiral, 1995
Ringu, 1991
Rakeun, 1990

Other books you might like:
Kobo Abe, *The Face of Another*, 1962
Alfred Birnbaum, *Monkey-Brain Sushi*, 1993
  editor

Horror

Gordon Linzner, *The Oni*, 1986
Tom Te-Wu Ma, *Chinese Ghost Stories for Adults*, 2000
Kelley Wilde, *Angel Kiss*, 1993

700
KAREN E. TAYLOR

Blood Red Dawn
(New York: Pinnacle, 2004)

Story type: Vampire Story
Series: Vampire Legacy. Book 7
Subject(s): Family; Supernatural; Vampires
Major character(s): Deirdre Griffin, Vampire; Mitch Greer, Saloon Keeper/Owner; Max, Vampire
Time period(s): 2000s
Locale(s): New Orleans, Louisiana; Whitby, England; New York, New York

Summary: Vampires Deirdre and Mitch have settled into domestic bliss in their adopted home in England, and the pregnant Deirdre is on the verge of kicking her vampire habit through a metamorphosis of her blood when she inexplicably disappears. All clues point to Deirdre being overpowered and kidnapped and Mitch, suspecting the Vampire Cadre that Deirdre has run afoul of before, travels to America for answers. Complicating matters is Deirdre's delicate health, which could prove fatal if not handled carefully.

Other books by the same author:
Resurrection, 2002
The Vampire Vivienne, 2001
Blood of My Blood, 2000
Blood Ties, 1995
Bitter Blood, 1994

Other books you might like:
Poppy Z. Brite, *Lost Souls*, 1992
Sherry Gottleib, *Worse than Death*, 1999
Pat Graversen, *Sweet Blood*, 1992
Brent Monahan, *The Book of Common Dread*, 1993
Steven Spruill, *Daughter of Darkness*, 1996

701
JAMES M. THOMPSON

Tainted Blood
(New York: Pinnacle, 2004)

Story type: Vampire Story
Series: Elijah Pike. Book 4
Subject(s): Horror; Supernatural; Vampires
Major character(s): Elijah Pike, Vampire; Theo Thantos, Vampire; John Ashby, Vampire
Time period(s): 2000s
Locale(s): North Waterford, Maine

Summary: Elijah Pike has nearly perfected the vaccine that will curb his vampirism and allow him to rejoin humanity. Although Elijah hopes to share his vaccine with others of his kind, an army led by Theo Thantos has no interest, and hopes instead to vampirize powerful businessmen and politicians in America to draw them into Theo's web. Unknown to Thantos,

Pike's serum also confers extraordinary strength on its user, setting the stage for a spectacular showdown between the two vampire factions.

Other books by the same author:
Immortal Blood, 2003
Dark Blood, 2002
Night Blood, 2001

Other books you might like:
Trisha Baker, *Crimson Kiss*, 2001
Michael Cecilione, *Thirst*, 1996
David Dvorkin, *Insatiable*, 1993
Steven Spruill, *Rulers of Darkness*, 1995
Karen E. Taylor, *Blood Secrets*, 1994

702
LISA TUTTLE

My Death
(Harrogate, England: PS Publishing, 2004)

Story type: Doppelganger
Subject(s): Horror; Love; Writing
Major character(s): Helen Elizabeth Ralston, Writer; Clarissa Breen, Writer; Selwyn, Agent
Time period(s): 2000s
Locale(s): Glasgow, Scotland

Summary: The unnamed narrator of this novella, a writer struggling to establish herself after her divorce, decides to write the biography of Helen Elizabeth Ralston. Helen was a former model turned writer who, in the 1920s, nearly committed suicide over her love for a painter, before going on to fame as an early feminist author. While interviewing the aged Helen for the book, the narrator begins to pick up on subtle parallels between Helen's life and her own. Published in simultaneous signed limited hardcover and softcover chapbook editions. Introduction by Thomas Tessier.

Other books by the same author:
Ghosts and Other Lovers, 2001
The Pillow Friend, 1996
Lost Futures, 1992
Gabriel, 1987
Familiar Spirit, 1983

Other books you might like:
Michael Cadnum, *Ghostwright*, 1992
    Martin H. Greenberg, co-editor
Elizabeth Hand, *Mortal Love*, 2004
Dan Simmons, *A Winter Haunting*, 2002
Peter Straub, *In the Night Room*, 2004
Thomas Tessier, *Fogheart*, 1997

703
STEVE VERNON

Long Horn, Big Shaggy
(Effort, Pennsylvania: Demonic Clown, 2004)

Story type: Reanimated Dead
Subject(s): Horror; Supernatural

Major character(s): Milton Leadbetter, Gunfighter; Jonah Walker, Gunfighter; Zacheus Boonehorn Tides, Gunfighter
Time period(s): 19th century
Locale(s): Devil's Anvil, Texas

Summary: In this episodic novel, an epic battle is fought between Milton Leadbetter and Zacheus Tides in a wild west populated by crawlers, zombie gunslingers, and all disgusting species of the reanimated dead. Dead gunslinger Jonah Walker becomes a pawn between the two in their frontier struggle for survival.

Other books by the same author:
Nightmare Dreams, 2004

Other books you might like:
Nancy A. Collins, *Dead Man's Hand*, 2004
Joe R. Lansdale, *Dead in the West*, 1986
Tim Lebbon, *Fears Unnamed*, 2004
S.P. Somtow, *Moon Dance*, 1989

704

DAN VINING

The Quick

(New York: Jove, 2004)

Story type: Mystery; Reanimated Dead
Subject(s): Detection; Mystery; Supernatural
Major character(s): Jimmy Miles, Detective—Private; Jean Kantke, Businesswoman; Angel Figueora, Mechanic
Time period(s): 2000s
Locale(s): Los Angeles, California

Summary: Jean Kantke contacts private eye Jimmy Miles in the hope that he can help her find the truth about her father, a district attorney. Decades before, he was executed for murdering his wife, Jean's mother, even though he protested his innocence until the end. Jimmy is the ideal detective for investigating such mysteries: he's a Sailor, a person who once died but who still walks the Earth, appearing as someone else to those who knew him in his lifetime. In the course of this blend of hard-boiled crime and horror fiction, Jimmy encounters Walkers, malevolent versions of Sailors, whose meddling is a clue to the mystery Jean wants cleared up. First novel.

Other books you might like:
Clive Barker, *Cabal*, 1988
Randall Boyll, *Darkman*, 1991
P.N. Elrod, *Cold Streets*, 2003
Simon R. Green, *Agents of Light and Darkness*, 2003
Ric Meyers, *Fear Itself*, 1991

705

JAMES C. WARDLAW

Pools of Dreams

(Baltimore: PublishAmerica, 2004)

Story type: Collection
Subject(s): Horror; Short Stories; Supernatural

Summary: Most of these 30 varied stories of horror and the supernatural are original to the volume, though some appeared in small press publications. Selections include the vampire tale ''On Wicked Wings We Fly;'' ''Recombinant Nightmare,'' a science fiction-horror hybrid about the perils of tampering with genetics; and ''Don't Go Near Neally Swamp,'' in which a reanimated corpse dishes out vengeance from beyond the grave. Although presented as a single-author collection, the book also includes ''Anna,'' a ''Special Guest Story'' by J.R. Cain. First book.

Other books you might like:
Gary A. Braunbeck, *From Beneath These Fields of Blood*, 2003
Gemma Files, *Kissing Carrion*, 2003
Angeline Hawkes-Craig, *Memento Mori*, 2003
Kurt Newton, *Dark Demons*, 2002
Mehitobel Wilson, *Dangerous Red*, 2003

706

F. PAUL WILSON

Crisscross

(New York: Forge, 2004)

Story type: Occult
Series: Repairman Jack. Book 8
Subject(s): Cults; Good and Evil; Supernatural
Major character(s): Repairman Jack, Mercenary; Jamie Grant, Journalist; Luther Brady, Religious
Time period(s): 2000s
Locale(s): New York, New York

Summary: Repairman Jack is an urban mercenary who offers his services as a last resort to those who cannot find justice within the traditional legal system. He accepts an assignment to infiltrate the Dormentalists, a religious cult with sinister associations, and make contact with a wealthy woman's son who has been drawn into their beliefs. To his shock, Jack discovers that the cult's pseudoreligious schemes have a basis in the machinations engineered by The Adversary, the formidable supernatural entity who has played a role in all of Jack's other adventures. Also published as a signed limited edition hardcover from Gauntlet Press.

Other books by the same author:
Gateways, 2003
The Haunted Air, 2002
Hosts, 2001
All the Rage, 2000
Conspiracies, 1999

Other books you might like:
David Bowker, *Death Prayer*, 1996
Nicholas Conde, *The Religion*, 1982
John Coyne, *Child of Shadows*, 1990
Dean R. Koontz, *The Servants of Twilight*, 1984
Simon Maginn, *Virgins and Martyrs*, 1995

707

L. MARIE WOOD, Editor

Be Mine

(Houston: Cyber-Pulp, 2004)

Story type: Anthology
Subject(s): Horror; Short Stories; Suspense

Summary: The 26 stories are all original to this compilation and are concerned with the dark side of love and passion. In John B. Rosenman's "Your Cold and Loving Arms," a man discovers that the statue with which he is obsessed is a living entity. Ken Kupstis' "Fight for the Last" is a tale of love under the duress of zombie attack. The editor's own "The Salacity of Death" is a suggestive tale of necrophilia.

Other books by the same author:
Carnival of Horror, 2004

Other books you might like:
Nancy A. Collins, *Dark Love*, 1995
    Edward E. Kramer, Martin H. Greenberg, co-editors
Ellen Datlow, *Little Deaths*, 1994
    editor
Jeff Gelb, *Hot Blood: Tales of Provocative Horror*, 1989
    Lonn Friend, co-editor
Rosalind Greenberg, *14 Vicious Valentines*, 1988
    Martin H. Greenberg, Charles G. Waugh, co-editors
Michele Slung, *I Shudder at Your Touch*, 1991

708

L. MARIE WOOD

Carnival of Horror

(Houston: Cyber-Pulp, 2004)

Story type: Anthology; Carnival/Circus Horror
Subject(s): Horror; Short Stories; Supernatural

Summary: These 19 new stories of horror and suspense all have carnival, circus, or fairground settings. Jason Brannon's "Pyro" concerns a fire-eater with a side to his personality even more strange than his profession. The editor's own story, "A Bat out of Hell," is a shocker set on a roller coaster ride. Foreword by Drew Williams.

Other books by the same author:
Be Mine, 2004

Other books you might like:
George Hatch, *Guignoir and Other Furies*, 1991
    editor
Bill Pronzini, *The Wickedest Show on Earth*, 1985
    Marcia Muller, co-editor
Gary L. Raisor, *Obsessions*, 1991
    editor
F. Paul Wilson, *Freak Show*, 1992
    editor

709

STEPHEN WOODWORTH

Through Violet Eyes

(New York: Dell, 2004)

Story type: Mystery; Serial Killer
Subject(s): Detection; Mystery; Supernatural
Major character(s): Dan Atwater, FBI Agent; Natalie Lindstrom, Mutant; Evan Markham, Murderer
Time period(s): 2000s
Locale(s): Los Angeles, California; Seattle, Washington

Summary: FBI agent Dan Atwater is used to working with Violets, genetic mutants (recognizable by the violet irises of their eyes) who are able to channel the dead, including murder victims, to help track down their murderers. Most Violets are employed by the federally protected North American Afterlife Communications Corps Now, an arm of law enforcement. In this first novel in a projected series, Dan is working to save the Violets themselves: a killer who has found a way to cloak his or her identity is systematically killing and disposing of the less than 200 Violets known to exist in America. First novel.

Other books by the same author:
With Red Hands, 2004

Other books you might like:
H.B. Gilmour, *The Eyes of Laura Mars*, 1978
Diana Graziunas, *Thinning the Predators*, 1996
    Jim Starling, co-author
Stephen King, *The Dead Zone*, 1979
Dean R. Koontz, *The Vision*, 1977
Brian Lumley, *Necroscope*, 1988

710

CHELSEA QUINN YARBRO

Dark of the Sun

(New York: Tor, 2004)

Story type: Vampire Story
Series: Chronicles of Saint-Germain. Book 17
Subject(s): China; History; Vampires
Major character(s): Comte de Saint-Germain, Vampire; Roshei, Monster (ghoul), Servant; Dukkai, Shaman
Time period(s): 6th century
Locale(s): Yang-Chou, China

Summary: Count St. Germain, a vampire for several millennia, is conducting business in 6th-century Shanghai (under the name Sangi-Ragozh) when the volcanic island of Krakatoa erupts, filling the atmosphere with dust that causes crop failure, premature winter, and other natural calamities. As the superstitious natives look for scapegoats to blame for their seemingly supernatural misfortune, foreigners in the country are treated as pariahs. St. Germain's efforts to return to his home in the Carpathian mountains becomes a desperate struggle for survival as he is deprived of his lover and food source, and the last sack of soil from his native land that gives him his vitality.

Other books by the same author:
Midnight Harvest, 2003
Night Blooming, 2002
A Feast in Exile, 2001
Come Twilight, 2000
Communion Blood, 1999

Other books you might like:
Les Daniels, *The Silver Skull*, 1979
Lafcadio Hearn, *Kwaidan*, 1904
Pierre Kast, *The Vampires of Alfama*, 1975
Anne Rice, *Queen of the Damned*, 1988
Brian Stableford, *The Empire of Fear*, 1988

Horror

Science Fiction in 2004
by
Don D'Ammassa

The mix of plot devices and themes in science fiction, as in any field, tends to evolve over time, and to reflect current events, as well as the changing tastes of editors and readers. These changes are almost always gradual, necessarily when the gap between selling a novel and seeing it appear in print can be a year or more. When an individual book enjoys noticeable success, it might be imitated a year or two later, but often the momentum has dissipated by then and the fluctuations tend to even out. If we compare 2004 to 1964, we can find some dramatic differences in the kind of stories that were published, but if we compare 2004 to 1984, it becomes more difficult to distinguish trends, and as the gap narrows further, the task becomes even more difficult.

For a variety of reasons, most of them probably external to the field, science fiction has generally become less panoramic in sscope in recent years. The majority of novels during the past decade have been set in the comparatively near future and have reflected contemporary events and preoccupations. The threat of a nuclear war and its aftermath have become less pressing, although the possibility of ecological catastrophes of various kinds have taken their place. Alien invaders, hostile mutations, and robotic or other artificially created enemies have given way to repressive and secretive government agencies, grasping corporations, and similar conspiracies. Alternate histories have grown dramatically in popularity, dwelling on alternate versions of the past or present, and similarly time travel stories have rarely taken their protagonists into the future. The apparent exception to this trend has been in stories of space travel, which are almost necessarily set in the future, but even in space opera there has been a noticeable reluctance to speculate too far into the future. Many of these are now set exclusively within our solar system, and the concept of the galactic empire is rarely seen outside of media tie-in novels.

The year 2004 broke this pattern fairly dramatically, although it is not clear whether this is simply an aberration or whether many writers are actively seeking to write something different, and to explore territory which has been largely overlooked in recent years. For whatever reason, a very large proportion of this year's novels—particularly the better ones—involve space travel and/or distant future settings, either as a central element in the plot or as background for a story set in a society very different from our own. Galactic empires are back, as well as mysterious and sometimes malevolent aliens. Military science fiction has kept the concept of interstellar war alive, but most stories in this subgenre have a very narrow focus on those individuals involved in the actual hostilities. Several of this year's novels use such conflict as a backdrop for a very different kind of story. The emphasis on hard science diminished dramatically, with only Ben Bova continuing to write detailed, realistic stories of space travel within the solar system. Dystopian futures, humorous science fiction, natural disasters, cloning, telepathy and other psi powers, virtual reality, genetic engineering, immortality, dramatic technological changes, and other familiar themes were largely abandoned by writers.

As we might expect, the authors most actively writing adventures in outer space are those who have used that setting in the past. Kevin J. Anderson's *Horizon Storms*, third in his Saga of the Seven Suns series, is the most grandiose of those published this year. An experiment in stellar manipulation initiated by human scientists inadvertently leads to war with a previously unknown intelligent race. As the death toll rises, the increasing number of factions among both human and various alien civilizations results in a constant state of flux. Anderson, who has also been extending the Dune series by the late Frank Herbert in collaboration with his son, Brian Herbert, continues to excel with this complex solo series. Similarly, Alastair Reynolds continued and, perhaps concluded, his history of a distant future with *Absolution Gap*, third in an unnamed trilogy. In this work, humanity has split into two separate strains and countless distinct cultures, although all face extinction because of the remnants of a malevolent alien technology.

269

Reynolds also incorporates a good deal of hard science in his fiction. Peter Hamilton, author of the very popular Reality Dysfunction series, launched a new sequence of large scale space operas with *Pandora's Star*, in which human space explorers visit a remote star system and unwittingly release a race of bellicose and highly advanced aliens from their imprisonment within a force field.

Several other 2004 novels dealt with the interaction between human and alien civilizations, although there were no traditional first contact stories. Nancy Kress demonstrates what might happen if humanity found itself caught in the middle of a conflict between two superior alien civilizations in *Crucible*, second in the Jake Holman series. Gregory Benford invites the reader to follow the voyage of the last surviving human being to the stars for a confrontation with enigmatic aliens in *Beyond Infinity*. An entire planet may be destroyed just to make a point about the balance of interstellar power in *Iron Sunrise* by Charles Stross, with only a teenage girl standing in the way.

Other space adventures demonstrate that we don't need aliens to menace us among the stars, that we might well prove capable of providing the threat all by ourselves. Allen Steele followed up his excellent *Coyote* with *Coyote Rising*, in which the refugees from a repressive government on Earth discover that their haven on a newly found planet is about to be engulfed by an influx of settlers from the home world. This is followed inevitably by all of the restrictions and complexities of the very authority they hoped to escape. Jack Vance returns after much too long an absence with *Lurulu*, a light, witty, inventive space adventure which rambles across a series of planets as a spaceship captain and his friend search for the man who swindled and abducted his mother. Vance's unique narrative style and unusual characterization have rarely been better showcased.

In *The Shores of Tomorrow* by Roger MacBride Allen, third and final volume in his Solace trilogy, space travel and time travel are interconnected. The immediate conflict arises primarily from the unsuspected complexities of terraforming other planets, and the efforts by some individuals in power to conceal the truth about an imminent collapse of the colonization effort. *Marque and Reprisal* by Elizabeth Moon, her second adventure of Ky Vatta, involves intrigue and risks in outer space with the danger coming from business rivals who are maneuvering to destroy the protagonist's family and its commercial empire. Susan Shwartz also mixes finances and outer space in *Hostile Takeover*, set on a remote colony world whose management has been concealing a sinister secret, unearthed only when an unlikely hero, a glorified accountant, is sent to audit their books. The always entertaining Jack McDevitt provides a sort of Mary Celeste story in outer space. *Polaris* is a mystery involving the unexplained disappearance of the entire crew of an interstellar research vessel, and the persistent efforts to prevent anyone from discovering the truth, orchestrated by parties unknown but very deadly.

Not all of the best science fiction of 2004 involved space travel. *Crux* by Albert Cowdrey, easily the best first novel of the year, is set in a very distant future in which human society has evolved into something approaching a Utopian state. There are inevitably dissidents unhappy with their lot, and some of them have stolen a time machine and hope to travel back and alter the past. Ian McDonald in *River of Gods* takes his readers to a fairly near future India, after that nation has begun to splinter into various smaller states, all interacting with varying degrees of hostility, and all trapped in an inevitable descent toward war. Kenneth Oppel's *Airborn* was the year's best science fiction novel for younger readers, set in an alternate reality where intercontinental travel is accomplished by means of giant zeppelins. Travelers are often preyed upon by sky pirates, and a young boy's early encounter with one such group changes his fate. Elizabeth Ann Scarborough continued her story of a genetically recreated Cleopatra in *Cleopatra 7.2*, mixing rationalized reincarnation with solid science. Two very different aliens hide among humans on Earth, surviving through countless generations before finally meeting in a battle to the death in Joe Haldeman's *Camouflage*, his best novel in several years. Kim Stanley Robinson tackled the possibility that global warming is real in *Forty Signs of Rain*, a thoughtful and intelligently written story of ecological disaster, with short sighted politicians ignoring the warnings provided by scientists. Although occasionally polemical and one sided, Robinson presents a strong indictment of the human tendency to refuse to act for the common good.

Alternate realities also play a large part in *The Atrocity Archives* by newcomer Charles Stross, two related short novels in one volume that involve alternate realities, aliens, and quantum physics. More significant was *The Separation* by Christopher Priest, which was previously published in England in what was apparently very limited quantities, and which only became generally available in the United States this year. Priest's novel, the best of his many excellent books, follows the career of two brothers who get caught up in World War II, one of them joining the military, the other becoming an unshakable pacifist. Their lives are interwoven not only with each other, but through two different versions of history: our own, and one in which England negotiated a separate peace with Hitler's subordinates and brought the war to an early end. One surprising alternate history title this year was *The Plot Against America* by Philip Roth, who has occasionally included fantastic elements in his work, but never to this extent. His premise is that Charles Lindbergh defeated Franklin Delano Roosevelt to become President of the United States, and that he turned the country away from England, improved relations with Nazi Germany, and remained neutral during the war. Although Roth's Lindbergh does not impose pogroms or other restrictions on Jews in America, the result is still an atmosphere of menace and unease, seen from the point of view of a very young "Philip Roth" growing up in New York.

There were also several excellent short story collections published in 2004. Among these were *TThumbprints* by Pamela Sargent, the very comprehensive *The John Varley Reader* by John Varley, *Collected Stories* by C.J. Cherryh, and *On Account of Darkness* by Barry Malzberg and Bill Pronzini. The usual flood of theme anthologies with original stories continued, but without producing any memorable collections.

The overall best science fiction novel of the year was hard to pick. *The Separation* would be the logical choice if it had not been published previously. *Absolution Gap* is another strong contender, although it is the weakest title in the trilogy. There are several other novels clustered at the top as well, but *Forty Signs of Rain* and *Polaris* are the two strongest contenders. 2004 was in general an above average year for the genre, and hopefully the harbinger of an even better 2005.

Recommended Titles

Entries for the following books are included in this volume.

Horizon Storms by Kevin J. Anderson

Crux by Albert Cowdrey

Crucible by Nancy Kress

Polaris by Jack McDevitt

River of Gods by Ian McDonald

Marque and Reprisal by Elizabeth Moon

Airborn by Kenneth Oppel

Absolution Gap by Alastair Reynolds

The Plot Against America by Philip Roth

Thumbprints by Pamela Sargent

Cleopatra 7.2 by Elizabeth Ann Scarborough

Hostile Takeover by Susan Shwartz

Coyote Rising by Allen Steele

Lurulu by Jack Vance

The John Varley Reader by John Varley

The entries for the following books can be found in *WDIRN? 2004. Volume 2.*

The Shores of Tomorrow by Roger MacBride Allen

Beyond Infinity by Gregory Benford

Collected Stories by C.J. Cherryh

Camouflage by Joe Haldeman

Pandora's Star by Peter Hamilton

On Account of Darkness by Barry Malzberg and Bill Pronzini

The Separation by Christopher Priest

Forty Signs of Rain by Kim Stanley Roobinson

The Atrocity Archives by Charles Stross

Iron Sunrise by Charles Stross

For More Information about Fantastic Fiction by Neil Barron

Born in Luxembourg in 1884, Hugo Gernsback immigrated to the U.S. in 1904 and founded and edited several electronic hobbyist magazines. In 1926 he founded and edited *Amazing Stories*, the first all-SF magazine. It was soon forced into bankruptcy and he later founded several other SF pulps. Historians of SF recognize the importance of Gernsback but differ sharply on his influence. The dominant view is that he was a disaster, untalented as both an editor and writer of SF, imposing a crippling philosophy on the early development of SF. Mike Ashley thinks more highly of Gernsback, and over two decades wrote a detailed study (250 of the book's 499 pages) in *The Gernsback Days: A Study of the Evolution of Modern Science Fiction*. Co-authored by Robert A.W. Lowndes, the book was published by Wildside Press in 2004. Ashley's research provides much detail not previously revealed or placed in context. Lowndes (1916-1998), an early pulp magazine editor, provides 132 pages of summaries of the fiction in Gernsback's magazines, 1926-1936. Most of the remaining pages list issue-by-issue contents of SF in Gernsback magazines published 1908-1936. Gernsback has been the subject of many articles and books (the selected bibliography runs 8 pages), including Gary Westfahl's favorable *The Mechanics of Wonder* (Liverpool University Press, 1998). But the final judgment is likely to be that of Everett F. Bleiler in *Science-Fiction: The Gernsback Years* (Kent State University Press, 1998), who concludes: ''In general, apart from an occasional story, one must look back at the authors of 1926-1936 mostly as predecessors, rather than as authors to be read today apart from historical reasons.''

Brian Stableford is perhaps the best qualifed scholar to compile a work like the *Historical Dictionary of Science Fiction Literature* (Scarecrow, 2004). His extensive scientific and literary knowledge is evident in the 16 page chronology and even more evident in the carefully argued 24 page introduction, in which he explores the problems of defining SF and how it differs in content, narrative strategies, and as a commercial product from mimetic/conventional fiction. The approximately 800 entries were selected on the basis of their historical importance. About 85% are for authors and include years, nationality, and key works with terse critical/descriptive information. Other entries explain terms (sense of wonder, space opera, sharecropping, etc.), a few coined by Stableford. Major magazines have entries, as do academic and a few fan organizations. All words/phrases in boldface have their own entries, an easy form of cross-referencing. The dictionary concludes with a detailed and current bibliography of secondary literature, divided into thirteen categories, from general reference works to writing guides. Stableford was a major contributor to John Clute and Peter Nicholls' *Encyclopedia of Science Fiction* (1979; 2nd ed., St. Martin's Press, 1993), which every library should own (it's now out of print). There is inevitably a lot of overlap in the coverage; Stableford's entries are much more succinct and a dozen years more current. Libraries with the encyclopedia's second edition can probably skip this volume, but it would be a good choice for libraries lacking the encyclopedia or other recent SF biographical guides.

Becky Siegel Spratford and Tammy Hennigh Clausen are readers' advisory librarians at the Berwyn Public Library in Illinois. Their *The Horror Reader's Advisory: The Librarian's Guide to Vampires, Killer Tomatoes, and Haunted Houses* (ALA, 2004) is a chatty, cliche-filled introduction for fellow librarians. A short potted history begins the 161 page book, whose list of horror authors, Gothic to contemporary, include most of the major figures, as well as many decidedly minor talents. The next chapter provides tips on matching horror fiction to widely varying readers, who are not, they emphasize, mostly teenage boys. A set of twenty-two books, all pre-Stephen King's *Carrie* (first published in 1974), are designated ''classics'' and briefly described. The following ten chapters focus on subgenres such as ghosts, were animals, serial killers, witches and demons, splatterpunk, etc. The final chapters discuss collection development (weeding little-used materials, as well as acquring new books), marketing the horror materials, and sources of more information, print and online. One source they praise is Anthony Fonseca and June Pulliam's *Hooked on Horror* (Libraries Unlimited, 1999; 2nd ed., 2003). It's a good guide for librarians.

The SF writer about whom more has been written than any other, with the possible exception of Ursula K. Le Guin, is Philip K. Dick. He and a twin sister were born prematurely in 1928, and her immediate death haunted Dick's entire life. Only one of his realistic novels was published during his lifetime; most of the others appeared after his death in 1982. Several of his stories have been filmed, of which the best and best known was *Blade Runner*, based very loosely on *Do Androids Dream of Electric Sheep?* (originally published in 1968), and the subject of many essays and several books. Dick was prolific, with more than fifty novels and 118 short stories published in a five-volume set. His anguish, recurrent psychological problems (including a lifetime addiction to amphetamines) and frequent paranoia were transmuted into his fiction. Perhaps his most intense concern was metaphysical, distinguishing between the real and the ersatz (this theme is prominent in *Blade Runner*). Whether you would learn this basic information from Emmanuel Carrere's *I Am Alive and You Are Dead: A Journey into the Mind of Philip K. Dick* (Metropolitan Books/Henry Holt, 2004, translated by Timothy Bent from the 1993 French original) is doubtful. The author, a novelist and screenplay writer, has talked to people who knew Dick and has read about him, but his account is not that of a biographer or even a literary critic, but more of a sympathetic observer. Most readers, possibly excluding Dick fans, will find this a bore and

unenlightening, in spite of Dick's importance to SF. Much better for almost anyone else is Lawrence Sutin's *Divine Invasions: A Life of Philip K. Dick* (Harmony Books, 1989), which is documented, critically balanced and has an index.

S.T. Joshi is one of the major critics of weird/supernatural/horror fiction, especially of the works of H.P. Lovecraft (1890-1937), who's attracted a cult following. Joshi's latest book is *The Evolution of the Weird Tale* (Hippocampus Press, 2004). Joshi has explored this territory before in *The Weird Tale* (University of Texas Press, 1990), which focuses on Lovecraft, Arthur Machen, Lord Dunsany, Algernon Blackwood, M.R. James, and Ambrose Bierce. *The Modern Weird Tale* (McFarland, 2001) covers contemporary writers such as Shirley Jackson, William Peter Blatty, Stephen King, Clive Barker, Ramsey Campbell, Peter Straub, and Anne Rice.

Joshi's latest book reprints and revises a number of specialty magazine essays and some book introductions. His subjects range from American and British writers of the ''golden age'' (roughly 1890 to 1930), including Robert W. Chambers, F. Marion Crawford, Rudyard Kipling, E.F. Benson, and L.P. Hartley. Lovecraft is discussed in moderate detail along with those he strongly influenced, such as Frank Belknap Long, Robert Bloch, and Fritz Leiber. Contemporary writers discussed include Rod Serling, L.P. Davies, Les Daniels, Dennis Etchison, David J. Schow, and Poppy Z. Brite. Joshi is a stern critic, dismissing as meretricious most of the work of the ''splatterpunks'' and trendy writers like Brite. Libraries owning works by the better writers Joshi discusses with insight and, generally, fairness, could broaden the horizons of weird/horror fiction readers with this inexpensive and clearly written survey.

If anyone could be appropriately tagged ''the father of science fiction,'' it would be H.G. Wells (1866-1946); W. Warren Wagar is one of many critics who argues this. Another candidate, Jules Verne (1828-1905) is sometimes suggested, but—perhaps because he was trained as a lawyer, unlike Wells, who had considerable science training—his many voyage extraordinaires rarely go beyond the knowledge of his day. While his tales are energetic, they are intellectually cautious. When he wrote of a moon voyage, he included more ballistics than most readers cared to know (and they were wrong as well). Wells, in spite of his scientific training, was content to substitute ''the ingenious use of scientific patter'' to gain credibility for his stories, or scientific romances as he reluctantly called them (the term science fiction did not become common until the 1930s). Verne was annoyed that Wells would use an obvious impossibility (Cavorite, which was impervious to gravitation) as the propulsive force for his moon ship.

Wagar says he was greatly influenced by Wells as a boy in the early 1930s. He wrote his 1956 doctoral thesis on Wells, published by Yale University Press in 1961 as *H.G. Wells and the World State* and wrote other books about Wells in subsequent years, including this new one, *H.G.*

Wells: Traversing Time (Wesleyan University Press, 2004). Wagar's emphasis here is on Wells' penchant for setting present day concerns (many of which are today's major problems) "within a framework of evolutionary time," to quote another Wells critic. Wagar's first chapter provides an overview of Wells' life and major works, not only the scientific romances but his other fiction, journalism and essays as well. Later chapters flesh out this summary. Just enough background detail is provided to orient the interested lay reader, while the notes, bibliography and index will serve the scholar.

If your library lacks either one of the two best biographies of Wells, David C. Smith's *H.G. Wellls: Desperately Mortal* (Yale University Press, 1986) or Norman and Jeanne MacKenzie's *H.G. Wells: A Biography* (Simon & Schuster, 1973; revised and published by Hogarth in 1987 as *The Life of H.G. Wells: The Time Traveller*), you should consider Wagar's balanced study, an excellent example of intellectual history rather than of literary criticism or straight biography. But first, you should own or acquire copies of *Seven Science Fiction Novels* in the bargain-priced Dover omnibus reprint (1994) and *The Complete Short Stories of H.G. Wells*, edited by John Hammond (Dent, 1998; Trafalgar Square, U.S. distributor).

If a poll were taken of representative book readers asking them to name SF authors, it's likely that Ray Bradbury (1920-) would be, if not the most frequently mentioned, certainly among the top three. *The Martian Chronicles* (published by Doubleday in 1950) synthesized from many earlier pulp magazine stories, has been a steady seller for more than half a century. His appeal extends well beyond the SF field. Not surprisingly, he has been the subject of a number of books, most recently *Ray Bradbury: The Life of Fiction* (Kent State University Press, 2004) by Jonathan R. Eller and William F. Touponce, both English professors at Indiana University. Their goal, in this lengthy and detailed study, is to explain the evolution of Bradbury's fiction by examining successive versions of his stories and books (including many unpublished works), and to show how he moved from the marginal field of SF to the literary mainstream. The authors use the carnival, in the broadest sense, as an explanatory metaphor intrinsic to much of Bradbury's fiction, poetry, and other writings. Myths and masks are also important elements in their analysis, which begins with *Dark Carnival* (Gauntlet, 1947), known to most in its revised version as *The October Country* (Ballantine, 1955). One of the eight chapters is devoted to his four crime novels. A 78 page appendix provides a listing, 1938-2003, of his published books (100), individual stories (400), plays, etc., citing both their original appearances and many reprints. A second appendix lists typescripts of his many unpublished works, long and short. Notes, a selected bibliography and an index complete the study, which will be valuable for serious students of Bradbury. Public libraries should select based on

likely reader interest, but many will judge this too scholarly. A good alternative choice, although a bit dated, is David Mogen's *Ray Bradbury* (Twayne, 1986). Jerry Weist's lightweight survey, *Ray Bradbury: An Illustrated Life* (Morrow, 2002) may suffice.

As Bradbury's popularity and appeal widened, he was the subject of an increasing number of interviews, twenty-one of which are collected in *Conversations with Ray Bradbury*, edited by Steven L. Aggelis (University Press of Mississippi, 2004). Aggelis says he has a list of 335 interviews, an emphatic measure of Bradbury's mainstream status. His selection is balanced and minimally repetitive, with Bradbury often providing multiple perspectives on the same work when questioned. The interviews are arranged chronologically from 1948, the year after the publication of his first book, to a concluding conversation with the editor in October 2002. The interviews range from two pages to the lengthiest, 20 pages (and one of the best) by Ken Kelley in the May 1996 *Playboy*. Collectively they cover Bradbury's short fiction, novels, plays and film, radio and music adaptations. A four-part bibliography of published books begins the book, followed by a balanced introduction by the editor, which includes brief quotes from many of the interviews. A useful ten-page chronology is followed by the "conversations" and an index. More readable and accessible than the Kent State study, this is a good choice for most public libraries. Bradbury, 84, received a National Medal of Arts, the government's highest honor for artistic excellence, in November 2004. Madeleine L'Engle, 85, also received this medal.

Tony Nourmand is co-owner of a London gallery specializing in vintage film posters. Graham Marsh is an art director, illustrator and writer. They co-edited six decade-long surveys of film posters from the 1930s through the 1980s and an excellent book of SF film posters. Their latest co-edited work is *Horror Poster Art* (Aurum, 2004; Trafalgar Square, U.S. distributor). Like its companion SF survey, it's a very well selected and annotated volume, reproducing about 200 posters of roughly 150 films, released 1922 to 2000, with film title, artist, designer, and photographer indexes. Foreign language (European, Japanese) posters can be compared with those from the United States/United Kingdom; the differences are often striking, with the former posters favoring more abstract design. The Polish and Hungarian posters for the brilliant 1974 comedy/horror film, *Young Frankenstein*, are intriguingly different. The reproductions are necessarily much smaller than the originals (roughly a fourth the size on average) but lose little of their power. Although many of the films were "exploitation" films, the posters, while often graphic, lack the gory and shock qualities of the movies. Sir Christopher Frayling, director of London's Royal College of Art, isn't slumming when he analyzes the often perverse appeal of such films. A good choice for film collections in larger public libraries.

Science Fiction Titles

DAN ABNETT

Double Eagle

(Nottingham, England: Black Library, 2004)

Story type: Space Opera; Military
Series: Warhammer
Subject(s): Military Life
Major character(s): August Kaminsky, Military Personnel; Bree Jagdea, Military Personnel; Anakwanar Sek, Nobleman, Warrior
Time period(s): Indeterminate Future
Locale(s): Outer Space; Enothis, Planet—Imaginary

Summary: A battle between the forces of order and humanity are hard pressed in their latest series of clashes, with a powerful enemy force gathered behind a brilliant and cruel leader. The novel concentrates primarily on describing a series of encounters among airborne fighting ships.

Other books by the same author:
Ravenor, 2004
Riders of the Dead, 2003
Sabbat Martyr, 2003
Hereticus, 2002
Xenos, 2001

Other books you might like:
Stephen Ames Berry, *The Final Assault*, 1988
Ben Counter, *Grey Knights*, 2004
William C. Dietz, *The Final Battle*, 1995
Matthew Farrer, *Legacy*, 2004
John Ringo, *Hell's Faire*, 2003

712

DAN ABNETT

Traitor General

(Nottingham, England: Black Library, 2004)

Story type: Space Opera; Military

Series: Warhammer
Subject(s): Military Life; Space Travel
Major character(s): Ibram Gaunt, Military Personnel (colonel-commissar); Landerson, Military Personnel; Mkvenner, Military Personnel
Time period(s): Indeterminate Future
Locale(s): Planet—Imaginary

Summary: A high ranking military officer with confidential information has been captured and is being held captive on a hostile planet. Colonel-Commissar Gaunt and a select group of soldiers must go in and rescue him if possible, or kill him if necessary to prevent him from revealing what he knows to the enemy.

Other books by the same author:
Ravenor, 2004
Riders of the Dead, 2003
Sabbat Martyr, 2003
Hereticus, 2002
The Guns of Tanith, 2002

Other books you might like:
John Dalmas, *The Regiment*, 1987
Richard Fawkes, *Face of the Enemy*, 1999
Elizabeth Moon, *Once a Hero*, 1997
Joel Rosenberg, *Not for Glory*, 1988
David Weber, *Ashes of Victory*, 2000

713

KEVIN J. ANDERSON

Horizon Storms

(New York: Aspect, 2004)

Story type: Space Opera; Hard Science Fiction
Series: Saga of Seven Sons. Book 3
Subject(s): Aliens
Major character(s): Jora'h, Alien; Nikki Chan Tylar, Pilot; Shelia Andez, Military Personnel, Prisoner
Time period(s): Indeterminate Future
Locale(s): Outer Space

Summary: The interstellar war that was inadvertently started by a human scientific experiment is spreading farther, sucking additional races into the conflict. Now a previously unknown race with extraordinarily advanced weapons has joined the conflict, and even those races which hoped to remain neutral find themselves in danger.

Where it's reviewed:
Chronicle, August 2004, page 24
Publishers Weekly, July 5, 2004, page 42

Other books by the same author:
A Forest of Stars, 2003
Captain Nemo, 2002
Hopscotch, 2002
Dogged Persistence, 2001
Ruins, 1996

Other books you might like:
C.J. Cherryh, *The Kif Strike Back*, 1986
Gordon R. Dickson, *Tactics of Mistake*, 1970
Joe Haldeman, *The Forever War*, 1974
Frank Herbert, *Dune Messiah*, 1969
Dan Simmons, *The Fall of Hyperion*, 1990

714

CATHERINE ASARO

Sunrise Alley
(New York: Baen, 2004)

Story type: Cyberpunk; Future Shock
Subject(s): Cyborgs
Major character(s): Samantha Bryton, Fugitive; Turner, Cyborg, Fugitive; Charon, Criminal
Time period(s): 2030s (2033)
Locale(s): United States

Summary: Samantha Bryton's life is turned upside down when she becomes a fugitive, pursued by the minions of an arch criminal 30 years in the future. Her only companion is Turner, a taciturn man whose body is partly artificial, and who may no longer think of himself as entirely human.

Where it's reviewed:
Booklist, August 2004, page 1912
Chronicle, August 2004, page 23

Other books by the same author:
The Charmed Sphere, 2004
Skyfall, 2003
Spherical Harmonic, 2001
The Quantum Rose, 2000
The Veiled Web, 1999

Other books you might like:
C.J. Cherryh, *The Pride of Chanur*, 1982
Denise Lopes Heald, *Mistwalker*, 1994
Frederik Pohl, *Man Plus*, 1976
S.L. Viehl, *Stardoc*, 2000
Jack Williamson, *Manseed*, 1982

715

KAGE BAKER

The Life of the World to Come
(New York: Tor, 2004)

Story type: Time Travel; Humor
Series: Company. Book 6
Subject(s): Time Travel
Major character(s): Mendoza, Cyborg, Scientist (botanist); Alec Chatterfield, Time Traveler, Criminal; Rutherford, Wealthy
Time period(s): Indeterminate Past; 24th century
Locale(s): Earth

Summary: The cyborg botanist Mendoza travels through time for an enigmatic 24th-century agency and has been marooned in the distant past after becoming a somewhat troublesome employee. Mendoza has fallen in love with the same man twice, in two different incarnations, and as she muses about his past life, she runs into a third incarnation.

Other books by the same author:
The Anvil of the World, 2003
Black Projects, White Knights, 2002
The Graveyard Game, 2001
Mendoza in Hollywood, 2000
Sky Coyote, 1999

Other books you might like:
Poul Anderson, *Corridors of Time*, 1965
Kathleen Ann Goonan, *The Bones of Time*, 1996
Robert Silverberg, *Hawksbill Station*, 1968
Michael Swanwick, *Bones of the Earth*, 2002
Connie Willis, *Doomsday Book*, 1992

716

BRUCE BALFOUR

Prometheus Road
(New York: Ace, 2004)

Story type: Post-Disaster; Alternate Intelligence
Subject(s): Artificial Intelligence; Disasters
Major character(s): Tom Eliot, Farmer; Magnus, Recluse; Uriah, Worker
Time period(s): Indeterminate Future
Locale(s): North America

Summary: A disaster resulted in the sinking of much of the West Coast, and the collapse of technological civilization. Tom is a farmer who has always been tempted to question the status quo despite the demonstrable presence of the ''gods,'' whom he will eventually discover are actually artificial intelligences which survived the cataclysm.

Where it's reviewed:
Booklist, November 1, 2004, page 471
Chronicle, October 2004, page 27

Other books by the same author:
The Digital Dead, 2003
The Forge of Mars, 2002
Star Crusader, 1995

Other books you might like:
William Barton, *When Heaven Fell*, 1995
Martin Caidin, *The God Machine*, 1968
D.F. Jones, *Colossus*, 1966
Thomas F. Monteleone, *Ozymandias*, 1981
Robert J. Sawyer, *The Terminal Experiment*, 1995

717

MARGARET BALL

Disappearing Act
(New York: Baen, 2004)

Story type: Space Opera; Mystery
Subject(s): Secrets
Major character(s): Calandra Vissi, Police Officer; Maris, Criminal; Chulayen Vajjandara, Government Official
Time period(s): Indeterminate Future
Locale(s): Outer Space; Tasman, Space Station

Summary: Calandra Vissi conducts a secret investigation into smuggling and other possible crimes on Tasman, an artificial world created at a strategic point in space. Her discoveries put her life in jeopardy and she assumes an alternate identity in order to escape, but finds herself in even worse trouble.

Other books by the same author:
Mathemagics, 1996
Lost in Translation, 1995
No Earthly Sunne, 1994
Changeweaver, 1993
Flameweaver, 1991

Other books you might like:
C.J. Cherryh, *The Hunter of Worlds*, 1977
Julie E. Czerneda, *To Trade the Stars*, 2002
Robert Hoskins, *To Control the Stars*, 1977
S.L. Viehl, *Stardoc*, 2000
Timothy Zahn, *The Icarus Hunt*, 1999

718

JOHN BARNES

Gaudeamus
(New York: Tor, 2004)

Story type: Humor; Satire
Subject(s): Time Travel; Humor
Major character(s): John Barnes, Writer, Historical Figure; Travis Bismark, Spy (industrial)
Time period(s): 2000s
Locale(s): United States

Summary: The author becomes a character in his own novel, relating stories told to him by a friend who works as an industrial spy. The friend has become aware of inventions that could make time travel and teleportation possible. Humorous and anecdotal adventures follow as the secret is stolen and efforts are made to recover it.

Where it's reviewed:
Chronicle, October 2004, page 24
Locus, October 2004, page 29

Other books by the same author:
In the Hall of the Martian King, 2003
The Sky So Big and Black, 2002
The Merchants of Souls, 2001
Candle, 2000
Finity, 1999

Other books you might like:
Arthur C. Clarke, *Tales from the White Hart*, 1957
L. Sprague de Camp, *Tales from Gavagan's Bar*, 1953
    Fletcher Pratt, co-author
John DeChancie, *Dr. Dimension*, 1993
    David Bischoff, co-author
Henry Kuttner, *Robots Have No Tails*, 1952
Spider Robinson, *Callahan's Touch*, 1993

719

NEAL BARRETT JR.

Prince of Christler-Coke
(Urbana, Illinois: Golden Gryphon, 2004)

Story type: Satire; Future Shock
Subject(s): Humor
Major character(s): Asel Iacoca, Nobleman, Prisoner; Sylvan Lee McCree, Prisoner
Time period(s): Indeterminate Future
Locale(s): North America

Summary: In a biting and often very funny satire, the executives of today have become the formal aristocracy of tomorrow, their positions passed down through their families for generations to come. A power play leaves Asel Iacoca not only deprived of his family inheritance, but imprisoned in a detention center from which he escapes to find out the truth about America.

Where it's reviewed:
Locus, September 2004, page 66

Other books by the same author:
The Prophecy Machine, 2001
The Treachery of Kings, 2001
Perpetuity Blues, 2000
Slightly Off Center, 1992
The Hereafter Gang, 1991

Other books you might like:
Brian W. Aldiss, *Enemies of the System*, 1978
Benjamin Appel, *The Funhouse*, 1959
Shepherd Mead, *The Big Ball of Wax*, 1959
Rebecca Ore, *Outlaw School*, 2000
Frederik Pohl, *The Age of the Pussyfoot*, 1968

720

STEPHEN BAXTER

Exultant
(London: Gollancz, 2004)

Story type: Space Opera; Hard Science Fiction
Series: Destiny's Children. Book 2
Subject(s): Aliens; Space Travel

Science Fiction

Major character(s): Pirius, Spaceship Captain; Enduring Hope, Spaceman; Nilis, Government Official
Time period(s): Indeterminate Future
Locale(s): Outer Space

Summary: In the very distant future, humans are locked in a vast interstellar war with the alien Xeelee, who have had a civilization since before humans evolved. A desperate mission is undertaken to penetrate deep into their regions of space and uncover the secrets of their latest military campaign, in the opening stages of what might well be the final battle.

Where it's reviewed:
Booklist, November 15, 2004, page 570
Locus, October 2004, page 25

Other books by the same author:
The Hunters of Pangaea, 2004
Coalescent, 2003
Evolution, 2002
Icebones, 2001
Longtusk, 2001

Other books you might like:
Kevin J. Anderson, *The Hidden Empire*, 2002
Gregory Benford, *Matter's End*, 1995
Brian Herbert, *The Battle of Corrin*, 2004
    Kevin J. Anderson, co-author
Fred Saberhagen, *Berserker Man*, 2004
Dan Simmons, *Endymion*, 1995

721

JAMES BEAUSEIGNEUR

Acts of God

(New York: Warner, 2004)

Story type: Religious; Disaster
Series: Christ Clone. Book 3
Subject(s): Disasters; Coming-of-Age
Major character(s): Christopher Goodman, Religious; Chaim Levin, Religious; Decker Hawthorne, Businessman
Time period(s): Indeterminate Future
Locale(s): Earth

Summary: After cloning cells on the Shroud of Turin, the birth and eventual maturity of Christopher Goodman coincides with a dramatic and violent restructuring of the world. Asteroids strike the planet and destroy many cities, while plagues and other phenomena seem to indicate that he is in fact the Second Coming.

Other books by the same author:
Birth of an Age, 2004
In His Image, 2003

Other books you might like:
Nancy Freedman, *Joshua, Son of None*, 1973
James Morrow, *Only Begotten Daughter*, 1990
Richard Sears, *First Born*, 2000
Ian Watson, *God's World*, 1979
Jane Yolen, *Armageddon Summer*, 1998
    Bruce Coville, co-author

722

DONALD J. BINGLE

Forced Conversion

(Waterville, Maine: Five Star, 2004)

Story type: Dystopian; Military
Subject(s): Virtual Reality; Military Life
Major character(s): Derek, Military Personnel; Maria Casini, Fugitive; Manning, Military Personnel
Time period(s): Indeterminate Future
Locale(s): Earth

Summary: Derek is a soldier in the army of the ruling government of Earth, which is in the process of forcibly putting people into a state of suspended animation while their minds function in a form of virtual reality. His experiences while separated from his unit convince him that he is fighting on the wrong side. First novel.

Other books you might like:
Dennis Danvers, *End of Days*, 1999
James P. Gunn, *The Joy Makers*, 1961
Nick Sagan, *Idlewild*, 2003
Neal Stephenson, *Snow Crash*, 1992
Chet Williamson, *Hell*, 1995

723

ERIC BROWN

Bengal Station

(Waterville, Maine: Five Star, 2004)

Story type: Mystery; Space Opera
Subject(s): Mental Telepathy
Major character(s): Jeff Vaughan, Telepath; Jimmy Chandra, Police Officer; Sukara, Teenager
Time period(s): Indeterminate Future
Locale(s): Verkerk's World, Planet—Imaginary; Thailand; Outer Space

Summary: Jeff Vaughan is a telepath who teams up with a police officer to investigate a religious cult that has spread across several colony worlds and which uses drugs and criminal activities to enforce obedience. Elsewhere, an orphan in Thailand is lured into space by another telepath.

Where it's reviewed:
Analog, December 2004, page 134
Chronicle, August 2004, page 24

Other books by the same author:
New York Blues, 2001
New York Nights, 2000
Penumbra, 1999
Walkabout, 1999
Engineman, 1994

Other books you might like:
Alfred Bester, *The Demolished Man*, 1951
Tara Harper, *Lightwing*, 1992
Christopher Hinz, *Anachronisms*, 1988
Lisanne Norman, *Turning Point*, 1993
F. Paul Wilson, *The Tery*, 1990

724

ERIC BROWN

New York Dreams
(London: Gollancz, 2004)

Story type: Mystery; Future Shock
Series: Virex. Book 3
Subject(s): Virtual Reality
Major character(s): Hal Halliday, Detective—Private; Suzie Charlesworthy, Child, Actress; Casey, Artificial Intelligence
Time period(s): 2040s (2041)
Locale(s): New York, New York

Summary: Hal Halliday's life is getting worse with each passing day. His partner is dead, his girlfriend has left him, and he spends most of his time with an artificial companion he created in a virtual reality world. When a child actress disappears, and there are hints that his dead partner might somehow have returned to life, Halliday's slow slide toward self-destruction is interrupted.

Other books by the same author:
Bengal Station, 2004
New York Blues, 2001
New York Nights, 2000
Penumbra, 1999
Engineman, 1994

Other books you might like:
Paul Levinson, *The Pixel Eye*, 2003
Mike McQuay, *The Odds Are Murder*, 1983
S. Andrew Swann, *Specters of Dawn*, 1994
Lawrence Watt-Evans, *Nightside City*, 1989
F. Paul Wilson, *Dydeetown World*, 1989

725

M.M. BUCKNER

Neurolink
(New York: Ace, 2004)

Story type: Dystopian; Political
Subject(s): Submarines
Major character(s): Dominic Jedes, Businessman; Klas Lorn, Businessman; Richter Jedes, Spirit
Time period(s): 23rd century
Locale(s): Earth; Undersea Environment/Habitat

Summary: When Richter Jedes dies in an accident, his electronic simulation continues as companion to his son, Dominic. Dominic is told that he must engineer the deaths of 2,000 lower-class citizens as a means to cut costs for the family corporation. He begins to have second thoughts once he has embarked on the project.

Other books by the same author:
Hyperthought, 2003

Other books you might like:
Neal Barrett Jr., *Prince of Christler-Coke*, 2004
Michael G. Coney, *Neptune's Cauldron*, 1981
Steven Gould, *Blind Waves*, 2000

Allen Steele, *Oceanspace*, 2000
Peter Watts, *Starfish*, 1999

726

MARK BUDZ

Crache
(New York: Bantam, 2004)

Story type: Disaster; Cyberpunk
Subject(s): Ecothriller; Technology
Major character(s): L. Marichi, Musician; Fola Hanani, Settler
Time period(s): Indeterminate Future
Locale(s): Mymercia, Asteroid; Earth

Summary: An accident that wipes out all but one member of a work team on the asteroid Mymercia is linked to a mysterious disease that literally leeches the souls of its victims. An unusual blend of technology, ecological awareness, and mysticism.

Where it's reviewed:
Booklist, November 15, 2004, page 570
Publishers Weekly, October 18, 2004, page 53

Other books by the same author:
Clade, 2003

Other books you might like:
Poul Anderson, *Tales of the Flying Mountains*, 1971
Ben Bova, *The Precipice*, 2001
Scott Mackay, *The Meek*, 2001
Mary Rosenblum, *The Stone Garden*, 1995
Joan D. Vinge, *The Outcasts of Heaven's Belt*, 1978

727

ROBERT BUETTNER

Orphanage
(New York: Aspect, 2004)

Story type: Military; Space Opera
Subject(s): Space Travel; Aliens
Major character(s): Jason Wander, Military Personnel, Teenager; Pooh Hart, Military Personnel; Druwan Parker, Military Personnel
Time period(s): Indeterminate Future
Locale(s): Outer Space; Jupiter

Summary: Aliens establish a base on Ganymede and begin a long range bombardment of the Earth. Although the situation is deteriorating badly, humanity is able to launch one warship. The crew is very inexperienced, but they cross the intervening space and manage to defeat the aliens and save the day. Although a little implausible, this first novel is still a rousing adventure.

Other books you might like:
William C. Dietz, *Freehold*, 1987
David Feintuch, *Midshipman's Hope*, 1994
William R. Forstchen, *Action Stations*, 1998
Robert A. Heinlein, *Starship Troopers*, 1959
John Ringo, *Gust Front*, 2001

728

CHRIS BUNCH

The Doublecross Program

(New York: Roc, 2004)

Story type: Military; Space Opera
Series: Star Risk. Book 3
Subject(s): Military Life
Major character(s): M'chel Riss, Mercenary; Jasmine King, Mercenary; Chaos Goodnight, Mercenary
Time period(s): Indeterminate Future
Locale(s): Roh Bahtrine, Planet—Imaginary; Outer Space

Summary: A group of mercenaries finds itself short on funds so they accept an unusual job performing a reverse bank robbery to cover up the illegal borrowing of some funds. Things become predictably more complicated, eventually landing them in the middle of an interstellar war.

Other books by the same author:
The Scoundrel Worlds, 2003
Star Risk, Ltd., 2002
Firemask, 2000
Storm Force, 2000
Hunt the Heavens, 1996

Other books you might like:
Lois McMaster Bujold, *Cetaganda*, 1996
William C. Dietz, *For More than Glory*, 2003
David Drake, *With the Lightnings*, 1998
Jerry Pournelle, *Falkenberg's Legion*, 1990
John Ringo, *Gust Front*, 2001

729

A.J. BUTCHER

Chaos Rising

(New York: Little, Brown, 2004)

Story type: Young Adult; Espionage Thriller
Series: Spy High. Book 2
Subject(s): Technology; Espionage; Spies
Major character(s): Benjamin Stanton Jr., Teenager, Spy; Elmore Grant, Teacher; Jennifer Chen, Teenager, Spy
Time period(s): 2000s
Locale(s): Massachusetts

Summary: Devereaux Academy poses as a private school but it is actually a training ground for new spies and has access to technology unknown to the general public. A group of terrorists attempt to hold the world hostage, but the young spies prove more than their match.

Other books by the same author:
Spy High: Mission One, 2004

Other books you might like:
K.A. Applegate, *Inside the Illusion*, 2000
Bruce Coville, *Robot Trouble*, 1986
James P. Hogan, *Bug Park*, 1997
Nancy Holder, *The Book of Fours*, 2002
Melinda Metz, *Outsider*, 1998

730

A.J. BUTCHER

Spy High: Mission One

(New York: Little, Brown, 2004)

Story type: Young Adult; Espionage Thriller
Series: Spy High. Book 1
Subject(s): Technology; Espionage; Spies
Major character(s): Benjamin Stanton Jr., Teenager, Spy; Elmore Grant, Teacher; Jennifer Chen, Teenager, Spy
Time period(s): 2000s
Locale(s): Massachusetts

Summary: Young people are trained at a special school as spies using advanced technological devices unknown to the rest of the world. In their first adventure, the spies are forced to respond to efforts by a megalomaniac to seize control of the world.

Other books by the same author:
Chaos Rising, 2004

Other books you might like:
K.A. Applegate, *Gateway to the Gods*, 2000
Bruce Coville, *Operation Sherlock*, 1986
Greg Cox, *Loose Ends*, 2001
Melinda Metz, *Seeker*, 1999
John Vornholt, *Seven Crows*, 2003

731

JAY CASELBERG

Metal Sky

(New York: Roc, 2004)

Story type: Mystery; Psychic Powers
Series: Jack Stein. Book 2
Subject(s): Psychic Powers
Major character(s): Jack Stein, Detective—Private; Bridgett Farrell, Wealthy
Time period(s): Indeterminate Future
Locale(s): Yorkstone, Planet—Imaginary

Summary: Psychic detective Jack Stein returns for a new futuristic adventure, this time on another distant world. A mysterious alien artifact has been stolen and Stein's new client wants it back. The investigation reveals that the object's value doesn't lie just with its antiquity.

Where it's reviewed:
Chronicle, August 2004, page 26

Other books by the same author:
Wyrmhole, 2003

Other books you might like:
Alfred Bester, *The Demolished Man*, 1951
Lee Killough, *Spider Play*, 1986
Mike McQuay, *When Trouble Beckons*, 1981
Larry Niven, *The Long Arm of Gil Hamilton*, 1976
S. Andrew Swann, *Forests of the Night*, 1993

732
ADAM CONNELL
Counterfeit Kings
(New York: Phobos, 2004)

Story type: Space Opera; Political
Subject(s): Space Colonies
Major character(s): Horrocks, Bodyguard; Sari, Bodyguard; Guilfoyle, Detective—Private
Time period(s): Indeterminate Future
Locale(s): Outer Space

Summary: The ruler of a group of colonies in the outer solar system is the object of an assassination plot by unknown forces. In the aftermath, the succession to the throne is confused by the existence of a number of surgically altered doubles and the further plotting of forces determined to seize power. First novel.

Other books you might like:
John Barnes, *In the Hall of the Martian King*, 2003
Colin Greenland, *Take Back Plenty*, 1990
Edmond Hamilton, *The Star Kings*, 1949
Alexander Jablokov, *Deepdrive*, 1998
Jack Vance, *The Star King*, 1964

733
STORM CONSTANTINE
The Shades of Time and Memory
(New York: Tor, 2004)

Story type: Political; Fantasy
Series: Wraethu Histories. Book 2
Subject(s): Fantasy; Genetic Engineering
Major character(s): Caeru har Aralis, Government Official; Velaxis, Alien (Wraethu); Pellaz, Alien (Wraethu)
Time period(s): Indeterminate Future
Locale(s): Planet—Imaginary

Summary: The Wraethu are a race of hermaphrodites who appear to have evolved from humanity. As they grow into a new civilization, they must discover their own unique way of dealing with politics, government, and other societal structures which they cannot necessarily adopt from the older race.

Where it's reviewed:
Library Journal, November 15, 2004, page 55
Publishers Weekly, October 25, 2004, page 32

Other books by the same author:
The Wraiths of Will and Pleasure, 2003
The Crown of Silence, 2001
The Way of Light, 2001
Sea Dragon Heir, 2000
Scenting Hallowed Blood, 1996

Other books you might like:
Karen Haber, *The Mutant Season*, 1989
    Robert Silverberg, co-author
Nancy Kress, *Beggar's Ride*, 1996
Henry Kuttner, *Mutant*, 1953
Kate Wilhelm, *Where Late the Sweet Birds Sang*, 1976

Chelsea Quinn Yarbro, *False Dawn*, 1978

734
STEPHEN COONTS
Saucer: The Conquest
(New York: St Martin's Griffin, 2004)

Story type: Techno-Thriller; Espionage Thriller
Series: Rip Cantrell. Book 2
Subject(s): Space Travel
Major character(s): Rip Cantrell, Pilot; Pierre Artois, Government Official; Charlotte Pine, Spacewoman
Time period(s): 2000s
Locale(s): United States; Outer Space

Summary: France has been establishing a space colony on the moon thanks to the discovery of an ancient flying saucer, but a power mad extremist decides to use the vessel to dominate the world. Rip Cantrell uses a second saucer to foil his plans in a fast-paced, exciting, but implausible and scientifically impossible, manner.

Where it's reviewed:
Booklist, August 2004, page 1868
Publishers Weekly, August 9, 2004, page 230

Other books by the same author:
Liberty, 2004
Deep Black, 2003
Saucer: The Conquest, 2002
Fortunes of War, 1998
Final Flight, 1989

Other books you might like:
Campbell Black, *Asterisk Destiny*, 1978
Martin Caidin, *The Mendelov Conspiracy*, 1969
Louis A. Goth, *Red-12*, 1979
Edward E. Smith, *The Skylark of Space*, 1928
Gene Snyder, *The Ogden Enigma*, 1980

735
ALBERT E. COWDREY
Crux
(New York: Tor, 2004)

Story type: Time Travel; Space Opera
Subject(s): Time Travel; Scientific Experiments
Major character(s): Hastings Max, Police Officer; Yost, Military Personnel (colonel); Dyeva, Criminal, Time Traveler
Time period(s): Indeterminate Future
Locale(s): Earth; Outer Space

Summary: Humanity almost wiped itself out in a great conflict, but survived and built an interstellar empire based on the principles of freedom. A group of well-meaning renegades steals a time machine and sets out to prevent the catastrophe in the past, even though that might alter the present. First novel.

Where it's reviewed:
Locus, December 2004, page 27

Other books you might like:
Poul Anderson, *The Time Patrol*, 1991
J.R. Dunn, *Days of Cain*, 1997
Gordon Eklund, *Serving in Time*, 1975
Fritz Leiber, *Changewar*, 1983
H. Beam Piper, *Paratime*, 1981

736

DON D'AMMASSA

Haven

(Waterville, Maine: Five Star, 2004)

Story type: Mystery; Space Colony
Subject(s): Space Colonies; Aliens
Major character(s): Wes Avery, Writer; Dona Tharmody, Computer Expert; Lydia Hanifer, Police Officer
Time period(s): Indeterminate Future
Locale(s): Haven, Planet—Imaginary

Summary: Wes Avery is vacationing on Haven while recovering from a long illness when he stumbles across a dead body that disappears before he can summon the authorities. Having made friends with another visitor to the planet, he attempts to uncover the truth, which involves the mysterious doings of a prominent politician and efforts to alter the status of the primitive but intelligent alien population.

Other books by the same author:
Scarab, 2004
Servants of Chaos, 2002
Blood Beast, 1988

Other books you might like:
Danny DeMartino, *Wayward Moon*, 2001
Joe Clifford Faust, *A Death of Honor*, 1987
Katherine Kurtz, *The Legacy of Lehr*, 1986
Mel Odom, *Lethal Interface*, 1992
John E. Stith, *Reunion on Neverend*, 1994

737

GUY D'ARMEN

City of Gold and Lepers

(Encino, California: Black Coat, 2004)

Story type: Adventure; Medical
Subject(s): Scientific Experiments; Biotechnology
Major character(s): Francis Ardan, Explorer, Prisoner; Louise Ducharme, Prisoner; Natas, Criminal, Scientist
Time period(s): 1920s (1927)
Locale(s): Tibet

Summary: Francis Ardan is traveling through a remote part of Tibet when he is captured by Natas, a criminal mastermind who has developed a way to inflict leprosy on the population of a small city of slaves. Ardan teams up with beautiful Louise Ducharme to outwit Natas in this novel, which has been translated into English for the first time from the 1928 French edition.

Other books you might like:
H. Rider Haggard, *The People of the Mist*, 1894
A. Merritt, *The Face in the Abyss*, 1931

James Rollins, *Excavation*, 2000
Rex Stout, *Under the Andes*, 1914
John Taine, *The Purple Sapphire*, 1924

738

BILL DESMEDT

Singularity

(Seattle: Per Aspera, 2004)

Story type: Hard Science Fiction; Espionage Thriller
Subject(s): Secrets; Scientific Experiments
Major character(s): Jack Adler, Scientist; Marianna Bonaventure, Spy; Arkady Grishin, Businessman
Time period(s): 2000s
Locale(s): At Sea

Summary: A scientist concludes that the Tunguska explosion resulted from a collision with a miniature black hole, and that the object is still inside the Earth, where it will eventually destroy the entire planet. His efforts to save the world are complicated by various business interests who place their own fortunes ahead of the welfare of the world. First novel.

Other books you might like:
David Brin, *Earth*, 1990
Elizabeth Hand, *Icarus Descending*, 1993
Fritz Leiber, *The Wanderer*, 1964
Yvonne Navarro, *Final Impact*, 1997
Thomas Wren, *The Doomsday Effect*, 1986

739

WILLIAM C. DIETZ

For Those Who Fell

(New York: Ace, 2004)

Story type: Military; Space Colony
Series: Legion of Damned. Book 6
Subject(s): Military Life
Major character(s): William Booly III, Military Personnel (general); Antonio Santana, Military Personnel (first lieutenant); Kuga-Ka, Alien
Time period(s): Indeterminate Future
Locale(s): Algeron, Planet—Imaginary; Outer Space

Summary: A military based society seeks a planetary home for its capital after the destruction of the old one by an implacable alien enemy. They establish one on an inhabited planet despite the objections of some of the indigenous aliens, causing problems behind their lines, as well as in space.

Where it's reviewed:
Booklist, September 1, 2004, page 74
Publishers Weekly, September 6, 2004, page 50

Other books by the same author:
For More than Glory, 2003
Earthrise, 2002
Deathday, 2001
By Force of Arms, 2000
Bodyguard, 1994

Other books you might like:
W. Michael Gear, *Starstrike*, 1990
Walter Hunt, *The Dark Wing*, 2001
Elizabeth Moon, *Once a Hero*, 1997
Joel Rosenberg, *Hero*, 1990
Rick Shelley, *Sucker Punch*, 2003

740

DAVID DRAKE, Editor
ERIC FLINT, Co-Editor
JIM BAEN, Co-Editor

The World Turned Upside Down
(New York: Baen, 2004)

Story type: Anthology
Subject(s): Short Stories

Summary: The classic science fiction stories in this very large collection were all originally published between the 1930s and 1960s. Among the many authors included are Theodore Sturgeon, H. Beam Piper, Fredric Brown, James H. Schmitz, Fritz Leiber, and A.E. van Vogt. There is no common theme as the stories are meant to illustrate a cross section of the field during those years.

Other books by the same author:
The Reaches, 2004
Grimmer than Hell, 2003
The Far Side of the Stars, 2003
Paying the Piper, 2002
With the Lightnings, 1998

Other books you might like:
Fredric Brown, *From These Ashes*, 2002
H. Beam Piper, *Federation*, 1981
James H. Schmitz, *Dangerous Territory*, 2001
Theodore Sturgeon, *And Now the News*, 2003
A.E. van Vogt, *The Best of A.E. van Vogt*, 1876

741

MATTHEW FARRER

Legacy
(Nottingham, England: Black Library, 2004)

Story type: Space Opera; Military
Series: Warhammer
Subject(s): Military Life
Major character(s): Shira Calpurnia, Military Personnel; Baron Mykal, Nobleman; Varro Phrax, Nobleman
Time period(s): Indeterminate Future
Locale(s): Hydraphur, Planet—Imaginary

Summary: The battle for power among the aristocrats on Hydraphur has grown so violent and bitter that they are no longer willing even to submit to offworld authority. That forces Shira Calpurnia and her small group of soldiers to be particularly innovative in putting down the ensuing unrest.

Other books by the same author:
Crossfire, 2003

Other books you might like:
Chris Bunch, *Firemask*, 2000
John Dalmas, *Soldiers*, 2001
William King, *Space Wolf*, 2000
John Ringo, *Hell's Faire*, 2003
Rick Shelley, *Holding the Line*, 2001

742

RICHARD FAWKES

Nature of the Beast
(New York: Eos, 2004)

Story type: Military; Space Opera
Subject(s): Military Life
Major character(s): Christoph Stone, Military Personnel; Anders Seaborg, Spaceship Captain, Military Personnel; Bartie Lars, Prisoner
Time period(s): 24th century (2319)
Locale(s): Spaceship; Outer Space

Summary: Human civilization has been attacked by the remorseless alien Remors and now the time has come to launch a military strike to recapture one of the lost colony worlds. The military expedition sent to do the job is about to make a startling discovery, however, because the aliens are turning their prisoners into a new weapon.

Other books by the same author:
Face of the Enemy, 1999

Other books you might like:
F.M. Busby, *Cage a Man*, 1973
Robert A. Heinlein, *Starship Troopers*, 1959
Barry B. Longyear, *Enemy Mine*, 1985
 David Gerrold, co-author
R.M. Meluch, *War Birds*, 1989
Timothy Zahn, *Conqueror's Legacy*, 1996

743

ERIC FLINT, Editor

Grantville Gazette
(New York: Baen, 2004)

Story type: Collection
Subject(s): Short Stories

Summary: This collection of original short stories is related to the novel *1632* by the editor, the story of a town that becomes displaced in time and ends up in an alternate history. Other than the contribution by the Flint, the stories are all by newcomers, in some cases their very first story.

Other books by the same author:
1634, 2004 (Andrew Dennis, co-author)
The Course of Empire, 2003 (K.D. Wentworth, co-author)
1633, 2002
1632, 2000
Mother of Demons, 1997

Other books you might like:
Fredric Brown, *What Mad Universe*, 1949
William R. Forstchen, *Band of Brothers*, 1999

Edmond Hamilton, *City at World's End*, 1951
Kirk Mitchell, *Cry Republic*, 1989
S.M. Stirling, *Island in the Sea of Time*, 1998

744

ERIC FLINT
DAVE FREER, Co-Author

The Rats, the Bats, and the Ugly

(New York: Baen, 2004)

Story type: Military; Space Opera
Series: Rats. Book 2
Subject(s): Military Life
Major character(s): Chip Connolly, Military Personnel; Longfang O'Neil, Alien, Military Personnel; Michaela Bronstein, Military Personnel
Time period(s): Indeterminate Future
Locale(s): Outer Space

Summary: In the distant future, war is still a commonplace event, and military units are made up of both sexes, as well as alien volunteers. An unlikely group of unusual characters is called upon to repeat their earlier victories, against impossible odds, in a fresh round of fighting.

Where it's reviewed:
Booklist, September 15, 2004, page 215
Locus, December 2004, page 31

Other books by the same author:
The Philosophical Strangler, 2001
1632, 2000
Fortune's Stroke, 2000 (David Drake, co-author)
Destiny's Shield, 1999 (David Drake, co-author)
Mother of Demons, 1997

Other books you might like:
William C. Dietz, *By Force of Arms*, 2000
David Drake, *With the Lightnings*, 1998
Leo Frankowski, *Kren of the Mitchegai*, 2004
    David Grossman, co-author
William H. Keith, *Jackers*, 1994
Rick Shelley, *Deep Strike*, 2002

745

ALAN DEAN FOSTER

Sliding Scales

(New York: Del Rey, 2004)

Story type: Space Opera; Space Colony
Series: Pip and Flinx. Book 10
Subject(s): Aliens
Major character(s): Philip "Flinx" Lynx, Vacationer, Fugitive; Pip, Alien (mini-dragon); Takuuna, Alien
Time period(s): Indeterminate Future
Locale(s): Jast, Planet—Imaginary

Summary: Flinx is still on the run from mysterious forces who want to harness his unusual abilities, but for the moment he's more interested in resting than in finding out the truth about his origins. He diverts to a supposedly peaceful, out of the way world for a short vacation, but it proves to be just as impossible to let down his guard there as everywhere else.

Where it's reviewed:
Booklist, September 15, 2004, page 215
Publishers Weekly, August 23, 2004, page 41

Other books by the same author:
Lost and Found, 2004
Drowning World, 2003
Flinx's Folly, 2003
Diuturnity's Dawn, 2002
Impossible Places, 2002

Other books you might like:
Poul Anderson, *The Rebel Worlds*, 1969
C.J. Cherryh, *Chanur's Venture*, 1984
Julie E. Czerneda, *Survival*, 2004
Keith Laumer, *Retief in the Ruins*, 1986
Andre Norton, *The Solar Queen*, 2003

746

C.S. FRIEDMAN

The Wilding

(New York: DAW, 2004)

Story type: Space Opera; Psychic Powers
Subject(s): Psychic Powers
Major character(s): Tathas, Warrior; Zara, Government Official; Rho, Psychic
Time period(s): Indeterminate Future
Locale(s): Outer Space

Summary: War has been the state of things between two vast human empires spread through the stars for as long as anyone can remember. One side has developed psychic powers, while the other relies on ever more advanced technology, and dissidents from both sides seek refuge where they can.

Other books by the same author:
This Alien Shore, 1998
Crown of Shadows, 1995
When the Night Falls, 1993
The Madness Season, 1990
In Conquest Born, 1986

Other books you might like:
Kevin J. Anderson, *The Hidden Empire*, 2002
Poul Anderson, *Star Ways*, 1956
Gordon R. Dickson, *Soldier, Ask Not*, 1967
Alastair Reynolds, *Redemption Ark*, 2002
Edward E. Smith, *First Lensman*, 1950

747

JAMES ALAN GARDNER

Radiant

(New York: Eos, 2004)

Story type: Space Opera; Space Colony
Series: Expendables. Book 3
Subject(s): Aliens

Major character(s): Youn Shee, Explorer; Festina Ramos, Military Personnel (admiral); Tut, Explorer
Time period(s): Indeterminate Future
Locale(s): Outer Space

Summary: Youn Shee is an explorer, one of a group charged with handling high risk situations which means that they are individually expendable as far as human society is concerned. Along with her partner and a famous military figure, she joins forces to combat the efforts by an alien intelligence known as the Balrog to increase its influence in human known space.

Where it's reviewed:
Locus, August 2004, page 27

Other books by the same author:
Trapped, 2002
Hunted, 2000
Vigilant, 1999
Commitment Hour, 1998
Expendable, 1997

Other books you might like:
Poul Anderson, *A Knight of Ghosts and Shadows*, 1975
John Brunner, *Polymath*, 1963
C.J. Cherryh, *The Fires of Azeroth*, 1979
Murray Leinster, *Invaders of Space*, 1964
Andre Norton, *Forerunner*, 1981

748

ROBERTA GELLIS

Overstars Mail: Imperial Challenge

(Waterville, Maine: Five Star, 2004)

Story type: Space Opera; Mystery
Subject(s): Space Travel
Major character(s): Cyn Lystris, Postal Worker; Frefem Aimee, Passenger; Fremale Demoson, Passenger
Time period(s): Indeterminate Future
Locale(s): Outer Space

Summary: Cyn Lystris is pursuing what is intended to be a quiet, safe career delivering mail and occasional passengers from one planet to the next. Unfortunately, one of his current passengers is a prominent political figure traveling incognito, and another is an assassin determined to cut short his career. Even more unfortunately, Cyn doesn't know who is who.

Other books by the same author:
Thrice Bound, 2001
Bull God, 2000
Enchanted Fire, 1996
Shimmering Splendor, 1995
Dazzling Brightness, 1994

Other books you might like:
David Brin, *The Postman*, 1985
C.J. Cherryh, *Chanur's Legacy*, 1992
Gordon R. Dickson, *Spacial Delivery*, 1961
John E. Stith, *Death Tolls*, 1987
Timothy Zahn, *The Icarus Hunt*, 1999

749

KURT GIAMBASTINI

Dreams of the Desert Wind

(Auburn, Washington: Fairwood, 2004)

Story type: Espionage Thriller; Psychic Powers
Subject(s): Political Thriller
Major character(s): David Fineblum, Scholar; Rivka Danilovitch, Military Personnel; Ghazayil, Aged Person
Time period(s): 2000s
Locale(s): Middle East

Summary: When an American scholar overhears an elderly woman speaking a language believed to be extinct for centuries, he decides to investigate and eventually discovers a closely held secret involving a variety of mental powers. An Israeli soldier falls in love with him and feels torn between her feelings and her duty.

Other books by the same author:
From the Heart of the Storm, 2003
Shadow of the Storm, 2003
The Spirit of Thunder, 2002
The Year the Cloud Fell, 2001

Other books you might like:
Steven Barnes, *The Kundalini Equation*, 1986
Timothy Benford, *Hitler's Daughter*, 1983
T. Ernesto Bethancourt, *Instruments of Darkness*, 1977
Bernhardt J. Hurwood, *The Invisibles*, 1971
Graham Joyce, *Requiem*, 1995

750

JONATHAN GREEN

Iron Hands

(Nottingham, England: Black Library, 2004)

Story type: Space Opera; Military
Series: Warhammer
Subject(s): Military Life
Major character(s): Brother-Apothecary Caduceus, Military Personnel; Iron-Father Gdolkin, Military Personnel
Time period(s): Indeterminate Future
Locale(s): Outer Space; Medusa, Planet—Imaginary

Summary: In the very distant future, a particularly dedicated band of space marines patrols the borders of civilized space. Their discipline is reinforced by a highly ritualized religious system that serves them in battle as well, although the latest round of attacks from external forces seems powerful enough to challenge even their abilities.

Other books by the same author:
Magestorm, 2004
The Dead and the Damned, 2002

Other books you might like:
Dan Abnett, *First and Only*, 2000
Stephen Ames Berry, *Battle for Terra Two*, 1986
Stephen Goldin, *The Eternity Brigade*, 1980
Victor Milan, *CLD*, 1995
Warren Norwood, *Midway Between*, 1984

751

STEVEN HARPER

Offspring
(New York: Roc, 2004)

Story type: Space Opera; Psychic Powers
Series: Silent Empire. Book 4
Subject(s): Mental Telepathy
Major character(s): Kendi Weaver, Telepath; Ben Rymar, Businessman; Salman Reza, Government Official (senator)
Time period(s): Indeterminate Future
Locale(s): Bellerophon, Planet—Imaginary

Summary: On Bellerophon, the natives are able to enter a telepathic dream reality inaccessible to normal humans. Their shared psychic community has been disrupted and that has led to political and civil turmoil as well, with telepath Kendi Weaver caught in the middle.

Other books by the same author:
Trickster, 2003
Nightmare, 2002
Dreamer, 2001

Other books you might like:
Lloyd Biggle, *The World Menders*, 1971
Stephen Goldin, *And Not Make Dreams Your Master*, 1981
Keith Laumer, *Night of Delusions*, 1972
Ann Maxwell, *Dead God Dancing*, 1979
Tricia Sullivan, *Dreaming in Smoke*, 1998

752

BRIAN HERBERT
KEVIN J. ANDERSON, Co-Author

The Battle of Corrin
(New York: Tor, 2004)

Story type: Space Opera; Political
Series: Dune. Book 6
Subject(s): Space Colonies
Major character(s): Vorian Atreides, Military Personnel; Quentin Butler, Military Personnel; Omnius, Artificial Intelligence
Time period(s): Indeterminate Future
Locale(s): Outer Space; Arrakis, Planet—Imaginary

Summary: This is presumably the last of six prequels to the Dune series written by Frank Herbert. The war between the human dominated worlds and the forces organized by inimical artificial intelligences seems to be drawing to a close, but the machines aren't quite ready to admit defeat. The climax involves the early history of the Fremen of Arrakis, who figure prominently in the Dune novels.

Where it's reviewed:
Booklist, August 2004, page 1871

Other books by the same author:
The Machine Crusade, 2003 (Kevin J. Anderson, co-author)
The Butlerian Jihad, 2002 (Kevin J. Anderson, co-author)
House Corrino, 2001 (Kevin J. Anderson, co-author)

House Harkonnen, 2000 (Kevin J. Anderson, co-author)
House Atreides, 1999 (Kevin J. Anderson, co-author)

Other books you might like:
Isaac Asimov, *Foundation*, 1951
C.J. Cherryh, *Downbelow Station*, 1984
Frank Herbert, *Dune*, 1965
Alastair Reynolds, *Chasm City*, 2001
Dan Simmons, *Hyperion*, 1989

753

NALO HOPKINSON, Editor
UPPINDER MEHAN, Co-Editor

So Long Been Dreaming
(Vancouver: Arsenal Pulp, 2004)

Story type: Anthology
Subject(s): Short Stories

Summary: This is an anthology of 20 original short stories by writers who either live outside the English speaking world or who are members of minority races. Their backgrounds often provide a fresh perspective on familiar genre themes. Although the quality of the writing varies, the majority are surprisingly good given such an inexperienced roster of authors.

Where it's reviewed:
Booklist, September 1, 2004, page 76

Other books by the same author:
The Salt Roads, 2003
Skin Folk, 2001
Midnight Robber, 2000
Brown Girl in the Ring, 1998

Other books you might like:
Alexander Besher, *Mir*, 1994
John Brunner, *Stand on Zanzibar*, 1968
Samuel R. Delany, *Distant Stars*, 1981
Ian McDonald, *River of Gods*, 2004
Maureen McHugh, *China Mountain Zhang*, 1992

754

MATTHEW HUGHES

Black Brillion
(New York: Tor, 2004)

Story type: Humor; Fantasy
Series: Archonate. Book 3
Subject(s): Fantasy
Major character(s): Baro Harkless, Security Officer; Luff Imbry, Criminal; Guth Bandar, Aged Person
Time period(s): Indeterminate Future
Locale(s): Earth

Summary: In a future so remote that technology almost seems magical and Earth has become unrecognizable, a security officer and a dashing, intelligent criminal engage in a battle of wits. A mostly humorous adventure story written in open imitation of Jack Vance, this is part of a loosely constructed series set in the Archonate.

Where it's reviewed:
Booklist, November 1, 2004, page 472
Locus, December 2004, page 65
Publishers Weekly, November 1, 2004, page 48

Other books by the same author:
Fool Me Twice, 2001
Fools Errant, 1994

Other books you might like:
Avram Davidson, *Rogue Dragon*, 1965
Philip Jose Farmer, *Dark Is the Sun*, 1979
Mick Farren, *The Song of Phaid the Gambler*, 1981
Michael Moorcock, *An Alien Heat*, 1972
Jack Vance, *Ecce and Old Earth*, 1991

755

GWYNETH JONES

Life

(Seattle: Aqueduct, 2004)

Story type: Literary; Future Shock
Subject(s): Women; Futuristic Fiction
Major character(s): Anna Senoz, Businesswoman; Ramone Holyrod, Businessman; Patrick Spencer Meade, Businessman
Time period(s): 2000s
Locale(s): United States

Summary: In the near future, a group of young professionals struggle to make a career for themselves. Anna is particularly troubled by sex discrimination, but she begins to notice a pervasive change in the structure of human society, which may make this less of an issue in the years to come.

Other books by the same author:
Midnight Lamp, 2003
Castles Made of Sand, 2002
Bold as Love, 2001
The Phoenix Cafe, 1998
Flowerdust, 1993

Other books you might like:
Helen Collins, *Mutagenesis*, 1993
Suzette Haden Elgin, *Native Tongue*, 1984
Pamela Sargent, *The Shore of Women*, 1986
Sheri S. Tepper, *The Gate to Women's Country*, 1988
Connie Willis, *The Bellwether*, 1996

756

THEODORE JUDSON

Fitzpatrick's War

(New York: DAW, 2004)

Story type: Post-Holocaust; Political
Subject(s): Military Life
Major character(s): Robert Bruce, Military Personnel; Isaac Fitzpatrick, Military Personnel; Tony Mason, Nobleman
Time period(s): 26th century
Locale(s): North America

Summary: This first novel is cast in the form of the memoirs of a soldier who served in the forces of a new nation that arose in North America after the collapse of our civilization. The narrator was an acquaintance of a man viewed years later as a heroic figure, although the memoir suggests that he had less noble motives.

Where it's reviewed:
Chronicle, August 2004, page 24
Library Journal, August 2004, page 72
Publishers Weekly, July 19, 2004, page 149

Other books you might like:
Poul Anderson, *Twilight World*, 1961
Leigh Brackett, *The Long Tomorrow*, 1955
C.C. MacApp, *Prisoners of the Sky*, 1969
Edgar Pangborn, *The Company of Glory*, 1975
Eric Vinicoff, *Maiden Flight*, 1988

757

NANCY KRESS

Crucible

(New York: Tor, 2004)

Story type: Space Colony; Political
Subject(s): Space Colonies
Major character(s): Alex Cutler, Settler; Julian Cabot Martin, Spaceship Captain; Jake Holman, Administrator
Time period(s): Indeterminate Future
Locale(s): Greentrees, Planet—Imaginary

Summary: The colonists on Greentrees thought they had successfully escaped the increasingly repressive government back on Earth, but another colony ship arrives, this one under the direct control of the authorities and with a complement large enough to overwhelm the previous wave of settlers. Their choice is whether to be absorbed or to abandon the original site and seek refuge elsewhere on the planet. This is the sequel to *Crossfire*.

Where it's reviewed:
Booklist, August 2004, page 1913
Chronicle, August 2004, page 23
Library Journal, August 2004, page 72

Other books by the same author:
Crossfire, 2003
Nothing Human, 2003
Probability Space, 2002
Beaker's Dozen, 1998
Oaths and Miracles, 1996

Other books you might like:
Poul Anderson, *The Day of Their Return*, 1973
Harry Harrison, *Planet of No Return*, 1982
Frederik Pohl, *O Pioneer!*, 1998
Robert Silverberg, *Starborne*, 1996
Clifford D. Simak, *A Heritage of Stars*, 1977

758

MERCEDES LACKEY
ERIC FLINT, Co-Author
DAVE FREER, Co-Author

The Wizard of Karres

(New York: Baen, 2004)

Story type: Space Opera; Humor
Subject(s): Space Travel; Psychic Powers
Major character(s): Pausert, Spaceship Captain; Leewit, Witch, Spacewoman; Hulik, Witch, Spacewoman
Time period(s): Indeterminate Future
Locale(s): Outer Space

Summary: An exasperated spaceship captain has a series of adventures involving three passengers aboard his ship, young women whose psychic powers make them the equivalent of witches, primarily dealing with the discovery that males may also possess these extraordinary abilities. This is the sequel to *The Witches of Karres* by James H. Schmitz.

Where it's reviewed:
Booklist, August 2004, page 1913
Chronicle, August 2004, page 23
Locus, August 2004, page 27

Other books by the same author:
Alta, 2004
Joust, 2003
Brightly Burning, 2000
Owlflight, 1997
Magic's Price, 1990

Other books you might like:
Ron Goulart, *Hawkshaw*, 1972
Keith Laumer, *Galactic Odyssey*, 1967
Andre Norton, *The Solar Queen*, 2003
James H. Schmitz, *The Witches of Karres*, 1966
Timothy Zahn, *The Icarus Hunt*, 1999

759

KEITH LAUMER

Legions of Space

(New York: Baen, 2004)

Story type: Collection
Subject(s): Short Stories

Summary: This retrospective collection of Keith Laumer's fiction includes four stories and two novels, all previously published and all adventures in space. The novels are *A Trace of Memory* from 1963, the story of the discovery of an abandoned alien starship, and *Planet Run*, written with Gordon R. Dickson and published in 1967, a planetary adventure story.

Other books by the same author:
A Plague of Demons and Other Stories, 2003
Future Imperfect, 2003
Odyssey, 2002
Retief, 2002
The Lighter Side, 2002

Other books you might like:
Poul Anderson, *The Enemy Stars*, 1958
Gordon R. Dickson, *Arcturus Landing*, 1956
Murray Leinster, *Med Ship*, 2002
Andre Norton, *Star Soldiers*, 2002
Robert Silverberg, *The Silent Invaders*, 1963

760

LIZ MAVERICK

The Shadow Runners

(New York: Love Spell, 2004)

Story type: Dystopian; Post-Disaster
Subject(s): Political Thriller; Princes and Princesses
Major character(s): Jenny Red, Fugitive; D'ekkar Han Valoren, Nobleman; Prince Kyber, Nobleman
Time period(s): 22nd century (2176)
Locale(s): Australia

Summary: Two centuries from now, civilization has broken down and Australia has once again become largely a penal colony, ruled by a decaying group of aristocrats who have partially recreated Regency England. Jenny Red, a fugitive with connections to the nobility, finds herself playing a dangerous game of deception and intrigue. This is the author's first science fiction novel.

Other books you might like:
A. Bertram Chandler, *Kelly Country*, 1983
Lee Harding, *Waiting for the End of the World*, 1983
David Ireland, *A Woman of the Future*, 1979
Sean McMullen, *The Eyes of the Calculor*, 2001
Wynne Whiteford, *Breathing Space Only*, 1980

761

MAXINE MCARTHUR

Less than Human

(New York: Aspect, 2004)

Story type: Mystery; Techno-Thriller
Subject(s): Computers; Secrets
Major character(s): Eleanor McGuire, Computer Expert; Tomihiro Sakaki, Businessman; Ishihara, Police Officer (inspector)
Time period(s): Indeterminate Future
Locale(s): Japan

Summary: A mysterious death is initially ruled an accident, but a computer expert has her doubts. Her thoughts are confirmed when she compares notes with a police inspector who has reservations about an apparent mass suicide. Together they uncover a group of fanatics using the Internet to wreak havoc against technological society.

Other books by the same author:
Time Past, 2002
Time Future, 2001

Other books you might like:
Joe Clifford Faust, *A Death of Honor*, 1987
Lee Killough, *Spider Play*, 1986
Mel Odom, *Lethal Interface*, 1992

K.D. Wentworth, *The Imperium Game*, 1994
Walter Jon Williams, *Voice of the Whirlwind*, 1987

762

JACK MCDEVITT

Polaris

(New York: Ace, 2004)

Story type: Space Opera; Mystery
Subject(s): Immortality
Major character(s): Chase Kolpath, Pilot, Businesswoman; Alex Benedict, Antiques Dealer; Maddy English, Spaceship Captain
Time period(s): Indeterminate Future
Locale(s): Rimway, Planet—Imaginary; Outer Space

Summary: As Alex Benedict and Chase Kolpath are in the process of purchasing artifacts connected to a mysterious disappearance in space, they notice several incidents that convince them someone is still trying to cover up what happened. Attempts are made on their lives as they pursue their investigation on other planets and on an abandoned space station.

Where it's reviewed:
Analog, December 2004, page 132
Booklist, November 1, 2004, page 472
Chronicle, October 2004, page 25
Library Journal, November 15, 2004, page 54
Locus, November 2004, page 25

Other books by the same author:
Omega, 2003
Chindi, 2002
Deepsix, 2001
Infinity Beach, 2000
Ancient Shores, 1996

Other books you might like:
Poul Anderson, *A Circus of Hells*, 1970
Joe Haldeman, *Buying Time*, 1989
Alastair Reynolds, *Chasm City*, 2001
John E. Stith, *Death Tolls*, 1987
Timothy Zahn, *The Icarus Hunt*, 1999

763

IAN MCDONALD

River of Gods

(London: Simon & Schuster, 2004)

Story type: Future Shock; Political
Subject(s): Political Thriller; Technology
Major character(s): Shaheen Badoor Khan, Consultant; Vishram Rey, Entertainer; Lisa Durnau, Scientist
Time period(s): 2040s (2047)
Locale(s): India

Summary: A few decades from now, India has collapsed into several smaller nations, each still militarily powerful. The author introduces a large cast of characters, mostly Indian with a few outsiders, and uses their personal stories to paint a picture of a possible future of the world's most populous

society. The various characters will find themselves all drawn together as a crisis threatens to reshape their part of the world.

Where it's reviewed:
Locus, July 2004, page 21

Other books by the same author:
The Ares Express, 2001
Tendeleo's Story, 2000
Kirinya, 1998
Evolution's Shore, 1995
Speaking in Tongues, 1992

Other books you might like:
Alexander Besher, *Mir*, 1994
John Brunner, *Stand on Zanzibar*, 1968
Paul J. McAuley, *White Devils*, 2004
Maureen McHugh, *China Mountain Zhang*, 1992
Liz Williams, *Nine Layers of Sky*, 2003

764

OISIN MCGANN

The Gods and Their Machines

(New York: Tor, 2004)

Story type: Military; Political
Subject(s): Technology; Space Colonies
Major character(s): Chamus Aronson, Pilot; Riadni Mocranen, Rebel; Master Elbeth, Religious
Time period(s): Indeterminate Future
Locale(s): Planet—Imaginary

Summary: Two cultures have developed on a distant colony world, one technological and dominant, the other more religious and dedicated to guerrilla warfare against what they see as a repressive regime. A pilot from the dominant culture is stranded in enemy territory and his relationship with a young woman changes the future for both nations. This is the author's first book for adults.

Where it's reviewed:
Library Journal, November 15, 2004, page 55

Other books you might like:
Poul Anderson, *People of the Wind*, 1973
Gordon R. Dickson, *Tactics of Mistake*, 1970
Keith Laumer, *Star Colony*, 1981
Barry B. Longyear, *Enemy Mine*, 1985
  David Gerrold, co-author
Mack Reynolds, *Trample an Empire Down*, 1978

765

GRAHAM MCNEILL

Dead Sky, Black Sun

(Nottingham, England: Black Library, 2004)

Story type: Space Opera; Military
Series: Warhammer
Subject(s): Military Life; Space Travel
Major character(s): Uriel Ventris, Military Personnel (captain); Pasanius, Military Personnel
Time period(s): Indeterminate Future

Science Fiction

Locale(s): Outer Space; Planet—Imaginary

Summary: The space marines are trained and equipped to fight in space or on alien worlds, and they are the most feared force in the galaxy. The Chaos Marine Legions, allied with the dark forces that plot the downfall of the human race, is their only rival. Two professional soldiers have a series of adventures that nearly cost them their lives many times over.

Other books by the same author:
Ursun's Teeth, 2004
The Ambassador, 2003
Warriors of Ultramar, 2003
Storm of Iron, 2002

Other books you might like:
Dan Abnett, *Traitor General*, 2004
Ben Counter, *Grey Knights*, 2004
Jonathan Green, *Iron Hands*, 2004
Gordon Rennie, *Shadow Point*, 2003
Gav Thorpe, *Angels of Darkness*, 2003

766

A. MERRITT

The Moon Pool

(Middletown, Connecticut: Wesleyan University Press, 2004)

Story type: Mystical; Psychic Powers
Subject(s): Psychic Powers
Major character(s): Walter Goodwin, Scientist; Olaf Huldricksson, Sea Captain; Yolara, Religious
Time period(s): 20th century
Locale(s): Underground Environment

Summary: A scientist, an aviator, and a sea captain are the primary members of a party who stumble on a strange lost civilization, dominated by a cruel religion that requires human sacrifice, and peopled by both human and inhuman creatures. Mike Levy provides a lengthy, informative introduction to this new edition of the 1919 lost world classic.

Other books by the same author:
The Metal Monster, 1946
Dwellers in the Mirage, 1932
The Face in the Abyss, 1931
Seven Footprints to Satan, 1928
The Ship of Ishtar, 1926

Other books you might like:
Edgar Rice Burroughs, *The Land That Time Forgot*, 1924
Ian Cameron, *The Lost Ones*, 1962
H. Rider Haggard, *The People of the Mist*, 1894
John Taine, *The Greatest Adventure*, 1929
Dennis Wheatley, *The Lost Continent*, 1938

767

MELISA MICHAELS

World-Walker

(Waterville, Maine: Five Star, 2004)

Story type: Alternate Universe; Science Fantasy
Subject(s): Alternate History

Major character(s): Suli Grail, Police Officer; Jesse Farrell, Musician, Criminal; Jud, Police Officer
Time period(s): Indeterminate
Locale(s): Alternate Universe

Summary: Suli Grail is part of an organization that polices activities across a series of parallel universes, regulating travel among them and preventing people from unauthorized meddling in other realities. When her lover steals the device that allows her to move across the barriers between worlds, she is given the job of tracking him down and recovering it before he can do any serious harm.

Other books by the same author:
Far Harbor, 1989
Floater Factor, 1988
Last War, 1986
First Battle, 1985
Skirmish, 1985

Other books you might like:
John Brunner, *Meeting at Infinity*, 1961
Kenneth Bulmer, *The Key to Venudine*, 1968
Keith Laumer, *The Galaxy Builder*, 1984
Bob Shaw, *A Wreath of Stars*, 1976
Roger Zelazny, *Roadmarks*, 1980

768

L.E. MODESITT JR.

Flash

(New York: Tor, 2004)

Story type: Political; Future Shock
Subject(s): Political Thriller; Technology
Major character(s): Jonat deVrai, Consultant; Juan Carlisimo, Political Figure; Tan uy-Smythe, Consultant
Time period(s): Indeterminate Future
Locale(s): North America

Summary: A political consultant is hired to find out if a politician is using high technology to influence voters illegally in an upcoming election. His investigation uncovers a much bigger problem, including someone who is prepared to kill to make sure that the secret is not revealed. This is set in the same universe as the author's *Archform: Beauty*.

Other books by the same author:
The Wellspring of Chaos, 2004
Darknesses, 2003
Archform: Beauty, 2002
Legacies, 2002
The Octagonal Raven, 2001

Other books you might like:
Ben Bova, *The Multiple Man*, 1976
D.G. Compton, *The Unsleeping Eye*, 1974
John Dalmas, *The General's President*, 1988
Mike McQuay, *The Puppetmaster*, 1991
Eric Frank Russell, *The Mindwarpers*, 1965

769

ELIZABETH MOON

Marque and Reprisal
(New York: Del Rey, 2004)

Story type: Military; Space Opera
Series: Ky Vatta. Book 2
Subject(s): Space Travel
Major character(s): Kylara Vatta, Spaceship Captain; Jim Hakusar, Stowaway; Gammis Turek, Criminal
Time period(s): Indeterminate Future
Locale(s): Slotter Key, Planet—Imaginary; Outer Space

Summary: An entire family of interstellar entrepreneurs is targeted by a criminal attack on them and their holdings. Ky Vatta finds herself in desperate straits as she is drawn into a power struggle involving a planet whose economy is based to a great extent on illegal activities.

Where it's reviewed:
Booklist, September 1, 2004, page 75
Publishers Weekly, August 2, 2004, page 56

Other books by the same author:
Trading in Danger, 2003
The Speed of Dark, 2002
Against the Odds, 2000
Rules of Engagement, 1999
Once a Hero, 1997

Other books you might like:
Lois McMaster Bujold, *Brother in Arms*, 1989
C.J. Cherryh, *The Kif Strike Back*, 1986
Julie E. Czerneda, *To Trade the Stars*, 2002
Andre Norton, *The Solar Queen*, 2003
Timothy Zahn, *The Icarus Hunt*, 1999

770

MICHAEL MOORCOCK, Editor

New Worlds: An Anthology
(New York: Thunder's Mouth, 2004)

Story type: Anthology
Subject(s): Short Stories

Summary: During the 1960s and 1970s the magazine *New Worlds* provided a haven for writers who were interested in experimenting with writing techniques, sometimes at the expense of traditional storytelling, sometimes adding a new dimension. This is a retrospective look at some of the best stories from that era, including those written by J.G. Ballard, Charles Platt, Barrington J. Bayley, Thomas Disch, Brian W. Aldiss, and many others.

Other books by the same author:
The Skrayling Tree, 2003
The Dreamthief's Daughter, 2001
Count Brass, 1998
Sailing to Utopia, 1996
Fabulous Harbors, 1995

Other books you might like:
Brian W. Aldiss, *Common Clay*, 1996

J.G. Ballard, *War Fever*, 1990
Barrington J. Bayley, *The Zen Gun*, 1983
Thomas M. Disch, *The Man Who Had No Idea*, 1982
Charles Platt, *The Silicon Man*, 1991

771

JAMES MORROW

The Cat's Pajamas and Other Stories
(San Francisco: Tachyon, 2004)

Story type: Collection
Subject(s): Short Stories

Summary: Of the 13 short stories in this collection, all but two were first published within the past two years, the others having appeared in the 1990s. Morrow frequently turns his satirical eye to institutions and habits of modern Americans, often involving religious matters. The best story in this collection, ''Auspicious Eggs,'' takes a rather jaundiced view of the Roman Catholic Church, and some of the others are almost equally controversial.

Where it's reviewed:
Locus, September 2004, page 25

Other books by the same author:
The Eternal Footman, 1999
Bible Stories for Adults, 1996
Blameless in Abaddon, 1996
Towing Jehovah, 1994
City of Truth, 1990

Other books you might like:
Avram Davidson, *What Strange Stars and Skies*, 1968
Paul Di Filippo, *The Steampunk Trilogy*, 1996
Harlan Ellison, *The Troublemakers*, 2001
Barry N. Malzberg, *In the Stone House*, 2000
Joanna Russ, *The Hidden Side of the Moon*, 1987

772

KEN OPPEL

Airborn
(New York: Eos, 2004)

Story type: Young Adult; Alternate Universe
Subject(s): Alternate History
Major character(s): Matt Cruse, Teenager; Kate DeVries, Teenager; Paul Rideau, Pilot
Time period(s): Indeterminate
Locale(s): Alternate Universe

Summary: In a version of our world that vaguely resembles the late 19th century, travel between continents is conducted in giant zeppelins. The protagonist is a cabin boy on one of these, who agrees to help a young girl prove that her dying grandfather's last words were not a delusion, although a band of predatory air pirates almost proves their undoing.

Where it's reviewed:
Booklist, June 1, 2004, page 172
Horn Book Magazine, July-August 2004, page 459
School Library Journal, July 2004, page 110

Other books by the same author:
Firewing, 2003
Sunwing, 2001
Silverwing, 1997
Dead Water Zone, 1992

Other books you might like:
Poul Anderson, *Maurai and Kith*, 1982
John Brosnan, *The Sky Lords*, 1991
Edmund Cooper, *Cloud Walker*, 1973
C.C. MacApp, *Prisoners of the Sky*, 1969
Jules Verne, *Master of the World*, 1904

773

FREDERIK POHL

The Boy Who Would Live Forever
(New York: Tor, 2004)

Story type: Space Opera; Space Colony
Series: Heechee. Book 6
Subject(s): Space Travel
Major character(s): Stan Avery, Teenager, Spaceman; Estrella Pancorbo, Spacewoman; Wan Enrique Santos-Smith, Zealot
Time period(s): Indeterminate Future
Locale(s): Outer Space

Summary: A teenaged boy and two companions travel into space just as it appears that the Gateway program, a transportation system inherited from an alien race, is about to be decommissioned. Their paths cross that of a fanatic determined to destroy the Heechee.

Where it's reviewed:
Booklist, September 15, 2004, page 216
Library Journal, September 15, 2004, page 52
Publishers Weekly, August 9, 2004, page 235

Other books by the same author:
The Far Shore of Time, 1999
O Pioneer!, 1998
Mining the Oort, 1992
Stopping at Slowyear, 1991
Outnumbering the Dead, 1990

Other books you might like:
Poul Anderson, *Starfarers*, 1998
Greg Bear, *Eon*, 1985
John DeChancie, *Red Limit Freeway*, 1984
Robert A. Heinlein, *Time for the Stars*, 1956
Andre Norton, *The Stars Are Ours*, 1954

774

IRENE RADFORD

The Dragon Circle
(New York: DAW, 2004)

Story type: Space Opera; Space Colony
Series: Stargods. Book 2
Subject(s): Space Colonies
Major character(s): Martin Konner O'Hara, Fugitive, Psychic; Irythros, Alien; Kat Talbot, Spacewoman

Time period(s): Indeterminate Future
Locale(s): Planet—Imaginary

Summary: Three brothers who have psychic powers are hiding from the galactic empire on a planet whose indigenous aliens welcome them for their intervention against a brutal ruler. Just when it appears that they may have found a refuge, the brothers discover that their presence has been detected and that a force has been sent against them.

Other books by the same author:
The Hidden Dragon, 2002
Guardians of the Trust, 2000
Guardians of the Balance, 1999
The Dragon's Touchstone, 1997
The Glass Dragon, 1994

Other books you might like:
Poul Anderson, *Starfarers*, 1998
Andre Norton, *Brother to Shadows*, 1993
Christopher Stasheff, *The Warlock Is Missing*, 1986
S.L. Viehl, *Endurance*, 2001
Timothy Zahn, *Angelmass*, 2001

775

ALASTAIR REYNOLDS

Absolution Gap
(New York: Ace, 2004)

Story type: Space Opera; Religious
Series: Revelation Space. Book 3
Subject(s): Aliens; Disasters
Major character(s): Rashmika Els, Teenager; Scorpio, Animal (pig); Clavain, Military Personnel, Aged Person
Time period(s): 27th century; 28th century
Locale(s): Outer Space; Ararat, Planet—Imaginary; Hela, Planet—Imaginary

Summary: Ancient, automated killing machines are advancing on human space, intent on exterminating our species. On the planet Hela, a mysterious artifact and a nearby planet that periodically disappears give rise to a variety of new religions. A large cast of characters pursue their individual destinies.

Where it's reviewed:
Chronicle, April 2004, page 34
Library Journal, June 15, 2004, page 62
Locus, February 2004, page 25
Publishers Weekly, May 31, 2004, page 56

Other books by the same author:
Diamond Dogs, Turquoise Days, 2003
Redemption Ark, 2002
Chasm City, 2001
Revelation Space, 2000

Other books you might like:
Gordon R. Dickson, *The Chantry Guild*, 1988
Frank Herbert, *Dune Messiah*, 1969
Cecelia Holland, *Floating Worlds*, 1975
Dan Simmons, *Endymion*, 1995
Joan D. Vinge, *The Summer Queen*, 1991

776

LEIGH RICHARDS

Califia's Daughters

(New York: Bantam, 2004)

Story type: Post-Nuclear Holocaust; Disaster
Subject(s): Apocalypse
Major character(s): Dian, Warrior; Tomas, Survivor; Judith, Artisan
Time period(s): Indeterminate Future
Locale(s): California

Summary: A global war has left civilization in ruins. A generation later, males are still in short supply, jealously protected by tribes of women living in scattered communities. Visitors from one community make a surprising offer to another, whose citizens are concerned that the gift might be the pretense for something less welcome.

Where it's reviewed:
Booklist, August 2004, page 1914

Other books you might like:
John Brosnan, *The Sky Lords*, 1991
Suzy McKee Charnas, *The Conqueror's Child*, 1999
George R. Stewart, *Earth Abides*, 1949
Sheri S. Tepper, *The Gate to Women's Country*, 1988
John Wyndham, *Re-Birth*, 1955

777

JOHN RINGO
JULIE COCHRANE, Co-Author

Cally's War

(New York: Baen, 2004)

Story type: Space Opera; Future Shock
Subject(s): Aliens
Major character(s): Cally O'Neal, Criminal (assassin); Tir, Alien (Darhel); John Earl Bill Stuart, Criminal (assassin)
Time period(s): Indeterminate Future
Locale(s): Chicago, Illinois; Moon (Earth's); Jupiter

Summary: Cally O'Neal is a professional assassin who uses multiple identities to perform her duties on a future Earth that has been contacted by representatives of an alien civilization including the Darhel, a race that has regular relations with humans. O'Neal's latest assignment proves to be more complicated, and dangerous, than anything she has done before.

Other books by the same author:
Emerald Sea, 2004
Hell's Faire, 2003
When the Devil Dances, 2002
Gust Front, 2001
A Hymn Before Battle, 2000

Other books you might like:
C.J. Cherryh, *The Faded Sun: Kesrith*, 1978
Denise Lopes Heald, *Mistwalker*, 1994
Robert A. Heinlein, *Friday*, 1982
Keith Laumer, *Knight of Delusions*, 1982
S.L. Viehl, *Bladerunner*, 2003

778

J.D. ROBB (Pseudonym of Nora Roberts)

Divided in Death

(New York: Putnam, 2004)

Story type: Mystery; Techno-Thriller
Series: Eve Dallas. Book 18
Subject(s): Political Thriller
Major character(s): Eve Dallas, Detective—Homicide; Roarke, Businessman, Spouse (Eve's husband); Reve Ewing, Security Officer
Time period(s): 2050s (2059)
Locale(s): New York, New York

Summary: Someone has murdered the husband of a prominent security specialist and framed her for the crime. Homicide detective Eve Dallas and her crew must untangle a complicated web of mysteries that are further obscured by the intervention of a future version of the Homeland Security Office, which has grown corrupt.

Other books by the same author:
Portrait in Death, 2003
Purity in Death, 2002
Reunion in Death, 2002
Betrayal in Death, 2001
Judgment in Death, 2001

Other books you might like:
Lynn S. Hightower, *Alien Blues*, 1992
Lee Killough, *Spider Play*, 1986
Mel Odom, *Lethal Interface*, 1992
Mary Rosenblum, *The Stone Garden*, 1995
Denise Vitola, *The Red Sky File*, 1999

779

SPIDER ROBINSON

Very Bad Deaths

(New York: Baen, 2004)

Story type: Mystery; Psychic Powers
Subject(s): Mental Telepathy
Major character(s): Russell, Writer; Zandor Zudenigo, Telepath; Hilda Mandic, Detective—Police
Time period(s): 2000s (2003)
Locale(s): British Columbia, Canada

Summary: Russell is startled when his old college roommate calls him after many years. Zandor informs him that he is an involuntary telepath, and he has overheard information about a serial killer. He enlists Russell's aid in contacting the police so they can identify the killer before he strikes again.

Other books by the same author:
Callahan's Cone, 2003
By Any Other Name, 2001
Free Lunch, 2001
Callahan's Key, 2000
User Friendly, 1998

Other books you might like:
Eric Brown, *Bengal Station*, 2004

Leonard Daventry, *A Man of Double Deed*, 1965
L.P. Davies, *The Artificial Man*, 1965
Frank M. Robinson, *Waiting*, 1999
Mary Stewart, *Touch Not the Cat*, 1976

780

JAMES ROLLINS

Sandstorm

(New York: William Morrow, 2004)

Story type: Espionage Thriller; Military
Subject(s): Secrets; Women
Major character(s): Omaha Dunn, Archaeologist; Safia al-Maaz, Scientist; Painter Crowe, Spy
Time period(s): 2000s
Locale(s): England; Oman

Summary: An anachronistic discovery inside an artifact at a museum in England launches two expeditions into the desert of Oman. One expedition is secretly supported by agents of the American intelligence services, who believe the lost city holds a new technology, and the other by a criminal organization intent upon securing that knowledge for themselves.

Where it's reviewed:
School Library Journal, November 2004, page 177

Other books by the same author:
Ice Hunt, 2003
Amazonia, 2002
Deep Fathom, 2001
Excavation, 2000
Subterranea, 1999

Other books you might like:
John Darnton, *Neanderthal*, 1997
Mark Frost, *The List of Seven*, 1993
Talbot Mundy, *The Nine Unknown*, 1923
Tim Powers, *Declare*, 2001
Wilbur Smith, *The Sunbird*, 1972

781

PHILIP ROTH

The Plot Against America

(Boston: Houghton, 2004)

Story type: Alternate History; Dystopian
Subject(s): Alternate History; Coming-of-Age
Major character(s): Charles Lindbergh, Historical Figure, Political Figure (president); Philip Roth, Child, Historical Figure; Walter Winchell, Historical Figure, Journalist
Time period(s): 1940s (1940-1944)
Locale(s): Newark, New Jersey; Danville, Kentucky

Summary: Franklin Delano Roosevelt is defeated in his bid for re-election by Charles Lindbergh, who chooses to remain neutral during World War II and is actually quite well disposed toward the Nazis. Although there are no pogroms in America, the climate of tolerance alters perceptibly under his administration. Author Roth describes his childhood in this alternate world.

Where it's reviewed:
Commentary, December 2004, page 65
New York Times Book Review, October 3, 2004, page 1
Newsweek, September 20, 2004, page 56
School Library Journal, November 2004, page 177
Time, September 27, 2004, page 67

Other books by the same author:
The Ghost Writer, 1979
The Breast, 1972
Our Gang, 1971
Portnoy's Complaint, 1969
Letting Go, 1962

Other books you might like:
Brian W. Aldiss, *The Year Before Yesterday*, 1987
John Barnes, *Finity*, 1999
Robert Harris, *Fatherland*, 1992
Brad Linaweaver, *Moon of Ice*, 1988
Christopher Priest, *The Separation*, 2003

782

NICK SAGAN

Edenborn

(New York: Putnam, 2004)

Story type: Post-Disaster; Genetic Manipulation
Subject(s): Genetic Engineering
Major character(s): Vashti, Genetically Altered Being; Champagne, Genetically Altered Being; Haji, Teenager, Genetically Altered Being
Time period(s): Indeterminate Future
Locale(s): Earth

Summary: Years after a virulent new plague has wiped out the old human race, a small number of genetically altered individuals attempt to create a series of small new communities scattered around the Earth, using virtual reality as a training device. This is a loosely connected sequel to *Idlewild*.

Where it's reviewed:
Booklist, September 1, 2004, page 75
Publishers Weekly, September 13, 2004, page 59

Other books by the same author:
Idlewild, 2003

Other books you might like:
Henry Wilson Allen, *Genesis Five*, 1968
Margaret Atwood, *Oryx and Crake*, 2003
T.J. Bass, *Half Past Human*, 1971
James Blish, *Titan's Daughter*, 1961
Robert Charles Wilson, *Bios*, 1999

783

PAMELA SARGENT

Thumbprints

(Urbana, Illinois: Golden Gryphon, 2004)

Story type: Collection
Subject(s): Short Stories

Summary: A selection of nine stories drawn from the period 1972 to 2004 illustrates the variety of themes the author uses in her work. The stories deal with alternate histories, other worlds and environments, and often have a feminist element. ''Climb the Wind'' later became the basis for a novel by the same title.

Other books by the same author:
Behind the Eyes of Dreamers, 2002
Child of Venus, 2001
Climb the Wind, 1999
Venus of Shadows, 1986
The Golden Space, 1983

Other books you might like:
Samuel R. Delany, *Distant Stars*, 1981
Ursula K. Le Guin, *Four Ways to Forgiveness*, 1996
Frederik Pohl, *In the Problem Pit*, 1976
Theodore Sturgeon, *And Now the News*, 2003
Kate Wilhelm, *Somerset Dreams*, 1978

784

AL SARRANTONIO

Haydn of Mars

(New York: Ace, 2004)

Story type: Space Opera; Alternate Universe
Subject(s): Aliens; Political Thriller
Major character(s): Princess Haydn, Alien (Martian), Fugitive; Frane, Alien (Martian), Warrior; Kerl, Alien (Martian)
Time period(s): Indeterminate Future
Locale(s): Mars

Summary: Martian Princess Haydn gets caught up in the turmoil when a warrior woman leads a successful revolt against the existing government of Mars. After becoming a fugitive, Princess Haydn gradually acquires the self-confidence and wisdom to actively serve as a focal point for the resistance and those who want to restore a free government to that planet.

Other books by the same author:
Orangefield, 2002
Return, 1998
Journey, 1997
Personal Agendas, 1997
Exile, 1996

Other books you might like:
Leigh Brackett, *Nemesis from Terra*, 1961
A. Bertram Chandler, *The Alternate Martians*, 1965
Charles L. Fontenay, *Rebels of the Red Planet*, 1961
Robert A. Heinlein, *Red Planet*, 1949
Wallace West, *The Bird of Time*, 1959

785

ELIZABETH ANN SCARBOROUGH

Cleopatra 7.2

(New York: Ace, 2004)

Story type: Genetic Manipulation; Religious
Series: Cleopatra. Book 2

Subject(s): Scientific Experiments; Genetic Engineering
Major character(s): Leda Hubbard, Anthropologist; Gabriella Farouk, Scientist (Egyptologist); Cleopatra, Artificial Intelligence
Time period(s): 2000s
Locale(s): United States; Egypt

Summary: Scientists have injected surviving cell material from Cleopatra into two modern women, who are able to communicate internally with Cleopatra's personality. While one pursues efforts to have Mark Antony cloned, the other returns to the United States as a wave of fundamentalism and anti-scientific thinking reaches the boiling point.

Where it's reviewed:
Publishers Weekly, November 15, 2004, page 45

Other books by the same author:
Channeling Cleopatra, 2002
The Godmother's Apprentice, 1995
The Godmother, 1994
The Last Refuge, 1992
Nothing Sacred, 1991

Other books you might like:
John Brunner, *Timescoop*, 1969
Hal Clement, *Needle*, 1950
T.W. Hard, *Sum VII*, 1979
Robert Sheckley, *Mindswap*, 1966
Timothy Zahn, *Dragon and Thief*, 2003

786

DAVID SHERMAN
DAN CRAGG, Co-Author

A World of Hurt

(New York: Del Rey, 2004)

Story type: Military; Space Opera
Series: Starfist. Book 10
Subject(s): Military Life; Aliens
Major character(s): Charlie Bass, Military Personnel (ensign); Hiram Birkenstock, Worker; Claypoole, Military Personnel (corporal)
Time period(s): Indeterminate Future
Locale(s): Maugham's Station, Planet—Imaginary

Summary: When it is suspected that the alien Skink have been meddling in affairs on the colony world of Maugham's Station, a unit of marines is dispatched to that world. They discover alien trouble, but it's not at all what they were suspecting, and Ensign Charlie Bass finds himself fighting for his life again.

Where it's reviewed:
Publishers Weekly, October 4, 2004, page 74

Other books by the same author:
Gulf Run, 2004
Lazarus Rising, 2003 (Dan Cragg, co-author)
Rally Point, 2003
Hangfire, 2001 (Dan Cragg, co-author)
Technokill, 2000 (Dan Cragg, co-author)

Other books you might like:
John Dalmas, *The Lizard War*, 1989

Roland Green, *The Painful Field*, 1993
John Ringo, *Gust Front*, 2001
Rick Shelley, *Side Show*, 1994
Timothy Zahn, *Conqueror's Pride*, 1994

787

SUSAN SHWARTZ

Hostile Takeover

(New York: Tor, 2004)

Story type: Hard Science Fiction; Space Colony
Subject(s): Space Colonies; Secrets
Major character(s): Caroline Cater Williams, Accountant (auditor); Marc Davidoff, Military Personnel; Margaret Lovat, Settler
Time period(s): Indeterminate Future
Locale(s): Vesta, Planet—Imaginary

Summary: Professional auditor CC Williams is sent to the remote colony world of Vesta to find out why its mining operation is in poor financial shape. She discovers the existence of criminal activity, the presence of aliens, and uncovers a number of other secrets, nearly losing her life in the process.

Other books by the same author:
Second Chances, 2001
Cross and Crescent, 1997
The Grail of Hearts, 1992

Other books you might like:
Poul Anderson, *Mayday Orbit*, 1961
Stephen Leigh, *Dark Water's Embrace*, 1998
Murray Leinster, *This World Is Taboo*, 1961
Frederik Pohl, *Stopping at Slowyear*, 1991
Allen Steele, *Coyote Rising*, 2004

788

JOHN SLADEK

The Complete Roderick

(New York: Overlook, 2004)

Story type: Robot Fiction; Satire
Subject(s): Humor
Major character(s): Roderick, Robot
Time period(s): Indeterminate Future
Locale(s): Earth

Summary: This is a combined edition of *Roderick*, and its sequel, *Roderick at Random*, both of which have been difficult to find for years, particularly in unexpurgated editions. Roderick is a robot who wanders through a future human society learning about the foibles of humanity as portrayed by Sladek's sharp, incisive, satirical humor.

Where it's reviewed:
Chronicle, October 2004, page 26

Other books by the same author:
Maps, 2002
Tik Tok, 1983
The Best of John Sladek, 1981
Keep the Giraffe Burning, 1977

Mechasm, 1968

Other books you might like:
Henry Kuttner, *Robots Have No Tails*, 1952
Fritz Leiber, *The Silver Eggheads*, 1962
Barry B. Longyear, *Naked Came the Robot*, 1988
Rudy Rucker, *The Hacker and the Ants*, 1994
Clifford D. Simak, *Shakespeare's Planet*, 1976

789

EMILE SOUVESTRE

The World as It Shall Be

(Middletown, Connecticut: Wesleyan University Press, 2004)

Story type: Satire; Future Shock
Subject(s): Technology
Major character(s): Maurice, Time Traveler; Marthe, Time Traveler; Monsieur Atout, Professor
Time period(s): 30th century (3000)
Locale(s): France

Summary: This is the first English translation of a satirical novel originally published in France in 1846. Two people find themselves in the year 3000 and are taken on a grand tour of the world, filled with technological wonders but with human foibles exaggerated, often quite humorously.

Other books you might like:
Karel Capek, *The War with the Newts*, 1936
Aldous Huxley, *Brave New World*, 1932
Albert Robida, *The Twentieth Century*, 1888
Jules Verne, *Paris in the Twentieth Century*, 1994
Eugene Zamyatin, *We*, 1924

790

WEN SPENCER

Dog Warrior

(New York: Roc, 2004)

Story type: First Contact; Mystery
Series: Ukiah Oregon. Book 4
Subject(s): Aliens; Secrets
Major character(s): Ukiah Oregon, Detective—Private, Alien; Atticus Steele, Alien; Zheng, Police Officer (special agent)
Time period(s): 2000s
Locale(s): Massachusetts

Summary: Ukiah Oregon meets his brother, Atticus Steele, and reveals to him the truth about their half-alien, half-human biochemistry. The two end up saving each other's lives after getting involved with violent biker gangs, dangerous drug trafficking, and a government agent with a determined personal agenda.

Other books by the same author:
Bitter Waters, 2003
Tinker, 2003
Tainted Trail, 2002
Alien Taste, 2001

Other books you might like:
Algis Budrys, *Hard Landing*, 1993

Octavia Butler, *Wild Seed*, 1980
Joe Haldeman, *Camouflage*, 2004
Stephen King, *Firestarter*, 1980
Scott Westerfeld, *Polymorph*, 1997

791

ALLEN STEELE

Coyote Rising
(New York: Ace, 2004)

Story type: Space Colony; Political
Subject(s): Space Colonies; Space Exploration
Major character(s): Zoltan Shirow, Religious; James Garcia, Architect; Allegria DiSilvio, Fugitive
Time period(s): 23rd century (2260)
Locale(s): Coyote, Planet—Imaginary

Summary: The fugitives from Earth who colonized Coyote find their freedom in jeopardy again. Along with a wave of colonists from the home world, an authoritarian government arrives that intends to rule all humans on the planet. Those unwilling to be dominated decide to take a desperate trek into the unknown interior.

Where it's reviewed:
Booklist, November 15, 2004, page 571
Publishers Weekly, November 8, 2004, page 40

Other books by the same author:
American Beauty, 2003
Coyote, 2002
Chronospace, 2001
Oceanspace, 2000
The Tranquility Alternative, 1996

Other books you might like:
Hal Clement, *Cycle of Fire*, 1957
Alan Dean Foster, *Icerigger*, 1974
Keith Laumer, *Star Colony*, 1981
Larry Niven, *The Legacy of Heorot*, 1987
  Jerry Pournelle, co-author
Frederik Pohl, *O Pioneer!*, 1998

792

TRAVIS S. TAYLOR

Warp Speed
(New York: Baen, 2004)

Story type: Future Shock; Hard Science Fiction
Subject(s): Space Travel
Major character(s): Neil Anson Clemons, Scientist; Tabitha Ames, Spacewoman; Jim Daniels, Scientist
Time period(s): Indeterminate Future
Locale(s): Moon (Earth's); Outer Space

Summary: A team of scientists working on the moon stumbles across a new discovery that could revolutionize space travel. When news of their invention leaks out, the furor in the international community over the potential change in the balance of power precipitates the early stages of a new world war. First novel.

Other books you might like:
Harry Harrison, *The Daleth Effect*, 1970
James P. Hogan, *The Genesis Machine*, 1978
Dean Ing, *The Big Lifters*, 1988
Duncan Long, *Anti-Grav Unlimited*, 1988
Edward E. Smith, *The Skylark of Space*, 1928

793

MASRK TIER, Editor

Visions of Liberty
(New York: Baen, 2004)

Story type: Anthology
Subject(s): Short Stories; Freedom

Summary: A collection of nine stories, each with a libertarian political bias. All the stories examine the loss of one or another form of liberty in varying future settings. The contributors include Jack Williamson, Mike Resnick, Robert Sawyer, Lloyd Biggle, and Brad Lineaweaver.

Other books you might like:
Lloyd Biggle, *Silence Is Deadly*, 1977
Brad Linaweaver, *Moon of Ice*, 1988
Mike Resnick, *Outpost*, 2001
Robert J. Sawyer, *Hominids*, 2002
Jack Williamson, *The Humanoids*, 1950

794

KAREN TRAVISS

City of Pearl
(New York: Eos, 2004)

Story type: Space Colony; Religious
Subject(s): Space Colonies; Aliens
Major character(s): Shan Frankland, Government Official (former), Spacewoman; Aras, Alien; Surendra Parekh, Settler
Time period(s): 23rd century; 24th century
Locale(s): Constantine, Planet—Imaginary

Summary: This first novel deals with the human colonization of a planet that is under the protection of a mysterious alien figure. Through the generations, he grows increasingly concerned about the influx of humans, which leads to a crisis when a new expedition arrives bearing a government official.

Where it's reviewed:
Chronicle, August 2004, page 26

Other books you might like:
Poul Anderson, *The Day of Their Return*, 1973
Michael Bishop, *Stolen Faces*, 1977
John Brunner, *The Rites of Ohe*, 1963
Anne McCaffrey, *Dinosaur Planet*, 1993
Andre Norton, *Janus*, 2003

Science Fiction

795

KAREN TRAVISS

Crossing the Line

(New York: Eos, 2004)

Story type: Space Opera; Space Colony
Series: Shan Frankland. Book 2
Subject(s): Aliens; Space Colonies
Major character(s): Shan Frankland, Government Official (former), Spacewoman; Aras, Alien; Malcolm Okurt, Military Personnel
Time period(s): 24th century (2376)
Locale(s): Planet—Imaginary

Summary: Shan Frankland has already risked her future by choosing to protect the complex alien society orbiting Cavanaugh's Star from the interference of outsiders, and the situation is only growing worse now that humans are arriving in larger numbers. This time some view her as a threat who must be killed if necessary to prevent further resistance.

Other books by the same author:
City of Pearl, 2004
Hard Contact, 2004

Other books you might like:
Marion Zimmer Bradley, *Rediscovery*, 1993
C.J. Cherryh, *Foreigner*, 1994
Doris Egan, *The Complete Ivory*, 2001
Denise Lopes Heald, *Mistwalker*, 1994
S.L. Viehl, *Eternity Row*, 2002

796

HARRY TURTLEDOVE

Curious Notions

(New York: Tor, 2004)

Story type: Young Adult; Alternate Universe
Series: Crosstime Traffic. Book 2
Subject(s): Alternate History
Major character(s): Paul Gomes, Teenager, Spy; Lawrence Gomes, Spy; Lucy Woo, Teenager
Time period(s): Indeterminate
Locale(s): Alternate Universe

Summary: Paul Gomes and his father are secret agents working in an alternate universe where the Germans won the first world war. Their job is to harvest raw materials and knowledge for use in our time line. When the occupation forces begin to suspect them of subversive activities, they have to become very inventive to preserve their freedom.

Where it's reviewed:
Booklist, October 15, 2004, page 395

Other books by the same author:
Out of the Darkness, 2004
In the Presence of Mine Enemies, 2003
Advance and Retreat, 2002
Ruled Britannia, 2002
Blood and Iron, 2001

Other books you might like:
Fredric Brown, *What Mad Universe*, 1949
F.M. Busby, *All These Earths*, 1978
Brad Ferguson, *The World Next Door*, 1990
James P. Hogan, *Paths to Otherwhere*, 1996
Murray Leinster, *The Other Side of Here*, 1955

797

HARRY TURTLEDOVE

Days of Infamy

(New York: New American Library, 2004)

Story type: Alternate Universe; Military
Subject(s): Alternate History
Major character(s): Fletch Armitage, Military Personnel; Jiro Takahashi, Fisherman; Oscar Van Der Kirk, Unemployed
Time period(s): 1940s (1941)
Locale(s): Hawaii

Summary: Instead of just bombing Pearl Harbor, the Japanese invade and capture the Hawaiian Islands in this alternate history novel. A large cast of characters from both the Japanese and American sides provides a detailed examination of Hawaii under military rule and the plans for military action against the west coast of North America.

Where it's reviewed:
Booklist, September 15, 2004, page 180
Library Journal, October 15, 2004, page 57
Publishers Weekly, October 1, 2004, page 60

Other books by the same author:
Conan of Venarium, 2004
In the Presence of Mine Enemies, 2003
Jaws of Darkness, 2003
The Victorious Opposition, 2003
Ruled Britannia, 2002

Other books you might like:
Brian W. Aldiss, *The Year Before Yesterday*, 1987
John Birmingham, *Weapons of Choice*, 2004
Alfred Coppel, *The Burning Mountain*, 1982
James P. Hogan, *The Prometheus Operation*, 1985
David Westheimer, *Downfall*, 1971

798

HARRY TURTLEDOVE

Homeward Bound

(New York: Del Rey, 2004)

Story type: Alternate History; Invasion of Earth
Subject(s): Aliens; Space Travel
Major character(s): Sam Yeager, Military Personnel (colonel); Atvar, Alien, Military Personnel; Kassquit, Alien
Time period(s): Indeterminate Future
Locale(s): Earth; Outer Space

Summary: Aliens have invaded and conquered part of Earth, but have been unable to expand their holdings, just as humans have been unable to eject them. When a group of humans develop the technology to travel to the aliens' home world, the possibility of expanding the war in that direction changes the balance of power. This is a sequel to the author's earlier Worldwar and Colonization trilogies.

Other books by the same author:
Conan of Venarium, 2004
Curious Notions, 2004
Return Engagement, 2004
The Gunpowder Empire, 2003
Advance and Retreat, 2002

Other books you might like:
William C. Dietz, *Deathday*, 2001
David Gerrold, *A Matter for Men*, 1983
Harry Harrison, *Invasion: Earth*, 1982
Robert Silverberg, *The Alien Years*, 1998
John Wyndham, *Out of the Deeps*, 1953

799

HARRY TURTLEDOVE

Return Engagement
(New York: Del Rey, 2004)

Story type: Alternate History; Military
Series: Settling Accounts Trilogy. Book 1
Subject(s): Alternate History
Major character(s): Flora Blackford, Political Figure; Clarence Porter, Military Personnel (general); Leonard O'Doull, Doctor
Time period(s): 20th century
Locale(s): United States; Confederate States of America, Fictional Country

Summary: In a world where the Confederacy remained independent and a long-standing enemy of the United States, the equivalent of our World War II opens with a sneak attack on Philadelphia, precipitating another war between North and South. A blend of historical and entirely fictional characters interact as the war expands to draw in the rest of the world.

Where it's reviewed:
Library Journal, August 2004, page 72
Publishers Weekly, July 19, 2004, page 149

Other books by the same author:
Conan of Venarium, 2004
In the Presence of Mine Enemies, 2003
Advance and Retreat, 2002
The Center Cannot Hold, 2002
Ruled Britannia, 2002

Other books you might like:
Ben Bova, *Triumph*, 1993
Gordon Eklund, *All Times Possible*, 1974
Jake Page, *Shatterhand*, 1996
David Poyer, *The Shiloh Project*, 1981
Ted White, *Sideslip*, 1968
   Dave Von Arnam, co-author

800

JACK VANCE

Lurulu
(New York: Tor, 2004)

Story type: Space Opera; Mystery
Subject(s): Space Travel; Space Colonies
Major character(s): Myron Tany, Spaceman; Adair Maloof, Spaceship Captain; Isel Wingo, Spaceman
Time period(s): Indeterminate Future
Locale(s): Fluter, Planet—Imaginary; Glicca, Planet—Imaginary

Summary: Myron Tany finds himself stranded on a backward world, so he takes a position as purser aboard a commercial starship. After becoming friends with the captain, Myron helps him track down the man who kidnapped the captain's mother, a search that takes them to several very odd worlds.

Where it's reviewed:
Booklist, November 15, 2004, page 572
Locus, November 2004, page 25
Publishers Weekly, October 1, 2004, page 60

Other books by the same author:
Ports of Call, 1998
The Night Lamp, 1996
Throy, 1992
Ecce and Old Earth, 1991
Araminta Station, 1988

Other books you might like:
Poul Anderson, *Three Worlds to Conquer*, 1964
C.J. Cherryh, *The Pride of Chanur*, 1982
Gordon R. Dickson, *Mission to Universe*, 1965
Andre Norton, *The Solar Queen*, 2003
Timothy Zahn, *The Icarus Hunt*, 1999

801

JOHN VARLEY

The John Varley Reader
(New York: Ace, 2004)

Story type: Collection
Subject(s): Short Stories

Summary: Thirty years ago, John Varley's short fiction created considerable excitement because of its fresh approach to old themes. This is a retrospective collection of the best of his work from the beginning of his career until quite recently, involving stories of murder, intrigue, adventures in outer space, body sculpting, and other unusual themes.

Other books by the same author:
Red Thunder, 2003
The Golden Globe, 1998
Steel Beach, 1992
Millennium, 1983
Titan, 1979

Other books you might like:
J.G. Ballard, *Chronopolis*, 1971
Samuel R. Delany, *Aye, and Gomorrah*, 2003

Paul Di Filippo, *Babylon Sisters and Other Posthumans*, 2003
Joanna Russ, *The Hidden Side of the Moon*, 1987
Roger Zelazny, *The Last Defender of Camelot*, 1980

Jack McDevitt, *Ancient Shores*, 1996
Wen Spencer, *Alien Taste*, 2001
Allen Steele, *Clarke County, Space*, 1990

802

DAVID WEBER

The Shadow of Saganami

(New York: Baen, 2004)

Story type: Military; Space Opera
Series: Saganami Island. Book 1
Subject(s): Space Colonies; Military Life
Major character(s): Helen Zilwicki, Military Personnel (captain); Aikawa Kagiyama, Military Personnel; Aivars Terekhov, Military Personnel
Time period(s): Indeterminate Future
Locale(s): Outer Space; Manticore, Planet—Imaginary

Summary: The Republic of Haven is embroiled in another interstellar war, but Captain Helen Zilwicki and her crew are sent to watch over an allied system that appears to have been virtually forgotten by both sides. They quickly discover that this is not the easy assignment they expected, when a variety of conspiracies begin to flower and the local space pirates turn out to have political and military support from the enemy.

Where it's reviewed:
Publishers Weekly, October 18, 2004, page 52

Other books by the same author:
Windrider's Oath, 2004
Empire from the Ashes, 2003
The Excalibur Alternative, 2002
Ashes of Victory, 2000
The Apocalypse Troll, 1999

Other books you might like:
Scott Gier, *Genellan: Planetfall*, 1995
R.M. Meluch, *War Birds*, 1989
Elizabeth Moon, *Once a Hero*, 1997
John Scalvi, *Old Man's War*, 2004
Diann Thornley, *Echoes of Issel*, 1996

803

T.H.F. WEISSKOPF, Editor

Cosmic Tales

(New York: Baen, 2004)

Story type: Anthology
Subject(s): Short Stories

Summary: Most of the 14 original short stories in this collection involve adventures and are all set within our own solar system. The contributors include Charles Sheffield, Gregory Benford, Wen Spencer, Allen Steele, Jack McDevitt, and James P. Hogan.

Where it's reviewed:
Chronicle, July 2004, page 44

Other books you might like:
Gregory Benford, *Cosm*, 1998
James P. Hogan, *Martian Knightlife*, 2001

804

SCOTT WESTERFELD

So Yesterday

(New York: Razorbill, 2004)

Story type: Satire; Future Shock
Subject(s): Secrets
Major character(s): Hunter, Advertising; Jennifer, Advertising; Mandy Wilkins, Advertising
Time period(s): 2000s
Locale(s): New York, New York

Summary: In this unusually structured novel, various people associated with the advertising industry slowly become aware that there are secretive groups living within normal humanity. Those groups are quietly reshaping human culture according to rules not visible to most people.

Other books by the same author:
The Killing of Worlds, 2003
The Risen Empire, 2003
Evolution's Darling, 2000
Fine Prey, 1998
Polymorph, 1997

Other books you might like:
Gerald Kersh, *The Secret Masters*, 1952
Fritz Leiber, *You're All Alone*, 1972
Eric Frank Russell, *The Mindwarpers*, 1965
Connie Willis, *The Bellwether*, 1996
Timothy Zahn, *The Green and the Gray*, 2004

805

LIZ WILLIAMS

Banner of Souls

(New York: Bantam, 2004)

Story type: Genetic Manipulation; Future Shock
Subject(s): Genetic Engineering
Major character(s): Dreams-of-War, Warrior; Yskatarina Lys, Genetically Altered Being, Spacewoman; Lunae, Child, Genetically Altered Being
Time period(s): Indeterminate Future
Locale(s): Earth

Summary: In the distant future, a warrior from the planet Mars and a genetically enhanced woman from another world both travel to Earth because of the advent of another genetically altered individual. This individual is a child that one is sworn to protect and the other to destroy. Their struggle may determine the future of intelligent life in the solar system.

Where it's reviewed:
Booklist, October 1, 2004, page 319
Library Journal, October 15, 2004, page 71
Publishers Weekly, August 23, 2004, page 42

Other books by the same author:
Nine Layers of Sky, 2003
The Poison Master, 2003
Empire of Bones, 2002
Ghost Sister, 2001

Other books you might like:
Anne Harris, *Accidental Creatures*, 2001
Scott Mackay, *The Meek*, 2001
Tricia Sullivan, *Lethe*, 1995
George Turner, *The Genetic Soldier*, 1994
Jim Young, *Armed Memory*, 1995

806

JENNIFER WINGERT

Grasp the Stars
(New York: DAW, 2004)

Story type: Space Opera; Espionage Thriller
Subject(s): Aliens
Major character(s): Rachel Ajmani, Administrator; Meris, Alien; Lafiya Duchamp, Technician
Time period(s): Indeterminate Future
Locale(s): Space Station

Summary: The administrator of a human operated space station in a distant solar system, which caters to a variety of races, goes through a series of crises almost simultaneously. The closing of another destination has doubled their traffic, there's an inspection underway, and a visiting alien is the focus of potentially violent conflicts. First novel.

Other books you might like:
John Brunner, *Sanctuary in the Sky*, 1960
C.J. Cherryh, *The Pride of Chanur*, 1982
Julie E. Czerneda, *Hidden in Sight*, 2003
Tanya Huff, *Valor's Choice*, 2000
Maxine McArthur, *Time Future*, 2001

807

N. LEE WOOD

Master of None
(New York: Aspect, 2004)

Story type: Space Colony; Dystopian
Subject(s): Utopia/Dystopia
Major character(s): Nathan Crewe, Criminal, Scientist (botanist); Yaenida Nga'esha, Wealthy; Vasant Subah, Government Official
Time period(s): Indeterminate Future
Locale(s): Vanar, Planet—Imaginary

Summary: A botanist lands on the reclusive planet of Vanar illegally, and is caught and convicted under a legal system he doesn't even understand. Fortunately, he is adopted by a wealthy family who introduce him to the intricacies of a matriarchal society that has been largely cut off from the rest of the human race.

Where it's reviewed:
Chronicle, November 2004, page 44
Publishers Weekly, September 27, 2004, page 43

Other books by the same author:
Bloodrights, 1999
Faraday's Orphans, 1997
Looking for the Mahdi, 1996

Other books you might like:
Catherine Asaro, *The Last Hawk*, 1997
Suzy McKee Charnas, *Walk to the End of the World*, 1974
Joanna Russ, *The Female Man*, 1975
Pamela Sargent, *The Shore of Women*, 1986
Sheri S. Tepper, *The Gate to Women's Country*, 1988

808

TIMOTHY ZAHN

The Green and the Gray
(New York: Tor, 2004)

Story type: Psychic Powers; First Contact
Subject(s): Aliens
Major character(s): Roger Whittier, Lawyer; Caroline Whittier, Real Estate Agent; Melantha Green, Teenager, Alien
Time period(s): 2000s
Locale(s): New York, New York

Summary: A human couple discover that two separate alien races are secretly living in Manhattan. Peace between the two appears to be dependent upon the fate of a teenaged girl with extraordinary psychic abilities who may maintain the balance of power between the two, but there are factions on both sides who differ about how she should be treated.

Where it's reviewed:
Library Journal, September 15, 2004, page 53
Publishers Weekly, August 9, 2004, page 235

Other books by the same author:
Dragon and Soldier, 2004
Survivor's Quest, 2004
Dragon and Thief, 2003
Manta's Gift, 2002
Angelmass, 2001

Other books you might like:
Michael Bishop, *A Little Knowledge*, 1977
Algis Budrys, *Hard Landing*, 1993
Robert J. Sawyer, *Illegal Alien*, 1998
Clifford D. Simak, *Way Station*, 1963
Walter Tevis, *The Man Who Fell to Earth*, 1963

809

GEORGE ZEBROWSKI, Editor

Synergy SF
(Waterville, Maine: Five Star, 2004)

Story type: Anthology
Subject(s): Short Stories

Summary: This anthology of original stories and essays is primarily by newer writers in the field. The essays include a discussion of Cele Goldsmith's days as an editor written by Barry Malzberg, and a reminiscence by William Tenn. The short stories include works by Charles L. Harness, Damien Broderick, and others.

Other books by the same author:
In the Distance, and Ahead in Time, 2002
Swift Thoughts, 2002
Brute Orbits, 1998
Stranger Suns, 1995

The Stars Will Speak, 1985

Other books you might like:
Damien Broderick, *Transcension*, 2002
Charles L. Harness, *Lurid Dreams*, 1990
Barry N. Malzberg, *In the Stone House*, 2000
Pamela Sargent, *Behind the Eyes of Dreamers*, 2002
William Tenn, *The Seven Sexes*, 1968

The Year in Historical Fiction
by
Daniel S. Burt

Since the inception of the bestseller list at the end of the nineteenth century, the most represented fictional genre has been the historical novel. Annually as well, historical novels appear more than any other genre on critics' best-of-the-year lists. Arguably, the world's most popular novel, Margaret Mitchell's *Gone with the Wind*, is a historical novel, as is what many consider the greatest novel ever written—Leo Tolstoy's *War and Peace*. Among both the top-selling novels each year and the most critically acclaimed, historical novels year-in and year-out have been the dominating genre. Why should this be?

The historical novel continues to appeal to writers, readers, and critics alike because the past is both inexhaustible and irresistible. You would think that after the countless historical novels that have appeared since Sir Walter Scott first transported his readers to the historical past in the early nineteenth century there would be nothing left for a historical novelist to shine fresh light on, no historical figures left unexamined, no historical era in need of an imaginative makeover. But you would be wrong.

The historical fiction collected here from the second half of 2004 makes clear that there is a great deal of life left in the genre, as well as strange new worlds to conquer and the well known to revisit and revise. Readers of the novels collected here can experience such diverse subjects as the Trojan War in Lindsay Clarke's *The War at Troy*, the U.S. South Seas Exploring Expedition of the 1830s in Joan Druett's *A Watery Grave*, Cuban revolutionary Jose Marti in Guatemala in Francisco Goldman's *The Divine Husband*, eighteenth-century Vietnam in Kien Nguyen's *Le Colonial*, the Krakatoa explosion in Chelsea Quinn Yarbro's *Dark of the Sun*, and the assassination of President William McKinley in Jonathan Lowy's *The Temple of Music*. Familiar historical faces seen from novel vantage points include Mary Todd Lincoln in Barbara Hambly's *The Emancipator's Wife*, King Arthur in Jack Whyte's *The Lance Thrower* and Allan Massie's *Arthur the King*, Anne Boleyn in Suzannah

Dunn's *The Queen of Subtleties*, and Sarah Bernhardt in Adam Braver's *Divine Sarah*. Several novels introduce readers to lesser known, but fascinating, people, places, and events: Boris, King of Bulgaria in Jan Benzely and Thom Lemmons' *King's Ransom*, Lord Derby in Emma Donoghue's *Life Mask*, sixteenth-century Brazil in Jean-Christophe Rufin's *Brazil Red*, the Cawnpore Massacre in Elisabeth McNeill's *The Lady of Cawnpore*, and the turbulent history of Iran in Marteza Baharloo's *The Quince Seed Potion*.

The power and persistence of historical fiction can be attributed to the form's ability to transport readers back in time to explore the unfamiliar intimately, while shocking with the strange and affirming the recognizable in the distant past. Good historical novelists bring the past to life; great historical novelists bridge the gap between eras and our own to uncover commonality and timeless relevance. If bridging distance is the motive of all historical novelists, in several books collected here it is also a central theme. Aliette Armel in *Love, the Painter's Wife and the Queen of Sheba* connects Renaissance painter, Piero della Francesco, his wife, and the Biblical Queen of Sheba; while Nina Schuyler in *The Painting* links Paris in the aftermath of the Franco-Prussian War with Japan on the verge of the modern era; and Jane Stevenson's *The Empress of the Last Days* draws a connection between events in seventeenth-century Holland and Barbados with the succession of the British monarchy. These and other historical novels collected here make clear that there is considerable imaginative life left and new worlds, eras, and individuals to conquer in this tried-and-true fictional work horse. Collected here are works from such distinguished writers as Philip Roth, Elizabeth Frank, Roddy Doyle, Ha Jin, Michael Chabon, Madison Smart Bell, and David Lodge. Included are novels by two acclaimed film directors, Neil Jordan and Allan Parker, a work by a Pulitzer Prize winning biographer (Elizabeth Frank's *Cheat and Charmer*) and a novel by a prince, Prince Michael of Greece (*The*

White Night of Petersburg). There are several impressive debuts, including a first novel from the octogenarian publisher Walter Zacharius, and a final bow, left, alas, incomplete, from one of the greatest of all contemporary historical novelists, Patrick O'Brian. All provide strong evidence that historical fiction as a form is thriving.

Despite finding favor with both reader and writer alike, the historical novel remains one of the most controversial of literary genres. Historical novels have been criticized both for their errors and falsification of history and for indulging in historical detail work at the expense of a novel's purported main job of plot and character development. The historical novelist by invading the province of the historian with an intention to elucidate the past, as well as to entertain, must serve two severe and opposite masters. Not bound by the same restrictions as the historian to report only what is known and verifiable, the historical novelist is free to look beneath the facts of history for insights, to fill in gaps in the historical record with speculation and surmise. The writer of historical fiction must satisfy both the impulses of the historian and the novelist that often diverge. It is not surprising that achieving the ideal balance between truth and invention makes success in the historical novel so difficult and elusive.

Selection Criteria

More than any other fictional genre, it is necessary to define exactly what constitutes a historical novel. All novels deal with the past, except science fiction that is set in the future, or fantasy novels set in an imagined, alternative world outside historical time. Yet not all novels set in the past are truly historical. Central to any workable definition of historical fiction is the degree to which the writer attempts not to recall the past but to recreate it. In some cases the time frame, setting, and customs of a novel's era are merely incidental to its action and characterization. In other cases, period details function as little more than a colorful backdrop for characters and situations that could as easily be played out in a different era with little alteration. So-called historical "costume dramas" could to a greater or lesser degree work as well with a change of costume in a different place and time. The novels that we can identify as truly historical, however, attempt much more than incidental period surface details or interchangeable historical eras. What justifies a designation as a historical novel is the writer's attempt at providing an accurate and believable representation of a particular historical era. The writer of historical fiction shares with the historian a verifiable depiction of past events, lives, and customs. In historical fiction, the past itself becomes as much a subject for the novelist as the characters and action.

Most of us use the phrase "historical novel" casually, never really needing an exact definition to make ourselves understood. We just know it when we see it. This listing, however, requires a set of criteria to determine what's in and what's out. Otherwise the list has no boundaries. If the

working definition of historical fiction is too loose, every novel set in a period before the present qualifies, and nearly every novel becomes a historical novel immediately upon publication. If the definition is so strict that only books set in a time before the author's birth, for example, make the cut, then countless works that critics, readers, librarians, and the authors themselves think of as historical novels would be excluded.

The challenge here, therefore, has been to fashion a definition or set of criteria flexible enough to include novels that pass what can be regarded as the litmus test for historical fiction: Did the author use his or her imagination—and often quite a bit of research—to evoke another and earlier time than the author's own? Walter Scott, who is credited with "inventing" the historical novel in English during the early nineteenth century provides a useful criterion in the subtitle of *Waverley*, his initial historical novel, the story of Scottish life at the time of the Jacobite Rebellion of 1745: "'Tis Sixty Years Since." This supplies a possible formula for separating the created past from the remembered past. What is unique and distinctive about the so-called historical novel is its attempt to imagine a distant period of time before the novelist's lifetime. Scott's sixty-year span (the same, incidentally, used by Tolstoy in *War and Peace*) between a novel's composition and its imagined era offers an arbitrary but useful means to distinguish between the personal and the historical past. The distance of two generations or nearly a lifetime provides a necessary span for the past to emerge as history and forces the writer to rely on more than recollection to uncover the patterns and textures of the past. I have, therefore, adopted Scott's formula but adjusted it to fifty years, including those books in which the significant portion of their plots is set in a period fifty years or more before the novel was written.

Because a rigid application of this fifty-year rule might disqualify quite a few books intended by their authors and regarded by their readers to be historical novels, another test has been applied to books written about more recent eras: Did the author use actual historical figures and events while setting out to recreate a specific, rather than a general or incidental, historical period? Although it is, of course, risky to speculate about a writer's intention, it is possible by looking at the book's approach, its use of actual historical figures, and its emphasis on a distinctive time and place that enhances the reader's knowledge of past lives, events, and customs to detect when a book conforms to what most would consider a central preoccupation of the historical novel.

I have tried to apply these criteria for the historical novel as a guide, not as an inflexible rule, and have allowed some exceptions when warranted by special circumstances. I hope I have been able to anticipate what most readers would consider historical novels, but I recognize that I may have overlooked some worthy representations of the past in the interest of dealing with a manageable list of titles. Finally, not every title in the Western, historical mystery, or historical romance genres has been included to avoid unnecessary duplication with the other sections of this book. I have included those novels that share characteristics with another genre—whether fantasy, Western, mystery, or romance—that seem to put the strongest emphasis on historical interest, detail, and accuracy.

Historical Fiction Highlights

In looking for trends among the listing of historical novels included here, I find the series remains perhaps the most noteworthy of contemporary handling of the historical novel genre. While the series is the rule in historical mysteries, multivolume historical novels with recurring characters in ongoing episodes continue in vogue in all types of historical novels. Writers increasingly seem to prefer telling their stories in a trilogy or some other multipart format rather than in a single stand-alone volume. This is likely as much a publishing and economic decision as an artistic one, since sequels capitalize on a novel's hard-earned success. Catering to an audience who demands more of the same can have its drawbacks, however, and some historical fiction series seem more like franchises than fresh and innovative reading experiences. While there is something to be said for the elbow room to follow a character's development over time and through multiple situations, or to examine a period's evolution, there are also certain benefits for letting a series close naturally before it has a chance to repeat itself.

The initial installment of projected series represented here include Christina Dodd's historical romance series set during the Napoleonic era, *Some Enchanted Evening*, and Sara Douglass' medieval fantasy, *The Nameless Day* (its second installment, *The Wounded Hawk*, is also included). Second installments include Roddy Doyle's *Oh, Play That Thing*, Dan O'Brien's *The Indian Agent*, and Thalassa Ali's *A Beggar at the Gate*. Several series closing installments also appear, including Madison Smartt Bell's towering trilogy on Toussaint L'Ouverture and the Haitian War of Independence, *The Stone the Builder Refused* and Rosalind Miles' feminist-inspired retelling of the Tristan and Isolde legend, *The Lady of the Sea*. Van Reid brings to a close, most reluctantly for his many fans, his entertaining Moosepath League series with *Fiddler's Green*. Other impressive debuts make one hopeful for a sequel, such as Peter Ackroyd's *The Clerkenwell Tales*, in which Chaucer's Canterbury pilgrims are recruited for a detailed look at fourteenth-century England, Jeff Shaara's chronicle of World War I, *To the Last Man*, and Susanna Clarke's entertaining and absorbing *Jonathan Strange & Mr. Norrell* that shows the revival of magic to help win the war against Napoleon.

Clarke's novel suggests a second trend among recent historical novels in incorporating fantasy or deliberate altering of the past as part of the fictional strategy. Alternate history remains popular with the current master of the form, Harry Turtledove, represented by two volumes, *Settling Accounts* and *Days of Infamy*, He also appears under the

pseudonym H.N. Turteltaub with the delightfully entertaining *Owls to Athens*. "What if" figures prominently in Jack Dann's *The Rebel* in which actor James Dean survives his fatal car crash to participate in the upheaval of the 1960s, and in *The Plot Against America*, Philip Roth's chronicling the impact of Charles Lindbergh's 1940 election as U.S. President on a Jewish family in Newark, New Jersey.

Among popular eras for fictional treatment, World War II dominates the field the war examined on multiple fronts: from the perspective of two German teenager Monique Charlesworth's *The Children's War*, in espionage in Alan Furst's *Dark Voyage* and Lily Powell's *The Devil in Buenos Aires*, in comb with David L. Robbins' *Liberation Road* and on the home front in Fred Har *Following the Harvest*, Mark Mills' *Amagansett*, and Max Allan Collins' *The London Blitz Murders*. India is a popular subject in several including Carolyn Slaughter's *The Black Englishman* and Barbara Cleverly' *The Damascened Blade*. It is also refreshing to see novels about somewhat neglected periods and subjects, including the Korean War (Ha Jin's *War Trash* Jews in the American South (Roy Hoffman's *Chicken Dreaming Corn*), and Hollywood during the McCarthy era (Elizabeth Frank's *Cheat and Charmer*). Finally, who would have thought that the magisterial and daunting Henry James wo require a second fictional biography as David Lodge's *Author, Author* fol closely on the heels of Colm Toibin's *The Master*, that appeared earlier In a similar literary vein, Robert Anderson follows a recent spate of novels on Sylvia Plath and Ted Hughes in *Little Fugue*.

Historical Mysteries

As in years past, the single largest subcategory of historical fiction remains historical mysteries, a genre that continues to attract a diverse group of writers who show that a key way to propel readers through the historical past is with secrets and suspense. The games afoot in Ancient Rome (Lindsey Davis' *Scandal Takes a Holiday*, Caroline Lawrence's *The Twelve Tasks of Flavia Gemina*, and David Wishart's *Parthian Shot*), the Middle Ages (Margaret Frazer's *The Widow's Tale*, Michael Jecks' *The Outlaw of Ennor* and *The Tolls of Death*), Bernard Knight's *Crowner's Quest*, Priscilla Royal's *Tyrant of the Mind*, John Sack's *The Franciscan Conspiracy*, and C.J. Sansom's *Dark Fire*), in the Elizabethan Period (Fiona Buckley's *The Siren Queen*), the Georgian Period (Deryn Lake's *Death in the Setting Sun*), throughout the nineteenth century (Gilles Bornais' *The Devil Lives in Glasgow*, Barbara Hambly's *Dead Water*, Jane Jakeman's *Let There Be Blood*, Joan Lock's *Dead End*), during World War I (Anne Perry's *Shoulder the Sky*, and in the 1920s, 1930s, and 1940s (Carola Dunn's *A Mourning Wedding*, Stuart Wood's *The Prince of Beverly Hills*, and Lee Irby's *7,000 Clams*). There are several strong debuts, including Joan Druett's *A Watery Grave*, Edwin Thomas' Napoleonic era mystery (*The Blighted Cliffs*), Pat McIntosh's Tudor era mystery *The Harper's Quine*, and

Philippa Morgan's mystery featuring Geoffrey Chaucer as sleuth (*Chaucer and the House of Fame*). Edgar Allan Poe returns as a detective in Harold Schechter's *The Mask of Red Death*, and Agatha Christie is recruited to track down a serial murderer in Max Allan Collins' *The London Blitz Murders*. Collins also provides a period crime sequel to his graphic novel (and acclaimed motion picture), *Road to Perdition*, with *Road to Purgatory*.

What would a listing of historical mysteries be without appearances by the greatest detective of all—Sherlock Holmes. There are two Holmesian inspired mysteries listed here. Carole Nelson Douglas brings back Holmes' heart-throb Irene Adler in *Spider Dance*, and Michael Chabon imagines Holmes in retirement during World War II in *The Final Solution*.

Fictional Biographies

Fictional biographies in which a historical figure's life, or a significant portion of it, is recreated, remains a staple subgenre of the historical novel. Listed here are fictional biographies or biographically-inspired fictions of such famous figures as Alexander the Great (Stephen Pressfield's *The Virtues of War*, Hannibal (David Anthony Durham's *Pride of Carthage*, Abelaird and Heloise (Antoine Audouard's *Farewell, My Only One*), Anne Boleyn (Susannah Dunn's *The Queen of Subtleties*), William Shakespeare (Bruce Cook's *Young Will*), and Sarah Bernhardt (Adam Braver's *Divine Sarah*). There are also biographical treatments of the lesser known such as Scottish warrior Robert the Bruce (Duncan A. Bruce's *The Great Scot*), Solomon and Sheba (India Edghill's *Wisdom's Daughter*), the Custer massacre scapegoat Marcus Reno (Richard S. Wheeler's *Obituary for Major Reno*), nineteenth-century actress Harriet Smithson and French composer Hector Berlioz (Christine Balint's *Ophelia's Fan*), presidential assassin Leon Czologosz (Jonathan Lowy's *The Temple of Music*), and Grand Duke Nicholas Konstantinovich (Prince Michael's *The White Night of Petersburg*).

Other novels feature intriguing cameo appearances by such historical figures as Catherine the Great and Benjamin Franklin in Randall Wallace's *Love and Honor*, Tecumseh in Rosanne Bittner's *Into the Prairie*, Louis Armstrong in Roddy Doyle's *Oh, Play That Thing*, and Babe Ruth in Lee Irby's *7,000 Clams*.

Unusual Eras, Events, and Oddities

Let me conclude this survey of the historical novels collected here with a round-up of the odd and the off beat, books that impressed with their unusual subjects and perspectives. Ellen Cooney breathes fresh life into the American Revolution by looking at events from the perspective of a remote Maine village in *Gun Ball Hill*. Philip Lee Williams' sheds new light on the Civil War's Battle of Atlanta in *A Distant Flame*. Adam Williams looks at China's Boxer Rebellion in *The Palace of Heavenly Pleasure*. John Sack examines the controversy surrounding St. Francis in *The Franciscan Conspiracy*, Emma Donoghue looks at a famous eighteenth- century scandal in *Life Mask*, and Louis de Bernieres covers the modern history of Turkey in *Birds Without Wings*.

Praise for the most inventive goes to David Mitchell's head-spinning juggling of various eras in *Cloud Atlas*, Thornton Lawrence's reunion between writer Joseph Conrad and the sailor who inspired his character Marlow in *Sailors on the Inward Sea*, and Paul Weidner's dwarf-eye view of the court of Louis XIV in *Memoir of a Dwarf*.

The historical novel is, as the books collected here make clear, many things, but few would describe the form as very conducive to comedy. Perhaps history as a consistent chronicle of death, destruction, and suffering defeats the comic instinct, and while there are exceptions to the rule, tragedy and pathos seem more congenial to the tone of most historical novels. Two exceptions are worth mentioning here. Gideon Defoe has written an exuberant, Monty Pythonesque adventure linking a pirate crew with English scientist Charles Darwin in *The Pirates! In an Adventure with Scientists*, and H.N. Turteltaub provides another installment of his amusing chronicle of misadventures in the Mediterranean world of the Ancient Greeks in *Owls to Athens*. Both are recommended as antidotes for novels that take themselves far too seriously or suggest that dutiful solemnity is the only appropriate response to the grand pageant of history.

Recommendations

Here are my selections of the twenty-five most accomplished and interesting historical novels for the last half of 2004:

Peter Ackroyd, *The Clerkenwell Tales*

Louis Auchincloss, *East Side Story*

Christine Balint, *Ophelia's Fan*

Madison Smartt Bell, *The Stone the Builder Refused*

Susanna Clarke, *Jonathan Strange & Mr. Norrell*

Louis de Bernieres, *Birds Without Wings*

Emma Donoghue, *Life Mask*

Roddy Doyle, *Oh, Play That Thing*

David Anthony Durham, *Pride of Carthage*

Elizabeth Frank, *Cheat and Charmer*

Alan Furst, *Dark Voyage*

Jennifer Haigh, *Baker Towers*

Ha Jin, *War Trash*

David Lodge, *Author, Author*

Jonathan Lowy, *The Temple of Music*

Allan Massie, *Arthur the King*

Steven Pressfield, *The Virtues of War*

Van Reid, *Fiddler's Green*

David L. Robbins, *Liberation Road*

Philip Roth, *The Plot Against America*

Jeff Shaara, *To the Last Man*

Carolyn Slaughter, *The Black Englishman*

Neal Stephenson, *The System of the World*

Jane Stevenson, *The Empress of the Last Days*

Richard S. Wheeler, *Obituary for Major Reno*

For More Information about Historical Fiction

Printed Sources

Lynda G. Adamson, *American Historical Fiction: An Annotated Guide to Novels for Adults and Young Adults*. Phoenix: Oryx Press, 1999.

Lynda G. Adamson, *World Historical Fiction: An Annotated Guide to Novels for Adults and Young Adults*. Phoenix: Oryx Press, 1999.

Daniel S. Burt, *What Historical Fiction Do I Read Next?* Detroit: Gale, Vols. 1-3, 1997-2003.

Daniel S. Burt, *The Biography Book*. Westport: Oryx/Greenwood Press, 2001.

Donald K Hartman, *Historical Figures in Fiction*. Phoenix: Oryx Press, 1994.

Electronic Sources

The Historical Novel Society (http//www.historicalnovel society.org). Includes articles, interviews, and reviews of historical novels.

Of Ages Past: The Online Magazine of Historical Fiction (http://www.angelfire.com/il/ofagespast/). Includes novel excerpts, short stories, articles, author profiles, and reviews.

Soon's Historical Fiction Site (http://uts.cc.utexas.edu/~soon/histfiction/). A rich source of information on the historical novel genre, including links to more specialized sites on particular authors and types of historical fiction.

Historical Titles

810

PETER ACKROYD

The Clerkenwell Tales

(New York: Nan A. Talese, 2004)

Story type: Historical/Medieval
Subject(s): Middle Ages; Pilgrims and Pilgrimages; Politics
Major character(s): William Exmewe, Religious (friar); Thomas Gunter, Doctor; Miles Vavasour, Lawyer
Time period(s): 14th century (1399)
Locale(s): London, England

Summary: Ackroyd inventively reassembles Geoffrey Chaucer's Canterbury pilgrims for a panoramic portrait of 1390s London. The political backdrop of the story is the dynastic conflict over the throne of Richard II, as detailed in Shakespeare's *Richard II* and the Henry IV plays. William Exmewe (the Friar) launches a terrorist campaign on behalf of Henry Bolingbroke that eventually affects Thomas Gunter (the Physician), Miles Vavasour (the Man of Law), and other Chaucerian pilgrims. The thriller aspect of the novel's plot provides the momentum for a knowledgeable and vivid depiction of the period and the place.

Where it's reviewed:
Booklist, September 1, 2004, page 54
Kirkus Reviews, July 1, 2004, page 587
Publishers Weekly, July 19, 2004, page 142

Other books by the same author:
The Plato Papers, 2000
Milton in America, 1997
The House of Doctor Dee, 1994
The Trial of Elizabeth Cree, 1994
English Music, 1992

Other books you might like:
Catherine Darby, *The Love Knot*, 1989
Judith Healey, *The Canterbury Papers*, 2004
Sheri Holman, *A Stolen Tongue*, 1997
Philip Lindsay, *The Gentle Knight*, 1942
Candace Robb, *A Gift of Sanctuary*, 1998

811

THALASSA ALI

A Beggar at the Gate

(New York: Bantam, 2004)

Story type: Historical/Victorian
Subject(s): Victorian Period; Cultural Conflict; Indian Empire
Major character(s): Marianna Givens, Gentlewoman, Spouse (of Hassan); Hassan Ali Khan, Nobleman, Spouse (of Marianna)
Time period(s): 1840s
Locale(s): Calcutta, India; Lahore, India

Summary: In this sequel to *A Singular Hostage*, Ali continues the saga of Marianna Givens, a young Englishwoman in 19th-century India. After marrying the Punjabi courtier Hassan Ali Khan, Marianna is forced to flee to Calcutta to protect Hassan's infant son from the Maharajah of Punjab. On her return to Lahore, intending to divorce Hassan and return to respectable British society, she finds herself caught between warring Punjabi factions.

Where it's reviewed:
Publishers Weekly, October 4, 2004, page 69

Other books by the same author:
A Singular Hostage, 2002

Other books you might like:
Philip Hensher, *The Mulberry Empire*, 2002
M.M. Kaye, *The Far Pavilions*, 1978
Allan Mallinson, *Honorable Company*, 2000
Rebecca Ryman, *The Veil of Illusions*, 1995
Carolyn Slaughter, *A Black Englishman*, 2004

812

DOUG ALLYN

The Burning of Rachel Hayes

(Waterville, Maine: Five Star, 2004)

Story type: Mystery

Subject(s): Mystery and Detective Stories; Small Town Life
Major character(s): David Westbrook, Veterinarian; Megan Keyes, Journalist
Time period(s): 2000s; 1870s
Locale(s): Michigan

Summary: Edgar-winning mystery writer Allyn shuttles between two eras as veterinarian Dr. David Westbrook moves to a small town in northern Michigan to start a new life. After he rescues a young boy from a well and discovers human remains, he investigates the disappearance of farm woman Rachel Hayes who vanished in 1871. Westbrook is aided by reporter Megan Keyes in his investigation, and the narrative shifts backwards in time to connect separate mysteries set 133 years apart.

Where it's reviewed:
Booklist, October 15, 2004, page 391
Kirkus Reviews, October 1, 2004, page 940
Publishers Weekly, October 25, 2004, page 31

Other books by the same author:
The Hard Luck Club, 2002
Welcome to Wolf Country, 2001
A Dance in Deep Water, 1997
Black Water, 1996
Ice Water Mansions, 1996

Other books you might like:
William Diehl, *Eureka*, 2002
Loren D. Estleman, *Thunder City*, 1999
William Heffernan, *Beulah Hill*, 2001
Joe R. Lansdale, *The Bottoms*, 2000
Jeffrey Lent, *Lost Nation*, 2002

813

ROBERT ANDERSON

Little Fugue

(New York: Ballantine, 2004)

Story type: Literary
Subject(s): Authors and Writers; Biography; Poetry
Major character(s): Ted Hughes, Historical Figure, Writer (poet); Assia Gutmann Wevill, Historical Figure, Writer (poet); Robert Anderson, Writer
Time period(s): 20th century; 2000s (1968-2001)
Locale(s): New York, New York; England

Summary: This is yet another fictionalized account of the relationship between poets Sylvia Plath and Ted Hughes. What's different here is that the novel looks at the aftermath of Plath's 1963 suicide and its effect on Hughes; his mistress Assia Gutmann Wevill; and a fictional character, aspiring writer Robert Anderson whose life is changed when he first reads Plath's poetry. Hughes' life and the controversies surrounding his relationship with Plath are counterpointed by Anderson's experiences that include the Columbia riots of 1968 and the terrorist attacks on 9/11.

Where it's reviewed:
Booklist, November 15, 2004, page 551
Kirkus Reviews, November 15, 2004, page 1059
Publishers Weekly, October 18, 2004, page 47

Other books by the same author:
Ice Age, 2000

Other books you might like:
Peter Carey, *My Life as a Fake*, 2003
Martin Corrick, *The Navigation Log*, 2003
Kate Moses, *Wintering*, 2003
Emma Tennant, *Sylvia and Ted*, 2001
Meg Wolitzer, *The Wife*, 2003

814

ALIETTE ARMEL

Love, the Painter's Wife and the Queen of Sheba

(New Milford, Connecticut: Toby, 2004)

Story type: Historical/Renaissance
Subject(s): Artists and Art; Biblical Fiction
Major character(s): Piero della Francesca, Historical Figure, Artist; Silvia della Francesca, Spouse (of Piero); Bilqis, Historical Figure, Ruler (Queen of Sheba)
Time period(s): 15th century; 10th century B.C.
Locale(s): Arezzo, Italy; Jerusalem, Israel

Summary: Armel weaves together two different stories from very different eras. The first scenes, from the life of actual Renaissance artist Piero della Francesca, are told through the perspective of his wife, Silvia. Anxious for him to remain home in Arezzo rather than answer a papal order to come to Rome, Silvia, Scheherazade-like, captivates him with the story of the Queen of Sheba. The story inspires the painter to undertake his most celebrated work.

Where it's reviewed:
Kirkus Reviews, June 1, 2004, page 504
Library Journal, June 15, 2004, page 56

Other books you might like:
Roberta Kells Dorr, *The Queen of Sheba*, 1990
India Edghill, *Wisdom's Daughter*, 2004
Faye Levine, *Solomon & Sheba*, 1980
Atle Naess, *Doubting Thomas*, 2000
Jay Williams, *Solomon & Sheba*, 1959

815

LOUIS AUCHINCLOSS

East Side Story

(Boston: Houghton Mifflin, 2004)

Story type: Family Saga
Subject(s): Family Relations; Social Classes
Major character(s): David Carnochan, Businessman
Time period(s): 19th century; 20th century
Locale(s): New York, New York

Summary: Auchincloss' 60th book takes up his usual subject: the history of a prominent New York City family. Scottish merchant David Carnochan immigrates to America in the 1830s and establishes a textile business. The novel traces the subsequent generations as they amass a family fortune and enter the upper reaches of New York society. Auchincloss is a master of this milieu, and the novel provides both a summary of American history in the 19th and 20th centuries, as well as an engaging family saga.

Where it's reviewed:
Booklist, November 1, 2004, page 462
Kirkus Reviews, September 15, 2004, page 879
Library Journal, October 1, 2004, page 66
New York Times Book Review, December 19, 2004, page 13
Publishers Weekly, October 4, 2004, page 66

Other books by the same author:
The Scarlet Letters, 2003
Manhattan Monologues, 2002
Her Infinite Variety, 2000
The Education of Oscar Fairfax, 1995
Three Lives, 1993

Other books you might like:
Elaine Bissell, *Family Fortune*, 1985
Diana Diamond, *The First Wife*, 2004
Dominick Dunn, *The Two Mrs. Grenvilles*, 1985
Roxana Robinson, *Sweetwater*, 2003
Jessica Shattuck, *The Hazards of Good Breeding*, 2003

816

ANTOINE AUDOUARD

Farewell, My Only One
(Boston: Houghton Mifflin, 2004)

Story type: Historical/Medieval
Subject(s): Middle Ages; Lovers; Biography
Major character(s): Peter Abelard, Historical Figure, Philosopher; Heloise, Historical Figure, Gentlewoman; William, Student
Time period(s): 12th century (1116)
Locale(s): Paris, France

Summary: Audouard's Goncourt Prize-nominated novel re-creates the famous and tragic medieval love story of Heloise and Abelard from the perspective of a young student named William who travels from Oxford to Paris in 1116. There he falls in love with the beautiful and passionate Heloise and comes under the intellectual spell of the brilliant, iconoclastic teacher Abelard. Through William's admiring eyes, the sad course of Abelard and Heloise's passion for one another and its persecution by the standards of the times are lyrically portrayed.

Where it's reviewed:
Booklist, May 15, 2004, page 1607
Publishers Weekly, June 14, 2004, page 41

Other books you might like:
Elisabeth McNeill, *A Garden of Briars*, 1993
Marion Meade, *Stealing Heaven*, 1979
George Moore, *Heloise and Abelard*, 1925
Sharan Newman, *Heresy*, 2002
Helen Waddell, *Peter Abelard*, 1933

817

MORTEZA BAHARLOO

The Quince Seed Potion
(Bridgehampton, New York: Bridge Works, 2004)

Story type: Historical/Exotic
Subject(s): Servants
Major character(s): Sarveali Jokar, Servant; Teimor Khan, Nobleman
Time period(s): 20th century (1928-1981)
Locale(s): Iran

Summary: This debut novel covers events in modern Iranian history from the 1920s to the 1980s from the perspective of an indentured servant, Sarveali Jokar, who serves one of Iran's great dynastic families. Sold by a relative into servitude as a youth, Sarveali is attached to the all-powerful Shirlu khans. Sarveali's fortunes are tied to the fate of Iran's ruling dynasty, and he must endure a spurned love for his khan's son, Teimor Khan. He must also deal with his marriage to his cousin, her murder, imprisonment, and opium addiction. This is a vivid look at Iran from a knowing but exotic perspective.

Where it's reviewed:
Booklist, October 15, 2004, page 388
Kirkus Reviews, September 15, 2004, page 879

Other books you might like:
James Buchan, *The Persian Bride*, 2000
James Clavell, *Whirlwind*, 1986
Anahita Firouz, *In the Walled Garden*, 2002
Dora Levy Mossaanen, *Harem*, 2002
Dorit Rabinyan, *Persian Bride*, 1998

818

CHRISTINE BALINT

Ophelia's Fan
(New York: Norton, 2004)

Story type: Historical/Regency
Subject(s): Actors and Actresses; Music and Musicians; Biography
Major character(s): Harriet Smithson, Historical Figure, Actress; Hector Berlioz, Historical Figure, Composer
Time period(s): 19th century
Locale(s): London, England; Paris, France

Summary: Balint's impressive novel animates the life and stage career of 19th-century Shakespearean actress Harriet Smithson. Born in Ireland, Smithson became a sensation on the London and Paris stages where she captivated composer Hector Berlioz, whom she eventually married. Although Smithson would inspire Berlioz's most famous work, the *Symphonie Fantastique*, their married life would be troubled, and Smithson provides her own perspective on it in imagined letters to her son. Balint succeeds in authentically recreating both the lives of Smithson and Berlioz, as well as the theatrical world of the early 19th century.

Where it's reviewed:
Booklist, July 2004, page 1815
Kirkus Reviews, June 15, 2004, page 547

Historical

Library Journal, June 15, 2004, page 56
Publishers Weekly, August 2, 2004, page 53

Other books by the same author:
The Salt Letters, 2001

Other books you might like:
Adam Braver, *Divine Sarah*, 2004
Stephanie Cowell, *Marrying Mozart*, 2004
J.D. Landis, *Longing*, 2000
Rose Tremain, *Music & Silence*, 2000
Sarah Waters, *Tipping the Velvet*, 1999

819

JON R. BAUMAN

Santa Fe Passage

(New York: St. Martin's Press, 2004)

Story type: Historical/American West
Subject(s): Frontier and Pioneer Life; Mexicans
Major character(s): Matthew Collins, Scout, Businessman; Edward Waterman, Businessman
Time period(s): 19th century
Locale(s): Santa Fe, New Mexico

Summary: Bauman chronicles the turbulent history of New Mexico in this novel that begins in 1822 when teenage orphan Matthew Collins runs away from Illinois to seek his fortune as a trader on the famed Santa Fe Trail. He becomes a teamster and a scout before becoming a prosperous Santa Fe businessman with his partner Edward Waterman. Matthew marries a Mexican woman and becomes a Mexican citizen. When war with Mexico comes in 1846, he is forced to choose which side to support. The novel serves to document the issues that divided New Mexico during this period.

Where it's reviewed:
Publishers Weekly, October 11, 2004, page 54

Other books you might like:
Terry C. Johnston, *Crack in the Sky*, 1997
James A. Michener, *The Eagle and the Raven*, 1990
P.G. Nagle, *The Guns of Valverde*, 2000
Charles Portis, *Gringos*, 1991
Richard S. Wheeler, *Santa Fe*, 1994

820

CARRIE A. BEBRIS

Suspense and Sensibility

(New York: Forge, 2005)

Story type: Historical/Regency; Mystery
Series: Mr. and Mrs. Darcy. Book 2
Subject(s): Mystery and Detective Stories
Major character(s): Fitzwilliam Darcy, Gentleman, Spouse (of Elizabeth); Elizabeth Bennet Darcy, Gentlewoman, Spouse (of Darcy); Kitty Bennet, Gentlewoman (Elizabeth's sister)
Time period(s): 1810s
Locale(s): London, England; Hertfordshire, England

Summary: Bebris provides a second sleuthing opportunity for newlyweds Fitzwilliam and Elizabeth Darcy, the protagonists of Jane Austen's classic *Pride and Prejudice*. Taking on the responsibility of finding a suitable husband for Elizabeth's sister Kitty, the couple must contend with a series of challenges and puzzles that threaten to stop another Bennet from getting to the altar safely.

Other books by the same author:
Pride and Prescience, 2004
Pool of Radiance, 2000
Shadowborn, 1998

Other books you might like:
Elizabeth Ashton, *Mr. Darcy's Daughters*, 2003
Ted Bader, *Desire and Duty*, 1997
   Marilyn Bader, co-author
Julia Barrett, *Presumption*, 1995
Stephanie Barron, *The Jane Austen Series*, 1996-
Emma Tennant, *Pemberley*, 1995

821

MADISON SMARTT BELL

The Stone That the Builder Refused

(New York: Pantheon, 2004)

Story type: Historical/Post-French Revolution
Series: Haitian Rebellion Trilogy. Book 3
Subject(s): Rebellions, Revolts, and Uprisings; Slavery; Haitians
Major character(s): Pierre Dominique Toussaint L'Ouverture, Historical Figure, Political Figure; Dr. Hebert, Narrator; Jean Jacques Dessalines, Military Personnel (Haitian general)
Time period(s): 1800s (1802-1803)
Locale(s): Haiti; France

Summary: Bell brings to a close his masterful Haitian rebellion trilogy with its concluding chapter, set in 1802, when a French army commanded by Napoleon's brother-in-law attempts to overthrow Toussaint's government and restore slavery to the island. The novel treats the defense mounted by Toussaint's black generals, including Dessalines, Henri Christophe, and Maurepas, as well as their betrayal of Toussaint and his downfall. The book's narrative focus comes from Dr. Hebert, who is able to pass between both sides in the conflict. Scenes of battle and politics are intercut with scenes from Toussaint's last days in a French jail. This is an impressive mix of historical fact and imaginative recreation, and a fitting conclusion to a major achievement by a skilled historical novelist.

Where it's reviewed:
Booklist, September 15, 2004, page 179
Kirkus Reviews, October 1, 2004, page 907
Library Journal, October 15, 2004, page 52
New York Times Book Review, November 14, 2004, page 49
Publishers Weekly, September 20, 2004, page 43

Other books by the same author:
Anything Goes, 2002
Master of the Crossroads, 2000
Ten Indians, 1996

All Souls' Rising, 1995
Save Me, Joe Louis, 1993

Other books you might like:
Peter Bourne, *Drums of Destiny*, 1947
Vina Delmar, *A Time for Titans*, 1974
Benjamin H. Levin, *Black Triumvirate*, 1972
James A. Michener, *Caribbean*, 1989
Anatolii Vinogradov, *The Black Consul*, 1935

822

JAN BENZELY
THOM LEMMONS, Co-Author

King's Ransom

(Colorado Springs, Colorado: WaterBrook, 2004)

Story type: Historical/World War II
Subject(s): Jews; World War II; Kings, Queens, Rulers, etc.
Major character(s): Boris III, Ruler (King of Bulgaria); Daria, Young Woman; Dobri, Military Personnel (sergeant)
Time period(s): 1940s
Locale(s): Bulgaria

Summary: Based on a true story, this is an account of the efforts made by Boris III, King of Bulgaria, to save the lives of his country's Jewish population from the Nazi Holocaust. The novel tells the inspiring tale of how Boris, along with members of the Orthodox Church, and Jewish leaders prevented the loss of a single Bulgarian Jew to Hitler's concentration camps. Boris' heroic efforts are interwoven with a love story between Daria, a Jewish woman, and Dobri, a sergeant in the king's guard.

Other books you might like:
Jenna Blum, *Those Who Saved Us*, 2004
Louise Doughty, *Fires in the Dark*, 2003
Ian MacMillan, *Village of a Million Spirits*, 1999
Daniel Silva, *A Death in Vienna*, 2004

823

NELLA BIELSKI

The Year Is '42

(New York: Pantheon, 2004)

Story type: Historical/World War II
Subject(s): World War II
Major character(s): Karl Bazinger, Military Personnel (German officer)
Time period(s): 1940s (1942)
Locale(s): Paris, France; Saxony, Germany; Kiev, Union of Soviet Socialist Republics

Summary: Ukrainian playwright and novelist Bielski looks at the occupation of Paris by the Nazis from the perspective of Karl Bazinger, a Wehrmacht officer, who plunges into the attractions of the city, and associates with such luminaries as Coco Chanel and Jean Cocteau. After arousing the suspicions of the SS, Bazinger is transferred to the Russian front where he is exposed to the harsh realities of the war.

Where it's reviewed:
Booklist, October 15, 2004, page 388

Kirkus Reviews, September 15, 2004, page 880
Publishers Weekly, October 4, 2004, page 66

Other books by the same author:
After Arkadia, 1991
Oranges for the Son of Alexander Levy, 1982

Other books you might like:
Frederick Busch, *A Memory of War*, 2003
Monique Charlesworth, *The Children's War*, 2004
Louise Doughty, *Fires in the Dark*, 2003
James Thackara, *The Book of Kings*, 1999
Walter Zacharius, *Songbird*, 2004

824

SANDRA BIRDSELL

Katya

(Minneapolis: Milkweed Editions, 2004)

Story type: Historical/Russian Revolution; Historical/World War I
Subject(s): Religious Traditions; Family Life; Revolutions
Major character(s): Katya Vogt, Immigrant
Time period(s): 1910s; 1920s
Locale(s): Russia; Canada

Summary: This novel looks at the impact of the Russian Revolution on the German Mennonite community that fled persecution in Germany in the 18th century to settle productively on the Russian steppes. Katya Vogt immigrates to Canada in the 1920s and recalls her past life and the breakup of her family and community with the outbreak of World War I. As pacifists, the Mennonites are considered unpatriotic, and, then as the revolution grows, bands of anarchists, Bolsheviks, and peasants, envious of the Mennonites' prosperity, pillage and plunder their properties. Katya manages to escape, but only after witnessing a brutal massacre in 1917. Birdsell documents an off-the-beaten-track aspect of the Russian Revolution.

Where it's reviewed:
Kirkus Reviews, August 15, 2004, page 757
Library Journal, August 2004, page 63

Other books by the same author:
The Chrome Suite, 1992
Agassiz, 1991
The Missing Child, 1989

Other books you might like:
Robert Alexander, *The Kitchen Boy*, 2003
Marilyn Bowering, *Visible Worlds*, 1998
Martha Brooks, *Confessions of a Heartless Girl*, 2003
Andrei Makine, *Dreams of My Russian Summers*, 1997
Aleksandr Solzhenitsyn, *November 1916*, 1999

825

ROSANNE BITTNER

Into the Prairie

(New York: Forge, 2004)

Story type: Historical/American West; Family Saga

Historical

Series: Westward America!. Book 3
Subject(s): Frontier and Pioneer Life; Indians of North America; Family Relations
Major character(s): Jonah Wilde, Settler, Spouse (of Sadie); Sadie Wilde, Settler, Spouse (of Jonah); Tecumseh, Historical Figure, Indian
Time period(s): 1810s (1810)
Locale(s): Fort Wayne, Indiana; Ohio

Summary: Jonah Wilde sets out from his farm in Ohio to claim land in the newly opened Indiana Territory. As Jonah, his wife Sadie, and their young son build their new homestead there, they are caught up in the Indian wars led by Tecumseh. After an Indian attack, Sadie and her son are taken hostage, and Jonah is left for dead. Sadie eventually falls in love with her Indian captor and faces a difficult decision when Jonah turns out to be alive.

Where it's reviewed:
Booklist, July 2004, page 1815

Other books by the same author:
Into the Valley, 2003
Into the Wilderness, 2002
The Mating Game, 2002
Mystic Warriors, 2001
Mystic Dreamers, 1999

Other books you might like:
Elizabeth Adler, *Crossing the Panther's Path*, 2002
Sara Donati, *Fire Along the Sky*, 2004
Larry McMurtry, *Boone's Lick*, 2000
James Alexander Thom, *Panther in the Sky*, 1989
Melanie Wallace, *Blue Horse Dreaming*, 2003

826

MICHAEL BLAINE

The Midnight Band of Mercy

(New York: Soho, 2004)

Story type: Historical/Victorian America; Mystery
Subject(s): Mystery and Detective Stories; City and Town Life
Major character(s): Max Greengrass, Detective—Amateur, Journalist (newspaper reporter)
Time period(s): 1890s (1893)
Locale(s): New York, New York

Summary: The discovery of four dead cats arranged in a row on a Greenwich Village sidewalk prompts newspaper reporter Max Greengrass to investigate. When leads turn up dead, Greengrass follows his story to an unusual source: the Catholic Church and a reformist group of women who prove to be not what they seem. The novel excels in its depiction of New York City in the 1890s.

Where it's reviewed:
Booklist, September 1, 2004, page 54
Kirkus Reviews, August 1, 2004, page 701
Library Journal, September 1, 2004, page 136
New York Times Book Review, September 26, 2004, page 24
Publishers Weekly, August 2, 2004, page 51

Other books by the same author:
The Desperate Season, 1999

Other books you might like:
Jon Boorstin, *The Newsboys' Lodging House*, 2003
Susanna Clarke, *Jonathan Strange & Mr. Norrell*, 2004
Paula Cohen, *Gramercy Park*, 2002
Harold Schechter, *The Mask of Red Death*, 2004
Victoria Thompson, *Murder on Marble Row*, 2004

827

WIN BLEVINS

Beauty for Ashes

(New York: Forge, 2004)

Story type: Historical/American West; Mountain Man
Series: Rendezvous. Book 2
Subject(s): Frontier and Pioneer Life; Fur Trade; Indians of North America
Major character(s): Sam Morgan, Trapper; Meadowlark, Indian (Crow), Lover (of Sam)
Time period(s): 1820s
Locale(s): Rocky Mountains

Summary: Blevins continues his series begun with *So Wild a Dream* concerning the fur trade in the American West in the 1820s. After a harrowing 700-mile journey alone and on foot into the western frontier, Sam Morgan has learned his craft as a trapper. After a disappointing visit home to Pennsylvania, Morgan sets out west again to find his beloved Crow Indian maiden Meadowlark. Finding her is only the beginning of the challenges he faces. To win her he must become a Crow himself, and he must endure capture by the Sioux that leaves him with nothing to win Meadowlark's family over.

Where it's reviewed:
Kirkus Reviews, August 15, 2004, page 757
Publishers Weekly, October 18, 2004, page 49

Other books by the same author:
So Wild a Dream, 2003
Ravenshadow, 1999
The Rock Child, 1998
Stone Song, 1995
The High Missouri, 1994

Other books you might like:
Terry C. Johnston, *Carry the Wind*, 1987
Frederick Manfred, *Lord Grizzly*, 1954
Jonathan Raymond, *The Half-Life*, 2004
Melanie Wallace, *Blue Horse Dreaming*, 2003
Richard S. Wheeler, *The Deliverance*, 2003

828

GILLES BORNAIS

The Devil Lives in Glasgow

(New York: Carnot USA, 2004)

Story type: Historical/Victorian; Mystery
Subject(s): Mystery and Detective Stories; Crime and Criminals
Major character(s): Joe Hackney, Detective—Police (Scotland Yard detective)
Time period(s): 1880s (1887)

Locale(s): Glasgow, Scotland

Summary: French journalist Bornais' first novel is a Victorian era mystery that has Scotland Yard detective Joe Hackney traveling to Glasgow to investigate two brutal murders. The unusual wounds of the victims link the murders to past cases, and Hackney finds himself dealing with a baffling set of circumstances surrounding a key witness who has disappeared. Bornais' period tale won France's Black Claw prize for best crime fiction.

Where it's reviewed:
Kirkus Reviews, July 1, 2004, page 605
Library Journal, June 1, 2004, page 108
Publishers Weekly, July 5, 2004, page 41

Other books you might like:
Dennis Burges, *Graves Gate*, 2003
Howard Engel, *Mr. Doyle and Dr. Bell*, 2003
Anthony O'Neill, *The Lamplighter*, 2003
Matthew Pearl, *The Dante Club*, 2003
David Pirie, *The Night Calls*, 2003

829

ADAM BRAVER

Divine Sarah

(New York: William Morrow, 2004)

Story type: Historical/Edwardian
Subject(s): Biography; Actors and Actresses
Major character(s): Sarah Bernhardt, Historical Figure, Actress; Thomas Edison, Historical Figure, Inventor; Vince Baker, Journalist (newspaper reporter)
Time period(s): 1900s (1906)
Locale(s): Venice Beach, California

Summary: Braver's novel follows a week in the life of renowned actress Sarah Bernhardt. The world's first superstar is in 1906 California on her Farewell Tour of America. The Divine Sarah must contend with charges of immorality from the citizenry and a complex personal life that includes a drug addiction. She is shown giving a cocaine-inspired recitation of *Hamlet* for Thomas Edison. Bernhardt's tangled life is connected with the story of newspaper reporter Vince Baker, assigned to cover her visit. Braver provides an evocative depiction that looks at American innocence through the offbeat lens of Bernhardt's decadence.

Where it's reviewed:
Booklist, July 2004, page 1815
Kirkus Reviews, April 15, 2004, page 344
Publishers Weekly, June 14, 2004, page 44

Other books by the same author:
Mr. Lincoln's War, 2003

Other books you might like:
Christine Balint, *Ophelia's Fan*, 2004
E.L. Doctorow, *Ragtime*, 1975
Joel Gross, *Sarah*, 1987
Francoise Sagan, *Dear Sarah Bernhardt*, 1988
Jean Stubbs, *Eleanora Duse*, 1970

830

DUNCAN A. BRUCE

The Great Scot

(New York: St. Martin's Press, 2004)

Story type: Historical/Medieval
Subject(s): Middle Ages; Kings, Queens, Rulers, etc.; Biography
Major character(s): Robert the Bruce, Historical Figure, Ruler (King of Scotland); David Crawford, Military Personnel
Time period(s): 14th century
Locale(s): Scotland

Summary: The author chronicles the life of Robert the Bruce of Scotland. Designated King of the Scots in 1306, Robert had to defend his crown under the threat of a harsh English invasion and occupation. Fighting both pitched battles and guerrilla warfare, Robert inspired his countrymen and gained an improbable victory against great odds at the Battle of Bannockburn in 1314. Robert's story is narrated by a soldier and confidant of the king, David Crawford, in a memoir that celebrates one of Scotland's greatest heroes.

Where it's reviewed:
Booklist, July 2004, page 1816
Kirkus Reviews, June 15, 2004, page 549

Other books you might like:
Dorothy Dunnett, *King Hereafter*, 1982
Virginia Henley, *A Year and a Day*, 1998
Katherine Kurtz, *The Temple and the Stone*, 1998
    Deborah Turner Harris, co-author
Jane Porter, *The Scottish Chiefs*, 1921
Nigel Tranter, *Robert the Bruce*, 1969

831

FIONA BUCKLEY (Pseudonym of Valerie Anand)

The Siren Queen

(New York: Scribner, 2004)

Story type: Historical/Elizabethan; Mystery
Series: Ursula Blanchard. Book 8
Subject(s): Mystery and Detective Stories; Kings, Queens, Rulers, etc.
Major character(s): Ursula Blanchard, Spy (espionage agent), Widow(er); Elizabeth I, Historical Figure, Ruler (Queen of England); Meg Blanchard, Gentlewoman (Ursula's daughter)
Time period(s): 16th century (1569)
Locale(s): England

Summary: Ursula Blanchard, Queen Elizabeth's half-sister and occasional secret agent, must insinuate herself into the household of an Italian banker who may be plotting against the queen. Meanwhile, Ursula's daughter is in love with a nobleman who could be part of the conspiracy. As the body count escalates, Ursula finds herself once again trying to protect Queen Elizabeth's throne.

Where it's reviewed:
Booklist, October 1, 2004, page 466
Library Journal, November 1, 2004, page 62

Publishers Weekly, October 4, 2004, page 73

Other books by the same author:
The Fugitive Queen, 2003
A Pawn for a Queen, 2002
Queen of Ambition, 2001
Queen's Ransom, 2000
The Doublet Affair, 1998

Other books you might like:
Patricia Finney, *Gloriana's Torch*, 2003
Philippa Gregory, *The Queen's Fool*, 2004
Karen Harper, *The Queene's Christmas*, 2003
Robin Maxwell, *The Wild Irish*, 2003
Fidelis Morgan, *The Rival Queens*, 2001

832

MICHAEL CHABON

The Final Solution

(New York: Fourth Estate, 2004)

Story type: Mystery; Historical/World War II
Subject(s): Mystery and Detective Stories; World War II; Small Town Life
Major character(s): Sherlock Holmes, Detective—Private
Time period(s): 1940s (1944)
Locale(s): Sussex, England

Summary: Chabon's period mystery novella employs as sleuth an 89-year-old retired pipe-smoking detective, who spends his time keeping bees. He is unnamed but unmistakably Sherlock Holmes. Here, "the old man" is asked to investigate circumstances surrounding a mute boy whose parrot mouths numbers in German. Chabon assembles a colorful cast of characters and presents an authentic recreation of wartime English country life.

Where it's reviewed:
Booklist, October 1, 2004, page 282
Kirkus Reviews, October 1, 2004, page 928
Publishers Weekly, November 1, 2004, page 43

Other books by the same author:
The Amazing Adventures of Kavalier & Clay, 2000
Werewolves in Their Youths, 1999
Wonder Boys, 1995
A Model World and Other Stories, 1991
The Mysteries of Pittsburgh, 1988

Other books you might like:
Max Allan Collins, *The London Blitz Murders*, 2004
Laurie R. King, *The Mary Russell/Sherlock Holmes Series*, 1994-
Michael Kurland, *The Great Game*, 2001
Larry Millett, *Sherlock Holmes and the Secret Alliance*, 2001
Donald Thomas, *Sherlock Holmes and the Voice from the Crypt*, 2002

833

ELIZABETH CHADWICK

The Falcons of Montabard

(New York: St. Martin's Press, 2004)

Story type: Historical/Medieval
Subject(s): Middle Ages; Knights and Knighthood; Crusades
Major character(s): Sabin FitzSimon, Knight; Edmund Strongfist, Knight; Annais, Young Woman
Time period(s): 12th century (1120)
Locale(s): Scotland; Jerusalem, Palestine

Summary: In this medieval adventure, Sabin FitzSimon accompanies the aging knight Sir Edmund Strongfist and his daughter Annais on a crusade to Jerusalem in the 12th century. There, amidst the intrigue of the court of King Baldwin, they experience a series of challenges, including kidnappings and a daring rescue from a Saracen fortress. Mixing the fictional and the historical, this is a colorful adventure tale showing knighthood in flower that will be enjoyed by any fan of historical romances.

Where it's reviewed:
Booklist, May 15, 2004, page 1607

Other books by the same author:
The White Mantle, 2003
Lords of the White Castle, 2002
The Love Knot, 1999
The Champion, 1998
The Conquest, 1997

Other books you might like:
David W. Ball, *Ironfire*, 2004
Evan S. Connell, *Deus lo Volt!*, 2000
Michael Alexander Eisner, *The Crusader*, 2001
Cecelia Holland, *Jerusalem*, 1997
James Patterson, *The Jester*, 2003
   Andrew Gross, co-author

834

MONIQUE CHARLESWORTH

The Children's War

(New York: Knopf, 2004)

Story type: Historical/World War II
Subject(s): World War II; Children and War; Jews
Major character(s): Ilse, Teenager; Nicolai, Teenager
Time period(s): 1930s; 1940s
Locale(s): Hamburg, Germany; Paris, France; Morocco

Summary: Charlesworth portrays the impact of World War II from the perspectives of two German teenagers. Ilse, a young girl with a Jewish father and a Protestant mother, is sent at the war's outbreak to relatives in Morocco for safety before reuniting with her father in Paris as the Germans arrive. Meanwhile, a German boy, Nicolai, a member of the Hitler Youth, befriends a family servant who turns out to be Ilse's mother as he begins to feel more and more alienated from his countrymen. The novel achieves both an original perspective on the war and a dramatic immediacy in this look at war through adolescent eyes.

Where it's reviewed:
Booklist, August 2004, page 1896
Kirkus Reviews, July 1, 2004, page 590
Library Journal, June 15, 2004, page 57
Publishers Weekly, August 16, 2004, page 43

Other books by the same author:
The Glass House, 1986

Other books you might like:
Lorenzo Carcaterra, *Street Boys*, 2002
Myla Goldberg, *Bee Season*, 2000
James Thackara, *The Book of Kings*, 1999
Philippe Tupon, *The Mistress*, 1999
Walter Zacharius, *Songbird*, 2004

835

STEFAN CHWIN

Death in Danzig

(Orlando, Florida: Harcourt, 2004)

Story type: Historical/World War II
Subject(s): War; World War II
Major character(s): Hanemann, Professor (anatomy)
Time period(s): 1940s (1945)
Locale(s): Danzig, Poland

Summary: This novel looks at life and conflict in the Polish port of Danzig during and after World War II. Hanemann, a German professor of anatomy, investigates the mysterious death of his lover in a ship accident before the war. He decides to stay in Danzig after most of the German population has fled and the city is occupied by the Russians and becomes the Polish city of Gdansk. His story is joined by that of the unnamed narrator's Polish family.

Where it's reviewed:
Booklist, September 15, 2004, page 206
Library Journal, August 2004, page 64
Publishers Weekly, October 25, 2004, page 28

Other books you might like:
Linda D. Cirino, *Eva's Story*, 1999
Gunter Grass, *The Call of the Toad*, 1992
Helaine G. Helmreich, *The Chimney Tree*, 2000
Ian MacMillan, *Village of a Million Spirits*, 1999
David L. Robbins, *The End of War*, 2000

836

LINDSAY CLARKE

The War at Troy

(New York: St. Martin's Press, 2004)

Story type: Historical/Ancient Greece; Legend
Subject(s): War; Legends; Ancient History
Major character(s): Paris, Royalty (Trojan prince); Helen, Royalty (Spartan queen); Achilles, Warrior
Time period(s): Indeterminate Past
Locale(s): Troy, Ancient Civilization; Greece

Summary: Clarke offers a lively retelling of Homer's *Iliad* and the Trojan War that, unlike Homer's account, supplies the full story. This includes King Menelaus' wife Helen's abduction by the Trojan Paris, the combat between the Greeks and Trojans before the walls of Troy, and the city's fall by the stratagem of the Trojan Horse. Despite a sometimes jarring modern idiom in the dialogue, Clarke manages a believable account of the most famous combat of all time, as well as credible human portraits of all the famous participants, including Achilles, Hector, Agamemnon, and Odysseus.

Where it's reviewed:
Kirkus Reviews, July 15, 2004, page 645

Other books by the same author:
Alice's Masque, 1994
The Chymical Wedding, 1989
Sunday Whiteman, 1987

Other books you might like:
Elizabeth Cook, *Achilles*, 2002
Richard Matturro, *Troy*, 1989
Colleen McCullough, *The Song of Troy*, 2001
Philip Parotti, *The Greek Generals Talk*, 1986
Richard Powell, *Whom the Gods Would Destroy*, 1970

837

SUSANNA CLARKE

Jonathan Strange & Mr. Norrell

(New York: Bloomsbury, 2004)

Story type: Historical/Napoleonic Wars; Historical/Fantasy
Subject(s): Magic; Fantasy; War
Major character(s): Mr. Norrell, Scholar, Magician; Jonathan Strange, Magician; Arthur Wellesley, Military Personnel, Historical Figure (Duke of Wellington)
Time period(s): 1800s
Locale(s): London, England; Yorkshire, England

Summary: In what has been described as a Harry Potter for adults, Clarke's story tells how the power of magic is revived in England during the Napoleonic Wars. Mr. Norrell is a reclusive bookworm whose scholarship gains him significant magical powers and makes him the toast of London society. Jonathan Strange, a young aristocrat, becomes Norrell's first pupil, and Strange uses his magic skill to serve Wellington in the campaigns against the French. Despite its fanciful premise, this impressive debut novel is an entertaining adventure story that achieves the captivating density that Harry Potter readers enjoy.

Where it's reviewed:
Booklist, September 1, 2004, page 1797
Kirkus Reviews, July 1, 2004, page 590
Library Journal, August 2004, page 64
New York Times Book Review, September 5, 2004, page 11
Publishers Weekly, July 12, 2004, page 41

Other books you might like:
Emma Donoghue, *Life Mask*, 2004
Glen David Gold, *Carter Beats the Devil*, 2001
David Liss, *A Spectacle of Corruption*, 2004
Lawrence Norfolk, *Lempiere's Dictionary*, 1992
Andrew Taylor, *An Unpardonable Crime*, 2004

Historical

838

BARBARA CLEVERLY

The Damascened Blade

(New York: Carroll & Graf, 2004)

Story type: Mystery; Historical/Roaring Twenties
Series: Joe Sandilands. Book 3
Subject(s): Mystery and Detective Stories
Major character(s): Joe Sandilands, Police Officer; Lily Coblenz, Heiress
Time period(s): 1920s (1922)
Locale(s): India

Summary: Joe Sandilands, a Scotland Yard commander based in India, takes charge of an American heiress, Lily Coblenz, who wants to tour India's dangerous northwest frontier with Afghanistan. At the frontier fort of Gor Khatri, a Pathan prince dies, British hostages are taken, and Sandilands has one week to identify and bring to justice the prince's killer to avoid war.

Where it's reviewed:
Booklist, July 2004, page 1823
Library Journal, July 2004, page 63
New York Times Book Review, August 8, 2004, page 15
Publishers Weekly, June 14, 2004, page 46

Other books by the same author:
Ragtime in Simla, 2002
The Last Kashmiri Rose, 2001

Other books you might like:
Thalassa Ali, *A Beggar at the Gate*, 2004
Philip Hensher, *The Mulberry Empire*, 2002
Susanna Moore, *One Last Look*, 2003
Rebecca Ryman, *Shalimar*, 1999
Carolyn Slaughter, *A Black Englishman*, 2004

839

EDWARD CLINE

Sparrowhawk. Book 3: Caxton

(San Francisco: MacAdam/Cage, 2004)

Story type: Historical/Colonial America
Series: Sparrowhawk. Book 3
Subject(s): Politics; American Colonies
Major character(s): Hugh Kenrick, Landowner; Jack Frake, Landowner
Time period(s): 1750s (1759)
Locale(s): Caxton, Virginia, American Colonies

Summary: In the aftermath of the French and Indian War, the American colonists celebrate their growing freedom in this third installment of Cline's depiction of the intellectual and cultural climate that helps to ignite the American Revolution. Set in the growing Virginia town of Caxton, the novel follows the growth of the spirit of independence as reflected from the perspective of landowners Hugh Kenrick and Jack Frake. Newcomers to the series are advised to start at the beginning for the necessary context for the characters and action here.

Other books by the same author:
Sparrowhawk. Book 2: Hugh Kenrick, 2002
Sparrowhawk. Book 1: Jack Frake, 2001
First Prize, 1988

Other books you might like:
Thomas Fleming, *Remember the Morning*, 1997
Ken Follett, *A Place Called Freedom*, 1995
Patrick McGrath, *Martha Peake*, 2001
Jeff Shaara, *The Glorious Cause*, 2002
Jeff Shaara, *Rise to Rebellion*, 2001

840

EDWARD CLINE

Sparrowhawk. Book 4: Empire

(San Francisco: MacAdam/Cage, 2004)

Story type: Historical/Georgian; Historical/Colonial America
Series: Sparrowhawk. Book 4
Subject(s): Politics
Major character(s): Hugh Kenrick, Political Figure; Patrick Henry, Historical Figure, Political Figure; Thomas Jefferson, Historical Figure, Political Figure
Time period(s): 1760s (1765)
Locale(s): Virginia, American Colonies; London, England

Summary: This installment of Cline's series about the political and cultural forces that produced the American Revolution deals with the anti-tax movement in the American colonies following the 1765 passage of the Stamp Act. Hugh Kenrick has become a burgess in the Virginia legislature and the political maneuvering in opposition to English control over the colonies on both sides of the Atlantic allows for appearances of such noteworthy historical figures as Patrick Henry, Thomas Jefferson, Adam Smith, and Samuel Johnson.

Where it's reviewed:
Publishers Weekly, November 15, 2004, page 41

Other books by the same author:
Sparrowhawk. Book 3: Caxton, 2004
Sparrowhawk. Book 2: Hugh Kenrick, 2002
Sparrowhawk. Book 1: Jack Frake, 2001
First Prize, 1988

Other books you might like:
Thomas Fleming, *Remember the Morning*, 1997
Ken Follett, *A Place Called Freedom*, 1995
Patrick McGrath, *Martha Peake*, 2001
Jeff Shaara, *The Glorious Cause*, 2002
Jeff Shaara, *Rise to Rebellion*, 2001

841

DON COLDSMITH

The Pipestone Quest

(Norman: University of Oklahoma Press, 2004)

Story type: Indian Culture; Historical/American West
Series: Spanish Bit Saga
Subject(s): Indians of North America; Cultures and Customs
Major character(s): Beaver, Indian
Time period(s): Indeterminate Past

Locale(s): Great Plains, North America

Summary: This is another chapter in the on-going Spanish Bit Saga depicting Native American life before the arrival of white settlers. Beaver sets out to discover the source of the red pipestone's power by going to the quarry where it is mined in what is now Minnesota. On the way, the small group he is traveling with suspects a curse has befallen them that can only be broken by uncovering the red pipestone's secret. Coldsmith is a master of Native American life and customs, and this novel will not disappoint those interested in an authentic depiction.

Other books by the same author:
The Long Journey Home, 2001
Tallgrass, 1997
Runestone, 1995
The Smoky Hill, 1989
The Spanish Bit Saga, 1980-

Other books you might like:
Joseph Bruchac, *Dawn Land*, 1993
W. Michael Gear, *The First North Americans Series*, 1990-
    Kathleen O'Neal Gear, co-author
Pamela Jekel, *She Who Hears the Sun*, 1999
Vella C. Munn, *Blackfeet Season*, 1999
Linda Lay Shuler, *She Who Remembers*, 1988

842

MAX ALLAN COLLINS

The London Blitz Murders
(New York: Berkley Prime Crime, 2004)

Story type: Mystery; Historical/World War II
Subject(s): Mystery and Detective Stories; World War II; Serial Killers
Major character(s): Sir Bernard Spilsbury, Doctor (pathologist); Agatha Christie, Historical Figure, Writer
Time period(s): 1940s (1942)
Locale(s): London, England

Summary: In 1942 as the German blitz pounds London, a serial killer is apparently on the loose. To catch the murderer, renowned pathologist Sir Bernard Spilsbury consults with Agatha Christie. The novel weaves together period details about wartime London and a good deal of information about Christie's life and works.

Other books by the same author:
Road to Purgatory, 2004
Body of Evidence, 2003
Cold Burn, 2003
Chicago Confidential, 2002
Sin City, 2002

Other books you might like:
Henning Boetius, *The Phoenix*, 2001
Francis Cottam, *The Fire Fighter*, 2001
John Gardner, *Bottled Spider*, 2002
John Lawton, *Black Out*, 1995
Molly Lefebure, *Blitz!*, 1998

843

MAX ALLAN COLLINS

Road to Purgatory
(New York: William Morrow, 2004)

Story type: Historical/World War II
Subject(s): Crime and Criminals
Major character(s): Michael O'Sullivan Jr., Military Personnel, Veteran; Patty Ann O'Hara, Young Woman; Eliot Ness, Historical Figure, FBI Agent
Time period(s): 1940s (1942)
Locale(s): Chicago, Illinois

Summary: Collins supplies a sequel to his graphic novel, *Road to Perdition*, that was made into an Oscar-winning 2002 movie. Here, Michael O'Sullivan, Jr., the boy who accompanied his gangster father on a murderous attack on Al Capone's Chicago mob, is now in his early 20s and recently returned home from combat with the war's first Congressional Medal of Honor and without his left eye. While trying to adjust to civilian life with his girlfriend Patty Ann O'Hara, he is asked by Eliot Ness to go undercover to infiltrate what remains of Capone's syndicate. Included is a flashback scene to 1922 showing Michael O'Sullivan, Sr. in action rescuing Irish crime boss John Looney.

Where it's reviewed:
Kirkus Reviews, November 1, 2004, page 1021
Publishers Weekly, November 22, 2004, page 39

Other books by the same author:
The London Blitz Murders, 2004
Body of Evidence, 2003
Florida Getaway, 2003
Sin City, 2002
Angel in Black, 2001

Other books you might like:
Calvin Baker, *Once Two Heroes*, 2003
Melvyn Bragg, *A Son of War*, 2003
Roddy Doyle, *Oh, Play That Thing*, 2004
Terry Gamble, *The Water Dancers*, 2003
Michael C. White, *The Garden of Martyrs*, 2004

844

MARYSE CONDE

Who Slashed Celanire's Throat?
(New York: Atria, 2004)

Story type: Historical/Exotic
Subject(s): Revenge; Cultural Conflict
Major character(s): Celanire, Crime Victim
Time period(s): 1900s
Locale(s): Cote d'Ivoire; Guadeloupe; Peru

Summary: This work was inspired by the actual event of an infant found with her throat cut on the French Caribbean island of Guadeloupe. The novel follows the mysterious Celanire, who has a massive scar across her neck, as she travels to the Ivory Coast, back to her native Guadeloupe, and on to Peru on a mission to learn the truth about her violent past and to exact revenge. The narrative allows Conde to explore the history of the French in the Ivory Coast and in Guadeloupe.

Where it's reviewed:
Kirkus Reviews, July 1, 2004, page 591
Library Journal, September 1, 2004, page 136
Publishers Weekly, July 19, 2004, page 143

Other books by the same author:
Desirada, 2000
Windward Heights, 1999
The Last of the African Kings, 1997
I, Tituba, Black Witch of Salem, 1992
The Children of Segu, 1989

Other books you might like:
Michelle de Kretser, *The Hamilton Case*, 2004
Christopher Nicole, *Mistress of Darkness*, 1976
Jennifer Patrick, *The Night She Died*, 2004
Jean Rhys, *Wide Sargasso Sea*, 1966
Andre Schwarz-Bart, *A Woman Named Solitude*, 1973

845

BRUCE COOK

Young Will

(New York: St. Martin's Press, 2004)

Story type: Historical/Elizabethan
Subject(s): Autobiography; Authors and Writers; Sexual Behavior
Major character(s): William Shakespeare, Historical Figure, Writer; Christopher Marlowe, Historical Figure, Writer; Anne Hathaway, Historical Figure, Spouse (of Shakespeare)
Time period(s): 16th century; 17th century
Locale(s): Stratford-upon-Avon, England; London, England

Summary: *Young Will* is the final novel of Cook, who wrote the popular Sir John Fielding mystery series as Bruce Alexander and who died in 2003. This memoir of William Shakespeare fills the gap in the biographical record of the Bard's youthful activities from 1582 to 1592, between his marriage to Anne Hathaway and his emergence as a London playwright and actor. The aging playwright in 1616 confesses his youthful sins, and they are many and varied. Included is Shakespeare's fateful meeting with Christopher Marlowe, the identity of the "dark lady" of the sonnets and the young man to whom many of the poems were addressed, as well as enough "life experience" to fill many plays. Cook's speculations and inventions are securely anchored by a credible backdrop of Elizabethan England and the London theater scene.

Where it's reviewed:
Booklist, September 1, 2004, page 59
Library Journal, September 1, 2004, page 138
Publishers Weekly, September 20, 2004, page 47

Other books by the same author:
The Sidewalk Hilton, 1994
Rough Cut, 1990
Sex Life, 1978

Other books you might like:
Stephanie Cowell, *The Players*, 1997

John Mortimer, *Will Shakespeare*, 1977
Robert Nye, *The Late Mr. Shakespeare*, 1999
Grace Tiffany, *Will*, 2004
Leonard Tourney, *Time's Fool*, 2004

846

ELLEN COONEY

Gun Ball Hill

(Hanover, New Hampshire: University Press of New England, 2004)

Story type: Historical/American Revolution; Historical/Colonial America
Subject(s): Revolutionary War; Small Town Life; Politics
Major character(s): William Mowlam, Settler; Lavinia Mowlam, Settler; John Avens, Religious (clergyman)
Time period(s): 1770s (1777)
Locale(s): Tibbetston, Maine

Summary: The outbreak of the Revolutionary War is depicted from the perspective of the inhabitants of a small village in Maine. The novel shows William and Lavinia Mowlam's growing commitment to the cause of independence, supported by her brother-in-law John Avens, a Boston clergyman and associate of Paul Revere and Samuel Adams. When the British retaliate against Lavinia's seditious writings, they inflame the region and recruit many to the colonists' cause. Cooney manages to dramatize the issues that led to the Revolutionary War by localizing them in the motives of ordinary people.

Where it's reviewed:
Booklist, August 2004, page 1897
Kirkus Reviews, June 15, 2004, page 549

Other books by the same author:
The White Palazzo, 2002
The Old Ballerina, 1999
All the Way Home, 1984
Small-Town Girl, 1983

Other books you might like:
Paul Bryers, *The Prayer of the Bone*, 2003
J.E. Fender, *Audacity*, 2003
Thomas Fleming, *Dreams of Glory*, 1983
John Gould, *The Wines of Pentagoet*, 1986
Jeff Shaara, *Rise to Rebellion*, 2001

847

M. ALLEN CUNNINGHAM

The Green Age of Asher Witherow

(Denver: Unbridled Books, 2004)

Story type: Historical/American West; Coming-of-Age
Subject(s): Miners and Mining; Coming-of-Age
Major character(s): Asher Witherow, Miner
Time period(s): 19th century (1860s-1880s)
Locale(s): Nortonville, California

Summary: This first novel examines 19th-century life in the coal-mining town of Nortonville, California. This community of mostly Welsh miners is seen from the perspective of young Asher Witherow, whose best friend is accidentally burned to death in front of him. The traumatic event haunts Asher's life and symbolizes the dangerous lot of the miners during the period. The novel excels at painting an authentic and haunting portrait of the harsh conditions in a frontier mining town.

Where it's reviewed:
Booklist, September 1, 2004, page 59
Kirkus Reviews, August 1, 2004, page 703
Library Journal, August 2004, page 66
Publishers Weekly, September 13, 2004, page 56

Other books you might like:
Pat Hughes, *The Breaker Boys*, 2004
Brad Kessler, *Lick Creek*, 2001
Tawni O'Dell, *Coal Run*, 2004
Richard S. Wheeler, *Sun Mountain*, 1999
Lauren Wolk, *Those Who Favor Fire*, 1998

848

JACK DANN

The Rebel: An Imagined Life of James Dean

(New York: William Morrow, 2004)

Story type: Alternate History; Historical/Fantasy
Subject(s): Biography; Actors and Actresses; Movie Industry
Major character(s): James Dean, Historical Figure, Actor; Pier Angeli, Historical Figure, Actress; Marilyn Monroe, Historical Figure, Actress
Time period(s): 1950s; 1960s
Locale(s): United States

Summary: Dann imagines what might have happened if 1950s Hollywood icon James Dean had survived his fatal car crash in 1955. In this fictional biography/fantasy, Dean's troubled relationship with actress Pier Angeli is dramatized, as well as his relationship with Marilyn Monroe, through whom Dean gets involved with the Kennedys. As Dean trades his superstardom for a political career, the novel provides glimpses of a veritable who's who of departed celebrities from odd angles, including Elvis Presley, Jack Kerouac, Frank Sinatra, and Bobby and Jack Kennedy. Often far-fetched and cartoonish, the novel's appeal rests in its outrageously alternate view of American pop and political history.

Where it's reviewed:
Booklist, June 1, 2004, page 1699
Kirkus Reviews, May 15, 2004, page 457
Publishers Weekly, June 21, 2004, page 42

Other books by the same author:
Jubilee, 2003
Visitations, 2003
Dreaming Down-Under, 2001
Counting Coup, 2000
Future War, 1999

Other books you might like:
Leslie Epstein, *Pandaemonium*, 1997
E.J. Gorman, *The Marilyn Tapes*, 1995
Geoff Nicholson, *The Hollywood Dodo*, 2004
Joyce Carol Oates, *Blonde*, 2000
Jerry Stahl, *I, Fatty*, 2004

849

JOHN R. DANN

Song of the Earth

(New York: Forge, 2005)

Story type: Historical/Pre-history; Adventure
Subject(s): Cultures and Customs; Family Relations
Major character(s): Grae, Prehistoric Human, Chieftain
Time period(s): 301st century B.C.
Locale(s): Europe; Africa

Summary: In a prequel to Dann's *Song of the Axe*, this novel, set in 30,000 B.C. chronicles the journey of a prehistoric tribe up from Africa into Europe, led by the tribe's chieftain, Grae. It takes several generations, all led by descendents of Grae, to finally reach their desired home. The novel, mixing legend, myth, and archaeology, shows how primitive peoples survived in the harsh environment they faced.

Other books by the same author:
Song of the Axe, 2001

Other books you might like:
Richard Adams, *Shardik*, 2002
Jean M. Auel, *The Shelters of Stone*, 2003
Kathleen O'Neal Gear, *People of the Raven*, 2004
    W. Michael Gear, co-author
Sue Harrison, *Call Down the Stars*, 2001
Robert J. Sawyer, *Hominids*, 2002

850

LINDSEY DAVIS

Scandal Takes a Holiday

(New York: Mysterious, 2004)

Story type: Historical/Ancient Rome; Mystery
Series: Marcus Didius Falco. Book 16
Subject(s): Mystery and Detective Stories; Roman Empire; Crime and Criminals
Major character(s): Marcus Didius Falco, Detective—Private
Time period(s): 1st century
Locale(s): Rome, Roman Empire; Ostia, Roman Empire

Summary: Ancient Roman private detective Marcus Didius Falco returns to investigate the disappearance of a gossip columnist in the seaport of Ostia. Falco uncovers a pirate-run kidnapping ring, and, as in all of Falco's cases, his extended, troublesome family members get in the way of his investigation. Ancient history purists may be put off by the mystery's deliberate anachronisms, but others who relish a humorous mystery set against a colorful period background should be delighted.

Where it's reviewed:
Booklist, September 1, 2004, page 68
Publishers Weekly, July 12, 2004, page 47

Other books by the same author:
The Accusers, 2004
The Jupiter Myth, 2003
A Body in the Bathhouse, 2002
Ode to a Banker, 2001

Historical

One Virgin Too Many, 2000
Other books you might like:
Ron Burns, *Roman Shadows*, 1992
Colleen McCullough, *The Masters of Rome Series*, 1990-
John Maddox Roberts, *The SPQR Series*, 1990-
Steven Saylor, *The Roma Sub Rosa Series*, 1991-
Marilyn Todd, *Second Act*, 2003

851

CATHY DAY

The Circus in Winter

(Orlando, Florida: Harcourt, 2004)

Story type: Historical/Americana; Collection
Subject(s): Small Town Life; Circus; Short Stories
Time period(s): 19th century; 20th century (1884-1939)
Locale(s): Lima, Indiana

Summary: Day's debut is a collection of linked short stories centered in Lima, Indiana, the winter home of the Great Porter Circus from 1884 to 1939. Based on the author's own background and familiarity with circus life, the stories look through the greasepaint and beyond the roar of the crowd at the complicated and often mundane and tragic lives of the performers, workers, and hangers-on that make up the circus world. Authentic in its evocation of its era and region, the collection provides an often fascinating and moving glimpse at a truly American subculture.

Where it's reviewed:
Booklist, July 2004, page 1817
Library Journal, May 1, 2004, page 139
New York Times Book Review, July 18, 2004, page 21
Publishers Weekly, May 17, 2004, page 33

Other books you might like:
Robert Chalmers, *Fortune's Bastard*, 2004
Robert Hough, *The Final Confession of Mabel Stark*, 2001
Norma Peterson, *Rhonda the Rubber Woman*, 1998
Michael Raleigh, *The Blue Moon Circus*, 2003
Richard Schmitt, *The Aerialist*, 2000

852

LOUIS DE BERNIERES

Birds Without Wings

(New York: Knopf, 2004)

Story type: Historical/World War I
Subject(s): Religious Conflict; War; Cultural Conflict
Major character(s): Kemal Ataturk, Historical Figure, Military Personnel; Rustum Bey, Businessman (merchant); Iskander, Artisan (potter)
Time period(s): 19th century; 20th century
Locale(s): Turkey (Anatolia)

Summary: In his first novel since the internationally acclaimed *Corelli's Mandolin*, de Bernieres chronicles the emergence of modern Turkey and the disasters facing a once ethnically harmonious town in Anatolia brought on by World War I and the breakup of the Ottoman Empire. Ranging from the late 19th century to the 1920s, the novel covers several inter-locking stories, including that of merchant Rustum Bey who kills his faithless wife's lover and has her stoned, and Iskander, a potter whose son supplies a harrowing account of the carnage of Gallipoli. The novel also follows the career of Kemal Ataturk who emerges from war hero to political leader and establishes Turkey as a modern nation. Ambitious and sweeping in its focus, the novel supplies an evocative portrait of its time and place.

Where it's reviewed:
Kirkus Reviews, August 15, 2004, page 759
Publishers Weekly, August 30, 2004, page 34

Other books by the same author:
Corelli's Mandolin, 1994
The Troublesome Offspring of Cardinal Guzman, 1994
The War of Don Emmanuel's Nether Parts, 1990

Other books you might like:
Martin Booth, *Islands of Silence*, 2003
Ann Bridge, *The Dark Moment*, 1952
Carol Edgarian, *Rise the Euphrates*, 1994
Micheline A. Marcom, *Three Apples Fell from Heaven*, 2001
Richard Reinhardt, *The Ashes of Smyrna*, 1971

853

GIDEON DEFOE

The Pirates! In an Adventure with Scientists

(New York: Pantheon, 2004)

Story type: Historical/Victorian
Subject(s): Pirates; Sea Stories; Science
Major character(s): Charles Darwin, Historical Figure, Scientist
Time period(s): 19th century
Locale(s): At Sea; England

Summary: This zany, over-the-top tale recounts what happens when an unnamed pirate captain and his crew mistake Charles Darwin's ship, *Beagle*, for a treasure ship and capture it. The pirate captain befriends Darwin, and together they head back to England to rescue Darwin's brother, who has been abducted by the Bishop of Oxford. Deliberately stuffed with anachronisms, the novel makes little attempt at believability, preferring an absurdist strategy of subverting conventional views.

Where it's reviewed:
Booklist, October 15, 2004, page 389
Kirkus Reviews, August 15, 2004, page 761

Other books you might like:
Nicholas Griffin, *The Requiem Shark*, 2000
Gene Hackman, *Wake of the Perdido Star*, 1999
   Daniel Lenihan, co-author
Roger McDonald, *Mr. Darwin's Shooter*, 1998
Joanna Catherine Scott, *Cassandra Lost*, 2004
Neal Stephenson, *The Confusion*, 2004

854

CHRISTINA DODD

Some Enchanted Evening

(New York: William Morrow, 2004)

Story type: Romance; Historical/Regency
Series: Lost Princesses. Book 1
Subject(s): Romance; Princes and Princesses
Major character(s): Clarice, Royalty (princess); Robert MacKenzie, Nobleman
Time period(s): 1800s
Locale(s): England; Scotland

Summary: The author launches a proposed Lost Princesses trilogy centered on three young women who, after a revolution, flee their small country during the Napoleonic Wars pursued by assassins. In Scotland, Princess Clarice comes to the attention of Robert MacKenzie, Earl of Hepburn. He tests her loyalty to her royal identity and her affection as he recruits her into playing a part in an elaborate scheme of vengeance.

Where it's reviewed:
Booklist, May 15, 2004, page 1603
Kirkus Reviews, May 15, 2004, page 471
Publishers Weekly, May 24, 2004, page 41

Other books by the same author:
Almost Like Being in Love, 2004
One Kiss from You, 2003
Scandalous Again, 2003
Lost in Your Arms, 2002
In My Wildest Dreams, 2001

Other books you might like:
Mary Balogh, *Slightly Dangerous*, 2004
Gaelen Foley, *Devil Takes a Bride*, 2004
Stephanie Laurens, *The Ideal Bride*, 2004
Amanda Quick, *The Paid Companion*, 2004
Julia Quinn, *When He Was Wicked*, 2004

855

SARA DONATI

Fire Along the Sky

(New York: Bantam, 2004)

Story type: Historical/War of 1812; Family Saga
Series: Bonner Family
Subject(s): War of 1812; Frontier and Pioneer Life; Family Relations
Major character(s): Nathaniel Bonner, Spouse (of Elizabeth), Farmer; Elizabeth Bonner, Spouse (of Nathaniel); Lily Bonner, Young Woman
Time period(s): 1810s (1812)
Locale(s): New York; Montreal, Quebec, Canada

Summary: Donati continues the saga of the pioneer Bonner family. The emphasis here is on Elizabeth and Nathaniel's children. Their precocious youngest child, Lily, pursues her artistic aspirations in Montreal; damaged elder daughter Hannah returns to the family's upper New York wilderness homestead; and 18-year-old Daniel Bonner takes up arms against the British. The impact of the War of 1812 on the family is dramatized, including the American invasion of French Canada.

Where it's reviewed:
Booklist, August 2004, page 1868
Publishers Weekly, August 16, 2004, page 44

Other books by the same author:
Lake in the Clouds, 2002
Dawn on a Distant Shore, 2001
Into the Wilderness, 1998

Other books you might like:
Elizabeth Adler, *Crossing the Panther's Path*, 2002
Michelle Black, *An Uncommon Enemy*, 2001
Ernest Hebert, *The Old American*, 2000
Deborah Larsen, *The White*, 2002
Robert Moss, *The Firekeeper*, 1995
David Nevin, *1812*, 1996

856

EMMA DONOGHUE

Life Mask

(Orlando, Florida: Harcourt, 2004)

Story type: Historical/Georgian; Lesbian/Historical
Subject(s): Homosexuality/Lesbianism; Sexual Behavior; Scandal
Major character(s): Eliza Farren, Historical Figure, Actress; Anne Seymour Damer, Historical Figure, Artist (sculptor); Edward Smith Stanley, Historical Figure, Nobleman (Earl of Derby)
Time period(s): 1780s; 1790s (1787-1797)
Locale(s): England

Summary: Based on an actual scandal, Donoghue's novel dramatizes the complicated sexual relations among Lord Derby, actress Eliza Farren, and sculptress Anne Damer. As gossip spreads that Eliza and Anne are enjoying an "unnatural" relationship, the French Revolution produces major upheavals among the British nobility. This is a fascinating look at the sexual and political intrigues among the upper classes in Britain at the end of the 18th century.

Where it's reviewed:
Booklist, September 1, 2004, page 60
Kirkus Reviews, July 1, 2004, page 592
Library Journal, May 1, 2004, page 86
New York Times Book Review, September 26, 2004, page 22
Publishers Weekly, July 26, 2004, page 38

Other books by the same author:
The Woman Who Gave Birth to Rabbits, 2002
Slammerkin, 2000
Kissing the Witch, 1997
Hood, 1995
Stir-Fry, 1994

Other books you might like:
Janet Gleeson, *The Grenadillo Box*, 2004
Sheri Holman, *The Dress Lodger*, 2000
David Liss, *A Spectacle of Corruption*, 2004
Charles Palliser, *The Unburied*, 2000
Sarah Waters, *Affinity*, 2000

Historical

857

CAROLE NELSON DOUGLAS

Spider Dance
(New York: Forge, 2004)

Story type: Historical/Victorian; Mystery
Series: Irene Adler. Book 8
Subject(s): Mystery and Detective Stories
Major character(s): Irene Adler, Detective—Amateur, Singer (opera); Nellie Bly, Journalist, Historical Figure; Nell Huxleigh, Young Woman
Time period(s): 1890s (1899)
Locale(s): New York, New York

Summary: ''That woman'' as she is known in the Sherlock Holmes canon—Irene Adler—returns for another adventure. Assisted by newspaper reporter Nellie Bly and British parson's daughter Nell Huxleigh, Irene continues to investigate her own past, which she cannot remember. Their investigation uncovers a complex political conspiracy, lost treasure, and the affairs of Lola Montez, the notorious Spanish dancer who romanced King Ludwig of Bavaria.

Where it's reviewed:
Publishers Weekly, November 29, 2004, page 27

Other books by the same author:
Femme Fatale, 2003
Castle Rouge, 2002
Chapel Noir, 2001
Irene's Last Waltz, 1994
Good Night, Mr. Holmes, 1990

Other books you might like:
Rhys Bowen, *Death of Riley*, 2002
Michael Chabon, *The Final Solution*, 2004
Laurie R. King, *The Game*, 2004
Michael Kurland, *Sherlock Holmes: The Hidden Years*, 2004
Larry Millett, *The Disappearance of Sherlock Holmes*, 2002

858

SARA DOUGLASS

The Nameless Day
(New York: Tor, 2004)

Story type: Historical/Medieval; Historical/Fantasy
Series: Crucible. Book 1
Subject(s): Middle Ages; Religious Life; Plague
Major character(s): Brother Thomas Neville, Religious (Dominican friar); Michael, Biblical Figure, Angel
Time period(s): 14th century (1378)
Locale(s): Europe

Summary: Mixing fantasy and history, Douglass imagines medieval Europe under the grip of the Black Death and the brutality of the Hundred Years War in the first installment of a proposed trilogy. A Dominican friar, Brother Thomas Neville, is summoned by St. Michael to combat the evil of the times that takes the form of shapeshifting demons infiltrating normal human society. Neville must round up the demons and help to restore order. Despite the reliance on supernatural

elements, the novel is firmly anchored in the cultural and historical details of 14th-century Europe.

Where it's reviewed:
Booklist, July 2004, page 1828
Library Journal, June 15, 2004, page 62
Publishers Weekly, June 21, 2004, page 47

Other books by the same author:
Gods' Concubine, 2004
Sinner, 2004
Beyond the Hanging Wall, 2003
Threshold, 2003
Starman, 2002

Other books you might like:
Ann Benson, *The Burning Road*, 1999
Geraldine Brooks, *Year of Wonder*, 2001
Jeff Long, *Year Zero*, 2002
Peter Millar, *Bleak Midwinter*, 2001
Steve White, *Demon's Gate*, 2004

859

SARA DOUGLASS

The Wounded Hawk
(New York: Tor, 2005)

Story type: Historical/Medieval; Historical/Fantasy
Series: Crucible. Book Two
Subject(s): Middle Ages; Religious Life; Plague
Major character(s): Brother Thomas Neville, Religious (former Dominican friar); Michael, Biblical Figure, Angel; Richard II, Ruler (King of England), Historical Figure
Time period(s): 14th century
Locale(s): Europe

Summary: Thomas Neville, a former Dominican friar, has been ordered by the Archangel Michael to help defeat the forces of hell who have invaded the world. His efforts bring him into conflict with Richard II and Henry Bolinbroke, while other historical figures, such as John of Gaunt and Joan of Arc, also appear.

Where it's reviewed:
Publishers Weekly, December 20, 2004, page 41

Other books by the same author:
Gods' Concubine, 2004
Sinner, 2004
The Nameless Day, 2004
Beyond the Hanging Wall, 2003
Hades' Daughter, 2003

Other books you might like:
Ann Benson, *The Burning Road*, 1999
Geraldine Brooks, *Year of Wonder*, 2001
Jeff Long, *Year Zero*, 2002
Peter Millar, *Bleak Midwinter*, 2001
Steve White, *Demon's Gate*, 2004

860

RODDY DOYLE

Oh, Play That Thing

(New York: Viking, 2004)

Story type: Historical/Roaring Twenties
Series: Last Roundup. Book 2
Subject(s): Music and Musicians
Major character(s): Henry Smart, Revolutionary (Irish); Louis Armstrong, Historical Figure, Musician
Time period(s): 1920s
Locale(s): New York, New York; Chicago, Illinois

Summary: Book two of Doyle's the Last Roundup series, following the acclaimed *A Star Called Henry*, sends former IRA assassin Henry Smart to America. Arriving in New York City in 1924, Henry tries advertising, bootlegging, pornography, and unlicensed dentistry before heading to Chicago where he becomes the manager of the young Louis Armstrong. As the duo ascend the burgeoning jazz scene in Chicago and New York, Smart's past comes back to haunt him. Somewhat overburdened by too many twists and turns of the plot and a crowded cast of characters who disappear too soon from attention, the novel is nevertheless full of Doyle's characteristic vitality and convincing animation of a past time and place.

Where it's reviewed:
Booklist, September 1, 2004, page 4
Library Journal, November 15, 2004, page 60
New York Times Book Review, November 14, 2004, page 62
Publishers Weekly, September 20, 2004, page 43

Other books by the same author:
Rory & Ita, 2002
A Star Called Henry, 2000
The Woman Who Walked into Doors, 1996
Paddy Clarke, Ha-Ha-Ha, 1993
The Van, 1991

Other books you might like:
Kevin Baker, *Dreamland*, 1999
Thomas Fleming, *A Passionate Girl*, 2004
Patrick Neate, *Twelve Bar Blues*, 2001
Frederick Turner, *1929*, 2003
Michael C. White, *The Garden of Martyrs*, 2004

861

JOAN DRUETT

A Watery Grave

(New York: St. Martin's Minotaur, 2004)

Story type: Mystery; Historical/Victorian
Series: Wiki Coffin. Book 1
Subject(s): Mystery and Detective Stories; Sea Stories
Major character(s): William ''Wiki'' Coffin, Linguist, Sailor; George Rochester, Sea Captain
Time period(s): 1830s (1838)
Locale(s): New Zealand; *Swallow*, At Sea; Virginia

Summary: Druett launches a historical mystery series based on the actual 1838-1842 United States South Seas Exploring Expedition. The novel introduces William ''Wiki'' Coffin, the son of a Maori mother and an American seafaring father who is recruited by Captain George Rochester to serve as the official translator on the voyage. Eventually cleared of the charge of murdering the wife of the expedition's astronomer, Coffin ships out, convinced that the killer is along on the voyage. The author is a respected maritime historian, and her expertise is evident in a great start to a series combining historical mystery and sea adventure.

Where it's reviewed:
Booklist, September 1, 2004, page 68
Kirkus Reviews, August 1, 2004, page 715
Library Journal, August 2004, page 59
Publishers Weekly, July 26, 2004, page 41

Other books by the same author:
Abigail, 1988

Other books you might like:
Clare Dudman, *One Day the Ice Will Reveal All Its Dead*, 2004
Stephanie Johnson, *Belief*, 2002
Patrick O'Brian, *The Aubrey/Maturin Series*, 1970-2004
Wilder Perkins, *Hoare and the Matter of Treason*, 2001
Diane Smith, *Pictures from an Expedition*, 2002

862

CAROLA DUNN

A Mourning Wedding

(New York: St. Martin's Minotaur, 2004)

Story type: Historical/Roaring Twenties; Mystery
Series: Daisy Dalrymple. Book 13
Subject(s): Mystery and Detective Stories; Crime and Criminals; Weddings
Major character(s): Daisy Dalrymple, Journalist, Detective—Amateur; Alec Fletcher, Police Officer, Spouse (of Daisy); Lucy Fotheringay, Gentlewoman
Time period(s): 1920s
Locale(s): Cambridgeshire, England

Summary: Daisy Dalrymple's childhood friend Lucy Fotheringay is about to be married at her family's country estate in rural Cambridgeshire. Daisy must solve the murder of Lady Eva Devenish, Lucy's great-aunt, who is found strangled in her bed, and the death of Lucy's uncle. Along with her husband, Scotland Yard Detective Alec Fletcher, Daisy must also cope with her pregnancy and try to make sense of the mysterious reluctance of her friend about her upcoming wedding.

Where it's reviewed:
Booklist, October 1, 2004, page 60
Library Journal, November 1, 2004, page 60

Other books by the same author:
Die Laughing, 2003
The Case of the Murdered Muckraker, 2002
To Davy Jones Below, 2001
Rattle His Bones, 2000
Styx and Stones, 1999

Historical

Other books you might like:
Dianne Day, *The Fremont Jones Series*, 1995-
Gillian Linscott, *The Nell Bray Series*, 1991-
Annette Meyers, *Murder Me Now*, 2001
Anne Perry, *Seven Dials*, 2003
David Roberts, *Dangerous Sea*, 2003

863

SUZANNAH DUNN

The Queen of Subtleties
(New York: William Morrow, 2004)

Story type: Historical/Renaissance
Subject(s): Kings, Queens, Rulers, etc.; Biography; Marriage
Major character(s): Anne Boleyn, Historical Figure, Royalty; Henry VIII, Historical Figure, Ruler (King of England); Lucy Cornwallis, Baker (confectioner)
Time period(s): 16th century
Locale(s): England

Summary: Dunn animates the rise and fall of Anne Boleyn by alternating between Anne's own account of her relationship with Henry VIII and the perspective of Lucy Cornwallis, confectioner to the king. Their link is a court musician who is loved by the women. Both supply fascinating access to the world of the Tudor court, its intrigues, rivalries, and dangers, and the role of women during the time, among the upper reaches of society and also at the lower.

Where it's reviewed:
Kirkus Reviews, August 15, 2004, page 761
Library Journal, September 1, 2004, page 138
Publishers Weekly, September 20, 2004, page 44

Other books by the same author:
Darker Days than Usual, 1990

Other books you might like:
Margaret George, *The Autobiography of Henry VIII*, 1986
Philippa Gregory, *The Other Boleyn Girl*, 2001
Francis Hackett, *Queen Anne Boleyn*, 1939
Norah Lofts, *The Concubine*, 1963
Robin Maxwell, *The Secret Diary of Anne Boleyn*, 1997

864

DAVID ANTHONY DURHAM

Pride of Carthage
(New York: Doubleday, 2005)

Story type: Historical/Ancient Rome
Subject(s): Ancient History; Biography; War
Major character(s): Hannibal, Historical Figure, Military Personnel; Imco Vaca, Military Personnel; Aradna, Young Woman
Time period(s): 3rd century B.C.; 2nd century B.C. (218-183 B.C.)
Locale(s): Roman Empire; Mediterranean

Summary: After two critically well-received novels about African-American life in the 19th century, Durham shifts his focus to the story of Hannibal and his march on Rome in the Second Punic War. In 218 B.C., Hannibal leads an army of 100,000 over the Pyrenees and through the Alps to invade the Roman Empire and wins victories over Roman forces at Lake Trasimene and at Cannae before his eventual defeat before the gates of Rome. Durham chronicles the military campaign and provides an intimate portrait of its commander. The novel also looks at events from the perspective of the soldier Imco Vaca and Aradna, a camp follower. First rate historical fiction.

Where it's reviewed:
Kirkus Reviews, October 15, 2004, page 976
Library Journal, November 1, 2004, page 72
Publishers Weekly, October 18, 2004, page 45

Other books by the same author:
Walk through Darkness, 2002
Gabriel's Story, 2001

Other books you might like:
Bryher, *The Coin of Carthage*, 1963
Robert S. Capps, *Hannibal's Lieutenant*, 1994
Ross Leckie, *Hannibal*, 1996
Ross Leckie, *Scipio*, 1998
John Maddox Roberts, *Hannibal's Children*, 2002

865

INDIA EDGHILL

Wisdom's Daughter
(New York: St. Martin's Press, 2004)

Story type: Legend
Subject(s): Biblical Fiction; Kings, Queens, Rulers, etc.; Jews
Major character(s): Solomon, Historical Figure (King of Israel), Biblical Figure; Bilqis, Historical Figure, Ruler (Queen of Sheba)
Time period(s): 10th century B.C.
Locale(s): Jerusalem, Israel

Summary: Edghill's story chronicles the relationship between King Solomon and Bilqis, Queen of Sheba. Weaving together numerous perspectives, including several of Solomon's 40 wives and his war general, the novel shows why the Queen of Sheba comes to Jerusalem and is able to win Solomon's love. An atmospheric tale, the emphasis here is on the court intrigue that besets Solomon's reign.

Where it's reviewed:
Booklist, September 15, 2004, page 207
Kirkus Reviews, August 15, 2004, page 761

Other books by the same author:
Queenmaker, 2002

Other books you might like:
Aliette Armel, *Love, the Painter's Wife and the Queen of Sheba*, 2004
Anita Diamant, *The Red Tent*, 1997
Roberta Kells Dorr, *The Queen of Sheba*, 1990
Rebecca Kohn, *The Gilded Chamber*, 2004
Faye Levine, *Solomon & Sheba*, 1980

866
MARGARET ELPHINSTONE
Voyageurs
(New York: Canongate, 2004)

Story type: Historical/War of 1812

Subject(s): Frontier, Canada; Frontier and Pioneer Life; War of 1812

Major character(s): Mark Greenhow, Young Man, Relative (Rachel's brother); Rachel Greenhow, Religious (Quaker missionary), Relative (Mark's sister)

Time period(s): 1810s (1811-1812)

Locale(s): United States; Canada; England

Summary: Set against a backdrop of the War of 1812, Elphinstone's novel describes the adventures of Englishman Mark Greenhow who ventures into the wilderness to find his Quaker missionary sister Rachel, who has disappeared in an Indian raid. As the war breaks out, Mark finds his pacifism tested as he accompanies a contingent of voyageurs, frontiersmen who navigate the North American fur-trade route by canoe, into the wild area along the U.S.-Canadian border.

Where it's reviewed:
Booklist, August 2004, page 1897
Kirkus Reviews, June 1, 2004, page 508
Library Journal, August 2004, page 66
Publishers Weekly, August 16, 2004, page 45

Other books you might like:
Michelle Black, *An Uncommon Enemy*, 2001
Edward Blair, *A Journey to the Interior*, 2001
Deborah Larsen, *The White*, 2002
David Nevin, *1812*, 1996
Willard M. Wallace, *Jonathan Dearborn*, 1967

867
ELIZABETH FRANK
Cheat and Charmer
(New York: Random House, 2004)

Story type: Political

Subject(s): Movie Industry; Communism

Major character(s): Dinah Lasker, Spouse (of Jake); Jake Lasker, Director, Producer

Time period(s): 1950s

Locale(s): Hollywood, California; Washington, District of Columbia; Paris, France

Summary: Frank, who won a Pulitzer Prize for her biography of poet Louise Bogan, offers a novel documenting the cultural and political life in Hollywood during the 1950s Red Scare. The narrative is centered by Dinah Lasker and her movie producer husband Jake. When she is called to name names based on her brief association with the Communist Party, Dinah faces the dilemma of staying true to her principles and allowing her husband to be blacklisted, or betraying her friends. The novel looks at the impact of her decision, while supplying a knowing depiction of its era.

Where it's reviewed:
Booklist, September 1, 2004, page 6

Kirkus Reviews, August 15, 2004, page 762
Library Journal, September 1, 2004, page 139
Publishers Weekly, August 16, 2004, page 40

Other books you might like:
William F. Buckley, *The Redhunter*, 1999
Jack Dann, *The Rebel: An Imagined Life of James Dean*, 2004
Leslie Epstein, *Pandaemonium*, 1997
Jerry Stahl, *I, Fatty*, 2004
Gore Vidal, *The Golden Age*, 1998

868
MARGARET FRAZER
The Widow's Tale
(New York: Berkley Prime Crime, 2005)

Story type: Historical/Medieval; Mystery

Series: Dame Frevisse. Book 14

Subject(s): Mystery and Detective Stories; Middle Ages

Major character(s): Dame Frevisse, Religious (nun); Cristiana, Widow(er); Henry VI, Historical Figure, Ruler (King of England)

Time period(s): 15th century (1449)

Locale(s): England

Summary: Dame Frevisse comes to the aid of a widow, Cristiana, who has been banished to St. Frideswide's nunnery and forced to undergo severe punishment for unspecified sins. She actually holds an important secret with significant political implications for the reign of King Henry VI, who comes on the scene for the novel's exciting climax.

Where it's reviewed:
Publishers Weekly, December 20, 2004, page 40

Other books by the same author:
The Hunter's Tale, 2004
The Bastard's Tale, 2003
The Clerk's Tale, 2002
The Squire's Tale, 2000
The Reeve's Tale, 1999
The Prioress' Tale, 1997

Other books you might like:
Edward Marston, *The Domesday Book Series*, 1993-
Ian Morson, *The William Falconer Series*, 1994-
Ellis Peters, *The Brother Cadfael Series*, 1977-1994
Priscilla Royal, *Tyrant of the Mind*, 2004
Peter Tremayne, *The Sister Fidelma Series*, 1994-

869
DAVID FULMER
Jass
(Orlando, Florida: Harcourt, 2004)

Story type: Historical/Americana; Mystery

Subject(s): Music and Musicians; Mystery and Detective Stories

Major character(s): Valentin St. Cyr, Detective—Private; Tom Anderson, Political Figure, Historical Figure

Time period(s): 1900s

Locale(s): New Orleans, Louisiana

Summary: Fulmer continues his atmospheric mystery series set in New Orleans' red-light district of Storyville in the early years of the 20th century. Creole detective Valentin St. Cyr investigates the brutal murders of four jazz musicians, while working for Tom Anderson, the so-called "King of Storyville." Historical figures, such as jazz great Jelly Roll Morton and New Orleans' legendary madam Miss Lulu, make appearances.

Where it's reviewed:
Kirkus Reviews, November 1, 2004, page 1030
Publishers Weekly, November 29, 2004, page 26

Other books by the same author:
Chasing the Devil's Tail, 2001

Other books you might like:
Kenneth Abel, *Cold Steel Rain*, 2000
Jonathan Kellerman, *A Cold Heart*, 2003
Robert Skinner, *Pale Shadow*, 2001
Julie Smith, *Mean Woman Blues*, 2003
Penelope Williamson, *Wages of Sin*, 2004

870

ALAN FURST

Dark Voyage

(New York: Random House, 2004)

Story type: Historical/World War II; Espionage
Subject(s): World War II; Espionage; Sea Stories
Major character(s): Eric DeHaan, Sea Captain, Spy
Time period(s): 1940s (1941)
Locale(s): *Noordendam*, At Sea; Mediterranean; Lisbon, Portugal

Summary: Dutch sea captain Eric DeHaan is recruited by Dutch Naval Intelligence to smuggle arms and spies in his unarmed tramp freighter past the watchful German Navy to Allied strongholds. Disguising his ship as a neutral Spanish freighter, DeHaan is shown taking British commandos on a North African raid, delivering ammunition to the beleaguered British garrison on Crete, and finally involved on a secret mission to Sweden's Baltic coast. Furst authentically captures shipboard life and the exotic ports and their back alleys along the way.

Where it's reviewed:
Booklist, July 2004, page 1798
Kirkus Reviews, July 1, 2004, page 594
Library Journal, July 2004, page 69
New York Times Book Review, August 15, 2004, page 7
Publishers Weekly, July 19, 2004, page 143

Other books by the same author:
Blood of Victory, 2002
Kingdom of Shadows, 2001
Red Gold, 1999
The World at Night, 1996
The Polish Officer, 1995

Other books you might like:
Ken Follett, *Jackdaws*, 2001
Joseph Kanon, *The Good German*, 2001
Lily Powell, *The Devil in Buenos Aires*, 2004

Daniel Silva, *The English Assassin*, 2002
Robert Wilson, *The Company of Strangers*, 2001

871

NICOLE GALLAND

The Fool's Tale

(New York: William Morrow, 2004)

Story type: Historical/Medieval
Subject(s): Middle Ages; Romance; Kings, Queens, Rulers, etc.
Major character(s): Isabel Mortimer, Royalty, Spouse (of Maelgwyn); Maelgwyn ap Cadwallon, Ruler (king), Spouse (of Isabel); Gwirion, Entertainer (jester)
Time period(s): 12th century
Locale(s): Wales

Summary: Screenwriter Galland's debut novel is a historical romance about a Welsh queen's love affair with a court jester. Isabel Mortimer is a young Englishwoman in a political marriage with King Maelgwyn ap Cadwallon of Wales. At first humiliated by the sharp wit of her husband's best friend and jester, Gwirion, Isabel eventually falls in love with him, and the pair must face the consequences of their illicit passion.

Where it's reviewed:
Booklist, November 15, 2004, page 553
Kirkus Reviews, November 15, 2004, page 1061

Other books you might like:
Elizabeth Chadwick, *The Marsh King's Daughter*, 2000
Virginia Henley, *The Marriage Bed*, 2000
Laura Kinsale, *For My Lady's Heart*, 1993
Morgan Llywelyn, *The Wind from Hastings*, 1978
Sharon Kay Penman, *Here Be Dragons*, 1985

872

R. GARCIA Y ROBERTSON

White Rose

(New York: Forge, 2004)

Story type: Historical/Medieval; Time Travel
Series: War of the Roses. Book 3
Subject(s): Time Travel; Romance
Major character(s): Robyn Stafford, Time Traveler; Edward Plantagenet, Royalty, Historical Figure; Owen Tudor, Historical Figure, Nobleman
Time period(s): 15th century (1461); 21st century
Locale(s): Wales; Hollywood, California

Summary: Time traveling Hollywood executive Robyn Stafford is now Lady Robyn of Pontefract, and is engaged to marry Edward Plantagenet, the Prince of Wales. Finding herself the captive of Owen Tudor, Edward's sworn enemy, Robyn must use all her wiles to gain her freedom, reunite with Edward, and contend with his many other deadly enemies. This is high-speed, page-turning costume adventure, mixing in historical details amid the romance.

Where it's reviewed:
Kirkus Reviews, August 15, 2004, page 762

Other books by the same author:
Lady Robyn, 2003
Knight Errant, 2001
American Woman, 1998
The Spiral Dance, 1991

Other books you might like:
Michael Crichton, *Timeline*, 1999
Diana Gabaldon, *The Fiery Cross*, 2001
Diana Gabaldon, *Voyager*, 1994
Linda Lael Miller, *Knights*, 1996
Diana Norman, *Fitzempress' Law*, 1980

873

KATHLEEN O'NEAL GEAR
W. MICHAEL GEAR, Co-Author

People of the Raven

(New York: Forge, 2004)

Story type: Historical/Pre-history
Series: First North Americans. Book 12
Subject(s): Indians of North America; Pre-Columbian History; Cultures and Customs
Major character(s): Rain Bear, Prehistoric Human, Chieftain; Evening Star, Prehistoric Human, Slave (escaped)
Time period(s): 10th century B.C. (c. 9300 B.C.)
Locale(s): Pacific Northwest, North America

Summary: Archaeologists W. Michael and Kathleen Gear supply another chapter in their First North Americans series chronicling prehistoric life. As inhabitants of North America struggle with the massive environmental changes of the Ice Age, Rain Bear, the chief of the Raven People, is faced with a dilemma. Should he provide sanctuary for Evening Star, an escaped slave from the North Wind People, his tribe's sworn enemies, or send her back to be tortured and possibly killed? Once again, the authors combine a dramatic story with credible details of prehistoric life.

Other books by the same author:
Dark Inheritance, 2001
The Summoning God, 2000
The Visitant, 1999

Other books you might like:
Jean M. Auel, *The Shelters of Stone*, 2003
W. Michael Gear, *The First North Americans Series*, 1990- Kathleen O'Neal Gear, co-author
Sue Harrison, *Call Down the Stars*, 2001
Charlotte Prentiss, *People of the Mesa*, 1995
William Sarabande, *The First Americans Series*, 1987-

874

FRANCISCO GOLDMAN

The Divine Husband

(New York: Atlantic Monthly, 2004)

Story type: Historical/Exotic
Subject(s): Biography

Major character(s): Jose Marti, Historical Figure, Writer (poet); Maria de las Nieves, Religious (former nun); Francisca "Paquita" Aparicio, Religious (former nun)
Time period(s): 19th century
Locale(s): Central America

Summary: Goldman imagines what might have happened during the year or so that Cuban poet and revolutionary Jose Marti spent in Guatemala. Maria de las Nieves, a former nun, gives birth to two children out of wedlock, and Marti, along with Maria's other suitors, are weighed as the suspected father. Meanwhile, the fate of an unnamed Central American country is dramatized in the experiences of Maria's best friend, Francisca "Paquita" Aparicio, who marries a revolutionary leader and becomes the country's first lady.

Where it's reviewed:
Booklist, August 2004, page 1899
Kirkus Reviews, June 1, 2004, page 509
Library Journal, July 2004, page 70
New York Times Book Review, September 26, 2004, page 29
Publishers Weekly, June 14, 2004, page 41

Other books by the same author:
The Ordinary Seaman, 1997
The Long Night of White Chickens, 1992

Other books you might like:
Carlos Fuentes, *The Years with Laura Diaz*, 2000
Gabriel Garcia Marquez, *The Autumn of the Patriarch*, 1992
Ana Menendez, *Loving Che*, 2003
Lily Tuck, *The News from Paraguay*, 2004
Mario Vargas Llosa, *The Feast of the Goat*, 2001

875

PIP GRANGER

Trouble in Paradise

(Scottsdale, Arizona: Poisoned Pen Press, 2005)

Story type: Mystery; Historical/World War II
Subject(s): Mystery and Detective Stories; City and Town Life; Family Relations
Major character(s): Zelda Fluck, Spouse; Zinnia Makepeace, Healer
Time period(s): 1940s (1945)
Locale(s): London, England

Summary: The prequel to the author's *Not All Tarts Are Apple* and *The Widow Ginger* is set in the aftermath of World War II in the neighborhood of Paradise Gardens in London's East End. For Zelda Fluck, the war's end means a return home of her abusive husband, Charlie. Meanwhile, Zelda's friend and healer, Zinnia Makepeace, is being threatened. The novel supplies a vivid look at London life following the war.

Where it's reviewed:
Publishers Weekly, December 20, 2004, page 40

Other books by the same author:
The Widow Ginger, 2003
Not All Tarts Are Apple, 2002

Other books you might like:
Jill Barnett, *Sentimental Journey*, 2001
Melvyn Bragg, *The Soldier's Return*, 2002

Historical

Mick Jackson, *Five Boys*, 2002
Christopher Petit, *Robinson*, 1994
Fay Weldon, *Rhode Island Blues*, 2000

876

JENNIFER HAIGH

Baker Towers

(New York: William Morrow, 2005)

Story type: Family Saga
Subject(s): Family Relations; Small Town Life; Miners and Mining
Major character(s): Rose Novak, Parent, Widow(er); Georgie Novak, Veteran (World War II); Dorothy Novak, Young Woman
Time period(s): 1940s
Locale(s): Bakerton, Pennsylvania

Summary: Set in a post-World War II era Pennsylvania mining town, Haigh's novel looks at the struggles of the Novak family. Rose Novak's husband has died; her eldest son Georgie has returned from the war; daughter Dorothy gives up her glamorous job in Washington; while another daughter comes home to care for the ailing Rose and the two youngest daughters. The climax of the novel is a mining disaster that unites the entire family.

Where it's reviewed:
Booklist, November 1, 2004, page 464
Library Journal, December 1, 2004, page 100
Publishers Weekly, November 22, 2004, page 38

Other books by the same author:
Mrs. Kimble, 2003

Other books you might like:
Alice Adams, *After the War*, 2000
Pat Hughes, *The Baker Boys*, 2004
Tawni O'Dell, *Coal Run*, 2004
Sharon Rolens, *Worthy's Town*, 2000
Amy Tan, *The Bonesetter's Daughter*, 2001

877

BARBARA HAMBLY

Dead Water

(New York: Bantam, 2004)

Story type: Mystery; Historical/Antebellum American South
Series: Benjamin January. Book 8
Subject(s): Mystery and Detective Stories; African Americans; Rivers
Major character(s): Benjamin January, Slave (former), Detective—Amateur; Rose January, Spouse (of Benjamin)
Time period(s): 1830s (1836)
Locale(s): New Orleans, Louisiana; Mississippi River

Summary: In this installment of Hambly's antebellum mystery series featuring former slave Benjamin January, the sleuth and his wife, Rose, pursue a bank employee who has absconded with their life savings, posing as slaves aboard an upriver Mississippi steamboat. When their quarry is killed, the pair must sort out the culprit among a colorful collection of slave dealers, abolitionists, and sundry passengers.

Where it's reviewed:
Booklist, July 2004, page 1798
Kirkus Reviews, June 1, 2004, page 519
Publishers Weekly, July 5, 2004, page 41

Other books by the same author:
Days of the Dead, 2003
Wet Grave, 2002
Die upon a Kiss, 2001
Sold Down the River, 2000
Graveyard Dust, 1999

Other books you might like:
Darren Coleman, *Before I Let Go*, 2004
Peter J. Heck, *Death on the Mississippi*, 1995
Michael Killian, *A Grave at Glorieta*, 2002
Ann McMillan, *The Civil War Mystery Series*, 1999-
Josh Russell, *Yellow Jack*, 1999

878

BARBARA HAMBLY

The Emancipator's Wife

(New York: Bantam, 2004)

Story type: Historical/American Civil War
Subject(s): Biography; Politics; Civil War
Major character(s): Mary Todd Lincoln, Historical Figure, Spouse (of Abraham Lincoln); Abraham Lincoln, Historical Figure, Political Figure
Time period(s): 19th century
Locale(s): United States

Summary: Hambly offers a fictional biography of Mary Todd Lincoln, one of the most maligned and controversial of America's First Ladies. The novel treats her upbringing in a prominent Lexington, Kentucky, home and marriage to a country lawyer with limited prospects. The Lincolns' life together would be marred by personal tragedies, as well as the Civil War that seriously affected Mrs. Lincoln's mental stability. Ultimately charged with lunacy by her son in 1875, Mary Todd Lincoln is shown revisiting key scenes from her past to come to terms with them and herself.

Other books by the same author:
Dead Water, 2004
Days of the Dead, 2003
Wet Grave, 2002
Die upon a Kiss, 2001
Sold Down the River, 2000

Other books you might like:
Anne Colver, *Mr. Lincoln's Wife*, 1943
William Safire, *Freedom*, 1987
Richard Slotkin, *Abe*, 2000
Irving Stone, *Love Is Eternal*, 1954
Gore Vidal, *Lincoln*, 1984

879

FRED HARRIS

Following the Harvest

(Norman: University of Oklahoma Press, 2004)

Story type: Historical/World War II; Coming-of-Age
Subject(s): Small Town Life; Farm Life; Migrant Labor
Major character(s): Will Haley, Worker (on harvesting crew), Teenager
Time period(s): 1940s (1943)
Locale(s): Vernon, Oklahoma; Nebraska; Rhame, North Dakota

Summary: Fred Harris, a former U.S. senator from Oklahoma and presidential candidate, has authored two well-received period mysteries. Here he presents a tale of life in a small southwestern Oklahoma town during World War II and the lot of the traveling wheat harvesters. Will Haley is a teenager who follows the wheat harvest through Oklahoma, Nebraska, and North Dakota. His experiences form a vivid coming-of-age lesson, set against a believable period and regional backdrop.

Where it's reviewed:
Publishers Weekly, September 27, 2004, page 37

Other books by the same author:
Easy Pickin's, 2000
Coyote Revenge, 1999

Other books you might like:
Clancy Carlile, *Children of the Dust*, 1995
Robert Gatewood, *The Sound of the Trees*, 2002
Stephen Hunter, *Hot Springs*, 2000
Joe R. Lansdale, *The Bottoms*, 2000
Heather Parkinson, *Across Open Ground*, 2002

880

DAVID HEWSON

Lucifer's Shadow

(New York: Delacorte, 2004)

Story type: Historical/Georgian
Subject(s): Suspense; Libraries; Music and Musicians
Major character(s): Daniel Forster, Scholar
Time period(s): 1730s; 21st century
Locale(s): Venice, Italy

Summary: Alternating between the present and 18th-century Venice, this thriller turns on a concerto composed by a young Jewish woman in 1733 and her unique violin. A present-day English scholar, Daniel Forster, slowly uncovers the secret of the concerto and the violin; while in the past, another naive young man gets involved with the source of a centuries-old intrigue. Despite the jarring time shifts, this is an ingenious puzzle in which past and present neatly dovetail, and all is sustained by Venice's powerful spell.

Where it's reviewed:
Booklist, May 1, 2004, page 1504

Other books by the same author:
A Season for the Dead, 2004

Solstice, 1999

Other books you might like:
James Gollin, *Eliza's Galiardo*, 1983
Tanith Lee, *Venus Preserved*, 2003
Michelle Louric, *The Floating Book*, 2003
Arturo Perez-Reverte, *The Flanders Panel*, 1994
Edward Sklepowich, *The Last Gondola*, 2003

881

ALICE HOFFMAN

Blackbird House

(New York: Doubleday, 2004)

Story type: Family Saga; Collection
Subject(s): Short Stories
Time period(s): Multiple Time Periods (18th-20th centuries)
Locale(s): Cape Cod, Massachusetts

Summary: Hoffman's collection of interconnected short stories is centered by a Cape Cod farmhouse whose history is told through its inhabitants from colonial American days through the 19th and 20th centuries. Woven into each atmospheric story is the haunting presence of a white blackbird, a fitting emblem for the oddity and grief of the stories' characters who must face adversity with a stoical determination.

Where it's reviewed:
Booklist, May 15, 2004, page 1579
Kirkus Reviews, May 15, 2004, page 461
Library Journal, July 2004, page 76
Publishers Weekly, June 21, 2004, page 42

Other books by the same author:
Seventh Heaven, 2003
The Probable Future, 2003
The Drowning Season, 2002
Blue Diary, 2001
The River King, 2000

Other books you might like:
Andrew Buckley, *The Bostoner*, 2000
Sarah Challis, *Blackthorn Winter*, 2004
Mindy Friddle, *The Garden Angel*, 2004
William Martin, *Cape Cod*, 1991
Nancy Zaroulis, *Massachusetts*, 1991

882

ROY HOFFMAN

Chicken Dreaming Corn

(Athens: University of Georgia Press, 2004)

Story type: Historical/World War I; Historical/Roaring Twenties
Subject(s): Jews
Major character(s): Morris Kleinman, Businessman, Spouse (of Miriam); Miriam Kleinman, Spouse (of Morris)
Time period(s): 20th century (1910s-1940s)
Locale(s): Mobile, Alabama

Summary: This is a charming novel about a Romanian Jew who settles in Mobile, Alabama. Morris Kleinman is driven

Historical

from his native country by pogroms. He meets his future wife, Miriam, before opening a general store in Mobile in 1907. The novel chronicles the Kleinman family fortunes through both world wars. This is an engaging look at Southern life and culture from an interesting, immigrant Jewish perspective.

Where it's reviewed:
Kirkus Reviews, August 1, 2004, page 705

Other books by the same author:
Almost Family, 1983

Other books you might like:
Hortense Calisher, *Tattoo for a Slave*, 2004
Jack Kerley, *The Hundredth Man*, 2004
Barth Landor, *A Week in Winter*, 2004
Joyce Carol Oates, *The Tattooed Girl*, 2003
Philip Roth, *The Plot Against America*, 2004

883

RICHARD HOYT

Sonja's Run
(New York: Forge, 2005)

Story type: Historical/Victorian; Adventure
Subject(s): Adventure and Adventurers; Russian Empire
Major character(s): Sonja Sankova, Writer (poet); Peter "Colonel Cut" Koslov, Adventurer; Jack Sandt, Photographer
Time period(s): 1850s
Locale(s): Russia

Summary: This spirited adventure tale is the story of half-Chinese, half-Russian poet Sonja Sankova. She falls in love with American photographer Jack Sandt, and runs afoul of Peter "Colonel Cut" Koslov, the infamous adventurer with a necklace of ears taken from the serfs and Jews he has killed. Koslov chases the couple across Russia in a series of exciting encounters. Meticulously researched in its period details, the novel features appearances by such historical figures as Tsar Nicholas I, Karl Marx, and writer Ivan Turgenev.

Other books by the same author:
Snake Eyes, 1995
Marimba, 1992
Darwin's Secret, 1989
Fish Story, 1985
Head of State, 1985

Other books you might like:
Thalassa Ali, *A Singular Hostage*, 2002
George MacDonald Fraser, *The Flashman Series*, 1969-
Philip Hensher, *The Mulberry Empire*, 2002
Michael, Prince of Greece, *The White Night of St. Petersburg*, 2004
Jean-Christophe Rufin, *The Siege of Isfahan*, 2001

884

LEE IRBY

7,000 Clams
(New York: Doubleday, 2004)

Story type: Historical/Roaring Twenties
Subject(s): Crime and Criminals; Sports/Baseball
Major character(s): Babe Ruth, Historical Figure, Sports Figure (baseball player); Frank Hearn, Criminal
Time period(s): 1920s
Locale(s): St. Petersburg, Florida; New Jersey

Summary: In this atmospheric crime novel, set in the 1920s during spring training for the Yankees in St. Petersburg, Florida, down-on-his-luck bootlegger and enforcer Frank Hearn acquires an I.O.U. for $7,000 signed by Babe Ruth. Hearn heads down to St. Petersburg to collect but finds himself among others scrambling to make their fortunes in the Florida boomtown. Irby, a St. Petersburg resident, draws on his home's colorful history to create this entertaining period novel.

Other books you might like:
James Carlos Blake, *A World of Thieves*, 2001
Darryl Brock, *Havana Heat*, 2000
Chistopher Cook, *Robbers*, 2000
Donald Honig, *The Last Great Season*, 1979
Mark Winegardner, *The Veracruz Blues*, 1996

885

JANE JAKEMAN

Let There Be Blood
(New York: Berkley Prime Crime, 2004)

Story type: Mystery; Historical/Regency
Subject(s): Mystery and Detective Stories; Crime and Criminals
Major character(s): Lord Ambrose, Nobleman
Time period(s): 1830s
Locale(s): West Country, England

Summary: Jakeman introduces a distinctive period sleuth, Lord Ambrose, who may remind readers of Lord Byron and Rochester in Charlotte Bronte's *Jane Eyre*. Badly scarred by wounds received in the Greek war for independence in 1830, Lord Ambrose returns to recuperate in his ancestral English West Country manor. He is forced out of seclusion to investigate the murders of one of his tenant farmers and the farmer's son. Solving the mystery surrounding these deaths slowly brings Lord Ambrose back to life. With an intriguing sleuth and solid period background, this is an entertaining mystery that deserves a second act.

Where it's reviewed:
Library Journal, September 1, 2004, page 122
Publishers Weekly, August 16, 2004, page 46

Other books by the same author:
In the Kingdom of Mists, 2003
Death at Versailles, 2002
Death in the South of France, 2001

Other books you might like:
Bruce Alexander, *The Sir John Fielding Series*, 1994-
Stephanie Barron, *The Jane Austen Series*, 1996-
Roberta Rogow, *The Charles Dodgson/Arthur Conan Doyle Series*, 1998-
Kate Ross, *The Julian Kestrel Series*, 1993-1997
Rosemary Stevens, *The Bloodied Cravat*, 2002

886

JOHN JAKES

Savannah: Or, A Gift for Mr. Lincoln

(New York: Dutton, 2004)

Story type: Historical/American Civil War
Subject(s): War; Civil War; Family Relations
Major character(s): Sara Lester, Widow(er), Plantation Owner; Stephen Hopewell, Journalist; William Tecumseh Sherman, Historical Figure, Military Personnel (Union general)
Time period(s): 1860s (1864)
Locale(s): Savannah, Georgia

Summary: Jakes chronicles the capture of Savannah by General William Tecumseh Sherman's Union Army during the Civil War. The center of the action is plantation owner and widow Sara Lester and her 12-year-old daughter Hattie. They are shown caught in the climactic last act of Sherman's infamous March to the Sea in which Savannah is to become ''a gift for Mr. Lincoln.'' Sara finds support from journalist Stephen Hopewell; while Hattie develops a relationship with Sherman himself.

Where it's reviewed:
Booklist, July 2004, page 1799
Library Journal, September 15, 2004, page 49
Publishers Weekly, August 16, 2004, page 40

Other books by the same author:
Charleston, 2002
On Secret Service, 2000
American Dreams, 1998
Homeland, 1993
California Gold, 1989

Other books you might like:
Cynthia Bass, *Sherman's March*, 1994
Diane Haeger, *My Dearest Cecelia*, 2003
William C. Harris Jr., *Delirium of the Brave*, 1999
James Reasoner, *Savannah*, 2003
Philip Lee Williams, *A Distant Flame*, 2004

887

MICHAEL JECKS

The Outlaws of Ennor

(London: Headline, 2004)

Story type: Historical/Medieval; Mystery
Series: Medieval West Country Mystery. Book 16
Subject(s): Mystery and Detective Stories; Middle Ages; Shipwrecks

Major character(s): Sir Baldwin de Furnshill, Knight, Government Official (keeper of the king's peace); Simon Puttock, Lawman (bailiff)
Time period(s): 14th century (1320s)
Locale(s): Scilly Islands, England

Summary: In this installment of Jecks' accomplished series, sleuths Baldwin and Simon Puttock are shipwrecked off the Scilly Islands, and Baldwin is believed lost. Simon finds himself on the tiny island of Ennor, where he is ordered to investigate the murder of the island's tax gatherer. Baldwin washes ashore on a different island and investigates the same murder with a very different result.

Other books by the same author:
The Tolls of Death, 2004
The Mad Monk of Gidleigh, 2003
The Templar's Penance, 2003
The Devil's Acolyte, 2002
The Sticklepath Strangler, 2001

Other books you might like:
Susanna Gregory, *A Killer in Winter*, 2003
Bernard Knight, *Crowner's Quest*, 2004
Sharon Kay Penman, *Time and Chance*, 2002
Priscilla Royal, *Wine of Violence*, 2003
Kate Sedley, *Nine Men Dancing*, 2003

888

MICHAEL JECKS

The Tolls of Death

(London: Headline, 2004)

Story type: Historical/Medieval; Mystery
Series: Medieval West Country Mystery. Book 17
Subject(s): Mystery and Detective Stories; Middle Ages; Small Town Life
Major character(s): Sir Baldwin de Furnshill, Knight, Government Official (keeper of the king's peace); Simon Puttock, Lawman (bailiff)
Time period(s): 14th century (1323)
Locale(s): Cornwall, England

Summary: Former Knight Templar Sir Baldwin de Furnshill and Bailiff Simon Puttock are called in to investigate the hanging death of a widow in a small Cornish village and the village's miller who has been caught embezzling money collected from tolls. The novel relies on a convincing depiction of period customs.

Where it's reviewed:
Publishers Weekly, September 27, 2004, page 41

Other books by the same author:
The Outlaws of Ennor, 2004
The Tolls of Death, 2004
The Mad Monk of Gidleigh, 2003
The Templar's Penance, 2003
The Devil's Acolyte, 2002

Other books you might like:
Margaret Frazer, *The Widow's Tale*, 2005
Jules Hardy, *Altered Land*, 2002
Janet Lawrence, *Death at the Table*, 1997

Historical

Sharon Kay Penman, *Time and Chance*, 2002
Priscilla Royal, *Tyrant of the Mind*, 2004

HA JIN

War Trash

(New York: Pantheon, 2004)

Story type: Psychological
Subject(s): Korean War; Prisoners of War
Major character(s): Yu Yuan, Military Personnel, Prisoner; Liu Tai-an, Prisoner; Pei Shan, Prisoner
Time period(s): 1950s
Locale(s): Korea, South

Summary: Ha Jin's novel of the Korean War takes the form of a memoir by Yu Yuan, a Chinese POW, who is captured fighting alongside the North Koreans. The American captors attempt to break their captives by reducing them to "war trash." Yu Yuan, who has no loyalty to the Communists and only wants to return home to his family and fiancee, finds himself in between two factions of Chinese prisoners: the pro-Nationalists, led by the sadistic Liu Tai-an, and the pro-Communists, commanded by Pei Shan. The novel offers a fresh look at the Korean War from an unusual perspective.

Where it's reviewed:
Booklist, August 2004, page 1872
Kirkus Reviews, August 15, 2004, page 763
Library Journal, August 2004, page 67
New York Times Book Review, October 10, 2004, page 1
Publishers Weekly, August 2, 2004, page 49

Other books by the same author:
The Crazed, 2002
The Bridegroom, 2000
Waiting, 1999
In the Pond, 1998
Ocean of Words, 1996

Other books you might like:
James Brady, *The Marines of Autumn*, 2000
James Hickey, *Chrysanthemum in the Snow*, 1990
John Katzenbach, *Hart's War*, 2000
James Salter, *The Hunters*, 1997
Edwin Howard Simmons, *Dog Company Six*, 2000

890

NEIL JORDAN

Shade

(New York: Bloomsbury, 2004)

Story type: Mystery; Ghost Story
Subject(s): Mystery and Detective Stories; Murder; Ghosts
Major character(s): Nina Hardy, Crime Victim, Spirit
Time period(s): 20th century (1900-1950)
Locale(s): River Boyne, Ireland

Summary: The ghost of the murdered Nina Hardy relives her life through the first half of the 20th century in Jordan's interesting experiment with atmospheric narrative point of view. Nina describes her circle of childhood friends and the

challenges they face as a result of the Great War, as well as her experiences as an actress. All are pieces of a complex puzzle to account for why she was killed by one of her closest friends.

Where it's reviewed:
Booklist, September 1, 2004, page 61
Kirkus Reviews, August 1, 2004, page 706
Publishers Weekly, August 30, 2004, page 30

Other books by the same author:
Nightlines, 1995
The Dream of a Beast, 1989
The Past, 1980

Other books you might like:
Christine Balint, *Ophelia's Fan*, 2004
Dicey Deere, *The Irish Village Murder*, 2004
Erin Hart, *Lake of Sorrows*, 2004
Regina McBride, *The Marriage Bed*, 2004
John McGahern, *The Barracks*, 2004

891

ELMER KELTON

Jericho's Road

(New York: Forge, 2004)

Story type: Historical/American West; Historical/Post-American Civil War
Series: Texas Rangers. Book 6
Subject(s): Law Enforcement; Feuds; Ranch Life
Major character(s): Andy Pickard, Lawman (Texas Ranger); Guadalupe Chavez, Rancher; Jericho Jackson, Rancher
Time period(s): 1870s
Locale(s): Nueces Strip, Texas; Mexico

Summary: Andy Pickard commands a small Ranger company along the Nueces Strip, land disputed by feuding Mexican rancher Guadalupe Chavez and Texan rancher Jericho Jackson. Pickard and fellow Ranger Farley Brackett find themselves caught up in the feud as violence escalates into a bloody battle for supremacy. Spur Award-winning author Kelton excels in delivering believable western action.

Where it's reviewed:
Booklist, October 15, 2004, page 390
Kirkus Reviews, August 15, 2004, page 767
Library Journal, October 15, 2004, page 54
Publishers Weekly, November 1, 2004, page 43

Other books by the same author:
Texas Vendetta, 2004
Lone Star Rising, 2003
Ranger's Trail, 2002
Badger Boy, 2001
The Smiling Country, 1998

Other books you might like:
Henry Chappell, *Blood Kin*, 2004
Larry McMurtry, *By Sorrow's River*, 2003
Diana Palmer, *Lawless*, 2003
Guy Vanderhaeghe, *The Last Crossing*, 2004
Richard S. Wheeler, *The Deliverance*, 2003

892

BERNARD KNIGHT

Crowner's Quest

(Sutton, England: Severn House, 2004)

Story type: Historical/Medieval; Mystery
Series: Crowner John Mystery
Subject(s): Mystery and Detective Stories; Middle Ages; Crime and Criminals
Major character(s): Sir John de Wolfe, Nobleman; Sir Richard de Revelle, Nobleman, Lawman (sheriff)
Time period(s): 12th century (1194)
Locale(s): England

Summary: In this installment of Knight's series, Sir John de Wolfe investigates the death of a canon who is found hanged. Although suicide is suspected, Sir John has his doubts. His investigation brings him into conflict with his brother-in-law the sheriff, Sir Richard de Revelle, who has his own secret motive for Sir John's inquiry to fail.

Where it's reviewed:
Kirkus Reviews, April 15, 2004, page 302

Other books by the same author:
The Poisoned Chalice, 2003
The Tinner's Corpse, 2001
The Awful Secret, 2000
The Sanctuary Seeker, 1998

Other books you might like:
Susanna Gregory, *A Summer of Discontent*, 2003
Michael Jecks, *The Outlaws of Ennor*, 2004
Sharon Kay Penman, *Time and Chance*, 2002
Priscilla Royal, *Wine of Violence*, 2003
Kate Sedley, *Nine Men Dancing*, 2003

893

DERYN LAKE

Death in the Setting Sun

(London: Allison & Busby, 2004)

Story type: Historical/Georgian; Mystery
Series: John Rawlings. Book 10
Subject(s): Mystery and Detective Stories
Major character(s): John Rawlings, Apothecary, Detective—Amateur; Emilia Rawlings, Spouse (of John)
Time period(s): 1760s
Locale(s): England

Summary: Apothecary John Rawlings and his wife Emilia are invited to a Christmas party on the grounds of Gunnersbury House, hosted by a close relation of King George II. After he discovers his wife stabbed through the heart, Rawlings is the prime suspect in her murder, and he must find the real murderer to avenge his wife and save himself from the gallows.

Other books by the same author:
Death in the Valley of the Shadows, 2003
Death at St. James's Palace, 2002
Death in the West Wind, 2002
Death at Apothecaries' Hall, 2000
Death in the Peerless Pool, 1999

Other books you might like:
Bruce Alexander, *Experiment in Treason*, 2002
Emma Donoghue, *Slammerkin*, 2000
Nicholas Griffin, *The House of Sight and Shadow*, 2001
David Liss, *A Conspiracy of Paper*, 2001
Fidelis Morgan, *The Rival Queens*, 2001

894

DEWEY LAMBDIN

The Captain's Vengeance

(New York: St. Martin's Press, 2004)

Story type: Historical/Napoleonic Wars; Military
Series: Alan Lewrie. Book 12
Subject(s): Sea Stories; Pirates; Adventure and Adventurers
Major character(s): Alan Lewrie, Military Personnel (naval captain); Charite, Pirate
Time period(s): 1790s (1799)
Locale(s): New Orleans, Louisiana

Summary: Lambdin's popular nautical adventure series continues with British captain Alan Lewrie dispatched to Spanish-held New Orleans in pursuit of pirates. There he encounters woman pirate Charite who is plotting an insurrection against the Spanish rulers on behalf of France. Lewrie gets entangled with Charite romantically and with the complex politics of the period in which no one is to be trusted.

Where it's reviewed:
Publishers Weekly, September 6, 2004, page 43

Other books by the same author:
The Alan Lewrie Series, 1989-

Other books you might like:
C.S. Forester, *The Horatio Hornblower Series*, 1933-1966
Alexander Kent, *The Richard Bolitho Series*, 1968-1986
Patrick O'Brian, *The Aubrey/Maturin Series*, 1970-2004
Dudley Pope, *The Nicholas Ramage Series*, 1965-
Richard Woodman, *An Eye of the Fleet*, 2001

895

CAROLINE LAWRENCE

The Twelve Tasks of Flavia Gemina

(Brookfield, Connecticut: Roaring Brook, 2004)

Story type: Historical/Ancient Rome; Mystery
Series: Roman Mysteries. Book VI
Subject(s): Mystery and Detective Stories; Crime and Criminals; Ancient History
Major character(s): Flavia Gemina, Detective—Private
Time period(s): 1st century (79 A.D.)
Locale(s): Ostia, Roman Empire

Summary: In this installment of Lawrence's entertaining Ancient Roman mystery series, featuring woman detective Flavia Gemina, a mysterious widow has designs on Flavia's father. As a lion roams the streets of Ostia, Flavia must complete 12 heroic tasks, echoing the achievement of the immortal Greek hero Hercules. Is she up to the challenge?

Other books by the same author:
The Assassins of Rome, 2003
The Dolphins of Larentum, 2003
The Pirates of Pompeii, 2003
The Thieves of Ostia, 2002
The Secrets of Vesuvius, 2001

Other books you might like:
Lindsey Davis, *The Marcus Didius Falco Series*, 1989-
John Maddox Roberts, *The SPQR Series*, 1990-
Steven Saylor, *The Roma Sub Rosa Series*, 1991-
Marilyn Todd, *Second Act*, 2003
David Wishart, *Parthian Shot*, 2004

896

JOAN LOCK

Dead End

(Sutton, England: Severn House, 2004)

Story type: Mystery; Historical/Victorian
Subject(s): Mystery and Detective Stories; Victorian Period; Crime and Criminals
Major character(s): Best, Detective—Police (detective inspector)
Time period(s): 19th century
Locale(s): London, England; Newcastle, England

Summary: Detective Inspector Best departs London for Newcastle to investigate the murder of a woman found surrounded by white roses in a four-poster bed in the furniture section of the world's first department store. The victim is the spoiled daughter of a nobleman whose participation in a spiritualist society might be connected to her demise. Best searches for the reasons behind the murder and why the corpse winds up on display at the department store. The novel is packed with period information about Victorian Newcastle.

Where it's reviewed:
Booklist, August 2004, page 1906
Kirkus Reviews, October 1, 2004, page 942

Other books by the same author:
Dead Letters, 2003
Dead Born, 2001

Other books you might like:
Dennis Burges, *Graves Gate*, 2003
Howard Engel, *Mr. Doyle and Dr. Bell*, 2003
Anthony O'Neill, *The Lamplighter*, 2003
Matthew Pearl, *The Dante Club*, 2003
David Pirie, *The Night Calls*, 2003

897

DAVID LODGE

Author, Author

(New York: Viking, 2004)

Story type: Historical/Victorian; Historical/World War I
Subject(s): Authors and Writers; Biography

Major character(s): Henry James, Historical Figure, Writer; George Du Maurier, Historical Figure, Artist; Constance Fenimore Woolson, Historical Figure, Writer
Time period(s): 19th century; 20th century (1880s-1915)
Locale(s): England

Summary: Close on the heels of Colm Toibin's *The Master*, Lodge supplies another fictional biography of novelist Henry James. Opening in 1915 with James on his deathbed, the novel moves back in time to the 1880s to explore James' career as a writer and relationships with such figures as George Du Maurier and Constance Fenimore Woolsey. Lodge suggests that James sublimated all his human needs and desires for his art, turning him into a relentless egomaniac. The novel provides a full account of James' disastrous attempt to achieve success as a playwright. The overwhelming self-centeredness of the Master does not permit a very sympathetic portrait, but Lodge compensates with a vivid and fascinating portrayal of the literary and theatrical life in England at the end of the 19th century and the beginning of the 20th. The author insists that nearly everything that happens in the novel is based on factual sources, and he supplies a list of his deviations from the record.

Where it's reviewed:
Kirkus Reviews, July 15, 2004, page 651
New York Times Book Review, October 10, 2004, page 30
Publishers Weekly, August 30, 2004, page 29

Other books by the same author:
Thinks, 2001
Therapy, 1995
The Picture Goers, 1993
Paradise News, 1991
Changing Places, 1975

Other books you might like:
Joan Aiken, *The Haunting of Lamb House*, 1993
Carol De Chellis Hill, *Henry James' Midnight Song*, 1993
Matthew Pearl, *The Dante Club*, 2003
Colm Toibin, *The Master*, 2004
Gore Vidal, *Empire*, 1987

898

JONATHAN LOWY

The Temple of Music

(New York: Crown, 2004)

Story type: Historical/Victorian America
Subject(s): Presidents; Crime and Criminals
Major character(s): Leon Czolgosz, Historical Figure, Murderer; William McKinley, Historical Figure, Political Figure; Ida McKinley, Historical Figure, Spouse (of William)
Time period(s): 1900s (1901)
Locale(s): Buffalo, New York; Washington, District of Columbia; New York, New York

Summary: Lowy's view of Gilded Age America at the turn of the century is focused on the assassination of William McKinley at the 1901 Pan American Exposition in Buffalo, New York, by immigrant factory worker Leon Czolgosz. The novel supplies a background and motive for the shadowy Czolgosz, as well as portraits of many of the key figures of the period, including William McKinley and his wife Ida; McKinley's chief political rival, William Jennings Bryan; newspaper magnate William Randolph Hearst; philanthropist Andrew Carnegie; socialite Morris Vandeveer; activist Emma Goldman; and one of the founders of the modern political campaign, Mark "Dollar" Hanna. Lowy manages to weave together his large cast and the drama of the assassination into an able reconstruction of a bygone and somewhat forgotten chapter in American history.

Where it's reviewed:
Kirkus Reviews, October 1, 2004, page 932
Publishers Weekly, November 29, 2004, page 24

Other books by the same author:
Elvis and Nixon, 2001

Other books you might like:
Kevin Baker, *Dreamland*, 1999
E.L. Doctorow, *Ragtime*, 1975
Guy Johnson, *Echoes of a Distant Summer*, 2002
Darin Straus, *The Real McCoy*, 2002
Gore Vidal, *Empire*, 1987

899

ROBERT N. MACOMBER

Honorable Mention
(Sarasota, Florida: Pineapple, 2004)

Story type: Historical/American Civil War; Military
Series: Honor. Book 3
Subject(s): War; Sea Stories; Civil War
Major character(s): Peter Wake, Military Personnel (Union naval commander)
Time period(s): 1860s (1864-1866)
Locale(s): *U.S.S. Hunt*, At Sea; Florida; Havana, Cuba

Summary: The third volume of Macomber's series dramatizing naval action during the Civil War is set between the re-election of Abraham Lincoln in 1864 and the relocation of former Confederates to Latin America in 1866. Lt. Peter Wake is in command of a steamer that is involved in a series of engagements, including chasing an escaping slave ship, confronting the Confederacy's most powerful warship in Havana's harbor, and tracking down a colony of former Confederates in Puerto Rico.

Other books by the same author:
Point of Honor, 2003
At the Edge of Honor, 2002

Other books you might like:
Jim Crace, *Signals of Distress*, 1994
Louise Meriwether, *Fragments of the Ark*, 1994
Christopher Nicole, *Iron Ships, Iron Men*, 1989
David Poyer, *Fire on the Waters*, 2001
Willard M. Wallace, *The Raiders*, 1970

900

JULIET MARILLIER

Foxmask
(New York: Tor, 2004)

Story type: Historical/Fantasy
Subject(s): Vikings; Islands
Major character(s): Thorvald, Teenager; Creidhe, Teenager
Time period(s): 8th century
Locale(s): Orkney Islands, Scotland

Summary: In a sequel to the author's *Wolfskin*, set in Britain and Norway during the Dark Ages, the Viking Thorvald travels to Scotland's Orkney Islands to search for his exiled father. Unbeknownst to him, he is accompanied by a stowaway, Creidhe, and together they encounter the Long Knife people and must play a role in restoring Foxmask, a powerful seer, to his people. Mixing history and folklore, romance and fantasy, the novel dramatizes the clash of cultures against the backdrop of the first Viking voyages from Norway to the Orkneys.

Where it's reviewed:
Booklist, July 2004, page 1829
Library Journal, August 2004, page 73
Publishers Weekly, July 12, 2004, page 48

Other books by the same author:
Wolfskin, 2003
Child of the Prophecy, 2002
Son of the Shadows, 2001
Daughter of the Forest, 2000

Other books you might like:
Michael Crichton, *Eaters of the Dead*, 1976
Cecelia Holland, *The Witches' Kitchen*, 2004
Rebecca Tingle, *The Edge of the Sword*, 2001
Henry Treece, *Viking's Dawn*, 1956
Anna Lee Waldo, *Circle of Stars*, 2001

901

ALLAN MASSIE

Arthur the King
(New York: Carroll & Graf, 2004)

Story type: Historical/Fantasy; Legend
Subject(s): Arthurian Legends; Knights and Knighthood
Major character(s): Arthur, Ruler; Merlin, Wizard; Guinevere, Spouse (of Arthur)
Time period(s): 5th century
Locale(s): England

Summary: Massie offers an at times offbeat retelling of the Arthurian legend. The novel keeps mainly to the familiar story of the young Arthur, schooled by Merlin, who claims the throne by pulling Excalibur from its stone, but provides an unusual look at Merlin's childhood and development. Arthur's marriage to Guinevere is one of convenience, while his true love is for his half-sister Morgan le Fay (and several pretty youths). Those interested in a different slant on a familiar story will be intrigued; purists may well be shocked.

Historical

Where it's reviewed:
Kirkus Reviews, October 15, 2004, page 979
Publishers Weekly, December 20, 2004, page 38

Other books by the same author:
The Evening of the World, 2002
Augustus, 1995
Caesar, 1994
Tiberius, 1993
The Sins of the Father, 1991

Other books you might like:
Marion Zimmer Bradley, *The Mists of Avalon*, 1982
Bernard Cornwell, *The Arthurian Warlord Chronicles*, 1996-1998
Parke Godwin, *Firelord*, 1980
Jack Whyte, *The Lance Thrower*, 2004
Persia Woolley, *The Guinevere Trilogy*, 1987-1991

902

TAKASHI MATSUOKA

Autumn Bridge
(New York: Delacorte, 2004)

Story type: Historical/Exotic
Subject(s): Samurai; Adventure and Adventurers
Major character(s): Lord Genji, Nobleman, Warlord; Emily Gibson, Religious (missionary); Lady Shizuka, Noble-woman
Time period(s): 19th century; 14th century
Locale(s): Japan

Summary: Matsuoka continues the story of Japanese noble-man Lord Genji begun in *Cloud of Sparrows*, focusing on his growing attraction to American missionary Emily Gibson. Genji, the head of the Okumichi clan, fights off conservative opposition to Western influence, while Emily learns more about Genji's 14th-century forebear, Shizuka, and her history of forbidden love that offers parallels with Emily's own circumstances. The author effortlessly and authentically shuffles between her eras in a gripping tale of passion and intrigue.

Where it's reviewed:
Booklist, July 2004, page 188
Kirkus Reviews, June 1, 2004, page 511
Publishers Weekly, July 19, 2004, page 144

Other books by the same author:
Cloud of Sparrows, 2002

Other books you might like:
James Clavell, *Gai-Jin*, 1993
Lynn Guest, *Yedo*, 1985
I.J. Parker, *Rashomon Gate*, 2002
Jeff Talarigo, *The Pearl Diver*, 2004
Eiji Yoshikawa, *Musashi*, 1981

903

PAT MCINTOSH

The Harper's Quine
(New York: Carroll & Graf, 2004)

Story type: Mystery
Series: Gil Cunningham. Book 1
Subject(s): Mystery and Detective Stories; Law
Major character(s): Gilbert Cunningham, Lawyer
Time period(s): 15th century (1492)
Locale(s): Glasgow, Scotland

Summary: McIntosh's historical mystery debut is set in 15th-century Glasgow and features lawyer and would-be priest Gilbert Cunningham, who investigates the murder of a young woman found on the grounds of a cathedral. The victim turns out to be the estranged wife of a nobleman. Cunningham must follow a complicated trail of clues to reveal the motive for the murder and its dangerous perpetrator.

Where it's reviewed:
Kirkus Reviews, July 1, 2004, page 607
Library Journal, July 2004, page 63
Publishers Weekly, July 12, 2004, page 47

Other books you might like:
Fiona Buckley, *A Pawn for a Queen*, 2002
Claudia Gross, *Scholarium*, 2004
Ian Morson, *The William Falconer Series*, 1994-
Robin Paige, *Death at Glamis Castle*, 2003
Ellis Peters, *The Brother Cadfael Series*, 1977-1994

904

ELISABETH MCNEILL

The Lady of Cawnpore
(Sutton, England: Severn House, 2004)

Story type: Historical/Victorian
Subject(s): Rebellions, Revolts, and Uprisings; Victorian Period; Indian Empire
Major character(s): Emily Maynard, Gentlewoman; Dowlah Ram, Servant; Jenny Garland, Widow(er)
Time period(s): 1850s (1857); 1910s (1919)
Locale(s): Cawnpore, India

Summary: McNeill's novel shifts between two eras in India's history, the horrific Cawnpore Mutiny of 1857 and 1919 when the drive for Indian independence gains momentum. The angle of view comes from Emily Maynard, who experiences the Mutiny. She is rescued by Dowlah Ram, a servant of her father, whom she marries and with whom she later lives happily as an Indian woman. The pain of her past returns with the arrival of widow Jenny Garland, whose husband has been killed in World War I. The novel manages both its historical eras with skill.

Where it's reviewed:
Booklist, September 1, 2004, page 62

Other books by the same author:
Press Relations, 2003
The Last Cocktail Party, 2002

The Golden Days, 2001
Money Troubles, 2000
Turn Back Time, 1998

Other books you might like:
J.G. Farrell, *The Siege of Krishnapur*, 1978
Valerie Fitzgerald, *Zemindar*, 1981
Tom Gibson, *A Soldier of India*, 1982
M.M. Kaye, *The Shadow of the Moon*, 1979
Vivian Stuart, *Massacre at Cawnpore*, 1992

905

MICHAEL, PRINCE OF GREECE

The White Night of St. Petersburg
(New York: Atlantic Monthly, 2004)

Story type: Historical/Russian Revolution
Subject(s): Kings, Queens, Rulers, etc.; Russian Empire; Biography
Major character(s): Nicholas Kostantinovich Romanov, Historical Figure, Nobleman; Fanny Lear, Historical Figure, Prostitute
Time period(s): 19th century; 20th century
Locale(s): Russia

Summary: Prince Michael of Greece, himself a distant relation to the Romanovs of Imperial Russia, tells the story of a long-forgotten Romanov, Grand Duke Nicholas Kostantinovich, based on the firsthand account of his granddaughter. Beginning in 1860, the story follows the career of the Grand Duke, including his scandalous affair with a beautiful American courtesan, Fanny Lear, and his implication in a plot to fund revolutionaries by stealing the Romanov family jewels. This leads to his banishment to faraway Tashkent, and disappearance from the official Romanov family record. Those interested in the Russian ruling family before the Revolution will be grateful for this attempt to reclaim an intriguing aspect of the family's history.

Where it's reviewed:
Booklist, September 15, 2004, page 209
Library Journal, October 1, 2004, page 72
Publishers Weekly, September 6, 2004, page 46

Other books by the same author:
Sultana, 1983

Other books you might like:
Robert Alexander, *The Kitchen Boy*, 2003
Allen Appel, *Time After Time*, 1985
Natasha Borovsky, *A Daughter of the Nobility*, 1985
True Bowen, *And the Stars Shall Fall*, 1951
Susanna Hoe, *God Save the Tsar*, 1978

906

ROSALIND MILES

The Lady of the Sea
(New York: Crown, 2004)

Story type: Historical/Medieval; Legend
Series: Tristan and Isolde Trilogy. Book 3

Subject(s): Knights and Knighthood; Romance; Arthurian Legends
Major character(s): Isolde, Royalty (princess); Tristan, Knight; Mark, Ruler (King of Cornwall)
Time period(s): Indeterminate Past
Locale(s): Cornwall, England; Ireland

Summary: Miles brings to a close her trilogy chronicling the legendary love affair between Tristan and Isolde. Trapped in a loveless marriage to King Mark of Cornwall and in love with her husband's nephew, Tristan of Lyonesse, Isolde returns home to Ireland to defend against an invasion by the Picts and the advances of the Pict king. Meanwhile, Tristan is torn between his love and his duty to his uncle as the story moves toward its stirring climax. Miles elaborates on the classic story from a decidedly feminist perspective.

Where it's reviewed:
Booklist, October 15, 2004, page 390
Library Journal, September 15, 2004, page 49
Publishers Weekly, October 11, 2004, page 53

Other books by the same author:
The Maid of the White Hands, 2002
The Child of the Holy Grail, 2001
The Knight of the Sacred Lake, 2000
Guenevere: Queen of the Summer Country, 1999
I, Elizabeth, 1994

Other books you might like:
Bernard Cornwell, *The Arthurian Warlord Chronicles*, 1996-1998
Kate Hawks, *The Lovers: The Legend of Trystan and Yseult*, 1990
Diana L. Paxson, *The White Raven*, 1988
Anna Taylor, *Drustan the Wanderer*, 1971
Persia Woolley, *The Guinevere Trilogy*, 1987-1991

907

MARK MILLS

Amagansett
(New York: Putnam, 2004)

Story type: Mystery
Subject(s): Mystery and Detective Stories; Fishing; Small Town Life
Major character(s): Conrad Labarde, Fisherman, Veteran; Tom Hollis, Police Officer (deputy chief)
Time period(s): 1940s (1947)
Locale(s): Amagansett, New York

Summary: Set in 1947 in the small Long Island fishing community of Amagansett, Mills' debut uses a murder investigation to uncover the class and ethnic rifts that divide the community. When Basque fisherman Conrad Labarde nets the body of a beautiful young woman, Deputy Chief of Police Tom Hollis takes up the investigation to determine the cause of her death. She turns out to be a daughter of privilege with a secret, the uncovering of which sheds light on the troubled history of Long Island's south shore.

Where it's reviewed:
Booklist, August 2004, page 1907
Kirkus Reviews, July 15, 2004, page 652

Historical

New York Times Book Review, August 29, 2004, page 12
Publishers Weekly, July 12, 2004, page 44

Other books you might like:
John Casey, *Spartina*, 1989
Dorothy Garlock, *The Edge of Town*, 2001
Norman G. Gautreau, *Sea Room*, 2002
John R. Hayes, *Catskill*, 2001
Tim Winton, *Dirt Music*, 2001

908
DAVID MITCHELL

Cloud Atlas
(New York: Random House, 2004)

Story type: Psychological; Collection
Subject(s): Short Stories

Summary: Mitchell's inventive narrative interweaves six separate but ultimately related stories, beginning with a 19th-century Pacific voyage, through the story of an early 20th-century counterfeiter, to a 1970s reporter pursued by hitmen, and an editor trapped in a home for the aged. There's method in all the madness, but it becomes the reader's task to discover the connecting threads and re-assemble them into a cohesive whole.

Where it's reviewed:
Kirkus Reviews, May 15, 2004, page 464
Library Journal, June 15, 2004, page 60
New York Times Book Review, August 29, 2004, page 7
Publishers Weekly, June 28, 2004, page 30

Other books by the same author:
Number9Dream, 2001
Ghostwritten, 2000

Other books you might like:
Susanna Clarke, *Jonathan Strange & Mr. Norrell*, 2004
Andrew Sean Greer, *The Confessions of Max Tivoli*, 2004
Orhan Pamuk, *Snow*, 2004
Arthur Phillips, *The Egyptologist*, 2004
David Foster Wallace, *Oblivion*, 2004

909
PHILIPPA MORGAN

Chaucer and the House of Fame
(New York: Carroll & Graf, 2004)

Story type: Historical/Medieval; Mystery
Subject(s): Mystery and Detective Stories; Authors and Writers
Major character(s): Geoffrey Chaucer, Historical Figure, Writer
Time period(s): 14th century (1370)
Locale(s): England; France

Summary: This medieval mystery debut shows Geoffrey Chaucer, the future author of *The Canterbury Tales*, journeying to France to try to prevent the loss of the valuable territory of Aquitaine. His mission to convince a French nobleman to remain loyal is complicated by a series of

mysterious deaths, including that of the French nobleman in a wild boar hunt. The novel draws on solid period details and achieves the necessary balance between puzzles and history to make a repeat performance eagerly anticipated.

Where it's reviewed:
Kirkus Reviews, August 1, 2004, page 717
Publishers Weekly, August 2, 2004, page 55

Other books you might like:
Peter Ackroyd, *The Clerkenwell Tales*, 2004
Catherine Darby, *The Love Knot*, 1989
Sara Douglass, *The Nameless Day*, 2004
Judith Healey, *The Canterbury Papers*, 2004
Candace Robb, *A Gift of Sanctuary*, 1998

910
BHARATI MUKHERJEE

The Tree Bride
(New York: Hyperion, 2004)

Story type: Family Saga
Subject(s): Family Relations; Emigration and Immigration
Major character(s): Tara Lata, Revolutionary; Tara Chatterjee, Immigrant
Time period(s): 19th century; 21st century
Locale(s): India; San Francisco, California

Summary: Mukherjee's second installment of a trilogy, begun with *Desirable Daughters* and narrated by Tara Chatterjee, living in present-day San Francisco, concerns her great-great-aunt Tara Lata. Born in 1874, Tara was married at the age of five to a tree because her fiance died. She would later play a significant role in the struggle for India's independence from Britain. When her house is firebombed, the narrator attempts to rebuild her life while uncovering the connection between the explosion and her legendary relative. A story about how the past remains powerfully present, the bridging of the gaps between the two supplies a compelling chronicle of Indo-British history and contemporary cultural conflicts.

Where it's reviewed:
Booklist, June 1, 2004, page 1671
Library Journal, August 2004, page 69
New York Times Book Review, September 26, 2004, page 24

Other books by the same author:
Desirable Daughters, 2002
Leave It to Me, 1997
The Tiger's Daughter, 1996
The Holder of the World, 1993
Jasmin, 1989

Other books you might like:
Samina Ali, *Madras on Rainy Days*, 2004
David Davidar, *The House of Blue Mangoes*, 2002
Chitra Banerjee Divakaruni, *Queen of Dreams*, 2004
Hari Kunzru, *The Impressionist*, 2002
Vikram Seth, *A Suitable Boy*, 1996

911

JAN NEEDLE

The Spithead Nymph

(Ithaca, New York: McBooks, 2004)

Story type: Historical/Georgian; Military
Series: William Bentley. Number 3
Subject(s): Sea Stories; Adventure and Adventurers; Slavery
Major character(s): William Bentley, Military Personnel (British midshipman)
Time period(s): 1790s
Locale(s): London, England; *Biter*, At Sea; Jamaica

Summary: Needle continues to chronicle realistic shipboard life from the perspective of the ordinary seaman in the age of sail. William Bentley, while awaiting trial for treason, is offered a chance to avoid prison by serving as first lieutenant aboard the *Biter* on a harrowing journey to Jamaica for a close-up look at the evils of slavery. Stripped of its glamour, life aboard a sailing ship is depicted with an authentic, sobering realism.

Other books by the same author:
The Wicked Trade, 2001
A Fine Boy for Killing, 2000

Other books you might like:
Alexander Kent, *The Richard Bolitho Series*, 1968-1986
Dewey Lambdin, *The Alan Lewrie Series*, 1989-
Patrick O'Brian, *The Aubrey/Maturin Series*, 1970-2004
Dudley Pope, *The Nicholas Ramage Series*, 1965-
Richard Woodman, *The Nathaniel Drinkwater Series*, 1984-

912

KIEN NGUYEN

Le Colonial

(New York: Little, Brown, 2004)

Story type: Historical/Exotic
Subject(s): Religious Life
Major character(s): Pierre de Behaine, Religious (Jesuit monsignor); Francois Gervaise, Artist, Religious (missionary); Henri Monange, Religious (missionary), Teenager
Time period(s): 18th century
Locale(s): Vietnam

Summary: Nguyen transports the reader to 18th-century Annam (now Vietnam) with the interlinked stories of three French missionaries—Jesuit Pierre de Behaine; a former artist, Francois Gervaise; and teenager Henri Monange. Each must test his values against the reality and alternative culture of the Vietnamese. Gervaise turns to Buddhism and joins a rebel force of peasants, Monange falls in love with a beautiful servant girl, while de Behaine, in service to a powerful prince, finds himself on opposite sides from his former missionary colleagues in a brutal civil war between the peasants and warlords. The Vietnamese-born Nguyen provides a fascinating and instructive look at her homeland.

Where it's reviewed:
Kirkus Reviews, July 15, 2004, page 653
Library Journal, September 1, 2004, page 141

Publishers Weekly, August 30, 2004, page 34

Other books by the same author:
The Tapestries, 2002
The Unwanted, 2001

Other books you might like:
Christie Dickason, *Indochine*, 1987
Thu Huong Duong, *Paradise of the Blind*, 1993
Marguerite Duras, *The Lover*, 1985
Catherine Texier, *Victorine*, 2004
Monique Truong, *The Book of Salt*, 2003

913

PATRICK O'BRIAN

21: The Final Unfinished Voyage of Jack Aubrey

(New York: Norton, 2004)

Story type: Historical/Napoleonic Wars
Series: Aubrey/Maturin. Book 21
Subject(s): Sea Stories; Military Life
Major character(s): Jack Aubrey, Military Personnel (British naval officer); Stephen Maturin, Doctor (ship's surgeon); Samuel Mputa, Diplomat, Bastard Son (of Jack)
Time period(s): 1810s (1816)
Locale(s): *Surprise*, At Sea; South Africa; Argentina

Summary: At the time of Patrick O'Brian's death in 2000, he left three chapters of an unfinished 21st novel in the acclaimed nautical series featuring British naval commander Jack Aubrey and his boon companion, surgeon and intelligence agent Stephen Maturin. Recently raised to the rank of rear admiral of the Blue, Aubrey heads to the South African station to assume his responsibilities via Argentina. There he meets up with the region's Papal Nuncio, Samuel Mputa, who happens to be Jack's illegitimate son. In Africa, Maturin meets an old university classmate, and their rivalry escalates into a duel. It is here that fans of the series will be left forever hanging. The book offers O'Brian's corrected typescript, handwritten portions of the corresponding text, and added notes and comments.

Where it's reviewed:
Booklist, October 15, 2004, page 390
Kirkus Reviews, August 15, 2004, page 770
Library Journal, November 15, 2004, page 51
Publishers Weekly, August 30, 2004, page 31

Other books by the same author:
Blue at the Mizzen, 1999
The Hundred Days, 1998
The Yellow Admiral, 1996
The Commodore, 1995
The Wine-Dark Sea, 1993

Other books you might like:
Joan Druett, *A Watery Grave*, 2004
Dewey Lambdin, *Havoc's Sword*, 2003
Jan Needle, *The Spithead Nymph*, 2004
Edwin Thomas, *The Blighted Cliffs*, 2004
Richard Woodman, *A King's Cutter*, 2001

Historical

914

DAN O'BRIEN

The Indian Agent

(Guilford, Connecticut: Lyons, 2004)

Story type: Historical/American West; Indian Wars
Subject(s): Indians of North America; Medicine; Biography
Major character(s): Valentine T. McGillycuddy, Doctor, Historical Figure; Red Cloud, Historical Figure, Indian; Fanny McGillycuddy, Spouse (of Valentine), Historical Figure
Time period(s): 1870s; 1880s
Locale(s): Great Plains; Black Hills, South Dakota

Summary: This sequel to O'Brien's award-winning *The Contract Surgeon* continues the fictional biography of the renowned western physician Valentine T. McGillycuddy, who became a friend of the great Sioux war chief Crazy Horse. Here he is shown becoming the youngest agent of the Pine Ridge Reservation and his experiences document the early days of the reservation system as the Sioux make a painful transition to ''civilized'' life. The novel shows the fate of war chief Red Cloud and his followers as they make a final stand against the whites who have poured into the Black Hills in search of gold. The tragic Battle of Wounded Knee, which McGillycuddy fails to prevent, is the novel's climax.

Where it's reviewed:
Kirkus Reviews, August 15, 2004, page 770
Publishers Weekly, October 4, 2004, page 68

Other books by the same author:
The Contract Surgeon, 1999
In the Center of the Nation, 1991
Spirit of the Hills, 1988
Eminent Domain, 1987

Other books you might like:
Frederick J. Chiaventone, *Moon of Bitter Cold*, 2002
Adrian C. Louis, *Skins*, 1995
Harold Burton Meyers, *Reservations*, 1999
James Welch, *The Heartsong of Charging Elk*, 2001
Richard S. Wheeler, *Dodging Red Cloud*, 1987

915

ROBIN PAIGE (Pseudonym of Bill Albert and Susan Wittig Albert)

Death at Blenheim Palace

(New York: Berkley Prime Crime, 2004)

Story type: Historical/Edwardian; Mystery
Series: Kathryn Ardleigh. Book 11
Subject(s): Mystery and Detective Stories
Major character(s): Lord Charles Sheridan, Nobleman; Lady Kathryn Sheridan, Noblewoman
Time period(s): 1900s (1903)
Locale(s): England

Summary: The Duke and Duchess of Marlborough invite husband-and-wife sleuths Lord Charles and Lady Kate Sheridan to Blenheim Palace to research a scandal that took place on the site in the 12th century involving the murder of the mistress of King Henry II. While the Sheridans try to solve this ancient mystery, a new one develops when a housemaid, the duke, and his mistress all disappear.

Other books by the same author:
Death in Hyde Park, 2004
Death at Glamis Castle, 2003
Death at Dartmoor, 2002
Death at Epsom Downs, 2001
Death at White Chapel, 2000

Other books you might like:
Marion Chesney, *Hasty Death*, 2004
Tracy Chevalier, *Falling Angels*, 2001
Robert Lee Hall, *The King Edward Plot*, 1980
J.P. Morrissey, *A Weekend at Blenheim*, 2002
Anne Perry, *The Thomas and Charlotte Pitt Series*, 1979-

916

ELIZABETH PALMER

The Distaff Side

(New York: St. Martin's Press, 2004)

Story type: Historical/World War I
Subject(s): World War I
Major character(s): Vera Kalanskaya, Dancer; Bertie Langham, Gentleman; Mai Binnington, Suffragette
Time period(s): 1910s (1917)
Locale(s): Paris, France; England

Summary: After former Russian dancer Vera Kalanskaya, who is stranded in Paris, steals the jewels and identity of her ailing employer, she emerges as the Princess Zhenia Dashkova in England where she gets involved with the rich Bertie Langham. His mother has chosen Mai Binnington for her son, but she loses favor through her activities as a suffragette. The ''princess'' must deal with the Russian secret police tracking the stolen jewels, while Mai endures an abusive marriage.

Where it's reviewed:
Booklist, November 1, 2004, page 465
Kirkus Reviews, September 15, 2004, page 887

Other books by the same author:
The Dark Side of the Sun, 2000
The Golden Rule, 1998
Flowering Judas, 1997
Old Money, 1996
Scarlet Angel, 1993

Other books you might like:
Charlotte Bingham, *The Chestnut Tree*, 2003
Anita Brookner, *The Rules of Engagement*, 2003
A.S. Byatt, *A Whistling Woman*, 2003
Hayden Gabriel, *Where the Light Remains*, 2003
Marcia Willett, *The Children's Hour*, 2004

917

ALAN PARKER

The Sucker's Kiss

(New York: St. Martin's Press, 2004)

Story type: Historical/American West Coast; Coming-of-Age
Subject(s): Crime and Criminals
Major character(s): Tommy Moran, Thief (pickpocket); Effie, Young Woman
Time period(s): 20th century
Locale(s): San Francisco, California

Summary: Alan Parker, British director of such films as *Midnight Express* and *Angela's Ashes*, makes his fictional debut with this story set in Northern California in the early years of the 20th century. It concerns expert pickpocket Tommy Moran whose career begins during the San Francisco earthquake of 1906 and continues through the Depression. Finding himself in the Napa Valley, he meets the love of his life, Effie, the daughter of an Armenian wine maker. She offers him a chance to go straight, but he faces challenges from his past criminal affiliations and from Italian and Chinese criminals. This is a strong period adventure, suffused with the particulars of place and the colorful patois of street life.

Where it's reviewed:
Booklist, September 1, 2004, page 63
Kirkus Reviews, August 15, 2004, page 770

Other books you might like:
Michael Chabon, *The Amazing Adventures of Kavalier & Clay*, 2000
Glen David Gold, *Carter Beats the Devil*, 2001
Philip Roth, *American Pastoral*, 1997
Darin Straus, *The Real McCoy*, 2002
Sarah Waters, *Fingersmith*, 2002

918

MICHAEL PEARCE

A Cold Touch of Ice

(Scottsdale, Arizona: Poisoned Pen Press, 2004)

Story type: Historical/Edwardian; Mystery
Series: Mamur Zapt. Book 13
Subject(s): Mystery and Detective Stories; Crime and Criminals
Major character(s): Gareth Owen, Police Officer
Time period(s): 1910s (1912)
Locale(s): Cairo, Egypt

Summary: In this installment of Pearce's popular Edwardian mystery series, Gareth Owen, the Mamur Zapt, the British head of Cairo's secret police, investigates the murder of an Italian businessman and long-time Cairo resident. It is 1912, and Italy is at war with Turkey. Could the murder be connected? Owen's investigation allows the reader an authentic look at period Cairo and the turbulent political climate preceding the outbreak of the Great War.

Where it's reviewed:
Booklist, August 2004, page 1907

Kirkus Reviews, July 1, 2004, page 607
Publishers Weekly, July 19, 2004, page 148

Other books by the same author:
Death of an Effendi, 2004
The Fig Tree Murder, 2003
The Snake Catcher's Daughter, 2003
The Camel of Destruction, 2002
The Mamur Zapt and the Spoils of Egypt, 1992

Other books you might like:
Olivia Manning, *The Danger Tree*, 1977
Glenn Meades, *The Sands of Sakkara*, 1999
Elizabeth Peters, *The Amelia Peabody Series*, 1975-
Robert Sole, *The Photographer's Wife*, 1999
David Stevens, *The Waters of Babylon*, 2000

919

MICHAEL PEARCE

A Dead Man in Trieste

(New York: Carroll & Graf, 2004)

Story type: Mystery; Historical/Edwardian
Subject(s): Mystery and Detective Stories
Major character(s): Sandor Seymour, Police Officer, Spy
Time period(s): 1900s (1906)
Locale(s): Trieste, Austria-Hungary

Summary: Pearce, the author of the popular Mamur Zapt mysteries, launches a new historical mystery series set in the Adriatic port city of Trieste in 1906. When the British consul disappears, Special Branch officer Sandor Seymour is dispatched to investigate. Finding the consul's corpse, Seymour tries to answer why he had been on the docks the evening he died and who had he attended the cinema with earlier that evening. Seymour is an intriguing sleuth, and Pearce succeeds in creating a fascinating atmospheric mystery.

Where it's reviewed:
Kirkus Reviews, October 1, 2004, page 943
Library Journal, November 1, 2004, page 58
New York Times Book Review, December 26, 2004, page 22
Publishers Weekly, October 4, 2004, page 73

Other books by the same author:
A Cold Touch of Ice, 2004
The Face in the Cemetery, 2004
The Fig Tree Murder, 2003
The Snake Catcher's Daughter, 2003
The Last Cut, 1998

Other books you might like:
Conrad Allen, *Murder on the Minnesota*, 2002
Clare Curzon, *Guilty Knowledge*, 2000
Dianne Day, *The Fremont Jones Series*, 1995-
Gillian Linscott, *The Perfect Knowledge*, 2001
Elliott Roosevelt, *A First Class Murder*, 1991

Historical

920

MICHAEL PEARCE

The Face in the Cemetery

(Scottsdale, Arizona: Poisoned Pen Press, 2004)

Story type: Mystery; Historical/World War I
Series: Mamur Zapt. Book 14
Subject(s): Mystery and Detective Stories; World War I
Major character(s): Gareth Owen, Police Officer
Time period(s): 1910s (1914)
Locale(s): Cairo, Egypt; Minya, Egypt

Summary: Gareth Owen, the Mamur Zapt, or head of the British secret police in Cairo, contends with the impact of World War I which has reached Egypt in 1914. While in the province of Minya, Owen finds the body of a German woman wrapped in bandages and surrounded by mummified cats. The murder might be connected with an uprising aimed at driving the British out of Egypt.

Where it's reviewed:
New York Times Book Review, December 26, 2004, page 22
Publishers Weekly, November 18, 2004, page 39

Other books by the same author:
A Cold Touch of Ice, 2004
A Dead Man in Trieste, 2004
The Fig Tree Murder, 2003
The Snake Catcher's Daughter, 2003
The Last Cut, 1998

Other books you might like:
Olivia Manning, *The Danger Tree*, 1977
Glenn Meades, *The Sands of Sakkara*, 1999
Elizabeth Peters, *The Amelia Peabody Series*, 1975-
Robert Sole, *The Photographer's Wife*, 1999
David Stevens, *The Waters of Babylon*, 2000

921

ANNE PERRY

Shoulder the Sky

(New York: Ballantine, 2004)

Story type: Historical/World War I; Mystery
Series: Joseph Reavley. Book 2
Subject(s): Mystery and Detective Stories; World War I
Major character(s): Joseph Reavley, Professor, Religious (chaplain); Matthew Reavley, Spy; Judith Reavley, Driver, Linguist
Time period(s): 1910s (1915)
Locale(s): London, England; France; Ypres, Belgium

Summary: Perry's period mystery series follows the careers of the Reavley siblings during World War I as they seek to bring to justice the murderer of their parents. Joseph, a military chaplain, is in the thick of trench warfare at Ypres; Judith is a driver for the commanding general; and Matthew, an intelligence officer, seeks the mysterious "Peacemaker." The murder of a war correspondent by one of his compatriots at the front provides a major clue to the facts behind their parents' deaths. The novel features a vivid depiction of the Great War battlefield.

Where it's reviewed:
Booklist, July 2004, page 1800
Kirkus Reviews, July 15, 2004, page 654
Library Journal, September 1, 2004, page 126
Publishers Weekly, July 26, 2004, page 41

Other books by the same author:
The Shifting Tide, 2004
No Graves as Yet, 2003
Seven Dials, 2003
Southampton Row, 2002
The Whitechapel Conspiracy, 2000

Other books you might like:
Rennie Airth, *River of Darkness*, 1999
Patricia Anthony, *Flanders*, 1998
Iain Lawrence, *Lord of the Nutcracker Men*, 2001
Gillian Linscott, *The Perfect Daughter*, 2001
Charles Todd, *The Ian Rutledge Series*, 1996-

922

ARTHUR PHILLIPS

The Egyptologist

(New York: Random House, 2004)

Story type: Historical/Roaring Twenties
Subject(s): Egyptian Antiquities; Archaeology; Ancient History
Major character(s): Ralph Trilipush, Archaeologist (Egyptologist); Harold Ferrell, Detective—Police
Time period(s): 1920s
Locale(s): Egypt

Summary: Phillips' creative follow-up to his critically-acclaimed first novel *Prague* follows the adventures of Egyptologist Ralph Trilipush who is trying to find the tomb of Egyptian King Atum-hadu. But why is an Australian detective, Harold Ferrell, on Trilipush's trail as a suspect in the case of the mysterious death of an Australian Egyptologist? This intriguing labyrinth ends with a shocking conclusion.

Where it's reviewed:
Booklist, June 1, 2004, page 1671
Library Journal, July 2004, page 73
New York Times Book Review, September 12, 2004, page 8
Publishers Weekly, July 5, 2004, page 35

Other books by the same author:
Prague, 2002

Other books you might like:
Rikki Ducornet, *Gazelle*, 2003
Kate Ellis, *The Bone Garden*, 2003
Olivia Manning, *The Danger Tree*, 1977
Michael Pearce, *The Mamur Zapt Series*, 1988-
Elizabeth Peters, *Children of the Storm*, 2003

923

LILY POWELL

The Devil in Buenos Aires
(Guilford, Connecticut: Lyons, 2004)

Story type: Historical/World War II; Espionage
Subject(s): World War II; Espionage
Major character(s): Antonie Herrnfeld, Immigrant; Stefan von der Heiden, Diplomat
Time period(s): 1940s
Locale(s): Buenos Aires, Argentina

Summary: This espionage thriller is set in Buenos Aires during World War II as German Jew Antonie Herrnfeld is recruited as a spy by Nazi diplomat Stefan von der Heiden to protect the lives of her parents in Germany. Learning from the British that her parents are dead, Antonie turns double agent in an increasingly dangerous espionage game. Atmospheric and packed with period details, the novel is an exciting read with some interesting twists along the way.

Other books by the same author:
The Bird of Paradise, 1971

Other books you might like:
John Altman, *A Gathering of Spies*, 2000
Ken Follett, *Jackdaws*, 2001
Alan Furst, *Dark Voyage*, 2004
Greg Iles, *Black Cross*, 1995
Robert Wilson, *The Company of Strangers*, 2001

924

STEVEN PRESSFIELD

The Virtues of War
(New York: Doubleday, 2004)

Story type: Historical/Ancient Greece
Subject(s): Autobiography; Kings, Queens, Rulers, etc.; Ancient History
Major character(s): Alexander the Great, Historical Figure, Military Personnel
Time period(s): 4th century B.C.
Locale(s): Macedonia; Middle East

Summary: Pressfield allows Alexander the Great to dictate the story of his life, as the Macedonian military commander looks back on his fabled career of conquest. This internal view of Alexander sheds light on his motives and passions, while Pressfield's remarkable expertise about the period's weapons, military strategies, and customs brings a distant era to vivid life.

Where it's reviewed:
Booklist, September 15, 2004, page 210
Library Journal, October 1, 2004, page 72
Publishers Weekly, October 11, 2004, page 57

Other books by the same author:
Last of the Amazons, 2002
Tides of War, 2000
Gates of Fire, 1999
The Legend of Bagger Vance, 1995

Other books you might like:
Maurice Druon, *Alexander the God*, 1954
Priscilla Galloway, *The Courtesan's Daughter*, 2002
Nikos Kazantazakis, *Alexander the Great*, 1982
Valerio Massimo Manfredi, *The Alexander the Great Trilogy*, 2001-2002
Mary Renault, *The Persian Boy*, 1972

925

NANCY RAWLES

My Jim
(New York: Crown, 2005)

Story type: Historical/Americana; Historical/Post-American Civil War
Subject(s): African Americans; Slavery
Major character(s): Sadie, Slave; Jim, Slave
Time period(s): 19th century
Locale(s): Missouri; Louisiana

Summary: Writing in dialect, Rawles intimately describes the impact of slavery from the perspective of Sadie, the wife of Jim from Mark Twain's *Adventures of Huckleberry Finn*. Sadie chronicles her life with Jim on Mas Watson's Missouri plantation and the circumstances that led to Jim's flight to freedom. She is punished for Jim's escape and persecuted as a witch. Convinced that Jim has died, Sadie must struggle on her own. The couple are not reunited, and Sadie continues her story after emancipation as her granddaughter prepares to head west with a Buffalo Soldier.

Where it's reviewed:
Booklist, November 15, 2004, page 563
Library Journal, December 1, 2004, page 102
Publishers Weekly, November 29, 2004, page 22

Other books by the same author:
Crawfish Dreams, 2003
Love Like Gumbo, 1997

Other books you might like:
Pam Durbin, *So Far Back*, 2000
Valerie Martin, *Property*, 2003
Greg Matthews, *The Further Adventures of Huckleberry Finn*, 1984
Toni Morrison, *Beloved*, 1987
Alice Randall, *The Wind Done Gone*, 2001

926

VAN REID

Fiddler's Green
(New York: Viking, 2004)

Story type: Historical/Victorian America; Mystery
Series: Moosepath League. Book 5
Subject(s): Small Town Life; Clubs; Feuds
Major character(s): Sundry Moss, Servant (valet); Tobias Walton, Gentleman
Time period(s): 1890s (1897)
Locale(s): Portland, Maine

Historical

Summary: This is the fifth and apparently final installment of Reid's picaresque series about 19th-century Maine's Pickwickian Moosepath League. The story concerns the wedding of Moosepath chairman Tobias Walton and its aftermath. There are other romantic encounters among League members, notably Walton's valet Sundry Moss, in addition to a kidnapping and a bitter family feud. Reid is a master of his era and region, and newcomers to the series, as well as veterans will have much to admire and enjoy here.

Where it's reviewed:
Booklist, July 2004, page 1819
Kirkus Reviews, May 15, 2004, page 467
Publishers Weekly, June 28, 2004, page 32

Other books by the same author:
Mrs. Roberto, 2003
Peter Loon, 2002
Daniel Plainway, 2000
Mollie Peer, 1999
Cordelia Underwood, 1998

Other books you might like:
Cynthia Applewhite, *Summer Dreams and the Kleig Light Gas Company*, 1982
Wendell Berry, *Jayber Crow*, 2000
Tony Earley, *Jim the Boy*, 2000
Brent Monahan, *The Manhattan Island Club*, 2003
Norma Peterson, *Rhonda the Rubber Woman*, 1998

927

DAVID L. ROBBINS

Liberation Road
(New York: Bantam, 2005)

Story type: Historical/World War II
Subject(s): War; World War II; Race Relations
Major character(s): Ben Kahn, Religious (Jewish chaplain); Joe Amos, Military Personnel (truck driver)
Time period(s): 1940s
Locale(s): France

Summary: Robbins tells the powerful (and overlooked) story of the 688th Truck Battalion, part of the famed Red Ball Express, a contingent of 23,000 men manning 6,000 trucks which had to supply the fast-moving combat troops in their rush to Germany following D-Day. Action is described from the perspective of Ben Kahn, a World War I veteran and now a Jewish army chaplain; Joe Amos, a young black truck driver; and a war profiteer, known as ''White Dog.'' Kahn is looking for his son, a B-17 pilot shot down over France, and the action rushes toward the liberation of Paris. Robbins is a master of his era, and this is an exciting novel that fills in details about a fascinating aspect of the war.

Where it's reviewed:
Kirkus Reviews, October 15, 2004, page 982
Publishers Weekly, November 29, 2004, page 23

Other books by the same author:
Last Citadel, 2003
Scorched Earth, 2002
The End of War, 2000
War of the Rats, 2000

Souls to Keep, 1998

Other books you might like:
Liam Callanan, *The Cloud Atlas*, 2004
Francis Cottam, *The Fire Fighter*, 2001
Andrew Greig, *The Clouds Above*, 2001
John Oliver Killens, *And Then We Heard Thunder*, 1963
Steve Yarbrough, *Prisoner of War*, 2003

928

MADELEINE E. ROBINS

Petty Treason
(New York: Forge, 2004)

Story type: Mystery; Historical/Regency
Series: Sarah Tolerance. Book 2
Subject(s): Mystery and Detective Stories; Crime and Criminals
Major character(s): Sarah Tolerance, Detective—Private
Time period(s): 1810s (1810)
Locale(s): London, England

Summary: Robins' second Regency mystery featuring unorthodox, gender-bending ''agent of inquiry'' Sarah Tolerance shows the sleuth investigating the murder of a French aristocrat inside his locked home. There is no end of suspects, but the how of the murder is as baffling as who is responsible. Tolerance's inquiry takes her on an intriguing tour of 1810 London, including the scandalous lifestyle of the royal family and the lot of emigres who fled France when Napoleon gained power.

Where it's reviewed:
Library Journal, September 1, 2004, page 126
Publishers Weekly, August 16, 2004, page 46

Other books by the same author:
Point of Honour, 2003
The Stone War, 1999
Lady John, 1982

Other books you might like:
T.F. Banks, *The Thief-Taker*, 2001
Stephanie Barron, *The Jane Austen Series*, 1996-
Fidelis Morgan, *The Rival Queens*, 2001
Kate Ross, *The Julian Kestrel Series*, 1993-1997
Rosemary Stevens, *The Beau Brummell Series*, 2000-

929

PHILIP ROTH

The Plot Against America
(Boston: Houghton Mifflin, 2004)

Story type: Alternate History; Historical/Fantasy
Subject(s): Politics; Anti-Semitism; Presidents
Major character(s): Charles Lindbergh, Historical Figure, Political Figure; Walter Winchell, Historical Figure, Journalist; Henry Ford, Historical Figure, Businessman
Time period(s): 1940s
Locale(s): United States

Summary: Roth tries his hand at alternate history by imagining Charles A. Lindbergh's defeat of FDR in the 1940 presidential election on a pro-Nazi, anti-Semitic platform. The changes in American life under Lindbergh's administration are measured in the lives of young narrator Philip Roth, and his Jewish family in Newark, New Jersey. Historical figures such as Walter Winchell, Henry Ford, and Fiorello La Guardia appear in this chillingly plausible political novel.

Where it's reviewed:
Booklist, August 2004, page 1874
Kirkus Reviews, July 15, 2004, page 655
New York Times Book Review, October 3, 2004, page 14
Publishers Weekly, July 12, 2004, page 44

Other books by the same author:
The Dying Animal, 2001
The Human Stain, 2000
I Married a Communist, 1998
American Pastoral, 1997
Sabbath's Theater, 1995

Other books you might like:
Reeve Lindbergh, *The Names of the Mountains*, 1992
Joyce Carol Oates, *The Tattooed Girl*, 2003
Steve Thayer, *Silent Snow*, 1999
Harry Turtledove, *Settling Accounts*, 2004
Kate Wenner, *Setting Fires*, 2000

930

PRISCILLA ROYAL

Tyrant of the Mind

(Scottsdale, Arizona: Poisoned Pen Press, 2004)

Story type: Historical/Medieval; Mystery
Subject(s): Mystery and Detective Stories; Middle Ages; Religious Life
Major character(s): Eleanor, Religious (prioress); Brother Thomas, Religious
Time period(s): 13th century (1271)
Locale(s): England

Summary: In Royal's second medieval mystery, Sister Eleanor, Prioress of Tyndal, and Brother Thomas visit her father's Wynethorpe Castle on the Welsh border. They intend to care for her brother's sick, illegitimate son, while her father arranges a marriage for Eleanor's brother, Robert. When someone winds up dead, Robert is blamed, and Eleanor and Thomas search for the real culprit.

Where it's reviewed:
Library Journal, November 1, 2004, page 60
Publishers Weekly, November 15, 2004, page 44

Other books by the same author:
Wine of Violence, 2003

Other books you might like:
Alys Clare, *Ashes of Elements*, 2001
Susanna Gregory, *The Matthew Bartholomew Series*, 1996-
Edward Marston, *The Domesday Book Series*, 1993-
Ian Morson, *The William Falconer Series*, 1994-
Candace Robb, *The Owen Archer Series*, 1993-

931

JEAN-CHRISTOPHE RUFIN

Brazil Red

(New York: Norton, 2004)

Story type: Adventure; Coming-of-Age
Subject(s): Orphans; Indians of South America; Coming-of-Age
Major character(s): Just, Orphan; Colombe, Orphan; Chevalier Durand de Villegagnon, Historical Figure, Nobleman
Time period(s): 16th century
Locale(s): France; Brazil

Summary: Prix Goncourt-winning author Rufin follows the adventures of two French orphan siblings—Just and Colombe—on a colonizing expedition to Brazil in the 16th century. Under the command of the historical Chevalier Durand de Villegagnon, whose memoir provides some of the novel's details, the expedition is soon locked in a deadly struggle with the native population and the Portuguese who claim sovereignty. The orphans find themselves caught between the often contradictory values of European civilization and an alternative Indian view that is under assault.

Where it's reviewed:
Booklist, August 2004, page 1902
Kirkus Reviews, July 1, 2004, page 602
Library Journal, July 2004, page 74
Publishers Weekly, July 5, 2004, page 36

Other books by the same author:
The Siege of Isfahan, 2001
The Abyssinian, 1999

Other books you might like:
David W. Ball, *Empires of Sand*, 1999
Alejo Carpentier, *The Kingdom of the World*, 1956
Colleen McCullough, *Morgan's Run*, 2000
Eduardo Sguiglia, *Fordlandia*, 2000
Karen Tei Yamashita, *Brazil-Maru*, 1992

932

JOHN R. SACK

The Franciscan Conspiracy

(Ashland, Oregon: White Cloud, 2004)

Story type: Mystery
Subject(s): Mystery and Detective Stories; Religious Life; Biography
Major character(s): Father Leo, Religious; Amata, Student
Time period(s): 13th century
Locale(s): Italy

Summary: This historical mystery novel explores the secrets behind an effort to conceal facts about St. Francis of Assisi in which the Franciscan Order destroyed all early biographies of the saint and hid his body. Set 30 years after Francis' death, the novel shows Father Leo and his student, Amata, searching for the truth about Francis.

Other books you might like:
Umberto Eco, *The Name of the Rose*, 1983

Historical

Claudia Gross, *Scholarium*, 2004
Ian Morson, *The William Falconer Series*, 1994-
Ellis Peters, *The Brother Cadfael Series*, 1977-1994
Candace Robb, *The Owen Archer Series*, 1993-

933

C.J. SANSOM

Dark Fire

(New York: Viking, 2004)

Story type: Mystery; Historical/Medieval
Series: Matthew Shardlake. Book 2
Subject(s): Mystery and Detective Stories
Major character(s): Thomas Cromwell, Historical Figure, Government Official; Matthew Shardlake, Lawyer
Time period(s): 16th century
Locale(s): London, England

Summary: Matthew Shardlake, the hunchbacked Tudor-era lawyer and sleuth introduced in Sansom's *Dissolution*, returns for a second adventure. Shardlake defends a girl accused of murder who refuses to speak, and under English law, will be slowly crushed to death. To win a stay of execution, he agrees to undertake a secret mission for Lord Thomas Cromwell, the king's high counselor, to learn the secret of a terrifying new weapon called Greek Fire from the alchemists who possess it. Sansom excels at rendering interesting period atmosphere, and Shardlake's investigation takes him on a fascinating tour of Tudor England.

Where it's reviewed:
Booklist, November 15, 2004, page 566
Kirkus Reviews, October 15, 2004, page 982
Publishers Weekly, November 15, 2004, page 40

Other books by the same author:
Dissolution, 2003

Other books you might like:
Iris Collier, *Day of Wrath*, 2002
Kathy Lynn Emerson, *Face Down Across the Western Sea*, 2002
Philippa Gregory, *The Other Boleyn Girl*, 2001
Karen Harper, *The Queene's Cure*, 2002
Priscilla Royal, *Tyrant of the Mind*, 2004

934

HAROLD SCHECHTER

The Mask of Red Death

(New York: Ballantine, 2004)

Story type: Historical/Americana; Mystery
Subject(s): Mystery and Detective Stories; City and Town Life; Indians of North America
Major character(s): Edgar Allan Poe, Historical Figure, Writer; Kit Carson, Scout, Historical Figure; John Johnson, Frontiersman, Historical Figure
Time period(s): 1840s (1845)
Locale(s): New York, New York

Summary: The author's third period mystery to make use of Edgar Allan Poe as sleuth has the writer joining forces with frontiersman Kit Carson to track down a serial killer on the loose in New York City in 1845. The scalped victims lead the terrified New Yorkers to suspect a Native American in P.T. Barnum's sideshow, but Carson puts Poe on the trail of real-life Indian killer John Johnson, who murdered Carson's Arapaho wife. Schechter takes some liberties with the facts surrounding Carson and Johnson, but compensates by his expert handling of period detail of the back alleyways of New York City.

Where it's reviewed:
Kirkus Reviews, June 15, 2004, page 556
Library Journal, July 2004, page 63
Publishers Weekly, May 31, 2004, page 54

Other books by the same author:
The Hum Bug, 2001
Nevermore, 1999
Outcry, 1997

Other books you might like:
George Egon Hatvary, *The Murder of Edgar Allan Poe*, 1997
John May, *Poe & Fanny*, 2004
Manny Meyers, *The Last Mystery of Edgar Allan Poe*, 1978
Randall Silvis, *Disquiet Heart*, 2002
Andrew Taylor, *An Unpardonable Crime*, 2004

935

NINA SCHUYLER

The Painting

(Chapel Hill, North Carolina: Algonquin Books, 2004)

Story type: Historical/Victorian
Subject(s): Artists and Art; War
Major character(s): Ayoshi, Artist; Hiyashi, Artist, Government Official; Jorgen, Veteran (Franco-Prussian War)
Time period(s): 1870s
Locale(s): Japan; Paris, France

Summary: This intriguing debut novel connects two separate, distant circles. One concerns Ayoshi, a Japanese artist trapped in a loveless marriage with Hiyashi, a government official and disabled potter; the other deals with Jorgen, a Danish soldier who lost his leg fighting for France in the Franco-Prussian War. Working for a Paris importer, Jorgen finds one of Hiyashi's ceramic bowls holding an erotic painting by Ayoshi. It causes him to reevaluate his life. Although Jorgen and Ayoshi never meet, the juxtaposition of their two worlds produces a fascinating journey of discovery and the universal language of art and love.

Where it's reviewed:
Booklist, August 2004, page 1902
Kirkus Reviews, August 15, 2004, page 773
Library Journal, September 1, 2004, page 142
Publishers Weekly, October 4, 2004, page 68

Other books you might like:
Sarah Dunant, *The Birth of Venus*, 2003
Lydia Y. Minatoya, *The Strangeness of Beauty*, 1999
Brian Moore, *The Magician's Wife*, 1997
Alyson Richman, *The Mask Carver's Son*, 2000
Susan Vreeland, *The Forest Lover*, 2004

936

HELEN SCULLY

In the Hope of Rising Again

(New York: Penguin, 2004)

Story type: Family Saga; Historical/Americana
Subject(s): Family Relations
Major character(s): Regina Riant, Spouse (of Charles Morrow); Charles Morrow, Spouse (of Regina); Camilla, Servant (maid)
Time period(s): 19th century; 20th century
Locale(s): Mobile, Alabama

Summary: Scully looks at American history from the aftermath of the Civil War through the Great Depression from the perspective of the prominent Alabama Riant family. The story is anchored by matriarch Regina Riant, the daughter of a Confederate veteran and newspaper magnate. She is married to Charles Morrow, a man she does not love, and is sustained by her devotion to her black maid Camilla and by her Catholic faith. Regina is shown coping with a series of losses while stoically carrying on against a backdrop of change that thoroughly alters life in the Deep South.

Where it's reviewed:
Booklist, July 2004, page 1820
Kirkus Reviews, June 1, 2004, page 515
Publishers Weekly, July 5, 2004, page 38

Other books you might like:
Justin Cronin, *The Summer Guest*, 2004
Elsie Burch Donald, *Nashborough*, 2001
Paul Jaskunas, *Hidden*, 2004
Mark Mills, *Amagansett*, 2004
Anne Tyler, *The Amateur Marriage*, 2004

937

JEFF SHAARA

To the Last Man

(New York: Ballantine, 2004)

Story type: Historical/World War I
Subject(s): World War I; War; Military Life
Major character(s): John J. Pershing, Military Personnel (American commander), Historical Figure; Manfred von Richthofen, Military Personnel (German aviator), Historical Figure; Raoul Lufbery, Military Personnel (American aviator)
Time period(s): 1910s
Locale(s): United States; France

Summary: Shaara shifts his attention from the Civil War and the Revolution to America's involvement in World War I, capturing the perspective of such historical figures as General Pershing and German air ace Manfred von Richthofen, as well as fictional combatants aviator Raoul Lufbery and Marine Roscoe Temple. Together the cast helps to illustrate the mass slaughter of the war and its continuing influence in forming modern history. The book is particularly strong in evoking the horror of trench warfare and the earliest days of aerial combat.

Where it's reviewed:
Booklist, September 15, 2004, page 180
Kirkus Reviews, September 15, 2004, page 888
Library Journal, October 1, 2004, page 73
Publishers Weekly, October 11, 2004, page 54

Other books by the same author:
The Glorious Cause, 2002
Rise to Rebellion, 2001
Gone for Soldiers, 2000
The Last Full Measure, 1998
Gods and Generals, 1996

Other books you might like:
Mark Goodman, *Hurrah for the Next Man Who Dies*, 1985
Frances Itani, *Deafening*, 2003
Judith Claire Mitchell, *The Last Day of War*, 2004
Robert L. O'Connell, *Fast Eddie*, 1999
Jacqueline Winspear, *Birds of a Feather*, 2004

938

MARY SHARRATT

The Real Minerva

(Boston: Houghton Mifflin, 2004)

Story type: Historical/Roaring Twenties
Subject(s): Women; Small Town Life
Major character(s): Penny Niebeck, Teenager; Barbara Niebeck, Servant (cleaning woman), Parent (of Penny); Cora Egan, Farmer
Time period(s): 1920s (1923)
Locale(s): Minnesota

Summary: Small town life in Minnesota during the 1920s is dramatized in this novel about women's lives. Fifteen-year-old Penny Niebeck, angered over her mother Barbara's affair with the man for whom she keeps house, becomes the hired girl for Cora Egan, a former Chicago society woman now pregnant and living alone on her grandfather's farm. All three women show different aspects of being victims of men, their society, and their pasts, and their stories illustrate the challenge of survival.

Where it's reviewed:
Booklist, September 1, 2004, page 64
Kirkus Reviews, August 15, 2004, page 774
Publishers Weekly, September 6, 2004, page 47

Other books by the same author:
Summit Avenue, 2000

Other books you might like:
Elizabeth Brundage, *The Doctor's Wife*, 2004
Jonatha Ceely, *Mina*, 2004
Terry Gamble, *The Water Dancers*, 2003
Helen Humphreys, *Afterimage*, 2000
William Riviere, *Kate Caterina*, 2001

Historical

939

CAROLYN SLAUGHTER

A Black Englishman

(New York: Farrar, Straus and Giroux, 2004)

Story type: Historical/Roaring Twenties
Subject(s): Marriage; Race Relations; Religious Conflict
Major character(s): Isabel Herbert, Spouse (of Neville); Neville Herbert, Spouse (of Isabel), Military Personnel (British army officer); Sam Singh, Doctor, Lover (of Isabel)
Time period(s): 1920s
Locale(s): India

Summary: Loosely based on incidents in the life of the author's maternal grandmother, the novel dramatizes what happens when Isabel Herbert accompanies her military husband to India and falls in love with Sam Singh, an Oxford-educated Indian doctor, the so-called black Englishman of the book's title. Their illicit affair is doomed from the start and becomes the locus for the author to explore the racial and religious prejudices of colonial India.

Where it's reviewed:
Booklist, October 1, 2004, page 312
Library Journal, October 15, 2004, page 56
Publishers Weekly, September 27, 2004, page 35

Other books by the same author:
Before the Knife, 2002
The Innocents, 1986
A Perfect Woman, 1984
Dreams of the Kalahari, 1981
Magdalene, 1978

Other books you might like:
Thalassa Ali, *A Beggar at the Gate*, 2004
Barbara Cleverly, *The Damascened Blade*, 2004
David Davidar, *The House of Blue Mangoes*, 2002
Amitav Ghosh, *The Glass Palace*, 2001
Susanna Moore, *One Last Look*, 2003

940

DANIELLE STEEL

Echoes

(New York: Delacorte, 2004)

Story type: Historical/World War I; Historical/World War II
Subject(s): War; Romance; Jews
Major character(s): Beata Wittgenstein, Spouse (of Antoine); Antoine de Vallerand, Spouse (of Beata), Nobleman
Time period(s): 20th century (1910s-1940s)
Locale(s): Germany; Switzerland

Summary: Steel's novel deals with the impact of World War I and World War II on the German beauty Beata Wittgenstein who falls in love with French nobleman Antoine de Vallerand while on vacation in Switzerland. Her orthodox Jewish parents disapprove, but Beata defies them and marries Antoine. When World War I ends, the couple returns to Germany only to get caught up in the Nazis' persecution of the Jews, in which even their daughter, Amadea, who has taken vows as a Carmelite nun, is not safe. Steel's usual glitz and glamour is missing here. Instead, the novel offers a multigenerational saga against the backdrop of 20th-century European history.

Where it's reviewed:
Booklist, October 1, 2004, page 233
Kirkus Reviews, October 1, 2004, page 936
Publishers Weekly, October 4, 2004, page 68

Other books by the same author:
Dating Game, 2004
Miracle, 2004
Second Chance, 2004
Ransom, 2004
Safe Harbor, 2003

Other books you might like:
William Brodrick, *The Sixth Lamentation*, 2003
Sebastian Faulks, *Charlotte Gray*, 1998
Ken Follett, *Jackdaws*, 2001
Alan Furst, *Blood of Victory*, 2002
Thomas Sanchez, *Day of the Bees*, 2000

941

NEAL STEPHENSON

The System of the World

(New York: William Morrow, 2004)

Story type: Historical/Georgian; Historical/Seventeenth Century
Series: Baroque Cycle. Volume 3
Subject(s): Adventure and Adventurers; Science
Major character(s): Daniel Waterhouse, Scientist; Eliza de la Zeur, Spy; Isaac Newton, Historical Figure, Scholar
Time period(s): 1710s
Locale(s): London, England

Summary: In the third volume of Stephenson's mind-expanding Baroque Cycle, Daniel Waterhouse travels from his Boston home to London to mediate the dispute between Sir Isaac Newton and Gottfried von Leibnitz over the origin of calculus. While there, he becomes involved in the search for a group of terrorists targeting the proponents of Natural Philosophy, including Waterhouse himself. Meanwhile, professional rogue Jack Shaftoe continues his scheming aimed at disrupting Britain's new monetary system, while Eliza de la Zeur asserts her influence over Caroline of Ansbach, consort of the next King of England. A liberal education in itself, the novel, like the series, is a triumph of capturing its era and the emergence of modern science and politics.

Where it's reviewed:
Booklist, September 15, 2004, page 180
Library Journal, September 15, 2004, page 51
Publishers Weekly, September 13, 2004, page 57

Other books by the same author:
The Confusion, 2004
Quicksilver, 2003
Cryptonomicon, 1999
The Diamond Age, 1995
Snow Crash, 1992

Other books you might like:
Susanna Clarke, *Jonathan Strange & Mr. Norrell*, 2004
Emma Donoghue, *Life Mask*, 2004
Lisa Goldstein, *The Alchemist's Door*, 2002
Philip Kerr, *Dark Matter*, 2002
Lawrence Norfolk, *The Pope's Rhinoceros*, 1996

942

JANE STEVENSON

The Empress of Last Days

(Boston: Houghton Mifflin, 2004)

Story type: Historical/Seventeenth Century
Subject(s): Biography; Kings, Queens, Rulers, etc.; Race Relations
Major character(s): Elizabeth of Bohemia, Historical Figure, Royalty; Pelagius, Slave (former); Balthasar, Heir
Time period(s): 17th century; 21st century
Locale(s): Netherlands; Barbados; England

Summary: Stevenson concludes her masterful trilogy set in 17th-century Europe concerning a queen and her former slave. Elizabeth of Bohemia, sister of Charles I of England, in exile in Holland, marries the once-enslaved African prince, Pelagius. The couple have a son, Balthasar, and the family's descendants up to the present are investigated by two professors who uncover the fact that a black woman from Barbados may be the true queen of England.

Where it's reviewed:
Booklist, October 15, 2004, page 39
Kirkus Reviews, October 1, 2004, page 936
Library Journal, November 15, 2004, page 52
Publishers Weekly, October 18, 2004, page 48

Other books by the same author:
The Shadow King, 2003
The Winter Queen, 2002
London Bridges, 2001
Several Deceptions, 1999

Other books you might like:
Christina Dodd, *Some Enchanted Evening*, 2004
Philippa Gregory, *The Queen's Fool*, 2004
Arthur Japin, *The Two Hearts of Kwasi Boachi*, 2000
David Liss, *The Coffee Trader*, 2003
Deborah Moggach, *Tulip Flower*, 2000

943

JULIAN STOCKWIN

Mutiny

(New York: Scribner, 2004)

Story type: Historical/Napoleonic Wars; Action/Adventure
Series: Thomas Kydd. Book 4
Subject(s): Sea Stories; Military Life; War
Major character(s): Thomas Kydd, Military Personnel (British sailor); Nicholas Renzi, Military Personnel (British sailor)
Time period(s): 1790s (1797)
Locale(s): Venice, Italy; *Bacchante*, At Sea

Summary: Stockwin's nautical adventure series chronicling the naval career of Thomas Kydd depicts both imagined and historical events during the Napoleonic Wars. Kydd, now a master's mate, joins the crew of the frigate *Bacchante* on a mission to rescue a British diplomat during Napoleon's siege of Venice. Kydd and companion Nicholas Renzi later participate in the most notorious fleet mutiny in British naval history.

Other books by the same author:
Seaflower, 2003
Artemis, 2002
Kydd, 2001

Other books you might like:
Dewey Lambdin, *Havoc's Sword*, 2003
Jan Needle, *The Spithead Nymph*, 2004
Dudley Pope, *Ramage's Mutiny*, 2001
Neal Stephenson, *The Confusion*, 2004
Richard Woodman, *A King's Cutter*, 2001

944

EDWIN THOMAS

The Blighted Cliffs

(New York: St. Martin's Press, 2004)

Story type: Historical/Napoleonic Wars; Mystery
Series: Reluctant Adventures of Lieutenant Martin Jerrold. Book 1
Subject(s): Mystery and Detective Stories; Military Life
Major character(s): Martin Jerrold, Military Personnel (British naval lieutenant)
Time period(s): 1800s (1806)
Locale(s): Dover, England

Summary: Set during the Napoleonic Wars, this mystery/adventure is the first in a projected trilogy dealing with carousing scapegrace Lt. Martin Jerrold. Having missed the Battle of Trafalgar while sleeping off a hangover below decks, Jerrold is consigned to intercept smuggling operations out of Dover. However, when he comes under suspicion in the murder of an unidentified man, Jerrold must solve the case and clear his name. This is an entertaining debut with a winning sleuth and solid period details.

Where it's reviewed:
Publishers Weekly, June 7, 2004, page 29

Other books you might like:
Bruce Alexander, *The Sir John Fielding Series*, 1994-
Joan Druett, *A Watery Grave*, 2004
Dewey Lambdin, *Havoc's Sword*, 2003
Jan Needle, *The Spithead Nymph*, 2004
Wilder Perkins, *The Bartholomew Hoare Series*, 1998-2001

945

LAWRENCE THORNTON

Sailors on the Inward Sea

(New York: Free Press, 2004)

Story type: Historical/World War I
Subject(s): Sea Stories; World War I; Authors and Writers

Major character(s): Jack Malone, Sea Captain; Joseph Conrad, Historical Figure, Writer
Time period(s): 1910s
Locale(s): England; At Sea

Summary: Thornton's inventive novel explores the friendship between novelist Joseph Conrad and merchant mariner Jack Malone, who is revealed to be the inspiration for Conrad's Marlow in *Heart of Darkness* and *Lord Jim*. Malone's attempt to understand his friend is tested by the implications of an event in World War I, witnessed by Conrad, when a British minesweeper crashes into a German submarine. Complex in its narrative strategy and depending on the reader's familiarity with Conrad and his works, the novel is often brilliant in penetrating the mind of a great novelist and the raw material out of which great novels are made.

Where it's reviewed:
Booklist, August 2004, page 1904
Kirkus Reviews, July 15, 2004, page 658
Library Journal, September 1, 2004, page 143
New York Times Book Review, September 26, 2004, page 24
Publishers Weekly, September 13, 2004, page 58

Other books by the same author:
Naming the Spirits, 1995
Ghost Woman, 1992
Under the Gypsy Moon, 1991
Imagining Argentina, 1987

Other books you might like:
Alexander Fullerton, *The Blooding of the Guns*, 2001
Gary Livingston, *Tears of Ice*, 2001
David Lodge, *Author, Author*, 2004
Steve Weiner, *The Yellow Sailor*, 2001
Meg Wolitzer, *The Wife*, 2003

946

H.N. TURTELTAUB (Pseudonym of Harry Turtledove)

Owls to Athens
(New York: Forge, 2004)

Story type: Historical/Ancient Greece; Adventure
Subject(s): Sea Stories; Business Enterprises
Major character(s): Menedemos, Trader; Sostratos, Trader
Time period(s): 4th century B.C.
Locale(s): Mediterranean; Athens, Greece

Summary: Turteltaub supplies a new installment of the ongoing adventures of Menedemos and Sostratos, merchant traders in the 4th century B.C. Mediterranean world. They journey to Athens with a worthless cargo of olive oil where they witness firsthand the bumpy transition to democracy. Along the way, the earthy Menedemos has an affair with a married woman, while the brainy Sostratos witnesses the drama festival known as the Greater Dionysia, and both men have enough misadventures to satisfy fans of this lighthearted and amusing series.

Where it's reviewed:
Kirkus Reviews, October 15, 2004, page 983

Other books by the same author:
The Sacred Land, 2003

The Gryphon's Skull, 2002
Over the Wine-Dark Sea, 2001
Justinian, 1998

Other books you might like:
Gillian Bradshaw, *The Sand-Reckoner*, 2000
Karen Essex, *Kleopatra*, 2001
Michael Curtis Ford, *The Ten Thousand*, 2001
Valerio Massimo Manfredi, *Spartan*, 2003
Steven Pressfield, *Last of the Amazons*, 2002

947

HARRY TURTLEDOVE

Days of Infamy
(New York: New American Library, 2004)

Story type: Historical/World War II; Alternate History
Subject(s): Alternate History; War
Major character(s): Fletch Armitage, Military Personnel (artillery officer); Jiro Takahashi, Fisherman; Joe Crosetti, Military Personnel (airman)
Time period(s): 1940s (1941)
Locale(s): Hawaii

Summary: Alternate history master Turtledove imagines a successful Japanese invasion of Hawaii after the attack on Pearl Harbor in 1941. Occupation of the islands is dramatized from multiple perspectives, including soldiers Fletch Armitage and Joe Crosetti, as well as Japanese fisherman Jiro Takahashi and his family. Alternating between their stories, the novel also imagines the military strategy of both the Japanese and the Americans with Hawaii changing hands.

Where it's reviewed:
Booklist, September 15, 2004, page 180
Library Journal, October 15, 2004, page 57
Publishers Weekly, October 1, 2004, page 60

Other books by the same author:
Curious Notions, 2004
Out of the Darkness, 2004
Return Engagement, 2004
The First Heroes, 2004
Jaws of Darkness, 2003

Other books you might like:
Kiana Davenport, *Song of the Exile*, 1999
Alison McLeay, *After Shanghai*, 1996
Nancy Morgan, *City of Women*, 1952
Martin Cruz Smith, *December 6*, 2002
Kathleen Tyau, *Makai*, 1999

948

HARRY TURTLEDOVE

Return Engagement
(New York: Del Rey, 2004)

Story type: Historical/Fantasy; Alternate History
Series: Settling Accounts Trilogy. Book 1
Subject(s): Alternate History; World War II; Politics

Major character(s): Al Smith, Historical Figure, Political Figure; Jake Featherston, Political Figure; Franklin Delano Roosevelt, Historical Figure, Political Figure
Time period(s): 1940s
Locale(s): United States

Summary: Turtledove, the reigning master of alternate history, begins a new trilogy that looks at the outbreak of World War II as it might have played out in a U.S. divided into North and South after the victory of the Confederacy in the Civil War. Jake Featherston, the ruthless Confederate leader, launches a surprise attack on the North, and its president, Al Smith, must respond to war at home and abroad, aided by an obscure assistant secretary of war, Franklin Delano Roosevelt. Readers fascinated by what-if scenarios will be captivated by Turtledove's inventiveness here. What-ifs delightfully give way to what's next.

Where it's reviewed:
Booklist, July 2004, page 1800
Kirkus Reviews, July 1, 2004, page 605
Library Journal, August 2004, page 72
Publishers Weekly, July 19, 2004, page 149

Other books by the same author:
Out of the Darkness, 2004
American Empire: The Victorious Opposition, 2003
In the Presence of Mine Enemies, 2003
American Empire: The Center Cannot Hold, 2002
Rulers of the Darkness, 2000

Other books you might like:
Steven Barnes, *Lion's Blood*, 2002
Robert Conroy, *1901*, 1995
Harry Harrison, *Stars & Stripes Triumphant*, 2003
Douglas Niles, *Fox on the Rhine*, 2000
    Michael Dobson, co-author

█ 949 █

PENNY VINCENZI

Something Dangerous
(New York: Overlook, 2004)

Story type: Historical/Roaring Twenties; Family Saga
Subject(s): Family Relations; Publishing; Business Enterprises
Major character(s): Giles Lytton, Heir; Kit Lytton, Heir; Venetia Lytton, Heiress
Time period(s): 20th century (1920s-1940s)
Locale(s): England

Summary: In a sequel to Vincenzi's family saga *No Angel* chronicling the Lyttons, a prominent British publishing family, it's 1928 and the heirs apparent—Giles, Kit, and their twin sisters, Venetia and Adele—are coming of age. Giles takes on a position in the firm, and the twins make their court debuts. Meanwhile the Lyttons' foster child, Barty Miller, shows the most aptitude for running the firm. The family and the business are shown enduring the Depression and the coming of World War II, with internal and external pressures breaking the family apart.

Where it's reviewed:
Booklist, September 1, 2004, page 8

Library Journal, September 15, 2004, page 51
Publishers Weekly, September 27, 2004, page 38

Other books by the same author:
Crossing the Pond, 2003
No Angel, 2003
Almost a Crime, 2000
Another Woman, 1994
Old Sins, 1989

Other books you might like:
Louis Auchincloss, *East Side Story*, 2004
Christine Balint, *The Salt Letters*, 2001
Jane Heller, *Best Enemies*, 2004
Suzanne Morris, *Wives and Mistresses*, 1986
Fred Mustard Stewart, *Savages in Love and War*, 2001

█ 950 █

RANDALL WALLACE

Love and Honor
(New York: Wheelhouse, 2004)

Story type: Historical/American Revolution; Historical/Colonial America
Subject(s): War; Revolutionary War; Russian Empire
Major character(s): Keiran Selkirk, Military Personnel; Catherine the Great, Historical Figure, Ruler (Empress of Russia); Benjamin Franklin, Historical Figure, Political Figure
Time period(s): 1770s (1774)
Locale(s): Virginia, American Colonies; Russia

Summary: This Revolutionary War adventure tale has Virginia colonist Keiran Selkirk sent by Benjamin Franklin on a mission to Russia and the court of Catherine the Great to persuade the Russians not to aid the British in the war for independence. Selkirk has multiple hair-raising adventures in Russia, including battling wolves, Cossacks, and protecting a group of aristocratic young women. Eventually, Selkirk impresses the Russians with his American pluck and is summoned to an audience in Catherine's bedchamber.

Where it's reviewed:
Kirkus Reviews, August 1, 2004, page 714
Publishers Weekly, August 30, 2004, page 33

Other books by the same author:
Pearl Harbor, 2001
Braveheart, 1995
Blood of the Lamb, 1990
So Late into the Night, 1983
The Russian Rose, 1980

Other books you might like:
Christian Cameron, *Washington and Caesar*, 2004
Jimmy Carter, *The Hornet's Nest*, 2003
Thomas Fleming, *Dreams of Glory*, 1983
John Ensor Harr, *Dark Eagle*, 1999
Jeff Shaara, *The Glorious Cause*, 2002

951

PAUL WEIDNER

Memoir of a Dwarf

(Madison: University of Wisconsin Press, 2004)

Story type: Historical/Seventeenth Century
Subject(s): Kings, Queens, Rulers, etc.
Major character(s): Louis XIV, Historical Figure, Ruler (King of France); Hugues, Courtier; Francoise d'Aubigne, Historical Figure, Noblewoman (Madame de Maintenon)
Time period(s): 17th century
Locale(s): Versailles, France

Summary: The artistic producer of the Hartford Stage debuts with a first novel that looks at the court of French King Louis XIV in Versailles from the vantage point of a dwarf named Hugues who manages to rise into the very highest court circles by catering to the nobles' vices. The novel offers glimpses of the king and such famous figures as Madame de Maintenon and the Marquise de Montespan, as well as some of the most notorious behavior of the decadent court at Versailles.

Other books you might like:
Louis Auchincloss, *The Cat and the King*, 1981
Mildred A. Butler, *Ward of the Sun King*, 1970
Ursula Hegi, *Stones from the River*, 1994
Vonda N. McIntyre, *The Moon and the Sun*, 1997
Judith Merkle Riley, *The Oracle Glass*, 1994

952

RICHARD S. WHEELER

An Obituary for Major Reno

(New York: Forge, 2004)

Story type: Historical/American West; Indian Wars
Subject(s): Indians of North America; Military Life; War
Major character(s): George Armstrong Custer, Historical Figure, Military Personnel; Marcus Reno, Historical Figure, Military Personnel; Joseph Richler, Journalist
Time period(s): 1870s (1876); 1880s (1889)
Locale(s): Little Big Horn, Montana

Summary: Wheeler supplies an account of Custer's Last Stand from the perspective of Major Marcus Reno, one of Custer's senior officers who survived the battle and then became the scapegoat for the disaster. In 1889, newspaperman Joseph Richler gets the dying Reno's side of the story, including his conduct during the battle and its later effects on Reno's career and life. This is a masterful revisionist view of the celebrated Battle of the Little Big Horn from a perspective that exposes the many myths surrounding it.

Where it's reviewed:
Publishers Weekly, December 6, 2004, page 45

Other books by the same author:
The Deliverance, 2003
The Exile, 2003
Eclipse, 2002
Downriver, 2001
The Fields of Eden, 2001

Other books you might like:
Michael Blake, *Marching to Valhalla*, 1997
Keith Coplin, *Crofton's Fire*, 2004
Edwin P. Hoyt, *The Last Stand*, 1995
Andrew Huebner, *American by Blood*, 2000
Robert Skimin, *The River and the Horseman*, 1999

953

JACK WHYTE

The Lance Thrower

(New York: Forge, 2004)

Story type: Historical/Fantasy; Legend
Series: Camulod Chronicles. Book 8
Subject(s): Arthurian Legends; Knights and Knighthood
Major character(s): Arthur, Ruler; Clothar, Scholar, Knight
Time period(s): 5th century
Locale(s): England

Summary: In the eighth, and purportedly last, installment of Whyte's epic retelling of Arthur Pendragon's early story, the young king faces the challenge of ruling. To assist him, Clothar of Gaul arrives to help Arthur establish the rule of law and prevent Arthur's kingdom from descending again into violence. Clothar, the Lance Thrower, is perhaps better known as Lancelot.

Other books by the same author:
Uther, 2000
The Fort at River's Bend, 1999
The Sorcerer, 1999
The Saxon Shore, 1998
The Eagles' Brood, 1997

Other books you might like:
Marion Zimmer Bradley, *The Mists of Avalon*, 1982
Bernard Cornwell, *The Arthurian Warlord Chronicles*, 1996-1998
Parke Godwin, *Firelord*, 1980
Rosalind Miles, *The Knight of the Sacred Lake*, 2000
Persia Woolley, *The Guinevere Trilogy*, 1987-1991

954

ADAM WILLIAMS

The Palace of Heavenly Pleasure

(New York: St. Martin's Press, 2004)

Story type: Historical/Victorian
Subject(s): China; Rebellions, Revolts, and Uprisings; War
Major character(s): Henry Manners, Spy; Helen Frances Delamere, Gentlewoman; Edward Airton, Religious (missionary)
Time period(s): 1890s (1899)
Locale(s): China

Summary: This first novel is a complex adventure tale set against the backdrop of the Boxer Rebellion in late 19th-century China. The inhabitants of the fictional Chinese city of Shishan find themselves swept up in the rebellion that has targeted Europeans. At the center of the story, British spy Henry Manners has fallen in love with Helen Frances

Delamere, who is betrothed to another, to the shock of missionary Edward Airton. Differences must be set aside if they are to survive the growing violence. The title of the novel refers to a notorious brothel that plays an important role in the outcome of this thrilling novel.

Where it's reviewed:
Library Journal, November 15, 2004, page 53

Other books you might like:
Robert S. Elegant, *Dynasty*, 1977
Anthony Esler, *Forbidden City*, 1977
Lisa Huang Fleischman, *Dream of the Walled City*, 2000
John Hamilton Lewis, *Opal Eye Devil*, 2000
Douglas Reeman, *The First to Land*, 1984

955

PHILIP LEE WILLIAMS

A Distant Flame

(New York: St. Martin's Press, 2004)

Story type: Historical/American Civil War
Subject(s): War; Civil War; Small Town Life
Major character(s): Charlie Merrill, Military Personnel (Confederate sharpshooter); William Tecumseh Sherman, Historical Figure, Military Personnel (Union general); Joe Johnston, Historical Figure, Military Personnel (Confederate general)
Time period(s): 1860s (1864); 1910s (1914)
Locale(s): Atlanta, Georgia

Summary: Williams chronicles the Civil War Battle of Atlanta from the perspective of a young Confederate sharpshooter, Charlie Merrill. As General Sherman leads his Union forces into the heart of Georgia, Merrill becomes notorious for his ability to kill the enemy on behalf of the Confederate cause that he begins to doubt. After careful accounts of the action of the Atlanta campaign, the novel fast forwards to 1914 when an aged Merrill tries to make sense of his war experiences. The weak link here is the protagonist, Merrill, whose behavior and speech do not match his adolescence, but Civil War buffs interested in a colorful depiction of the Battle of Atlanta will be satisfied.

Where it's reviewed:
Kirkus Reviews, July 15, 2004, page 660

Other books by the same author:
Blue Crystal, 1993
Final Heat, 1992
Perfect Timing, 1991
The Song of Daniel, 1989
The Heat of a Distant Forest, 1984

Other books you might like:
Cynthia Bass, *Sherman's March*, 1994
Frederick Busch, *The Night Inspector*, 1999
Thomas Cullinan, *The Besieged*, 1970
Diane Haeger, *My Dearest Cecelia*, 2003
Miriam Freeman Rawl, *From the Ashes of Ruin*, 1999

956

DAVID WISHART

Parthian Shot

(London: Hodder & Stoughton, 2004)

Story type: Historical/Ancient Rome; Mystery
Series: Marcus Corvinus
Subject(s): Mystery and Detective Stories; Roman Empire
Major character(s): Marcus Corvinus, Nobleman
Time period(s): 1st century
Locale(s): Rome, Roman Empire

Summary: Wishart supplies another delightful case for Ancient Roman detective Marcus Corvinus who is asked to investigate an attack on a Parthian prince and the murder of one of the Parthian delegates to Rome. Despite intentional anachronisms of modern slang, the mystery, by a British classical scholar, is firmly and authentically grounded in the colorful details of its era.

Where it's reviewed:
Kirkus Reviews, June 1, 2004, page 521
Library Journal, July 2004, page 63

Other books by the same author:
A Vote for Murder, 2003
Germanicus, 2002
White Murder, 2002
Ovid, 2002
Last Rites, 2001

Other books you might like:
Lindsey Davis, *The Marcus Didius Falco Series*, 1989-
Mary Reed, *Five for Silver*, 2004
    Eric Mayer, co-author
John Maddox Roberts, *The SPQR Series*, 1990-
Rosemary Rowe, *Germanicus Mosaic*, 1999
Steven Saylor, *The Roma Sub Rosa Series*, 1991-

957

STUART WOODS

The Prince of Beverly Hills

(New York: Putnam, 2004)

Story type: Historical/Depression Era; Mystery
Subject(s): Movie Industry; Mystery and Detective Stories
Major character(s): Rick Barron, Detective—Homicide (former), Security Officer; Clete Barrow, Actor
Time period(s): 1930s (1939)
Locale(s): Hollywood, California

Summary: In this atmospheric period mystery, Rick Barron is a recently demoted homicide detective in 1939 Hollywood. When he comes to the assistance of movie star Clete Barrow, he is rewarded by becoming head of security at Centurion Studios. Barron's film career as a fledgling producer hits a snag when he must investigate a murder cover-up and a blackmail scam. The vintage Hollywood setting is enhanced by cameo appearances by such stars as Clark Gable, Jack Benny, Greta Garbo, and Spencer Tracy, and mobster Bugsy Siegel.

Historical

Where it's reviewed:
Booklist, September 1, 2004, page 8
Library Journal, October 1, 2004, page 74
Publishers Weekly, September 20, 2004, page 45

Other books by the same author:
Reckless Abandon, 2004
Capital Crimes, 2003
Dirty Words, 2003
Blood Orchid, 2002
Cold Paradise, 2002

Other books you might like:
Elizabeth Frank, *Cheat and Charmer*, 2004
Alan Parker, *The Sucker's Kiss*, 2004
Deborah Smith, *Charming Grace*, 2004
Jerry Stahl, *I, Fatty*, 2004
Robin Lynn Williams, *The Assistants*, 2004

958

CHELSEA QUINN YARBRO

Dark of the Sun

(New York: Tor, 2004)

Story type: Vampire Story
Series: Chronicles of Saint-Germain. Book 17
Subject(s): Vampires; Fantasy; Volcanoes
Major character(s): Comte de Saint-Germain, Vampire; Dukkai, Shaman
Time period(s): 6th century
Locale(s): Asia

Summary: The vampire Saint-Germain, here known as Sangi-Ragozh, is in Asia when Krakatoa explodes, causing massive tidal waves and world-wide darkness as the massive plume of ash and dust spreads around the globe. As the world tries to discover the reason that the sun has disappeared and illness, starvation, and social unrest has spread, Sangi-Ragozh seeks answers and safety with a nomadic tribe led by a female shaman, Dukkai, as he tries to reach his home in the Carpathian Mountains to protect his immortality.

Where it's reviewed:
Publishers Weekly, November 1, 2004, page 48

Other books by the same author:
In the Face of Death, 2004

Midnight Harvest, 2003
Night Blooming, 2002
The Palace, 2002
A Feast in Exile, 2001

Other books you might like:
Barbara Hambly, *Those Who Hunt the Night*, 1988
Karen Harbaugh, *The Vampire Viscount*, 1995
Eyvind Johnson, *The Days of His Grace*, 1970
Anne Rice, *Blood and Gold*, 2001
Flora Speer, *A Love Beyond Time*, 1994

959

WALTER ZACHARIUS

Songbird

(New York: Atria, 2004)

Story type: Historical/World War II; Espionage
Subject(s): Nazis; Holocaust; Espionage
Major character(s): Mia Levy, Spy, Refugee
Time period(s): 1930s; 1940s
Locale(s): Poland; New York, New York (Brooklyn); Paris, France

Summary: After her family is sent to Treblinka, Mia Levy, a young Polish Jew, manages to take refuge with the Resistance and escapes to America. She is then recruited by American military intelligence and returns to Europe as a spy. There she joins a Paris brothel catering to high-ranking Nazis. The best portion of the novel is Zacharius' meticulous recreation of Polish Jewish life under the Nazi occupation. First novel.

Where it's reviewed:
Booklist, June 1, 2004, page 1704
Kirkus Reviews, July 15, 2004, page 660
Publishers Weekly, July 26, 2004, page 37

Other books you might like:
Jenna Blum, *Those Who Saved Us*, 2004
Louise Doughty, *Fires in the Dark*, 2003
Binnie Kirshenbaum, *A Disturbance in One Place*, 2004
Ian MacMillan, *Village of a Million Spirits*, 1999
Daniel Silva, *A Death in Vienna*, 2004

Inspirational Fiction in Review
by
Melissa Hudak

As the old saying goes, the more things change, the more they stay the same. This is especially true in the world of inspirational fiction publishing. For years, the cornerstones of this area of genre fiction were contemporary romances and historical novels that were usually set in the nineteenth-century American West. Over the past few years, this situation has changed and more and more other types of subgenres are being published by the inspirational fiction market. Unfortunately, as certain types of newcomers to the field gained in popularity, imitators began to emerge. Sometimes the followers were just as good or better than their predecessors. Other times they were not.

Although many inspirational fiction mysteries have been published in the past, it has only been in the past few years that the subgenre has gained momentum, with many new authors entering the field. This may be due to the wild success of Dee Henderson's romantic suspense novels over the past few years. Very much in the vein of Henderson's titles are Terri Blackstock's Cape Refuge series, which features police chief Matt Cade and his reporter friend Blair Owens. The Cape Refuge books are fairly dark, something still rare in inspirational fiction. The latest title, *Breaker's Reef*, revolves around the deaths and disappearances of teenagers, certainly not a common topic in inspirational mysteries. Blackstock also has some of the more well written characters in the genre. She tends to create real people rather than caricatures, something that is (unfortunately) still a rarity in inspirational fiction.

There are a few caricatures in the latest title from mystery writing duo Ron and Janet Benrey, but their first installment in a new series is so entertaining that it doesn't really matter. *Dead as a Scone*, the first book of the Royal Tunbridge Wells Mysteries, has as many stock British characters as an Agatha Christie novel, such as the seemingly dotty old lady, the staid banker, and a vicar, along with oceans of tea and tons of scones. The Benreys wanted to create a homage to the old-fashioned cozy mystery, and they

have done so. If some readers are put off by the use of old-fashioned words, such as "twaddle" and "poppycock," many more will be thrilled at the lack of more offensive words.

Another throwback to the kinder and gentler mystery is Lorena McCourtney's new series featuring older widow Ivy Malone, a woman who has discovered that as she has gotten up in years she has also become invisible to those around her, especially younger people. Taking advantage of this, Ivy decides to use her natural curiosity to find out who is vandalizing a local cemetery. In the process, she gets involved in the investigation of the murder of a young woman. While nothing groundbreaking, McCourtney's *Invisible* has a light humor that is engaging enough to make readers look forward to future installments in the series.

Less successful is Rick Dewhurst's *Bye Bye Bertie*, a parody of hard-boiled private detective novels. Although you have to give Dewhurst credit for trying, the book really doesn't work well. It is funny at times, but much more often just seems to be trying too hard. This is a shame since something new is always needed in the world of inspirational fiction. Parodies are always difficult to pull off however, and Dewhurst is hampered by the restrictions of the genre. When writing a parody of private eye novels, a subgenre known for its use of sex and violence, it is difficult to work within the limitations of inspirational fiction, which demand writers use scenes of sex and violence subtly, if at all. That said, Dewhurst does what he can and does manage to get a few laughs out of the misadventures of a private detective that lives with his mother and wants desperately to find a wife.

Another man desperate to marry is Jay Jarvis, the lead character in Ray Blackston's *Lost in Rooville*. In this third book in the series tracking the romantic entanglements of Jay and his friends, Jay heads off for Australia intending to propose to his girlfriend at some point. The trouble is that something always gets in the way. Jay's misadventures are so reminiscent of those found in many chick lit books that I tend to think of this series as a male variation of those books. Inspirational fiction publishers did take the plunge into the world of chick lit last year, and are continuing to publish books in this subgenre with a certain amount of success.

Kristin Billerbeck's *She's Out of Control* is the follow-up to *What a Girl Wants*, the debut of hapless patent attorney Ashley Stockingdale. In the sequel, Ashley has seemingly found the man of her dreams, but he doesn't seem to be anxious to move their relationship towards marriage. So Ashley does what any good chick lit gal does—she hangs around with her friends and makes humorous commentary about whatever is going on in her life. While Billerbeck's books will probably never make fans of Bridget Jones forget that particular young woman, Ashley is a good substitute for readers who don't care for Bridget's much more casual attitude towards sex.

A more serious bent on the chick lit phenomenon as filtered by the inspirational fiction market was the Yada Yada Prayer Group series. Featuring a mix of ages, with most in their middle years, the series focuses on Jodi Baxter, a wife and mother who bonds with the members of her racially diverse prayer group. Unlike a great deal of material published under the banner of chick lit, author Neta Jackson tries to delve deeper into the lives of her characters by involving them in problems that would never happen to Ashley Stockingdale. The second title in the series, *The Yada Yada Prayer Group Gets Down*, deals with racism, lynching, guilt, death, drug addiction, and robbery. The series, while laudable for attempting a racially diverse cast, tends to focus mainly on the white characters, which limits its scope a bit. The books also tend to be overladen with plots, with the list of what goes on in this book alone a perfect example. Just having Jodi Baxter attempt to deal with her guilt over her accidental killing of a child in a car accident would have been enough for one book. The additions of layer upon layer of plots tends to make the book unwieldy. The Yada Yada books are certainly enjoyable, but in this case, less would have been more.

Just as Neta Jackson has attempted to create a racially diverse cast in her books, more and more inspirational fiction publishers are trying to reach a wider market by publishing titles written by and featuring African Americans. Among the groundbreakers in this subgenre is Sharon Ewell Foster, a wonderfully unpredictable writer who never backs away from a tough topic, and always laces her novels with optimism and hope. In her latest book, *Ain't No Mountain*, Foster takes a couple of stereotypes (the husband growing emotionally distant and his confused wife), turns them around, makes a reader laugh and think, then wraps her story up in a graceful and charming manner. Books don't come much better than those written by Foster, and in the inspirational fiction market hers stand out like a shining beacon.

Among the other titles written by African Americans in recent months is a debut novel from Stacy Hawkins Adams

called *Speak to My Heart*. The plot, focusing on a woman's struggle to come to terms with the secrets inflicted upon her by her parents, is one not often touched upon in inspirational fiction. Serena Jasper is on the top of the world. She has been accepted into a prestigious graduate program in advertising and is thrilled that her career is going the way she wants it to. Then she gets a blow from an unexpected source—her beloved mother. Serena's mother decides to tell her the truth about her parentage after many years of silence. Her biological father is actually the man she had thought was just a family friend. A married family friend. Distraught by what she sees as the hypocrisy of her elders, Serena not only pulls away from her family, but begins to question her faith as well. Her journey back to her faith takes up the majority of the book, and it is a well-written and emotional portrayal of a woman who can no longer accept the status quo, but has learned the hard way to question, rather than accept things blindly. While having characters go through a spiritual crisis is nothing new in inspirational fiction, it is still rare for a character to delve into her beliefs with the depth Serena does. At times, it even seems doubtful that Serena will ever fully regain her faith. Even when she does return to Christianity, she is a changed person, and her new level of beliefs reflect that change.

Another African-American character undergoing a crisis is Jermaine Hill in Derek Jackson's novel *A Man Inspired*. Jermaine Hill is a successful motivational speaker with a great deal of wealth and all the things money can provide, a fast car, great house, and lots of women. The old saying about money not providing happiness has proven true for Jermaine, however. A long-standing guilt over the death of two friends in a car crash has left him depressed and all the money in the world can't help him cope. A suicide attempt finally forces Jermaine to accept treatment for his depression. It is commendable for Jackson to write about depression, something rarely mentioned in inspirational fiction. Unfortunately, the book is littered with cliched characters, such as a beautiful woman who saves Jermaine from his inner demons and an evil tabloid journalist who wants to bring Jermaine down at any cost. Coupling the lack of believable characters with Jermaine's far too simplistic (and sudden) finding of faith, the book simply doesn't work overall, regardless of its good intentions.

Although not writing from an African American viewpoint, another author with the intention of introducing a taboo topic to inspirational fiction is Melody Carlson. Her book, *Crystal Lies*, tells the story of a family disintegrating due to their son's drug addiction. Glennis Harmon is living the perfect upper middle-class suburban existence until her whole world comes crumbling down due to her son's methamphetamine addiction. While scrambling around to find help for her son, Glennis soon realizes the rest of her family is in trouble, too. Her husband, always stern and distant, is having an affair and their daughter is too self-righteous to want to help her brother. Soon Glennis is forced to confront how her own overindulgent mothering may have contributed to her family's problems. Carlson doesn't sugarcoat the realities here. There are no easy answers for Glennis and her family. The author deserves kudos for not only tackling a subject usually ignored by inspirational fiction, but pulling it off so well.

Obviously, Melody Carlson's *Crystal Lies* is on my list of recommended books, but there were many other wonderful books written in the inspirational fiction genre in the past few months, including some stellar debuts by authors Denise Hildreth and Patti Ann Hill. The top twenty-five titles are listed in alphabetical order by author.

Ron Benrey and Janet Benrey, *Dead as a Scone*

Terri Blackstock, *Breaker's Reef*

Ray Blackston, *Lost in Rooville*

Vonette Z. Bright and Nancy Moser, *A Place to Belong*

Terry Burns, *Mysterious Ways*

Melody Carlson, *Crystal Lies*

Colleen Coble, *Distant Echoes*

Robert Elmer, *The Celebrity*

Sharon Ewell Foster, *Ain't No Mountain*

Louise M. Gouge, *Hannah Rose*

Margaret A. Graham, *Land Sakes*

Rene Gutteridge, *Boo Who*

Veronica Heley, *The Lady of the Hall*

Denise Hildreth, *Savannah from Savannah*

Patti Ann Hill, *Like a Watered Garden*

Joseph H. Hilley, *Sober Justice*

Lorena McCourtney, *Invisible*

Kathleen Morgan, *Child of the Mist*

Kathleen Morgan, *The Christkindl's Gift*

Lisa Samson, *Tiger Lillie*

Debra White Smith, *Reason and Romance*

Lauraine Snelling, *Opal*

Jamie Langston Turner, *No Dark Valley*

Thomas Williams, *The Bride of Stone*

Linda Windsor, *Paper Moon*

Inspirational Titles

960

STACY HAWKINS ADAMS

Speak to My Heart

(Grand Rapids, Michigan: Fleming H. Revell, 2004)

Story type: Contemporary
Subject(s): African Americans; Mothers and Daughters; Secrets
Major character(s): Serena Jasper, Advertising
Time period(s): 2000s
Locale(s): Richmond, Virginia

Summary: Serena Jasper is excited to learn of her acceptance to graduate school. Furthering her career has been a life-long dream, and achieving the first of her goals is thrilling. Then her mother tells her a family secret that devastates her. The man she had thought was her biological father had been married to her mother at the time of her conception, but she was actually fathered by another man. Horrified at the lies, Serena decides she needs some time away from her family. Devoting herself to her career, Serena becomes more successful and then meets a handsome young seminary student named Micah and grows close to him. However, the past continues to haunt her and soon Serena realizes she must make peace with her mother before she can continue on with her life. First novel.

Other books you might like:
Michele Andrea Bowen, *Church Folk*, 2001
Judy Candis, *All Things Hidden*, 2004
Jamellah Ellis, *That Faith, That Trust, That Love*, 2003
Felicia Mason, *Testimony*, 2002
Michelle Stimpson, *Boaz Brown*, 2004

961

GINNY AIKEN

Spring of My Love

(Grand Rapids, Michigan: Fleming H. Revell, 2005)

Story type: Historical/American West

Series: Silver Hills. Book 3
Subject(s): Drought; Orphans; Ranch Life
Major character(s): Angel Rogers, Orphan, Rancher; Jeremy Johnson, Rancher, Neighbor (of Angel)
Time period(s): 1890s
Locale(s): Hartville, Colorado

Summary: Left orphaned, Angel Rogers is determined to run the family ranch on her own. With a drought devastating the countryside surrounding Angel's ranch, the water on her land has become a hot commodity. Among the neighboring ranchers hoping to gain access to Angel's water is Jeremy Johnson. At first, Jeremy's only concern is to get enough water to sustain his cattle through the drought, but once he gets to know his pretty neighbor, he decides he would like to share the rest of his life with her.

Other books by the same author:
Light of My Heart, 2004
Song of My Soul, 2004
Camellia, 2001
Lark, 2000
Magnolia, 2000

Other books you might like:
Dianna Crawford, *The Frontier Women Series*, 2000-
Kristen Heitzmann, *The Rocky Mountain Legacy Series*, 1998-
Kathleen Morgan, *The Brides of Culdee Creek Series*, 1999-
Diane Noble, *The California Chronicles*, 1999-
Lauraine Snelling, *The Dakotah Treasures Series*, 2003-

962

MARK AMMERMAN

The Rain from God

(Colorado Springs, Colorado: RiverOak, 2005)

Story type: Historical/Seventeenth Century
Series: Cross and the Tomahawk. Book 2
Subject(s): Indians of North America
Major character(s): Katanaquat, Indian
Time period(s): 17th century

Locale(s): Rhode Island

Summary: A warrior from the Narragansett tribe of Rhode Island, Katanaquat is satisfied to live his life in the traditional way of his people. He worships many gods and is allowed more than one wife. When the white men arrive in Katanaquat's territory and threaten his way of life, the warrior resists their attempts to change his beliefs. Then Katanaquat meets Roger Williams and begins to change his ways. Originally published in 1997 by Horizon Books.

Other books by the same author:
Longshot, 2000
The Ransom, 1997

Other books you might like:
Angela Elwell Hunt, *The Keepers of the Ring Series*, 1996-
Alan Morris, *The Guardians of the North Series*, 1996-
Judith Pella, *Warrior's Song*, 1996
Marlo M. Schalesky, *The Winds of Freedom Series*, 2000-
Stephanie Grace Whitson, *The Dakota Moons Series*, 2001-

963

LYNN AUSTIN

Gods and Kings

(Minneapolis: Bethany House, 2005)

Story type: Biblical Fiction
Series: Chronicles of the Kings. Book 1
Subject(s): Biblical Fiction
Major character(s): Hezekiah, Royalty (prince, later king)
Time period(s): Indeterminate Past
Locale(s): Middle East

Summary: Hoping to pacify his idol Molech and win a war, King Ahaz decides to sacrifice his son Hezekiah. Hezekiah's mother, Abijah, is distraught over her son's imminent demise and is greatly awed when a miracle saves his life. When Hezekiah becomes king, he rules with the only two people he knows he can trust—his mother and his wife. As he faces an invading army, Hezekiah relies on his belief in the true god Yahweh to survive.

Other books by the same author:
A Light to My Path, 2004
Fire by Night, 2003
Candle in the Darkness, 2002
Hidden Places, 2001
Wings of Refuge, 2000

Other books you might like:
Gene Edwards, *The First Century Diaries Series*, 1998-
John Hagee, *The Apocalypse Diaries Series*, 2001-
Gilbert Morris, *The Lion of Judah Series*, 2002-
Francine Rivers, *The Mark of the Lion Series*, 1993-
James R. Shott, *The People of the Promise Series*, 1992-

964

JUDY BAER

The Whitney Chronicles

(New York: Steeple Hill Cafe, 2004)

Story type: Contemporary
Subject(s): Dating (Social Customs); Friendship; Women
Major character(s): Whitney Blake, Public Relations
Time period(s): 2000s
Locale(s): Minnesota

Summary: Written in diary format, this book chronicles the life and misadventures of Whitney Blake, a single young woman, as she deals with friendships, career, and romance. Whitney's mother thinks she should be married and constantly dredges up unappealing men for her to date. Since Whitney is able to find unappealing men on her own, she sees no good reason for her mother's interference. Her life is complicated by a demanding boss, who is intent on having his product featured at a conference in Las Vegas. Whitney's life takes a dramatic turn when her best friend Kim is diagnosed with breast cancer. While helping Kim through the treatment process, she can't help noticing Kim's doctor is both attractive and single. He also comes with some emotional baggage, as most of Whitney's men do.

Where it's reviewed:
Publishers Weekly, September 20, 2004, page 48

Other books by the same author:
Libby's Story, 2001
Tia's Story, 2001
Jenny's Story, 2000
Country Bride, 1989
Bid for My Heart, 1987

Other books you might like:
Kristin Billerbeck, *The Ashley Stockingdale Series*, 2004-
Ray Blackston, *Flabbergasted*, 2003
Penny Culliford, *The Theodora Series*, 2004-
Robin Jones Gunn, *The Sisterchicks Series*, 2003-
Neta Jackson, *The Yada Yada Prayer Group Series*, 2003-

965

RON BENREY
JANET BENREY, Co-Author

Dead as a Scone

(Uhrichsville, Ohio: Barbour, 2004)

Story type: Mystery
Series: Royal Tunbridge Mysteries. Book 1
Subject(s): Museums
Major character(s): Nigel Owen, Museum Curator (tea museum); Flick Adams, Scientist (forensic chemist), Museum Curator (tea museum)
Time period(s): 2000s
Locale(s): Tunbridge Wells, England

Summary: Being director of a tea museum is not a career path Nigel Owen would have chosen for himself, but since he was made redundant after ten years with an insurance company, Nigel is willing to take anything. Although the position is a temporary one, Nigel has high hopes for the future. Then Dame Elspeth Hawker, one of the museum's trustees, tells Nigel she suspects there is a thief at the museum. Before Dame Elspeth can tell what she knows, she is poisoned at a meeting of the trustees. Joining forces with Flick Adams, a forensic chemist and one of the museum's curators, Nigel begins to investigate what happened to Dame Elspeth.

Other books by the same author:
Humble Pie, 2004
The Second Mile, 2002
Little White Lies, 2001

Other books you might like:
Mindy Starns Clark, *The Million Dollar Mysteries Series*, 2002-
Mary-Jane Deeb, *Murder on the Riviera*, 2004
Ellen Edwards Kennedy, *Irregardless of Murder*, 2001
Kathi Mills-Macias, *The Toni Matthews Series*, 2001-
Gayle Roper, *The Amhearst Series*, 1997-
Patricia H. Rushford, *The Helen Bradley Series*, 1997-

966

KRISTIN BILLERBECK

She's Out of Control

(Nashville: WestBow, 2004)

Story type: Romance
Series: Ashley Stockingdale. Book 2
Subject(s): Animals/Dogs; Dating (Social Customs)
Major character(s): Ashley Stockingdale, Lawyer (patent attorney); Seth Greenwood, Boyfriend (of Ashley)
Time period(s): 2000s
Locale(s): Silicon Valley, California

Summary: Although patent attorney Ashley Stockingdale has been dating Seth Greenwood for nine months, she is no closer to getting the commitment she wants. His idea of a great gift isn't an engagement ring, but a boisterous puppy. Seth's commitment phobia, along with a new job, a new roommate, and new ownership of half of a house, soon leave Ashley feeling as if her life is spinning out of control.

Other books by the same author:
What a Girl Wants, 2004
An Unbreakable Hope, 2003
Grace in Action, 2001
The Prodigal's Welcome, 2001
The Landlord Takes a Bride, 2000

Other books you might like:
Judy Baer, *The Whitney Chronicles*, 2004
Ray Blackston, *Flabbergasted*, 2003
Penny Culliford, *The Theodora Series*, 2004-
Robin Jones Gunn, *The Sisterchicks Series*, 2003-
Neta Jackson, *The Yada Yada Prayer Group Series*, 2003-

967

TERRI BLACKSTOCK

Breaker's Reef

(Grand Rapids, Michigan: Zondervan, 2005)

Story type: Mystery
Series: Cape Refuge. Book 4
Subject(s): Murder; Writing
Major character(s): Matthew Cade, Police Officer (police chief); Sheila Caruso, Convict (ex-con), Parent
Time period(s): 2000s
Locale(s): Cape Refuge, Georgia

Summary: When a teenage girl is found murdered, the residents of Cape Refuge are stunned that such a hideous crime has occurred in their community. Sheila Caruso, an ex-convict trying to go straight, realizes that the murder mirrors one in a book written by her employer, a famous mystery writer. Then a second teenager is killed, again in a way similar to a fictional crime, the police aren't sure what to think. Evidence turns up in Police Chief Matthew Cade's truck, and as Cade fights to clear his name, Sheila's teenage daughter disappears.

Other books by the same author:
River's Edge, 2004
Line of Duty, 2003
Southern Storm, 2003
Cape Refuge, 2002
Covenant Child, 2002

Other books you might like:
Colleen Coble, *The Rock Harbor Series*, 2003-
Athol Dickson, *The Garr Reed Series*, 1996-
Alton Gansky, *The Ridgeline Series*, 1998-
Kathi Mills-Macias, *The Toni Matthews Series*, 2001-
Patricia H. Rushford, *The Angel Delaney Series*, 2004-
Audrey Stallsmith, *The Thyme Will Tell Series*, 1998-

968

RAY BLACKSTON

Lost in Rooville

(Grand Rapids, Michigan: Fleming H. Revell, 2005)

Story type: Contemporary
Series: Jay Jarvis. Book 3
Subject(s): Romance; Travel
Major character(s): Jay Jarvis, Religious (missionary), Traveler; Steve Cole, Friend (of Jay)
Time period(s): 2000s
Locale(s): Australia

Summary: Jay Jarvis didn't realize what he was getting into when he headed off to Australia with his girlfriend Allie, best friend Steve, and Steve's girlfriend Darcy. The Australian outback has plenty of adventures in store for the quartet, including errant kangaroos and temperamental transportation. Both Jay and Steve intend to add to the drama by proposing to their girlfriends, if they can only find the perfect spot for a proposal.

Other books by the same author:
A Delirious Summer, 2004

Inspirational

Flabbergasted, 2003

Other books you might like:
Judy Baer, *The Whitney Chronicles*, 2004
Kristin Billerbeck, *The Ashley Stockingdale Series*, 2004-
Robin Jones Gunn, *The Sisterchicks Series*, 2003-
Debra White Smith, *To Rome with Love*, 2001
Linda Windsor, *Paper Moon*, 2005

969

ANDREA BOESHAAR

Precious Things

(Uhrichsville, Ohio: Barbour, 2004)

Story type: Contemporary
Series: Faded Photographs. Book 3
Subject(s): Adoption; Reunions
Major character(s): Blythe Severson, Antiques Dealer; Kylie Rollins, Young Woman
Time period(s): 2000s
Locale(s): Chicago, Illinois

Summary: Blythe Severson is unprepared for the shock she receives when Kylie Rollins walks into her antiques shop. Kylie's mother has recently died and now the young woman is on a quest to find the truth. After receiving a photograph taken in 1969 of her mother in the mail, Kylie realized that the slender young woman in the picture could not have been pregnant and was not her birth mother. Blythe, who had thought she had put the past well behind her, is unable and unwilling to deal with Kylie's questions. Soon though, Blythe realizes Kylie deserves to know the truth about her parentage.

Other books by the same author:
The Long Ride Home, 2004
Broken Things, 2003
Hidden Things, 2003
The Summer Girl, 2003
An Unmasked Heart, 2001

Other books you might like:
Terri Blackstock, *Never Again Good-Bye*, 1996
Robin Lee Hatcher, *Firstborn*, 2002
Thomas Kinkade, *Home Song*, 2003
Lisa Samson, *Songbird*, 2003
Debra White Smith, *The Key*, 2003

970

VONETTE Z. BRIGHT
NANCY MOSER, Co-Author

A Place to Belong

(Wheaton, Illinois: Tyndale House, 2005)

Story type: Contemporary
Series: Sister Circle. Book 4
Subject(s): Boarding Houses; Friendship; Widows/Widowers
Major character(s): Evelyn Peerbaugh, Landlord (boarding house owner), Widow(er)
Time period(s): 2000s
Locale(s): United States

Summary: After her husband's sudden death left her nearly penniless, Evelyn Peerbaugh turned her home into a boarding house. As women filled her empty rooms, they also transformed Evelyn's lonely life into one filled with love and laughter. This final book wraps up the stories of Evelyn and her boarders.

Other books by the same author:
An Undivided Heart, 2004
Round the Corner, 2003
The Sister Circle, 2003

Other books you might like:
Robin Jones Gunn, *The Sisterchicks Series*, 2003-
Roxanne Henke, *The Coming Home to Brewster Series*, 2002-
Neta Jackson, *The Yada Yada Prayer Group Series*, 2003-
Sally John, *The Other Way Home Series*, 2002-
Beverly LaHaye, *The Seasons Series*, 1999-
Lauraine Snelling, *The Healing Quilt*, 2002

971

TERRY BURNS

Mysterious Ways

(Colorado Springs, Colorado: RiverOak, 2005)

Story type: Historical/American West
Subject(s): African Americans; Identity, Concealed; Robbers and Outlaws
Major character(s): Amos Taylor, Imposter (disguised as a preacher), Thief; Joseph Washington, Aged Person, Handicapped (blind)
Time period(s): 1860s
Locale(s): Quiet Valley, Texas

Summary: When Amos Taylor sees a preacher's suit hanging on a clothesline, he steals it, knowing it will be useful. Amos takes a stagecoach out of town, robs the passengers, and then dons the suit. With his new persona of preacher, nobody expects the newcomer in Quiet Valley of being the cruel man who robbed the stage. Joseph Washington, a blind former slave, realizes Amos is not a religious man, let alone a man of the cloth. However, he believes God has plans for Amos and doesn't let on that he knows the truth. First novel.

Other books you might like:
Paul Bagdon, *The West Texas Sunrise Series*, 2003-
Stephen Bly, *The Fortunes of the Black Hills Series*, 1999-
Al Lacy, *The Journeys of the Stranger Series*, 1994-
Gilbert Morris, *The Reno Western Saga Series*, 1992-
James Walker, *The Wells Fargo Trail Series*, 1994-

972

JUDY CANDIS

All Things Hidden

(West Bloomfield, Michigan: Walk Worthy, 2004)

Story type: Mystery
Subject(s): African Americans; Kidnapping; Racism
Major character(s): Jael Reynolds, Detective—Homicide, Single Parent; Grant Lewis, FBI Agent
Time period(s): 2000s

Locale(s): Dadesville, Florida

Summary: Jael Reynolds is finding it difficult to juggle the roles of single mother and homicide detective, but she is determined to do the best job possible in all areas of her life. Jael's ex-husband Virgil is of little help, as he constantly complains of the influence her work has on their son Ramon. When Ramon is kidnapped by the Ku Klux Klan, it appears as if Virgil might have been right. Jael, though, is determined to get her son back and, teamed up with FBI Agent Grant Lewis, prepares for the battle of her life.

Where it's reviewed:
Library Journal, September 1, 2004, page 130
Publishers Weekly, July 19, 2004, page 143

Other books by the same author:
Blood Offering, 2002
Still Rage, 2001
Colorblind, 1998

Other books you might like:
Sharon Ewell Foster, *Passing by Samaria*, 2000
Sally John, *Moment of Truth*, 2005
Lorena McCourtney, *The Julesburg Mysteries*, 2002-
Patricia H. Rushford, *Deadly Aim*, 2004
Jacquelin Thomas, *The Prodigal Husband*, 2002

973

MELODY CARLSON

Crystal Lies

(Colorado Springs, Colorado: WaterBrook, 2004)

Story type: Contemporary
Subject(s): Drugs; Family Problems; Mothers and Sons
Major character(s): Glennis Harmon, Parent, Spouse
Time period(s): 2000s
Locale(s): United States

Summary: Glennis Harmon is proud of her upscale lifestyle and believes her family is immune from such things as drug abuse. Then Glennis learns her seemingly perfect son Jacob is addicted to drugs. Glennis' husband, a city attorney, wants to hide the problem, thinking it will hurt his career by shattering their image as a perfect family. Glennis, however, is determined to find help for Jacob, even if it means the end of her marriage.

Other books by the same author:
The Gift of Christmas Present, 2004
Armando's Treasure, 2003
Hidden History, 2003
Finding Alice, 2003
Looking for Cassandra Jane, 2002

Other books you might like:
Deborah Bedford, *A Rose by the Door*, 2001
Robin Lee Hatcher, *Beyond the Shadows*, 2004
Bette Nordberg, *A Season of Grace*, 2004
Jane Orcutt, *The Living Stone*, 2000
Dawn Ringling, *Jumping in Sunset*, 2003

974

MELODY CARLSON

The Gift of Christmas Present

(Grand Rapids, Michigan: Fleming H. Revell, 2004)

Story type: Contemporary
Subject(s): Adoption; Christmas; Secrets
Major character(s): Christine Bradley, Care Giver, Adoptee; Esther Daniels, Grandparent (of Christine)
Time period(s): 2000s
Locale(s): United States

Summary: Christine Bradley is stunned when her father tells her that she was adopted. Though her father says that her biological mother is dead, Christine feels a need to track down somebody from her birth family. She goes to visit a cranky older woman named Mrs. Daniels, whom she believes is her grandmother. When Mrs. Daniels assumes Christine is her new companion/caregiver/housekeeper, sent to help her while she recovers from a sprained ankle, Christine decides to keep her identity secret. As the two women grow closer, Christine learns that Mrs. Daniels had always regretted the way she treated her daughter. Still, when Christine reveals who she is, Mrs. Daniels struggles to accept the truth.

Where it's reviewed:
Library Journal, September 1, 2004, page 134

Other books by the same author:
Crystal Lies, 2004
Armando's Treasure, 2003
Hidden History, 2003
Finding Alice, 2003
Looking for Cassandra Jane, 2002

Other books you might like:
Andrea Boeshaar, *Precious Things*, 2004
Robin Lee Hatcher, *Firstborn*, 2002
Kristen Heitzmann, *The Still of Night*, 2003
Sally John, *In a Heartbeat*, 2004
Carole Gift Page, *In Search of Her Own*, 1997

975

MELODY CARLSON

Three Days

(Grand Rapids, Michigan: Fleming H. Revell, 2005)

Story type: Biblical Fiction
Subject(s): Bible; Biblical Fiction; Mothers and Sons
Major character(s): Mary, Biblical Figure, Historical Figure
Time period(s): 1st century
Locale(s): Middle East

Summary: The story of Mary, the mother of Jesus, is told in this short but touching book. As Mary witnesses the struggles of her son's last days on earth and his eventual Resurrection, she reflects on her life and her great love and devotion to her beloved child. She also contemplates her childhood and life, and how she became the mother of Jesus.

Other books by the same author:
Crystal Lies, 2004

Inspirational

The Gift of Christmas Present, 2004
Armando's Treasure, 2003
Finding Alice, 2003
Angels in the Snow, 2002

Other books you might like:
Roberta Kells Dorr, *Honored*, 2003
Marjorie Holmes, *Two from Galilee*, 1986
Norah Lofts, *How Far to Bethlehem?*, 1965
Calvin Miller, *A Symphony in Sand*, 1990
Francine Rivers, *Unafraid*, 2001

976

COLLEEN COBLE

Distant Echoes

(Nashville: WestBow, 2005)

Story type: Mystery
Series: Aloha Reef. Book 1
Subject(s): Animals/Dolphins; Terrorism
Major character(s): Kaia Ohana, Scientist (dolphin researcher); Jesse Matthews, Security Officer (at naval base), Military Personnel
Time period(s): 2000s
Locale(s): Kauai, Hawaii

Summary: Off the coast of Hawaii, a missile test goes horribly wrong and destroys a tourist boat, killing several passengers. Jesse Matthews, head of security at the U.S. naval base, begins to look into the situation to see just what went wrong. He suspects terrorism may be behind the incident, but cannot be sure. When Jesse is unable to find any definite leads, he turns to dolphin researcher Kaia Ohana for help. With the assistance of dolphins she has been teaching to communicate, Kaia and Jesse try to stop the terrorists before they can strike again.

Other books by the same author:
Beyond a Doubt, 2004
Into the Deep, 2004
The Cattle Baron's Wife, 2004
Without a Trace, 2003
Red River Bride, 2002

Other books you might like:
Lisa Tawn Bergren, *Chosen*, 1996
Robin Jones Gunn, *Whispers*, 1995
Dee Henderson, *True Honor*, 2002
Lauraine Snelling, *Hawaiian Sunrise*, 1999
Lori Wick, *Bamboo and Lace*, 2001

977

TED DEKKER

Obsessed

(Nashville: WestBow, 2005)

Story type: Mystery
Subject(s): Nazis
Major character(s): Stephen Friedman, Businessman (real estate tycoon); Gerhard Braun, Military Personnel (concentration camp commander)

Time period(s): 1940s; 1970s
Locale(s): Los Angeles, California; Poland

Summary: In the 1970s, Los Angeles is an exciting place to live and real estate mogul Stephen Friedman is enjoying his swinging lifestyle. Something is missing from his life though. Stephen lost his family in the concentration camps of Nazi-controlled Poland and he has never fully recovered from this trauma. Then Stephen finds the papers of a dead woman he believes was his mother and begins a quest to find the truth.

Where it's reviewed:
Publishers Weekly, November 1, 2004, page 41

Other books by the same author:
Black, 2004
Red, 2004
White, 2004
Thr3e, 2003
Blink, 2002

Other books you might like:
John Bayer, *The Lazarus Project*, 1999
Linda L. Chaikin, *The Day to Remember Series*, 1999-
Alton Gansky, *A Ship Possessed*, 1999
Frank Simon, *Trial by Fire*, 1999
Bodie Thoene, *The Zion Covenant Series*, 1989-

978

TED DEKKER

Red

(Nashville: WestBow, 2004)

Story type: Action/Adventure; Science Fiction
Series: Circle Trilogy. Book 2
Subject(s): Terrorism
Major character(s): Thomas Hunter, Writer
Time period(s): 2000s
Locale(s): United States; Alternate Universe

Summary: The second book in the Circle Trilogy follows Thomas Hunter as he continues to battle evil in two worlds. When he falls asleep in one world, he awakes in a second world. Both of the worlds are on the brink of despair. In one, a group called the New Allegiance has spread a deadly virus into the world. Hunter believes the only way to save the world is to find the scientist who has the vaccine for the virus. Meanwhile, in Hunter's second world, the Horde is coming closer to victory over the Forest People.

Where it's reviewed:
Library Journal, June 1, 2004, page 114

Other books by the same author:
Black, 2004
White, 2004
Thr3e, 2003
Blink, 2002
Thunder of Heaven, 2002

Other books you might like:
T. Davis Bunn, *The Dream Voyagers*, 1999
Alton Gansky, *Dark Moon*, 2002
Karen Hancock, *Arena*, 2002
Shane Johnson, *The Last Guardian*, 2001

Stephen R. Lawhead, *Dream Thief*, 1996

Gilbert Morris, *The Dani Ross Series*, 2000-
Patricia H. Rushford, *The Helen Bradley Series*, 1997-

979
TED DEKKER

White
(Nashville: WestBow, 2004)

Story type: Action/Adventure; Science Fiction
Series: Circle Trilogy. Book 3
Subject(s): Terrorism
Major character(s): Thomas Hunter, Writer
Time period(s): 2000s
Locale(s): United States; Alternate Universe

Summary: The Circle Trilogy ends with this title. Thomas Hunter continues to battle evil in two worlds. As a war rages in one of his worlds, a virus threatens to overcome another. Just as Thomas believes he is reaching a solution to one crisis, he falls asleep and faces new battles in the other world.

Other books by the same author:
Black, 2004
Red, 2004
Thr3e, 2003
Blink, 2002
Thunder of Heaven, 2002

Other books you might like:
T. Davis Bunn, *The Dream Voyagers*, 1999
Alton Gansky, *Dark Moon*, 2002
Karen Hancock, *Arena*, 2002
Shane Johnson, *The Last Guardian*, 2001
Stephen R. Lawhead, *Dream Thief*, 1996

980
RICK DEWHURST

Bye Bye Bertie
(Nashville: Broadman & Holman, 2005)

Story type: Mystery
Series: Joe LaFlam. Book 1
Subject(s): Cults; Kidnapping; Missing Persons
Major character(s): Joe LaFlam, Detective—Private
Time period(s): 2000s
Locale(s): United States

Summary: Single private eye Joe LaFlam would like to get married, so when a beautiful young woman comes into his office asking for help, he is more interested in her than her problem. Soon, though, her case begins to intrigue Joe. Her sister is missing and is believed to have joined a cult. Before Joe knows what is happening, he is looking for two missing people. First novel.

Where it's reviewed:
Publishers Weekly, December 13, 2004, page 49

Other books you might like:
Ron Benrey, *The Pippa Hunnechurch Series*, 2001-
Tim Downs, *The Bug Man Series*, 2003-
Alton Gansky, *The J.D. Stanton Series*, 1999-
Kathi Mills-Macias, *The Toni Matthews Series*, 2001-

981
DEBBIE DIGIOVANNI

Concessions
(Colorado Springs, Colorado: RiverOak, 2004)

Story type: Contemporary
Subject(s): Marriage; Moving, Household
Major character(s): Karen LaRue, Spouse (of Jack), Parent; Jack LaRue, Spouse (of Karen)
Time period(s): 2000s
Locale(s): Alaska; California

Summary: Karen LaRue is happy with her life in Alaska and is stunned when her husband Jack tells her he wants to move. The long winters and constant struggle to make a living have become too much for him. With Karen's reluctant agreement, the LaRues pack up their two daughters and their belongings and move to California. Jack loves the warm climate and his new lifestyle, but Karen desperately misses her old way of life. As Jack continues to change, Karen wonders if she can keep up with him. First novel.

Other books you might like:
Lisa Tawn Bergren, *Pathways*, 2001
Roxanne Henke, *The Coming Home to Brewster Series*, 2002-
Beverly LaHaye, *The Seasons Series*, 1999-
Bonnie Leon, *A Sacred Place*, 2000
Debra White Smith, *The Seven Sisters Series*, 2000-

982
SUSAN K. DOWNS
SUSAN MAY WARREN, Co-Author

Marina
(Uhrichsville, Ohio: Barbour, 2005)

Story type: Historical/World War II
Series: Heirs of Anton. Book 3
Subject(s): Russians; World War II
Major character(s): Marina Vasileva, Widow(er); Edward Neumann, Military Personnel (OSS agent)
Time period(s): 1940s
Locale(s): Union of Soviet Socialist Republics

Summary: Left widowed after her husband is killed fighting the Nazis during World War II, Marina Vasileva takes up his fight as a sharpshooter for a covert band of partisans. She is teamed with Edward Neumann, a disgraced OSS agent. The two must destroy German supply lines to Moscow.

Other books by the same author:
Nadia, 2004
Ekaterina, 2003

Other books you might like:
Bonnie Leon, *A Sacred Place*, 2000
Judith Pella, *The Daughters of Fortune Series*, 2002-
Michael Phillips, *The Secret of the Roses Series*, 1993-
Noreen Riols, *The House of Annanbrae Series*, 1994-
Frank Simon, *Trial by Fire*, 1999

Inspirational

Bodie Thoene, *The Zion Covenant Series*, 1989-

983
TIM DOWNS

Chop Shop
(West Monroe, Louisiana: Howard, 2004)

Story type: Mystery
Series: Bug Man. Book 2
Subject(s): Medical Thriller; Transplants
Major character(s): Nick Polchak, Scientist (forensic entomologist); Riley McKay, Doctor (medical examiner)
Time period(s): 2000s
Locale(s): Pittsburgh, Pennsylvania

Summary: After being suspended by his college for threatening a student, entomologist Nick Polchak heads to Pittsburgh to help out Dr. Riley McKay. Riley is certain something suspicious is going on at the Allegheny County coroner's office. Autopsies are being mismanaged, bodies appear with unexplained wounds, and evidence turns up missing. Speaking to her superiors is out of the question since Riley is certain her boss is involved in the odd occurrences. Nick and Riley soon learn that a black market in organs has led to people being targeted for murder.

Where it's reviewed:
Publishers Weekly, June 7, 2004, page 30

Other books by the same author:
Shoofly Pie, 2003

Other books you might like:
Athol Dickson, *The Garr Reed Series*, 1996-
Alton Gansky, *The Ridgeline Series*, 1998-
Gayle Roper, *The Amhearst Series*, 1997-
Patricia H. Rushford, *The Angel Delaney Series*, 2004-
Sally S. Wright, *The Ben Reese Series*, 1997-

984
PAIGE LEE ELLISTON

Changes of Heart
(Grand Rapids, Michigan: Fleming H. Revell, 2005)

Story type: Contemporary
Series: Montana Skies. Book 1
Subject(s): Grief; Ranch Life
Major character(s): Maggie Locke, Widow(er); Ian Lane, Religious (minister); Danny Pulver, Veterinarian
Time period(s): 2000s
Locale(s): Montana

Summary: After being left a widow suddenly, Maggie Locke tries to go on with her life but finds her new single status to be challenging. Maggie develops friendships with the local minister, Ian Lane, and veterinarian Danny Pulver, but is dismayed when she realizes both men have romantic feelings for her. When a blizzard hits unexpectedly and Maggie must find a way to get back to her ranch, she has to depend on both men for help. Doing so allows Maggie to come to conclusions about her future. First novel.

Other books you might like:
Lynn Austin, *Hidden Places*, 2001
Cathleen Connors, *A Home of Her Own*, 2002
Patricia Hickman, *Sandpebbles*, 2002
Patti Ann Hill, *Like a Watered Garden*, 2005
Karen Kingsbury, *Maggie's Miracle*, 2003
Jane Orcutt, *The Living Stone*, 2000

985
ROBERT ELMER

The Celebrity
(Colorado Springs, Colorado: WaterBrook, 2005)

Story type: Contemporary
Subject(s): Memory Loss; Mothers and Sons; Singing
Major character(s): Jamie D. Lane, Singer (pop star); Anne Stewart, Teacher, Accident Victim (car accident)
Time period(s): 2000s
Locale(s): Riverdale, Washington

Summary: Pop star Jamie D. Lane is riding a wave of success when he takes a break to visit his mother in Los Angeles. To his surprise, his mother, who has Alzheimer's disease, requests that they return to their hometown of Riverdale, Washington. Knowing he would be mobbed if he appears as the celebrity Jamie D. Lane, he cuts off his signature blonde hair and goes undercover as Joe Bradley. He meets Anne Stewart, a teacher who is recovering from a car accident. As the two become close, Jamie wonders what will happen when he reveals his true self to her.

Other books by the same author:
The Duet, 2004

Other books you might like:
Judy Baer, *Libby's Story*, 2001
James Scott Bell, *Breach of Promise*, 2004
Robin Jones Gunn, *Waterfalls*, 2004
Tracie Peterson, *A Slender Thread*, 2000
Patricia H. Rushford, *Morningsong*, 1998

986
AISHA FORD

Flippin' the Script
(West Bloomfield, Michigan: Walk Worthy, 2004)

Story type: Contemporary
Subject(s): African Americans; Television Programs
Major character(s): Sabrina Bradley, Television (assistant producer); Darci Oliver, Television Personality (talk show host)
Time period(s): 2000s
Locale(s): United States

Summary: Sabrina Bradley's job may seem glamorous to outsiders, but working as the assistant producer for a talk show largely consists of doing errands for her tyrannical boss, Darci Oliver. Then Darci finds Sabrina's list of New Year's resolutions and sees a potential ratings bonanza. Her idea is to follow Sabrina on-air for a year to see if she follows through on the resolutions. If Sabrina succeeds, she will get a bonus and a promotion. If she fails, she will have no job at all. Not really seeing an option, Sabrina agrees. Soon she is in the middle of a media frenzy, and Sabrina realizes that Darci is more than willing to fight dirty if it looks as if Sabrina might meet her goals.

Where it's reviewed:
Library Journal, September 1, 2004, page 130

Other books by the same author:
Missouri Getaways, 2003
Whole in One, 2002
Pride and Pumpernickel, 2001
The Wife Degree, 2000
Stacy's Wedding, 1999

Other books you might like:
Angela Benson, *The Genesis House Series*, 2000-
Venise Berry, *Colored Sugar Water*, 2002
Kristin Billerbeck, *The Ashley Stockingdale Series*, 2004-
Felicia Mason, *Testimony*, 2002
Michelle Stimpson, *Boaz Brown*, 2004
Jacquelin Thomas, *Singsation*, 2001

987

SHARON EWELL FOSTER

Ain't No Mountain

(Minneapolis: Bethany House, 2004)

Story type: Contemporary
Subject(s): Dating (Social Customs); Internet
Major character(s): Mary, Postal Worker; Eleanore "Puddin" Jenkins, Counselor (advisor to lovelorn); Moor, Student—College
Time period(s): 2000s
Locale(s): Baltimore, Maryland

Summary: Mary is a single woman who misses her old life in New Orleans and has had a run of bad dates. Moor is a young African student who misses his life in Lesotho. Puddin is a middle aged married woman who has come to believe her husband has some interests she considers abhorrent. The lives of these three people converge when Puddin decides her husband's sudden need for secret video viewing might lead to her having to support herself in the near future. She obtains a job as an advisor to the lovelorn who place Internet personal ads in the Charm City News Personals. She advises both Mary and Moor while juggling her own marital problems. Sequel to *Ain't No River*.

Other books by the same author:
Passing into Light, 2002
Ain't No River, 2001
Riding through Shadows, 2001
Passing by Samaria, 2000

Other books you might like:
Venise Berry, *Colored Sugar Water*, 2002
Michele Andrea Bowen, *Church Folk*, 2001
Aisha Ford, *Flippin' the Script*, 2004
Stephanie Perry Moore, *A Lova' Like No Otha'*, 2003
Jacquelin Thomas, *A Change Is Gonna Come*, 2003

988

ALTON GANSKY

The Incumbent

(Grand Rapids, Michigan: Zondervan, 2005)

Story type: Mystery; Political
Subject(s): Political Thriller; Politics
Major character(s): Madison "Maddy" Glenn, Political Figure (mayor)
Time period(s): 2000s
Locale(s): Santa Rita, California

Summary: Mayor Maddy Glenn is satisfied with the job she is doing in her small California town, certain she is making a difference. Then one of her campaign workers disappears, leaving behind a teenage daughter, Celeste. When a second worker disappears, it seems as if somebody is targeting those individuals the mayor loves and respects. As Maddy struggles to take care of Celeste while still performing her mayoral duties, she is forced to face the question of who is behind the disappearances.

Other books by the same author:
Beneath the Ice, 2004
A Treasure Deep, 2003
Out of Time, 2003
Dark Moon, 2002
The Prodigy, 2001

Other books you might like:
John Bayer, *Satan's Ring*, 2002
T. Davis Bunn, *The Ultimatum*, 1999
Glyn J. Godwin, *Body Politic*, 2003
Angela Elwell Hunt, *The Justice*, 2001
Clay Jacobsen, *Circle of Seven*, 2000

989

SHARON GILLENWATER

Twice Blessed

(New York: Steeple Hill, 2004)

Story type: Historical/American West
Subject(s): Gambling
Major character(s): Camille Dupree, Gambler, Publisher (newspaper owner); Tyler McKinnon, Businessman (owner of stagecoach line)
Time period(s): 1880s
Locale(s): Willow Grove, Texas

Summary: Camille Dupree is traveling to Willow Grove, Texas, to take a job as a card dealer in the saloon of her friends Nate and Bonnie. On the stagecoach to Willow Grove, Camille meets Tyler McKinnon. Tyler owns the stagecoach line, but is temporarily driving. He and Camille flirt, but both believe the flirtation will never amount to anything. Once in Willow Grove, Camille learns that Nate and Bonnie don't actually want her to work in the saloon. They just want her to turn her back on her dubious profession of gambler. Tyler agrees to help her and soon Camille is able to buy the town's newspaper. However, when a figure from her past arrives in

Inspirational

town, Camille soon realizes she may not be able to run away from past mistakes.

Other books by the same author:
Highland Call, 1999
Texas Tender, 1997
Song of the Highlands, 1996
Antiques, 1995
Love Song, 1995

Other books you might like:
Stephen Bly, *The Heroines of the Golden West Series*, 1998-
Lori Copeland, *The Brides of the West Series*, 1998-
Al Lacy, *The Mail Order Bride Series*, 1998-
Tracie Peterson, *The Heirs of Montana Series*, 2004-
Lori Wick, *The Rocky Mountain Memories Series*, 1996-

990

JOSEPH F. GIRZONE

Joshua in a Troubled World

(New York: Doubleday, 2005)

Story type: Contemporary/Fantasy
Series: Joshua. Book 8
Subject(s): Peace
Major character(s): Joshua, Religious (prophet)
Time period(s): Indeterminate Future
Locale(s): Washington, District of Columbia; Middle East

Summary: Joshua, a modern day Jesus, arrives in Washington, D.C. His Middle Eastern appearance, coupled with his numerous visits to churches, synagogues, and mosques soon attracts attention of the wrong sort. Brought into custody by government agents, Joshua is questioned and released, but remains under suspicion for covert activities. When Joshua begins to organize a diverse group of Christians, Muslims, and Jews for a peaceful mission to the Middle East, it is again thought that he is up to no good.

Where it's reviewed:
Booklist, November 15, 2004, page 531
Publishers Weekly, November 29, 2004, page 21

Other books by the same author:
The Messenger, 2002
The Parables of Joshua, 2001
Joshua: The Homecoming, 1999
Joshua and the Shepherd, 1996
Joshua and the City, 1995

Other books you might like:
T. Davis Bunn, *The Messenger*, 1995
Jack Cavanaugh, *Postmarked Heaven*, 2002
Roger Elwood, *The Angelwalk Series*, 1989-
Sally-Ann Roberts, *Angelvision*, 2002
D. Brian Shafer, *Chronicles of the Host*, 2002

991

LOUISE M. GOUGE

Hannah Rose

(Colorado Springs, Colorado: RiverOak, 2005)

Story type: Historical
Series: Ahab. Book 2
Subject(s): Slavery; Widows/Widowers
Major character(s): Hannah Ahab, Widow(er)
Time period(s): 1840s
Locale(s): Boston, Massachusetts

Summary: Captain Ahab is dead, leaving behind a widow and a young son. Hannah Ahab decides to move on with her life by leaving the whaling village of Nantucket and taking a journey abroad. She and her son go to Boston to prepare for their trip. While visiting friends in that city, Hannah meets Captain Lazarus and Captain Longwood, both of whom make the widow realize she might like to marry again. Hannah is also confronted with the realities of slavery and the slave trade, leaving her to question her long-held beliefs about that institution.

Other books by the same author:
Ahab's Bride, 2004
The Homecoming, 1998
Once There Was a Way Back Home, 1994

Other books you might like:
Dianna Crawford, *The Frontier Women Series*, 2000-
B.J. Hoff, *The Song of Erin Series*, 1997-
Jim Kraus, *The Circle of Destiny Series*, 2000-
Delia Parr, *The Trinity Series*, 2002-
Jake Thoene, *The Portraits of Destiny Series*, 1998-

992

MARGARET A. GRAHAM

Good Heavens

(Grand Rapids, Michigan: Fleming H. Revell, 2004)

Story type: Contemporary
Series: Esmeralda. Book 2
Subject(s): Drugs; Women
Major character(s): Esmeralda, Care Giver (housemother), Widow(er)
Time period(s): 2000s
Locale(s): North Carolina

Summary: Esmeralda is a feisty Southern widow who is used to the slow pace of life in Live Oaks, South Carolina. Dealing with female addicts is something she is not used to, but when she is asked to take a job as housemother at a Christian halfway house for addicts, Esmeralda agrees. Arriving at an isolated spot in North Carolina, Esmeralda is dismayed to see that the Priscilla House desperately needs help. The bills haven't been paid in months, food is scarce, and the new director is unable to cope with her charges. Esmeralda plunges in and soon has things running smoothly enough that she can begin taking an interest in the young women under her care.

Other books by the same author:
Mercy Me, 2003

Other books you might like:
Ginny Aiken, *The Bellamy's Blossoms Series*, 2000-
Ray Blackston, *Flabbergasted*, 2003
Linda Dorrell, *True Believers*, 2001
Annie Jones, *Deep Dixie*, 1999
Lisa Samson, *The Church Ladies*, 2001

993

MARGARET A. GRAHAM

Land Sakes

(Grand Rapids, Michigan: Fleming H. Revell, 2005)

Story type: Contemporary
Series: Esmeralda. Book 3
Subject(s): Cruise Ships; Travel
Major character(s): Esmeralda, Care Giver, Widow(er); Winifred Winchuster, Wealthy, Employer (of Esmeralda)
Time period(s): 2000s
Locale(s): At Sea

Summary: Having left her job as a housemother at a halfway house for drug addicts, Esmeralda takes a position as a companion to a wealthy woman. Mrs. Winifred Winchuster, her Afghan hound, and Esmeralda all set off on an Alaskan cruise. Esmeralda is determined to bring her new employer to Christianity, but finds the process more difficult than she had imagined it would be.

Other books by the same author:
Good Heavens, 2004
Mercy Me, 2003
Anna, 1986

Other books you might like:
Charlene Ann Baumbich, *The Dearest Dorothy Series*, 2004-
Peggy Darty, *Getaways*, 2000
Lisa Samson, *The Church Ladies*, 2001
Debra White Smith, *To Rome with Love*, 2001
Linda Windsor, *It Had to Be You*, 2001

994

RENE GUTTERIDGE

Boo Who

(Colorado Springs, Colorado: WaterBrook, 2004)

Story type: Contemporary
Subject(s): Small Town Life
Major character(s): Christian Wolfe ''Boo'' Boone, Writer (retired), Salesman (cars and books)
Time period(s): 2000s
Locale(s): Skary, Indiana

Summary: Horror novelist Boo Boone has quit writing and has turned to sales to pay the bills, first taking a job selling cars, then moving on to a bookstore. Meanwhile, Boo's hometown of Skary, Indiana, is reeling from the shock of losing Boo's fans. Tourism from fans of the one-time novelist's books has fallen off drastically. As the town struggles to find a new source of income, Boo's fiancee is distracted from their upcoming wedding when she gets the chance to become the country's next homemaking guru. Sequel to *Boo*.

Where it's reviewed:
Publishers Weekly, July 26, 2004, page 38

Other books by the same author:
The Splitting Storm, 2004
Boo, 2003
Troubled Waters, 2003
Ghost Writer, 2000

Other books you might like:
Stephen Bly, *Paperback Writer*, 2003
Lori Copeland, *The Heavenly Daze Series*, 2001-
Philip Gulley, *The Harmony Series*, 2000-
Robin Jones Gunn, *The Glenbrooke Series*, 1995-
Robert Waldron, *Blue Hope*, 2002

995

RENE GUTTERIDGE

Storm Gathering

(Wheaton, Illinois: Tyndale House, 2005)

Story type: Mystery
Subject(s): Murder
Major character(s): Mick Kline, Fugitive
Time period(s): 2000s
Locale(s): Texas

Summary: Mick Kline wakes up in a strange woman's apartment and finds himself the main suspect in a murder investigation. Thinking he won't be able to convince the police of his innocence, Mick runs away. With the police on his trail, Mick begins to realize the truth may lie with his estranged brother. This book is the prequel to *The Splitting Storm*.

Other books by the same author:
Boo Who, 2004
The Splitting Storm, 2004
Boo, 2003
Troubled Waters, 2003
Ghost Writer, 2000

Other books you might like:
Terri Blackstock, *The Cape Refuge Series*, 2002-
Colleen Coble, *The Rock Harbor Series*, 2003-
Brandilyn Collins, *The Hidden Faces Series*, 2004-
Dee Henderson, *The O'Malley Series*, 2001-
Patricia H. Rushford, *The Angel Delaney Series*, 2004-

996

HANK HANEGRAAFF
SIGMUND BROUWER, Co-Author

The Last Disciple

(Wheaton, Illinois: Tyndale House, 2004)

Story type: Biblical Fiction
Subject(s): Roman Empire; End-Times
Major character(s): Vitas, Political Figure (advisor to Emperor Nero)
Time period(s): 1st century

Inspirational

Locale(s): Roman Empire

Summary: Vitas, a trusted advisor to Nero, is concerned because the emperor's behavior is becoming increasingly erratic. Followers of Christ are convinced that Nero is the Antichrist and they are going through the Tribulation. As things in Rome become more turbulent, Vitas escapes to Jerusalem. There he marries a young Jewish slave named Sophia, who has converted to Christianity. Realizing her religious beliefs would cause her great trouble in Rome, Vitas insists she hide her faith. Although authors Sigmund Brouwer and Hank Hanegraaff have published other books, this is their first book as co-authors.

Other books you might like:
Irene Brand, *The Legacies of Faith Series*, 1996-
Tim F. LaHaye, *The Left Behind Series*, 1995-
Mel Odom, *Apocalypse Dawn*, 2003
Francine Rivers, *The Mark of the Lion Series*, 1993-
Andrew M. Seddon, *Imperial Legions*, 2000

997

VALERIE HANSEN

Everlasting Love
(New York: Steeple Hill, 2004)

Story type: Romance
Subject(s): Animals; Divorce; Homeless People
Major character(s): Megan White, Health Care Professional (animal therapist); James Harris, Administrator (camp director)
Time period(s): 2000s
Locale(s): Ozarks

Summary: Megan White has combined her love of animals and her love of helping others into the perfect career. She is an animal therapist for a camp in the Ozarks. The camp gives disturbed and homeless children time away from their troubles. While Megan believes animals will give the children something to love, the camp director, James Harris, does not. In fact, he thinks Megan's program will cause nothing but problems. He is even more concerned when he discovers that Megan's teenage sister Roxy will be joining the camp. Roxy is distraught over her parents' divorce and her father's subsequent remarriage.

Other books by the same author:
Blessings of the Heart, 2003
Samantha's Gift, 2003
Love One Another, 2001
Second Chances, 2001
The Perfect Couple, 2000

Other books you might like:
Hannah Alexander, *Hideaway*, 2003
Irene Brand, *The Test of Love*, 2000
Margaret Daley, *A Family for Tory*, 2004
Teresa Hill, *Someone to Watch over Me*, 2004
Lois Richer, *The Camp Hope Series*, 2004-

998

NEESA HART

Impeachable Offense
(Wheaton, Illinois: Tyndale House, 2004)

Story type: End of the World
Series: End of State. Book 2
Subject(s): End-Times; Political Thriller
Major character(s): Brad Benton, Government Official (White House chief of staff)
Time period(s): Indeterminate Future
Locale(s): Washington, District of Columbia

Summary: It is the End Times and people all over the world are disappearing. The crisis is deeply felt in Washington, D.C., as members of the political world attempt to calm the growing concerns of the citizens of the United States. White House Chief of Staff Brad Benton has survived two attempts on his life after trying to investigate the mysterious death of the White House press secretary. Realizing he is in over his head, Brad teams up with a close-knit band of friends to try to find out what is going on. This series is an off-shoot of the popular Left Behind series by Tim F. LaHaye and Jerry B. Jenkins.

Other books by the same author:
Want Ad Wedding, 2004
End of State, 2003
Her Passionate Pirate, 2001
Who Gets to Marry Max?, 2000
You Made Me Love You, 2000

Other books you might like:
Ken Abraham, *The Prodigal Project Series*, 2003-
T. Davis Bunn, *The Ultimatum*, 1999
Clay Jacobsen, *Circle of Seven*, 2000
Shane Johnson, *A Form of Godliness*, 2004
Mel Odom, *Apocalypse Dawn*, 2003
Robert L. Wise, *The Tail of the Dragon*, 2000

999

VERONICA HELEY

The Lady of the Hall
(Grand Rapids, Michigan: Zondervan, 2005)

Story type: Contemporary
Series: Eden Hall. Book 2
Subject(s): Family Problems; Inheritance
Major character(s): Minty Cardale, Heiress; Patrick, Boyfriend (of Minty)
Time period(s): 2000s
Locale(s): England

Summary: After a long struggle, Minty Cardale has inherited Eden Hall, a magnificent estate in England. Unfortunately, her problems are not yet over. Her stepfamily is determined to prove Minty has no right to the estate and battles any changes she tries to implement. There is also little money, so necessary improvements to the estate cannot be made. The one bright spot in Minty's life is Patrick, her boyfriend. When he suggests they might not have a future together, Minty begins to wonder if she should stay at Eden Hall, or just give up her fight and leave.

Other books by the same author:
Eden Hall, 2004
Murder in the Garden, 2004
Murder by Accident, 2003
Murder of Innocence, 2003
Murder by Suicide, 2002

Other books you might like:
Lynn Austin, *Eve's Daughters*, 1999
T. Davis Bunn, *The Book of Hours*, 2000
Michael Phillips, *The Heathersleigh Hall Series*, 1998-
Adrian Plass, *Ghosts*, 2003
Sally Brice Winterbourn, *Autumn Return*, 2001

1000

KATHY HERMAN

A Shred of Evidence

(Sisters, Oregon: Multnomah, 2005)

Story type: Mystery
Series: Seaport. Book 1
Subject(s): Child Abuse
Major character(s): Ellen Jones, Editor (newspaper)
Time period(s): 2000s
Locale(s): United States

Summary: Ellen Jones is eating lunch at a restaurant when she overhears some disturbing gossip about her new friend Sue Ann's husband. Not thinking the rumors could possibly be true, Ellen does some researching through old newspaper files and learns that the man was once accused of pedophilia. The charges were never proven, however. Ellen finds herself in the dilemma of having to decide whether to tell others of her discoveries. If the charges are true, Ellen might protect other children. If they are lies, she is merely spreading gossip and ruining a man's life.

Other books by the same author:
Poor Mrs. Rigsby, 2004
A Fine Line, 2003
High Stakes, 2003
Day of Reckoning, 2002
Vital Signs, 2002

Other books you might like:
Kristen Heitzmann, *A Rush of Wings*, 2003
Dee Henderson, *The O'Malley Series*, 2001-
David Ryan Long, *Ezekiel's Shadow*, 2001
Catherine Palmer, *Fatal Harvest*, 2003
Gayle Roper, *The Seaside Seasons Series*, 2001-

1001

DENISE HILDRETH

Savannah from Savannah

(Nashville: WestBow, 2004)

Story type: Contemporary
Subject(s): Beauty Contests; Mothers and Daughters; Writing
Major character(s): Savannah Phillips, Journalist
Time period(s): 2000s
Locale(s): Savannah, Georgia

Summary: Since childhood, Savannah Phillips has dreamed of becoming a published author. When she learns that her novel, written as a graduate thesis, has won a prestigious literary award and is to be published, Savannah is thrilled. Then she learns that her mother engineered her win. Crushed by the duplicity, Savannah decides to return to her hometown of Savannah, Georgia, and work to expose lies and deceit wherever she can. Taking a job at the local newspaper, Savannah is soon hard at work exposing what she thinks is a rigged beauty contest. First novel.

Where it's reviewed:
Library Journal, June 1, 2004, page 111

Other books you might like:
Ginny Aiken, *The Bellamy's Blossoms Series*, 2000-
Ray Blackston, *Flabbergasted*, 2003
Annie Jones, *Deep Dixie*, 1999
Lisa Samson, *The Church Ladies*, 2001
Augusta Trobaugh, *Praise Jerusalem!*, 1997

1002

PATTI ANN HILL

Like a Watered Garden

(Minneapolis: Bethany House, 2005)

Story type: Contemporary
Series: Garden Gates. Book 1
Subject(s): Gardens and Gardening; Grief; Widows/Widowers
Major character(s): Mibby Garrett, Gardener (garden designer), Widow(er)
Time period(s): 2000s
Locale(s): Colorado

Summary: Garden designer Mibby Garrett is still reeling from the shock of her husband's sudden death in a bike accident. She has decided that the best way to get through life is to avoid anything that reminds her of married life, such as her son's baseball games and grocery shopping. Soon, though, the groceries run out and her friends move on and Mibby is left alone with her dog and son for companionship. Realizing something has to change, Mibby decides to venture out into the world again. First novel.

Where it's reviewed:
Publishers Weekly, November 15, 2004, page 40

Other books you might like:
Paige Lee Elliston, *Changes of Heart*, 2005
Robin Lee Hatcher, *Beyond the Shadows*, 2004
Patricia Hickman, *Sandpebbles*, 2002
Karen Kingsbury, *Maggie's Miracle*, 2003
Jane Orcutt, *The Living Stone*, 2000

Inspirational

1003

TERESA HILL

Someone to Watch over Me

(New York: Steeple Hill, 2004)

Story type: Romance
Subject(s): Animals/Dogs; Death; Grief
Major character(s): Gwen Moss, Crime Victim, Businesswoman (florist); William Jackson "Jax" Cassidy, Police Officer
Time period(s): 2000s
Locale(s): Magnolia Falls, Georgia

Summary: When policeman Jax Cassidy loses his mother to cancer, he is grief-stricken. However, he also has to care for three younger sisters and a dog named Romeo. The dog is a bit of a problem. Originally intended to be trained as a search and rescue dog, Romeo flunked out of the training program because he would rather follow women than learn his job. Adopted by Jax's family, Romeo was soon thoroughly spoiled by his mother and sisters. When Gwen Moss moves to Magnolia Falls, she befriends the Cassidy family and soon takes over the care of Romeo. Although Jax doesn't particularly care for Romeo, he is soon spending more and more time with Gwen. Soon the two realize that they are both grieving, although for different reasons, and begin to fall in love.

Other books by the same author:
Bed of Lies, 2003
Heard It through the Grapevine, 2003
The Edge of Heaven, 2002
Unbreak My Heart, 2001
Twelve Days, 2000

Other books you might like:
Hannah Alexander, *Safe Haven*, 2004
Shelley Bates, *Grounds to Believe*, 2004
J.F. Margos, *Shattered Image*, 2004
Shirlee McCoy, *Still Waters*, 2004
Lenora Worth, *After the Storm*, 2004

1004

JOSEPH H. HILLEY

Sober Justice

(Colorado Springs, Colorado: RiverOak, 2004)

Story type: Mystery
Subject(s): Alcoholism; Legal Thriller
Major character(s): Mike Connolly, Lawyer, Alcoholic
Time period(s): 2000s
Locale(s): Mobile, Alabama

Summary: Mike Connolly's life has settled into a rut of alcoholic despair. His law practice has dwindled down to nearly nothing, he hasn't seen his daughter in over a year, and his dependence on gin has overtaken his life. Then Mike is appointed to a capital murder case. His client is a homeless man named Avery Thompson who allegedly robbed and murdered a prominent local attorney. As Mike becomes immersed in the case, he begins to believe there is a conspiracy keeping his client behind bars. First novel.

Other books you might like:
James Scott Bell, *Blind Justice*, 2000
Chuck Chitwood, *The Trial of Job*, 2000
Michael Farris, *Guilty by Association*, 1997
Craig Parshall, *The Chambers of Justice Series*, 2002-
Randy Singer, *Dying Declaration*, 2004

1005

ANGELA ELWELL HUNT

The Awakening

(Nashville: WestBow, 2004)

Story type: Contemporary
Subject(s): Death; Mothers and Daughters; Phobias
Major character(s): Aurora Norquest, Handicapped (agoraphobic)
Time period(s): 2000s
Locale(s): New York, New York

Summary: After a long illness, Mary Elizabeth Norquest dies, leaving her daughter Aurora bereft. Due to her agoraphobia, Aurora has not left the New York City apartment she shared with her mother for years. Aurora has depended on delivery services and the overwhelming kindness of her mother's oldest friend Clara to maintain her secluded existence. After her mother's death, though, Aurora begins to question her life. Her new neighbor Philip Cannon helps her to connect to the outside world via the Internet. Soon Aurora is looking for her long-lost father and making tentative steps back to the outside world.

Where it's reviewed:
Publishers Weekly, June 7, 2004, page 31

Other books by the same author:
Unspoken, 2005
The Debt, 2004
The Canopy, 2003
The Pearl, 2003
The Shadow Women, 2002

Other books you might like:
Melody Carlson, *Angels in the Snow*, 2002
Brandilyn Collins, *Cast a Road Before Me*, 2001
Elizabeth Musser, *The Swan House*, 2001
Susan Oliver, *Once upon a Gulf Coast Summer*, 2004
Tracie Peterson, *A Slender Thread*, 2000

1006

DEREK JACKSON

A Man Inspired

(West Bloomfield, Michigan: Walk Worthy, 2005)

Story type: Contemporary
Subject(s): Depression
Major character(s): Jermaine Hill, Television Personality (motivational speaker)
Time period(s): 2000s
Locale(s): Los Angeles, California

Summary: Jermaine Hill is a motivational speaker who can make anybody feel better about themselves. With a top rated television show and money pouring in, Jermaine should feel good about himself as well. However, he is haunted by a depression he cannot escape. Having lost many people close to him, Jermaine is now surrounded by people who are only there because of his wealth and celebrity. With the depression growing worse daily, Jermaine turns to a God he never thought existed for help. First novel.

Where it's reviewed:
Publishers Weekly, November 22, 2004, page 39

Other books you might like:
Angela Benson, *The Genesis House Series*, 2000-
Michele Andrea Bowen, *Second Sunday*, 2001
Aisha Ford, *Flippin' the Script*, 2004
Felicia Mason, *Testimony*, 2002
Jacquelin Thomas, *The Prodigal Husband*, 2002

1007
NETA JACKSON

The Yada Yada Prayer Group Gets Down
(Nashville: Integrity, 2004)

Story type: Contemporary
Series: Yada Yada Prayer Group. Book 2
Subject(s): Crime and Criminals; Friendship; Prayer
Major character(s): Jodi Baxter, Spouse, Parent
Time period(s): 2000s
Locale(s): Chicago, Illinois

Summary: Jodi Baxter's once quiet life is slowly spinning out of control. Wracked with guilt after causing the death of a child in a car accident, Jodi is traumatized when the boy's mother refuses to forgive her. Jodi's life is further complicated when the mother of a close friend accuses her husband Denny of being involved in a lynching years before. When a heroin addict robs Jodi's prayer group at knifepoint, she realizes forgiveness is difficult for anybody, even a devout Christian like herself.

Where it's reviewed:
Library Journal, September 1, 2004, page 132
Publishers Weekly, August 9, 2004, page 233

Other books by the same author:
The Yada Yada Prayer Group, 2003

Other books you might like:
Vonette Z. Bright, *The Sister Circle Series*, 2003-
Robin Jones Gunn, *The Sisterchicks Series*, 2003-
Roxanne Henke, *After Anne*, 2002
Beverly LaHaye, *The Seasons Series*, 1999-
Lauraine Snelling, *The Healing Quilt*, 2002

1008
ARLENE JAMES

The Heart's Voice
(New York: Steeple Hill, 2004)

Story type: Romance
Subject(s): Deafness; Widows/Widowers

Major character(s): Becca Kinder, Clerk, Widow(er); Dan Holden, Carpenter, Handicapped (deaf)
Time period(s): 2000s
Locale(s): Rain Dance, Oklahoma

Summary: After her husband dies in a rodeo accident, Becca Kinder takes a job at her in-laws' store to try to make ends meet. Unfortunately, the job doesn't pay enough for the costly repairs her rundown house needs, so Becca looks for a carpenter who will be willing to charge her reasonable rates for the repairs. She believes Dan Holden, a quiet man who shops at the store, might help, but when she asks if he has time, Dan seems taciturn and distant. What Becca doesn't know is that Dan suffered a hearing loss while serving in the military and is keeping the condition hidden. What people perceive as rudeness or shyness is actually Dan's inability to hear what they are saying.

Other books by the same author:
Beautician Gets Million Dollar Tip, 2004
Fortune Finds Florist, 2004
Tycoon Meets Texan, 2004
Her Secret Affair, 2003
The Detective's Dilemma, 2003

Other books you might like:
Carolyne Aarsen, *Ever Faithful*, 1998
Marcy Froemke, *A Family Man*, 1999
Deb Kastner, *A Perfect Match*, 2002
Mae Nunn, *Hearts in Bloom*, 2004
Lois Richer, *Heaven's Kiss*, 2004

1009
JERRY B. JENKINS

Silenced: The Wrath of God Descends
(Wheaton, Illinois: Tyndale House, 2004)

Story type: End of the World
Series: Underground Zealot. Book 2
Subject(s): End-Times
Major character(s): Paul Stepola, Spy (double agent)
Time period(s): Indeterminate Future
Locale(s): United Seven States of America, Fictional Country

Summary: A drought has transformed Los Angeles, a main city in the United Seven States of America, into a wasteland. Since the underground movement composed of true believers in God has plenty of water, unbelievers have started to see the religious truths the government wants to hide. An official named Paul Stepola has long been an operative for the government, but his belief system has broken down. He now works for both the underground movement of believers, and the government whose task it is to stop them from gaining power. When three major cities are attacked by terrorists in the name of God, Paul realizes he must find out who is behind the horrors and expose them, all without blowing his cover.

Other books by the same author:
Soon, 2003
The Youngest Hero, 2002
Hometown Legend, 2001
Though None Go with Me, 2000
Twas the Night Before, 1998

Inspirational

Other books you might like:
Ken Abraham, *The Prodigal Project Series*, 2003-
Neesa Hart, *The Left Behind Political Series*, 2004-
Paul Meier, *The Millennium Series*, 1993-
Mel Odom, *Apocalypse Dawn*, 2003
Robert L. Wise, *The Tribulation Survival Series*, 2004-

1010

SALLY JOHN

Moment of Truth

(Eugene, Oregon: Harvest House, 2005)

Story type: Contemporary
Series: In a Heartbeat. Book 3
Subject(s): Abuse; Arson; Homeless People
Major character(s): Cara Fleming, Police Officer; Bryan O'Shaugnessy, Religious (Episcopal priest)
Time period(s): 2000s
Locale(s): Chicago, Illinois

Summary: Before becoming a police officer, Cara Fleming had a hard life in which she was often homeless and abused. After her apartment is destroyed in a fire believed to be arson, Cara returns to life on the streets in an attempt to protect both herself and an eyewitness. While volunteering at a homeless shelter, Cara meets an overworked Episcopal priest named Bryan O'Shaugnessy. Bryan is drawn to his new volunteer, but soon realizes she has secrets that might keep them apart.

Other books by the same author:
Flash Point, 2004
In a Heartbeat, 2004
After All These Years, 2003
Just to See You Smile, 2003
The Winding Road Home, 2003

Other books you might like:
Judy Candis, *All Things Hidden*, 2004
Colleen Coble, *The Rock Harbor Series*, 2003-
Dee Henderson, *The O'Malley Series*, 2001-
Kathi Mills-Macias, *The Toni Matthews Series*, 2001-
Patricia H. Rushford, *The Angel Delaney Series*, 2004-

1011

ANNIE JONES

Sadie-in-Waiting

(New York: Steeple Hill, 2004)

Story type: Contemporary; Humor
Subject(s): Cemeteries; Mothers
Major character(s): Sadie Pickett, Maintenance Worker (graveyard superintendent)
Time period(s): 2000s
Locale(s): Wileyville, Kentucky

Summary: Sadie Pickett is a woman with a great many responsibilities. She is the wife of a pharmacist, mother of two teenagers, primary caretaker of her father, and president of a local woman's group. So when the mayor of Wileyville, Kentucky, shows up on her doorstep and asks her to take the job of graveyard superintendent, she doesn't exactly jump at

the offer. All of her friends think the job is just what she needs, though. Against her better judgment, Sadie jumps into yet another responsibility.

Other books by the same author:
The Snowbirds, 2001
Lost Romance Ranch, 2000
Cupid's Corner, 1999
The Double Heart Diner, 1999

Other books you might like:
Charlene Ann Baumbich, *The Dearest Dorothy Series*, 2004-
Kristin Billerbeck, *The Ashley Stockingdale Series*, 2004-
Ray Blackston, *The Jay Jarvis Series*, 2003-
Penny Culliford, *The Theodora Series*, 2004-
Robin Jones Gunn, *The Sisterchicks Series*, 2003-

1012

DEB KASTNER

Undercover Blessings

(New York: Steeple Hill, 2005)

Story type: Romance
Subject(s): Crime and Criminals; Mothers and Daughters
Major character(s): Lily Montague, Single Parent; Kevin "Mack" MacCormack, FBI Agent
Time period(s): 2000s
Locale(s): Georgia

Summary: After 7-year-old Abigail witnesses a crime, her mother Lily flees with her daughter to Abigail's grandmother's home in Georgia to hide. Not too thrilled about returning home, Lily must protect her daughter while continuing life-long battles with her own mother. Lily and Abigail are accompanied by FBI Agent Mack MacCormack, who usually dislikes undercover work. However, being with little Abigail and her beautiful mother makes Mack enjoy his latest assignment, perhaps a bit too much.

Other books by the same author:
Hart's Harbor, 2003
A Perfect Match, 2002
The Christmas Groom, 2002
A Daddy at Heart, 2001
Black Hills Bride, 2000

Other books you might like:
Cynthia Cooke, *Luck and a Prayer*, 2004
Margaret Daley, *The Power of Love*, 2002
Gail Gaymer Martin, *A Love for Safekeeping*, 2002
Felicia Mason, *Sweet Devotion*, 2004
Marta Perry, *Desperately Seeking Dad*, 2000

1013

LEISHA KELLY

Katie's Dream

(Grand Rapids, Michigan: Fleming H. Revell, 2004)

Story type: Historical/Depression Era
Series: Wortham Family. Book 3
Subject(s): Children; Depression (Economic)

Major character(s): Sam Wortham, Farmer; Julia Wortham, Spouse
Time period(s): 1930s
Locale(s): Dearing, Illinois

Summary: Sam and Julia Wortham return home after enjoying a cheerful Fourth of July celebration, only to be confronted with bad news. Sam's ex-con brother Edward has turned up with a surprise in tow—a little girl named Katie whom he claims was fathered by Sam. Sam protests his innocence and Julia struggles to believe him as Edward revels in the trouble that he has caused the Worthams.

Other books by the same author:
Emma's Gift, 2003
Julia's Hope, 2002

Other books you might like:
Lynn Austin, *Hidden Places*, 2001
Patricia Hickman, *The Millwood Hollow Series*, 2003-
Calvin Miller, *Snow*, 1998
Gary E. Parker, *The Blue Ridge Legacy Series*, 2001-
Lance Wubbels, *The Gentle Hills Series*, 1994-

1014

KAREN KINGSBURY

Beyond Tuesday Morning

(Grand Rapids, Michigan: Zondervan, 2005)

Story type: Contemporary
Subject(s): Terrorism; Widows/Widowers
Major character(s): Jamie Bryan, Volunteer, Widow(er)
Time period(s): 2000s
Locale(s): New York, New York

Summary: It has been three years since terrorists destroyed the Twin Towers in New York City. Since then, Jamie Bryan has been mourning her firefighter husband and honoring his memory by volunteering at a chapel across the street from the site of the destruction. There she meets two men with whom she feels a connection, a firefighter and a police officer. When Jamie learns that the police officer is the brother of Eric Michaels, a man with amnesia who resembled her husband and ended up taking his place for three months after 9/11, Jamie wants nothing more to do with him. The pain of learning Eric was not her husband was more than she could bear. As Jamie reads her husband's journal, she realizes he would want her to move on with her life. Sequel to *One Tuesday Morning*.

Other books by the same author:
Oceans Apart, 2004
Sarah's Song, 2004
Maggie's Miracle, 2003
One Tuesday Morning, 2003
Halfway to Forever, 2002

Other books you might like:
Lisa Tawn Bergren, *Chosen*, 1996
Dee Henderson, *True Honor*, 2002
Patricia Hickman, *Sandpebbles*, 2002
Jane Orcutt, *The Living Stone*, 2000
Michael Phillips, *King's Crossroads*, 2003

1015

KAREN KINGSBURY

Sarah's Song

(New York: Warner, 2004)

Story type: Contemporary
Series: Red Gloves. Book 3
Subject(s): Christmas; Friendship; Old Age
Major character(s): Sarah Lindeman, Aged Person
Time period(s): 20th century; 2000s (1940-2004)
Locale(s): United States

Summary: As an old woman, Sarah reflects on her long life. She had dreamed of escaping from her small hometown via a singing career. However, her other dream was to marry Sam Lindeman. Sam wanted nothing more than to settle down in their hometown, teach at the local school, and maybe someday become principal. Now, years later, Sarah performs a ritual for the 12 days of Christmas and ponders what might have been, and what was.

Other books by the same author:
Oceans Apart, 2004
Maggie's Miracle, 2003
One Tuesday Morning, 2003
Gideon's Gift, 2002
Halfway to Forever, 2002

Other books you might like:
T. Davis Bunn, *The Gift*, 1994
Thomas J. Davis, *The Christmas Quilt*, 2000
Jerry B. Jenkins, *Twas the Night Before*, 1998
Paul McCusker, *Epiphany*, 1998
Diane Noble, *Come My Little Angel*, 2001

1016

AL LACY

JOANNA LACY, Co-Author

The Heart Remembers

(Sisters, Oregon: Multnomah, 2004)

Story type: Historical/American West
Series: Frontier Doctors. Book 3
Subject(s): Indians of North America; Memory Loss
Major character(s): Dane Logan, Doctor, Amnesiac; Tharyn Logan, Spouse (of Dane)
Time period(s): 1880s
Locale(s): Colorado

Summary: Dane and Tharyn Logan have settled into life in the rugged West. Dane, a devoted doctor, has cared for most of his neighbors and many have become his close friends. He even practices among the local Indian tribe and counts many of the tribe as his friends, too. When a stagecoach he is riding in crashes, Dane survives, but is left with amnesia. Not remembering Tharyn or any of his friends, Dane can only hope that someday he will be found by somebody who knows him.

Other books by the same author:
Beloved Physician, 2004
One More Sunrise, 2004
All My Tomorrows, 2003

Inspirational

Whispers in the Wind, 2003
Let There Be Light, 2002

Other books you might like:
Ginny Aiken, *Light of My Heart*, 2004
Kristen Heitzmann, *The Rocky Mountain Legacy Series*, 1998-
Kathleen Morgan, *Child of Promise*, 2002
Lynn Morris, *The Cheney Duvall Series*, 1994-
Delia Parr, *The Trinity Series*, 2002-
Peggy Stoks, *Olivia's Touch*, 2000

1017

AL LACY
JOANNA LACY, Co-Author

Wings of Riches

(Sisters, Oregon: Multnomah, 2005)

Story type: Historical/American West
Series: Dreams of Gold. Book 1
Subject(s): Gold; Gold Discoveries; Miners and Mining
Major character(s): Craig Turley, Prospector; Kathy Ross, Governess
Time period(s): 1840s
Locale(s): California

Summary: Craig Turley is the son of a wealthy man, but he wants to succeed without his father's help. Hearing of fabulous gold discoveries in California, he heads west. Mining proves to be more difficult than Craig thought, but he discovers some gold. When his gold is stolen, Craig begins to realize how the lust for gold has changed his personality.

Other books by the same author:
Beloved Physician, 2004
One More Sunrise, 2004
The Heart Remembers, 2004
All My Tomorrows, 2003
Whispers in the Wind, 2003

Other books you might like:
Stephen Bly, *Fool's Gold*, 2000
Jim Kraus, *The Price*, 2000
Gilbert Morris, *The Yukon Queen*, 1995
Elaine L. Schulte, *With Wings as Eagles*, 1990
Bodie Thoene, *Winds of Promise*, 1997

1018

YVONNE LEHMAN

Coffee Rings

(Uhrichsville, Ohio: Barbour, 2004)

Story type: Contemporary
Subject(s): Accidents; Guilt; Secrets
Major character(s): Eunice Hogan, Aged Person
Time period(s): 2000s
Locale(s): North Carolina

Summary: When Eunice Hogan learns that she has only a few months left to live, she decides to delve into the mystery surrounding her daughter's death. Nineteen years earlier, Dove had gone swimming with three friends. Dove drowned and Ruby, Lara, and Annette all gave different stories to the police. Needing to know the facts about Dove's death, Eunice tracks down the three women in a desperate search for the truth.

Other books by the same author:
His Hands, 2003
On a Clear Day, 2003
Past the Ps Please, 2002
The Stranger's Kiss, 2001
Secret Ballot, 2000

Other books you might like:
Kathy Herman, *Day of Reckoning*, 2002
Karen Kingsbury, *Waiting for Morning*, 1999
Nancy Moser, *The Seat Beside Me*, 2002
Bette Nordberg, *Thin Air*, 2002
Deborah Raney, *After the Rains*, 2002
Travis Thrasher, *The Watermark*, 2001

1019

THOM LEMMONS

Sunday Clothes

(Nashville: Broadman & Holman, 2004)

Story type: Historical
Subject(s): Marriage; Religion
Major character(s): Addie Caswell Douglas, Spouse (of Zeb), Parent; Zeb Douglas, Salesman (traveling)
Time period(s): 1890s; 20th century (1898-1920)
Locale(s): United States

Summary: Addie Caswell falls desperately in love with handsome traveling salesman Zeb Douglas, much to her father's disapproval. Addie's father, a strict Methodist, disapproves of the Church of Christ, to which Zeb belongs. He also feels selling is not a steady enough career to support a wife. Addie disobeys her father and marries Zeb. For awhile, they are happy, but as their family grows Zeb begins to feel the strain of the pressures of marriage and family life.

Where it's reviewed:
Booklist, April 1, 2004, page 1347

Other books by the same author:
Jabez, 2001
Mother of Faith, 2001
Woman of Means, 2000
Daughter of Jerusalem, 1999
Once upon a Cross, 1992

Other books you might like:
Jack Cavanaugh, *The American Family Portrait Series*, 1994-
B.J. Hoff, *The Song of Erin Series*, 1997-
Sara Mitchell, *The Sinclair Legacy Series*, 2001-
Gilbert Morris, *The House of Winslow Series*, 1986-
Diane Noble, *The California Chronicles*, 1999-
Delia Parr, *The Trinity Series*, 2002-

1020

F.P. LIONE

The Deuce

(Grand Rapids, Michigan: Fleming H. Revell, 2005)

Story type: Mystery
Series: Midtown Blues. Book 1
Subject(s): Police Procedural
Major character(s): Tony Cavalucci, Police Officer; Joe Fiore, Police Officer
Time period(s): 2000s
Locale(s): New York, New York

Summary: As a New York City cop Tony Cavalucci has seen it all—vice, murder, and corruption. In his night shift on 42nd Street, Tony sees only the sordid parts of life and has come to believe that the world is unfixable. His cynicism has begun to infect his personal life. Then his partner is injured and Tony gets a new one. Joe Fiore sees the same things Tony does, but has a strength that gives him the courage to keep believing in God. First novel.

Other books you might like:

Terri Blackstock, *The Cape Refuge Series*, 2002-
Brandilyn Collins, *The Hidden Faces Series*, 2004-
Dee Henderson, *The O'Malley Series*, 2001-
Lorena McCourtney, *The Julesburg Mysteries*, 2002-
Kathi Mills-Macias, *The Toni Matthews Series*, 2001-

1021

KATHRYN MACKEL

The Departed

(Nashville: WestBow, 2005)

Story type: Mystery
Subject(s): Magicians; Paranormal
Major character(s): Joshua Lazarus, Television Personality (medium), Magician; Maggie Lazarus, Spouse
Time period(s): 2000s
Locale(s): United States

Summary: Joshua Lazarus is a magician struggling to get by in the entertainment industry when he stumbles onto a project that provides more money than he had ever thought possible. He becomes a medium on television and gives grieving people messages supposedly from their deceased loved ones. At first, Joshua and his wife Maggie revel in their newfound wealth. Then Maggie begins to realize there is something terribly wrong with what Joshua is doing. When Joshua begins to hear voices, he realizes he is in far over his head.

Other books by the same author:
The Surrogate, 2004

Other books you might like:

Terri Blackstock, *The Newpointe 911 Series*, 1998-
Athol Dickson, *The Garr Reed Series*, 1996-
Alton Gansky, *The Ridgeline Series*, 1998-
Kathi Mills-Macias, *The Toni Matthews Series*, 2001-
Sally S. Wright, *The Ben Reese Series*, 1997-

1022

J.F. MARGOS

Shattered Image

(New York: Steeple Hill, 2004)

Story type: Contemporary
Subject(s): Murder; Veterans
Major character(s): Toni Sullivan, Artist (forensic sculptor)
Time period(s): 2000s
Locale(s): Austin, Texas

Summary: Toni Sullivan is a forensic sculptor. She takes a skull and uses her artistic skills and medical knowledge to create a lifelike portrait of how the person looked when they were alive. Two bodies found on Red Bud Isle disturb Toni as never before. As she does her best to help track down their killer, Toni is asked to perform a favor for a close friend. Irini's husband was declared missing in action in Vietnam. Now he may have been found, but Irini wants Toni to find out for sure. First novel.

Other books you might like:

Ron Benrey, *The Pippa Hunnechurch Series*, 2001-
Colleen Coble, *The Rock Harbor Series*, 2003-
Tim Downs, *The Bug Man Series*, 2003-
Kathi Mills-Macias, *The Toni Matthews Series*, 2001-
Gilbert Morris, *The Dani Ross Series*, 2000-
Patricia H. Rushford, *The Angel Delaney Series*, 2004-

1023

L.A. MARZULLI

The Revealing

(Grand Rapids, Michigan: Zondervan, 2005)

Story type: Science Fiction
Series: Nephilim. Book 3
Subject(s): Aliens
Major character(s): Art MacKenzie, Journalist; Johanen, Religious (spiritual mentor)
Time period(s): Indeterminate Future
Locale(s): Middle East

Summary: A race of alien hybrids is attempting to take over the earth. A small band of humans fights to save the world. Their one chance of succeeding is to find a disk containing the work of Cardinal Fiorre, who was murdered by the hybrids. Art MacKenzie and his spiritual mentor Johanen are searching for the disk, but others are also looking and those individuals will stop at nothing in their quest to find it first.

Other books by the same author:
The Unholy Deception, 2002
Nephilim, 1999

Other books you might like:

T. Davis Bunn, *The Dream Voyagers*, 1999
Karen Hancock, *Arena*, 2002
Robert Don Hughes, *The Fallen*, 1995
Shane Johnson, *The Last Guardian*, 2001
Bill Myers, *Eli*, 2000

Inspirational

1024

FELICIA MASON

Gabriel's Discovery

(New York: Steeple Hill, 2004)

Story type: Romance
Subject(s): Abuse; African Americans; Drugs
Major character(s): Susan Carter, Administrator (runs abused women's shelter), Single Parent; Gabriel Dawson, Religious (pastor)
Time period(s): 2000s
Locale(s): Colorado Springs, Colorado

Summary: Susan Carter has twin daughters to raise and a women's shelter to run. Consequently, she has little time for romance. That comes as a breath of fresh air to pastor Gabriel Dawson, who is used to fending off setups from friends and family of single women in his congregation. When Susan informs Gabriel of the battered women in his parish, and the drug dealing activities of their men, he gets more involved in the problems of his parishioners. He also gets more involved in Susan's life and the two soon begin to fall in love.

Other books by the same author:
Enchanted Heart, 2004
Sweet Devotion, 2004
Sweet Harmony, 2004
Sweet Accord, 2003
Testimony, 2002

Other books you might like:
Hannah Alexander, *Hideaway*, 2003
Angela Benson, *The Genesis House Series*, 2000-
Michele Andrea Bowen, *Church Folk*, 2001
Cheryl Wolverton, *Healing Hearts*, 2000
Lenora Worth, *After the Storm*, 2004

1025

LORENA MCCOURTNEY

Invisible

(Grand Rapids, Michigan: Fleming H. Revell, 2004)

Story type: Mystery; Amateur Detective
Series: Ivy Malone. Book 1
Subject(s): Cemeteries; Old Age
Major character(s): Ivy Malone, Aged Person, Detective—Amateur
Time period(s): 2000s
Locale(s): United States

Summary: Ivy Malone is disturbed when vandals attack a local cemetery. She goes to the police to report the incident, but her concerns are ignored. In fact, Ivy understands that as a stereotypical little old lady, most people tend to ignore her. Realizing her status as an ''invisible'' person might come in handy in detective work, Ivy decides to find out who is behind the vandalism on her own. Unfortunately, the case involves more than vandalism and she is soon in the middle of a murder investigation.

Other books by the same author:
Undertow, 2003

Riptide, 2002
Whirlpool, 2002
Searching for Stardust, 1999
Canyon, 1998

Other books you might like:
Ron Benrey, *The Pippa Hunnechurch Series*, 2001-
Colleen Coble, *The Rock Harbor Series*, 2003-
Dudley J. Delffs, *The Father Grif Series*, 1998-
Ellen Edwards Kennedy, *Irregardless of Murder*, 2001
Patricia H. Rushford, *The Helen Bradley Series*, 1997-

1026

SUSAN MEISSNER

Why the Sky Is Blue

(Eugene, Oregon: Harvest House, 2004)

Story type: Contemporary
Subject(s): Adoption; Family Problems; Rape
Major character(s): Claire Holland, Parent, Spouse
Time period(s): 1980s; 2000s
Locale(s): Blue Prairie, Minnesota

Summary: Claire Holland's quiet life is suddenly turned upside down when she is brutally attacked and raped by a stranger. Claire is further traumatized when she discovers she is pregnant. Her husband Dan is supportive, but does not want her to keep the baby. Although realizing giving up the child will be difficult, Claire agrees to put the baby up for adoption. The aftereffects of the attack reverberate continually throughout Claire's life and greatly impact her daughter Kate, who is only 12 when her mother is raped. First novel.

Other books you might like:
Sylvia Bambola, *Tears in a Bottle*, 2001
Brandilyn Collins, *The Bradleyville Series*, 2001-
Beverly LaHaye, *The Seasons Series*, 1999-
Victoria Christopher Murray, *Joy*, 2001
Francine Rivers, *The Atonement Child*, 1999

1027

KATHLEEN MORGAN

Child of the Mist

(Grand Rapids, Michigan: Fleming H. Revell, 2005)

Story type: Historical
Series: These Highland Hills. Book 1
Subject(s): Feuds; Marriage
Major character(s): Anne MacGregor, Healer; Niall Campbell, Laird
Time period(s): 16th century
Locale(s): Scotland

Summary: Anne MacGregor never thought she would be forced into an arranged betrothal, but that is just what has happened. When her father explains that a match between their clan and that of the Campbells would bring a truce between the fighting families, Anne agrees to the commitment. Even before Anne arrives at the home of Niall Campbell, she realizes the peace will not come easily. Her safety is threatened more than once and nobody appears to care much for the match, or the peace it will bring. As a traitor begins to work against Niall, his position as leader of the clan is threatened. This is a rewritten version of a 1993 work of the same title that author Kathleen Morgan wrote for the secular market.

Other books by the same author:
Giver of Roses, 2005
The Christkindl's Gift, 2004
All Good Gifts, 2003
Consuming Fire, 2003
Child of Promise, 2002

Other books you might like:
Sharon Gillenwater, *The Song of the Highlands Series*, 1996-
Angela Elwell Hunt, *The Heirs of Cahira O'Connor Series*, 1998-
Grace Johnson, *The Scottish Shores Series*, 1997-
Stephen R. Lawhead, *The Celtic Crusades Series*, 1999-
Bodie Thoene, *The Galway Chronicles*, 1997-

1028

KATHLEEN MORGAN

The Christkindl's Gift

(Grand Rapids, Michigan: Fleming H. Revell, 2004)

Story type: Historical
Subject(s): Christmas; Widows/Widowers
Major character(s): Anna Hannack, Widow(er)
Time period(s): 1910s
Locale(s): Wolffsburg, Colorado

Summary: Anna Hannack has struggled to get by since her husband's death, but she sees no need to marry again. Her children, Erich and Rosa, think differently, however. Rosa decides to write a letter to Christkindl asking for a new father. When Anna's father-in-law brings home a stranger to share Christmas with them, Rosa is convinced he is the new father sent by Christkindl.

Other books by the same author:
Child of the Mist, 2005
All Good Gifts, 2003
Consuming Fire, 2003
Child of Promise, 2002
Embrace the Dawn, 2002

Other books you might like:
Thomas J. Davis, *The Christmas Quilt*, 2000
Karen Kingsbury, *The Red Gloves Series*, 2002-
Jane Kirkpatrick, *The Kinship and Courage Series*, 2000-
Diane Noble, *Come My Little Angel*, 2001
Lauraine Snelling, *The Red River of the North Series*, 1996-

---

1029

KATHLEEN MORGAN

Giver of Roses

(Grand Rapids, Michigan: Fleming H. Revell, 2005)

Story type: Fantasy
Series: Guardians of Gadiel. Book 1
Subject(s): War

Major character(s): Vartan Karayan, Warrior
Time period(s): Indeterminate
Locale(s): Astara, Fictional City

Summary: A three-year siege has left the city of Astara in ruins. The only person standing between the invaders and complete domination is the heir to Astara, Vartan Karayan. Critically wounded, Vartan escapes with the help of Danae. Called to join the Dragonmaids, Danae must decide what path to take in life. Vartan also has some difficult choices to make as he attempts to preserve his beloved Astara.

Other books by the same author:
Child of the Mist, 2005
The Christkindl's Gift, 2004
All Good Gifts, 2003
Consuming Fire, 2003
Child of Promise, 2002

Other books you might like:
Shaunti Feldhahn, *The Veritas Conflict*, 2001
Nancy Moser, *The Mustard Seed Series*, 1998-
Michael Phillips, *The Caledonia Series*, 1999-
Chris Walley, *The Lamb Among the Stars Series*, 2004-
Linda Wichman, *Legend of the Emerald Rose*, 2005

1030

GILBERT MORRIS

Charade

(Grand Rapids, Michigan: Zondervan, 2005)

Story type: Mystery
Subject(s): Computers; Revenge
Major character(s): Oliver Benson, Computer Expert (programmer)
Time period(s): 2000s
Locale(s): Los Angeles, California

Summary: Oliver Benson is a brilliant computer programmer, but is unhappy. His problems include out of control weight and an inability to find love or romance. When Oliver invents a computer program that becomes wildly successful, he has more money to spend then he had ever thought imaginable but he is still not a happy man. His manager introduces him to a beautiful young woman who is soon in love with him. The two marry and Oliver thinks he has it all until he discovers his wife and manager together. When they attack Oliver, he barely escapes with his life. Recovering from his injuries, Oliver vows to avenge himself.

Other books by the same author:
The Eyes of Texas, 2005
The Virtuous Woman, 2005
Till Shiloh Comes, 2005
God's Handmaiden, 2004
The Royal Handmaid, 2004

Other books you might like:
Larry Burkett, *The Illuminati*, 1991
Chuck Chitwood, *The Trial of Job*, 2000
Kathy Herman, *Day of Reckoning*, 2002
Jefferson Scott, *Terminal Logic*, 1997
Robert L. Wise, *Deleted*, 2003

Inspirational

1031

GILBERT MORRIS
LYNN MORRIS, Co-Author

The Immortelles

(Nashville: Thomas Nelson, 2004)

Story type: Historical/Antebellum American South
Series: Creoles. Book 2
Subject(s): Friendship
Major character(s): Damita De Salvedo y Madariaga, Southern Belle; Rissa, Slave
Time period(s): 1830s
Locale(s): South

Summary: Spoiled and headstrong, Damita De Salvedo y Madariaga has always been given whatever she wants and never considers the feelings of others. Damita buys a slave girl named Rissa and treats the girl with a haughty disdain. On a voyage to Savannah, Damita is involved in a shipwreck. Rescued by Yancy Devereaux, she is at first thrilled to have such a handsome man in her life, but loses interest quickly due to his race. The two part and soon afterwards, Damita's family loses most of their fortune. Damita is forced to give up her wealthy lifestyle and even sells Rissa. Luckily, Rissa is bought by Dr. Jefferson Whitman, who is actually her brother. Jefferson frees Rissa and gives her the same type of wealthy lifestyle Damita once enjoyed. With the situations of the women reversed, they meet again with intriguing consequences.

Other books by the same author:
The Alchemy, 2004
The Moon by Night, 2004
The Exiles, 2003
Where Two Seas Met, 2001
Driven with the Wind, 2000

Other books you might like:
Roger Elwood, *The Plantation Letters Series*, 1997-
Virginia Gaffney, *The Richmond Chronicles*, 1996-
Sara Mitchell, *The Sinclair Legacy Series*, 2001-
Michael Phillips, *The Shenandoah Sisters Series*, 2003-
Lauraine Snelling, *The Secret Refuge Series*, 2000-

1032

GILBERT MORRIS

Till Shiloh Comes

(Minneapolis: Bethany House, 2005)

Story type: Biblical Fiction
Series: Lions of Judah. Book 4
Subject(s): Brothers; Jealousy
Major character(s): Joseph, Biblical Figure
Time period(s): Indeterminate Past
Locale(s): Middle East

Summary: Joseph is the beloved 11th son of Jacob. In Jacob's eyes, Joseph can do nothing wrong. This causes immense jealousy among the other sons, who believe they will never be able to attain their father's love. Disturbed by the thought that Jacob will name Joseph the next patriarch, the brothers plot to murder their sibling. One brother has a change of heart and, in a compromise, Joseph is sold into slavery.

Other books by the same author:
Charade, 2005
The Eyes of Texas, 2005
The Virtuous Woman, 2005
God's Handmaiden, 2004
The Royal Handmaid, 2004

Other books you might like:
Gene Edwards, *The First Century Diaries Series*, 1998-
Tracy Groot, *The Brother's Keeper*, 2003
Thom Lemmons, *The Daughters of Faith Series*, 1999-
Francine Rivers, *The Lineage of Grace Series*, 2000-
Robert L. Wise, *The People of the Covenant Series*, 1991-

1033

MARK STANLEIGH MORRIS

Billy Goat Hill

(Sisters, Oregon: Multnomah, 2005)

Story type: Contemporary
Subject(s): Brothers
Major character(s): Wade Parker, Child
Time period(s): 1950s
Locale(s): Los Angeles, California

Summary: It is the 1950s, supposedly a time of great peace and tranquility throughout America. The Parker family, however, is not enjoying this time of peace. Always troubled, the family becomes involved in a terrible crisis. Eight-year-old Wade Parker is determined to keep the crisis from spinning out of control. Unfortunately, his little brother is in on the family secret, and he can't keep a secret to save his life. First novel.

Other books you might like:
Phil Callaway, *Growing Up on the Edge of the World*, 2004
W. Dale Cramer, *Bad Ground*, 2004
Patricia Hickman, *Fallen Angels*, 2003
Catherine Palmer, *The Happy Room*, 2001
Brad Whittington, *The Fred Series*, 2003-

1034

MICHAEL MORRIS

Live Like You Were Dying

(Nashville: WestBow, 2005)

Story type: Contemporary
Subject(s): Family; Family Problems; Relationships
Major character(s): Nathan Bishop, Construction Worker (supervisor)
Time period(s): 2000s
Locale(s): United States

Summary: Construction supervisor Nathan Bishop has built a successful career. He is one of the top men in his field and seems to have it all. Then an accident sends him to the hospital and tests reveal a growth on his lungs. Aware he might not have long to live, Nathan reconnects with his wife and daughter, who were always second to his career. When he goes on a cross-country journey with his father, Nathan realizes some dreams he'd never really known he had. This book is based on the country music song performed by Tim McGraw.

Other books by the same author:
Slow Way Home, 2003
A Place Called Wiregrass, 2002

Other books you might like:
T. Davis Bunn, *The Gift*, 1994
Karen Kingsbury, *Gideon's Gift*, 2002
Paul McCusker, *Epiphany*, 1998
Bill Myers, *When the Last Leaf Falls*, 2001
Lauraine Snelling, *The Healing Quilt*, 2002

1035

TOM MORRISEY

Deep Blue

(Grand Rapids, Michigan: Zondervan, 2005)

Story type: Action/Adventure
Series: Beck Easton. Book 1
Subject(s): Diving; Treasure
Major character(s): Beck Easton, Store Owner (dive shop); Jennifer Cassidy, Student—Graduate
Time period(s): 2000s
Locale(s): United States; Bahamas

Summary: Graduate student Jennifer Cassidy is researching the history of a Southern family when she learns of the existence of a treasure hidden in a spring near the family's ancestral home. Jennifer asks dive shop owner Beck Easton to help her locate the treasure. Beck is dubious, but when he finds a map confirming Jennifer's findings, the two head off on a treasure hunt that takes them across the United States and to the Bahamas.

Where it's reviewed:
Publishers Weekly, November 29, 2004, page 24

Other books by the same author:
Turn Four, 2004
Yucatan Deep, 2002

Other books you might like:
Alton Gansky, *A Treasure Deep*, 2003
Dee Henderson, *The Uncommon Heroes Series*, 2000-
Paul McHenry, *Code Name Antidote*, 2000
Oliver North, *The Peter Newman Series*, 2002-
Jefferson Scott, *The Operation Firebrand Series*, 2002-

1036

BILL MYERS

Soul Tracker

(Grand Rapids, Michigan: Zondervan, 2004)

Story type: Science Fiction
Series: Soul Tracker. Book 1
Subject(s): Death; Grief; Single Parent Families
Major character(s): David Kauffman, Writer, Single Parent
Time period(s): 2000s
Locale(s): United States

Summary: David Kauffman is a single father grieving for his teenage daughter Emily, who died suddenly. Since David is an agnostic, he doesn't have the comfort of believing in heaven. In desperation, he turns to a group called Life After Life, a scientific group that claims to study what really happens to people after death. He meets Gita Patekar, a Christian woman employed by the group. As David becomes more involved in the doings of the group, he becomes aware of more evil than he had ever expected to find.

Where it's reviewed:
Library Journal, September 1, 2004, page 132
Publishers Weekly, August 16, 2004, page 43

Other books by the same author:
The Bloodstone Chronicles, 2003
The Wager, 2003
The Face of God, 2002
When the Last Leaf Falls, 2001
Eli, 2000

Other books you might like:
Randy Alcorn, *Lord Foulgrin's Letters*, 2000
Roger Elwood, *The Angelwalk Series*, 1989-
Shaunti Feldhahn, *The Veritas Conflict*, 2001
Karen Hancock, *Arena*, 2002
Angela Elwell Hunt, *The Pearl*, 2003
Randall Scott Ingermanson, *Transgression*, 2000

1037

DIANE NOBLE

The Last Storyteller

(Colorado Springs, Colorado: WaterBrook, 2004)

Story type: Contemporary
Subject(s): Abortion; Aging; Grandmothers
Major character(s): Taite Abbott, Young Woman; Naini, Aged Person, Grandparent (of Taite); Sam Wellington, Student (medical), Boyfriend (of Taite)
Time period(s): 2000s
Locale(s): California

Summary: When Taite Abbott learns she is pregnant, she is unsure how to react. Then her boyfriend Sam announces that he has gotten a fellowship in Boston studying stem cells. He invites her to come with him, but Taite refuses, thinking a pregnant girlfriend is the last thing he needs. Taite decides to have an abortion, but before she goes through with it, goes to visit her grandmother Naini. As Naini shares stories of her past and their family's heritage, she also encourages Taite to tell Sam of the pregnancy and to reconcile with her mother.

Where it's reviewed:
Library Journal, September 1, 2004, page 134

Other books by the same author:
Phoebe, 2003
Heart of Glass, 2002
At Play in the Promised Land, 2001
Come My Little Angel, 2001
The Blossom and the Nettle, 2000

Other books you might like:
Sylvia Bambola, *Tears in a Bottle*, 2001

Inspirational

Lori Copeland, *Child of Grace*, 2001
Karen Kingsbury, *Halfway to Forever*, 2002
Beverly LaHaye, *Showers in Season*, 2000
Victoria Christopher Murray, *Joy*, 2001
Francine Rivers, *The Atonement Child*, 1999

1038

CRAIG PARSHALL

The Last Judgment

(Eugene, Oregon: Harvest House, 2005)

Story type: Legal; Mystery
Series: Chambers of Justice. Book 5
Subject(s): Muslims; Oil; Terrorism
Major character(s): Will Chambers, Lawyer
Time period(s): 2000s
Locale(s): Virginia; Middle East

Summary: A mysterious cult, hoping to undermine the political situation in the Middle East, sets off an explosion that rocks Jerusalem. With the Temple Mount in ruins and hundreds of Muslims dead, the always shaky situation in the region grows grimmer. In the United States, attorney Will Chambers becomes involved when his client Gilead Amahn, a Christian convert from Islam, becomes the prime suspect in the bombing.

Other books by the same author:
Missing Witness, 2004
Custody of the State, 2003
The Accused, 2003
The Resurrection File, 2002

Other books you might like:
James Scott Bell, *Final Witness*, 1999
Chuck Chitwood, *The Trial of Job*, 2000
Christopher A. Lane, *Appearance of Evil*, 1997
Jake Thoene, *Shaiton's Fire*, 2002
Robert Whitlow, *The Sacrifice*, 2002

1039

TRACIE PETERSON

The Hope Within

(Minneapolis: Bethany House, 2005)

Story type: Historical/American West
Series: Heirs of Montana. Book 4
Subject(s): Pioneers; Ranch Life
Major character(s): Dianne Selby, Rancher
Time period(s): 1880s
Locale(s): Montana; Kansas

Summary: Dianne Selby and her family are forced to leave their beloved Montana ranch, the Diamond V. Always brave, Dianne is determined to start fresh. Then her husband Cole learns his father is ill and the family travels to Kansas to be with him. Cole's family is unwelcoming, causing Dianne to feel left out. With Cole showing her little support, Dianne begins to miss Montana. Finally, she is forced into making a decision that will change her life forever.

Other books by the same author:
Castles, 2004
Land of My Heart, 2004
The Coming Storm, 2004
To Dream Anew, 2004
Silent Star, 2003

Other books you might like:
Kristen Heitzmann, *The Rocky Mountain Legacy Series*, 1998-
Al Lacy, *The Mail Order Bride Series*, 1998-
Kathleen Morgan, *The Brides of Culdee Creek Series*, 1999-
Diane Noble, *The California Chronicles*, 1999-
Lauraine Snelling, *The Dakotah Treasures Series*, 2003-

1040

TRACIE PETERSON
JUDITH MILLER, Co-Author

A Love Woven True

(Minneapolis: Bethany House, 2005)

Story type: Historical
Series: Lights of Lowell. Book 2
Subject(s): Animals/Horses; Slavery
Major character(s): Jasmine Houston, Widow(er)
Time period(s): 1840s
Locale(s): Lowell, Massachusetts

Summary: Having been left widowed after enduring an unhappy arranged marriage, Jasmine Houston is glad to be free to raise her son as she sees fit. A staunch abolitionist, Jasmine agrees to hide escaped slaves on her farm outside of Lowell, Massachusetts—something she realizes would greatly anger her father-in-law, a plantation owner. With the help of her brother-in-law Nolan, Jasmine helps a slave family escape. However, something goes horribly wrong and both the slaves and Jasmine's son disappear.

Other books by the same author:
A Tapestry of Hope, 2004
A Fragile Design, 2003
Daughter of the Loom, 2003
These Tangled Threads, 2003
Kansas, 2001

Other books you might like:
Lynn Austin, *The Refiner's Fire Series*, 2002-
Virginia Gaffney, *The Richmond Chronicles*, 1996-
Gilbert Morris, *The Bonnets and Bugles Series*, 1995-
Michael Phillips, *The Shenandoah Sisters Series*, 2003-
Lauraine Snelling, *The Secret Refuge Series*, 2000-

1041

TRACIE PETERSON

To Dream Anew

(Minneapolis: Bethany House, 2004)

Story type: Historical
Series: Heirs of Montana. Book 3
Subject(s): Pioneers; Ranch Life

Major character(s): Dianne Selby, Rancher; Cole Selby, Rancher
Time period(s): 1860s
Locale(s): Montana

Summary: Dianne and Cole Selby have settled into life on the Diamond V Ranch in Montana. The relocation to the pioneer life of the West was difficult for Dianne, but she wouldn't want to live anywhere else. She is troubled, then, when new neighbors threaten the Selbys' lifestyle. To make matters worse, the local Indian tribes are resisting the white settlers. Dianne's Blackfoot friend Koko remains loyal to her, but Koko's brother Takes Many Horses sees nothing good about the white presence.

Other books by the same author:
Castles, 2004
Land of My Heart, 2004
The Coming Storm, 2004
Across the Years, 2003
Beneath a Harvest Sky, 2003

Other books you might like:
Lisa Tawn Bergren, *The Northern Lights Series*, 1998-
Kristen Heitzmann, *The Rocky Mountain Legacy Series*, 1998-
Lynn Morris, *The Cheney Duvall Series*, 1994-
Diane Noble, *The California Chronicles*, 1999-
Lauraine Snelling, *The Dakotah Treasures Series*, 2003-

`1042`

KEL RICHARDS

Dark Storm

(Colorado Springs, Colorado: RiverOak, 2004)

Story type: Action/Adventure
Subject(s): Archaeology; Hurricanes; Islands
Major character(s): Nick Hamilton, Journalist
Time period(s): 2000s
Locale(s): Cavendish Island, Australia

Summary: Australian journalist Nick Hamilton goes to Cavendish Island, 800 kilometers northeast of Sydney, to join an archaeological expedition. Once home to one of the most brutal prisons in Australia, the island has a cruel history and a reputation for Satanism. Now, as the archaeologists study the island's past, it appears as if current day Satanists have an interest in the island, as does a secret military group.

Other books by the same author:
Murder in the Mummy's Tomb, 2002
An Outbreak of Darkness, 1996
Death in Egypt, 1996
The Case of the Dead Certainty, 1995
The Third Bloodstain, 1995

Other books you might like:
Lisa Tawn Bergren, *Chosen*, 1996
T.L. Higley, *Marduk's Tablet*, 2003
C.J. Illinik, *The Tablets of Ararat*, 2002
Christoper A. Lane, *Eden's Gate*, 1994
Michael Phillips, *The Rift in Time Series*, 1997-

`1043`

LOIS RICHER

Forgotten Justice

(Wheaton, Illinois: Tyndale House, 2004)

Story type: Romantic Suspense
Series: Camp Hope. Book 2
Subject(s): Memory Loss; Physically Handicapped
Major character(s): John Riddle, Amnesiac; Christa Anderson, Handicapped (paralyzed)
Time period(s): 2000s
Locale(s): Canada

Summary: John Riddle shows up at Camp Hope, a summer camp deep in the north of Canada. He has lost his memory and has no idea who he is or how he got to the camp. At the camp, he meets Christa Anderson who was paralyzed in a swimming accident. She had thought the possibility of love was gone forever, but when she meets John she begins to hope again. Then mysterious incidents start to plague Christa and the camp. John wonders if somebody from his past is causing the threatening incidents and if the best move he can make is to go away before Christa gets hurt.

Other books by the same author:
A Time to Remember, 2004
Dangerous Sanctuary, 2004
Heaven's Kiss, 2004
Blessings, 2003
Inner Harbor, 2003

Other books you might like:
Lori Copeland, *Roses Will Bloom Again*, 2002
Lyn Cote, *Summer's End*, 2003
Dee Henderson, *The O'Malley Series*, 2001-
Debra White Smith, *The Seven Sisters Series*, 2000-
Susan May Warren, *The Perfect Match*, 2004

`1044`

PATRICIA H. RUSHFORD
HARRISON JAMES, Co-Author

Deadfall

(Nashville: Integrity, 2004)

Story type: Mystery
Series: McAllister Files. Book 2
Subject(s): Missing Persons
Major character(s): Antonio "Mac" McAllister, Detective—Police
Time period(s): 2000s
Locale(s): Oregon

Summary: When a ski instructor mysteriously disappears, police detective Mac McAllister is assigned to the case. Suicide is considered a strong possibility, but the man's parents insist their son would never kill himself. They suspect their son's girlfriend is somehow involved in his disappearance. As Mac struggles with the case, he also faces problems in his personal life and makes a major decision about his future with his fiancee.

Inspirational

Other books by the same author:
Secrets, Lies, and Alibis, 2003

Other books you might like:
Tim Downs, *The Bug Man Series*, 2003-
Alton Gansky, *The Ridgeline Series*, 1998-
Linda Hall, *The Royal Canadian Mounted Police Series*, 1998-
Kathi Mills-Macias, *The Toni Matthews Series*, 2001-
Sally S. Wright, *The Ben Reese Series*, 1997-

1045

CYNTHIA RUTLEDGE

Love Enough for Two

(New York: Steeple Hill, 2004)

Story type: Romance
Subject(s): Single Parent Families
Major character(s): Sierra Summers, Single Parent; Matthew Dixon, Lawyer
Time period(s): 2000s
Locale(s): Santa Barbara, California

Summary: Sierra Summers, a struggling single mother, leaps at the opportunity to change places with her wealthy friend Libby for the summer. Then handsome lawyer Matt Dixon walks into the antiques store where Sierra is working under Libby's name and asks the store owner about Libby. Sierra recognizes Matt's name from her own past and wants nothing to do with him. Once the two meet, however, sparks fly. Sequel to *Two Hearts*.

Other books by the same author:
Two Hearts, 2004
A Love to Keep, 2003
Kiss Me Kaitlyn, 2003
Trish's Not-So-Little Secret, 2002
Wedding Bell Blues, 2002

Other books you might like:
Carolyne Aarsen, *A Mother at Heart*, 2000
Dana Corbit, *A Blessed Life*, 2002
Lyn Cote, *Testing His Patience*, 2004
Marta Perry, *A Mother's Wish*, 2002
Ruth Scofield, *Loving Thy Neighbor*, 2001

1046

LISA SAMSON

Tiger Lillie

(Colorado Springs, Colorado: WaterBrook, 2004)

Story type: Contemporary
Subject(s): Abuse; Dating (Social Customs)
Major character(s): Lillie Bauer, Businesswoman (wedding planner)
Time period(s): 2000s
Locale(s): Baltimore, Maryland

Summary: Lillie Bauer prides herself on being afraid of nothing and living life to its fullest. She goes bungee jumping on her birthday dressed in an evening gown, runs a wedding planning company called Extreme Weddings and Extremely Odd Occasions, and loves her friend and business partner Cristoff, an epileptic, celibate gay man. One thing Lillie does not enjoy is dating. She has never recovered from the loss of her childhood sweetheart Ted, who disappeared 15 years earlier under mysterious circumstances. However, thanks to the love of her friends and her beloved younger sister Tacy, Lillie feels no lack in her life. When she learns that Tacy is being abused by her husband, Lillie goes all out to save her little sister.

Where it's reviewed:
Publishers Weekly, August 23, 2004, page 36

Other books by the same author:
Songbird, 2003
The Living End, 2003
Women's Intuition, 2002
The Church Ladies, 2001
Fields of Gold, 2000

Other books you might like:
Margaret A. Graham, *Mercy Me*, 2003
Linda Hall, *Sadie's Song*, 2001
Patricia Hickman, *Katrina's Wings*, 2000
Annie Jones, *The Snowbirds*, 2001
Bette Nordberg, *Serenity Bay*, 2000
Vinita Hampton Wright, *Velma Still Cooks in Leeway*, 2000

1047

RUTH SCOFIELD

Love Came Unexpectedly

(New York: Steeple Hill, 2005)

Story type: Romance
Subject(s): Animals/Horses; Foster Children
Major character(s): Sunny Merrill, Nurse, Heiress; Grant Prentiss, Businessman (runs riding stable)
Time period(s): 2000s
Locale(s): Ozarks

Summary: Sunny Merrill grew up in foster care, so she is surprised to learn that she has inherited her grandfather's resort, Sunshine Acres. The resort is prime property in the Ozarks and Sunny must live there for one year before entertaining thoughts of selling. Once Sunny meets her neighbor Grant, the owner of a riding stable, she is no longer certain she even wants to leave.

Other books by the same author:
Take My Hand, 2003
Loving Thy Neighbor, 2001
Wonders of the Heart, 2001
Whispers of the Heart, 2000
The Perfect Groom, 1999

Other books you might like:
Irene Brand, *Heiress*, 1998
Lyn Cote, *Summer's End*, 2003
Robin Jones Gunn, *Woodlands*, 2000
Catherine Palmer, *Finders Keepers*, 1999
Allie Pleiter, *Bad Heiress Day*, 2004

1048
ANNETTE GAIL SMITH

A New Day at Tanglewood
(Chicago: Moody, 2005)

Story type: Contemporary
Series: Coming Home to Ruby Prairie. Book 2
Subject(s): Foster Homes; Small Town Life; Widows/Widowers
Major character(s): Charlotte Carter, Widow(er); Treasure Evans, Masseuse (massage therapist)
Time period(s): 2000s
Locale(s): Ruby Prairie, Texas

Summary: Charlotte Carter came to the small town of Ruby Prairie, Texas, to open a home for troubled girls called Tanglewood. After some initial misgivings by the local townsfolk, Tanglewood has proved to be a solid addition to the community. Massage therapist Treasure Evans comes to town to help Charlotte out. Treasure finds romance with another newcomer to Ruby Prairie, Jasper Jones.

Other books by the same author:
A Town Called Ruby Prairie, 2004
Watermelon Days and Firefly Nights, 2002

Other books you might like:
Mary Carlson, *The Whispering Pines Series*, 1999-
Lori Copeland, *The Heavenly Daze Series*, 2001-
Philip Gulley, *The Harmony Series*, 2000-
Robin Jones Gunn, *The Glenbrooke Series*, 1995-
Jan Karon, *The Mitford Series*, 1994-

1049
DEBRA WHITE SMITH

Reason and Romance
(Eugene, Oregon: Harvest House, 2004)

Story type: Romance
Series: Austen. Book 2
Subject(s): College Life; Inheritance; Literature
Major character(s): Elaina Woods, Professor (of literature); Ted Farris, Student—College
Time period(s): 2000s
Locale(s): Lakeland, Oklahoma

Summary: Elaina Woods' excitement at getting her first college teaching job is tempered by the death of her father. With issues of money and inheritance threatening to tear her family apart, Elaina retreats to the relative calm of her classroom. One of her students is Ted Farris and Elaina is immediately attracted to the handsome and intelligent man. Meanwhile, her sister Anna is throwing reason to the winds in her pursuit of Willis Kenney.

Other books by the same author:
First Impressions, 2004
Let's Begin Again, 2003
The Key, 2003
For Your Heart Only, 2002
This Time Around, 2002

Other books you might like:
Eileen Berger, *A Family for Jana*, 2002
Lyn Cote, *Summer's End*, 2003
Robin Jones Gunn, *Woodlands*, 2000
Melanie M. Jeschke, *Inklings*, 2004
Catherine Palmer, *Finders Keepers*, 1999

1050
LAURAINE SNELLING

Opal
(Minneapolis: Bethany House, 2005)

Story type: Historical/American West
Series: Dakotah Treasures. Book 3
Subject(s): Sisters
Major character(s): Opal Torvald, Young Woman; Jacob Chandler, Religious (minister)
Time period(s): 1880s
Locale(s): West

Summary: Opal Torvald is thrilled when her sister Ruby marries rancher Rand Harrison. Loving the freedom of ranch life, Opal learns to shoot and ride. She thinks she can do anything. Then her actions cost her a dear friend and Opal begins to doubt herself. When a young minister named Jacob Chandler arrives in town, he is drawn to the beautiful and troubled Opal. However, she believes the tragedies of her past have cost her the right to love anybody.

Other books by the same author:
Pearl, 2004
The Way of Women, 2004
More than a Dream, 2003
Ruby, 2003
The Healing Quilt, 2002

Other books you might like:
Lori Copeland, *The Brides of the West Series*, 1998-
Catherine Palmer, *The Town Called Hope Series*, 1997-
Judith Pella, *The Ribbons of Steel Series*, 1997-
Tracie Peterson, *The Heirs of Montana Series*, 2004-
Lori Wick, *The Yellow Rose Trilogy*, 1999-2001

1051
JAMIE LANGSTON TURNER

No Dark Valley
(Minneapolis: Bethany House, 2004)

Story type: Contemporary
Subject(s): Death; Neighbors and Neighborhoods
Major character(s): Celia Coleman, Art Dealer
Time period(s): 2000s
Locale(s): Derby, South Carolina; Dunmore, Georgia

Summary: Left orphaned as a teenager, Celia Coleman was raised by her strict and deeply religious grandmother in Dunmore, Georgia. After escaping the hardscrabble life via college, Celia avoids returning to Dunmore. She settles in South Carolina and runs an art gallery. Keeping her social relationships to an absolute minimum, Celia has found a drab existence that, in her mind, is good because it keeps her from the pain of failed relationships. When Celia's grandmother dies, she reluctantly returns to Dunmore. Learning she has inherited her grandmother's estate, a rundown house and store, Celia resolves to sell both and get out of town as soon as possible. Then she meets the new neighbor, Bruce Healey, and begins a tentative friendship.

Where it's reviewed:
Publishers Weekly, July 5, 2004, page 37

Other books by the same author:
A Garden to Keep, 2001
By the Light of a Thousand Stars, 1999
Some Wildflower in My Heart, 1998
Suncatchers, 1995

Other books you might like:
Charlene Ann Baumbich, *The Dearest Dorothy Series*, 2004-
W. Dale Cramer, *Sutter's Cross*, 2003
Linda Dorrell, *True Believers*, 2001
Lisa Samson, *The Church Ladies*, 2001
Vinita Hampton Wright, *Velma Still Cooks in Leeway*, 2000

1052

ROBERT VAUGHAN

Light of Hope

(New York: Forge, 2004)

Story type: Contemporary
Subject(s): Environment; Oil; Single Parent Families
Major character(s): Galen Scobey, Single Parent, Business-man (oil company executive); Ellie Springer, Teacher
Time period(s): 2000s
Locale(s): Point Hope, Alaska

Summary: After his wife's death, Galen Scobey has devoted his life to his career and his son. When his firm, an oil company, sends him to a small town in Alaska, Galen is surprised to find himself attracted to a schoolteacher named Ellie Springer. Unfortunately, the oil company and its disastrous environmental effects are not wanted in Alaska and the locals have started a protest movement against Galen and his company. Ellie takes the side of the townspeople and Galen finds himself fighting both the environmentalists and the woman he has grown to love.

Other books by the same author:
His Truth Is Marching On, 2004
Christmas Past, 2003
Whose Voice the Waters Heard, 2003
Trailback, 2003
Touch the Face of God, 2002

Other books you might like:
Lisa Tawn Bergren, *Pathways*, 2001
Debbie DiGiovanni, *Concessions*, 2004
Deb Kastner, *Hart's Harbor*, 2003
Karen Kingsbury, *Gideon's Gift*, 2002
Adrian Plass, *Ghosts*, 2003

1053

CHRIS WALLEY

The Shadow at Evening

(Wheaton, Illinois: Tyndale House, 2004)

Story type: Science Fiction
Series: Lamb Among the Stars. Book 1
Subject(s): Good and Evil
Major character(s): Merral Stefan D'Avanos, Woodsman
Time period(s): Indeterminate Future
Locale(s): Farholme, Planet—Imaginary

Summary: Many years in the future, war and evil have long been things of the past and all people live in harmony. That is about to change. On the planet Farholme, strange things are happening and it appears as if evil is entering the once peaceful world. A forester named Merral sees the evil for himself, and realizes he must join the fight against it. First novel.

Other books you might like:
Ted Dekker, *The Color Trilogy*, 2004-
Karen Hancock, *The Legends of the Guardian King Series*, 2003-
L.A. Marzulli, *Nephilim*, 1999
Michael Phillips, *The Caledonia Series*, 1999-
Kathy Tyers, *The Firebird Trilogy*, 1987-2000

1054

SUSAN MAY WARREN

Flee the Night

(Wheaton, Illinois: Tyndale House, 2005)

Story type: Mystery
Subject(s): Espionage
Major character(s): Lacey Galloway, Fugitive, Parent; Jim Micah, Military Personnel (Green Beret)
Time period(s): 2000s
Locale(s): United States

Summary: Lacey Galloway is on the run. She hopes that she can turn over an encryption/decryption program to the U.S. National Security Agency and then be free from the entanglements she got herself in during her younger days. Now a mother, Lacey only wants to settle down someplace safe. That doesn't seem likely to happen, though, and soon Lacey is struggling for her life once again.

Other books by the same author:
Letters from the Enemy, 2004
The Perfect Match, 2004
Happily Ever After, 2003
Tying the Knot, 2003

Other books you might like:
Ted Dekker, *Thr3e*, 2003
Alton Gansky, *A Treasure Deep*, 2003
Lois Richer, *Shadowed Secrets*, 2005
Jake Thoene, *Shaiton's Fire*, 2002
Travis Thrasher, *Gun Lake*, 2004

1055

ROBERT WHITLOW

Life Everlasting

(Nashville: WestBow, 2004)

Story type: Mystery
Series: Santee. Book 2
Subject(s): Family Problems
Major character(s): Baxter Richardson, Crime Victim; Rena Richardson, Spouse; Alexia Lindale, Lawyer
Time period(s): 2000s
Locale(s): Charleston, South Carolina

Summary: Baxter Richardson is in a coma after his wife Rena pushed him off a cliff. As Baxter clings to life, Rena tries desperately to cover up her crime. Baxter's brother and father, meanwhile, are attempting to cover up crimes of their own. In an attempt to buy Rena's silence, they bribe her to keep quiet about her knowledge of the Richardson family fortune. Rena's lawyer, Alexia Lindale, is becoming more and more disturbed over her client's lies and no longer knows if she can trust her.

Where it's reviewed:
Publishers Weekly, August 23, 2004, page S16

Other books by the same author:
Life Support, 2003
The Sacrifice, 2002
The Trial, 2001
The List, 2000

Other books you might like:
James Scott Bell, *Final Witness*, 1999
Chuck Chitwood, *The Trial of Job*, 2000
Michael Farris, *Guilt by Association*, 1997
Joseph H. Hilley, *Sober Justice*, 2004
Christopher A. Lane, *Appearance of Evil*, 1997
Craig Parshall, *The Chambers of Justice Series*, 2002-

1056

STEPHANIE GRACE WHITSON

Watchers on the Hill

(Minneapolis: Bethany House, 2004)

Story type: Historical/American West
Series: Pine Ridge Portraits. Book 2
Subject(s): Military Life; Widows/Widowers
Major character(s): Charlotte Valentine Bishop, Widow(er); Nathan Boone, Military Personnel
Time period(s): 1880s
Locale(s): Fort Robinson, Nebraska

Summary: Although Charlotte Bishop presents a grieving face to the world, she is secretly relieved when her tyrannical and abusive husband dies. Left to raise her son Will, Charlotte doesn't want to continue living with her mother-in-law, who is as tyrannical as her son was. Desperate to escape, Charlotte returns to her father's home in Fort Robinson, Nebraska. She had hated living there as a young woman, but is now glad for the serenity the surroundings provide her. Charlotte is re-

united with her old flame, Lieutenant Nathan Boone, and the two begin to fall in love again.

Other books by the same author:
Secrets on the Wind, 2003
Heart of the Sandhills, 2002
Edge of the Wilderness, 2001
Valley of the Shadows, 2000
Nora's Ribbon of Memories, 1999

Other books you might like:
Lisa Tawn Bergren, *The Northern Lights Series*, 1998-
Lori Copeland, *The Brides of the West Series*, 1998-
Tracie Peterson, *The Westward Chronicles*, 1998-
Kay D. Rizzo, *The Serenity Inn Series*, 1998-
Lauraine Snelling, *The Red River of the North Series*, 1996-

1057

BRAD WHITTINGTON

Living with Fred

(Nashville: Broadman & Holman, 2005)

Story type: Contemporary
Series: Fred. Book 2
Subject(s): Religious Life; Small Town Life
Major character(s): Mark Cloud, Teenager
Time period(s): 1970s
Locale(s): Fred, Texas

Summary: When young Mark Cloud returns to the small town of Fred, Texas, after spending some time in California, he learns that many things have changed since he was there. Left adrift, Mark runs across an old book that makes him doubt his long-held religious beliefs. Soon he is asking questions about God and Jesus that nobody, not even his preacher father, can answer to his satisfaction. As Mark embarks on a spiritual journey, he soon learns that the townspeople aren't too thrilled with his challenges of beliefs they hold dear. He must face up to the fact that his newfound questions may cost his father his job.

Other books by the same author:
Welcome to Fred, 2003

Other books you might like:
Charlene Ann Baumbich, *The Dearest Dorothy Series*, 2004-
Traci DePree, *The Lake Emily Series*, 2002-
Philip Gulley, *The Harmony Series*, 2000-
Thomas Kinkade, *The Cape Light Series*, 2002-
Lance Wubbels, *The Gentle Hills Series*, 1994-

1058

LINDA WICHMAN

Legend of the Emerald Rose

(Grand Rapids, Michigan: Kregel, 2005)

Story type: Fantasy
Subject(s): Arthurian Legends; Knights and Knighthood
Major character(s): Emerald Rose Rayn, Warrior
Time period(s): Indeterminate Past
Locale(s): England

Summary: The days of Camelot are over. After the deaths of King Arthur and Queen Guinevere, the wizard Merlin has disappeared. With evil forces threatening all they hold dear, the remaining Knights of the Round Table come up with a plan that even they believe is unlikely to succeed. Emerald Rose Rayn is a warrior with a strong faith in God. She has also been kept in ignorance of her true birthright. Can she save England from the dark forces that threaten to envelop it? First novel.

Other books you might like:

T. Davis Bunn, *The Dream Voyagers*, 1999

Karen Hancock, *The Legends of the Guardian King Series*, 2003-

Shane Johnson, *The Last Guardian*, 2001

Kathy Tyers, *The Firebird Trilogy*, 1987-2000

Chris Walley, *The Lamb Among the Stars Series*, 2004-

1059

THOMAS WILLIAMS

The Bride of Stone

(Grand Rapids, Michigan: Fleming H. Revell, 2004)

Story type: Fantasy
Subject(s): Princes and Princesses
Major character(s): Avelessa, Royalty (princess); Davian, Artist (sculptor); Perivale, Ruler (king)
Time period(s): Indeterminate
Locale(s): Seven Kingdoms, Fictional Country

Summary: The Seven Kingdoms are ruled by a domineering king named Perival. Fearful of the effects of his daughter's beauty, the king scars the Princess Avelessa and imprisons her in her room. With music as her only comfort, Avelessa can only dream of escape. On the other side of the Seven Kingdoms, sculptor Davian pursues his craft. He falls in love with a barmaid and is distraught when he realizes she is only interested in his money. Fates manage to bring Avelessa and Davian together and they fall desperately in love.

Other books by the same author:
The Devil's Mouth, 2001
The Crown of Eden, 1999

Other books you might like:

Karen Hancock, *The Legends of the Guardian King Series*, 2003-

John Houghton, *A Distant Shore*, 1994

Gilbert Morris, *The Far Fields Series*, 1994-

Michael Phillips, *The Caledonia Series*, 1999-

Kathy Tyers, *The Firebird Trilogy*, 1987-2000

Chris Walley, *The Lamb Among the Stars Series*, 2004-

1060

LINDA WINDSOR

Paper Moon

(Nashville, Tennessee: WestBow, 2005)

Story type: Romance
Series: Moonstruck. Book 1
Subject(s): Single Parent Families; Vacations

Major character(s): Caroline Spencer, Child-Care Giver (day care center owner), Single Parent; Blaine Madison, Single Parent, Businessman
Time period(s): 2000s
Locale(s): Mexico

Summary: When Caroline Spencer agrees to chaperone her daughter Annie's class trip to Mexico, she has no idea what she is getting into. The grandmother of Annie's best friend Karen was supposed to be her co-chaperone, but when she injures herself, Karen's busy father agrees to take over. Blaine Madison, a workaholic who is deeply devoted to his daughter, doesn't know how to relate to her as a teenager. Soon Caroline's faith and humor soften Blaine's tough attitude towards life and the two single parents find themselves falling in love.

Other books by the same author:
Along Came Jones, 2003
Deirdre, 2002
It Had to Be You, 2001
Riona, 2001
Maire, 2000

Other books you might like:

Terri Blackstock, *The Second Chances Series*, 1996-

Mary Davis, *Newlywed Games*, 2000

Annie Jones, *The Route 66 Series*, 1999-

Suzy Pizzuti, *The Halo Hattie's Boarding House Series*, 1998-

Karen Rispin, *Rustlers*, 1998

Debra White Smith, *To Rome with Love*, 2001

1061

ROBERT L. WISE

Tagged

(New York: Warner Faith, 2005)

Story type: Apocalyptic Horror
Series: Tribulation Survival. Book 2
Subject(s): End-Times
Major character(s): Graham Peck, Fugitive
Time period(s): Indeterminate Future
Locale(s): United States

Summary: Once the assistant to Chicago's mayor, Graham Peck is now a fugitive. Hiding out in northern Wisconsin with his family, Graham hopes to keep them together and safe. The world outside is a dangerous place—disasters, war, and famine are taking their toll on the world's population. It is believed the world is going through the Tribulation. When Graham's daughter disappears, the Pecks must find her before she is killed.

Other books by the same author:
Narrow Door at Colditz, 2004
Wired, 2004
Deleted, 2003
The Dead Detective, 2002
The Empty Coffin, 2001

Other books you might like:

Alton Gansky, *Dark Moon*, 2002

Hank Hanegraaff, *The Last Disciple*, 2004

Tim F. LaHaye, *The Left Behind Series*, 1995-

Bill Myers, *Fire of Heaven*, 1999
Mel Odom, *The Apocalypse Series*, 2003-

1062

LENORA WORTH

A Tender Touch

(New York: Steeple Hill, 2004)

Story type: Romance
Subject(s): Animals/Dogs
Major character(s): Fredrica Hayes, Veterinarian; Clay Dempsey, Police Officer
Time period(s): 2000s
Locale(s): Sunset Island, Georgia

Summary: When Atlanta policeman Clay Dempsey's K-9 dog is injured in the line of duty, he decides they both need time off to recuperate. Clay goes to Sunset Island, Georgia, for some rest. Needing to find a veterinarian who can help his dog Samson during his rehabilitation, Clay visits the office of Fredrica Hayes. Soon Clay is falling in love with the pretty vet and wondering if he might make his stay permanent.

Other books by the same author:
After the Storm, 2004
Heart of Stone, 2003
The Carpenter's Wife, 2003
Lacey's Retreat, 2002
Something Beautiful, 2002

Other books you might like:
Irene Brand, *Autumn's Awakening*, 2001
Margaret Daley, *A Family for Keeps*, 2002
Gena Dalton, *Stranger at the Crossroads*, 2002
Gail Gaymer Martin, *A Love for Safekeeping*, 2002
Carol Steward, *Her Kind of Hero*, 1999

Inspirational

Popular Fiction in Review
by
Tom Barton

What's new in popular fiction?

Thankfully, there are some familiar threads in the current batch of stories and overall, I think, it's fair to say that popular fiction is alive, well and thriving. There's enough variety and quality writing in popular fiction to satisfy almost every taste. Yes, some themes have been reworked, but each generation needs to put their own spin on things and, in so doing, update stories for contemporary audiences. The following is a brief round-up of popular fiction in this edition of *What Do I Read Next?*.

Spy stories and thrillers are still very prominent. Such stories offer authors an opportunity for delivering insight to thoughtful readers, as well as entertainment. Take for instance World War II. While everyone knows that the Allied forces (Great Britain, the United States, and their allies) defeated the Axis powers (Germany, Italy, and Japan) in World War II, many people might take the victory against fascism for granted. After all, the war has been over since 1945. However, it's unlikely that anyone reading Alan Furst's work would come to such an ill-informed conclusion. Furst's stories are set during and just before World War II and dispel any notion of an easy victory for the Allies. His novel *Dark Voyage* is set in 1941, the year that Great Britain and her allies lost more than 1,500 merchant ships, mostly to German submarines. Furst, I believe, captures the suspense and heroic effort required to win the war.

Although not specifically about World War II, spying is a family affair in Charles McCarry's *Old Boys*, which draws upon Cold War experiences in an updated tale involving terrorists with plans to obtain a nuclear weapon. Paul Christopher, who last appeared in McCarry's 1991 work *Second Sight*, is at the center of the story and he gets help from his cousin Horace Hubbard. Fortunately, Horace can call upon retired CIA colleagues for assistance. If you like spy stories, you will probably like Martin Cruz Smith's Arkady Renko series. Readers follow an honest Russian cop in Moscow, amid a sea of political and social corruption. Smith tells a good yarn and he gives readers a look inside contemporary Russia. This is a country, one can argue, that has gotten more complicated, since the Cold War ended. *Wolves Eat Dogs* was published in 2004.

World War II figures very prominently in Nella Bielski's *The Year Is '42*. The novel unfolds around a doomed love affair between a German officer and an Ukrainian doctor, who is married to a patriot. Although *The Children's War* by Monique Charlesworth is set during World War II, it deals with the war's human complications rather than the war itself. The story unfolds from the perspective of a young girl growing up in Germany with a Jewish father and a Protestant mother.

Having directed his talents toward the American Revolutionary War and the Civil War, Jeff Shaara's epic, *To the Last Man*, tackles whatt was called at the time, the Great War because of the death and destruction it produced in the early part of the twentieth century. Now, of course, we refer to it as World War I and know it was only a preview for the horrors of World War II. Using a very broad scope, Shaara manages to place readers inside headquarters with the bickering officer corps, as well as in the trenches with the doomed foot soldiers.

Although *War Trash* has an unusual spin, the Korean War takes center stage in Ha Jin's latest work. The story follows an officer in the Red Chinese Army. He is captured and spends the war in a prisoner of war camp, where he struggles to maintain his self worth. Ha Jin, readers will remember, won the National Book Award in 2000 for his collection *The Bridegroom*.

Speaking of awards, author Alan Hollinghurst came up with a successful formula for his book *The Line of Beauty*, which won the 2004 Man Booker Prize. The book deals with upper-class decadence and political scandal in 1980s England, during Margaret Thatcher's tour as prime minister. Although Hollinghurst made the short-list for the Booker

Prize 10 years ago, some observers were surprised when he won this year. His book's protagonist is gay and a scholar at Oxford. The work has been called a Jamesian drama, referring, of course, to the American writer Henry James.

This reminds me. I've included, two fictional biographies of Henry James: *Author, Author* by David Lodge and *The Master* by Colm Toibin. While contemporary critics view James as a giant in American literature, this was not the case at the beginning of the twentieth century. To begin with, his works didn't sell very well. At one point, his lack of success caused him to try his hand as a playwright. Fortunately, he wasn't successful and went back to writing novels. Toibin's novel was a finalist for the Man Booker Prize.

In this year's competition for the National Book Award, Lily Tuck walked away with the prize for her novel, *The News from Paraguay*. The fictionalized work follows the life of Irish courtesan Ella Lynch, the mistress of Francisco Solano Lopez, dictator of Paraguay. Lopez led his country into a disastrous war against Brazil, Argentina, and Uruguay. Another novel, *The Stone That the Builder Refused*, is also based on historical events south of the border. The book is the final volume in Madison Smartt Bell's trilogy about Toussaint L'Ouverture. A former slave, L'Ouverture consolidated a slave rebellion into a revolution on the French colony island of Saint Domingue, now known as Haiti. As far as the historical record is concerned, this is the only successful slave rebellion. While Margaret Drabble's book *The Red Queen* doesn't have the broad sweep of a revolution, it does have an historical twist. The story evolves as a modern woman scholar finds parallels in her own life with the life of Korean princess who lived more than two hundred years ago.

Hollywood stories, featuring people who make their living in the movie industry, are still very popular. The reading public seems to have an inexhaustible appetite for stories about movie stars and/or celebrities. Interest tends to increase with details about wild parties featuring sex, drugs, and liquor. Take for instance, Jerry Stahl's work, *I, Fatty*, a story about the rise and fall of Roscoe "Fatty" Arbuckle, a star from the silent movie era. While most people are likely to have heard about silent movie great Charlie Chaplin, not many people are familiar with Fatty Arbuckle, although some might argue Chaplin and Arbuckle shared the same spotlight. That was before a young starlet died during a wild party. Unfortunately for Arbuckle, he was charged and stood trial for the rape and murder of the starlet. Although the jury acquitted him, his career did not survive testimony about sex, drugs, and liquor, which came out during his trial. You might say he was convicted in the court of public opinion.

On a similar note, *Cheat and Charmer* by Elizabeth Frank, deals with careers destroyed, during the 1950s, when there was some concern that the movie industry was infested with Communists intent on overthrowing the United States government. The story deals with the process by which more

than a few people found themselves unable to work in the movies. Apparently, if a person was called a Communist, during a government hearing that was enough to put them on a de facto blacklist and keep them from getting a job. On a lighter note, another star from the silent era is at the center of *The Silver Screen* by Maureen Howard. When sound was added to movies, the star left the business for a more conventional life, which turns the story into more of a family drama. Speaking of sound, Larry McMurtry's *Loop Group* has been called by some observers a kinder and gentler *Thelma and Louise*. For the record, the title of McMurtry's book refers to the last step in the movie editing process, which adds necessary sounds.

There's an old saying: Fame and fortune go hand-in-hand. This of course isn't always true but having a famous name can help, at least initially. Take for instance, Kristin Gore, daughter of former Vice President Al Gore. She has written a novel, *Sammy's Hill*, from the perspective of a youthful career woman, working in government, who has a healthy interest in romance. Some critics have called it a fun, fast read. Two other authors with famous names are, Nick Sagan and Benjamin Cheever. Sagan is the son of the late Carl Sagan, a scientist whose writing and narration helped popularize science on public television. It shouldn't come as a surprise that Nick Sagan has written a story that some might call science fiction. However, the story has more to do with the social sciences than it does with the physical sciences. *Edenborn*, a sequel to his first novel *Idlewild*, is set in the future after the world as we know it has been obliterated by plague. Cheever is the son of the late John Cheever, a writer of short stories and novels delving into the lives of upper-class suburbanites. It's fair to say that Benjamin Cheever is in the process of becoming successful in his own right. His book *The Good Nanny* is a satirical comedy about nannies and their employers.

Another writer, who has made a career of examining middle-class mores, is John Updike. His book, *Villages*, follows Owen Mackenzie from cradle to retirement, showing changes in social attitudes and their consequences from the Great Depression up to the present. There aren't many authors that can be mentioned in the same sentence with John Updike. However, no such restriction applies to Philip Roth, who has carved out his own impressive niche. Roth's *The Plot Against America* takes a thread from the historical record, but with a slightly offbeat twist. The work is what might be called an alternate history. The story speculates about what might have happened if Charles Lindbergh ran against and defeated Franklin Delano Roosevelt in the 1940 presidential election. According to the book's scenario, President Lindbergh would have kept the U.S. out of World War II and Hitler's Germany would have won the war. While the plot sounds a bit far-fetched, in Roth's capable hands the story becomes plausible and frightening.

Another contemporary writer, Joyce Carol Oates, is arguably in the same class with Updike and Roth. Oates can and does it all. Her book, *The Falls*, includes a suicide at Niagara Falls, relationships between men and women, family secrets, curses and a scandal involving a polluted subdivision. In short, she covers a lot of social landscape and keeps the story credible. Also showing promise when it comes to the social landscape is Marilynne Robinson. *Gilead* spans multiple time periods from just before the Civil War until 1956. It's a family saga about God-fearing men of the cloth, detailing what they did and how they felt about it.

Another author working in the social landscape, although from a slightly different perspective is Tom Wolfe. His book *I Am Charlotte Simmons* examines life on contemporary college campuses. As one might guess, one thing hasn't changed; sex is still the biggest preoccupation among young people attending college. However, Wolfe maintains that unlike their parents or grandparents before them, young people are a good deal more out in the open about sex. A term used in the book, sexiled, Wolfe maintains, is easily recognized by students everywhere. It means having to leave your room because your roommate needs it for romance. A former journalist, Wolfe researched his book by visiting various campuses across the country and talking to students. He also allowed his children, one still attending college and one having graduated, to read his manuscript before he submitted it to his publisher. Although Nicholas Delbanco's *The Vagabonds* emanates from a sexual act, it has more to do with attitudes children have about their parents. I mean how would you feel if you found out your grandmother's sexual indiscretion left you very well off? The story involves, in a surprising way, three men who were luminary giants of the early 20th century, Thomas Edison, Harvey Firestone, and Henry Ford.

Nelson DeMille's *Night Fall* builds a story around a real live disaster, the crash of TWA flight 800. More than 200 passengers and crew died when the plane crashed off the coast of Long Island in July 1996. John Corey, a character from DeMille's *Lion's Game*, reappears to investigate the cause of the crash. There has been much speculation about the cause of the crash: friendly fire, shoulder-fired missile, and mechanical failure.

Maria Flook, who made a name for herself writing true crime non-fiction, no doubt draws on this experience in *Lux* which is an unusual murder story. Namely, the killer courts the victim's wife. Speaking of true crime, Indra Sinha's debut novel, *The Death of Mr. Love*, is structured around a notorious murder trial that occurred circa 1950 in India, involving a British officer, his English wife, and her Indian lover. The book adds some spin to the scenario, combining family history with another scandalous love affair, murder, and blackmail. One might also call the book an immigrant story laced with colonialism. An interracial love affair amid colonial tension is also at the center of Carolyn Slaughter's *A Black Englishman*. The story is set in India just after World War I. An English officer is posted there and his English wife joins him. Subsequently, the couple becomes estranged

and she takes an Indian lover. The social backdrop with its religious, political, and social strife makes life very difficult for the lovers. Another story related to colonialism is *The In-Between World of Vikram Lall* by M.G. Vassanji. Winner of Canada's Giller Prize, the story follows an Indian man who grew up in Kenya, during the Mau Mau rebellion. His middle-class upbringing positioned him for a career in government. There he developed a knack for corrupt practices and made a fortune. He then left Kenya and immigrated to Canada.

Stories about immigration and assimilation still hit a familiar chord, although they have changed slightly over the years, or so it would seem. Nowadays, one might find relatively middle-class individuals looking at the experience in terms of a family history. Take for example *The Turk and My Mother* by Mary Helen Stefaniak. The story revolves around a family of Croatian-Americans, who settled in Milwaukee shortly after World War I. The family matriarch holds center stage, filling in the details of events that occurred before the family left the old country for America. A central feature of grandma's tale is the interest her daughter-in-law had in a Turkish prisoner of war. Another book about the immigration experience is *The Queen of the Big Time* by Adriana Trigiani. The story follows characters in a small Pennsylvania village settled by Italian immigrants almost 100 years ago. In addition to the problems of modern life, they struggle to maintain their ancestral traditions. Author Gish Jen gives us a slightly different twist on the problem of immigration and assimilation by mixing cultures and races. *The Love Wife* deals with a Chinese American man who has a mother determined to find him a Chinese wife. The problem is that he already has a wife, but she isn't Chinese. Things really get interesting when the couple begin having children.

To say the least, marriage is very complicated and challenging. Some might argue that modern society doesn't make it any easier, either. However, one might like to try, one just can't turn the clock back. Although things might be unpleasant, you can survive or at least that might be the message readers will come away with from the book *Shifting through Neutral* by Bridgett M. Davis. The story follows a working-class African-American family living in Detroit during the late 1960s and early 1970s. Although there are changes occurring in the outside world, the family's survival depends on issues in their inside world. Survival is also an issue in Walter Mosley's *Little Scarlet*, which is the eighth book in the Easy Rawlings series. This time around, the Los Angeles police enlist Easy's help to find a serial killer. The hitch is that the murders are occurring during the riots in Watts and the killer is using the riots for cover. Easy struggles, but he knows how to survive.

The fact is, everyone struggles for survival. However, it can be especially challenging for the working class, or that might be the message readers take from Jennifer Haigh's second novel *Baker Towers*. Set in a coal mining town just after World War II, the story follows members of a single-parent family as they attempt to take advantage of various economic and social opportunities. Ironically, the only member of the family happy with their social position is the daughter, who reluctantly goes away to college. Another portrait about working class life is painted in *The Mercy Killers* by Lisa Reardon. In this novel, child abuse plays a role in the motivation of a younger brother taking the blame for a crime his older brother committed. The story is set in Michigan.

Moral obligations can get complicated but, generally speaking, people try to do the right thing. However, actions are open to interpretation. Take for instance a repairman, who witnesses a young woman's suicide in Steven Sherrill's book *Visits from the Drowned Girl*. Although he's too far away to do anything about it, he doesn't notify the authorities. At the center of the story is the notion that he was the woman's last living witness. The last living witness having a moral obligation is, I think, an interesting notion. Apparently, Alexander McCall Smith and by extension social philosopher Isabel Dalhousie takes the notion very seriously, too. Isabel is a character from Smith's new series. Unlike his earlier series, which is set in Zimbabwe and features the private detective Precious Ramotswe, the new series is set in Edinburgh, Scotland. The first series book is *The Sunday Philosophy Club*. In the story, Isabel witnesses the death of a stockbroker at a public concert. In fact, she was the last person he looked at before he jumped from the balcony. As his last living witness, she feels obligated to investigate. Considering his success with detective stories set in Zimbabwe, fans may worry why he's trying a new series, but I wouldn't fret about it. Sometimes authors need to try something new to keep up their enthusiasm. This may be the case for Smith, and don't be surprised if he returns to the earlier series at a later date.

A case in point is Janet Evanovich. She is the creator of the Stephanie Plum series, which has been very successful. However, after ten books, perhaps it's time for a change. This may explain why *Metro Girl* doesn't feature Stephanie. Although the book does include a very strong woman character, she's not looking for bail jumpers but for her missing brother who happens to be a NASCAR driver. Speaking of NASCAR, how about combining it with an updated version of *The Canterbury Tales*. That's an interesting notion, which is how one can describe *St. Dale* by Sharyn McCrumb. The title refers to Dale Earnhardt, the late great race car driver, and the story is organized around a secular pilgrimage or bus tour of race tracks where Earnhardt made racing history.

Taking something old and making it new is quite a challenge. I think it's doubly difficult because readers are likely to view the new with their notions of the old. This, I think, is the situation that faces Eric Van Lustbader and Mark Winegardner as they try to pick up where two popular fiction giants left off. Van Lustbader's *The Bourne Legacy* is the latest chapter in the life of former CIA agent Jason Bourne, the character created by the late Robert Ludlum. Many would argue that Bourne is the most successful character in Ludlum's very successful career. This, of course, adds to the challenge. An equally daunting task faced Winegardner, who wrote *The Godfather Returns*, picking up where Mario Puzo left off with the now infamous Corleone Family, which is a contemporary icon thanks to the movies, *The Godfather* and *The Godfather II*. Both writers, Van Lustbader and Winegardner, appear to be well-grounded and up to the challenge.

There's one other title that I think is worth mentioning, *The Send-Away Girl* by Barbara Sutton. It's a collection of short stories and it won a Flannery O'Connor Award, given out by the University of Georgia. Now, I must admit that I flat out love Flannery O'Connor's work, but that's not why I wast to mention *The Send-Away Girl*. You see, the reason is that the title makes me smile. It refers to someone who works as a gofer, as in, go for coffee, go for the paper, etc. I think the title is a wonderful use of language. For me, the title touches upon the magic language can convey.

In case you're wondering, I do believe this is a very good time to be a reader.

Recommended Titles

The Stone That the Builder Refused by Madison Smartt Bell

The Year Is '42 by Nella Bielski

The Children's War by Monique Charlesworth

Metro Girl by Janet Evanovich

Cheat and Charmer by Elizabeth Frank

Dark Voyage by Alan Furst

Sammy's Hill by Kristin Gore

Baker Towers by Jennifer Haigh

The Love Wife by Gish Jen

The Ninth Life of Louis Drax by Liz Jensen

War Trash by Ha Jin

St. Dale by Sharyn McCrumb

Loop Group by Larry McMurtry

The Falls by Joyce Carol Oates

The Mercy Killers by Lisa Reardon

Gilead by Marilynne Robinson

The Death of Mr. Love by Indra Sinha

A Black Englishman by Carolyn Slaughter

The Sunday Philosophy Club by Alexander McCall Smith

I, Fatty by Jerry Stahl

The Turk and My Mother by Mary Helen Stefaniak

The Send-Away Girl by Barbara Sutton

The Last King by Nichelle C. Tramble

The Queen of the Big Time by Adriana Trigiani

The News from Paraguay by Lily Tuck

Popular Fiction Titles

1063

MARC ACITO

How I Paid for College
(New York: Broadway, 2004)

Story type: Coming-of-Age; Humor
Subject(s): Friendship; College Life; Actors and Actresses
Major character(s): Edward Zanni, Teenager, Actor (in training); Al Zanni, Parent (Edward's father)
Time period(s): 1980s (1983)
Locale(s): Wallingford, New Jersey

Summary: High school senior Edward Zanni wants to attend Juilliard and study acting, and ultimately become a star. During his audition, he has a nervous breakdown. Ironically, the school officials think he's acting and are so impressed they admit him. Edward's father doesn't support his son's ambitions and refuses to pay his tuition. The school won't grant him a scholarship, since his father makes too much money. Edward is resourceful, however, and has some equally resourceful friends who help him embezzle the money from his father. In the course of their scheme, they have a good time, although a few glitches occur. Edward is also confused about his sexual identity, being attracted to both his girlfriend, Kelly, and a good-looking football player.

Where it's reviewed:
Booklist, August 2004, page 1895
Kirkus Reviews, June 15, 2004, page 547
Library Journal, October 1, 2004, page 66
Publishers Weekly, September 6, 2004, page 47

Other books you might like:
Mike Albo, *Hornito*, 2000
Russell Banks, *Rule of the Bone*, 1995
A.S. Byatt, *The Biographers's Tale*, 2000
Jonathan Coe, *The Rotters Club*, 2001
Jonathan Safran Foer, *Everything Is Illuminated*, 2002

1064

JONATHAN AMES

Wake Up, Sir
(New York: Scribner, 2004)

Story type: Psychological
Subject(s): Men; Alcoholism; Authors and Writers
Major character(s): Alan Blair, Writer, Alcoholic; Jeeves, Servant (a valet)
Time period(s): 2000s
Locale(s): Montclair, New Jersey; Saratoga Springs, New York

Summary: Thirty-something novelist Alan Blair is Jewish, an alcoholic, and lives with his aunt and uncle. When Alan refuses to get help, they show him the door. Having just received a huge insurance settlement, Alan is independent. He hires Jeeves, a personal valet, and the two move to an artists' colony. Through all of Alan's various trials and tribulations, Jeeves is there to counsel him, in this madcap adventure that owes more than a little to the spirit of humorist P.G. Wodehouse.

Where it's reviewed:
Kirkus Reviews, April 15, 2004, page 343
Library Journal, July 2004, page 66
New York Times Book Review, August 1, 2004, page 10
Publishers Weekly, May 10, 2004, page 33

Other books by the same author:
What's Not to Love, 2000
The Extra Man, 1998
I Pass Like Night, 1989

Other books you might like:
Martin Amis, *The Information*, 1995
Thomas Berger, *Being Invisible*, 1987
Richard Flanigan, *The Sound of One Hand Clapping*, 1997
Alice McDermott, *Charming Billy*, 1998
John O'Brien, *Leaving Las Vegas*, 1995

1065

MARY KAY ANDREWS

Hissy Fit

(New York: HarperCollins, 2004)

Story type: Humor; Contemporary
Subject(s): Women; Relationships; Revenge
Major character(s): Keeley Murdock, Bride (called off her wedding), Interior Decorator; A.J. Jernigan, Fiance(e) (Keeley's former); Will Mahoney, Wealthy, Businessman
Time period(s): 2000s
Locale(s): Madison, Georgia

Summary: In Keeley Murdock's world, good manners and decorum reign supreme. So, when Keeley catches her fiance having sex with her maid of honor at the rehearsal dinner, she pitches a fit. Despite warnings to the contrary, Keeley cancels the wedding. Her actions bring unwanted notoriety to her reputation and pressure from her ex-fiance's family. They own the local bank, and almost force Keeley's interior decorating business into financial ruin. Salvation appears on the horizon in the person of Will Mahoney. He purchases a local factory and hires Keeley to redo an old antebellum mansion he fancies.

Where it's reviewed:
Library Journal, July 2004, page 66
Publishers Weekly, July 5, 2004, page 36

Other books by the same author:
Little Bitty Lies, 2003
Savannah Blues, 2002

Other books you might like:
E.M. Forster, *A Room with a View*, 1908
Olivia Goldsmith, *Dumping Billy*, 2004
Allegra Goodman, *Paradise Park*, 2001
Barbara Kingsolver, *The Bean Trees*, 1988
Steve Martin, *Shopgirl*, 2000

1066

ALIETTE ARMEL

Love, the Painter's Wife and the Queen of Sheba

(New Milford, Connecticut: Toby, 2004)

Story type: Historical
Subject(s): Artists and Art; Relationships; Storytelling
Major character(s): Piero della Francesca, Historical Figure, Artist; Silvia della Francesca, Spouse (Piero's wife); Bilqis, Historical Figure, Ruler (Queen of Sheba)
Time period(s): 15th century
Locale(s): Arezzo, Italy

Summary: A critic and historian in France, this is Armel's fictional debut in English. The story follows the life of the Renaissance painter Piero della Francesca, although the focus of the story is his wife, Silvia. They are childless and she fears that he will leave her. When the Pope summons Piero, Silvia intervenes by making up a story about the Queen of Sheba, who ascended the throne at age 16, when her father died.

Subsequently, the young queen must confront and deal with a sexist King Solomon. Silvia's plan works as her husbands falls under the spell of her captivating story and stays home. Translated by Alison Anderson.

Where it's reviewed:
Kirkus Reviews, June 1, 2004, page 504
Library Journal, June 15, 2004, page 56

Other books you might like:
Barbara Taylor Bradford, *Three Weeks in Paris*, 2002
Tracy Chevalier, *Girl with a Pearl Earring*, 1999
Sarah Dunant, *The Birth of Venus*, 2003
Penelope Fitzgerald, *Innocence*, 1986
E.M. Forster, *A Room with a View*, 1908

1067

KATE ATKINSON

Case Histories

(New York: Little, Brown, 2004)

Story type: Domestic; Romance
Subject(s): Fate; Crime and Criminals; Psychological
Major character(s): Jackson Brodie, Detective—Private
Time period(s): 2000s
Locale(s): Cambridge, England

Summary: Atkinson offers three detective stories in this work. The stories are set in Cambridge, England, and involve crimes that police regard as cold cases. Connecting the stories is Jackson Brodie, a private investigator who cultivates a taste for French culture. In the first story, two sisters, Amelia and Julie, hire Brodie to find out the truth about their sister Olivia's disappearance more than 30 years ago. The second case calls for Brodie to find the murderer of Laura Wyre, a young woman, who was stabbed to death. For the third case, Brodie is hired to find a niece, whose mother was sent to prison for murdering her husband. The backdrop for these stories is Brodie's personal life, including an ex-wife, who uses their daughter to make life miserable for the somewhat offbeat detective.

Where it's reviewed:
Booklist, August 2004, page 1870
Kirkus Reviews, August 15, 2004, page 755
Library Journal, September 15, 2004, page 47
New York Times, November 15, 2004, page B10

Other books by the same author:
Not the End of the World, 2002
Abandonment, 2000
Emotionally Weird, 2000
Human Croquet, 1997
Behind the Scenes at the Museum, 1996 (Whitbread Prize winner)

Other books you might like:
Elizabeth Berg, *Open House*, 2000
Dan Chaon, *You Remind Me of Me*, 2004
Pearl Cleage, *Some Things I Never Thought I'd Do*, 2003
A.L. Kennedy, *Indelible Acts*, 2003
Zadie Smith, *White Teeth*, 2000

1068

DEAN BAKOPOULOS

Please Don't Come Back from the Moon
(Orlando, Florida: Harcourt, 2005)

Story type: Domestic; Coming-of-Age
Subject(s): Single Parent Families; Adolescence; Working Mothers
Major character(s): Michael Smolij, Young Man
Time period(s): 1990s (1991)
Locale(s): Maple Rock, Michigan

Summary: Magic and myth combine in this debut novel about growing up in a working class Detroit suburb where dreams die early and expectations are rarely realized. Michael is 16 when his father disappears without any warning and is never heard from again. Dozens of other men in the neighborhood also disappear, although not all at once, tearing apart the social fabric of the community. Michael's mother is forced to work two jobs to support him and his brother, as are most of the other abandoned wives. Subsequently, Michael's brother enlists in the military, and his mother remarries and moves away, leaving Michael alone in the family home. Although Michael's life—a job, college classes, and a girlfriend—offers him a semblance of normalcy, he wrestles with a restless urge to leave.

Where it's reviewed:
Booklist, November 15, 2004, page 551
Kirkus Reviews, November 1, 2004, page 1019
Library Journal, November 15, 2004, page 49
Publishers Weekly, November 15, 2004, page 7

Other books you might like:
Clare Boylan, *Last Resorts*, 1986
Catherine Cookson, *The Bailey Chronicles*, 1988
Judith Guest, *Errands*, 1997
D.H. Lawrence, *Sons and Lovers*, 1913
Joyce Carol Oates, *Them*, 1969

1069

JULIAN BARNES

The Lemon Table
(New York: Knopf, 2004)

Story type: Collection
Subject(s): Short Stories; Aging; Relationships
Locale(s): United States

Summary: Critically acclaimed stylist Barnes offers a collection of 11 short stories that look beyond the surface of aging and facing death. The stories are ''Appetite,'' ''The Things You Know,'' ''The Fruit Cage,'' ''The Revival,'' ''Hygiene,'' ''The Silence,'' ''The Story of Mat Israelson,'' ''Vigilance,'' ''A Short History of Hairdressing,'' ''Knowing French,'' and ''Old Folkery.'' Six of these stories were published in the *New Yorker*. Barnes' ability to cover a wide range of subjects from the 19th century to the 21st century with wit and conviction is on display. The characters muse about relationships, marriage, gossip, lost love, devotion, reflections, and other issues they face.

Where it's reviewed:
Kirkus Reviews, April 1, 2004, page 283
Library Journal, June 1, 2004, page 128
New York Times Book Review, June 27, 2004, page 7
Publishers Weekly, May 10, 2004, page 33

Other books by the same author:
Love, etc., 2001
Talking It Over, 1991
A History of the World in Ten and One-Half Chapters, 1990
Staring at the Sun, 1986
Metroland, 1980

Other books you might like:
Carrie Brown, *Rose's Garden*, 1998
Andrew Sean Greer, *The Confessions of Max Tivoli*, 2004
Bobbie Ann Mason, *Spence and Lila*, 1988
Alix Kates Shulman, *Memoirs of an Ex-Prom Queen*, 1972
Nicholas Sparks, *The Notebook*, 1996

1070

RICHARD BARRE

Echo Bay
(Santa Barbara, California: Capra, 2004)

Story type: Psychological Suspense
Subject(s): Accidents; Family Relations; Shipwrecks
Major character(s): Shawn Rainey, Sports Figure (ex-downhill skier); Catherine Mulvhill, Wealthy
Time period(s): 2000s
Locale(s): Lake Tahoe, Nevada

Summary: Action, secrets, and guilt from a misspent youth haunt Shawn Rainey, who was once a champion downhill skier. To make matters worse, Shawn's wife is living with Terry, his former business partner. Shawn and Terry are both interested in a scheme designed to get investors to finance the raising of a sunken ship. Terry gives Shawn an ultimatum: get the money or lose visitation rights to his children. Reluctantly, Shawn agrees, but to succeed he must match wits with Catherine Mulvhill, a self-appointed, elderly guardian of the local old money set.

Where it's reviewed:
Library Journal, May 15, 2004, page 113

Other books by the same author:
Wind on the River, 2004
Bethany, 2003
Burning Moon, 2003
Star, 2002
Blackheart Highway, 1999

Other books you might like:
Harlan Coben, *Tell No One*, 2001
Richard Flanagan, *Death of a River Guide*, 1994
Margaret Leroy, *Postcards from Berlin*, 2003
James Patterson, *The Beach House*, 2002
    Peter de Jonge, co-author
Christina Schwarz, *Drowning Ruth*, 2000

1071

CHRISTINA BARTOLOMEO

Snowed In

(New York: St. Martin's Press, 2004)

Story type: Humor; Romance
Subject(s): Marriage; Relatives; Artists and Art
Major character(s): Sophie Quinn, Artist (freelance); Paul Quinn, Spouse (Sophie's husband); Ned, Friend (of Sophie's)
Time period(s): 2000s
Locale(s): Portland, Maine

Summary: Sophie Quinn wakes up one morning feeling trapped, or at least in a mental funk. She has just moved to Portland, Maine. It's winter, the pipes are frozen, and she supects her husband, Paul, is fooling around. His assistant seems to be sending come-hither looks his way, at least in Sophie's opinion, and her best friend agrees with her. Sophie is a freelance artist who works out of her home, and work has been scarce lately, another problem. Her mother-in-law also seems intent on driving her crazy. Things pick up when Sophie joins a walkers group and begins to make new friends. One of the men, Ned, is especially nice, and she contemplates trading Paul for him.

Where it's reviewed:
Booklist, October 15, 2004, page 388
Kirkus Reviews, November 1, 2004, page 1019
Publishers Weekly, October 11, 2004, page 55

Other books by the same author:
The Side of the Angels, 2002
Cupid and Diana, 1998

Other books you might like:
Megan Chance, *An Inconvenient Wife*, 2004
Joyce Carol Oates, *American Appetites*, 1989
Jodi Picoult, *Picture Perfect*, 2002
Danielle Steel, *Answered Prayers*, 2002
Anne Tyler, *The Amateur Marriage*, 2004

1072

MADISON SMARTT BELL

The Stone That the Builder Refused

(New York: Pantheon, 2004)

Story type: Historical; Saga
Series: Haitian Rebellion Trilogy. Book 3
Subject(s): Biography; Revolutions; Haitians
Major character(s): Pierre Dominique Toussaint L'Ouverture, Historical Figure, Political Figure; Dr. Hebert, Narrator
Time period(s): 1800s (1801-1803)
Locale(s): Haiti (then French colony of Saint Domingue)

Summary: This is third volume in Bell's trilogy following *All Souls' Rising* (1995), and *Master of the Crossroads* (2000). This epic work follows the career of Toussaint L'Ouverture, the leader of the Haitian Revolution of 1791. What starts out as an uprising of African slaves against their cruel European masters soon turns into a revolution as the former slaves drive their white masters from the French colony known as Saint

Domingue. By 1793, Toussaint proves himself to be an astute politician, as well as a military commander. After stabilizing the country and abolishing slavery in 1801, Toussaint realizes the country's economy needs to be rebuilt and he invites the white planters back. Along the way, he makes compromises that ultimately lead to his downfall. However, the historical record shows this is the only slave rebellion that was successful and it wouldn't have been possible without Toussaint L'Ouverture.

Where it's reviewed:
Booklist, September 15, 2004, page 179
Kirkus Reviews, October 1, 2004, page 927
Library Journal, October 15, 2004, page 52
New York Times Book Review, November 14, 2004, page 49
Publishers Weekly, September 20, 2004, page 43

Other books by the same author:
Anything Goes, 2002
Master of the Crossroads, 2000
Ten Indians, 1996
All Souls' Rising, 1995
Doctor Sleep, 1991

Other books you might like:
Edwidge Danticat, *The Dew Breaker*, 2004
Edward P. Jones, *The Known World*, 2003
Valerie Martin, *Property*, 2003
Kate McCafferty, *Testimony of an Irish Slave Girl*, 2002
David Pesci, *Amistad*, 1997

1073

TED BELL

Assassin

(New York: Atria, 2004)

Story type: Adventure; Psychological Suspense
Series: Alexander Hawke. Book 2
Subject(s): Revenge; Terrorism; Sea Stories
Major character(s): Alexander Hawke, Spy; Snay bin Wazir, Terrorist; Victoria Sweet, Spouse (Alex's wife), Crime Victim (murdered)
Time period(s): 2000s
Locale(s): London, England; New England; Indonesia

Summary: In his second work featuring his character Alexander Hawke, Bell cannot escape comparisons to Ian Fleming and his superhero, James Bond. However, Hawke is an American whose forebears were pirates and he resembles a modern day privateer more than he does the gentlemanly Bond. As the story opens, he is about to wed the beautiful Victoria Sweet. After the ceremony, a sniper kills her and Hawke is emotionally devastated. The U.S. Secretary of State intervenes, bringing Hawke evidence of a network that is responsible for terrorizing American diplomats overseas and is planning to bring the terror to U.S. shores. Hawke correctly suspects that the network is also responsible for the death of his beloved Victoria, and sets out to bring them to justice and exact his own personal revenge. A cast of colorful characters provides Hawke with the necessary support for accomplishing his goal.

Where it's reviewed:
Booklist, July 2004, page 1823

Publishers Weekly, June 21, 2004, page 43

Other books by the same author:
Hawke, 2003

Other books you might like:
Tom Clancy, *Rainbow Six*, 1998
Nelson DeMille, *The Lion's Game*, 2000
Frederick Forsyth, *Avenger*, 2003
John Le Carre, *The Little Drummer Girl*, 1983
Robert Ludlum, *The Janson Directive*, 2002

1074

STEVE BERRY

The Romanov Prophecy
(New York: Ballantine, 2004)

Story type: Historical; Saga
Subject(s): Murder; Revolutions; Kings, Queens, Rulers, etc.
Major character(s): Miles Lord, Lawyer; Stefan Baklanov, Relative (of the royal family); Akilina Petrovna, Entertainer
Time period(s): 20th century; 21st century
Locale(s): Moscow, Russia

Summary: Berry uses the historical record to play a what if game, putting an interesting spin on what could happen in Russia. American Miles Lord, who speaks fluent Russian, finds himself in Moscow on the eve of the restoration of the Russian monarchy, which was abolished during the Russian Revolution in the early part of the 20th century. When the Communists took over, the royal family—Nicholas II, his wife Alexandra, and their children—was assassinated. After the Communist government collapsed in the later part of the 20th century, it was succeeded by a series of inept governments unable to address the problems in a modern society. This explains the voters 21st century decision to restore the monarchy. Now, Lord has been selected to head the commission that will select the new monarch from relatives of the murdered Nicholas. To fully discharge his responsibilities, Lord must investigate what really happened on the day Nicholas died. Were there any survivors?

Where it's reviewed:
Kirkus Reviews, July 15, 2004, page 644
Library Journal, July 2004, page 66

Other books by the same author:
The Amber Room, 2003

Other books you might like:
Robert Alexander, *The Kitchen Boy*, 2003
J.M. Coetzee, *The Master of Petersburg*, 1994
Helen Dunmore, *The Siege*, 2002
Robert Harris, *Archangel*, 1999
Shirley Hazzard, *The Great Fire*, 2003

1075

DAVID BEZMOZGIS

Natasha: And Other Stories
(New York: Farrar, Straus and Giroux, 2004)

Story type: Collection; Ethnic
Subject(s): Short Stories; Emigration and Immigration; Jews
Major character(s): Mark Berman, Narrator
Time period(s): 2000s
Locale(s): Toronto, Ontario, Canada

Summary: This debut collection of six loosely linked short stories introduces the Berman family, Russian Jewish immigrants who left Latvia and have landed in Toronto, Canada. Some of the stories have been previously published. In ''Tapka,'' six-year-old Mark confronts the difficulty of speaking English. A dinner party given to promote the family business has the opposite effect in ''Roman Berman, Massage Therapist.'' In ''Natasha,'' an older cousin gives Mark's sexual education a jump start. The other stories in the collection are ''The Second Strongest Man,'' ''An Animal to the Memory,'' and ''Choynski.''

Where it's reviewed:
Kirkus Reviews, April 1, 2004, page 284
Library Journal, March 15, 2004, page 109
New York Times Book Review, June 27, 2004, page 6
Publishers Weekly, April 19, 2004, page 36

Other books you might like:
Nicholas Delbanco, *What Remains*, 2000
E.L. Doctorow, *The Book of Daniel*, 1971
Nathan Englander, *For the Relief of Unbearable Urges*, 1999
Nomi Eve, *The Family Orchard*, 2000
Adam Haslett, *You Are Not a Stranger*, 2002

1076

NELLA BIELSKI

The Year Is '42
(New York: Pantheon, 2004)

Story type: Historical/World War II
Subject(s): Relationships; Guilt; Doctors
Major character(s): Karl Bazinger, Military Personnel (German officer); Katia, Doctor (Ukrainian)
Time period(s): 1940s (1942)
Locale(s): Paris, France; Kiev, Union of Soviet Socialist Republics

Summary: Ukrainian author Bielski tells a story about life, love, and war. Karl Bazinger, an outspoken German army officer, is stationed in occupied Paris. In a city for the most part untouched by the war, Karl soaks up French culture but he soon runs afoul of his superiors and is shipped to the Eastern front. There the carnage of war is everywhere. After developing a skin disease, Karl seeks help and the doctor who treats him is Ukrainian. Her name is Katia and her husband has just been sent to prison by the Nazis. A doomed relationship develops between Karl and Katia, who shows him that the Ukrainians have culture, too. Translated by John Berger and Lisa Appignanesi.

Popular Fiction

Where it's reviewed:

Booklist, October 15, 2004, page 388
Kirkus Reviews, September 15, 2004, page 880
Publishers Weekly, October 4, 2004, page 66

Other books you might like:

C.S. Forester, *The African Queen*, 1935
Adam Hall, *Quiller Solitaire*, 1992
John Le Carre, *Absolute Friends*, 2003
Boris Pasternak, *Doctor Zhivago*, 1958
Rebecca West, *The Return of the Soldier*, 1918

1077

MAEVE BINCHY

Nights of Rain and Stars

(New York: Dutton, 2004)

Story type: Psychological
Subject(s): Friendship; Travel; Relationships
Major character(s): Thomas, Divorced Person; David, Tourist; Elsa, Journalist (TV reporter)
Time period(s): 2000s
Locale(s): Aghia Anna, Greece

Summary: Four tourists are brought together in Greece when their tour boat catches on fire, killing 24 people. In the aftermath, the four are thrown together with other survivors, seeking refuge in the local tavern, owned by Andreas. Each of them are running from problems they have at home. Elsa, a German, is trying to escape from a love affair gone sour, while Fiona, from Ireland, has brought her boyfriend to get him away from her disapproving family. David, an Englishman, is trying to keep from going into the family business. Thomas, an American, is running away from complications of a failed marriage. As the four become friends, Andreas and a woman named Vonni attempt to guide them through their difficulties.

Where it's reviewed:

Booklist, July 2004, page 1796
Library Journal, August 2004, page 63
Publishers Weekly, July 19, 2004, page 142

Other books by the same author:

Quentins, 2002
Scarlet Feather, 2000
Tara Road, 1998
Evening Class, 1996
Circle of Friends, 1990

Other books you might like:

Jonathan Franzen, *The Corrections*, 2001
Alice McDermott, *Child of My Heart*, 2002
Larry McMurtry, *Loop Group*, 2004
Nuala O'Faolain, *My Dream of You*, 2001
Carol Shields, *Unless*, 2002

1078

T. CORAGHESSAN BOYLE

The Inner Circle

(New York: Viking, 2004)

Story type: Adult
Subject(s): Erotica; Sexual Behavior; Teacher-Student Relationships
Major character(s): Alfred Kinsey, Historical Figure, Scientist (researcher of sex practices); John Milk, Researcher (Kinsey's assistant); Iris Milk, Spouse (John's wife)
Time period(s): 1940s; 1950s
Locale(s): Bloomington, Indiana

Summary: Boyle fictionalizes the life of Alfred Kinsey, author of the Kinsey Reports, which in the 1940s and 1950s scandalized the country by making public American sexual behavior. The story is narrated by John Milk, who meets Kinsey as a student at Indiana University. After graduating, Kinsey recruits John to help him research human sexual behavior. Quickly learning the nuts and bolts of research, interviewing, and recording data, John soon becomes one of Kinsey's closest advisors. By incremental steps, Kinsey begins pushing the boundaries of research from recording to participating in sexual behavior. John not only participates but recruits his wife, too.

Where it's reviewed:

Library Journal, July 15, 2004, page 66
Publishers Weekly, July 5, 2004, page 34

Other books by the same author:

Drop City, 2003
After the Plague, 2001
A Friend of the Earth, 2000
Riven Rock, 1998
The Road to Wellville, 1993

Other books you might like:

Tracy Chevalier, *Girl with a Pearl Earring*, 1999
John Fowles, *A Maggot*, 1985
Joyce Carol Oates, *Beasts*, 2002
Philip Roth, *The Dying Animal*, 2001
Irving Wallace, *The Chapman Report*, 1960

1079

EDNA BUCHANAN

Cold Case Squad

(New York: Simon & Schuster, 2004)

Story type: Mystery; Contemporary
Subject(s): Police Procedural; Murder; Relationships
Major character(s): Craig Burch, Detective—Police (sergeant); K.C. Riley, Detective—Police (lieutenant); Sam Stone, Detective—Police
Time period(s): 2000s
Locale(s): Miami, Florida

Summary: Buchanan's novel picks up where *The Ice Maiden* (2002) left off, with the special police unit working cold unsolved crimes. In the previous book, Miami Police Sgt. Craig Burch helped crime reporter Britt Montero. This time out Burch, who takes police work very seriously, gets star billing. He's a decent man with a good heart but his occupation has a tragic effect on his personal life. While the squad works several cases, the focal point is a 12-year-old case involving a man blown to bits, while he was doing routine maintenance on his car. Although his death had been regarded as accidental, new evidence suggests it was murder.

Where it's reviewed:
Booklist, April 1, 2004, page 1330
Kirkus Reviews, April 15, 2004, page 363
Publishers Weekly, April 19, 2004, page 37

Other books by the same author:
The Ice Maiden, 2002
You Only Die Twice, 2001
Garden of Evil, 1999
Pulse, 1998
Margin of Error, 1997

Other books you might like:
John Grisham, *The Last Juror*, 2004
Patricia Highsmith, *The Boy Who Followed Ripley*, 1993
Elmore Leonard, *Pronto*, 1993
Lisa Scottoline, *Killer Smile*, 2004
Charles Willeford, *Miami Blues*, 1984

1080

JAMES LEE BURKE

In the Moon of Red Ponies
(New York: Simon & Schuster, 2004)

Story type: Psychological Suspense; Mystery
Series: Billy Bob Holland. Book 2
Subject(s): Trials; Veterans; Indians of North America
Major character(s): Billy Bob Holland, Lawyer, Lawman (ex-Texas Ranger); Johnny American Horse, Activist (for Indian rights), Indian; Amber Finley, Girlfriend (Johnny's)
Time period(s): 2000s
Locale(s): Missoula, Montana

Summary: Ex-Texas Ranger Billy Bob Holland is alive and well and living in Montana, where he now practices law. Johnny American Horse, a Native American activist, becomes Billy Bob's client after the state charges him with a double murder. From Billy Bob's perspective, things just don't add up. For one thing, the murder victims attempted to kill Johnny. A local cop appears to be obsessed with Johnny's girlfriend, the daughter of a U.S. senator. Of course, this doesn't even consider why a federal agent dispatched from Washington, D.C., is snooping around. Before Billy Bob can get a handle on things, more bodies begin to show up. Despite death threats, Billy Bob lands on his feet but it does take some doing.

Where it's reviewed:
Chicago Tribune Books, June 27, 2004, page 2
Kirkus Reviews, May 1, 2004, page 408
Library Journal, June 1, 2004, page 118
Publishers Weekly, May 24, 2004, page 44

Other books by the same author:
Last Car to Elysian Fields, 2003
Jolie Blon's Bounce, 2002

White Doves at Morning, 2002
Bitterroot, 2001
Purple Cane Road, 2000

Other books you might like:
David Baldacci, *The Simple Truth*, 1998
Patricia Cornwell, *Cause of Death*, 1996
Richard Dooling, *Brain Storm*, 1998
William Faulkner, *Intruder in the Dust*, 1948
John Grisham, *The Client*, 1993

1081

CAROLE CADWALLADR

The Family Tree
(New York: Dutton, 2005)

Story type: Domestic; Psychological
Subject(s): Secrets; Pregnancy; Mothers and Daughters
Major character(s): Rebecca Monroe, Researcher (pop culture); Alistair Monroe, Spouse (Rebecca's husband), Scientist (geneticist)
Time period(s): 20th century
Locale(s): England

Summary: In her first novel, journalist Cadwalladr delivers a family saga that spans three generations. Rebecca Monroe narrates a story about her life, her mother's suicide, and her grandmother's affair that crossed the color line. Rebecca, an expert on pop culture and married to a geneticist, takes a hard look at her family and its history. She wonders about whether or not to have children and analyzes the pros and cons from both the genetic and environmental perspectives. Several factors, including her husband's use of her in his work, the fact that her grandmother suffered from Alzheimer's, and her own loveless marriage, play a large role in her decision.

Where it's reviewed:
Kirkus Reviews, September 15, 2004, page 881
Library Journal, October 1, 2004, page 66
Publishers Weekly, November 8, 2004, page 33

Other books you might like:
Julianna Baggott, *Girl Talk*, 2001
Carrie Fisher, *Delusions of Grandma*, 1994
Ethan Hawke, *Ash Wednesday*, 2002
Patrick Neate, *The London Pigeon Wars*, 2004
William Trevor, *Felicia's Journey*, 1994

1082

LAN SAMANTHA CHANG

Inheritance
(New York: Norton, 2004)

Story type: Historical; Family Saga
Subject(s): Chinese Americans; Sisters; War
Major character(s): Junan, Spouse (Li Ang's wife); Yinan, Relative (Junan's sister), Lover (Li Ang's); Li Ang, Military Personnel, Spouse (Junan's husband)
Time period(s): 20th century
Locale(s): China; Taiwan; United States

Summary: Chang weaves together a story that features family relations and personal compromises amid struggles to survive the political upheavals of 20th-century China. Junan and Yinan are inseparable sisters. Li Ang, a soldier, marries Junan; however, when the Japanese invade China, the couple is separated. Junan sends her sister Yinan to look after Li Ang but the arrangement soon becomes complicated when Yinan and Li Ang fall in love and have a child. After the defeat of Japan, the Communists divide the country and Junan immigrates to the United States with her two daughters. Yinan and Li Ang stay in China with their son.

Where it's reviewed:
Library Journal, June 15, 2004, page 57
Publishers Weekly, July 5, 2004, page 36

Other books by the same author:
Hunger, 1998

Other books you might like:
Monica Ali, *Brick Lane*, 2003
Sarah Dunant, *The Birth of Venus*, 2003
C.Y. Lee, *The Flower Drum Song*, 1957
Chang-rae Lee, *Aloft*, 2004
Amy Tan, *The Bonesetter's Daughter*, 2001

1083

MONIQUE CHARLESWORTH

The Children's War

(New York: Knopf, 2004)

Story type: Historical/World War II
Subject(s): Children and War; Family Relations; Nazis
Major character(s): Ilse, Teenager; Otto, Parent (Ilse's father); Lore, Parent (Ilse's mother)
Time period(s): 1930s (1939)
Locale(s): Morocco; Paris, France; Marseilles, France

Summary: Growing up is difficult enough in the best of times; throw in tyranny, ideology, and a world war and things get really complicated. This is the situation Ilse, a young girl, faces in 1939 Nazi Germany. Her father is Jewish and her mother is Protestant. Her father, a Communist, plans to stay in Germany to fight the Fascists. Her mother is beside herself. She sends Ilse to Morroco to visit an uncle but when the uncle enlists to fight Hitler, Ilse travels to Paris. Her father, tricked into leaving Germany, meets Ilse. Now, mom wants Ilse to return home to Germany but she stays with her father. When Paris falls to the Germans, they join the underground. Her father is captured by the Germans and dies a hero. Meanwhile, her mother is killed when the Allies bomb Hamburg.

Where it's reviewed:
Kirkus Reviews, July 1, 2004, page 590
Library Journal, June 15, 2004, page 57

Other books by the same author:
Foreign Exchange, 1995
The Glass House, 1986

Other books you might like:
Edna Ferber, *Fanny Herself*, 1917
Alan Furst, *Dark Voyage*, 2004
Tess Uriza Holthe, *When the Elephants Dance*, 2002

Helen Humphreys, *Leaving Earth*, 1998
Nora Okja Keller, *Fox Girl*, 2002

1084

BENJAMIN CHEEVER

The Good Nanny

(New York: Bloomsbury, 2004)

Story type: Humor; Contemporary
Subject(s): Authorship; Kidnapping; Satire
Major character(s): Stuart Cross, Spouse (of Andie); Andie Cross, Parent (mother of Ginny and Jane); Louise, Child-Care Giver (nanny)
Time period(s): 2000s
Locale(s): New York, New York

Summary: This a black comedy about a professional couple with children who find out the hard way that although good help is hard to find, don't hire perfect help. Stuart and Andie Cross are thrilled with Louise. She's a good cook, wonderful with their two daughters, a good housekeeper, and she still finds time to paint, wonderfully. Things start to unravel when Stuart finds himself between jobs. Rather than find a new job, he decides to stay home and write the great American novel. Andie is in full support. Soon he develops writer's block and becomes envious of Louise's skill as a painter. Andie, who is keeping the household afloat with her job, longs to be at home with her daughters. Tensions build until they explode in a surprising conclusion, involving kidnapping and a lucrative book deal.

Where it's reviewed:
Kirkus Reviews, May 15, 2004, page 456
Library Journal, June 15, 2004, page 57
New York Times Book Review, July 18, 2004, page 22
Publishers Weekly, May 3, 2004, page 166

Other books by the same author:
Famous After Death, 1999
The Plagiarist, 1992

Other books you might like:
John Banville, *Athena*, 1995
Ann Beattie, *Chilly Scenes of Winter*, 1976
Saul Bellow, *More Die of Heartbreak*, 1987
Carl Hiaasen, *Tourist Season*, 1986
John Irving, *Setting Free the Bears*, 2003

1085

SUSANNA CLARKE

Jonathan Strange & Mr. Norrell

(New York: Bloomsbury, 2004)

Story type: Historical; Fantasy
Subject(s): Teacher-Student Relationships; Magicians; Fairy Tales
Major character(s): Mr. Norrell, Magician, Wealthy; Jonathan Strange, Scholar, Magician
Time period(s): 1800s
Locale(s): London, England

Summary: Clarke combines history and magic in a debut novel that makes pure fantasy plausible. The premise is that English magicians ruled the ancient world but through time their art was lost or forgotten. In the early 19th century, Mr. Norrell, a wealthy eccentric, sets out to bring back the magic. He compiles the works of the early magicians in a library at his estate and soon succeeds. When Napoleon threatens, Mr. Norrell uses his magic to help England defeat France. Complications develop when he learns of another magician, Jonathan Strange, who also helps the English. Although Mr. Norrell is more advanced, he teams up with Jonathan. However, the two men approach the art from different perspectives and trouble follows. Jonathan is much more interested in the more dangerous rituals than Mr. Norrell.

Where it's reviewed:
Publishers Weekly, July 12, 2004, page 41

Other books you might like:
Mitch Albom, *The Five People You Meet in Heaven*, 2003
Paul Auster, *Mr. Vertigo*, 1994
Catherine Cookson, *Riley*, 1998
Andrew Sean Greer, *The Confessions of Max Tivoli*, 2004
Paul Theroux, *Millroy the Magician*, 1994

1086

PATRICIA CORNWELL

Trace

(New York: Putnam, 2004)

Story type: Mystery
Series: Kay Scarpetta. Book 13
Subject(s): Doctors; Women; Violence
Major character(s): Kay Scarpetta, Consultant, Doctor (forensic pathologist); Joel Marcus, Doctor, Government Official (medical examiner); Gilly Paulsson, Crime Victim, Teenager
Time period(s): 2000s
Locale(s): Richmond, Virginia

Summary: As the story opens, Kay Scarpetta, recently fired from her position as the Virginia state medical examiner, is licking her wounds in Florida. Her replacement, Dr. Joel Marcus, needs help and soon asks Scarpetta to come back. A 14-year-old girl has died and Marcus can't figure out the cause. Scarpetta's usual supporting cast is present to lend her a hand. They include her friend Pete Marino, a former cop, and her niece Lucy Farinelli, a private detective. Then there's Edgar Allen, a man with an abnormal interest in dead bodies. It's another tough case, but Scarpetta is up to the challenge.

Where it's reviewed:
Booklist, August 2004, page 1868
Kirkus Reviews, August 1, 2004, page 715
Library Journal, September 15, 2004, page 48
Publishers Weekly, August 2, 2004, page 50

Other books by the same author:
Blow Fly, 2003
The Last Precinct, 2000
Point of Origin, 1998
Unnatural Exposure, 1997
From Potter's Field, 1995

Other books you might like:
Barbara Taylor Bradford, *The Triumph of Katie Byrne*, 2001
Sandra Brown, *The Crush*, 2002
Sue Grafton, *R Is for Ricochet*, 2004
Lisa Scottoline, *Killer Smile*, 2004
Alice Sebold, *The Lovely Bones*, 2002

1087

BRIDGETT M. DAVIS

Shifting through Neutral

(New York: Amistad, 2004)

Story type: Coming-of-Age
Subject(s): African Americans; Women; Family Relations
Major character(s): Rae Dodson, Narrator; Kimmie, Relative (Rae's half sister)
Time period(s): 1960s; 1970s
Locale(s): Detroit, Michigan

Summary: Rae Dodson, the narrator, grows up in Detroit during the 1960s and 1970s. The Motown sound is everywhere and the automobile factories provide jobs for an African-American middle class. Nevertheless, Rae's household is divided. Her mother's nerves have pushed her father away. Migraine headaches have crippled him and he has taken refuge in the basement. Kimmie, Rae's older half-sister, returns from New Orleans. Heartbreak ensues, but it is tempered by love.

Where it's reviewed:
Booklist, April 15, 2004, page 1423
Publishers Weekly, April 19, 2004, page 39

Other books you might like:
Rainelle Burton, *The Root Worker*, 2001
Stephen L. Carter, *The Emperor of Ocean Park*, 2002
David Anthony Durham, *Gabriel's Story*, 2001
Patricia Jones, *Red on a Rose*, 2001
Omar Tyree, *Flyy Girl*, 1993

1088

JEFFERY DEAVER

Garden of Beasts

(New York: Simon & Schuster, 2004)

Story type: Historical; Psychological Suspense
Subject(s): Crime and Criminals; Murder; Olympic Games
Major character(s): Paul Schumann, Murderer (for hire), Spy; Reinhard Ernst, Government Official (Nazi); Willie Kohl, Police Officer
Time period(s): 1930s (1936)
Locale(s): New York, New York; Berlin, Germany

Summary: In a departure from his very popular Lincoln Rhyme series, Deaver deals here with the 1936 Olympics, held in Nazi Germany's Berlin. The story opens in New York City when Paul Schumann, a German American and mob assassin, is arrested. He is given a choice—face life in prison or take a dangerous secret assignment. If he is successful, Schumann is promised a pardon for his previous crimes. Schumann's mission is to assassinate Adolf Hitler. What fol-

Popular Fiction

lows is a cat and mouse game as the American hitman attempts to track down the Nazi dictator and eliminate him. Although history tells us that Schumann failed, it's a credit to Deaver's imagination and writing talent that he keeps the story interesting.

Where it's reviewed:
Booklist, May 1, 2004, page 1504
Kirkus Reviews, June 1, 2004, page 507
Library Journal, May 15, 2004, page 113
Publishers Weekly, May 3, 2004, page 166

Other books by the same author:
The Stone Monkey, 2002
The Blue Nowhere, 2001
The Empty Chair, 2000
The Devil's Teardrop, 1999
The Coffin Dancer, 1998

Other books you might like:
Len Deighton, *Winter*, 1987
Frederick Forsyth, *The Day of the Jackal*, 1971
Alan Furst, *Dark Voyage*, 2004
James Patterson, *The Thomas Berryman Number*, 1976
Daniel Silva, *The Mark of the Assassin*, 1998

1089

NICHOLAS DELBANCO

The Vagabonds
(New York: Warner, 2004)

Story type: Psychological; Domestic
Subject(s): Brothers and Sisters; Secrets; Inheritance
Major character(s): Joanna Saperstone, Single Parent; Claire Saperstone, Relative (sister of Joanna and David); David Saperstone, Relative (brother of Joanna and Claire)
Time period(s): 2000s; 1910s (1916)
Locale(s): Saratoga Springs, New York

Summary: When Alice Saperstone dies, she leaves each of her three children $500,000.00. The children, Joanna, Claire, and David, are shocked, then determined to find out where the money came from. The story goes back to Alice's mother, Elizabeth, who in her youth meets ''the vagabonds''— Thomas Edison, Henry Firestone, and Henry Ford—at a dinner party. The vagabonds take an annual vacation that is a high point of the social season. When Elizabeth becomes pregnant, the vagabonds put stock in trust for her. Her baby dies, and she later gives birth to Alice, but neither of them ever touches the stock.

Where it's reviewed:
Booklist, October 1, 2004, page 307
Chicago Tribune Books, December 5, 2004, page 3
Kirkus Reviews, September 1, 2004, page 822
Library Journal, October 1, 2004, page 66
Publishers Weekly, November 8, 2004, page 36

Other books by the same author:
What Remains, 2000
Old Scores, 1997
Writers Trade and Other Stories, 1990
Stillness, 1980

Other books you might like:
Reed Arvin, *The Will*, 2000
Anita Brookner, *Undue Influence*, 1999
Carrie Brown, *Confinement*, 2004
F. Scott Fitzgerald, *This Side of Paradise*, 1920
Nadine Gordimer, *The Pickup*, 2001

1090

NELSON DEMILLE

Night Fall
(New York: Warner, 2004)

Story type: Psychological Suspense; Political
Subject(s): Airplane Accidents; Terrorism; Mystery
Major character(s): John Corey, Detective—Police (anti-terrorist unit); Kate Mayfield, FBI Agent (anti-terrorist unit), Spouse (Corey's wife)
Time period(s): 1990s; 2000s (1996-2001)
Locale(s): Long Island, New York

Summary: This is a fictional account of a factual event—TWA Flight 800, which exploded just off Long Island in July 1996. The plane's crew and all 230 passengers died. The story picks up five years later, after a government task force blames mechanical failure for the crash. However, two members of a special anti-terrorist task force, John Corey and Kate Mayfield, don't believe the government's conclusion. A husband and wife team, Corey, a detective, and Mayfield, an FBI agent, set out to uncover the truth. Resolution will depend on a video recording of a couple making illicit love on the beach with what appears to be a large explosion in the background.

Where it's reviewed:
Booklist, September 1, 2004, page 4
Kirkus Reviews, September 15, 2004, page 882
Library Journal, October 1, 2004, page 68
Publishers Weekly, September 20, 2004, page 43

Other books by the same author:
Up Country, 2001
The Lion's Gate, 2000
Plum Island, 1997
The General's Daughter, 1992
The Gold Coast, 1990

Other books you might like:
David Baldacci, *Last Man Standing*, 2001
Richard Barth, *Jumper*, 2000
John Grisham, *The Pelican Brief*, 1992
John Le Carre, *Absolute Friends*, 2003
Daniel Silva, *The Kill Artist*, 2000

1091

STACEY D'ERASMO

A Seahorse Year
(Boston: Houghton Mifflin, 2004)

Story type: Psychological; Gay/Lesbian Fiction
Subject(s): Runaways; Family Problems; Homosexuality/Lesbianism

Major character(s): Christopher, Teenager, Mentally Ill Person; Hal, Parent (Christopher's father), Homosexual; Nan, Parent (Christopher's mother), Lesbian
Time period(s): 2000s
Locale(s): San Francisco, California

Summary: D'Erasmo paints her characters into very tight emotional corners, then steps back to see what will happen. Two gay people, Hal and Nan, who are both confused over their sexuality, meet. Nan wants a child and Hal agrees to father one for her. Their son Christopher is born, and although both are concerned and loving parents, they eventually split up. Nan pairs up with a woman named Marina, but Marina plays around, infuriating Nan. Then Christopher is diagnosed with schizophrenia and disappears at the age of 16. A frantic search for the mentally ill teenager ensues.

Where it's reviewed:
Kirkus Reviews, May 1, 2004, page 409
Library Journal, June 15, 2004, page 57
New York Times Book Review, August 15, 2004, page 18
Publishers Weekly, May 17, 2004, page 33

Other books by the same author:
Tea, 2000

Other books you might like:
Carol Anshaw, *Lucky in the Corner*, 2002
Mark Haddon, *The Curious Incident of the Dog in the Night-Time*, 2003
J.D. Salinger, *The Catcher in the Rye*, 1951
William Trevor, *The Story of Lucy Gault*, 2002
Anne Tyler, *The Amateur Marriage*, 2004

1092

JANET DESAULNIERS

What You've Been Missing

(Iowa City: University of Iowa Press, 2004)

Story type: Collection; Contemporary Realism
Subject(s): Short Stories; Fear; Parent and Child
Time period(s): 2000s
Locale(s): United States

Summary: This debut collection of ten fast-paced short stories won the John Simmons Short Fiction Award. Most of the stories are set in the Midwest and three have been published previously. In ''Where We All Should Have Been,'' a mother worries about her daughter, who likes to get high with men. ''Everyone Is Wearing a Hat'' concerns a mother who mourns after her child has been killed in a hit-and-run accident. ''Who Knows More than You'' examines the relationship between two sisters. A man, who is in love with a younger woman, listens in ''The Good Fight'' as a woman friend complains about being dumped by her husband for a younger woman. Women commiserate with each other about children stolen by estranged mates in ''Mother Without Children.'' ''After Rosa Parks'' deals with the bond between a brother and sister.

Where it's reviewed:
Chicago Tribune Books, October 3, 2004, page 1
Kirkus Reviews, August 15, 2004, page 760
Library Journal, August 2004, page 71

Other books you might like:
Richard Bausch, *Someone to Watch over Me*, 2000
Amy Bloom, *A Blind Man Can See How Much I Love You*, 2001
Robert Olen Butler, *Had a Good Time*, 2004
Gary Fincke, *Sorry I Worried You*, 2004
Bobbie Ann Mason, *Zigzagging Down a Wild Trail*, 2001

1093

ERIC JEROME DICKEY

Drive Me Crazy

(New York: Dutton, 2004)

Story type: Psychological Suspense; Contemporary Realism
Subject(s): Marriage; Interpersonal Relations; Secrets
Major character(s): Driver, Chauffeur, Convict (ex-con); Wolf, Employer (Driver's boss); Lisa, Spouse (Wolf's wife), Lover (Driver's)
Time period(s): 2000s
Locale(s): Los Angeles, California

Summary: Driver is an ex-con with a heart who is trying to go straight. He is gainfully employed as a chauffeur for a man named Wolf and entertains Wolf's wife, Lisa, in bed on the side. Trouble rears its ugly head when Lisa pays Driver $1,500 to kill her husband. He takes the money, but can't bring himself to do the deed. However, Driver can't give the money back either, since he has used it to pay for his mother's funeral. Lisa agrees to forgive the debt if Driver keeps her happy in the bedroom.

Where it's reviewed:
Publishers Weekly, June 28, 2004, page 31

Other books by the same author:
Naughty or Nice, 2003
The Other Woman, 2003
Thieves' Paradise, 2002
Between Lovers, 2001
Liar's Game, 2000

Other books you might like:
Margaret Atwood, *Oryx and Crake*, 2003
Julian Barnes, *Love, etc.*, 2001
Larry Brown, *Father and Son*, 1996
James Lee Burke, *The Lost Get-Back Boogie*, 1987
Austin Clarke, *The Question*, 1999

1094

EMMA DONOGHUE

Life Mask

(Orlando, Florida: Harcourt, 2004)

Story type: Historical; Romance
Subject(s): Interpersonal Relations; Biography; Actors and Actresses
Major character(s): Anne Seymour Damer, Historical Figure, Artist (sculptress); Edward Smith Stanley, Historical Figure, Nobleman (Earl of Derby); Eliza Farren, Historical Figure, Actress
Time period(s): 18th century (1775-1799)

Locale(s): London, England

Summary: Eighteenth-century London is a time and place of excitement and uncertainty, as great fortunes are made in the midst of great threats both natural and man-made. The story revolves around three characters and their relationships. Lord Derby is the richest man in the House of Lords but he is also the ugliest. Actress Eliza Farren is the queen of London theater but she is a commoner. Widow Anne Seymour Damer is a sculptress but she is rumored to be a lesbian. Eliza longs to become part of high society and Derby's courtship offers her an opportunity to achieve her goal. Complications set in when Eliza becomes friends with Anne, and Derby objects.

Where it's reviewed:
Booklist, September 1, 2004, page 60
Chicago Tribune Books, October 10, 2004, page 3
Kirkus Reviews, July 1, 2004, page 592
Library Journal, September 15, 2004, page 48
Publishers Weekly, July 26, 2004, page 38

Other books by the same author:
The Woman Who Gave Birth to Rabbits, 2002
Slammerkin, 2000
We Are Michael Field, 1998
Kissing the Witch, 1997
Hood, 1995

Other books you might like:
Louis Auchincloss, *The Cat and the King*, 1981
Elizabeth Byrd, *Maid of Honour*, 1978
Austin Clarke, *The Question*, 1999
Francine Prose, *Primitive People*, 1992
Nora Roberts, *Divine Evil*, 1992

1095

MARGARET DRABBLE

The Red Queen
(Orlando, Florida: Harcourt, 2004)

Story type: Psychological
Subject(s): Books and Reading; Grief; Women
Major character(s): Barbara Halliwell, Scholar; Hyegyong, Royalty (crown princess); Dr. Oo, Scholar
Time period(s): 2000s; 18th century
Locale(s): Oxford, England; Seoul, Korea, South

Summary: The story switches back and forth between modern times and the distant past, shifting from a modern day English scholar to an 18th-century Korean crown princess. On the eve of a conference in Korea, Barbara Halliwell anonymously receives the Crown Princess Hyegyong's memoir. Barbara reads the book on the flight to Seoul. The princess lived when women ruled only through men, which didn't stop her. She manipulated and outlived all the men in her life, and survived numerous palace plots. Barbara's own experience has parallels to that of the princess. When Barbara arrives in Korea, a mysterious Dr. Oo acts as a tour guide, taking her to places familiar to the princess. Barbara has an affair with another scholar. Her experience becomes very intense and Barbara almost comes apart mentally.

Where it's reviewed:
Booklist, September 1, 2004, page 4

Kirkus Reviews, August 15, 2004, page 761
Library Journal, September 1, 2004, page 138
New York Times Book Review, October 10, 2004, page 15
Publishers Weekly, September 6, 2004, page 44

Other books by the same author:
The Seven Sisters, 2002
The Peppered Moth, 2001
The Witch of Exmoor, 1996
The Middle Ground, 1980
Ice Age, 1977

Other books you might like:
Elizabeth Berg, *Durable Goods*, 1993
Catherine Bush, *The Rules of Engagement*, 2000
Nora Okja Keller, *Fox Girl*, 2002
A.L. Kennedy, *Indelible Acts*, 2003
Chang-rae Lee, *Aloft*, 2004

1096

SARAH DUNN

The Big Love
(New York: Little, Brown, 2004)

Story type: Humor; Romance
Subject(s): Relationships; Women; Dating (Social Customs)
Major character(s): Alison Hopkins, Journalist (newspaper columnist); Tom, Boyfriend (Alison's ex), Lover (Kate's); Kate Pearce, Lover (Tom's)
Time period(s): 2000s
Locale(s): Philadelphia, Pennsylvania

Summary: Dunn presents a story about how a good girl gets on with her life when her boyfriend dumps her for another woman. When Alison Hopkins throws a party, she sends her live-in boyfriend Tom to the store for some last minute items. He never comes back. Instead, he calls to say he's leaving Alison for another woman. Although Tom's not really the love of her life, he's better than no one and Alison is knocked for a loop. While others might seek refuge in alcohol, drugs, or sex, Alison can't do that because she is a good girl whose strict upbringing would never allow her to do such things. Besides, such personal vices cost money, which she can't afford. As a struggling columnist on a near bankrupt newspaper, Alison can barely make ends meet. No, she must find her own way in the world of the desperately single. On the journey, she finds that words of wisdom laced with large amounts of humor can be a big help.

Where it's reviewed:
New York Times, June 25, 2004, page B35
Publishers Weekly, May 10, 2004, page 34

Other books you might like:
Cheryl Benard, *Turning on the Girls*, 2001
Thomas Berger, *Best Friends*, 2003
Helen Fielding, *Bridget Jones's Diary*, 1996
Fannie Flagg, *Standing in the Rainbow*, 2002
Karen Joy Fowler, *The Jane Austen Book Club*, 2004

1097
TONY EPRILE

The Persistence of Memory
(New York: Norton, 2004)

Story type: Coming-of-Age; Satire
Subject(s): Biography; Jews; Africa
Major character(s): Paul Sweetbread, Military Personnel; Lyddie, Military Personnel (captain)
Time period(s): 1980s
Locale(s): South Africa; Angola; Zambia

Summary: Memory, unlike history, which is a record of the past, can be independent from winners and losers. This is the situation facing Eprile's main character Paul Sweetbread, when he is called before South Africa's Truth and Reconciliation Commission. Paul was not a very good student at the university. Growing up as a fat boy, he wasn't popular. This didn't change when he joined the army. However, everything changed when he was assigned to a movie crew that filmed the secret war in Nambia and Angola. Some army actions Paul's crew captured on film now appear to be morally questionable if not outright criminal. When the film becomes public, Paul's superior officers question his sanity in an attempt to discredit him.

Where it's reviewed:
Kirkus Reviews, April 1, 2004, page 285
Library Journal, May 15, 2004, page 114
New York Times, July 30, 2004, page B36
Publishers Weekly, June 21, 2004, page 45

Other books by the same author:
Temporary Sojourner, 1989

Other books you might like:
Sybille Bedford, *A Legacy*, 1957
Anita Brookner, *Family and Friends*, 1985
E.L. Doctorow, *The Book of Daniel*, 1971
Jeffrey Eugenides, *The Virgin Suicides*, 1993
John Updike, *Seek My Face*, 2002

1098
JANET EVANOVICH

Metro Girl
(New York: HarperCollins, 2004)

Story type: Mystery; Psychological Suspense
Subject(s): Murder; Missing Persons; Brothers and Sisters
Major character(s): Alexandra Barnaby, Mechanic (former), Young Woman (Wild Bill's sister); William "Wild Bill" Barnaby, Sailor; Sam Hooker, Sports Figure (NASCAR driver)
Time period(s): 2000s
Locale(s): Miami, Florida; Key West, Florida; Cuba

Summary: Janet Evanovich, veteran writer of the Stephanie Plum series, tries her hand at something different. An action-thriller, it features a brother and sister team of Wild Bill Barnaby and Alex Barnaby, his older sister. Ever since he was a child, Wild Bill has put action before thinking, mainly because Alex has always been around to bail him out. This

time Wild Bill may have gone too far. He has "borrowed" his friend Sam Hooker's yacht and disappeared into the Gulf of Mexico. Alex suspects foul play and heads to Miami to get to the bottom of things. Sam attaches himself to Alex, figuring she will lead him to his missing boat. The search for Bill ends up involving a group of Evanovich's customary colorful characters, Cuban politics, missing gold, and a possible weapon of mass destruction.

Where it's reviewed:
Booklist, November 1, 2004, page 443
Publishers Weekly, November 8, 2004, page 36

Other books by the same author:
Ten Big Ones, 2004
To the Nines, 2003
Visions of Sugar Plums, 2002
Seven Up, 2001
Four to Score, 1998

Other books you might like:
Sue Grafton, *R Is for Ricochet*, 2004
Dennis Lehane, *Prayers for Rain*, 1999
Laura Lippman, *The Last Place*, 2002
Sara Paretsky, *Windy City Blues*, 1995
Julie Smith, *Louisiana Hotshot*, 2001

1099
JANET EVANOVICH

Ten Big Ones
(New York: St. Martin's Press, 2004)

Story type: Mystery; Contemporary Realism
Series: Stephanie Plum. Book 10
Subject(s): Women; Murder; Family
Major character(s): Stephanie Plum, Bounty Hunter; Joe Morelli, Police Officer, Boyfriend (Stephanie's); Carlos "Ranger" Manoso, Bounty Hunter
Time period(s): 2000s
Locale(s): Trenton, New Jersey

Summary: New readers and fans will be delighted that Stephanie Plum, bond enforcer or bounty hunter, depending on one's point of view, returns with another adventure on the streets of Trenton, New Jersey. A cast of unforgettable characters, including ex-hooker Lula and ace bounty hunter Ranger, is back with our heroine. Stephanie's on-again, off-again lover, Joe Morelli, is there, too. The story revolves around a gang-style robbery, which Stephanie happens to witness. This becomes a problem for the robbery's mastermind and he takes it upon himself to eliminate Stephanie. Not to worry, how could Stephanie lose? She's got her grandmother in her corner.

Where it's reviewed:
Library Journal, June 1, 2004, page 107
New York Times Book Review, June 27, 2004, page 21
Publishers Weekly, June 7, 2004, page 35

Other books by the same author:
Full Speed, 2003
Full Tilt, 2003
To the Nines, 2003 (Stephanie Plum. Book 9)
Hard Eight, 2002 (Stephanie Plum. Book 8)

Popular Fiction

Visions of Sugar Plums, 2002 (Christmas fantasy novella featuring Stephanie Plum)

Other books you might like:
James Lee Burke, *In the Electric Mist with Confederate Dead*, 1993
Harlan Coben, *Dropshot*, 1996
Jeffery Deaver, *The Empty Chair*, 2000
Elmore Leonard, *Pagan Babies*, 2000
Robert B. Parker, *Family Honor*, 1999

1100
PERCIVAL EVERETT

Damned If I Do
(St. Paul, Minnesota: Graywolf, 2004)

Story type: Collection
Subject(s): Short Stories; Humor; Racial Conflict
Time period(s): 2000s
Locale(s): United States

Summary: Everett's second collection of 12 short stories, which are set in the South and West, offers a satirical look at the human condition especially when it comes to issues of race and prejudice. In ''Alluvial Deposits,'' a rude rancher refuses to cooperate with a black government expert. A fisherman gets marriage counseling from a talking fish in ''Epigenesis.'' A young black musician causes quite a stir when he buys a pickup truck with a Confederate flag on it in ''The Appropriation of Cultures.'' Everett also provides a host of eccentric characters, including Chicken Lady, a man in ''True Romance;'' an escaped patient from a mental institution; and a character calming a horse with a flashlight in ''Afraid of the Dark.'' The stories are insightful and humorous, despite the seriousness of their subject.

Where it's reviewed:
Booklist, October 15, 2004, page 389
Library Journal, November 15, 2004, page 53
Publishers Weekly, October 25, 2004, page 27

Other books by the same author:
My Existing Condition, 2004
Erasure, 2001
Grand Canyon, Inc., 2001
Watershed, 1996
Cutting Lisa, 1986

Other books you might like:
James Lee Burke, *Half of Paradise*, 1965
Pete Dexter, *Train*, 2003
Eric Jerome Dickey, *Thieves' Paradise*, 2002
Jack Fuller, *The Best of Jackson Payne*, 2000
E. Lynn Harris, *Any Way the Wind Blows*, 2001

1101
MICHEL FABER

The Courage Consort
(Orlando, Florida: Harcourt, 2004)

Story type: Collection; Psychological
Subject(s): Twins; Archaeology; Singing

Summary: This is the first American edition of three novellas, although two of them were previously published in Scotland. The title novella revolves around a singing group practicing in a remote castle. The tension is very high as the group tries to master a very difficult new piece. After perfecting it, a sudden death prevents them from performing. In *The Hundred and Ninety-Nine Steps* an archaeologist meets an attractive man while working at a site to uncover evidence of an ancient murder. Subsequently, she incorporates clues from the site into dreams that someone is murdering her. The final novella, *The Fahrenheit Twins* is about fraternal twins living in the Arctic with their parents. When their mother dies suddenly, the brother and sister take her corpse into the wilderness. Their journey becomes an odyssey of self-discovery.

Where it's reviewed:
Booklist, September 1, 2004, page 60
Kirkus Reviews, September 1, 2004, page 824
Library Journal, September 1, 2004, page 144
New York Times, October 25, 2004, page B6
Publishers Weekly, August 23, 2004, page 35

Other books by the same author:
The Crimson Petal and the White, 2002
The Hundred and Ninety-Nine Steps, 2001
Some Rain Must Fall, 2000
Under the Skin, 2000

Other books you might like:
Jeffrey Archer, *Sons of Fortune*, 2003
Edward Carey, *Alva & Irva*, 2003
Lisa Carey, *In the Country of the Young*, 2000
Zakes Mda, *She Plays with the Darkness*, 1995
Joanna Trollope, *A Spanish Lover*, 1997

1102
JON FASMAN

The Geographer's Library
(New York: Penguin, 2004)

Story type: Mystery
Subject(s): Authorship; Journalism; Murder
Major character(s): Paul Tomm, Journalist (reporter)
Time period(s): 2000s
Locale(s): Lincoln, Connecticut

Summary: Fasman's debut novel is a mystery story with an academic spin. Paul Tomm, a middle-aged cub reporter for a local newspaper, really gets into an assignment writing an obituary, a chore most journalists regard as mundane. As it turns out, Tomm's assignment unfolds into a very large story. A local professor has been found dead in his home. In most jurisdictions, this makes it a coroner's case since local authorities want to make sure no foul play is involved. Subsequently, the coroner in charge of the investigation is killed in a hit-and-run traffic accident. Also, the call reporting the good professor's death was anonymous and was made from a pay phone. The narrative switches back and forth between the murder investigation and a robbery at the home of the king's geographer, which occurred in the year 1154.

Where it's reviewed:
Booklist, November 15, 2004, page 553

Library Journal, November 15, 2004, page 49

Other books you might like:
Barbara Taylor Bradford, *Dangerous to Know*, 1995
Michael Connelly, *The Poet*, 1996
John Grisham, *The Pelican Brief*, 1992
Carl Hiaasen, *Basket Case*, 2002
Joseph Kanon, *The Good German*, 2001

1103

KATIE FFORDE

Paradise Fields
(New York: St. Martin's Press, 2004)

Story type: Romance; Contemporary/Mainstream
Subject(s): Widows/Widowers; Inheritance; Single Parent Families
Major character(s): Nel Innes, Widow(er), Parent (three children); Jake Demerand, Lawyer; Fleur Innes, Teenager (Nel's daughter)
Time period(s): 2000s
Locale(s): Cotswold Hills, England

Summary: After her husband dies, Nel raises three children alone. Although she remains unattached, she is very active in the town's civic and charitable affairs, particularly a farmer's market. Her life is satisfying and secure, but things are about to change, a little too quickly for Nel's taste. Her daughter Fleur is now a teenager with a mind of her own. Sir Gerald, owner of the land on which the farmer's market stands, dies and his son, Pierce, plans to develop the property. Nel also develops a crush on Jake, Pierce's solicitor. Things don't look promising, but Nel is nothing if not resilient.

Where it's reviewed:
Booklist, November 1, 2004, page 462
Kirkus Reviews, October 1, 2004, page 930
Library Journal, October 15, 2004, page 53
Publishers Weekly, November 8, 2004, page 35

Other books by the same author:
Artistic License, 2002
Highland Fling, 2002
Life Skills, 1999
Stately Pursuits, 1998
Wild Designs, 1997

Other books you might like:
Elizabeth Berg, *Open House*, 2000
Judy Blume, *Smart Women*, 1983
Barbara Delinsky, *The Vineyard*, 2000
Chitra Banerjee Divakaruni, *The Vine of Desire*, 2002
Sarah Dunant, *Mapping the Edge*, 1999

1104

HELEN FIELDING

Olivia Joules and the Overactive Imagination
(New York: Viking, 2004)

Story type: Contemporary/Mainstream; Humor

Subject(s): Women; Spies; Terrorism
Major character(s): Olivia Joules, Journalist (freelance); Pierre Feramo, Spy
Time period(s): 2000s
Locale(s): London, England; Miami, Florida

Summary: Some consider Helen Fielding's character Bridget Jones to be the one who got the ball rolling with chick lit, stories featuring young, urban, professional, single women looking for happiness and fulfillment in the modern era. Here Fielding takes a quantum leap from that genre, or maybe just gives it a quick makeover with an Ian Fleming touch (think James Bond). Rachel Pixley changes her name to Olivia Joules and has a promising career as a London journalist. Then, she gets demoted to the ho-hum style pages. On assignment in Miami, she uncovers a terrorist plot and embarks on a round-the-world adventure. She deals with kidnappings, bomb plots, serial killers, and scuba diving, all of which lead to her recruitment by MI6 (the English counterpart to the CIA).

Where it's reviewed:
New York Times Book Review, June 20, 2004, page 9
Newsweek, June 14, 2004, page 59
Publishers Weekly, June 7, 2004, page 31

Other books by the same author:
Cause Celeb, 2001
Bridget Jones: The Edge of Reason, 1999
Bridget Jones's Diary, 1996

Other books you might like:
Dave Barry, *Tricky Business*, 2002
Tristan Egolf, *Skirt and Fiddle*, 2002
Dorothy Gilman, *The Amazing Mrs. Pollifax*, 1970
Mabel Maney, *Kiss the Girls and Make Them Spy*, 2001
Tim Parks, *Mimi's Ghost*, 2001

1105

FANNIE FLAGG

A Redbird Christmas
(New York: Random House, 2004)

Story type: Inspirational; Americana
Subject(s): City and Town Life; Christmas; Illness
Major character(s): Oswald T. Campbell, Orphan, Patient (emphysema); Jack, Animal (cardinal); Patsy Casey, Child (abandoned), Handicapped (crippled)
Time period(s): 2000s
Locale(s): Lost River, Alabama; Chicago, Illinois

Summary: Flagg weaves the magic of Christmas into a story about a dying man, a crippled child, and a pet bird. After a doctor tells Oswald Campbell that he has a year to live, he leaves Chicago for a small town in Alabama to spend his last Christmas. There he finds a cast of eccentric characters, including Roy Grimmit, a macho storekeeper, who hand feeds a sick cardinal named Jack, known locally as a redbird. Jack is popular and loved by the town's residents, especially by young Patsy Casey, a disabled orphan. As the story unfolds, Oswald settles in and the spirit of Christmas takes over.

Where it's reviewed:
Booklist, October 1, 2004, page 282

Kirkus Reviews, October 1, 2004, page 939
Library Journal, November 1, 2004, page 72
Publishers Weekly, September 27, 2004, page 35

Other books by the same author:
Standing in the Rainbow, 2002
Welcome to the World Baby Girl, 1998
Daisy Fay and the Miracle Man, 1992
Fried Green Tomatoes at the Whistle-Stop Cafe, 1987
Coming Attractions, 1981

Other books you might like:
David Baldacci, *The Christmas Train*, 2002
Jude Deveraux, *The Blessing*, 1998
John Grisham, *Skipping Christmas*, 2001
Jan Karon, *The Mitford Snowmen*, 2001
Jill McCorkle, *Carolina Moon*, 1996

1106

SUSAN FLETCHER

Eve Green

(New York: Norton, 2004)

Story type: Domestic; Coming-of-Age
Subject(s): Friendship; Women; Missing Persons
Major character(s): Eve Green, Young Woman, Orphan; Billy Macklin, Recluse; Daniel, Worker (hired hand)
Time period(s): 2000s
Locale(s): Cae Tresaint, Wales

Summary: This debut novel takes place in a small Welsh village and is told from the perspective of a young woman reminiscing about her life. After her mother dies suddenly, Eve comes to the village as an orphan to live with her grandparents on the family farm. At first, things are difficult but Eve soon adjusts to farm life. Some of the edges are smoothed by Daniel, a hired hand, and Billy, a large gentle giant, who is shunned by local villagers. Eve eventually learns the circumstances surrounding her father's desertion of her mother. An added twist concerns the disappearance and presumed abduction of young Rosie Hughes.

Where it's reviewed:
Chicago Tribune Books, October 10, 2004, page 1
Kirkus Reviews, July 1, 2004, page 593
Library Journal, August 2004, page 66
Publishers Weekly, July 26, 2004, page 37

Other books you might like:
Bridgett M. Davis, *Shifting through Neutral*, 2004
Carol Goodman, *The Seduction of Water*, 2003
Sue Monk Kidd, *The Secret Life of Bees*, 2002
Margot Livesey, *Eva Moves the Furniture*, 2001
Daniel Wallace, *The Watermelon King*, 2003

1107

MARIA FLOOK

Lux

(New York: Little, Brown, 2004)

Story type: Humor; Mystery
Subject(s): Relationships; Murder; Nature

Major character(s): Alden Warren, Worker (for park service), Spouse (of missing husband); Lux Davis, Murderer, Landscaper
Time period(s): 2000s
Locale(s): Cape Cod, Massachusetts

Summary: Flook draws on her background as a true crime writer in a gritty realistic story that revolves around a murder in Cape Cod. Alden, a young woman, who works for the park service, has been dealing with bouts of depression for two years, ever since her husband Monty disappeared without a trace. Although a good teacher, authorities take his disappearance with a grain of salt because of his reputation for chasing women. In fact, Alden herself is having an affair with a married man. However, things really get complicated when Lux Davis shows up and begins courting Alden. Lux has a secret that will affect their future relationship.

Where it's reviewed:
Booklist, October 1, 2004, page 310
Kirkus Reviews, September 1, 2004, page 824
Library Journal, October 1, 2004, page 68
Publishers Weekly, September 6, 2004, page 44

Other books by the same author:
You Have the Wrong Man, 1996
Open Water, 1994
Family Night, 1993

Other books you might like:
Martin Amis, *The Rachel Papers*, 1973
John Berger, *Corker's Freedom*, 1964
Mary Higgins Clark, *The Lottery Winner*, 1994
Elizabeth McCracken, *The Giant's House*, 1996
Marge Piercy, *Summer People*, 1989

1108

VINCE FLYNN

Memorial Day

(New York: Atria, 2004)

Story type: Psychological Suspense; Political
Series: Mitch Rapp. Book 5
Subject(s): Terrorism; Veterans; Spies
Major character(s): Mitch Rapp, Spy (counterterrorist)
Time period(s): 2000s (2004)
Locale(s): Washington, District of Columbia; Afghanistan; Pakistan

Summary: In Flynn's thriller, the main character, Mitch Rapp, is out to protect the world from terrorism. The story opens in Washington, D.C., a week before Memorial Day and the dedication of the World War II memorial. When the CIA learns about a terrorist plot to attack the United States, Rapp is given the job of stopping them. From then on, it's off to the races as Rapp heads to Afghanistan. He picks up a commando unit and they attack a terrorist camp in Pakistan. The raid gives them the necessary information to foil the terrorist plot. The action is non-stop; the results are predictable, but the fun is in getting there.

Where it's reviewed:
Publishers Weekly, May 10, 2004, page 35

Other books by the same author:
Executive Power, 2003
Separation of Power, 2001
Third Option, 2000
Transfer of Power, 1999

Other books you might like:
Molly Cochran, *Third Magic*, 2003
Nelson DeMille, *The Lion's Game*, 2000
Ken Follett, *Hammer of Eden*, 1998
Jack Higgins, *Drink with the Devil*, 1996
John Le Carre, *The Little Drummer Girl*, 1983

1109

ELIZABETH FRANK

Cheat and Charmer
(New York: Random House, 2004)

Story type: Historical; Domestic
Subject(s): Relationships; Family Saga; Infidelity
Major character(s): Dinah Lasker, Spouse (Jake's wife); Jake Lasker, Director, Producer; Genevieve ''Veevi'' Milligan, Actress, Relative (Dinah's sister)
Time period(s): 20th century (1935-1955)
Locale(s): Hollywood, California; Paris, France

Summary: Frank, an accomplished writer of non-fiction, tries her hand at fiction with a family saga that delves beyond Hollywood glamour and examines social and political forces that influenced the movie industry during the 20th century. In the works for 25 years, the novel opens amid the tumultuous 1930s social upheaval. Dinah and her younger sister Veevi dabble in radical politics. Veevi, a successful, beautiful actress, marries a Communist film director and moves to Paris. Meanwhile, Dinah marries Jake Lasker, who also becomes a successful film director and they enjoy a comfortable Hollywood lifestyle. After World War II, when a fervent wave of anti-Communism sweeps across the country, the U.S. Congress convenes hearings to investigate alleged communist activities in Hollywood. Dinah is called to testify about Communists she knew. If she refuses, her husband will be blacklisted and banned from working in the film industry. Dinah testifies and names Veevi. Subsequently, Veevi gets dumped by her second husband and moves back to the U.S. However, Veevi's career as an actress is over thanks to Dinah's testimony.

Where it's reviewed:
Booklist, September 1, 2004, page 5
Kirkus Reviews, August 15, 2004, page 762
Library Journal, September 1, 2004, page 139
New York Times Book Review, November 14, 2004, page 52
Publishers Weekly, August 16, 2004, page 40

Other books you might like:
Joan Didion, *Play It as It Lays*, 1970
John Gregory Dunne, *Playland*, 1994
F. Scott Fitzgerald, *The Last Tycoon*, 1941
William Goldman, *Tinsel*, 1979
Jerry Stahl, *I, Fatty*, 2004

1110

ALAN FURST

Dark Voyage
(New York: Random House, 2004)

Story type: Historical/World War II
Subject(s): Refugees; War; Spies
Major character(s): Eric DeHaan, Sea Captain, Spy
Time period(s): 1940s (1941)
Locale(s): Lisbon, Portugal

Summary: In 1941, England is at war with the Axis Powers and German U-boats have sunk more than 1,500 merchant ships during the last year. The Royal Navy and British Intelligence (also known as spy services) are charged with stemming the tide. This is the backdrop as the *Santa Rosa*, a tramp freighter, steams into Lisbon, Portugal. Although flying neutral Spain's flag en route to pick up cooking oil and sardines for delivery to a Baltic port, the ship is in the employ of the British and is really picking up spy equipment to be used in a secret mission off the coast of Sweden. This is a desperate battle for survival. If the British don't stop the U-boats from sinking their merchant ships, Germany will win the war. Although the outcome isn't in doubt now, it's a tribute to Furst that he keeps up the suspense in the retelling of events from the perspective of those who lived them.

Where it's reviewed:
Booklist, July 2004, page 1798
Kirkus Reviews, July 1, 2004, page 594
Library Journal, July 2004, page 69
New York Times Book Review, August 15, 2004, page 7
Publishers Weekly, July 19, 2004, page 143

Other books by the same author:
Blood of Victory, 2002
Kingdom of Shadows, 2001
Red Gold, 1999
The World at Night, 1996
The Polish Officer, 1995

Other books you might like:
Ken Follett, *The Key to Rebecca*, 1980
Jack Higgins, *The Eagle Has Landed*, 1975
Greg Iles, *Black Cross*, 1995
John Le Carre, *Absolute Friends*, 2003
Robert Ludlum, *The Bourne Identity*, 1980

1111

LISA GLATT

A Girl Becomes a Comma Like That
(New York: Simon & Schuster, 2004)

Story type: Contemporary/Mainstream
Subject(s): Mothers and Daughters; Aging; Modern Life
Major character(s): Rachel Spark, Professor (poetry); Ella Bloom, Clerk (at an abortion clinic); Georgia Carter, Teenager
Time period(s): 2000s
Locale(s): Los Angeles, California

Summary: Rachel Sparks is a single, thirty-something professional woman who teaches poetry. She has been looking for love, without success, since she lost her virginity at age 13. When her mother is stricken with breast cancer, Rachel moves back home to help out. While facing up to her mother's mortality, Rachel distracts herself by bedding a steady stream of men and predictably, she gets pregnant. She visits an abortion clinic where Ella, one of her students, works. Ella, recently married, is concerned about her husband's fidelity. Teenager Georgia, a frequent visitor to the women's clinic, possesses copious amounts of street smarts but she comes up short when it comes to boys. Through it all, Rachel's mother provides comic relief and a good example of how not to be overwhelmed by life or death.

Where it's reviewed:
Kirkus Reviews, April 15, 2004, page 348
Publishers Weekly, April 5, 2004, page 34

Other books by the same author:
Shelter, 2000
Monsters and Other Lovers, 1996

Other books you might like:
James Kelman, *You Have to Be Careful in the Land of the Free*, 2004
Chang-rae Lee, *Aloft*, 2004
George Minot, *The Blue Bowl*, 2004
Rohinton Mistry, *Family Matters*, 2001
Alice Randall, *Pushkin and the Queen of Spades*, 2004

1112

MARY GORDON

Pearl

(New York: Pantheon, 2004)

Story type: Psychological; Domestic
Subject(s): Students, Foreign; Mothers and Daughters; Political Movements
Major character(s): Maria Meyers, Parent (Pearl's mother); Pearl Meyers, Student—College (studying in Ireland); Joseph, Friend (of Maria)
Time period(s): 2000s
Locale(s): New York, New York; Dublin, Ireland

Summary: Maria Meyers is raised a devout Catholic, the daughter of a Jewish father who converted. As she grows up in the 1960s, Maria largely abandons her faith. Now, her life is turned upside down when she gets a call from the State Department concerning her daughter, Pearl. Pearl is supposedly studying linguistics abroad, but Maria is informed that Pearl has chained herself to a flagpole in front of the U.S. Embassy in Dublin. She is also on a hunger strike, and in danger of dying. Maria is forced to reexamine her own life as she works to save her daughter.

Where it's reviewed:
Booklist, October 1, 2004, page 282
Kirkus Reviews, October 15, 2004, page 977
Library Journal, October 15, 2004, page 53
Publishers Weekly, October 18, 2004, page 45

Other books by the same author:
Spending, 1998

The Other Side, 1989
Men and Angels, 1985
The Company of Women, 1980
Final Payments, 1978

Other books you might like:
Susan Choi, *American Woman*, 2003
Jack Higgins, *A Prayer for Dying*, 1973
Patrick McCabe, *Call Me the Breeze*, 2003
Julie Parsons, *Eager to Please*, 2000
William Trevor, *The Story of Lucy Gault*, 2002

1113

KRISTIN GORE

Sammy's Hill

(New York: Miramax, 2004)

Story type: Political; Humor
Subject(s): Women; Relationships; Modern Life
Major character(s): Samantha Joyce, Assistant (to Senator Gary); Robert Gary, Political Figure (senator); Aaron Driver, Assistant (to Senator Bramer), Boyfriend (Sammy's)
Time period(s): 2000s
Locale(s): Washington, District of Columbia

Summary: This tongue-in-cheek debut novel, written by former Vice President Al Gore's daughter, follows an idealistic young woman working in Washington, D.C. Sammy, who works on Ohio Senator Robert Gary's staff, is responsible for crafting reform health care legislation. When Senator Gary collaborates with New Jersey Senator John Bramer, romance develops between Sammy and Aaron, a Bramer staff worker. Complications set in when Sammy accidentally sends out a blanket e-mail about her romance with Aaron. The e-mail soon gets into the hands of the press and a minor scandal develops.

Where it's reviewed:
Booklist, August 2004, page 1871
Kirkus Reviews, July 1, 2004, page 595
Library Journal, August 2004, page 67
New York Times Book Review, September 12, 2004, page 23
Publishers Weekly, July 12, 2004, page 42

Other books you might like:
Anonymous, *Primary Colors*, 1996
Sarah Dunn, *The Big Love*, 2004
Helen Fielding, *Bridget Jones's Diary*, 1996
Jeff Greenfield, *The People's Choice*, 1995
Mario Vargas Llosa, *The Feast of the Goat*, 2001

1114

SUE GRAFTON

R Is for Ricochet

(New York: Putnam, 2004)

Story type: Contemporary; Mystery
Series: Kinsey Millhone. Book 18
Subject(s): Crime and Criminals; Sexual Behavior; Women

Major character(s): Kinsey Millhone, Detective—Private; Reba Lafferty, Convict (newly paroled), Socialite; Alan Beckwith, Businessman
Time period(s): 2000s
Locale(s): California

Summary: Grafton hasn't quite run out of letters of the alphabet and Kinsey Millhone hasn't run out of energy from dodging bullets and catching evil doers. The story revolves around socialite Reba Lafferty, who has just been paroled from prison. Confined to her home, Reba's parole calls for her to avoid her sinful ways by walking the straight and narrow. However, her appetite seems limitless and the odds of her staying away from booze, gambling, and illicit sex appear remote. When Reba's former love interest runs afoul of the feds, she enlists Kinsey's help to get the goods on him. Complications set in, thanks to the high-strung Reba, but Kinsey comes through in the end.

Where it's reviewed:
Kirkus Reviews, June 1, 2004, page 519
Library Journal, July 2004, page 64
Publishers Weekly, June 14, 2004, page 47

Other books by the same author:
Q Is for Quarry, 2002
P Is for Peril, 2001
O Is for Outlaw, 1999
N Is for Noose, 1998
M Is for Malice, 1996

Other books you might like:
Michael Connelly, *The Narrows*, 2004
Patricia Cornwell, *Blow Fly*, 2003
Stephen King, *The Green Mile*, 1997
Dennis Lehane, *Mystic River*, 2001
Scott Turow, *Reversible Errors*, 2002

1115

JENNIFER HAIGH

Baker Towers

(New York: William Morrow, 2005)

Story type: Historical; Domestic
Subject(s): Social Classes; Miners and Mining; Small Town Life
Major character(s): Rose Novak, Parent (of five), Widow(er); Georgie Novak, Veteran (of World War II); Lucy Novak, Relative (Georgie's sister)
Time period(s): 1940s; 1950s
Locale(s): Bakerton, Pennsylvania

Summary: In her novel, Haigh takes a hard look at a working class life in a mining town in Pennsylvania just after World War II. Rose Novak becomes a single parent when her husband dies in a mining accident. Although Rose is Italian, she lives in a company-owned house in the Polish section because her husband was Polish. Raising five children by herself is not easy. None of her children are interested in mining, but getting out is a challenge. Her oldest son Georgie succeeds when he finds a wealthy wife. However, Rose's daughters aren't as lucky. After a breakdown, Dorothy leaves a job in the nation's capitol and returns home. When Rose's health

begins to fail, Joyce comes home to care for her. Lucy, the youngest, goes off to college but would rather be home with her family and friends.

Where it's reviewed:
Booklist, November 1, 2004, page 464
Kirkus Reviews, September 15, 2004, page 883
Library Journal, December 1, 2004, page 100
New York Times, January 13, 2005, page B10
Publishers Weekly, November 22, 2004, page 38

Other books by the same author:
Mrs. Kimble, 2003 (2003 Pen/Hemingway Award winner)

Other books you might like:
Larry Brown, *Joe*, 1991
William Kennedy, *Roscoe*, 2002
D.H. Lawrence, *Women in Love*, 1920
Richard Russo, *Nobody's Fool*, 1993
Martin Cruz Smith, *Rose*, 1996

1116

LAURELL K. HAMILTON

Incubus Dreams

(New York: Berkley, 2004)

Story type: Mystery; Horror
Series: Anita Blake, Vampire Hunter. Book 9
Subject(s): Serial Killers; Vampires; Fantasy
Major character(s): Anita Blake, Vampire Hunter; Jean-Claude, Vampire (master of the city); Richard Zeeman, Werewolf
Time period(s): 2000s
Locale(s): St. Louis, Missouri

Summary: A gang of vampire serial killers is murdering women who work in local striptease clubs. Vampire hunter Anita Blake, whose power comes from sex, which gives her the energy that fuels her physical and psychic powers, will need all her strength to bring the murderous vampires to justice. Along the way, she will need help from her current boyfriend Jean-Claude, the city's master vampire; her ex-boyfriend Richard, a werewolf chieftain; and Micah, king of the wereleopards.

Where it's reviewed:
Kirkus Reviews, September 1, 2004, page 825
Library Journal, October 1, 2004, page 69

Other books by the same author:
Circus of the Damned, 2004
Cerulean Sins, 2003
A Caress of Twilight, 2002
Narcissus in Chains, 2001
Guilty Pleasures, 1993

Other books you might like:
Ray Bradbury, *From the Dust Returned*, 2001
Stephen King, *The Dark Tower*, 2004
Dean R. Koontz, *Odd Thomas*, 2003
James Patterson, *Violets Are Blue*, 2001
Anne Rice, *Interview with the Vampire*, 1976

Popular Fiction

1117

MIMI HARE
CLARE NAYLOR, Co-Author

The Second Assistant

(New York: Viking, 2004)

Story type: Coming-of-Age; Contemporary
Subject(s): Women; Movie Industry; Satire
Major character(s): Elizabeth Miller, Agent (for talent agency); Scott Wagner, Agent (Liz's boss)
Time period(s): 2000s
Locale(s): Hollywood, California

Summary: This novel explores the notion that politics and show business are very similar. Elizabeth Miller works in Washington, D.C., as an aide to a prominent U.S. senator. When an offer to join a high-powered talent agency in Hollywood comes up, Elizabeth jumps at the chance. Complications set in almost immediately because she doesn't have a scorecard on the various movie stars, directors, producers, and other power moguls in Tinsel Town. Of course, it doesn't help that her supervisor has several addictions, including sex and drugs. The story gives an insider's view of the behind-the-scenes machinery that makes Hollywood, well, Hollywood.

Where it's reviewed:
Booklist, March 1, 2004, page 1101
Kirkus Reviews, March 15, 2004, page 247
Publishers Weekly, March 8, 2004, page 45

Other books you might like:
Robert Coover, *The Adventures of Lucky Pierre*, 2002
Carrie Fisher, *Postcards from the Edge*, 1987
William Goldman, *Tinsel*, 1979
Emma McLaughlin, *The Nanny Diaries*, 2002
    Nicola Kraus, co-author
Lauren Weisberger, *The Devil Wears Prada*, 2003

1118

JOHN HARWOOD

The Ghost Writer

(Orlando, Florida: Harcourt, 2004)

Story type: Gothic; Psychological
Subject(s): Mothers and Sons; Death; Authorship
Major character(s): Gerard Freeman, Librarian, Young Man (Alice's pen pal); Alice Jessel, Young Woman (English), Handicapped (wheelchair-bound)
Time period(s): 19th century; 20th century
Locale(s): Mawson, Australia; London, England

Summary: Family secrets and adolescent fantasies, with a little help from the spirit world, drive this debut novel. Gerard and Alice have been pen pals for years—he lives in Australia and she lives in England. He would like a conventional relationship but she is confined to a wheelchair and refuses to meet him. Meanwhile, he finds some ghost short stories written by his great-grandmother. He reads the stories and begins to unravel a web of family secrets that show connections between his family and Alice. His grandmother's stories suggest knowledge of events before they happen, and the stories also predict tragedy for Gerard, which he sets out to avoid.

Where it's reviewed:
Chicago Tribune Books, August 8, 2004, page 7
Kirkus Reviews, May 1, 2004, page 413
Library Journal, July 2004, page 70
Publishers Weekly, June 7, 2004, page 30

Other books you might like:
John Banville, *Eclipse*, 2001
Clive Barker, *Coldheart Canyon*, 2001
Lisa Carey, *In the Country of the Young*, 2000
Stephen King, *Bag of Bones*, 1998
Stewart O'Nan, *The Night Country*, 2003

1119

MARK HELPRIN

The Pacific and Other Stories

(New York: Penguin, 2004)

Story type: Collection
Subject(s): Short Stories; Good and Evil; Grief

Summary: There are 16 short stories in this collection by Helprin. When the manager of an opera company in ''Il Colore Ritrovato'' hears an amateur singer with talent, he hesitates. Would the singer be able to handle success? In ''Monday,'' a contractor considers sacrificing other commitments in order to help a woman whose husband was killed when the World Trade Center was attacked on September 11th. In ''Perfection,'' an orthodox Jewish boy goes to Yankee Stadium intent on saving Mickey Mantle. A rancher's unrequited love for his neighbor's wife blooms in ''Passchendaele.'' Love is also dealt with in ''Last Tea with the Armorers'' and ''Prelude.'' The other stories are: ''A Brilliant Idea and His Own,'' ''Vandevere's House,'' ''Sidney Balbion,'' ''Mar Nueva,'' ''Rain,'' ''Jacob Bayer and the Telephone,'' ''Sail Shining in White,'' ''Charlotte of the Utrechtseweg,'' and ''The Pacific.''

Where it's reviewed:
Booklist, October 1, 2004, page 312
Kirkus Reviews, August 15, 2004, page 764
Library Journal, September 1, 2004, page 145
New York Times, November 1, 2004, page E8
Publishers Weekly, August 23, 2004, page 36

Other books by the same author:
A Soldier of the Great War, 1991
Winter's Tale, 1983
Ellis Island and Other Stories, 1981
Refiner's Fire, 1977
A Dove of the East, 1975

Other books you might like:
Michel Faber, *The Courage Consort*, 2004
Yann Martel, *The Facts Behind the Helsinki Roccamatios*, 2004
Alice Munro, *Runaway*, 2004
Annie Proulx, *Bad Dirt*, 2004
Neal Stephenson, *Quicksilver*, 2003

1120

CARL HIAASEN

Skinny Dip

(New York: Knopf, 2004)

Story type: Contemporary
Subject(s): Revenge; Marriage; Crime and Criminals
Major character(s): Chaz Perrone, Scientist (marine biologist); Joey Perrone, Spouse (Chaz's wife); Mick Stranahan, Police Officer (ex-cop)
Time period(s): 2000s
Locale(s): Miami, Florida

Summary: Hiaasen has a knack for writing about the horrible things people do without making them seem horrible. Here Chaz Perrone, a misguided marine biologist, has a scheme that will allow an evil businessman to continue polluting the Everglades. When Chaz's wife finds out about the scheme, she threatens to stop it, so Chaz tosses her off a luxury cruise ship in the middle of the Atlantic. Unfortunately for Chaz, she doesn't die. Instead she is rescued by ex-cop Mick Stranahan. From then on Chaz and the evil man are doomed, as his wife and her new friend make plans to save the Everglades and to get revenge.

Where it's reviewed:
Kirkus Reviews, May 15, 2004, page 460
Library Journal, June 1, 2004, page 122
New York Times, July 12, 2004, page E1
Publishers Weekly, May 10, 2004, page 34

Other books by the same author:
Basket Case, 2002
Sick Puppy, 2000
Lucky You, 1997
Strip Tease, 1993
Tourist Season, 1986

Other books you might like:
Margaret Atwood, *The Robber Bride*, 1993
Susan Coll, *Karlmarx.com*, 2001
Richard Condon, *Prizzi's Money*, 1994
John Gregory Dunne, *Playland*, 1994
Ken Wells, *Junior's Leg*, 2001

1121

JACK HIGGINS

Dark Justice

(New York: Putnam, 2004)

Story type: Psychological Suspense; Political
Series: Sean Dillon. Book 13
Subject(s): Terrorism; Spies; Violence
Major character(s): Charles Ferguson, Military Personnel (general); Sean Dillon, Criminal (assassin); Josef Belov, Government Official
Time period(s): 2000s
Locale(s): United States; Ireland

Summary: Higgins here tackles the topic du jour, counterterrorism, as Gen. Charles Ferguson, leader of Britain's Private Army, matches wits with some shadowy characters from the Middle East. The story jump-starts when Ferguson learns of a plot to assassinate the president of the United States. From then on, it's off to the races as Ferguson enlists the services of IRA hit man Sean Dillon and an associate of Vladimir Putin. With Ferguson on the job, the action is fierce and the terrorists don't have a chance.

Where it's reviewed:
Publishers Weekly, July 26, 2004, page 40

Other books by the same author:
Bad Company, 2003
Midnight Runner, 2002
Edge of Danger, 2001
Day of Reckoning, 2000
Pay the Devil, 1999

Other books you might like:
Eric Ambler, *Doctor Frigo*, 1974
Ted Bell, *Assassin*, 2004
Tom Clancy, *Red Rabbit*, 2002
Adam Hall, *The Quiller Memorandum*, 1965
John Le Carre, *Call for the Dead*, 1961

1122

ALAN HOLLINGHURST

The Line of Beauty

(New York: Bloomsbury, 2004)

Story type: Coming-of-Age; Domestic
Subject(s): Friendship; Social Classes; Homosexuality/Lesbianism
Major character(s): Nick Guest, Homosexual, Student—College (at Oxford); Gerald Feddens, Political Figure; Toby Feddens, Friend (of Nick), Relative (Gerald's son)
Time period(s): 1980s (1983-1987)
Locale(s): London, England (Notting Hill)

Summary: Hollinghurst takes a hard look at class nuance and class differences in 1980s England when Margaret Thatcher was prime minister. Nick Guest, a gay student, takes a summer room in the mansion of an Oxford classmate, Toby Feddens. Toby's father Gerald is a member of parliament and a minister in the Thatcher government. Nick, who has a crush on the straight Toby, becomes fast friends with his sister Catherine, which gives him free rein in the household and access into the drug and alcohol use of this upper-class family. Subsequently, Nick has affairs with a black clerk and an Lebanese millionaire. Then public scandal overtakes Gerald and Nick gets entangled, too.

Where it's reviewed:
Booklist, October 15, 2004, page 389
Kirkus Reviews, August 15, 2004, page 765
New York Times Book Review, October 31, 2004, page 19
Publishers Weekly, September 20, 2004, page 51

Other books by the same author:
The Spell, 1998
The Folding Star, 1994
The Swimming Pool Library, 1988

Other books you might like:
Louis Auchincloss, *Manhattan Monologues*, 2002

Popular Fiction

Patricia Highsmith, *The Talented Mr. Ripley*, 1955
Khaled Hosseini, *The Kite Runner*, 2003
David Leavitt, *Martin Bauman*, 2000
Jamie O'Neill, *At Swim, Two Boys*, 2001

1123

MAUREEN HOWARD

The Silver Screen
(New York: Viking, 2004)

Story type: Psychological
Subject(s): Marriage; Women; Movie Industry
Major character(s): Isabel Maher, Actress (silent films); Rita Maher, Relative (Isabel's daughter); Joseph Maher, Religious (a priest), Relative (Isabel's son)
Time period(s): 2000s
Locale(s): Providence, Rhode Island

Summary: Isabel Maher, a silent film star, abandoned Hollywood when technology enabled movie makers to add sound tracks. Then, she moved east and slipped into a conventional life with a husband and two children. When Isabel dies, her loved ones, a daughter, a son, and a best friend, must reevaluate the choices they face. Rita, her daughter, abruptly disappears when the mobster she married is taken into the witness protection program. Her son, Joseph, a Jesuit priest who suffers from the horrors of war, retreats to a boarding house, and moves in with Gemma, a neighbor who in their youth lived next door.

Where it's reviewed:
Kirkus Reviews, June 1, 2004, page 510
Library Journal, June 15, 2004, page 58
Publishers Weekly, May 17, 2004, page 31

Other books by the same author:
Big as Life, 2001
A Lover's Almanac, 1998
Natural History, 1992
Expensive Habits, 1986
Bridgeport Bus, 1965

Other books you might like:
John Gregory Dunne, *Playland*, 1994
Clifford Irving, *Tom Mix and Pancho Villa*, 1982
John Jakes, *American Dreams*, 1998
Joyce Carol Oates, *Blonde*, 2000
Jerry Stahl, *I, Fatty*, 2004

1124

SUSAN ISAACS

Any Place I Hang My Hat
(New York: Scribner, 2004)

Story type: Political; Domestic
Subject(s): Mothers and Daughters; Campaigns, Political; Journalism
Major character(s): Amy Lincoln, Journalist; Freddy Carrasco, Student—College, Bastard Son
Time period(s): 2000s
Locale(s): New York, New York

Summary: Amy Lincoln is a hard-nosed journalist working for a weekly news magazine. Although she possesses Ivy League degrees from Harvard and Columbia, Amy came up the hard way. She was abandoned by her mother shortly after her father was sent to prison. Raised by a quirky grandmother, who ardently practiced shoplifting, Amy was rescued by a scholarship to a boarding school. She's been able to keep her early life from intruding, but now that's about to change. While covering the presidential campaign, Amy meets a college student claiming to be the illegitimate son of a presidential candidate. As she sets out to find the truth of the student's claim, she begins to search for her mother.

Where it's reviewed:
Booklist, July 2004, page 1799
Kirkus Reviews, August 15, 2004, page 765
Library Journal, September 1, 2004, page 140
New York Times Book Review, October 24, 2004, page 23
Publishers Weekly, August 2, 2004, page 49

Other books by the same author:
Long Time No See, 2001
Red, White, and Blue, 1998
Lily White, 1996
Shining Through, 1988
Compromising Positions, 1978

Other books you might like:
Margaret Atwood, *Bodily Harm*, 1981
Sandra Brown, *Standoff*, 2000
Joan Didion, *The Last Thing He Wanted*, 1996
Margaret Drabble, *The Middle Ground*, 1980
Kristin Gore, *Sammy's Hill*, 2004

1125

J.A. JANCE

Day of the Dead
(New York: William Morrow, 2004)

Story type: Mystery; Contemporary
Subject(s): Indians of North America; Police Procedural; Murder
Major character(s): Brandon Walker, Police Officer (ex-sheriff); Emma Orozco, Indian, Parent (Roseanne's mother); Roseanne Orozco, Crime Victim (murdered)
Time period(s): 2000s
Locale(s): Southwest

Summary: Ex-sheriff Brandon Walker, protagonist of some of Jance's earlier novels, sets out to solve the murder of Roseanne Orozco whose body was dismembered and left alongside a road. He takes the case at the request of her mother Emma, an old Indian woman. Brandon is a member of The Last Chance Club, a privately funded ad hoc agency that investigates unsolved crimes. In the course of his investigation, Brandon uncovers several similar unsolved crimes, which are the handiwork of an evil couple, Larry and Gayle Stryker. Although not Native American himself, Brandon's adopted daughter is, as are many of his friends, and Native American mythology and wisdom play a large part in the story.

Where it's reviewed:
Publishers Weekly, April 12, 2004, page 34

Other books by the same author:
Exit Wounds, 2003
Partner in Crime, 2002
Birds of Prey, 2001
Devil's Claw, 2000
Outlaw Mountain, 2000

Other books you might like:
Nevada Barr, *Hunting Season*, 2002
Tony Hillerman, *The Sinister Pig*, 2003
Phillip Margolin, *Wild Justice*, 2000
Craig Nova, *Cruisers*, 2004
Danielle Steel, *Ransom*, 2004

1126

GISH JEN

The Love Wife
(New York: Knopf, 2004)

Story type: Contemporary; Ethnic
Subject(s): Chinese Americans; Interracial Marriage; Assimilation
Major character(s): Carnegie Wong, Spouse (Janie's husband); Janie Wong, Spouse (Carnegie's wife); Lan Lin, Relative (Carnegie's), Child-Care Giver
Time period(s): 2000s
Locale(s): United States

Summary: An interracial marriage, cultural differences, and parental interference are just some of the things covered in Gish Jen's work. When Carnegie marries Janie, Mama Wong doesn't approve. She wants Carnegie to marry a Chinese girl, if for no other reason than to respect his heritage. Of course, as a second generation American, Carnegie doesn't see it that way. However, he doesn't completely turn his back on his mother's wishes. When the couple has trouble having children, they adopt two Chinese girls. When Mama dies, her will has provisions for a distant relative to come to the United States to care for Carnegie's children as a nanny. Then, Janie has a child, too, leading to some interesting complications.

Where it's reviewed:
Booklist, July 2004, page 1799
Kirkus Reviews, July 1, 2004, page 598
Library Journal, July 2004, page 70
New York Times, September 7, 2004, page B1
Publishers Weekly, July 26, 2004, page 35

Other books by the same author:
Who's Irish?, 1999
Mona in the Promised Land, 1996
Typical American, 1991

Other books you might like:
Chang-rae Lee, *Aloft*, 2004
Kate Manning, *Whitegirl*, 2002
Zadie Smith, *White Teeth*, 2000
Amy Tan, *The Bonesetter's Daughter*, 2001
Anne Tyler, *Back When We Were Grownups*, 2001

1127

LIZ JENSEN

The Ninth Life of Louis Drax
(New York: Tin House/Bloomsbury, 2004)

Story type: Domestic; Psychological
Subject(s): Accidents; Hospitals; Doctors
Major character(s): Louis Drax, Child, Patient (in a coma); Pascal Dannachet, Doctor (runs clinic); Pierre Drax, Parent (Louis' father)
Time period(s): 2000s
Locale(s): Provence, France

Summary: For his first eight years, Louis Drax has had an annual life-threatening accident. He's like a cat with nine lives. Then, while at picnic in his ninth year, Louis falls off of a cliff. The question is did he fall or was he pushed? Louis survives but he is in a coma. Although his father disappears, his mother takes him to Dr. Dannachet, who runs a clinic for coma patients where a doctor attempts to revive Louis. However, it's a harder task than one might think: Louis doesn't want to be revived. In his comatose state, he has found a friend, who has welcomed him to his ninth life. Louis reveals his reasons for not wanting to come back.

Where it's reviewed:
Booklist, November 15, 2004, page 561
Kirkus Reviews, November 1, 2004, page 1025
Publishers Weekly, November 8, 2004, page 34

Other books by the same author:
War Crimes for the Home, 2002
Ark Baby, 1998
Egg Dancing, 1996

Other books you might like:
Robin Cook, *Coma*, 1977
Mark Haddon, *The Curious Incident of the Dog in the Night-Time*, 2003
Chuck Palahniuk, *Diary*, 2003
Alice Sebold, *The Lovely Bones*, 2002
Tim Winton, *That Eye, the Sky*, 2002

1128

HA JIN

War Trash
(New York: Pantheon, 2004)

Story type: Historical
Subject(s): Korean War; Chinese; Prisoners of War
Major character(s): Yu Yuan, Military Personnel (Chinese officer), Prisoner (of war)
Time period(s): 1950s (1950-1953)
Locale(s): Korea, South

Summary: This work is a novel in the form of a memoir written by a Chinese officer captured by the Americans during the Korean War. The officer, Yu Yuan, serves in a Red Chinese army unit sent to Korea at the time when United Nations forces, led by Americans, are able to turn the tide against the North Koreans, who had invaded South Korea. Yu describes his struggle to maintain his human dignity as a prisoner of war, while remaining loyal to himself and his country.

Where it's reviewed:
Booklist, August 2004, page 1872
Kirkus Reviews, August 15, 2004, page 763
Library Journal, August 2004, page 67
New York Times Book Review, October 10, 2004, page 1
Publishers Weekly, August 2, 2004, page 49

Other books by the same author:
The Crazed, 2002
The Bridegroom, 2000 (National Book Award winner)
Waiting, 1999
Under the Red Flag, 1997
Ocean of Words, 1996

Other books you might like:
Frederick Busch, *War Babies*, 1989
Margaret Drabble, *The Red Queen*, 2004
Xingjian Gao, *Soul Mountain*, 2000
Nora Okja Keller, *Fox Girl*, 2002
James A. Michener, *The Bridges at Toko-Ri*, 1953

1129

SETH KANTNER

Ordinary Wolves

(Minneapolis: Milkweed Editions, 2004)

Story type: Coming-of-Age; Psychological
Subject(s): Wilderness; Eskimos; Grief
Major character(s): Abe Hawcly, Parent (Cutuk's father), Artist; Cutuk Hawcly, Relative (Jerry's younger brother); Jerry Hawcly, Relative (Abe's son)
Time period(s): 2000s
Locale(s): Alaska

Summary: When Abe Hawcly decides to go native, he moves his wife and three children to a sod hut in Alaska. While his family survives from hunting and fishing, Abe paints. Soon after, his wife becomes disillusioned, leaving Abe and the children. Jerry, the oldest boy, decides to live in Fairbanks; while Iris leaves for college and then becomes a teacher. Cutuk, the youngest son, grows up learning to hunt and fish from local Native Americans. He loves and respects the wilderness, where he decides to make his life, eschewing the confusion of the city.

Where it's reviewed:
Kirkus Reviews, April 15, 2004, page 350
Library Journal, March 15, 2004, page 106
Publishers Weekly, May 3, 2004, page 170

Other books you might like:
Rick Bass, *Where the Sea Used to Be*, 1998
Sallie Bissell, *A Darker Justice*, 2002
Nicholas Evans, *The Smoke Jumper*, 2001
Jim Harrison, *True North*, 2004
Annie Proulx, *That Old Ace in the Hole*, 2002

1130

THOMAS KENEALLY

The Tyrant's Novel

(New York: Nan A. Talese, 2004)

Story type: Political
Subject(s): Dictators; Authors and Writers; Political Prisoners
Major character(s): Alan Sheriff, Refugee, Writer (novelist)
Time period(s): Indeterminate Future
Locale(s): United States

Summary: Keneally, who is known for taking historical events and making them into unforgettable novels, offers a story based upon recent events in a thinly disguised Saddam Hussein-era Iraq. In a detention camp of an unnamed country, a man is interviewed about his past life. He tells of being a successful writer with a wonderful life. Then, one day the country's dictator summons him and orders him to ghostwrite a novel, which the dictator will put his name on. The subject of the novel is pure fantasy. The object of the novel is to encourage the world to remove economic sanctions from the dictator's country. To do this, the novel must convince readers that the dictator is not a ruthless tyrant but a visionary who is being unjustly persecuted by his enemies.

Where it's reviewed:
New York Times, June 17, 2004, page B1
Publishers Weekly, May 24, 2004, page 42

Other books by the same author:
The Office of Innocence, 2003
Bettany's Book, 2000
A River Town, 1995
Jacko, 1994
Schindler's List, 1982

Other books you might like:
Margaret Atwood, *The Blind Assassin*, 2000
Paul Auster, *Oracle Night*, 2003
Sandra Brown, *Envy*, 2001
Percival Everett, *Erasure*, 2001
Arthur Koestler, *Darkness at Noon*, 1941

1131

STEPHEN KING

Song of Susannah

(New York: Simon & Schuster, 2004)

Story type: Gothic; Contemporary
Series: Dark Tower. Book 6
Subject(s): Horror; Suspense; Supernatural
Major character(s): Mia, Demon; Susannah Dean, Young Woman; Eddie Dean, Addict, Spouse (Susannah's husband)
Time period(s): 1990s (1999); 1970s (1977)
Locale(s): New York, New York; Maine

Summary: In 1999, Susannah Dean has been impregnated and taken to New York City. The boy in Susannah's womb was placed there by the spirit Mia, who intends for the boy to kill the gunslinger Roland Deschain. Roland and Susannah's husband, Eddie Dean, fell into an ambush in 1977 in New

England. Meanwhile, Father Don Callahan and Jake Chambers, 11, continue to search for Stephen King. Callahan, readers will remember, was the priest in *Salems' Lot*. The goal is to either destroy or save the Dark Tower, depending on the character's disposition. Of course, this all makes perfect sense to fans who are familiar with the time-space continuum King uses and how his characters travel back and forth.

Where it's reviewed:
Booklist, May 1, 2004, page 1483
Kirkus Reviews, May 1, 2004, page 406
Library Journal, May 15, 2004, page 115
Publishers Weekly, April 19, 2004, page 37

Other books by the same author:
Everything's Eventual, 2002
From a Buick 8, 2002
Black House, 2001
Dreamcatcher, 2001
The Girl Who Loved Tom Gordon, 1999

Other books you might like:
Eric Bogosian, *The Mall*, 2000
Dean R. Koontz, *The Taking*, 2004
Ira Levin, *Rosemary's Baby*, 1967
Chuck Palahniuk, *Lullaby*, 2002
Omar Tyree, *Leslie*, 2002

1132

SOPHIE KINSELLA

Shopaholic and Sister
(New York: Dial, 2004)

Story type: Humor
Series: Becky Bloomwood. Book 4
Subject(s): Marriage; Sisters; Shopping
Major character(s): Becky Brandon, Spouse (of Luke); Luke Brandon, Spouse (of Becky)
Time period(s): 2000s
Locale(s): London, England

Summary: Becky returns to London from a globe-trotting shopping spree with her new husband, Luke, in tow. Luke is shocked when two trucks show up shortly afterwards—all full of Becky's purchases. Then Becky finds out she has a previously unknown sister, Jessica, the result of a fling her father had in the 1970s. Becky can hardly wait to bond with her, but Jessica turns out to be an environmentalist who distains conspicuous consumption. Luke becomes preoccupied with work and a stranger shows up with murky intentions. A satisfactory resolution is pretty much a given, but the real fun is getting there.

Where it's reviewed:
Booklist, September 15, 2004, page 208
Kirkus Reviews, August 1, 2004, page 707
Library Journal, September 15, 2004, page 49
Publishers Weekly, August 30, 2004, page 32

Other books by the same author:
Can You Keep a Secret?, 2004
Shopaholic Ties the Knot, 2003
Shopaholic Takes Manhattan, 2002
Confessions of a Shopaholic, 2001

Other books you might like:
Jennifer Crusie, *Welcome to Temptation*, 2000
Nick Hornby, *How to Be Good*, 2001
Elinor Lipman, *The Ladies' Man*, 1999
Jeanne Ray, *Step-Ball-Change*, 2002
Jennifer Weiner, *In Her Shoes*, 2002

1133

JAYNE ANN KRENTZ

Falling Awake
(New York: Putnam, 2004)

Story type: Romantic Suspense
Subject(s): Dreams and Nightmares; Sleep; Crime and Criminals
Major character(s): Isabel Wright, Researcher (sleep analyst); Randolph Belvedere, Businessman (Isabel's boss); Ellis Cutler, Businessman (venture capitalist)
Time period(s): 2000s
Locale(s): California

Summary: Isabel Wright works for a sleep research laboratory as a sleep analyst and she uses her expertise to analyze dreams and interpret them. Her abilities are developed to the point where she can solve crimes and other problems just by sleeping. When the owner of the sleep research lab turns up murdered, his son takes over. Isabel soon runs afoul of her new boss and is fired. She then sets out to become a motivational speaker. As it turns out, the lab begins to flounder because her skills brought in most of the lab's revenue. Her interest in Ellis Cutler and his dreams develops into a romantic interest.

Where it's reviewed:
Booklist, October 1, 2004, page 283
Kirkus Reviews, September 15, 2004, page 884
Library Journal, October 15, 2004, page 54
Publishers Weekly, October 11, 2004, page 55

Other books by the same author:
Truth or Dare, 2003
Lost and Found, 2001
Dawn in Eclipse Bay, 2000
Eye of the Beholder, 1999
Flash, 1998

Other books you might like:
Stephen J. Cannell, *The Viking Funeral*, 2002
Michael Crichton, *Prey*, 2002
Linda Howard, *White Lies*, 1988
Margaret Truman, *Murder in Havana*, 2001
Marianne Wiggins, *Evidence of Things Unseen*, 2003

1134

NEIL LABUTE

Seconds of Pleasure
(New York: Grove, 2004)

Story type: Contemporary Realism; Collection
Subject(s): Relationships; Short Stories
Time period(s): 2000s

Locale(s): United States

Summary: Although he is a successful playwright and film-maker, this is LaBute's debut collection. There are 20 stories dealing with subjects both edgy and dark, including pleasure, humiliation, cruelty, regret, guilt, and insight. A wife discovers infidelity in "Time Share." In "Opportunity," a woman is haunted by her sister's disappearance. A husband makes his wife's blemish in "Perfect" take center stage, while in "Maraschino," a man wonders about the identity of a woman in bed with him. A screen test for a prostitute is described in "Ravishing" and a man is obsessed with a sore on a woman's leg in "Boo Boo." At an airport a married man enjoys a passing flirtation in "Layover," while a flight attendant serves the wife of her lover in "Whitecap." A car stalls outside a strip club in "Helping Hand" and a woman mechanic puts a condescending customer in his place in "Full Service."

Where it's reviewed:
Booklist, August 2004, page 1899
Kirkus Reviews, August 1, 2004, page 707
Library Journal, September 1, 2004, page 145
New York Times, October 25, 2004, page B6
Publishers Weekly, June 28, 2004, page 29

Other books you might like:
Julian Barnes, *Love, etc.*, 2001
John Biguenet, *The Torturer's Apprentice*, 2001
Ruth Prawer Jhabvala, *My Nine Lives*, 2004
Penelope Lively, *The Photograph*, 2003
Chuck Palahniuk, *Choke*, 2001

1135

DON LEE

Country of Origin
(New York: Norton, 2004)

Story type: Mystery; Multicultural
Subject(s): Police Procedural; Sexual Behavior; Missing Persons
Major character(s): Lisa Countryman, Student—Graduate; Tom Hurley, Diplomat (U.S. Embassy); Kenzo Ota, Police Officer (inspector)
Time period(s): 1980s
Locale(s): Tokyo, Japan

Summary: Set in Tokyo, the story follows a police investigation into the disappearance of an American graduate student, Lisa Countryman, who is half-Japanese and half-black. While working on her dissertation, Countryman had been employed as a hostess at a men's night club. When Inspector Kenzo Ota, receives the case, he conducts an energetic investigation with an eye toward salvaging his stalled career. The inquiry reveals Countryman's efforts to uncover her family heritage. The author uses the threads of the story to examine race, personal identity as filtered through social conventions, and the sex trade.

Where it's reviewed:
Library Journal, February 1, 2004, page 124
Publishers Weekly, April 12, 2004, page 34

Other books by the same author:
Yellow, 2001

Other books you might like:
Sara Backer, *American Fuji*, 2001
John Burdett, *Bangkok 8*, 2003
Graham Greene, *Honorary Consul*, 1973
Julie Parsons, *Mary, Mary*, 1998
Martin Cruz Smith, *December 6*, 2002

1136

JEFF LINDSAY

Darkly Dreaming Dexter
(New York: Doubleday, 2004)

Story type: Psychological Suspense; Contemporary
Subject(s): Murder; Secrets; Serial Killers
Major character(s): Dexter Morgan, Scientist, Serial Killer
Time period(s): 2000s
Locale(s): Miami, Florida

Summary: Dexter Morgan has a special talent for profiling criminals. However, unlike the stereotype of the tortured, sensitive man who is kept awake nights by the knowledge of what evil men do and how the legal system is often at odds to address it, Dexter is undisturbed. One might say he's a man of action; he rids society of those who might slip between the cracks, or one might call him a sociopathic serial killer with some redeeming qualities. For a while, thanks to Dexter, the world is a very orderly place. This all changes when someone begins to copy Dexter. Now, he must set out to bring to justice someone who is not only as cunning as he is, but someone who is equally crazy.

Where it's reviewed:
Kirkus Reviews, June 1, 2004, page 511
Library Journal, June 15, 2004, page 59
Publishers Weekly, April 19, 2004, page 36

Other books by the same author:
Tropical Depression, 1994

Other books you might like:
Jeffery Deaver, *The Bone Collector*, 1997
Bret Easton Ellis, *American Psycho*, 1991
Thomas Harris, *The Silence of the Lambs*, 1988
Edna O'Brien, *In the Forest*, 2002
James Patterson, *Cat & Mouse*, 1997

1137

MARGOT LIVESEY

Banishing Verona
(New York: Henry Holt, 2004)

Story type: Domestic; Romance
Subject(s): Radio Broadcasting; Pregnancy; Family Problems
Major character(s): Zeke Cafarelli, Carpenter; Verona Mac-Intyre, Radio Personality
Time period(s): 2000s
Locale(s): London, England; Boston, Massachusetts; New York, New York

Summary: Romance, mystery, class differences, and suspense are key features in this story about an older woman and a younger man. The story opens in London where Zeke, 29, is a tradesman and Verona, 37, is a successful radio personality. He is quite handsome, while she is single and seven months pregnant. After meeting coincidentally at a building he is working on, they fall madly in love but she leaves for Boston. Each has family concerns: Verona's brother is involved in some shady financial dealings and Zeke's family is pressuring him to take over the family business. Zeke follows Verona to Boston, but the path of true love is not without its twists and turns.

Where it's reviewed:
Booklist, September 1, 2004, page 6
Kirkus Reviews, September 15, 2004, page 885
Library Journal, October 1, 2004, page 71
New York Times Book Review, December 5, 2004, page 80
Publishers Weekly, August 30, 2004, page 29

Other books by the same author:
Eva Moves the Furniture, 2001
The Missing World, 2000
Criminals, 1996
Homework, 1990
Learning by Heart, 1986

Other books you might like:
Betsy Berne, *Bad Timing*, 2001
Ethan Hawke, *Ash Wednesday*, 2002
Mary Lawson, *Crow Lake*, 2002
Jennifer Weiner, *In Her Shoes*, 2002
Daniel Woodrell, *The Death of Sweet Mister*, 2001

1138

DAVID LODGE

Author, Author
(New York: Viking, 2004)

Story type: Historical; Literary
Subject(s): Biography; Authors and Writers; Writing
Major character(s): Henry James, Historical Figure, Writer; George Du Maurier, Historical Figure, Artist; Constance Fenimore Woolson, Historical Figure, Writer
Time period(s): 19th century; 20th century
Locale(s): London, England

Summary: This is a fictionalized biography of Henry James, the great American writer, who spent most of his life in England. The story focuses on James' personal relationships, especially with his friend George Du Maurier, an English magazine artist, and Constance Fenimore Woolson, an American writer. Although James is now regarded as a literary giant, this wasn't always so. In the late 19th century, James feels that he is a failure at writing novels and decides to become a playwright. He does this in consultation with Du Maurier, who himself decides to try his hand at writing. In one of history's ironies, Du Maurier's effort produces *Trilby*, which is thought by many to be the novel of the century, while, James' stage play, *Guy Domville*, is considered a failure, forcing James to resume his work as a novelist.

Where it's reviewed:
Booklist, September 15, 2004, page 179
Kirkus Reviews, July 15, 2004, page 651
New York Times Book Review, October 10, 2004, page 30
Publishers Weekly, August 30, 2004, page 29

Other books by the same author:
Thinks, 2001
Home Truths, 2000
Therapy, 1995
Paradise News, 1991
Nice Work, 1989

Other books you might like:
Leonore Fleischer, *Shadowlands*, 1993
Henry James, *The Wings of the Dove*, 1902
Brian Morton, *A Window Across the River*, 2003
Emma Tennant, *Sylvia and Ted*, 2001
Colm Toibin, *The Master*, 2004

1139

TAKASHI MATSUOKA

Autumn Bridge
(New York: Delacorte, 2004)

Story type: Psychological; Historical
Subject(s): Lovers; Women; Missionaries
Major character(s): Lord Genji, Nobleman, Warlord; Emily Gibson, Religious
Time period(s): 19th century
Locale(s): Japan

Summary: Modernization runs up against fierce resistance in mid-19th-century Japan in Matsuoka's family saga as Lord Genji struggles to prepare his country for the 20th century. Genji's affair with Emily Gibson, a Western missionary, provides him with strength, but they must keep it secret or risk giving his enemies the means to destroy him. While she translates the clan's history from ancient scrolls dating back to the 14th century, Emily is astounded to find Genji's ancestors making specific references to her existence years before her parents were born. It seems Genji has inherited his visionary skills, which show him the future without the ability to alter it.

Where it's reviewed:
Chicago Tribune Books, August 8, 2004, page 2
Kirkus Reviews, June 1, 2004, page 511
Publishers Weekly, July 19, 2004, page 144

Other books by the same author:
Cloud of Sparrows, 2002

Other books you might like:
Sarah Dunant, *Transgressions*, 1998
C.S. Forester, *The African Queen*, 1935
Ellen Gilchrist, *Annunciation*, 1983
James A. Michener, *Sayonara*, 1954
Martin Cruz Smith, *December 6*, 2002

Popular Fiction

1140

MARGARET MAZZANTINI

Don't Move

(New York: Nan A. Talese/Doubleday, 2004)

Story type: Contemporary Realism; Romance
Subject(s): Sexual Behavior; Accidents; Infidelity
Major character(s): Angela, Accident Victim, Relative (Timoteo's daughter); Timoteo, Doctor, Lover (of Italia); Italia, Young Woman, Impoverished
Time period(s): 2000s
Locale(s): Italy

Summary: Mazzantini's second novel (the first one hasn't been translated into English) deals with parental guilt, eroticism, and sexual behavior. The story opens when a young woman riding a motor scooter collides with a car. Angela, the young woman, is transported to a hospital where she lies in a coma, and her father Timoteo, a prominent doctor, tries desperately to communicate with her. During this one-sided conversation, he confesses to a love affair that began with a rape and ended poorly. While on the way to meet Elsa, his wife and Angela's mother, Timoteo meets Italia, a lower-class woman. She's not beautiful like his wife but he's enthralled by her earthiness and can't or won't control himself. Subsequently, he's torn between his stable upper-class existence with Elsa and his obsession with Italia. Translated from the Italian by John Cullen.

Where it's reviewed:
Kirkus Reviews, April 1, 2004, page 290
Library Journal, May 1, 2004, page 141
New York Times Book Review, July 4, 2004, page 16
Publishers Weekly, April 12, 2004, page 38

Other books you might like:
John Fowles, *Mantissa*, 1982
David Galef, *Flesh*, 1995
Erica Jong, *Fear of Flying*, 1973
D.H. Lawrence, *Lady Chatterly's Lover*, 1928
Claire Tristram, *After*, 2004

1141

ALEXANDER MCCALL SMITH

The Sunday Philosophy Club

(New York: Pantheon, 2004)

Story type: Mystery
Subject(s): Women; Journalism; Ethics
Major character(s): Isabel Dalhousie, Philosopher, Editor (ethics journal); Mark Fraser, Stock Broker; Grace, Housekeeper (Isabel's)
Time period(s): 2000s
Locale(s): Edinburgh, Scotland

Summary: McCall Smith, author of the Botswana based No. 1 Ladies' Detective Agency series, tries his hand at a new series. Set in Edinburgh, Scotland, the heroine is Isabel Dalhousie, a philosopher and editor of a prestigious journal, *Review of Applied Ethics*. The story revolves around an alleged suicide at the local concert hall. Mark Fraser, a stock broker, dies when he falls from a balcony. Isabel witnesses Fraser's death and feels morally obligated to investigate because she was the last person he saw. As in the previous series, McCall Smith uses plot as a device to introduce a cast of delightful characters.

Where it's reviewed:
Booklist, August 2004, page 1872
Kirkus Reviews, August 1, 2004, page 717
Library Journal, August 2004, page 62
Publishers Weekly, August 2, 2004, page 51

Other books by the same author:
The Full Cupboard of Life, 2003
The Kalahari Typing School for Men, 2002
Morality for Beautiful Girls, 2001
The No. 1 Ladies' Detective Agency, 1998

Other books you might like:
Peter Carey, *My Life as a Fake*, 2003
Yann Martel, *Life of Pi*, 2001
Jessica Shattuck, *The Hazards of Good Breeding*, 2003
Muriel Spark, *A Far Cry from Kensington*, 1988
Danielle Steel, *Second Chance*, 2004

1142

CHARLES MCCARRY

Old Boys

(New York: Overlook, 2004)

Story type: Political; Contemporary
Series: Paul Christopher
Subject(s): Spies; Missing Persons; Espionage
Major character(s): Horace Hubbard, Spy (CIA agent), Cousin (Paul Christopher's); Zarah Christopher, Relative (Paul's daughter); Paul Christopher, Spy, Crime Victim (assassinated)
Time period(s): 2000s
Locale(s): United States; Asia; Europe

Summary: Horace Hubbard works for the CIA, as does his cousin Paul Christopher. When the Chinese government reports that Paul has been killed, a memorial service is held for him, but Horace doesn't believe his cousin is dead. When Paul's daughter also has doubts, Horace sets out to find the truth. To help in his search, he enlists the aid of some former colleagues who are now retired from the spy service. Along the way, Horace encounters a Chinese slave labor camp, ex-Nazi agents, some ex-KGB agents, and Muslim terrorists who possess nuclear bombs.

Where it's reviewed:
Chicago Tribune Books, June 13, 2004, page 3
Kirkus Reviews, April 15, 2004, page 353
Library Journal, May 1, 2004, page 140
Publishers Weekly, May 3, 2004, page 169

Other books by the same author:
Lucky Bastard, 1998
Shelley's Heart, 1995
Second Sight, 1991
The Bride of the Wilderness, 1988
The Last Supper, 1983

Other books you might like:
Milton Bearden, *The Black Tulip*, 1998
Dan Brown, *Digital Fortress*, 1998
Tom Clancy, *Red Rabbit*, 2002
John Le Carre, *The Russia House*, 1989
Robert Littell, *The Company*, 2002

1143

SHARYN MCCRUMB

St. Dale
(New York: Kensington, 2004)

Story type: Mystery
Subject(s): Quest; Sports/Auto Racing; Biography
Major character(s): Harry Bailey, Travel Agent; Harley Claymore, Tour Guide, Sports Figure (ex-race car driver); Bill Knight, Religious (minister)
Time period(s): 2000s (2001)
Locale(s): Southeast

Summary: A modern day pilgrimage finds 13 characters on a bus tour of the NASCAR circuit where the late Dale Earnhardt made auto racing history and, in the minds of many, became a secular saint. The tour stops at tracks throughout the Southeast: Bristol, Martinsville, Mooresville, Rockingham, Lowe's, Talladega, Atlanta, Daytona, and Darlington. The narrative mixes the exploits of Earnhardt with the colorful characters riding the bus. The tour guide, a former race car driver, wants to rekindle his career. A terminally ill child is fulfilling a dying wish. Another young man is trying to reconnect with his dead father. Others are just enjoying the ride.

Where it's reviewed:
Kirkus Reviews, December 1, 2004, page 1109
Library Journal, November 15, 2004, page 50

Other books by the same author:
Ghost Riders, 2003
The Songcatcher, 2001
The PMS Outlaws, 2000
Foggy Mountain Breakdown and Other Stories, 1997
Zombies of the Gene Pool, 1992

Other books you might like:
Rita Mae Brown, *Riding Shotgun*, 1996
Frederick Exley, *A Fan's Notes*, 1968
Mark Harris, *Bang the Drum Slowly*, 1984
W.P. Kinsella, *Shoeless Joe Jackson Comes to Iowa*, 1980
Bernard Malamud, *The Natural*, 1961

1144

ELIZABETH MCKENZIE

Stop That Girl
(New York: Random House, 2004)

Story type: Contemporary; Domestic
Subject(s): Divorce; Mothers and Daughters; Grandmothers
Major character(s): Ann Ransom, Heroine; Roy Weeks, Real Estate Agent, Step-Parent (of Ann); Dr. Frost, Grandparent (Ann's grandmother)

Time period(s): 2000s
Locale(s): United States

Summary: This is a novel, told in nine stories, about relations and reconstituted families. Ann Ransom is eight when her mother remarries. Although her stepfather is a decent sort, Ann is sent off on a European vacation with her grandmother, who is annoying. When Ann returns, her mother withdraws from her. When Ann is 16, her mother tries unsuccessfully to reenter her daughter's life. Ann tries to get away. She receives a college scholarship, after giving a sob story to an admissions officer. However, any thoughts that she might get on with her life without interference from her slightly weird family are soon quashed when her grandmother comes back into her life.

Where it's reviewed:
Kirkus Reviews, November 15, 2004, page 1064
Library Journal, November 15, 2004, page 50
Publishers Weekly, November 1, 2004, page 40

Other books you might like:
Carole Cadwalladr, *The Family Tree*, 2005
Sandra Cisneros, *Caramelo*, 2002
Henry James, *What Maisie Knew*, 1897
Stephen King, *The Girl Who Loved Tom Gordon*, 1999
Jessica Shattuck, *The Hazards of Good Breeding*, 2003

1145

EMMA MCLAUGHLIN
NICOLA KRAUS, Co-Author

Citizen Girl
(New York: Simon & Schuster, 2004)

Story type: Satire; Americana
Subject(s): Women; Careers; Employment
Major character(s): Girl, Businesswoman; Buster, Boyfriend (of Girl); Guy, Businessman (Girl's boss)
Time period(s): 2000s
Locale(s): New York, New York

Summary: The authors of *The Nanny Diaries* take aim at corporate America in a lightweight satire. The story, which is told from a feminist perspective, follows a young career woman named Girl who struggles with corporate culture. After she is fired, she sets out to find a job that will utilize her full potential. Surprisingly, she finds an ideal job with an ideal boss and that's the problem—the job turns out to be too good to be true. Although it utilizes her marketing and promotional talent, the sex industry isn't exactly respectable. However, there are compensations: she makes a fabulous salary and meets Buster, a sensitive new age guy.

Where it's reviewed:
Kirkus Reviews, October 1, 2004, page 934
Library Journal, November 1, 2004, page 76
Publishers Weekly, October 11, 2004, page 53

Other books by the same author:
The Nanny Diaries, 2002

Other books you might like:
Alice Randall, *Pushkin and the Queen of Spades*, 2004
Lee Smith, *The Last Girls*, 2002
Alisa Valdes-Rodriguez, *The Dirty Girls Social Club*, 2003

Debra Weinstein, *Apprentice to the Flower Poet Z*, 2004
Irene Zabytko, *When Luba Leaves Home*, 2003

1146

LARRY MCMURTRY

Loop Group

(New York: Simon & Schuster, 2004)

Story type: Domestic; Humor
Subject(s): Travel; Women; Friendship
Major character(s): Maggie Clary, Widow(er); Connie, Friend (of Maggie)
Time period(s): 2000s
Locale(s): Los Angeles, California

Summary: Widow Maggie Clary, 60, is depressed. She hasn't felt right since undergoing a hysterectomy and can't help wondering if life has passed her by. Despite objections from her three married daughters, Maggie decides to embark upon an adventure with her lifelong friend Connie. Aside from growing up and chasing men together, the two women have Hollywood careers, dubbing movies with sound. Maggie and Connie travel cross-country to see Maggie's aunt, who owns a chicken farm in Texas. They encounter a cast of unforgettable characters, including hitchhikers who are interesting and dangerous. McMurtry's skill at drawing eccentric but fascinating characters drives the story.

Where it's reviewed:
Booklist, October 15, 2004, page 363
Kirkus Reviews, September 15, 2004, page 886
Library Journal, October 15, 2004, page 54
Publishers Weekly, November 8, 2004, page 35

Other books by the same author:
By Sorrow's River, 2003
The Wandering Hill, 2003
The Sin Killer, 2002
Lonesome Dove, 1985
Terms of Endearment, 1975

Other books you might like:
Margaret Atwood, *Life Before Man*, 1996
Elizabeth Berg, *Never Change*, 2001
Elizabeth Buchan, *Revenge of the Middle-Aged Woman*, 2002
Margaret Drabble, *The Seven Sisters*, 2002
Molly Giles, *Iron Shoes*, 2000

1147

DAVID MEANS

The Secret Goldfish

(New York: Fourth Estate, 2004)

Story type: Collection
Subject(s): Short Stories; Humor
Time period(s): 2000s
Locale(s): United States

Summary: In this collection, Means writes about the contemporary American experience, which includes, drugs, violence, boredom, and death. The stories are character-driven and the plots are slightly offbeat. For the most part, the stories are set in the Midwest and on the east coast. The subjects are varied and include: lightning chasing a man, a car blown off the Mackinac Bridge, a woman murdering her boyfriend after consulting with God and the devil, a marriage disintegrating while a pet goldfish watches, oversexed teenagers on a crime spree, farm hands sniffing glue, adultery in New York, and accidental death from skiing while using drugs.

Where it's reviewed:
Booklist, September 1, 2004, page 62
Chicago Tribune Books, October 10, 2004, page 6
Kirkus Reviews, July 15, 2004, page 652
Library Journal, August 2004, page 73
Publishers Weekly, July 5, 2004, page 34

Other books by the same author:
Assorted Fire Events, 2000
A Quick Kiss of Redemption, 1991

Other books you might like:
David Benioff, *When the Nines Roll Over*, 2004
David Bezmozgis, *Natasha: And Other Stories*, 2004
Dan Chaon, *You Remind Me of Me*, 2004
Courtney Eldridge, *Unkempt*, 2004
Naama Goldstein, *The Place Will Comfort You*, 2004

1148

DEON MEYER

Heart of the Hunter

(New York: Little, Brown, 2004)

Story type: Psychological Suspense; Political
Subject(s): Terrorism; Loyalty; Friendship
Major character(s): Thobela ''Tiny'' Mpayipheli, Revolutionary (ANC hero), Maintenance Worker; Miriam Nzuluwazi, Spouse (Tiny's wife); Monica Kleintjes, Young Woman (Tiny's best friend's daughter)
Time period(s): 2000s
Locale(s): Cape Town, South Africa; Lusaka, Zambia

Summary: Despite adjustment to a peaceful existence, spending years in an armed revolutionary movement makes it very hard to resist requests to return to the violent ways when friends need you. This is the situation faced by Thobela ''Tiny'' Mpayipheli, a giant of a man, who is happily married and living in Cape Town. Complications set in when Tiny's friend Johnny Kleintjes is kidnapped and held hostage. Johnny's daughter asks Tiny to help her father. To accomplish the task, Tiny must leave his home and do battle with the villains, while matching wits with the CIA and other institutions in post-apartheid South Africa. The author, a South African, is well-known in France, although this is his American debut. Translated by K.L. Seegers.

Where it's reviewed:
Chicago Tribune Books, July 25, 2004, page 3
Kirkus Reviews, June 15, 2004, page 553
Library Journal, May 15, 2004, page 115

Other books by the same author:
Dead at Daybreak, 2000 (Madeleine Van Biljon, translator)

Other books you might like:
John Burdett, *Bangkok 8*, 2003

Jack Higgins, *Dark Justice*, 2004
Michael Simon, *Dirty Sally*, 2004
Jeff Stetson, *Blood on the Leaves*, 2004
Kevin Wignall, *For the Dogs*, 2004

1149

MARK MILLS

Amagansett

(New York: Putnam, 2004)

Story type: Historical; Romance
Subject(s): Fishing; Murder; Social Classes
Major character(s): Conrad Labarde, Fisherman, Veteran; Lillian Wallace, Socialite, Crime Victim (murdered); Tom Hollis, Police Officer (chief)
Time period(s): 1940s (1947)
Locale(s): Long Island, New York

Summary: In his debut novel, screenwriter Mills offers a post-World War II story that details the friction in the social fabric of the Hamptons, a community on Long Island where rich and privileged New York City residents vacation in their summer mansions. However, these seasonal visits aren't well received by the community's year-round residents, who are mostly working class and ethnic. The story opens when the body of a young heiress is hauled out of the water in the net of a local fisherman. When a subsequent investigation suggests that the woman was murdered, the chief of police and a local fisherman are determined to solve the crime. The dead woman's relatives and a former boyfriend get caught up in the process.

Where it's reviewed:
Booklist, August 2004, page 1907
Kirkus Reviews, July 15, 2004, page 652
Library Journal, July 2004, page 72
New York Times Book Review, August 29, 2004, page 12
Publishers Weekly, July 12, 2004, page 44

Other books you might like:
Ernest Hemingway, *The Old Man and the Sea*, 1952
Cormac McCarthy, *Suttree*, 1979
Donna Tartt, *The Secret History*, 1992
Tim Winton, *Dirt Music*, 2001
Tom Wolfe, *I Am Charlotte Simmons*, 2004

1150

HOWARD FRANK MOSHER

Waiting for Teddy Williams

(Boston: Houghton Mifflin, 2004)

Story type: Americana; Coming-of-Age
Subject(s): Single Parent Families; Sports/Baseball; Family Relations
Major character(s): E.A. Allen, Young Man; Gypsy Lee, Parent (E.A.'s mother); Teddy, Drifter (with baseball skills), Friend (of E.A.)
Time period(s): 20th century
Locale(s): Kingdom Common, Vermont

Summary: In Kingdom Common, a village in Vermont, Boston Red Sox fever isn't an ailment; it's part of the culture. So, it's no surprise that devotion to the Red Sox can be a life and death matter. Gran has been confined to a wheelchair since 1978, when the Yankees whipped the Red Sox in a playoff and she takes her frustration out on daughter Gypsy Lee and her grandson E.A. (Ethan Allen). Life is pretty dull until one day a drifter named Teddy comes to town. He has his own problems but he is determined to redeem himself by doing one good thing. Teddy decides to help E.A., who is a bit of a social outcast, become a baseball star. As E.A. grows up, he finds the fate of his beloved Red Sox in his hands.

Where it's reviewed:
Kirkus Reviews, July 1, 2004, page 600
Publishers Weekly, June 14, 2004, page 42

Other books by the same author:
The True Account, 2003
Northern Borders, 1994
A Stranger in the Kingdom, 1989
Marie Blythe, 1983
Where the Rivers Flow North, 1978

Other books you might like:
Percival Everett, *Suder*, 1983
Mark Harris, *The Southpaw*, 1953
Stephen King, *The Girl Who Loved Tom Gordon*, 1999
W.P. Kinsella, *Shoeless Joe Jackson Comes to Iowa*, 1980
Bill Littlefield, *Prospect*, 1989

1151

WALTER MOSLEY

Little Scarlet

(Boston: Little, Brown, 2004)

Story type: Mystery; Ethnic
Series: Easy Rawlings. Book 8
Subject(s): African Americans; Riots; Serial Killers
Major character(s): Easy Rawlins, Detective—Amateur (freelances); Melvin Suggs, Detective—Police; Nola Payne, Crime Victim (murdered)
Time period(s): 1960s (1965)
Locale(s): Los Angeles, California

Summary: In 1965 Los Angeles, African Americans are rioting in Watts and Easy Rawlins, 45, like the other sensible people in the neighborhood has hunkered down to ride things out. However, there is evidence that a murderer is loose in the neighborhood. Someone is using the riots to cover up the trail of his crimes. When Detective Melvin Suggs contacts Easy to help the police catch the murderer, Easy agrees. Subsequently, he will be assisted by a cast of very colorful characters.

Where it's reviewed:
Kirkus Reviews, June 1, 2004, page 521
Library Journal, June 1, 2004, page 108
New York Times, July 5, 2004, page B1
Publishers Weekly, May 24, 2004, page 47

Other books by the same author:
The Man in My Basement, 2004
Walkin' the Dog, 1999
A Little Yellow Dog, 1996
White Butterfly, 1992

Popular Fiction

Devil in a Blue Dress, 1990

Other books you might like:
Stephen L. Carter, *The Emperor of Ocean Park*, 2002
Pete Dexter, *Train*, 2003
Eric Jerome Dickey, *Cheaters*, 1999
Percival Everett, *Watershed*, 1996
Jack Fuller, *The Best of Jackson Payne*, 2000

1152

SABINA MURRAY

A Carnivore's Inquiry

(New York: Grove, 2004)

Story type: Psychological; Contemporary
Subject(s): Women; Murder; Horror
Major character(s): Katherine Shea, Young Woman; Boris Naryshkin, Writer, Boyfriend (Katherine's)
Time period(s): 2000s
Locale(s): New York, New York; Maine; Mexico

Summary: A tale of cannibalism and serial murders follows Katherine as she attempts to satisfy her various appetites. After she meets Boris in the New York subway, she seduces him and moves in with him. Unsatisfied with him, she then begins sleeping around and eventually leaves him. Taking a trip across the country to Mexico, she meets two men who are subsequently murdered in a horrible fashion. Katherine becomes obsessed with cannibalism. The story raises many questions about modern society and individual appetites.

Where it's reviewed:
Booklist, May 15, 2004, page 1598
Kirkus Reviews, May 15, 2004, page 464
Library Journal, April 1, 2004, page 123
New York Times, August 17, 2004, page B6
Publishers Weekly, May 31, 2004, page 49

Other books by the same author:
The Caprices, 2002 (Pen/Faulkner Award winner)
Slow Burn, 1990

Other books you might like:
Pat Barker, *Blow Your House Down*, 1984
Madison Smartt Bell, *Doctor Sleep*, 1991
Ian Caldwell, *The Rule of Four*, 2004
    Dustin Thomason, co-author
Mary Higgins Clark, *Daddy's Little Girl*, 2002
Thomas Harris, *The Silence of the Lambs*, 1988

1153

V.S. NAIPAUL

Magic Seeds

(New York: Knopf, 2004)

Story type: Political; Psychological
Subject(s): Identity; Social Issues; Political Crimes and Offenses
Major character(s): Willie Chandran, Revolutionary; Sarojini, Relative (Willie's sister); Roger, Lawyer, Friend (of Willie)
Time period(s): 2000s

Locale(s): Berlin, Germany; London, England; India

Summary: V.S. Naipaul, who won the 2001 Nobel Prize for literature, picks up where *Half a Life* (2001) left off. After leaving his wife in Africa, Willie Chandran is in Berlin with his sister and her husband. Always ready to assume another identity, Willie allows his sister to hook him up with a radical group in India. The Communist-led group is fomenting revolution allegedly to overthrow the caste system and Willie dives in with both feet but soon becomes disillusioned and is captured by the police. He goes to prison and writes a book that develops a following in intellectual circles. Roger, an old friend, gets Willie out of jail and takes him back to London, where he settles in as a darling of intellectual circles. However, he still feels like an outsider.

Where it's reviewed:
Booklist, November 15, 2004, page 531
Kirkus Reviews, October 15, 2004, page 980
New York Times Book Review, November 28, 2004, page 14
Publishers Weekly, October 18, 2004, page 49

Other books by the same author:
Half a Life, 2001
A Way in the World, 1994
The Enigma of Arrival, 1987
A Bend in the River, 1979
A House for Mr. Biswas, 1961

Other books you might like:
Madison Smartt Bell, *The Stone That the Builder Refused*, 2004
Susan Choi, *American Woman*, 2003
Hari Kunzru, *The Impressionist*, 2002
Norman Rush, *Mortals*, 2003
Salman Rushdie, *The Satanic Verses*, 1988

1154

ANITA NAIR

Ladies Coupe

(New York: St. Martin's Griffin, 2004)

Story type: Contemporary
Subject(s): Travel; Women; Relationships
Major character(s): Akhila, Spinster
Time period(s): 2000s
Locale(s): India

Summary: This story gives chick lit a different perspective, that of an Indian woman. As she enters middle age, the never married Akhila decides to take charge of her life. Who will oppose her? That's simple—her family—the same loving family that she has supported ever since her father died 26 years ago. To get away, Akhila takes a train to a resort. On the way, she meets several other women. The group develops a camaraderie and shares observations about their lives, eventually deciding that while life isn't always nice and tidy, it is worth living.

Where it's reviewed:
Kirkus Reviews, May 1, 2004, page 418
Library Journal, June 15, 2004, page 60

Other books by the same author:
The Better Man, 2000

Other books you might like:
Monica Ali, *Brick Lane*, 2003
Anita Diamant, *The Red Tent*, 1997
Ruth Prawer Jhabvala, *My Nine Lives*, 2004
Heidi Julavits, *The Effect of Living Backwards*, 2003
Barbara Kingsolver, *The Bean Trees*, 1988

1155

PATRICK NEATE

The London Pigeon Wars
(New York: Farrar, Straus and Giroux, 2004)

Story type: Psychological Suspense; Satire
Subject(s): Animals/Birds; Relationships; Modern Life
Major character(s): Murray, Lover (of Karen and Emma), Friend (of Tom Dare); Tom Dare, Boyfriend (of Karen); Tariq, Spouse (Emma's husband), Businessman (software)
Time period(s): 2000s
Locale(s): London, England

Summary: If he's your friend, Murray is a special kind of guy. There isn't anything he wouldn't do for his friends and they know it. So what if he doesn't have a last name or his ethnic background is hidden? You can count on Murray. Things happen around him and appear to resolve favorably. Take for instance, his affair with Tariq's wife Emma. Murray raised the money to save their house when Tariq's business went south. OK, so maybe he goes overboard sometimes, but don't forget about those killer pigeons that were attacking people in the street. Yeah, Murray had something to do with it, but don't forget, he also came up with a solution.

Where it's reviewed:
Kirkus Reviews, April 1, 2004, page 291
Library Journal, April 15, 2004, page 125
New York Times Book Review, June 13, 2004, page 19

Other books by the same author:
Twelve Bar Blues, 2001

Other books you might like:
Benjamin Anastas, *The Faithful Narrative of a Pastor's Disappearance*, 2001
Dan Chaon, *Fitting Ends and Other Stories*, 1995
Susan Minot, *Lust & Other Stories*, 1989
Han Ong, *Fixer Chao*, 2001
Arthur Phillips, *Prague*, 2002

1156

GEOFF NICHOLSON

The Hollywood Dodo
(New York: Simon & Schuster, 2004)

Story type: Humor; Romance
Subject(s): Fathers and Daughters; Movie Industry; Satire
Major character(s): Dorothy Cadwallader, Actress, Relative (Henry's daughter); Henry Cadwallader, Doctor, Widow(er); Rick McCartney, Director
Time period(s): 2000s

Locale(s): Hollywood, California; London, England

Summary: When Dorothy Cadwallader, a talented young British actress, decides Hollywood is calling her, her father Henry, a recent widower, decides to go along. Henry, of course, is out to protect his daughter from the predators in the movie industry. On the plane, they make the acquaintance of Rick, an up-and-coming director. As luck would have it, Dorothy's career prospects evaporate quickly. Henry begins to develop some new appetites. He lusts after a socialite real estate agent and decides to try his hand at acting. Subsequently, he hooks up with Rick, who is attempting to combine his efforts into two films, a 17th-century costume drama and a porn movie. Father may not know best, but he does keep it interesting.

Where it's reviewed:
Kirkus Reviews, April 1, 2004, page 293
New York Times Book Review, June 13, 2004, page 22
Publishers Weekly, May 3, 2004, page 168

Other books by the same author:
Bedlam Burning, 2002
Female Ruins, 2000
Flesh Guitar, 1999
Footsucker, 1995
The Foodchain, 1992

Other books you might like:
Steve Allen, *Die Laughing*, 1998
Jen Banbury, *Like a Hole in the Head*, 1998
Gigi Levangie Grazer, *Maneater*, 2003
Jane Heller, *Lucky Stars*, 2003
Rita Rudner, *Tickled Pink*, 2001

1157

THISBE NISSEN

Osprey Island
(New York: Knopf, 2004)

Story type: Psychological
Subject(s): Accidents; Single Parent Families; Summer
Major character(s): Bud Chizek, Hotel Owner, Parent (Suzi's father); Nancy Chizek, Spouse (Bud's wife), Hotel Owner; Suzi Chizek, Single Parent (Mia's mother)
Time period(s): 1980s (1988)
Locale(s): New York

Summary: The Chizek family owns and operates a resort. Besides attending to the guests, Bud and Nancy Chizek must also cope with a cast of colorful characters who help them run the hotel. This includes their rebellious daughter, Suzi, and her six-year-old daughter, Mia. Secrets create tension which is fueled by alcoholic frenzies. The drunk housekeeper dies in an accidental fire. Her husband, also with a taste for alcohol, tends to be a bully. Their son, Squee, is forced to seek refuge with his father's friend, who is trying to cope with being dumped by his girlfriend. At the end of the summer, everyone is changed, some for the better.

Where it's reviewed:
Kirkus Reviews, May 15, 2004, page 464
Library Journal, June 15, 2004, page 61

Popular Fiction

Other books by the same author:
The Good People of New York, 2001
Out of the Girls' Room and into the Night, 1999

Other books you might like:
Amit Chaudhuri, *A New World*, 2000
Barbara Delinsky, *A Woman's Place*, 1997
Margaret Drabble, *The Needle's Eye*, 1972
Stephen King, *Bag of Bones*, 1998
Sue Miller, *The Good Mother*, 1986

1158

CRAIG NOVA

Cruisers

(New York: Shaye Areheart, 2004)

Story type: Psychological Suspense; Contemporary
Subject(s): Murder; Fate; Emotional Problems
Major character(s): Russell Boyd, Police Officer (highway trooper); Zofia, Girlfriend (Russell's); Frank Kohler, Computer Expert
Time period(s): 2000s
Locale(s): Vermont

Summary: Russell Boyd is a state trooper in a mill town in Vermont. His laid-back, easygoing demeanor hides the horrors that he has witnessed during his career enforcing society's laws. Zofia, his girlfriend, understands his need to take things slow and this, of course, is what makes her so attractive to him. Frank Kohler, a computer technician who is temperamentally wound too tight, barely clings to his sanity. He lives alone in the woods and is paranoid about hunters and fishermen trespassing on his land. At some level, Frank recognizes his difficulty and decides to remedy the problem with a mail-order bride from Russia. Unfortunately, his bride Katryna doesn't help, instead she seems to wind Frank even tighter. Meanwhile, Frank has an encounter with Russell and Zofia, when they wander on his land during an outing with some school children. This sets the stage for a final confrontation, when Frank finally snaps.

Where it's reviewed:
Chicago Tribune Books, July 18, 2004, page 1
Kirkus Reviews, May 15, 2004, page 465
Publishers Weekly, July 5, 2004, page 39

Other books by the same author:
Wetware, 2001
The Universal Donor, 1997
The Book of Dreams, 1994
Trombone, 1992
Tornado Alley, 1989

Other books you might like:
Mary Higgins Clark, *Daddy's Little Girl*, 2002
Harlan Coben, *No Second Chance*, 2003
Reynolds Price, *Noble Norfleet*, 2002
Alice Sebold, *The Lovely Bones*, 2002
Donna Tartt, *The Little Friend*, 2002

1159

JOSIP NOVAKOVICH

April Fool's Day

(New York: HarperCollins, 2004)

Story type: Psychological; Coming-of-Age
Subject(s): Political Prisoners; Men; War
Major character(s): Ivan Dolinar, Student—Graduate, Military Personnel
Time period(s): 20th century (1948-1999)
Locale(s): Croatia; Serbia

Summary: In his debut novel, Novakovich, an accomplished short story writer, offers readers a political satire. The story follows the trials and tribulations of Ivan Dolinar, whose life continually gets turned upside down. Born in 1948 in what is now Croatia (previously part of Yugoslavia), Ivan grows up a fierce patriot and supporter of Marshal Tito, the Yugoslavian dictator. Although he graduates from medical school in Serbia, he never becomes a doctor. When a prank backfires, Ivan is convicted of a political crime and sent to prison. After his release, he is drafted into the Serbian army and fights against Croatia. Subsequently, he also serves in the Croatian army and fights against the Serbs. Later, he marries a woman he raped during his military service.

Where it's reviewed:
Booklist, September 1, 2004, page 63
Kirkus Reviews, August 1, 2004, page 708
New York Times Book Review, September 19, 2004, page 20
Publishers Weekly, August 23, 2004, page 37

Other books by the same author:
Salvation and Other Disasters, 1998
Yolk, 1995

Other books you might like:
Pat Barker, *Regeneration*, 1991
Thomas Berger, *Crazy in Berlin*, 1958
Stephen Crane, *The Red Badge of Courage*, 2004
John Dos Passos, *Three Soldiers*, 1921
Joseph Heller, *Catch-22*, 1961

1160

JOYCE CAROL OATES

The Falls

(New York: Ecco, 2004)

Story type: Americana; Family Saga
Subject(s): Relationships; Men; Women
Major character(s): Ariah Littrell, Widow(er), Spouse (Dirk's wife); Dirk Burnaby, Wealthy
Time period(s): 20th century (1950-1980)
Locale(s): Niagra Falls, New York

Summary: On Ariah Littrell's wedding night, her new husband jumps into Niagara Falls. Her religious upbringing causes Ariah to believe herself damned. Dirk Burnaby, a wealthy, gentle young man, falls in love with her and they subsequently marry and have a family. Nevertheless, Ariah's mistrust fuels her fears and becomes a self-fulfilling curse. When Dirk becomes involved in the plight of the residents of Love

Canal, a subdivision where homeowners were sold property on dangerously polluted land, things begin to come undone. Ariah doesn't believe Dirk's motives are altruistic; she thinks he's become involved with another woman also involved with the case. When the suit fails, Dirk is ruined financially and socially, and dies a broken man.

Where it's reviewed:
Booklist, May 1, 2004, page 1483
Kirkus Reviews, June 15, 2004, page 555
Library Journal, May 15, 2004, page 116
Publishers Weekly, July 5, 2004, page 35

Other books by the same author:
Rape, 2003
The Tattooed Girl, 2003
I'll Take You There, 2002
Middle Age, 2001
Blonde, 2000

Other books you might like:
Richard Bausch, *In the Night Season*, 1998
Elizabeth Benedict, *Almost*, 2001
Judith Guest, *Ordinary People*, 1981
Fannie Hurst, *Imitation of Life*, 1933
John Irving, *A Widow for One Year*, 1998

1161

CYTHIA OZICK

Heir to the Glimmering World
(Boston: Houghton Mifflin, 2004)

Story type: Historical; Domestic
Subject(s): Inheritance; Orphans; Refugees
Major character(s): Rose Meadows, Orphan; Anneliese Mitwisser, Young Woman; James Abair, Wealthy, Boyfriend (Anneliese's)
Time period(s): 1930s
Locale(s): New York, New York (Bronx)

Summary: Ozick's story is set in the middle of the Depression in New York City. The story's narrator, Rose Meadows, is orphaned and adrift. She takes a job as a research assistant to an exiled German, Professor Mitwisser and soon becomes embroiled in his family affairs. The family's sole means of support is erratic as it comes from James, an eccentric millionaire. The family's precarious existence drives the professor's wife to a nervous breakdown. Rose helps nurse her and tends to the couple's five children with some assistance from the family's oldest daughter, the beautiful Anneliese, who is only a couple of years Rose's junior. Meanwhile, a romance develops between Anneliese and James but it's not untroubled. James, whose father made the family fortune writing children's books, about James' childhood, has become embittered from his unwanted celebrity and needs to work this out.

Where it's reviewed:
Booklist, July 2004, page 1800
Kirkus Reviews, July 1, 2004, page 600
Library Journal, July 2004, page 73
New York Times Book Review, September 5, 2004, page 12
Publishers Weekly, August 9, 2004, page 228

Other books by the same author:
The Puttermesser Papers, 1997
The Shawl, 1989
The Messiah of Stockholm, 1987
The Cannibal Galaxy, 1983
Trust, 1966

Other books you might like:
Anita Brookner, *Family and Friends*, 1985
Nicholas Delbanco, *What Remains*, 2000
E.L. Doctorow, *The Book of Daniel*, 1971
Nomi Eve, *The Family Orchard*, 2000
Jonathan Safran Foer, *Everything Is Illuminated*, 2002

1162

ORHAN PAMUK

Snow
(New York: Knopf, 2004)

Story type: Contemporary Realism
Subject(s): Suicide; Poverty; Resistance Movements
Major character(s): Kerim Alakusoglu, Writer (poet), Expatriate; Ipek, Young Woman; Kadife, Young Woman (Ipek's sister)
Time period(s): 2000s
Locale(s): Kars, Turkey

Summary: Kerim, an expatriate and poet, returns to his Turkish village after living in Germany for 12 years. Ostensibly, he is trying to reconnect with Ipek, a beautiful woman. Also, he's curious about the disturbing news that several young women have committed suicide. Kerim finds the village a hotbed of political intrigue, as radical Islamists and Kurd separatists flex their muscles. He finds himself caught in the mix. The radicals, the idealists, and the government all want a piece of him. In short, the traditional Eastern ways are being assaulted by a modern world. To maintain his sanity, Kerim is forced to leave. However, his experience ignites a burst of creative energy.

Where it's reviewed:
Kirkus Reviews, June 1, 2004, page 512
Library Journal, July 2004, page 73
New York Times, August 10, 2004, page B6
Publishers Weekly, July 19, 2004, page 144

Other books by the same author:
My Name Is Red, 2001
The New Life, 1997
The Black Book, 1994
The White Castle, 1991

Other books you might like:
Boris Akunin, *The Winter Queen*, 2003
Alev Lytle Croutier, *Seven Houses*, 2002
Kurban Said, *Ali and Nino*, 1996
Janet Wallach, *Seraglio*, 2003
A.B. Yehoshua, *The Liberated Bride*, 2003

Popular Fiction

1163

JAMES PATTERSON

Sam's Letters to Jennifer
(New York: Little, Brown, 2004)

Story type: Romance; Contemporary/Mainstream
Subject(s): Relationships; Family; Letters
Major character(s): Jennifer, Widow(er), Journalist; Samantha, Aged Person (in coma), Grandparent (of Jennifer)
Time period(s): 2000s
Locale(s): Chicago, Illinois; Lake Geneva, Wisconsin

Summary: Jennifer, a grieving widow, writes for a Chicago newspaper. When her grandmother Samantha becomes deathly ill, Jennifer goes to her bedside. At Samantha's house, Jennifer finds a packet of letters addressed to her. In the letters, her grandmother writes about her life and Jennifer is astounded at what she learns. Although married to the same man for 26 years, he was abusive. However, Samantha found other compensations, including a wonderful lover. The letters coax Jennifer out of her grief-stricken haze. She reconnects with her first love and helps nurse him through a terminal illness. Despite its sadness and beauty, life goes on.

Where it's reviewed:
Kirkus Reviews, June 1, 2004, page 513
Publishers Weekly, June 7, 2004, page 33

Other books by the same author:
The Jester, 2003 (Andrew Gross, co-author)
The Lake House, 2003
Four Blind Mice, 2002
The Beach House, 2002 (Peter de Jonge, co-author)
Suzanne's Diary for Nicholas, 2001

Other books you might like:
Valerie Martin, *Italian Fever*, 1999
Margaret Mazzantini, *Don't Move*, 2004
Jill McCorkle, *Carolina Moon*, 1996
Bernhard Schlink, *Flights of Love*, 2001
Lee Smith, *News of the Spirit*, 1997

1164

ARTURO PEREZ-REVERTE

The Queen of the South
(New York: Putnam, 2004)

Story type: Contemporary; Psychological Suspense
Subject(s): Drugs; Crime and Criminals; Women
Major character(s): Teresa Mendoza, Drug Dealer
Time period(s): 2000s
Locale(s): Mexico; Spain; Morocco

Summary: Perez-Reverte's novel tells the story of Teresa Mendoza, a woman who recognizes opportunity when it presents itself. Teresa is also capable of taking advantage of opportunity, despite competition from dangerous men. When her drug dealing boyfriend is killed, Teresa is forced to run for her life. She leaves Mexico and heads to Morocco where she finds a new boyfriend and earns a living transporting drugs. Fate deals her a setback and she is sent to prison. When she is released, she more or less picks up where she left off only this

time, she's the boss. In 12 short years, she becomes the brains behind the largest drug operation in the Mediterranean. Translated by Andrew Hurley.

Where it's reviewed:
Booklist, April 1, 2004, page 1331
Chicago Tribune Books, June 27, 2004, page 2
Kirkus Reviews, April 15, 2004, page 356
Library Journal, May 15, 2004, page 116
Publishers Weekly, May 10, 2004, page 37

Other books by the same author:
The Nautical Chart, 2001 (Margaret Sayers Peden, translator)
The Seville Communion, 1998 (Sonia Soto, translator)
The Club Dumas, 1996 (Sonia Soto, translator)
The Fencing Master, 1994 (Margaret Costa, translator)

Other books you might like:
Dan Brown, *The Da Vinci Code*, 2003
Ian Caldwell, *The Rule of Four*, 2004
    Dustin Thomason, co-author
Tom Clancy, *Red Rabbit*, 2002
Michael Crichton, *Prey*, 2002
Umberto Eco, *The Name of the Rose*, 1983

1165

ARTHUR PHILLIPS

The Egyptologist
(New York: Random House, 2004)

Story type: Historical; Adventure
Subject(s): Archaeology; Mystery; Murder
Major character(s): Ralph Trilipush, Archaeologist; Harold Farrell, Detective—Police; Paul Caldwell, Archaeologist (a missing person)
Time period(s): 1920s (1922)
Locale(s): Egypt

Summary: Phillips uses two unreliable narrators in a story about missing persons, murder, and the fame and fortune associated with great archaeological discoveries in the early 20th century. Ralph Trilipush, an Oxford educated archaeologist, believes he is on the brink of a discovery equal to King Tut's tomb. Ralph, who translated a pornographic verse written by King Atum-hadu, believes that he can find his tomb. He obtains financial backing from his girlfriend's father and sets out to make the discovery. Meanwhile, Harold Farrell, an Australian detective, tries to find a missing archaeologist, Paul Caldwell, uncovering a couple of murders along the way. Resolution arrives when the efforts of Ralph and Harold collide.

Where it's reviewed:
Kirkus Reviews, August 1, 2004, page 710
Library Journal, July 2004, page 73
New York Times, August 24, 2004, page B1
Publishers Weekly, July 5, 2004, page 35

Other books by the same author:
The Empty Chamber, 2004
Prague, 2002

Other books you might like:
Dan Brown, *The Da Vinci Code*, 2003

Ian Caldwell, *The Rule of Four*, 2004
  Dustin Thomason, co-author
Michael Crichton, *Timeline*, 1999
Umberto Eco, *Foucault's Pendulum*, 1989
Winfried Georg Sebald, *Austerlitz*, 2001

1166

ANNIE PROULX

Bad Dirt

(New York: Scribner, 2004)

Story type: Collection
Subject(s): Short Stories; Cultures and Customs; Ranch Life
Time period(s): 2000s
Locale(s): Wyoming

Summary: Proulx offers ten short stories in this collection, picking up where she left off in her Pulitzer Prize-winning book *Close Range*. Set in Wyoming, the work offers a cast of unforgettable characters struggling for existence against a harsh landscape. In the story "What Kind of Furniture Would Jesus Pick?," a man struggles to save his ranch despite drought and debt. Men aren't the only ones who are beset with hardships; women face disaster, too. In "The Trickle Down Effect," a woman is almost undone when a hired hand doesn't work out. There's an emotional toll exacted as well. A couple's marriage takes a hit when their dream of retiring on a ranch turns into an emotional nightmare in "Man Crawling Out of Trees." In "The Hellhole," a game warden has a creative solution for poachers. In "Florida Rental," a woman solves a problem with her neighbor. A magic kettle grants three wishes, two of which end badly, in "Dump Jack."

Where it's reviewed:
Booklist, October 1, 2004, page 283
Chicago Tribune Books, November 28, 2004, page 3
Kirkus Reviews, October 1, 2004, page 935
Library Journal, November 1, 2004, page 79
Publishers Weekly, October 4, 2004, page 67

Other books by the same author:
That Old Ace in the Hole, 2002
Close Range, 1999
Accordion Crimes, 1996
The Shipping News, 1993
Postcards, 1992

Other books you might like:
Thomas McGuane, *The Cadence of Grass*, 2002
Larry McMurtry, *Horseman, Pass By*, 1961
Danielle Steel, *The Ranch*, 1997
John Steinbeck, *Of Mice and Men*, 1938
John Updike, *Licks of Love*, 2000

1167

PATRICK RAMBAUD

The Retreat

(New York: Atlantic Monthly, 2004)

Story type: Historical/Napoleonic Wars
Series: Napoleonic Wars. Book 2

Subject(s): Biography; Napoleonic Wars; Winter
Major character(s): Napoleon Bonaparte, Historical Figure, Military Personnel (French general and emperor); Prince Mikhail Kutuzof, Historical Figure, Military Personnel (Russian field marshal)
Time period(s): 1810s (1812)
Locale(s): Moscow, Russia

Summary: This is the second book in a proposed trilogy about Napoleon. The book opens just after Napoleon has defeated the Russians at Borodino in 1812, with Napoleon at the gates of Moscow. He expects that the Russians will sue for peace and he will return to France in triumph. Instead, the Russians retreat, leaving Moscow empty. Napoleon hunkers down and waits. While he waits, winter approaches, the city catches fire, and food supplies are exhausted, but the Russians still don't surrender. Thus, Napoleon is forced to retreat back to France. Along the way, his army must battle the Russians, the cold winter, and starvation. The retreat is disastrous and only a small fraction of the French army survives. The author shifts the perspective between Napoleon, his staff, his soldiers, a troupe of actors, and the Russians. Translated by Will Hobson.

Where it's reviewed:
Kirkus Reviews, September 1, 2004, page 831
Publishers Weekly, October 11, 2004, page 54

Other books by the same author:
The Battle, 2000

Other books you might like:
Robert Alexander, *The Kitchen Boy*, 2003
Madison Smartt Bell, *Master of the Crossroads*, 2000
Bernard Cornwell, *Sharpe's Siege*, 1987
Helen Dunmore, *The Siege*, 2002
Khaled Hosseini, *The Kite Runner*, 2003

1168

JAY RAYNER

Eating Crow

(New York: Simon & Schuster, 2004)

Story type: Psychological; Satire
Subject(s): Writing; Restaurants; Guilt
Major character(s): Marc Basset, Critic (restaurant)
Time period(s): 2000s
Locale(s): London, England

Summary: Rayner, the restaurant critic for the *London Observer*, makes his fictional debut with a novel about a food critic who works for a London paper. The main character, Marc Basset, has quite a reputation for devastating reviews aimed at restaurants that dare not measure up to his standards. Complications set in when a chef kills himself after receiving one of Basset's vitriolic appraisals. At first unmoved by the chef's desperate act, Basset almost comes apart, when he watches TV and sees the chef's little daughter console her mother. Basset approaches the widow and apologizes, then sets out to individually apologize to everyone who has been victimized by his unkind words.

Where it's reviewed:
Kirkus Reviews, June 1, 2004, page 513

Popular Fiction

New York Times Book Review, August 1, 2004, page 11

Other books you might like:
Maeve Binchy, *Quentins*, 2002
Anthony Bourdain, *Bobby Gold*, 2002
Nora Ephron, *Heartburn*, 1983
Fannie Flagg, *Fried Green Tomatoes at the Whistle-Stop Cafe*, 1987
Richard Russo, *Empire Falls*, 2001

1169

LISA REARDON

The Mercy Killers

(New York: Counterpoint, 2004)

Story type: Psychological Suspense
Subject(s): Serial Killers; Aging; Family Relations
Major character(s): Charlie Simpkins, Relative (P.T.'s younger brother), Veteran; Gabriel "P.T." Simpkins, Mentally Ill Person (brain damaged), Abuse Victim (by his father); Gil McGurk, Saloon Keeper/Owner (of McGurk's Tap)
Time period(s): 1960s; 1970s (1967-1972)
Locale(s): Ypsilanti, Michigan

Summary: Set in Ypsilanti, Michigan, the story revolves around Charlie Simpkins as he interacts with his family and friends. Charlie isn't a bad guy, although trouble seems to follow him. While growing up, Charlie's older brother P.T. protected him from the vicious beatings handed out by their alcoholic father. P.T. is good natured but the beatings leave him mentally disabled. When their grandfather is smothered to death, Charlie confesses rather than allow P.T. to take the blame. The prosecutor offers a deal, prison or the army. Charlie opts for the army and is promptly shipped to Vietnam. After a two-year stint, Charlie returns to marry Diane, a sweet young woman. However, before he can turn over a new leaf, Charlie finds himself drawn back to the crowd that gathers at McGurk's tavern. When the tavern owner's estranged wife turns up murdered, most of the evidence points toward P.T., leaving Charlie in a dilemma.

Where it's reviewed:
Chicago Tribune Books, September 19, 2004, page 1
Kirkus Reviews, July 15, 2004, page 654

Other books by the same author:
Blameless, 2000
Billy Dead, 1998

Other books you might like:
Larry Brown, *Joe*, 1991
Jere Hoar, *The Hit*, 2003
Raj Kamal Jha, *The Blue Bedspread*, 1999
Dennis Lehane, *A Drink Before the War*, 1994
Laura Lippman, *The Last Place*, 2002

1170

ELWOOD REID

D.B.

(New York: Doubleday, 2004)

Story type: Psychological Suspense; Historical

Subject(s): Hijackers and Hijacking; Retirement; Police Procedural
Major character(s): D.B. Cooper, Historical Figure (airplane hijacker), Fugitive; Frank Marshall, Aged Person, FBI Agent (now retired)
Time period(s): 1970s (1971)
Locale(s): Portland, Oregon; Mexico

Summary: A man called D.B. Cooper (no one is really sure if this is his real name) hijacks an airplane back in 1971. He ransoms the passengers for $200,000 and two parachutes. Then, Cooper disappears when he jumps from the airplane with the money somewhere over Oregon or northern California. The money is never recovered and Cooper is never apprehended for the crime. This story imagines that Cooper retired to Mexico, where he would have lived happily ever after if his identity had remained secret. However, the truth has a way of slipping out. When it does, Cooper is forced to return to the U.S. to retrieve his stash of cash. Along the way, he is pursued by a retired FBI agent who is obsessed with the case.

Where it's reviewed:
Kirkus Reviews, May 1, 2004, page 419
Library Journal, June 1, 2004, page 124
New York Times Book Review, August 8, 2004, page 9
Publishers Weekly, May 31, 2004, page 50

Other books by the same author:
Midnight Sun, 2000
What Salmon Know, 1999
If I Don't Six, 1998

Other books you might like:
Louis Begley, *About Schmidt*, 1996
Tom Franklin, *Hell at the Breech*, 2003
Janette Turner Hospital, *Due Preparations for the Plague*, 2003
Heidi Julavits, *The Effect of Living Backwards*, 2003
Toby Olson, *Write Letter to Billy*, 2000

1171

NANCY REISMAN

The First Desire

(New York: Pantheon, 2004)

Story type: Historical; Domestic
Subject(s): Jews; Missing Persons; Family
Major character(s): Abe Cohen, Store Owner (jewelry store), Parent (five children); Goldie Cohen, Relative (Abe's eldest daughter)
Time period(s): 20th century (1929-1950)
Locale(s): Buffalo, New York

Summary: Reisman's debut novel, set in Buffalo, is a family saga. The story isn't about what happens, but how and why everyone feels the way they do. Abe Cohen runs a jewelry store while his wife Rebecca raises their five children. When Rebecca dies, everyone expects Goldie, their oldest daughter, to be responsible for her younger siblings; instead she disappears. Sadie, the married younger sister, is forced to step in, but the task is overwhelming since Abe is a tyrant and the other children are uncooperative. For various reasons, everyone is unhappy in some way; all are conflicted. They all want to escape from the family, while at the same time staying connected to it.

Where it's reviewed:
Kirkus Reviews, July 15, 2004, page 654
Library Journal, August 2004, page 69
New York Times Book Review, September 12, 2004, page 17
Publishers Weekly, August 30, 2004, page 49

Other books by the same author:
House Fires, 1999

Other books you might like:
Binnie Kirshenbaum, *An Almost Perfect Moment*, 2004
Chaim Potok, *The Chosen*, 1967
Henry Roth, *Call It Sleep*, 1934
Philip Roth, *The Plot Against America*, 2004
Kate Wenner, *Setting Fires*, 2000

1172
KEITH RIDGWAY

The Parts
(New York: Thomas Dunne, 2004)

Story type: Psychological Suspense
Subject(s): Widows/Widowers; Conspiracies; Wealth
Major character(s): Delly Roche, Widow(er), Wealthy; Kitty Flood, Friend (of Delly), Lesbian; George Addison-Blake, Doctor, Relative (Delly's adopted son)
Time period(s): 2000s
Locale(s): Dublin, Ireland

Summary: The story, set in current day Ireland, develops from the lives of several different characters. The narrative is tied together by a radio talk show, when Joe Kavanagh, the show's host, becomes preoccupied with conspiracy theory, as a way of boosting the ratings on his show. Eccentric widow Delly Roche is about to die or so she believes. Kitty Flood, a lesbian author, is taking care of Delly. Delly's husband, Daniel Gilmore, a successful businessman, and her lover Frank Cullen, who was Daniel's assistant, were killed when their helicopter crashed more than ten years ago. Meanwhile, Dr. George Addison-Blake, the caretaker of Delly's estate, kidnaps Kevin, a gay prostitute, who was scheduled to appear on the radio talk show.

Where it's reviewed:
Kirkus Reviews, April 15, 2004, page 359
Library Journal, June 15, 2004, page 61
New York Times Book Review, June 13, 2004, page 23

Other books by the same author:
Standard Time, 2001
The Long Falling, 1998

Other books you might like:
Reed Arvin, *The Will*, 2000
Robin Cook, *Harmful Intent*, 1990
John Irving, *The Fourth Hand*, 2001
Terry Southern, *The Magic Christian*, 1960
Colm Toibin, *The Master*, 2004

1173
MARILYNNE ROBINSON

Gilead
(New York: Farrar, Straus and Giroux, 2004)

Story type: Domestic; Inspirational
Subject(s): Fathers and Sons; Clergy; Aging
Major character(s): John Ames, Religious (minister)
Time period(s): 19th century; 20th century
Locale(s): Gilead, Iowa

Summary: Robinson's novel is a family saga that starts just before the Civil War and continues until the mid-1950s. The story opens in 1956, when Rev. John Ames, 77, realizes that his days are numbered. Married with a six-year-old son, Ames writes a letter to the boy, hoping the child will read it when he is a young man. The letter details the good reverend's life, and the lives of his preacher father, a confirmed pacifist and his preacher grandfather, a passionate abolitionist. In addition to providing his son with a family history and descriptions of a preacher's life on the prairie, the narrative also describes historical forces that swept the country, including the bloody abolitionist struggle to keep Kansas from becoming a slave state, the Civil War, World War I, and the Spanish influenza epidemic.

Where it's reviewed:
Booklist, August 2004, page 1874
Chicago Tribune Books, November 28, 2004, page 1
Kirkus Reviews, August 15, 2004, page 772
Newsweek, December 6, 2004, page 87
Publishers Weekly, September 27, 2004, page 36

Other books by the same author:
Housekeeping, 1980

Other books you might like:
Richard Babcock, *Bow's Boy*, 2002
Sandra Brown, *White Hot*, 2004
James M. Cain, *Mildred Pierce*, 1945
Ursula Hegi, *Sacred Time*, 2003
Maile Meloy, *Liars and Saints*, 2003

1174
JONATHAN ROSEN

Joy Comes in the Morning
(New York: Farrar, Straus and Giroux, 2004)

Story type: Psychological
Subject(s): Women; Clergy; Holocaust
Major character(s): Henry Friedman, Holocaust Victim; Deborah Green, Religious (rabbi); Lev Friedman, Relative (Henry's son)
Time period(s): 2000s
Locale(s): New York, New York

Summary: The importance of ritual and tradition is examined in Rosen's novel. Henry Friedman, fearing that his health is failing, attempts suicide. While recovering, Rabbi Deborah Green tries to comfort Henry. A Holocaust survivor, Henry reflects on the meaning of his life, including his views of religion. Meanwhile, the good rabbi makes a connection with

Henry's wife and his son Lev, with whom she falls in love. However, life has a way of getting complicated. Lev comes from an almost anti-religious perspective and Deborah's family is very secular, making their emotional relationship anything but easy.

Where it's reviewed:
Booklist, August 2004, page 1902
Chicago Tribune Books, September 19, 2004, page 3
Kirkus Reviews, July 15, 2004, page 655
Library Journal, September 1, 2004, page 141
Publishers Weekly, July 12, 2004, page 43

Other books by the same author:
Eve's Apple, 1997

Other books you might like:
Martin Amis, *Time's Arrow, or, the Nature of the Offense*, 1991
Saul Bellow, *Mr. Sammler's Planet*, 1970
Gwen Edelman, *War Story*, 2001
William Styron, *Sophie's Choice*, 1979
Simone Zelitch, *Louisa*, 2000

PHILIP ROTH

The Plot Against America
(Boston: Houghton Mifflin, 2004)

Story type: Historical/World War II; Americana
Subject(s): Alternate History; Politics; Jews
Major character(s): Charles Lindbergh, Historical Figure, Political Figure; Franklin Delano Roosevelt, Historical Figure, Political Figure; Philip Roth, Child, Historical Figure
Time period(s): 1940s (1940-1944)
Locale(s): Newark, New Jersey

Summary: Roth plays the what if game with an alternate history tale. Instead of Roosevelt winning the 1940 election and guiding the United States through World War II and the defeat of Nazi Germany, the very popular Charles Lindbergh defeats Roosevelt with a promise to keep the country out of the European war. After his election, Lindbergh cuts a deal with Hitler, who then completes the conquest of Europe. This sets the stage in the United States for the rise of fascism and the persecution of the Jews. Young Philip Roth, who is growing up in New Jersey, watches as his cousin goes to Canada to enlist in the fight against Hitler. Various segments in the Jewish community take sides, some supporting Lindbergh and some opposing him. In the author's capable hands, this implausible story becomes frighteningly plausible.

Where it's reviewed:
Booklist, August 2004, page 1874
Kirkus Reviews, July 15, 2004, page 655
New York Times Book Review, October 3, 2004, page 1
Publishers Weekly, July 12, 2004, page 44

Other books by the same author:
The Dying Animal, 2001
The Human Stain, 2000
I Married a Communist, 1998
The Great American Novel, 1973
Portnoy's Complaint, 1969

Other books you might like:
Anonymous, *Primary Colors*, 1996
Joan Didion, *Democracy*, 1984
E.L. Doctorow, *The Book of Daniel*, 1971
Jack Higgins, *The President's Daughter*, 1997
Gore Vidal, *Burr*, 1973

1176

CARLOS RUIZ ZAFON

The Shadow of the Wind
(New York: Penguin, 2004)

Story type: Coming-of-Age; Literary
Subject(s): Books and Reading; Fantasy; Censorship
Major character(s): Daniel Sempere, Guardian (of a forgotten book)
Time period(s): 1950s
Locale(s): Barcelona, Spain

Summary: Shortly after World War II, Daniel Sempere travels with his father to an unusual sanctuary, a resting place for forgotten books. A bookseller, Daniel's father insists that his son choose a book. A dutiful son, Daniel does as he is told. Then, he must guard it from all danger. This turns out to be quite a trick because the forces of destruction, led by the Lucifer-like Julian Carax, are determined to burn the forgotten books. As he grows up, Daniel crosses paths with Carax. Daniel also meets the enigmatic Clara Barcelo and the beautiful Beatriz Aguilar. Lucia Graves did the translation. Although well-known in Spain, this is Ruiz Zafon's first book to be translated into English.

Where it's reviewed:
Booklist, March 1, 2004, page 1102
Kirkus Reviews, March 1, 2004, page 200
Library Journal, February 1, 2004, page 126
Publishers Weekly, February 16, 2004, page 148

Other books you might like:
Emilia Pardo Bazan, *The House of Ulloa*, 1990
Ian Caldwell, *The Rule of Four*, 2004
   Dustin Thomason, co-author
John Dunning, *The Bookman's Promise*, 2004
Carlos Fuentes, *The Years with Laura Diaz*, 2000
Arturo Perez-Reverte, *The Queen of the South*, 2004

1177

NICK SAGAN

Edenborn
(New York: Putnam, 2004)

Story type: Dystopian; Science Fiction
Subject(s): Human Behavior; Plague; Endangered Species
Time period(s): Indeterminate Future
Locale(s): Earth

Summary: Sagan, a successful screenwriter, has written a novel with a dystopian theme. The work is a sequel to his 2003 novel *Idlewild* in which a plague ravaged the earth. Now, the survivors prepare to make a brave new world but human nature being what it is, there are difficulties, including annoying people, governments, and other untidy human institutions. The constantly mutating plague, technology, and genetic engineering add spice to the mix. When murder and politics enter the scene, things really come apart. The science is edgy and the pace is quick.

Where it's reviewed:
Kirkus Reviews, July 15, 2004, page 666
New York Times Book Review, August 29, 2004, page 12

Other books by the same author:
Idlewild, 2003

Other books you might like:
Margaret Atwood, *Oryx and Crake*, 2003
Russell Banks, *The Darling*, 2004
Clive Barker, *Sacrament*, 1996
Philip K. Dick, *The Penultimate Truth*, 1967
Valerie Martin, *A Recent Martyr*, 1987

1178
BART SCHNEIDER

The Beautiful Inez
(New York: Shaye Areheart, 2004)

Story type: Historical; Psychological
Subject(s): Marriage; Women; Homosexuality/Lesbianism
Major character(s): Inez Roseman, Musician (violinist), Parent (two children); Jake Roseman, Spouse (Inez's husband), Lawyer; Sylvia Bran, Imposter, Musician
Time period(s): 1960s
Locale(s): San Francisco, California

Summary: Schneider's novel is a prequel to 2001's *Secret Love*. Inez Roseman, a 40ish, modestly successful classical violinist possesses classical blonde good looks. A mother of two children, she is married to Jake, a successful lawyer with an interest in civil rights. On the surface, Inez has an idyllic life but her marriage has become stale and love has become tedious. This all changes when Sylvia Bran, posing as a reporter, enters her life. The two women hit it off and enter into a passionate affair.

Where it's reviewed:
Kirkus Reviews, December 1, 2004, page 1112
Library Journal, November 15, 2004, page 52
Publishers Weekly, November 22, 2004, page 36

Other books by the same author:
Secret Love, 2001
Blue Bossa, 1998

Other books you might like:
Sylvia Brownrigg, *Pages for You*, 2001
Percival Everett, *My Existing Condition*, 2004
Alison Lurie, *The Last Resort*, 1998
Chuck Palahniuk, *Choke*, 2001
Joanna Trollope, *A Village Affair*, 1989

1179
LESLIE SCHNUR

The Dog Walker
(New York: Atria, 2004)

Story type: Humor; Contemporary
Subject(s): Identity, Concealed; Relationships; Modern Life
Major character(s): Nina Shepard, Animal Trainer (walks dogs); Daniel Maguire, Lawyer, Twin (of Billy); Billy Maguire, Twin (of Daniel)
Time period(s): 2000s
Locale(s): New York, New York

Summary: Nina Shepard is single, unattached, and living in Manhattan. While reality hasn't been kind to her—she doesn't have a boyfriend but wants one—she has a job that ruthlessly feeds her imagination with plenty of fantasy. Nina is a dog walker. She has the keys to her clients' apartments, giving her access to their homes and personal space. This is how she meets Daniel and falls for him. Complications set in when she discovers that Daniel isn't really Daniel, but rather Daniel's twin brother Billy. As it turns out, Nina has a few secrets of her own. Nina's clients and friends add lively bits of color.

Where it's reviewed:
Kirkus Reviews, June 1, 2004, page 514
Library Journal, June 15, 2004, page 66
Publishers Weekly, June 14, 2004, page 42

Other books you might like:
Peter Carey, *Illywhacker*, 1985
Karen Joy Fowler, *The Jane Austen Book Club*, 2004
Jane Heller, *Female Intelligence*, 2001
Anne Tyler, *A Patchwork Planet*, 1998
Jennifer Weiner, *Good in Bed*, 2001

1180
LISA SCOTTOLINE

Killer Smile
(New York: HarperCollins, 2004)

Story type: Mystery; Ethnic
Subject(s): Italian Americans; Internment; Legal Thriller
Major character(s): Mary DiNunzio, Lawyer, Widow(er); Amadeo Brandolini, Businessman (interned during WWII)
Time period(s): 2000s
Locale(s): Philadelphia, Pennsylvania; Missoula, Montana

Summary: Although still grieving, Mary DiNunzio is back on the job. In point of fact, her friends need her. Her first case is a pro bono representation for a family who suffered at the hands of the U.S. government during World War II. The result was that an Italian immigrant, Amadeo Brandolini, a small businessman, lost everything, including his life. After he was arrested and sent to an internment camp, Brandolini fell into a deep depression and committed suicide. Now, his family is attempting to make the government accountable. As layers of the official story are peeled back, there is reason to believe that Brandolini may not have committed suicide. Of course,

Mary is up to the task. Before all is said and done, her life will be threatened and she will have to travel to Montana.

Where it's reviewed:
Kirkus Reviews, May 1, 2004, page 420
Library Journal, May 15, 2004, page 116
Publishers Weekly, March 22, 2004, page 58

Other books by the same author:
Dead Ringer, 2003
Courting Trouble, 2002
The Vendetta Defense, 2001
Moment of Truth, 2000
Mistaken Identity, 1999

Other books you might like:
Robert Harris, *Fatherland*, 1992
Julie Otsuka, *When the Emperor Was Divine*, 2002
Richard North Patterson, *Degree of Guilt*, 1993
Danielle Steel, *Silent Honor*, 1996
Scott Turow, *The Burden of Proof*, 1990

1181

HELEN SCULLY

In the Hope of Rising Again

(New York: Penguin, 2004)

Story type: Historical; Family Saga
Subject(s): Relationships; Inheritance; Depression (Economic)
Major character(s): Colonel Riant, Publisher (newspaper); Regina Riant, Spouse (of Charles); Charles Morrow, Spouse (Regina's husband)
Time period(s): 19th century; 20th century
Locale(s): Mobile, Alabama

Summary: In her debut novel, Scully presents a family saga set in the American South that runs from the end of the Civil War to the beginning of the Great Depression in 1929. Colonel Riant owns a newspaper in Mobile, Alabama. He attempts to instruct his children in the notion of social responsibility, or using wealth and position for the benefit of everyone, especially those less fortunate. However, his daughter Regina is the only one who hears the message. Her four brothers take the opposite view; they believe that wealth is for their personal benefit and squander their inheritance.

Where it's reviewed:
Kirkus Reviews, June 1, 2004, page 515
Publishers Weekly, July 5, 2004, page 38

Other books you might like:
Alice Adams, *Families and Survivors*, 1974
Ellen Douglas, *Can't Quit You Baby*, 1988
Kaye Gibbons, *Ellen Foster*, 1987
Ellen Gilchrist, *Net of Jewels*, 1992
Margaret Mitchell, *Gone with the Wind*, 1936

1182

JOHN SEARLES

Strange but True

(New York: William Morrow, 2004)

Story type: Contemporary/Mainstream
Subject(s): Accidents; Mothers and Sons; Death
Major character(s): Melissa Moody, Pregnant Teenager, Girlfriend (Ronnie's); Philip Chase, Young Man (Ronnie's older brother); Charlene Chase, Parent (mother of Philip and Ronnie)
Time period(s): 2000s
Locale(s): Pennsylvania

Summary: Philip Chase grows up knowing his younger brother Ronnie is their parents' favorite. When Ronnie dies in a car crash on his prom night, Philip's mother blames him. Philip leaves home until an injury forces him to move back. Life is very unpleasant as he and his mother continually bicker with each other. Five years after Ronnie's death, his girlfriend Melissa shows up claiming to be carrying Ronnie's child. Philip is dumbfounded, but Philip's mother has a different view. She desperately wants to believe Melissa and sets out to prove that the child is Ronnie's. Meanwhile, Melissa's landlady, Gail, wants to evict her. Gail, who is also pregnant, fears that her husband, Bill, has been using date rape drugs to have sexual relations with young women. When Bill gets wind of his wife's suspicions, Melissa disappears.

Where it's reviewed:
Kirkus Reviews, July 1, 2004, page 602
New York Times, July 22, 2004, page B7
Publishers Weekly, July 5, 2004, page 37

Other books by the same author:
Boy Still Missing, 2001

Other books you might like:
Dan Chaon, *You Remind Me of Me*, 2004
Jane Hamilton, *Disobedience*, 2000
Adam Langer, *Crossing California*, 2004
James Patterson, *Sam's Letters to Jennifer*, 2004
Alice Randall, *Pushkin and the Queen of Spades*, 2004

1183

JEFF SHAARA

To the Last Man

(New York: Ballantine, 2004)

Story type: Historical/World War I
Subject(s): War; Politics; Death
Major character(s): Manfred von Richthofen, Military Personnel (German pilot), Historical Figure; Raoul Lufbery, Military Personnel (American pilot); Roscoe Temple, Military Personnel (American marine)
Time period(s): 1910s (1916-1918)
Locale(s): Europe

Summary: Shaara's work is an epic story about World War I. Diplomats jockey to draw the United States into the conflict on the side of England and France against Germany. American General John ''Blackjack'' Pershing struggles to maintain command of his ill-equipped troops against British and French efforts to absorb the Americans into their armies. The terrible reality of trench warfare—the advances and retreats, and death—is seen through the eyes of soldiers, who experience the mud and the blood. Airplanes have also been added to the mix and the airborne knights from each side fight for supremacy in the sky, while delivering death to the ground forces below.

Where it's reviewed:
Booklist, September 15, 2004, page 180
Kirkus Reviews, September 15, 2004, page 888
Library Journal, October 1, 2004, page 73
Publishers Weekly, October 11, 2004, page 54

Other books by the same author:
The Glorious Cause, 2002
Rise to Rebellion, 2001
Gone for Soldiers, 2000
The Last Full Measure, 1998
Gods and Generals, 1996

Other books you might like:
Pat Barker, *Regeneration*, 1991
Humphrey Cobb, *Paths of Glory*, 1935
Jim Harrison, *Legends of the Fall*, 1979
Ian McEwan, *Atonement*, 2001
Michael Ondaatje, *The English Patient*, 1992

1184

SIDNEY SHELDON

Are You Afraid of the Dark?
(New York: William Morrow, 2004)

Story type: Mystery; Espionage
Subject(s): Spies; Murder; Widows/Widowers
Major character(s): Kelly Harris, Widow(er); Diane Stevens, Widow(er); Tanner Kingsley, Businessman (chief executive)
Time period(s): 2000s
Locale(s): New York, New York; Paris, France; Berlin, Germany

Summary: Sheldon's thriller opens with four seemingly unrelated deaths: a woman disappears in Berlin, a man falls from the Eiffel Tower, a man dies in a plane crash in Denver, and a body is recovered in New York. However, each of the victims worked for a think tank called Kingsley International Group (KIG) and two victims left behind wives. Tanner Kingsley tries to reassure the widows—Kelly Harris and Diane Stevens—that his firm is doing everything it can to bring the criminals to justice. However, Tanner loses credibility when the widows find themselves targeted by the assassins.

Where it's reviewed:
Booklist, August 2004, page 1872
Kirkus Reviews, July 1, 2004, page 603

Other books by the same author:
Tell Me Your Dreams, 1998
Morning, Noon, and Night, 1995
Windmills of the Gods, 1987
Bloodline, 1977

Other books you might like:
Mary Higgins Clark, *Nighttime Is My Time*, 2004
Patricia Cornwell, *Trace*, 2004
John Grisham, *The Last Juror*, 2004
John Le Carre, *Absolute Friends*, 2003
Danielle Steel, *Ransom*, 2004

1185

STEVEN SHERRILL

Visits from the Drowned Girl
(New York: Random House, 2004)

Story type: Psychological
Subject(s): Suicide; Secrets; American South
Major character(s): Benny Poteat, Repairman (of broadcast towers); Jenna, Artist (makes videos), Mentally Ill Person (commits suicide); Rebecca, Relative (Jenna's sister)
Time period(s): 2000s
Locale(s): Buffalo, North Carolina

Summary: Benny Poteat makes his living high above the ground, working on power lines. One day he witnesses a young woman who throws herself in the river and drowns. Benny is too high up and too far away to do anything to stop the tragedy. Instead of calling the authorities, he tells no one, but does take the woman's things, including a video camera she set up to record her demise. Then, he sets out to find her family. When he does, he slips into their lives in such a way that it makes it impossible for him to tell them what happened to the girl. Soon, however, the secret begins to drive him crazy.

Where it's reviewed:
Booklist, May 15, 2004, page 1602
Chicago Tribune Books, August 22, 2004, page 7
Kirkus Reviews, April 1, 2004, page 295
Publishers Weekly, March 29, 2004, page 35

Other books by the same author:
The Minotaur Takes a Cigarette Break, 2000

Other books you might like:
Richard Flanagan, *Death of a River Guide*, 1994
John Grisham, *The Client*, 1993
Carson McCullers, *The Heart Is a Lonely Hunter*, 1940
John O'Hara, *Appointment in Samarra*, 1934
Donna Tartt, *The Little Friend*, 2002

1186

MICHAEL SIMON

Dirty Sally
(New York: Viking, 2004)

Story type: Ethnic; Mystery
Subject(s): Murder; Jews; Police Procedural
Major character(s): Dan Reles, Detective—Homicide
Time period(s): 2000s
Locale(s): Austin, Texas

Summary: Although this is Simon's debut novel, it's not like he's a new kid on the block, or at least, he's not an inexperienced new kid on the block. His previous work, acting,

Popular Fiction (sidebar)

ghostwriting, and playwriting may have provided him with the stepping stones for a long career. The novel is set in Austin, Texas, and opens with the brutal murder of a prostitute. Her body is dismembered with certain parts sent to prominent citizens. Police Detective Dan Reles, who was recently suspended, needs this type of case to redeem a career that has been deteriorating. After his marriage broke up and his partner was killed in a car crash, Reles turned to alcohol and violence. To make matters worse, Reles is an outsider—he's Jewish and didn't grow up in the South.

Where it's reviewed:
Chicago Tribune Books, July 25, 2004, page 3
Kirkus Reviews, June 1, 2004, page 515
Publishers Weekly, May 31, 2004, page 46

Other books you might like:
Saul Bellow, *Mr. Sammler's Planet*, 1970
James Lee Burke, *In the Moon of Red Ponies*, 2004
Stephen L. Carter, *The Emperor of Ocean Park*, 2002
Michael Connelly, *The Narrows*, 2004
Carl Hiaasen, *Skinny Dip*, 2004

1187

INDRA SINHA

The Death of Mr. Love

(New York: William Morrow, 2004)

Story type: Psychological; Domestic
Subject(s): Mothers and Daughters; Friendship; Trials
Major character(s): Bhalu, Businessman (bookseller); Maya, Aged Person (dying), Parent (Bhalu's mother); Phoebe, Friend (of Bhalu)
Time period(s): 20th century (1950-1998)
Locale(s): London, England; Bombay, India

Summary: This debut novel is based in part on a 1950 murder that occurred in India. Mr. Love, an Indian playboy who seduced married women, was murdered by a enraged husband, a British officer. The narrative begins in 1998 and weaves back and forth between the past and the present. On her deathbed, Maya tells her son Bhalu a cryptic story about their departure from India. The story doesn't make any sense, until Bhalu's childhood friend Phoebe lets him read her deceased mother's diary. Phoebe's mother, Sylvia, had an affair with Mr. Love and was blackmailed. The blackmailer forced Sylvia and Maya to leave India. Bhalu and Phoebe decide to find and punish the blackmailer.

Where it's reviewed:
Kirkus Reviews, September 15, 2004, page 889
Library Journal, November 15, 2004, page 52

Other books you might like:
Monica Ali, *Brick Lane*, 2003
Ann Beattie, *My Life, Starring Dara Falcon*, 1997
Ruth Prawer Jhabvala, *My Nine Lives*, 2004
Jhumpa Lahiri, *Interpreter of Maladies*, 1999
Carol Shields, *The Stone Diaries*, 1997

1188

CAROLYN SLAUGHTER

A Black Englishman

(New York: Farrar, Straus and Giroux, 2004)

Story type: Historical/Roaring Twenties; Romance
Subject(s): Race Relations; Doctors; Women
Major character(s): Isabel Herbert, Spouse (Neville's wife); Sam Singh, Doctor, Lover (Isabel's); Neville Webb, Military Personnel (career officer)
Time period(s): 1920s
Locale(s): India

Summary: This is a love story laced with heavy doses of social and historical reality. After the love of her life is killed in World War I, Isabel settles for Neville, a career officer. When Neville is posted to India, Isabel follows. At the time, India is taking the first steps towards independence from England. The social scene is a cauldron of racial, religious, and political differences that are often acted out violently. Against this backdrop, the sensitive Isabel becomes estranged from Neville and falls in love with Sam, an English-educated Indian doctor. The consequences for both Sam and Isabel are frightening when their affair is uncovered.

Where it's reviewed:
Booklist, October 1, 2004, page 312
Kirkus Reviews, September 1, 2004, page 834
Library Journal, October 15, 2004, page 56
Publishers Weekly, September 27, 2004, page 35

Other books by the same author:
The Widow, 1989
The Innocents, 1986
A Perfect Woman, 1984
Dreams of the Kalahari, 1981
Magdalene, 1978

Other books you might like:
Margaret Atwood, *The Blind Assassin*, 2000
Desmond Barry, *Cressida's Bed*, 2004
Peter Carey, *Oscar and Lucinda*, 1988
J.M. Coetzee, *Disgrace*, 1999
Ruth Prawer Jhabvala, *Heat and Dust*, 1975

1189

ELLEN SLEZAK

All These Girls

(New York: Hyperion, 2004)

Story type: Psychological; Domestic
Subject(s): Women; Grief; Travel
Major character(s): Candy Golden, Sports Figure (high school basketball player), Orphan; Gloria Dreslinski, Relative (Candy's aunt), Widow(er); Elizabeth Brannigan, Relative (Candy's aunt), Divorced Person (three failed marriages)
Time period(s): 2000s
Locale(s): Lovely, Michigan

Summary: The story in Slezak's debut novel swirls around personal crises in the lives of three women. Candy, a high school sophomore and star basketball player, becomes an orphan suddenly. She goes to live with relatives but the transition isn't smooth. Her Aunt Glo, a recent widow, is still dealing with the loss of her husband. Another aunt, Elizabeth, is recently divorced and, after the breakup of this third marriage, is emotionally wounded herself. Neither aunt feels prepared to be responsible for their young niece. Things come to a head when Candy quits basketball. Her aunts do come around, but it takes a pilgrimage for the three women to get back on the same page.

Where it's reviewed:
Booklist, August 1, 2004, page 1903
Chicago Tribune Books, September 19, 2004, page 1
Kirkus Reviews, June 15, 2004, page 556
Publishers Weekly, August 23, 2004, page 38

Other books by the same author:
Last Year's Jesus, 2002 (short stories)

Other books you might like:
Graham Greene, *Travels with My Aunt*, 1969
Jim Harrison, *The Women Lit by Fireflies*, 1990
Barbara Kingsolver, *The Bean Trees*, 1988
Joyce Carol Oates, *You Must Remember This*, 1987
Donna Tartt, *The Little Friend*, 2002

1190

MARTIN CRUZ SMITH

Wolves Eat Dogs

(New York: Simon & Schuster, 2004)

Story type: Mystery
Series: Arkady Renko. Book 5
Subject(s): Police Procedural; Russians; Wealth
Major character(s): Arkady Renko, Police Officer (special investigator)
Time period(s): 2000s
Locale(s): Moscow, Russia; Chernobyl, Ukraine; Pripyat, Ukraine

Summary: Smith's memorable character Arkady Renko, an honest Russian police investigator, returns in the fifth book of the series. Renko is called to the scene when millionaire Pasha Ivanov falls ten stories to his death. Was this a suicide or a murder? Renko's boss wants him to declare the death a suicide but evidence on the scene, including a bloody hand print on the windowsill, the bloody nose of one of Ivanov's men, and salt in the closet raises questions. Renko's investigation will take him to the Ukraine, where he will visit the abandoned towns of Chernobyl and Pripyat. As his investigation proceeds, Renko will find another body. Suicide won't be an issue—the victim's throat was cut.

Where it's reviewed:
Booklist, September 1, 2004, page 8
Kirkus Reviews, September 1, 2004, page 834
Library Journal, October 15, 2004, page 56
New York Times Book Review, November 14, 2004, page 50
Publishers Weekly, September 6, 2004, page 43

Other books by the same author:
December 6, 2002
Havana Bay, 1999
Red Square, 1992

Polar Star, 1989
Gorky Park, 1981

Other books you might like:
Tom Clancy, *The Cardinal of the Kremlin*, 1988
Alan Furst, *Night Soldiers*, 1988
Stuart M. Kaminsky, *Murder on the Trans-Siberian Express*, 2001
John Le Carre, *Absolute Friends*, 2003
Robert Ludlum, *The Tristan Betrayal*, 2003

1191

MARK SPRAGG

An Unfinished Life

(New York: Knopf, 2004)

Story type: Psychological; Domestic
Subject(s): Veterans; Pregnancy; Friendship
Major character(s): Jean Gilkyson, Widow(er), Single Parent (Griff's mother); Griff Gilkyson, Child (Jean's daughter); Einar Gilkyson, Rancher, Grandparent (Griff's grandfather)
Time period(s): 2000s
Locale(s): Iowa; Ishawooa, Wyoming

Summary: Spragg's novel centers on a family reunion that has a rocky start. After the accidental death of her husband, Jean has awful luck picking boyfriends. Her latest choice is a real loser, who forces Jean to leave Iowa to protect her young daughter, Griff. They seek refuge with Jean's father-in-law Einar. Jean and Griff are desperate and the old man reluctantly takes them in, even though he blames Jean for his son's death and isn't happy to see her. When Griff makes friends with Einar's old army buddy, she soon wins over her grandfather, too. Meanwhile, Jean develops a relationship with the local sheriff, which proves very helpful when her ex-boyfriend comes looking for her.

Where it's reviewed:
Booklist, August 2004, page 1901
Library Journal, June 1, 2004, page 126
Publishers Weekly, August 9, 2004, page 231

Other books by the same author:
The Fruit of Stone, 2002

Other books you might like:
Richard Bausch, *Rebel Powers*, 1993
Richard Condon, *The Manchurian Candidate*, 1959
Edna Ferber, *Giant*, 1952
Carrie Fisher, *Delusions of Grandma*, 1994
Annie Proulx, *Close Range*, 1999

1192

JERRY STAHL

I, Fatty

(New York: Bloomsbury, 2004)

Story type: Historical/Depression Era; Americana
Subject(s): Actors and Actresses; Movie Industry; Trials
Major character(s): Roscoe ''Fatty'' Arbuckle, Entertainer (comic), Historical Figure (movie star)

Time period(s): 1930s (1933)
Locale(s): Hollywood, California

Summary: Stahl's book is based on the historical events surrounding the rise to fame and fall from grace of Roscoe "Fatty" Arbuckle. Arbuckle grows up in abject poverty, but becomes one of the cinema's greatest comic actors, rivaling Charlie Chaplin and Buster Keaton in popularity. Things come to a crashing halt when he is charged with the rape and murder of a starlet. Although he is acquitted of all charges in court, the public is not so forgiving when it learns about Arbuckle's debauched lifestyle. His career comes to an ignominious end, a lesson in the fickleness of fate.

Where it's reviewed:
Kirkus Reviews, May 1, 2004, page 422
Library Journal, June 1, 2004, page 126
Publishers Weekly, May 24, 2004, page 42

Other books by the same author:
Plainclothes Naked, 2001
Perv: A Love Story, 1999

Other books you might like:
Joan Didion, *Play It as It Lays*, 1970
Carrie Fisher, *Postcards from the Edge*, 1987
Judith Krantz, *Scruples*, 1978
Terry Southern, *Blue Movie*, 1970
Robert Stone, *Children of Light*, 1986

1193

MARY HELEN STEFANIAK

The Turk and My Mother

(New York: Norton, 2004)

Story type: Ethnic; Family Saga
Subject(s): Grandmothers; Storytelling; Family Relations
Major character(s): Staramajka, Grandparent (George's grandmother); George, Relative (son of Josef and Agnes)
Time period(s): 20th century; 21st century
Locale(s): Croatia; Milwaukee, Wisconsin

Summary: The saga of a Croatian-American family is told in several interlocking stories recounted on his deathbed by a man named George. The family immigrates to Milwaukee shortly after World War I. George recounts tales of his grandmother, Staramajka, the family matriarch; her son Josef, who avoids the war by coming to America; Josef's wife, Agnes, and her forbidden love for a Turkish prisoner of war; and Staramajka's other son, Marko, who disappears during the war, but later turns up alive. The author paints a vivid picture of the family's life in the old country, and their struggles to survive, both there and in their adopted land.

Where it's reviewed:
Kirkus Reviews, April 15, 2004, page 361
Publishers Weekly, April 26, 2004, page 39

Other books by the same author:
Self Storage and Other Stories, 1997

Other books you might like:
Robert Boswell, *Century's Son*, 2002
George Hagen, *The Laments*, 2004
Adam Langer, *Crossing California*, 2004

Gary Shteyngart, *The Russian Debutante's Handbook*, 2002
Irene Zabytko, *When Luba Leaves Home*, 2003

1194

BARBARA SUTTON

The Send-Away Girl

(Athens: University of Georgia Press, 2004)

Story type: Collection; Americana
Subject(s): Friendship; Cultures and Customs; Short Stories
Time period(s): 2000s
Locale(s): United States

Summary: This is Sutton's debut short story collection and it won her a Flannery O'Connor Award for short fiction. There are ten stories and most are darkly comic. "Tra Il Devoto Et Profano" features a neglected child and a minister who likes alcohol. In "Maybe, Maybe Not," a pie throwing memory helps a couple get married. A woman anxiously waits for surgery in "The Brotherhood of Healing." An incorrigible child rescues a woman in "Rabbit Punch." In "The Send-Away Girl," a woman reflects on her many jobs, while poetry is used to treat a heartbroken man in "Tenants." In "The Rest of Esther," an elderly woman is plied for a bequest. The other stories are: "The Art of Getting Real," "Risk Merchants," and "The Empire of Light."

Where it's reviewed:
Booklist, August 2004, page 1898
Kirkus Reviews, August 1, 2004, page 713
Publishers Weekly, September 6, 2004, page 44

Other books you might like:
Ed Allen, *Ate It Anyway*, 2003
Catherine Brady, *Curled in the Bed of Love*, 2003
Gary Fincke, *Sorry I Worried You*, 2004
Gina Ochsner, *The Necessary Grace to Fall*, 2002
Kellie Wells, *Compression Scars*, 2002

1195

COLM TOIBIN

The Master

(New York: Scribner, 2004)

Story type: Historical
Subject(s): Biography; Authors and Writers; Loneliness
Major character(s): Henry James, Historical Figure, Writer
Time period(s): 19th century; 20th century (1843-1916)
Locale(s): New York, New York; London, England; Venice, Italy

Summary: This is a fictional account of the life of Henry James, the man some critics consider to be the best American writer. Born in 1843 in the United States, James lived most of his life abroad in Paris, Venice, Rome, and London among intellectuals, artists, writers, and the aristocracy. Although his work is known for psychological insight, James himself is portrayed as lonely and longing. Despite his best efforts to fully connect with another, James failed miserably, perhaps explaining his ability to probe the psyche of his characters.

Where it's reviewed:
Kirkus Reviews, April 1, 2004, page 297
Library Journal, May 1, 2004, page 142
Publishers Weekly, April 19, 2004, page 39

Other books by the same author:
The Blackwater Lightship, 1999
The Story of the Night, 1996
The Heather Blazing, 1992
The South, 1990

Other books you might like:
Jim Crace, *Signals of Distress*, 1994
Helen Dewitt, *The Last Samurai*, 2000
John Griesemer, *Signal & Noise*, 2003
Henry James, *The Wings of the Dove*, 1902
Joanna Trollope, *Girl from the South*, 2002

1196

TOURE

Soul City
(New York: Little, Brown, 2004)

Story type: Humor; Utopia
Subject(s): African Americans; Fantasy; Campaigns, Political
Major character(s): Cadillac Jackson, Journalist; Mahogany Sunflower, Radio Personality (DJ); Lil Mo Love, Religious (preacher)
Time period(s): 2000s
Locale(s): Soul City

Summary: Toure's satirical first novel looks at racial stereotypes, power, and greed. Cadillac Jackson, a hard-bitten journalist, writes for the magazine *Chocolate City*. When he is assigned to cover the mayoral election in Soul City, he is stunned with what he finds. Although the geography is vague, it seems the city was founded by escaped slaves who could fly. Now, the place is a utopia for blacks. The political campaign is all about music: that is who controls the city's music track. Parents encourage their children to buy records and a sense of unity pervades the entire community. Then Cadillac meets the local DJ, a beautiful young woman named Mahogany. Reality does intrude, but the author introduces it laced with a good deal of humor.

Where it's reviewed:
Booklist, September 1, 2004, page 66
Kirkus Reviews, July 15, 2004, page 659
Library Journal, October 1, 2004, page 74
Publishers Weekly, August 9, 2004, page 231

Other books by the same author:
The Portable Promised Land, 2002

Other books you might like:
T. Coraghessan Boyle, *Drop City*, 2003
Don DeLillo, *Cosmopolis*, 2003
Ursula K. Le Guin, *The Dispossessed*, 1974
Walter Mosley, *Futureland*, 2001
Alice Randall, *Pushkin and the Queen of Spades*, 2004

1197
NICHELLE D. TRAMBLE

The Last King
(New York: Ballantine, 2004)

Story type: Mystery; Ethnic
Series: Maceo Redfield. Book 2
Subject(s): African Americans; Rape; Friendship
Major character(s): Maceo Redfield, Sports Figure (ex-baseball player), Friend (of Billy Crane); Billy Crane, Drug Dealer, Crime Victim (murdered); Felicia Bennett, Girlfriend (Billy's)
Time period(s): 1980s (1989); 1990s (1991)
Locale(s): Oakland, California; San Francisco, California

Summary: This is Tramble's second novel featuring Maceo Redfield, a washed-up baseball player. Told against a backdrop of a crack cocaine epidemic in Oakland, the story picks up where the first book, *The Dying Ground* (2001), left off. After spending two years on the road, Maceo, a little worse for wear—his face is scarred—is back in town. He stops at the barbershop to get caught up. He learns that pro basketball star Cotton Knox is under suspicion for the murder of a woman found in a hotel room. Witnesses place Cotton and his wife outside the hotel arguing over the woman. However, forces are afoot to pin the murder on someone else. At issue is a very lucrative drug trade. Things get really complicated when Maceo sets out to find his friends. After he gets mugged, he tries to find Cotton. He arrives just in time to rescue a woman friend of the murdered woman. The story moves quickly with numerous twists.

Where it's reviewed:
Chicago Tribune Books, June 13, 2004, page 3
Kirkus Reviews, April 1, 2004, page 298

Other books by the same author:
The Dying Ground, 2001

Other books you might like:
Richard Babcock, *Bow's Boy*, 2002
Zora Neale Hurston, *Every Tongue Got to Confess*, 2001
Walter Mosley, *Bad Boy Brawly Brown*, 2002
ZZ Packer, *Drinking Coffee Elsewhere*, 2002
Suzan-Lori Parks, *Getting Mother's Body*, 2003

1198
WILLIAM TREVOR

A Bit on the Side
(New York: Viking, 2004)

Story type: Collection
Subject(s): Relationships; Psychological; Short Stories
Time period(s): 2000s
Locale(s): Ireland

Summary: Trevor's collection offers 12 stories that deal with death, adultery, loneliness, inheritance, guilt, bitterness, and regret. The sharply drawn characters and psychological nuance more than make up for the bleakness. The lovers in ''A Bit on the Side'' decide to end their affair, despite an enduring love for each other. The widow in ''Sitting with the

Dead'' appears relieved at the death of her husband. A teenage girl in ''Rose Wept'' becomes upset when she learns her tutor's wife has been unfaithful. A woman in ''Solitude'' reveals the details surrounding an accident that altered her life. A librarian mourns the deaths of his wife and his former lover in ''Graillis's Legacy.''

Where it's reviewed:
Booklist, September 1, 2004, page 65
Chicago Tribune Books, November 28, 2004, page 3
Kirkus Reviews, September 1, 2004, page 835
Publishers Weekly, August 16, 2004, page 40

Other books by the same author:
The Story of Lucy Gault, 2002
The Hill Bachelors, 2000
Death in Summer, 1998
After Rain, 1996
Outside Ireland, 1995

Other books you might like:
Elizabeth Berg, *Ordinary Life*, 2002
Ellen Gilchrist, *I Cannot Get You Close Enough*, 1990
Bobbie Ann Mason, *Zigzagging Down a Wild Trail*, 2001
Alice Munro, *Runaway*, 2004
John Updike, *The Afterlife and Other Stories*, 1994

1199

ADRIANA TRIGIANI

The Queen of the Big Time

(New York: Random House, 2004)

Story type: Historical; Ethnic
Subject(s): Italian Americans; Love; Emigration and Immigration
Major character(s): Nella Castelluca, Heroine; Renato Lanzara, Boyfriend (Nella's)
Time period(s): 19th century; 20th century
Locale(s): Bari, Italy; Roseto, Pennsylvania

Summary: Once upon a time, it was thought that immigrants left the old country behind when they came to the United States and became citizens. Currently, many scholars think the process of becoming American is a little more complicated. Trigiani's novel is a reflection of the current thinking. In the late 19th century, residents from a small Italian village come to the U.S. and settle in a small town in Pennsylvania that they make into a mirror image of the village they left behind in Italy. For more than 100 years, they support each other, cherishing and keeping alive the old culture in their adopted land. Nella Castelluca, is determined to keep this tradition alive and she struggles to reconcile her responsibility with her personal dreams. The result is an interesting portrait of some Italian-American families.

Where it's reviewed:
Publishers Weekly, July 12, 2004, page 45

Other books by the same author:
Lucia, Lucia, 2003
Milk Glass Moon, 2002
Big Cherry Holler, 2001
Big Stone Gap, 2000

Other books you might like:
Roland Merullo, *Revere Beach Boulevard*, 1998
John Murray, *A Few Short Notes on Tropical Butterflies*, 2003
Olaf Olafsson, *Walking into the Night*, 2003
Marge Piercy, *Fly Away Home*, 1984
Erich Segal, *Love Story*, 1970

1200

LILY TUCK

The News from Paraguay

(New York: HarperCollins, 2004)

Story type: Political; Historical/Victorian
Subject(s): Women; Dictators; Relationships
Major character(s): Ella Lynch, Historical Figure, Lover (of Lopez); Francisco Solano Lopez, Political Figure (dictator), Historical Figure
Time period(s): 19th century
Locale(s): Paris, France; Asuncion, Paraguay

Summary: Ella Lynch, an Irish courtesan, is the main character of Tuck's fictional biography, a story of epic scope in a 19th-century Latin American country. Francisco Solano Lopez, the future dictator of Paraguay, first sets eyes on the young Ella Lynch, in Paris in 1854. Soon an item of gossip, they fall in love and she follows him to Paraguay, where she becomes his mistress. In this exotic world, where Europeans, North Americans, native Guaran Indians, and a tired Spanish aristocracy clash and jockey for power and influence, life can be interesting and unpredictable. Despite Lopez's ill-fated dreams of conquest, which bring his country into disastrous wars with Brazil and Argentina, Ella totally remains loyal, bears him children, supports his dreams, and tolerates his wanton philandering.

Where it's reviewed:
Booklist, March 15, 2004, page 1268
Kirkus Reviews, February 15, 2004, page 153
Library Journal, February 15, 2004, page 164
New York Times Book Review, May 2, 2004, page 24
Publishers Weekly, May 3, 2004, page 172

Other books by the same author:
Limbo, and Other Places I Have Lived, 2002
Siam, or, the Woman Who Shot a Man, 1999
The Woman Who Walked on Water, 1996
Interviewing Matisse, or, the Woman Who Died Standing Up, 1991

Other books you might like:
Austin Clarke, *The Polished Hoe*, 2003
Anne Enright, *The Pleasure of Eliza Lynch*, 2002
Binnie Kirshenbaum, *Hester Among the Ruins*, 2002
Valerie Martin, *Property*, 2003
Charles Webb, *The Graduate*, 1963

1201

JOHN UPDIKE

Villages

(New York: Knopf, 2004)

Story type: Coming-of-Age; Psychological
Subject(s): Relationships; Small Town Life; Computers
Major character(s): Owen Mackenzie, Computer Expert; Phyllis Mackenzie, Spouse (Owen's first wife); Julia Mackenzie, Spouse (Owen's second wife)
Time period(s): 20th century; 21st century
Locale(s): Willow, Pennsylvania; Middle Falls, Connecticut; Haskells Crossing, Massachusetts

Summary: *Villages* follows the life of Owen Mackenzie from his birth during the Depression to his retirement, and his story can be read as a social history of a generation. He grows up an only child in a Pennsylvania village, lives in a Connecticut village for most of his adult working life, and retires to a Massachusetts village. As an adult, Owen develops a successful software business, marries his first wife, Phyllis, and has four children. Along the way, Owen takes more than a passing interest in other women and sex, leading to his divorce and subsequent remarriage to Julia.

Where it's reviewed:
Kirkus Reviews, September 1, 2004, page 836
Library Journal, October 1, 2004, page 74
New York Times Book Review, October 31, 2004, page 13
Publishers Weekly, September 6, 2004, page 44

Other books by the same author:
The Early Stories, 1953-1975, 2003
Licks of Love, 2000
Memories of the Ford Administration, 1992
Rabbit at Rest, 1990
Couples, 1968

Other books you might like:
Margaret Atwood, *The Edible Woman*, 1969
Saul Bellow, *More Die of Heartbreak*, 1987
Thomas Berger, *Best Friends*, 2003
Charles Dickens, *Great Expectations*, 1861
John Irving, *The Water-Method Man*, 1972

1202

ERIC VAN LUSTBADER

The Bourne Legacy

(New York: St. Martin's Press, 2004)

Story type: Mystery; Contemporary
Series: Jason Bourne. Book 4
Subject(s): Suspense; Violence; Espionage
Major character(s): Jason Bourne, Spy (retired), Professor (of Eastern Studies); Alex Conklin, Spy (Jason's boss), Crime Victim (murdered); Mo Panov, Crime Victim (murdered)
Time period(s): 2000s
Locale(s): Washington, District of Columbia

Summary: When bestselling author Robert Ludlum passed away in March 2004, fans the world over mourned. Perhaps, his most memorable character was Jason Bourne who ap-

peared in several books. New readers and fans alike will be happy at the news of another book about Ludlum's hero thanks to the diligent work of writer Eric Van Lustbader. As the story opens, David Webb (real name Jason Bourne), an indestructible CIA agent, has retired and is a college professor. When an assassin sets his sights on Webb, he seeks help from friends, and violence and murder soon follow. Despite his mild mannered personality, Webb is up to the task.

Where it's reviewed:
Publishers Weekly, June 7, 2004, page 32

Other books by the same author:
Mistress of the Pearl, 2004
Art Kills, 2002
The Veil of a Thousand Tears, 2002
The Ring of Five Dragons, 2001
Dragons of the Sea of Night, 1998

Other books you might like:
Tom Clancy, *Patriot Games*, 1987
John Le Carre, *Absolute Friends*, 2003
Charles McCarry, *Old Boys*, 2004
Daniel Silva, *The Confessor*, 2003
James H. Webb, *Lost Soldiers*, 2001

1203

M.G. VASSANJI

The In-Between World of Vikram Lall

(New York: Knopf, 2004)

Story type: Psychological; Political
Subject(s): Brothers and Sisters; Friendship; Africa
Major character(s): Vikram Lall, Government Official; Njoroge, Friend
Time period(s): 1950s; 1960s (1950-1965)
Locale(s): Nairobi, Kenya

Summary: Vassanji examines the effects of colonialism, changing countries, and changing cultures on an individual's identity. Vikram Lall, a man of Indian ancestry, grows up in Kenya. When some English neighbors become victims of the Mau Mau rebellion, Vikram's family moves to Nairobi. Eventually he enters government service and becomes rich through corruption. As an older man, he lives in Canada in exile and reflects back on his life, one filled with ethnic conflicts. His English friends regard the Mau Maus as rebels, while his Kenyan friends see them as freedom fighters. His parents discourage a Kenyan friend from courting his sister. Although his family has lived in Kenya for three generations, Vikram never thinks of himself as an African. This book won Vassanji Canada's Giller Prize for the second time.

Where it's reviewed:
Booklist, September 1, 2004, page 66
Kirkus Reviews, August 1, 2004, page 713
Library Journal, August 2004, page 71
Publishers Weekly, July 26, 2004, page 37

Other books by the same author:
Amriika, 1999
The Book of Secrets, 1996 (Giller Prize winner)
Uhuru Street, 1992
No New Land, 1991

The Gunny Sack, 1989

Other books you might like:
Chimamanda Ngozi Adichie, *Purple Hibiscus*, 2003
Nadine Gordimer, *The Pickup*, 2001
Patrick McGrath, *Port Mungo*, 2004
Zakes Mda, *She Plays with the Darkness*, 1995
Shashi Tharoor, *Riot*, 2001

1204

VLADIMIR VOINOVICH

Monumental Propaganda

(New York: Knopf, 2004)

Story type: Political; Satire
Subject(s): Terror; Russians; Communism
Major character(s): Aglaya Stepanovna Revkina, Zealot (Stalin supporter)
Time period(s): 20th century
Locale(s): Dolgov, Russia

Summary: The story follows the life of Aglaya Stepanovna Revkina, a true believer in Josef Stalin. When Stalin is denounced in 1956, Revkina is expelled from the Communist Party. Despite this setback, Revkina remains steadfast in her devotion to the dictator. She rescues a discarded statue of her hero from a garbage dump and installs it in her apartment. The author contrasts the events in her life with historical events in Russia. On one level, her actions appear to be sheer lunacy. Stalin used the state to terrorize both innocent people and his enemies. On another level, her actions appear rational. State repression and tyranny has been replaced with decadence and crime. Translated by Andrew Bromfield.

Where it's reviewed:
Kirkus Reviews, May 15, 2004, page 469
Library Journal, April 15, 2004, page 127
New York Times Book Review, August 8, 2004, page 6
Publishers Weekly, May 24, 2004, page 41

Other books by the same author:
The Fur Hat, 1989 (Susan Brownsberger, translator)
Moscow 2042, 1987 (Richard Lourie, translator)
Pretender to the Throne, 1981 (Richard Lourie, translator)
In Plain Russian, 1979 (Richard Lourie, translator)
The Life and Extraordinary Adventures of Private Ivan Chonkina, 1977 (Richard Lourie, translator)

Other books you might like:
Anonymous, *Primary Colors*, 1996
Anthony Burgess, *A Clockwork Orange*, 1962
Jaroslav Hasek, *The Good Soldier Schweik*, 1930
Joseph Heller, *Catch-22*, 1961
Kurt Vonnegut, *Slaughterhouse-Five*, 1969

1205

AMANDA EYRE WARD

How to Be Lost

(San Francisco: MacAdam/Cage, 2004)

Story type: Psychological
Subject(s): Missing Persons; Sisters; Travel

Major character(s): Ellie Winters, Relative (Caroline's lost sister); Caroline Winters, Waiter/Waitress; Madeline Winters, Relative (Caroline's estranged sister)
Time period(s): 2000s
Locale(s): New Orleans, Louisiana; Montana

Summary: Caroline and Madeline Winters are haunted by their five-year-old sister, Ellie, who disappeared 15 years ago on the day the three girls planned to run away together. Her disappearance sent the family into a tailspin from which it never recovered. Their father drank himself to death, and their mother is very bitter. Now Madeline is unhappily married and Caroline has abandoned a once promising musical career. When Caroline sees a picture of a young woman in a popular magazine who resembles Ellie, she sets out for Montana in search of her lost sister.

Where it's reviewed:
Booklist, September 1, 2004, page 66
Chicago Tribune Books, October 10, 2004, page 1
Kirkus Reviews, August 15, 2004, page 776

Other books by the same author:
Sleep Toward Heaven, 2003

Other books you might like:
Edwidge Danticat, *The Dew Breaker*, 2004
Diane Johnson, *L'Affaire*, 2003
Heidi Julavits, *The Effect of Living Backwards*, 2003
Anita Nair, *Ladies Coupe*, 2004
Donna Tartt, *The Little Friend*, 2002

1206

JENNIFER WEINER

Little Earthquakes

(New York: Atria, 2004)

Story type: Contemporary/Mainstream; Romance
Subject(s): Friendship; Forgiveness; Pregnancy
Major character(s): Rebecca ''Becky'' Rothstein-Rabinowitz, Cook; Ayinde Towne, Housewife; Kelly Day, Businesswoman (event planner)
Time period(s): 2000s
Locale(s): Philadelphia, Pennsylvania

Summary: The impact of pregnancy and motherhood on four modern career women is examined in Weiner's novel. Becky, a successful chef, meets Kelly, an event planner, and Ayinde, wife of an NBA star, at a prenatal yoga class. Lia, a successful actress, joins the group after leaving her husband. Becky, who has an adoring husband, deals with a chronic weight problem and a difficult mother-in-law. Ayinde's husband strays at a most inappropriate time, and Kelly's husband takes up watching television seriously, after he is laid off. Everything becomes magnified as each woman gives birth. Weiner taps into numerous emotional chords that these women face as new parents. While the subject is quite serious, the author uses humor to keep the story from becoming overbearing.

Where it's reviewed:
Booklist, September 1, 2004, page 66
Kirkus Reviews, July 15, 2004, page 659
Library Journal, August 2004, page 71
Publishers Weekly, September 13, 2004, page 59

Other books by the same author:
In Her Shoes, 2002
Good in Bed, 2001

Other books you might like:
Melissa Bank, *The Girl's Guide to Hunting and Fishing*, 1999
Megan Chance, *An Inconvenient Wife*, 2004
Helen Fielding, *Bridget Jones: The Edge of Reason*, 1999
John Irving, *The 158-Pound Marriage*, 1974
Anne Tyler, *The Amateur Marriage*, 2004

1207

FAY WELDON

Mantrapped

(New York: Grove, 2004)

Story type: Psychological
Subject(s): Gender Roles; Relationships; Fantasy
Major character(s): Trisha, Aged Person; Peter, Young Man; Doralee, Spouse (Peter's wife)
Time period(s): 2000s
Locale(s): London, England

Summary: Weldon's work deals with gender roles and identity. Trisha was an up and coming actress when she won the lottery and gave up acting for a life of conspicuous consumption. Now, she is older and broke. To support herself, she moves to an unfashionable part of town and gets a job in a dry cleaners where she meets a happy yuppie couple, Doralee and Peter. One day, Trisha brushes past Peter in the hall and they switch souls. Doralee seeks professional help to redress the problem. Although a resolution is at hand, the experts don't have the answers. Weldon's observations, mostly about her own unsuccessful marriage, add interest.

Where it's reviewed:
Booklist, September 1, 2004, page 8
Kirkus Reviews, September 15, 2004, page 891
Library Journal, October 15, 2004, page 56
Publishers Weekly, September 27, 2004, page 35

Other books by the same author:
The Bulgari Connection, 2001
Rhode Island Blues, 2000
Bad Girls Don't Cry, 1997
Wicked Women, 1997
Worst Fears, 1996

Other books you might like:
Margaret Atwood, *Lady Oracle*, 1976
Barbara Taylor Bradford, *Her Own Rules*, 1996
Dan Chaon, *You Remind Me of Me*, 2004
Harlan Coben, *Just One Look*, 2004
Don DeLillo, *The Body Artist*, 2001

1208

LAUREN WILLIG

The Secret History of the Pink Carnation

(New York: Dutton, 2004)

Story type: Historical; Romance
Subject(s): Spies; Napoleonic Wars; Students, Foreign

Major character(s): Eloise Kelly, Student—Graduate; Arabella Selwick-Aderly, Noblewoman; Richard Selwick, Scholar, Spy (for England)
Time period(s): 2000s; 1800s (1801)
Locale(s): London, England; Paris, France

Summary: Romance and suspense drive this historical novel that includes a contemporary story with an early 19th-century twist. An American doctoral candidate, Eloise, starts the ball rolling when she shows up in modern day London intent on doing research on Richard Selwick, an English spy called the Pink Carnation during the Napoleonic Wars. Luckily, Eloise is given access to Selwick's papers by his descendant, Arabella. As Eloise reads the papers she discovers a complicated romance that develops when Richard meets Amy Balcourt, a young woman who becomes the spy called the Purple Gentian. Together Richard and Amy are out to foil Napoleon Bonaparte. While Richard wants to protect England, Amy wants to avenge the death of her father, who was sent to the guillotine in France. In the midst of her research, Eloise runs into objections from another Selwick relative, an attractive man named Colin, seeking to protect the family's privacy. Of course, romance allows Eloise to continue her research and complete Richard and Amy's story.

Where it's reviewed:
Booklist, November 15, 2004, page 558
Kirkus Reviews, November 1, 2004, page 1028
Library Journal, November 15, 2004, page 53

Other books you might like:
Sylvia Brownrigg, *The Metaphysical Touch*, 2000
Susan Coll, *Karlmarx.com*, 2001
Robin Cook, *Shock*, 2001
Catherine Coulter, *The Aristocrat*, 2002
Penelope Lively, *Moon Tiger*, 1987

1209

SARAH WILLIS

A Good Distance

(New York: Berkley, 2004)

Story type: Contemporary/Mainstream
Subject(s): Mothers and Daughters; Death; Guilt
Major character(s): Jennifer, Parent, Spouse (of Todd); Todd, Spouse (Jennifer's second husband)
Time period(s): 2000s
Locale(s): United States

Summary: The pursuit of happiness has built-in obstacles under the best of circumstances. Add a second marriage, a teenage girl from a first marriage, and a demented mother into the mix and happiness becomes a real challenge. Jennifer faces this challenge when she decides to take care of her mother who suffers from Alzheimer's disease. Jennifer's mom grew up in the Depression and didn't have an easy time raising her family. That is one reason for Jennifer bringing her home; another is Jennifer's guilt over a family secret. As the three females more or less bond with each other, things get very complicated. Todd, Jennifer's second husband, feels ignored and seeks refuge in Internet chat rooms.

Where it's reviewed:
Kirkus Reviews, February 1, 2004, page 109
New York Times Book Review, June 13, 2004, page 18

Other books by the same author:
The Rehearsal, 2001
Some Things That Stay, 2000

Other books you might like:
Lynette Brasfield, *Nature Lessons*, 2003
Anita Brookner, *The Bay of Angels*, 2001
Jacquelyn Mitchard, *Twelve Times Blessed*, 2003
Nicholas Sparks, *Message in a Bottle*, 1998
Anne Tyler, *Back When We Were Grownups*, 2001

1210

MARK WINEGARDNER

The Godfather Returns
(New York: Random House, 2004)

Story type: Americana; Family Saga
Subject(s): Crime and Criminals; Organized Crime; Family
Major character(s): Michael Corleone, Organized Crime Figure (Mafia boss); Nick Geraci, Organized Crime Figure (rival to Corleone family); Tom Hagen, Political Figure, Lawyer (for Corleone family)
Time period(s): 1950s; 1960s (1955-1962)
Locale(s): Las Vegas, Nevada; New York, New York

Summary: Mario Puzo, author of *The Godfather*, died in 1999 but his legacy, which was helped along by Francis Ford Coppola's movies, *The Godfather* and *The Godfather II* lives on. Mark Winegardner, author of two novels and a collection, was chosen to continue the saga. The story largely picks up where Puzo left off, with flashbacks that take advantage of gaps in the original work. Michael Corleone decides two things: to relocate the family to Las Vegas and move out of criminal activity into legitimate businesses. Tom Hagen, who becomes an elected official in Nevada, is on hand to help. Michael's brother Fredo, who has a few sexual hang-ups, and other familiar characters make appearances. Of course, complications occur, especially with another gangster, Nick Geraci, who is out to get Michael.

Where it's reviewed:
New York Times, November 12, 2004, page B39
Newsweek, November 8, 2004, page 55
Time, November 22, 2004, page 88

Other books by the same author:
That's True of Everybody, 2002
Crooked River Burning, 2001
The Veracruz Blues, 1996

Other books you might like:
James Lee Burke, *Burning Angel*, 1995
Richard Condon, *Prizzi's Family*, 1982
Pete Dexter, *Brotherly Love*, 1991
George V. Higgins, *At End of Day*, 2000
Elmore Leonard, *Pronto*, 1993
Mario Puzo, *The Godfather*, 1969

1211

TOM WOLFE

I Am Charlotte Simmons
(New York: Farrar, Straus and Giroux, 2004)

Story type: Coming-of-Age; Contemporary/Mainstream
Subject(s): Women; Social Classes; College Life
Major character(s): Charlotte Simmons, Student—College; Jojo Johanssen, Student—College, Sports Figure (basketball player); Adam Geller, Student—College, Editor (college newspaper)
Time period(s): 2000s
Locale(s): North Carolina

Summary: Wolfe turns his discerning eye on college life in this work set in North Carolina at fictional Dupont University. Charlotte Simmons, a bright young woman from a conservative Southern family, is experiencing contemporary college life with its pervasive sex, drugs, booze, and sports, to say nothing of social jockeying tinged with class and racial overtones. JoJo, the only starting white on the basketball team, struggles to keep his position, which is threatened by a freshman African American. Fraternity boys get in a brawl with bodyguards of a prominent politician, who has been caught in a compromising position with a coed. Beverly sets out to bed the lacrosse team. Somehow Charlotte's experiences bring all the threads together.

Where it's reviewed:
New York Times Book Review, November 28, 2004, page 13
Publishers Weekly, November 8, 2004, page 35

Other books by the same author:
A Man in Full, 1998
The Bonfire of the Vanities, 1987

Other books you might like:
Alice Adams, *Superior Women*, 1984
Sylvia Brownrigg, *Pages for You*, 2001
Jill McCorkle, *The Cheer Leader*, 1984
Joyce Carol Oates, *I'll Take You There*, 2002
Philip Roth, *The Dying Animal*, 2001

1212

MEG WOLITZER

The Position
(New York: Scribner, 2005)

Story type: Adult; Domestic
Subject(s): Sexual Behavior; Parent and Child; Psychological
Major character(s): Paul Mellow, Spouse (Roz's husband); Roz Mellow, Spouse (Paul's wife)
Time period(s): 2000s; 1970s (1975)
Locale(s): United States

Summary: *The Position* chronicles attitude changes that occur over 30 years for a married couple, their family, and to some extent, society as a whole. Roz and Paul are madly in love with each other and they especially enjoy sex, often and creatively. They write a comprehensive book on the subject, including illustrations of themselves having sex and are pleased when the book becomes a runaway bestseller. After reading the book, their children aren't happy. Some 30 years later, a publisher wants to reissue the book. However, at this time Paul and Roz are married but not to each other; their children are grown but not well-adjusted.

Where it's reviewed:
Publishers Weekly, November 8, 2004, page 32

Other books by the same author:
Surrender, Dorothy, 1999

Friends for Life, 1994
This Is Your Life, 1988
Hidden Pictures, 1986

Other books you might like:
T. Coraghessan Boyle, *The Inner Circle*, 2004
Bonnie Burnard, *A Good House*, 1999
Lisa Glatt, *A Girl Becomes a Comma Like That*, 2004
Robert H. Rimmer, *Come Live My Life*, 1998
Edmund Wilson, *Memoirs of Hecate County*, 1946

Series Index

This index alphabetically lists series to which books featured in the entries belong. Beneath each series name, book titles are listed alphabetically with author names and genre codes. The genre codes are as follows: *c* Popular Fiction, *f* Fantasy, *h* Horror, *i* Inspirational, *m* Mystery, *r* Romance, *s* Science Fiction, *t* Historical, and *w* Western. Numbers refer to the entries that feature each title.

Time Period Index

This index chronologically lists the time settings in which the featured books take place. Main headings refer to a century; where no specific time is given, the headings MULTIPLE TIME PERIODS, INDETERMINATE PAST, INDETERMINATE FUTURE, and INDETER-MINATE are used. The 18th through 21st centuries are broken down into decades when possible. (Note: 1800s, for example, refers to the first decade of the 19th century.) Featured titles are listed alphabetically beneath time headings, with author names and genre codes. The genre codes are as follows: c Popular Fiction, f Fantasy, h Horror, i Inspirational, m Mystery, r Romance, s Science Fiction, t Historical, and w Western. Numbers refer to the entries that feature each title.

20th CENTURY

Geographic Index

This index provides access to all featured books by geographic settings—such as countries, continents, oceans, and planets. States and provinces are indicated for the United States and Canada. Also interfiled are headings for fictional place names (Spaceships, Imaginary Planets, etc.). Sections are further broken down by city or the specific name of the imaginary locale. Book titles are listed alphabetically under headings, with author names and genre codes. The genre codes are as follows: *c* Popular Fiction, *f* Fantasy, *h* Horror, *i* Inspirational, *m* Mystery, *r* Romance, *s* Science Fiction, *t* Historical, and *w* Western. Numbers refer to the entries that feature each title.

GUADELOUPE

Who Slashed Celanire's Throat? - Maryse
  Conde   *t*   844

HAITI

The Stone That the Builder Refused - Madison Smartt
  Bell   *t*   821
The Stone That the Builder Refused - Madison Smartt
  Bell   *c*   1072

Cap Misere
American Gothic - Michael Romkey   *h*   687

INDIA

A Black Englishman - Carolyn Slaughter   *c*   1188
A Black Englishman - Carolyn Slaughter   *t*   939
The Damascened Blade - Barbara Cleverly   *t*   838
The Damascened Blade - Barbara Cleverly   *m*   32
Ladies Coupe - Anita Nair   *c*   1154
Magic Seeds - V.S. Naipaul   *c*   1153
Night of Sin - Julia Ross   *r*   374
River of Gods - Ian McDonald   *s*   763
The Tree Bride - Bharati Mukherjee   *t*   910

Bombay
The Death of Mr. Love - Indra Sinha   *c*   1187

Calcutta
A Beggar at the Gate - Thalassa Ali   *t*   811

Cawnpore
The Lady of Cawnpore - Elisabeth McNeill   *t*   904

Lahore
A Beggar at the Gate - Thalassa Ali   *t*   811

Pune
The Cosmic Clues - Manjiri Prabhu   *m*   164

INDONESIA

Assassin - Ted Bell   *c*   1073

IRAN

The Quince Seed Potion - Morteza Baharloo   *t*   817

IRELAND

A Bit on the Side - William Trevor   *c*   1198
Dark Justice - Jack Higgins   *c*   1121
The Lady of the Sea - Rosalind Miles   *t*   906

Clifden
In Like Flynn - Dorien Kelly   *r*   308

County Offaly
Lake of Sorrows - Erin Hart   *m*   99

Dublin
The Parts - Keith Ridgway   *c*   1172
Pearl - Mary Gordon   *c*   1112

River Boyne
Shade - Neil Jordan   *t*   890

ISRAEL

Jerusalem
Bethlehem Road Murder - Batya Gur   *m*   94
Love, the Painter's Wife and the Queen of Sheba -
  Aliette Armel   *t*   814
Wisdom's Daughter - India Edghill   *t*   865

ITALY

Don't Move - Margaret Mazzantini   *c*   1140
The Franciscan Conspiracy - John R. Sack   *t*   932
The Nameless Day - Sara Douglass   *f*   525

Arezzo
Love, the Painter's Wife and the Queen of Sheba -
  Aliette Armel   *t*   814
Love, the Painter's Wife and the Queen of Sheba -
  Aliette Armel   *c*   1066

Bari
The Queen of the Big Time - Adriana
  Trigiani   *c*   1199

Florence
Brimstone - Douglas Preston   *h*   683
Pasta Imperfect - Maddy Hunter   *m*   107

Pisa
Pasta Imperfect - Maddy Hunter   *m*   107

Rome
Pasta Imperfect - Maddy Hunter   *m*   107

Trieste
A Dead Man in Trieste - Michael Pearce   *m*   159

Venice
Lucifer's Shadow - David Hewson   *t*   880
The Master - Colm Toibin   *c*   1195
Mutiny - Julian Stockwin   *t*   943

JAMAICA

The Spithead Nymph - Jan Needle   *t*   911

JAPAN

Autumn Bridge - Takashi Matsuoka   *t*   902
Autumn Bridge - Takashi Matsuoka   *c*   1139
Less than Human - Maxine McArthur   *s*   761
The Painting - Nina Schuyler   *t*   935

Tokyo
Country of Origin - Don Lee   *c*   1135

JUPITER

Cally's War - John Ringo   *s*   777
Orphanage - Robert Buettner   *s*   727

KENYA

Derati
Exorcist: The Beginning - Steven Piziks   *h*   682

Nairobi
The In-Between World of Vikram Lall - M.G.
  Vassanji   *c*   1203

KOREA, SOUTH

War Trash - Ha Jin   *c*   1128
War Trash - Ha Jin   *t*   889

Seoul
The Red Queen - Margaret Drabble   *c*   1095

LAOS

Vientiane
The Coroner's Lunch - Colin Cotterill   *m*   41

MACEDONIA

The Virtues of War - Steven Pressfield   *t*   924

MARS

Haydn of Mars - Al Sarrantonio   *s*   784

MEDITERRANEAN

Dark Voyage - Alan Furst   *t*   870
Owls to Athens - H.N. Turteltaub   *t*   946
Pride of Carthage - David Anthony Durham   *t*   864

MEXICO

A Carnivore's Inquiry - Sabina Murray   *c*   1152
D.B. - Elwood Reid   *c*   1170
Jericho's Road - Elmer Kelton   *t*   891
Jericho's Road - Elmer Kelton   *w*   458
Paper Moon - Linda Windsor   *i*   1060
The Queen of the South - Arturo Perez-
  Reverte   *c*   1164

Mexico City
The Puzzle of the Blue Banderilla - Stuart
  Palmer   *m*   156

Nogales
Choke Point - James C. Mitchell   *m*   144

Santa Alana
Johnny Blue and the Texas Rangers - Joseph A.
  West   *w*   493

Sierra Madre Mountains
The Last Campaign - Tim Champlin   *w*   424

MIDDLE EAST

Dreams of the Desert Wind - Kurt
  Giambastini   *s*   749
Gods and Kings - Lynn Austin   *i*   963
Joshua in a Troubled World - Joseph F.
  Girzone   *i*   990
The Last Judgment - Craig Parshall   *i*   1038
The Revealing - L.A. Marzulli   *i*   1023
Three Days - Melody Carlson   *i*   975
Till Shiloh Comes - Gilbert Morris   *i*   1032
The Virtues of War - Steven Pressfield   *t*   924

MOON (EARTH'S)

Cally's War - John Ringo   *s*   777
Warp Speed - Travis S. Taylor   *s*   792

MOROCCO

The Children's War - Monique Charlesworth   *t*   834
The Children's War - Monique
  Charlesworth   *c*   1083
The Queen of the South - Arturo Perez-
  Reverte   *c*   1164

MYTHICAL PLACE

The Winter Oak - James A. Hetley   *f*   544

Algul Sient
The Dark Tower - Stephen King   *h*   649

Avalon
Ancestors of Avalon - Diana L. Paxson   *f*   574

Faldorrah
Ghosts in the Snow - Tamara Siler Jones   *h*   646

The Hold
Lost Truth - Dawn Cook   *f*   518

Mephistopolis
Infernal Angel - Edward Lee   *h*   656

Ypsilanti

The Mercy Killers - Lisa Reardon   *c*   1169

MIDWEST

Sander's City

Hot Summer Nights - LuAnn McLane   *r*   340

MINNESOTA

The Real Minerva - Mary Sharratt   *t*   938
The Whitney Chronicles - Judy Baer   *i*   964

Blue Prairie

Why the Sky Is Blue - Susan Meissner   *i*   1026

Excelsior

Crewel Yule - Monica Ferris   *m*   76

Great Falls

Phi Beta Bimbo - Trish Jensen   *r*   300

Lake Eden

Sugar Cookie Murder - Joanne Fluke   *m*   80

Minneapolis

Alone at Night - K.J. Erickson   *m*   71
Undead and Unemployed - MaryJanice
   Davidson   *r*   248

Redstone

Alone at Night - K.J. Erickson   *m*   71

St. Paul

Undead and Unemployed - MaryJanice
   Davidson   *h*   625
Undead and Unemployed - MaryJanice
   Davidson   *r*   248

Tyson's Corner

Phi Beta Bimbo - Trish Jensen   *r*   300

MISSISSIPPI RIVER

Dead Water - Barbara Hambly   *t*   877

MISSOURI

My Jim - Nancy Rawles   *t*   925

Cordelia

Follow Me Home - Jerri Corgiat   *r*   244

St. Louis

Friday, the Arapaho Boy - Marc Simmons   *w*   483
Incubus Dreams - Laurell K. Hamilton   *h*   637
Incubus Dreams - Laurell K. Hamilton   *c*   1116
Ring around My Heart - Pat White   *r*   404

MONTANA

Calder Promise - Janet Dailey   *r*   245
Changes of Heart - Paige Lee Elliston   *i*   984
The Hope Within - Tracie Peterson   *i*   1039
How to Be Lost - Amanda Eyre Ward   *c*   1205
To Dream Anew - Tracie Peterson   *i*   1041

Blackfoot Reservation

Indian Why Stories - Frank B. Linderman   *w*   461

Deer Lodge

McKeag's Mountain - L.J. Martin   *w*   462

Fire Creek

War at Fire Creek - Cameron Judd   *w*   457

Helena

McKeag's Mountain - L.J. Martin   *w*   462

Little Big Horn

An Obituary for Major Reno - Richard S.
   Wheeler   *t*   952

Missoula

In the Moon of Red Ponies - James Lee
   Burke   *c*   1080
Killer Smile - Lisa Scottoline   *c*   1180

Redhorse Butte

Judgment Day - Frank Roderus   *w*   479

Shady Hills

Starlight Comes Home - Janet Muirhead
   Hill   *w*   450

NEBRASKA

Following the Harvest - Fred Harris   *t*   879

Fort Robinson

Watchers on the Hill - Stephanie Grace
   Whitson   *i*   1056

Omaha

Yonnondio from the Thirties - Tillie Olsen   *w*   470

NEVADA

Lake Tahoe

Echo Bay - Richard Barre   *c*   1070

Las Vegas

Cat in an Orange Twist - Carole Nelson
   Douglas   *m*   60
Chill Factor - Rachel Caine   *f*   514
The Godfather Returns - Mark
   Winegardner   *c*   1210
The Nerd Who Loved Me - Vicki Lewis
   Thompson   *r*   397
Wiley's Shuffle - Lono Waiwaiole   *m*   204

NEW ENGLAND

Assassin - Ted Bell   *c*   1073

Cobb's Landing

Death of a Trickster - Kate Borden   *m*   18

NEW HAMPSHIRE

Tyler

Buried Dreams - Brendan DuBois   *m*   63

NEW JERSEY

7,000 Clams - Lee Irby   *t*   884

Bayfield

Satan's Pony - Robin Hathaway   *m*   101

Harborport

As You Wish - Francine Matthews   *r*   334

Harton

Thieves Break In - Cristina Sumners   *m*   192

Hendersonia

In the Night Room - Peter Straub   *h*   697

Montclair

Wake Up, Sir - Jonathan Ames   *c*   1064

Newark

Dying in the Dark - Valerie Wilson Wesley   *m*   207
The Plot Against America - Philip Roth   *c*   1175
The Plot Against America - Philip Roth   *s*   781

Paradise Point

Chances Are - Barbara Bretton   *r*   231

Rellingford

Afterlife - Douglas Clegg   *h*   616

Trenton

Ten Big Ones - Janet Evanovich   *c*   1099

Troutville

Dying to Marry - Janelle Taylor   *r*   392

Wallingford

How I Paid for College - Marc Acito   *c*   1063

NEW MEXICO

Agua Bendita

Tortuga - Rudolfo Anaya   *w*   413

Albuquerque

Delivery - Ben Daitz   *w*   434

Bernalillo

Thief in Retreat - Aimee Thurlo   *m*   199

Ceremony

Backshooter - Robert J. Randisi   *w*   475

Mogote

Delivery - Ben Daitz   *w*   434

Navajo Reservation

Blood Retribution - David Thurlo   *m*   200
Skeleton Man - Tony Hillerman   *w*   451
Skeleton Man - Tony Hillerman   *m*   106

Posadas County

Convenient Disposal - Steven F. Havill   *m*   102
Convenient Disposal - Steven F. Havill   *w*   448

Santa Fe

The Alias Man - Bill Pronzini   *m*   165
Santa Fe Passage - Jon R. Bauman   *w*   415
Santa Fe Passage - Jon R. Bauman   *t*   819
Serafina's Stories - Rudolfo Anaya   *w*   412
Slowkill - Michael McGarrity   *w*   463

Taos

Dead Man's Canyon - Ralph Cotton   *w*   432
Friday, the Arapaho Boy - Marc Simmons   *w*   483

Valle Bosque

Coyote Morning - Lisa Lenard-Cook   *w*   460

Window Rock

Skeleton Man - Tony Hillerman   *w*   451

NEW YORK

The Black House - Constance Little   *m*   130
Fire Along the Sky - Sara Donati   *t*   855
Osprey Island - Thisbe Nissen   *c*   1157
The Shaughnessey Accord - Alison Kent   *r*   311
Tall, Dark, and Hungry - Lynsay Sands   *r*   377

Amagansett

Amagansett - Mark Mills   *m*   143
Amagansett - Mark Mills   *t*   907

Bromptons

Putting on the Dog - Cynthia Baxter   *m*   7

Buffalo

The First Desire - Nancy Reisman   *c*   1171
The Temple of Music - Jonathan Lowy   *t*   898

Centerville

Deficiency - Andrew Neiderman   *h*   674

Hemlock Falls

Buried by Breakfast - Claudia Bishop   *m*   12

Isola

Hark! A Novel of the 87th Precinct - Ed
   McBain   *m*   138

Long Island

Amagansett - Mark Mills   *c*   1149
Night Fall - Nelson DeMille   *c*   1090

New York

Absent Friends - S.J. Rozan   *m*   177
Afterlife - Douglas Clegg   *h*   616

Genre Index

This index lists the books featured as main entries in *What Do I Read Next?* by genre and story type within each genre. Beneath each of the nine genres, the story types appear alphabetically, and titles appear alphabetically under story type headings. The name of the primary author, genre code and the book entry number also appear with each title. The genre codes are as follows: *c* Popular Fiction, *f* Fantasy, *h* Horror, *i* Inspirational, *m* Mystery, *r* Romance, *s* Science Fiction, *t* Historical, and *w* Western. For definitions of the story types, see the "Key to Genre Terms" following the Introduction.

FANTASY

Adventure

Freedom's Gate - Naomi Kritzer *f* 557
Wolf Captured - Jane Lindskold *f* 561

Alternate History

Kindling - Mick Farren *f* 531
Strange Cargo - Jeffrey E. Barlough *f* 504

Alternate Universe

Black Water - D.J. MacHale *f* 565
The Finest Creation - Jean Rabe *f* 577
The Runes of the Earth - Stephen R. Donaldson *f* 524

Anthology

Crossroads - F. Brett Cox *f* 521
In Lands That Never Were - Gordon Van Gelder *f* 586
Little Red Riding Hood in the Big Bad City - Martin H. Greenberg *f* 540
Masters of Fantasy - Bill Fawcett *f* 532
Powers of Detection - Dana Stabenow *f* 583
Swords of the Empire - Marc Gascoigne *f* 537
Turn the Other Chick - Esther Friesner *f* 535
The Year's Best Fantasy and Horror: Seventeenth Annual Collection - Ellen Datlow *f* 523

Collection

The Bloody Crown of Conan - Robert E. Howard *f* 546
The Savage Tales of Solomon Kane - Robert E. Howard *f* 547
Secret Life - Jeff Vandermeer *f* 587

Contemporary

The Autumn Castle - Kim Wilkins *f* 593
Chill Factor - Rachel Caine *f* 514
Ghostlands - Marc Zicree *f* 598
Industrial Magic - Kelley Armstrong *f* 501
The King of Ice Cream - Robert Wayne McCoy *f* 567
The Last Guardian of Everness - John C. Wright *f* 596
The Seadragon's Daughter - Alan F. Troop *f* 585

Shadows in the Darkness - Elaine Cunningham *f* 522
Twilight Rising, Serpent's Dream - Diana Marcellas *f* 566
The Winter Oak - James A. Hetley *f* 544

Historical

Ancestors of Avalon - Diana L. Paxson *f* 574
Child of the Dark Prophecy - T.A. Barron *f* 505
A Cold Summer Night - Trystam Kith *f* 554
Jonathan Strange & Mr. Norrell - Susanna Clarke *f* 517
The Lance Thrower - Jack Whyte *f* 592
The Nameless Day - Sara Douglass *f* 525
One King, One Soldier - Alexander C. Irvine *f* 549
Rite of Conquest - Judith Tarr *f* 584
Seraphim - Michele Hauf *f* 541

Horror

The King of Ice Cream - Robert Wayne McCoy *f* 567

Humor

Currant Events - Piers Anthony *f* 500
A Hat Full of Sky - Terry Pratchett *f* 576
Heroics for Beginners - John Moore *f* 570

Legend

Child of the Dark Prophecy - T.A. Barron *f* 505
The Lance Thrower - Jack Whyte *f* 592
The Seadragon's Daughter - Alan F. Troop *f* 585

Light Fantasy

The Autumn Castle - Kim Wilkins *f* 593
Clovermead - David Randall *f* 578
Lost Truth - Dawn Cook *f* 518
Luna - Julie Anne Peters *f* 575
The Mountain's Call - Caitlin Brennan *f* 508
Strange Cargo - Jeffrey E. Barlough *f* 504
The Winter Oak - James A. Hetley *f* 544
The Wizard - Gene Wolfe *f* 595

Magic Conflict

Ancestors of Avalon - Diana L. Paxson *f* 574
Banewreaker - Jacqueline Carey *f* 515

Blood of the Dragon - C.L. Werner *f* 590
The Bright and the Dark - Michele M. Welch *f* 589
The Charnel Prince - J. Gregory Keyes *f* 552
Chill Factor - Rachel Caine *f* 514
A Cold Summer Night - Trystam Kith *f* 554
The Covenant Rising - Stan Nicholls *f* 572
Dawn of Night - Paul S. Kemp *f* 551
A Day Dark as Night - Carl Bowen *f* 507
Demonstorm - James Barclay *f* 503
Dragon's Treasure - Elizabeth A. Lynn *f* 563
Elegy for a Lost Star - Elizabeth Haydon *f* 542
Exile's Return - Raymond E. Feist *f* 533
The Fifth Dawn - Cory J. Herndon *f* 543
The Firebird's Vengeance - Sarah Zettel *f* 597
The First Stone - Mark Anthony *f* 499
Furies of Calderon - Jim Butcher *f* 512
Gifts - Ursula K. Le Guin *f* 560
The Glasswright's Master - Mindy L. Klasky *f* 555
Grey Knights - Ben Counter *f* 520
The Hidden Stars - Madeline Howard *f* 545
Iron Council - China Mieville *f* 569
Jonathan Strange & Mr. Norrell - Susanna Clarke *f* 517
Kindling - Mick Farren *f* 531
Lady of Poison - Bruce R. Cordell *f* 519
The Language of Power - Rosemary Kirstein *f* 553
Lost Truth - Dawn Cook *f* 518
Master of the Cauldron - David Drake *f* 527
Outlaw: Champions of Kanigawa - Scott McGough *f* 568
Paladins - Joel Rosenberg *f* 580
Paths of Evil - Richard C. White *f* 591
Prisoner of Haven - Nancy Varian Berberick *f* 506
The Queen's Knight - Deborah Chester *f* 516
The Rage - Richard Lee Byers *f* 513
Raven's Shadow - Patricia Briggs *f* 510
The Return of Nightfall - Mickey Zucker Reichert *f* 579
Rite of Conquest - Judith Tarr *f* 584
The Runes of the Earth - Stephen R. Donaldson *f* 524
Sacred Flesh - Robin D. Laws *f* 559
Scabbard's Song - Kim Hunter *f* 548
The Scrolls of the Ancients - Robert Newcomb *f* 571
The Shadow Roads - Sean Russell *f* 581
Shadowmarch. Volume 1 - Tad Williams *f* 594
Sinner - Sara Douglass *f* 526
Tanequil - Terry Brooks *f* 511
The Three Sisters - Rebecca Locksley *f* 562
To Light a Candle - Mercedes Lackey *f* 558
Treason Keep - Jennifer Fallon *f* 530

HORROR

INSPIRATIONAL

Genre Index

Romance

Everlasting Love - Valerie Hansen   *i*   997
Gabriel's Discovery - Felicia Mason   *i*   1024
The Heart's Voice - Arlene James   *i*   1008
Love Came Unexpectedly - Ruth Scofield   *i*   1047
Love Enough for Two - Cynthia Rutledge   *i*   1045
Paper Moon - Linda Windsor   *i*   1060
Reason and Romance - Debra White Smith   *i*   1049
She's Out of Control - Kristin Billerbeck   *i*   966
Someone to Watch over Me - Teresa Hill   *i*   1003
A Tender Touch - Lenora Worth   *i*   1062
Undercover Blessings - Deb Kastner   *i*   1012

Romantic Suspense

Forgotten Justice - Lois Richer   *i*   1043

Science Fiction

Red - Ted Dekker   *i*   978
The Revealing - L.A. Marzulli   *i*   1023
The Shadow at Evening - Chris Walley   *i*   1053
Soul Tracker - Bill Myers   *i*   1036
White - Ted Dekker   *i*   979

MYSTERY

Action/Adventure

Cross Current - Christine Kling   *m*   120
Heart of the Hunter - Deon Meyer   *m*   142
Hot Plastic - Peter Craig   *m*   43
Metro Girl - Janet Evanovich   *m*   72
Pyro - Earl Emerson   *m*   70
Red Tide - G.M. Ford   *m*   81
The Romanov Prophecy - Steve Berry   *m*   11
Skinny Dip - Carl Hiaasen   *m*   103
Tampa Burn - Randy Wayne White   *m*   209
Trophy Hunt - C.J. Box   *m*   19
The Warlord's Son - Dan Fesperman   *m*   77

Amateur Detective

The Actor's Guide to Adultery - Rick Copp   *m*   39
And a Puzzle to Die On - Parnell Hall   *m*   95
Bitch Creek - William G. Tapply   *m*   196
The Black House - Constance Little   *m*   130
The Blue Rose - Anthony Eglin   *m*   69
A Bond with Death - Bill Crider   *m*   45
Booked for Murder - Tim Myers   *m*   152
Bound for Murder - Laura Childs   *m*   28
Buried by Breakfast - Claudia Bishop   *m*   12
Buried Dreams - Brendan DuBois   *m*   63
Buried Stuff - Sharon Fiffer   *m*   78
Burning Bridges - Troy Soos   *m*   188
Bye, Bye Love - Virginia Swift   *m*   194
Carnage on the Committee - Ruth Dudley Edwards   *m*   68
Cat in an Orange Twist - Carole Nelson Douglas   *m*   60
A Catered Wedding - Isis Crawford   *m*   44
The Christmas Thief - Mary Higgins Clark   *m*   31
Courting Disaster - Joanne Pence   *m*   161
Crewel Yule - Monica Ferris   *m*   76
Cross Current - Christine Kling   *m*   120
Dead for the Winter - Betsy Thornton   *m*   198
The Deadly Dance - M.C. Beaton   *m*   8
Death by Deep Dish Pie - Sharon Short   *m*   184
Death by Inferior Design - Leslie Caine   *m*   26
Death of a Trickster - Kate Borden   *m*   18
Death Takes a Gander - Christine Goff   *m*   86
Died Blonde - Nancy J. Cohen   *m*   34
Dr. Poggioli: Criminologist - T.S. Stribling   *m*   191
Double Shot - Diane Mott Davidson   *m*   52
Dying to Call You - Elaine Viets   *m*   203
The Famous Flower of Serving Men - Deborah Grabien   *m*   88

Forged - Laura Crum   *m*   47
Four on the Floor - Deborah Morgan   *m*   147
Green Thumb - Ralph McInerny   *m*   139
The Gun in Daniel Webster's Bust - Margaret Scherf   *m*   182
The Hanging in the Hotel - Simon Brett   *m*   21
Headhunter - Roy Lewis   *m*   127
High Country Fall - Margaret Maron   *m*   133
A Hoe Lot of Trouble - Heather Webber   *m*   206
Holy Guacamole! - Nancy Fairbanks   *m*   73
Home Body - Gerry Boyle   *m*   20
Jack in the Pulpit - Cynthia Riggs   *m*   170
The Jasmine Moon Murder - Laura Childs   *m*   29
Jingle Bell Bark - Laurien Berenson   *m*   10
Killer Blonde - Laura Levine   *m*   126
Lake of Sorrows - Erin Hart   *m*   99
Mansions of the Dead - Sarah Stewart Taylor   *m*   197
A Midsummer Night's Scream - Jill Churchill   *m*   30
Moth and Flame - John Morgan Wilson   *m*   210
A Mourning Wedding - Carola Dunn   *m*   65
Mrs. Hudson and the Spirits' Curse - Martin Davies   *m*   53
Mum's the Word - Kate Collins   *m*   36
Murder of a Pink Elephant - Denise Swanson   *m*   193
On Thin Ice - Alina Adams   *m*   1
Pale as the Dead - Fiona Mountain   *m*   150
Pasta Imperfect - Maddy Hunter   *m*   107
The Pearl Diver - Sujata Massey   *m*   135
Please Do Feed the Cat - Marian Babson   *m*   4
Putting on the Dog - Cynthia Baxter   *m*   7
The Puzzle of the Blue Banderilla - Stuart Palmer   *m*   156
Requiem for a Realtor - Ralph McInerny   *m*   140
Satan's Pony - Robin Hathaway   *m*   101
Snuffed Out - Tim Myers   *m*   153
Speak Now - Margaret Dumas   *m*   64
Sugar Cookie Murder - Joanne Fluke   *m*   80
Tagged for Murder - Elaine Flinn   *m*   79
Taking the Wrap - Dolores Johnson   *m*   110
The Tale of Hill Top Farm - Susan Wittig Albert   *m*   2
Thief in Retreat - Aimee Thurlo   *m*   199
Thieves Break In - Cristina Sumners   *m*   192
This Old Souse - Mary Daheim   *m*   50
Through the Grinder - Cleo Coyle   *m*   42
Till the End of Tom - Gillian Roberts   *m*   172
To Collar a Killer - Lee Charles Kelley   *m*   116
Tropic of Murder - Lev Raphael   *m*   167
Uncommon Grounds - Sandra Balzo   *m*   5
The Vanished Priestess - Meredith Blevins   *m*   17
Verse of the Vampyre - Diana Killian   *m*   117
Which Big Giver Stole the Chopped Liver? - Sharon Kahn   *m*   111
Wife of Moon - Margaret Coel   *m*   33
Winter of Discontent - Jeanne M. Dams   *m*   51
Wrapped Up in Crosswords - Nero Blanc   *m*   15

Anthology

The Best American Mystery Stories 2004 - Nelson DeMille   *m*   56
The Mammoth Book of Roaring Twenties Whodunnits - Mike Ashley   *m*   3
Sherlock Holmes: The Hidden Years - Michael Kurland   *m*   124
The World's Finest Mystery and Crime Stories: Fifth Annual Collection - Ed Gorman   *m*   87

Collection

The Danger Zone and Other Stories - Erle Stanley Gardner   *m*   84
Dr. Poggioli: Criminologist - T.S. Stribling   *m*   191
Whispers of the Dead - Peter Tremayne   *m*   202

Domestic

Double Shot - Diane Mott Davidson   *m*   52

Espionage

A Dead Man in Trieste - Michael Pearce   *m*   159
Garden of Beasts - Jeffery Deaver   *m*   55
Heart of the Hunter - Deon Meyer   *m*   142
Into the Volcano - Forrest DeVoe Jr.   *m*   57

Historical

Amagansett - Mark Mills   *m*   143
The Castlemaine Murders - Kerry Greenwood   *m*   91
The Damascened Blade - Barbara Cleverly   *m*   32
A Mourning Wedding - Carola Dunn   *m*   65
Murder in Montparnasse - Kerry Greenwood   *m*   92
Now You See It - Stuart M. Kaminsky   *m*   113
Queer Street - Curt Colbert   *m*   35

Historical/Ancient Rome

The Judgment of Caesar - Steven Saylor   *m*   180
Scandal Takes a Holiday - Lindsey Davis   *m*   54

Historical/Antebellum American South

Dead Water - Barbara Hambly   *m*   96

Historical/Depression Era

The More Deceived - David Roberts   *m*   171

Historical/Edwardian

A Dead Man in Trieste - Michael Pearce   *m*   159
Death of an Effendi - Michael Pearce   *m*   160
Hasty Death - Marion Chesney   *m*   27
The Tale of Hill Top Farm - Susan Wittig Albert   *m*   2

Historical/Elizabethan

The Counterfeit Crank - Edward Marston   *m*   134
The Siren Queen - Fiona Buckley   *m*   24
Time's Fool - Leonard Tourney   *m*   201

Historical/Medieval

Chaucer and the House of Fame - Philippa Morgan   *m*   148
Consolation for an Exile - Caroline Roe   *m*   175
A Feast of Poisons - C.L. Grace   *m*   89
The Hangman's Hymn - P.C. Doherty   *m*   58
The Harper's Quine - Pat McIntosh   *m*   141
A Play of Isaac - Margaret Frazer   *m*   83
Tyrant of the Mind - Priscilla Royal   *m*   176
Whispers of the Dead - Peter Tremayne   *m*   202
The Witch in the Well - Sharan Newman   *m*   154

Historical/Napoleonic Wars

Petty Treason - Madeleine E. Robins   *m*   173

Historical/Roaring Twenties

The Mammoth Book of Roaring Twenties Whodunnits - Mike Ashley   *m*   3

Historical/Victorian

A Christmas Visitor - Anne Perry   *m*   162
The Midnight Band of Mercy - Michael Blaine   *m*   14

POPULAR FICTION

Genre Index

Subject Index

This index lists subjects which are covered in the featured titles. Beneath each subject heading, titles are arranged alphabetically with the author names, genre codes, and entry numbers also indicated. The genre codes are as follows: *c* Popular Fiction, *f* Fantasy, *h* Horror, *i* Inspirational, *m* Mystery, *r* Romance, *s* Science Fiction, *t* Historical, and *w* Western.

Apartheid

Heart of the Hunter - Deon Meyer   *m*   142

Apocalypse

Califia's Daughters - Leigh Richards   *s*   776

Arab-Israeli Wars

Bethlehem Road Murder - Batya Gur   *m*   94

Archaeology

Buried Dreams - Brendan DuBois   *m*   63
Buried Stuff - Sharon Fiffer   *m*   78
The Courage Consort - Michel Faber   *c*   1101
The Cretan Counterfeit - Katharine Farrer   *m*   74
The Dark Lord - Patricia Simpson   *r*   381
Dark Storm - Kel Richards   *i*   1042
The Egyptologist - Arthur Phillips   *m*   922
The Egyptologist - Arthur Phillips   *c*   1165
Exorcist: The Beginning - Steven Piziks   *h*   682
Headhunter - Roy Lewis   *m*   127
Lake of Sorrows - Erin Hart   *m*   99

Arson

Fire When Ready - Kate Kingsbury   *m*   119
In a Dark House - Deborah Crombie   *m*   46
Moment of Truth - Sally John   *i*   1010
Pyro - Earl Emerson   *m*   70

Art

Color Blind - Jonathan Santlofer   *m*   179
Mansions of the Dead - Sarah Stewart
   Taylor   *m*   197
Pale as the Dead - Fiona Mountain   *m*   150

Arthurian Legends

Arthur the King - Allan Massie   *t*   901
Child of the Dark Prophecy - T.A. Barron   *f*   505
The Lady of the Sea - Rosalind Miles   *t*   906
The Lance Thrower - Jack Whyte   *t*   953
The Lance Thrower - Jack Whyte   *f*   592
Legend of the Emerald Rose - Linda
   Wichman   *i*   1058

Artificial Intelligence

Prometheus Road - Bruce Balfour   *s*   716

Artists and Art

Love, the Painter's Wife and the Queen of Sheba -
   Aliette Armel   *c*   1066
Love, the Painter's Wife and the Queen of Sheba -
   Aliette Armel   *t*   814
The Manor - Scott Nicholson   *h*   676
The Painting - Nina Schuyler   *t*   935
Snowed In - Christina Bartolomeo   *c*   1071

Assimilation

The Love Wife - Gish Jen   *c*   1126

Astrology

The Cosmic Clues - Manjiri Prabhu   *m*   164

Authors and Writers

Author, Author - David Lodge   *t*   897
Author, Author - David Lodge   *c*   1138

Carnage on the Committee - Ruth Dudley
   Edwards   *m*   68
Chaucer and the House of Fame - Philippa
   Morgan   *t*   909
Killer Blonde - Laura Levine   *m*   126
Little Fugue - Robert Anderson   *t*   813
The Master - Colm Toibin   *c*   1195
Pasta Imperfect - Maddy Hunter   *m*   107
Please Do Feed the Cat - Marian Babson   *m*   4
Sailors on the Inward Sea - Lawrence
   Thornton   *t*   945
The Tale of Hill Top Farm - Susan Wittig
   Albert   *m*   2
The Tyrant's Novel - Thomas Keneally   *c*   1130
Wake Up, Sir - Jonathan Ames   *c*   1064
Young Will - Bruce Cook   *t*   845

Authorship

The Geographer's Library - Jon Fasman   *c*   1102
The Ghost Writer - John Harwood   *c*   1118
The Good Nanny - Benjamin Cheever   *c*   1084

Autobiography

The Virtues of War - Steven Pressfield   *t*   924
Young Will - Bruce Cook   *t*   845

Automobiles

Four on the Floor - Deborah Morgan   *m*   147

Babies

The Babe Magnet - Robin Wells   *r*   403
A Christmas Baby - Annette Blair   *r*   226
The Missing Link - Katharine Farrer   *m*   75
My Long, Tall Texas Heartthrob - Geralyn
   Dawson   *r*   249

Bands

Murder of a Pink Elephant - Denise
   Swanson   *m*   193

Bar Mitzvah/Bat Mitzvah

The Last Dark Place - Stuart M. Kaminsky   *m*   112

Beaches

Buried Dreams - Brendan DuBois   *m*   63

Beauty

The Painted Rose - Donna Birdsell   *r*   223

Beauty Contests

Savannah from Savannah - Denise Hildreth   *i*   1001

Behavior

The Price of Pleasure - Kresley Cole   *r*   243

Bible

Three Days - Melody Carlson   *i*   975

Biblical Fiction

Gods and Kings - Lynn Austin   *i*   963
Love, the Painter's Wife and the Queen of Sheba -
   Aliette Armel   *t*   814
Three Days - Melody Carlson   *i*   975
Wisdom's Daughter - India Edghill   *t*   865

Biography

Author, Author - David Lodge   *c*   1138
Author, Author - David Lodge   *c*   897
The Divine Husband - Francisco Goldman   *t*   874
Divine Sarah - Adam Braver   *t*   829
The Emancipator's Wife - Barbara Hambly   *t*   878
The Empress of Last Days - Jane Stevenson   *t*   942
Farewell, My Only One - Antoine Audouard   *t*   816
The Franciscan Conspiracy - John R. Sack   *t*   932
The Great Scot - Duncan A. Bruce   *t*   830
The Indian Agent - Dan O'Brien   *t*   914
Life Mask - Emma Donoghue   *c*   1094
Little Fugue - Robert Anderson   *t*   813
The Master - Colm Toibin   *c*   1195
Ophelia's Fan - Christine Balint   *t*   818
The Persistence of Memory - Tony Eprile   *c*   1097
Pride of Carthage - David Anthony Durham   *t*   864
The Queen of Subtleties - Suzannah Dunn   *t*   863
The Rebel: An Imagined Life of James Dean - Jack
   Dann   *t*   848
The Retreat - Patrick Rambaud   *c*   1167
St. Dale - Sharyn McCrumb   *c*   1143
The Stone That the Builder Refused - Madison Smartt
   Bell   *c*   1072
The White Night of St. Petersburg - Michael, Prince of
   Greece   *t*   905

Biological Warfare

Red Tide - G.M. Ford   *m*   81

Biotechnology

City of Gold and Lepers - Guy D'Armen   *s*   737

Birthdays

And a Puzzle to Die On - Parnell Hall   *m*   95

Blackmail

The Damascened Blade - Barbara Cleverly   *m*   32
Duke of Sin - Adele Ashworth   *r*   215
Time's Fool - Leonard Tourney   *m*   201

Blindness

A Mourning in Autumn - Harker Moore   *m*   146

Boarding Houses

A Place to Belong - Vonette Z. Bright   *i*   970

Boats and Boating

Cross Current - Christine Kling   *m*   120
Metro Girl - Janet Evanovich   *m*   72

Books and Reading

The Marine Meets His Match - Cathie Linz   *r*   323
The Overnight - Ramsey Campbell   *h*   611
The Red Queen - Margaret Drabble   *c*   1095
Sawyer's Quest - Will Cade   *w*   423
The Shadow of the Wind - Carlos Ruiz
   Zafon   *c*   1176

Brothers

Billy Goat Hill - Mark Stanleigh Morris   *i*   1033
California Girl - T. Jefferson Parker   *m*   158
Till Shiloh Comes - Gilbert Morris   *i*   1032

Brothers and Sisters

Darkly Dreaming Dexter - Jeff Lindsay   *m*   128

Character Name Index

This index alphabetically lists the major characters in each featured title. Each character name is followed by a description of the character. Citations also provide titles of the books featuring the character, listed alphabetically if there is more than one title; author names and genre codes. The genre codes are as follows: *c* Popular Fiction, *f* Fantasy, *h* Horror, *i* Inspirational, *m* Mystery, *r* Romance, *s* Science Fiction, *t* Historical, and *w* Western. Numbers refer to the entries that feature each title.

A

Abair, James (Wealthy; Boyfriend)
Heir to the Glimmering World - Cythia Ozick   *c*   1161

Abbott, Taite (Young Woman)
The Last Storyteller - Diane Noble   *i*   1037

Abelard, Peter (Historical Figure; Philosopher)
Farewell, My Only One - Antoine Audouard   *t*   816

Able (Knight)
The Wizard - Gene Wolfe   *f*   595

Achilles (Warrior)
The War at Troy - Lindsay Clarke   *t*   836

Aching, Tiffany (Witch; Apprentice)
A Hat Full of Sky - Terry Pratchett   *f*   576

Achmed (Ruler)
Elegy for a Lost Star - Elizabeth Haydon   *f*   542

Ackenzac, Leovigild (Composer)
The Charnel Prince - J. Gregory Keyes   *f*   552

Ackerman, Johnny (Cowboy)
Judgment Day - Frank Roderus   *w*   479

Acosta, Carmen (Teenager; Crime Victim)
Convenient Disposal - Steven F. Havill   *w*   448

Adams, Flick (Scientist; Museum Curator)
Dead as a Scone - Ron Benrey   *i*   965

Adams, Lindsey (Police Officer; Spouse)
Dry Heat - Jon Talton   *m*   195

Addams, Alcea O'Malley (Divorced Person; Baker)
Follow Me Home - Jerri Corgiat   *r*   244

Addison-Blake, George (Doctor; Relative)
The Parts - Keith Ridgway   *c*   1172

Adler, Irene (Detective—Amateur; Singer)
Spider Dance - Carole Nelson Douglas   *m*   61
Spider Dance - Carole Nelson Douglas   *t*   857

Adler, Jack (Scientist)
Singularity - Bill DeSmedt   *s*   738

Agatha (Religious)
The Last Dark Place - Stuart M. Kaminsky   *m*   112
Thief in Retreat - Aimee Thurlo   *m*   199

Aguilar, Miguel (Rancher)
The Baron Honor - Jory Sherman   *w*   481

Ahab, Hannah (Widow(er))
Hannah Rose - Louise M. Gouge   *i*   991

Aimee (Passenger)
Overstars Mail: Imperial Challenge - Roberta Gellis   *s*   748

Aimery (Nobleman)
Maiden of Fire - Deborah Johns   *r*   301

Airton, Edward (Religious)
The Palace of Heavenly Pleasure - Adam Williams   *t*   954

Ajam, Najeeb (Guide; Linguist)
The Warlord's Son - Dan Fesperman   *m*   77

Ajmani, Rachel (Administrator)
Grasp the Stars - Jennifer Wingert   *s*   806

Akhila (Spinster)
Ladies Coupe - Anita Nair   *c*   1154

al-Maaz, Safia (Scientist)
Sandstorm - James Rollins   *s*   780

Alakusoglu, Kerim (Writer; Expatriate)
Snow - Orhan Pamuk   *c*   1162

Alaric (Religious)
Grey Knights - Ben Counter   *f*   520

Albion, Brian (Warrior)
The Winter Oak - James A. Hetley   *f*   544

Alder, Sally (Professor; Detective—Amateur)
Bye, Bye Love - Virginia Swift   *m*   194

Alexander, Rachel (Detective—Private; Animal Trainer)
Fall Guy - Carol Lea Benjamin   *m*   9

Alexander, Simon (FBI Agent)
Dating Is Murder - Harley Jane Kozak   *r*   319

Alexander the Great (Historical Figure; Military Personnel)
The Virtues of War - Steven Pressfield   *t*   924

Ali Khan, Hassan (Nobleman; Spouse)
A Beggar at the Gate - Thalassa Ali   *t*   811

Alissa (Sorceress)
Lost Truth - Dawn Cook   *f*   518

Allard, Frank (Rancher)
Mountains Against the Sun - Perry Holmes   *w*   452

Allen, E.A. (Young Man)
Waiting for Teddy Williams - Howard Frank Mosher   *c*   1150

Allerton, Matthew (Nobleman; Military Personnel)
Cordelia's Corinthian - Victoria Hinshaw   *r*   294

Alviso, Jaime (Friend; Immigrant)
North with De Anza - Dorothy Ward Erskine   *w*   439

Amalfi, Angelina (Journalist; Detective—Amateur)
Courting Disaster - Joanne Pence   *m*   161

Amara (Spy)
Furies of Calderon - Jim Butcher   *f*   512

Amata (Student)
The Franciscan Conspiracy - John R. Sack   *t*   932

Ambrewster, Harry (Accountant; Babysitter)
The Nerd Who Loved Me - Vicki Lewis Thompson   *r*   397

Ambrose (Nobleman)
Let There Be Blood - Jane Jakeman   *t*   885

American Horse, Johnny (Activist; Indian)
In the Moon of Red Ponies - James Lee Burke   *c*   1080

Ames, John (Religious)
Gilead - Marilynne Robinson   *c*   1173

Ames, Tabitha (Spacewoman)
Warp Speed - Travis S. Taylor   *s*   792

Amiss, Robert (Writer; Detective—Amateur)
Carnage on the Committee - Ruth Dudley Edwards   *m*   68

Amos, Joe (Military Personnel)
Liberation Road - David L. Robbins   *t*   927

Anderson, Christa (Handicapped)
Forgotten Justice - Lois Richer   *i*   1043

Anderson, Robert (Writer)
Little Fugue - Robert Anderson   *t*   813

Anderson, Serena (Store Owner)
The Marine Meets His Match - Cathie Linz   *r*   323

Anderson, Tess (Agent; Child-Care Giver)
My Long, Tall Texas Heartthrob - Geralyn Dawson   *r*   249

Anderson, Tom (Political Figure; Historical Figure)
Jass - David Fulmer   *t*   869

Andez, Shelia (Military Personnel; Prisoner)
Horizon Storms - Kevin J. Anderson   *s*   713

Andrew, Emily (Tour Guide; Detective—Amateur)
Pasta Imperfect - Maddy Hunter   *m*   107

Andrews, Rachel (Spouse; Employer)
Bloody Hills - Charles G. West   *w*   490

Angela (Accident Victim; Relative)
Don't Move - Margaret Mazzantini   *c*   1140

Angelese (Angel)
Infernal Angel - Edward Lee *h* 656

Angeli, Pier (Historical Figure; Actress)
The Rebel: An Imagined Life of James Dean - Jack Dann *t* 848

Annais (Young Woman)
The Falcons of Montabard - Elizabeth Chadwick *t* 833

Anybody, Rob (Thief)
A Hat Full of Sky - Terry Pratchett *f* 576

Anza, Juan Bautista de (Military Personnel; Historical Figure)
North with De Anza - Dorothy Ward Erskine *w* 439

Aparicio, Francisca "Paquita" (Religious)
The Divine Husband - Francisco Goldman *t* 874

Aradna (Young Woman)
Pride of Carthage - David Anthony Durham *t* 864

Aras (Alien)
City of Pearl - Karen Traviss *s* 794
Crossing the Line - Karen Traviss *s* 795

Arbuckle, Roscoe "Fatty" (Entertainer; Historical Figure)
I, Fatty - Jerry Stahl *c* 1192

Ardacris, Serrah (Fugitive)
The Covenant Rising - Stan Nicholls *f* 572

Ardan, Francis (Explorer; Prisoner)
City of Gold and Lepers - Guy D'Armen *s* 737

Argeneau, Bastien (Vampire; Businessman)
Tall, Dark, and Hungry - Lynsay Sands *r* 377

Ariana of Clairmont (Noblewoman)
Heart of the Hunter - Tina St. John *r* 386

Armitage, Fletch (Military Personnel)
Days of Infamy - Harry Turtledove *s* 797
Days of Infamy - Harry Turtledove *t* 947

Armstrong, Louis (Historical Figure; Musician)
Oh, Play That Thing - Roddy Doyle *t* 860

Arnthor (Ruler)
The Wizard - Gene Wolfe *f* 595

Aron (Nobleman)
The Bright and the Dark - Michele M. Welch *f* 589

Aronson, Chamus (Pilot)
The Gods and Their Machines - Oisin McGann *s* 764

Arthur (Ruler)
Arthur the King - Allan Massie *t* 901
The Lance Thrower - Jack Whyte *t* 953

Artois, Pierre (Government Official)
Saucer: The Conquest - Stephen Coonts *s* 734

Arvin (Warrior)
Venom's Taste - Lisa Smedman *f* 582

Ascension, Kim (Banker)
The Secret Beau - Annette Mahon *r* 331

Ashby, John (Vampire)
Tainted Blood - James M. Thompson *h* 701

Ashby, Ria (Teacher; Ward)
Beyond a Wicked Kiss - Jo Goodman *r* 273

Atani, Karadur (Nobleman; Mythical Creature)
Dragon's Treasure - Elizabeth A. Lynn *f* 563

Ataturk, Kemal (Historical Figure; Military Personnel)
Birds Without Wings - Louis de Bernieres *t* 852

Atout (Professor)
The World as It Shall Be - Emile Souvestre *s* 789

Atreides, Vorian (Military Personnel)
The Battle of Corrin - Brian Herbert *s* 752

Atvar (Alien; Military Personnel)
Homeward Bound - Harry Turtledove *s* 798

Atwater, Dan (FBI Agent)
Through Violet Eyes - Stephen Woodworth *h* 709

Aubrey, Jack (Military Personnel)
21: The Final Unfinished Voyage of Jack Aubrey - Patrick O'Brian *t* 913

Audrey (Spouse)
The Haunted Hillbilly - Derek McCormack *h* 665

Austen, Jaine (Writer; Detective—Amateur)
Killer Blonde - Laura Levine *m* 126

Austin, Port (Outlaw; Murderer)
Vengeance Rider - Ralph Compton *w* 431

Avare, Simeon (Supernatural Being)
The Dark Lord - Patricia Simpson *r* 381

Avelessa (Royalty)
The Bride of Stone - Thomas Williams *i* 1059

Avens, John (Religious)
Gun Ball Hill - Ellen Cooney *t* 846

Avery, Linden (Doctor)
The Runes of the Earth - Stephen R. Donaldson *f* 524

Avery, Stan (Teenager; Spaceman)
The Boy Who Would Live Forever - Frederik Pohl *s* 773

Avery, Wes (Writer)
Haven - Don D'Ammassa *s* 736

Aylesgarth, Roman (Nobleman)
The Heiress of Hyde Park - Jacqueline Navin *r* 351

Ayoshi (Artist)
The Painting - Nina Schuyler *t* 935

B

Bahnakson, Bahzell (Barbarian; Diplomat)
Windrider's Oath - David Weber *f* 588

Bahr, Marshall "Mars" (Detective—Police; Divorced Person)
Alone at Night - K.J. Erickson *m* 71

Bai-sha, Kevla (Worker)
On Fire's Wings - Christie Golden *f* 539

Bailey, Harry (Travel Agent)
St. Dale - Sharyn McCrumb *c* 1143

Bainbridge, Maddy (Single Parent; Bride)
Chances Are - Barbara Bretton *r* 231

Baker, Vince (Journalist)
Divine Sarah - Adam Braver *t* 829

Baklanov, Stefan (Relative)
The Romanov Prophecy - Steve Berry *c* 1074

Baldwin, Joanne (Witch)
Chill Factor - Rachel Caine *f* 514

Baldwin de Furnshill (Knight; Government Official)
The Outlaws of Ennor - Michael Jecks *t* 887
The Tolls of Death - Michael Jecks *t* 888

Ballinger, Nina (Journalist)
Invitation to a Hanging - Robert J. Randisi *w* 476

Balthasar (Heir)
The Empress of Last Days - Jane Stevenson *t* 942

Bandar, Guth (Aged Person)
Black Brillion - Matthew Hughes *s* 754

Banks, Jo (Doctor; Detective—Amateur)
Satan's Pony - Robin Hathaway *m* 101

Banner, Sophie Lindel (Widow(er))
A Duke for Christmas - Cynthia Pratt *r* 362

Bardin, Billy (Teenager)
Billy Bardin and the Witness Tree - Mary E. Penson *w* 472

Bardin, William (Surveyor; Farmer)
Billy Bardin and the Witness Tree - Mary E. Penson *w* 472

Barnaby, Alexandra (Mechanic; Young Woman)
Metro Girl - Janet Evanovich *m* 72
Metro Girl - Janet Evanovich *c* 1098

Barnaby, Tom (Police Officer)
A Ghost in the Machine - Caroline Graham *m* 90

Barnaby, William "Wild Bill" (Sailor)
Metro Girl - Janet Evanovich *c* 1098

Barnard, Terri (Doctor)
Deficiency - Andrew Neiderman *h* 674

Barndollar, Sarah (Police Officer; Single Parent)
The Rivals - Joan Johnston *r* 303

Barnes, Dylan (Martial Arts Expert)
The Darkening - Chandler McGrew *h* 667

Barnes, John (Writer; Historical Figure)
Gaudeamus - John Barnes *s* 718

Barnett, Terry (Carpenter; Crime Victim)
Dead for the Winter - Betsy Thornton *w* 488

Baron, Anson (Rancher)
The Baron Honor - Jory Sherman *w* 481

Baron, Martin (Rancher; Lawman)
The Baron Honor - Jory Sherman *w* 481

Barr, Temple (Public Relations; Detective—Amateur)
Cat in an Orange Twist - Carole Nelson Douglas *m* 60

Barret, Roarke (Knight)
The Knight's Redemption - Joanne Rock *r* 371

Barrett, Cathy (Secretary)
Nightingale's Lament - Simon R. Green *h* 636

Barron, Rick (Detective—Homicide; Security Officer)
The Prince of Beverly Hills - Stuart Woods *t* 957

Barrow, Clete (Actor)
The Prince of Beverly Hills - Stuart Woods *t* 957

Bass, Charlie (Military Personnel)
A World of Hurt - David Sherman *s* 786

Basset, Marc (Critic)
Eating Crow - Jay Rayner *c* 1168

Bauer, Lillie (Businesswoman)
Tiger Lillie - Lisa Samson *i* 1046

Baxter, Jodi (Spouse; Parent)
The Yada Yada Prayer Group Gets Down - Neta Jackson *i* 1007

Bays, Buddy (Saloon Keeper/Owner; Criminal)
Skin River - Steven Sidor *m* 185

Bazinger, Karl (Military Personnel)
The Year Is '42 - Nella Bielski *c* 1076
The Year Is '42 - Nella Bielski *t* 823

Bear (Indian; Friend)
Blood River - Jory Sherman *w* 482

Bear (Warrior)
Paladins - Joel Rosenberg *f* 580

Beauprix, Anthony (Detective—Police)
A Perfect Cover - Maureen Tan *r* 390

Beaver (Indian)
The Pipestone Quest - Don Coldsmith *t* 841

Becha, Rilsin Sae (Government Official; Noblewoman)
The Blood of the Land - Noel-Anne Brennan *f* 509

Becker, Andy (Journalist)
California Girl - T. Jefferson Parker *m* 158

Becker, David (Religious)
California Girl - T. Jefferson Parker *m* 158

Becker, Nick (Detective—Homicide)
California Girl - T. Jefferson Parker *m* 158

Beckett, Grace (Adventurer)
The First Stone - Mark Anthony *f* 499

Beckwith, Alan (Businessman)
R Is for Ricochet - Sue Grafton *c* 1114

Beezo, Punchinello (Criminal)
Life Expectancy - Dean R. Koontz *h* 652

Behaine, Pierre de (Religious)
Le Colonial - Kien Nguyen *t* 912

Behan, John (Lawman; Friend)
Trouble in Tombstone - Richard S. Wheeler *w* 494

Bel (Agent)
The Language of Power - Rosemary Kirstein *f* 553

Belov, Josef (Government Official)
Dark Justice - Jack Higgins *c* 1121

Belvedere, Randolph (Businessman)
Falling Awake - Jayne Ann Krentz *c* 1133

Benedict, Alex (Antiques Dealer)
Polaris - Jack McDevitt *s* 762

Bennet, Kitty (Gentlewoman)
Suspense and Sensibility - Carrie A. Bebris *t* 820

Bennett, Celeste (Wealthy; Public Relations)
Killer Curves - Roxanne St. Claire *r* 383

Bennett, Felicia (Girlfriend)
The Last King - Nichelle D. Tramble *c* 1197

Benoliel, Joseph Adrian (Wealthy)
Dead Lines - Greg Bear *h* 603

Benson, Oliver (Computer Expert)
Charade - Gilbert Morris *i* 1030

Bentley, William (Military Personnel)
The Spithead Nymph - Jan Needle *t* 911

Benton, Brad (Government Official)
Impeachable Offense - Neesa Hart *i* 998

Benton, Delilah (Writer)
Loving Delilah - Candice Poarch *r* 361

Berger, Mitch (Critic; Widow(er))
The Burnt Orange Sunrise - David Handler *m* 98

Bergman, Chris (Teenager; Friend)
Starlight Comes Home - Janet Muirhead
  Hill *w* 450

Berlioz, Hector (Historical Figure; Composer)
Ophelia's Fan - Christine Balint *t* 818

Berman, Mark (Narrator)
Natasha: And Other Stories - David
  Bezmozgis *c* 1075

Bernhardt, Sarah (Historical Figure; Actress)
Divine Sarah - Adam Braver *t* 829

Bertrand (Religious)
The Nameless Day - Sara Douglass *f* 525

Bertrand, Carmela (Store Owner; Detective—
  Amateur)
Bound for Murder - Laura Childs *m* 28

Best (Detective—Police)
Dead End - Joan Lock *t* 896

Beverly, Vincent (Gentleman)
The Christmas Matchmaker - Jeanne Savery *r* 378

Bey, Rustum (Businessman)
Birds Without Wings - Louis de Bernieres *t* 852

Bhalu (Businessman)
The Death of Mr. Love - Indra Sinha *c* 1187

Bigelow, Kevin (Nobleman)
Heroics for Beginners - John Moore *f* 570

Bill the First (Rancher)
The American Cowboy - Will James *w* 454

Bill the Second (Rancher)
The American Cowboy - Will James *w* 454

Bill the Third (Rancher)
The American Cowboy - Will James *w* 454

Billy (Orphan; Frontierswoman)
The Lutheran - Jack Britton Sullivan *w* 486

Bilqis (Historical Figure; Ruler)
Love, the Painter's Wife and the Queen of Sheba -
  Aliette Armel *c* 1066
Love, the Painter's Wife and the Queen of Sheba -
  Aliette Armel *t* 814
Wisdom's Daughter - India Edghill *t* 865

bin Wazir, Snay (Terrorist)
Assassin - Ted Bell *c* 1073

Binnington, Mai (Suffragette)
The Distaff Side - Elizabeth Palmer *t* 916

Birchspring (Mythical Creature; Aged Person)
The Secret of Shabaz - Jennifer Macaire *f* 564

Birkenstock, Hiram (Worker)
A World of Hurt - David Sherman *s* 786

Bishop, Charlotte Valentine (Widow(er))
Watchers on the Hill - Stephanie Grace
  Whitson *i* 1056

Bishop, Natalie (Doctor)
All She Ever Wanted - Barbara Freethy *r* 268

Bishop, Nathan (Construction Worker)
Live Like You Were Dying - Michael Morris *i* 1034

Bismark, Travis (Spy)
Gaudeamus - John Barnes *s* 718

Black, Fletcher (Artist)
Meant to Be - Edie Claire *r* 241

Black, Harrison (Store Owner; Detective—Amateur)
Snuffed Out - Tim Myers *m* 153

Black, Mordichai (Hero)
Aphrodite's Flame - Julie Kenner *r* 309

Black-spot (Indian)
Friday, the Arapaho Boy - Marc Simmons *w* 483

Blackburne, Ashford (Nobleman)
A Christmas Baby - Annette Blair *r* 226

Blackford, Flora (Political Figure)
Return Engagement - Harry Turtledove *s* 799

Blackstone, Harry (Magician)
Now You See It - Stuart M. Kaminsky *m* 113

Blacksword, Tanaros (Warrior)
Banewreaker - Jacqueline Carey *f* 515

Blair, Alan (Writer; Alcoholic)
Wake Up, Sir - Jonathan Ames *c* 1064

Blake, Anita (Vampire Hunter)
Incubus Dreams - Laurell K. Hamilton *h* 637
Incubus Dreams - Laurell K. Hamilton *c* 1116

Blake, Natasha (Genealogist; Detective—Amateur)
Pale as the Dead - Fiona Mountain *m* 150

Blake, Sam (Carpenter)
American Idle - Alesia Holliday *r* 295

Blake, Whitney (Public Relations)
The Whitney Chronicles - Judy Baer *i* 964

Blake, Woody (Businessman)
The Overnight - Ramsey Campbell *h* 611

Blakeney, Cordelia (Noblewoman)
Kindling - Mick Farren *f* 531

Blanchard, Meg (Gentlewoman)
The Siren Queen - Fiona Buckley *t* 831

Blanchard, Ursula (Spy; Widow(er))
The Siren Queen - Fiona Buckley *m* 24
The Siren Queen - Fiona Buckley *t* 831

Blevins, Billy Ray (Outlaw; Murderer)
Bloody Hills - Charles G. West *w* 490

Blind Seer (Animal)
Wolf Captured - Jane Lindskold *f* 561

Bloom, Ella (Clerk)
A Girl Becomes a Comma Like That - Lisa
  Glatt *c* 1111

Blue, Carolyn (Journalist; Detective—Amateur)
Holy Guacamole! - Nancy Fairbanks *m* 73

Blue Quartz, Chert (Mythical Creature)
Shadowmarch. Volume 1 - Tad Williams *f* 594

Blume, Molly (Writer; Divorced Person)
Grave Endings - Rochelle Krich *m* 123

Bly, Nellie (Journalist; Historical Figure)
Spider Dance - Carole Nelson Douglas *m* 61
Spider Dance - Carole Nelson Douglas *t* 857

Bob (Computer Expert)
The Atrocity Archives - Charles Stross *h* 698

Boleyn, Anne (Historical Figure; Royalty)
The Queen of Subtleties - Suzannah Dunn *t* 863

Bonaparte, Napoleon (Historical Figure; Military
  Personnel)
The Retreat - Patrick Rambaud *c* 1167

Bonaventure, Marianna (Spy)
Singularity - Bill DeSmedt *s* 738

Bone, Slayton (Rancher; Thief)
A Bad Day to Die - J. Lee Butts *w* 422

Bonner, Elizabeth (Spouse)
Fire Along the Sky - Sara Donati *t* 855

Bonner, Lily (Young Woman)
Fire Along the Sky - Sara Donati *t* 855

Bonner, Nathaniel (Spouse; Farmer)
Fire Along the Sky - Sara Donati *t* 855

Booly, William III (Military Personnel)
For Those Who Fell - William C. Dietz *s* 739

Boom (Animal)
Black Water - D.J. MacHale *f* 565

Boone, Christian Wolfe "Boo" (Writer; Salesman)
Boo Who - Rene Gutteridge *i* 994

Boone, Nathan (Military Personnel)
Watchers on the Hill - Stephanie Grace
  Whitson *i* 1056

Booth, John Wilkes (Actor; Murderer)
The Curse of Cain - J. Mark Powell *w* 473

Boris III (Ruler)
King's Ransom - Jan Benzely *t* 822

Bourne, Jason (Spy; Professor)
The Bourne Legacy - Eric Van Lustbader *c* 1202

Bowman, Bruce (Crime Suspect)
Through the Grinder - Cleo Coyle *m* 42

Bowmaster, Leeana (Teenager; Noblewoman)
Windrider's Oath - David Weber *f* 588

Boyd, Russell (Police Officer)
Cruisers - Craig Nova *c* 1158

Bracewell, Nicholas (Producer)
The Counterfeit Crank - Edward Marston *m* 134

Brackett, Farley (Lawman; Military Personnel)
Jericho's Road - Elmer Kelton *w* 458

Bradley, Christine (Care Giver; Adoptee)
The Gift of Christmas Present - Melody
  Carlson *i* 974

Bradley, Sabrina (Television)
Flippin' the Script - Aisha Ford *i* 986

Brady, Luther (Religious)
Crisscross - F. Paul Wilson *h* 706

Bran, Sylvia (Imposter; Musician)
The Beautiful Inez - Bart Schneider   c   1178

Brancaster Talbot, Claire (Businesswoman; Heiress)
Highland Rogue - Deborah Hale   r   282

Brand, Luke (Widow(er); Farmer)
Dark Harvest - Karen Harper   r   285

Brandolini, Amadeo (Businessman)
Killer Smile - Lisa Scottoline   c   1180

Brandon, Becky (Spouse)
Shopaholic and Sister - Sophie Kinsella   c   1132

Brandon, Luke (Spouse)
Shopaholic and Sister - Sophie Kinsella   c   1132

Brannigan, Elizabeth (Relative; Divorced Person)
All These Girls - Ellen Slezak   c   1189

Brannon, Hugh (Advertising)
Not Quite as Advertised - Tanya Michaels   r   346

Bransford, Cordelia "Corey" (Gentlewoman; Governess)
Cordelia's Corinthian - Victoria Hinshaw   r   294

Branson, Cade (Rancher)
Winter Kill - Cotton Smith   w   484

Branson, Titus (Rancher)
Winter Kill - Cotton Smith   w   484

Brant (Police Officer)
Blitz - Ken Bruen   m   23

Braun, Gerhard (Military Personnel)
Obsessed - Ted Dekker   i   977

Breen, Clarissa (Writer)
My Death - Lisa Tuttle   h   702

Brewster, Ray (Professor)
When Christmas Comes - Debbie Macomber   r   330

Brewydd (Ruler)
Raven's Shadow - Patricia Briggs   f   510

Brighton, Glory (Restaurateur)
The Shaughnessey Accord - Alison Kent   r   311

Brinker (Detective—Private)
Choke Point - James C. Mitchell   m   144

Brodie, Jackson (Detective—Private)
Case Histories - Kate Atkinson   c   1067

Bronstein, Michaela (Military Personnel)
The Rats, the Bats, and the Ugly - Eric Flint   s   744

Brooks, Colleen (Survivor)
Ghostlands - Marc Zicree   f   598

Brown, Floyd (Detective—Homicide)
Color Blind - Jonathan Santlofer   m   179

Brown, Nancy (Prostitute)
Donovan's Dove - Joseph A. West   w   492

Browne, Martha (Writer)
The First Cut - Peter Robinson   m   174

Browne, Verity (Journalist; Activist)
The More Deceived - David Roberts   m   171

Browning, Richard (Gentleman; Guardian)
The Affair at Greengage Manor - Mona Gedney   r   269

Browning, Theodosia (Store Owner; Detective—Amateur)
The Jasmine Moon Murder - Laura Childs   m   29

Broxigar (Mythical Creature)
The Well of Eternity - Richard A. Knaak   f   556

Bruce, Robert (Military Personnel)
Fitzpatrick's War - Theodore Judson   s   756

Bruenna (Wizard)
The Fifth Dawn - Cory J. Herndon   f   543

Brunner (Bounty Hunter)
Blood of the Dragon - C.L. Werner   f   590

Bryan, Jamie (Volunteer; Widow(er))
Beyond Tuesday Morning - Karen Kingsbury   i   1014

Bryant, Arthur (Detective—Police)
Full Dark House - Christopher Fowler   m   82

Bryce, Henry (Interior Decorator; Detective—Amateur)
The Gun in Daniel Webster's Bust - Margaret Scherf   m   182

Bryerly, Dubric (Detective—Private)
Ghosts in the Snow - Tamara Siler Jones   h   646

Bryton, Samantha (Fugitive)
Sunrise Alley - Catherine Asaro   s   714

Buchanan, Thaddeus (Gambler; Veteran)
Loving Mercy - Teresa Bodwell   r   230

Burby, Nick (Detective—Private; Boyfriend)
Putting on the Dog - Cynthia Baxter   m   7

Burch, Craig (Detective—Police)
Cold Case Squad - Edna Buchanan   c   1079

Burke, Nate (Police Officer)
Northern Lights - Nora Roberts   r   368

Burke, Shan (Teenager)
When the Sky Rained Dust - Patrick Dearen   w   436

Burkett, Ken (Lawman)
Branded - Ed Gorman   w   442

Burnaby, Dirk (Wealthy)
The Falls - Joyce Carol Oates   c   1160

Burnham, Francis (Nobleman)
A Rakish Spy - Laura Paquet   r   358

Burns, Amos (Lawman; Crime Victim)
Mountains Against the Sun - Perry Holmes   w   452

Burns, Marty (Detective—Private)
Apocalypse Now, Voyager - Jay Russell   h   688

Burrack, Sam (Lawman)
Dead Man's Canyon - Ralph Cotton   w   432

Buster (Boyfriend)
Citizen Girl - Emma McLaughlin   c   1145

Butler, Charles (Psychologist)
Winter House - Carol O'Connell   m   155

Butler, Jacob (Police Officer)
As Good as Dead - Beverly Barton   r   219

Butler, Quentin (Military Personnel)
The Battle of Corrin - Brian Herbert   s   752

Byrne, Christy (Widow(er); Single Parent)
Silver Bells - Luanne Rice   r   363

C

Cabot, Belinda "Billy" (Computer Expert; Baker)
Raspberry Crush - Jill Winters   r   407

Cade, Matthew (Police Officer)
Breaker's Reef - Terri Blackstock   i   967

Cadotte, Will (Professor; Werewolf)
Blue Moon - Lori Handeland   r   283

Caduceus (Military Personnel)
Iron Hands - Jonathan Green   s   750

Cadwallader, Dorothy (Actress; Relative)
The Hollywood Dodo - Geoff Nicholson   c   1156

Cadwallader, Henry (Doctor; Widow(er))
The Hollywood Dodo - Geoff Nicholson   c   1156

Caesar, Julius (Historical Figure; Ruler)
The Judgment of Caesar - Steven Saylor   m   180

Cafarelli, Zeke (Carpenter)
Banishing Verona - Margot Livesey   c   1137

Caldason, Reeth (Warrior)
The Covenant Rising - Stan Nicholls   f   572

Calder, Laura (Socialite)
Calder Promise - Janet Dailey   r   245

Caldwell, Paul (Archaeologist)
The Egyptologist - Arthur Phillips   c   1165

Cale, Erevis (Sorcerer)
Dawn of Night - Paul S. Kemp   f   551

Calhoun, Stoney (Fisherman; Amnesiac)
Bitch Creek - William G. Tapply   m   196

Callahan, Connor (Doctor; Widow(er))
Snap Shot - Meg Chittenden   r   240

Callahan, Donald (Religious)
The Dark Tower - Stephen King   h   649

Calpurnia, Shira (Military Personnel)
Legacy - Matthew Farrer   s   741

Calverson, Timona "Timmy" (Young Woman)
Somebody Wonderful - Kate Rothwell   r   375

Camilla (Servant)
In the Hope of Rising Again - Helen Scully   t   936

Campbell, Daisy (Divorced Person)
Wild in the Moment - Jennifer Greene   r   278

Campbell, Niall (Laird)
Child of the Mist - Kathleen Morgan   i   1027

Campbell, Oswald T. (Orphan; Patient)
A Redbird Christmas - Fannie Flagg   c   1105

Campbell, Violet (Businesswoman)
Wild in the Moonlight - Jennifer Greene   r   279

Campion, Peregrine (Gentleman)
A Worthy Opponent - Louise Bergin   r   220

Cantrell, Rip (Pilot)
Saucer: The Conquest - Stephen Coonts   s   734

Cardale, Minty (Heiress)
The Lady of the Hall - Veronica Heley   i   999

Carella, Steve (Police Officer)
Hark! A Novel of the 87th Precinct - Ed McBain   m   138

Cargo, Frederick (Traveler)
Strange Cargo - Jeffrey E. Barlough   f   504

Carlisimo, Juan (Political Figure)
Flash - L.E. Modesitt Jr.   s   768

Carlson, Sam (Restaurateur; Divorced Person)
Espresso for Two - Courtni Wright   r   411

Carly, Abel (Twin)
Dead Man's Canyon - Ralph Cotton   w   432

Carly, Blake (Outlaw; Twin)
Dead Man's Canyon - Ralph Cotton   w   432

Carnochan, David (Businessman)
East Side Story - Louis Auchincloss   t   815

Carrasco, Freddy (Student—College; Bastard Son)
Any Place I Hang My Hat - Susan Isaacs   c   1124

Carrigan, Joseph (Relative; Cowboy)
War at Fire Creek - Cameron Judd   w   457

Carrigan, Liam (Relative; Cowboy)
War at Fire Creek - Cameron Judd   w   457

Carrigan, Patrick (Rancher)
War at Fire Creek - Cameron Judd   w   457

Carruthers, Mitchell (Bodyguard; Detective—Private)
Nerd Gone Wild - Vicki Lewis Thompson   r   396

Carson, Kit (Scout; Historical Figure)
The Mask of Red Death - Harold Schechter   m   181
The Mask of Red Death - Harold Schechter   t   934

Carter, Charlotte (Widow(er))
A New Day at Tanglewood - Annette Gail Smith   i   1048

Carter, Derian (Adventurer)
Wolf Captured - Jane Lindskold *f* 561

Carter, Georgia (Teenager)
A Girl Becomes a Comma Like That - Lisa
Glatt *c* 1111

Carter, Madeline (Stock Broker; Detective—
Amateur)
Mad Money - Linda L. Richards *r* 365

Carter, Sherry (Divorced Person; Relative)
And a Puzzle to Die On - Parnell Hall *m* 95

Carter, Susan (Administrator; Single Parent)
Gabriel's Discovery - Felicia Mason *i* 1024

Caruso, Sheila (Convict; Parent)
Breaker's Reef - Terri Blackstock *i* 967

Case, Tucker (Pilot)
The Stupidest Angel - Christopher Moore *h* 671

Casey (Artificial Intelligence)
New York Dreams - Eric Brown *s* 724

Casey, Patsy (Child; Handicapped)
A Redbird Christmas - Fannie Flagg *c* 1105

Cashel (Shepherd)
Master of the Cauldron - David Drake *f* 527

Casini, Maria (Fugitive)
Forced Conversion - Donald J. Bingle *s* 722

Cassidy, Jennifer (Student—Graduate)
Deep Blue - Tom Morrisey *i* 1035

Cassidy, William Jackson "Jax" (Police Officer)
Someone to Watch over Me - Teresa Hill *i* 1003

Castelluca, Nella (Heroine)
The Queen of the Big Time - Adriana
Trigiani *c* 1199

Cates, William (Nobleman; Diplomat)
An Honorable Match - Laura Paquet *r* 357

Cathcart, Harry (Detective—Private)
Hasty Death - Marion Chesney *m* 27

Cather, Audrey (Scientist)
The Dry Salvages - Caitlin R. Kiernan *h* 647

Catherine the Great (Historical Figure; Ruler)
Love and Honor - Randall Wallace *t* 950

Cavalucci, Tony (Police Officer)
The Deuce - F.P. Lione *i* 1020

Cecily (Ruler)
Silver's Edge - Anne Kelleher *f* 550

Celanire (Crime Victim)
Who Slashed Celanire's Throat? - Maryse
Conde *t* 844

Cerelinde (Noblewoman)
Banewreaker - Jacqueline Carey *f* 515

Cesare, Giselle (Cook)
Girl Gone Wild - Joanne Rock *r* 370

Chaisa, Selene (Noblewoman)
A Day Dark as Night - Carl Bowen *f* 507

Chambers, Will (Lawyer)
The Last Judgment - Craig Parshall *i* 1038

Champagne (Genetically Altered Being)
Edenborn - Nick Sagan *s* 782

Champion, Ed (Outlaw; Thief)
Staring Down the Devil - Peter Brandvold *w* 420

Champion, Reece (Businessman; Vampire)
Master of the Night - Angela Knight *r* 318

Chandler, Jacob (Religious)
Opal - Lauraine Snelling *i* 1050

Chandra, Jimmy (Police Officer)
Bengal Station - Eric Brown *s* 723

Chandran, Willie (Revolutionary)
Magic Seeds - V.S. Naipaul *c* 1153

Charite (Pirate)
The Captain's Vengeance - Dewey Lambdin *t* 894

Charles, Gillian (Socialite; Heiress)
Sweetheart, Indiana - Suzanne Simmons *r* 380

Charlesworthy, Suzie (Child; Actress)
New York Dreams - Eric Brown *s* 724

Charon (Criminal)
Sunrise Alley - Catherine Asaro *s* 714

Chartwell, William (Military Personnel; Sea
Captain)
The Captain's Mermaid - Mary Blayney *r* 228

Chase, Charlene (Parent)
Strange but True - John Searles *c* 1182

Chase, Philip (Young Man)
Strange but True - John Searles *c* 1182

Chatterfield, Alec (Time Traveler; Criminal)
The Life of the World to Come - Kage Baker *s* 715

Chatterjee, Tara (Immigrant)
The Tree Bride - Bharati Mukherjee *t* 910

Chaucer, Geoffrey (Historical Figure; Writer)
Chaucer and the House of Fame - Philippa
Morgan *m* 148
Chaucer and the House of Fame - Philippa
Morgan *t* 909

Chavez, Guadalupe (Rancher)
Jericho's Road - Elmer Kelton *t* 891

Chee, Jim (Police Officer; Indian)
Skeleton Man - Tony Hillerman *w* 451
Skeleton Man - Tony Hillerman *m* 106

Chen, Jennifer (Teenager; Spy)
Chaos Rising - A.J. Butcher *s* 729
Spy High: Mission One - A.J. Butcher *s* 730

Chen Cao (Police Officer)
When Red Is Black - Xiaolong Qiu *m* 166

Chetwynde, Courtney (Teenager)
Black Water - D.J. MacHale *f* 565

Chief (Animal)
Rabbit Goes Duck Hunting - Deborah L.
Duvall *w* 438

Childe, Christina Malcolm (Psychic; Noblewoman)
This Magic Moment - Patricia Rice *r* 364

Chilton (Agent)
A Cold Summer Night - Trystam Kith *f* 554

Chizek, Bud (Hotel Owner; Parent)
Osprey Island - Thisbe Nissen *c* 1157

Chizek, Nancy (Spouse; Hotel Owner)
Osprey Island - Thisbe Nissen *c* 1157

Chizek, Suzi (Single Parent)
Osprey Island - Thisbe Nissen *c* 1157

Chopin, Jim (Police Officer)
A Taint in the Blood - Dana Stabenow *m* 189

Christie, Agatha (Historical Figure; Writer)
The London Blitz Murders - Max Allan
Collins *t* 842

Christmas, Tim (Apprentice)
Strange Cargo - Jeffrey E. Barlough *f* 504

Christopher (Teenager; Mentally Ill Person)
A Seahorse Year - Stacey D'Erasmo *c* 1091

Christopher, Paul (Spy; Crime Victim)
Old Boys - Charles McCarry *c* 1142

Christopher, Zarah (Relative)
Old Boys - Charles McCarry *c* 1142

Chung, Lin (Businessman; Lover)
The Castlemaine Murders - Kerry
Greenwood *m* 91

Cisco, Loretta (Businesswoman; Widow(er))
Family Blessings - Fern Michaels *r* 344

Claire of Foix (Religious)
Maiden of Fire - Deborah Johns *r* 301

Clarice (Royalty)
Some Enchanted Evening - Christina Dodd *t* 854

Clark, Megan (Archaeologist; Librarian)
Tome of Murder - D.R. Meredith *w* 464

Clarke, Mercy (Rancher; Widow(er))
Loving Mercy - Teresa Bodwell *r* 230

Clary, Maggie (Widow(er))
Loop Group - Larry McMurtry *c* 1146

Clavain (Military Personnel; Aged Person)
Absolution Gap - Alastair Reynolds *s* 775

Claymore, Harley (Tour Guide; Sports Figure)
St. Dale - Sharyn McCrumb *c* 1143

Claypoole (Military Personnel)
A World of Hurt - David Sherman *s* 786

Cleary, Lilly Bell Rose (Lawyer)
Skinny-Dipping - Claire Matturro *m* 136

Cleaver, James (Accountant)
All the Lonely People - David B. Silva *h* 692

Clemons, Neil Anson (Scientist)
Warp Speed - Travis S. Taylor *s* 792

Cleopatra (Artificial Intelligence)
Cleopatra 7.2 - Elizabeth Ann Scarborough *s* 785

Cleopatra (Historical Figure; Ruler)
The Judgment of Caesar - Steven Saylor *m* 180

Clio (Historian)
Currant Events - Piers Anthony *f* 500

Clothar (Scholar; Knight)
The Lance Thrower - Jack Whyte *t* 953
The Lance Thrower - Jack Whyte *f* 592

Cloud (Mythical Creature)
The Wizard - Gene Wolfe *f* 595

Cloud, Mark (Teenager)
Living with Fred - Brad Whittington *i* 1057

Coblenz, Lily (Heiress)
The Damascened Blade - Barbara Cleverly *t* 838

Cody, Diane (Businesswoman)
Shadows in the Darkness - Elaine
Cunningham *f* 522

Cody, Ryan (Lawyer)
Shadows in the Darkness - Elaine
Cunningham *h* 623

Cody, William F. "Buffalo Bill" (Entertainer;
Historical Figure)
East of the Border - Johnny D. Boggs *w* 417

Coffin, William "Wiki" (Linguist; Sailor)
A Watery Grave - Joan Druett *m* 62
A Watery Grave - Joan Druett *t* 861

Cohen, Abe (Store Owner; Parent)
The First Desire - Nancy Reisman *c* 1171

Cohen, Goldie (Relative)
The First Desire - Nancy Reisman *c* 1171

Coldheart, Hirad (Barbarian; Warrior)
Demonstorm - James Barclay *f* 503

Coldwell, Eliot (Writer; Professor)
Banquet for the Damned - Adam L.G. Nevill *h* 675

Cole, Lewis (Journalist; Detective—Amateur)
Buried Dreams - Brendan DuBois *m* 63

Cole, Steve (Friend)
Lost in Rooville - Ray Blackston *i* 968

Coleman, Celia (Art Dealer)
No Dark Valley - Jamie Langston Turner *i* 1051

Colette (Con Artist; Runaway)
Hot Plastic - Peter Craig *m* 43

Collins, Matthew (Scout; Businessman)
Santa Fe Passage - Jon R. Bauman   *t*   819
Santa Fe Passage - Jon R. Bauman   *w*   415

Collins, Maxwell (Businessman)
See Isabelle Run - Elizabeth Bloom   *r*   229

Collins, Sarah (Store Owner)
The Alias Man - Bill Pronzini   *m*   165

Colombe (Orphan)
Brazil Red - Jean-Christophe Rufin   *t*   931

Colon, Ignacio (Outlaw; Murderer)
Invitation to a Hanging - Robert J. Randisi   *w*   476

Colson, Mark (Businessman)
Phi Beta Bimbo - Trish Jensen   *r*   300

Compton, Elizabeth Hartleigh (Noblewoman; Widow(er))
Fire When Ready - Kate Kingsbury   *m*   119

Conan (Barbarian)
The Bloody Crown of Conan - Robert E. Howard   *f*   546

Conklin, Alex (Spy; Crime Victim)
The Bourne Legacy - Eric Van Lustbader   *c*   1202

Connen-Neute (Teacher)
Lost Truth - Dawn Cook   *f*   518

Conner, Jane (Journalist)
The Eggnog Chronicles - Carly Alexander   *r*   211

Conner, Ricki (Store Owner)
The Eggnog Chronicles - Carly Alexander   *r*   211

Connie (Friend)
Loop Group - Larry McMurtry   *c*   1146

Connolly, Chip (Military Personnel)
The Rats, the Bats, and the Ugly - Eric Flint   *s*   744

Connolly, Mike (Lawyer; Alcoholic)
Sober Justice - Joseph H. Hilley   *i*   1004

Connor, Bridget (Assistant)
Who Wants to Marry a Heartthrob? - Stephanie Doyle   *r*   255

Conrad, Joseph (Historical Figure; Writer)
Sailors on the Inward Sea - Lawrence Thornton   *t*   945

Coolidge, Vance (Rancher)
West of Rock River - John D. Nesbitt   *w*   468

Cooper, D.B. (Historical Figure; Fugitive)
D.B. - Elwood Reid   *c*   1170

Corbus (Vampire)
Blood of the Dragon - C.L. Werner   *f*   590

Cord, Morgan (Teacher)
The Alias Man - Bill Pronzini   *m*   165

Corey, John (Detective—Police)
Night Fall - Nelson DeMille   *c*   1090

Corinth, Edward (Nobleman)
The More Deceived - David Roberts   *m*   171

Corleone, Michael (Organized Crime Figure)
The Godfather Returns - Mark Winegardner   *c*   1210

Cornwallis, Lucy (Baker)
The Queen of Subtleties - Suzannah Dunn   *t*   863

Corso, Frank (Journalist)
Red Tide - G.M. Ford   *m*   81

Cortez, Benicio (Businessman; Sorcerer)
Industrial Magic - Kelley Armstrong   *h*   601
Industrial Magic - Kelley Armstrong   *f*   501

Cortez, Lucas (Lawyer; Sorcerer)
Industrial Magic - Kelley Armstrong   *h*   601
Industrial Magic - Kelley Armstrong   *f*   501

Corvinus, Marcus (Nobleman)
Parthian Shot - David Wishart   *t*   956

Cosi, Clare (Restaurateur; Detective—Amateur)
Through the Grinder - Cleo Coyle   *m*   42

Costas, Stefos (Director)
Turn Me On - Kristin Hardy   *r*   284

Cotterill, Simon (Carpenter)
The Hangman's Hymn - P.C. Doherty   *m*   58

Coulter, Zeke (Store Owner; Rancher)
Bright Eyes - Catherine Anderson   *r*   213

Countryman, Lisa (Student—Graduate)
Country of Origin - Don Lee   *c*   1135

Covenant, Roger (Murderer)
The Runes of the Earth - Stephen R. Donaldson   *f*   524

Cowper, Fred (Military Personnel)
Xombies - Walter Greatshell   *h*   635

Craddock, Billy Don (Hunter; Sidekick)
Flat Crazy - Ben Rehder   *w*   478

Crandall, Harry (Publisher; Editor)
A Hard Man Is Good to Find - Jane Blackwood   *r*   225

Crane, Billy (Drug Dealer; Crime Victim)
The Last King - Nichelle D. Tramble   *c*   1197

Crank (Spy)
The Darkening - Chandler McGrew   *h*   667

Crawford, Cheryl (Spouse; Teacher)
Kissed - Carmen Green   *r*   277

Crawford, David (Military Personnel)
The Great Scot - Duncan A. Bruce   *t*   830

Crawford, Justin (Diplomat)
Kissed - Carmen Green   *r*   277

Creidhe (Teenager)
Foxmask - Juliet Marillier   *t*   900

Crewe, Nathan (Criminal; Scientist)
Master of None - N. Lee Wood   *s*   807

Cristiana (Widow(er))
The Widow's Tale - Margaret Frazer   *t*   868

Cromwell, Thomas (Historical Figure; Government Official)
Dark Fire - C.J. Sansom   *t*   933

Crosetti, Joe (Military Personnel)
Days of Infamy - Harry Turtledove   *t*   947

Cross, Andie (Parent)
The Good Nanny - Benjamin Cheever   *c*   1084

Cross, Stuart (Spouse)
The Good Nanny - Benjamin Cheever   *c*   1084

Crowe, Painter (Spy)
Sandstorm - James Rollins   *s*   780

Crowe, Theo (Police Officer)
The Stupidest Angel - Christopher Moore   *h*   671

Cruse, Matt (Teenager)
Airborn - Ken Oppel   *s*   772

Cully (Knight; Religious)
Paladins - Joel Rosenberg   *f*   580

Culver, Clay (Scout)
Bloody Hills - Charles G. West   *w*   490

Cunningham, Gilbert (Lawyer)
The Harper's Quine - Pat McIntosh   *m*   141
The Harper's Quine - Pat McIntosh   *t*   903

Custer, George Armstrong (Historical Figure; Military Personnel)
An Obituary for Major Reno - Richard S. Wheeler   *t*   952

Cutler, Alex (Settler)
Crucible - Nancy Kress   *s*   757

Cutler, Ellis (Businessman)
Falling Awake - Jayne Ann Krentz   *c*   1133

Cutter (Rebel)
Iron Council - China Mieville   *f*   569

Cutter, Jamie (Doctor; Fiance(e))
To Collar a Killer - Lee Charles Kelley   *m*   116

Czolgosz, Leon (Historical Figure; Murderer)
The Temple of Music - Jonathan Lowy   *t*   898

D

Dace (Military Personnel)
A Day Dark as Night - Carl Bowen   *f*   507

D'Agosta, Vincent (Police Officer)
Brimstone - Douglas Preston   *h*   683

Dagstaff, Felix (Rancher)
The Palo Duro Trail - Ralph Compton   *w*   430

Dalamar (Wizard)
Wizards' Conclave - Douglas Niles   *f*   573

Dalhousie, Isabel (Philosopher; Editor)
The Sunday Philosophy Club - Alexander McCall Smith   *c*   1141

Dallas, Eve (Detective—Homicide)
Divided in Death - J.D. Robb   *s*   778

Dalrymple, Daisy (Journalist; Detective—Amateur)
A Mourning Wedding - Carola Dunn   *m*   65
A Mourning Wedding - Carola Dunn   *t*   862

Dalziel, Andy (Police Officer)
Good Morning, Midnight - Reginald Hill   *m*   104

Damer, Anne Seymour (Historical Figure; Artist)
Life Mask - Emma Donoghue   *t*   856
Life Mask - Emma Donoghue   *c*   1094

Damisa (Noblewoman)
Ancestors of Avalon - Diana L. Paxson   *f*   574

Danford, Ezra (Widow(er))
Family Blessings - Fern Michaels   *r*   344

D'Ange, Seraphim (Warrior)
Seraphim - Michele Hauf   *f*   541

Daniel (Worker)
Eve Green - Susan Fletcher   *c*   1106

Daniels, Catherine (Runaway)
Tempting the Highlander - Janet Chapman   *r*   239

Daniels, Esther (Grandparent)
The Gift of Christmas Present - Melody Carlson   *i*   974

Daniels, Jacqueline (Detective—Homicide)
Whiskey Sour - J.A. Konrath   *m*   121

Daniels, Jim (Scientist)
Warp Speed - Travis S. Taylor   *s*   792

Danilovitch, Rivka (Military Personnel)
Dreams of the Desert Wind - Kurt Giambastini   *s*   749

Dannachet, Pascal (Doctor)
The Ninth Life of Louis Drax - Liz Jensen   *c*   1127

Dante (Musician)
Banquet for the Damned - Adam L.G. Nevill   *h*   675

Danvers, Zachary (Wealthy; Contractor)
See How She Dies - Lisa Jackson   *r*   299

Darcy, Elizabeth Bennet (Gentlewoman; Spouse)
Suspense and Sensibility - Carrie A. Bebris   *t*   820

Darcy, Fitzwilliam (Gentleman; Spouse)
Suspense and Sensibility - Carrie A. Bebris   *t*   820

Dare, Anne (Noblewoman)
The Charnel Prince - J. Gregory Keyes   *f*   552

Dare, Tom (Boyfriend)
The London Pigeon Wars - Patrick Neate   *c*   1155

Character Name Index

Gdolkin (Military Personnel)
Iron Hands - Jonathan Green   *s*   750

Geddes, Ewan (Businessman)
Highland Rogue - Deborah Hale   *r*   282

Geller, Adam (Student—College; Editor)
I Am Charlotte Simmons - Tom Wolfe   *c*   1211

Gelman, Gwen "GiGi" (Detective—Private)
Shadows in the Darkness - Elaine
    Cunningham   *h*   623
Shadows in the Darkness - Elaine
    Cunningham   *f*   522

Gemina, Flavia (Detective—Private)
The Twelve Tasks of Flavia Gemina - Caroline
    Lawrence   *t*   895

Genji (Nobleman; Warlord)
Autumn Bridge - Takashi Matsuoka   *c*   1139
Autumn Bridge - Takashi Matsuoka   *t*   902

Genosa, Arturo (Director)
Blood Rites - Jim Butcher   *h*   608

George (Relative)
The Turk and My Mother - Mary Helen
    Stefaniak   *c*   1193

Geraci, Nick (Organized Crime Figure)
The Godfather Returns - Mark
    Winegardner   *c*   1210

Geronimo (Indian; Historical Figure)
The Last Campaign - Tim Champlin   *w*   424

Gervaise, Francois (Artist; Religious)
Le Colonial - Kien Nguyen   *t*   912

Ghazayil (Aged Person)
Dreams of the Desert Wind - Kurt
    Giambastini   *s*   749

Gibson, Emily (Religious)
Autumn Bridge - Takashi Matsuoka   *c*   1139
Autumn Bridge - Takashi Matsuoka   *t*   902

Gilbert, Erin (Interior Decorator; Detective—
Amateur)
Death by Inferior Design - Leslie Caine   *m*   26

Gilkyson, Einar (Rancher; Grandparent)
An Unfinished Life - Mark Spragg   *c*   1191
An Unfinished Life - Mark Spragg   *w*   485

Gilkyson, Griff (Child)
An Unfinished Life - Mark Spragg   *w*   485
An Unfinished Life - Mark Spragg   *c*   1191

Gilkyson, Jean (Widow(er); Single Parent)
An Unfinished Life - Mark Spragg   *c*   1191
An Unfinished Life - Mark Spragg   *w*   485

Gillespie, Claire (Police Officer)
Last Seen in Aberdeen - M.G. Kincaid   *m*   118

Girl (Businesswoman)
Citizen Girl - Emma McLaughlin   *c*   1145

Givens, Marianna (Gentlewoman; Spouse)
A Beggar at the Gate - Thalassa Ali   *t*   811

Glamorgan, Ariana (Noblewoman)
The Knight's Redemption - Joanne Rock   *r*   371

Glenn, Madison "Maddy" (Political Figure)
The Incumbent - Alton Gansky   *i*   988

Glissa (Mythical Creature)
The Fifth Dawn - Cory J. Herndon   *f*   543

Gobineau (Criminal)
Blood of the Dragon - C.L. Werner   *f*   590

Golden, Candy (Sports Figure; Orphan)
All These Girls - Ellen Slezak   *c*   1189

Goldman, Herman (Survivor)
Ghostlands - Marc Zicree   *f*   598

Gomes, Lawrence (Spy)
Curious Notions - Harry Turtledove   *s*   796

Gomes, Paul (Teenager; Spy)
Curious Notions - Harry Turtledove   *s*   796

Good, Sally (Professor; Detective—Amateur)
A Bond with Death - Bill Crider   *m*   45

Goodman, Christopher (Religious)
Acts of God - James Beauseigneur   *s*   721

Goodman, Natalie (Accountant)
The Pleasure Principle - Shirley Harrison   *r*   286

Goodnight, Chaos (Mercenary)
The Doublecross Program - Chris Bunch   *s*   728

Goodrow, Charlie (Mechanic)
The Attraction - Douglas Clegg   *h*   617

Goodwin, Walter (Scientist)
The Moon Pool - A. Merritt   *s*   766

Gordianus the Finder (Detective—Private)
The Judgment of Caesar - Steven Saylor   *m*   180

Gordon, Diana (Detective—Private; Photographer)
Snap Shot - Meg Chittenden   *r*   240

Gough, Jimmy (Cowboy)
The Palo Duro Trail - Ralph Compton   *w*   430

Governor (Government Official)
Serafina's Stories - Rudolfo Anaya   *w*   412

Grace (Housekeeper)
The Sunday Philosophy Club - Alexander McCall
    Smith   *c*   1141

Grae (Prehistoric Human; Chieftain)
Song of the Earth - John R. Dann   *t*   849

Graham, Belle (Editor; Detective—Amateur)
Wrapped Up in Crosswords - Nero Blanc   *m*   15

Graham, Devlin (Bounty Hunter; Wealthy)
As You Wish - Francine Matthews   *r*   334

Grail, Suli (Police Officer)
World-Walker - Melisa Michaels   *s*   767

Grant, Darius (Artist)
Wonderful and Wild - Simona Taylor   *r*   393

Grant, Elmore (Teacher)
Chaos Rising - A.J. Butcher   *s*   729
Spy High: Mission One - A.J. Butcher   *s*   730

Grant, Jamie (Journalist)
Crisscross - F. Paul Wilson   *h*   706

Graves, Harry (Businessman)
Taking Time - Lynn Abbey   *f*   498

Gray, Aisling (Courier)
You Slay Me - Katie MacAlister   *r*   329

Gray, Jordan (Farmer)
Devil's Kin - Charles G. West   *w*   491

Graybrook, Dorn (Hunter; Mythical Creature)
The Rage - Richard Lee Byers   *f*   513

Grayling, Joshua (Nobleman)
Paladins - Joel Rosenberg   *f*   580

Grayson, Erin (FBI Agent; Witch)
Master of the Night - Angela Knight   *r*   318

Grayson, John (Military Personnel)
The Improper Wife - Diane Perkins   *r*   360

Green, Deborah (Religious)
Joy Comes in the Morning - Jonathan
    Rosen   *c*   1174

Green, Eve (Young Woman; Orphan)
Eve Green - Susan Fletcher   *c*   1106

Green, Melantha (Teenager; Alien)
The Green and the Gray - Timothy Zahn   *s*   808

Green, Tom (Police Officer)
The Last Dark Place - Stuart M. Kaminsky   *m*   112
Thief in Retreat - Aimee Thurlo   *m*   199

Greene, Sonia (Businesswoman)
Lovecraft - Hans Rodionoff   *h*   686

Greengrass, Max (Detective—Amateur; Journalist)
The Midnight Band of Mercy - Michael
    Blaine   *m*   14
The Midnight Band of Mercy - Michael
    Blaine   *t*   826

Greenhow, Mark (Young Man; Relative)
Voyageurs - Margaret Elphinstone   *t*   866

Greenhow, Rachel (Religious; Relative)
Voyageurs - Margaret Elphinstone   *t*   866

Greenwood, Seth (Boyfriend)
She's Out of Control - Kristin Billerbeck   *i*   966

Greer, Mitch (Saloon Keeper/Owner)
Blood Red Dawn - Karen E. Taylor   *h*   700

Gregory, Charlotte (Teacher)
A Rakish Spy - Laura Paquet   *r*   358

Gregory, Michael (Architect)
The Dark Lord - Patricia Simpson   *r*   381

Grey, Walter (Young Man)
Infernal Angel - Edward Lee   *h*   656

Grier, Cash (Police Officer)
Renegade - Diana Palmer   *r*   356

Griffin, Cal (Lawyer; Survivor)
Ghostlands - Marc Zicree   *f*   598

Griffin, Deirdre (Vampire)
Blood Red Dawn - Karen E. Taylor   *h*   700

Grimes, Davina (Amnesiac)
Forgotten Destiny - Janet Tanner   *r*   391

Grishin, Arkady (Businessman)
Singularity - Bill DeSmedt   *s*   738

Gruber, Jim (Farmer)
Following the Harvest - Fred Harris   *w*   447

Grunthor (Warrior)
Elegy for a Lost Star - Elizabeth Haydon   *f*   542

Gry (Teenager; Psychic)
Gifts - Ursula K. Le Guin   *f*   560

Gudrun (Mythical Creature)
Snow-Walker - Catherine Fisher   *f*   534

Guest, Nick (Homosexual; Student—College)
The Line of Beauty - Alan Hollinghurst   *c*   1122

Guidry, Todd (Patient)
Family Inheritance - Deborah LeBlanc   *h*   655

Guilfoyle (Detective—Private)
Counterfeit Kings - Adam Connell   *s*   732

Guinevere (Spouse)
Arthur the King - Allan Massie   *t*   901

Gunderson, Charley (Foreman)
Territorial Rough Rider - Tim Champlin   *w*   425

Gunter, Thomas (Doctor)
The Clerkenwell Tales - Peter Ackroyd   *t*   810

Gunther, Joe (Police Officer; Widow(er))
The Surrogate Thief - Archer Mayor   *m*   137

Guy (Businessman)
Citizen Girl - Emma McLaughlin   *c*   1145

Gwirion (Entertainer)
The Fool's Tale - Nicole Galland   *t*   871

H

Hablet (Ruler)
Treason Keep - Jennifer Fallon   *f*   530

Hackney, Joe (Detective—Police)
The Devil Lives in Glasgow - Gilles Bornais   *t*   828

Hades (Deity)
Goddess of Spring - P.C. Cast   *r*   238

Hafydd (Knight)
The Shadow Roads - Sean Russell   *f*   581

Hagen, Tom (Political Figure; Lawyer)
The Godfather Returns - Mark
   Winegardner   *c*   1210

Haji (Teenager; Genetically Altered Being)
Edenborn - Nick Sagan   *s*   782

Hakusar, Jim (Stowaway)
Marque and Reprisal - Elizabeth Moon   *s*   769

Hal (Parent; Homosexual)
A Seahorse Year - Stacey D'Erasmo   *c*   1091

Halaravilli (Ruler)
The Glasswright's Master - Mindy L. Klasky   *f*   555

Haley, Bob (Farmer; Alcoholic)
Following the Harvest - Fred Harris   *w*   447

Haley, Will (Worker; Teenager)
Following the Harvest - Fred Harris   *w*   447
Following the Harvest - Fred Harris   *t*   879

Hallbrooke, Jack (FBI Agent)
Always - Jude Deveraux   *r*   253

Halliday, Hal (Detective—Private)
New York Dreams - Eric Brown   *s*   724

Halliday, Travis (Gentleman)
On the Twelfth Day of Christmas - Mona
   Gedney   *r*   270

Halliwell, Barbara (Scholar)
The Red Queen - Margaret Drabble   *c*   1095

Halmus, Pete (Appraiser)
Viator - Lucius Shepard   *h*   691

Hamilton, Joakim (Scientist)
The Dry Salvages - Caitlin R. Kiernan   *h*   647

Hamilton, Kate (Detective—Private)
The Trouble with Valentine's Day - Rachel
   Gibson   *r*   272

Hamilton, Nick (Journalist)
Dark Storm - Kel Richards   *i*   1042

Hanani, Fola (Settler)
Crache - Mark Budz   *s*   726

Hanemann (Professor)
Death in Danzig - Stefan Chwin   *t*   835

Hanford, Chase (Saloon Keeper/Owner)
All the Lonely People - David B. Silva   *h*   692

Hanifer, Lydia (Police Officer)
Haven - Don D'Ammassa   *s*   736

Hank (Musician)
The Haunted Hillbilly - Derek McCormack   *h*   665

Hanna, Charley (Lawman)
Bad Night at Dry Creek - Cameron Judd   *w*   456

Hannack, Anna (Widow(er))
The Christkindl's Gift - Kathleen Morgan   *i*   1028

Hannibal (Historical Figure; Military Personnel)
Pride of Carthage - David Anthony Durham   *t*   864

Hannibal, Joe (Lawman)
Backshooter - Robert J. Randisi   *w*   475

Hanrahan, Bill (Detective—Homicide)
The Last Dark Place - Stuart M. Kaminsky   *m*   112

har Aralis, Caeru (Government Official)
The Shades of Time and Memory - Storm
   Constantine   *s*   733

Hardington, Tess James (Widow(er); Single Parent)
Mostly Mayhem - Lisa Manuel   *r*   332

Hardrada, Harald (Warrior)
Rite of Conquest - Judith Tarr   *f*   584

Hardy, Nina (Crime Victim; Spirit)
Shade - Neil Jordan   *t*   890

Harkless, Baro (Security Officer)
Black Brillion - Matthew Hughes   *s*   754

Harlech (Warrior)
Child of the Dark Prophecy - T.A. Barron   *f*   505

Harmon, Glennis (Parent; Spouse)
Crystal Lies - Melody Carlson   *i*   973

Harold, Natalie (Activist)
Coyote Morning - Lisa Lenard-Cook   *w*   460

Harper, Ben (Security Officer)
Breathe: Everyone Has to Do It - Christopher
   Fowler   *h*   630

Harris, Chris (Architect)
Aloha Love - Alice Wootson   *r*   410

Harris, James (Administrator)
Everlasting Love - Valerie Hansen   *i*   997

Harris, Kelly (Widow(er))
Are You Afraid of the Dark? - Sidney
   Sheldon   *c*   1184

Harrison, Mace (Police Officer)
The Lake - Richard Laymon   *h*   653

Harrison, Sarah (Noblewoman; Impoverished)
An Honorable Match - Laura Paquet   *r*   357

Hart, Pooh (Military Personnel)
Orphanage - Robert Buettner   *s*   727

Hathaway, Anne (Historical Figure; Spouse)
Young Will - Bruce Cook   *t*   845

Hawcly, Abe (Parent; Artist)
Ordinary Wolves - Seth Kantner   *c*   1129

Hawcly, Cutuk (Relative)
Ordinary Wolves - Seth Kantner   *c*   1129

Hawcly, Jerry (Relative)
Ordinary Wolves - Seth Kantner   *c*   1129

Hawke, Alexander (Spy)
Assassin - Ted Bell   *c*   1073

Hawkes, Grenville (Vampire)
Hawkes Harbor - S.E. Hinton   *h*   641

Hawkins, Danielle "Danni" (Detective—Private)
Arouse Suspicion - Maureen McKade   *r*   337

Hawkins, Leo (Military Personnel; Nobleman)
Captain Hawkins' Dilemma - Maria Greene   *r*   280

Hawthorn, Fiona (Noblewoman; Debutante)
Lady Fiasco - Kathleen Baldwin   *r*   218

Hawthorne, Decker (Businessman)
Acts of God - James Beauseigneur   *s*   721

Hawthorne, Helen (Fugitive; Detective—Amateur)
Dying to Call You - Elaine Viets   *m*   203

Haydn (Alien; Fugitive)
Haydn of Mars - Al Sarrantonio   *s*   784

Hayes, Alexandra (Public Relations; Single Parent)
Ring around My Heart - Pat White   *r*   404

Hayes, Fredrica (Veterinarian)
A Tender Touch - Lenora Worth   *i*   1062

Hayes, Lucinda "Cinda" (Lawyer)
Chilling Effect - Marianne Wesson   *m*   208

Hayle, Tamara (Detective—Private; Single Parent)
Dying in the Dark - Valerie Wilson Wesley   *m*   207

Hayward, Laura (Police Officer)
Brimstone - Douglas Preston   *h*   683

Hayworth, May (Noblewoman)
The Heiress of Hyde Park - Jacqueline Navin   *r*   351

Hearn, Frank (Criminal)
7,000 Clams - Lee Irby   *t*   884

Hebert (Narrator)
The Stone That the Builder Refused - Madison Smartt
   Bell   *t*   821

The Stone That the Builder Refused - Madison Smartt
   Bell   *c*   1072

Heiden, Stefan von der (Diplomat)
The Devil in Buenos Aires - Lily Powell   *t*   923

Helen (Royalty)
The War at Troy - Lindsay Clarke   *t*   836

Heloise (Historical Figure; Gentlewoman)
Farewell, My Only One - Antoine Audouard   *t*   816

Henderson, Jim (Guard)
The Prison - R. Patrick Gates   *h*   633

Henley, Will (Businessman; Financier)
Too Close to the Sun - Diana Dempsey   *r*   251

Hennessey, Russell Tremayne (Businessman; Parent)
Chesapeake Tide - Jeanette Baker   *r*   217

Henry, Patrick (Historical Figure; Political Figure)
Sparrowhawk. Book 4: Empire - Edward
   Cline   *t*   840

Henry VI (Historical Figure; Ruler)
The Widow's Tale - Margaret Frazer   *t*   868

Henry VIII (Historical Figure; Ruler)
The Queen of Subtleties - Suzannah Dunn   *t*   863

Hepburn, Patrick (Nobleman; Psychic)
Insatiable - Virginia Henley   *r*   289

Herbert, Isabel (Spouse)
A Black Englishman - Carolyn Slaughter   *c*   1188
A Black Englishman - Carolyn Slaughter   *t*   939

Herbert, Neville (Spouse; Military Personnel)
A Black Englishman - Carolyn Slaughter   *t*   939

Herrnfeld, Antonie (Immigrant)
The Devil in Buenos Aires - Lily Powell   *t*   923

Heydon, Cassie (Patient)
Infernal Angel - Edward Lee   *h*   656

Heywood, Parker (Artist; Teacher)
Say Yes - Donna Hill   *r*   292

Hezekiah (Royalty)
Gods and Kings - Lynn Austin   *i*   963

Hickok, James Butler "Wild Bill" (Gunfighter;
   Historical Figure)
East of the Border - Johnny D. Boggs   *w*   417

Hicks, Lorrie (Spouse)
Life Expectancy - Dean R. Koontz   *h*   652

Higgins, Steve (Police Officer)
Messenger - Edward Lee   *h*   657

Hill, Jermaine (Television Personality)
A Man Inspired - Derek Jackson   *i*   1006

Hiyashi (Artist; Government Official)
The Painting - Nina Schuyler   *t*   935

Hoffman, Nick (Professor; Detective—Amateur)
Tropic of Murder - Lev Raphael   *m*   167

Hogan, Eunice (Aged Person)
Coffee Rings - Yvonne Lehman   *i*   1018

Hogwood, Dolores (Government Official)
The Jaguar Knights - Dave Duncan   *f*   528

Holbrook, Anna (Parent; Abuse Victim)
Yonnondio from the Thirties - Tillie Olsen   *w*   470

Holbrook, Jim (Miner; Bully)
Yonnondio from the Thirties - Tillie Olsen   *w*   470

Holbrook, Mazie (Child; Abuse Victim)
Yonnondio from the Thirties - Tillie Olsen   *w*   470

Holden, Dan (Carpenter; Handicapped)
The Heart's Voice - Arlene James   *i*   1008

Holden, Tom (Police Officer)
Thieves Break In - Cristina Sumners   *m*   192

Holden, Vicky (Lawyer; Indian)
Wife of Moon - Margaret Coel   *m*   33
Wife of Moon - Margaret Coel   *w*   427

M

Norrell (Magician; Wealthy)
Jonathan Strange & Mr. Norrell - Susanna Clarke   *c*   1085

Northman, Eric (Vampire; Amnesiac)
Dead to the World - Charlaine Harris   *h*   638

Norwood, Russell (Courier)
The Last Campaign - Tim Champlin   *w*   424

Novack, Sarah (Doctor)
Exorcist: The Beginning - Steven Piziks   *h*   682

Novak, Dorothy (Young Woman)
Baker Towers - Jennifer Haigh   *t*   876

Novak, Georgie (Veteran)
Baker Towers - Jennifer Haigh   *t*   876
Baker Towers - Jennifer Haigh   *c*   1115

Novak, Lucy (Relative)
Baker Towers - Jennifer Haigh   *c*   1115

Novak, Rose (Parent; Widow(er))
Baker Towers - Jennifer Haigh   *c*   1115
Baker Towers - Jennifer Haigh   *t*   876

Nowack, Shelley (Friend; Detective—Amateur)
A Midsummer Night's Scream - Jill Churchill   *m*   30

Nudie (Vampire)
The Haunted Hillbilly - Derek McCormack   *h*   665

Nzuluwazi, Miriam (Spouse)
Heart of the Hunter - Deon Meyer   *c*   1148

O

O'Bannon, Brogan (Nobleman; Twin)
In a Wild Wood - Sasha Lord   *r*   327

O'Brien, Dan (Military Personnel)
The Hidden Valley - Jeanne Williams   *w*   496

O'Brien, Dan (Orphan; Friend)
The Underground River - Jeanne Williams   *w*   497

O'Doull, Leonard (Doctor)
Return Engagement - Harry Turtledove   *s*   799

Ohana, Kaia (Scientist)
Distant Echoes - Colleen Coble   *i*   976

O'Hara, Martin Konner (Fugitive; Psychic)
The Dragon Circle - Irene Radford   *s*   774

O'Hara, Patty Ann (Young Woman)
Road to Purgatory - Max Allan Collins   *t*   843

Ohayon, Michael (Police Officer)
Bethlehem Road Murder - Batya Gur   *m*   94

Ohmsford, Pen (Wizard)
Tanequil - Terry Brooks   *f*   511

Okurt, Malcolm (Military Personnel)
Crossing the Line - Karen Traviss   *s*   795

Oliver, Darci (Television Personality)
Flippin' the Script - Aisha Ford   *i*   986

Oliver, Flynn (Investigator; Gentleman)
Miss Fortune - Julia London   *r*   326

O'Malley, Aidan (Bridegroom)
Chances Are - Barbara Bretton   *r*   231

O'Malley, John (Religious; Detective—Amateur)
Wife of Moon - Margaret Coel   *w*   427
Wife of Moon - Margaret Coel   *m*   33

Omnius (Artificial Intelligence)
The Battle of Corrin - Brian Herbert   *s*   752

Omohundro, Texas Jack (Scout; Actor)
East of the Border - Johnny D. Boggs   *w*   417

O'Neal, Blackie (Saloon Keeper/Owner; Rake)
To Tempt a Texan - Georgina Gentry   *r*   271

O'Neal, Cally (Criminal)
Cally's War - John Ringo   *s*   777

O'Neil, Longfang (Alien; Military Personnel)
The Rats, the Bats, and the Ugly - Eric Flint   *s*   744

Oo (Scholar)
The Red Queen - Margaret Drabble   *c*   1095

or-Reiss, Garric (Ruler)
Master of the Cauldron - David Drake   *f*   527

Oregon, Ukiah (Detective—Private; Alien)
Dog Warrior - Wen Spencer   *s*   790

Ori (Worker)
Iron Council - China Mieville   *f*   569

Orlova, Astasia (Noblewoman)
Prisoner of the Iron Tower - Sarah Ash   *f*   502

Ormond, Peter (Postal Worker; Drifter)
Territorial Rough Rider - Tim Champlin   *w*   425

O'Rourke, Meara (Adoptee; Teacher)
Meant to Be - Edie Claire   *r*   241

Orozco, Emma (Indian; Parent)
Day of the Dead - J.A. Jance   *c*   1125

Orozco, Roseanne (Crime Victim)
Day of the Dead - J.A. Jance   *c*   1125

Orrec (Teenager; Psychic)
Gifts - Ursula K. Le Guin   *f*   560

O'Shaugnessy, Bryan (Religious)
Moment of Truth - Sally John   *i*   1010

O'Shea, Magdalene "Maggie" (Supernatural Being; Store Owner)
Shifting Love - Constance O'Day-Flannery   *r*   353

O'Sullivan, Michael Jr. (Military Personnel; Veteran)
Road to Purgatory - Max Allan Collins   *m*   37
Road to Purgatory - Max Allan Collins   *t*   843

Otter (Animal)
Rabbit Goes Duck Hunting - Deborah L. Duvall   *w*   438

Otto (Parent)
The Children's War - Monique Charlesworth   *c*   1083

Ouriana (Ruler)
The Hidden Stars - Madeline Howard   *f*   545

Overton, Lynette (Noblewoman)
The Duke's Scandalous Secret - Connie Lane   *r*   321

Owen, Gareth (Police Officer)
A Cold Touch of Ice - Michael Pearce   *t*   918
Death of an Effendi - Michael Pearce   *m*   160
The Face in the Cemetery - Michael Pearce   *t*   920

Owen, Nigel (Museum Curator)
Dead as a Scone - Ron Benrey   *i*   965

Owens, Brandi (Store Owner)
Espresso for Two - Courtni Wright   *r*   411

P

Pagliano, Maria (Young Woman)
The Devil Served Tortellini - Shirley Jump   *r*   306

Paiboun, Siri (Doctor)
The Coroner's Lunch - Colin Cotterill   *m*   41

Pale Moon (Indian)
Little Brother Real Snake - Billy Moore   *w*   466

Pancorbo, Estrella (Spacewoman)
The Boy Who Would Live Forever - Frederik Pohl   *s*   773

Pangloss, Lulu (Young Woman)
Xombies - Walter Greatshell   *h*   635

Panov, Mo (Crime Victim)
The Bourne Legacy - Eric Van Lustbader   *c*   1202

Pantolini, Sabrina (Producer)
Turn Me On - Kristin Hardy   *r*   284

Parekh, Surendra (Settler)
City of Pearl - Karen Traviss   *s*   794

Paris (Royalty)
The War at Troy - Lindsay Clarke   *t*   836

Parish, Cole (Editor)
All She Ever Wanted - Barbara Freethy   *r*   268

Parker (Criminal; Thief)
Nobody Runs Forever - Richard Stark   *m*   190

Parker, Daria (Musician)
Murder of Angels - Caitlin R. Kiernan   *h*   648

Parker, Druwan (Military Personnel)
Orphanage - Robert Buettner   *s*   727

Parker, Wade (Child)
Billy Goat Hill - Mark Stanleigh Morris   *i*   1033

Parrish, Matt (Lawyer)
Beauty Queen - Julia London   *r*   325

Pasanius (Military Personnel)
Dead Sky, Black Sun - Graham McNeill   *s*   765

Pascoe, Peter (Police Officer)
Good Morning, Midnight - Reginald Hill   *m*   104

Patrick (Boyfriend)
The Lady of the Hall - Veronica Heley   *i*   999

Patrick, Willy Bryce (Writer)
In the Night Room - Peter Straub   *h*   697

Patterson, Mary Lee (Spouse; Parent)
Dancing with Lyndon - Donley Watt   *w*   489

Patterson, Natalie (Restaurateur; Divorced Person)
Bright Eyes - Catherine Anderson   *r*   213

Patterson, Thomas (Lawyer; Political Figure)
Dancing with Lyndon - Donley Watt   *w*   489

Patterson, Tommy (Teenager)
Dancing with Lyndon - Donley Watt   *w*   489

Paulsson, Gilly (Crime Victim; Teenager)
Trace - Patricia Cornwell   *c*   1086

Pausert (Spaceship Captain)
The Wizard of Karres - Mercedes Lackey   *s*   758

Payne, Nola (Crime Victim)
Little Scarlet - Walter Mosley   *c*   1151

Pearce, Kate (Lover)
The Big Love - Sarah Dunn   *c*   1096

Peck, Graham (Fugitive)
Tagged - Robert L. Wise   *i*   1061

Peerbaugh, Evelyn (Landlord; Widow(er))
A Place to Belong - Vonette Z. Bright   *i*   970

Pei Shan (Prisoner)
War Trash - Ha Jin   *t*   889

Pelagius (Slave)
The Empress of Last Days - Jane Stevenson   *t*   942

Pelindrake, Arra (Filmmaker; Wizard)
Smoke and Shadows - Tanya Huff   *h*   642

Pellaz (Alien)
The Shades of Time and Memory - Storm Constantine   *s*   733

Pendaar "Father Daar" (Religious; Time Traveler)
Tempting the Highlander - Janet Chapman   *r*   239

Pendergast, Aloysius (FBI Agent)
Brimstone - Douglas Preston   *h*   683

Pendragon, Arthur (Ruler)
The Lance Thrower - Jack Whyte   *f*   592

Pendragon, Bobby (Teenager)
Black Water - D.J. MacHale   *f*   565

Pennington, Dorothy (Spouse; Store Owner)
Haven - Julie Marshall   *r*   333

Pepper, Amanda (Teacher; Fiance(e))
Till the End of Tom - Gillian Roberts   *m*   172

Peralta, Pedro (Child; Immigrant)
North with De Anza - Dorothy Ward
Erskine   *w*   439

Peregrine, Nathaniel (Vampire)
American Gothic - Michael Romkey   *h*   687

Perika, Daisy (Shaman; Relative)
The Witch's Tongue - James D. Doss   *m*   59
The Witch's Tongue - James D. Doss   *w*   437

Perivale (Ruler)
The Bride of Stone - Thomas Williams   *i*   1059

Perrone, Chaz (Scientist)
Skinny Dip - Carl Hiaasen   *c*   1120

Perrone, Joey (Spouse)
Skinny Dip - Carl Hiaasen   *c*   1120
Skinny Dip - Carl Hiaasen   *m*   103

Perry, Lincoln (Detective—Private)
Tonight I Said Goodbye - Michael Kortya   *m*   122

Pershing, John J. (Military Personnel; Historical
Figure)
To the Last Man - Jeff Shaara   *t*   937

Peter (Young Man)
Mantrapped - Fay Weldon   *c*   1207

Peter de Montselm (Knight; Religious)
Hidden Honor - Anne Stuart   *r*   388

Peters, Toby (Detective—Private)
Now You See It - Stuart M. Kaminsky   *m*   113

Petrovna, Akilina (Entertainer)
The Romanov Prophecy - Steve Berry   *c*   1074
The Romanov Prophecy - Steve Berry   *m*   11

Pevsner, Phil (Detective—Private)
Now You See It - Stuart M. Kaminsky   *m*   113

Peyton, Annabelle (Impoverished; Noblewoman)
Secrets of a Summer Night - Lisa Kleypas   *r*   317

Pheresa (Ruler)
The Queen's Knight - Deborah Chester   *f*   516

Philips, Adrian (Detective—Police; Cyborg)
The Demon's Daughter - Emma Holly   *r*   296

Phillips, Savannah (Journalist)
Savannah from Savannah - Denise Hildreth   *i*   1001

Phoebe (Friend)
The Death of Mr. Love - Indra Sinha   *c*   1187

Phrax, Varro (Nobleman)
Legacy - Matthew Farrer   *s*   741

Pickard, Andy (Lawman)
Jericho's Road - Elmer Kelton   *t*   891
Jericho's Road - Elmer Kelton   *w*   458

Pickett, Joe (Game Warden)
Trophy Hunt - C.J. Box   *m*   19

Pickett, Sadie (Maintenance Worker)
Sadie-in-Waiting - Annie Jones   *i*   1011

Pierce, Maureen (Witch)
The Winter Oak - James A. Hetley   *f*   544

Pierce, Todd Baxter (Student)
The King of Ice Cream - Robert Wayne
McCoy   *h*   666

Piero della Francesca (Historical Figure; Artist)
Love, the Painter's Wife and the Queen of Sheba -
Aliette Armel   *c*   1066
Love, the Painter's Wife and the Queen of Sheba -
Aliette Armel   *t*   814

Pierre (Artisan)
The Harper's Quine - Pat McIntosh   *m*   141

Pike, Elijah (Vampire)
Tainted Blood - James M. Thompson   *h*   701

Pilgrim, John (FBI Agent; Crime Victim)
Dry Heat - Jon Talton   *w*   487

Pine, Charlotte (Spacewoman)
Saucer: The Conquest - Stephen Coonts   *s*   734

Pip (Alien)
Sliding Scales - Alan Dean Foster   *s*   745

Piper, Oscar (Detective—Homicide)
The Puzzle of the Blue Banderilla - Stuart
Palmer   *m*   156

Pirius (Spaceship Captain)
Exultant - Stephen Baxter   *s*   720

Plant, Melrose (Professor; Sidekick)
Winds of Change - Martha Grimes   *m*   93

Plantagenet, Edward (Royalty; Historical Figure)
White Rose - R. Garcia y Robertson   *f*   536
White Rose - R. Garcia y Robertson   *t*   872

Plum, Stephanie (Bounty Hunter)
Ten Big Ones - Janet Evanovich   *c*   1099

Poe, Edgar Allan (Historical Figure; Writer)
The Mask of Red Death - Harold Schechter   *m*   181
The Mask of Red Death - Harold Schechter   *t*   934

Poggioli, Henry (Psychologist; Detective—Amateur)
Dr. Poggioli: Criminologist - T.S. Stribling   *m*   191

Polchak, Nick (Scientist)
Chop Shop - Tim Downs   *i*   983

Polycrates, Rosco (Detective—Private; Spouse)
Wrapped Up in Crosswords - Nero Blanc   *m*   15

Pomeroy (Rebel)
Iron Council - China Mieville   *f*   569

Poor Boy, Gideon (Mountain Man; Sidekick)
Beauty for Ashes - Win Blevins   *w*   416

Popper, Jessica (Veterinarian; Detective—Amateur)
Putting on the Dog - Cynthia Baxter   *m*   7

Porter, Clarence (Military Personnel)
Return Engagement - Harry Turtledove   *s*   799

Porter, Lance (Military Personnel)
One King, One Soldier - Alexander C. Irvine   *f*   549

Poteat, Benny (Repairman)
Visits from the Drowned Girl - Steven
Sherrill   *c*   1185

Potter, Beatrix (Historical Figure; Detective—
Amateur)
The Tale of Hill Top Farm - Susan Wittig
Albert   *m*   2

Power, Kate (Police Officer)
Staying Power - Judith Cutler   *m*   49

Prager, Bertoldus (Rancher; Thief)
McKeag's Mountain - L.J. Martin   *w*   462

Pratt, Cyril (Repairman)
Walpuski's Typewriter - Frank Darabont   *h*   624

Prentiss, Grant (Businessman)
Love Came Unexpectedly - Ruth Scofield   *i*   1047

Prescott, Katrina (Widow(er); Foster Parent)
As You Wish - Francine Matthews   *r*   334

Preston (Vampire)
Bride of the Fat White Vampire - Andrew
Fox   *h*   631

Preston, Calder (FBI Agent; Lover)
Dangerous Curves - Jacey Ford   *r*   266

Preston, Davies (Nobleman; Agent)
The Christmas Wedding - Laurie Brown   *r*   233

Preston, Guy (Actor)
Apocalypse Now, Voyager - Jay Russell   *h*   688

Pritchard, Joe (Detective—Private)
Tonight I Said Goodbye - Michael Kortya   *m*   122

Pritchard, Rhys (Religious; Researcher)
A.K.A. Goddess - Evelyn Vaughn   *r*   399

Prophet, Lou (Bounty Hunter; Guide)
Staring Down the Devil - Peter Brandvold   *w*   420

Pudding, Katherine Elizabeth (Caterer)
A Man in a Kilt - Sandy Blair   *r*   227

Pulver, Danny (Veterinarian)
Changes of Heart - Paige Lee Elliston   *i*   984

Puttock, Simon (Lawman)
The Outlaws of Ennor - Michael Jecks   *t*   887
The Tolls of Death - Michael Jecks   *t*   888

Q

Quarles, Malachai (Sea Captain)
A Perfect Romance - Anne Robins   *r*   369

Quilliam, Margaret "Meg" (Cook; Detective—
Amateur)
Buried by Breakfast - Claudia Bishop   *m*   12

Quilliam, Sarah "Quill" (Innkeeper; Detective—
Amateur)
Buried by Breakfast - Claudia Bishop   *m*   12

Quinn, Mike (Detective—Police)
Through the Grinder - Cleo Coyle   *m*   42

Quinn, Nina (Landscaper; Detective—Amateur)
A Hoe Lot of Trouble - Heather Webber   *m*   206

Quinn, Paul (Spouse)
Snowed In - Christina Bartolomeo   *c*   1071

Quinn, Sophie (Artist)
Snowed In - Christina Bartolomeo   *c*   1071

R

Rael-Lamont, Vivian (Businesswoman; Widow(er))
Duke of Sin - Adele Ashworth   *r*   215

Rain, Phoebe (Abuse Victim; Psychic)
Midnight Rain - Holly Lisle   *r*   324

Rain Bear (Prehistoric Human; Chieftain)
People of the Raven - Kathleen O'Neal Gear   *t*   873

Rainey, Shawn (Sports Figure)
Echo Bay - Richard Barre   *c*   1070

Raisin, Agatha (Detective—Private)
The Deadly Dance - M.C. Beaton   *m*   8

Raleigh, William (Nobleman)
Duke of Sin - Adele Ashworth   *r*   215

Ralston, Helen Elizabeth (Writer)
My Death - Lisa Tuttle   *h*   702

Ram, Dowlah (Servant)
The Lady of Cawnpore - Elisabeth McNeill   *t*   904

Ramey, Jed (Lawman)
Devil's Kin - Charles G. West   *w*   491

Ramos, Festina (Military Personnel)
Radiant - James Alan Gardner   *s*   747

Randall, Marian (Gentlewoman; Nurse)
The General's Daughter - Kate Huntington   *r*   298

Randall, Sunny (Detective—Private; Divorced
Person)
Melancholy Baby - Robert B. Parker   *m*   157

Randolph, Cai (Military Personnel)
The Power of Two - Patti O'Shea   *r*   354

Ransom, Ann (Heroine)
Stop That Girl - Elizabeth McKenzie   *c*   1144

Raphat (Nobleman)
The Blood of the Land - Noel-Anne Brennan   *f*   509

Rapp, Mitch (Spy)
Memorial Day - Vince Flynn   *c*   1108

Rathbone, Henry (Inventor; Scientist)
A Christmas Visitor - Anne Perry   *m*   162

Ravenson, Raven (Warrior)
The Last Guardian of Everness - John C. Wright   *f*   596

Ravenson, Wendy (Housewife)
The Last Guardian of Everness - John C. Wright   *f*   596

Ravenwood, Jane (Noblewoman)
An Enchanting Minx - Sharon Stancavage   *r*   387

Rawlings, Emilia (Spouse)
Death in the Setting Sun - Deryn Lake   *t*   893

Rawlings, John (Apothecary; Detective—Amateur)
Death in the Setting Sun - Deryn Lake   *t*   893

Rawlins, Easy (Detective—Amateur)
Little Scarlet - Walter Mosley   *c*   1151

Ray, Elizabeth (Child)
The Hidden - Sarah Pinborough   *h*   681

Rayn, Emerald Rose (Warrior)
Legend of the Emerald Rose - Linda Wichman   *i*   1058

Reagan, Abe (Detective—Police)
I'm Watching You - Karen Rose   *r*   372

Reavley, Joseph (Professor; Religious)
Shoulder the Sky - Anne Perry   *m*   163
Shoulder the Sky - Anne Perry   *t*   921

Reavley, Judith (Driver; Linguist)
Shoulder the Sky - Anne Perry   *m*   163
Shoulder the Sky - Anne Perry   *t*   921

Reavley, Matthew (Spy)
Shoulder the Sky - Anne Perry   *m*   163
Shoulder the Sky - Anne Perry   *t*   921

Rebecca (Nurse)
The Lipstick Diaries - Lori Soard   *r*   382

Rebecca (Relative)
Visits from the Drowned Girl - Steven Sherrill   *c*   1185

Rebecca (Royalty)
Heroics for Beginners - John Moore   *f*   570

Red, Jenny (Fugitive)
The Shadow Runners - Liz Maverick   *s*   760

Red Cloud (Historical Figure; Indian)
The Indian Agent - Dan O'Brien   *t*   914
The Indian Agent - Dan O'Brien   *w*   469

Red Squirrel (Indian)
Little Brother Real Snake - Billy Moore   *w*   466

Redding, Sarah (Widow(er))
Bad Night at Dry Creek - Cameron Judd   *w*   456

Redfield, Maceo (Sports Figure; Friend)
The Last King - Nichelle D. Tramble   *c*   1197

Reed, Lacie (Investigator; Spy)
A Perfect Cover - Maureen Tan   *r*   390

Regan (Teenager)
Luna - Julie Anne Peters   *f*   575

Reilly, Regan (Detective—Private)
The Christmas Thief - Mary Higgins Clark   *m*   31

Reles, Dan (Detective—Homicide)
Dirty Sally - Michael Simon   *c*   1186

Renault, Gabriel (Military Personnel; Amnesiac)
Forget Me Not - Marliss Melton   *r*   341

Renault, Helen (Widow(er))
Forget Me Not - Marliss Melton   *r*   341

Renko, Arkady (Police Officer)
Wolves Eat Dogs - Martin Cruz Smith   *m*   187
Wolves Eat Dogs - Martin Cruz Smith   *c*   1190

Reno, Marcus (Historical Figure; Military Personnel)
An Obituary for Major Reno - Richard S. Wheeler   *t*   952

Renslow, Athena (Young Woman)
The Duel - Barbara Metzger   *r*   342

Renzi, Nicholas (Military Personnel)
Mutiny - Julian Stockwin   *t*   943

Repairman Jack (Mercenary)
Crisscross - F. Paul Wilson   *h*   706

Revelle, Richard de (Nobleman; Lawman)
Crowner's Quest - Bernard Knight   *t*   892

Revkina, Aglaya Stepanovna (Zealot)
Monumental Propaganda - Vladimir Voinovich   *c*   1204

Rey, Vishram (Entertainer)
River of Gods - Ian McDonald   *s*   763

Reyes-Guzman, Estelle (Police Officer)
Convenient Disposal - Steven F. Havill   *w*   448
Convenient Disposal - Steven F. Havill   *m*   102

Reynaud, Natalie (Police Officer)
Ice Run - Steve Hamilton   *m*   97

Reynolds, Catherine (Debutante; Gentlewoman)
A Hint of Seduction - Amelia Grey   *r*   281

Reynolds, Jael (Detective—Homicide; Single Parent)
All Things Hidden - Judy Candis   *i*   972

Reza, Salman (Government Official)
Offspring - Steven Harper   *s*   751

Rhapsody (Singer)
Elegy for a Lost Star - Elizabeth Haydon   *f*   542

Rho (Psychic)
The Wilding - C.S. Friedman   *s*   746

Rhonin (Wizard)
The Well of Eternity - Richard A. Knaak   *f*   556

Riant (Publisher)
In the Hope of Rising Again - Helen Scully   *c*   1181

Riant, Regina (Spouse)
In the Hope of Rising Again - Helen Scully   *c*   1181
In the Hope of Rising Again - Helen Scully   *t*   936

Richard II (Ruler; Historical Figure)
The Wounded Hawk - Sara Douglass   *t*   859

Richardson, Baxter (Crime Victim)
Life Everlasting - Robert Whitlow   *i*   1055

Richardson, Rena (Spouse)
Life Everlasting - Robert Whitlow   *i*   1055

Richelieu, Rory "Doodlebug" (Vampire)
Bride of the Fat White Vampire - Andrew Fox   *h*   631

Richler, Joseph (Journalist)
An Obituary for Major Reno - Richard S. Wheeler   *t*   952

Richmond, Scott (Wealthy; Fiance(e))
Caught in the Act - Pam McCutcheon   *r*   336

Richthofen, Manfred von (Military Personnel; Historical Figure)
To the Last Man - Jeff Shaara   *c*   1183
To the Last Man - Jeff Shaara   *t*   937

Riddle, John (Amnesiac)
Forgotten Justice - Lois Richer   *i*   1043

Rideau, Paul (Pilot)
Airborn - Ken Oppel   *s*   772

Rieux, Gabrielle Robichon (Businesswoman; Smuggler)
White Horses - Joan Wolf   *r*   408

Riker (Detective—Homicide)
Winter House - Carol O'Connell   *m*   155

Riley, K.C. (Detective—Police)
Cold Case Squad - Edna Buchanan   *c*   1079

Riley, Simon (Photojournalist)
Return to Me - Shannon McKenna   *r*   339

Rimbaud, Arthur (Writer; Historical Figure)
One King, One Soldier - Alexander C. Irvine   *f*   549

Ringwood, Claire Liddicote (Spouse)
The Cretan Counterfeit - Katharine Farrer   *m*   74

Ringwood, Richard (Police Officer)
The Cretan Counterfeit - Katharine Farrer   *m*   74
The Missing Link - Katharine Farrer   *m*   75

Riss, M'chel (Mercenary)
The Doublecross Program - Chris Bunch   *s*   728

Rissa (Slave)
The Immortelles - Gilbert Morris   *i*   1031

Rivers, Margaret (Noblewoman)
The Nameless Day - Sara Douglass   *f*   525

Ro-shei (Monster; Servant)
Dark of the Sun - Chelsea Quinn Yarbro   *h*   710

Roarke (Businessman; Spouse)
Divided in Death - J.D. Robb   *s*   778

Robbins, Chad (Young Man)
House of Blood - Bryan Smith   *h*   693

Robert (Writer)
Children of Epiphany - Frances Oliver   *h*   678

Robert the Bruce (Historical Figure; Ruler)
The Great Scot - Duncan A. Bruce   *t*   830

Roberts (Police Officer)
Blitz - Ken Bruen   *m*   23

Robey, Raine (Businesswoman; Computer Expert)
Dangerous Curves - Jacey Ford   *r*   266

Robin Hood (Vampire)
A Cold Summer Night - Trystam Kith   *h*   651

Roche, Delly (Widow(er); Wealthy)
The Parts - Keith Ridgway   *c*   1172

Rochester, George (Sea Captain)
A Watery Grave - Joan Druett   *t*   861

Roderick (Robot)
The Complete Roderick - John Sladek   *s*   788

Roger (Lawyer; Friend)
Magic Seeds - V.S. Naipaul   *c*   1153

Rogers, Angel (Orphan; Rancher)
Spring of My Love - Ginny Aiken   *i*   961

Rollins, Kylie (Young Woman)
Precious Things - Andrea Boeshaar   *i*   969

Rolvaag, Karl (Detective—Homicide)
Skinny Dip - Carl Hiaasen   *m*   103

Romanov, Nicholas Kostantinovich (Historical Figure; Nobleman)
The White Night of St. Petersburg - Michael, Prince of Greece   *t*   905

Roosevelt, Franklin Delano (Historical Figure; Political Figure)
The Plot Against America - Philip Roth   *c*   1175
Return Engagement - Harry Turtledove   *t*   948

Rose, Julie (Heiress; Crime Victim)
Just a Hint—Clint - Lori Foster   *r*   267

Rose of Valinor (Royalty)
The Prince - Elizabeth Minogue   *r*   347

Roseman, Inez (Musician; Parent)
The Beautiful Inez - Bart Schneider   *c*   1178

Roseman, Jake (Spouse; Lawyer)
The Beautiful Inez - Bart Schneider   *c*   1178

Rosenzweig (Religious)
The King of Ice Cream - Robert Wayne McCoy   *f*   567

Character Description Index

This index alphabetically lists descriptions of the major characters in featured titles. The descriptions may be occupations (astronaut, lawyer, etc.) or may describe persona (amnesiac, runaway, teenager, etc.). For each description, character names are listed alphabetically. Also provided are book titles, author names, genre codes and entry numbers. The genre codes are as follows: *c* Popular Fiction, *f* Fantasy, *h* Horror, *i* Inspirational, *m* Mystery, *r* Romance, *s* Science Fiction, *t* Historical, and *w* Western.

ABUSE VICTIM

Holbrook, Anna
Yonnondio from the Thirties - Tillie Olsen   *w*   470

Holbrook, Mazie
Yonnondio from the Thirties - Tillie Olsen   *w*   470

Moore, Tippy
Renegade - Diana Palmer   *r*   356

Rain, Phoebe
Midnight Rain - Holly Lisle   *r*   324

Shiflett, Clarisse
Delivery - Ben Daitz   *w*   434

Simpkins, Gabriel "P.T."
The Mercy Killers - Lisa Reardon   *c*   1169

ACCIDENT VICTIM

Angela
Don't Move - Margaret Mazzantini   *c*   1140

Stewart, Anne
The Celebrity - Robert Elmer   *i*   985

Tortuga
Tortuga - Rudolfo Anaya   *w*   413

ACCOUNTANT

Ambrewster, Harry
The Nerd Who Loved Me - Vicki Lewis Thompson   *r*   397

Cleaver, James
All the Lonely People - David B. Silva   *h*   692

Goodman, Natalie
The Pleasure Principle - Shirley Harrison   *r*   286

Williams, Caroline Cater
Hostile Takeover - Susan Shwartz   *s*   787

ACTIVIST

American Horse, Johnny
In the Moon of Red Ponies - James Lee Burke   *c*   1080

Browne, Verity
The More Deceived - David Roberts   *m*   171

Davies, Rebecca
Burning Bridges - Troy Soos   *m*   188

Harold, Natalie
Coyote Morning - Lisa Lenard-Cook   *w*   460

Newcombe, Chloe
Dead for the Winter - Betsy Thornton   *w*   488
Dead for the Winter - Betsy Thornton   *m*   198

ACTOR

Barrow, Clete
The Prince of Beverly Hills - Stuart Woods   *t*   957

Booth, John Wilkes
The Curse of Cain - J. Mark Powell   *w*   473

Dean, James
The Rebel: An Imagined Life of James Dean - Jack Dann   *t*   848

Jarvis, Jarrod
The Actor's Guide to Adultery - Rick Copp   *m*   39

Joliffe
A Play of Isaac - Margaret Frazer   *m*   83

Montez, Rafe
Ghost of a Chance - Flo Fitzpatrick   *r*   265

Mueller, Don
Ghost of a Chance - Flo Fitzpatrick   *r*   265

Omohundro, Texas Jack
East of the Border - Johnny D. Boggs   *w*   417

Preston, Guy
Apocalypse Now, Voyager - Jay Russell   *h*   688

Zanni, Edward
How I Paid for College - Marc Acito   *c*   1063

ACTRESS

Angeli, Pier
The Rebel: An Imagined Life of James Dean - Jack Dann   *t*   848

Bernhardt, Sarah
Divine Sarah - Adam Braver   *t*   829

Cadwallader, Dorothy
The Hollywood Dodo - Geoff Nicholson   *c*   1156

Charlesworthy, Suzie
New York Dreams - Eric Brown   *s*   724

Earp, Josie
Tombstone Travesty - Jane Candia Coleman   *w*   428

Falshaw, Kate
Dangerous Deceptions - Lynn Kerstan   *r*   314

Farren, Eliza
Life Mask - Emma Donoghue   *t*   856
Life Mask - Emma Donoghue   *c*   1094

Maher, Isabel
The Silver Screen - Maureen Howard   *c*   1123

Milligan, Genevieve "Veevi"
Cheat and Charmer - Elizabeth Frank   *c*   1109

Monroe, Marilyn
The Rebel: An Imagined Life of James Dean - Jack Dann   *t*   848

Smithson, Harriet
Ophelia's Fan - Christine Balint   *t*   818

ADDICT

Dean, Eddie
The Dark Tower - Stephen King   *h*   649
Song of Susannah - Stephen King   *c*   1131

Shiflett, Junior
Delivery - Ben Daitz   *w*   434

ADMINISTRATOR

Ajmani, Rachel
Grasp the Stars - Jennifer Wingert   *s*   806

Carter, Susan
Gabriel's Discovery - Felicia Mason   *i*   1024

Harris, James
Everlasting Love - Valerie Hansen   *i*   997

Holman, Jake
Crucible - Nancy Kress   *s*   757

Troutbeck, Jack
Carnage on the Committee - Ruth Dudley Edwards   *m*   68

ADOPTEE

Bradley, Christine
The Gift of Christmas Present - Melody Carlson   *i*   974

Nash, Adria
See How She Dies - Lisa Jackson   *r*   299

O'Rourke, Meara
Meant to Be - Edie Claire   *r*   241

ADVENTURER

Beckett, Grace
The First Stone - Mark Anthony   *f*   499

Carter, Derian
Wolf Captured - Jane Lindskold   *f*   561

Jak
Dawn of Night - Paul S. Kemp   *f*   551

Kalrakin
Wizards' Conclave - Douglas Niles   *f*   573

Kane, Solomon
The Savage Tales of Solomon Kane - Robert E. Howard   *f*   547

Koslov, Peter "Colonel Cut"
Sonja's Run - Richard Hoyt   *t*   883

St. George, Jonathan Devoran
Night of Sin - Julia Ross   *r*   374

Tolan, Maggie
Wind Walker - Cassie Edwards   *r*   257

ADVERTISING

Brannon, Hugh
Not Quite as Advertised - Tanya Michaels   *r*   346

Hunter
So Yesterday - Scott Westerfeld   *s*   804

Jasper, Serena
Speak to My Heart - Stacy Hawkins Adams   *i*   960

Jennifer
So Yesterday - Scott Westerfeld   *s*   804

McBride, Jocelyn "Joss"
Not Quite as Advertised - Tanya Michaels   *r*   346

Vogler, Michael
The Bride Wore Chocolate - Shirley Jump   *r*   305

Wells, Richard
Who Wants to Marry a Heartthrob? - Stephanie Doyle   *r*   255

Wilkins, Mandy
So Yesterday - Scott Westerfeld   *s*   804

AGED PERSON

Bandar, Guth
Black Brillion - Matthew Hughes   *s*   754

Birchspring
The Secret of Shabaz - Jennifer Macaire   *f*   564

Clavain
Absolution Gap - Alastair Reynolds   *s*   775

Felton, Cora
And a Puzzle to Die On - Parnell Hall   *m*   95

Ghazayil
Dreams of the Desert Wind - Kurt Giambastini   *s*   749

Hogan, Eunice
Coffee Rings - Yvonne Lehman   *i*   1018

Lindeman, Sarah
Sarah's Song - Karen Kingsbury   *i*   1015

Lovecraft, Sarah
Lovecraft - Hans Rodionoff   *h*   686

Malone, Ivy
Invisible - Lorena McCourtney   *i*   1025

Marshall, Frank
D.B. - Elwood Reid   *c*   1170

Maya
The Death of Mr. Love - Indra Sinha   *c*   1187

Naini
The Last Storyteller - Diane Noble   *i*   1037

Samantha
Sam's Letters to Jennifer - James Patterson   *c*   1163

Trisha
Mantrapped - Fay Weldon   *c*   1207

Trumbull, Victoria
Jack in the Pulpit - Cynthia Riggs   *m*   170

Washington, Joseph
Mysterious Ways - Terry Burns   *w*   421
Mysterious Ways - Terry Burns   *i*   971

Waxmelt
Clovermead - David Randall   *f*   578

AGENT

Anderson, Tess
My Long, Tall Texas Heartthrob - Geralyn Dawson   *r*   249

Bel
The Language of Power - Rosemary Kirstein   *f*   553

Chilton
A Cold Summer Night - Trystam Kith   *f*   554

Feinwold, Iggy
Walpuski's Typewriter - Frank Darabont   *h*   624

Lopez, Alexis
Playing with Boys - Alisa Valdes-Rodriguez   *r*   398

Miller, Elizabeth
The Second Assistant - Mimi Hare   *c*   1117

Preston, Davies
The Christmas Wedding - Laurie Brown   *r*   233

Selwyn
My Death - Lisa Tuttle   *h*   702

Wagner, Scott
The Second Assistant - Mimi Hare   *c*   1117

ALCOHOLIC

Blair, Alan
Wake Up, Sir - Jonathan Ames   *c*   1064

Connolly, Mike
Sober Justice - Joseph H. Hilley   *i*   1004

Haley, Bob
Following the Harvest - Fred Harris   *w*   447

Malloy, Tom
Branded - Ed Gorman   *w*   442

Rupert, Framp
Sawyer's Quest - Will Cade   *w*   423

Sweet, Mason
Wanting What You Get - Kathy Love   *r*   328

ALIEN

Aras
City of Pearl - Karen Traviss   *s*   794
Crossing the Line - Karen Traviss   *s*   795

Atvar
Homeward Bound - Harry Turtledove   *s*   798

Frane
Haydn of Mars - Al Sarrantonio   *s*   784

Green, Melantha
The Green and the Gray - Timothy Zahn   *s*   808

Haydn
Haydn of Mars - Al Sarrantonio   *s*   784

Irythros
The Dragon Circle - Irene Radford   *s*   774

Jora'h
Horizon Storms - Kevin J. Anderson   *s*   713

Kassquit
Homeward Bound - Harry Turtledove   *s*   798

Kerl
Haydn of Mars - Al Sarrantonio   *s*   784

Kuga-Ka
For Those Who Fell - William C. Dietz   *s*   739

Meris
Grasp the Stars - Jennifer Wingert   *s*   806

O'Neil, Longfang
The Rats, the Bats, and the Ugly - Eric Flint   *s*   744

Oregon, Ukiah
Dog Warrior - Wen Spencer   *s*   790

Pellaz
The Shades of Time and Memory - Storm Constantine   *s*   733

Pip
Sliding Scales - Alan Dean Foster   *s*   745

Steele, Atticus
Dog Warrior - Wen Spencer   *s*   790

Takuuna
Sliding Scales - Alan Dean Foster   *s*   745

Tir
Cally's War - John Ringo   *s*   777

Velaxis
The Shades of Time and Memory - Storm Constantine   *s*   733

AMNESIAC

Calhoun, Stoney
Bitch Creek - William G. Tapply   *m*   196

Grimes, Davina
Forgotten Destiny - Janet Tanner   *r*   391

Logan, Dane
The Heart Remembers - Al Lacy   *i*   1016

Northman, Eric
Dead to the World - Charlaine Harris   *h*   638

Renault, Gabriel
Forget Me Not - Marliss Melton   *r*   341

Riddle, John
Forgotten Justice - Lois Richer   *i*   1043

Soldier
Scabbard's Song - Kim Hunter   *f*   548

Wright, McKenna
The Cat's Meow - Emily Carmichael   *r*   236

Wright, Rachel
The Hidden - Sarah Pinborough   *h*   681

ANGEL

Angelese
Infernal Angel - Edward Lee   *h*   656

Michael
The Nameless Day - Sara Douglass   *t*   858
The Wounded Hawk - Sara Douglass   *t*   859

ANIMAL

Blind Seer
Wolf Captured - Jane Lindskold   *f*   561

Boom
Black Water - D.J. MacHale   *f*   565

Chief
Rabbit Goes Duck Hunting - Deborah L. Duvall   *w*   438

Dashiell
Fall Guy - Carol Lea Benjamin   *m*   9

Character Description Index

Gallant-Stallion
The Finest Creation - Jean Rabe *f* 577

Jack
A Redbird Christmas - Fannie Flagg *c* 1105

Ji-Stu
Rabbit Goes Duck Hunting - Deborah L. Duvall *w* 438

Midnight Louie
Cat in an Orange Twist - Carole Nelson Douglas *m* 60

Nefertiti "Titi"
The Cat's Meow - Emily Carmichael *r* 236

Otter
Rabbit Goes Duck Hunting - Deborah L. Duvall *w* 438

Scorpio
Absolution Gap - Alastair Reynolds *s* 775

Starlight
Starlight Comes Home - Janet Muirhead Hill *w* 450

ANIMAL LOVER

Stevens, Miranda
Starlight Comes Home - Janet Muirhead Hill *w* 450

ANIMAL TRAINER

Alexander, Rachel
Fall Guy - Carol Lea Benjamin *m* 9

Field, Jack
To Collar a Killer - Lee Charles Kelley *m* 116

Shepard, Nina
The Dog Walker - Leslie Schnur *c* 1179

ANTHROPOLOGIST

Hubbard, Leda
Cleopatra 7.2 - Elizabeth Ann Scarborough *s* 785

Miller, Hart
Banquet for the Damned - Adam L.G. Nevill *h* 675

ANTIQUES DEALER

Benedict, Alex
Polaris - Jack McDevitt *s* 762

Doyle, Molly
Tagged for Murder - Elaine Flinn *m* 79

Ferry, Inez
The Rottweiler - Ruth Rendell *m* 169

Fox, Peter
Verse of the Vampyre - Diana Killian *m* 117

Keene, Jessie
The Alias Man - Bill Pronzini *m* 165

Lowry, Tim
Buried Stuff - Sharon Fiffer *m* 78

Severson, Blythe
Precious Things - Andrea Boeshaar *i* 969

Sheppard, Kate
The Blue Rose - Anthony Eglin *m* 69

Shimura, Rei
The Pearl Diver - Sujata Massey *m* 135

Talbot, Jeff
Four on the Floor - Deborah Morgan *m* 147

Wheel, Jane
Buried Stuff - Sharon Fiffer *m* 78

APOTHECARY

Rawlings, John
Death in the Setting Sun - Deryn Lake *t* 893

APPRAISER

Halmus, Pete
Viator - Lucius Shepard *h* 691

APPRENTICE

Aching, Tiffany
A Hat Full of Sky - Terry Pratchett *f* 576

Christmas, Tim
Strange Cargo - Jeffrey E. Barlough *f* 504

Kutch
The Covenant Rising - Stan Nicholls *f* 572

ARCHAEOLOGIST

Caldwell, Paul
The Egyptologist - Arthur Phillips *c* 1165

Clark, Megan
Tome of Murder - D.R. Meredith *w* 464

Dunn, Omaha
Sandstorm - James Rollins *s* 780

Jeffries, Trenton
Exorcist: The Beginning - Steven Piziks *h* 682

Landon, Arnold
Headhunter - Roy Lewis *m* 127

Maguire, Cormac
Lake of Sorrows - Erin Hart *m* 99

Trilipush, Ralph
The Egyptologist - Arthur Phillips *c* 1165
The Egyptologist - Arthur Phillips *t* 922

ARCHITECT

Garcia, James
Coyote Rising - Allen Steele *s* 791

Gregory, Michael
The Dark Lord - Patricia Simpson *r* 381

Harris, Chris
Aloha Love - Alice Wootson *r* 410

Sheppard, Alex
The Blue Rose - Anthony Eglin *m* 69

Westray, Arthur
The Nebuly Coat - John Meade Falkner *h* 627

ART DEALER

Coleman, Celia
No Dark Valley - Jamie Langston Turner *i* 1051

ART HISTORIAN

McKinnon, Kate
Color Blind - Jonathan Santlofer *m* 179

St. George, Sweeney
Mansions of the Dead - Sarah Stewart Taylor *m* 197

ARTIFICIAL INTELLIGENCE

Casey
New York Dreams - Eric Brown *s* 724

Cleopatra
Cleopatra 7.2 - Elizabeth Ann Scarborough *s* 785

Omnius
The Battle of Corrin - Brian Herbert *s* 752

ARTISAN

Iskander
Birds Without Wings - Louis de Bernieres *t* 852

Judith
Califia's Daughters - Leigh Richards *s* 776

Nash, Trista Josephine
The Heiress of Hyde Park - Jacqueline Navin *r* 351

Pierre
The Harper's Quine - Pat McIntosh *m* 141

Trader, Rani
The Glasswright's Master - Mindy L. Klasky *f* 555

ARTIST

Ayoshi
The Painting - Nina Schuyler *t* 935

Black, Fletcher
Meant to Be - Edie Claire *r* 241

Damer, Anne Seymour
Life Mask - Emma Donoghue *t* 856
Life Mask - Emma Donoghue *c* 1094

Davian
The Bride of Stone - Thomas Williams *i* 1059

Delacourte, Lucien
The Painted Rose - Donna Birdsell *r* 223

Du Maurier, George
Author, Author - David Lodge *t* 897
Author, Author - David Lodge *c* 1138

Duncan, Eve
Blind Alley - Iris Johansen *m* 109

Gervaise, Francois
Le Colonial - Kien Nguyen *t* 912

Grant, Darius
Wonderful and Wild - Simona Taylor *r* 393

Hawcly, Abe
Ordinary Wolves - Seth Kantner *c* 1129

Heywood, Parker
Say Yes - Donna Hill *r* 292

Hiyashi
The Painting - Nina Schuyler *t* 935

Jackson, Mason
The Manor - Scott Nicholson *h* 676

Jenna
Visits from the Drowned Girl - Steven Sherrill *c* 1185

Lisa
Children of Epiphany - Frances Oliver *h* 678

Mitry, Desiree
The Burnt Orange Sunrise - David Handler *m* 98

Nagarian, Gavril
Prisoner of the Iron Tower - Sarah Ash *f* 502

Piero della Francesca
Love, the Painter's Wife and the Queen of Sheba - Aliette Armel *t* 814
Love, the Painter's Wife and the Queen of Sheba - Aliette Armel *c* 1066

Quinn, Sophie
Snowed In - Christina Bartolomeo *c* 1071

Shelley, Wollstonecraft "Wollie"
Dating Is Murder - Harley Jane Kozak *r* 319

Stephens, Heather
Dead for the Winter - Betsy Thornton *w* 488

Stuyvesant, Pam
The Course of the Heart - M. John Harrison   *h*   639

Sullivan, Toni
Shattered Image - J.F. Margos   *i*   1022

Z, Immanuel
The Autumn Castle - Kim Wilkins   *f*   593

ASSISTANT

Connor, Bridget
Who Wants to Marry a Heartthrob? - Stephanie Doyle   *r*   255

Driver, Aaron
Sammy's Hill - Kristin Gore   *c*   1113

Jenkins
Queer Street - Curt Colbert   *m*   35

Joyce, Samantha
Sammy's Hill - Kristin Gore   *c*   1113

ASTROLOGER

Samarth, Sonia
The Cosmic Clues - Manjiri Prabhu   *m*   164

AVENGER

Lassiter
Lassiter - Loren Zane Grey   *w*   444
Riders of the Purple Sage: The Restored Edition - Zane Grey   *w*   445

Morgan, Chip
Blood River - Jory Sherman   *w*   482

BABY

Landen, Isabelle
The Babe Magnet - Robin Wells   *r*   403

BABYSITTER

Ambrewster, Harry
The Nerd Who Loved Me - Vicki Lewis Thompson   *r*   397

BAKER

Addams, Alcea O'Malley
Follow Me Home - Jerri Corgiat   *r*   244

Cabot, Belinda "Billy"
Raspberry Crush - Jill Winters   *r*   407

Cornwallis, Lucy
The Queen of Subtleties - Suzannah Dunn   *t*   863

Santoro, Carolina "Lina"
Goddess of Spring - P.C. Cast   *r*   238

Swensen, Hannah
Sugar Cookie Murder - Joanne Fluke   *m*   80

BANKER

Ascension, Kim
The Secret Beau - Annette Mahon   *r*   331

Dombrowski, Emma
The Eggnog Chronicles - Carly Alexander   *r*   211

Swift, William
Ghosts of Albion: Astray - Amber Benson   *h*   604

BARBARIAN

Bahnakson, Bahzell
Windrider's Oath - David Weber   *f*   588

Coldheart, Hirad
Demonstorm - James Barclay   *f*   503

Conan
The Bloody Crown of Conan - Robert E. Howard   *f*   546

Evan
The Mountain's Call - Caitlin Brennan   *f*   508

BASTARD DAUGHTER

Kazanov, Amber
To Love a Princess - Patricia Grasso   *r*   275

McAllister, Roxanne
The Demon's Daughter - Emma Holly   *r*   296

BASTARD SON

Carrasco, Freddy
Any Place I Hang My Hat - Susan Isaacs   *c*   1124

Fitzroy, William
Hidden Honor - Anne Stuart   *r*   388

Mputa, Samuel
21: The Final Unfinished Voyage of Jack Aubrey - Patrick O'Brian   *t*   913

BIBLICAL FIGURE

Joseph
Till Shiloh Comes - Gilbert Morris   *i*   1032

Mary
Three Days - Melody Carlson   *i*   975

Michael
The Nameless Day - Sara Douglass   *t*   858
The Wounded Hawk - Sara Douglass   *t*   859

Solomon
Wisdom's Daughter - India Edghill   *t*   865

BODYGUARD

Carruthers, Mitchell
Nerd Gone Wild - Vicki Lewis Thompson   *r*   396

Horrocks
Counterfeit Kings - Adam Connell   *s*   732

Sari
Counterfeit Kings - Adam Connell   *s*   732

BOUNTY HUNTER

Brunner
Blood of the Dragon - C.L. Werner   *f*   590

Graham, Devlin
As You Wish - Francine Matthews   *r*   334

Locke, John
Invitation to a Hanging - Robert J. Randisi   *w*   476

Manoso, Carlos "Ranger"
Ten Big Ones - Janet Evanovich   *c*   1099

Plum, Stephanie
Ten Big Ones - Janet Evanovich   *c*   1099

Prophet, Lou
Staring Down the Devil - Peter Brandvold   *w*   420

Threadbare the Lutheran
The Lutheran - Jack Britton Sullivan   *w*   486

BOYFRIEND

Abair, James
Heir to the Glimmering World - Cythia Ozick   *c*   1161

Burby, Nick
Putting on the Dog - Cynthia Baxter   *m*   7

Buster
Citizen Girl - Emma McLaughlin   *c*   1145

Dare, Tom
The London Pigeon Wars - Patrick Neate   *c*   1155

Driver, Aaron
Sammy's Hill - Kristin Gore   *c*   1113

Greenwood, Seth
She's Out of Control - Kristin Billerbeck   *i*   966

Lanzara, Renato
The Queen of the Big Time - Adriana Trigiani   *c*   1199

Morelli, Joe
Ten Big Ones - Janet Evanovich   *c*   1099

Naryshkin, Boris
A Carnivore's Inquiry - Sabina Murray   *c*   1152

Patrick
The Lady of the Hall - Veronica Heley   *i*   999

Stuart, Alexander "Lex" Rothschild III
A.K.A. Goddess - Evelyn Vaughn   *r*   399

Tom
The Big Love - Sarah Dunn   *c*   1096

Wellington, Sam
The Last Storyteller - Diane Noble   *i*   1037

BRIDE

Bainbridge, Maddy
Chances Are - Barbara Bretton   *r*   231

Larson, Lacy
A Texan's Luck - Jodi Thomas   *r*   394

Leonard, Isabelle
See Isabelle Run - Elizabeth Bloom   *r*   229

Morrow, Lizbeth
Dying to Marry - Janelle Taylor   *r*   392

Murdock, Keeley
Hissy Fit - Mary Kay Andrews   *r*   214
Hissy Fit - Mary Kay Andrews   *c*   1065

BRIDEGROOM

Dunhill, Dylan III
Dying to Marry - Janelle Taylor   *r*   392

Larson, Walker
A Texan's Luck - Jodi Thomas   *r*   394

O'Malley, Aidan
Chances Are - Barbara Bretton   *r*   231

BULLY

Holbrook, Jim
Yonnondio from the Thirties - Tillie Olsen   *w*   470

BUSINESSMAN

Argeneau, Bastien
Tall, Dark, and Hungry - Lynsay Sands   *r*   377

Beckwith, Alan
R Is for Ricochet - Sue Grafton   *c*   1114

Belvedere, Randolph
Falling Awake - Jayne Ann Krentz   *c*   1133

Bey, Rustum
Birds Without Wings - Louis de Bernieres   *t*   852

Bhalu
The Death of Mr. Love - Indra Sinha   *c*   1187

Blake, Woody
The Overnight - Ramsey Campbell   *h*   611

Brandolini, Amadeo
Killer Smile - Lisa Scottoline   c   1180

Carnochan, David
East Side Story - Louis Auchincloss   t   815

Champion, Reece
Master of the Night - Angela Knight   r   318

Chung, Lin
The Castlemaine Murders - Kerry
  Greenwood   m   91

Collins, Matthew
Santa Fe Passage - Jon R. Bauman   t   819
Santa Fe Passage - Jon R. Bauman   w   415

Collins, Maxwell
See Isabelle Run - Elizabeth Bloom   r   229

Colson, Mark
Phi Beta Bimbo - Trish Jensen   r   300

Cortez, Benicio
Industrial Magic - Kelley Armstrong   h   601
Industrial Magic - Kelley Armstrong   f   501

Cutler, Ellis
Falling Awake - Jayne Ann Krentz   c   1133

Eddie
Lucious Lemon - Heather Swain   r   389

Faber, Mitchell
In the Night Room - Peter Straub   h   697

Ford, Henry
The Plot Against America - Philip Roth   t   929

Forest, Ian
Shadows in the Darkness - Elaine
  Cunningham   h   623

Frants, Oliver
Staying Dead - Laura Anne Gilman   f   538

Friedman, Stephen
Obsessed - Ted Dekker   i   977

Geddes, Ewan
Highland Rogue - Deborah Hale   r   282

Graves, Harry
Taking Time - Lynn Abbey   f   498

Grishin, Arkady
Singularity - Bill DeSmedt   s   738

Guy
Citizen Girl - Emma McLaughlin   c   1145

Hawthorne, Decker
Acts of God - James Beauseigneur   s   721

Henley, Will
Too Close to the Sun - Diana Dempsey   r   251

Hennessey, Russell Tremayne
Chesapeake Tide - Jeanette Baker   r   217

Holyrod, Ramone
Life - Gwyneth Jones   s   755

Hunt, Simon
Secrets of a Summer Night - Lisa Kleypas   r   317

Jarvis, Adam Rafael
Very Truly Sexy - Dawn Atkins   r   216

Jedes, Dominic
Neurolink - M.M. Buckner   s   725

Kingsley, Tanner
Are You Afraid of the Dark? - Sidney
  Sheldon   c   1184

Kleinman, Morris
Chicken Dreaming Corn - Roy Hoffman   t   882

Lannigan, Seth
Raspberry Crush - Jill Winters   r   407

Longleigh, Redmond
Taking Time - Lynn Abbey   f   498

Lorn, Klas
Neurolink - M.M. Buckner   s   725

MacFarlane, Angus
The Silver Yoke - Roland Cheek   w   426

Maddox, Luke
Fatal Error - Colleen Thompson   r   395

Madison, Blaine
Paper Moon - Linda Windsor   i   1060

Mahoney, Will
Hissy Fit - Mary Kay Andrews   r   214
Hissy Fit - Mary Kay Andrews   c   1065

McDonald, Julian
Shifting Love - Constance O'Day-Flannery   r   353

McKinnon, Tyler
Twice Blessed - Sharon Gillenwater   i   989

McNeal, Ian
A Berry Merry Christmas - Marcia Evanick   r   258

Meade, Patrick Spencer
Life - Gwyneth Jones   s   755

Morgan, Eric
Sweet Justice - Shirley Harrison   r   287

Prentiss, Grant
Love Came Unexpectedly - Ruth Scofield   i   1047

Roarke
Divided in Death - J.D. Robb   s   778

Rutledge, Boone
Calder Promise - Janet Dailey   r   245

Rymar, Ben
Offspring - Steven Harper   s   751

Sakaki, Tomihiro
Less than Human - Maxine McArthur   s   761

Scobey, Galen
Light of Hope - Robert Vaughan   i   1052

Stuart, Alexander "Lex" Rothschild III
A.K.A. Goddess - Evelyn Vaughn   r   399

Sutter, Rob
The Trouble with Valentine's Day - Rachel
  Gibson   r   272

Tariq
The London Pigeon Wars - Patrick Neate   c   1155

Thurman, Lowell
The Resort - Bentley Little   h   658

Trevelyan, Benedict
The Mistress of Trevelyan - Jennifer St. Giles   r   385

Waterman, Edward
Santa Fe Passage - Jon R. Bauman   t   819
Santa Fe Passage - Jon R. Bauman   w   415

Weinstein, Stanley
Dead Lines - Greg Bear   h   603

Wilander, Thomas
Viator - Lucius Shepard   h   691

BUSINESSWOMAN

Bauer, Lillie
Tiger Lillie - Lisa Samson   i   1046

Brancaster Talbot, Claire
Highland Rogue - Deborah Hale   r   282

Campbell, Violet
Wild in the Moonlight - Jennifer Greene   r   279

Cisco, Loretta
Family Blessings - Fern Michaels   r   344

Cody, Diane
Shadows in the Darkness - Elaine
  Cunningham   f   522

Day, Kelly
Little Earthquakes - Jennifer Weiner   c   1206

Dyer, Mandy
Taking the Wrap - Dolores Johnson   m   110

Girl
Citizen Girl - Emma McLaughlin   c   1145

Greene, Sonia
Lovecraft - Hans Rodionoff   h   686

Kantke, Jean
The Quick - Dan Vining   h   704

Kolpath, Chase
Polaris - Jack McDevitt   s   762

LeJeune, Jessica
Family Inheritance - Deborah LeBlanc   h   655

McAllister, Amber
A Berry Merry Christmas - Marcia Evanick   r   258

Moss, Gwen
Someone to Watch over Me - Teresa Hill   i   1003

Rael-Lamont, Vivian
Duke of Sin - Adele Ashworth   r   215

Rieux, Gabrielle Robichon
White Horses - Joan Wolf   r   408

Robey, Raine
Dangerous Curves - Jacey Ford   r   266

Ross, Viola
The Irish Devil - Diane Whiteside   r   405

Rothchild, Stella
Blue Dahlia - Nora Roberts   r   366

Rutherford, Annie
In Like Flynn - Dorien Kelly   r   308

Senoz, Anna
Life - Gwyneth Jones   s   755

Talbot, Jazzy
As Good as Dead - Beverly Barton   r   219

Toadfern, Josie
Death by Deep Dish Pie - Sharon Short   m   184

Woodrow, Candace
The Bride Wore Chocolate - Shirley Jump   r   305

Wynn, Nora
Sweet Revenge - Kate Clemens   r   242

CAPTIVE

Tolan, Maggie
Wind Walker - Cassie Edwards   r   257

CARE GIVER

Bradley, Christine
The Gift of Christmas Present - Melody
  Carlson   i   974

Esmeralda
Good Heavens - Margaret A. Graham   i   992
Land Sakes - Margaret A. Graham   i   993

Gale, Marvin
Murder of Angels - Caitlin R. Kiernan   h   648

Ismelda
Tortuga - Rudolfo Anaya   w   413

CARPENTER

Barnett, Terry
Dead for the Winter - Betsy Thornton   w   488

Blake, Sam
American Idle - Alesia Holliday   r   295

Cafarelli, Zeke
Banishing Verona - Margot Livesey   c   1137

Cotterill, Simon
The Hangman's Hymn - P.C. Doherty   m   58

Holden, Dan
The Heart's Voice - Arlene James   *i*   1008

Larson, Teague
Wild in the Moment - Jennifer Greene   *r*   278

CATERER

Pudding, Katherine Elizabeth
A Man in a Kilt - Sandy Blair   *r*   227

Schulz, Goldy Bear
Double Shot - Diane Mott Davidson   *m*   52

Simmons, Bernadette "Bernie"
A Catered Wedding - Isis Crawford   *m*   44

Simmons, Libby
A Catered Wedding - Isis Crawford   *m*   44

CHAUFFEUR

Driver
Drive Me Crazy - Eric Jerome Dickey   *c*   1093

CHIEFTAIN

Grae
Song of the Earth - John R. Dann   *t*   849

Rain Bear
People of the Raven - Kathleen O'Neal Gear   *t*   873

Summer Day
Trouble's Messenger - Max Brand   *w*   419

CHILD

Casey, Patsy
A Redbird Christmas - Fannie Flagg   *c*   1105

Charlesworthy, Suzie
New York Dreams - Eric Brown   *s*   724

Drax, Louis
The Ninth Life of Louis Drax - Liz Jensen   *c*   1127

Gilkyson, Griff
An Unfinished Life - Mark Spragg   *c*   1191
An Unfinished Life - Mark Spragg   *w*   485

Holbrook, Mazie
Yonnondio from the Thirties - Tillie Olsen   *w*   470

Jorgen
Exile's Return - Raymond E. Feist   *f*   533

Liliana
The Vampire de Sade - Mary Ann Mitchell   *h*   668

Lomez, Rachel
Coyote Morning - Lisa Lenard-Cook   *w*   460

Lunae
Banner of Souls - Liz Williams   *s*   805

Mefell, Megan
Twilight Rising, Serpent's Dream - Diana Marcellas   *f*   566

Parker, Wade
Billy Goat Hill - Mark Stanleigh Morris   *i*   1033

Peralta, Pedro
North with De Anza - Dorothy Ward Erskine   *w*   439

Ray, Elizabeth
The Hidden - Sarah Pinborough   *h*   681

Roth, Philip
The Plot Against America - Philip Roth   *c*   1175
The Plot Against America - Philip Roth   *s*   781

Thurman, Ryan
The Resort - Bentley Little   *h*   658

CHILD-CARE GIVER

Anderson, Tess
My Long, Tall Texas Heartthrob - Geralyn Dawson   *r*   249

Lan Lin
The Love Wife - Gish Jen   *c*   1126

Louise
The Good Nanny - Benjamin Cheever   *c*   1084

Spencer, Caroline
Paper Moon - Linda Windsor   *i*   1060

CIVIL SERVANT

Seddon, Carole
The Hanging in the Hotel - Simon Brett   *m*   21

CLERK

Bloom, Ella
A Girl Becomes a Comma Like That - Lisa Glatt   *c*   1111

Kinder, Becca
The Heart's Voice - Arlene James   *i*   1008

Malloy, Andy
Branded - Ed Gorman   *w*   442

Sawyer, Billy
Sawyer's Quest - Will Cade   *w*   423

Summer, Rose
Hasty Death - Marion Chesney   *m*   27

COMPANION

Nash, Helena
My Pleasure - Connie Brockway   *r*   232

COMPOSER

Ackenzac, Leovigild
The Charnel Prince - J. Gregory Keyes   *f*   552

Berlioz, Hector
Ophelia's Fan - Christine Balint   *t*   818

COMPUTER EXPERT

Benson, Oliver
Charade - Gilbert Morris   *i*   1030

Bob
The Atrocity Archives - Charles Stross   *h*   698

Cabot, Belinda "Billy"
Raspberry Crush - Jill Winters   *r*   407

Fischer, Jeff
What Phoebe Wants - Cindi Myers   *r*   350

Kohler, Frank
Cruisers - Craig Nova   *c*   1158

Mackenzie, Owen
Villages - John Updike   *c*   1201

Maddox, Luke
Fatal Error - Colleen Thompson   *r*   395

McGuire, Eleanor
Less than Human - Maxine McArthur   *s*   761

Robey, Raine
Dangerous Curves - Jacey Ford   *r*   266

Rothman, Ruby
Which Big Giver Stole the Chopped Liver? - Sharon Kahn   *m*   111

Tharmody, Dona
Haven - Don D'Ammassa   *s*   736

Winterbourne, Paige
Industrial Magic - Kelley Armstrong   *h*   601
Industrial Magic - Kelley Armstrong   *f*   501

CON ARTIST

Colette
Hot Plastic - Peter Craig   *m*   43

Fortune
Johnny Blue and the Texas Rangers - Joseph A. West   *w*   493

Fritz-Allan, Gerda
Children of the Glens - Gwen Kirkwood   *r*   316

Swift, Jerry
Hot Plastic - Peter Craig   *m*   43

Swift, Kevin
Hot Plastic - Peter Craig   *m*   43

CON MAN

Waldrip, Duke
Flat Crazy - Ben Rehder   *w*   478

CONSTRUCTION WORKER

Bishop, Nathan
Live Like You Were Dying - Michael Morris   *i*   1034

CONSULTANT

deVrai, Jonat
Flash - L.E. Modesitt Jr.   *s*   768

Flynn, Daniel
In Like Flynn - Dorien Kelly   *r*   308

Khan, Shaheen Badoor
River of Gods - Ian McDonald   *s*   763

Landen, Holt
The Babe Magnet - Robin Wells   *r*   403

Lannigan, Seth
Raspberry Crush - Jill Winters   *r*   407

Scarpetta, Kay
Trace - Patricia Cornwell   *c*   1086
Trace - Patricia Cornwell   *m*   40

uy-Smythe, Tan
Flash - L.E. Modesitt Jr.   *s*   768

CONTRACTOR

Danvers, Zachary
See How She Dies - Lisa Jackson   *r*   299

Larson, Teague
Wild in the Moment - Jennifer Greene   *r*   278

CONVICT

Caruso, Sheila
Breaker's Reef - Terri Blackstock   *i*   967

Driver
Drive Me Crazy - Eric Jerome Dickey   *c*   1093

Lafferty, Reba
R Is for Ricochet - Sue Grafton   *c*   1114

Miller, Darrell
Haven - Julie Marshall   *r*   333

Waldrip, Duke
Flat Crazy - Ben Rehder   *w*   478

COOK

Cesare, Giselle
Girl Gone Wild - Joanne Rock   *r*   370

Del Rosso, Dante
The Devil Served Tortellini - Shirley Jump   *r*   306

Johnson, Millard
Territorial Rough Rider - Tim Champlin   *w*   425

Manelli, Ellie "Lemon"
Lucious Lemon - Heather Swain   *r*   389

Quilliam, Margaret "Meg"
Buried by Breakfast - Claudia Bishop   *m*   12

Rothstein-Rabinowitz, Rebecca "Becky"
Little Earthquakes - Jennifer Weiner   *c*   1206

Tock, Jimmy
Life Expectancy - Dean R. Koontz   *h*   652

COUNSELOR

Frost, Isole
Aphrodite's Flame - Julie Kenner   *r*   309

Jenkins, Eleanore "Puddin"
Ain't No Mountain - Sharon Ewell Foster   *i*   987

COURIER

Gray, Aisling
You Slay Me - Katie MacAlister   *r*   329

Lauria
Freedom's Gate - Naomi Kritzer   *f*   557

Norwood, Russell
The Last Campaign - Tim Champlin   *w*   424

COURTIER

Hugues
Memoir of a Dwarf - Paul Weidner   *t*   951

COUSIN

Hubbard, Horace
Old Boys - Charles McCarry   *c*   1142

COWBOY

Ackerman, Johnny
Judgment Day - Frank Roderus   *w*   479

Carrigan, Joseph
War at Fire Creek - Cameron Judd   *w*   457

Carrigan, Liam
War at Fire Creek - Cameron Judd   *w*   457

Donner, Jess
Bucked Out in Dodge - Ralph Compton   *w*   429

Dupree, Johnny Blue
Johnny Blue and the Texas Rangers - Joseph A. West   *w*   493

Ellsworth, Steve
Bucked Out in Dodge - Ralph Compton   *w*   429

Gough, Jimmy
The Palo Duro Trail - Ralph Compton   *w*   430

Wilkins, Stu
Bucked Out in Dodge - Ralph Compton   *w*   429

CRIME SUSPECT

Bowman, Bruce
Through the Grinder - Cleo Coyle   *m*   42

CRIME VICTIM

Acosta, Carmen
Convenient Disposal - Steven F. Havill   *w*   448

Barnett, Terry
Dead for the Winter - Betsy Thornton   *w*   488

Burns, Amos
Mountains Against the Sun - Perry Holmes   *w*   452

Celanire
Who Slashed Celanire's Throat? - Maryse Conde   *t*   844

Christopher, Paul
Old Boys - Charles McCarry   *c*   1142

Conklin, Alex
The Bourne Legacy - Eric Van Lustbader   *c*   1202

Crane, Billy
The Last King - Nichelle D. Tramble   *c*   1197

Hardy, Nina
Shade - Neil Jordan   *t*   890

Larson, Lacy
A Texan's Luck - Jodi Thomas   *r*   394

Maddux, Kyle
Backshooter - Robert J. Randisi   *w*   475

McKeag, Dan
McKeag's Mountain - L.J. Martin   *w*   462

Moss, Gwen
Someone to Watch over Me - Teresa Hill   *i*   1003

Orozco, Roseanne
Day of the Dead - J.A. Jance   *c*   1125

Panov, Mo
The Bourne Legacy - Eric Van Lustbader   *c*   1202

Paulsson, Gilly
Trace - Patricia Cornwell   *c*   1086

Payne, Nola
Little Scarlet - Walter Mosley   *c*   1151

Pilgrim, John
Dry Heat - Jon Talton   *w*   487

Richardson, Baxter
Life Everlasting - Robert Whitlow   *i*   1055

Rose, Julie
Just a Hint—Clint - Lori Foster   *r*   267

Sweet, Victoria
Assassin - Ted Bell   *c*   1073

Wallace, Lillian
Amagansett - Mark Mills   *c*   1149

CRIMINAL

Bays, Buddy
Skin River - Steven Sidor   *m*   185

Beezo, Punchinello
Life Expectancy - Dean R. Koontz   *h*   652

Charon
Sunrise Alley - Catherine Asaro   *s*   714

Chatterfield, Alec
The Life of the World to Come - Kage Baker   *s*   715

Crewe, Nathan
Master of None - N. Lee Wood   *s*   807

Dillon, Sean
Dark Justice - Jack Higgins   *c*   1121

Dyeva
Crux - Albert E. Cowdrey   *s*   735

Farrell, Jesse
World-Walker - Melisa Michaels   *s*   767

Fleischer, Angelika
Sacred Flesh - Robin D. Laws   *f*   559

Gobineau
Blood of the Dragon - C.L. Werner   *f*   590

Hearn, Frank
7,000 Clams - Lee Irby   *t*   884

Hood, Robin
A Cold Summer Night - Trystam Kith   *f*   554

Imbry, Luff
Black Brillion - Matthew Hughes   *s*   754

Jamison, Carl
Shadows in the Darkness - Elaine Cunningham   *f*   522

Maris
Disappearing Act - Margaret Ball   *s*   717

Natas
City of Gold and Lepers - Guy D'Armen   *s*   737

Naulg
Venom's Taste - Lisa Smedman   *f*   582

O'Neal, Cally
Cally's War - John Ringo   *s*   777

Parker
Nobody Runs Forever - Richard Stark   *m*   190

Stuart, John Earl Bill
Cally's War - John Ringo   *s*   777

SunSoar, Dragonstar
Sinner - Sara Douglass   *f*   526

Tarleton, Basil
The Curse of Cain - J. Mark Powell   *w*   473

Turek, Gammis
Marque and Reprisal - Elizabeth Moon   *s*   769

Wiley
Wiley's Shuffle - Lono Waiwaiole   *m*   204

CRITIC

Basset, Marc
Eating Crow - Jay Rayner   *c*   1168

Berger, Mitch
The Burnt Orange Sunrise - David Handler   *m*   98

Schlaegel, Patrick
The Resort - Bentley Little   *h*   658

CYBORG

Mendoza
The Life of the World to Come - Kage Baker   *s*   715

Philips, Adrian
The Demon's Daughter - Emma Holly   *r*   296

Turner
Sunrise Alley - Catherine Asaro   *s*   714

DANCER

Davlin, Kiely
Ghost of a Chance - Flo Fitzpatrick   *r*   265

Kalanskaya, Vera
The Distaff Side - Elizabeth Palmer   *t*   916

Terrell, Lainie
The Nerd Who Loved Me - Vicki Lewis Thompson   *r*   397

DEBUTANTE

Hawthorn, Fiona
Lady Fiasco - Kathleen Baldwin   *r*   218

Reynolds, Catherine
A Hint of Seduction - Amelia Grey   *r*   281

DEITY

Hades
Goddess of Spring - P.C. Cast   *r*   238

Satoris
Banewreaker - Jacqueline Carey   *f*   515

DEMON

Mia
Song of Susannah - Stephen King   *c*   1131

Theron
Dream of Me - Lisa Cach   *r*   234

Yasammez
Shadowmarch. Volume 1 - Tad Williams   *f*   594

DETECTIVE

Shaughnessey, Tripp
The Shaughnessey Accord - Alison Kent   *r*   311

Tanner, Jack
The Curse of Cain - J. Mark Powell   *w*   473

DETECTIVE—AMATEUR

Adler, Irene
Spider Dance - Carole Nelson Douglas   *t*   857
Spider Dance - Carole Nelson Douglas   *m*   61

Alder, Sally
Bye, Bye Love - Virginia Swift   *m*   194

Amalfi, Angelina
Courting Disaster - Joanne Pence   *m*   161

Amiss, Robert
Carnage on the Committee - Ruth Dudley
    Edwards   *m*   68

Andrew, Emily
Pasta Imperfect - Maddy Hunter   *m*   107

Austen, Jaine
Killer Blonde - Laura Levine   *m*   126

Banks, Jo
Satan's Pony - Robin Hathaway   *m*   101

Barr, Temple
Cat in an Orange Twist - Carole Nelson
    Douglas   *m*   60

Bertrand, Carmela
Bound for Murder - Laura Childs   *m*   28

Black, Harrison
Snuffed Out - Tim Myers   *m*   153

Blake, Natasha
Pale as the Dead - Fiona Mountain   *m*   150

Blue, Carolyn
Holy Guacamole! - Nancy Fairbanks   *m*   73

Browning, Theodosia
The Jasmine Moon Murder - Laura Childs   *m*   29

Bryce, Henry
The Gun in Daniel Webster's Bust - Margaret
    Scherf   *m*   182

Carter, Madeline
Mad Money - Linda L. Richards   *r*   365

Cole, Lewis
Buried Dreams - Brendan DuBois   *m*   63

Cosi, Clare
Through the Grinder - Cleo Coyle   *m*   42

Dalrymple, Daisy
A Mourning Wedding - Carola Dunn   *t*   862
A Mourning Wedding - Carola Dunn   *m*   65

Davies, Rebecca
Burning Bridges - Troy Soos   *m*   188

Debbon, Henry
The Black House - Constance Little   *m*   130

Devonshire, Betsy
Crewel Yule - Monica Ferris   *m*   76

Dimato, Angela
Death Takes a Gander - Christine Goff   *m*   86

Dowling, Roger
Requiem for a Realtor - Ralph McInerny   *m*   140

Doyle, Molly
Tagged for Murder - Elaine Flinn   *m*   79

Dyer, Mandy
Taking the Wrap - Dolores Johnson   *m*   110

Felton, Cora
And a Puzzle to Die On - Parnell Hall   *m*   95

Field, Jack
To Collar a Killer - Lee Charles Kelley   *m*   116

Flynn, Judith McMonigle
This Old Souse - Mary Daheim   *m*   50

Gavin, Nora
Lake of Sorrows - Erin Hart   *m*   99

Gilbert, Erin
Death by Inferior Design - Leslie Caine   *m*   26

Good, Sally
A Bond with Death - Bill Crider   *m*   45

Graham, Belle
Wrapped Up in Crosswords - Nero Blanc   *m*   15

Greengrass, Max
The Midnight Band of Mercy - Michael
    Blaine   *m*   14
The Midnight Band of Mercy - Michael
    Blaine   *t*   826

Hawthorne, Helen
Dying to Call You - Elaine Viets   *m*   203

Hoffman, Nick
Tropic of Murder - Lev Raphael   *m*   167

Hollister, Grace
Verse of the Vampyre - Diana Killian   *m*   117

Hudson
Mrs. Hudson and the Spirits' Curse - Martin
    Davies   *m*   53

January, Benjamin
Dead Water - Barbara Hambly   *m*   96
Dead Water - Barbara Hambly   *t*   877

Jarvis, Jarrod
The Actor's Guide to Adultery - Rick Copp   *m*   39

Jeffry, Jane
A Midsummer Night's Scream - Jill Churchill   *m*   30

Kane, Ellianne
A Perfect Gentleman - Barbara Metzger   *r*   343

Knight, Abby
Mum's the Word - Kate Collins   *m*   36

Knight, Roger
Green Thumb - Ralph McInerny   *m*   139

Knott, Deborah
High Country Fall - Margaret Maron   *m*   133

Koerney, Kathryn
Thieves Break In - Cristina Sumners   *m*   192

Landon, Arnold
Headhunter - Roy Lewis   *m*   127

Levy, Rebecca "Bex"
On Thin Ice - Alina Adams   *m*   1

Lowry, Tim
Buried Stuff - Sharon Fiffer   *m*   78

Lucas, Lorinda
Please Do Feed the Cat - Marian Babson   *m*   4

Maguire, Cormac
Lake of Sorrows - Erin Hart   *m*   99

Malone, Ivy
Invisible - Lorena McCourtney   *i*   1025

Martin, Dorothy
Winter of Discontent - Jeanne M. Dams   *m*   51

McCarthy, Gail
Forged - Laura Crum   *m*   47

McMorrow, Jack
Home Body - Gerry Boyle   *m*   20

Meehan, Alvirah
The Christmas Thief - Mary Higgins Clark   *m*   31

Midnight Louie
Cat in an Orange Twist - Carole Nelson
    Douglas   *m*   60

Murdock, Emily
The Gun in Daniel Webster's Bust - Margaret
    Scherf   *m*   182

Newcombe, Chloe
Dead for the Winter - Betsy Thornton   *m*   198
Dead for the Winter - Betsy Thornton   *w*   488

Nichol, Jude
The Hanging in the Hotel - Simon Brett   *m*   21

Nowack, Shelley
A Midsummer Night's Scream - Jill Churchill   *m*   30

O'Malley, John
Wife of Moon - Margaret Coel   *m*   33
Wife of Moon - Margaret Coel   *w*   427

Poggioli, Henry
Dr. Poggioli: Criminologist - T.S. Stribling   *m*   191

Popper, Jessica
Putting on the Dog - Cynthia Baxter   *m*   7

Potter, Beatrix
The Tale of Hill Top Farm - Susan Wittig
    Albert   *m*   2

Quilliam, Margaret "Meg"
Buried by Breakfast - Claudia Bishop   *m*   12

Quilliam, Sarah "Quill"
Buried by Breakfast - Claudia Bishop   *m*   12

Quinn, Nina
A Hoe Lot of Trouble - Heather Webber   *m*   206

Rawlings, John
Death in the Setting Sun - Deryn Lake   *t*   893

Rawlins, Easy
Little Scarlet - Walter Mosley   *c*   1151

St. George, Sweeney
Mansions of the Dead - Sarah Stewart
    Taylor   *m*   197

Schulz, Goldy Bear
Double Shot - Diane Mott Davidson   *m*   52

Seddon, Carole
The Hanging in the Hotel - Simon Brett   *m*   21

Shelley, Wollstonecraft "Wollie"
Dating Is Murder - Harley Jane Kozak   *r*   319

Sheppard, Alex
The Blue Rose - Anthony Eglin   *m*   69

Sheppard, Kate
The Blue Rose - Anthony Eglin   *m*   69

Shimura, Rei
The Pearl Diver - Sujata Massey   *m*   135

Shore, Marla
Died Blonde - Nancy J. Cohen   *m*   34

Simmons, Bernadette "Bernie"
A Catered Wedding - Isis Crawford   *m*   44

Simmons, Libby
A Catered Wedding - Isis Crawford   *m*   44

Spotted Tongue
Tome of Murder - D.R. Meredith *w* 464

Sullivan, Seychelle
Cross Current - Christine Kling *m* 120

Summer, Rose
Hasty Death - Marion Chesney *m* 27

Swensen, Hannah
Sugar Cookie Murder - Joanne Fluke *m* 80

Swinbrooke, Kathryn
A Feast of Poisons - C.L. Grace *m* 89

Talbot, Jeff
Four on the Floor - Deborah Morgan *m* 147

Thorsen, Maggy
Uncommon Grounds - Sandra Balzo *m* 5

Toadfern, Josie
Death by Deep Dish Pie - Sharon Short *m* 184

Travis, Melanie
Jingle Bell Bark - Laurien Berenson *m* 10

Troutbeck, Jack
Carnage on the Committee - Ruth Dudley
    Edwards *m* 68

Trumbull, Victoria
Jack in the Pulpit - Cynthia Riggs *m* 170

Turner, Peggy
Death of a Trickster - Kate Borden *m* 18

Webb, Marshall
Burning Bridges - Troy Soos *m* 188

Wheel, Jane
Buried Stuff - Sharon Fiffer *m* 78

Winston, Alex
Booked for Murder - Tim Myers *m* 152

Wintercraft-Hawkes, Penelope "Penny"
The Famous Flower of Serving Men - Deborah
    Grabien *m* 88

Withers, Hildegarde
The Puzzle of the Blue Banderilla - Stuart
    Palmer *m* 156

DETECTIVE—HOMICIDE

Barron, Rick
The Prince of Beverly Hills - Stuart Woods *t* 957

Becker, Nick
California Girl - T. Jefferson Parker *m* 158

Brown, Floyd
Color Blind - Jonathan Santlofer *m* 179

Dallas, Eve
Divided in Death - J.D. Robb *s* 778

Daniels, Jacqueline
Whiskey Sour - J.A. Konrath *m* 121

Hanrahan, Bill
The Last Dark Place - Stuart M. Kaminsky *m* 112

Jessenovik *Matthew* "Vic"
A Cold and Silent Dying - Eleanor Taylor
    Bland *m* 16

Lieberman, Abe
The Last Dark Place - Stuart M. Kaminsky *m* 112

MacAlister, Marti
A Cold and Silent Dying - Eleanor Taylor
    Bland *m* 16

Mallory, Kathleen
Winter House - Carol O'Connell *m* 155

Piper, Oscar
The Puzzle of the Blue Banderilla - Stuart
    Palmer *m* 156

Reles, Dan
Dirty Sally - Michael Simon *c* 1186

Reynolds, Jael
All Things Hidden - Judy Candis *i* 972

Riker
Winter House - Carol O'Connell *m* 155

Rolvaag, Karl
Skinny Dip - Carl Hiaasen *m* 103

Sakura, Jimmy
A Mourning in Autumn - Harker Moore *m* 146

Vail, Dalton
Died Blonde - Nancy J. Cohen *m* 34

Voort, Conrad
At Hell's Gate - Ethan Black *m* 13

DETECTIVE—POLICE

Bahr, Marshall "Mars"
Alone at Night - K.J. Erickson *m* 71

Beauprix, Anthony
A Perfect Cover - Maureen Tan *r* 390

Best
Dead End - Joan Lock *t* 896

Bryant, Arthur
Full Dark House - Christopher Fowler *m* 82

Burch, Craig
Cold Case Squad - Edna Buchanan *c* 1079

Corey, John
Night Fall - Nelson DeMille *c* 1090

Dresden, Harry
Blood Rites - Jim Butcher *h* 608

Farrell, Harold
The Egyptologist - Arthur Phillips *c* 1165

Ferrell, Harold
The Egyptologist - Arthur Phillips *t* 922

Frisch, Nettie
Alone at Night - K.J. Erickson *m* 71

Gannon, Joe
Out of the Storm - JoAnn Ross *r* 373

Hackney, Joe
The Devil Lives in Glasgow - Gilles Bornais *t* 828

Mandic, Hilda
Very Bad Deaths - Spider Robinson *s* 779

May, John
Full Dark House - Christopher Fowler *m* 82

McAllister, Antonio "Mac"
Deadfall - Patricia H. Rushford *i* 1044

Philips, Adrian
The Demon's Daughter - Emma Holly *r* 296

Quinn, Mike
Through the Grinder - Cleo Coyle *m* 42

Reagan, Abe
I'm Watching You - Karen Rose *r* 372

Riley, K.C.
Cold Case Squad - Edna Buchanan *c* 1079

Stone, Sam
Cold Case Squad - Edna Buchanan *c* 1079

Suggs, Melvin
Little Scarlet - Walter Mosley *c* 1151

Yu, Lily
Tempting Danger - Eileen Wilks *r* 406

Yu Guangming
When Red Is Black - Xiaolong Qiu *m* 166

DETECTIVE—PRIVATE

Alexander, Rachel
Fall Guy - Carol Lea Benjamin *m* 9

Brinker
Choke Point - James C. Mitchell *m* 144

Brodie, Jackson
Case Histories - Kate Atkinson *c* 1067

Bryerly, Dubric
Ghosts in the Snow - Tamara Siler Jones *h* 646

Burby, Nick
Putting on the Dog - Cynthia Baxter *m* 7

Burns, Marty
Apocalypse Now, Voyager - Jay Russell *h* 688

Carruthers, Mitchell
Nerd Gone Wild - Vicki Lewis Thompson *r* 396

Cathcart, Harry
Hasty Death - Marion Chesney *m* 27

Devereau, Lucy
The Darkening - Chandler McGrew *h* 667

Falco, Marcus Didius
Scandal Takes a Holiday - Lindsey Davis *t* 850
Scandal Takes a Holiday - Lindsey Davis *m* 54

Farinelli, Lucy
Trace - Patricia Cornwell *m* 40

Farrell, Elspeth Brodie
The Depths of Solitude - Jo Bannister *m* 6

Fisher, Phryne
The Castlemaine Murders - Kerry
    Greenwood *m* 91
Murder in Montparnasse - Kerry Greenwood *m* 92

Gelman, Gwen "GiGi"
Shadows in the Darkness - Elaine
    Cunningham *h* 623
Shadows in the Darkness - Elaine
    Cunningham *f* 522

Gemina, Flavia
The Twelve Tasks of Flavia Gemina - Caroline
    Lawrence *t* 895

Gordianus the Finder
The Judgment of Caesar - Steven Saylor *m* 180

Gordon, Diana
Snap Shot - Meg Chittenden *r* 240

Guilfoyle
Counterfeit Kings - Adam Connell *s* 732

Halliday, Hal
New York Dreams - Eric Brown *s* 724

Hamilton, Kate
The Trouble with Valentine's Day - Rachel
    Gibson *r* 272

Hawkins, Danielle "Danni"
Arouse Suspicion - Maureen McKade *r* 337

Hayle, Tamara
Dying in the Dark - Valerie Wilson Wesley *m* 207

Holmes, Sherlock
The Final Solution - Michael Chabon *t* 832
Mrs. Hudson and the Spirits' Curse - Martin
    Davies *m* 53
Sherlock Holmes: The Hidden Years - Michael
    Kurland *m* 124
Spider Dance - Carole Nelson Douglas *m* 61

Jones, Lena
Desert Shadows - Betty Webb *m* 205

Kiernan, Top
Buzz Riff - Sam Hill *m* 105

Knight, Philip
Green Thumb - Ralph McInerny *m* 139

LaFlam, Joe
Bye Bye Bertie - Rick Dewhurst *i* 980

Leaphorn, Joe
Skeleton Man - Tony Hillerman *m* 106
Skeleton Man - Tony Hillerman *w* 451

DIPLOMAT

DIRECTOR

DIVORCED PERSON

DOCTOR

Swinbrooke, Kathryn
A Feast of Poisons - C.L. Grace   *m*   89

Templeman, Hyman
Deficiency - Andrew Neiderman   *h*   674

Timoteo
Don't Move - Margaret Mazzantini   *c*   1140

Washington, David
Loving Delilah - Candice Poarch   *r*   361

DRIFTER

Donovan, Zeke
Donovan's Dove - Joseph A. West   *w*   492

Dugan, Chester
All the Lonely People - David B. Silva   *h*   692

Ormond, Peter
Territorial Rough Rider - Tim Champlin   *w*   425

Teddy
Waiting for Teddy Williams - Howard Frank
    Mosher   *c*   1150

DRIVER

Filomon
Tortuga - Rudolfo Anaya   *w*   413

Reavley, Judith
Shoulder the Sky - Anne Perry   *m*   163
Shoulder the Sky - Anne Perry   *t*   921

DRUG DEALER

Crane, Billy
The Last King - Nichelle D. Tramble   *c*   1197

Mendoza, Teresa
The Queen of the South - Arturo Perez-
    Reverte   *c*   1164

Shiflett, Junior
Delivery - Ben Daitz   *w*   434

EDITOR

Crandall, Harry
A Hard Man Is Good to Find - Jane
    Blackwood   *r*   225

Dalhousie, Isabel
The Sunday Philosophy Club - Alexander McCall
    Smith   *c*   1141

Geller, Adam
I Am Charlotte Simmons - Tom Wolfe   *c*   1211

Graham, Belle
Wrapped Up in Crosswords - Nero Blanc   *m*   15

Jones, Ellen
A Shred of Evidence - Kathy Herman   *i*   1000

McLane, Jaimie
A Hard Man Is Good to Find - Jane
    Blackwood   *r*   225

Parish, Cole
All She Ever Wanted - Barbara Freethy   *r*   268

Van Schuyler Durango, Lacey
To Tempt a Texan - Georgina Gentry   *r*   271

Wright, Rachel
The Hidden - Sarah Pinborough   *h*   681

EMPLOYER

Andrews, Rachel
Bloody Hills - Charles G. West   *w*   490

Winchuster, Winifred
Land Sakes - Margaret A. Graham   *i*   993

Wolf
Drive Me Crazy - Eric Jerome Dickey   *c*   1093

ENGINEER

Mannschlieter, Otto
The Silver Yoke - Roland Cheek   *w*   426

ENTERTAINER

Arbuckle, Roscoe "Fatty"
I, Fatty - Jerry Stahl   *c*   1192

Cody, William F. "Buffalo Bill"
East of the Border - Johnny D. Boggs   *w*   417

Gwirion
The Fool's Tale - Nicole Galland   *t*   871

Petrovna, Akilina
The Romanov Prophecy - Steve Berry   *m*   11
The Romanov Prophecy - Steve Berry   *c*   1074

Rey, Vishram
River of Gods - Ian McDonald   *s*   763

EXPATRIATE

Alakusoglu, Kerim
Snow - Orhan Pamuk   *c*   1162

Horolfsdaughter, Jessa
Snow-Walker - Catherine Fisher   *f*   534

Julian
The Bright and the Dark - Michele M.
    Welch   *f*   589

Kaspar
Exile's Return - Raymond E. Feist   *f*   533

Martin, Dorothy
Winter of Discontent - Jeanne M. Dams   *m*   51

EXPLORER

Ardan, Francis
City of Gold and Lepers - Guy D'Armen   *s*   737

Shee, Youn
Radiant - James Alan Gardner   *s*   747

Tut
Radiant - James Alan Gardner   *s*   747

FARMER

Bardin, William
Billy Bardin and the Witness Tree - Mary E.
    Penson   *w*   472

Bonner, Nathaniel
Fire Along the Sky - Sara Donati   *t*   855

Brand, Luke
Dark Harvest - Karen Harper   *r*   285

Egan, Cora
The Real Minerva - Mary Sharratt   *t*   938

Eliot, Tom
Prometheus Road - Bruce Balfour   *s*   716

Gray, Jordan
Devil's Kin - Charles G. West   *w*   491

Gruber, Jim
Following the Harvest - Fred Harris   *w*   447

Haley, Bob
Following the Harvest - Fred Harris   *w*   447

Maxwell, Ewan
Children of the Glens - Gwen Kirkwood   *r*   316

Watson, Luke
When the Sky Rained Dust - Patrick Dearen   *w*   436

Wortham, Sam
Katie's Dream - Leisha Kelly   *i*   1013

FBI AGENT

Alexander, Simon
Dating Is Murder - Harley Jane Kozak   *r*   319

Atwater, Dan
Through Violet Eyes - Stephen Woodworth   *h*   709

Grayson, Erin
Master of the Night - Angela Knight   *r*   318

Hallbrooke, Jack
Always - Jude Deveraux   *r*   253

Lewis, Grant
All Things Hidden - Judy Candis   *i*   972

Lopez, Diane
Blood Retribution - David Thurlo   *m*   200

MacCormack, Kevin "Mack"
Undercover Blessings - Deb Kastner   *i*   1012

Marshall, Frank
D.B. - Elwood Reid   *c*   1170

Mayfield, Kate
Night Fall - Nelson DeMille   *c*   1090

McTeague, Lila
The Witch's Tongue - James D. Doss   *w*   437
The Witch's Tongue - James D. Doss   *m*   59

Ness, Eliot
Road to Purgatory - Max Allan Collins   *t*   843

Pendergast, Aloysius
Brimstone - Douglas Preston   *h*   683

Pilgrim, John
Dry Heat - Jon Talton   *w*   487

Preston, Calder
Dangerous Curves - Jacey Ford   *r*   266

FEMME FATALE

Fritz-Allan, Gerda
Children of the Glens - Gwen Kirkwood   *r*   316

FIANCE(E)

Cutter, Jamie
To Collar a Killer - Lee Charles Kelley   *m*   116

Dreyfuss, Nicole
Caught in the Act - Pam McCutcheon   *r*   336

Faber, Mitchell
In the Night Room - Peter Straub   *h*   697

Garcia, Leonida
Mokelumne Gold - Major Mitchell   *w*   465

Jernigan, A.J.
Hissy Fit - Mary Kay Andrews   *c*   1065

Liddicote, Clare
The Missing Link - Katharine Farrer   *m*   75

Pepper, Amanda
Till the End of Tom - Gillian Roberts   *m*   172

Richmond, Scott
Caught in the Act - Pam McCutcheon   *r*   336

Woodrow, Candace
The Bride Wore Chocolate - Shirley Jump   *r*   305

FILMMAKER

Foster, Tony
Smoke and Shadows - Tanya Huff   *h*   642

Pelindrake, Arra
Smoke and Shadows - Tanya Huff   *h*   642

Character Description Index

Roth, William
The Manor - Scott Nicholson   *h*   676

FINANCIER

Henley, Will
Too Close to the Sun - Diana Dempsey   *r*   251

FIRE FIGHTER

Wollf, Paul
Pyro - Earl Emerson   *m*   70

FISHERMAN

Calhoun, Stoney
Bitch Creek - William G. Tapply   *m*   196

Labarde, Conrad
Amagansett - Mark Mills   *m*   143
Amagansett - Mark Mills   *c*   1149
Amagansett - Mark Mills   *t*   907

Takahashi, Jiro
Days of Infamy - Harry Turtledove   *t*   947
Days of Infamy - Harry Turtledove   *s*   797

FOREMAN

Gunderson, Charley
Territorial Rough Rider - Tim Champlin   *w*   425

FOSTER PARENT

McBain, Robbie
Tempting the Highlander - Janet Chapman   *r*   239

Prescott, Katrina
As You Wish - Francine Matthews   *r*   334

FRIEND

Alviso, Jaime
North with De Anza - Dorothy Ward
   Erskine   *w*   439

Bear
Blood River - Jory Sherman   *w*   482

Behan, John
Trouble in Tombstone - Richard S. Wheeler   *w*   494

Bergman, Chris
Starlight Comes Home - Janet Muirhead
   Hill   *w*   450

Cole, Steve
Lost in Rooville - Ray Blackston   *i*   968

Connie
Loop Group - Larry McMurtry   *c*   1146

Ellsworth, Steve
Bucked Out in Dodge - Ralph Compton   *w*   429

Fassig, Roger
Billy Bardin and the Witness Tree - Mary E.
   Penson   *w*   472

Feddens, Toby
The Line of Beauty - Alan Hollinghurst   *c*   1122

Flood, Anna
The Green Age of Asher Witherow - M. Allen
   Cunningham   *w*   433

Flood, Kitty
The Parts - Keith Ridgway   *c*   1172

Jenning, Michael
Chasing Destiny - Stephen Overholser   *w*   471

Joseph
Pearl - Mary Gordon   *c*   1112

Lessing, Henry
Trouble's Messenger - Max Brand   *w*   419

Manko, Bass
Winter Kill - Cotton Smith   *w*   484

Me
Johnny Blue and the Texas Rangers - Joseph A.
   West   *w*   493

Murray
The London Pigeon Wars - Patrick Neate   *c*   1155

Ned
Snowed In - Christina Bartolomeo   *c*   1071

Nichol, Jude
The Hanging in the Hotel - Simon Brett   *m*   21

Njoroge
The In-Between World of Vikram Lall - M.G.
   Vassanji   *c*   1203

Nowack, Shelley
A Midsummer Night's Scream - Jill Churchill   *m*   30

O'Brien, Dan
The Underground River - Jeanne Williams   *w*   497

Phoebe
The Death of Mr. Love - Indra Sinha   *c*   1187

Redfield, Maceo
The Last King - Nichelle D. Tramble   *c*   1197

Roger
Magic Seeds - V.S. Naipaul   *c*   1153

Simpson, Terri
Tall, Dark, and Hungry - Lynsay Sands   *r*   377

Standing Bear, Henry
The Cold Dish - Craig Johnson   *w*   455

Teddy
Waiting for Teddy Williams - Howard Frank
   Mosher   *c*   1150

FRONTIERSMAN

Johnson, John
The Mask of Red Death - Harold Schechter   *t*   934

Lessing, Henry
Trouble's Messenger - Max Brand   *w*   419

FRONTIERSWOMAN

Billy
The Lutheran - Jack Britton Sullivan   *w*   486

Morgan, Mercy
Blood River - Jory Sherman   *w*   482

FUGITIVE

Ardacris, Serrah
The Covenant Rising - Stan Nicholls   *f*   572

Bryton, Samantha
Sunrise Alley - Catherine Asaro   *s*   714

Casini, Maria
Forced Conversion - Donald J. Bingle   *s*   722

Cooper, D.B.
D.B. - Elwood Reid   *c*   1170

DiSilvio, Allegria
Coyote Rising - Allen Steele   *s*   791

Elzith
The Bright and the Dark - Michele M.
   Welch   *f*   589

Galloway, Lacey
Flee the Night - Susan May Warren   *i*   1054

Hawthorne, Helen
Dying to Call You - Elaine Viets   *m*   203

Haydn
Haydn of Mars - Al Sarrantonio   *s*   784

Kline, Mick
Storm Gathering - Rene Gutteridge   *i*   995

Lynx, Philip "Flinx"
Sliding Scales - Alan Dean Foster   *s*   745

O'Hara, Martin Konner
The Dragon Circle - Irene Radford   *s*   774

Peck, Graham
Tagged - Robert L. Wise   *i*   1061

Red, Jenny
The Shadow Runners - Liz Maverick   *s*   760

Spring, Jethro
The Silver Yoke - Roland Cheek   *w*   426

Turner
Sunrise Alley - Catherine Asaro   *s*   714

GAMBLER

Buchanan, Thaddeus
Loving Mercy - Teresa Bodwell   *r*   230

Donovan, Zeke
Donovan's Dove - Joseph A. West   *w*   492

Dupree, Camille
Twice Blessed - Sharon Gillenwater   *i*   989

Holliday, John Henry "Doc"
The Hebrew Kid and the Apache Maiden - Robert J.
   Avrech   *w*   414
Trouble in Tombstone - Richard S. Wheeler   *w*   494
Vengeance Rider - Ralph Compton   *w*   431

Vance, Ike
Donovan's Dove - Joseph A. West   *w*   492

Wiley
Wiley's Shuffle - Lono Waiwaiole   *m*   204

GAME WARDEN

Marlin, John
Flat Crazy - Ben Rehder   *m*   168
Flat Crazy - Ben Rehder   *w*   478

Marquez, John
Night Game - Kirk Russell   *m*   178

Pickett, Joe
Trophy Hunt - C.J. Box   *m*   19

GARDENER

Garrett, Mibby
Like a Watered Garden - Patti Ann Hill   *i*   1002

GENEALOGIST

Blake, Natasha
Pale as the Dead - Fiona Mountain   *m*   150

GENETICALLY ALTERED BEING

Champagne
Edenborn - Nick Sagan   *s*   782

Haji
Edenborn - Nick Sagan   *s*   782

Lunae
Banner of Souls - Liz Williams   *s*   805

Lys, Yskatarina
Banner of Souls - Liz Williams   *s*   805

Vashti
Edenborn - Nick Sagan   *s*   782

GENIUS

Tomlinson, Sighurdhr
Tampa Burn - Randy Wayne White   *m*   209

GENTLEMAN

Beverly, Vincent
The Christmas Matchmaker - Jeanne Savery   *r*   378

Browning, Richard
The Affair at Greengage Manor - Mona
    Gedney   *r*   269

Campion, Peregrine
A Worthy Opponent - Louise Bergin   *r*   220

Darcy, Fitzwilliam
Suspense and Sensibility - Carrie A. Bebris   *t*   820

Halliday, Travis
On the Twelfth Day of Christmas - Mona
    Gedney   *r*   270

Langham, Bertie
The Distaff Side - Elizabeth Palmer   *t*   916

Oliver, Flynn
Miss Fortune - Julia London   *r*   326

Sutherland, Grant
The Price of Pleasure - Kresley Cole   *r*   243

Walton, Tobias
Fiddler's Green - Van Reid   *t*   926

Whittaker, Derek
Under a Lucky Star - Diane Farr   *r*   259

GENTLEWOMAN

Bennet, Kitty
Suspense and Sensibility - Carrie A. Bebris   *t*   820

Blanchard, Meg
The Siren Queen - Fiona Buckley   *t*   831

Bransford, Cordelia "Corey"
Cordelia's Corinthian - Victoria Hinshaw   *r*   294

Darcy, Elizabeth Bennet
Suspense and Sensibility - Carrie A. Bebris   *t*   820

Dearborn, Annabelle
Deceiving Miss Dearborn - Laurie Bishop   *r*   224

Delamere, Helen Frances
The Palace of Heavenly Pleasure - Adam
    Williams   *t*   954

Delaney, Maggie
The Improper Wife - Diane Perkins   *r*   360

Dunsworthy, Bianca
The Perfect Bride - Jo Ann Ferguson   *r*   263

Eckersley, Sarah
Hardly a Husband - Rebecca Hagan Lee   *r*   322

Fotheringay, Lucy
A Mourning Wedding - Carola Dunn   *t*   862

Givens, Marianna
A Beggar at the Gate - Thalassa Ali   *t*   811

Heloise
Farewell, My Only One - Antoine Audouard   *t*   816

Leigh, Violet
On the Twelfth Day of Christmas - Mona
    Gedney   *r*   270

Lytton, Alexandra
The Affair at Greengage Manor - Mona
    Gedney   *r*   269

Lytton, Eliza
Captain Hawkins' Dilemma - Maria Greene   *r*   280

Marsh, Anne
Night of Sin - Julia Ross   *r*   374

Maynard, Emily
The Lady of Cawnpore - Elisabeth McNeill   *t*   904

Nash, Helena
My Pleasure - Connie Brockway   *r*   232

Randall, Marian
The General's Daughter - Kate Huntington   *r*   298

Reynolds, Catherine
A Hint of Seduction - Amelia Grey   *r*   281

Shelton, Judith
A Worthy Opponent - Louise Bergin   *r*   220

Stewart, Lavinia
The Captain's Mermaid - Mary Blayney   *r*   228

Thorncroft, Mariah
Moonlight and Mischief - Rhonda Woodward   *r*   409

Tucker, Arabella
A Wicked Wench - Anne Herries   *r*   291

Tucker, Nan
A Wicked Wench - Anne Herries   *r*   291

Valentine, Judy
Mysterious Ways - Terry Burns   *w*   421

Wesley, Evelina
An Adventurous Lady - Valerie King   *r*   315

GIRLFRIEND

Bennett, Felicia
The Last King - Nichelle D. Tramble   *c*   1197

Finley, Amber
In the Moon of Red Ponies - James Lee
    Burke   *c*   1080

Moody, Melissa
Strange but True - John Searles   *c*   1182

Young, Sarah
Judgment Day - Frank Roderus   *w*   479

Zofia
Cruisers - Craig Nova   *c*   1158

GOVERNESS

Bransford, Cordelia "Corey"
Cordelia's Corinthian - Victoria Hinshaw   *r*   294

Lovell, Titania "Ann"
The Mistress of Trevelyan - Jennifer St. Giles   *r*   385

Lytton, Alexandra
The Affair at Greengage Manor - Mona
    Gedney   *r*   269

Ross, Kathy
Wings of Riches - Al Lacy   *i*   1017

GOVERNMENT OFFICIAL

Artois, Pierre
Saucer: The Conquest - Stephen Coonts   *s*   734

Baldwin de Furnshill
The Outlaws of Ennor - Michael Jecks   *t*   887
The Tolls of Death - Michael Jecks   *t*   888

Becha, Rilsin Sae
The Blood of the Land - Noel-Anne Brennan   *f*   509

Belov, Josef
Dark Justice - Jack Higgins   *c*   1121

Benton, Brad
Impeachable Offense - Neesa Hart   *i*   998

Cromwell, Thomas
Dark Fire - C.J. Sansom   *t*   933

Diamond, Venus
The Good Diamond - Skye Kathleen Moody   *m*   145

Dimato, Angela
Death Takes a Gander - Christine Goff   *m*   86

Ernst, Reinhard
Garden of Beasts - Jeffery Deaver   *c*   1088

Frankland, Shan
City of Pearl - Karen Traviss   *s*   794
Crossing the Line - Karen Traviss   *s*   795

Governor
Serafina's Stories - Rudolfo Anaya   *w*   412

har Aralis, Caeru
The Shades of Time and Memory - Storm
    Constantine   *s*   733

Hiyashi
The Painting - Nina Schuyler   *t*   935

Hogwood, Dolores
The Jaguar Knights - Dave Duncan   *f*   528

Lall, Vikram
The In-Between World of Vikram Lall - M.G.
    Vassanji   *c*   1203

Marcus, Joel
Trace - Patricia Cornwell   *c*   1086

Miller, John "Jack"
Undercover with the Mob - Elizabeth
    Bevarly   *r*   222

Nilis
Exultant - Stephen Baxter   *s*   720

Reza, Salman
Offspring - Steven Harper   *s*   751

Sage, Ramsey
The Thing about Men - Elizabeth Bevarly   *r*   221

Subah, Vasant
Master of None - N. Lee Wood   *s*   807

Vajjandara, Chulayen
Disappearing Act - Margaret Ball   *s*   717

Valinov, Gholic
Grey Knights - Ben Counter   *f*   520

Zara
The Wilding - C.S. Friedman   *s*   746

Ziegler, Kevin
Convenient Disposal - Steven F. Havill   *w*   448

GRANDPARENT

Daniels, Esther
The Gift of Christmas Present - Melody
    Carlson   *i*   974

Frost
Stop That Girl - Elizabeth McKenzie   *c*   1144

Gilkyson, Einar
An Unfinished Life - Mark Spragg   *c*   1191
An Unfinished Life - Mark Spragg   *w*   485

Naini
The Last Storyteller - Diane Noble   *i*   1037

Samantha
Sam's Letters to Jennifer - James Patterson   *c*   1163

Staramajka
The Turk and My Mother - Mary Helen
    Stefaniak   *c*   1193

GUARD

Garcia, Gaspar
Serafina's Stories - Rudolfo Anaya   *w*   412

Henderson, Jim
The Prison - R. Patrick Gates   *h*   633

Saget, Tim
The Prison - R. Patrick Gates   *h*   633

Roth, Philip
The Plot Against America - Philip Roth   *c*   1175
The Plot Against America - Philip Roth   *s*   781

Ruth, Babe
7,000 Clams - Lee Irby   *t*   884

Shakespeare, William
Time's Fool - Leonard Tourney   *m*   201
Young Will - Bruce Cook   *t*   845

Sherman, William Tecumseh
A Distant Flame - Philip Lee Williams   *t*   955
Savannah: Or, A Gift for Mr. Lincoln - John
   Jakes   *t*   886

Smith, Al
Return Engagement - Harry Turtledove   *t*   948

Smith Stanley, Edward
Life Mask - Emma Donoghue   *t*   856
Life Mask - Emma Donoghue   *c*   1094

Smithson, Harriet
Ophelia's Fan - Christine Balint   *t*   818

Solomon
Wisdom's Daughter - India Edghill   *t*   865

Spicer, Jack
One King, One Soldier - Alexander C. Irvine   *f*   549

Tecumseh
Into the Prairie - Rosanne Bittner   *t*   825

Toussaint L'Ouverture, Pierre Dominique
The Stone That the Builder Refused - Madison Smartt
   Bell   *t*   821
The Stone That the Builder Refused - Madison Smartt
   Bell   *c*   1072

Tudor, Owen
White Rose - R. Garcia y Robertson   *t*   872

Villegagnon, Durand de
Brazil Red - Jean-Christophe Rufin   *t*   931

Wellesley, Arthur
Jonathan Strange & Mr. Norrell - Susanna
   Clarke   *t*   837

Wevill, Assia Gutmann
Little Fugue - Robert Anderson   *t*   813

Winchell, Walter
The Plot Against America - Philip Roth   *s*   781
The Plot Against America - Philip Roth   *t*   929

Woolson, Constance Fenimore
Author, Author - David Lodge   *t*   897
Author, Author - David Lodge   *c*   1138

HOLOCAUST VICTIM

Friedman, Henry
Joy Comes in the Morning - Jonathan
   Rosen   *c*   1174

HOMOSEXUAL

DuBois, Isaiah
Domino - J. Lea Koretsky   *w*   459

Guest, Nick
The Line of Beauty - Alan Hollinghurst   *c*   1122

Hal
A Seahorse Year - Stacey D'Erasmo   *c*   1091

Justice, Benjamin
Moth and Flame - John Morgan Wilson   *m*   210

HORSE TRAINER

Kerrec
The Mountain's Call - Caitlin Brennan   *f*   508

Valeria
The Mountain's Call - Caitlin Brennan   *f*   508

HOTEL OWNER

Chizek, Bud
Osprey Island - Thisbe Nissen   *c*   1157

Chizek, Nancy
Osprey Island - Thisbe Nissen   *c*   1157

HOUSEKEEPER

Grace
The Sunday Philosophy Club - Alexander McCall
   Smith   *c*   1141

Hudson
Mrs. Hudson and the Spirits' Curse - Martin
   Davies   *m*   53

Jeffries
Mrs. Jeffries Stalks the Hunter - Emily
   Brightwell   *m*   22

Watkins, Jane
The Prayer of the Night Shepherd - Phil
   Rickman   *h*   684

HOUSEWIFE

Ravenson, Wendy
The Last Guardian of Everness - John C.
   Wright   *f*   596

Starchild, Elena
The Three Sisters - Rebecca Locksley   *f*   562

Towne, Ayinde
Little Earthquakes - Jennifer Weiner   *c*   1206

HUNTER

Craddock, Billy Don
Flat Crazy - Ben Rehder   *w*   478

Graybrook, Dorn
The Rage - Richard Lee Byers   *f*   513

Locke, Noah
Chasing Destiny - Stephen Overholser   *w*   471

Mandenauer, Edward
Blue Moon - Lori Handeland   *r*   283

Turnstone, Will
The Rage - Richard Lee Byers   *f*   513

IMMIGRANT

Alviso, Jaime
North with De Anza - Dorothy Ward
   Erskine   *w*   439

Chatterjee, Tara
The Tree Bride - Bharati Mukherjee   *t*   910

Herrnfeld, Antonie
The Devil in Buenos Aires - Lily Powell   *t*   923

Isaacson, Ariel
The Hebrew Kid and the Apache Maiden - Robert J.
   Avrech   *w*   414

Peralta, Pedro
North with De Anza - Dorothy Ward
   Erskine   *w*   439

Vogt, Katya
Katya - Sandra Birdsell   *t*   824

IMPOSTER

Bran, Sylvia
The Beautiful Inez - Bart Schneider   *c*   1178

Lindley, Kat
Dark Harvest - Karen Harper   *r*   285

Taylor, Amos
Mysterious Ways - Terry Burns   *w*   421
Mysterious Ways - Terry Burns   *i*   971

Yamamoto, Greg
The Secret Beau - Annette Mahon   *r*   331

IMPOVERISHED

Harrison, Sarah
An Honorable Match - Laura Paquet   *r*   357

Italia
Don't Move - Margaret Mazzantini   *c*   1140

Peyton, Annabelle
Secrets of a Summer Night - Lisa Kleypas   *r*   317

Tucker, Arabella
A Wicked Wench - Anne Herries   *r*   291

Tucker, Nan
A Wicked Wench - Anne Herries   *r*   291

Wellstone, Stony
A Perfect Gentleman - Barbara Metzger   *r*   343

INDIAN

American Horse, Johnny
In the Moon of Red Ponies - James Lee
   Burke   *c*   1080

Bear
Blood River - Jory Sherman   *w*   482

Beaver
The Pipestone Quest - Don Coldsmith   *t*   841

Black-spot
Friday, the Arapaho Boy - Marc Simmons   *w*   483

Chee, Jim
Skeleton Man - Tony Hillerman   *w*   451
Skeleton Man - Tony Hillerman   *m*   106

Geronimo
The Last Campaign - Tim Champlin   *w*   424

Holden, Vicky
Wife of Moon - Margaret Coel   *m*   33
Wife of Moon - Margaret Coel   *w*   427

Katanaquat
The Rain from God - Mark Ammerman   *i*   962

Leaphorn, Joe
Skeleton Man - Tony Hillerman   *m*   106
Skeleton Man - Tony Hillerman   *w*   451

Lone Eagle, Adam
Wife of Moon - Margaret Coel   *w*   427
Wife of Moon - Margaret Coel   *m*   33

Lozen
The Hebrew Kid and the Apache Maiden - Robert J.
   Avrech   *w*   414

Manuelito, Bernadette "Bernie"
Skeleton Man - Tony Hillerman   *m*   106

Meadowlark
Beauty for Ashes - Win Blevins   *t*   827
Beauty for Ashes - Win Blevins   *w*   416

Orozco, Emma
Day of the Dead - J.A. Jance   *c*   1125

Pale Moon
Little Brother Real Snake - Billy Moore   *w*   466

Red Cloud
The Indian Agent - Dan O'Brien   *w*   469
The Indian Agent - Dan O'Brien   *t*   914

Red Squirrel
Little Brother Real Snake - Billy Moore   *w*   466

Serafina
Serafina's Stories - Rudolfo Anaya   *w*   412

Standing Bear, Henry
The Cold Dish - Craig Johnson   *w*   455

Tecumseh
Into the Prairie - Rosanne Bittner   *t*   825

Tuve, Billy
Skeleton Man - Tony Hillerman   *w*   451

Wild Fire
Little Brother Real Snake - Billy Moore   *w*   466

Wind Walker
Wind Walker - Cassie Edwards   *r*   257

INNKEEPER

Flynn, Judith McMonigle
This Old Souse - Mary Daheim   *m*   50

Foley, Ben
The Prayer of the Night Shepherd - Phil Rickman   *h*   684

Kent, Ellen
Return to Me - Shannon McKenna   *r*   339

Quilliam, Sarah "Quill"
Buried by Breakfast - Claudia Bishop   *m*   12

Winston, Alex
Booked for Murder - Tim Myers   *m*   152

INTERIOR DECORATOR

Bryce, Henry
The Gun in Daniel Webster's Bust - Margaret Scherf   *m*   182

Gilbert, Erin
Death by Inferior Design- Leslie Caine   *m*   26

Murdock, Emily
The Gun in Daniel Webster's Bust - Margaret Scherf   *m*   182

Murdock, Keeley
Hissy Fit - Mary Kay Andrews   *c*   1065
Hissy Fit - Mary Kay Andrews   *r*   214

Sullivan, Steve
Death by Inferior Design- Leslie Caine   *m*   26

INVALID

Holden, Wesley
Missing - Sharon Sala   *r*   376

Starlight, Christine
The Autumn Castle - Kim Wilkins   *f*   593

INVENTOR

Edison, Thomas
Divine Sarah - Adam Braver   *t*   829

Mudrin, Sola Dira
The Blood of the Land - Noel-Anne Brennan   *f*   509

Rathbone, Henry
A Christmas Visitor - Anne Perry   *m*   162

INVESTIGATOR

Oliver, Flynn
Miss Fortune - Julia London   *r*   326

Reed, Lacie
A Perfect Cover - Maureen Tan   *r*   390

Russell, Josiah
Mokelumne Gold - Major Mitchell   *w*   465

JOURNALIST

Amalfi, Angelina
Courting Disaster - Joanne Pence   *m*   161

Baker, Vince
Divine Sarah - Adam Braver   *t*   829

Ballinger, Nina
Invitation to a Hanging - Robert J. Randisi   *w*   476

Becker, Andy
California Girl - T. Jefferson Parker   *m*   158

Blue, Carolyn
Holy Guacamole! - Nancy Fairbanks   *m*   73

Bly, Nellie
Spider Dance - Carole Nelson Douglas   *m*   61
Spider Dance - Carole Nelson Douglas   *t*   857

Browne, Verity
The More Deceived - David Roberts   *m*   171

Cole, Lewis
Buried Dreams - Brendan DuBois   *m*   63

Conner, Jane
The Eggnog Chronicles - Carly Alexander   *r*   211

Corso, Frank
Red Tide - G.M. Ford   *m*   81

Dalrymple, Daisy
A Mourning Wedding - Carola Dunn   *m*   65
A Mourning Wedding - Carola Dunn   *t*   862

Duncan, Hugh
Girl Gone Wild - Joanne Rock   *r*   370

Elsa
Nights of Rain and Stars - Maeve Binchy   *c*   1077

Flurry, Katrina
The Samms Agenda - Alison Kent   *r*   310

Grant, Jamie
Crisscross - F. Paul Wilson   *h*   706

Greengrass, Max
The Midnight Band of Mercy - Michael Blaine   *t*   826
The Midnight Band of Mercy - Michael Blaine   *m*   14

Hamilton, Nick
Dark Storm - Kel Richards   *i*   1042

Hopewell, Stephen
Savannah: Or, A Gift for Mr. Lincoln - John Jakes   *t*   886

Hopkins, Alison
The Big Love - Sarah Dunn   *c*   1096

Jackson, Cadillac
Soul City - Toure   *c*   1196

Jennifer
Sam's Letters to Jennifer - James Patterson   *c*   1163

Joules, Olivia
Olivia Joules and the Overactive Imagination - Helen Fielding   *c*   1104

Justice, Benjamin
Moth and Flame - John Morgan Wilson   *m*   210

Kelly, Stanford J. "Skelly"
The Warlord's Son - Dan Fesperman   *m*   77

Keyes, Megan
The Burning of Rachel Hayes - Doug Allyn   *t*   812

Lincoln, Amy
Any Place I Hang My Hat - Susan Isaacs   *c*   1124

MacKenzie, Art
The Revealing - L.A. Marzulli   *i*   1023

Masterson, Bat
The Funeral of Tanner Moody - John Jakes   *w*   453

McLane, Jaimie
A Hard Man Is Good to Find - Jane Blackwood   *r*   225

McMorrow, Jack
Home Body - Gerry Boyle   *m*   20

Monaghan, Tess
By a Spider's Thread - Laura Lippman   *m*   129

Phillips, Savannah
Savannah from Savannah - Denise Hildreth   *i*   1001

Richler, Joseph
An Obituary for Major Reno - Richard S. Wheeler   *t*   952

Samuels, Elizabeth
Very Truly Sexy - Dawn Atkins   *r*   216

Stewart, Laurel
Out of the Storm - JoAnn Ross   *r*   373

Stone, Laura
Absent Friends - S.J. Rozan   *m*   177

Szabo, Annie
The Vanished Priestess - Meredith Blevins   *m*   17

Tomm, Paul
The Geographer's Library - Jon Fasman   *c*   1102

Van Schuyler Durango, Lacey
To Tempt a Texan - Georgina Gentry   *r*   271

Webb, Marshall
Burning Bridges - Troy Soos   *m*   188

Winchell, Walter
The Plot Against America - Philip Roth   *s*   781
The Plot Against America - Philip Roth   *t*   929

JUDGE

Knott, Deborah
High Country Fall - Margaret Maron   *m*   133

KNIGHT

Able
The Wizard - Gene Wolfe   *f*   595

Baldwin de Furnshill
The Outlaws of Ennor - Michael Jecks   *t*   887
The Tolls of Death - Michael Jecks   *t*   888

Barret, Roarke
The Knight's Redemption - Joanne Rock   *r*   371

Clothar
The Lance Thrower - Jack Whyte   *t*   953
The Lance Thrower - Jack Whyte   *f*   592

Cully
Paladins - Joel Rosenberg   *f*   580

deSteny, Hugh
A Cold Summer Night - Trystam Kith   *h*   651
A Cold Summer Night - Trystam Kith   *f*   554

FitzSimon, Sabin
The Falcons of Montabard - Elizabeth Chadwick   *t*   833

Hafydd
The Shadow Roads - Sean Russell   *f*   581

Jermayan
To Light a Candle - Mercedes Lackey   *f*   558

Kellen
To Light a Candle - Mercedes Lackey   *f*   558

Lynx
The Jaguar Knights - Dave Duncan   *f*   528

MeqVren, Neil
The Charnel Prince - J. Gregory Keyes   *f*   552

Peter de Montselm
Hidden Honor - Anne Stuart   *r*   388

Strongfist, Edmund
The Falcons of Montabard - Elizabeth
   Chadwick   *t*   833

Talmor
The Queen's Knight - Deborah Chester   *f*   516

Tristan
The Lady of the Sea - Rosalind Miles   *t*   906

Wolf
The Jaguar Knights - Dave Duncan   *f*   528

LAIRD

Campbell, Niall
Child of the Mist - Kathleen Morgan   *i*   1027

MacDougall, Duncan Angus
A Man in a Kilt - Sandy Blair   *r*   227

LANDLORD

Ferry, Inez
The Rottweiler - Ruth Rendell   *m*   169

Joliffe, Euphemia
The Nebuly Coat - John Meade Falkner   *h*   627

Peerbaugh, Evelyn
A Place to Belong - Vonette Z. Bright   *i*   970

LANDOWNER

Frake, Jack
Sparrowhawk. Book 3: Caxton - Edward
   Cline   *t*   839

Kenrick, Hugh
Sparrowhawk. Book 3: Caxton - Edward
   Cline   *t*   839

LANDSCAPER

Davis, Lux
Lux - Maria Flook   *c*   1107

Kitridge, Logan
Blue Dahlia - Nora Roberts   *r*   366

Quinn, Nina
A Hoe Lot of Trouble - Heather Webber   *m*   206

LAWMAN

Baron, Martin
The Baron Honor - Jory Sherman   *w*   481

Behan, John
Trouble in Tombstone - Richard S. Wheeler   *w*   494

Brackett, Farley
Jericho's Road - Elmer Kelton   *w*   458

Burkett, Ken
Branded - Ed Gorman   *w*   442

Burns, Amos
Mountains Against the Sun - Perry Holmes   *w*   452

Burrack, Sam
Dead Man's Canyon - Ralph Cotton   *w*   432

deSteny, Hugh
A Cold Summer Night - Trystam Kith   *f*   554
A Cold Summer Night - Trystam Kith   *h*   651

Dodge, Lucius "By God"
A Bad Day to Die - J. Lee Butts   *w*   422

Earp, Wyatt
Tombstone Travesty - Jane Candia Coleman   *w*   428
Trouble in Tombstone - Richard S. Wheeler   *w*   494

Hanna, Charley
Bad Night at Dry Creek - Cameron Judd   *w*   456

Hannibal, Joe
Backshooter - Robert J. Randisi   *w*   475

Holland, Billy Bob
In the Moon of Red Ponies - James Lee
   Burke   *c*   1080

Locke, John
Invitation to a Hanging - Robert J. Randisi   *w*   476

Maddux, Kyle
Backshooter - Robert J. Randisi   *w*   475

Masterson, Bat
The Funeral of Tanner Moody - John Jakes   *w*   453

Moody, Tanner
The Funeral of Tanner Moody - John Jakes   *w*   453

Pickard, Andy
Jericho's Road - Elmer Kelton   *w*   458
Jericho's Road - Elmer Kelton   *t*   891

Puttock, Simon
The Outlaws of Ennor - Michael Jecks   *t*   887
The Tolls of Death - Michael Jecks   *t*   888

Ramey, Jed
Devil's Kin - Charles G. West   *w*   491

Revelle, Richard de
Crowner's Quest - Bernard Knight   *t*   892

Russell, Josiah
Mokelumne Gold - Major Mitchell   *w*   465

Shaye, Daniel
Leaving Epitaph - Robert J. Randisi   *w*   477

Shaye, Matthew
Leaving Epitaph - Robert J. Randisi   *w*   477

Spratte, Johnny
Devil's Kin - Charles G. West   *w*   491

Tatum, Boz
A Bad Day to Die - J. Lee Butts   *w*   422

LAWYER

Chambers, Will
The Last Judgment - Craig Parshall   *i*   1038

Cleary, Lilly Bell Rose
Skinny-Dipping - Claire Matturro   *m*   136

Cody, Ryan
Shadows in the Darkness - Elaine
   Cunningham   *h*   623

Connolly, Mike
Sober Justice - Joseph H. Hilley   *i*   1004

Cortez, Lucas
Industrial Magic - Kelley Armstrong   *h*   601
Industrial Magic - Kelley Armstrong   *f*   501

Cunningham, Gilbert
The Harper's Quine - Pat McIntosh   *t*   903
The Harper's Quine - Pat McIntosh   *m*   141

Debbon, Henry
The Black House - Constance Little   *m*   130

Demerand, Jake
Paradise Fields - Katie Fforde   *c*   1103

DeWitt, Drew
The Rivals - Joan Johnston   *r*   303

DiNunzio, Mary
Killer Smile - Lisa Scottoline   *c*   1180

Dixon, Matthew
Love Enough for Two - Cynthia Rutledge   *i*   1045

Flowers, Jackie
Seeds of Doubt - Stephanie Kane   *m*   114

Griffin, Cal
Ghostlands - Marc Zicree   *f*   598

Hagen, Tom
The Godfather Returns - Mark
   Winegardner   *c*   1210

Hayes, Lucinda "Cinda"
Chilling Effect - Marianne Wesson   *m*   208

Holden, Vicky
Wife of Moon - Margaret Coel   *m*   33
Wife of Moon - Margaret Coel   *w*   427

Holland, Billy Bob
In the Moon of Red Ponies - James Lee
   Burke   *c*   1080

Kincaid, Samantha
Missing Justice - Alafair Burke   *m*   25

Law, Samuel
Sweetheart, Indiana - Suzanne Simmons   *r*   380

Levitt, Curt
Deficiency - Andrew Neiderman   *h*   674

Lindale, Alexia
Life Everlasting - Robert Whitlow   *i*   1055

Lone Eagle, Adam
Wife of Moon - Margaret Coel   *m*   33
Wife of Moon - Margaret Coel   *w*   427

Lord, Miles
The Romanov Prophecy - Steve Berry   *c*   1074
The Romanov Prophecy - Steve Berry   *m*   11

Madigan, Harry
Maximum Security - Rose Connors   *m*   38

Maguire, Daniel
The Dog Walker - Leslie Schnur   *c*   1179

Markham, Tom
The Cat's Meow - Emily Carmichael   *r*   236

Mayhew, Kristen
I'm Watching You - Karen Rose   *r*   372

Millner, Ethan
Light My Fire - Jane Graves   *r*   276

Nickerson, Marty
Maximum Security - Rose Connors   *m*   38

Parrish, Matt
Beauty Queen - Julia London   *r*   325

Patterson, Thomas
Dancing with Lyndon - Donley Watt   *w*   489

Roger
Magic Seeds - V.S. Naipaul   *c*   1153

Roseman, Jake
The Beautiful Inez - Bart Schneider   *c*   1178

Rumpole, Horace
Rumpole and the Penge Bungalow Murders - John
   Mortimer   *m*   149

Sawyer, B.L.
A Soldier Returns - Fred Grove   *w*   446

Shardlake, Matthew
Dark Fire - C.J. Sansom   *t*   933

Spenser, David
The Pleasure Principle - Shirley Harrison   *r*   286

Stockingdale, Ashley
She's Out of Control - Kristin Billerbeck   *i*   966

Sutherland, Nicholas
My Long, Tall Texas Heartthrob - Geralyn
   Dawson   *r*   249

Vavasour, Miles
The Clerkenwell Tales - Peter Ackroyd   *t*   810

Whittier, Roger
The Green and the Gray - Timothy Zahn   *s*   808

Williams, Dallas
Out of Order - Barbara Dunlop   *r*   256

Wright, McKenna
The Cat's Meow - Emily Carmichael   *r*   236

LEADER

Yeshi
On Fire's Wings - Christie Golden *f* 539

LESBIAN

Flood, Kitty
The Parts - Keith Ridgway *c* 1172

Nan
A Seahorse Year - Stacey D'Erasmo *c* 1091

LIBRARIAN

Clark, Megan
Tome of Murder - D.R. Meredith *w* 464

Dreyfuss, Nicole
Caught in the Act - Pam McCutcheon *r* 336

Freeman, Gerard
The Ghost Writer - John Harwood *c* 1118
The Ghost Writer - John Harwood *h* 640

Stepp, Ellie
Wanting What You Get - Kathy Love *r* 328

Tierney, Catherine
Silver Bells - Luanne Rice *r* 363

LINGUIST

Ajam, Najeeb
The Warlord's Son - Dan Fesperman *m* 77

Coffin, William "Wiki"
A Watery Grave - Joan Druett *m* 62
A Watery Grave - Joan Druett *t* 861

Reavley, Judith
Shoulder the Sky - Anne Perry *t* 921
Shoulder the Sky - Anne Perry *m* 163

LOVER

Chung, Lin
The Castlemaine Murders - Kerry
  Greenwood *m* 91

Foster, Tony
Smoke and Shadows - Tanya Huff *h* 642

Lattimore, Susan Andrews
A Soldier Returns - Fred Grove *w* 446

Lisa
Drive Me Crazy - Eric Jerome Dickey *c* 1093

Lynch, Ella
The News from Paraguay - Lily Tuck *c* 1200

Meadowlark
Beauty for Ashes - Win Blevins *w* 416
Beauty for Ashes - Win Blevins *t* 827

Murray
The London Pigeon Wars - Patrick Neate *c* 1155

Pearce, Kate
The Big Love - Sarah Dunn *c* 1096

Preston, Calder
Dangerous Curves - Jacey Ford *r* 266

Singh, Sam
A Black Englishman - Carolyn Slaughter *t* 939
A Black Englishman - Carolyn Slaughter *c* 1188

Timoteo
Don't Move - Margaret Mazzantini *c* 1140

Tom
The Big Love - Sarah Dunn *c* 1096

Yinan
Inheritance - Lan Samantha Chang *c* 1082

MAGICIAN

Blackstone, Harry
Now You See It - Stuart M. Kaminsky *m* 113

Humfrey
Currant Events - Piers Anthony *f* 500

Kellen
To Light a Candle - Mercedes Lackey *f* 558

Lazarus, Joshua
The Departed - Kathryn Mackel *i* 1021

Norrell
Jonathan Strange & Mr. Norrell - Susanna
  Clarke *c* 1085
Jonathan Strange & Mr. Norrell - Susanna
  Clarke *f* 517
Jonathan Strange & Mr. Norrell - Susanna
  Clarke *t* 837

Segundus, John
Jonathan Strange & Mr. Norrell - Susanna
  Clarke *f* 517

Strange, Jonathan
Jonathan Strange & Mr. Norrell - Susanna
  Clarke *f* 517
Jonathan Strange & Mr. Norrell - Susanna
  Clarke *t* 837
Jonathan Strange & Mr. Norrell - Susanna
  Clarke *c* 1085

MAINTENANCE WORKER

Mpayipheli, Thobela "Tiny"
Heart of the Hunter - Deon Meyer *m* 142
Heart of the Hunter - Deon Meyer *c* 1148

Pickett, Sadie
Sadie-in-Waiting - Annie Jones *i* 1011

MARTIAL ARTS EXPERT

Barnes, Dylan
The Darkening - Chandler McGrew *h* 667

Messenger, Peter
Trouble's Messenger - Max Brand *w* 419

Morse, Laura
Into the Volcano - Forrest DeVoe Jr. *m* 57

MASSEUSE

Evans, Treasure
A New Day at Tanglewood - Annette Gail
  Smith *i* 1048

MECHANIC

Barnaby, Alexandra
Metro Girl - Janet Evanovich *m* 72
Metro Girl - Janet Evanovich *c* 1098

Figueora, Angel
The Quick - Dan Vining *h* 704

Goodrow, Charlie
The Attraction - Douglas Clegg *h* 617

MENTALLY ILL PERSON

Christopher
A Seahorse Year - Stacey D'Erasmo *c* 1091

Jenna
Visits from the Drowned Girl - Steven
  Sherrill *c* 1185

Simpkins, Gabriel "P.T."
The Mercy Killers - Lisa Reardon *c* 1169

MERCENARY

D'Artaud, Florinn
The Burning Shore - Robert Earl *f* 529

Evans, Clint
Just a Hint—Clint - Lori Foster *r* 267

Goodnight, Chaos
The Doublecross Program - Chris Bunch *s* 728

King, Jasmine
The Doublecross Program - Chris Bunch *s* 728

Lorenzo
The Burning Shore - Robert Earl *f* 529

Mordicio
The Burning Shore - Robert Earl *f* 529

Repairman Jack
Crisscross - F. Paul Wilson *h* 706

Riss, M'chel
The Doublecross Program - Chris Bunch *s* 728

MILITARY PERSONNEL

Alexander the Great
The Virtues of War - Steven Pressfield *t* 924

Allerton, Matthew
Cordelia's Corinthian - Victoria Hinshaw *r* 294

Amos, Joe
Liberation Road - David L. Robbins *t* 927

Andez, Shelia
Horizon Storms - Kevin J. Anderson *s* 713

Anza, Juan Bautista de
North with De Anza - Dorothy Ward
  Erskine *w* 439

Armitage, Fletch
Days of Infamy - Harry Turtledove *t* 947
Days of Infamy - Harry Turtledove *s* 797

Ataturk, Kemal
Birds Without Wings - Louis de Bernieres *t* 852

Atreides, Vorian
The Battle of Corrin - Brian Herbert *s* 752

Atvar
Homeward Bound - Harry Turtledove *s* 798

Aubrey, Jack
21: The Final Unfinished Voyage of Jack Aubrey -
  Patrick O'Brian *t* 913

Bass, Charlie
A World of Hurt - David Sherman *s* 786

Bazinger, Karl
The Year Is '42 - Nella Bielski *t* 823
The Year Is '42 - Nella Bielski *c* 1076

Bentley, William
The Spithead Nymph - Jan Needle *t* 911

Bonaparte, Napoleon
The Retreat - Patrick Rambaud *c* 1167

Booly, William III
For Those Who Fell - William C. Dietz *s* 739

Boone, Nathan
Watchers on the Hill - Stephanie Grace
  Whitson *i* 1056

Brackett, Farley
Jericho's Road - Elmer Kelton *w* 458

Braun, Gerhard
Obsessed - Ted Dekker *i* 977

Bronstein, Michaela
The Rats, the Bats, and the Ugly - Eric Flint *s* 744

Bruce, Robert
Fitzpatrick's War - Theodore Judson *s* 756

Lopez, Ramon
Blood for Brother - Mackey Murdock *w* 467

NOBLEMAN

Aimery
Maiden of Fire - Deborah Johns *r* 301

Ali Khan, Hassan
A Beggar at the Gate - Thalassa Ali *t* 811

Allerton, Matthew
Cordelia's Corinthian - Victoria Hinshaw *r* 294

Ambrose
Let There Be Blood - Jane Jakeman *t* 885

Aron
The Bright and the Dark - Michele M. Welch *f* 589

Atani, Karadur
Dragon's Treasure - Elizabeth A. Lynn *f* 563

Aylesgarth, Roman
The Heiress of Hyde Park - Jacqueline Navin *r* 351

Bigelow, Kevin
Heroics for Beginners - John Moore *f* 570

Blackburne, Ashford
A Christmas Baby - Annette Blair *r* 226

Burnham, Francis
A Rakish Spy - Laura Paquet *r* 358

Cates, William
An Honorable Match - Laura Paquet *r* 357

Corinth, Edward
The More Deceived - David Roberts *m* 171

Corvinus, Marcus
Parthian Shot - David Wishart *t* 956

D'Artaud, Florinn
The Burning Shore - Robert Earl *f* 529

de Morte, Lucifer
Seraphim - Michele Hauf *f* 541

Dering, Jarrett
Dangerous Deceptions - Lynn Kerstan *r* 314

Dunshill, Sebastian
Calder Promise - Janet Dailey *r* 245

Eugene of Tielen
Prisoner of the Iron Tower - Sarah Ash *f* 502

Evan
The Mountain's Call - Caitlin Brennan *f* 508

Exeter, Benjamin Edward
He Said Never - Patricia Waddell *r* 400

Flanders, Thomas
The Duke's Scandalous Secret - Connie Lane *r* 321

Genji
Autumn Bridge - Takashi Matsuoka *c* 1139
Autumn Bridge - Takashi Matsuoka *t* 902

Grayling, Joshua
Paladins - Joel Rosenberg *f* 580

Hawkins, Leo
Captain Hawkins' Dilemma - Maria Greene *r* 280

Hepburn, Patrick
Insatiable - Virginia Henley *r* 289

Hughes, Richard
An Enchanting Minx - Sharon Stancavage *r* 387

Iacoca, Asel
Prince of Christler-Coke - Neal Barrett Jr. *s* 719

Jashemi-kha-Tahmu
On Fire's Wings - Christie Golden *f* 539

Kaspar
Exile's Return - Raymond E. Feist *f* 533

Kyber
The Shadow Runners - Liz Maverick *s* 760

MacKenzie, Robert
Some Enchanted Evening - Christina Dodd *t* 854

Maclean, Lachlan
Highland Princess - Amanda Scott *r* 379

Maddox, Ian
The Duel - Barbara Metzger *r* 342

Madraga, Wolf
The Three Sisters - Rebecca Locksley *f* 562

Mallory, Richard
Her Scandalous Affair - Candice Hern *r* 290

Marchman, Evan "West"
Beyond a Wicked Kiss - Jo Goodman *r* 273

Mason, Tony
Fitzpatrick's War - Theodore Judson *s* 756

Middleford, Theodore
A Rake's Redemption - Susannah Carleton *r* 235

Montgomery, Miles
To Love a Princess - Patricia Grasso *r* 275

Morley, Nicholas
Moonlight and Mischief - Rhonda Woodward *r* 409

Mykal
Legacy - Matthew Farrer *s* 741

O'Bannon, Brogan
In a Wild Wood - Sasha Lord *r* 327

Phrax, Varro
Legacy - Matthew Farrer *s* 741

Preston, Davies
The Christmas Wedding - Laurie Brown *r* 233

Raleigh, William
Duke of Sin - Adele Ashworth *r* 215

Raphat
The Blood of the Land - Noel-Anne Brennan *f* 509

Revelle, Richard de
Crowner's Quest - Bernard Knight *t* 892

Romanov, Nicholas Kostantinovich
The White Night of St. Petersburg - Michael, Prince of Greece *t* 905

Rotherstone
An Adventurous Lady - Valerie King *r* 315

St. George, Jonathan Devoran
Night of Sin - Julia Ross *r* 374

Sek, Anakwanar
Double Eagle - Dan Abnett *s* 711

Shepherdston, Jarrod
Hardly a Husband - Rebecca Hagan Lee *r* 322

Sheridan, Charles
Death at Blenheim Palace - Robin Paige *t* 915

Smith Stanley, Edward
Life Mask - Emma Donoghue *c* 1094
Life Mask - Emma Donoghue *t* 856

Standish, Leo
White Horses - Joan Wolf *r* 408

Swain, Gregory Alden
Deceiving Miss Dearborn - Laurie Bishop *r* 224

Swift, Dominic
A Duke for Christmas - Cynthia Pratt *r* 362

Teimor Khan
The Quince Seed Potion - Morteza Baharloo *t* 817

Tenragen, Tarja
Treason Keep - Jennifer Fallon *f* 530

Tudor, Owen
White Rose - R. Garcia y Robertson *t* 872

Tyrell
Lady Fiasco - Kathleen Baldwin *r* 218

Ursus
Clovermead - David Randall *f* 578

Vallerand, Antoine de
Echoes - Danielle Steel *t* 940

Valoren, D'ekkar Han
The Shadow Runners - Liz Maverick *s* 760

Varsah
The Return of Nightfall - Mickey Zucker Reichert *f* 579

Villegagnon, Durand de
Brazil Red - Jean-Christophe Rufin *t* 931

Wandersee, Lucian
The Perfect Bride - Jo Ann Ferguson *r* 263

Warburton, August
Courting Trouble - Nonnie St. George *r* 384

Wellstone, Stony
A Perfect Gentleman - Barbara Metzger *r* 343

Wickenham-Thickenham-Fines, John
A Hint of Seduction - Amelia Grey *r* 281

William of Normandy
Rite of Conquest - Judith Tarr *f* 584

Winchester, Harry
This Magic Moment - Patricia Rice *r* 364

Winston, Gervase
A Wicked Wench - Anne Herries *r* 291

Wolfblade, Damin
Treason Keep - Jennifer Fallon *f* 530

Wolfe, John de
Crowner's Quest - Bernard Knight *t* 892

NOBLEWOMAN

Ariana of Clairmont
Heart of the Hunter - Tina St. John *r* 386

Becha, Rilsin Sae
The Blood of the Land - Noel-Anne Brennan *f* 509

Blakeney, Cordelia
Kindling - Mick Farren *f* 531

Bowmaster, Leeana
Windrider's Oath - David Weber *f* 588

Cerelinde
Banewreaker - Jacqueline Carey *f* 515

Chaisa, Selene
A Day Dark as Night - Carl Bowen *f* 507

Childe, Christina Malcolm
This Magic Moment - Patricia Rice *r* 364

Compton, Elizabeth Hartleigh
Fire When Ready - Kate Kingsbury *m* 119

Damisa
Ancestors of Avalon - Diana L. Paxson *f* 574

Dare, Anne
The Charnel Prince - J. Gregory Keyes *f* 552

d'Aubigne, Francoise
Memoir of a Dwarf - Paul Weidner *t* 951

De Beauchamp, Marian
A Cold Summer Night - Trystam Kith *h* 651

Dearbourne, Victoria Anne
The Price of Pleasure - Kresley Cole *r* 243

Delphinea
Silver's Edge - Anne Kelleher *f* 550

Elizabeth
White Rose - R. Garcia y Robertson *f* 536

Elizabeth of Bredon
Hidden Honor - Anne Stuart *r* 388

Essington, Sarah
The Painted Rose - Donna Birdsell *r* 223

Fitzwilliam, Cynthia
Under a Lucky Star - Diane Farr   *r*   259

Glamorgan, Ariana
The Knight's Redemption - Joanne Rock   *r*   371

Harrison, Sarah
An Honorable Match - Laura Paquet   *r*   357

Hawthorn, Fiona
Lady Fiasco - Kathleen Baldwin   *r*   218

Hayworth, May
The Heiress of Hyde Park - Jacqueline Navin   *r*   351

MacDonald, Mairi
Highland Princess - Amanda Scott   *r*   379

Mallory, Sarah
A Rake's Redemption - Susannah Carleton   *r*   235

Maxwell, Matilda "Matty"
The Christmas Wedding - Laurie Brown   *r*   233

Micail
Ancestors of Avalon - Diana L. Paxson   *f*   574

Orlova, Astasia
Prisoner of the Iron Tower - Sarah Ash   *f*   502

Overton, Lynette
The Duke's Scandalous Secret - Connie Lane   *r*   321

Peyton, Annabelle
Secrets of a Summer Night - Lisa Kleypas   *r*   317

Ravenwood, Jane
An Enchanting Minx - Sharon Stancavage   *r*   387

Rivers, Margaret
The Nameless Day - Sara Douglass   *f*   525

Roskov, Natasha
Staring Down the Devil - Peter Brandvold   *w*   420

Seldansdaughter, Kaeritha
Windrider's Oath - David Weber   *f*   588

Selwick-Aderly, Arabella
The Secret History of the Pink Carnation - Lauren Willig   *c*   1208

Sheridan, Kathryn
Death at Blenheim Palace - Robin Paige   *t*   915

Shizuka
Autumn Bridge - Takashi Matsuoka   *t*   902

Sinderian
The Hidden Stars - Madeline Howard   *f*   545

Spencer, Catherine Seton
Insatiable - Virginia Henley   *r*   289

Weymouth, Isabel
Her Scandalous Affair - Candice Hern   *r*   290

Wills, Elise
The Shadow Roads - Sean Russell   *f*   581

NURSE

Hutchinson, Julie
Afterlife - Douglas Clegg   *h*   616

Merrill, Sunny
Love Came Unexpectedly - Ruth Scofield   *i*   1047

Randall, Marian
The General's Daughter - Kate Huntington   *r*   298

Rebecca
The Lipstick Diaries - Lori Soard   *r*   382

OCCULTIST

Dhevic, Alexander
Messenger - Edward Lee   *h*   657

OFFICE WORKER

Frame, Phoebe
What Phoebe Wants - Cindi Myers   *r*   350

Jameson, Miranda
Breathe: Everyone Has to Do It - Christopher Fowler   *h*   630

Mangeshkar, Meera
Breathe: Everyone Has to Do It - Christopher Fowler   *h*   630

Wade, Janna
Missing Monday - Matthew Costello   *h*   620

ORGANIZED CRIME FIGURE

Corleone, Michael
The Godfather Returns - Mark Winegardner   *c*   1210

Geraci, Nick
The Godfather Returns - Mark Winegardner   *c*   1210

ORPHAN

Billy
The Lutheran - Jack Britton Sullivan   *w*   486

Campbell, Oswald T.
A Redbird Christmas - Fannie Flagg   *c*   1105

Colombe
Brazil Red - Jean-Christophe Rufin   *t*   931

Dearbourne, Victoria Anne
The Price of Pleasure - Kresley Cole   *r*   243

Golden, Candy
All These Girls - Ellen Slezak   *c*   1189

Green, Eve
Eve Green - Susan Fletcher   *c*   1106

Just
Brazil Red - Jean-Christophe Rufin   *t*   931

Meadows, Rose
Heir to the Glimmering World - Cythia Ozick   *c*   1161

O'Brien, Dan
The Underground River - Jeanne Williams   *w*   497

Rogers, Angel
Spring of My Love - Ginny Aiken   *i*   961

Tania
The Secret of Shabaz - Jennifer Macaire   *f*   564

OUTCAST

McAllister, Roxanne
The Demon's Daughter - Emma Holly   *r*   296

OUTLAW

Austin, Port
Vengeance Rider - Ralph Compton   *w*   431

Blevins, Billy Ray
Bloody Hills - Charles G. West   *w*   490

Carly, Blake
Dead Man's Canyon - Ralph Cotton   *w*   432

Champion, Ed
Staring Down the Devil - Peter Brandvold   *w*   420

Colon, Ignacio
Invitation to a Hanging - Robert J. Randisi   *w*   476

Langer, Ethan
Leaving Epitaph - Robert J. Randisi   *w*   477

Lenifee, Ben
Mountains Against the Sun - Perry Holmes   *w*   452

Moody, Tanner
The Funeral of Tanner Moody - John Jakes   *w*   453

Murphy, Noah
Bad Night at Dry Creek - Cameron Judd   *w*   456

Spratte, Johnny
Devil's Kin - Charles G. West   *w*   491

PARANORMAL INVESTIGATOR

Galloway, Anna
The Manor - Scott Nicholson   *h*   676

PARENT

Baxter, Jodi
The Yada Yada Prayer Group Gets Down - Neta Jackson   *i*   1007

Caruso, Sheila
Breaker's Reef - Terri Blackstock   *i*   967

Chase, Charlene
Strange but True - John Searles   *c*   1182

Chizek, Bud
Osprey Island - Thisbe Nissen   *c*   1157

Cohen, Abe
The First Desire - Nancy Reisman   *c*   1171

Cross, Andie
The Good Nanny - Benjamin Cheever   *c*   1084

Delacourte, Elizabeth Jane
Chesapeake Tide - Jeanette Baker   *r*   217

Douglas, Addie Caswell
Sunday Clothes - Thom Lemmons   *i*   1019

Drax, Pierre
The Ninth Life of Louis Drax - Liz Jensen   *c*   1127

Galloway, Lacey
Flee the Night - Susan May Warren   *i*   1054

Hal
A Seahorse Year - Stacey D'Erasmo   *c*   1091

Harmon, Glennis
Crystal Lies - Melody Carlson   *i*   973

Hawcly, Abe
Ordinary Wolves - Seth Kantner   *c*   1129

Hennessey, Russell Tremayne
Chesapeake Tide - Jeanette Baker   *r*   217

Holbrook, Anna
Yonnondio from the Thirties - Tillie Olsen   *w*   470

Holland, Claire
Why the Sky Is Blue - Susan Meissner   *i*   1026

Innes, Nel
Paradise Fields - Katie Fforde   *c*   1103

Jennifer
A Good Distance - Sarah Willis   *c*   1209

LaRue, Karen
Concessions - Debbie DiGiovanni   *i*   981

Lattimore, Susan Andrews
A Soldier Returns - Fred Grove   *w*   446

Lee, Gypsy
Waiting for Teddy Williams - Howard Frank Mosher   *c*   1150

Lore
The Children's War - Monique Charlesworth   *c*   1083

Maya
The Death of Mr. Love - Indra Sinha   *c*   1187

McAdams, Larkin
A Christmas Baby - Annette Blair   *r*   226

POLITICAL FIGURE

POSTAL WORKER

PREGNANT TEENAGER

Moody, Melissa
Strange but True - John Searles   *c*   1182

PREHISTORIC HUMAN

Evening Star
People of the Raven - Kathleen O'Neal Gear   *t*   873

Grae
Song of the Earth - John R. Dann   *t*   849

Rain Bear
People of the Raven - Kathleen O'Neal Gear   *t*   873

PRISONER

Andez, Shelia
Horizon Storms - Kevin J. Anderson   *s*   713

Ardan, Francis
City of Gold and Lepers - Guy D'Armen   *s*   737

Ducharme, Louise
City of Gold and Lepers - Guy D'Armen   *s*   737

Iacoca, Asel
Prince of Christler-Coke - Neal Barrett Jr.   *s*   719

Lars, Bartie
Nature of the Beast - Richard Fawkes   *s*   742

Liu Tai-an
War Trash - Ha Jin   *t*   889

Majere, Dezra
Prisoner of Haven - Nancy Varian Berberick   *f*   506

Majere, Usha
Prisoner of Haven - Nancy Varian Berberick   *f*   506

McCree, Sylvan Lee
Prince of Christler-Coke - Neal Barrett Jr.   *s*   719

Nagarian, Gavril
Prisoner of the Iron Tower - Sarah Ash   *f*   502

Pei Shan
War Trash - Ha Jin   *t*   889

Wilder, Jesse Alden
A Soldier Returns - Fred Grove   *w*   446

Yu Yuan
War Trash - Ha Jin   *t*   889
War Trash - Ha Jin   *c*   1128

PRODUCER

Bracewell, Nicholas
The Counterfeit Crank - Edward Marston   *m*   134

Lasker, Jake
Cheat and Charmer - Elizabeth Frank   *t*   867
Cheat and Charmer - Elizabeth Frank   *c*   1109

Pantolini, Sabrina
Turn Me On - Kristin Hardy   *r*   284

PROFESSOR

Alder, Sally
Bye, Bye Love - Virginia Swift   *m*   194

Atout
The World as It Shall Be - Emile Souvestre   *s*   789

Bourne, Jason
The Bourne Legacy - Eric Van Lustbader   *c*   1202

Brewster, Ray
When Christmas Comes - Debbie Macomber   *r*   330

Cadotte, Will
Blue Moon - Lori Handeland   *r*   283

Coldwell, Eliot
Banquet for the Damned - Adam L.G. Nevill   *h*   675

Good, Sally
A Bond with Death - Bill Crider   *m*   45

Hanemann
Death in Danzig - Stefan Chwin   *t*   835

Hoffman, Nick
Tropic of Murder - Lev Raphael   *m*   167

Knight, Roger
Green Thumb - Ralph McInerny   *m*   139

Lambert, Rae
The Dark Lord - Patricia Simpson   *r*   381

Montgomery, Adam
Always - Jude Deveraux   *r*   253

Plant, Melrose
Winds of Change - Martha Grimes   *m*   93

Reavley, Joseph
Shoulder the Sky - Anne Perry   *m*   163
Shoulder the Sky - Anne Perry   *t*   921

Simpson, Terri
Tall, Dark, and Hungry - Lynsay Sands   *r*   377

Singer, Magdalene "Maggi"
A.K.A. Goddess - Evelyn Vaughn   *r*   399

Spark, Rachel
A Girl Becomes a Comma Like That - Lisa Glatt   *c*   1111

Stern, Caryn
Missing Monday - Matthew Costello   *h*   620

Woods, Elaina
Reason and Romance - Debra White Smith   *i*   1049

PROSPECTOR

Turley, Craig
Wings of Riches - Al Lacy   *i*   1017

Yancy, Will
Vengeance Valley - Richard S. Wheeler   *w*   495

PROSTITUTE

Brown, Nancy
Donovan's Dove - Joseph A. West   *w*   492

Lear, Fanny
The White Night of St. Petersburg - Michael, Prince of Greece   *t*   905

PSYCHIC

Childe, Christina Malcolm
This Magic Moment - Patricia Rice   *r*   364

Diamond, Michael
Afterlife - Douglas Clegg   *h*   616

Erroy, Brantor
Gifts - Ursula K. Le Guin   *f*   560

Firekeeper
Wolf Captured - Jane Lindskold   *f*   561

Gry
Gifts - Ursula K. Le Guin   *f*   560

Hepburn, Patrick
Insatiable - Virginia Henley   *r*   289

LeBlanc, Dahlia
Mind Game - Christine Feehan   *r*   261

Magadon
Dawn of Night - Paul S. Kemp   *f*   551

Montgomery, Darci Monroe
Always - Jude Deveraux   *r*   253

O'Hara, Martin Konner
The Dragon Circle - Irene Radford   *s*   774

Orrec
Gifts - Ursula K. Le Guin   *f*   560

Rain, Phoebe
Midnight Rain - Holly Lisle   *r*   324

Rho
The Wilding - C.S. Friedman   *s*   746

Trevane, Nicolas
Mind Game - Christine Feehan   *r*   261

PSYCHOLOGIST

Butler, Charles
Winter House - Carol O'Connell   *m*   155

Denison, Skye
Murder of a Pink Elephant - Denise Swanson   *m*   193

Poggioli, Henry
Dr. Poggioli: Criminologist - T.S. Stribling   *m*   191

PUBLIC RELATIONS

Barr, Temple
Cat in an Orange Twist - Carole Nelson Douglas   *m*   60

Bennett, Celeste
Killer Curves - Roxanne St. Claire   *r*   383

Blake, Whitney
The Whitney Chronicles - Judy Baer   *i*   964

Hayes, Alexandra
Ring around My Heart - Pat White   *r*   404

Lopez, Alexis
Playing with Boys - Alisa Valdes-Rodriguez   *r*   398

PUBLISHER

Crandall, Harry
A Hard Man Is Good to Find - Jane Blackwood   *r*   225

Dupree, Camille
Twice Blessed - Sharon Gillenwater   *i*   989

Riant
In the Hope of Rising Again - Helen Scully   *c*   1181

RADIO PERSONALITY

MacIntyre, Verona
Banishing Verona - Margot Livesey   *c*   1137

Stedquest, Stevie
The Babe Magnet - Robin Wells   *r*   403

Sunflower, Mahogany
Soul City - Toure   *c*   1196

RAKE

O'Neal, Blackie
To Tempt a Texan - Georgina Gentry   *r*   271

RANCHER

Aguilar, Miguel
The Baron Honor - Jory Sherman   *w*   481

Allard, Frank
Mountains Against the Sun - Perry Holmes   *w*   452

Baron, Anson
The Baron Honor - Jory Sherman   *w*   481

Baron, Martin
The Baron Honor - Jory Sherman   *w*   481

Bill the First
The American Cowboy - Will James   *w*   454

Bill the Second
The American Cowboy - Will James   *w*   454

Bill the Third
The American Cowboy - Will James   *w*   454

Bone, Slayton
A Bad Day to Die - J. Lee Butts   *w*   422

Branson, Cade
Winter Kill - Cotton Smith   *w*   484

Branson, Titus
Winter Kill - Cotton Smith   *w*   484

Carrigan, Patrick
War at Fire Creek - Cameron Judd   *w*   457

Chavez, Guadalupe
Jericho's Road - Elmer Kelton   *t*   891

Clarke, Mercy
Loving Mercy - Teresa Bodwell   *r*   230

Coolidge, Vance
West of Rock River - John D. Nesbitt   *w*   468

Coulter, Zeke
Bright Eyes - Catherine Anderson   *r*   213

Dagstaff, Felix
The Palo Duro Trail - Ralph Compton   *w*   430

Durham, Fred
West of Rock River - John D. Nesbitt   *w*   468

Durham, Tip
West of Rock River - John D. Nesbitt   *w*   468

Fletcher, Buck
Vengeance Rider - Ralph Compton   *w*   431

Gilkyson, Einar
An Unfinished Life - Mark Spragg   *c*   1191
An Unfinished Life - Mark Spragg   *w*   485

Jackson, Jericho
Jericho's Road - Elmer Kelton   *w*   458
Jericho's Road - Elmer Kelton   *t*   891

Johnson, Jeremy
Spring of My Love - Ginny Aiken   *i*   961

Kerney, Kevin
Slowkill - Michael McGarrity   *w*   463

Kerrington, Allie
Lassiter - Loren Zane Grey   *w*   444

Lopez, Ramon
Blood for Brother - Mackey Murdock   *w*   467

McKeag, Dan
McKeag's Mountain - L.J. Martin   *w*   462

Moon, Charlie
The Witch's Tongue - James D. Doss   *w*   437
The Witch's Tongue - James D. Doss   *m*   59

Morgan, Chip
Blood River - Jory Sherman   *w*   482

Prager, Bertoldus
McKeag's Mountain - L.J. Martin   *w*   462

Rogers, Angel
Spring of My Love - Ginny Aiken   *i*   961

Rudd, Joe
Lassiter - Loren Zane Grey   *w*   444

Selby, Cole
To Dream Anew - Tracie Peterson   *i*   1041

Selby, Dianne
The Hope Within - Tracie Peterson   *i*   1039
To Dream Anew - Tracie Peterson   *i*   1041

Slaton, Marcus
Blood for Brother - Mackey Murdock   *w*   467

Slaton, Rawls
Blood for Brother - Mackey Murdock   *w*   467

Tull
Riders of the Purple Sage: The Restored Edition -
   Zane Grey   *w*   445

Withersteen, Jane
Riders of the Purple Sage: The Restored Edition -
   Zane Grey   *w*   445

REAL ESTATE AGENT

Lieberman, Madison
Cold Feet - Brenda Novak   *r*   352

Morgan, Eric
Sweet Justice - Shirley Harrison   *r*   287

Weeks, Roy
Stop That Girl - Elizabeth McKenzie   *c*   1144

Whittier, Caroline
The Green and the Gray - Timothy Zahn   *s*   808

REBEL

Cutter
Iron Council - China Mieville   *f*   569

Jashemi-kha-Tahmu
On Fire's Wings - Christie Golden   *f*   539

Mocranen, Riadni
The Gods and Their Machines - Oisin
   McGann   *s*   764

Pomeroy
Iron Council - China Mieville   *f*   569

SunSoar, Dragonstar
Sinner - Sara Douglass   *f*   526

RECEPTIONIST

Jacobs, Shelby
Out of Order - Barbara Dunlop   *r*   256

RECLUSE

Macklin, Billy
Eve Green - Susan Fletcher   *c*   1106

Magnus
Prometheus Road - Bruce Balfour   *s*   716

REFUGEE

Levy, Mia
Songbird - Walter Zacharius   *t*   959

Sheriff, Alan
The Tyrant's Novel - Thomas Keneally   *c*   1130

RELATIVE

Addison-Blake, George
The Parts - Keith Ridgway   *c*   1172

Angela
Don't Move - Margaret Mazzantini   *c*   1140

Baklanov, Stefan
The Romanov Prophecy - Steve Berry   *c*   1074

Brannigan, Elizabeth
All These Girls - Ellen Slezak   *c*   1189

Cadwallader, Dorothy
The Hollywood Dodo - Geoff Nicholson   *c*   1156

Carrigan, Joseph
War at Fire Creek - Cameron Judd   *w*   457

Carrigan, Liam
War at Fire Creek - Cameron Judd   *w*   457

Carter, Sherry
And a Puzzle to Die On - Parnell Hall   *m*   95

Christopher, Zarah
Old Boys - Charles McCarry   *c*   1142

Cohen, Goldie
The First Desire - Nancy Reisman   *c*   1171

Dreslinski, Gloria
All These Girls - Ellen Slezak   *c*   1189

Eckstrum, Destiny
Chasing Destiny - Stephen Overholser   *w*   471

Farinelli, Lucy
Trace - Patricia Cornwell   *m*   40

Feddens, Toby
The Line of Beauty - Alan Hollinghurst   *c*   1122

Friedman, Lev
Joy Comes in the Morning - Jonathan
   Rosen   *c*   1174

George
The Turk and My Mother - Mary Helen
   Stefaniak   *c*   1193

Greenhow, Mark
Voyageurs - Margaret Elphinstone   *t*   866

Greenhow, Rachel
Voyageurs - Margaret Elphinstone   *t*   866

Hawcly, Cutuk
Ordinary Wolves - Seth Kantner   *c*   1129

Hawcly, Jerry
Ordinary Wolves - Seth Kantner   *c*   1129

Kimmie
Shifting through Neutral - Bridgett M.
   Davis   *c*   1087

Knight, Philip
Green Thumb - Ralph McInerny   *m*   139

Lan Lin
The Love Wife - Gish Jen   *c*   1126

Lozen
The Hebrew Kid and the Apache Maiden - Robert J.
   Avrech   *w*   414

Maher, Joseph
The Silver Screen - Maureen Howard   *c*   1123

Maher, Rita
The Silver Screen - Maureen Howard   *c*   1123

Malloy, Andy
Branded - Ed Gorman   *w*   442

Milligan, Genevieve "Veevi"
Cheat and Charmer - Elizabeth Frank   *c*   1109

Novak, Lucy
Baker Towers - Jennifer Haigh   *c*   1115

Perika, Daisy
The Witch's Tongue - James D. Doss   *w*   437
The Witch's Tongue - James D. Doss   *m*   59

Rebecca
Visits from the Drowned Girl - Steven
   Sherrill   *c*   1185

Rupert, Framp
Sawyer's Quest - Will Cade   *w*   423

Saperstone, Claire
The Vagabonds - Nicholas Delbanco   *c*   1089

Saperstone, David
The Vagabonds - Nicholas Delbanco   *c*   1089

Sarojini
Magic Seeds - V.S. Naipaul   *c*   1153

Sawyer, Laurel
Sawyer's Quest - Will Cade   *w*   423

Shaye, Matthew
Leaving Epitaph - Robert J. Randisi   *w*   477

Simpkins, Charlie
The Mercy Killers - Lisa Reardon   *c*   1169

Winters, Ellie
How to Be Lost - Amanda Eyre Ward   *c*   1205

Winters, Madeline
How to Be Lost - Amanda Eyre Ward   *c*   1205

Yinan
Inheritance - Lan Samantha Chang   *c*   1082

RELIGIOUS

Agatha
The Last Dark Place - Stuart M. Kaminsky   *m*   112
Thief in Retreat - Aimee Thurlo   *m*   199

Airton, Edward
The Palace of Heavenly Pleasure - Adam Williams   *t*   954

Alaric
Grey Knights - Ben Counter   *f*   520

Ames, John
Gilead - Marilynne Robinson   *c*   1173

Aparicio, Francisca "Paquita"
The Divine Husband - Francisco Goldman   *t*   874

Avens, John
Gun Ball Hill - Ellen Cooney   *t*   846

Becker, David
California Girl - T. Jefferson Parker   *m*   158

Behaine, Pierre de
Le Colonial - Kien Nguyen   *t*   912

Bertrand
The Nameless Day - Sara Douglass   *f*   525

Brady, Luther
Crisscross - F. Paul Wilson   *h*   706

Callahan, Donald
The Dark Tower - Stephen King   *h*   649

Chandler, Jacob
Opal - Lauraine Snelling   *i*   1050

Claire of Foix
Maiden of Fire - Deborah Johns   *r*   301

Cully
Paladins - Joel Rosenberg   *f*   580

Dawson, Gabriel
Gabriel's Discovery - Felicia Mason   *i*   1024

Dowling, Roger
Requiem for a Realtor - Ralph McInerny   *m*   140

Elbeth
The Gods and Their Machines - Oisin McGann   *s*   764

Eleanor
Tyrant of the Mind - Priscilla Royal   *t*   930
Tyrant of the Mind - Priscilla Royal   *m*   176

Exmewe, William
The Clerkenwell Tales - Peter Ackroyd   *t*   810

Fidelma
Whispers of the Dead - Peter Tremayne   *m*   202

Frevisse
The Widow's Tale - Margaret Frazer   *t*   868

Gervaise, Francois
Le Colonial - Kien Nguyen   *t*   912

Gibson, Emily
Autumn Bridge - Takashi Matsuoka   *t*   902
Autumn Bridge - Takashi Matsuoka   *c*   1139

Goodman, Christopher
Acts of God - James Beauseigneur   *s*   721

Green, Deborah
Joy Comes in the Morning - Jonathan Rosen   *c*   1174

Greenhow, Rachel
Voyageurs - Margaret Elphinstone   *t*   866

Jarvis, Jay
Lost in Rooville - Ray Blackston   *i*   968

Johanen
The Revealing - L.A. Marzulli   *i*   1023

Joshua
Joshua in a Troubled World - Joseph F. Girzone   *i*   990

Kahn, Ben
Liberation Road - David L. Robbins   *t*   927

Knight, Bill
St. Dale - Sharyn McCrumb   *c*   1143

Koerney, Kathryn
Thieves Break In - Cristina Sumners   *m*   192

Lane, Ian
Changes of Heart - Paige Lee Elliston   *i*   984

Leo
The Franciscan Conspiracy - John R. Sack   *t*   932

Levin, Chaim
Acts of God - James Beauseigneur   *s*   721

Love, Lil Mo
Soul City - Toure   *c*   1196

Maher, Joseph
The Silver Screen - Maureen Howard   *c*   1123

Merrin, Lankester
Exorcist: The Beginning - Steven Piziks   *h*   682

Micail
Ancestors of Avalon - Diana L. Paxson   *f*   574

Monange, Henri
Le Colonial - Kien Nguyen   *t*   912

Neville, Thomas
The Nameless Day - Sara Douglass   *t*   858
The Nameless Day - Sara Douglass   *f*   525
The Wounded Hawk - Sara Douglass   *t*   859

Nieves, Maria de las
The Divine Husband - Francisco Goldman   *t*   874

O'Malley, John
Wife of Moon - Margaret Coel   *w*   427
Wife of Moon - Margaret Coel   *m*   33

O'Shaugnessy, Bryan
Moment of Truth - Sally John   *i*   1010

Pendaar "Father Daar"
Tempting the Highlander - Janet Chapman   *r*   239

Peter de Montselm
Hidden Honor - Anne Stuart   *r*   388

Pritchard, Rhys
A.K.A. Goddess - Evelyn Vaughn   *r*   399

Reavley, Joseph
Shoulder the Sky - Anne Perry   *m*   163
Shoulder the Sky - Anne Perry   *t*   921

Rosenzweig
The King of Ice Cream - Robert Wayne McCoy   *f*   567

Shirow, Zoltan
Coyote Rising - Allen Steele   *s*   791

Siritalanu
The Glasswright's Master - Mindy L. Klasky   *f*   555

Thomas
Tyrant of the Mind - Priscilla Royal   *t*   930

Tiriki
Ancestors of Avalon - Diana L. Paxson   *f*   574

Tull
Riders of the Purple Sage: The Restored Edition - Zane Grey   *w*   445

Ware, Jonathan
The Hidden Valley - Jeanne Williams   *w*   496

Watkins, Merrily
The Prayer of the Night Shepherd - Phil Rickman   *h*   684

Yolara
The Moon Pool - A. Merritt   *s*   766

REPAIRMAN

Poteat, Benny
Visits from the Drowned Girl - Steven Sherrill   *c*   1185

Pratt, Cyril
Walpuski's Typewriter - Frank Darabont   *h*   624

RESCUER

Stewart, Jeanine
Aloha Love - Alice Wootson   *r*   410

RESEARCHER

Levy, Rebecca "Bex"
On Thin Ice - Alina Adams   *m*   1

Milk, John
The Inner Circle - T. Coraghessan Boyle   *c*   1078

Monroe, Rebecca
The Family Tree - Carole Cadwalladr   *c*   1081

Pritchard, Rhys
A.K.A. Goddess - Evelyn Vaughn   *r*   399

Wright, Isabel
Falling Awake - Jayne Ann Krentz   *c*   1133

RESTAURATEUR

Brighton, Glory
The Shaughnessey Accord - Alison Kent   *r*   311

Carlson, Sam
Espresso for Two - Courtni Wright   *r*   411

Cosi, Clare
Through the Grinder - Cleo Coyle   *m*   42

Del Rosso, Dante
The Devil Served Tortellini - Shirley Jump   *r*   306

Manelli, Ellie "Lemon"
Lucious Lemon - Heather Swain   *r*   389

Patterson, Natalie
Bright Eyes - Catherine Anderson   *r*   213

Thorsen, Maggy
Uncommon Grounds - Sandra Balzo   *m*   5

REVOLUTIONARY

Chandran, Willie
Magic Seeds - V.S. Naipaul   *c*   1153

Lata, Tara
The Tree Bride - Bharati Mukherjee   *t*   910

Mpayipheli, Thobela "Tiny"
Heart of the Hunter - Deon Meyer   *c*   1148
Heart of the Hunter - Deon Meyer   *m*   142

Smart, Henry
Oh, Play That Thing - Roddy Doyle   *t*   860

Varden, Kane
The Sun Witch - Linda Winstead Jones   *r*   304

ROBOT

Roderick
The Complete Roderick - John Sladek   *s*   788

Character Description Index

Selwick, Richard
The Secret History of the Pink Carnation - Lauren Willig   *c*   1208

Strange, Jonathan
Jonathan Strange & Mr. Norrell - Susanna Clarke   *c*   1085

SCIENTIST

Adams, Flick
Dead as a Scone - Ron Benrey   *i*   965

Adler, Jack
Singularity - Bill DeSmedt   *s*   738

al-Maaz, Safia
Sandstorm - James Rollins   *s*   780

Cather, Audrey
The Dry Salvages - Caitlin R. Kiernan   *h*   647

Clemons, Neil Anson
Warp Speed - Travis S. Taylor   *s*   792

Crewe, Nathan
Master of None - N. Lee Wood   *s*   807

Daniels, Jim
Warp Speed - Travis S. Taylor   *s*   792

Darwin, Charles
The Pirates! In an Adventure with Scientists - Gideon Defoe   *t*   853

Delacourte, Elizabeth Jane
Chesapeake Tide - Jeanette Baker   *r*   217

Durnau, Lisa
River of Gods - Ian McDonald   *s*   763

Farouk, Gabriella
Cleopatra 7.2 - Elizabeth Ann Scarborough   *s*   785

Ford, Marion "Doc"
Tampa Burn - Randy Wayne White   *m*   209

Goodwin, Walter
The Moon Pool - A. Merritt   *s*   766

Hamilton, Joakim
The Dry Salvages - Caitlin R. Kiernan   *h*   647

Kinsey, Alfred
The Inner Circle - T. Coraghessan Boyle   *c*   1078

Lachlan, Cameron
Wild in the Moonlight - Jennifer Greene   *r*   279

Mendoza
The Life of the World to Come - Kage Baker   *s*   715

Monroe, Alistair
The Family Tree - Carole Cadwalladr   *c*   1081

Morgan, Dexter
Darkly Dreaming Dexter - Jeff Lindsay   *c*   1136
Darkly Dreaming Dexter - Jeff Lindsay   *m*   128

Murdin, Umachandra
The Dry Salvages - Caitlin R. Kiernan   *h*   647

Natas
City of Gold and Lepers - Guy D'Armen   *s*   737

Ohana, Kaia
Distant Echoes - Colleen Coble   *i*   976

Perrone, Chaz
Skinny Dip - Carl Hiaasen   *c*   1120

Polchak, Nick
Chop Shop - Tim Downs   *i*   983

Rathbone, Henry
A Christmas Visitor - Anne Perry   *m*   162

Swan, Mark
Missing Monday - Matthew Costello   *h*   620

Waterhouse, Daniel
The System of the World - Neal Stephenson   *t*   941

Wheel, Charley
Buried Stuff - Sharon Fiffer   *m*   78

SCOUT

Carson, Kit
The Mask of Red Death - Harold Schechter   *t*   934
The Mask of Red Death - Harold Schechter   *m*   181

Collins, Matthew
Santa Fe Passage - Jon R. Bauman   *t*   819
Santa Fe Passage - Jon R. Bauman   *w*   415

Culver, Clay
Bloody Hills - Charles G. West   *w*   490

Omohundro, Texas Jack
East of the Border - Johnny D. Boggs   *w*   417

SEA CAPTAIN

Chartwell, William
The Captain's Mermaid - Mary Blayney   *r*   228

DeHaan, Eric
Dark Voyage - Alan Furst   *c*   1110
Dark Voyage - Alan Furst   *t*   870

Huldricksson, Olaf
The Moon Pool - A. Merritt   *s*   766

Malone, Jack
Sailors on the Inward Sea - Lawrence Thornton   *t*   945

Quarles, Malachai
A Perfect Romance - Anne Robins   *r*   369

Rochester, George
A Watery Grave - Joan Druett   *t*   861

Sutherland, Grant
The Price of Pleasure - Kresley Cole   *r*   243

SECRETARY

Barrett, Cathy
Nightingale's Lament - Simon R. Green   *h*   636

Whittaker, Derek
Under a Lucky Star - Diane Farr   *r*   259

SECURITY OFFICER

Barron, Rick
The Prince of Beverly Hills - Stuart Woods   *t*   957

Ewing, Reve
Divided in Death - J.D. Robb   *s*   778

Harkless, Baro
Black Brillion - Matthew Hughes   *s*   754

Harper, Ben
Breathe: Everyone Has to Do It - Christopher Fowler   *h*   630

Matthews, Jesse
Distant Echoes - Colleen Coble   *i*   976

SERIAL KILLER

Morgan, Dexter
Darkly Dreaming Dexter - Jeff Lindsay   *c*   1136
Darkly Dreaming Dexter - Jeff Lindsay   *m*   128

SERVANT

Camilla
In the Hope of Rising Again - Helen Scully   *t*   936

Flotsam "Flottie"
Mrs. Hudson and the Spirits' Curse - Martin Davies   *m*   53

Jeeves
Wake Up, Sir - Jonathan Ames   *c*   1064

Johnson, Millard
Territorial Rough Rider - Tim Champlin   *w*   425

Jokar, Sarveali
The Quince Seed Potion - Morteza Baharloo   *t*   817

Moss, Sundry
Fiddler's Green - Van Reid   *t*   926

Nella
Ghosts in the Snow - Tamara Siler Jones   *h*   646

Niebeck, Barbara
The Real Minerva - Mary Sharratt   *t*   938

Ram, Dowlah
The Lady of Cawnpore - Elisabeth McNeill   *t*   904

Ro-shei
Dark of the Sun - Chelsea Quinn Yarbro   *h*   710

SETTLER

Cutler, Alex
Crucible - Nancy Kress   *s*   757

Hanani, Fola
Crache - Mark Budz   *s*   726

Lovat, Margaret
Hostile Takeover - Susan Shwartz   *s*   787

Mowlam, Lavinia
Gun Ball Hill - Ellen Cooney   *t*   846

Mowlam, William
Gun Ball Hill - Ellen Cooney   *t*   846

Parekh, Surendra
City of Pearl - Karen Traviss   *s*   794

Wilde, Jonah
Into the Prairie - Rosanne Bittner   *t*   825

Wilde, Sadie
Into the Prairie - Rosanne Bittner   *t*   825

SHAMAN

Dukkai
Dark of the Sun - Chelsea Quinn Yarbro   *t*   958
Dark of the Sun - Chelsea Quinn Yarbro   *h*   710

Eli
Family Inheritance - Deborah LeBlanc   *h*   655

Perika, Daisy
The Witch's Tongue - James D. Doss   *m*   59
The Witch's Tongue - James D. Doss   *w*   437

Summer Day
Trouble's Messenger - Max Brand   *w*   419

War Eagle
Indian Why Stories - Frank B. Linderman   *w*   461

SHEPHERD

Cashel
Master of the Cauldron - David Drake   *f*   527

SHIPOWNER

Sullivan, Seychelle
Cross Current - Christine Kling   *m*   120

SIDEKICK

Craddock, Billy Don
Flat Crazy - Ben Rehder   *w*   478

Dupree, Johnny Blue
Johnny Blue and the Texas Rangers - Joseph A. West   *w*   493

Flotsam "Flottie"
Mrs. Hudson and the Spirits' Curse - Martin Davies   *m*   53

Character Description Index

Martin, Julian Cabot
Crucible - Nancy Kress   *s*   757

Pausert
The Wizard of Karres - Mercedes Lackey   *s*   758

Pirius
Exultant - Stephen Baxter   *s*   720

Seaborg, Anders
Nature of the Beast - Richard Fawkes   *s*   742

Vatta, Kylara
Marque and Reprisal - Elizabeth Moon   *s*   769

SPACEWOMAN

Ames, Tabitha
Warp Speed - Travis S. Taylor   *s*   792

Frankland, Shan
City of Pearl - Karen Traviss   *s*   794
Crossing the Line - Karen Traviss   *s*   795

Hulik
The Wizard of Karres - Mercedes Lackey   *s*   758

Leewit
The Wizard of Karres - Mercedes Lackey   *s*   758

Lys, Yskatarina
Banner of Souls - Liz Williams   *s*   805

Pancorbo, Estrella
The Boy Who Would Live Forever - Frederik Pohl   *s*   773

Pine, Charlotte
Saucer: The Conquest - Stephen Coonts   *s*   734

Talbot, Kat
The Dragon Circle - Irene Radford   *s*   774

SPINSTER

Akhila
Ladies Coupe - Anita Nair   *c*   1154

Morgan, Madeline
The Marryin' Kind - Nancy J. Parra   *r*   359

SPIRIT

Hardy, Nina
Shade - Neil Jordan   *t*   890

Jedes, Richter
Neurolink - M.M. Buckner   *s*   725

MacDougall, Duncan Angus
A Man in a Kilt - Sandy Blair   *r*   227

Mueller, Don
Ghost of a Chance - Flo Fitzpatrick   *r*   265

SPORTS FIGURE

Claymore, Harley
St. Dale - Sharyn McCrumb   *c*   1143

Golden, Candy
All These Girls - Ellen Slezak   *c*   1189

Hooker, Sam
Metro Girl - Janet Evanovich   *c*   1098
Metro Girl - Janet Evanovich   *m*   72

Johanssen, Jojo
I Am Charlotte Simmons - Tom Wolfe   *c*   1211

Lansing, Beau
Killer Curves - Roxanne St. Claire   *r*   383

Rainey, Shawn
Echo Bay - Richard Barre   *c*   1070

Redfield, Maceo
The Last King - Nichelle D. Tramble   *c*   1197

Ruth, Babe
7,000 Clams - Lee Irby   *t*   884

Silverspoon, Timothy Lucas
Ring around My Heart - Pat White   *r*   404

SPOUSE

Adams, Lindsey
Dry Heat - Jon Talton   *m*   195

Ali Khan, Hassan
A Beggar at the Gate - Thalassa Ali   *t*   811

Andrews, Rachel
Bloody Hills - Charles G. West   *w*   490

Audrey
The Haunted Hillbilly - Derek McCormack   *h*   665

Baxter, Jodi
The Yada Yada Prayer Group Gets Down - Neta Jackson   *i*   1007

Bonner, Elizabeth
Fire Along the Sky - Sara Donati   *t*   855

Bonner, Nathaniel
Fire Along the Sky - Sara Donati   *t*   855

Brandon, Becky
Shopaholic and Sister - Sophie Kinsella   *c*   1132

Brandon, Luke
Shopaholic and Sister - Sophie Kinsella   *c*   1132

Chizek, Nancy
Osprey Island - Thisbe Nissen   *c*   1157

Crawford, Cheryl
Kissed - Carmen Green   *r*   277

Cross, Stuart
The Good Nanny - Benjamin Cheever   *c*   1084

Darcy, Elizabeth Bennet
Suspense and Sensibility - Carrie A. Bebris   *t*   820

Darcy, Fitzwilliam
Suspense and Sensibility - Carrie A. Bebris   *t*   820

Dean, Eddie
The Dark Tower - Stephen King   *h*   649
Song of Susannah - Stephen King   *c*   1131

Doralee
Mantrapped - Fay Weldon   *c*   1207

Douglas, Addie Caswell
Sunday Clothes - Thom Lemmons   *i*   1019

Earp, Allie
Tombstone Travesty - Jane Candia Coleman   *w*   428

Earp, Josie
Tombstone Travesty - Jane Candia Coleman   *w*   428

Fletcher, Alec
A Mourning Wedding - Carola Dunn   *m*   65
A Mourning Wedding - Carola Dunn   *t*   862

Fluck, Zelda
Trouble in Paradise - Pip Granger   *t*   875

Givens, Marianna
A Beggar at the Gate - Thalassa Ali   *t*   811

Guinevere
Arthur the King - Allan Massie   *t*   901

Harmon, Glennis
Crystal Lies - Melody Carlson   *i*   973

Hathaway, Anne
Young Will - Bruce Cook   *t*   845

Herbert, Isabel
A Black Englishman - Carolyn Slaughter   *t*   939
A Black Englishman - Carolyn Slaughter   *c*   1188

Herbert, Neville
A Black Englishman - Carolyn Slaughter   *t*   939

Hicks, Lorrie
Life Expectancy - Dean R. Koontz   *h*   652

Holland, Claire
Why the Sky Is Blue - Susan Meissner   *i*   1026

January, Rose
Dead Water - Barbara Hambly   *t*   877

Jennifer
A Good Distance - Sarah Willis   *c*   1209

Junan
Inheritance - Lan Samantha Chang   *c*   1082

Kleinman, Miriam
Chicken Dreaming Corn - Roy Hoffman   *t*   882

Kleinman, Morris
Chicken Dreaming Corn - Roy Hoffman   *t*   882

LaRue, Jack
Concessions - Debbie DiGiovanni   *i*   981

LaRue, Karen
Concessions - Debbie DiGiovanni   *i*   981

Lasker, Dinah
Cheat and Charmer - Elizabeth Frank   *t*   867
Cheat and Charmer - Elizabeth Frank   *c*   1109

Lazarus, Maggie
The Departed - Kathryn Mackel   *i*   1021

Li Ang
Inheritance - Lan Samantha Chang   *c*   1082

Lincoln, Mary Todd
The Emancipator's Wife - Barbara Hambly   *t*   878

Lisa
Drive Me Crazy - Eric Jerome Dickey   *c*   1093

Littrell, Ariah
The Falls - Joyce Carol Oates   *c*   1160

Logan, Tharyn
The Heart Remembers - Al Lacy   *i*   1016

Mackenzie, Julia
Villages - John Updike   *c*   1201

Mackenzie, Phyllis
Villages - John Updike   *c*   1201

Maelgwyn ap Cadwallon
The Fool's Tale - Nicole Galland   *t*   871

Mapstone, Lindsey
Dry Heat - Jon Talton   *w*   487

Marquez, Lena
The Stupidest Angel - Christopher Moore   *h*   671

Mayfield, Kate
Night Fall - Nelson DeMille   *c*   1090

McGillycuddy, Fanny
The Indian Agent - Dan O'Brien   *w*   469
The Indian Agent - Dan O'Brien   *t*   914

McKinley, Ida
The Temple of Music - Jonathan Lowy   *t*   898

Mellow, Paul
The Position - Meg Wolitzer   *c*   1212

Mellow, Roz
The Position - Meg Wolitzer   *c*   1212

Milk, Iris
The Inner Circle - T. Coraghessan Boyle   *c*   1078

Monroe, Alistair
The Family Tree - Carole Cadwalladr   *c*   1081

Morrow, Charles
In the Hope of Rising Again - Helen Scully   *c*   1181
In the Hope of Rising Again - Helen Scully   *t*   936

Mortimer, Isabel
The Fool's Tale - Nicole Galland   *t*   871

Murtagh, Colum
A Feast of Poisons - C.L. Grace   *m*   89

Nzuluwazi, Miriam
Heart of the Hunter - Deon Meyer   *c*   1148

Patterson, Mary Lee
Dancing with Lyndon - Donley Watt   *w*   489

Pennington, Dorothy
Haven - Julie Marshall   *r*   333

Perrone, Joey
Skinny Dip - Carl Hiaasen   *c*   1120
Skinny Dip - Carl Hiaasen   *m*   103

Polycrates, Rosco
Wrapped Up in Crosswords - Nero Blanc   *m*   15

Quinn, Paul
Snowed In - Christina Bartolomeo   *c*   1071

Rawlings, Emilia
Death in the Setting Sun - Deryn Lake   *t*   893

Riant, Regina
In the Hope of Rising Again - Helen Scully   *c*   1181
In the Hope of Rising Again - Helen Scully   *t*   936

Richardson, Rena
Life Everlasting - Robert Whitlow   *i*   1055

Ringwood, Claire Liddicote
The Cretan Counterfeit - Katharine Farrer   *m*   74

Roarke
Divided in Death - J.D. Robb   *s*   778

Roseman, Jake
The Beautiful Inez - Bart Schneider   *c*   1178

Shiflett, Clarisse
Delivery - Ben Daitz   *w*   434

Silvia della Francesca
Love, the Painter's Wife and the Queen of Sheba - Aliette Armel   *t*   814
Love, the Painter's Wife and the Queen of Sheba - Aliette Armel   *c*   1066

Stephens, Heather
Dead for the Winter - Betsy Thornton   *w*   488

Sweet, Victoria
Assassin - Ted Bell   *c*   1073

Tariq
The London Pigeon Wars - Patrick Neate   *c*   1155

Todd
A Good Distance - Sarah Willis   *c*   1209

Vallerand, Antoine de
Echoes - Danielle Steel   *t*   940

Warren, Alden
Lux - Maria Flook   *c*   1107

Wheel, Charley
Buried Stuff - Sharon Fiffer   *m*   78

Wilde, Jonah
Into the Prairie - Rosanne Bittner   *t*   825

Wilde, Sadie
Into the Prairie - Rosanne Bittner   *t*   825

Wittgenstein, Beata
Echoes - Danielle Steel   *t*   940

Wong, Carnegie
The Love Wife - Gish Jen   *c*   1126

Wong, Janie
The Love Wife - Gish Jen   *c*   1126

Wortham, Julia
Katie's Dream - Leisha Kelly   *i*   1013

SPY

Amara
Furies of Calderon - Jim Butcher   *f*   512

Bismark, Travis
Gaudeamus - John Barnes   *s*   718

Blanchard, Ursula
The Siren Queen - Fiona Buckley   *t*   831
The Siren Queen - Fiona Buckley   *m*   24

Bonaventure, Marianna
Singularity - Bill DeSmedt   *s*   738

Bourne, Jason
The Bourne Legacy - Eric Van Lustbader   *c*   1202

Chen, Jennifer
Chaos Rising - A.J. Butcher   *s*   729
Spy High: Mission One - A.J. Butcher   *s*   730

Christopher, Paul
Old Boys - Charles McCarry   *c*   1142

Conklin, Alex
The Bourne Legacy - Eric Van Lustbader   *c*   1202

Crank
The Darkening - Chandler McGrew   *h*   667

Crowe, Painter
Sandstorm - James Rollins   *s*   780

de la Zeur, Eliza
The System of the World - Neal Stephenson   *t*   941

DeHaan, Eric
Dark Voyage - Alan Furst   *t*   870
Dark Voyage - Alan Furst   *c*   1110

Dering, Jarrett
Dangerous Deceptions - Lynn Kerstan   *r*   314

Falshaw, Kate
Dangerous Deceptions - Lynn Kerstan   *r*   314

Feramo, Pierre
Olivia Joules and the Overactive Imagination - Helen Fielding   *c*   1104

Gomes, Lawrence
Curious Notions - Harry Turtledove   *s*   796

Gomes, Paul
Curious Notions - Harry Turtledove   *s*   796

Hawke, Alexander
Assassin - Ted Bell   *c*   1073

Hubbard, Horace
Old Boys - Charles McCarry   *c*   1142

Lauria
Freedom's Gate - Naomi Kritzer   *f*   557

Levy, Mia
Songbird - Walter Zacharius   *t*   959

Mallory, Jack
Into the Volcano - Forrest DeVoe Jr.   *m*   57

Manners, Henry
The Palace of Heavenly Pleasure - Adam Williams   *t*   954

Morse, Laura
Into the Volcano - Forrest DeVoe Jr.   *m*   57

Rapp, Mitch
Memorial Day - Vince Flynn   *c*   1108

Reavley, Matthew
Shoulder the Sky - Anne Perry   *m*   163
Shoulder the Sky - Anne Perry   *t*   921

Reed, Lacie
A Perfect Cover - Maureen Tan   *r*   390

Samms, Julian
The Samms Agenda - Alison Kent   *r*   310

Schumann, Paul
Garden of Beasts - Jeffery Deaver   *c*   1088
Garden of Beasts - Jeffery Deaver   *m*   55

Selwick, Richard
The Secret History of the Pink Carnation - Lauren Willig   *c*   1208

Seymour, Sandor
A Dead Man in Trieste - Michael Pearce   *m*   159
A Dead Man in Trieste - Michael Pearce   *t*   919

Shaughnessey, Tripp
The Shaughnessey Accord - Alison Kent   *r*   311

Stanton, Benjamin Jr.
Chaos Rising - A.J. Butcher   *s*   729
Spy High: Mission One - A.J. Butcher   *s*   730

Stepola, Paul
Silenced: The Wrath of God Descends - Jerry B. Jenkins   *i*   1009

STEP-PARENT

Weeks, Roy
Stop That Girl - Elizabeth McKenzie   *c*   1144

STOCK BROKER

Carter, Madeline
Mad Money - Linda L. Richards   *r*   365

Fraser, Mark
The Sunday Philosophy Club - Alexander McCall Smith   *c*   1141

STORE OWNER

Anderson, Serena
The Marine Meets His Match - Cathie Linz   *r*   323

Bertrand, Carmela
Bound for Murder - Laura Childs   *m*   28

Black, Harrison
Snuffed Out - Tim Myers   *m*   153

Browning, Theodosia
The Jasmine Moon Murder - Laura Childs   *m*   29

Cohen, Abe
The First Desire - Nancy Reisman   *c*   1171

Collins, Sarah
The Alias Man - Bill Pronzini   *m*   165

Conner, Ricki
The Eggnog Chronicles - Carly Alexander   *r*   211

Coulter, Zeke
Bright Eyes - Catherine Anderson   *r*   213

Dauphinee, Arlene
Viator - Lucius Shepard   *h*   691

DeMarco, Sandy
Light My Fire - Jane Graves   *r*   276

Devonshire, Betsy
Crewel Yule - Monica Ferris   *m*   76

Doug
Dead Man's Hand - Tim Lebbon   *h*   654

Easton, Beck
Deep Blue - Tom Morrisey   *i*   1035

Everette, Regina
Say Yes - Donna Hill   *r*   292

Knight, Abby
Mum's the Word - Kate Collins   *m*   36

Malloy, Tom
Branded - Ed Gorman   *w*   442

Moon, Penelope
Where You Least Expect It - Tori Carrington   *r*   237

O'Shea, Magdalene "Maggie"
Shifting Love - Constance O'Day-Flannery   *r*   353

Owens, Brandi
Espresso for Two - Courtni Wright   *r*   411

Pennington, Dorothy
Haven - Julie Marshall   *r*   333

Sarah
The Lipstick Diaries - Lori Soard   *r*   382

Simpson, Graham
She'll Never Live - Hunter Morgan   *r*   349

STORYTELLER

Serafina
Serafina's Stories - Rudolfo Anaya   *w*   412

War Eagle
Indian Why Stories - Frank B. Linderman   *w*   461

STOWAWAY

Hakusar, Jim
Marque and Reprisal - Elizabeth Moon   *s*   769

STUDENT

Amata
The Franciscan Conspiracy - John R. Sack   *t*   932

Jones, Tina
The King of Ice Cream - Robert Wayne
   McCoy   *f*   567

Josh
The Attraction - Douglas Clegg   *h*   617

Kalantha
The Finest Creation - Jean Rabe   *f*   577

Meven
The Finest Creation - Jean Rabe   *f*   577

Pierce, Todd Baxter
The King of Ice Cream - Robert Wayne
   McCoy   *h*   666

Shapiro, Bronwyn
The Attraction - Douglas Clegg   *h*   617

Wellington, Sam
The Last Storyteller - Diane Noble   *i*   1037

William
Farewell, My Only One - Antoine Audouard   *t*   816

STUDENT—COLLEGE

Carrasco, Freddy
Any Place I Hang My Hat - Susan Isaacs   *c*   1124

Farris, Ted
Reason and Romance - Debra White Smith   *i*   1049

Geller, Adam
I Am Charlotte Simmons - Tom Wolfe   *c*   1211

Guest, Nick
The Line of Beauty - Alan Hollinghurst   *c*   1122

Johanssen, Jojo
I Am Charlotte Simmons - Tom Wolfe   *c*   1211

Kirsten
The First Cut - Peter Robinson   *m*   174

Meyers, Pearl
Pearl - Mary Gordon   *c*   1112

Moor
Ain't No Mountain - Sharon Ewell Foster   *i*   987

Simmons, Charlotte
I Am Charlotte Simmons - Tom Wolfe   *c*   1211

Yeager, Luke
The King of Ice Cream - Robert Wayne
   McCoy   *f*   567
The King of Ice Cream - Robert Wayne
   McCoy   *h*   666

STUDENT—GRADUATE

Cassidy, Jennifer
Deep Blue - Tom Morrisey   *i*   1035

Countryman, Lisa
Country of Origin - Don Lee   *c*   1135

Dolinar, Ivan
April Fool's Day - Josip Novakovich   *c*   1159

Kelly, Eloise
The Secret History of the Pink Carnation - Lauren
   Willig   *c*   1208

Lear, Rachel
Miss Fortune - Julia London   *r*   326

Mackenzie, C.K.
Till the End of Tom - Gillian Roberts   *m*   172

SUFFRAGETTE

Binnington, Mai
The Distaff Side - Elizabeth Palmer   *t*   916

SUPERNATURAL BEING

Avare, Simeon
The Dark Lord - Patricia Simpson   *r*   381

O'Shea, Magdalene "Maggie"
Shifting Love - Constance O'Day-Flannery   *r*   353

SURVEYOR

Bardin, William
Billy Bardin and the Witness Tree - Mary E.
   Penson   *w*   472

SURVIVOR

Brooks, Colleen
Ghostlands - Marc Zicree   *f*   598

Goldman, Herman
Ghostlands - Marc Zicree   *f*   598

Griffin, Cal
Ghostlands - Marc Zicree   *f*   598

Linden, Loretta
A Perfect Romance - Anne Robins   *r*   369

Tomas
Califia's Daughters - Leigh Richards   *s*   776

TEACHER

Ashby, Ria
Beyond a Wicked Kiss - Jo Goodman   *r*   273

Connen-Neute
Lost Truth - Dawn Cook   *f*   518

Cord, Morgan
The Alias Man - Bill Pronzini   *m*   165

Crawford, Cheryl
Kissed - Carmen Green   *r*   277

Delacourte, Lucien
The Painted Rose - Donna Birdsell   *r*   223

Dorset, Natalie
Undercover with the Mob - Elizabeth
   Bevarly   *r*   222

Flynn, Mike
The Hidden - Sarah Pinborough   *h*   681

Foster, Edwin
Judgment Day - Frank Roderus   *w*   479

Grant, Elmore
Chaos Rising - A.J. Butcher   *s*   729
Spy High: Mission One - A.J. Butcher   *s*   730

Gregory, Charlotte
A Rakish Spy - Laura Paquet   *r*   358

Heywood, Parker
Say Yes - Donna Hill   *r*   292

Hollister, Grace
Verse of the Vampyre - Diana Killian   *m*   117

Hood, Daniel
The Depths of Solitude - Jo Bannister   *m*   6

Kendall, Aidan
Where You Least Expect It - Tori Carrington   *r*   237

Keribdis
Lost Truth - Dawn Cook   *f*   518

Maddox, Susan
Fatal Error - Colleen Thompson   *r*   395

Mathilda of Flanders
Rite of Conquest - Judith Tarr   *f*   584

Medlar, Lucas
The Course of the Heart - M. John Harrison   *h*   639

Munro, Ramsey
My Pleasure - Connie Brockway   *r*   232

O'Rourke, Meara
Meant to Be - Edie Claire   *r*   241

Pepper, Amanda
Till the End of Tom - Gillian Roberts   *m*   172

Springer, Ellie
Light of Hope - Robert Vaughan   *i*   1052

Springer, Emily
When Christmas Comes - Debbie Macomber   *r*   330

Stewart, Anne
The Celebrity - Robert Elmer   *i*   985

Travis, Melanie
Jingle Bell Bark - Laurien Berenson   *m*   10

Withers, Hildegarde
The Puzzle of the Blue Banderilla - Stuart
   Palmer   *m*   156

TECHNICIAN

Duchamp, Lafiya
Grasp the Stars - Jennifer Wingert   *s*   806

TEENAGER

Acosta, Carmen
Convenient Disposal - Steven F. Havill   *w*   448

Avery, Stan
The Boy Who Would Live Forever - Frederik
   Pohl   *s*   773

Bardin, Billy
Billy Bardin and the Witness Tree - Mary E.
   Penson   *w*   472

Bergman, Chris
Starlight Comes Home - Janet Muirhead
   Hill   *w*   450

Bowmaster, Leeana
Windrider's Oath - David Weber   *f*   588

Burke, Shan
When the Sky Rained Dust - Patrick Dearen   *w*   436

Carter, Georgia
A Girl Becomes a Comma Like That - Lisa
   Glatt   *c*   1111

Chen, Jennifer
Chaos Rising - A.J. Butcher   *s*   729
Spy High: Mission One - A.J. Butcher   *s*   730

Chetwynde, Courtney
Black Water - D.J. MacHale   *f*   565

Christopher
A Seahorse Year - Stacey D'Erasmo   *c*   1091

Cloud, Mark
Living with Fred - Brad Whittington   *i*   1057

Creidhe
Foxmask - Juliet Marillier   *t*   900

Cruse, Matt
Airborn - Ken Oppel   *s*   772

DeVries, Kate
Airborn - Ken Oppel   *s*   772

Drummond, Ashley
She'll Never Live - Hunter Morgan   *r*   349

Els, Rashmika
Absolution Gap - Alastair Reynolds   *s*   775

Fassig, Roger
Billy Bardin and the Witness Tree - Mary E.
   Penson   *w*   472

Fuentes, Lake
Tampa Burn - Randy Wayne White   *m*   209

Gomes, Paul
Curious Notions - Harry Turtledove   *s*   796

Green, Melantha
The Green and the Gray - Timothy Zahn   *s*   808

Gry
Gifts - Ursula K. Le Guin   *f*   560

Haji
Edenborn - Nick Sagan   *s*   782

Haley, Will
Following the Harvest - Fred Harris   *t*   879
Following the Harvest - Fred Harris   *w*   447

Hutchinson, Matt
Afterlife - Douglas Clegg   *h*   616

Ilse
The Children's War - Monique Charlesworth   *t*   834
The Children's War - Monique
   Charlesworth   *c*   1083

Innes, Fleur
Paradise Fields - Katie Fforde   *c*   1103

Kevin
Chill Factor - Rachel Caine   *f*   514

Liam
Luna - Julie Anne Peters   *f*   575

Luna
Luna - Julie Anne Peters   *f*   575

McKeag, Roan
McKeag's Mountain - L.J. Martin   *w*   462

Michiko
Outlaw: Champions of Kanigawa - Scott
   McGough   *f*   568

Monange, Henri
Le Colonial - Kien Nguyen   *t*   912

Nessa
Silver's Edge - Anne Kelleher   *f*   550

Nicolai
The Children's War - Monique Charlesworth   *t*   834

Niebeck, Penny
The Real Minerva - Mary Sharratt   *t*   938

Orrec
Gifts - Ursula K. Le Guin   *f*   560

Patterson, Tommy
Dancing with Lyndon - Donley Watt   *w*   489

Paulsson, Gilly
Trace - Patricia Cornwell   *c*   1086

Pendragon, Bobby
Black Water - D.J. MacHale   *f*   565

Regan
Luna - Julie Anne Peters   *f*   575

Stanton, Benjamin Jr.
Chaos Rising - A.J. Butcher   *s*   729
Spy High: Mission One - A.J. Butcher   *s*   730

Stevens, Miranda
Starlight Comes Home - Janet Muirhead
   Hill   *w*   450

Sukara
Bengal Station - Eric Brown   *s*   723

Swift, Kevin
Hot Plastic - Peter Craig   *m*   43

Tamsin
Children of Epiphany - Frances Oliver   *h*   678

Tavi
Furies of Calderon - Jim Butcher   *f*   512

Thorvald
Foxmask - Juliet Marillier   *t*   900

Toldane, Ashdla
Twilight Rising, Serpent's Dream - Diana
   Marcellas   *f*   566

Tortuga
Tortuga - Rudolfo Anaya   *w*   413

Wander, Jason
Orphanage - Robert Buettner   *s*   727

Ware, Christy
The Underground River - Jeanne Williams   *w*   497

Watson, Josh
When the Sky Rained Dust - Patrick Dearen   *w*   436

Weaver, Argo
Kindling - Mick Farren   *f*   531

West, Deana
The Lake - Richard Laymon   *h*   653

Wickward, Clovermead
Clovermead - David Randall   *f*   578

Woo, Lucy
Curious Notions - Harry Turtledove   *s*   796

Yeager, Luke
The King of Ice Cream - Robert Wayne
   McCoy   *h*   666
The King of Ice Cream - Robert Wayne
   McCoy   *f*   567

Young, Sarah
Judgment Day - Frank Roderus   *w*   479

Zanni, Edward
How I Paid for College - Marc Acito   *c*   1063

TELEPATH

Vaughan, Jeff
Bengal Station - Eric Brown   *s*   723

Weaver, Kendi
Offspring - Steven Harper   *s*   751

Zudenigo, Zandor
Very Bad Deaths - Spider Robinson   *s*   779

TELEVISION

Bradley, Sabrina
Flippin' the Script - Aisha Ford   *i*   986

Vernon, Jules
American Idle - Alesia Holliday   *r*   295

TELEVISION PERSONALITY

Hill, Jermaine
A Man Inspired - Derek Jackson   *i*   1006

Kind, Daniel
The Coffin Trail - Martin Edwards   *m*   67

Lazarus, Joshua
The Departed - Kathryn Mackel   *i*   1021

Oliver, Darci
Flippin' the Script - Aisha Ford   *i*   986

St. Clair, Aislyn
Sweet Justice - Shirley Harrison   *r*   287

Willoughby, Claire
The Thing about Men - Elizabeth Bevarly   *r*   221

TERRORIST

bin Wazir, Snay
Assassin - Ted Bell   *c*   1073

THIEF

Anybody, Rob
A Hat Full of Sky - Terry Pratchett   *f*   576

Bone, Slayton
A Bad Day to Die - J. Lee Butts   *w*   422

Champion, Ed
Staring Down the Devil - Peter Brandvold   *w*   420

Fortune
Johnny Blue and the Texas Rangers - Joseph A.
   West   *w*   493

Fox, Peter
Verse of the Vampyre - Diana Killian   *m*   117

Langer, Ethan
Leaving Epitaph - Robert J. Randisi   *w*   477

Moran, Tommy
The Sucker's Kiss - Alan Parker   *t*   917

Parker
Nobody Runs Forever - Richard Stark   *m*   190

Prager, Bertoldus
McKeag's Mountain - L.J. Martin   *w*   462

Rudd, Joe
Lassiter - Loren Zane Grey   *w*   444

Sommers, Jamie
Hawkes Harbor - S.E. Hinton   *h*   641

Sudian
The Return of Nightfall - Mickey Zucker
   Reichert   *f*   579

Taylor, Amos
Mysterious Ways - Terry Burns   *w*   421
Mysterious Ways - Terry Burns   *i*   971

TIME TRAVELER

Chatterfield, Alec
The Life of the World to Come - Kage Baker   *s*   715

Dyeva
Crux - Albert E. Cowdrey   *s*   735

Magnusson, Ragnor
Wet and Wild - Sandra Hill   *r*   293

Marthe
The World as It Shall Be - Emile Souvestre   *s*   789

Maurice
The World as It Shall Be - Emile Souvestre   *s*   789

McBain, Robbie
Tempting the Highlander - Janet Chapman   *r*   239

Merrigan, Emma
Taking Time - Lynn Abbey   *f*   498

Pendaar "Father Daar"
Tempting the Highlander - Janet Chapman   *r*   239

Santoro, Carolina "Lina"
Goddess of Spring - P.C. Cast   *r*   238

Stafford, Robyn
White Rose - R. Garcia y Robertson   *t*   872
White Rose - R. Garcia y Robertson   *f*   536

TOUR GUIDE

Andrew, Emily
Pasta Imperfect - Maddy Hunter   *m*   107

Claymore, Harley
St. Dale - Sharyn McCrumb   *c*   1143

Tyler, Kate
The Lipstick Diaries - Lori Soard   *r*   382

TOURIST

David
Nights of Rain and Stars - Maeve Binchy   *c*   1077

TRADER

Menedemos
Owls to Athens - H.N. Turteltaub   *t*   946

Sostratos
Owls to Athens - H.N. Turteltaub   *t*   946

TRAPPER

Morgan, Sam
Beauty for Ashes - Win Blevins   *t*   827
Beauty for Ashes - Win Blevins   *w*   416

TRAVEL AGENT

Bailey, Harry
St. Dale - Sharyn McCrumb   *c*   1143

TRAVELER

Cargo, Frederick
Strange Cargo - Jeffrey E. Barlough   *f*   504

Eugen
Sacred Flesh - Robin D. Laws   *f*   559

Franziskus
Sacred Flesh - Robin D. Laws   *f*   559

Jarvis, Jay
Lost in Rooville - Ray Blackston   *i*   968

Kara
The Rage - Richard Lee Byers   *f*   513

Rowan
The Language of Power - Rosemary Kirstein   *f*   553

San Juste, Dominique
Seraphim - Michele Hauf   *f*   541

Wastefield, Jane
Strange Cargo - Jeffrey E. Barlough   *f*   504

TWIN

Carly, Abel
Dead Man's Canyon - Ralph Cotton   *w*   432

Carly, Blake
Dead Man's Canyon - Ralph Cotton   *w*   432

Maguire, Billy
The Dog Walker - Leslie Schnur   *c*   1179

Maguire, Daniel
The Dog Walker - Leslie Schnur   *c*   1179

O'Bannon, Brogan
In a Wild Wood - Sasha Lord   *r*   327

Shailiha
The Scrolls of the Ancients - Robert
  Newcomb   *f*   571

Sorrell, Reve
As Good as Dead - Beverly Barton   *r*   219

Talbot, Jazzy
As Good as Dead - Beverly Barton   *r*   219

Tristan
The Scrolls of the Ancients - Robert
  Newcomb   *f*   571

UNEMPLOYED

Van Der Kirk, Oscar
Days of Infamy - Harry Turtledove   *s*   797

VACATIONER

Lynx, Philip "Flinx"
Sliding Scales - Alan Dean Foster   *s*   745

VAGRANT

Yaxley
The Course of the Heart - M. John Harrison   *h*   639

VAMPIRE

Argeneau, Bastien
Tall, Dark, and Hungry - Lynsay Sands   *r*   377

Ashby, John
Tainted Blood - James M. Thompson   *h*   701

Champion, Reece
Master of the Night - Angela Knight   *r*   318

Corbus
Blood of the Dragon - C.L. Werner   *f*   590

Duchon, Jules
Bride of the Fat White Vampire - Andrew
  Fox   *h*   631

Fitzroy, Henry
Smoke and Shadows - Tanya Huff   *h*   642

Griffin, Deirdre
Blood Red Dawn - Karen E. Taylor   *h*   700

Hawkes, Grenville
Hawkes Harbor - S.E. Hinton   *h*   641

Jean-Claude
Incubus Dreams - Laurell K. Hamilton   *h*   637
Incubus Dreams - Laurell K. Hamilton   *c*   1116

Max
Blood Red Dawn - Karen E. Taylor   *h*   700

Nez, Lee
Blood Retribution - David Thurlo   *m*   200

Northman, Eric
Dead to the World - Charlaine Harris   *h*   638

Nudie
The Haunted Hillbilly - Derek McCormack   *h*   665

Peregrine, Nathaniel
American Gothic - Michael Romkey   *h*   687

Pike, Elijah
Tainted Blood - James M. Thompson   *h*   701

Preston
Bride of the Fat White Vampire - Andrew
  Fox   *h*   631

Richelieu, Rory "Doodlebug"
Bride of the Fat White Vampire - Andrew
  Fox   *h*   631

Robin Hood
A Cold Summer Night - Trystam Kith   *h*   651

Sade, Louis
The Vampire de Sade - Mary Ann Mitchell   *h*   668

Saint-Germain
Dark of the Sun - Chelsea Quinn Yarbro   *h*   710
Dark of the Sun - Chelsea Quinn Yarbro   *t*   958

Sinclair, Eric
Undead and Unemployed - MaryJanice
  Davidson   *r*   248
Undead and Unemployed - MaryJanice
  Davidson   *h*   625

Taylor, Betsy
Undead and Unemployed - MaryJanice
  Davidson   *h*   625
Undead and Unemployed - MaryJanice
  Davidson   *r*   248

Thantos, Theo
Tainted Blood - James M. Thompson   *h*   701

Thomas
Blood Rites - Jim Butcher   *h*   608

VAMPIRE HUNTER

Blake, Anita
Incubus Dreams - Laurell K. Hamilton   *h*   637
Incubus Dreams - Laurell K. Hamilton   *c*   1116

Van Helsing, Abraham
The Many Faces of Van Helsing - Jeanne
  Cavelos   *h*   612

VETERAN

Buchanan, Thaddeus
Loving Mercy - Teresa Bodwell   *r*   230

Jorgen
The Painting - Nina Schuyler   *t*   935

Labarde, Conrad
Amagansett - Mark Mills   *c*   1149
Amagansett - Mark Mills   *m*   143
Amagansett - Mark Mills   *t*   907

Novak, Georgie
Baker Towers - Jennifer Haigh   *t*   876
Baker Towers - Jennifer Haigh   *c*   1115

O'Sullivan, Michael Jr.
Road to Purgatory - Max Allan Collins   *m*   37
Road to Purgatory - Max Allan Collins   *t*   843

Simpkins, Charlie
The Mercy Killers - Lisa Reardon   *c*   1169

Varden, Kane
The Sun Witch - Linda Winstead Jones   *r*   304

VETERINARIAN

Hayes, Fredrica
A Tender Touch - Lenora Worth   *i*   1062

McCarthy, Gail
Forged - Laura Crum   *m*   47

Popper, Jessica
Putting on the Dog - Cynthia Baxter   *m*   7

Pulver, Danny
Changes of Heart - Paige Lee Elliston   *i*   984

Westbrook, David
The Burning of Rachel Hayes - Doug Allyn   *t*   812

Yamamoto, Greg
The Secret Beau - Annette Mahon   *r*   331

VINTNER

DeLuca, Gabriela "Gabby"
Too Close to the Sun - Diana Dempsey   *r*   251

VOLUNTEER

Bryan, Jamie
Beyond Tuesday Morning - Karen
  Kingsbury   *i*   1014

WAITER/WAITRESS

Leonard, Isabelle
See Isabelle Run - Elizabeth Bloom   *r*   229

Stackhouse, Sookie
Dead to the World - Charlaine Harris   *h*   638

Winters, Caroline
How to Be Lost - Amanda Eyre Ward   *c*   1205

WARD

Ashby, Ria
Beyond a Wicked Kiss - Jo Goodman   *r*   273

Tamhill, Prudence
He Said Never - Patricia Waddell   *r*   400

WARLORD

Genji
Autumn Bridge - Takashi Matsuoka   *c*   1139
Autumn Bridge - Takashi Matsuoka   *t*   902

Konda
Outlaw: Champions of Kanigawa - Scott
McGough   *f*   568

WARRIOR

Achilles
The War at Troy - Lindsay Clarke   *t*   836

Albion, Brian
The Winter Oak - James A. Hetley   *f*   544

Arvin
Venom's Taste - Lisa Smedman   *f*   582

Bear
Paladins - Joel Rosenberg   *f*   580

Blacksword, Tanaros
Banewreaker - Jacqueline Carey   *f*   515

Caldason, Reeth
The Covenant Rising - Stan Nicholls   *f*   572

Coldheart, Hirad
Demonstorm - James Barclay   *f*   503

D'Ange, Seraphim
Seraphim - Michele Hauf   *f*   541

Dian
Califia's Daughters - Leigh Richards   *s*   776

Diviner, Madoc
Prisoner of Haven - Nancy Varian Berberick   *f*   506

Dreams-of-War
Banner of Souls - Liz Williams   *s*   805

Frane
Haydn of Mars - Al Sarrantonio   *s*   784

Grunthor
Elegy for a Lost Star - Elizabeth Haydon   *f*   542

Hardrada, Harald
Rite of Conquest - Judith Tarr   *f*   584

Harlech
Child of the Dark Prophecy - T.A. Barron   *f*   505

Jade, Harmonious
A Day Dark as Night - Carl Bowen   *f*   507

Karayan, Vartan
Giver of Roses - Kathleen Morgan   *i*   1029

Kore
Paths of Evil - Richard C. White   *f*   591

Layla
Paths of Evil - Richard C. White   *f*   591

Maclean, Lachlan
Highland Princess - Amanda Scott   *r*   379

Magnusson, Ragnor
Wet and Wild - Sandra Hill   *r*   293

Marrec
Lady of Poison - Bruce R. Cordell   *f*   519

McGoin
Exile's Return - Raymond E. Feist   *f*   533

Mochi
Outlaw: Champions of Kanigawa - Scott
McGough   *f*   568

Ravenson, Raven
The Last Guardian of Everness - John C.
Wright   *f*   596

Rayn, Emerald Rose
Legend of the Emerald Rose - Linda
Wichman   *i*   1058

Sek, Anakwanar
Double Eagle - Dan Abnett   *s*   711

Spotted Tongue
Tome of Murder - D.R. Meredith   *w*   464

Stave
The Runes of the Earth - Stephen R.
Donaldson   *f*   524

Tamar
Freedom's Gate - Naomi Kritzer   *f*   557

Tathas
The Wilding - C.S. Friedman   *s*   746

Toren
The Shadow Roads - Sean Russell   *f*   581

Ulmarra, Gunggari
Lady of Poison - Bruce R. Cordell   *f*   519

Yani
The Three Sisters - Rebecca Locksley   *f*   562

WEALTHY

Abair, James
Heir to the Glimmering World - Cythia
Ozick   *c*   1161

Bennett, Celeste
Killer Curves - Roxanne St. Claire   *r*   383

Benoliel, Joseph Adrian
Dead Lines - Greg Bear   *h*   603

Burnaby, Dirk
The Falls - Joyce Carol Oates   *c*   1160

Danvers, Zachary
See How She Dies - Lisa Jackson   *r*   299

Donovan, William
The Irish Devil - Diane Whiteside   *r*   405

Dunhill, Dylan III
Dying to Marry - Janelle Taylor   *r*   392

Eddie
Lucious Lemon - Heather Swain   *r*   389

Fairweather, Helen
American Gothic - Michael Romkey   *h*   687

Farrell, Bridgett
Metal Sky - Jay Caselberg   *s*   731

Graham, Devlin
As You Wish - Francine Matthews   *r*   334

Hunt, Simon
Secrets of a Summer Night - Lisa Kleypas   *r*   317

Maddox, Ian
The Duel - Barbara Metzger   *r*   342

Mahoney, Will
Hissy Fit - Mary Kay Andrews   *r*   214
Hissy Fit - Mary Kay Andrews   *c*   1065

McDonald, Julian
Shifting Love - Constance O'Day-Flannery   *r*   353

Mulvhill, Catherine
Echo Bay - Richard Barre   *c*   1070

Nga'esha, Yaenida
Master of None - N. Lee Wood   *s*   807

Norrell
Jonathan Strange & Mr. Norrell - Susanna
Clarke   *c*   1085

Richmond, Scott
Caught in the Act - Pam McCutcheon   *r*   336

Roche, Delly
The Parts - Keith Ridgway   *c*   1172

Rutherford
The Life of the World to Come - Kage Baker   *s*   715

Rutledge, Boone
Calder Promise - Janet Dailey   *r*   245

Vogler, Michael
The Bride Wore Chocolate - Shirley Jump   *r*   305

Wentworth, Daniel Eli IV
Sleep Tight - Laura Marie Altom   *r*   212

Winchuster, Winifred
Land Sakes - Margaret A. Graham   *i*   993

WEREWOLF

Cadotte, Will
Blue Moon - Lori Handeland   *r*   283

Turner, Rule
Tempting Danger - Eileen Wilks   *r*   406

Zeeman, Richard
Incubus Dreams - Laurell K. Hamilton   *c*   1116
Incubus Dreams - Laurell K. Hamilton   *h*   637

WIDOW(ER)

Ahab, Hannah
Hannah Rose - Louise M. Gouge   *i*   991

Banner, Sophie Lindel
A Duke for Christmas - Cynthia Pratt   *r*   362

Berger, Mitch
The Burnt Orange Sunrise - David Handler   *m*   98

Bishop, Charlotte Valentine
Watchers on the Hill - Stephanie Grace
Whitson   *i*   1056

Blanchard, Ursula
The Siren Queen - Fiona Buckley   *m*   24
The Siren Queen - Fiona Buckley   *t*   831

Brand, Luke
Dark Harvest - Karen Harper   *r*   285

Bryan, Jamie
Beyond Tuesday Morning - Karen
Kingsbury   *i*   1014

Byrne, Christy
Silver Bells - Luanne Rice   *r*   363

Cadwallader, Henry
The Hollywood Dodo - Geoff Nicholson   *c*   1156

Callahan, Connor
Snap Shot - Meg Chittenden   *r*   240

Carter, Charlotte
A New Day at Tanglewood - Annette Gail
Smith   *i*   1048

Cisco, Loretta
Family Blessings - Fern Michaels   *r*   344

Clarke, Mercy
Loving Mercy - Teresa Bodwell   *r*   230

Clary, Maggie
Loop Group - Larry McMurtry   *c*   1146

Compton, Elizabeth Hartleigh
Fire When Ready - Kate Kingsbury   *m*   119

Cristiana
The Widow's Tale - Margaret Frazer   *t*   868

WITCH

WIZARD

WOODSMAN

WORKER

Wilf
The Overnight - Ramsey Campbell *h* 611

WRITER

Alakusoglu, Kerim
Snow - Orhan Pamuk *c* 1162

Amiss, Robert
Carnage on the Committee - Ruth Dudley
 Edwards *m* 68

Anderson, Robert
Little Fugue - Robert Anderson *t* 813

Austen, Jaine
Killer Blonde - Laura Levine *m* 126

Avery, Wes
Haven - Don D'Ammassa *s* 736

Barnes, John
Gaudeamus - John Barnes *s* 718

Benton, Delilah
Loving Delilah - Candice Poarch *r* 361

Blair, Alan
Wake Up, Sir - Jonathan Ames *c* 1064

Blume, Molly
Grave Endings - Rochelle Krich *m* 123

Boone, Christian Wolfe "Boo"
Boo Who - Rene Gutteridge *i* 994

Breen, Clarissa
My Death - Lisa Tuttle *h* 702

Browne, Martha
The First Cut - Peter Robinson *m* 174

Chaucer, Geoffrey
Chaucer and the House of Fame - Philippa
 Morgan *m* 148
Chaucer and the House of Fame - Philippa
 Morgan *t* 909

Christie, Agatha
The London Blitz Murders - Max Allan
 Collins *t* 842

Coldwell, Eliot
Banquet for the Damned - Adam L.G. Nevill *h* 675

Conrad, Joseph
Sailors on the Inward Sea - Lawrence
 Thornton *t* 945

Derwood, Mahalia "Hailie"
Wonderful and Wild - Simona Taylor *r* 393

Flynn, Daniel
In Like Flynn - Dorien Kelly *r* 308

Hughes, Ted
Little Fugue - Robert Anderson *t* 813

Hunter, Thomas
Red - Ted Dekker *i* 978
White - Ted Dekker *i* 979

James, Henry
Author, Author - David Lodge *t* 897
Author, Author - David Lodge *c* 1138
The Master - Colm Toibin *c* 1195

Jones, Dakota
Follow Me Home - Jerri Corgiat *r* 244

Kauffman, David
Soul Tracker - Bill Myers *i* 1036

Ladd, Diana
Day of the Dead - J.A. Jance *m* 108

Lovecraft, Howard Phillips
Lovecraft - Hans Rodionoff *h* 686

Lucas, Lorinda
Please Do Feed the Cat - Marian Babson *m* 4

Marlowe, Christopher
Young Will - Bruce Cook *t* 845

Marti, Jose
The Divine Husband - Francisco Goldman *t* 874

Naryshkin, Boris
A Carnivore's Inquiry - Sabina Murray *c* 1152

Patrick, Willy Bryce
In the Night Room - Peter Straub *h* 697

Poe, Edgar Allan
The Mask of Red Death - Harold Schechter *t* 934
The Mask of Red Death - Harold Schechter *m* 181

Ralston, Helen Elizabeth
My Death - Lisa Tuttle *h* 702

Rimbaud, Arthur
One King, One Soldier - Alexander C. Irvine *f* 549

Robert
Children of Epiphany - Frances Oliver *h* 678

Russell
Very Bad Deaths - Spider Robinson *s* 779

Russell, Peter
Dead Lines - Greg Bear *h* 603

Sankova, Sonja
Sonja's Run - Richard Hoyt *t* 883

Shakespeare, William
Time's Fool - Leonard Tourney *m* 201
Young Will - Bruce Cook *t* 845

Sheriff, Alan
The Tyrant's Novel - Thomas Keneally *c* 1130

Sirocco, Nick
Arouse Suspicion - Maureen McKade *r* 337

Spicer, Jack
One King, One Soldier - Alexander C. Irvine *f* 549

Swift, Tamara
Ghosts of Albion: Astray - Amber Benson *h* 604

Trovato, Caleb
Cold Feet - Brenda Novak *r* 352

Underhill, Tim
In the Night Room - Peter Straub *h* 697

Wallis, Talba
Louisiana Lament - Julie Smith *m* 186

Walpuski, Howard
Walpuski's Typewriter - Frank Darabont *h* 624

Wevill, Assia Gutmann
Little Fugue - Robert Anderson *t* 813

Willoughby, Claire
The Thing about Men - Elizabeth Bevarly *r* 221

Woolson, Constance Fenimore
Author, Author - David Lodge *t* 897
Author, Author - David Lodge *c* 1138

YOUNG MAN

Allen, E.A.
Waiting for Teddy Williams - Howard Frank
 Mosher *c* 1150

Chase, Philip
Strange but True - John Searles *c* 1182

Freeman, Gerard
The Ghost Writer - John Harwood *c* 1118
The Ghost Writer - John Harwood *h* 640

Greenhow, Mark
Voyageurs - Margaret Elphinstone *t* 866

Grey, Walter
Infernal Angel - Edward Lee *h* 656

Peter
Mantrapped - Fay Weldon *c* 1207

Robbins, Chad
House of Blood - Bryan Smith *h* 693

Smolij, Michael
Please Don't Come Back from the Moon - Dean
 Bakopoulos *c* 1068

YOUNG WOMAN

Abbott, Taite
The Last Storyteller - Diane Noble *i* 1037

Annais
The Falcons of Montabard - Elizabeth
 Chadwick *t* 833

Aradna
Pride of Carthage - David Anthony Durham *t* 864

Barnaby, Alexandra
Metro Girl - Janet Evanovich *c* 1098
Metro Girl - Janet Evanovich *m* 72

Bonner, Lily
Fire Along the Sky - Sara Donati *t* 855

Calverson, Timona "Timmy"
Somebody Wonderful - Kate Rothwell *r* 375

Daria
King's Ransom - Jan Benzely *t* 822

Dean, Susannah
Song of Susannah - Stephen King *c* 1131

DelaSangre, Chloe
The Seadragon's Daughter - Alan F. Troop *f* 585

Effie
The Sucker's Kiss - Alan Parker *t* 917

Emerson, Jenny
Haven - Julie Marshall *r* 333

Finnerty, Jo
The Palo Duro Trail - Ralph Compton *w* 430

Green, Eve
Eve Green - Susan Fletcher *c* 1106

Huxleigh, Nell
Spider Dance - Carole Nelson Douglas *t* 857

Ipek
Snow - Orhan Pamuk *c* 1162

Italia
Don't Move - Margaret Mazzantini *c* 1140

Jackson, Alicia
House of Blood - Bryan Smith *h* 693

Jessel, Alice
The Ghost Writer - John Harwood *h* 640
The Ghost Writer - John Harwood *c* 1118

Kadife
Snow - Orhan Pamuk *c* 1162

Kleintjes, Monica
Heart of the Hunter - Deon Meyer *c* 1148

Ky, Nikki
Murder of Angels - Caitlin R. Kiernan *h* 648

Mitwisser, Anneliese
Heir to the Glimmering World - Cythia
 Ozick *c* 1161

Novak, Dorothy
Baker Towers - Jennifer Haigh *t* 876

O'Hara, Patty Ann
Road to Purgatory - Max Allan Collins *t* 843

Pagliano, Maria
The Devil Served Tortellini - Shirley Jump *r* 306

Pangloss, Lulu
Xombies - Walter Greatshell *h* 635

Renslow, Athena
The Duel - Barbara Metzger *r* 342

Rollins, Kylie
Precious Things - Andrea Boeshaar *i* 969

Shea, Katherine
A Carnivore's Inquiry - Sabina Murray   *c*   1152

Torvald, Opal
Opal - Lauraine Snelling   *i*   1050

Weaver, Dream
House of Blood - Bryan Smith   *h*   693

ZEALOT

Revkina, Aglaya Stepanovna
Monumental Propaganda - Vladimir
   Voinovich   *c*   1204

Santos-Smith, Wan Enrique
The Boy Who Would Live Forever - Frederik
   Pohl   *s*   773

Author Index

This index is an alphabetical listing of the authors of books featured in entries and those listed within entries under the rubrics "Other books by the same author" and "Other books you might like." For each author, the titles of books described or listed in this edition and their entry numbers appear. Bold numbers indicate a featured main entry; light-face numbers refer to books recommended for further reading.

B

Babb, Sandra
Where Names Are Unknown 434, 436, 447, 470

Babcock, Richard
Bow's Boy 1173, 1197

Babson, Marian
Canapes for the Kitties 4
The Cat Next Door 4
The Cat Who Wasn't a Dog 4
The Company of Cats 4
The Diamond Cat 60
Please Do Feed the Cat **4**
To Catch a Cat 4

Backer, Sara
American Fuji 1135

Bader, Ted
Desire and Duty 820

Baen, Jim
The World Turned Upside Down **740**

Baer, Judy
Bid for My Heart 964
Country Bride 964
Jenny's Story 964
Libby's Story 964, 985
Tia's Story 964
The Whitney Chronicles **964**, 966, 968

Bagdon, Paul
The Stranger from Medina 467
The West Texas Sunrise Series 971

Baggott, Julianna
Girl Talk 1081

Baharloo, Morteza
The Quince Seed Potion **817**

Bailey, Robin Wayne
Swords Against the Shadowlands 551

Baines, Candice Poarch
Loving Delilah **361**

Baker, Calvin
Once Two Heroes 843

Baker, Jeanette
Blood Roses 217
Chesapeake Tide **217**
The Delaney Woman 217
Irish Lady 217
Nell 217
Spellbound 217

Baker, Kage
The Anvil of the World 715
Black Projects, White Knights 715
The Graveyard Game 715
The Life of the World to Come **715**
Mendoza in Hollywood 715
Sky Coyote 715

Baker, Kevin
Dreamland 860, 898

Baker, Madeline
Enchanted Crossings 250

Baker, Megan Sybil
An Accidental Goddess 274

Baker, Trisha
Crimson Kiss 701

Bakopoulos, Dean
Please Don't Come Back from the Moon **1068**

Baldacci, David
The Christmas Train 1105

Last Man Standing 1090
The Simple Truth 1080

Baldwin, Kathleen
Cut from the Same Cloth 218
Lady Fiasco **218**, 387
Mistaken Kiss 218

Balfour, Bruce
The Digital Dead 716
The Forge of Mars 716
Prometheus Road **716**
Star Crusader 716

Balint, Christine
Ophelia's Fan **818**, 829, 890
The Salt Letters 818, 949

Ball, David W.
Empires of Sand 931
Ironfire 833

Ball, Margaret
Changeweaver 717
Disappearing Act **717**
Flameweaver 717
Lost in Translation 717
Mathemagics 717
No Earthly Sunne 717

Ballard, J.G.
Chronopolis 801
War Fever 770

Ballard, Mignon
An Angel to Die For 522

Balogh, Mary
Beyond the Sunrise 408
The Famous Heroine 218
One Night for Love 314
A Regency Christmas Feast 335
The Secret Pearl 351
Slightly Dangerous 854
Thief of Dreams 290

Balzo, Sandra
Uncommon Grounds **5**, 29, 42

Bambola, Sylvia
Tears in a Bottle 1026, 1037

Banbury, Jen
Like a Hole in the Head 1156

Bancroft, Blair
The Indifferent Earl 358

Bangs, Nina
From Boardwalk with Love 310, 311
Men at Work **252**
An Original Sin 252

Bank, Melissa
The Girl's Guide to Hunting and Fishing 1206

Banks, Carolyn
The Robin Vaughan Series 47

Banks, L.A.
The Hunted 601
Minion 637
Stroke of Midnight **313**

Banks, Leanne
Some Girls Do 249

Banks, Russell
The Darling 1177
Rule of the Bone 1063

Banks, T.F.
The Thief-Taker 173, 928

Banning, Lynna
One Starry Christmas **247**

Bannister, Jo
The Depths of Solitude **6**
Echoes of Lies 6

The Frank Shapiro Series 48
Reflections 6
True Witness 6

Banville, John
Athena 1084
Eclipse 1118

Barbour, Anne
A Wedding Bouquet 254

Barclay, James
Demonstorm **503**
Elfsorrow 503
Light Stealer 503, 526
Nightchild 503, 548
Noonshade 503, 556
Shadowheart 503

Barclay, Suzanne
The Knights of Christmas 348
Knight's Ransom 386
Lion's Legacy 379

Barker, Clive
Cabal 704
Coldheart Canyon 1118
The Great and Secret Show 649, 657
Sacrament 1177
Tapping the Vein 600, 686
Weaveworld 681

Barker, Pat
Blow Your House Down 1152
Regeneration 1159, 1183

Barlough, Jeffrey E.
Dark Sleeper 504
The House in the High Woods 504
Strange Cargo **504**

Barnard, Robert
The Charlie Peace/Mike Odhams Series 90
Death of an Old Goat 68, 167
A Little Local Murder 8, 21
Out of the Blackout 82, 119
Skeleton in the Grass 171

Barnes, John
Candle 718
Finity 718, 781
Gaudeamus **718**
In the Hall of the Martian King 718, 732
The Merchants of Souls 718
The Sky So Big and Black 718

Barnes, Julian
A History of the World in Ten and One-Half Chapters 1069
The Lemon Table **1069**
Love, etc. 1069, 1093, 1134
Metroland 1069
Staring at the Sun 1069
Talking It Over 1069

Barnes, Linda
The Carlotta Carlyle Series 129, 151, 157

Barnes, Steven
The Kundalini Equation 749
Lion's Blood 948

Barnett, David G.
Damned: An Anthology of the Lost **602**

Barnett, Jill
Sentimental Journey 875

Barr, Nevada
The Anna Pigeon Series 120, 145, 189
Blood Lure 178
Hunting Season 1125

Barre, Richard
Bethany 1070
Blackheart Highway 1070
Burning Moon 1070
Echo Bay **1070**
Star 1070
Wind on the River 1070

Barrett, Julia
Presumption 820

Barrett, Neal Jr.
The Hereafter Gang 719
The Leaves of Time 531
Perpetuity Blues 719
Prince of Christler-Coke **719**, 725
The Prophecy Machine 719
Slightly Off Center 719
The Treachery of Kings 719

Barron, Stephanie
The Jane Austen Series 173, 820, 885, 928

Barron, T.A.
The Ancient One 505
Child of the Dark Prophecy **505**
The Fires of Merlin 505
The Mirror of Merlin 505
The Tree Girl 505
The Wings of Merlin 505

Barry, Dave
Tricky Business 1104

Barry, Desmond
Cressida's Bed 1188

Barth, Richard
Jumper 1090

Bartholomew, Nancy
The Sierra Lavatoni Series 34, 72

Bartolomeo, Christina
Cupid and Diana 1071
The Side of the Angels 1071
Snowed In **1071**

Barton, Beverly
After Dark 219
As Good as Dead **219**, 349
The Fifth Victim 219, 349, 372
Keeping Annie Safe 219
The Last to Die 219
What She Doesn't Know 219

Barton, William
When Heaven Fell 716

Bass, Cynthia
Sherman's March 886, 955

Bass, Rick
Where the Sea Used to Be 1129

Bass, T.J.
Half Past Human 782

Bates, Shelley
Grounds to Believe 1003

Baudino, Gael
Branch and Crown 525
Maze of Moonlight 541

Baum, Thomas
Out of Body 633

Bauman, Jon R.
Santa Fe Passage **415**, 819

Baumbich, Charlene Ann
The Dearest Dorothy Series 993, 1011, 1051, 1057

Baumgardner, Cathie
The Marine Meets His Match **323**

Bausch, Richard
In the Night Season 1160

Author Index

Author Index

Author Index

Goldberg, Myla
Bee Season 834

Golden, Christie
Dance of the Dead 539
The Enemy Within 539
Instrument of Fate 539
Lord of the Clans 539
On Fire's Wings **539**
Vampire of the Mists 539

Golden, Christopher
Ghosts of Albion: Astray **604**

Goldin, Stephen
*And Not Make Dreams Your
    Master* 751
The Eternity Brigade 750

Goldman, Francisco
The Divine Husband **874**
*The Long Night of White
    Chickens* 874
The Ordinary Seaman 874

Goldman, William
Tinsel 1109, 1117

Goldring, Kat
Death Medicine 458
The Willi Gallagher Series 193

Goldsmith, Olivia
Dumping Billy 1065

Goldstein, Lisa
The Alchemist's Door 941
Travellers in Magic 690

Goldstein, Naama
The Place Will Comfort You 1147

Gollin, James
Eliza's Galiardo 880

Golling, Diane Farr
Under a Lucky Star **259**

Gonzales, Jovita
Caballero 415

Gooden, Philip
Mask of Night 201
The Sleep of Death 134

Goodger, Jane
A Hard Man Is Good to Find **225**
The Perfect Wife 215

Goodman, Allegra
Paradise Park 1065

Goodman, Carol
The Seduction of Water 1106

Goodman, Jo
All I Ever Needed 273
Beyond a Wicked Kiss **273**, 321
Everything I Wanted 273
Let Me Be the One 273
More than You Wished 273
Tempting Torment 273

Goodman, Mark
*Hurrah for the Next Man Who
    Dies* 937

Goonan, Kathleen Ann
The Bones of Time 715

Gordimer, Nadine
The Pickup 1089, 1203

Gordon, Mary
The Company of Women 1112
Final Payments 1112
Men and Angels 1112
The Other Side 1112
Pearl **1112**
Spending 1112

Gore, Kristin
Sammy's Hill **1113**, 1124

Gores, Joe
32 Cadillacs 17
Hammett 37

Gorman, E.J.
The Marilyn Tapes 848

Gorman, Ed
*The Blue and the Gray
    Undercover* 443
Branded **442**
The Fatal Frontier 443
Gun Truth 442, 467
Gunslinger 443
Lawless 442, 443
The Long Ride Back 440, 441, 442
Night of Shadows 442, 475, 479,
    491
Storm Riders 443
Texas Rangers 422, 442, **443**
*The World's Finest Mystery and Crime
    Stories: Fifth Annual Collection* **87**
*The World's Finest Mystery and Crime
    Stories: First Annual Collection* 87
*The World's Finest Mystery and Crime
    Stories: Fourth Annual
    Collection* 87
*The World's Finest Mystery and Crime
    Stories: Second Annual
    Collection* 87
*The World's Finest Mystery and Crime
    Stories Series* 56
*The World's Finest Mystery and Crime
    Stories: Third Annual Collection* 87

Goth, Louis A.
Red-12 734

Gottleib, Sherry
Worse than Death 700

Gouge, Louise M.
Ahab's Bride 991
Hannah Rose **991**
The Homecoming 991
*Once There Was a Way Back
    Home* 991

Goulart, Ron
Hawkshaw 758

Gould, John
The Wines of Pentagoet 846

Gould, Steven
Blind Waves 725

Gower, Daniel H.
The Orpheus Process 603

Grabien, Deborah
Eyes in the Fire 88
*The Famous Flower of Serving
    Men* **88**
The Weaver and the Factory Maid 88,
    150

Grace, C.L.
The Book of Shadows 89
The Eye of God 89
A Feast of Poisons **89**, 141
The Kathryn Swinbrooke Series 83
A Maze of Murders 89
The Merchant of Death 89
Saintly Murders 89

Grafton, Sue
The Kinsey Millhone Series 129, 151,
    157
M Is for Malice 1114
N Is for Noose 1114
O Is for Outlaw 1114
P Is for Peril 1114

Q Is for Quarry 1114
R Is for Ricochet 1086, 1098, **1114**

Graham, Caroline
Death in Disguise 90
Death of a Hollow Man 90
Faithful Unto Death 90
A Ghost in the Machine **90**
The Inspector Tom Barnaby Series 46
A Place of Safety 90
Written in Blood 90

Graham, Heather
Tall, Dark, and Deadly 324

Graham, Margaret A.
Anna 993
Good Heavens **992**, 993
Land Sakes **993**
Mercy Me 992, 993, 1046

Granger, Ann
*The Alan Markby/Meredith Mitchell
    Series* 6

Granger, Pip
Not All Tarts Are Apple 17, 875
Trouble in Paradise **875**
The Widow Ginger 875

Grant, Anne Underwood
The Sydney Teague Series 133

Grant, Charles L.
The Black Carousel 657
The Nestling 617
Shadows 606
Tales from the Nightside 669

Grant, Gavin J.
*The Year's Best Fantasy and Horror:
    Seventeenth Annual Collection* **523**

Grant, Linda
The Catherine Sayler Series 151

Grant, Maxwell
Norgil the Magician 84

Grant, Susan
Contact 274, 354
The Legend of Banzai Maguire 261,
    274, 354
Once a Pirate 274
The Scarlet Empress **274**
The Star Prince 274
The Star Princess 274

Grass, Gunter
The Call of the Toad 835

Grasso, Patricia
To Catch a Countess 275
To Charm a Prince 275
To Love a Princess **275**
To Tame a Duke 275
To Tame an Angel 275
Violets in the Snow 275, 351

Graversen, Pat
Sweet Blood 700

Graves, Jane
Flirting with Disaster 276
I Got You, Babe 276
Light My Fire **276**
Wild at Heart 276

Graves, Sarah
The Jacobia Tiptree Series 18, 26,
    203

Gray, Ginna
For the Love of Grace 376
The Witness 246

Grayson, Kristin
Simply Irresistible 329
Utterly Charming 309

Grazer, Gigi Levangie
Maneater 1156

Graziunas, Diana
Thinning the Predators 709

Greatshell, Walter
Xombies 635

Greber, Judith
Till the End of Tom **172**

Greeley, Andrew M.
The Blackie Ryan Series 140

Green, Carmen
Doctor, Doctor 277
Endless Love 277
Island Bliss 277
Keeping Secrets 277
Kissed **277**
Silken Love 277

Green, Jonathan
The Dead and the Damned 537, 750
Iron Hands **750**, 765
Magestorm 590, 750

Green, Michael
The Jimjams 658

Green, Roland
The Painful Field 786

Green, Sharon
Convergence 589

Green, Simon R.
Agents of Light and Darkness 636,
    704
Beyond the Blue Moon 543, 552, 555
Blue Moon Rising 533
The Bones of Haven 507
The God Killer 551
Hex and the City 636
Nightingale's Lament 583, **636**
Something from the Nightside 636

Greenberg, Martin H.
Against the King 540
Dracula: Prince of Darkness 612
Elf Fantastic 540
Elf Magic 540
Holmes for the Holidays 124
*Little Red Riding Hood in the Big Bad
    City* **540**
Merlin 540
Murder Most Medieval 202
Murder, My Dear Watson 124
*The New Adventures of Sherlock
    Holmes* 124
*New Stories from the Twilight
    Zone* 610, 689
A Taste for Blood 645
Texas Rangers **443**
Vampire Detectives 612
Wizard Fantastic 540
*The World's Finest Mystery and Crime
    Stories: Fifth Annual Collection* **87**

Greenberg, Rosalind
14 Vicious Valentines 707

Greene, Elena
His Blushing Bride 254, 320

Greene, Graham
Honorary Consul 1135
Travels with My Aunt 1189

Greene, Jennifer
Kiss Your Prince Charming 323
Millionaire M.D. 279, 403
Rock Solid 278, 279
Where Is He Now? 221, 237, 278,
    279
Wild in the Field 278, 279
Wild in the Moment **278**

H

Author Index

Author Index

Author Index

Author Index

Author Index

Author Index

Author Index

Author Index

Title Index

This index alphabetically lists all titles featured in entries and those listed within entries under "Other books by the same author" and "Other books you might like." Each title is followed by the author's name and the number of the entry where the book is described or listed. Bold numbers indicate featured main entries; light-face numbers refer to books recommended for further reading.

A

A 5th Avenue Christmas
Cozzens, Tracy   233

7 Days and 7 Nights
Wax, Wendy   255

11 Harrowhouse
Browne, Gerald   145

13 Horrors
Hopkins, Brian   615, 679

13 Short Horror Novels
Waugh, Charles G.   622

14 Vicious Valentines
Greenberg, Rosalind   707

16 Lighthouse Road
Macomber, Debbie   330

21: The Final Unfinished Voyage of Jack Aubrey
O'Brian, Patrick   **913**

28 Days Later
Garland, Alex   635

32 Cadillacs
Gores, Joe   17

The 37th Mandala
Laidlaw, Marc   523

.45-Caliber Revenge
Brandvold, Peter   420

65mm
Hoover, Dale   608, 642

The 87th Precinct Series
McBain, Ed   121

The 158-Pound Marriage
Irving, John   1206

204 Rosewood Lane
Macomber, Debbie   330

311 Pelican Court
Macomber, Debbie   330

1610
Gentle, Mary   504

1632
Flint, Eric   743, 744

1633
Flint, Eric   743

1634
Flint, Eric   743

1812
Nevin, David   855, 866

1901
Conroy, Robert   948

1929
Turner, Frederick   860

2001: A Space Odyssey
Clarke, Arthur C.   647

7,000 Clams
Irby, Lee   **884**

A.K.A. Goddess
Vaughn, Evelyn   **399**

The Abandoned
Clegg, Douglas   616, 618

Abandonment
Atkinson, Kate   1067

The Abbess Helewise Series
Clare, Alys   83, 154, 176, 202

The Abducted Heiress
Scott, Amanda   379

Abe
Slotkin, Richard   878

Abigail
Druett, Joan   861

The Abigail Timberlake Series
Myers, Tamar   28, 29, 76, 78, 79, 147

Abilene Gundown
Sherman, Jory   481, 482

The Abilene Trail
Compton, Ralph   429, 430, 431

About Face
Michaels, Fern   341

About Schmidt
Begley, Louis   1170

Absent Friends
Rozan, S.J.   **177**

Absolute Certainty
Connors, Rose   38

Absolute Friends
Le Carre, John   77, 1076, 1090, 1110, 1184, 1190, 1202

Absolute Zero
Logan, Chuck   97

Absolution Gap
Reynolds, Alastair   **775**

The Abyssinian
Rufin, Jean-Christophe   931

Accidental Creatures
Harris, Anne   805

An Accidental Goddess
Baker, Megan Sybil   274

Accordion Crimes
Proulx, Annie   1166

The Accused
Parshall, Craig   1038

The Accusers
Davis, Lindsey   54, 850

Achilles
Cook, Elizabeth   836

Acquainted with the Night
Roden, Barbara   643, **685**

Across a Wild Sea
Lord, Sasha   327

Across a Wine Dark Sea
Bryan, Jessica   238, 541

Across Open Ground
Parkinson, Heather   879

Across the Years
Peterson, Tracie   1041

Act of Mercy
Tremayne, Peter   202

Acting on Impulse
Thompson, Vicki Lewis   397

Action Stations
Forstchen, William R.   727

The Actor's Guide to Adultery
Copp, Rick   **39**

The Actor's Guide to Murder
Copp, Rick   39

Acts of God
Beauseigneur, James   **721**

Adam and Eve and Pinch Me
Rendell, Ruth   169

Adam and Evil
Roberts, Gillian   172

The Adam Dalgliesh Series
James, P.D.   93, 104

Advance and Retreat
Turtledove, Harry   796, 798, 799

The Adventures of Lucky Pierre
Coover, Robert   1117

The Adventures of Max Latin
Davis, Norbert   84

The Adventures of Paul Pry. Vols. 1-2
Gardner, Erle Stanley   84

An Adventurous Lady
King, Valerie   **315**

The Aerialist
Schmitt, Richard   851

The Affair at Greengage Manor
Gedney, Mona   **269**, 270

An Affair of Honor
Hern, Candice   387

The Affair of the 39 Cufflinks
Anderson, James   171

The Affair of the Blood-Stained Egg Cozy
Anderson, James   3, 65

The Affair of the Incognito Tenant
Roberts, Lora   53

L'Affaire
Johnson, Diane   1205

Affinity
Waters, Sarah   856

The African Queen
Forester, C.S.   1076, 1139

Title Index

Title Index

Title Index

Title Index

Title Index

Title Index

E

Title Index

Title Index

Title Index

Title Index

Title Index

Title Index

Title Index

Title Index

Title Index

Title Index

Title Index

Title Index

Title Index

Title Index

Title Index

Title Index

Title Index